॥ श्रीमत्कुञ्जबिहारिणे नमः ॥

GWB
Dedicated to
H.N.A.M.E-I.
H.K.A.K.

TAXMANN®'S

Supplement to

Direct Taxes Ready Reckoner

As Amended by
Taxation Laws (Amendment)
Ordinance 2019

Dr. Vinod K. Singhania
Jeewan Singhania

Asst. Years
2019-20 & 2020-21

First published : May 1978

Forty-third edition : July 2019

Free with Direct Taxes Ready Reckoner, 43rd Edition

Law stated in this book is as amended by the Taxation Laws (Amendment) Ordinance 2019

Published by :
Taxmann Publications (P.) Ltd.

Sales & Marketing :
59/32, New Rohtak Road, New Delhi-110 005 India
Phone : +91-11-45562222
Website : www.taxmann.com
E-mail : sales@taxmann.com

Regd. Office :
21/35, West Punjabi Bagh, New Delhi-110 026 India

Printed at :
Tan Prints (India) Pvt. Ltd.
44 Km. Mile Stone, National Highway, Rohtak Road
Village Rohad, Distt. Jhajjar (Haryana) India
E-mail : sales@tanprints.com

Contents

PAGE

1 Surcharge for the assessment year 2020-21

Surcharge for the assessment year 2020-21 in the case of individual/HUF/AOP/BOI/artificial juridical person

101. The Taxation Laws (Amendment) Ordinance, 2019 (hereinafter referred to as Ordinance) has amended provisions regulating surcharge on income-tax for the assessment year 2020-21. The amended version of surcharge for the assessment year 2020-21 for an individual, HUF, AOP, BOI or an artificial juridical person is as follows –

Different situations	*Nature and quantum of income of the assessee (i.e., individual, HUF, AOP, BOI or an artificial juridical person)*	*Surcharge on amount of income-tax computed on that part of income which is taxable under sections 111A and 112A*	*Surcharge on amount of income-tax computed on other incomes*
Situation 1	Total income (including income under sections 111A and 112A) does not exceed Rs. 50 lakh	*Nil*	*Nil*
Situation 2	Total income (including income under sections 111A and 112A) exceeds Rs. 50 lakh but does not exceed Rs. 1 crore	10%	10%
Situation 3	Total income (including income under sections 111A and 112A) exceeds Rs. 1 crore but does not exceed Rs. 2 crore	15%	15%
Situation 4	Total income (excluding income under sections 111A and 112A) exceeds Rs. 2 crore but does not exceed Rs. 5 crore	15%	25%
Situation 5	Total income (excluding income under sections 111A and 112A) exceeds Rs. 5 crore	15%	37%
Situation 6	Total income (including income under sections 111A and 112A) exceeds Rs. 2 crore (but it is not covered by *Situation 4* and *Situation 5*)	15%	15%

Note - Where the total income includes any income chargeable under section 111A and section 112A, the rate of surcharge on the amount of income-tax computed on that part of income shall not exceed 15 per cent.

101-E1 X Find out the tax liability in the cases given below for the assessment year 2020-21 –

Different taxpayers	*Capital gain under sections –*		*Other incomes*	*Total*
	111A	*112A*		
	Rs.	*Rs.*	*Rs.*	*Rs.*
X (46 years) resident	9,00,000	7,00,000	59,00,000	75,00,000
Y (62 years) resident	10,00,000	14,00,000	1,56,00,000	1,80,00,000
Z (24 years) resident	4,00,000	2,00,000	3,34,00,000	3,40,00,000
A (52 years) resident	3,00,000	8,00,00,000	6,59,00,000	14,62,00,000
B (41 years) resident	1,68,00,000	2,00,000	70,00,000	2,40,00,000

Different taxpayers	*Capital gain under sections –*		*Other incomes*	*Total*
	111A	*112A*		
	Rs.	*Rs.*	*Rs.*	*Rs.*
C (40 years) resident	8,90,00,000	–	60,00,000	9,50,00,000
D (32 years) resident	90,000	5,10,000	48,00,000	54,00,000
E (64 years) non-resident	5,80,000	1,20,000	97,00,000	1,04,00,000
F (28 years) resident	42,00,000	70,000	6,00,000	48,70,000
G (59 years) resident	–	6,01,00,000	9,00,000	6,10,00,000

- *Tax liability in the case of X* - Total income of X (including income taxable under sections 111A and 112A) exceeds Rs. 50 lakh but does not exceed Rs. 1 crore. It is covered by *Situation 2.* Applicable surcharge in this case is 10% (on income-tax pertaining to income taxable under sections 111A and 112A as well as other incomes). Tax liability will be as follows –

	Section 111A (IT rate : 15%)	*Section 112A (IT rate : 10% on capital gain exceeding Rs. 1 lakh)*	*Other incomes*	*Total*
	Rs.	*Rs.*	*Rs.*	*Rs.*
Income-tax	1,35,000	60,000	15,82,500	17,77,500
Surcharge	13,500	6,000	1,58,250	1,77,750
Income-tax and surcharge	1,48,500	66,000	17,40,750	19,55,250
Health and education cess (@ 4% of income-tax and surcharge)	5,940	2,640	69,630	78,210
Tax liability	1,54,440	68,640	18,10,380	20,33,460

Tax liability in the case of Y - Total income of Y (including income taxable under sections 111A and 112A) exceeds Rs. 1 crore but does not exceed Rs. 2 crore. It is covered by *Situation 3.* Applicable surcharge in this case is 15% (on income-tax pertaining to income taxable under sections 111A and 112A as well as other incomes). Tax liability will be as follows –

	Section 111A (IT rate : 15%)	*Section 112A (IT rate : 10% on capital gain exceeding Rs. 1 lakh)*	*Other incomes*	*Total*
	Rs.	*Rs.*	*Rs.*	*Rs.*
Income-tax	1,50,000	1,30,000	44,90,000	47,70,000
Surcharge	22,500	19,500	673,500	7,15,500
Income-tax and surcharge	1,72,500	1,49,500	51,63,500	54,85,500
Health and education cess (@ 4% of income-tax and surcharge)	6,900	5,980	2,06,540	2,19,420
Tax liability	1,79,400	1,55,480	53,70,040	57,04,920

Tax liability in the case of Z - Total income of Z (excluding income taxable under sections 111A and 112A) exceeds Rs. 2 crore but does not exceed Rs. 5 crore. It is covered by *Situation 4.* Applicable surcharge in this case is 15% on income-tax pertaining to income taxable under sections 111A and 112A and 25% on other incomes. Tax liability will be as follows –

	Section 111A (IT rate : 15%)	*Section 112A (IT rate : 10% on capital gain exceeding Rs. 1 lakh)*	*Other incomes*	*Total*
	Rs.	*Rs.*	*Rs.*	*Rs.*
Income-tax	60,000	10,000	98,32,500	99,02,500
Surcharge	9,000	1,500	24,58,125	24,68,625

	Section 111A (IT rate : 15%)	*Section 112A (IT rate : 10% on capital gain exceeding Rs. 1 lakh)*	*Other incomes*	*Total*
	Rs.	*Rs.*	*Rs.*	*Rs.*
Income-tax and surcharge	69,000	11,500	1,22,90,625	1,23,71,125
Health and education cess (@ 4% of income-tax and surcharge)	2,760	460	4,91,625	4,94,845
Tax liability	71,760	11,960	1,27,82,250	1,28,65,970

Tax liability in the case of A - Total income of A (excluding income taxable under sections 111A and 112A) exceeds Rs. 5 crore. It is covered by *Situation 5.* Applicable surcharge in this case is 15% on income-tax pertaining to income taxable under sections 111A and 112A and 37% on other incomes. Tax liability will be as follows –

	Section 111A (IT rate : 15%)	*Section 112A (IT rate : 10% on capital gain exceeding Rs. 1 lakh)*	*Other incomes*	*Total*
	Rs.	*Rs.*	*Rs.*	*Rs.*
Income-tax	45,000	79,90,000	1,95,82,500	2,76,17,500
Surcharge	6,750	11,98,500	72,45,525	84,50,775
Income-tax and surcharge	51,750	91,88,500	2,68,28,025	3,60,68,275
Health and education cess (@ 4% of income-tax and surcharge)	2,070	3,67,540	10,73,121	14,42,731
Tax liability (rounded off)	53,820	95,56,040	2,79,01,146	3,75,11,010

Tax liability in the case of B - Total income of B (including income taxable under sections 111A and 112A) exceeds Rs. 2 crore. It is not covered by *Situations 1, 2* or *3.* His total income (excluding income taxable under sections 111A and 112A) does not exceed Rs. 2 crore. Even *Situations 4* and *5* are not applicable. Consequently, it is covered by *Situation 6.* Applicable surcharge in this case is 15% on income-tax pertaining to income taxable under sections 111A and 112A and 15% on other incomes. Tax liability will be as follows –

	Section 111A (IT rate : 15%)	*Section 112A (IT rate : 10% on capital gain exceeding Rs. 1 lakh)*	*Other incomes*	*Total*
	Rs.	*Rs.*	*Rs.*	*Rs.*
Income-tax	25,20,000	10,000	19,12,500	44,42,500
Surcharge	3,78,000	1,500	2,86,875	6,66,375
Income-tax and surcharge	28,98,000	11,500	21,99,375	51,08,875
Health and education cess (@ 4% of income-tax and surcharge)	1,15,920	460	87,975	2,04,355
Tax liability	30,13,920	11,960	22,87,350	53,13,230

Tax liability in the case of C - Total income of C (including income taxable under sections 111A and 112A) exceeds Rs. 5 crore. However, it is not covered by *Situations 4* and *5.* Consequently, *Situation 6* is applicable. Surcharge in this case is 15% on income-tax pertaining to income taxable under sections 111A and 112A and 15% on other incomes. Tax liability will be as follows –

	Section 111A (IT rate : 15%)	*Section 112A (IT rate : 10% on capital gain exceeding Rs. 1 lakh)*	*Other incomes*	*Total*
	Rs.	*Rs.*	*Rs.*	*Rs.*
Income-tax	1,33,50,000	*Nil*	16,12,500	1,49,62,500
Surcharge	20,02,500	*Nil*	2,41,875	22,44,375

	Section 111A (IT rate : 15%)	*Section 112A (IT rate : 10% on capital gain exceeding Rs. 1 lakh)*	*Other incomes*	*Total*
	Rs.	*Rs.*	*Rs.*	*Rs.*
Income-tax and surcharge	1,53,52,500	*Nil*	18,54,375	1,72,06,875
Health and education cess (@ 4% of income-tax and surcharge)	6,14,100	*Nil*	74,175	6,88,275
Tax liability	1,59,66,600	*Nil*	19,28,550	1,78,95,150

Tax liability in the case of D - Total income of D (including income taxable under sections 111A and 112A) exceeds Rs. 50 lakh but does not exceed Rs. 1 crore. It is covered by *Situation 2*. Applicable surcharge in this case is 10% (on income-tax pertaining to income taxable under sections 111A and 112A as well as other incomes). Tax liability will be as follows –

	Section 111A (IT rate : 15%)	*Section 112A (IT rate : 10% on capital gain exceeding Rs. 1 lakh)*	*Other incomes*	*Total*
	Rs.	*Rs.*	*Rs.*	*Rs.*
Income-tax	13,500	41,000	1,252,500	1,307,000
Surcharge	1,350	4,100	125,250	130,700
Income-tax and surcharge	14,850	45,100	1,377,750	1,437,700
Health and education cess (@ 4% of income-tax and surcharge)	594	1,804	55,110	57,508
Tax liability (rounded off)	15,444	46,904	1,432,860	1,495,210

Tax liability in the case of E - Total income of E (including income taxable under sections 111A and 112A) exceeds Rs. 1 crore but does not exceed Rs. 2 crore. It is covered by *Situation 3*. Applicable surcharge in this case is 15% (on income-tax pertaining to income taxable under sections 111A and 112A as well as other incomes). He is non-resident. His tax liability will be as follows –

	Section 111A (IT rate : 15%)	*Section 112A (IT rate : 10% on capital gain exceeding Rs. 1 lakh)*	*Other incomes*	*Total*
	Rs.	*Rs.*	*Rs.*	*Rs.*
Income-tax	87,000	2,000	27,22,500	28,11,500
Surcharge	13,050	300	4,08,375	4,21,725
Income-tax and surcharge	1,00,050	2,300	31,30,875	32,33,225
Health and education cess (@ 4% of income-tax and surcharge)	4,002	92	1,25,235	1,29,329
Tax liability (rounded off)	1,04,052	2,392	32,56,110	33,62,550

Tax liability in the case of F - Total income of F (including income taxable under sections 111A and 112A) does not exceed Rs. 50 lakh. It is covered by *Situation 1*. Surcharge is not applicable in this case and tax liability will be as follows –

	Section 111A (IT rate : 15%)	*Section 112A (IT rate : 10% on capital gain exceeding Rs. 1 lakh)*	*Other incomes*	*Total*
	Rs.	*Rs.*	*Rs.*	*Rs.*
Income-tax	6,30,000	*Nil*	32,500	6,62,500
Surcharge	*Nil*	*Nil*	*Nil*	*Nil*
Income-tax and surcharge	6,30,000	*Nil*	32,500	6,62,500
Health and education cess (@ 4% of income-tax and surcharge)	25,200	*Nil*	1,300	26,500
Tax liability	6,55,200	*Nil*	33,800	6,89,000

Tax liability in the case of G - Total income of G (including income taxable under sections 111A and 112A) exceeds Rs. 5 crore. However, it is not covered by *Situations 4* and *5*. Consequently, *Situation 6* is applicable. Surcharge in this case is 15% (on income-tax pertaining to section 112A as well as other incomes). Tax liability will be as follows –

	Section 111A (IT rate : 15%) *Rs.*	*Section 112A (IT rate : 10% on capital gain exceeding Rs. 1 lakh)* *Rs.*	*Other incomes* *Rs.*	*Total* *Rs.*
Income-tax	–	60,00,000	92,500	60,92,500
Surcharge	–	9,00,000	13,875	9,13,875
Income-tax and surcharge	–	69,00,000	1,06,375	70,06,375
Health and education cess (@ 4% of income-tax and surcharge)	–	2,76,000	4,255	2,80,255
Tax liability	–	71,76,000	1,10,630	72,86,630

101-E2 Gross income of X (61 years), a resident individual, for the assessment year 2020-21 is Rs. 5,14,50,000 [salary (before standard deduction) : Rs. 10,90,000, lottery winnings : Rs. 92,00,000, long-term capital gain under section 112A : Rs. 1,60,000 and dividend from domestic companies : Rs. 4,10,00,000]. X is entitled to deduction of Rs. 1,50,000 under section 80C and Rs. 50,000 under section 80CCD(1B).

•

	Rs.
Salary income (after standard deduction)	10,40,000
Long-term capital gain (under section 112A)	1,60,000
Lottery winnings	92,00,000
Dividend from domestic companies [Rs. 4,10,00,000 – exemption under section 10(*34*) : Rs. 10,00,000]	4,00,00,000
Gross total income	5,04,00,000
Less: Deduction under sections 80C and 80CCD(1B)	2,00,000
Net income	5,02,00,000
Tax computation under normal provisions	
Tax on lottery winnings of Rs. 92,00,000 @ 30%	27,60,000
Tax on long-term capital gain of Rs. 1,60,000 under section 112A (10% of Rs. 60,000)	6,000
Tax on dividend income of Rs. 4,00,00,000 under section 115BBDA (10% of Rs. 4,00,00,000)	40,00,000
Tax on remaining income of Rs. 8,40,000 (first Rs. 3,00,000: *Nil*, next Rs. 2,00,000 @ 5% : Rs. 10,000 and on the balance of Rs. 3,40,000 @ 20% : Rs. 68,000)	78,000
Tax	68,44,000
Add: Surcharge [surcharge on tax on long-term capital gain of Rs. 6,000 @ 15% + 37% of remaining tax, *Situation 5* is applicable]	25,30,960
Total	93,74,960
Tax computation under marginal relief	
Step 1 - Tax payable if income is Rs. 5 crore [it may be assumed that salary is Rs. 8,40,000 (*i.e.*, Rs. 10,40,000 *minus* deduction under sections 80C and 80CCD), lottery winning is Rs. 90,00,000, long-term capital gain is Rs. 1,60,000 and dividend income is Rs. 4,00,00,000] –	
Tax on lottery income of Rs. 90,00,000 @ 30%	27,00,000
Tax on long-term capital gain of Rs. 1,60,000 under section 112A (10% of Rs. 60,000)	6,000
Tax on dividend income of Rs. 4,00,00,000 under section 115BBDA (10% of Rs. 1,00,00,000)	40,00,000
Tax on balance of Rs. 8,40,000	78,000
Tax on Rs. 5,00,00,000	67,84,000

	Rs.
Add: Surcharge [surcharge on tax on long-term capital gain of Rs. 6,000 @ 15% + 25% of remaining tax, *Situation 4* is applicable]	16,95,400
Total (*i.e.*, tax and surcharge on income of Rs. 2,00,00,000)	84,79,400
Step 2 - To the amount of tax and surcharge determined on Rs. 5 crore under *Step 1*, *add* tax @ 100% in respect of income exceeding Rs. 5 crore (*i.e.*, 100% of Rs. 2,00,000)	2,00,000
The aggregate tax and surcharge is Rs. 86,79,400 which is lower than the regular tax and surcharge of Rs. 93,74,960. Therefore, tax liability will be calculated in this case as follows –	
Tax and surcharge as computed above	86,79,400
Add: Health and education cess @ 4%	3,47,176
Tax liability (rounded off)	90,26,580

101-E3 X (40 years) is a resident individual for the assessment year 2020-21. His estimated income for the previous year 2019-20 is Rs. 5.40 crore (it includes long-term capital gain under section 112A on transfer of equity shares on June 1, 2019 of Rs. 4 crore). He has paid advance tax on June 15, 2019 and September 15, 2019 as follows –

	Rs.
Long-term capital gain under section 112A	4,00,00,000
Other income	1,40,00,000
Net income	5,40,00,000
Income-tax –	
- Tax under section 112A (10% of Rs. 3,99,00,000)	39,90,000
- Tax on other incomes of Rs. 1,40,00,000	40,12,500
Total	80,02,500
Add: Surcharge @ 37%	29,60,925
Tax and surcharge	1,09,63,425
Add: Health and education cess	4,38,537
Tax liability	1,14,01,962
Advance tax paid on June 15, 2019 (15% of Rs. 1,14,01,962, rounded off)	17,11,000
Advance tax paid on September 15, 2019 (30% of Rs. 1,14,01,962, rounded off)	34,21,000

Find out the amount of advance tax payable on December 15, 2019 and March 15, 2020 without attracting interest liability under sections 234B and 234C.

•

After the revision of surcharge by the Ordinance, surcharge has been reduced. This case is covered by *Situation 6*. Revised rate of surcharge is 15% on long-term capital gain as well as other income. Advance tax payable on December 15, 2019 and March 15, 2020 will be as follows –

	Rs.
Income-tax as calculated above	80,02,500
Add: Surcharge @ 15%	12,00,375
Tax and surcharge	92,02,875
Add: Health and education cess	3,68,115
Tax liability	95,70,990
Advance tax payable on December 15, 2019 [75% of Rs. 95,70,990 – (instalments paid on June 15, 2019 and September 15, 2019, *i.e.*, Rs. 51,32,000), rounded off]	20,47,000
Advance tax payable on March 15, 2020 [100% of Rs. 95,70,990 – (instalments paid on June 15, 2019, September 15, 2019 and December 15, 2019, *i.e.*, Rs. 71,79,000)]	23,91,990

Surcharge on advance tax in the case of AOP/BOI having income under section 115AD(1)(*b*)

102. Section 115AD(1)(*b*) covers income by way of short-term or long-term capital gains arising from the transfer of certain securities by Foreign Institution Investors (FIIs). The Ordinance has amended provisions regulating surcharge on such income by way of capital gains for the assessment year 2020-21. The amended version of surcharge for such FIIs is as follows –

Different situations	*Nature and quantum of income of AOP/BOI whether incorporated or not having income under section 115AD*	*Surcharge on tax on income by way of short-term or long-term capital gain on transfer of certain securities under section 115AD(1)(b)*	*Surcharge on tax on other incomes*
Situation 1	Total income does not exceed Rs. 50 lakh	*Nil*	*Nil*
Situation 2	Total income exceeds Rs. 50 lakh but does not exceed Rs. 1 crore	10%	10%
Situation 3	Total income exceeds Rs. 1 crore but does not exceed Rs. 2 crore	15%	15%
Situation 4	Total income [excluding income under section 115AD(1)(*b*)] exceeds Rs. 2 crore but does not exceed Rs. 5 crore	15%	25%
Situation 5	Total income [excluding income under section 115AD(1)(*b*)] exceeds Rs. 5 crore	15%	37%
Situation 6	Total income [including income under section 115AD(1)(*b*)] exceeds Rs. 2 crore (but it is not covered by *Situation 4* and *Situation 5*)	15%	15%

Surcharge on income taxable under section 115BAA or section 115BAB

103. In respect of income taxable within the parameters of section 115BAA or section 115BAB, the applicable surcharge will be 10 per cent (irrespective of quantum of income). For detailed discussion, *see* paras 201 and 202.3.

Surcharge in the case of TDS

104. Provisions regulating surcharge on TDS have been amended by the Ordinance with effect from September 20, 2019. The amendment is applicable if the following conditions are satisfied –

1. The recipient is non-resident in India.

2. The recipient is an individual or HUF or AOP or BOI (whether incorporated or not) or artificial juridical person.

3. Tax is deductible by the payer on short-term capital gain (which is calculated as per section 111A) or long-term capital gain (which is calculated as per section 112A).

If the above conditions are satisfied, surcharge on TDS (with effect from September 20, 2019) will be as follows –

Different situations	*Surcharge on TDS*
If the aforesaid payment/credit subject to TDS does not exceed Rs. 50 lakh during the financial year	*Nil*
If the aforesaid payment/credit subject to TDS exceeds Rs. 50 lakh but does not exceed Rs. 1 crore during the financial year	10%
If the aforesaid payment/credit subject to TDS exceeds Rs. 1 crore during the financial year	15%

2 Special provisions pertaining to taxation of certain companies

Tax on income of certain domestic companies [Sec. 115BAA]

201. Section 115BAA has been inserted by the Ordinance with effect from the assessment year 2020-21.

• *Conditions* - The following conditions should be satisfied in order to avail the benefit of lower tax rate under section 115BAA –

1. The assessee is a domestic company. It may be a public limited company or private limited company or listed company or unlisted company. There is no restriction on the amount of annual turnover. Shareholders of the company may be resident or non-resident. Such company may be controlled by a domestic entity or a foreign entity. It may be a company newly incorporated or an existing domestic company. There is no restriction on formation of such company. For instance, if a sole proprietary concern is converted into a company (or a firm is converted into a company), the converted company will be qualified for the purpose of this section.

2. Total income of the company is computed without claiming the following deductions –

- Deduction under section 10AA.
- Additional depreciation under section 32(1)(*iia*).
- Deduction under section 32AD.
- Deduction under section 33AB.
- Deduction under section 33ABA.
- Deduction under section 35(1)(*ii*)/(*iia*)/(*iii*)/35(2AA)/(2AB).
- Deduction under section 35AD.
- Deduction under section 35CCC.
- Deduction under section 35CCD.
- Deduction under any provisions of Chapter VI-A(*C*) [*i.e.,* sections 80HH to 80RRB] but other than the provisions of section 80JJAA.

3. The total income of the company is calculated without adjusting brought forward loss from any earlier year (if such loss pertains to any deduction under the aforesaid sections). Moreover, such loss will not be carried forward.

4. Total income of the company is calculated after claiming depreciation (determined in such manner as may be prescribed).

• *Tax rate* - If the aforesaid conditions are satisfied, income of the company will be taxable at the rate of 22 per cent (+SC+HEC). If such company has other incomes which are taxable under other provisions of Chapter XII (*i.e.,* sections 110 to 115BBG but other than sections 115BA and 115BAB), then tax on such other incomes will be calculated as per the rate(s) specified by these sections and balance amount of income will be taxable under section 115BAA at the rate of 22 per cent.

• *Surcharge (SC) and health and education cess (HEC)* - The above rate of 22 per cent is subject to surcharge at the rate of 10 per cent of income-tax (irrespective of quantum of total income) and health and education cess of 4 per cent (of income-tax + SC). In respect of income taxable under other provisions of Chapter XII (*i.e.*, sections 110 to 115BBG but other than sections 115BA and 115BAB), normal surcharge depending upon quantum of total income will be applicable. The table given below, summarises surcharge rates in different situations –

Domestic company which opts for lower taxation under section 115BAA	*Surcharge on tax on income chargeable under section 115BAA*	*Surcharge on tax on income taxable under other provisions of Chapter XII (i.e., sections 110 to 115BBG but other than sections 115BA and 115BAB)*
If total income of the domestic company does not exceed Rs. 1 crore	10%	*Nil*
If total income of the domestic company exceeds Rs. 1 crore but does not exceed Rs. 10 crore	10%	7%
If total income of the domestic company exceeds Rs. 10 crore	10%	12%

• *Option* - The aforesaid lower rate is applicable if the option is exercised in the prescribed manner on or before the due date of submission of return of income as given under section 139(1). This option can be exercised for any previous year relevant to the assessment year 2020-21 (or any subsequent year). However, once the company has exercised the option for any previous year, it cannot be subsequently withdrawn for the same or any other previous year.

• *MAT not applicable* - If a domestic company has exercised the option under section 115BAA, the provisions of minimum alternate tax under section 115JB are not applicable. However, the benefit of adjustment of brought forward tax credit (*i.e.*, MAT credit) under section 115JAA(2A)/(4) shall be available.

201-E1 Taxpayer is a domestic company. It wants to opt for lower tax rate under section 115BAA. The option will be submitted by the company before September 30, 2020 for the assessment year 2020-21 in the prescribed manner. Find out the tax liability in the following different cases for the assessment year 2020-21 –

Domestic company opted for lower tax under section 115BAA	*Business income computed under section 115BAA (including interest of Rs. 20,000 on bank deposit taxable under section 56)* *Rs.*	*Long-term capital gain under section 112A* *Rs.*	*Total* *Rs.*
X Ltd.	80,00,000	5,00,000	85,00,000
Y Ltd.	3,00,00,000	70,00,000	3,70,00,000
Z Ltd.	4,00,00,000	8,00,00,000	12,00,00,000
A Ltd.	90,00,000	*Nil*	90,00,000
B Ltd.	1,20,00,000	*Nil*	1,20,00,000
C Ltd.	14,00,00,000	*Nil*	14,00,00,000

C Ltd. has a brought forward business loss pertaining to textile trading business (assessment year 2017-18, amount of brought forward loss as per assessment order : Rs. 30,00,000).

•

	Business income including interest on bank deposits (IT rate : 22%) *Rs.*	*Section 112A (IT rate : 10% on capital gain exceeding Rs. 1 lakh)* *Rs.*	*Total* *Rs.*
Tax computation of X Ltd.			
Income-tax	17,60,000	40,000	18,00,000

	Business income including interest on bank deposits (IT rate : 22%) *Rs.*	*Section 112A (IT rate : 10% on capital gain exceeding Rs. 1 lakh)* *Rs.*	*Total* *Rs.*
Surcharge	1,76,000	-	1,76,000
Income-tax and surcharge	19,36,000	40,000	19,76,000
Health and education cess (@ 4% of income-tax and surcharge)	77,440	1,600	79,040
Tax liability	20,13,440	41,600	20,55,040
Tax computation of Y Ltd.			
Income-tax	66,00,000	6,90,000	72,90,000
Surcharge	6,60,000	48,300	7,08,300
Income-tax and surcharge	72,60,000	7,38,300	79,98,300
Health and education cess (@ 4% of income-tax and surcharge)	2,90,400	29,532	3,19,932
Tax liability (rounded off)	75,50,400	7,67,832	83,18,230
Tax computation of Z Ltd.			
Income-tax	88,00,000	79,90,000	1,67,90,000
Surcharge	8,80,000	9,58,800	18,38,800
Income-tax and surcharge	96,80,000	89,48,800	1,86,28,800
Health and education cess (@ 4% of income-tax and surcharge)	3,87,200	3,57,952	7,45,152
Tax liability (rounded off)	1,00,67,200	93,06,752	1,93,73,950
Tax computation of A Ltd.			
Income-tax	19,80,000	–	19,80,000
Surcharge	1,98,000	–	1,98,000
Income-tax and surcharge	21,78,000	–	21,78,000
Health and education cess (@ 4% of income-tax and surcharge)	87,120	–	87,120
Tax liability	22,65,120	–	22,65,120
Tax computation of B Ltd.			
Income-tax	26,40,000	–	26,40,000
Surcharge	2,64,000	–	2,64,000
Income-tax and surcharge	29,04,000	–	29,04,000
Health and education cess (@ 4% of income-tax and surcharge)	1,16,160	–	1,16,160
Tax liability	30,20,160	–	30,20,160
Tax computation of C Ltd.			
Income-tax [*i.e.,* 22% of (Rs. 14,00,00,000 – brought forward loss : Rs. 30,00,000)]	3,01,40,000	–	3,01,40,000
Surcharge	30,14,000	–	30,14,000
Income-tax and surcharge	3,31,54,000	–	3,31,54,000
Health and education cess (@ 4% of income-tax and surcharge)	13,26,160	–	13,26,160
Tax liability	3,44,80,160	–	3,44,80,160

201-E2 X Ltd. and Y Ltd. started business operation during April 2016. From the records of the company, the following data is noted –

Different assessment years	*X Ltd.*			*Y Ltd.*		
	Normal tax liability	*MAT liability*	*MAT carried forward under section 115JAA(2A) (cumulative figure)*	*Normal tax liability*	*MAT liability*	*MAT carried forward under section 115JAA(2A) (cumulative figure)*
	Rs.	*Rs.*	*Rs.*	*Rs.*	*Rs.*	*Rs.*
2017-18	4,00,000	32,00,000	28,00,000	12,00,000	8,00,000	*Nil*
2018-19	6,00,000	16,00,000	38,00,000	33,70,000	40,00,000	6,30,000
2019-20	8,00,000	7,00,000	37,00,000	18,10,000	42,30,000	30,50,000

The following information is available for the assessment year 2020-21 –

	Business income computed under section 115BAA	*Short-term capital gain under section 111A*	*Total*	*Book profit under section 115JB*
	Rs.	*Rs.*	*Rs.*	*Rs.*
X Ltd.	1,40,00,000	10,00,000	1,50,00,000	2,70,00,000
Y Ltd.	1,10,00,000	18,00,000	1,28,00,000	4,35,90,000

X Ltd. and Y Ltd. want to opt for lower tax rate under section 115BAA. The option will be submitted by these companies before September 30, 2020 for the assessment year 2020-21 in the prescribed manner. Find out the tax liability for the assessment year 2020-21.

•

Minimum alternate tax provisions of section 115JB are not applicable in the case of a domestic company which opts for lower tax scheme under section 115BAA. Consequently, in the case of X Ltd. and Y Ltd. minimum alternate tax is not applicable for the assessment year 2020-21 onwards. No amendment has, however, been made in the scheme of section 115JAA which regulates carried forward and set off of MAT credit. Consequently, the benefit of adjustment of brought forward tax credit (*i.e.*, MAT credit) under section 115JAA(2A)/(4) will be available to X Ltd. and Y Ltd.

Computation of tax under section 115BAA for the assessment year 2020-21 –

	X Ltd.			*Y Ltd.*		
	Business income (IT rate : 22%)	*Short-term capital gain under section 111A (IT rate : 15%)*	*Total*	*Business income (IT rate : 22%)*	*Short-term capital gain under section 111A (IT rate : 15%)*	*Total*
	Rs.	*Rs.*	*Rs.*	*Rs.*	*Rs.*	*Rs.*
Income-tax	30,80,000	1,50,000	32,30,000	24,20,000	2,70,000	26,90,000
Surcharge	3,08,000	10,500	3,18,500	2,42,000	18,900	2,60,900
Income-tax and surcharge	33,88,000	1,60,500	35,48,500	26,62,000	2,88,900	29,50,900
Health and education cess (@ 4% of income-tax and surcharge)	1,35,520	6,420	1,41,940	1,06,480	11,556	1,18,036
Tax liability	35,23,520	1,66,920	36,90,440	27,68,480	3,00,456	30,68,936

MAT credit under section 115JAA for the assessment year 2020-21 –

		X Ltd.	*Y Ltd.*
		Rs.	*Rs.*
Cumulative MAT credit available up to the assessment year 2019-20 under section 115JAA(2A)	(*a*)	37,00,000	30,50,000
Tax liability for the assessment year 2020-21 under normal provisions (*i.e.*, after ignoring section 115JB)	(*b*)	36,90,440	30,68,936

		X Ltd. Rs.	Y Ltd. Rs.
Tax liability for the assessment year 2020-21 under minimum alternate tax (*i.e.*, under section 115JB)	(*c*)	*Nil*	*Nil*
MAT credit adjustment available for the assessment year 2020-21 under section 115JAA(5) [*i.e.*, excess of (*b*) over (*c*), subject to maximum of (*a*)]	(*d*)	36,90,440	30,50,000
Tax payable for the assessment year 2020-21 [*i.e.*, (*b*) – (*d*)] (rounded off)	(*e*)	*Nil*	18,940
MAT credit to be carried forward under section 115JAA(3) [*i.e.*, (*a*) – (*d*)]	(*f*)	9,560	*Nil*

201-E3 X Ltd. has a manufacturing unit in Meghalaya. It is eligible for 100 per cent deduction under section 80-IE up to the assessment year 2021-22. Projected taxable income and book profit from manufacturing activity of the company for different years is as follows –

Previous year	*Assessment year*	*Taxable income before deduction under section 80-IE* Rs.	*Book profit* Rs.
2019-20	2020-21	50,00,000	85,00,000
2020-21	2021-22	40,00,000	1,09,50,156
2021-22	2022-23	65,00,000	86,33,333
2022-23	2023-24	48,00,000	88,80,000
2023-24	2024-25	88,50,000	93,73,333

Discuss whether (or not) X Ltd. should opt for lower tax regime of section 115BAA from the assessment year 2020-21 onwards. Annual turnover of the company is not more than Rs. 100 crore. Normal corporate tax applicable for the company is 25 per cent (not 30 per cent). X Ltd. has MAT credit available (cumulative amount up to the assessment year 2019-20 is Rs. 9,00,000).

•

	Normal tax under existing provisions			*Tax liability under new regime of section 115BAA****
	*Normal tax** Rs.	*Minimum alternate tax*** Rs.	*Tax payable* Rs.	Rs.
Assessment year 2020-21	*Nil*	13,26,000	13,26,000	12,58,400
Assessment year 2021-22	*Nil*	18,27,800	18,27,800	10,06,720
Assessment year 2022-23	16,90,000	13,46,800	16,90,000	16,35,920
Assessment year 2023-24	12,48,000	13,85,280	13,85,280	12,08,064
Assessment year 2024-25	23,01,000	14,62,240	23,01,000	22,27,368

*Corporate tax rate : 25%, health and education cess : 4%.

**MAT : 15%, surcharge : 7% (applicable for the assessment year 2021-22), health and education cess : 4%.

***Tax under section 115BAA : 22%, surcharge : 7%, health and education cess : 4%.

Tax liability of X Ltd. if it opts for lower tax regime of section 115BAA from the assessment year 2020-21 (or from a subsequent year) –

	AY 2020-21 Rs.	*AY 2021-22* Rs.	*AY 2022-23* Rs.	*AY 2023-24* Rs.	*AY 2024-25* Rs.	*Total* Rs.
Tax liability if lower tax regime of section 115BAA is opted from the assessment year 2020-21 (after adjusting MAT credit)	12,58,400 – 9,00,000 = 3,58,400	10,06,720	16,35,920	12,08,064	22,27,368	64,36,472

	AY 2020-21 Rs.	*AY 2021-22 Rs.*	*AY 2022-23 Rs.*	*AY 2023-24 Rs.*	*AY 2024-25 Rs.*	*Total Rs.*
Tax liability if lower tax regime of section 115BAA is opted from the assessment year 2021-22 (after adjusting MAT credit)	13,26,000	10,06,720 – 9,00,000 – 13,26,000 = (–) 12,19,280 (tax payable *zero*)	16,35,920 – 12,19,280 = 4,16,640	12,08,064	22,27,368	51,78,072
Tax liability if lower tax regime of section 115BAA is opted from the assessment year 2022-23 (after adjusting MAT credit)	13,26,000	18,27,800	16,35,920 – 9,00,000 – 13,26,000 – 18,27,800 = (–) 24,17,880 (tax payable *zero*)	12,08,064 – 24,17,880 = – 12,09,816 (tax payable *zero*)	22,27,368 – 12,09,816 = 10,17,552	41,71,352

Tax liability for the assessment years 2020-21 and 2021-22 is lower under section 115BAA as compare to tax under normal provisions. However, X Ltd. should opt for lower tax regime of section 115BAA only from the assessment year 2022-23 (as the aggregate tax bill of the assessment years 2020-21 to 2024-25 is the lowest under this option as shown above).

Tax on income of certain new domestic manufacturing companies [Sec. 115BAB]

202. Section 115BAB has been inserted by the Ordinance with effect from the assessment year 2020-21.

202.1 ***Conditions*** - The following conditions should be satisfied in order to avail the benefit of lower tax rate under section 115BAB –

• *Assessee* - The assessee is a domestic company. It may be a public limited company or private limited company or listed company or unlisted company. There is no restriction on the amount of annual turnover. Shareholders of the company may be resident or non-resident. Such company may be controlled by a domestic entity or a foreign entity.

• *Registration and commencement* - The company has been set up and registered on or after October 1, 2019 and has commenced manufacturing on or before March 31, 2023.

• *New undertaking* - The company is not formed by splitting up, or the reconstruction, of a business already in existence. However, this condition is not applicable in respect of an undertaking which is formed as a result of the re-establishment, reconstruction or revival by the person of the business of any such undertaking as referred to in section 33B.

• *Does not use old plant and machinery* - The company does not use any machinery or plant previously used for any purpose. However, there are two exceptions –

- *20 per cent old machinery is permitted* - If the value of the transferred assets does not exceed 20 per cent of the total value of the machinery or plant used in the business, this condition is deemed to have been satisfied.
- *Second-hand imported machinery is treated as new* - Any machinery or plant which was used outside India by any person other than the assessee shall not be regarded as machinery or plant previously used for any purpose, if the following conditions are fulfilled :—
  1. Such machinery or plant was not, at any time previous to the date of the installation by the assessee, used in India.
  2. Such machinery or plant is imported into India from any country outside India.
  3. No deduction on account of depreciation in respect of such machinery or plant has been allowed or is allowable under the Act in computing the total income of any person for any period prior to the date of the installation of the machinery or plant by the assessee.

• *Does not use hotel/convention centre building* - The company does not use any building previously used as a hotel or a convention centre, as the case may be.

• *Not engaged in any business other than manufacturing* - The company is not engaged in any business other than the business of manufacture or production of any article or thing and research in relation to, or distribution of, such article or thing manufactured or produced by it.

202.2 ***Mode of computation of income*** - If the above conditions are satisfied, income of the company will be calculated as follows –

• *A few tax incentives not available* - Total income of the company will be computed without claiming the following deductions –

- Deduction under section 10AA.
- Additional depreciation under section 32(1)(*iia*).
- Deduction under section 32AD.
- Deduction under section 33AB.
- Deduction under section 33ABA.
- Deduction under section 35(1)(*ii*)/(*iia*)/(*iii*)/35(2AA)/(2AB).
- Deduction under section 35AD.
- Deduction under section 35CCC.
- Deduction under section 35CCD.
- Deduction under any provisions of Chapter VI-A(*C*) [*i.e.*, sections 80HH to 80RRB] but other than the provisions of section 80JJAA.

• *No adjustment of brought forward losses pertaining to above sections* - The total income of the company will be calculated without adjusting brought forward loss from any earlier year (if such loss pertains to any deduction under the aforesaid sections). Moreover, such loss will not be carried forward.

• *Depreciation to be computed under a prescribed mode* - Total income of the company will be calculated after claiming depreciation (determined in such manner as may be prescribed).

• *Computation of reasonable profit by Assessing Officer in certain cases* - Where it appears to the Assessing Officer that, owing to the close connection between the company and any other person (or for any other reason), the course of business between them is so arranged that the business transacted between them produces to the company more than the ordinary profits which might be expected to arise, the Assessing Officer shall, in computing the profits and gains of such company, take the amount of profits as may be reasonably deemed to have been derived therefrom. For this purpose, the Assessing Officer may invoke the provisions of section 92BA pertaining to specified domestic transactions in order to calculate arm's length price. However, the rule of section 92BA is applicable if the aggregate value of such domestic transactions pertaining to the assessee for the relevant previous year exceeds Rs. 20 crore. Arm's length price is defined in section 92F(*ii*).

202.3 ***Computation of tax liability at the rate of 15 per cent*** - If the aforesaid conditions are satisfied, income of the company will be taxable at the rate of 15 per cent (+SC+HEC). If such company has other incomes which are taxable under other provisions of Chapter XII (*i.e.*, sections 110 to 115BBG but other than sections 115BA and 115BAA), then tax on such other incomes will be calculated as per the rate(s) specified by these sections and balance amount of income will be taxable under section 115BAB at the rate of 15 per cent.

• *Surcharge (SC) and health and education cess (HEC)* - The above rate of 15 per cent is subject to surcharge at the rate of 10 per cent of income-tax (irrespective of quantum of total income) and health and education cess of 4 per cent (of income-tax + SC). In respect of income taxable under other provisions of Chapter XII (*i.e.*, sections 110 to 115BBG but other than sections 115BA and 115BAA), normal surcharge depending upon quantum of total income will be applicable. The table given below, summarises surcharge rates in different situations –

Domestic company which opts for lower taxation under section 115BAB	*Surcharge on tax on income chargeable under section 115BAB*	*Surcharge on tax on income taxable under other provisions of Chapter XII (i.e., sections 110 to 115BBG but other than sections 115BA and 115BAA)*
If total income of the domestic company does not exceed Rs. 1 crore	10%	*Nil*
If total income of the domestic company exceeds Rs. 1 crore but does not exceed Rs. 10 crore	10%	7%
If total income of the domestic company exceeds Rs. 10 crore	10%	12%

• *Option* - The aforesaid lower rate is applicable if the option is exercised in the prescribed manner on or before the due date specified under section 139(1) for furnishing "the first of the returns of income for any previous year relevant to the assessment year commencing on or after April 1, 2020".

Meaning of "the first of the returns" - Under section 115BAB, the assessee-company is required to opt for the lower tax regime in the first year itself. If the company does not opt for section 115BAB in the first year, then it will become ineligible to opt for the same in a subsequent year. For instance, a company is incorporated on October 6, 2020 (and the business of manufacturing is commenced on December 1, 2020) and it wants to opt for lower tax regime of section 115BAB, then the option should be exercised from the first year (*i.e.*, from the assessment year 2021-22). If it is not so exercised for the assessment year 2021-22, then the company will become disqualified to opt for section 115BAB for the assessment year 2022-23 (or any subsequent year).

It may be noted that under the provisions of section 115BAA (*i.e.*, lower tax regime of 22 per cent) the option can be exercised in any year (*i.e.*, assessment year 2020-21 or in a subsequent year).

Option exercised under section 115BAB cannot be withdrawn - Once the company has exercised the option under section 115BAB, it cannot be subsequently withdrawn for the same or any other previous year. To put it differently, option once exercised under this section will be applicable in perpetuity to the company.

• *MAT not applicable* - If a domestic company has exercised the option under section 115BAB, the provisions of minimum alternate tax under section 115JB are not applicable. As the company (opting for section 115BAB) is a new company and option is required to be exercised in the first year, there is no possibility of having brought forward MAT credit.

Comparative corporate income-tax incidence under different provisions

203. The table summarises corporate tax incidence under existing and new provisions for the assessment year 2020-21 –

	Normal provisions if turnover of the previous year 2017-18 does not exceed Rs. 400 crore	*Normal provisions if turnover of the previous year 2017-18 exceeds Rs. 400 crore*	*Under section 115BA*	*Under section 115BAA*	*Under section 115BAB*
Mode of computation of income	With incentives	With incentives	Without incentives	Without incentives	Without incentives

	Normal provisions if turnover of the previous year 2017-18 does not exceed Rs. 400 crore	*Normal provisions if turnover of the previous year 2017-18 exceeds Rs. 400 crore*	*Under section 115BA*	*Under section 115BAA*	*Under section 115BAB*
Manufacturing activity is required	*No*	*No*	*Yes*	*No*	*Yes*
Any limit on annual turnover of the current year (to become disqualified)	*No*	*No*	*No*	*No*	*No*
Any limit on annual turnover of a preceding year (to become disqualified)	*Yes*	*No*	*No*	*No*	*No*
MAT applicable	Applicable	Applicable	Applicable	Not applicable	Not applicable
Whether any option is required to be exercised	*No*	*No*	*Yes*	*Yes*	*Yes*
Basic tax rates	25%	30%	25%	22%	15%
Effective tax rate (including SC + HEC) –					
- If total income does not exceed Rs. 1 crore	26%	31.2%	26%	25.168%	17.16%
- If total income exceeds Rs. 1 crore but does not exceed Rs. 10 crore	27.82%	33.384%	27.82%	25.168%	17.16%
- If total income exceeds Rs. 10 crore	29.12%	34.944%	29.12%	25.168%	17.16%

3 Other amendments

Lower minimum alternate tax

301. Minimum alternate tax under section 115JB has been reduced from 18.5 per cent to 15 per cent from the assessment year 2020-21. However, there is no change in surcharge and health and education cess. The effective rate of minimum alternate tax for the assessment year 2020-21 will be as follows –

	If book profit does not exceed Rs.1 crore				*If book profit is in the range of Rs. 1 crore – Rs. 10 crore*				*If book profit exceeds Rs. 10 crore*			
	IT	*SC*	*HEC*	*Total*	*IT*	*SC*	*HEC*	*Total*	*IT*	*SC*	*HEC*	*Total*
Domestic company	15%	–	0.60%	15.60%	15%	1.05%	0.642%	16.692%	15%	1.80%	0.672%	17.472%
Foreign company	15%	–	0.60%	15.60%	15%	0.30%	0.612%	15.912%	15%	0.75%	0.63%	16.38%

Note - Basic MAT rate is 9%, if the assessee is a unit located in an International Financial Services Centre and derives its income solely in convertible foreign exchange.

301.1 ***Marginal relief*** - If book profit of a company exceeds Rs. 1 crore but does not exceed Rs. 10 crore, the minimum alternate tax cannot exceed the following : (Rs. 15 lakh + book profit – Rs. 1 crore) + HEC. If, however, book profit exceeds Rs. 10 crore, the minimum alternate tax cannot exceed the following –

a. in the case of domestic company, (Rs. 160.50 lakh + book profit – Rs. 10 crore) + HEC; or

b. in the case of a foreign company, (Rs. 153 lakh + book profit – Rs. 10 crore) + HEC.

This marginal relief is applicable for the assessment year 2020-21 if book profit false in the following range –

Domestic company	Rs. 100 lakh – Rs. 101.2507 lakh
	Rs. 1000 lakh – Rs. 1009.0144 lakh
Foreign company	Rs. 100 lakh – Rs. 100.35419 lakh
	Rs. 1000 lakh – Rs. 1005.3412 lakh

MAT not applicable in the case of new lower corporate tax regime

302. Section 115JB has been amended with effect from the assessment year 2020-21 to provide that minimum alternate tax will not be applicable in the case of a person who has exercised the option referred to under section 115BAA or section 115BAB.

Amendment to section 92BA

303. Section 92BA provides the meaning of "specified domestic transaction" with reference to which the income is to be computed under section 92, having regard to arm's length price. The following transactions are covered within the meaning of "specified domestic transactions" if the aggregate of these transactions entered into by the assessee in a previous year exceeds Rs. 20 crore –

a. any transaction referred to in section 80A;

b. any transfer of goods or services referred to in section 80-IA(8);

c. any business transacted between the assessee and other person as referred to in section 80-IA(10);

d. any transaction, referred to in any other section under Chapter VI-A or section 10AA, to which provisions of section 80-IA(8)/(10) are applicable; or

e. any other transaction as may be prescribed.

• *Amendment* - With effect from the assessment year 2020-21, the aforesaid provisions of specified domestic transaction will also be applicable in the case of any business between the persons referred to in section 115BAB(4) [*see* para 202.2].

Amendment to section 115BA

304. Section 115BA was inserted by the Finance Act, 2016. It provides for lower tax rate of 25 per cent in the case of certain domestic manufacturing companies (incorporated on or after March 1, 2016). To get the benefit of this section, the assessee is required to submit an option. In this section, there is a provision to the effect that option (if once exercised) cannot be subsequently withdrawn for the same (or any other) assessment year. If this provision is continued, a domestic company which has opted for 25 per cent tax rate under section 115BA, will not be able to opt for lower tax regime of 22 per cent under section 115BAA.

• *Amendment* - In order to address the aforesaid issue, the Ordinance has amended section 115BA by inserting the following proviso in sub-section (4) –

> "Provided further that where the person exercises option under section 115BAB, the option under this section may be withdrawn".

However, there appears to be an apparent error as option under section 115BAB can be exercised only by a domestic company which is incorporated on or after October 1, 2019. If a company (which has already opted for section 115BA) cannot switch over to section 115BAB. It appears that the amendment is intended to permit switch over to lower tax regime of section 115BAA and inadvertently section 115BAB has been printed in the ordinance.

Amendment to section 115QA

305. Section 115QA provides for the levy of additional income-tax at the rate of 20 per cent (effective rate after surcharge and cess : 23.296 per cent) of the distributed income on account of buy-back of unlisted shares by the company. As additional income-tax has been levied at the level of company, the consequential income arising in the hands of shareholders has been exempted from tax under section 10(*34A*).

• *Amendment by the Finance (No. 2) Act, 2019* - In order to curb tax avoidance practices adopted by the listed companies, the scope of section 115QA was extended to all companies (including companies listed on a recognised stock exchange) by the Finance (No. 2) Act, 2019. However, the amendment is applicable if buy-back of shares takes place on or after July 5, 2019.

• *Further amendment by the Ordinance* - In order to provide relief to listed companies, which have made a public announcement of the buy-back of shares before July 5, 2019 but actual buy-back takes place on or after July 5, 2019, section 115QA has been amended. After the amendment (which is applicable with effect from July 5, 2019), provisions of section 115QA will not be applicable if the following conditions are satisfied –

1. It is buy-back of shares of listed company.

2. Public announcement pertaining to buy-back has been made before July 5, 2019 in accordance with the provisions of the SEBI (Buy-back of Securities) Regulations, 2018.

New depreciation rate for cars, buses, lorries or taxies

306. Depreciation rates have been revised *vide* Notification No. 69/2019, dated September 20, 2019. These rates are applicable form the assessment year 2020-21.

Nature of assets	*Depreciation rate*
Motor cars (other than those used in a business of running them on hire) acquired on or after August 23, 2019 but before April 1, 2020 and is put to use before April 1, 2020	30%
Motor buses, motor lorries and motor taxis used in a business of running them on hire, acquired on or after August 23, 2019 but before April 1, 2020 and is put to use before April 1, 2020	45%

306-E1 X & Co., LLP, engaged in technical consultancy. On April 1, 2019, it owns 2 cars (depreciated value of the block : Rs. 18,15,000, depreciation rate 15 per cent). One of the cars is transferred on August 10, 2019 for Rs. 4,50,000. Another car is purchased on September 1, 2019 for Rs. 42,00,000. There is no other depreciable asset owned by the assessee. Does it make any difference if the car purchased on September 1, 2019 is an old car ?

•

	Block of assets (15% depreciation rate) *Rs.*	*Block of assets (30% depreciation rate)* *Rs.*
Depreciated value of the block on April 1, 2019	18,15,000	*Nil*
Add: Actual cost of asset acquired during the financial year 2019-20	–	42,00,000
Less: Sale proceeds of asset transferred during the financial year 2019-20	4,50,000	–
Written down value of the block on March 31, 2020	13,65,000	42,00,000
Less: Depreciation for the previous year 2019-20	2,04,750	12,60,000
Depreciated value of the block on April 1, 2020	11,60,250	29,40,000
Add: Actual cost of asset acquired during the financial year 2020-21	–	–
Less: Sale proceeds of asset transferred during the financial year 2020-21	–	–
Written down value of the block on March 31, 2021	11,60,250	29,40,000
Less: Depreciation for the previous year 2020-21	1,74,038	8,82,000

Note - In the aforesaid Notification No. 69/2019, dated September 20, 2019, there is no requirement that to avail depreciation at the enhanced rate of 30% or 45%, the depreciable asset (*i.e.*, motor car, bus, lorry, etc.) should be a new asset. Consequently, the above calculations will be valid, even if the car purchased on September 1, 2019 is an old car.

Appendix 1 Taxation Laws (Amendment) Ordinance, 2019

[15 OF 2019]

Promulgated by the President in the Seventieth Year of the Republic of India.

An Ordinance further to amend the Income-tax Act, 1961 and the Finance (No. 2) Act, 2019.

WHEREAS Parliament is not in session and the President is satisfied that circumstances exist which render it necessary for him to take immediate action;

NOW, THEREFORE, in exercise of the powers conferred by clause (1) of article 123 of the Constitution, the President is pleased to promulgate the following Ordinance:—

CHAPTER I

PRELIMINARY

Short title and commencement.

1. (1) This Ordinance may be called the Taxation Laws (Amendment) Ordinance, 2019.

(2) Save as otherwise provided, this Ordinance shall come into force at once.

CHAPTER II

AMENDMENTS IN THE INCOME-TAX ACT, 1961

Amendment of section 92BA.

2. In section 92BA of the Income-tax Act, 1961 (43 of 1961) (hereafter in this Chapter referred to as the Income-tax Act), after clause (*v*), the following clause shall be inserted with effect from the 1st day of April, 2020, namely:—

"(*va*) any business transacted between the persons referred to in sub-section (4) of section 115BAB;".

Amendment of section 115BA.

3. In section 115BA of the Income-tax Act with effect from the 1st day of April, 2020,—

(*a*) for the marginal heading "Tax on income of certain domestic companies", the marginal heading "Tax on income of certain domestic manufacturing companies" shall be substituted;

(*b*) in sub-section (1), for the words "subject to the other provisions of this Chapter", the words, figures and letters "subject to the other provisions of this Chapter, other than those mentioned under section 115BAA and section 115BAB" shall be substituted;

(*c*) in sub-section (4), after the proviso, the following proviso shall be inserted, namely:—

"**Provided further** that where the person exercises option under section 115BAB, the option under this section may be withdrawn.".

Insertion of new sections 115BAA and 115BAB.

4. After section 115BA of the Income-tax Act, the following sections shall be inserted with effect from the 1st day of April, 2020, namely:—

'115BAA. *Tax on income of certain domestic companies.*—(1) Notwithstanding anything contained in this Act but subject to the provisions of this Chapter, other than those mentioned under section 115BA and section 115BAB, the income-tax payable in respect of the total income of a person, being a domestic company, for any previous year relevant to the assessment year beginning on or after the 1st day of April, 2020, shall, at the option of such person, be computed at the rate of twenty-two per cent, if the conditions contained in sub-section (2) are satisfied.

(2) For the purposes of sub-section (1), the following conditions shall apply subject to the condition that the total income of the company has been computed,—

(*i*) without any deduction under the provisions of section 10AA or clause (*iia*) of sub-section (1) of section 32 or section 32AD or section 33AB or section 33ABA or sub-clause (*ii*) or sub-clause (*iia*) or sub-clause (*iii*) of sub-section (1) or sub-section (2AA) or sub-section (2AB) of section 35 or section 35AD or section 35CCC or section 35CCD or under any provisions of Chapter VI-A under the heading *"C.— Deductions in respect of certain incomes"* other than the provisions of section 80JJAA;

(*ii*) without set off of any loss carried forward from any earlier assessment year if such loss is attributable to any of the deductions referred to in sub-clause (*i*); and

(*iii*) by claiming the depreciation, if any, under section 32, other than clause (*iia*) of sub-section (1) of the said section, determined in such manner as may be prescribed.

(3) The loss referred to in sub-clause (*ii*) of sub-section (2) shall be deemed to have been already given full effect to and no further deduction for such loss shall be allowed for any subsequent year.

(4) Nothing contained in this section shall apply unless the option is exercised by the person in the prescribed manner on or before the due date specified under sub-section (1) of section 139 for furnishing the returns of income for any previous year relevant to the assessment year commencing on or after 1st day of April, 2020 and such option once exercised shall apply to subsequent assessment years:

Provided that once the option has been exercised for any previous year, it cannot be subsequently withdrawn for the same or any other previous year.

115BAB. *Tax on income of certain new domestic manufacturing companies.*—(1) Notwithstanding anything contained in this Act but subject to the provisions of this Chapter, other than those mentioned under section 115BA and section 115BAA, the income-tax payable in respect of the total income of a person, being a domestic company, for any previous year relevant to the assessment year beginning on or after the 1st day of April, 2020, shall, at the option of such person, be computed at the rate of fifteen per cent, if the conditions contained in sub-section (2) are satisfied.

(2) For the purposes of sub-section (1), the following conditions shall apply, namely:—

(*a*) the company has been set-up and registered on or after the 1st day of October, 2019, and has commenced manufacturing on or before the 31st day of March, 2023, and,—

(*i*) is not formed by splitting up, or the reconstruction, of a business already in existence:

Provided that this condition shall not apply in respect of an undertaking which is formed as a result of the re-establishment, reconstruction or revival by the person of the business of any such undertaking as is referred to in section 33B, in the circumstances and within the period specified in the said section;

(*ii*) does not use any machinery or plant previously used for any purpose.

Explanation 1.—For the purposes of sub-clause (*ii*), any machinery or plant which was used outside India by any other person shall not be regarded as machinery or plant previously used for any purpose, if the following conditions are fulfilled, namely:—

(*A*) such machinery or plant was not, at any time previous to the date of the installation by the person, used in India;

(*B*) such machinery or plant is imported into India from any country outside India; and

(*C*) no deduction on account of depreciation in respect of such machinery or plant has been allowed or is allowable under the provisions of this Act in computing the total income of any person for any period prior to the date of the installation of machinery or plant by the person.

Explanation 2.—Where in the case of a person, any machinery or plant or any part thereof previously used for any purpose is put to use by the company and the total value of such machinery or plant or part thereof does not exceed twenty per cent of the total value of the machinery or plant used by the company, then, for the purposes of sub-clause (*ii*) of this clause, the condition specified therein shall be deemed to have been complied with;

(*iii*) does not use any building previously used as a hotel or a convention centre, as the case may be.

Explanation.—For the purposes of this sub-clause, the expressions "convention centre" and "hotel" shall have the meanings respectively assigned to them in clause (*a*) and clause (*b*) of sub-section (6) of section 80-ID;

(*b*) the company is not engaged in any business other than the business of manufacture or production of any article or thing and research in relation to, or distribution of, such article or thing manufactured or produced by it; and

(*c*) the total income of the company has been computed,—

(*i*) without any deduction under the provisions of section 10AA or clause (*iia*) of sub-section (1) of section 32 or section 32AD or section 33AB or section 33ABA or sub-clause (*ii*) or sub-clause (*iia*) or sub-clause (*iii*) of sub-section (1) or sub-section (2AA) or sub-section (2AB) of section 35 or section 35AD or section 35CCC or section 35CCD or under any provisions of Chapter VI-A under the heading "*C.—Deductions in respect of certain incomes*" other than the provisions of section 80JJAA;

(*ii*) without set off of any loss carried forward from any earlier assessment year if such loss is attributable to any of the deductions referred to in sub-clause (*i*); and

(*iii*) by claiming the depreciation under section 32, other than clause (*iia*) of sub-section (1) of the said section, determined in such manner as may be prescribed.

(3) The loss referred to in sub-clause (*ii*) of clause (*c*) of sub-section (2) shall be deemed to have been already given full effect to and no further deduction for such loss shall be allowed for any subsequent year.

(4) Where it appears to the Assessing Officer that, owing to the close connection between the company and any other person, or for any other reason, the course of business between them is so arranged that the business transacted between them produces to the company more than the ordinary profits which might be expected to arise, the Assessing Officer shall, in computing the profits and gains of such company for the purposes of this section, take the amount of profits as may be reasonably deemed to have been derived therefrom:

Provided that in case the aforesaid arrangement involves a specified domestic transaction referred to in section 92BA, the amount of profits from such transaction shall be determined having regard to arm's length price as defined in clause (*ii*) of section 92F.

(5) Nothing contained in this section shall apply unless the option is exercised by the person in the prescribed manner on or before the due date specified under sub-section (1) of section 139 for furnishing the first of the returns of income for any previous year relevant to the assessment year commencing on or after 1st day of April, 2020 and such option once exercised shall apply to subsequent assessment years:

Provided that once the option has been exercised for any previous year, it cannot be subsequently withdrawn for the same or any other previous year.'

Amendment of section 115JB.

5. In section 115JB of the Income-tax Act, with effect from the 1st day of April, 2020,—

(*a*) in sub-section (1), the following proviso shall be inserted, namely:—

"**Provided** that for the previous year relevant to the assessment year commencing on or after the 1st day of April, 2020, the provisions of this sub-section shall have effect as if for the words "eighteen and one-half per cent", occurring at both the places, the words "fifteen per cent" had been substituted.";

(*b*) for sub-section (5A), the following sub-section shall be substituted, namely:—

"(5A) The provisions of this section shall not apply to,—

(*i*) any income accruing or arising to a company from life insurance business referred to in section 115B;

(*ii*) a person who has exercised the option referred to under section 115BAA or section 115BAB.".

Amendment of section 115QA.

6. In section 115QA of the Income-tax Act, in sub-section (1), the following proviso shall be inserted and shall be deemed to have been inserted with effect from the 5th day of July, 2019, namely:—

"**Provided** that the provisions of this sub-section shall not apply to such buy-back of shares (being the shares listed on a recognised stock exchange), in respect of which public announcement has been made before 5th day of July, 2019 in accordance with the provisions of the Securities and Exchange Board of India (Buy-back of Securities) Regulations, 2018 made under the Securities and Exchange Board of India Act, 1992 (15 of 1992) as amended from time to time.

CHAPTER III

AMENDMENTS IN THE FINANCE (NO. 2) ACT, 2019

Amendment of Act No. 23 of 2019.

7. In section 2 of the Finance (No. 2) Act, 2019 [hereafter in this Chapter referred to as the Finance (No. 2) Act], in sub-section (9), with effect from the 1st day of April, 2019,—

(*a*) in third proviso,—

(*i*) in clause (*a*) for the words "the Income-tax Act", the words, figures and letters "the Income-tax Act, not having any income under section 115AD of the Income-tax Act" shall be inserted and shall be deemed to have been inserted;

(*ii*) after clause (*a*), the following clause shall be inserted and shall be deemed to have been inserted, namely:—

'(*aa*) in the case of every association of persons or body of individuals, whether incorporated or not, having income under section 115AD of the Income-tax Act,—

(*i*) at the rate of ten per cent of such "advance tax", where the total income exceeds fifty lakh rupees, but does not exceed one crore rupees;

(*ii*) at the rate of fifteen per cent of such "advance tax", where the total income exceeds one crore rupees but does not exceed two crore rupees;

(*iii*) at the rate of twenty five per cent of such "advance tax", where the total income [excluding the income of the nature referred to in clause (*b*) of sub-section (1) of section 115AD of the Income-tax Act] exceeds two crore rupees but does not exceed five crore rupees;

(*iv*) at the rate of thirty-seven per cent of such "advance tax", where the total income [excluding the income of the nature referred to in clause (*b*) of sub-section (1) of section 115AD of the Income-tax Act] exceeds five crore rupees;

(*v*) at the rate of fifteen per cent of such "advance tax", where the total income [including the income of the nature referred to in clause (*b*) of sub-section (1) of section 115AD of the Income-tax Act] exceeds two crore rupees but is not covered in sub-clauses (*iii*) and (*iv*):

Provided that in case where the total income includes any income chargeable under clause (*b*) of sub-section (1) of section 115AD of the Income-tax Act, the rate of surcharge on the advance tax computed on that part of income shall not exceed fifteen per cent;';

(*b*) in the fourth proviso, for the words, brackets and letter "in (*a*) above", the words, brackets and letters "in (*a*) and (*aa*) above" shall be substituted;

(*c*) after the eighth proviso, the following proviso shall be inserted, namely:—

'**Provided also** that in respect of any income chargeable to tax under section 115BAA or section 115BAB of the Income-tax Act, the tax computed under the first proviso shall be increased by a surcharge, for the purposes of the Union, calculated at the rate of ten per cent of such "advance tax".'

Amendment of Part II* of First Schedule.

8. In the First Schedule of the Finance (No. 2) Act, with effect from the 1st day of April, 2019,—

(*A*) in PART II, under the sub-heading "Surcharge on income-tax", in paragraph (*i*), in clause (*a*),—

(*i*) in sub-clauses I and II, after the words "aggregate of such incomes", the brackets, figures and letters "(including the income under the provisions of section 111A and section 112A of the Income-tax Act)" shall be inserted and shall be deemed to have been inserted;

*"and Part III" be added after "Part II".

(*ii*) in sub-clauses III and IV, after the words "aggregate of such incomes" the brackets, figures and letters "(excluding the income under the provisions of section 111A and section 112A of the Income-tax Act)" shall be inserted and shall be deemed to have been inserted;

(*iii*) after sub-clause IV, the following sub-clause shall be inserted and shall be deemed to have been inserted, namely:—

"*V.* at the rate of fifteen per cent of such tax, where the income or aggregate of such incomes (including the income under the provisions of section 111A and section 112A of the Income-tax Act) paid or likely to be paid and subject to the deduction exceeds two crore rupees, but is not covered under sub-clauses III and IV:

Provided that in case where the total income includes any income chargeable under section 111A and section 112A of the Income-tax Act, the rate of surcharge on the amount of income-tax deducted in respect of that part of income shall not exceed fifteen per cent;";

(*B*) in PART III, in Paragraph A, under the sub-heading "Surcharge on income-tax", after the opening portion,—

(*i*) in clauses (*a*) and (*b*), after the words "having a total income", the brackets, words, figures and letters "(including the income under the provisions of section 111A and section 112A)" shall be inserted;

(*ii*) in clauses (*c*) and (*d*), after the words "having a total income", the brackets, words, figures and letters "(excluding the income under the provisions of section 111A and section 112A)" shall be inserted;

(*iii*) after clause (*d*) and before the proviso, the following clause shall be inserted, namely:—

"(*e*) having a total income (including the income under the provisions of section 111A and section 112A) exceeding two crore rupees, but is not covered under clauses (*c*) and (*d*), shall be applicable at the rate of fifteen per cent of such income-tax:

Provided that in case where the total income includes any income chargeable under section 111A and section 112A of the Income-tax Act, the rate of surcharge on the amount of income-tax computed on that part of income shall not exceed fifteen per cent;".

Appendix 2 Modified Depreciation Rates

Block of Assets	*Depreciation allowed as per percentage of written down value*
1	2
(2) (*i*) Motor cars, other than those used in a business of running them on hire, acquired or put to use on or after the 1st day of April, 1990 except those covered under entry (*ii*);	15
(*ii*) Motor cars, other than those used in a business of running them on hire, acquired on or after the 23rd day of August, 2019 but before the 1st day of April, 2020 and is put to use before the 1st day of April, 2020.	30

Block of Assets	*Depreciation allowed as per percentage of written down value*
1	2
(*ii*) (*a*) Motor buses, motor lorries and motor taxis used in a business of running them on hire other than those covered under entry (*b*).	30
(*b*) Motor buses, motor lorries and motor taxis used in a business of running them on hire, acquired on or after the 23rd day of August, 2019 but before the 1st day of April, 2020 and is put to use before the 1st day of April, 2020.	45

॥ श्रीमत्कुञ्जबिहारिणे नमः ॥

GWB
Dedicated to
H.N.A.M.E-I.
H.K.A.K.

AMENDMENTS MADE BY FINANCE ACT, 2019 AND FINANCE (NO. 2) BILL, 2019

- Amendments made by the **Finance Act, 2019** and the **Finance (No. 2) Bill, 2019**, are duly incorporated in respective ***Chapters*** of the **Reckoner** and are appropriately highlighted.
- Comprehensive analysis of **amendments with illustrations** is given separately in ***Referencer 2 : Amendments at a glance.***

TAXMANN®'S

Direct Taxes Ready Reckoner

Dr. Vinod K. Singhania
Jeewan Singhania

Asst. Years
2019-20 & 2020-21
43rd Edition

First published : May 1978
Forty-third edition : July 2019
Price : ₹ 1375
Law stated in this book is as amended by the Finance (No. 2) Bill, 2019 (as passed by Lok Sabha)
Published by :
Taxmann Publications (P.) Ltd.
Sales & Marketing :
59/32, New Rohtak Road, New Delhi-110 005 India
Phone : +91-11-45562222
Website : www.taxmann.com
E-mail : sales@taxmann.com
Regd. Office :
21/35, West Punjabi Bagh, New Delhi-110 026 India
Printed at :
Tan Prints (India) Pvt. Ltd.
44 Km. Mile Stone, National Highway, Rohtak Road
Village Rohad, Distt. Jhajjar (Haryana) India
E-mail : sales@tanprints.com

Contents

PART B

TAX TABLES

PART C

MARKET QUOTATIONS

PART D

TAX TABLES OF PAST SIX YEARS

(*Assessment years 2013-14 to 2018-19*)

About the Author

Dr. Vinod K. Singhania got his Ph.D. from the Delhi School of Economics in 1976. His fields of special interest include all facets of corporate legislation and corporate economics especially the tax laws. Associated in different capacities with several professional institutes and business houses in India and abroad, Dr. Singhania is author of many popular books and software published by *Taxmann*. He has to his credit more than 300 research articles which have appeared in leading journals. He has been a resource person in over 750 seminars in India and abroad. He can be reached at *vks@taxmann.com*.

Abbreviations

AAR	:	*Authority for Advance Rulings*
ADT	:	*Avoidance of Double Taxation Agreement*
AIF	:	*Alternative investment fund*
AMT	:	*Alternate minimum tax under section 115JC*
AOPs	:	*Association of persons*
AY	:	*Assessment year*
BOI	:	*Body of individuals*
BSE	:	*Bombay Stock Exchange*
CBDT	:	*Central Board of Direct Taxes*
CCIT	:	*Chief Commissioner of Income-tax*
CII	:	*Cost Inflation Index*
CIT	:	*Commissioner of Income-tax*
CSR	:	*Corporate social responsibility*
CTT	:	*Commodities transaction tax*
DPIIT	:	*Department for Promotion of Industry and Internal Trade*
DTAA	:	*Double Taxation Avoidance Agreement*
EC	:	*Education cess*
FBT	:	*Fringe benefit tax*
FIFO	:	*First in First out*
FII	:	*Foreign Institutional Investor*
FITL	:	*Funded Interest Term Loan*
FMV	:	*Fair market value*
FY	:	*Financial year*
GAAR	:	*General Anti-Avoidance Rules*
GST	:	*Goods and services tax*
GTI	:	*Gross total income*
HEC	:	*Health and education cess*
HUF	:	*Hindu undivided family*
ICDS	:	*Income Computation and Disclosure Standards notified by the Central Government under section 145(2)*
Inv IT	:	*Infrastructure Investment Trust*
IT	:	*Income-tax*
IT + HEC	:	*Income-tax* plus *health and education cess*
IT + SC	:	*Income-tax* plus *surcharge on income-tax*
IT + SC + EC	:	*Income-tax* plus *surcharge on income-tax* plus *education cess on income-tax and surcharge*
IT + SC + EC + SHEC	:	*Income-tax* plus *surcharge on income-tax* plus *education cess* plus *secondary and higher education cess on income-tax and surcharge*
IT + SC + HEC	:	*Income-tax* plus *surcharge on income-tax* plus *health and education cess on income-tax and surcharge*
IT RATE	:	*Income-tax rate*
ITAT	:	*Income Tax Appellate Tribunal*
KVP	:	*Kisan Vikas Patra*
LLP	:	*Limited liability partnership*
LTC	:	*Leave travel concession*
MAT	:	*Minimum alternate tax under section 115JB*

NAV	:	*Net asset value*
NI	:	*Net income*
NPS	:	*National Pension System*
NSC	:	*National Stock Exchange*
PAN	:	*Permanent Account Number*
POEM	:	*Place of Effective Management*
PPF	:	*Public Provident Fund*
RBI	:	*Reserve Bank of India*
REIT	:	*Real Estate Investment Trust*
SI	:	*Salary income*
SEBI	:	*Security and Exchange Board of India*
SEZ	:	*Special Economic Zone*
SC	:	*Surcharge*
SHEC	:	*Secondary and higher education cess*
STT	:	*Securities transaction tax*
TAN	:	*Tax deduction/collection account number*
TCS	:	*Tax collection at source*
TDS	:	*Tax deduction at source*
VCC	:	*Venture capital company*
VCF	:	*Venture capital fund*
VCU	:	*Venture capital undertaking*
WT	:	*Wealth-tax*

(*All section references are to the Income-tax Act, 1961, unless otherwise stated*)

Section-wise Index

R-1

Tax rates

ASSESSMENT YEARS 2019-20 AND 2020-21

Tax liability - How to find out

Tax liability for the assessment years 2019-20 and 2020-21 shall be calculated as follows :—

	Rs.	*Rs.*
1. Find out gross total income	—	
2. Less: Deductions under sections 80C to 80U	—	
3. Find out net income [(*1*) – (*2*)]		—
4. Divide the net income into the following—		
4.1 Income subject to special tax rates mentioned in para 0.1-6	—	
4.2 Remaining income subject to normal rates	—	
5. Find out income-tax on net income—		
5.1 Tax on income specified in 4.1 (*supra*) at the rates given in para 0.1-6	—	
5.2 Tax on remaining income at the normal rate given in para 0.1-1 or 0.1-2 or 0.1-3 or 0.1-4 or 0.1-5	—	—
6. Less: Rebate under section 87A [applicable in the case of a resident individual having net income not exceeding Rs. 3.50 lakh (for the assessment year 2019-20) or Rs. 5 lakh (for the assessment year 2020-21)]		—
7. Income-tax after rebate under section 87A [(*5*) – (*6*)]		—
8. Add : Surcharge[2] @ 0%, 2%, 5%, 7%, 10%, 12%, 15%, 25% or 37% of (*7*)		—
9. Find out the total [(*7*)+(*8*)]		—
10. Add : Health and education cess (HEC) [4% of (*9*)]		
11. Find out the total [(*9*) + (*10*)]		—
12. Deduct : Rebate under section 86, 89, 90, 90A or 91		—
13. Tax liability [(*11*)–(*12*)]*		—
14. Add: Interest/penalty, etc.		—
15. Less: Pre-paid taxes [*i.e.*, advance tax, self-assessment tax, TDS, TCS, MAT/AMT credit]		—
16. Tax payable [(*13*) + (*14*) – (*15*)]		—

Notes :

1. (*2*) cannot exceed (*1*).

2. Surcharge is applicable as a % of income-tax [*i.e.*, (*7*)]. These rates are—

* In the case of a corporate-assessee, it cannot be less than minimum alternate tax. In the case of any other taxpayer, it cannot be less than alternate minimum tax.

	Net income range	*Assessment year 2019-20*	*Assessment year 2020-21*
Individuals/HUF/AOP/BOI/ artificial juridical person	0 – Rs. 50 lakh Rs. 50 lakh – Rs. 1 crore Rs. 1 crore – Rs. 2 crore Rs. 2 crore – Rs. 5 crore Above Rs. 5 crore	*Nil* 10% 15% 15% 15%	*Nil* 10% 15% 25% 37%
Firm/co-operative society/ local authority	0 – Rs. 1 crore Above Rs. 1 crore	*Nil* 12%	*Nil* 12%
Domestic company	0 – Rs. 1 crore Rs. 1 crore – Rs. 10 crore Above Rs. 10 crore	*Nil* 7% 12%	*Nil* 7% 12%
Foreign company	0 – Rs. 1 crore Rs. 1 crore – Rs. 10 crore Above Rs. 10 crore	*Nil* 2% 5%	*Nil* 2% 5%

Income-tax

0.1-1 ***Individuals, Hindu undivided families, AOPs, BOIs*** - The tax rates applicable to individuals are also applicable to a Hindu undivided family, an association of persons, body of individuals or an artificial juridical person. The rates applicable for the assessment years 2019-20 and 2020-21 are as follows :

0.1-1a *ASSESSMENT YEAR 2019-20* - Tax rates for the assessment year 2019-20 are given below—

• For a resident senior citizen (who is 60 years or more at any time during the previous year but less than 80 years on the last day of the previous year, *i.e.*, born on or after April 2, 1939 but before April 2, 1959)–

Net income range	*Income-tax rates‡*	*Surcharge*	*Health and education cess (HEC)*	*Tax table (page No.)*
Up to Rs. 3,00,000	*Nil*	*Nil*	*Nil*	—
Rs. 3,00,000 – Rs. 5,00,000	5% of (total income *minus* Rs. 3,00,000) [*see* Note 1]	*Nil*	4% of income-tax	B-3 to B-8
Rs. 5,00,000 – Rs. 10,00,000	Rs. 10,000 + 20% of (total income *minus* Rs. 5,00,000)	*Nil*	4% of income-tax	B-9 to B-12
Rs. 10,00,000 – Rs. 50,00,000	Rs. 1,10,000 + 30% of (total income *minus* Rs. 10,00,000)	*Nil*	4% of income-tax	B-13
Rs. 50,00,000 - Rs. 1,00,00,000	Rs. 13,10,000 + 30% of (total income *minus* Rs. 50,00,000)	10% of income-tax [*see* Note 2]	4% of income-tax and surcharge	B-14 and B-15
Above Rs.1,00,00,000	Rs. 28,10,000 + 30% of (total income *minus* Rs.1,00,00,000)	15% of income-tax [*see* Note 2]	4% of income-tax and surcharge	B-16 and B-17

• For a resident super senior citizen (who is 80 years or more at any time during the previous year, *i.e.*, born before April 2, 1939)—

Net income range	*Income-tax rates‡*	*Surcharge*	*Health and education cess (HEC)*	*Tax table (page No.)*
Up to Rs. 5,00,000	*Nil*	*Nil*	*Nil*	—
Rs. 5,00,000 – Rs. 10,00,000	20% of (total income *minus* Rs. 5,00,000)	*Nil*	4% of income-tax	B-9 to B-12
Rs. 10,00,000 – Rs. 50,00,000	Rs. 1,00,000 + 30% of (total income *minus* Rs. 10,00,000)	*Nil*	4% of income-tax	B-13

‡*See* also para 0.1-6.

Net income range	*Income-tax rates‡*	*Surcharge*	*Health and education cess (HEC)*	*Tax table (page No.)*
Rs. 50,00,000 - Rs. 1,00,00,000	Rs. 13,00,000 + 30% of (total income *minus* Rs. 50,00,000)	10% of income-tax [*see* Note 2]	4% of income-tax and surcharge	B-14 and B-15
Above Rs. 1,00,00,000	Rs. 28,00,000 + 30% of (total income *minus* Rs. 1,00,00,000)	15% of income-tax [*see* Note 2]	4% of income-tax and surcharge	B-16 and B-17

• For any other resident individual (born on or after April 2, 1959), any non-resident individual, every HUF/AOP/BOI/artificial juridical person—

Net income range	*Income-tax rates‡*	*Surcharge*	*Health and education cess (HEC)*	*Tax table (page No.)*
Up to Rs. 2,50,000	*Nil*	*Nil*	*Nil*	—
Rs. 2,50,000 – Rs. 5,00,000	5% of (total income *minus* Rs. 2,50,000) [*see* Note 1]	*Nil*	4% of income-tax	B-2 to B-8
Rs. 5,00,000 – Rs. 10,00,000	Rs. 12,500 + 20% of (total income *minus* Rs. 5,00,000)	*Nil*	4% of income-tax	B-9 to B-12
Rs. 10,00,000 – Rs. 50,00,000	Rs. 1,12,500 + 30% of (total income *minus* Rs. 10,00,000)	*Nil*	4% of income-tax	B-13
Rs. 50,00,000 - Rs. 1,00,00,000	Rs. 13,12,500 + 30% of (total income *minus* Rs. 50,00,000)	10% of income-tax [*see* Note 2]	4% of income-tax and surcharge	B-14 and B-15
Above Rs. 1,00,00,000	Rs. 28,12,500 + 30% of (total income *minus* Rs. 1,00,00,000)	15% of income-tax [*see* Note 2]	4% of income-tax and surcharge	B-16 and B-17

Notes :

1. Rebate under section 87A - A resident individual (whose net income does not exceed Rs. 3,50,000) can avail rebate under section 87A. It is deductible from income-tax before calculating health and education cess. The amount of rebate is 100 per cent of income-tax or Rs. 2,500, whichever is less.

2. Surcharge - Surcharge is 10 per cent of income-tax if net income is more than Rs. 50 lakh but not more than Rs. 1 crore. If net income is more than Rs. 1 crore, surcharge is 15 per cent of income-tax. Surcharge is subject to a marginal relief. If net income exceeds Rs. 50 lakh, the amount payable as income-tax and surcharge shall not exceed the total amount payable as income-tax on total income of Rs. 50 lakh by more than the amount of income that exceeds Rs. 50 lakh. Likewise, if net income exceeds Rs. 1 crore, the amount payable as income-tax and surcharge shall not exceed the total amount payable as income-tax and surcharge on total income of Rs. 1 crore by more than the amount of income that exceeds Rs. 1 crore.

3. Health and education cess (HEC) - It is 4 per cent of income-tax and surcharge.

TAX TABLES : For tax tables, *see* pages B-1 to B-17.

• *Alternate minimum tax* - Tax payable by a non-corporate assessee cannot be less than 18.5 per cent† (+SC+HEC) of "adjusted total income" as per section 115JC

0.1-1b *ASSESSMENT YEAR 2020-21* - Tax rates for the assessment year 2020-21 are given below—

• For a resident senior citizen (who is 60 years or more at any time during the previous year but less than 80 years on the last day of the previous year, *i.e.*, born on or after April 2, 1940 but before April 2, 1960)–

Net income range	*Income-tax rates‡*	*Surcharge*	*Health and education cess (HEC)*	*Tax table (page No.)*
Up to Rs. 3,00,000	*Nil*	*Nil*	*Nil*	—
Rs. 3,00,000 – Rs. 5,00,000	5% of (total income *minus* Rs. 3,00,000) [*see* Note 1]	*Nil*	4% of income-tax	B-19 to B-24

‡*See* also para 0.1-6.

† 9 per cent, if the assessee is a unit located in an International Financial Services Centre and derives its income solely in convertible foreign exchange.

Net income range	*Income-tax rates‡*	*Surcharge*	*Health and education cess (HEC)*	*Tax table (page No.)*
Rs. 5,00,000 – Rs. 10,00,000	Rs. 10,000 + 20% of (total income *minus* Rs. 5,00,000)	*Nil*	4% of income-tax	B-25 to B-28
Rs. 10,00,000 – Rs. 50,00,000	Rs. 1,10,000 + 30% of (total income *minus* Rs. 10,00,000)	*Nil*	4% of income-tax	B-29
Rs. 50,00,000 - Rs. 1,00,00,000	Rs. 13,10,000 + 30% of (total income *minus* Rs. 50,00,000)	10% of income-tax [*see* Note 2]	4% of income-tax and surcharge	B-30 and B-31
Rs. 1,00,00,000 - Rs. 2,00,00,000	Rs. 28,10,000 + 30% of (total income *minus* Rs.1,00,00,000)	15% of income-tax [*see* Note 2]	4% of income-tax and surcharge	B-32 and B-33
Rs. 2,00,00,000 - Rs. 5,00,00,000	Rs. 58,10,000 + 30% of (total income *minus* Rs. 2,00,00,000)	25% of income-tax [*see* Note 2]	4% of income-tax and surcharge	B-34 and B-35
Above Rs. 5,00,00,000	Rs. 1,48,10,000 + 30% of (total income *minus* Rs. 5,00,00,000)	37% of income-tax [*see* Note 2]	4% of income-tax and surcharge	B-36 and B-37

• For a resident super senior citizen (who is 80 years or more at any time during the previous year, *i.e.*, born before April 2, 1940)—

Net income range	*Income-tax rates‡*	*Surcharge*	*Health and education cess (HEC)*	*Tax table (page No.)*
Up to Rs. 5,00,000	*Nil*	*Nil*	*Nil*	—
Rs. 5,00,000 – Rs. 10,00,000	20% of (total income *minus* Rs. 5,00,000)	*Nil*	4% of income-tax	B-25 to B-28
Rs. 10,00,000 – Rs. 50,00,000	Rs. 1,00,000 + 30% of (total income *minus* Rs. 10,00,000)	*Nil*	4% of income-tax	B-29
Rs. 50,00,000 - Rs. 1,00,00,000	Rs. 13,00,000 + 30% of (total income *minus* Rs. 50,00,000)	10% of income-tax [*see* Note 2]	4% of income-tax and surcharge	B-30 and B-31
Rs. 1,00,00,000 – Rs. 2,00,00,000	Rs. 28,00,000 + 30% of (total income *minus* Rs.1,00,00,000)	15% of income-tax [*see* Note 2]	4% of income-tax and surcharge	B-32 and B-33
Rs. 2,00,00,000 – Rs. 5,00,00,000	Rs. 58,00,000 + 30% of (total income *minus* Rs. 2,00,00,000)	25% of income-tax [*see* Note 2]	4% of income-tax and surcharge	B-34 and B-35
Above Rs. 5,00,00,000	Rs. 1,48,00,000 + 30% of (total income *minus* Rs. 5,00,00,000)	37% of income-tax [*see* Note 2]	4% of income-tax and surcharge	B-36 and B-37

• For any other resident individual (born on or after April 2, 1960), any non-resident individual, every HUF/AOP/BOI/artificial juridical person—

Net income range	*Income-tax rates‡*	*Surcharge*	*Health and education cess (HEC)*	*Tax table (page No.)*
Up to Rs. 2,50,000	*Nil*	*Nil*	*Nil*	—
Rs. 2,50,000 – Rs. 5,00,000	5% of (total income *minus* Rs. 2,50,000) [*see* Note 1]	*Nil*	4% of income-tax	B-18 to B-24
Rs. 5,00,000 – Rs. 10,00,000	Rs. 12,500 + 20% of (total income *minus* Rs. 5,00,000)	*Nil*	4% of income-tax	B-25 to B-28
Rs. 10,00,000 – Rs. 50,00,000	Rs. 1,12,500 + 30% of (total income *minus* Rs. 10,00,000)	*Nil*	4% of income-tax	B-29
Rs. 50,00,000 - Rs. 1,00,00,000	Rs. 13,12,500 + 30% of (total income *minus* Rs. 50,00,000)	10% of income-tax [*see* Note 2]	4% of income-tax and surcharge	B-30 and B-31

‡*See* also para 0.1-6.

Net income range	*Income-tax rates‡*	*Surcharge*	*Health and education cess (HEC)*	*Tax table (page No.)*
Rs. 1,00,00,000 – Rs. 2,00,00,000	Rs. 28,12,500 + 30% of (total income *minus* Rs.1,00,00,000)	15% of income-tax [*see* Note 2]	4% of income-tax and surcharge	B-32 and B-33
Rs. 2,00,00,000 – Rs. 5,00,00,000	Rs. 58,12,500 + 30% of (total income *minus* Rs. 2,00,00,000)	25% of income-tax [*see* Note 2]	4% of income-tax and surcharge	B-34 and B-35
Above Rs. 5,00,00,000	Rs. 1,48,12,500 + 30% of (total income *minus* Rs. 5,00,00,000)	37% of income-tax [*see* Note 2]	4% of income-tax and surcharge	B-36 and B-37

Notes :

1. Rebate under section 87A - A resident individual (whose net income does not exceed Rs. 5,00,000) can avail rebate under section 87A. It is deductible from income-tax before calculating health and education cess. The amount of rebate is 100 per cent of income-tax or Rs. 12,500, whichever is less.

2. Surcharge - Surcharge is 10 per cent of income-tax if net income is more than Rs. 50 lakh but not more than Rs. 1 crore. If net income is more than Rs. 1 crore but not more than Rs. 2 crore, surcharge is 15 per cent of income-tax. If net income is more than Rs. 2 crore but not more than Rs. 5 crore, surcharge is 25 per cent of income-tax. If net income is more than Rs. 5 crore, surcharge is 37 per cent of income-tax. Surcharge is subject to a marginal relief. If net income exceeds Rs. 50 lakh, the amount payable as income-tax and surcharge shall not exceed the total amount payable as income-tax on total income of Rs. 50 lakh by more than the amount of income that exceeds Rs. 50 lakh. Moreover, if net income is in the range of Rs. 1 crore – Rs. 2 crore, the amount payable as income-tax and surcharge shall not exceed the total amount payable as income-tax and surcharge on total income of Rs. 1 crore by more than the amount of income that exceeds Rs. 1 crore. Similarly, if net income is in the range of Rs. 2 crore – Rs. 5 crore, the amount payable as income-tax and surcharge shall not exceed the total amount payable as income-tax and surcharge on total income of Rs. 2 crore by more than the amount of income that exceeds Rs. 2 crore. Likewise, if net income is above Rs. 5 crore, the amount payable as income-tax and surcharge shall not exceed the total amount payable as income-tax and surcharge on total income of Rs. 5 crore by more than the amount of income that exceeds Rs. 5 crore.

3. Health and education cess (HEC) - It is 4 per cent of income-tax and surcharge.

TAX TABLES : For tax tables, *see* pages B-1 and B-18 to B-37.

- *Alternate minimum tax* - Tax payable by a non-corporate assessee cannot be less than 18.5 per cent† (+SC+HEC) of "adjusted total income" as per section 115JC

0.1-2 ***Firms*** - A firm is taxable at the rate of 30 per cent for the assessment years 2019-20 and 2020-21 [*see* also para 0.1-6].

Surcharge - Surcharge is 12 per cent of income-tax if net income exceeds Rs. 1 crore. It is subject to marginal relief (in the case of a firm having a net income of exceeding Rs. 1 crore, the amount payable as income tax and surcharge shall not exceed the total amount payable as income-tax on total income of Rs. 1 crore by more than the amount of income that exceeds Rs. 1 crore).

Health and education cess - It is 4 per cent of income-tax and surcharge.

TAX TABLES : For tax tables, *see* pages B-38 to B-40.

- *Alternate minimum tax* - Tax payable by firm cannot be less than 18.5 per cent† [+ SC + HEC] of "adjusted total income" as per section 115JC.

0.1-3 ***Companies*** - For the assessment years 2019-20 and 2020-21 the following rates of income-tax are applicable:

‡*See* also para 0.1-6.

† 9 per cent, if the assessee is a unit located in an International Financial Services Centre and derives its income solely in convertible foreign exchange.

Company	*Rate of income-tax (per cent) [see also para 0.1-6]*	
	Assessment year 2019-20	*Assessment year 2020-21*
In the case of a domestic company -		
- where its total turnover or gross receipt during the previous year 2016-17 does not exceed Rs. 250 crore	25	*NA*
- where its total turnover or gross receipt during the previous year 2017-18 does not exceed Rs. 400 crore	*NA*	25
- any other domestic company	30	30
In the case of a foreign company -		
- royalty received from Government or an Indian concern in pursuance of an agreement made by it with the Indian concern after March 31, 1961, but before April 1, 1976, or fees for rendering technical services in pursuance of an agreement made by it after February 29, 1964 but before April 1, 1976 and where such agreement has, in either case, been approved by the Central Government	50	50
- other income	40	40

Surcharge - Surcharge is applicable at the rates given below—

	If net income does not exceed Rs. 1 crore	*If net income is in the range of Rs. 1 crore – Rs. 10 crore*	*If net income exceeds Rs. 10 crore*
Domestic company	*Nil*	7%*	12%**
Foreign company	*Nil*	2%*	5%**

**Marginal relief* - In the case of a company having a net income of exceeding Rs. 1 crore, the amount payable as income-tax and surcharge shall not exceed the total amount payable as income-tax on total income of Rs. 1 crore by more than the amount of income that exceeds Rs. 1 crore.

***Marginal relief* - In the case of a company having a net income of exceeding Rs. 10 crore, the amount payable as income-tax and surcharge shall not exceed the total amount payable as income-tax and surcharge on total income of Rs. 10 crore by more than the amount of income that exceeds Rs. 10 crore.

Health and education cess - It is 4 per cent of income-tax and surcharge.

TAX TABLES : For tax tables, *see* pages B-41 to B-48.

0.1-3a *MINIMUM ALTERNATE TAX* - The following rate of minimum alternate tax shall be applicable—

	If book profit does not exceed Rs.1 crore				*If book profit is in the range of Rs. 1 crore – Rs. 10 crore*				*If book profit exceeds Rs. 10 crore*			
	IT	*SC*	*HEC*	*Total*	*IT*	*SC*	*HEC*	*Total*	*IT*	*SC*	*HEC*	*Total*
Domestic company	18.5†	–	0.74	19.24	18.5†	1.295	0.7918	20.5868	18.5†	2.22	0.8288	21.5488
Foreign company	18.5†	–	0.74	19.24	18.5†	0.37	0.7548	19.6248	18.5†	0.925	0.777	20.202

Note - If book profit of a company exceeds Rs. 1 crore but does not exceed Rs. 10 crore, the minimum alternate tax cannot exceed the following : (Rs. 18.5 lakh + book profit – Rs. 1 crore) + HEC. If, however, book profit exceeds Rs. 10 crore, the minimum alternate tax cannot exceed the following –

a. in the case of domestic company, (Rs. 197.95 lakh + book profit – Rs. 10 crore) + HEC; or

b. in the case of a foreign company, (Rs. 188.7 lakh + book profit – Rs. 10 crore) + HEC.

† 9 per cent, if the assessee is a unit located in an International Financial Services Centre and derives its income solely in convertible foreign exchange.

0.1-4 ***Co-operative societies*** - The following rates are applicable to a co-operative society for the assessment years 2019-20 and 2020-21—

(Per cent)

Net income range	*Rate of income-tax [See also 0.1-6]*
Up to Rs. 10,000	10
Rs. 10,000 - Rs. 20,000	20
Above Rs. 20,000	30

Surcharge - Surcharge is 12 per cent of income-tax if net income exceeds Rs. 1 crore. It is subject to marginal relief (in the case of a co-operative society having a net income of exceeding Rs. 1 crore, the amount payable as income tax and surcharge shall not exceed the total amount payable as income-tax on total income of Rs. 1 crore by more than the amount of income that exceeds Rs. 1 crore).

Health and education cess - It is 4 per cent of income-tax and surcharge.

TAX TABLES : For tax tables, *see* pages B-49 and B-50.

• *Alternate minimum tax* - Tax payable by firm cannot be less than 18.5 per cent† [+ SC + HEC] of "adjusted total income" as per section 115JC.

0.1-5 ***Local authorities*** - Local authorities are taxable at the rate of 30 per cent.

Surcharge - Surcharge is 12 per cent of income-tax if net income exceeds Rs. 1 crore. It is subject to marginal relief (in the case of a local authority having a net income of exceeding Rs. 1 crore, the amount payable as income tax and surcharge shall not exceed the total amount payable as income-tax on total income of Rs. 1 crore by more than the amount of income that exceeds Rs. 1 crore).

Health and education cess - It is 4 per cent of income-tax and surcharge.

• *Alternate minimum tax* - Tax payable by firm cannot be less than 18.5 per cent† [+ SC + HEC] of "adjusted total income" as per section 115JC.

0.1-6 ***Tax rates specified in the Income-tax Act*** - The following incomes are taxable at the rates specified by the Income-tax Act and not at the rates mentioned in paras 0.1-1 to 0.1-5 *supra* :

Section	*Income*	*Income-tax rates**
(1)	*(2)*	*(3)*
111A	Short-term capital gains	15
112	Long-term capital gains	20‡
112A	Long-term capital gain in excess of Rs. 1 lakh	10
115A(1) (*a*)(*i*)	Dividend received by a foreign company or a non-resident non-corporate assessee [*it is not applicable in the case of dividends referred to in section 115-O]	20*
115A(1) (*a*)(*ii*)	Interest received by a foreign company or a non-resident non-corporate assessee from Government or an Indian concern on moneys borrowed or debt incurred by Government or the Indian concern in foreign currency	20
115A(1) (*a*)(*iia*)	Interest received from an infrastructure debt fund referred to in section 10(*47*)	5
115A(1) (*a*)(*iiaa*)	Interest received from an Indian company specified in section 194LC	5
115A(1) (*a*)(*iiab*)/ (*iiac*)	Interest of the nature and extent referred to in section 194LD or section 194LBA	5
115A (1)(*b*)	Royalty or fees for technical services (not referred to in section 44DA) received by a foreign company or non-resident non-corporate assessee from an Indian concern or Government in pursuance of an agreement approved by the Central Government if such agreement is made at any time after March 31, 1976	10

† 9 per cent, if the assessee is a unit located in an International Financial Services Centre and derives its income solely in convertible foreign exchange.

*These rates are subject to SC + HEC [*see* Notes at the end of Table].

‡In some cases, tax rate is 10% [*see* para 72.1]

Section	*Income*	*Income-tax rates*†
(1)	*(2)*	*(3)*
115AB	Income of an overseas financial organisation on transfer of units purchased in foreign currency being long-term capital gains	10
115AC	Income from bonds or Global Depository Receipts[1] or on bonds or Global Depository Receipts[1] of a public sector company sold by the Government and purchased in foreign currency or long-term capital gains arising from their transfer *[not applicable in the case of dividends referred to in section 115-O]	10*
115ACA	Income from Global Depository Receipts held by a resident individual who is an employee of an Indian company engaged in information technology software/services††	
	❑ Dividend [other than dividend referred to in section 115-O] on Global Depository Receipts issued under employees stock option scheme and purchased in foreign currency	10
	❑ Long-term capital gain on transfer of such receipts	10
115AD	Income in respect of securities received by a Foreign Institutional Investor as specified[2] by the Government	
	❑ Short-term capital gain covered by section 111A	15
	❑ Any other short-term capital gain	30
	❑ Long-term capital gain	10
	❑ Long-term capital gain (referred to in section 112A) in excess of Rs. 1 lakh	10
	❑ Interest referred to in section 194LD	5
	❑ Other income [*not applicable in the case of dividends referred to in section 115-O]	20*
115B	Profits and gains of life insurance business	12.5
115BA	Income of certain domestic companies‡	25
115BB	Winnings from lotteries, crossword puzzles, or race including horse race (not being income from the activity of owning and maintaining race horse) or card game and other game of any sort or from gambling or betting of any form or nature	30

†These rates are subject to SC + HEC [*see* Notes at the end of Table].

††An employee of an Indian company engaged in specified knowledge based industry or service or an employee of its subsidiary engaged in specified knowledge based industry or service.

1. Issued by an Indian company in accordance with the Foreign Currency Convertible Bonds and Ordinary Shares (Through Depository Receipt Mechanism) Scheme, 1993/Issue of Foreign Currency Exchangeable Bonds Scheme, 2008.

2. For notified Foreign Institutional Investor, *see* Taxmann's *Direct Taxes Circulars,* 2011 edition.

‡ Under section 115BA, a domestic company (which satisfies the following conditions) may opt for tax rate of 25 per cent -

- It is a set-up and registered on or after March 1, 2016.
- The company is not engaged in any business other than the business of manufacture or production of any article or thing and research in relation to (or distribution of) such article or thing manufactured or produced by it.
- Total income of the company is computed without claiming additional depreciation and deduction under sections 10AA, 32AC, 32AD, 33AB, 33ABA, 35(1)(*ii*)/(*iia*)/(*iii*)/35(2AA)/(2AB), 35AC, 35AD, 35CCC, 35CCD, sections 80H to 80TT (not being section 80JJAA).
- Total income of the company is calculated after claiming depreciation (rate cannot be more than 40 per cent) and without adjusting brought forward loss from any earlier year (if such loss pertains to any deduction under the aforesaid sections). Moreover, such loss will not be carried forward.
- This option shall be exercised on or before the due date for furnishing the first of the returns of income, which the company is required to furnish under the Act. This option should be exercised by electronically furnishing Form No. 10-IB (under digital signature or electronic verification code). Once the company has exercised the option for any previous year, it cannot be subsequently withdrawn for the same or any other previous year.

Section	Income	Income-tax rates†
(1)	*(2)*	*(3)*
115BBA(1) (*a*)/(*b*)	Income of a non-resident foreign citizen sportsman for participation in any game in India or received by way of advertisement or for contribution of articles relating to any game or sport in India or income of a non-resident sport association by way of guarantee money	20
115BBA(1) (*c*)	Income of non-resident foreign citizen (being an entertainer) for performance in India	20
115BBC	Anonymous donation	30
115BBD	Income of an Indian company by way of dividends declared, distributed or paid by a specified foreign company (in which the Indian company holds 26 per cent or more of equity share capital)	15
115BBDA	Aggregate dividend from domestic companies in excess of Rs. 10 lakh [excluding deemed dividend under section 2(*22*)(*e*)]	10
115BBE	Income referred to in sections 68, 69, 69A, 69B, 69C and 69D	60
115BBF	Income by way of royalty in respect of a patent developed and registered in India (received by a resident assessee who is a patentee)	10
115BBG	Income from transfer of carbon credits	10
115E	Income from foreign exchange assets and capital gains of non-resident Indian *a.* income from foreign exchange asset [*not applicable in the case of dividends referred to in section 115-O] *b.* long-term capital gain	 20* 10
115JB	Minimum alternate tax - Book profit of a company (not being a company given below) - Book profit of a company located in an International Financial Services Centre and derives its income solely in convertible foreign exchange	 18.5 9
115JC	Alternative minimum tax in the case of non-corporate taxpayer – - Adjusted total income (not being a unit given below) - Adjusted total income of a unit located in an International Financial Services Centre and derives its income solely in convertible foreign exchange	 18.5 9
115TD	Accreted income of certain trusts and institutions [*taxable at maximum marginal rate (MMR) of tax which is 35.88 per cent (for the assessment year 2019-20) and 42.744 per cent (for the assessment year 2020-21)]	MMR*
115UB(4)	Business income of a investment fund – ❑ Where investment fund is a domestic company or firm ❑ Where investment fund is a foreign company ❑ Where investment fund is any other person [*taxable at maximum marginal rate (MMR) of tax which is 35.88 per cent (for the assessment year 2019-20) and 42.744 per cent (for the assessment year 2020-21)]	 30 40 MMR*
161(1A)	Profits and gains of a business in the case of a trust	30
164	Income of private discretionary trust where shares of beneficiaries are indeterminate	30
164A	Income of an oral trust	30
167A	Income of a firm	30

† These rates are subject to SC + HEC [*see* Notes at the end of Table].

Section	*Income*	*Income-tax rates*†
(1)	*(2)*	*(3)*
167B	Income of an association of persons or body of individuals if shares of members are unknown	30
167B(2)	Income of an association of persons (AOP) or body of individuals (BOI) if total income of any member (excluding share from AOP/BOI) exceeds the maximum amount not chargeable to tax [*if total income of any member of the AOP /BOI is chargeable to tax at a rate higher than maximum marginal rate, then tax shall be charged on that portion of the total income of the AOP/BOI which is relatable to the share of such member at such higher rate and the balance of the total income is taxable at a maximum marginal rate] [maximum marginal rate of tax is 35.88 per cent (for the assessment year 2019-20) and 42.744 per cent (for the assessment year 2020-21)]	30*

Notes :

1. *Surcharge* - The above income-tax rates are subject to surcharge. Surcharge under section 115BBE is 25 per cent of income-tax. In other cases, surcharge is calculated as a percentage (given below) of income-tax –

	Net income‡ *range*	*Assessment year 2019-20*	*Assessment year 2020-21*
Individuals/HUF/AOP/BOI/ artificial juridical person	0 – Rs. 50 lakh	*Nil*	*Nil*
	Rs. 50 lakh – Rs. 1 crore	10%	10%
	Rs. 1 crore – Rs. 2 crore	15%	15%
	Rs. 2 crore – Rs. 5 crore	15%	25%
	Above Rs. 5 crore	15%	37%
Firm/co-operative society/ local authority	0 – Rs. 1 crore	*Nil*	*Nil*
	Above Rs. 1 crore	12%	12%
Domestic company	0 – Rs. 1 crore	*Nil*	*Nil*
	Rs. 1 crore – Rs. 10 crore	7%	7%
	Above Rs. 10 crore	12%	12%
Foreign company	0 – Rs. 1 crore	*Nil*	*Nil*
	Rs. 1 crore – Rs. 10 crore	2%	2%
	Above Rs. 10 crore	5%	5%

‡or book profit (for the purpose of section 115JB) or adjusted total income (for the purpose of section 115JC).

2. *Health and education cess* - It is 4 per cent of income-tax and surcharge.

Compulsory deposit

0.2 From the assessment year 1986-87, the scheme of compulsory deposit has been abolished.

❑

Wealth-tax

0.3 No wealth-tax from the assessment year 2016-17.

❑

Gift-tax

0.4 Gifts made after September 30, 1998 are not chargeable to gift-tax.

❑

Estate duty

0.5 The levy of estate duty has been abolished in respect of estates passing on death occurring on or after March 16, 1985.

❑

† These rates are subject to SC + HEC [*see* Notes *1* and *2* at the end of Table].

Rates for tax deduction at source

0.6 Tax is deductible at source at the rates given in table (*infra*). If PAN of the deductee is not intimated to the deductor, tax will be deducted at source by virtue of section 206AA either at the rate given in the table or at the rate of 20 per cent, whichever is higher†. Further, under section 94A(5), if payment or credit is made or given to a deductee who is located in a notified jurisdictional area‡, tax is deductible at the rate given in the table or at the rate of 30 per cent, whichever is higher. TDS rates for the financial year 2019-20 are as follows –

Category A - ***When recipient is resident***	
Nature of payment	*TDS (SC : Nil, HEC : Nil)*
• **Sec. 192** - Payment of salary [normal tax rates are applicable – *see* para 0.1-1b, SC : 10% (if total income exceeds Rs. 50 lakh but does not exceed Rs. 1 crore), 15% (if total income exceeds Rs. 1 crore but does not exceed Rs. 2 crore), 25% (if total income exceeds Rs. 2 crore but does not exceed Rs. 5 crore) or 37% (if total income exceeds Rs. 5 crore), HEC : 4%]	—
• **Sec. 192A** - Payment of taxable accumulated balance of provident fund	10
• **Sec. 193** - Interest on securities—	
a. interest on (*a*) debentures/securities for money issued by or on behalf of any local authority/statutory corporation, (*b*) listed debentures of a company [not being listed securities in demat form], (*c*) any security of the Central or State Government [*i.e.*, 8% Savings (taxable) Bonds, 2003 and 7.75% Savings (taxable) Bonds, 2018 but not any other Government security]	10
b. any other interest on securities (including interest on non-listed debentures)	10
• **Sec. 194** - Dividend—	
a. deemed dividend under section 2(*22*)(*e*)	*Nil*
b. any other dividend	*Nil*
• **Sec. 194A** - Interest other than interest on securities	10
• **Sec. 194B** - Winnings from lottery or crossword puzzle or card game or other game of any sort	30
• **Sec. 194BB** - Winnings from horse races	30
• **Sec. 194C** - Payment or credit to a resident contractor/sub-contractor—	
a. payment/credit to an individual or a Hindu undivided family	1
b. payment/credit to any person other than an individual or a Hindu undivided family	2

†However, this rule is subject to following modifications –

- *Case 1* - The provisions of section 206AA are not applicable in respect of payment of interest on long-term bonds to a non-resident under section 194LC.
- *Case 2* - Where tax is deductible on the strength of the provisions of DTAAs which is lower than 20 per cent, the provisions of section 206AA cannot be invoked (to compel the assessee to deduct tax at the rate of 20 per cent) even if the recipient does not have PAN – *DIT* v. *Serum Institute of India Ltd.* [2015] 56 taxmann.com 1 (Pune - Trib.), *CIT (International Taxation)* v. *Infosys BPO Ltd.* [2015] 60 taxmann.com 465 (Bang.).
- *Case 3* - If the recipient does not furnish PAN, tax will be deducted under section 192A at the maximum marginal rate of tax (*i.e.*, 42.744 per cent) and not at the rate of 20 per cent given by section 206AA.
- *Case 4* - The provisions of section 206AA are not be applicable, if a few conditions prescribed by rule 37BC$ are satisfied. Under this rule, the deductee is required to submit the following to deductor (to avoid application of section 206AA) – (*a*) name, e-mail id, contact number; (*b*) address in the foreign country; (*c*) tax residency certificate issued by the foreign Government; and (*d*) Tax Identification Number issued by the foreign country.

‡ 'Cyprus' was specified as notified jurisdictional area for purposes of section 94A *vide* Notification No. SO 3307(E)$, dated November 1, 2013. However, this notification has been rescinded with effect from November 1, 2013 (except as respects things done or omitted to be done before such rescission) *vide* Notification No. SO 4033(E), dated December 14, 2016$.

$ For rule 37BC, Notification No. SO 3307(E), dated November 1, 2013 and Notification No. SO 4033(E), dated December 14, 2016, log on to *taxmann.com/readyreckoner.aspx.*

Category A - ***When recipient is resident***	
Nature of payment	*TDS (SC* : Nil, *HEC* : Nil*)*
• **Sec. 194D** - Insurance commission— - if recipient is a resident (other than a company) - if recipient is a domestic company	 5 10
• **Sec. 194DA** - Payment in respect of life insurance policy [when exemption is not available under section 10(*10D*)] – - Up to August 31, 2019 : 1% of amount payable - With effect from September 1, 2019 : 5% of the amount of income comprised in payment	 1 5
• **Sec. 194EE** - Payment in respect of deposits under National Savings Scheme, 1987	10
• **Sec. 194F** - Payment on account of repurchase of units of MF or UTI	20
• **Sec. 194G** - Commission on sale of lottery tickets	5
• **Sec. 194H** - Commission or brokerage	5
• **Sec. 194-I** - Rent— *a.* rent of plant and machinery *b.* rent of land or building or furniture or fitting	 2 10
• **Sec. 194-IA** - Payment/credit of consideration to a resident transferor for transfer of any immovable property (other than rural agricultural land)	1
• **Sec. 194-IB** - Payment/credit of rent by an individual/HUF (if not subject to tax audit under section 44AB in the immediately preceding financial year)	5
• **Sec. 194-IC** - Payment under joint development agreement to a resident individual/ HUF (who transfers land/building)	10
• **Sec. 194J** - Professional fees, technical fees, royalty or remuneration to a director – - If payee is engaged only in the business of operation of call centre - Any other payment/credit	 2 10
• **Sec. 194LA** - Payment of compensation on acquisition of certain immovable property	10
• **Sec. 194LBA(1)** - Payment of the nature referred to in section 10(*23FC*) section 10(*23FC*)(*a*)/(*23FCA*) by business trust to resident unit holders	10
• **Sec. 194LBB** - Payment in respect of units of investment fund specified in section 115UB	10
• **Sec. 194LBC(1)** - Payment in respect of an investment in a securitisation trust specified in clause (*d*) of the *Explanation* occurring after section 115TCA— - if recipient is an individual or a Hindu undivided family - if recipient is any other person	 25 30
• **Sec. 194M** - Payment/credit to a resident contractor or resident professional or payment/credit by way of commission/brokerage (applicable with effect from September 1, 2019)	5
• **Sec. 194N** - Payment from one or more accounts to an account holder in cash by bank/co-operative bank/post office in excess of Rs. 1 crore in the financial year (applicable with effect from September 1, 2019)	2

Category B - *When recipient is non-resident or foreign company*										
	If recipient is non-resident individual/HUF/AOP/BOI/ artificial juridical person					*If recipient is non-resident co-operative society/firm*		*If recipient is non-domestic company*		
Aggregate payment or credit subject to TDS during the financial year 2019-20 →	*0 – Rs. 50 lakh*	*Rs. 50 lakh – Rs. 1 crore*	*Rs. 1 crore – Rs. 2 crore*	*Rs. 2 crore – Rs. 5 crore*	*Above Rs. 5 crore*	*0 – Rs. 1 crore*	*Above Rs. 1 crore*	*0 – Rs. 1 crore*	*Rs. 1 crore – Rs. 10 crore*	*Above Rs. 10 crore*
Nature of payment	*TDS + HEC : 4%*	*TDS + SC : 10% + HEC : 4%*	*TDS + SC : 15% + HEC : 4%*	*TDS + SC : 25% + HEC : 4%*	*TDS + SC : 37% + HEC : 4%*	*TDS + HEC : 4%*	*TDS + SC : 12% + HEC : 4%*	*TDS + HEC : 4%*	*TDS + SC : 2% + HEC : 4%*	*TDS + SC : 5% + HEC : 4%*
• **Sec. 192** - Payment of salary [normal tax rates are applicable – *see* para 0.1-1b SC : 10% (if total income exceeds Rs. 50 lakh but does not exceed Rs. 1 crore), 15% (if total income exceeds Rs. 1 crore but does not exceed Rs. 2 crore), 25% (if total income exceeds Rs. 2 crore but does not exceed Rs. 5 crore) or 37% (if total income exceeds Rs. 5 crore), HEC : 4%]	–	–	–	–	–	–	–	–	–	–
• **Sec. 192A** - Payment of taxable accumulated balance of provident fund	10.4	11.44	11.96	13	14.248	–	–	–	–	–
• **Sec. 194B** - Winnings from lottery or crossword puzzle or card game or other game of any sort	31.2	34.32	35.88	39	42.744	31.2	34.944	31.2	31.824	32.76
• **Sec. 194BB** - Winnings from horse races	31.2	34.32	35.88	39	42.744	31.2	34.944	31.2	31.824	32.76
• **Sec. 194E** - Payment to a non-resident foreign citizen sportsman/entertainer or non-resident sports association	20.8	22.88	23.92	26	28.496	20.8	23.296	20.8	21.216	21.84
• **Sec. 194EE** - Payment in respect of deposits under National Saving Scheme, 1987	10.4	11.44	11.96	13	14.248	*NA*	*NA*	*NA*	*NA*	*NA*
• **Sec. 194F** - Re-purchase of units of MF or UTI	20.8	22.88	23.92	26	28.496	*NA*	*NA*	*NA*	*NA*	*NA*
• **Sec. 194G** - Commission on sale of lottery tickets	5.2	5.72	5.98	6.5	7.124	5.2	5.824	5.2	5.304	5.46
• **Sec. 194LB** - Payment/credit by way of interest by infrastructure debt fund	5.2	5.72	5.98	6.5	7.124	5.2	5.824	5.2	5.304	5.46
• **Sec. 194LBA(2)** - Payment of the nature referred to in section 10(*23FC*) or section 10(*23FC*)(*a*) by business trust to unit holders	5.2	5.72	5.98	6.5	7.124	5.2	5.824	5.2	5.304	5.46
• **Sec. 194LBA(3)** - Payment of the nature referred to in section 10(*23FCA*) by business trust to unit holders	31.2	34.32	35.88	39	42.744	31.2	34.944	41.6	42.432	43.68
• **Sec. 194LBB** - Payment in respect of units of investment fund specified in section 115UB	31.2	34.32	35.88	39	42.744	31.2	34.944	41.6	42.432	43.68
• **Sec. 194LBC(2)** - Payment in respect of an investment in a securitisation trust specified in clause (*d*) of the *Explanation* occurring after section 115TCA	31.2	34.32	35.88	39	42.744	31.2	34.944	41.6	42.432	43.68
• **Sec. 194LC** - Payment/credit of interest by an Indian specified company on foreign currency approved loan/long-term bonds from outside India	5.2	5.72	5.98	6.5	7.124	5.2	5.824	5.2	5.304	5.46
• **Sec. 194LD** - Interest on a rupee denominated bond of an Indian company or Government security	5.2	5.72	5.98	6.5	7.124	5.2	5.824	5.2	5.304	5.46

Category B - *When recipient is non-resident or foreign company*										
	If recipient is non-resident individual/HUF/AOP/BOI/ artificial juridical person					*If recipient is non-resident co-operative society/firm*		*If recipient is non-domestic company*		
Aggregate payment or credit subject to TDS during the financial year 2019-20 →	*0 – Rs. 50 lakh*	*Rs. 50 lakh – Rs. 1 crore*	*Rs. 1 crore – Rs. 2 crore*	*Rs. 2 crore – Rs. 5 crore*	*Above Rs. 5 crore*	*0 – Rs. 1 crore*	*Above Rs. 1 crore*	*0 – Rs. 1 crore*	*Rs. 1 crore – Rs. 10 crore*	*Above Rs. 10 crore*
Nature of payment	*TDS + HEC : 4%*	*TDS + SC : 10% + HEC : 4%*	*TDS + SC : 15% + HEC : 4%*	*TDS + SC : 25% + HEC : 4%*	*TDS + SC : 37% + HEC : 4%*	*TDS + HEC : 4%*	*TDS + SC : 12% + HEC : 4%*	*TDS + HEC : 4%*	*TDS + SC : 2% + HEC : 4%*	*TDS + SC : 5% + HEC : 4%*
• **Sec. 194N** - Payment from one or more accounts to an account holder in cash by bank/co-operative bank/post office in excess of Rs. 1 crore in the financial year (applicable with effect from September 1, 2019)	2.08	2.288	2.392	2.6	2.8496	2.08	2.3296	2.08	2.1216	2.184
• **Sec. 195** - Payment/credit of other sum to a non-resident —										
a. income of foreign exchange assets payable to an Indian citizen	20.8	22.88	23.92	26	28.496	*NA*	*NA*	*NA*	*NA*	*NA*
b. income by way of long-term capital gains referred to in section 115E or section 112(1)(*c*)(*iii*)	10.4	11.44	11.96	13	14.248	10.4	11.648	10.4	10.608	10.92
c. income by way of long-term capital gains referred to in section 112A	10.4	11.44	11.96	13	14.248	10.4	11.648	10.4	10.608	10.92
d. short-term capital gains under section 111A	15.6	17.16	17.94	19.5	21.372	15.6	17.472	15.6	15.912	16.38
e. any other long-term capital gains [not being covered by sections 10(*33*), 10(*36*) and 112A]	20.8	22.88	23.92	26	28.496	20.8	23.296	20.8	21.216	21.84
f. income by way of interest payable by Government/Indian concern on money borrowed or debt incurred by Government or Indian concern in foreign currency (not being interest referred to in section 194LB or 194LC)	20.8	22.88	23.92	26	28.496	20.8	23.296	20.8	21.216	21.84
g. royalty [*see* Note 5]	10.4	11.44	11.96	13	14.248	10.4	11.648	10.4	10.608	10.92
h. royalty [not being royalty of the nature referred to in (*f*) *supra*] [*see* Note 6] –										
❑ where the agreement is made after March 31, 1961 but before April 1, 1976	10.4	11.44	11.96	13	14.248	10.4	11.648	52	53.04	54.6
❑ where the agreement is made on or after April 1, 1976	10.4	11.44	11.96	13	14.248	10.4	11.648	10.4	10.608	10.92
i. fees for technical services [*see* Note 7] –										
❑ where the agreement is made after February 29, 1964 but before April 1, 1976	10.4	11.44	11.96	13	14.248	10.4	11.648	52	53.04	54.6
❑ where the agreement is made on or after April 1, 1976	10.4	11.44	11.96	13	14.248	10.4	11.648	10.4	10.608	10.92
j. any other income	31.2	34.32	35.88	39	42.744	31.2	34.944	41.6	42.432	43.68
• **Sec. 196B** - Payment/credit of income from units (including long-term capital gains on transfer of such units) to an offshore fund	10.4	11.44	11.96	13	14.248	10.4	11.648	10.4	10.608	10.92
• **Sec. 196C** - Payment/credit of interest of foreign currency bonds or GDR (including long-term capital gains on transfer of such bonds) (not being dividend referred to in section 115-O)	10.4	11.44	11.96	13	14.248	10.4	11.648	10.4	10.608	10.92
• **Sec. 196D** - Payment/credit of income from securities (not being dividend, short-term or long-term capital gain) to Foreign Institutional Investors	20.8	22.88	23.92	26	28.496	20.8	23.296	20.8	21.216	21.84

Notes :

1. Under section 192 tax is deductible from salary. The payer shall calculate salary taxable in the hands of recipient. The amount so determined is subject to tax deduction under section 192. Under section 192A, tax is deductible on taxable accumulated balance of provident fund. Under section 195, tax is deductible only if income is taxable in the hands of recipient in India. In any other case, gross payment or credit (without GST, if GST is shown separately) is subject to tax deduction.

2. In *Category B*, tax is deductible at the above rates or the rates specified in ADT agreements entered into by the Central Government under section 90 (whichever is lower) [section 2(*37A*)(*iii*)] [*see* Referencer 10].

3. Tax is not deductible under section 192A, 193, 194, 194A, 194D, 194DA, 194-I, or 194EE if the recipient makes a declaration in Form No. 15G/15H under the provisions of section 197A [*see* para 175.4].

4. Under section 197 the recipient can apply the Assessing Officer in Form No. 13 to get a certificate of lower/no tax deduction. This benefit is, however, not available if tax is deductible under section 192A, 194B, 194BB, 194E, 194EE, 194F, 194-IA, 194LB, 194LBA, 194LC, 194M, 196B, 196C or 196D [*see* para 175.5].

5. Royalty payable by Government or an Indian concern in pursuance of an agreement made by non-resident with the Government or the Indian concern after March 31, 1976, where such royalty is in consideration for the transfer of all or any rights (including the granting of a licence) in respect of copyright in any book on a subject referred to in the first proviso to section 115A(1A) to the Indian concern or in respect of computer software referred to in the second proviso to section 115(1A), to a person resident in India.

6. Not being royalty of the nature referred to above, payable by Government or an Indian concern in pursuance of an agreement made by non-resident with the Government or the Indian concern and where such agreement is with an Indian concern, the agreement is approved by the Central Government or where it relates to matter included in the industrial policy, the agreement is in accordance with that policy.

7. Fees for technical services payable by Government or an Indian concern in pursuance of an agreement made by non-resident with the Government or the Indian concern and where such agreement is with an Indian concern, the agreement is approved by the Central Government or where it relates to matter included in the industrial policy, the agreement is in accordance with that policy.

Rates for tax collection at source

0.7 During the financial year 2019-20, tax shall be collected under section 206C at the rates given in the table (*infra*). If PAN of collectee is not intimated to the collector, tax will be collected by virtue of section 206CC either at twice the rate specified in the table (*infra*) or at the rate of 5 per cent, whichever is higher†.

Aggregate amount subject to TCS during the financial year 2019-20 → / *Different nature of goods*	*Status of purchaser or licensee or lessee*										
	Resident	*Non-resident individual/HUF/AOP/BOI/artificial juridical person*					*Non-resident co-operative society/firm*		*Non-domestic company*		
	Any amount	*0 – Rs. 50 lakh*	*Rs. 50 lakh – Rs. 1 crore*	*Rs. 1 crore – Rs. 2 crore*	*Rs. 2 crore – Rs. 5 crore*	*Above Rs. 5 crore*	*0 – Rs. 1 crore*	*Above Rs. 1 crore*	*0 – Rs. 1 crore*	*Rs. 1 crore – Rs. 10 crore*	*Above Rs. 10 crore*
	TCS	*TCS + HEC : 4%*	*TCS + SC : 10% + HEC : 4%*	*TCS + SC : 15% + HEC : 4%*	*TCS + SC : 25% + HEC : 4%*	*TCS + SC : 37% + HEC : 4%*	*TCS + HEC : 4%*	*TCS + SC : 12% + HEC : 4%*	*TCS + HEC : 4%*	*TCS + SC : 2% + HEC : 4%*	*TCS + SC : 5% + HEC : 4%*
Category A (sale of the following) -											
A1. Alcoholic liquor for human consumption (other than Indian made foreign liquor)	1	1.04	1.144	1.196	1.3	1.4248	1.04	1.1648	1.04	1.0608	1.092
A2. Indian made foreign liquor	1	1.04	1.144	1.196	1.3	1.4248	1.04	1.1648	1.04	1.0608	1.092
A3. Tendu leaves	5	5.2	5.72	5.98	6.5	7.124	5.2	5.824	5.2	5.304	5.46
A4. Timber obtained under a forest lease	2.5	2.6	2.86	2.99	3.25	3.562	2.6	2.912	2.6	2.652	2.73
A5. Timber obtained by any mode other than a forest lease	2.5	2.6	2.86	2.99	3.25	3.562	2.6	2.912	2.6	2.652	2.73

† However, the provisions of section 206CC shall not apply in the case of a non-resident collectee who does not have any permanent establishment in India.

Aggregate amount subject to TCS during the financial year 2019-20 → / *Different nature of goods*	*Status of purchaser or licensee or lessee*										
	Resident	*Non-resident individual/HUF/AOP/BOI/artificial juridical person*					*Non-resident co-operative society/firm*		*Non-domestic company*		
	Any amount	*0 – Rs. 50 lakh*	*Rs. 50 lakh – Rs. 1 crore*	*Rs. 1 crore – Rs. 2 crore*	*Rs. 2 crore – Rs. 5 crore*	*Above Rs. 5 crore*	*0 – Rs. 1 crore*	*Above Rs. 1 crore*	*0 – Rs. 1 crore*	*Rs. 1 crore – Rs. 10 crore*	*Above Rs. 10 crore*
	TCS	*TCS + HEC : 4%*	*TCS + SC : 10% + HEC : 4%*	*TCS + SC : 15% + HEC : 4%*	*TCS + SC : 25% + HEC : 4%*	*TCS + SC : 37% + HEC : 4%*	*TCS + HEC : 4%*	*TCS + SC : 12% + HEC : 4%*	*TCS + HEC : 4%*	*TCS + SC : 2% + HEC : 4%*	*TCS + SC : 5% + HEC : 4%*
A6. Any other forest produce (not being timber/tendu leaves)	2.5	2.6	2.86	2.99	3.25	3.562	2.6	2.912	2.6	2.652	2.73
A7. Scrap	1	1.04	1.144	1.196	1.3	1.4248	1.04	1.1648	1.04	1.0608	1.092
A8. Minerals, being coal or lignite or iron ore	1	1.04	1.144	1.196	1.3	1.4248	1.04	1.1648	1.04	1.0608	1.092
Category B (grant of lease/license of the following) -											
B1. Parking lot, toll plaza, mining and quarrying	2	2.08	2.288	2.392	2.6	2.8496	2.08	2.3296	2.08	2.1216	2.184
Category C (not applicable with effect from April 1, 2017)	–	–	–	–	–	–	–	–	–	–	–
Category D (sale of the following whether payment is received by cheque or by any other mode) –											
D1. Motor vehicle of the value exceeding Rs. 10 lakh	1	1.04	1.144	1.196	1.3	1.4248	1.04	1.1648	1.04	1.0608	1.092

Tax on dividend distribution, distribution by way of buy-back of shares and non-repatriation of excess money in secondary adjustment [Secs. 115-O, 115QA and 92CE]

0.8 These rates are given below –

0.8-1 ***Under sections 115-O and 115QA*** - Tax rates applicable on distribution under sections 115-O and 115QA during the financial year 2019-20 are as follows –

	Distribution tax (as a % of amount distributed)	*Surcharge (as a % of distribution tax)*	*HEC (as a % of distribution tax and surcharge)*	*Total (as a % of amount distributed)*
• Tax on dividend under section 115-O [not applicable in the case of deemed dividend under section 2(*22*)(*e*)]	17.647*	12	4	20.5552941
• Tax on dividend under section 115-O [applicable in the case of deemed dividend under section 2(*22*)(*e*)]	30	12	4	34.944
• Tax on distributed income of domestic company under section 115QA for buy- back of unlisted shares (up to July 4, 2019) or **any shares** (on or after July 5, 2019)	20	12	4	23.296

0.8-2 ***Under section 92CE*** - Under section 92CE(2A), additional income-tax is payable at the rate of 18 per cent of excess money (+ surcharge : 12 per cent of tax + HEC : 4 per cent of tax and surcharge). Effective rate of tax is 20.9664 per cent.

*15/85 of amount distributed.

Tax on income distributed by UTI/Mutual Fund under section 115R

0.9 Tax on income distributed by UTI/mutual fund[1] shall be charged during the financial year 2019-20 as follows—

	Distribution tax (as a % of amount distributed)	*Surcharge (as a % of distribution tax)*	*HEC (as a % of distribution tax and surcharge)*	*Total (as a % of amount distributed)*
• Any income distributed by the Administrator of the specified undertaking to unit-holder	*Nil*	*Nil*	*Nil*	*Nil*
• Any income distributed (on or after September 1, 2019) by a "specified mutual fund", out of its income derived from transactions made on a recognised stock exchange located in any International Financial Services Centre and where the consideration for such transaction is paid/payable in convertible foreign exchange	*Nil*	*Nil*	*Nil*	*Nil*
• Income distribution by money market mutual fund or a liquid fund or any other fund (not being equity oriented fund)				
- Unit-holder is individual/HUF	33.33[1]	12	4	38.8267
- Unit-holder is any other person	42.857[2]	12	4	49.92
• Income distribution to any person by equity oriented fund	11.1111[3]	12	4	12.9422
• Income distribution by a mutual fund under an infrastructure debt fund scheme to a non-resident/foreign company	5.26[4]	12	4	6.1305

Notes –

1. "Specified mutual fund" means a mutual fund specified under section 10(*23D*) —

- located in any International Financial Services Centre;
- of which all the units are held by non-residents.

2. "Equity oriented fund" means a fund set up under a scheme of a mutual fund specified under section 10(*23D*) and, —

a. in a case where the fund invests in the units of another fund which is traded on a recognised stock exchange, —

- a minimum of 90 per cent of the total proceeds of such fund is invested in the units of such other fund; and
- such other fund also invests a minimum of 90 per cent of its total proceeds in the equity shares of domestic companies listed on a recognised stock exchange; and

b. in any other case, a minimum of 65 per cent of the total proceeds of such fund is invested in the equity shares of domestic companies listed on a recognised stock exchange.

The percentage of equity shareholding or unit held in respect of the fund, as the case may be, shall be computed with reference to the annual average of the monthly averages of the opening and closing figures.

3. Tax under section 115R is applicable only on income distributed by way of dividend to unit-holders of mutual funds or UTI. It is not applicable on payments pertaining to redemption/repurchase of units or allotment of additional units by way of bonus units – Circular No. 6/2014, dated February 11, 2014.

---

1. 25/75 of amount distributed.
2. 30/70 of amount distributed.
3. 10/90 of amount distributed.
4. 5/95 of amount distributed.

Other taxes

0.10 Some other tax rates are given below—

0.10-1 ***Securities transaction tax*** - Securities transaction tax (STT) rates and other related issues are given below:

	Transaction in recognized stock exchange in India							
	Purchase of equity shares, units of equity oriented mutual fund or (with effect from October 1, 2014) units of a business trust (delivery based)		*Sale of equity shares, units of equity oriented mutual fund or (with effect from October 1, 2014) units of a business trust (delivery based)*		*Sale of equity shares, units of equity oriented mutual fund or (with effect from October 1, 2014) units of a business trust (non-delivery based)*	*Sale of derivative*	*Sale of unit of an equity oriented fund to the mutual fund*	*Sale of unlisted equity shares under an offer for sale to public [or, with effect from June 1, 2015, sale of unlisted units of a business trust by a unitholder which were acquired in consideration of a transfer referred to in section 47(xvii)]*
Whether securities transaction tax (STT) is applicable	Yes		Yes		Yes	Yes	Yes	Yes
Who has to pay STT	Purchaser		Seller		Seller	Seller	Seller	Seller
Rate of STT*	*Shares or units of a business trust*	*Units*	*Shares or units of a business trust*	*Units*				
- from June 1, 2016	0.1%	*Nil*	0.1%	0.001%	0.025%	0.05%,0.125%,0.01%.#	0.001%	0.2%
- from June 1, 2013 to May 31, 2016	0.1%	*Nil*	0.1%	0.001%	0.025%	0.017%, 0.125%, 0.01%†	0.001%	0.2%
- from July 1, 2012 to May 31, 2013	0.1%	0.1%	0.1%	0.1%	0.025%	0.017%, 0.125%, 0.017%‡	0.25%	0.2%
- from June 1, 2008 to June 30, 2012	0.125%	0.125%	0.125%	0.125%	0.025%	0.017%, 0.125%, 0.017%‡	0.25%	—

*Surcharge : *Nil*, HEC : *Nil*

0.05% of option premium in the case of sale of option (payable by seller), 0.125% of settlement price [with effect from September 1, 2019, 0.125% of (settlement price *minus* strike price)] in the case of sale of an option where option is exercised (payable by purchaser), 0.01% of the price in the case of sale of futures (payable by seller).

†0.017% of option premium in the case of sale of option (payable by seller), 0.125% of settlement price in the case of sale of an option where option is exercised (payable by purchaser), 0.01% of the price in the case of sale of futures (payable by seller).

‡0.017% of option premium in the case of sale of option (payable by seller), 0.125% of settlement price in the case of sale of an option where option is exercised (payable by purchaser), 0.017% of the price in the case of sale of futures (payable by seller).

	Transaction in recognized stock exchange in India						Sale of unit of an equity oriented fund to the mutual fund	Sale of unlisted equity shares under an offer for sale to public [or, with effect from June 1, 2015, sale of unlisted units of a business trust by a unitholder which were acquired in consideration of a transfer referred to in section 47(xvii)]
	Purchase of equity shares, units of equity oriented mutual fund or (with effect from October 1, 2014) units of a business trust (delivery based)		Sale of equity shares, units of equity oriented mutual fund or (with effect from October 1, 2014) units of a business trust (delivery based)		Sale of equity shares, units of equity oriented mutual fund or (with effect from October 1, 2014) units of a business trust (non-delivery based)	Sale of derivative		
- from June 1, 2006 to May 31, 2008	0.125%	0.125%	0.125%	0.125%	0.025%	0.017%	0.25%	—
- from June 1, 2005 to May 31, 2006	0.1%	0.1%	0.1%	0.1%	0.02%	0.0133%	0.2%	—
- during October 1, 2004 and May 31, 2005	0.075%	0.075%	0.075%	0.075%	0.015%	0.01%	0.15%	—
Who will collect STT	Stock exchange		Stock exchange		Stock exchange	Stock exchange	Mutual fund	Lead merchant banker

Note : STT is not applicable in case of preference shares, Government securities, bonds, debentures, units of mutual fund other than equity oriented mutual fund and in such cases, tax treatment of short-term and long-term capital gains shall be as per normal provisions of law.

0.10-2 ***Fringe benefits tax*** - Fringe benefit tax is not applicable from the assessment year 2010-11 onwards.

0.10-3 ***Banking cash transaction tax*** - It is not applicable after March 31, 2009.

0.10-4 ***Commodities transaction tax*** - Commodities transaction tax is chargeable as follows –

Taxable commodities transaction	*Value of taxable transaction*	*Rate*	*Payable by*
Sale of a commodity derivative	Price at which the commodity derivative is traded	0.01%	Seller
Sale of an option on commodity derivative	Option premium	0.05%	Seller
Sale of an option on commodity derivative, where option is exercised	Settlement price	0.0001%	Purchaser

R-2

Amendments at a glance

PART A - EFFECTED BY THE FINANCE (NO. 2) BILL, 2019*

Tax rates

0.11 Tax rates for the assessment years 2019-20 and 2020-21 are given in Referencer 1.

0.11-1 ***Income-tax*** - The following are income-tax rates for the assessment years 2019-20 and 2020-21 –

0.11-1a *INDIVIDUAL, HUF, AOP, BOI* - Exemption limit is Rs. 2,50,000† (it is applicable even in the case of a resident woman). Higher exemption limit is provided in the case of a senior citizen or super senior citizen. The slab rate of 5 per cent is applicable on net income up to Rs. 5,00,000; the slab rate of 20 per cent is applicable on net income between Rs. 5,00,000 and Rs. 10,00,000 and the slab rate of 30 per cent is applicable in respect of net income exceeding Rs. 10,00,000.

• *Senior citizen* - Senior citizen is a resident individual who is at least 60 years of age at any time during the previous year but of less than 80 years on the last day of previous year [assessment year 2019-20 (date of birth: on or after April 2, 1939 but before April 2, 1959) or assessment year 2020-21 (date of birth: on or after April 2, 1940 but before April 2, 1960)].

In the case of a senior citizen, exemption limit is Rs. 3,00,000†. Net income in the range of Rs. 3,00,000 to Rs. 5,00,000 is taxable at the rate of 5 per cent. Between Rs. 5,00,000 and Rs. 10,00,000, the slab rate is 20 per cent and the income exceeding Rs. 10,00,000 is taxable at the rate of 30 per cent. These rates will be applicable only in the case of a resident (ordinarily or otherwise) senior citizen. In the case of a non-resident senior citizen, the exemption limit is Rs. 2,50,000 as given below.

• *Super senior citizen* - A super senior citizen is a resident individual who is at least 80 years of age at any time during the previous year [assessment year 2019-20 (date of birth: before April 2, 1939) or assessment year 2020-21 (date of birth: before April 2, 1940)].

In the case of super senior citizen, first Rs. 5,00,000 of net income is exempt from tax. Net income in the range of Rs. 5,00,000 to Rs. 10,00,000 is taxable at the rate of 20 per cent. Net income exceeding Rs. 10,00,000 is taxable at the rate of 30 per cent. These rates will be applicable only in the case of a resident (ordinarily or otherwise) super senior citizen. In the case of a non-resident, the exemption limit will be Rs. 2,50,000 as given below.

• *Any other individual, HUF, AOP, BOI* - This category includes the following taxpayers –

1. Any other resident individual [assessment year 2019-20 (date of birth: on or after April 2, 1959) or assessment year 2020-21 (date of birth: on or after April 2, 1960)].

2. Any non-resident individual irrespective of age.

3. Any HUF, AOP, BOI, artificial juridical person.

In case of any of these persons, first Rs. 2,50,000† of net income is exempt from tax. Net income in the range of Rs. 2,50,000 to Rs. 5,00,000 is taxable at the rate of 5 per cent. On net income between Rs. 5,00,000 and Rs. 10,00,000, the slab rate is 20 per cent and income exceeding Rs. 10,00,000 is taxable at the rate of 30 per cent.

0.11-1b *FIRM* - There is no change in the tax rate. A partnership firm (including a limited liability partnership firm) is taxable at the rate of 30 per cent.

0.11-1c *COMPANY* - A domestic company is taxable at the rate of 30 per cent and a non-domestic company is taxable at the rate of 40 per cent. Different rates are, however, applicable in the following cases –

*As passed by Lok Sabha.

† Rebate under section 87A is available in the case of a resident individual if his/her taxable income does not exceed Rs. 3,50,000 (for the assessment year 2019-20) or Rs. 5,00,000 (for the assessment year 2020-21). The rebate has been discussed in para 111.

• A domestic company (which satisfies the conditions of section 115BA) is taxable at the rate of 25 per cent from the assessment year 2017-18 onwards. For section 115BA, *see* para 0.1-6.

• A domestic company (where its total turnover or gross receipt in the previous year 2016-17 does not exceed Rs. 250 crore) is taxable at the rate of 25 per cent (not 30 per cent) for the assessment year 2019-20.

• A domestic company (where its total turnover or gross receipt in the previous year 2017-18 does not exceed Rs. 400 crore) will be taxable at the rate of 25 per cent (not 30 per cent) for the assessment year 2020-21.

0.11-1d *CO-OPERATIVE SOCIETY AND LOCAL AUTHORITY* - In the case of a co-operative society/local authority, there is no change in the income-tax rate.

0.11-2 ***Surcharge on income-tax*** - Applicable surcharge (as a percentage of income-tax) for the assessment years 2019-20 and 2020-21 is as follows –

	Net income range	*Assessment year 2019-20*	*Assessment year 2020-21*
Individuals/HUF/AOP/BOI/artificial juridical person	0 – Rs. 50 lakh	*Nil*	*Nil*
	Rs. 50 lakh – Rs. 1 crore	10%	10%
	Rs. 1 crore – Rs. 2 crore	15%	15%
	Rs. 2 crore – Rs. 5 crore	15%	25%
	Above Rs. 5 crore	15%	37%
Firm/co-operative society/local authority	0 – Rs. 1 crore	*Nil*	*Nil*
	Above Rs. 1 crore	12%	12%
Domestic company	0 – Rs. 1 crore	*Nil*	*Nil*
	Rs. 1 crore – Rs. 10 crore	7%	7%
	Above Rs. 10 crore	12%	12%
Foreign company	0 – Rs. 1 crore	*Nil*	*Nil*
	Rs. 1 crore – Rs. 10 crore	2%	2%
	Above Rs. 10 crore	5%	5%

Note - The above surcharge is subject to a marginal relief [*see* para 0.11-5].

0.11-3 ***Health and education cess on income-tax*** - For the assessment years 2019-20 and 2020-21, health and education cess (HEC) is 4 per cent of income-tax and surcharge.

0.11-4 ***Minimum alternate tax/alternate minimum tax*** - A corporate-assessee is covered by minimum alternate tax under section 115JB. A non-corporate assessee is covered by alternate minimum tax under section 115JC.

• *Tax rate* - Basic rate for minimum alternate tax/alternate minimum tax is 18.5 per cent for the assessment years 2019-20 and 2020-21. If a unit is located in an International Financial Services Centre† and derives its income solely in convertible foreign exchange, the minimum alternate tax/alternate minimum tax is 9 per cent of book profit.

• *Surcharge* - Surcharge on minimum alternate tax/alternate minimum tax is as follows –

Adjusted total income/book profit range	*Individuals/HUF/AOP/BOI/artificial juridical person*		*Firm/co-operative society/local authority*	*Domestic company*	*Foreign company*
	AY 2019-20	*AY 2020-21*	*AYs 2019-20 and 2020-21*	*AYs 2019-20 and 2020-21*	*AYs 2019-20 and 2020-21*
0 – Rs. 50 lakh	*Nil*	*Nil*	*Nil*	*Nil*	*Nil*
Rs. 50 lakh – Rs. 1 crore	10%	10%	*Nil*	*Nil*	*Nil*
Rs. 1 crore – Rs. 2 crore	15%	15%	12%	7%	2%
Rs. 2 crore – Rs. 5 crore	15%	25%	12%	7%	2%
Rs. 5 crore – Rs. 10 crore	15%	37%	12%	7%	2%
Above Rs. 10 crore	15%	37%	12%	12%	5%

Note - The above surcharge is subject to a marginal relief [*see* para 0.11-5].

• *HEC* - HEC is 4 per cent of minimum alternate tax/alternate minimum tax and surcharge.

†"International Financial Services Centre" means an International Financial Services Centre which is set-up in a special economic zone and approved by the Central Government under section 18(1) of Special Economic Zones Act, 2005.

0.11-5 ***Marginal relief*** - The provisions pertaining to marginal relief (for the assessment year 2019-20) are given below –

• *Individual/HUF/AOP/artificial juridical person having income above Rs. 50 lakh* - In the case of these taxpayers, if income is slightly higher than Rs. 50 lakh, a provision has been made to provide for relief in marginal cases. The said relief is as follows –

If the net income exceeds Rs. 50 lakh, the total amount payable as income-tax and surcharge on such income shall not exceed the total amount payable as income-tax on a net income of Rs. 50 lakh by more than the amount of income that exceeds Rs. 50 lakh.

• *Individual/HUF/AOP/artificial juridical person having income above Rs. 1 crore* - In the case of these taxpayers, if income is more than Rs. 1 crore, the applicable surcharge will increase from 10 per cent to 15 per cent. Consequently, another marginal relief is provided when net income is slightly higher than Rs. 1 crore which is as given below –

If net income of these taxpayers exceeds Rs. 1 crore, the total amount payable as income-tax and surcharge on such income shall not exceed the total amount payable as income-tax and surcharge on net income of Rs. 1 crore by more than the amount of income that exceeds Rs. 1 crore.

• *Firms/co-operative societies/local authorities having income above Rs. 1 crore* - To avoid hardship, in the case of these taxpayers (having income of above Rs. 1 crore), a provision has been made to provide for relief in marginal cases. The said relief is as follows –

If the net income exceeds Rs. 1 crore, the total amount payable as income-tax and surcharge on such income shall not exceed the total amount payable as income-tax on a net income of Rs. 1 crore by more than the amount of income that exceeds Rs. 1 crore.

• *Domestic company/foreign company having income above Rs. 1 crore* - In the case of a company, surcharge is not applicable if net income does not exceed Rs. 1 crore. If net income exceeds Rs. 1 crore, surcharge is applicable.

To avoid hardship, in the case of a company whose income is slightly higher than Rs. 1 crore, a provision has been made to provide for relief in marginal cases. The said relief is as follows –

If the net income exceeds Rs. 1 crore, the total amount payable as income-tax and surcharge on such income shall not exceed the total amount payable as income-tax on a net income of Rs. 1 crore by more than the amount of income that exceeds Rs. 1 crore.

• *Domestic company/foreign company having income above Rs. 10 crore* - In the case of a corporate-assessee, if net income is more than Rs. 10 crore, the applicable surcharge will increase from 7 per cent to 12 per cent (in the case of foreign company, it increases from 2 per cent to 5 per cent). Consequently, another marginal relief is provided when net income is slightly higher than Rs. 10 crore which is as given below –

If the net income of a corporate-assessee exceeds Rs. 10 crore, the total amount payable as income-tax and surcharge on such income shall not exceed the total amount payable as income-tax and surcharge on net income of Rs. 10 crore by more than the amount of income that exceeds Rs. 10 crore.

0.11-5a *MARGINAL RELIEF FOR THE ASSESSMENT YEAR 2020-21* - In addition to above marginal relief, similar marginal relief will be available for the assessment year 2020-21 when in the case of individual/HUF/AOP/artificial juridical person, net income is above Rs. 2 crore and above Rs. 5 crore.

0.11-5b *INCOME RANGE WHEN MARGINAL RELIEF IS APPLICABLE* - Marginal relief will be applicable in case net income falls in the following range –

	Income range to attract marginal relief	*Page No. of tax table*	
		AY 2019-20	*AY 2020-21*
Resident senior citizen	Rs. 50 lakh – Rs. 51.9552 lakh	B-14	B-30
	Rs. 100 lakh – Rs. 102.145 lakh	B-16	B-32
	Rs. 200 lakh – Rs. 209.296 lakh	Not applicable	B-34
	Rs. 500 lakh – Rs. 530.173 lakh	Not applicable	B-36
Resident super senior citizen	Rs. 50 lakh – Rs. 51.9402 lakh	B-14	B-30
	Rs. 100 lakh – Rs. 102.1374 lakh	B-16	B-32
	Rs. 200 lakh – Rs. 209.28 lakh	Not applicable	B-34
	Rs. 500 lakh – Rs. 530.1528 lakh	Not applicable	B-36

	Income range to attract marginal relief	*Page No. of tax table*	
		AY 2019-20	*AY 2020-21*
Any other resident individual, any non-resident individual, any HUF or AOP/BOI	Rs. 50 lakh – Rs. 51.9589 lakh	B-14	B-30
	Rs. 100 lakh – Rs. 102.1469 lakh	B-16	B-32
	Rs. 200 lakh – Rs. 209.30 lakh	Not applicable	B-34
	Rs. 500 lakh – Rs. 530.1782 lakh	Not applicable	B-36
Firm	Rs. 100 lakh – Rs. 105.4216 Lakh	B-39	B-39
Co-operative society	Rs. 100 lakh – Rs. 105.4162 lakh	–	–
Domestic company (tax rate : 25%)	Rs. 100 lakh – Rs. 102.389 lakh	B-42	B-42
	Rs. 1000 lakh – Rs. 1017.3611 lakh	B-44	B-44
Domestic company (tax rate : 30%)	Rs. 100 lakh – Rs. 103.0927 lakh	B-42	B-42
	Rs. 1000 lakh – Rs. 1022.59030 lakh	B-44	B-44
Foreign company	Rs. 100 lakh – Rs. 101.3513 lakh	–	–
	Rs. 1000 lakh – Rs. 1020.6896 lakh	–	–

Note: The above net income ranges will remain valid only if the assessee does not have any income which is chargeable to tax at special rate(s) of tax (*e.g.*, long-term capital gains, short-term capital gains under section 111A, lottery income, etc.).

In the case of alternate minimum tax/minimum alternate tax, the marginal relief will be applicable in case adjusted total income/book profit falls in the following range for the assessment years 2019-20 and 2020-21 –

	Income range
Individual/HUF/AOP/BOI/artificial juridical person	Rs. 50 lakh – Rs. 51.16133 lakh
	Rs. 100 lakh – Rs. 101.174976 lakh
	Rs. 200 lakh – Rs. 204.813 lakh [*see* Note]
	Rs. 500 lakh – Rs. 514.8684 lakh [*see* Note]
Co-operative society/firm/local authority	Rs. 100 lakh – Rs. 102.8002 lakh
Domestic company	Rs. 100 lakh – Rs. 101.6146 lakh
	Rs. 1000 lakh – Rs. 1011.6675 lakh
Foreign company	Rs. 100 lakh – Rs. 100.4560 lakh
	Rs. 1000 lakh – Rs. 1006.8879 lakh

Note - Not applicable for the assessment year 2019-20.

0.11-6 ***Maximum marginal tax rates*** - Maximum marginal tax rates (at highest level) for the assessment years 2019-20 and 2020-21 are given in the table below –

	AY 2019-20	*AY 2020-21*
Individual/HUF/BOI/AOP/artificial juridical person	35.88%	42.744%
Firm (including limited liability partnership)	34.944%	34.944%
Co-operative society	34.944%	34.944%
Domestic company	29.12%, 34.944%	29.12%, 34.944%
Foreign company	43.68%	43.68%

0.11-7 ***Rates for tax deduction/collection at source*** - During the financial year 2019-20, tax will be deducted at source from salary at the rate given in para 0.1-1b. TDS rates for payments other than salary are given in para 0.6 of Referencer 1. TCS rates are given in para 0.7 of Referencer 1.

0.11-7a *SURCHARGE, EDUCATION CESS, ETC., IN THE CASE OF TDS/TCS* - For the financial year 2019-20, these rates are as follows –

TDS/TCS	*Nature of payment*	*Recipient/collectee*	*Whether health and education cess @ 4% applicable*	*Whether surcharge applicable*	
TDS	Salary	Resident/non-resident	*Yes*	*Yes*	Note 1
TDS	Other than salary	Resident	*No*	*No*	
TDS	Other than salary	Non-resident/foreign company	*Yes*	*Yes*	Note 2
TCS	Any	Resident	*No*	*No*	
TCS	Any	Non-resident/foreign company	*Yes*	*Yes*	Note 3

Notes –

1. If amount subject to TDS exceeds Rs. 50 lakh but does not exceed Rs. 1 crore, surcharge is 10 per cent of TDS. If it exceeds Rs. 1 crore but does not exceed Rs. 2 crore, surcharge is 15 per cent of TDS. If it exceeds Rs. 2 crore but does not exceed Rs. 5 crore, surcharge is 25 per cent of TDS. If it exceeds Rs. 5 crore, surcharge is 37% of TDS.

2. If the recipient is a non-resident (individual/HUF/AOP/artificial juridical person) and the payment/credit subject to TDS exceeds Rs. 50 lakh but does not exceed Rs. 1 crore, surcharge is 10 per cent of TDS. If it exceeds Rs. 1 crore but does not exceed Rs. 2 crore, surcharge is 15 per cent of TDS. If it exceeds Rs. 2 crore but does not exceed Rs. 5 crore, surcharge is 25 per cent of TDS. If it exceeds Rs. 5 crore, surcharge is 37% of TDS. If the recipient is a non-resident (firm/co-operative society) and the payment/credit subject to TDS exceeds Rs. 1 crore, surcharge is 12 per cent of TDS. If the recipient is a foreign company and the payment subject to TDS exceeds Rs. 1 crore but does not exceed Rs. 10 crore, surcharge is 2 per cent of TDS (it is 5 per cent of TDS if the payment/credit exceeds Rs. 10 crore).

3. If the purchaser/licensee/lessee is a non-resident (individual/HUF/AOP/artificial juridical person) and the amount subject to TCS exceeds Rs. 50 lakh but does not exceed Rs. 1 crore, surcharge is 10 per cent of TCS. If it exceeds Rs. 1 crore but does not exceed Rs. 2 crore, surcharge is 15 per cent of TCS. If it exceeds Rs. 2 crore but does not exceed Rs. 5 crore, surcharge is 25 per cent of TCS. If it exceeds Rs. 5 crore, surcharge is 37% of TCS. If the purchaser/licensee/lessee is a non-resident (firm/co-operative society) and the amount subject to TCS exceeds Rs. 1 crore, surcharge is 12 per cent of TCS. If the purchaser/licensee/lessee is a foreign company and the amount subject to TCS exceeds Rs. 1 crore but does not exceed Rs. 10 crore, surcharge is 2 per cent of TCS (it is 5 per cent of TCS if the amounts subject to TCS exceeds Rs. 10 crore).

0.11-E1 X (33 years) is a resident individual. His net income for the assessment year 2020-21 is Rs. 51,95,000 (*Situation 1*), or Rs. 51,98,000 (*Situation 2*).

•

	Situation 1 *Rs.*	*Situation 2* *Rs.*
Income-tax on net income	13,71,000	13,71,900
Add: Surcharge @10%	1,37,100	1,37,190
Income-tax and surcharge under normal computation (*a*)	15,08,100	15,09,090
Computation for marginal relief		
Step 1 - Income-tax on Rs. 50 lakh	13,12,500	13,12,500
Step 2 - Tax @ 100% of income in excess of Rs. 50 lakh	1,95,000	1,98,000
Tax under marginal relief computation (*b*)	15,07,500	15,10,500
Normal tax or tax under marginal relief, whichever is lower [(*a*) or (*b*), whichever is lower] (*c*)	15,07,500	15,09,090
Add: Health and education cess @ 4% of (*c*)	60,300	60,364
Tax liability (rounded off)	15,67,800	15,69,450

0.11-E2 X (41 years) is a resident individual. His net income for the assessment year 2020-21 is Rs. 5,30,00,000 (*Situation 1*), or Rs. 5,31,00,000 (*Situation 2*).

•

	Situation 1 *Rs.*	*Situation 2* *Rs.*
Income-tax on net income	1,57,12,500	1,57,42,500
Add: Surcharge @ 37%	58,13,625	58,24,725
Income-tax and surcharge under normal computation (*a*)	2,15,26,125	2,15,67,225
Computation for marginal relief		
Step 1 - Income-tax on Rs. 5 crore	1,48,12,500	1,48,12,500
Step 2 - Surcharge on income-tax @ 25% (if income is Rs. 5 crore)	37,03,125	37,03,125
Step 3 - Tax @ 100% of income in excess of Rs. 5 crore	30,00,000	31,00,000
Tax under marginal relief computation (*b*)	2,15,15,625	2,16,15,625
Normal tax or tax under marginal relief, whichever is lower [(*a*) or (*b*), whichever is lower] (*c*)	2,15,15,625	2,15,67,225
Add: Health and education cess @ 4% of (*c*)	8,60,625	8,62,689
Tax liability (rounded off)	2,23,76,250	2,24,29,910

0.11-E3 Gross income of X (61 years), a resident individual, for the assessment year 2020-21 is Rs. 2,14,50,000 [salary (before standard deduction) : Rs. 8,50,000, lottery winnings : Rs. 92,00,000, long-term capital gain under section 112A : Rs. 4,00,000 and dividend from domestic companies : Rs. 1,10,00,000]. X is entitled to deduction of Rs. 1,50,000 under section 80C and Rs. 50,000 under section 80CCD(1B).

•

	Rs.
Salary income (after standard deduction)	8,00,000
Long-term capital gain (under section 112A)	4,00,000
Lottery winnings	92,00,000
Dividend from domestic companies [Rs. 1,10,00,000 – exemption under section 10(*34*) : Rs. 10,00,000]	1,00,00,000
Gross total income	2,04,00,000
Less: Deduction under sections 80C and 80CCD(1B)	2,00,000
Net income	2,02,00,000
Tax computation under normal provisions	
Tax on lottery winnings of Rs. 92,00,000 @ 30%	27,60,000
Tax on long-term capital gain of Rs. 4,00,000 under section 112A (10% of Rs. 3,00,000)	30,000
Tax on dividend income of Rs. 1,00,00,000 under section 115BBDA (10% of Rs. 1,00,00,000)	10,00,000
Tax on remaining income of Rs. 6,00,000 (first Rs. 3,00,000: *Nil*, next Rs. 2,00,000 @ 5% : Rs. 10,000 and on the balance of Rs. 1,00,000 @ 20% : Rs. 20,000)	30,000
Tax	38,20,000
Add: Surcharge @ 25%	9,55,000
Total	47,75,000
Tax computation under marginal relief	
Step 1 - Tax payable if income is Rs. 2 crore [it may be assumed that salary is Rs. 6,00,000 (*i.e.*, Rs. 8,00,000 *minus* deduction under sections 80C and 80CCD), lottery winning is Rs. 90,00,000, long-term capital gain is Rs. 4,00,000 and dividend income is Rs. 1,00,00,000] –	
Tax on lottery income of Rs. 90,00,000 @ 30%	27,00,000
Tax on long-term capital gain of Rs. 4,00,000 under section 112A (10% of Rs. 3,00,000)	30,000
Tax on dividend income of Rs. 1,00,00,000 under section 115BBDA (10% of Rs. 1,00,00,000)	10,00,000
Tax on balance of Rs. 6,00,000	30,000
Tax on Rs. 2,00,00,000	37,60,000
Add: Surcharge @ 15% on income-tax of Rs. 37,60,000	5,64,000
Total (*i.e.*, tax and surcharge on income of Rs. 2,00,00,000)	43,24,000
Step 2 - To the amount of tax and surcharge determined on Rs. 2 crore under *Step 1*, *add* tax @ 100% in respect of income exceeding Rs. 2 crore (*i.e.*, 100% of Rs. 2,00,000)	2,00,000
The aggregate tax and surcharge is Rs. 45,24,000 which is lower than the regular tax and surcharge of Rs. 47,75,000. Therefore, tax liability will be calculated in this case as follows –	
Tax and surcharge as computed above	45,24,000
Add: Health and education cess @ 4%	1,80,960
Tax liability	47,04,960

0.11-E4 X Ltd. is a domestic company. Its turnover during the previous years 2017-18 and 2018-19 was Rs. 398 crore and Rs. 415 crore respectively. Net income of the company for the assessment year 2020-21 is Rs. 10.15 crore (*Situation 1*), or Rs. 10.20 crore (*Situation 2*). Minimum alternate tax is not applicable as book profit is Rs. 21,00,000.

•

	Situation 1 *Rs.*	*Situation 2* *Rs.*
Income-tax on net income @ 25%	2,53,75,000	2,55,00,000
Add: Surcharge @ 12%	30,45,000	30,60,000
Income-tax and surcharge under normal computation (*a*)	2,84,20,000	2,85,60,000
Computation for marginal relief		

	Situation 1 Rs.	Situation 2 Rs.
Step 1 - Income-tax and surcharge if income is Rs. 10 crore (*i.e.*, income-tax @ 25% and surcharge @ 7%)	2,67,50,000	2,67,50,000
Step 2 - Tax @ 100% of income in excess of Rs. 10 crore	15,00,000	20,00,000
Tax under marginal relief computation (*b*)	2,82,50,000	2,87,50,000
Normal tax or tax under marginal relief, whichever is lower [(*a*) or (*b*), whichever is lower] (*c*)	2,82,50,000	2,85,60,000
Add: Health and education cess @ 4%	11,30,000	11,42,400
Tax liability	2,93,80,000	2,97,02,400

0.11-E5 X Ltd. is a domestic company. The company has a manufacturing unit situated in Maharashtra. Turnover of the company in the previous year 2017-18 exceeded Rs. 400 crore. Income of the company for the assessment year 2020-21 is as follows –

	Situation 1 Rs.	Situation 2 Rs.
Income from manufacturing (computed under the Income-tax Act)	1,04,00,000	1,01,00,000
Book profit	10,10,50,000	10,25,50,000
•		
Net income	1,04,00,000	1,01,00,000
Income-tax	31,20,000	30,30,000
Add: Surcharge @ 7%	2,18,400	2,12,100
Income-tax and surcharge (*a*)	33,38,400	32,42,100
Computation for marginal relief		
Step 1 - Income-tax if income is Rs. 1 crore	30,00,000	30,00,000
Step 2 - Tax @ 100% of income in excess of Rs. 1 crore	4,00,000	1,00,000
Tax under marginal relief computation (*b*)	34,00,000	31,00,000
Normal tax or tax under marginal relief, whichever is lower [(*a*) or (*b*), whichever is lower] (*c*)	33,38,400	31,00,000
Minimum alternate tax (under normal provisions)		
Tax on book profit of Rs. 10,10,50,000/Rs. 10,25,50,000 @ 18.5%	1,86,94,250	1,89,71,750
Add: Surcharge @ 12%	22,43,310	22,76,610
Tax on book profit and surcharge (*d*)	2,09,37,560	2,12,48,360
Minimum alternate tax (under marginal relief)		
Tax on book profit if book profit is Rs. 10,00,00,000 [book profit @ 18.5% and surcharge @ 7%]	1,97,95,000	1,97,95,000
Add: 100% of book profit in excess of Rs. 1,00,00,000	10,50,000	25,50,000
Total (*e*)	2,08,45,000	2,23,45,000
Minimum alternate tax (including surcharge) after marginal relief [(*d*) or (*e*), whichever is lower] (*f*)	2,08,45,000	2,12,48,360
Normal tax or minimum alternate tax, whichever is higher [(*c*) or (*f*), whichever is higher]	2,08,45,000	2,12,48,360
Add: Health and education cess	8,33,800	8,49,934
Tax liability of the company (*g*)	2,16,78,800	2,20,98,294
Less: Tax liability, if minimum alternate tax is ignored [(*c*) + HEC] (*h*)	34,71,936	32,24,000
Tax credit available under section 115JAA(2A)	1,82,06,864	1,88,74,294

Amendment to section 2(*19AA*)

0.12 Section 2(*19AA*) provides for the definition of the expression "demerger" for the purpose of providing tax neutrality where assets and liabilities of an undertaking are transferred pursuant to the demerger. One of the existing conditions for tax-neutral demergers is that the resulting company should record the property and the liabilities of the undertaking at the value appearing in the books of account of the demerged company.

• *Amendment* - Indian Accounting Standards (Ind-AS) compliant companies are required to record the property and the liabilities of the undertaking at a value different from the book value of the demerged company. In order to accommodate such companies, section 2(*19AA*) has been amended with effect from the assessment year 2020-21. The amended provisions provide that the requirement of recording property and liabilities at book value by the resulting company shall not be applicable in a case where the property and liabilities of the undertakings received by it, are recorded at a value different from the value appearing in the books of account of the demerged company immediately before the demerger in compliance of the Indian Accounting Standards specified in Annexure to the Companies (Indian Accounting Standards) Rules, 2015.

Deemed accrual of gift of money to a non-resident/foreign company [Sec. 9(1)(*viii*)]

0.13 A person (who is non-resident in India) is taxable in India in respect of income that accrues or arises in India or is received in India or is deemed to accrue or arise in India or is deemed to be received in India. A gift of money is chargeable to tax in the hands of recipient, except for certain exceptions provided in section 56(2)(*x*).

• *Amendment* - In a few cases, gift received by a non-resident/foreign company from a resident person, is not taxable in India [even if it is not covered by exceptions specified in section 56(2)(*x*)]. There is no deeming provision under section 9 for this purpose.

To plug in this loophole, clause (*viii*) has been inserted in section 9(1) with effect from the assessment year 2020-21. This clause is applicable if the following conditions are satisfied –

1. Payer is resident in India (or money is received from a person resident in India). Payer may be resident and ordinarily resident in India or resident but not ordinarily resident in India. Payer may be an individual, HUF, AOP, BOI, artificial juridical person, firm, LLP, company or any other person.

2. Recipient is non-resident/foreign company (or money is received by a non-resident/foreign company).

3. A sum of money is received by non-resident/foreign company on or after July 5, 2019.

4. Income arises outside India. The transaction is not covered by any of the exceptions specified by section 56(2)(*x*).

If these conditions are satisfied, money received by a non-resident/foreign company, shall be deemed to accrue or arise in India.

• *Provisions illustrated* - X is resident in India. He transfers the following assets to his friend Y (a non-resident Indian or foreign citizen currently located in USA) or to Y Ltd. (a foreign company) –

1. Gift of Rs. 9 lakh by NEFT transfer from X's bank account (SBI, Mumbai) to Y's bank account in California.

2. Gift of Rs. 10 lakh to Y (this money is gifted to Y in India by an account-payee cheque when Y visited India on a short trip).

3. Gift of Rs. 11 lakh to Y (X has a bank account in Citibank, New York. Permission of RBI has taken for this purpose. This gift is transferred from Citibank, New York account of X to the account of Y in Deutsche Bank, New Jersey).

4. Gift of house property situated in Pune (stamp duty value : Rs. 45 lakh).

5. Gift of house property situated in New Jersey (market value : Rs. 2.70 crore).

6. Shares in Reliance Industries Ltd. (market value as per stock exchange quotation : Rs. 20 lakh).

7. Shares in a US company, not having any tangible/intangible assets in India (market value : Rs. 18 lakh).

8. Shares in Malaysian company (net worth of the company : Rs. 900 crore, more than 95 per cent assets located in India) (market value of shares gifted : Rs. 10.5 crore).

9. Jewellery (market value : Rs. 30 lakh) (it is given as gift to Y when he visited India).

10. Diamonds (market value : Rs. 10 lakh) (given as gift outside India from X's locker in a foreign bank).

11. Tagore painting (market value : Rs. 6 crore) (it is given as gift to Y when he visited India).

12. Raja Ravi Verma painting (market value : Rs. 2 crore) (taken from India by X when he visited USA and given as a gift on birthday of Y in California).

13. Computer and car (market value : Rs. 8 lakh) (given as gift to Y when he visited India).

14. Gift of Rs. 11 lakh by electronic transfer from Indian bank account of X to Y's bank account in USA (gift given on the occasion of marriage of Y).

15. Transfer of a plot of land in Nagpur to Y (stamp duty value : Rs. 62.8 lakh, sale consideration : Rs. 60 lakh).

In these cases, amount taxable in India in the hands of Y will be as follows –

Assets	*If transfer takes place before July 5, 2019*	*If transfer takes place on or after July 5, 2019*	*Sections*
Gift of Rs. 9 lakh by way of NEFT to foreign bank	Not taxable	Taxable†	9(1)(*viii*), 56(2)(*x*)
Gift of Rs. 10 lakh in India	Taxable†	Taxable†	5, 56(2)(*x*)
Gift of Rs. 11 lakh by bank transfer in New Jersey	Not taxable	Taxable†	9(1)(*viii*), 56(2)(*x*)
Pune property	Taxable†	Taxable†	5, 56(2)(*x*)
New Jersey property	Not taxable	Not taxable	5
Shares in Reliance	Taxable†	Taxable†	9(1)(*i*), 56(2)(*x*)
Shares in US company	Not taxable	Not taxable	9(1)(*i*), 56(2)(*x*)
Shares in a Malaysian company	Taxable†	Taxable†	9(1)(*i*), 56(2)(*x*)
Jewellery	Taxable†	Taxable†	5, 56(2)(*x*)
Diamonds	Not taxable	Not taxable	5, 56(2)(*x*)
Tagore painting	Taxable†	Taxable†	5, 56(2)(*x*)
Raja Ravi Verma painting	Not taxable	Not taxable	5, 56(2)(*x*)
Computer and car	Not taxable	Not taxable	5, 56(2)(*x*)
Marriage gift	Not taxable	Not taxable	5, 56(2)(*x*)
Transfer of Nagpur land (stamp duty value does not exceed 105% of sale consideration)	Not taxable	Not taxable	5, 56(2)(*x*)

†Subject to provisions of relevant Double Taxation Avoidance agreement.

Amendment to section 9A

0.14 In order to facilitate location of fund managers of off-shore funds in India, section 9A provides a specific tax regime for this purpose with the following objectives –

a. the tax liability in respect of income arising to the Fund from investment in India would be neutral to the fact as to whether the investment is made directly by the fund or through engagement of Fund manager located in India; and

b. that income of the fund from the investments outside India would not be taxable in India solely on the basis that the Fund management activity in respect of such investments have been undertaken through a fund manager located in India.

In the case of an "eligible investment fund", the fund management activity carried out through an "eligible fund manager" acting on behalf of such fund, shall not constitute business connection in India of the said fund. Further, an "eligible investment fund" shall not be said to be resident in India merely because the "eligible fund manager" undertaking fund management activities on its behalf, is located in India.

These benefits of section 9A are available subject to the conditions provided in sub-section (3)/(4)/(5) of the said section. These provisions, *inter-alia,* are related to residence of fund, corpus, size, investor broad basing, investment diversification and payment of remuneration to fund manager at arm's length.

• *Amendment* - Section 9A(3)(*j*) provides that the monthly average of the corpus of the fund shall not be less than Rs. 100 crore. Where the fund has been established or incorporated in the previous year, the corpus of fund shall not be less than Rs. 100 crore at the end of such previous year. This condition has been amended with effect from the assessment year 2019-20 to provide that where the fund has been established or incorporated in the previous year, the fund shall be required to fulfil the condition of maintaining the corpus of Rs. 100 crore within a period of 6 months from the last day of the month of its establishment or incorporation, or at the end of such previous year, whichever is later.

Further, section 9A(3)(*m*) provides that the remuneration paid by the fund to an eligible fund manager in respect of fund management activity undertaken by him on its behalf is not less than the arm's length price of the said activity. This condition has been amended to provide that the remuneration paid by the fund to an eligible fund manager in respect of fund management activity undertaken by him on its behalf is not less than the amount calculated in such manner as may be prescribed (instead of the arm's length price of the said activity).

Exemption of interest income of rupee denominated bonds [Sec. 10(*4C*)]

0.15 Clause (*4C*) has been inserted in section 10 with effect from the assessment year 2019-20. It is applicable if the following conditions are satisfied –

1. Interest is payable to a non-resident or a foreign company.

2. It is payable by an Indian company or a business trust.

3. It is payable in respect of money borrowed from a source outside India by way of issue of rupee denominated bonds [as referred to in section 194LC(2)(*ia*)].

4. The aforesaid bonds are issued during September 17, 2018 and March 31, 2019.

If these conditions are satisfied, interest income will be exempt under section 10(*4C*).

Exemption of certain income received by a specified fund [Sec. 10(*4D*)]

0.16 Clause (*4D*) has been inserted with effect from the assessment year 2020-21. It is applicable if the following conditions are satisfied –

1. Income is accrued or arises to, or received by a specified fund. For this purpose, "specified fund" means a fund which satisfies the following conditions –

- It is a fund established or incorporated in India in the form of a trust or a company or a limited liability partnership or a body corporate.
- It has a certificate of registration as a Category III Alternative Investment Fund and is regulated under SEBI (Alternative Investment Fund) Regulations, 2012.
- It is located in any International Financial Services Centre.
- All units of fund are held by non-residents.

2. Income arises as a result of transfer of capital asset referred to in section 47(*viiab*).

3. Income arises as a result of transfer of a capital asset on a recognised foreign exchange located in any International Financial Services Centre.

4. Consideration for transfer is paid or payable in convertible foreign exchange.

If the above conditions are satisfied, exemption will be available under section 10(*4D*) to the extent such income is accrued or arises or received in respect of units held by non-resident.

Amendment to section 10(*12A*)

0.17 Section 10(*12A*) provides that any payment from the National Pension System (NPS) Trust to an employee on closure of account or his opting out of the pension scheme referred to in section 80CCD, to the extent it does not exceed 40 per cent of the total amount payable to him at the time of closure or at the time of his opting out of the scheme, shall be exempt from tax.

• *Amendment* - With a view to enable the pensioner to have more disposable funds, the aforesaid exemption has been increased from 40 per cent to 60 per cent. After this amendment (which is applicable from the assessment year 2020-21) 60 per cent of the total amount payable to the person at the time of closure or at the time of his opting out of NPS, shall be exempt from tax under section 10(*12A*).

Amendment to section 10(*15*)

0.18 With a view to facilitate external borrowing by the units located in International Financial Services Centre, sub-clause (*ix*) has been inserted in section 10(*15*) with effect from the assessment year 2020-21. It is applicable if the following conditions are satisfied –

1. Recipient of interest is a non-resident.

2. Interest is payable by a unit located in an International Financial Service Centre.

3. Interest pertains to money borrowed by it on or after September 1, 2019.

If the aforesaid conditions are satisfied, interest income will be exempt under section 10(*15*)(*ix*).

Conditions governing exemption under section 10(*23C*)(*iv*)/(*v*)/(*vi*)/(*via*)

0.19 For availing of the exemption under the aforesaid sub-clauses of section 10(*23C*), the trust/institution is required to make an online application to the prescribed authority. The prescribed authority, before approving of the fund/institution, may call for such documents (including audited annual accounts) or information, which it may consider necessary in order to satisfy himself about the genuineness of the activities of the fund or trust or institution.

• *Amendment* - The above provisions have been amended with effect from September 1, 2019 on the following lines –

Enquiry at the time of approval - Under the amended version, the prescribed authority has been empowered to satisfy himself about the compliance of the trust or institution to requirements of any other law which is material for the purpose of achieving its objects.

Enquiry at the time of rescinding of notification - Where a trust or an institution has been granted approval under the aforesaid provisions and, subsequently, it is noticed that the trust or institution has violated requirements of any other law which was material for the purpose of achieving its objects, and the order (or direction or decree), holding that such violation has occurred, has not been disputed (or has attained finality), the prescribed authority/Central Government may, rescind the notification or withdraw the approval and forward a copy of the order rescinding the notification or withdrawing the approval to such fund or institution or trust or university, etc., and to the Assessing Officer.

Amendment to section 10(*34A*)

0.20 Any income arising to a shareholder (on account of buy-back of shares) is exempt from tax under section 10(*34A*). However, tax is payable by the company (which buys-back its own shares) under section 115QA. These two provisions are applicable only in the case of buy-back of unlisted shares.

• *Amendment* - The aforesaid provisions will be applicable (on or after July 5, 2019) even in the case of buy-back of listed shares. Consequently, in the case of buy-back of shares (listed or unlisted) on or after July 5, 2019 –

a. income of shareholder will be exempt under section 10(*34A*); and

b. the company (with buys-back its own shares), will be liable for tax on distributed income under section 115QA.

Cancellation of registration of charitable trust/institution [Sec. 12AA]

0.21 Section 12AA prescribes for manner of granting registration in case of trust or institution for the purpose of availing of exemption under section 11. Further, section 12AA provides procedure for cancellation of registration on the basis of the following two grounds –

- CIT/PCIT is satisfied that activities of trust/institute are not genuine or are not being carried out in accordance with its objects; and
- it is noticed that the activities of trust/institute are being carried out in a manner that either whole or any part of its income would cease to be exempt.

In many cases, courts/Tribunal have held that violation of provisions of the Prohibition of Capitation Fees Act, Foreign Contribution Regulation Act, or any other Act, by a charitable trust could not be a ground to take away the aforesaid registration of the entity – *Padanilam Welfare Trust* v. *CIT* [2012] 20 taxmann.com 113 (Chennai), *Global Academy of Emergency Medicine* v. *CIT* [2019] 101 taxmann.com 394 (Delhi), *CIT* v. *Maria Social Service Society* [2018] 99 taxmann.com 381 (Kar.), *Maria Social Service Society* v. *CIT* [2018] 99 taxmann.com 380 (Bang.), *Bharati Vidyapeeth* v. *ITO* [2009] 28 SOT 32 (Pune).

• *Amendment* - To supersede the aforesaid rulings, section 12AA has been amended with effect from September 1, 2019. The amended provisions provide the following –

Enquiry at the time of registration - At the time of granting the registration to a trust or institution, the CIT/PCIT shall, *inter alia,* also satisfy himself about the compliance of the trust or institution to requirements of any other law which is material for the purpose of achieving its objects.

Violation requirement for cancellation - Where a trust or an institution has been granted registration under section 12AA(1)(*b*) (or has obtained registration at any time under section 12A) and, subsequently, it is noticed that the trust or institution has violated requirements of any other law which was material for the purpose of achieving its objects, and the order (or direction or decree), holding that such violation has occurred, has not been disputed (or has attained finality), CIT/PCIT may, by an order in writing, cancel the registration of such trust or institution after affording a reasonable opportunity of being heard.

Prescription of electronic mode of payment [Sec. 13A]

0.22 To claim exemption under section 13A, a political party is required to receive donation (exceeding Rs. 2,000) only through an account-payee cheque/draft or using the electronic clearing system through a bank account.

• *Amendment to section 13A* - In order to encourage other electronic modes of payment, section 13A has been amended (with effect from the assessment year 2020-21) so as to include such other electronic mode as may be prescribed, in addition to the already existing permissible modes of payment in the form of an account-payee cheque or an account-payee bank draft or the electronic clearing system through a bank account.

• *Amendment to other sections* - There are several provisions in other sections [list given in the Table (*infra*)] which prohibit cash transactions and allow/encourage payment or receipt only through account-payee cheque, account-payee draft or electronic clearing system through a bank account. To promote other electronic modes of payment, identical modifications have been made in the scheme of these sections so as to include such other electronic mode as may be prescribed, in addition to the already existing permissible modes of payment in the form of an account-payee cheque or an account-payee bank draft or the electronic clearing system through a bank account. A list of similar amendment in other sections is as follows –

Section	*Amount in excess of which payment/ receipt is required by an account-payee cheque/draft/electronic clearing system through a bank*	*Other electronic modes (as may be prescribed) will be applicable from –*
35AD : Expenditure of capital nature	Rs. 10,000	Assessment year 2020-21
40A(3)/(3A)/(4) : Any business expenditure	Rs. 10,000	Assessment year 2020-21
43(*1*) : Actual cost	Rs. 10,000	Assessment year 2020-21
43CA : Consideration for transfer	Full consideration or part thereof	Assessment year 2020-21
44AD : Turnover	–	Assessment year 2020-21
50C : Consideration for transfer	Full consideration or part thereof	Assessment year 2020-21
56(2)(*x*) : Consideration for transfer	Full consideration or part thereof	Assessment year 2020-21
80JJAA : Cost in the case of existing business	–	Assessment year 2020-21
269SS : Loan or deposit	Rs. 20,000	September 1, 2019
269ST : Transactions	Rs. 2,00,000	September 1, 2019
269T : Repayment of loan/deposit	Rs. 20,000	September 1, 2019

Amendment to section 35AD

0.23 *See* para 0.22.

Disallowance of business expenditure on account of non-deduction of tax on payment to non-resident payee [Sec. 40(*a*)(*i*)]

0.24 In case of payment/credit to a non-resident/foreign company or payment/credit to a person outside India, tax deduction provisions are applicable, if the following conditions are satisfied –

a. the amount paid/payable is interest, royalty, technical fees or any other sum (but not salary), and

b. in the hands of the recipient, it is chargeable to tax in India.

Disallowance under section 40(*a*)(*i*) is applicable in the following two cases –

Case 1 - Tax is deductible from aforesaid payment/credit to a non-resident/foreign company, but it is not deducted.

Case 2 - Tax is deductible (and it is so deducted) on the aforesaid payment/credit but the tax deducted is not deposited by the deductor till the due date of submission of his return of income.

In the above two cases, 100 per cent of payment/credit is disallowed under section 40(*a*)(*i*). Consequently, no deduction is available in the year of payment /credit. If, however, tax is deducted in a subsequent year, expenditure [*i.e.*, amount disallowed under section 40(*a*)(*i*)] will be allowed as deduction in the year in which TDS is deposited by the deductor with the Government.

• *Amendment to section 40*(a)(i) - The above provisions have been amended with effect from the assessment year 2020-21. Under the amended provisions, a relief is given in *Case 1* (and not in *Case 2*). This relief will be available if the following conditions are satisfied –

1. Tax is deductible on the aforesaid payments but it is not deducted (wholly or partly) by the payer (*i.e.*, *Case 1*).

2. The payer is not deemed to be an assessee-in-default under the first proviso to section 201(1).

If the above conditions are satisfied, then for the purpose of section 40(*a*)(*i*) it shall be deemed that the payer has deducted and paid the tax on such amount on the date of the furnishing of return of income by the recipient.

• *Amendment to section 201* - Currently, relief is available under section 201 in the case of TDS default when recipient is resident. To accommodate the aforesaid modification in the scheme of section 40(*a*)(*i*), section 201 has been simultaneously amended with effect from the assessment year 2020-21.

After the amendment, by virtue of first proviso to section 201(1), the payer is not deemed to be an assessee-in-default if –

a. the recipient has furnished his return of income under section 139;

b. the recipient has taken into account the above income in such return of income;

c. the recipient has paid the tax due on the income declared in such return of income, and

d. the payer furnishes a certificate to this effect from a chartered accountant in a prescribed form.

• *Amendment applicable with retrospective effect or prospective effect* - The aforesaid amendments are applicable with effect from the assessment year 2020-21. However, courts have been unanimous in holding that amendments, which are intended to remove unintended hardships, are declaratory in nature and, therefore, operate retrospectively – *CIT* v. *Calcutta Export Company* [2018] 255 Taxman 293 (SC), *CIT* v. *Alom Extrusions Ltd.* [2009] 185 Taxman 416 (SC), *CIT* v. *Amrit Banaspati Co. Ltd.* [2002] 123 Taxman 74 (SC), *Allied Motors (P.) Ltd.* v. *CIT* [1997] 91 Taxman 205 (SC).

0.24-E1 X Ltd. pays a sum of Rs. 9,00,000 as commission to Y Inc. (a US company) on October 15, 2019. Tax is deductible under section 195 (read with Indo-US tax treaty) but it is not deducted by X Ltd. Y Inc. pays advance tax on the due dates on its income (including Rs. 9,00,000). Entire tax liability is paid by Y Inc. during the financial year 2019-20 by way of advance tax. Return of income of Y Inc. for the assessment year 2020-21 is submitted on September 20, 2020. X Ltd. has a certificate to this effect from a chartered accountant in the prescribed form.

•

In this case, tax is not deducted by X Ltd. in the financial year 2019-20. By virtue of section 40(*a*)(*i*), the payment of Rs. 9,00,000 will be disallowed in computing the income for the assessment year 2020-21. However, X Ltd. cannot be treated as an assessee-in-default under the amended provisions of first proviso to section 201(1), as the following conditions are satisfied –

a. Y Inc. has furnished its return of income under section 139;

b. Y Inc. has taken into account the above income in such return of income;

c. Y Inc. has paid the tax due on the income declared in such return of income, and

d. X Ltd. has a certificate to this effect from a chartered accountant in a prescribed form.

Under the amended provisions, it will be assumed that X Ltd. has deducted and paid tax on September 20, 2020. As a consequence, Rs. 45,000 will be allowed as deduction in the hands of X Ltd. for the financial year 2020-21 (*i.e.*, assessment year 2021-22).

0.24-E2 On December 8, 2019, Z Ltd. pays Rs. 4,00,000 as royalty to C (a non-resident individual) after deducting tax at the rate of 10 per cent under section 195, read with section 115A. The tax so deducted by Z Ltd. is not deposited till November 30, 2020. However, C submits his return of income on July 31, 2020 after including Rs. 4,00,000 in his income. As per his return of income, a refund of Rs. 82,000 is due to him.

•

In this case, the amended provisions are not applicable (the amended provisions are applicable only when the payer fails to deduct the whole or any part of tax). If tax is deducted but not paid, the amended provisions [as well as the first proviso to section 201(1)] are not applicable. Z Ltd. cannot claim any deduction for the previous year 2019-20 or 2020-21 in respect of royalty payment of Rs. 40,00,000.

Amendment to sections 40A and 43(*1*)

0.25 *See* para 0.22.

Section 43B extended to non-banking finance companies

0.26 Section 43B is applicable only if the taxpayer maintains books of account on the basis of mercantile system of accounting. Provisions of section 43B have been amended (with effect from the assessment year 2020-21) by inserting clause (*da*). After this amendment, the scope of section 43B has been extended to cover interest payable on loan or borrowing from –

a. "systemically important non-deposit taking non-banking financial company (NBFC)"; or

b. "deposit taking NBFC".

• *Impact of amendment* - Outcome of the amendment is as follows –

1. Deduction on payment basis - Interest payable on loan or borrowing to the aforesaid entities will be deductible on payment basis in the year in which interest is actually paid.

2. When deductible on accrual basis - If, however, interest is paid after the end of the previous year but on or before the due date of submission of return of income, interest will be deductible on "accrual" basis in the year in which it becomes due for payment.

3. Double deduction not allowed - *Explanation 3AA* has been inserted to provide that where a deduction in respect of aforesaid interest is allowed as deduction in any earlier year (*i.e.*, prior to the assessment year 2020-21) on accrual basis, such interest is not again deductible on payment basis in the year in which the payment is made.

4. Conversion of interest into loan - *Explanation 3CA* has been inserted to provide that if an outstanding interest is converted into loan, conversion will not be treated as payment of interest.

5. Systemically important non-deposit taking NBFC - It means a non-banking financial company (NBFC) which is not accepting or holding public deposits and is having total assets of not less than Rs. 500 crore as per the last audited balance sheet and is registered with RBI under the provisions of the Reserve Bank of India Act.

6. Deposit taking NBFC - "Deposit taking NBFC" means a non-banking financial company which is accepting or holding public deposits and is registered with RBI under the provisions of the Reserve Bank of India Act.

Amendment to section 43CA

0.27 *See* para 0.22.

Incentives to non-banking finance companies [Sec. 43D]

0.28 The existing provisions of section 43D, *inter alia,* provide that interest income in relation to certain categories of bad or doubtful debts received by certain institutions (or banks or corporations or companies), shall be chargeable to tax in the previous year in which it is credited to its profit and loss account or in the year in which it is actually received, whichever is earlier. This provision of section 43D gives a relief to the aforesaid taxpayers by specifically providing for taxability of interest on non-performing assets (NPA) on receipt basis.

Interest on NPAs of NBFCs - The aforesaid relaxation of section 43D is not available to interest on NPAs of non-banking finance companies (NBFCs). RBI governs the functioning of banks and NBFCs in India. According to RBI guidelines, NBFCs are only required to recognize income from NPAs, only when such income is actually received by NBFCs. However, the Apex Court in the case of *Southern Technologies Ltd.* v. *CIT* [2010] 187 Taxman 346 held that RBI guidelines would not have an overriding effect on income-tax provisions. Currently, interest on NPAs of NBFC is taxable on accrual basis. Even Income Computation and Disclosure Standard (ICDS) - IV requires that interest income should be recognised on the time basis determined by the amount outstanding and the rate applicable.

Amendment - Section 43D has been amended so as to insert reference of a "deposit-taking NBFC" or a "systemically important non-deposit taking NBFC" in it in order to extend the benefit of the provision of this section to the said entities. For meaning of "deposit-taking NBFC" and "systemically important non-deposit taking NBFC", *see* para 0.26.

Amendment applicable with retrospective effect or prospective effect - The aforesaid amendment is applicable with effect from the assessment year 2020-21. However, courts have been unanimous in holding that amendments, which are intended to remove unintended hardships, are declaratory in nature and, therefore, operate retrospectively – *CIT* v. *Calcutta Export Company* [2018] 255 Taxman 293 (SC), *CIT* v. *Alom Extrusions Ltd.* [2009] 185 Taxman 416 (SC), *CIT* v. *Amrit Banaspati Co. Ltd.* [2002] 123 Taxman 74 (SC), *Allied Motors (P.) Ltd.* v. *CIT* [1997] 91 Taxman 205 (SC).

Amendment to section 44AD

0.29 *See* para 0.22.

Amendment to section 47(*viiab*)

0.30 Section 47 provides that any transfer of a capital asset, being bonds or Global Depository Receipts [referred to in section 115AC(1)] or rupee denominated bond of an Indian company or derivative, made by a non-resident shall not be regarded as transfer.

• *Amendment* - The above provision of section 47(*viiab*) has been amended (with effect from the assessment year 2020-21) to provide that transfer of securities (as may be notified by the Central Government) shall not be regarded as transfer in the hands of a non-resident.

Amendment to section 50C

0.31 *See* para 0.22.

Amendment to sections 50CA and 56(2)(*x*)

0.32 Shares received by a person for inadequate consideration (or without consideration) are chargeable to tax in the hands of recipient under section 56(2)(*x*) to the extent of inadequacy of consideration (or absence of consideration), if a few conditions are satisfied (this section is also applicable for receipt of money or property without consideration or for inadequate consideration). Conversely, section 50CA provides that if unquoted shares are transferred for inadequate consideration, capital gain is calculated in the hands of transferor by taking fair market value of shares as "full value of consideration".

Fair market value - For these provisions, the fair market value is determined based on the prescribed method. Determination of fair market value based on the prescribed rules may result into genuine hardships in certain cases where the consideration for transfer of shares is approved by certain authorities and the person transferring the share has no control over such determination.

Exemption - Currently, the provisions of section 56(2)(*x*) are not applicable to certain specified transactions. However, no such exemption is available under section 50CA. For instance, if X transfers shares (fair market value : Rs. 10 lakh) to Y for Rs. 4 lakh, Rs. 6 lakh is taxable as income of Y (*i.e.*, recipient) under section 56(2)(*x*). Capital gain of X (*i.e.*, transferor) will be calculated by taking Rs. 10 lakh as full value of consideration under section 50C. If X and Y are relatives, section 56(2)(*x*) is not applicable [there are a few more such cases where section 56(2)(*x*) is not applicable]. However, no such exemption is available under section 50CA.

• *Amendment* - In order to provide relief to such types of transactions (as given above) from the applicability of sections 56(2)(*x*) and 50CA, these sections have been amended with effect from the assessment year 2020-21. The amended provisions empower the Board to prescribe transactions undertaken by certain class of persons to whom the provisions of sections 56(2)(*x*) and 50CA shall not be applicable.

Amendment to section 54GB

0.33 The existing provisions of the section 54GB, *inter alia*, provide for rollover benefit in respect of capital gain arising from the transfer of a residential property owned by an individual or a HUF. To be able to get benefit of this provision, the assessee is required to utilise the net consideration for subscription in the equity shares of an eligible company (*i.e.*, a company which owns an eligible start-up) before the due date of filing of the return of income. The assessee is required to have more than 50 per cent share capital (or more than 50 per cent voting rights) after the subscription in shares in the eligible company. The said section, *inter alia*, puts restriction on transfer of assets acquired by the company for 5 years from the date of acquisition. Currently, the benefit of this section is only available for investment in the equity shares of eligible start-up and that period ends on March 31, 2019 (in other words, at present no benefit is available for residential property transferred after March 31, 2019).

• *Amendment* - The following amendments have been made to the scheme of section 54GB with effect from the assessment year 2020-21 –

1. The sun set date of transfer of residential property (for investment in eligible start-up company) has been extended from March 31, 2019 to March 31, 2021.

2. The condition of minimum shareholding of 50 per cent of share capital or voting rights has been reduced to 25 per cent.

3. The condition restricting transfer of new asset (being computer or computer software) has been relaxed from the current 5 years to 3 years.

Amendment to section 56(2)(*viib*)

0.34 Section 56(2)(*viib*) is applicable if a closely held company (*i.e.*, a company in which the public are not substantially interested) receives consideration for issue of shares at a premium from resident persons. The aggregate consideration received for such shares (as exceeds the fair market value of shares) shall be chargeable to tax in the hands of recipient company.

• *Amendment to Category II AIF* - Exemption from this provision has been provided for the consideration for issue of shares received by a venture capital undertaking from a venture capital company or a venture capital fund or by a company from a class or classes of persons as may be notified by the Central Government in this behalf (*i.e.*, a start-up company). Currently, the benefit of exemption is available to Category I Alternate Investment Fund (AIF). With a view to facilitate venture capital undertakings to receive funds from Category II AIF, section 56(2)(*viib*) has been amended (with effect from the assessment year 2020-21). After this amendment, the benefit of exemption will be available to fund received by venture capital undertakings from Category I or Category II AIF.

• *Amendment to compliance with the notification of exemption issued under section 56(2)(*viib*)* - Under section 56(2)(*viib*), the Central Government is empowered to notify that the provisions of this section shall not be applicable to consideration received by a notified company. For the purpose of section 56(2)(*viib*), exemption is available to a "startup" if a few conditions, given by Notification No. GSR 127(E), dated February 19, 2019, are satisfied. With a view to ensure compliance with the conditions specified in the notification, the scheme of section 56(2)(*viib*) has been amended (with effect from the assessment year 2020-21) to provide that in case of failure to comply with the aforesaid conditions, the consideration received for issue of shares (which exceeds the fair market value of such shares), shall be deemed to be the income of the company chargeable to tax for the previous year in which the failure to comply with any of the aforesaid conditions has taken place. Further, it shall be deemed that the company has under-reported the said income in consequence of the misreporting referred to in section 270A(8)/(9) for the said previous year.

0.34-E1 X Ltd. is incorporated as a private limited company to set up a professional website for digital marketing in India and abroad. It is recognised as startup by the Department for Promotion of Industry and Internal Trade (DPIIT). After this recognition, shares are issued at premium to Y Ltd. on July 25, 2019 (face value : Rs. 1 crore, issue price : Rs. 11 crore, fair market value of shares : Rs. 3 crore). X Ltd. and Y Ltd. satisfy all conditions given by Notification No. GSR 127(E), dated February 19, 2019. X Ltd. has not invested, during the financial year 2019-20, in any of the assets (*e.g.*, land, shares, securities, jewellery, painting, etc.) given in the aforesaid notification. Tax consequences are examined if X Ltd. makes investment in shares, securities, land, paintings during the financial year 2021-22.

• *Assessment year 2020-21* - Shares are issued by X Ltd. at premium during the previous year 2019-20. Normally, the amount received from shareholders in excess of fair market value (*i.e.*, Rs. 11 crore – Rs. 3 crore which comes to Rs. 8 crore in this case), is chargeable to tax under section 56(2)(*viib*) in the hands of the recipient company. However, exemption is available from the operation of section 56(2)(*viib*) to a startup if conditions given by Notification No. GSR 127(E), dated February 19, 2019 are satisfied. In this case, these conditions are satisfied by X Ltd. which is a startup. Consequently, the excess amount of Rs. 8 crore is not chargeable to tax for the assessment year 2020-21.

Assessment year 2022-23 - After availing of the benefit of exemption under the aforesaid notification, startup company cannot make investment during 7 years (from the end of latest financial year in which shares are issued at premium) in a few assets (*e.g.*, land, shares, securities, jewellery, painting, etc.). In this case, 7 years period ends on March 31, 2027. However, X Ltd. has invested in these assets during the financial year 2021-22. Consequently, the exemption will be taken back. Amount chargeable to tax in the hands of X Ltd. for the previous year 2021-22 will be Rs. 8 crore (*i.e.*, the issue price in excess of fair market value).

0.34-E2 In the above example, X Ltd. submits return of income under section 139(1) on July 20, 2022 for the assessment year 2022-23 as follows –

Situation 1 - Deemed income of Rs. 8 crore, as calculated above, is not included.

Situation 2 - Deemed income of only Rs. 2 crore is included.

Situation 3 - Deemed income of Rs. 8 crore is fully included in the return.

The case is taken up for scrutiny assessment by issue of notice under section 143(2). Regular assessment under 143(3) is completed by adding the above deemed income (in *Situation 1* and *Situation 2*). An addition of Rs. 1 lakh is made by the Assessing Officer (in all situations) (this addition is made on estimation basis, accounts are correct and complete, but method employed is such that income cannot be properly deduced therefrom). Besides, an addition of Rs. 4 lakh is made by the Assessing Officer (in all situations) (this addition is on account of under-reported income).

Amount of penalty will be calculated on the following basis under section 270A –

	Situation 1 Rs.	*Situation 2* Rs.	*Situation 3* Rs.
Non-reporting of deemed income under second proviso to section 56(2)(*viib*) (it is treated as misreporting of income)	8 crore	6 crore	*Nil*
Addition of Rs. 1 lakh on estimated basis (not treated as under-reported income)	*Nil*	*Nil*	*Nil*
Addition of Rs. 4 lakh (it is under-reported income)	4 lakh	4 lakh	4 lakh

Amount of penalty will be 50% of tax payable on under-reported income and 200% of tax payable on misreporting of income.

Amendment to section 56(2)(*x*)

0.35 *See* paras 0.22 and 0.32.

Amendment to section 79

0.36 Section 79 regulates carry forward and set off of losses in case of a closely held company (*i.e.*, not being a company in which the public are substantially interested). Clause (*a*) of section 79 applies to all such companies (except an eligible start-up as referred to in section 80-IAC), while clause (*b*) applies only to such eligible start-up. These provisions are as follows –

• *Clause (a) of section 79 : Loss of a closely held company* - Where a change in shareholding has taken place during the previous year in the case of a closely held company, earlier year losses shall be carried forward and set off against the income of the current previous year, only if the persons beneficially holding 51 per cent of the voting power on the following two dates are same –

a. on the last day of the previous year in which the loss was incurred;

b. on the last day of the previous year in which the company wants to set off the brought forward loss.

• *Clause (b) of section 79 : Loss of a start-up* - In case of a closely held start-up (as referred to in section 80-IAC), brought forward loss can be set off against current year's income only if all the shareholders of the company (who held shares carrying voting power on the last day of the previous year in which the loss was incurred), continue to hold shares on the last day of the current year (*i.e.*, the year in which the company wants to set off the brought forward loss). This restriction is applicable only for such loss which is incurred during the period of 7 years beginning from the year in which such company is incorporated.

0.36-1 ***Amendment for eligible start-up*** - Currently, a closely held company (which owns an eligible start-up) cannot carry forward and set off loss under section 79(*a*).

To further facilitate ease of doing business in the case of an eligible start-up, the scheme of section 79 has been modified (with effect from the assessment year 2020-21) so as to provide that brought forward loss of a closely held eligible start-up shall be carried forward and set off against the income of current previous year on satisfaction of either of the two conditions stipulated currently under clause (*a*) or clause (*b*) as given above.

For other closely held companies, there would be no change, and loss incurred in any year prior to the previous year shall be carried forward and set off only on satisfaction of condition currently provided at clause (*a*).

0.36-2 ***Amendment to resolution of distressed companies*** - The existing provisions of section 79 are not applicable to a company where any change in shareholding takes place in a previous year pursuant to a resolution plan approved under the Insolvency and Bankruptcy Code, 2016 (IBC) subject to the condition that jurisdictional PCIT/CIT is provided a reasonable opportunity of being heard. Thus, loss in such cases can be carried forward and set off even if there is change in voting power or shareholding. This benefit has been extended to certain companies (with effect from the assessment year 2020-21). Thus, it has been provided in newly substituted section 79 that the provision of this section shall not apply to those companies, and their subsidiary and the subsidiary of such subsidiary, where –

- the National Company Law Tribunal (NCLT) on a petition moved by the Central Government under section 241 of the Companies Act has suspended the Board of Directors of such company and has appointed new directors, who are nominated by the Central Government, under section 242 of the Companies Act; and
- a change in shareholding of such company, and its subsidiaries and the subsidiary of such subsidiary, has taken place in a previous year pursuant to a resolution plan approved by NCLT under section 242 of the Companies Act, after affording a reasonable opportunity of being heard to the jurisdictional PCIT/CIT.

Amendment to section 80C

0.37 Section 80C has been amended with effect from the assessment year 2020-21. The amended version is applicable if the following conditions are satisfied –

1. The taxpayer is an employee of the Central Government.

2. He contributes to his NPS (Tier-II) account.

3. Such contribution is for a fixed period of not less than 3 years.

4. Such contribution is in accordance with the scheme as may be notified by the Central Government for this purpose.

If these conditions are satisfied, the aforesaid contribution will be deductible within the overall limit of Rs. 1,50,000 under section 80C.

Amendment to section 80CCD

0.38 The Union Cabinet in its meeting on December 6, 2018 has approved enhancement of the mandatory contribution by the Central Government for its employees covered under NPS Tier-I from 10 per cent to 14 per cent (minimum contribution by employees to remain 10 per cent). To avoid any adverse tax treatment in the hands of employees, section 80CCD(2) has been amended with effect from the assessment year 2020-21. The impact of amended version is as follows –

1. Contribution by the Central Government (or by any other employer) to NPS is first included under the head "Salaries" in hands of employees under section 15, read with section 17(*1*)(*viii*). After the above Union Cabinet's decision, the Central Government will continue 14 per cent of salary for its employees. To put it differently, 14 per cent contribution by the Central Government will be included in the salary of concerned employee under section 15, read with section 17(1)(*viii*).

2. Employer's contribution to NPS is deductible under section 80CCD(2) (the ceiling limit of Rs. 1,50,000 is not applicable). However, amount deductible under section 80CCD(2) on account of employer's contribution to NPS cannot exceed 10 per cent of "salary" of the concerned employee. This limit of 10 per cent has been extended to 14 per cent in the case of Central Government employees (with effect from the assessment year 2020-21). There is no amendment pertaining to non-Government employees.

Deduction in respect of interest on loan taken for certain house property [Sec. 80EEA]

0.39 Section 80EEA has been inserted with effect from the assessment year 2020-21. Deduction under this section is available if the following conditions are satisfied –

1. The assessee is an individual.

2. He is not eligible to claim any deduction under section 80EE.

3. He has taken a loan for the purpose of acquisition of residential house property.

4. The loan is sanctioned by a financial institution (*i.e.*, a bank or banking institution or a housing finance company) during April 1, 2019 and March 31, 2020.

5. The stamp duty value of the residential house property does not exceed Rs. 45 lakh. The expression "stamp duty value" means value adopted (or assessed or assessable) by any authority of the Central Government or a State Government for the purpose of payment of stamp duty in respect of an immovable property.

6. The assessee does not own any residential house property on the date of sanction of loan.

• *Amount of deduction* - If the above conditions are satisfied, the assessee can claim deduction under section 80EEA. Deduction is available in respect of interest payable on the above loan or Rs. 1,50,000, whichever is less. Deduction is available for the assessment year 2020-21 and subsequent assessment years.

• *Same interest is not deductible twice* - If interest is claimed as deduction under section 80EEA, such interest (or such portion of interest) is not again deductible under section 24(*b*) or under any other provision of the Act for the same or any other assessment year.

0.39-E1 Find out the amount of deduction under section 80EEA for the assessment year 2020-21 in the following cases (in all cases taxpayers are individuals, loan is taken from Punjab National Bank for acquisition of a residential property) –

Name of assessee (Case No.)	*Date of filing loan application to bank*	*Date on which loan sanctioned*	*Amount of loan sanctioned*	*Stamp duty value of property*	*Whether assessee owns any residential house property on date of sanction of loan*	*Interest payable for the previous year 2019-20*
			Rs.	*Rs.*		*Rs.*
X (Case 1)	March 6, 2019	June 12, 2019	42 lakh	45 lakh	No	94,500
Y (Case 2)	March 7, 2019	June 12, 2019	42 lakh	45 lakh	No	2,70,000
Z (Case 3)	March 12, 2019	June 12, 2019	42 lakh	43 lakh	No	2,40,000
A (Case 4)	March 15, 2019	June 12, 2019	42 lakh	44 lakh	No	90,000

Name of assessee (Case No.)	*Date of filing loan application to bank*	*Date on which loan sanctioned*	*Amount of loan sanctioned*	*Stamp duty value of property*	*Whether assessee owns any residential house property on date of sanction of loan*	*Interest payable for the previous year 2019-20*
B (Case 5)	March 25, 2020	April 8, 2020	42 lakh	45 lakh	No	1,50,000
C (Case 6)	March 8, 2019	June 12, 2019	42 lakh	48 lakh	No	1,50,000
D (Case 7)	March 21, 2019	June 12, 2019	42 lakh	45 lakh	Yes	1,70,000

In these cases, only one house is purchased (by utilising the sanctioned loan) by the aforesaid persons. However, Y has purchased another house on March 10, 2020 (by taking another loan or out of his past savings).

•

Case 1 - X satisfies all conditions of section 80EEA. Rs. 94,500 is deductible under section 80EEA. In respect of this interest, deduction under section 24 (or any other section) is not available. Date of making loan application is irrelevant. Date on which residential property is acquired is not considered for the purpose of deduction under section 80EEA. Suppose, in this case rate of interest is 9 per cent and loan of Rs. 42 lakh is released on January 1, 2020 but the property is acquired (or construction of property is completed) on June 1, 2021. Interest liability of the previous year 2019-20 is Rs. 94,500 which is deductible under section 80EEA. Interest liability of the previous year 2020-21 is Rs. 3,78,000, out of which Rs. 1,50,000 is deductible under section 80EEA.

Pre-construction period for the purpose of section 24(*b*) will be January 1, 2020 to March 31, 2021. Interest liability of pre-construction period comes to Rs. 4,72,500. Out of which Rs. 2,44,500 is claimed as deduction under section 80EEA for the previous years 2019-20 and 2020-21. The balance of Rs. 2,28,000 is deductible as pre-construction period's interest in 5 years in 5 equal instalments. The first instalment of Rs. 45,600 will be deductible in the previous year 2021-22 along with current year's interest of the previous year 2021-22 (*i.e.*, Rs. 3,78,000) as follows –

Deduction pertaining to interest available under different sections	*If property of X is –*	
	Self-occupied Rs.	*Let out* Rs.
Deduction under section 24(*b*)	2,00,000	4,23,600
Deduction under section 80EEA	1,50,000	*Nil*

Case 2 - Y can claim deduction of Rs. 1,50,000 under section 80EEA. On the date of sanction of loan, Y does not own a residential house property. It does not make any difference if he purchases second house property in the financial year 2019-20 or any other subsequent year.

Case 3 - Z can claim deduction of Rs. 1,50,000 under section 80EEA. The balance of Rs. 1,20,000 can be claimed as deduction under section 24, if the relevant conditions are satisfied.

Case 4 - A can claim deduction of Rs. 90,000 under section 80EEA.

Case 5 - Loan is not sanctioned during the previous year 2019-20. Date of application is irrelevant. Deduction under section 80EEA is not available. However, deduction can be claimed under section 24.

Case 6 - As the stamp duty value of the property is more than Rs. 45 lakh, deduction under section 80EEA is not available. This rule is applicable even if amount of loan actually released during the previous year 2019-20 is Rs. 45 lakh or less. However, C can claim deduction under section 24.

Case 7 - Deduction under section 80EEA is not available as E owns a residential property on the date of sanction of loan. E can, however, claim deduction under section 24.

Deduction in respect of interest on loan taken for purchase of electric vehicle [Sec. 80EEB]

0.40 Section 80EEB has been inserted from the assessment year 2020-21. Under this section, deduction is available if the following conditions are satisfied –

1. The assessee is an individual.

2. He has taken a loan for the purpose of purchase of an electric vehicle. For this purpose, "electric vehicle" means –

- a vehicle which is powered "exclusively" by an electric motor whose traction energy is supplied exclusively by traction battery installed in the vehicle, and
- it has such electric regenerative braking system, which during braking provides for the conversion of vehicle kinetic energy into electrical energy.

As the word "exclusive" is used, interest on loan taken for purchase of a "hybrid car" (which derives some of its power from conventional engine) is not eligible for deduction.

3. Loan is taken from a financial institution (*i.e.*, a bank or any deposit taking NBFC or a systematically important non-deposit taking NBFC).

4. Loan is sanctioned during April 1, 2019 and March 31, 2023.†

Amount of deduction - If the above conditions are satisfied, the assessee can claim deduction under section 80EEB. Deduction is available in respect of interest payable on the above loan or Rs. 1,50,000, whichever is less. Deduction is available for the assessment year 2020-21 and subsequent assessment years.

Same interest is not deductible twice - If interest is claimed as deduction under section 80EEB, such interest (or such portion of interest) is not again deductible under any other provision of the Act for the same or any other assessment year.

0.40-E1 X, an individual, takes a loan of Rs. 25 lakh on April 10, 2019 from SBI to purchase an electric car. Car will be delivered during April-May 2020. Interest liability (before subsidy) for the previous years 2019-20 and 2020-21 is Rs. 2,10,000 and Rs. 1,90,000 respectively. One-time interest subsidy of Rs. 70,000 is given by the Maharashtra Government on March 1, 2020. The following situations are considered –

Situation 1 - X is a salaried employee. His annual salary income (before standard deduction) is Rs. 40,50,000. Every year, X is entitled to deduction under sections 80C and 80D of Rs. 1,70,000.

Situation 2 - X is a businessman. His annual business income is Rs. 15,00,000. Electric vehicle will be used by him for personal purposes. Every year, X is entitled to deduction under sections 80C and 80G of Rs. 2,40,000.

Situation 3 - X is a businessman. His annual business income is Rs. 15,00,000 (before interest and expenditure pertaining to vehicle). Electric vehicle will be used by him for business purposes. Maintenance expenditure pertaining to electronic vehicle (including depreciation) for the previous year 2020-21 is Rs. 3,10,000. Every year X is entitled to deduction under sections 80C and 80CCD of Rs. 2,00,000.

Situation 4 - X is a retired private sector employee. He does not have any pension income. His taxable rental and interest income is Rs. 8,00,000 per annum. Electric vehicle will be used by him for personal purposes. Every year X is entitled to deduction under sections 80C of Rs. 1,50,000.

•

Interest payable is deductible up to Rs. 1,50,000 under section 80EEB. Subsidy received should be deducted to find out "interest payable". However, there is no specific provision in section 80EEB. Interest payable on loan (after State Government's subsidy) is Rs. 1,40,000 and Rs. 2,90,000. Income of X will be calculated as follows –

(Rs. in lakh)

	Situation 1		*Situation 2*		*Situation 3*		*Situation 4*	
	Assessment years							
	2020-21	*2021-22*	*2020-21*	*2021-22*	*2020-21*	*2021-22*	*2020-21*	*2021-22*
Salary	40.00	40.00	–	–	–	–	–	–
Business income	–	–	15.00	15.00	15.00	15.00	–	–
Less: Vehicle maintenance	–	–	–	–	–	(–)3.10	–	–
Less: Interest on loan under section 36	–	–	–	–	–	(–)1.90	–	–
Interest/rent	–	–	–	–	–	–	8.00	8.00
Gross total income	40.00	40.00	15.00	15.00	15.00	10.00	8.00	8.00
Less: Deduction under sections 80C, 80CCD, 80D and 80G	1.70	1.70	2.40	2.40	2.00	2.00	1.50	1.50
Less: Deduction under section 80EEB	1.40	1.50	1.40	1.50	1.40	–	1.40	1.50
Net income	36.90	36.80	11.20	11.10	11.60	8.00	5.10	5.00

Tax incentive for construction of affordable housing projects [Sec. 80-IBA]

0.41 The existing provisions of section 80-IBA, *inter alia*, provide that where the gross total income of an assessee includes any profits and gains derived from the business of developing and building housing projects, there shall, subject to certain conditions, be allowed, a deduction of an amount equal to 100 per cent of the profits and gains derived from such business.

†Memorandum explaining provisions of the Finance (No. 2) Bill, 2019 specifies one additional condition that the assessee should not own any other electric vehicle on the date of sanction of loan.

0.41-1 ***Existing conditions pertaining to plot size, area of residential unit, etc.*** - Under the existing provisions of section 80-IBA, deduction is available only if the size of the plot, area of residential unit and utilization of FAR, should not exceed the following –

Location of project	*Area of plot of land on which project is situated*	*Carpet area of residential units comprised in the housing project*	*Utilisation of permissible FAR*
Project is located within the cities of Chennai, Delhi, Kolkata or Mumbai	Not less than 1,000 square metres	Not to exceed 30 square metres	Not less than 90%
Project is located in any other place	Not less than 2,000 square metres	Not to exceed 60 square metres	Not less than 80%

0.41-2 ***Alignment of the definition of "affordable housing" with GST Act*** - The above parameters of "affordable housing" under section 80-IBA are different from "affordable housing" under GST Act. To align the aforesaid parameters with GST regulations, section 80-IBA has been amended (with effect from the assessment year 2020-21). The amended provisions (which are applicable for the projects approved on or after September 1, 2019) are as follows –

Size of the plot, area of residential unit, etc. - The size of the plot, area of residential unit and utilization of FAR should not exceed the following –

Location of project	*Area of plot of land on which project is situated*	*Carpet area of residential units comprised in the housing project*	*Utilisation of permissible FAR*
Project is located within the metropolitan cities of Bengaluru, Chennai, Delhi NCR (limited to Delhi, Noida, Greater Noida, Ghaziabad, Gurugram, Faridabad), Hyderabad, Kolkata and Mumbai (whole of Mumbai Metropolitan Region)	Not less than 1,000 square metres	Not to exceed 60 square metres	Not less than 90%
Project is located in any other place	Not less than 2,000 square metres	Not to exceed 90 square metres	Not less than 80%

• *Stamp duty value not exceeding Rs. 45 lakh* - The stamp duty value of a residential unit in the housing project does not exceed Rs. 45 lakh. The expression "stamp duty value" means value adopted (or assessed or assessable) by any authority of the Central Government or a State Government for the purpose of payment of stamp duty in respect of an immovable property.

Amendment to section 80JJAA

0.42 *See* para 0.22.

Amendment to section 80LA

0.43 Under the existing provisions of section 80LA, deduction is available to –

a. a scheduled bank and having an offshore banking unit in a special economic zone; or

b. a foreign bank and having an offshore banking unit in a special economic zone; or

c. a unit of International Financial Services Centre.

These assessees can claim deductions pertaining to (*a*) any income from the offshore banking unit in a Special Economic Zone; (*b*) income from the business referred to in section 6(1) of the Banking Regulation Act, with an undertaking located in Special Economic Zone or any other undertaking which develops, develops and operates or operates and maintains a Special Economic Zone; (*c*) income from any unit of the International Financial Services Centre from its business for which it has been approved for setting up in such a centre in a Special Economic Zone. The amount of deduction is 100 per cent of the aforesaid income for first 5 years and 50 per cent for next 5 years.

• *Amendment* - Under the amended version (which is applicable from the assessment year 2020-21), deduction available to a unit of International Financial Services Centre shall be increased to 100 per cent for any 10 consecutive years. The assessee, at his option, may claim the said deduction for any 10 consecutive assessment years out of 15 years beginning with the year in which the necessary permission is obtained.

Power of AO in respect of modified return of income filed in pursuance to signing of APA [Sec. 92CD]

0.44 Advance Pricing Agreement (APA) is an agreement between a taxpayer and a taxing authority on an appropriate transfer pricing methodology for a set of transactions over a fixed period of time in future.

The APA offers better assurance on transfer pricing methods and are conducive in providing certainty and unanimity of approach. Sections 92CC and 92CD provide a framework to empower the Board (with the approval of the Central Government) to enter into an APA with any person for determining the arm's length price (ALP) or specifying the manner in which ALP is to be determined in relation to an international transaction which is to be entered into by that person. The APA is valid for a period, not exceeding 5 previous years, as may be specified therein. These sections also provide for rollback of the APA for 4 years. In order to give effect to the APA, section 92CD also provides for mechanism, including filing of modified return of income by the taxpayer and manner of completion of assessments by the Assessing Officer having regard to terms of the APA.

Sub-section (3) of this section deals with a situation where assessment or re-assessment has already been completed, before expiry of the time allowed for filing of modified return. There is a view that due to the use of words "assess or reassess or recompute", the Assessing Officer may start fresh assessment or reassessment in respect of completed assessments or reassessments of the assessees who have modified their returns of income in accordance with the APA entered into by them, while the intention of the legislature is that Assessing Officer should merely modify the total income consequent to modification of return of income in pursuance of APA.

• *Amendment* - The scheme of section 92CD has been amended to clarify that in cases where assessment or reassessment has already been completed and modified return of income has been filed by the taxpayer, the Assessing Officers shall pass an order modifying the total income of the relevant assessment year (determined in such assessment/reassessment) having regard to and in accordance with the APA. Consequential amendment has also been made to section 246A(1)(*bb*). These amendments are applicable with effect from September 1, 2019. However, courts have been unanimous in holding that amendments, which are intended to remove unintended hardships, are declaratory in nature and, therefore, operate retrospectively.

Clarifications pertaining to secondary adjustment and option to assessee to make one-time payment [Sec. 92CE]

0.45 Section 92CE regulates provisions pertaining to secondary adjustment in international transactions. It was inserted with effect from the assessment year 2018-19. Secondary adjustment under section 92CE is applicable in the following situations –

1. Where a primary adjustment to transfer price has been made *suo motu* by the assessee in his return of income.

2. Where a primary adjustment to transfer price made by the Assessing Officer has been accepted by the assessee.

3. Where a primary adjustment to transfer price is determined by an APA (advance pricing agreement) entered into by the assessee under section 92CC.

4. Where a primary adjustment to transfer price is made as per the safe harbour rules framed under section 92CB.

5. Where a primary adjustment to transfer price is arising as a result of resolution of an assessment by way of the mutual agreement procedure under DTAA entered into under section 90/90A.

• *Threshold limit* - If the following two conditions are not satisfied, secondary adjustment is not required –

a. the amount of primary adjustment made in the case of an assessee in any previous year does not exceed Rs. 1 crore; and

b. the primary adjustment is made in respect of the assessment year 2016-17 (or any earlier assessment year).

0.45-1 ***Amendments (with effect from the assessment year 2018-19)*** - The following amendments have been made to the above scheme of secondary adjustment under section 92CE (with effect from the date of insertion of section 92CE, *i.e.*, assessment year 2018-19 onwards) –

• *Threshold limit* - The condition of threshold [*i.e.*, (*a*) and (*b*) given above] of Rs. 1 crore and of the primary adjustment made up to assessment year 2016-17, are alternate conditions.

• *Excess money* - The assessee shall be required to calculate interest on the excess money or part thereof.

• *APA agreements* - The provision of section 92CE pertaining to APA [*i.e.*, (3) given above] shall apply to the agreements which have been signed on or after April 1, 2017. However, no refund of the taxes already paid till date under the pre-amended section would be allowed.

• *Repatriation of excess money* - The excess money may be repatriated from any of the associated enterprises of the assessee which is not resident in India.

0.45-2 ***Amendment (applicable with effect from September 1, 2019)*** - Sub-sections (2A) to (2D) have been inserted in section 92CE with effect from September 1, 2019. These provisions are given below –

• *Additional income-tax* - In a case, where the excess money or part thereof has not been repatriated in time, the assessee will have the option to pay additional income-tax at the rate of 18 per cent on such excess money (or part thereof). It will be increased by surcharge at the rate of 12 per cent and health and education cess at the rate of 4 per cent (effective tax rate : 20.9664 per cent). The following points should be noted –

- If the assessee pays the additional income-tax, he will not be required to make secondary adjustment or compute interest from the date of payment of such tax. However, he is required to make secondary adjustment pertaining to interest till the date of payment of additional tax.
- The tax so paid shall be the final payment of tax and no credit shall be allowed in respect of the amount of tax so paid.
- The deduction in respect of the amount on which such tax has been paid, shall not be allowed under any other provision.

0.45-2E1 X Ltd. is an Indian company. It renders services to Y Inc. (an American company which is an associated enterprise of X Ltd. within the parameters of section 92A). During the previous year 2017-18, X Ltd. charges 8 per cent on cost for providing services to Y Inc. However, X Ltd. would have earned a margin of 11 per cent on cost if similar services were provided to unconnected foreign entities. The Assessing Officer makes transfer pricing adjustments to the tune of 3 per cent which comes to an addition of Rs. 12 crore to the reported income of X Ltd. (date of assessment order : December 20, 2018). The adjustment is accepted by X Ltd.

•

The addition of Rs. 12 crore is known as primary adjustment. However, the primary adjustment to the income of X Ltd. does not address the benefit obtained by Y Inc. by retaining Rs. 12 crore in cash. Provisions of section 92CE on secondary adjustment seek to target such cash benefit by applying a tax charge on the excess benefit in the hands of foreign entity. Under this section, Rs. 12 crore will be considered as a separate transaction as a deemed loan (in the language of section 92CE it is known as "secondary adjustment") given by X Ltd. to Y Inc. This deemed loan would exist for tax purposes only and would not appear in the books of account of X Ltd. Arm's length value of interest on deemed loan will be calculated as per rule 10CB [*i.e.*, where international transaction is denominated in Indian rupee : MCLR of SBI (1 year) + 3.25%]. This interest will be taxable in the hands of X Ltd. annually till Rs. 12 crore is repatriated by Y Inc. (of America) to X Ltd. (in India). Tax consequences in this case will be as follows on the assumption that (*a*) MCLR (1 year) of SBI + 3.25% comes to 11.7%, and (*b*) Y Inc. has not repatriated Rs. 12 crore to X Ltd. –

Previous year 2018-19 - Date of final assessment order (no appeal by X Ltd.) is December 20, 2018. Excess money is Rs. 12 crore. Time-limit for repatriation is 90 days from the date of final order (*i.e.*, December 20, 2018 + 90 days, last date for repatriation is March 20, 2019). Deemed interest on Rs. 12 crore will start from March 21, 2019 at the rate of 11.7%. For the previous year ending March 31, 2019, it comes to Rs. 4,23,123 (*i.e.*, amount of secondary adjustment for the previous year 2018-19). X Ltd. will pay income-tax on Rs. 4,23,123 at the applicable rate (*i.e.*, 25% or 30% + applicable surcharge + HEC).

Previous year 2019-20 - The following calculations are given on the assumption that income of X Ltd. before the aforesaid secondary adjustment is Rs. 2 crore. Tax on secondary adjustment is calculated under two different situations : *Situation 1* - X Ltd. does not pay additional income-tax as per section 92CE(2A), *Situation 2* - X Ltd. pays additional income-tax on the entire excess money on October 31, 2019 under section 92CE(2A) –

	Situation 1	*Situation 2*
Primary adjustment for the previous year 2018-19	12,00,00,000	12,00,00,000
Add: Secondary adjustment for the previous year 2018-19	4,23,123	4,23,123
Total (*a*)	12,04,23,123	12,04,23,123
Secondary adjustment for the previous year 2019-20 –		
- In *Situation 1* [*i.e.*, interest @ 11.7% on (*a*) from April 1, 2019 to March 31, 2020]	1,40,89,505	–
- In *Situation 2* [*i.e.*, interest @ 11.7% on (*a*) from April 1, 2019 to October 31, 2019]	–	82,18,878
Other income	2,00,00,000	2,00,00,000
Net income	3,40,89,510	2,82,18,880
Tax @ 30% + SC : 7% + HEC : 4%	1,13,80,440	94,20,590
Additional income-tax under section 92CE(2A) –		
Income-tax (18% of Rs. 12,00,00,000)	–	2,16,00,000

	Situation 1	Situation 2
Add: Surcharge @ 12% (always applicable, even if net income is below Rs. 1 crore)	–	25,92,000
Total	–	2,41,92,000
Add: Health and education cess @ 4%	–	9,67,680
Additional tax under section 92CE(2A)	–	2,51,59,680

Note - If the aforesaid additional tax is not paid, secondary adjustment for the previous year 2020-21 will be notional interest [@ MCLR (1 year) of SBI + 3.25%] on (Rs. 12,04,23,123 + 1,40,89,505).

Amendment to section 92D

0.46 The scheme of section 92D (relating to maintenance and keeping of information and document by persons entering into an international transaction or specified domestic transition) has been modified with effect from the assessment year 2020-21 on following lines –

- Sub-section (1) provides for keeping and maintaining of prescribed information and document by the person entering into an international transaction or specified domestic transaction, and by the constituent entity of an international group referred to in section 286. The requirement of information and document to be kept and maintained by a constituent entity of an international group (and filing of required form) shall be applicable even when there is no international transaction undertaken by such constituent entity.
- Sub-section (2) empowers the Board to prescribe the period for which said information and document shall be kept and maintained.
- Sub-section (3) provides that the Assessing Officer or the Commissioner (Appeals) may, in the course of any proceeding under the Act, require a person who has entered into an international transaction (or specified domestic transaction) to furnish any information or document referred to therein, within a period of 30 days from the date of receipt of a notice issued in this regard. The period of 30 days may be further extended up to 30 days on such person's application.
- Sub-section (4) provides that the constituent entity shall furnish the information and document referred to therein to the authority prescribed in such manner, on or before such date as may be prescribed.

Amendment to section 111A

0.47 Section 111A has been amended (with effect from the assessment year 2020-21) so as to provide that "equity oriented fund" shall have the meaning assigned to it in clause (*a*) of the *Explanation* to section 112A.

Amendment to section 115A

0.48 Section 115A provides the method of calculation of income-tax payable by a non-resident/foreign company where the total income includes any income by way of dividend (other than referred in section 115-O), interest, royalty and fees for technical services; etc. Section 80LA, provides for deduction in respect of certain incomes to a unit located in an International Financial Services Centre (IFSC). However, section 115A(4) prohibits any deduction under Chapter VIA (which includes section 80LA).

In order to ensure that units located in IFSC claim full deduction under section 80LA, the scheme of section 115A has been amended (with effect from the assessment year 2020-21) to provide that the aforesaid provision of section 115A(4) shall not apply to a unit of an IFSC for claiming deduction under section 80LA.

Book profit under section 115JB

0.49 Book profit for the purpose of calculation of minimum alternate tax is regulated by *Explanation 1* to section 115JB. Clause (*iih*) of the *Explanation* provides that in case of a company, against which an application for corporate insolvency resolution process has been admitted by the Adjudicating Authority under section 7/9/10 of the Insolvency and Bankruptcy Code, the aggregate amount of unabsorbed depreciation and loss (before depreciation) brought forward shall be allowed to be reduced from the net profit to calculate book profit. This clause has been amended (with effect from the assessment year 2020-21) so as to provide that the aggregate amount of unabsorbed depreciation and loss (excluding depreciation) brought forward shall also be allowed to be reduced from net profit to calculate book profit in case of a company, and its subsidiary and the subsidiary of such subsidiary, where, the National Company Law Tribunal, on an application moved by the Central Government under section 241 of the Companies Act, 2013 has suspended the Board of Directors of such company and has appointed new directors who are nominated by the Central Government, under section 242 of the said Act.

• *Meaning of subsidiary company* - A company shall be a subsidiary of another company, if such other company holds more than half in nominal value of the equity share capital of the company.

Tax on income distributed by way of dividend by a unit of International Financial Services Centre [Sec. 115-O(8)]

0.50 Section 115-O(8) provides that no tax on distributed profits shall be chargeable in respect of the total income of a company, being a unit of an International Financial Services Centre (IFSC), deriving income solely in convertible foreign exchange, for any assessment year on any amount declared, distributed or paid by such company, by way of dividends (whether interim or otherwise), on or after April 1, 2017, out of its current income, either in the hands of the company or the person receiving such dividend.

• *Amendment* - To facilitate distribution of dividend by companies operating in IFSC, the above provisions of section 115-O(8) have been amended (with effect from September 1, 2019) to provide that any dividend paid out of accumulated income derived from operations in IFSC, after April 1, 2017 shall also not be liable for tax on distributed profits.

Tax on income distributed by way of buy-back of shares [Sec. 115QA]

0.51 Section 115QA provides for the levy of additional income-tax at the rate of 20 per cent (effective rate after surcharge and cess : 23.296 per cent) of the distributed income on account of buy-back of unlisted shares by the company. As additional income-tax has been levied at the level of company, the consequential income arising in the hands of shareholders has been exempted from tax under section 10(*34A*).

• *Anti-abuse provision* - Section 115QA was introduced as an anti-abuse provision to check the practice of unlisted companies resorting to buy-back of shares instead of payment of dividends. This practice of widespread abuse was noted, in the past, amongst unlisted companies where the taxpayers preferred it for tax avoidance, as tax rate for capitals gains was lower than the rate of dividend distribution tax. However, instances of similar tax arbitrage have now come to notice in case of listed shares as well, whereby the listed companies are also indulging in such practice of resorting to buy-back of shares, instead of payment of dividends. Some of these cases are given below (facts are imaginary, only for illustration purpose) –

Case 1 - Mac Consultancy Ltd. is engaged in technical consultancy and provides consultancy services in India and abroad. 70 per cent of the shares in Mac Consultancy are held by Mac Holding Ltd. (date of allotment : April 1, 2001, issue price : Rs. 10 per share). Both are Indian companies and shares of Mac Consultancy are listed on Bombay Stock Exchange. Buy-back offer is given by Mac Consultancy on February 1, 2017 to distribute Rs. 1,000 crore to its shareholders. As shares of Mac Consultancy are listed shares, it is not liable for tax on distributed income under section 115QA. Securities transaction tax is applicable in the case of buy-back of shares of listed companies. Shareholders (including Mac Holding Ltd.) will get exemption under section 10(*38*), even if exemption under section 10(*34A*) is not available. In this case, Mac Consultancy has transferred Rs. 1,000 crore to shareholders (including Rs. 700 crore to Mac Holding Ltd.), but there is no income-tax liability on the payer or recipient.

Case 2 - Exemption is not available under section 10(*38*) if shares are transferred on or after April 1, 2018. Suppose in the above case, another buy-back offer is given by Mac Consultancy on June 6, 2018 to distribute Rs. 1,600 crore to shareholders. Additional information is as follows –

Market value of shares in Mac Consultancy on January 31, 2018 : Rs. 2,800 per share. 1:1 bonus shares offer is given to shareholders on May 1, 2018 (market quotation, cum-bonus : Rs. 3,000 per share, ex-bonus : Rs. 1,600). Offer price for buy-back on June 6, 2018 : Rs. 1,700 per share.

For this buy-back, Mac Consultancy will not pay any tax on distributed tax under section 115QA. Shareholders (including Mac Holdings Ltd.) will not have any exemption under section 10(*34A*) or 10(*38*). Income of shareholders (on account of this buy-back) will be taxable under section 112A as follows –

	Rs.
Full value of consideration (buy-back of 1 share)	1,700
Less: Cost of acquisition under section 55(2)(*ac*) [in case of demat, FIFO method is followed. Consequently, original shares are transferred by shareholders in buy-back. Cost of acquisition is – cost of original share : Rs. 10, fair market value on January 31, 2018 (but it cannot be more than sale consideration) : Rs. 1,700, whichever is higher]	1,700
Long-term capital gain	*Nil*

No tax on shareholders on transfer by way of buy-back of shares, in this case, under section 112A [even after withdrawal of exemption under section 10(*38*)].

• *Amendment* - In order to curb such tax avoidance practices adopted by the listed companies, the scope of existing anti-abuse provision under section 115QA has been extended to all companies (including companies listed on a recognised stock exchange). Thus, any buy-back of shares (on or after July 5, 2019) from a shareholder by a company listed on recognised stock exchange, shall also be covered by the provision of section 115QA. Accordingly, the scope of exemption under section 10(*34A*) has been extended to shareholders of the listed company on account of buy-back of shares. The table given below summarises the impact of amendments made to sections 10(*34A*) and 115QA.

	Exemptions to shareholders under section 10(34A)	*Tax on distributed income under section 115QA payable by a company which buy-backs its own shares*
Buy-back of unlisted shares (during June 1, 2013 and July 4, 2019)	Exemption available	Tax payable by company under section 115QA
Buy-back of listed shares (during June 1, 2013 and March 31, 2018)	Exemption not available under section 10(*34A*). However, exemption may be available under section 10(*38*)	Tax on distributed income under section 115QA, not applicable
Buy-back of listed shares (during April 1, 2018 and July 4, 2019)	Exemption not available under section 10(*34A*). However, tax is payable by shareholders in the case of long-term capital gain within the parameters of section 112A	Tax on distributed income under section 115QA, not applicable
Buy-back of listed/unlisted shares (on or after July 5, 2019)	Exemption available	Tax payable by company under section 115QA

Amendment to section 115R

0.52 The existing provisions of the section 115R provide that any amount of income distributed by the specified company or a mutual fund to its unitholders shall be chargeable to tax and such specified company or mutual fund shall be liable to pay additional income-tax on such distributed income.

• *Amendment* - In order to incentivize relocation of mutual fund in International Financial Services Centre (IFSC), the above provisions of section 115R have been amended with effect from September 1, 2019. The amended version provides that no additional income-tax shall be chargeable under section 115R if the following conditions are satisfied –

1. Income is distributed by "specified mutual fund". "Specified mutual fund" for this purpose is –

- It is a mutual fund specified under section 10(*23D*).
- It is located in any IFSC.
- All the units are held by non-residents

2. Such income is distributed out of its income derived from transactions made on a recognised stock exchange located in any IFSC and where the consideration for such transaction is paid or payable in convertible foreign exchange.

3. Such income is distributed on or after September 1, 2019.

Amendment to section 115UB

0.53 Section 115UB, *inter alia*, provides for pass through of income earned by the Category I and II Alternative Investment Fund (AIF), except for business income which is taxed at AIF level. Pass through of profits (other than profit and gains from business) has been allowed to individual investors so as to give them benefit of lower rate of tax, if applicable. Pass through of losses are not provided under the existing regime and are retained at AIF level to be carried forward and set off in accordance with Chapter VI. Provisions regulating adjustment of losses have been amended. Legal provision, before and after amendment, is summarised below –

Adjustment of losses up to the assessment year 2019-20 - If in any year there is a loss at the fund level (either current loss or the loss which remained to be set off), the loss shall not be allowed to be passed through to the investors but would be carried over at fund level to be set off against income of the next year in accordance with the provisions of Chapter VI.

Adjustment of losses with effect from the assessment year 2020-21 - From the assessment year 2020-21, section 115UB(2) has been amended to provide that –

- the business loss of the investment fund shall be allowed to be carried forward by the fund and it shall not be passed onto the unit holder;
- the loss (other than business loss) shall also be ignored for the purposes of pass through to its unit holders, if such loss has arisen in respect of a unit which has not been held by the unit holder for a period of at least 12 months;
- the loss (other than business loss) accumulated at the level of investment fund as on March 31, 2019, shall be deemed to be the loss of a unit holder who held the unit on March 31, 2019 in respect of the investments made by him in the investment fund and allowed to be carried forward by him for the remaining period calculated from the year in which the loss had occurred for the first time taking that year as the first year and it shall be set-off by him in accordance with the provisions of Chapter VI;
- the loss so deemed in the hands of unit holders shall not be available to the investment fund for the purposes of Chapter VI.

Mandatory furnishing of return of income by certain persons [Sec. 139]

0.54 The following amendments have been made to the provisions of section 139 –

• *High value transactions* - Currently, a person (other than a company or a firm) is required to furnish the return of income only if his total income exceeds the maximum amount not chargeable to tax, subject to certain exceptions. Therefore, a person entering into certain high value transactions is not necessarily required to furnish his return of income. In order to ensure that persons who enter into certain high value transactions do furnish their return of income, section 139 has been amended with effect from April 1, 2020 (*i.e.*, from the assessment year 2020-21 onwards). Under the amended version, a person (other than a company or a firm) shall be mandatorily required to file his return of income, if during the previous year, he –

a. has deposited an amount (or aggregate of the amounts) exceeding Rs. 1 crore in one or more current account maintained with a banking company or a co-operative bank; or

b. has incurred expenditure of an amount (or aggregate of the amounts) exceeding Rs. 2 lakh for himself or any other person for travel to a foreign country; or

c. has incurred expenditure of an amount (or aggregate of the amounts) exceeding Rs. 1 lakh towards consumption of electricity; or

d. fulfils such other prescribed conditions, as may be prescribed.

• *Persons claiming exemption under sections 54, 54B, etc.* - Currently, a person claiming rollover benefit of exemption from capital gains tax on investment in specified assets like house, bonds, etc., is not required to furnish a return of income, if after claim of such rollover benefits, his total income is not more than the exemption limit. In order to make furnishing of return compulsory for such persons, sixth proviso to section 139(1) has been amended with effect from April 1, 2020 (*i.e.*, from the assessment year 2020-21 onwards). Impact of sixth proviso (before and after amendment) is given below –

Who is covered by sixth proviso	*Individual/HUF/AOP/BOI/artificial juridical person*
When return is required to be submitted on compulsory basis	If total income (or net income or taxable income) exceeds the exemption limit without claiming the following exemptions or deductions –
	1. Deduction under sections 10A, 10B, 10BA, 80C to 80U.
	2. Exemption under section 10(*38*) [applicable only for the assessment years 2017-18 and 2018-19].
	3. Exemption under sections 54, 54B, 54D, 54EC, 54F, 54G, 54GA and 54GB [applicable from the assessment year 2020-21 onwards]

Inter-changeability of PAN and Aadhaar and mandatory quoting in prescribed transactions [Sec. 139A]

0.55 Section 139A, *inter alia*, provides that every person specified therein, who has not been allotted a PAN, shall apply to the Assessing Officer for allotment of PAN.

• In many cases, persons entering into high value transactions (such as purchase of foreign currency or huge withdrawal from the banks), do not possess a PAN. In order to keep an audit trail of such transactions, for widening and deepening of the tax base, new clause (*vii*) has been inserted (with effect from September 1, 2019) in section 139A(1) so as to provide that every person, who intends to enter into certain prescribed transactions and has not been allotted a PAN, shall also apply for allotment of a PAN.

• To ensure ease of compliance, modifications have been made to provide for inter-changeability of PAN with the Aadhaar number. For this purpose, provisions of section 139A have been amended (with effect from September 1, 2019) as follows –

1. Every person who is required to furnish or intimate or quote his PAN under the Act, and who has not been allotted a PAN but possesses the Aadhaar number, may furnish or intimate or quote his Aadhaar number in lieu of PAN, and such person shall be allotted a PAN in the prescribed manner.

2. Every person who has been allotted a PAN, and who has linked his Aadhaar number under section 139AA, may furnish or intimate or quote his Aadhaar number in lieu of a PAN.

• Section 139A, *inter alia*, provides that every person, receiving a document relating to a transaction for which PAN is required to be quoted, shall ensure that the PAN has been duly quoted therein. This provision has been amended (with effect from September 1, 2019) to provide that every person receiving such documents shall also ensure that the PAN or the Aadhaar number, as the case may be, has been duly quoted. Moreover, sub-section (6A) has been inserted in section 139A (with effect from September 1, 2019) to ensure quoting of PAN or Aadhaar number for entering into prescribed transactions and authentication thereof in the prescribed manner. Moreover, sub-section (6B) has been inserted to provide that the person receiving any document relating to such transactions, shall ensure that PAN/Aadhaar number is duly quoted and authenticated.

Amendment to section 139AA

0.56 Section 139AA(2) provides that the PAN allotted to a person shall be deemed to be invalid, in case the person fails to intimate the Aadhaar number, on or before the notified date.

In order to protect validity of transactions previously carried out through such PAN, the scheme of section 139AA has been modified (with effect from September 1, 2019) to provide that if a person fails to intimate the Aadhaar number, the PAN allotted to such person shall be made inoperative in the prescribed manner.

Provision of credit of relief provided under section 89 [Secs. 140A, 143, 234A, 234B and 234C]

0.57 Section 89 contains provisions for providing relief where salary (or family pension) is paid in arrears or in advance. The existing provisions of sections 140A, 143, 234A, 234B and 234C contain provisions pertaining to tax computation after allowing credit for prepaid taxes and certain admissible reliefs, credits, etc. However, the relief under section 89 is not specifically mentioned in these sections.

• *Amendment* - With a view to avoiding genuine hardship in the case of a person who is eligible for relief under section 89, the provisions of sections 140A, 143, 234A, 234B and 234C have been amended (with retrospective effect from the assessment year 2007-08) to provide that computation of tax liability shall be made under these sections after allowing relief under section 89.

TDS on non-exempt portion of life insurance pay-out on net basis [Sec. 194DA]

0.58 Under section 194DA, a person is required to deduct tax at source, if it pays any sum to a resident under a life insurance policy, which is not exempt under section 10(*10D*). The present requirement is to deduct tax at the rate of 1 per cent of amount payable [*i.e.*, sum payable by way of a life insurance policy including the sum allocated by way of bonus on such life insurance policy but excluding the amount exempted under section 10(*10D*)].

• *Amendment* - The aforesaid provision has been amended with effect from September 1, 2019 to provide tax deduction at the rate of 5 per cent of income component of the sum payable by the deductor.

0.58-E1 X takes an insurance policy on September 1, 2015 (single insurance premium paid at the time of taking policy : Rs. 40 lakh, sum assured : Rs. 50 lakh, amount payable by insurance company on maturity along with bonus : Rs. 55 lakh). Suppose date of maturity (and payment by insurance company) is August 20, 2019 (*Situation 1*) or September 1, 2019 (*Situation 2*).

•

Annual insurance premium is more than 10% of sum assured. Consequently, exemption under section 10(*10D*) is not available to X. Payment by insurance company is subject to TDS provisions of section 194DA as follows –

Situation 1 - Date of payment is August 20, 2019. Provisions of section 194DA, before the aforesaid amendment, are applicable. Insurance company will deduct tax at the rate of 1% of Rs. 55 lakh.

Situation 2 - Date of payment is September 1, 2019. Section 194DA is applicable (after the aforesaid amendment). Tax will be deducted by the insurance company as follows –

	Rs.
Amount payable by insurance company	55,00,000
Less: Indexed cost of acquisition [Rs. 40 lakh × CII of 2019-20 : 290 (assumed figure) ÷ CII of 2015-16 : 254]	45,66,929
Long-term capital gain of X (which is "income comprised" in payment of Rs. 55 lakh by insurance company)	9,33,071
Tax deductible by insurance company under section 194DA (5% of Rs. 9,33,071)	46,654

Amendment to section 194-IA

0.59 Section 194-IA relates to payment on transfer of certain immovable property (other than agricultural land) and provides for levy of TDS at the rate of 1 per cent on the amount of consideration paid or credited for transfer of such property.

• *Amendment* - The term "consideration for transfer of any immovable property" is not defined for the purposes of section 194-IA. In the case of purchase of immovable property, there are other types of payments made besides the sales consideration and the buyer is contractually bound to make such payments to the builder/seller, either under the same agreement or under a different agreement. Some of these payments are those for rights to amenities like club membership fee, car parking fee, electricity and water facility fees, maintenance fee, advance fee, etc. Accordingly, section 194-IA has been amended (with effect from September 1, 2019) to provide that the term "consideration for immovable property" shall include all charges of the nature of club membership fee, car parking fee, electricity and water facility fees, maintenance fee, advance fee or any other charges of similar nature, which are incidental to transfer of the immovable property.

TDS on certain payments by individual/HUF [Sec. 194M, applicable from September 1, 2019]

0.60 Section 194M has been inserted with effect from September 1, 2019. Provisions of this section are given below –

• *Who is deductor* - An individual/HUF (who is not required to deduct tax at source under sections 194C, 194H or 194J) is required to deduct tax under section 194M. Consequently, an individual/HUF is required to deduct tax at source in respect of the following under section 194M –

- Payment/credit to a resident contractor or resident professional, when such payment is for personal use.
- Payment/credit to a resident contractor or resident professional or to a resident by way of commission (not being insurance commission) or brokerage [where payer is an individual/HUF who carries on business or profession and books of account are not subject to tax audit under section 44AB(*a*)/(*b*) in the immediately preceding financial year].

• *Threshold limit* - Tax is not deductible if aggregate amount paid or payable during the financial year to a resident does not exceed Rs. 50 lakh.

• *Payment covered* - TDS under section 194M is applicable in respect of amount paid/payable to a resident for carrying out any work (including supply of labour for carrying out any work) in pursuance of a contract or by way of commission (not being insurance commission) or brokerage or by way of fees for professional services.

• *When deductible* - Tax is deductible at the time of credit of aforesaid sum or at the time of payment of the aforesaid sum in cash or by issue of a cheque or draft or by any other mode, whichever is earlier.

• *Rate of TDS* - Tax is deductible at the rate of 5 per cent of the aforesaid payment or credit.

• *Lower TDS certificate* - Recipient can apply for *nil*/lower TDS certificate under section 197.

• *TAN not necessary* - Individual/HUF (who is required to deduct tax under section 194M) shall be able to deposit the tax deducted using his PAN and shall not be required to obtain TAN.

0.60-E1 X is an individual. He makes the following payments to a resident consultant (or to a resident contractor for a work contract or to a resident by way of commission/brokerage). Amount of payment is Rs. 27,00,000 on August 10, 2019 and Rs. 26,00,000 on November 22, 2019. The following situations are examined –

Situation 1 - X is a businessman. His books of account are audited every year under section 44AB. Payment to consultant (or contractor or broker) is for business purposes.

Situation 2 - X is a businessman. His books are not audited in the immediately preceding financial year (as turnover is lower than the threshold limit of Rs. 1 crore). Payment to consultant (or contractor or broker) is for business purposes.

Situation 3 - Payment to consultant (or contractor) is for personal purposes [not deductible under section 37(1)].

Situation 4 - X is a non-resident Indian (or foreign citizen). He does not have any income in India. Payment to consultant (or contractor) is for personal purposes.

Situation 5 - X is a farmer. His entire income is exempt under section 10(*1*). Payment to consultant (or contractor) is for personal purposes.

•

Situation 1 - Tax is deductible under section 194J (if the recipient is consultant) or under section 194C (if recipient is a contractor) or under section 194H (if recipient is a broker). Consequently, TDS provisions of section 194M are not applicable. If it is payment to a consultant, amount of TDS under section 194J is 10% of Rs. 27,00,000 on August 10, 2019 and 10% of Rs. 26,00,000 on November 22, 2019.

Situation 2 - Provisions of sections 194C, 194H and 194J are not applicable. Aggregate payment to the recipient during the financial year 2019-20 is Rs. 53,00,000 (more than the threshold of Rs. 50,00,000 under section 194M). Tax is deductible under section 194M. Payment of Rs. 27,00,000 is made prior to September 1, 2019 (*i.e.*, before the application of section 194M). Therefore, tax deduction is not required at the time of payment of Rs. 27,00,000 on August 10, 2019. However, payment on November 22, 2019 is subject to TDS under section 194M (amount of TDS will be Rs. 1,30,000, being 5% of Rs. 26,00,000).

Situation 3 - It is payment to a consultant or contractor. Payment is for personal purposes. Tax is not deductible under section 194C or 194J. Consequently, tax is deductible under section 194M. No tax deduction at the time of payment of Rs. 27,00,000 on August 10, 2019. Tax of Rs. 1,30,000 will be deducted by X at the time of payment of Rs. 26,00,000 on November 22, 2019.

Situation 4 - Even if X is non-resident (not having income in India), TDS provisions of section 194M are applicable (as given above, no TDS on August 10, 2019 and Rs. 1,30,000 will be deducted on November 22, 2019).

Situation 5 - Even if income of X is exempt under section 10(*1*), TDS provisions of section 194M (as given above) are applicable.

TDS on payment of certain amounts in cash [Sec. 194N, applicable from September 1, 2019]

0.61 Section 194N has been inserted with effect from September 1, 2019. Provisions of section 194N are given below –

• *Who is deductor* - A bank, co-operative bank or a post office, who is responsible for paying any sum in cash to an accountholder, is required to deduct tax at source under section 194N.

• *Threshold limit* - It is Rs. 1 crore. In other words, tax is deductible by a bank (or co-operative bank or post office) if aggregate payment in cash from one or more accounts during a previous year to an accountholder, exceeds Rs. 1 crore.

• *When deductible* - Tax is deductible at the time of payment in cash.

• *Rate of TDS* - Tax is deductible at the rate of 2 per cent of payment (or aggregate payment) in cash exceeding Rs. 1 crore.

• *Lower TDS certificate* - Not possible.

• *Cash payment to certain recipients without TDS* - Exemption is available, when cash payment is made to certain recipients, such as the Government, banking company, co-operative society engaged in carrying on the business of banking, post office. Exemption is also available when cash payment is made to the following persons –

- Any business correspondent of a banking company or co-operative bank in accordance with the guidelines issued in this regard by RBI.
- Any white label ATM operator of a banking company/co-operative bank in accordance with the authorisation issued by RBI under the Payment and Settlement Systems Act, 2007.
- Such other person or class of persons notified by the Central Government in consultation with RBI.

• *Tax deducted under section 194N, not to be treated as deemed receipt* - Tax deducted (under section 194N) shall not be deemed to be income received (for the purpose of section 198) for computing income of recipient.

0.61-E1 X Ltd. is a manufacturing company (having head office at Mumbai and branch office at Kolkata). X Ltd. has a current account with SBI Mumbai and overdraft account with SBI Kolkata. The two accounts are separately operated by head office and branch office. Head office and branch office have separate TAN and GSTIN. Cash withdrawn by head office and branch office from these two accounts is as follows –

- from SBI Mumbai by head office on July 10, 2019 : Rs. 10 lakh
- from SBI Kolkata by branch office on October 10, 2019 : Rs. 60 lakh
- from SBI Mumbai by head office on January 10, 2020 : Rs. 35 lakh

•

Total cash payment to X Ltd. (head office and branch office) during the financial year 2019-20 is Rs. 1.05 crore. Cash payment by SBI up to January 9, 2020 does not exceed Rs. 1 crore. It exceeds Rs. 1 crore only after cash payment of Rs. 35 lakh on January 10, 2020. The excess amount is Rs. 5 lakh. Tax deductible by SBI on January 10, 2020 is Rs. 10,000 (being 2% of the excess amount of Rs. 5 lakh).

0.61-E2 Suppose cash payment by SBI to X Ltd. in the above example is as follows –

- from SBI Mumbai by head office on July 10, 2019 : Rs. 1.1 crore
- from SBI Kolkata by branch office on October 10, 2019 : Rs. 30 lakh
- from SBI Mumbai by head office on January 10, 2020 : Rs. 20 lakh

•

Cash payment exceeds Rs. 1 crore on July 10, 2019. No tax is, however, deductible on July 10, 2019 (as section 194N is applicable only from September 1, 2019). Up to October 10, 2019, cash payment by SBI to X Ltd. is Rs. 1.40 crore. Amount in excess of Rs. 1 crore (up to October 10, 2019) is Rs. 40 lakh (this includes cash payment of Rs. 10 lakh by SBI to X Ltd. prior to September 1, 2019). Therefore, tax deductible by SBI on October 10, 2019 is Rs. 60,000 (being 2% of Rs. 30 lakh). Further SBI will deduct tax at source under section 194N on January 10, 2020 which comes to Rs. 40,000 (*i.e.*, 2% of Rs. 20 lakh).

Online filing of application seeking determination of tax to be deducted at source on payment to non-residents [Sec. 195(2)]

0.62 Under section 195(2), a person (who is responsible for tax deduction on payment of any sum to a non-resident) considers that the whole of such sum would not be income chargeable in the case of the recipient, he can make an application to the Assessing Officer to determine the appropriate proportion of such sum (chargeable to tax in the hands of recipient) which is subject to TDS. This provision is used by a person making payment to a non-resident to obtain certificate/order from the Assessing Officer for lower or *nil* withholding tax.

• *Amendment* - The process of obtaining above certificate/order is currently manual. In order to use technology to streamline the process, the scheme of section 195 has been amended (with effect from November 1, 2019) to allow for prescribing the form and manner of application to the Assessing Officer and also for the manner of determination of appropriate portion of sum chargeable to tax by the Assessing Officer.

Amendment to section 197

0.63 Section 197 regulates the provisions pertaining to certificate of lower/*nil* tax deduction. It has been amended (with effect from September 1, 2019 so as to provide that the sums on which tax is deductible under section 194M, shall also be eligible for certificate for deduction at lower rate or *nil* rate.

Amendment to section 198

0.64 Section 198 has been amended with effect from September 1, 2019. The amended version provides that tax deducted under section 194N shall not be deemed to be income received (for the purpose of section 198) for computing income of recipient.

Amendment to section 201

0.65 *See* para 0.24.

Electronic filing of statement of transactions on which tax has not been deducted [Sec. 206A]

0.66 Section 206A relates to furnishing of statement in respect of payment of interest to residents where no tax has been deducted at source. At present, the section provides for filing of such statements on a floppy, diskette, magnetic tape, CD-ROM, or any other computer readable media.

• *Amendment* - To enable online filing of aforesaid statements, the scheme of section 206A has been modified (with effect from September 1, 2019) so as to provide for filing of statement (where tax has not been deducted on payment of interest to residents) in prescribed form in the prescribed manner. The modified scheme also provides for –

- correction of such statements for rectification of any mistake or to add, delete or update the information furnished,
- consequential amendment arising out of amendment carried out by the Finance Act, 2019 whereby threshold for TDS on certain payment of interest has been increased from Rs. 10,000 to Rs. 40,000.

Recovery of tax in pursuance of agreements with foreign countries [Sec. 228A]

0.67 Section 228A regulates recovery of tax in pursuance of agreements with foreign countries. It, *inter alia*, provides that where an agreement is entered into by the Central Government with a foreign Government for recovery of income-tax under the Income-tax Act and the corresponding law in force in that country and where such foreign country sends a certificate for the recovery of any tax due under such corresponding law from a person having any property in India, the Board, on receipt of such certificate may, forward it to the Tax Recovery Officer within whose jurisdiction such property is situated. This provision has been amended (with effect from September 1, 2019) so as to provide for tax recovery in cases where details of property of such person are not available but the said person is a resident in India. Further, section 228A(2) has been amended so as to provide for tax recovery where details of property of assessee in default are not available but the said assessee is a resident in a foreign country.

Amendment to sections 234A, 234B and 234C

0.68 *See* para 0.57.

Claim for refund [Sec. 239]

0.69 Section 239 provides, *inter alia*, that every claim of refund under Chapter XIX shall be made in the prescribed form and verified in the prescribed manner. In order to simplify the procedure for claim of refund, the scheme of section 239 has been modified (with effect from September 1, 2019) to provide that every claim for refund under Chapter XIX shall be made by furnishing return in accordance with the provisions of section 139. Moreover, sub-section (2) has been omitted.

Amendment to section 246A(1)(*bb*)

0.70 *See* para 0.44.

Amendment to sections 269SS and 269ST

0.71 *See* para 0.22.

Mandating acceptance of payments through prescribed electronic modes [Sec. 269SU]

0.72 Section 269SU has been inserted with effect from November 1, 2019, in order to achieve the mission of the Government to move towards a less cash economy to reduce generation and circulation of black money and to promote digital economy. It requires that every person, carrying on business, shall, arrange facility for accepting payment through the prescribed electronic modes, in addition to the facility for other electronic modes of payment, if any, being provided by such person. However, this provision is applicable only if total sales, turnover or gross receipts of the person in business exceed Rs. 50 crore during the immediately preceding previous year.

• *Penalty under section 271DB* - In order to ensure compliance of the aforesaid provisions, section 271DB has been inserted with effect from November 1, 2019. It provides that the failure to provide facility for electronic modes of payment prescribed under section 269SU, shall attract penalty of a sum of Rs. 5,000, for every day during which such failure continues. However, the penalty shall not be imposed if the person proves that there were good and sufficient reasons for such failure. Any such penalty shall be imposed by the Joint Commissioner.

• *Consequential amendment* - A consequential amendment has been made to the Payment and Settlement Systems Act, 2007 so as to provide that no bank or system provider shall impose any charge upon anyone, either directly or indirectly, for using the modes of electronic payment prescribed under section 269SU.

Provisions relating to under-reporting of income [Sec. 270A]

0.73 Section 270A contains provisions relating to penalty for under-reporting and misreporting of income. The existing provisions provide for various situations for the purposes of levy of penalty under this section. However, these provisions do not contain the mechanism for determining under-reporting of income and quantum of penalty to be levied in the case where the person has under-reported income and furnished the return of income for the first time under section 148.

• *Amendment* - The aforesaid provisions of section 270A have been amended (with retrospective effect from April 1, 2017) to provide for manner of computing the quantum of penalty in a case where the person has under-reported income and furnished his return for the first time under section 148.

Penalty for failure to comply with provisions of section 269SU [Sec. 271DB]

0.74 *See* para 0.72.

Amendment to section 271FAA

0.75 Section 271FAA regulates penalty for furnishing inaccurate statement of financial transaction or reportable account. It, *inter alia*, provides for penalty of a sum of Rs. 50,000, if a person referred to in section 285BA(1)(*k*) furnishes inaccurate information in the statement. Presently, penalty under section 271FAA cannot be imposed if inaccurate information is furnished by a person referred to in clauses (*a*) to (*j*) of section 285BA(1).

• *Amendment* - The above provisions of section 271FAA have been amended (with effect from September 1, 2019) so as to extend the penalty for furnishing inaccurate information in the statement to all the persons referred to in section 285BA(1).

Amendment to section 272B

0.76 The following amendments have been made to the provisions pertaining to section 272B with effect from September 1, 2019 –

• Section 272B(2) has been suitably amended so that penalty may also be levied on false quoting or non-intimation of Aadhaar number.

• Penalty of Rs. 10,000 shall be levied for each default under section 272B(2).

• New sub-section (2A) has been inserted to provide that if a person, who is required to quote and also authenticate his PAN/Aadhaar number, fails to do so, the Assessing Officer may direct that such person shall pay, by way of penalty, a sum of Rs. 10,000 for each such default.

• New sub-section (2B) has been inserted to provide that if a person who is required to ensure that PAN/ Aadhaar has been quoted/authenticated, fails to do so, the Assessing Officer may direct that such person shall pay, by way of penalty, a sum of Rs. 10,000 for each such default.

• Before passing a penalty order under sub-section (2A) or (2B), the person (on whom the penalty is proposed to be imposed) shall be given an opportunity of being heard.

Rationalisation of the provisions of section 276CC

0.77 Section 276CC, *inter alia*, provides that prosecution proceedings for failure to furnish returns of income against a person shall not proceeded against, for failure to furnish the return of income in due time, if the tax payable by such person, not being a company, on the total income determined on regular assessment does not exceed Rs. 3,000. For determining this monitoring ceiling, tax credit pertaining to TCS/ self-assessment tax is not considered.

• *Amendment* - In order to rationalise the aforesaid provisions of section 276CC, the following amendment have been made with effect from the assessment year 2020-21 –

1. The aforesaid threshold ceiling of Rs. 3,000 has been increased to Rs. 10,000.

2. The threshold ceiling of Rs. 10,000 shall be calculated as follows –

- Tax payable by the defaulter (not being a company) on total income determined on regular assessment
- *Less:* Advance tax or self-assessment tax paid before the expiry of assessment year.
- *Less:* Tax deducted or collected at source.

If the balance is Rs. 10,000 or less, section 276CC will not be applicable.

Widening the scope of Statement of Financial Transactions (SFT) [Sec. 285BA]

0.78 Section 285BA, *inter alia,* provides for furnishing of statement of financial transaction (SFT) or reportable account by person specified therein. In order to enable pre-filling of return of income, section 285BA has been amended (with effect from September 1, 2019) as follows –

1. These provisions have been modified to obtain information by widening the scope of furnishing of statement of financial transactions by compulsory furnishing of statement by certain prescribed persons (other than those who are currently furnishing the same).

2. The current threshold of Rs. 50,000 on aggregate value of transactions during a financial year, has been removed for furnishing of information, with a view to ensure pre-filling of information relating to small amount of transactions as well.

3. Sub-section (4) has been amended so as provide that if the defect in the statement is not rectified within the time specified therein, the provisions of the Act shall apply as if such person had furnished inaccurate information in the statement.

4. Penalty provisions under section 271FAA have been amended so as to ensure correct furnishing of information in the SFT and widen the scope of penalty to cover all the reporting entities under section 285BA.

Clarification regarding definition of the "accounting year" in section 286

0.79 Section 286 contains provisions relating to specific reporting regime in the form of Country-by-Country Report (CbCR) in respect of an international group. It provides that every parent entity or the alternate reporting entity (ARE), resident in India, shall, for every reporting accounting year, in respect of the international group of which it is a constituent, furnish a report, to the prescribed authority within a period of 12 months from the end of the said reporting accounting year, in the prescribed form. For this purpose, "accounting year" means a previous year in a case where the parent entity or ARE is resident in India.

• *Amendment* - In case of an alternate reporting entity (ARE) resident in India whose ultimate parent entity is not resident in India, the accounting year would always be the accounting year applicable in the country where such ultimate parent entity is resident and cannot be the previous year of the entity resident in India. Accordingly, the above provisions have been amended (with retrospectively effect from the assessment year 2017-18) as to provide that the accounting year in case of ARE, resident in India, whose ultimate parent entity is outside India, shall not mean the previous year but an annual accounting period, with respect to which the parent entity of the international group prepares its financial statements under any law for the time being in force or the applicable accounting standards of the country of which such entity is resident.

Time-limit for sale of attached property [Rule 68B of Second Schedule]

0.80 Rule 68B of the Second Schedule provides that no sale of immovable property attached towards the recovery of tax, penalty, etc., shall be made after the expiry of 3 years from the end of the financial year in which the order in consequence of which any tax, penalty, etc., becomes final.

• *Amendment* - The aforesaid time-limit has been extended to 7 years. The table given below highlights the above provision before and after amendment –

	Time-limit for sale of immovable property attached towards recovery of tax, penalty, etc.
Up to August 31, 2019	Within 3 years (4 years in some cases as specified in the first proviso to rule 68B) from the end of the financial year in which order giving rise to a demand becomes final
From September 1, 2019	Within 7 years (8 years in some cases as specified in the first proviso to rule 68B) from the end of the financial year in which order giving rise to a demand becomes final (Board may extend, for reasons to be recorded in writing, the aforesaid period of 7 years for a further period not exceeding 3 years)

Rationalisation of the Income Declaration Scheme, 2016

0.81 The existing provisions of section 187 of the Finance Act, 2016 provide, *inter alia,* that the tax, surcharge and penalty in respect of the undisclosed income, declared under the Income Declaration Scheme, 2016 (the Scheme) shall be paid on or before a notified due date.

• *Amendment (for late payment)* - The above provision of section 187 of the Finance Act, 2016 has been amended. Amended version (applicable with effect from June 1, 2016) provides as follows –

- The amount of tax, surcharge and penalty is not paid within the due date,

- The Central Government may notify the class of persons who may make the payment of the aforesaid amount on or before a notified date, along with the interest on such amount,
- Interest will be calculated at the rate of 1 per cent of every month (or part of a month),
- Interest will be payable for the period commencing on the date immediately following the due date and ending on the date of such payment.

• *Amendment (for claiming refund)* - Section 191 of the Finance Act, 2016 provides, *inter alia,* that any amount of tax, surcharge or penalty paid in pursuance of a declaration made under the Scheme shall not be refundable. This provision has been modified (with effect from June 1, 2016) so as to provide that the Central Government may notify the class of persons to whom the amount of tax, surcharge and penalty, paid in excess of the amount payable under the scheme, shall be refundable.

Settlement price in the case of securities transaction tax

0.82 As per the existing provisions section 99 of the Finance (No. 2) Act, 2004, the value of taxable securities transaction in respect of sale of an option in securities (where option is exercised) is settlement price.

• *Amendment* - Section 99 has been amended (with effect from September 1, 2019) on the following lines –

- The value of taxable securities transaction in respect of sale of an option in securities (where option is exercised) will be intrinsic value.
- For this purpose, intrinsic value means the difference between the settlement price and the strike price.

PART B - EFFECTED BY THE FINANCE ACT, 2019

Standard deduction to salaried employees [Sec. 16(*ia*)]

0.83 Clause (*ia*) was inserted in section 16 by the Finance Act, 2018 to provide standard deduction to salaried employees. Under this provision, standard deduction is Rs. 40,000 or salary income, whichever is lower, for the assessment year 2019-20. With effect from the assessment year 2020-21, the quantum of standard deduction has been increased to Rs. 50,000.

• *Provisions illustrated* - X (32 years) is a computer programmer and employed by Y Ltd., Bengaluru. He gets Rs. 1,80,000 per month as salary and Rs. 3,00,000 per annum as bonus. Besides, A Ltd. provides the following –

- Conveyance allowance for official purposes : Rs. 1,000 per month (expenditure for official use for the previous year is Rs. 11,500).
- Transport allowance (to cover journey between office and residence) : Rs. 1,600 per month (actual expenditure is not more than Rs. 1,200 per month).
- Fixed medical allowance : Rs. 500 per month (X claims that the entire amount is used for medical treatment of his family).
- Medical facility in a hospital which is owned by Y Ltd. Cost to Y Ltd. for providing this facility to X : Rs. 25,000.
- Medical facility in a State Government/Central Government hospital : Rs. 20,000.
- Medical facility in a private hospital in Bengaluru (the same hospital is recommended by the Government of Karnataka for the medical treatment of Government employees) : Rs. 24,000.
- Medical facility (rule 3A) in an hospital approved by the Chief Commissioner of Income-tax : Rs. 42,000.
- Medi-claim insurance premium paid by Y Ltd. for X and his family : Rs. 28,000.
- Reimbursement by A Ltd. of other medical expenditure : Rs. 19,000.

Income of X from salary will be calculated as follows –

	If AY is 2018-19 *Rs.*	*If AY is 2019-20* *Rs.*	*If AY is 2020-21* *Rs.*
Basic salary (Rs. 1,80,000 × 12)	21,60,000	21,60,000	21,60,000
Bonus	3,00,000	3,00,000	3,00,000

	If AY is 2018-19 Rs.	*If AY is 2019-20* Rs.	*If AY is 2020-21* Rs.
Conveyance allowance for official use [(Rs. 1,000 × 12) – Rs. 11,500]	500	500	500
Transport allowance (Rs. 1,600 × 12)	*Nil*	19,200	19,200
Fixed medical allowance (Rs. 500 × 12)	6,000	6,000	6,000
Medical facility in Y Ltd.'s hospital	*Nil*	*Nil*	*Nil*
Medical facility in Government hospital	*Nil*	*Nil*	*Nil*
Medical facility in private hospital (which is also recommended for the medical treatment of Government employees by the Government)	*Nil*	*Nil*	*Nil*
Medical facility (rule 3A) in a hospital recommended by the Chief Commissioner of Income-tax	*Nil*	*Nil*	*Nil*
Medi-claim insurance premium paid by Y Ltd.	*Nil*	*Nil*	*Nil*
Reimbursement of other medical expenditure (reimbursement up to Rs. 15,000 is not chargeable to tax for the assessment year 2018-19)	4,000	19,000	19,000
Gross salary	24,70,500	25,04,700	25,04,700
Less: Standard deduction under section 16(*ia*)	*Nil*	40,000	50,000
Income under the head "Salaries"	24,70,500	24,64,700	24,54,700

Notional rent on second self-occupied property exempt from tax [Secs. 23 and 24]

0.84 If a person has occupied one house property for his own residential purposes, it is not chargeable to income-tax. Annual value of such property is taken as *nil* and interest on capital which was borrowed to finance purchase, construction, etc., of such property is deductible (subject to satisfaction of a few conditions) up to Rs. 2,00,000. If a person has occupied more than one house property for his residential purposes, only one property (according to his own choice) is treated as self-occupied property (annual value of such property is taken as *nil*, interest liability is deductible up to Rs. 2,00,000 subject to a few conditions). In such a case, income from other self-occupied property/properties will be calculated as if such property/properties are "deemed to be let out".

• *Amendment* - The aforesaid provision has been amended to exempt notional income pertaining to two self-occupied residential house properties. Salient features of the amendment (applicable from the assessment year 2020-21) are given below –

1. If a person occupies only one house property for his own residential purposes, annual value of such property will be *nil* (as earlier). Interest on borrowed capital will be deductible up to Rs. 2,00,000 (subject to a few conditions).

2. If a person occupies two house properties for his own residential purposes, annual value of both the properties will be taken as *nil*. Aggregate interest on capital borrowed for the purpose of purchase/construction of these properties, will be deductible up to Rs. 2,00,000 (subject to similar conditions as were applicable earlier).

3. If a person occupies more than two house properties for his own residential purposes, only two properties (according to his own choice) will be treated as self-occupied properties and other houses will be "deemed to be let out". In the case of two self-occupied properties (as selected by the assessee), annual value will be *nil* and aggregate interest on borrowed capital will be deductible up to Rs. 2,00,000 (subject to similar conditions as were applicable earlier). In the case of "deemed to be let out" properties, taxable income will be calculated as if such properties are let out properties.

0.84-E1 X owns two house properties. These properties are used for own residential purposes throughout the previous year (not let out at all, not put to any other use, no other benefit is derived). Relevant data pertaining to these properties is given below –

	House 1 *Rs.*	*House 2* *Rs.*
Municipal value	4,10,000	16,20,000
Fair rent	4,30,000	16,50,000
Standard rent	3,90,000	15,80,000
Municipal tax (paid by X during the previous year)	40,000	70,000
Interest (on loan taken in 2013-14 to purchase these properties)	2,10,000	8,70,000

Business income of X is Rs. 20,00,000. He annually contributes Rs. 2,00,000 in NPS. Compute taxable income if assessment year is 2019-20 or 2020-21.

•

If assessment year is 2019-20 - Only one property (according to the choice of X) will be treated as "self-occupied property" and the other property will be taken as "deemed to be let out property". Bigger house is *House 2*. It may be taken as self-occupied property and income will be calculated as follows –

	House 1 *Rs.*	*House 2* *Rs.*
Gross annual value (municipal value or fair rent, whichever is higher but subject to a maximum of standard rent) (*nil* in the case of "self-occupied property")	3,90,000	*Nil*
Less: Municipal tax (not deductible in the case of "self-occupied property")	40,000	*Nil*
Net annual value	3,50,000	*Nil*
Less: Deductions under section 24		
Standard deduction (@ 30% of net annual value)	1,05,000	*Nil*
Interest on borrowed capital (in the case of "self-occupied property", maximum deductible amount is Rs. 2,00,000)	2,10,000	2,00,000
Income from properties	35,000	(–)2,00,000

Computation of income –

	Rs.
Income from house property (Rs. 35,000 – Rs. 2,00,000)	(–)1,65,000
Business income	20,00,000
Gross total income	18,35,000
Less: Deduction under Chapter VI-A	2,00,000
Net income	16,35,000

If assessment year is 2020-21 - From the assessment year 2020-21, two house properties can be taken as "self-occupied properties" and income will be calculated as follows –

	Rs.
Gross annual value of *House 1* and *House 2*	*Nil*
Less: Municipal tax (not deductible in the case of "self-occupied properties")	*Nil*
Net annual value	*Nil*
Less: Deduction under section 24	
Standard deduction	*Nil*
Interest on borrowed capital (Rs. 2,10,000 + Rs. 8,10,000, subject to maximum of Rs. 2,00,000)	2,00,000
Income from *House 1* and *House 2*	(–)2,00,000
Business income	20,00,000
Gross total income	18,00,000
Less: Deduction under Chapter VI-A	2,00,000
Net income	16,00,000

0.84-E2 Y owns two house properties. These properties are used for own residential purposes throughout the previous year (not let out at all, not put to any other use, no other benefit is derived). Relevant data pertaining to these properties is given below –

	House 1 Rs.	House 2 Rs.
Municipal value	10,00,000	18,00,000
Fair rent	9,00,000	19,00,000
Standard rent	11,00,000	18,50,000
Municipal tax (paid by Y during the previous year)	1,00,000	50,000
Interest (on loan taken in 2013-14 to purchase these properties)	12,00,000	10,00,000

Business income of Y is Rs. 30,00,000. He annually contributes Rs. 1,50,000 in public provident fund. Compute taxable income if assessment year is 2019-20 or 2020-21.

•

If assessment year is 2019-20 - Only one property (according to the choice of Y) will be treated as "self-occupied property" and the other property will be taken as "deemed to be let out property". *House 2* is selected by Y to be treated as "self-occupied property". Income will be calculated as follows –

	House 1 Rs.	House 2 Rs.
Gross annual value (municipal value or fair rent, whichever is higher but subject to a maximum of standard rent) (*nil* in the case of "self-occupied property")	9,00,000	*Nil*
Less: Municipal tax (not deductible in the case of "self-occupied property")	1,00,000	*Nil*
Net annual value	8,00,000	*Nil*
Less: Deductions under section 24		
Standard deduction (@ 30% of net annual value)	2,40,000	*Nil*
Interest on borrowed capital (in the case of "self-occupied property", maximum deductible amount is Rs. 2,00,000)	12,00,000	2,00,000
Income from properties	(–)6,40,000	(–)2,00,000

Computation of income –

	Rs.
Income from house property [Rs. (–) 6,40,000 + Rs. (–) 2,00,000]	(–)8,40,000
Business income	30,00,000
Gross total income (house property loss up to Rs. 2,00,000 can be set off against other incomes, balance will be carried forward)	28,00,000
Less: Deduction under Chapter VI-A	1,50,000
Net income	26,50,000

Note - House property loss up to Rs. 2,00,000 can be set off against business income (or any other income) in the current year by virtue of section 71(3A). Balance house property loss of Rs. 6,40,000 will be carried forward.

If assessment year is 2020-21 - From the assessment year 2020-21, two house properties can be taken as "self-occupied properties" and income will be calculated as follows –

	Rs.
Gross annual value of *House 1* and *House 2*	*Nil*
Less: Municipal tax (not deductible in the case of "self-occupied properties")	*Nil*
Net annual value	*Nil*
Less: Deduction under section 24	
Standard deduction	*Nil*
Interest on borrowed capital (Rs. 12,00,000 + Rs. 10,00,000, subject to maximum of Rs. 2,00,000)	2,00,000
Income from *House 1* and *House 2*	(–)2,00,000
Business income	30,00,000
Gross total income	28,00,000
Less: Deduction under Chapter VI-A	1,50,000
Net income	26,50,000

Note - Income under the head "Income from house property" is Rs. (–) 2,00,000. Loss of Rs. 2,00,000 can be set off against business income or any other income in the current year. Nothing will be carried forward.

0.84-E3 In example 0.84-E2, Y does not want to utilise the benefit of new amendment for the assessment year 2020-21 to treat *House 1* as well as *House 2* as "self-occupied properties". He wants to treat *House 2* as "self-occupied property" and *House 1* as "deemed to be let out property" so that he can carry forward house property loss of Rs. 6,40,000. Can he do so ?

•

After the new amendment to section 23(4)(*a*) (with effect from the assessment year 2020-21), the concept of "deemed to be let out property" will be applicable only if an assessee has occupied more than two houses for his residential purposes. In the above example, Y has occupied two houses for his residential purposes. For the assessment year 2020-21, *House 1* and *House 2* will be treated as "self-occupied properties". Y does not have any option to treat one of them as "deemed to be let out property".

0.84-E4 Z owns 5 houses. These houses are used by him for his residential purposes. These houses are not let out during any part of the previous year 2019-20. No other benefit is derived from these houses. The following information is noted from the records of Z –

	House 1 Rs.	*House 2* Rs.	*House 3* Rs.	*House 4* Rs.	*House 5* Rs.
Municipal value or fair rent, whichever is higher (but subject to maximum of standard rent)	12,00,000	12,70,000	27,60,000	4,90,000	15,90,000
Municipal taxes paid by Z	40,000	1,20,000	1,90,000	30,000	1,20,000
Interest on capital borrowed to purchase properties (date of borrowing in all cases is after April 1, 1999)	–	11,000	1,70,000	2,00,000	2,30,000
Interest on capital borrowed to finance repair, renewal or reconstruction of house properties	2,10,000	7,89,000	14,00,000	–	–

Business income of Z is Rs. 32,00,000. He is entitled for a deduction of Rs. 2,40,000 under Chapter VI-A. Compute net income for the assessment year 2020-21.

•

Z has occupied 5 properties for his own residential purposes. Only two houses (according to the choice of Z) will be treated as self-occupied properties. Other 3 houses will be "deemed to be let out". He has the following options –

Different options	*Houses to be treated as self-occupied*	*Houses deemed to be let out*
Option 1	House 1 and House 2	House 3, House 4 and House 5
Option 2	House 1 and House 3	House 2, House 4 and House 5
Option 3	House 1 and House 4	House 2, House 3 and House 5
Option 4	House 1 and House 5	House 2, House 3 and House 4
Option 5	House 2 and House 3	House 1, House 4 and House 5
Option 6	House 2 and House 4	House 1, House 3 and House 5
Option 7	House 2 and House 5	House 1, House 3 and House 4
Option 8	House 3 and House 4	House 1, House 2 and House 5
Option 9	House 3 and House 5	House 1, House 2 and House 4
Option 10	House 4 and House 5	House 1, House 2 and House 3

In order to minimise taxable income (and maximise loss to be carried forward), one may proceed as follows –

Step 1 - Find out income of 5 houses as if these are treated as "self-occupied property".

Step 2 - Find out income of 5 houses as if these are "deemed to be let out".

Step 3 - Find out the difference between income of each house computed under *Step 1* and *Step 2*.

Step 4 - Two houses (reporting highest difference as per *Step 3*) may be taken as "self-occupied properties". Other remaining houses will be "deemed to be let out".

	House 1 Rs.	*House 2* Rs.	*House 3* Rs.	*House 4* Rs.	*House 5* Rs.
Step 1 - Computation of income if these are self-occupied properties –					
Net annual value	*Nil*	*Nil*	*Nil*	*Nil*	*Nil*
Less: Interest on borrowed capital	30,000	41,000	2,00,000	2,00,000	2,00,000
Income from property (*a*)	(–)30,000	(–)41,000	(–)2,00,000	(–)2,00,000	(–)2,00,000
Step 2 - Computation of income if these are deemed to be let out –					
Gross annual value (being municipal value or fair rent, whichever is lower but subject to maximum of standard rent)	12,00,000	12,70,000	27,60,000	4,90,000	15,90,000
Less: Municipal tax	40,000	1,20,000	1,90,000	30,000	1,20,000
Net annual value	11,60,000	11,50,000	25,70,000	4,60,000	14,70,000
Less: Deduction under section 24					
Standard deduction	3,48,000	3,45,000	7,71,000	1,38,000	4,41,000
Interest on borrowed capital	2,10,000	8,00,000	15,70,000	2,00,000	2,30,000
Income from property (*b*)	6,02,000	5,000	2,29,000	1,22,000	7,99,000
Step 3 - Step 1 minus Step 2 [(*a*) – (*b*)]	(–)6,32,000	(–)46,000	(–)4,29,000	(–)3,22,000	(–)9,99,000
Step 4 - Selection : House 1 and House 5 (to be taken as self-occupied properties)					
Income of House 1 and House 5 (self-occupied properties) (*total interest pertaining to self-occupied properties cannot exceed Rs. 2,00,000)	(–)30,000	–	–	–	(–)1,70,000*
Income of House 2, House 3 and House 4 (deemed to be let out properties)	–	5,000	2,29,000	1,22,000	–
Income from properties	(–)30,000	5,000	2,29,000	1,22,000	(–)1,70,000

Income computation of Z –

	Rs.
Income from house property [Rs. (–)30,000 + Rs. 5,000 + Rs. 2,29,000 + Rs. 1,22,000 + Rs. (–)1,70,000]	1,56,000
Business income	32,00,000
Gross total income	33,56,000
Less: Deduction under Chapter VI-A	2,40,000
Net income	31,16,000

No notional income up to 2 years for house property held as stock-in-trade [Sec. 23(5)]

0.85 Sub-section (5) was inserted in section 23 by the Finance Act, 2017 with effect from the assessment year 2018-19. This sub-section is applicable if the following conditions are satisfied –

1. The property (consisting of any building and land appurtenant thereto) is held as stock-in-trade by the owner of the property.

2. The property (or any part of the property) is not let out during the whole (or any part) of the previous year.

If the above conditions are satisfied, annual value of such property (or part of the property) shall be taken to be *nil*. However, this concession is available only for the period up to 1 year from the end of the financial year in which the certificate of completion of construction of the property is obtained from the competent authority.

• *Amendment* - The aforesaid period of 1 year has been extended to 2 years with effect from the assessment year 2020-21. Consequently, if the above two conditions are satisfied, annual value of the aforesaid properties shall be taken to be *nil* for 2 years from the end of the financial year in which the certificate of completion of construction of the property is obtained from the competent authority.

Exemption under section 54 extended to purchase/construction of two residential houses

0.86 Capital gain arising from transfer of a house property is exempt under section 54, if the following conditions are satisfied –

1. The property (which is transferred) is a residential house property.

2. Transferor is an individual or a Hindu undivided family.

3. The property (which is transferred) is a long-term capital asset.

4. To avail of exemption, the assessee will have to purchase/construct one residential house property in India within a specified time-limit. If the new property is not purchased/constructed till the due date of submission of return of income, the amount should be deposited in Capital Gains Deposit Account Scheme and investment in new property can be made by withdrawing from the deposit account.

Exemption under section 54 is the amount of investment in the new property or the capital gain, whichever is lower.

• *Amendment* - Currently, exemption under section 54 is available for investment in construction/purchase of one residential house property. With effect from the assessment year 2020-21, the following amendments have been made to the scheme of section 54 –

1. To get exemption, one can purchase/construct two residential house properties (specified time-limit for construction/purchase will remain the same).

2. The aforesaid option (of investment in two residential house properties) will be available only where the amount of capital gain does not exceed Rs. 2 crore. To put it differently, if long-term capital asset (being a residential house property) is transferred by an individual (or HUF) and the amount of long-term capital gain (after indexation) exceeds Rs. 2 crore, the assessee cannot claim the benefit of investment in construction/ purchase of two residential house properties.

3. The aforesaid option can be exercised only once in a lifetime. In other words, if an assessee exercises the aforesaid option (of investment in two residential house properties) for the assessment year 2020-21, he shall not be subsequently entitled to exercise the same option for the assessment year 2021-22 (or any subsequent assessment year). However, in future he can continue to claim section 54 exemption by investing in purchase/construction of one residential house property.

0.86-E1 The following information is given by X and Y for the previous year 2019-20 –

	X *Rs.*	*Y* *Rs.*
Sale consideration of a residential house property situated in Kolkata	3,30,00,000	9,40,00,000
Stamp duty value on the date of transfer	3,50,00,000	9,50,00,000
Cost of acquisition in 1996-97	28,00,000	1,60,00,000
Fair market value on April 1, 2001	29,00,000	2,30,00,000
Cost of improvement incurred in 2002-03	40,000	50,00,000
Expenditure on transfer borne by transferor	40,000	50,000
Purchase of residential house property in Cochin on December 1, 2019	60,70,000	20,10,000
Purchase of another residential house property in Mumbai on July 10, 2020	2,02,00,000	1,20,00,000

•

Computation of capital gain –

	X *Rs.*	*Y* *Rs.*
Full value of consideration (stamp duty value is taken if it exceeds 105% of sale consideration)	3,50,00,000	9,40,00,000
Less:		
Indexed cost of acquisition (it is assumed that CII of 2019-20 is 290)		
- In the case of X (Rs. 29,00,000 × 290 ÷ 100)	84,10,000	–
- In the case of Y (Rs. 2,30,00,000 × 290 ÷ 100)	–	6,67,00,000
Indexed cost of improvement (it is assumed that CII of 2019-20 is 290)		

	X Rs.	Y Rs.
- In the case of X (Rs. 40,000 × 290 ÷ 105)	1,10,476	–
- In the case of Y (Rs. 50,00,000 × 290 ÷ 105)	–	1,38,09,524
Expenditure on transfer	40,000	50,000
Long-term capital gain before exemption	2,64,39,524	1,34,40,476
Less: Exemption under section 54		
- In the case of X (as long-term capital gain exceeds Rs. 2 crore, X can avail section 54 exemption only for investment in one residential house property)	2,02,00,000	–
- In the case of Y (as long-term capital gain does not exceed Rs. 2 crore, Y can claim section 54 exemption for investment in two residential house properties) (Rs. 20,10,000 + Rs. 1,20,00,000, subject to maximum of long-term capital gain of Rs. 1,34,40,476)	–	1,34,40,476
Income under the head "Capital gains"	62,39,524	*Nil*

0.86-E2 Y transfers a residential house property located in Mumbai for Rs. 18 crore (stamp duty value on the date of transfer is Rs 18.90 crore) on April 6, 2019. This property was purchased in 1998-99. Indexed cost of acquisition is Rs. 8.75 crore. Cost of improvement incurred during 1999-2000 is Rs. 18 lakh. Expenditure on transfer is Rs. 6 lakh. However, it is reimbursed by the purchaser. To get the benefit of exemption under section 54, Y deposits Rs. 8 crore in Capital Gain Deposit Account Scheme with SBI on July 1, 2020. On the same day, he invests Rs. 50 lakh in REC bonds for claiming exemption under section 54EC.

By withdrawing from the deposit account, he purchases/constructs the following house properties –

- On April 3, 2021, purchase of a residential house property in Delhi for Rs. 3.2 crore.
- On December 20, 2021, construction of another residential house property in Ahmedabad (investment in construction including cost of land : Rs. 3.5 crore).

Discuss tax consequences of these transactions.

•

Assessment year 2020-21 –

	Rs. in crore
Full value of consideration (stamp duty value is not taken, as it does not exceed 105% of actual sale consideration)	18.00
Less:	
Indexed cost of acquisition	8.75
Indexed cost of improvement (improvement expenditure incurred prior to April 1, 2001, not to be considered)	*Nil*
Expenditure on transfer (not deductible, as borne by purchaser)	*Nil*
Long-term capital gain	9.25
Less:	
Exemption under section 54 (amount deposited in Capital Gain Deposit Account Scheme)	8.00
Exemption under section 54EC (not available, investment made after 6 months from the date of transfer)	*Nil*
Long-term capital gain	1.25

Assessment year 2023-24 - As the amount of capital gain (before any exemption) is more than Rs. 2 crore, the assessee can purchase/construct one residential house property in India. He has deposited Rs. 8 crore in Capital Gain Deposit Account Scheme to claim exemption under section 54 for the assessment year 2020-21. Deposit account can be utilised for purchase/construction of one residential house within the specified time-limit (*i.e.*, for purchase : within 2 years from the date of transfer, for construction : within 3 years from the date of transfer). Y has purchased one residential house and constructed another house by withdrawing from the deposit account. Even if the two houses are purchased/constructed within the specified time-limit, only one of them is qualified for exemption under section 54 (the amount of original capital gain being more than Rs. 2 crore). Non-utilisation/misutilisation of deposit account attracts reversal of section 54 exemption. Such reversal is applicable after the expiry of 3 years from the date of transfer of house property. The 3 year time-limit expires on April 5, 2022. Consequently, the following amount will be chargeable to long-term capital gain for the previous year 2022-23 (*i.e.*, assessment year 2023-24) –

	Rs. in crore
Amount deposited in deposit account	8.00
Less:	
Withdrawal for construction of Ahmedabad property	3.50
Withdrawal for purchase of Delhi property (second house is not eligible for exemption under section 54)	*Nil*
Notional long-term capital gain chargeable to tax for assessment year 2023-24	4.50

Amendment to section 80-IBA

0.87 Deduction under section 80-IBA is available in respect of profits and gains derived from the business of developing and building affordable housing projects. This deduction is available if the project is approved by the competent authority after June 1, 2016 but on or before March 31, 2019.

• *Amendment* - The time-limit for approval has been extended by one year (with effect from the assessment year 2020-21). After this amendment, deduction under section 80-IBA will be available if the project is approved by the competent authority after June 1, 2016 but on or before March 31, 2020.

Rebate from income-tax in the case of resident individual [Sec. 87A]

0.88 A resident individual can claim a rebate from income-tax under section 87A. Currently, this rebate is available only if his total income does not exceed Rs. 3,50,000. The quantum of rebate for the assessment year 2019-20 is limited to Rs. 2,500. From the assessment year 2020-21, this rebate will be available if total income of the resident individual is Rs. 5,00,000 (or less). The quantum of maximum rebate will be Rs. 12,500. The following table summarises provisions of section 87A before and after this amendment –

Different years	*Total income of resident individual should not exceed the amount given below*	*Amount of rebate under section 87A*
Assessment years 2014-15 to 2016-17	Rs. 5,00,000	100% of income-tax or Rs. 2,000, whichever is less
Assessment year 2017-18	Rs. 5,00,000	100% of income-tax or Rs. 5,000, whichever is less
Assessment years 2018-19 and 2019-20	Rs. 3,50,000	100% of income-tax or Rs. 2,500, whichever is less
Assessment year 2020-21 onwards	Rs. 5,00,000	100% of income-tax or Rs. 12,500, whichever is less

0.88-E1 Taxable income or total income (*i.e.*, gross total income *minus* deduction under sections 80C to 80U) of X for the assessment year 2020-21 is Rs. 5,00,000 (*Situation 1*) or Rs. 5,10,000 (*Situation 2*). Tax liability of X is calculated in different cases – age of X at any time during the previous year 2019-20 is 40 years (*Case 1*), 60 years (*Case 2*) or 80 years (*Case 3*).

•

	Age of X : 40 years		*Age of X : 60 years*		*Age of X : 80 years*	
	Situation 1	*Situation 2*	*Situation 1*	*Situation 2*	*Situation 1*	*Situation 2*
	Rs.	*Rs.*	*Rs.*	*Rs.*	*Rs.*	*Rs.*
Total income	5,00,000	5,10,000	5,00,000	5,10,000	5,00,000	5,10,000
Income-tax on total income	12,500	14,500	10,000	12,000	*Nil*	2,000
Less: Rebate under section 87A	12,500	*Nil*	10,000	*Nil*	*Nil*	*Nil*
Balance	*Nil*	14,500	*Nil*	12,000	*Nil*	2,000
Add: Health and education cess	*Nil*	580	*Nil*	480	*Nil*	80
Tax liability	*Nil*	15,080	*Nil*	12,480	*Nil*	2,080

Increase in threshold limit for TDS from interest other than interest on securities [Sec. 194A]

0.89 Tax deduction at source is required under section 194A if interest (other than interest on securities) paid or payable to a resident exceeds the threshold limit given below –

Who is payer	*Interest is paid/payable on* ↓	*When recipient is a senior citizen* *Rs.*	*When recipient is any other person* *Rs.*
Banking company	Time deposit/recurring deposit	50,000	10,000
A co-operative society engaged in carrying on the banking business	Time deposit/recurring deposit	50,000	10,000

Who is payer	*Interest is paid/payable on* ↓	*When recipient is a senior citizen* *Rs.*	*When recipient is any other person* *Rs.*
Post office	Notified scheme (*i.e.*, Senior Citizen Savings Scheme, 2004)	50,000	10,000
Any other person	–	5,000	5,000

- *Amendment* - With effect from April 1, 2019, the aforesaid limit of Rs. 10,000 has been increased to Rs. 40,000. Consequently, if recipient of interest is a person (other than a senior citizen), tax will be deducted by bank/co-operative bank/post office (on or after April 1, 2019) only if aggregate interest payable during the financial year exceeds Rs. 40,000. There is no change in the threshold limit if recipient is a senior citizen. Moreover, there is no change in the threshold limit of Rs. 5,000. There is no amendment in respect of taxability of interest in the hands of recipient.

Increase in threshold limit for TDS from rent under section 194-I

0.90 Tax is deductible under section 194-I only if rent paid/payable during the financial year exceeds Rs. 1,80,000. The threshold limit has been increased to Rs. 2,40,000 with effect from April 1, 2019.

R-2A

Income Computation and Disclosure Standards

The Central Board of Direct Taxes has notified the Income Disclosure and Tax Accounting Standards *vide* Notification No. 87/2016[$], dated September 29, 2016. These standards are to be followed by all assessees (other than an individual/HUF who is not required to get his account of the previous year audited under section 44AB) following mercantile system of accounting. These standards are applicable for computation of income chargeable under the head "Profits and gains of business or profession" or "Income from other sources" and not for the purpose of maintenance of books of account. These standards are applicable for the assessment year 2017-18 onwards. In case of conflict between the provisions of the Income-tax Act (the Act) and this Income Computation and Disclosure Standard, the provisions of the Act shall prevail to that extent.

The following Income Computation and Disclosure Standards (ICDS) have been notified –

ICDS-I	Accounting policies
ICDS-II	Valuation of inventories
ICDS-III	Construction contracts
ICDS-IV	Revenue recognition
ICDS-V	Tangible fixed assets
ICDS-VI	Effects of changes in foreign exchange rates
ICDS-VII	Government grants
ICDS-VIII	Securities
ICDS-IX	Borrowing costs
ICDS-X	Contingent assets

Salient features of these standards are given below –

• Income Computation and Disclosure Standard I relating to accounting policies	
Considerations in the selection of accounting policies	■ Accounting policies adopted by a person shall be such so as to represent a true and fair view of the state of affairs and income of the business, profession or vocation. [Para 4]
	■ The treatment and presentation of transactions and events shall be governed by their substance and not merely by the legal form. [Para 4(*i*)]
	■ Marked to market loss or an expected loss shall not be recognised unless the recognition of such loss is in accordance with the provisions of any other Income Computation and Disclosure Standard. [Para 4(*ii*)]
Change of accounting policies	■ An accounting policy shall not be changed without reasonable cause. [Para 5]
Disclosure of accounting policies	■ All significant accounting policies adopted by a person shall be disclosed. [Para 6]
	■ Any change in an accounting policy which has a material effect shall be disclosed. The amount by which any item is affected by such change shall also be disclosed to the extent ascertainable. Where such amount is not ascertainable, wholly or in part, the fact shall be indicated. If a change is made in the accounting policies which has no material effect for the current previous year but which is reasonably expected to have a material

[$] For Notification No. 87/2016, log on to *taxmann.com/readyreckoner.aspx.*

	effect in later previous years, the fact of such change shall be appropriately disclosed in the previous year in which the change is adopted and also in the previous year in which such change has material effect for the first time. [Para 7]
	■ If the fundamental accounting assumptions of Going Concern, Consistency and Accrual are followed, specific disclosure is not required. If a fundamental accounting assumption is not followed, the fact shall be disclosed. [Para 9]
Transitional provisions	■ All contract or transaction existing on April 1, 2016 or entered into on or after April 1, 2016 shall be dealt with in accordance with the provisions of this standard after taking into account the income, expense or loss, if any, recognised in respect of the said contract or transaction for the previous year 2015-16 (or any earlier year). [Para 10]
• Income Computation and Disclosure Standard II relating to valuation of inventories	
Scope	Valuation of all inventories are covered, except the following – - Work-in-progress under construction contracts. - Work-in-progress covered by other standards. - Share, debentures and other financial instruments held as stock-in-trade. - Producers' inventories of livestock, agriculture and forest products, mineral oils, ores and gases to the extent that they are measured at net realisable value. - Machinery spares, which can be used only in connection with a tangible fixed asset and their use is expected to be irregular. [Para 1]
Measurement	Inventories shall be valued at cost, or net realisable value, whichever is lower. [Para 3]
Cost of inventories, purchase, services	Cost of inventories shall comprise of all costs of purchase, costs of services, costs of conversion and other costs incurred in bringing the inventories to their present location and condition. The costs of purchase shall consist of purchase price including duties and taxes, freight inwards and other expenditure directly attributable to the acquisition. Trade discounts, rebates and other similar items shall be deducted in determining the costs of purchase. The costs of services in the case of a service provider shall consist of labour and other costs of personnel directly engaged in providing the service including supervisory personnel and attributable overheads. [Paras 3 to 6]
Other costs	Interest and other borrowing costs shall not be included in the costs of inventories, unless they meet the criteria for recognition of interest as a component of the cost as specified in the Income Computation and Disclosure Standard on borrowing costs. [Para 11]
Exclusion from cost of inventories	The following costs shall be excluded and recognised as expenses of the period in which they are incurred, namely – - Abnormal amounts of wasted materials, labour, or other production costs; - Storage costs, unless those costs are necessary in the production process prior to a further production stage; - Administrative overheads that do not contribute to bringing the inventories to their present location and condition ; - Selling costs. [Para 12]
First-in-first-out and weighted average cost formula	Cost of inventories shall be assigned by using the First-in First-out (FIFO), or weighted average cost formula. The formula used shall reflect the fairest possible approximation to the cost incurred in bringing the items of inventory to their present location and condition. [Para 16]

Change of method of valuation	The method of valuation of inventories once adopted by a person in any previous year shall not be changed without reasonable cause. [Para 23]
Dissolution of firm/AOP	In case of dissolution of a partnership firm or association of person or body of individuals, notwithstanding whether business is discontinued or not, the inventory on the date of dissolution shall be valued at the net realisable value. [Para 24]
Disclosure	The following aspects shall be disclosed, namely – - the accounting policies adopted in measuring inventories including the cost formulae used; and - the total carrying amount of inventories and its classification appropriate to a person. [Para 26]
Transitional provision	Interest and other borrowing costs, which do not meet the criteria for recognition of interest as a component of the cost as per para 11, but included in the cost of the opening inventory as on April 1, 2016, shall be taken into account for determining cost of such inventory for valuation as on March 31, 2017 if such inventory continue to remain part of inventory as on the close of the previous year 2016-17. [Para 25]
• Income Computation and Disclosure Standard III relating to construction contracts	
Contract revenue	Contract revenue shall be recognised when there is reasonable certainty of its ultimate collection. Contract revenue shall comprise of the initial amount of revenue agreed in the contract, including retentions; and variations in contract work, claims and incentive payments – - to the extent that it is probable that they will result in revenue; and - they are capable of being reliably measured. [Paras 9 and 10]
Subsequent adjustment	Where contract revenue already recognised as income is subsequently written off in the books of account as uncollectible, the same shall be recognised as an expense and not as an adjustment of the amount of contract revenue. [Para 11]
Contract costs	Contract costs shall comprise of - - costs that relate directly to the specific contract; - costs that are attributable to contract activity in general and can be allocated to the contract; - such other costs as are specifically chargeable to the customer under the terms of the contract; and - allocated borrowing costs in accordance with the Income Computation and Disclosure Standard on Borrowing Costs. These costs shall be reduced by any incidental income, not being in the nature of interest, dividends or capital gains, that is not included in contract revenue. [Para 12] Contract costs include the costs attributable to a contract for the period from the date of securing the contract to the final completion of the contract. [Para 14]
Recognition of contract revenue and expenses	▪ Contract revenue and contract costs associated with the construction contract should be recognised as revenue and expenses respectively by reference to the stage of completion of the contract activity at the reporting date. [Para 16] ▪ The recognition of revenue and expenses by reference to the stage of completion of a contract is referred to as the percentage of completion method. Under this method, contract revenue is matched with the contract costs incurred in reaching the stage of completion, resulting in the

	reporting of revenue, expenses and profit which can be attributed to the proportion of work completed. [Para 17] ▪ The stage of completion of a contract shall be determined with reference to – - the proportion that contract costs incurred for work performed up to the reporting date bear to the estimated total contract costs; or - surveys of work performed; or - completion of a physical proportion of the contract work. Progress payments and advances received from customers are not determinative of the stage of completion of a contract. [Para 18] ▪ During the early stages of a contract, where the outcome of the contract cannot be estimated reliably contract revenue is recognised only to the extent of costs incurred. The early stage of a contract shall not extend beyond 25 per cent of the stage of completion. [Para 20]
Changes in estimates	The percentage of completion method is applied on a cumulative basis in each previous year to the current estimates of contract revenue and contract costs. Where there is change in estimates, the changed estimates shall be used in determination of the amount of revenue and expenses in the period in which the change is made and in subsequent periods. [Para 21]
Disclosure	▪ A person shall disclose – - the amount of contract revenue recognised as revenue in the period; and - the methods used to determine the stage of completion of contracts in progress. [Para 23] ▪ A person shall disclose the following for contracts in progress at the reporting date, namely – - amount of costs incurred and recognised profits (*less* recognised losses) up to the reporting date; - the amount of advances received; and - the amount of retentions. [Para 24]
Transitional provisions	Contract revenue and contract costs associated with the construction contract, which commenced on or after April 1, 2016 shall be recognised in accordance with the provisions of this standard. Contract revenue and contract costs associated with the construction contract, which commenced on or before March 31, 2016 but not completed by the said date, shall be recognised based on the method regularly followed by the person prior to the previous year 2016-17.
• Income Computation and Disclosure Standard IV relating to revenue recognition	
Scope	This standard covers activities of a person from sale of goods, rendering of services or income pertaining to interest, royalty, or dividends. [Para 1]
Revenue	"Revenue" is the gross inflow of cash, receivables or other consideration arising in the course of the ordinary activities of a person from the aforesaid activities. In an agency relationship, the revenue is the amount of commission and not the gross inflow of cash, receivables or other consideration. [Para 2]
Sale of goods	▪ In sale of goods the revenue shall be recognised when the seller has transferred to the buyer the property in the goods for a price or all significant risks and rewards of ownership have been transferred to the buyer and the seller retains no effective control of the goods transferred to a degree usually associated with ownership. In a situation, where transfer

	of property in goods does not coincide with the transfer of significant risks and rewards of ownership, revenue in such a situation shall be recognised at the time of transfer of significant risks and rewards of ownership to the buyer. [Para 3] ▪ Revenue shall be recognised when there is reasonable certainty of its ultimate collection. [Para 4] ▪ Where the ability to assess the ultimate collection with reasonable certainty is lacking at the time of raising any claim for escalation of price and export incentives, revenue recognition in respect of such claim shall be postponed to the extent of uncertainty involved. [Para 5]
Rendering of service	Revenue from service transactions shall be recognised by the percentage completion method. Income Computation and Disclosure Standard on construction contract also requires the recognition of revenue on this basis. The requirements of that Standard shall *mutatis mutandis* apply to the recognition of revenue and the associated expenses for a service transaction. [Para 6]
Interest	Interest shall accrue on the time basis determined by the amount outstanding and the rate applicable. Discount or premium on debt securities held is treated as though it were accruing over the period to maturity. [Para 7]
Royalty	Royalties shall accrue in accordance with the terms of the relevant agreement and shall be recognised on that basis unless, having regard to the substance of the transaction, it is more appropriate to recognise revenue on some other systematic and rational basis. [Para 8]
Dividend	Dividends are recognised in accordance with the provisions of the Act. [Para 9]
Disclosure	Following disclosures shall be made in respect of revenue recognition, namely – - in sale of goods amount not recognised as revenue during the previous year; - the amount of revenue from service transactions recognised as revenue during the previous year; - the method used to determine the stage of completion of service transactions in progress; and - for service transactions in progress at the end of previous year: amount of costs incurred and recognised profits (*less* recognised losses) up to end of previous year, amount of advances received, and amount of retentions. [Para 12]
Transitional provisions	▪ The transitional provisions of ICDS on construction contract shall *mutatis mutandis* apply to the recognition of revenue and the associated costs for a service transaction undertaken on or before March 31, 2016 but not completed by the said date. [Para 10] ▪ Revenue for a transaction (other than a service transaction) undertaken on or before March 31, 2016 but not completed by the said date, shall be recognised in accordance with the provisions of this standard for the previous year 2016-17 (or subsequent year). The amount of revenue, if any, recognised for the said transaction for the previous year 2015-16 (or earlier year) shall be taken into account for recognising revenue for the said transaction for the previous year 2016-17 (or subsequent year). [Para 11]
• Income Computation and Disclosure Standard V relating to tangible fixed assets	
Tangible fixed assets	Land, building, machinery, plant or furniture held with the intention of being used for the purpose of producing or providing goods or services and is not held for sale in the normal course of business. [Para 2]

Identification	Stand-by equipment and servicing equipment are to be capitalised. Machinery spares shall be charged to the revenue as and when consumed. When such spares can be used only in connection with an item of tangible fixed asset and their use is expected to be irregular, they shall be capitalised. [Para 4]
Actual cost components	■ *Positive list* - The following shall be part of actual cost – - purchase price, import duties and other taxes (excluding those subsequently recoverable) - any directly attributable expenditure on making the asset ready for its intended use - expenses which are specifically attributable to construction of a project or to the acquisition of a tangible fixed asset or bringing it to its working condition - expenditure incurred on start-up and commissioning of the project, including the expenditure incurred on test runs and experimental production. [Paras 5 to 8]
	■ *Negative list* - The following shall not be part of actual cost – - any trade discounts and rebates - administration and other general overhead expenses if they do not relate to a specific tangible fixed asset - expenditure incurred after the plant has begun commercial production (*i.e.*, production intended for sale or captive consumption) [such expenditure shall be treated as revenue expenditure]. [Paras 5 to 8]
Self-constructed tangible fixed assets	In arriving at the actual cost of self-constructed tangible fixed assets, the same principles shall apply as those described in paragraphs 5 to 8. Cost of construction that relate directly to the specific tangible fixed asset and costs that are attributable to the construction activity in general and can be allocated to the specific tangible fixed asset shall be included in actual cost. Any internal profits shall be eliminated in arriving at such costs. [Para 9]
Non-monetary consideration	■ When a tangible fixed asset is acquired in exchange for another asset, the fair value of the tangible fixed asset so acquired shall be its actual cost. [Para 10] ■ When a tangible fixed asset is acquired in exchange for shares or other securities, the fair value of the tangible fixed asset so acquired shall be its actual cost. [Para 11]
Improvements and repairs	Expenditure that increases the future benefits from the existing asset beyond its previously assessed standard of performance is added to the actual cost. [Para 12]
Transitional provisions	The actual cost of tangible fixed assets, acquisition or construction of which commenced on or before March 31, 2016 but not completed by the said date, shall be recognised in accordance with the provisions of this standard. The amount of actual cost, if any, recognised for the said assets for the previous year 2015-16 (or earlier year) shall be taken into account for recognising actual cost of the said assets for the previous year 2016-17 (or subsequent year).
• Income Computation and Disclosure Standard VI relating to changes in foreign exchange rates	
Initial recognition, conversion, recognition of exchange difference	■ *If covered by section 43A or rule 115* - It shall be subject to the provisions of section 43A of the Act and rule 115 read with rule 26 of Income-tax Rules. [Para 6] [*see* **Annex 1** and **Annex 2** at the end of this Referencer]
	■ *If not covered* - A foreign currency transaction shall be recorded, on initial recognition in the reporting currency, by applying to the foreign

	currency amount the exchange rate between the reporting currency and the foreign currency at the date of the transaction. [Para 3(1)] - An average rate for a week or a month that approximates the actual rate at the date of the transaction may be used for all transaction in each foreign currency occurring during that period. If the exchange rate fluctuates significantly, the actual rate at the date of the transaction shall be used. [Para 3(2)] - In respect of monetary items, exchange differences arising on the settlement thereof or on conversion thereof at last day of the previous year shall be recognised as income or as expense in that previous year. [Para 5]
Forward exchange contracts	▪ *For trading/speculation purposes or to hedge foreign currency risk* - Premium, discount or exchange difference on contracts that are intended for trading or speculation purposes, or that are entered into to hedge the foreign currency risk of a firm commitment or a highly probable forecast transaction shall be recognised at the time of settlement. [Para 11(5)] ▪ *In other cases* - Any premium or discount arising at the inception of a forward exchange contract shall be amortised as expense or income over the life of the contract. Exchange differences on such a contract shall be recognised as income or as expense in the previous year in which the exchange rates change. Any profit or loss arising on cancellation or renewal shall be recognised as income or as expense for the previous year. [Para 11(1)]
Transitional provisions	▪ All foreign currency transactions undertaken on or after April 1, 2016 shall be recognised in accordance with the provisions of this standard. [Para 12(1)]
	▪ Exchange differences arising in respect of monetary or non-monetary items on the settlement thereof during the previous year 2016-17 or on conversion thereof at March 31, 2017 shall be recognised in accordance with the provisions of this standard after taking into account the amount recognised on March 31, 2016 for an item, if any, which is carried forward from the previous year 2015-16. [Para 12(2)]
	▪ The financial statements of foreign operations for the previous year 2016-17 shall be translated using the principles and procedures specified in this standard after taking into account the amount recognised on March 31, 2016 for an item, if any, which is carried forward from the previous year 2015-16. [Para 12(3)]
	▪ All forward exchange contracts existing on April 1, 2016 or entered on or after the said date shall be dealt with in accordance with the provisions of this standard after taking into account the income or expenses, if any, recognised in respect of said contracts for the previous year 2015-16 (or earlier year). [Para 12(4)]
• Income Computation and Disclosure Standard VII relating to Government grants	
Scope	This Standard deals with the treatment of Government grants. The Government grants are sometimes called by other names such as subsidies, cash incentives, duty drawbacks, waiver, concessions, reimbursements, etc. However, it does not cover Government assistance (other than in the form of Government grants) and Government participation in the ownership of the enterprise. [Paras 1 and 2]
Meaning of Government	"Government" refers to the Central Government, State Governments, agencies and similar bodies, whether local, national, or international. [Para 3(1)]
Recognition of Government grants	▪ Government grants should not be recognised until there is reasonable assurance that the person shall comply with the conditions attached to them, and the grants shall be received. [Para 4(1)]

	▪ Recognition of Government grant shall not be postponed beyond the date of actual receipt. [Para 4(2)]
Treatment of Government grants	▪ *Grant relating to depreciable assets* - It shall be deducted from actual cost of the asset or written down value of the block of assets. [Para 5]
	▪ *Grant relating to non-depreciable assets* - Where the Government grant relates to non-depreciable assets of a person requiring fulfilment of certain obligations, the grant shall be recognised as income over the same period over which the cost of meeting such obligations is charged to income. [Para 6]
	▪ *Grant not directly relatable to an asset acquired* - Such grant shall be deducted on proportionate basis from the actual cost of the asset. [Para 7]
	▪ *Grant received as compensation for expenses/losses* - Government grant that is receivable as compensation for expenses or losses incurred in a previous financial year or for the purpose of giving immediate financial support to the person with no further related costs, shall be recognised as income of the period in which it is receivable. [Para 8]
	▪ *Other grants* - Any other Government grant (other than covered by above provisions) shall be recognised as income over the periods necessary to match them with the related costs, which they are intended to compensate. [Para 9]
	▪ *Non-monetary grants* - Government grants in the form of non-monetary assets, given at a concessional rate, shall be accounted for on the basis of their acquisition cost. [Para 10]
Refund of Government grants	▪ *Grant related to depreciable assets* - Refund relating to depreciable assets shall be recorded by increasing the actual cost or written down value of the block of assets by the amount refundable. Where the actual cost of the asset is increased, depreciation on the revised actual cost or written down value shall be provided prospectively at the prescribed rate. [Para 12]
	▪ *Grant not related to depreciable assets* - Amount refundable shall be applied first against any unamortised deferred credit remaining in respect of the Government grant. To the extent that the amount refundable exceeds any such deferred credit, or where no deferred credit exists, the amount shall be charged to profit and loss statement. [Para 11]
Disclosure	Nature and extent of Government grants recognised during the year by way of deduction from actual cost/written down value of block or recognised during the year as income, shall be disclosed. Further, nature and extent of Government grants not recognised during the year shall also be disclosed. [Para 14]
Transitional provisions	All Government grants which meet the recognition criteria of para 4 on or after April 1, 2016 shall be recognised for the previous year 2016-17 in accordance with the provisions of this standard after taking into account the amount, if any, of the said Government grant recognised for the previous year 2015-16 or earlier year. [Para 13]
• Income Computation and Disclosure Standard VIII relating to Securities	
Scope	This standard deals with securities held as stock-in-trade. However, it does not cover securities held by a person who is engaged in the business of insurance or securities held by mutual funds, venture capital funds, banks and public financial institutions. [Paras 1 and 2]
Recognition and initial measurement of securities	A security on acquisition shall be recognised at actual cost (*i.e.*, purchase price, acquisition charges, brokerage, fees, tax, duty or cess). Where a security is acquired in exchange for other securities/assets, the fair value of

	the security so acquired shall be its actual cost. Where unpaid interest has accrued before the acquisition of an interest-bearing security and is included in the price paid for the security, the subsequent receipt of interest is allocated between pre-acquisition and post-acquisition periods; the pre-acquisition portion of the interest is deducted from the actual cost. [Paras 4 to 8]
Subsequent measurement of listed securities	▪ Securities (held as stock-in-trade) shall be valued at the end of the previous year at actual cost initially recognised or net realisable value at the end of that previous year, whichever is lower. [Para 9]
	▪ For above purpose, the comparison of actual cost initially recognised and net realisable value shall be done category-wise and not for each individual security [for this purpose, securities shall be classified into following categories – (*a*) shares; (*b*) debt securities; (*c*) convertible securities; and (*d*) any other securities not covered above]. [Para 10]
Subsequent measurement of unlisted securities	▪ At the end of any previous year, securities not listed on a recognised stock exchange (or listed but not quoted on a recognised stock exchange with regularity from time to time) shall be valued at actual cost initially recognised. [Para 12]
• Income Computation and Disclosure Standard IX relating to borrowing costs	
Definitions	▪ *Borrowing costs* - "Borrowing costs" are interest and other costs incurred by a person in connection with the borrowing of funds and include (*a*) commitment charges on borrowings; (*b*) amortised amount of discounts or premiums relating to borrowings; (*c*) amortised amount of ancillary costs incurred in connection with the arrangement of borrowings; (*d*) finance charges in respect of assets acquired under finance leases or under other similar arrangements. [Para 2(1)(*a*)]
	▪ *Qualifying assets* - It means – - land, building, machinery, plant or furniture, being tangible assets; - know-how, patents, copyrights, trademarks, licences, franchises or any other business or commercial rights of similar nature, being intangible assets; - inventories that require a period of twelve months or more to bring them to a saleable condition. [Para 2(1)(*b*)]
Recognition	Borrowing costs (directly attributable to the acquisition, construction or production of a qualifying asset) shall be capitalized. In the case of inventory, such borrowing costs shall be added to the cost of inventory. [Para 3]
Borrowing costs eligible for capitalisation	▪ *Specific borrowing* - To the extent the funds are borrowed specifically for the purposes of acquisition, construction or production of a qualifying asset, the amount of borrowing costs to be capitalised on that asset shall be the actual borrowing costs incurred on the funds so borrowed. [Para 5]
	▪ *Other than specific borrowing* - To the extent the funds are borrowed generally and utilised for the purposes of acquisition, construction or production of a qualifying asset, the amount of borrowing costs to be capitalised shall be computed on proportionate basis. [Para 6] Formula for working out proportionate borrowing cost : $A \times B \div C$. A = Borrowing cost incurred during the previous year (except on borrowings directly relatable to specific purposes) B = The average of costs of qualifying asset as appearing in the balance sheet of a person on the first day and the last day of the previous year (excluding qualifying assets which are directly funded out of specific borrowings)

	C = The average of the amount of total assets as appearing in the balance sheet of a person on the first day and the last day of the previous year (excluding qualifying assets which are directly funded out of specific borrowings) Some modification are specified for B as follows – - *Value of B (when the qualifying asset does not appear in the balance sheet of a person on the first day or both on the first day and the last day of previous year) :* Half of the cost of qualifying asset - *Value of B (when the qualifying asset does not appear in the balance sheet of a person on the last day of previous year) :* Average of the costs of qualifying asset as appearing in the balance sheet of a person on the first day of the previous year and on the date of put to use or completion
Commencement of capitalisation	In the case of specific borrowing, the capitalisation of borrowing costs shall commence from the date on which funds were borrowed. Otherwise (when general funds are utilized), capitalisation of costs shall commence from the date on which funds were utilised. [Para 7]
Cessation of capitalisation	In the case of tangible and intangible assets (*i.e.*, all qualifying assets other than inventory), capitalisation of borrowing costs shall cease when the asset* is first put to use. In the case of inventory, capitalisation of borrowing costs shall cease when substantially all the activities necessary to prepare such inventory* for its intended sale are complete. [Para 8] *Part of asset or part of inventory when the construction of a qualifying asset is completed in parts and a completed part is capable of being used while construction continues for the other parts.
Disclosure	The accounting policy adopted for borrowing costs and the amount of borrowing costs capitalised during the previous year, shall be disclosed. [Para 11]
Transitional provisions	All the borrowing costs incurred on or after April 1, 2016 shall be capitalised for the previous year 2016-17 (or subsequent year) in accordance with the provisions of this standard after taking into account the amount of borrowing costs capitalised, if any, for the same borrowing for the previous year 2015-16 (or earlier year). [Para 10]
• Income Computation and Disclosure Standard X relating to contingent assets	
Definitions	▪ *Provision* - "Provision" is a liability which can be measured only by using a substantial degree of estimation. [Para 4(1)(*a*)]
	▪ *Contingent liability* - It is a possible obligation that arises from past events and the existence of which will be confirmed only by the occurrence or non-occurrence of one or more uncertain future events (not wholly within the control of the person). Further, it includes a present obligation that arises from past events but is not recognised because reliable estimate cannot be made (or it is not reasonably certain that an outflow of resources embodying economic benefits will be required to settle the obligation). [Para 4(1)(*d*)]
Recognition - Provisions	A provision shall be recognised when – - a person has a present obligation as a result of a past event; - it is reasonably certain that an outflow of resources embodying economic benefits will be required to settle the obligation; and - a reliable estimate can be made of the amount of the obligation. If these conditions are satisfied, provision shall be recognised and it shall be used in future for incurring expenditure for which the provision is

	originally made. It is only those obligations arising from past events existing independently of a person's future actions (*i.e.*, the future conduct of its business) that are recognised as provisions. Where details of a proposed new law have yet to be finalised, an obligation arises only when the legislation is enacted. [Paras 5 to 8 and 19]
Recognition - Contingent liabilities	A person shall not recognise a contingent liability. [Para 9]
Recognition - Contingent assets	A person shall not recognise a contingent asset. Contingent assets are assessed continually and when it becomes reasonably certain that inflow of economic benefit will arise, the asset and related income are recognised in the previous year in which the change occurs. [Paras 10 and 11]
Measurement	■ *Best estimate* - The amount recognised as a provision shall be the best estimate of the expenditure required to settle the present obligation at the end of the previous year. The amount of a provision shall not be discounted to its present value. [Para 12]
Reimbursement	■ Where some or all of the expenditure required to settle a provision is expected to be reimbursed by another party, the reimbursement shall be recognised when it is reasonably certain that reimbursement will be received if the person settles the obligation. The amount recognised for the reimbursement shall not exceed the amount of the provision. [Para 14]
	■ Where a person is not liable for payment of costs in case the third party fails to pay, no provision shall be made for those costs. [Para 15]
	■ An obligation, for which a person is jointly and severally liable, is a contingent liability to the extent that it is expected that the obligation will be settled by the other parties. [Para 16]
Review	■ Provisions shall be reviewed at the end of each previous year and adjusted to reflect the current best estimate. If it is no longer reasonably certain that an outflow of resources embodying economic benefits will be required to settle the obligation, the provision should be reversed. [Para 17]
	■ An asset and related income recognised shall be reviewed at the end of each previous year and adjusted to reflect the current best estimate. If it is no longer reasonably certain that an inflow of economic benefits will arise, the asset and related income shall be reversed. [Para 18]
Disclosure	Following disclosure shall be made in respect of each class of provision (or each class of asset and related income), namely – - brief description of the nature of the obligation/nature of assets and related income; - the carrying amount of provision (or asset) at the beginning and end of the previous year; - additional provisions of made (or additional amount of asset and related income recognised) during the previous year; - amounts used, that is incurred and charged against the provision, during the previous year; - unused amounts of provision (or assets and related income) reversed during the previous year; and - the amount of any expected reimbursement, stating the amount of any asset that has been recognised for that expected reimbursement. [Para 21]

Transitional provisions	All the provisions or assets and related income shall be recognised for the previous year 2016-17 (or subsequent year) in accordance with the provisions of this standard after taking into account the amount recognised, if any, for the same for the previous year 2015-16 (or any earlier year).

Annex 1 - *Provisions of section 43A*

Loss/gain due to exchange fluctuation	*Adjustment (whether books are maintained on mercantile basis or cash basis)*
▪ *Section 32 read with section 43(1)* - Increase/decrease in the cost of asset due to exchange fluctuation [*see* Note]	Added/deducted in the block in the year of actual payment
▪ *Section 35(1)(*iv*), 35A or 36(1)*(ix) - Increase/decrease in the amount of capital expenditure due to exchange fluctuation	Taken into account in the year of payment
▪ *Section 48* - Increase/decrease in cost of acquisition of a capital asset	Added to, or deducted from, the cost of acquisition in the year of payment

Note - Any increase/decrease in the cost of a depreciable asset due to exchange fluctuation is added (deducted) in the block of asset in the year of payment.

If the aforesaid increase/decrease in cost due to exchange fluctuation arises after the depreciable asset is transferred (but block of asset exists), then the increase/decrease in the cost will be adjusted in the written down value of block of asset. If, however, the increase/decrease in cost due to exchange fluctuation arises after the depreciable asset is transferred and the block of asset does not exist, then increase/decrease will be capital receipt/expenditure which is not chargeable/deductible under any other provision of the Act.

Annex 2 - *Provisions of rule 115 read with rule 26*

The rate of exchange for the calculation of the value in rupees of any income arising in foreign currency, shall be the telegraphic transfer buying rate of such currency adopted by SBI on the dates given below—

Different cases	*The telegraphic transfer buying rate adopted by SBI on the dates given below for the purpose of conversion of foreign income into Indian currency*
▪ *Case 1* - If tax is deducted at source under the provisions of sections 192 to 196D	On the date on which tax is required to be deducted
▪ *Case 2* - If tax is not deducted at source—	
- *Case 2.1* - Income case of salary income	The last day of the month immediately preceding the month in which salary is due (or is paid in advance/arrears)
- *Case 2.2* - Interest on securities	The last day of the month immediately preceding the month in which the income is due
- *Case 2.3* - Income from house property, business/ professional income and income from other sources (where foreign income is brought into India before the end of the previous year)	*Rule 115 is not applicable*
- *Case 2.4* - Income from house property, business/ professional income and income from other sources (where foreign income is not brought into India before the end of the previous year)	On the last date of the previous year

Different cases	*The telegraphic transfer buying rate adopted by SBI on the dates given below for the purpose of conversion of foreign income into Indian currency*
- *Case 2.5* - Income of non-resident engaged in the business of operation of ships	The last day of the month immediately preceding the month in which such income is deemed to accrue or arise in India
- *Case 2.6* - Dividend from non-Indian companies [and deemed dividend under section 2(*22*)(*e*) from any company]	The last day of the month immediately preceding the month in which such dividend is declared, distributed or paid
- *Case 2.7* - Capital gains	The last day of the month immediately preceding the month in which the capital asset is transferred.

R-3

Tax rates for the last ten assessment years

INCOME-TAX RATES* FOR INDIVIDUALS, HUFs, ASSOCIATIONS OF PERSONS AND BODY OF INDIVIDUALS

(in percentage)

	Assessment year 2009-10		
	Resident woman	*Resident senior citizen***	*Any other*
First Rs. 1,50,000	*Nil*	*Nil*	*Nil*
Next Rs. 30,000	*Nil*	*Nil*	10%
Next Rs. 45,000	10%	*Nil*	10%
Next Rs. 75,000	10%	10%	10%
Next Rs. 2,00,000	20%	20%	20%
Above Rs. 5,00,000	30%	30%	30%

	Assessment year 2010-11		
	Resident woman	*Resident senior citizen***	*Any other*
First Rs. 1,60,000	*Nil*	*Nil*	*Nil*
Next Rs. 30,000	*Nil*	*Nil*	10%
Next Rs. 50,000	10%	*Nil*	10%
Next Rs. 60,000	10%	10%	10%
Next Rs. 2,00,000	20%	20%	20%
Above Rs. 5,00,000	30%	30%	30%

	Assessment year 2011-12		
	Resident woman	*Resident senior citizen***	*Any other*
First Rs. 1,60,000	*Nil*	*Nil*	*Nil*
Next Rs. 30,000	*Nil*	*Nil*	10%
Next Rs. 50,000	10%	*Nil*	10%
Next Rs. 2,60,000	10%	10%	10%
Next Rs. 3,00,000	20%	20%	20%
Above Rs. 8,00,000	30%	30%	30%

	Assessment year 2012-13			
	Resident woman	Resident senior citizen***	Resident super senior citizen****	Any other
First Rs. 1,80,000	Nil	Nil	Nil	Nil
Next Rs. 10,000	Nil	Nil	Nil	10%
Next Rs. 60,000	10%	Nil	Nil	10%
Next Rs. 2,50,000	10%	10%	Nil	10%
Next Rs. 3,00,000	20%	20%	20%	20%
Above Rs. 8,00,000	30%	30%	30%	30%

	Assessment years 2013-14 and 2014-15		
	Resident senior citizen***	Resident super senior citizen****	Any other
First Rs. 2,00,000	Nil	Nil	Nil
Next Rs. 50,000	Nil	Nil	10%
Next Rs. 2,50,000	10%	Nil	10%
Next Rs. 5,00,000	20%	20%	20%
Above Rs. 10,00,000	30%	30%	30%

	Assessment years 2015-16 to 2017-18		
	Resident senior citizen***	Resident super senior citizen****	Any other
First Rs. 2,50,000	Nil	Nil	Nil
Next Rs. 50,000	Nil	Nil	10%
Next Rs. 2,00,000	10%	Nil	10%
Next Rs. 5,00,000	20%	20%	20%
Above Rs. 10,00,000	30%	30%	30%

	Assessment year 2018-19		
	Resident senior citizen***	Resident super senior citizen****	Any other
First Rs. 2,50,000	Nil	Nil	Nil
Next Rs. 50,000	Nil	Nil	5%
Next Rs. 2,00,000	5%	Nil	5%
Next Rs. 5,00,000	20%	20%	20%
Above Rs. 10,00,000	30%	30%	30%

*Certain incomes of non-resident Indians are taxable at the flat rate of 20 per cent [for details *see* para 179.1].

**65 years or more at any time during the previous year.

***60 years or more at any time during the previous year but less than 80 years on the last day of the previous year.

****80 years or more at any time during the previous year.

Union surcharge on income-tax

a. For the assessment year 2009-10 : 10% of income-tax if taxable income exceeds Rs. 10,00,000 (surcharge is payable whether the taxpayer is resident or non-resident).

b. For the assessment years 2010-11 to 2013-14 : *Nil.*

c. For the assessment years 2014-15 and 2015-16, 10 per cent of income-tax if taxable income exceeds Rs. 1 crore (surcharge is payable whether taxpayer is resident or non-resident).

d. For the assessment year 2016-17, 12 per cent of income-tax if taxable income exceeds Rs. 1 crore (surcharge is payable whether taxpayer is resident or non-resident).

e. For the assessment year 2017-18, 15 per cent of income-tax if taxable income exceeds Rs. 1 crore (surcharge is payable whether taxpayer is resident or non-resident).

f. For the assessment year 2018-19, 10 per cent of income-tax if taxable income exceeds Rs. 50 lakh or 15 per cent of income-tax if taxable income exceeds Rs. 1 crore (surcharge is payable whether taxpayer is resident or non-resident).

Education cess : 2% of income-tax and surcharge for the assessment years 2009-10 to 2018-19.
Secondary and higher education cess: 1% of income-tax and surcharge for the assessment years 2009-10 to 2018-19.

INCOME-TAX RATES FOR FIRMS

(in percentage)

	Assessment years			
	2009-10	*2010-11 and 2013-14*	*2014-15 and 2015-16*	*2016-17 to 2018-19*
Income-tax	30	30	30	30
Surcharge (as a percentage of income-tax)	10*	*Nil*	10*	12*
Total	33	30	33	33.6
Education cess (as a percentage of income-tax and surcharge)	3	3	3	3
Tax	33.99	30.9	33.99	34.608

*For the assessment years 2009-10, 2014-15 to 2018-19 surcharge is applicable only if net income exceeds Rs. 1 crore.

INCOME-TAX RATES FOR COMPANIES

RATES OF INCOME-TAX

(in percentage)

	Assessment years 2009-10 to 2018-19
a. In the case of a domestic company	30†
b. In the case of a foreign company :	
i. royalties received from an Indian concern in pursuance of an agreement made by it with the Indian concern after March 31, 1961; or fees for rendering technical services received from an Indian concern in pursuance of an agreement made by it with the Indian concern after February 29, 1964, but before April 1, 1976 and where such agreement has, in either case been approved by the Central Government	50
ii. other income	40

Union surcharge on income-tax : For the assessment years 2009-10 to 2010-11 (if net income exceeds Rs. 1 crore) : 10% of income-tax in the case of a domestic company and 2.5 per cent of income-tax in the case of a foreign company; for the assessment year 2011-12 (if net income exceeds Rs. 1 crore) : 7.5% of income-tax in the case of a domestic company and 2.5 per cent of income-tax in the case of a foreign company, for the assessment years 2012-13 and 2013-14 (if net income exceeds Rs. 1 crore) : 5 per cent of income-tax in the case of a domestic company and 2 per cent of income-tax in the case of a foreign company, for the assessment years 2014-15 and 2015-16 (if net income exceeds Rs. 1 crore but does not exceed Rs. 10 crore) : 5 per cent in the case of a domestic company and 2 per cent in the case of a foreign company [if net income exceeds Rs. 10 crore : 10 per cent in the case of a domestic company and 5 per cent in the case of a foreign company], for the assessment years 2016-17 to 2018-19 (if net income exceeds Rs. 1 crore but does not exceed Rs. 10 crore) : 7 per cent in the case of a domestic company and 2 per cent in the case of a foreign company [if net income exceeds Rs. 10 crore : 12 per cent in the case of a domestic company and 5 per cent in the case of a foreign company].
Education cess : 2% of income-tax and surcharge for the assessment years 2009-10 to 2018-19.
Secondary and higher education cess: 1% of income-tax and surcharge for the assessment years 2009-10 to 2018-19.

† 29 per cent for the assessment year 2017-18 (where the total turnover or gross receipt during the previous year 2014-15 does not exceed Rs. 5 crore) and 25 per cent for the assessment year 2018-19 (where the total turnover or gross receipt during the previous year 2015-16 does not exceed Rs. 50 crore).

DIVIDEND TAX RATES UNDER SECTION 115-O

	Dividend tax (as a % of dividend)	*Surcharge (as a % of dividend tax)*	*Education cess (as a % of dividend tax and surcharge)*	*Total (as a % of dividend)*
• From April 1, 2007 to March 31, 2010	15	10	3	16.995
• From April 1, 2010 to March 31, 2011	15	7.5	3	16.60875
• From April 1, 2011 to March 31, 2013	15	5	3	16.2225
• From April 1, 2013 to September 30, 2014	15	10	3	16.995
• From October 1, 2014 to March 31, 2015	17.64706	10	3	19.99412
• From April 1, 2015 to March 31, 2018	17.64706	12	3	20.357647
• From April 1, 2018 to March 31, 2019 [not being deemed dividend under section 2(*22*)(*e*)]	17.64706	12	4	20.555294
• From April 1, 2018 to March 31, 2019 [being deemed dividend under section 2(*22*)(*e*)]	30	12	4	34.944

INCOME-TAX RATES FOR CO-OPERATIVE SOCIETIES

For the assessment years 2009-10 to 2018-19—first Rs. 10,000 : 10%; next Rs. 10,000 : 20% and the balance : 30%.

Union surcharge on income-tax—

Assessment year	*Surcharge (as % of income-tax)*
2009-10 to 2013-14	*Nil*
2014-15 and 2015-16	10% (if income exceeds Rs. 1 crore)
2016-17 to 2018-19	12% (if income exceeds Rs. 1 crore)

Education cess : 2% of income-tax and surcharge for the assessment years 2009-10 to 2018-19.

Secondary and higher education cess: 1% of income-tax for the assessment years 2009-10 to 2018-19.

RATES OF WEALTH-TAX

FOR INDIVIDUALS, HUFs AND COMPANIES

(For the assessment years 2006-07 to 2015-16)

1 per cent of the amount by which net wealth exceeds Rs. 15,00,000 up to the assessment year 2009-10 and Rs. 30,00,000 from the assessment year 2010-11 (surcharge : *Nil,* education cess : *Nil,* secondary and higher education cess : *Nil*)

RATES OF GIFT-TAX

For the assessment years 1997-98 to 1999-2000 gift-tax is payable at the rate of 30 per cent (gifts made after September 30, 1998 are not chargeable to gift-tax)

Basic exemption : Rs. 30,000 for the assessment years 1997-98 to 1999-2000.

R-4

Gold and silver rates for the current year, last ten assessment years and on April 1, 1981/April 1, 2001

Assessment year/ valuation date	*Gold rates[1] (standard 24 carats) (per 10 gms.)* *Rs.*	*Silver rates (9,960 touch) (per 1 kg.)* *Rs.*	*Assessment year/ valuation date*	*Gold rates[1] (standard 24 carats) (per 10 gms.)* *Rs.*	*Silver rates (9,960 touch) (per 1kg.)* *Rs.*
1-4-1981	1,670	2,715	*Asst. Yr. 2014-15 31-3-2014*	28,470	43,070
1-4-2001	4,190	7,215	*Asst. Yr. 2015-16 31-3-2015*	26,245	37,825
Asst. Yr. 2009-10 31-3-2009	15,105	22,165	*Asst. Yr. 2016-17† 31-3-2016*	28,340	36,990
Asst. Yr. 2010-11 31-3-2010	16,320	27,255	*Asst. Yr. 2017-18† 31-3-2017*	28,950	42,000
Asst. Yr. 2011-12 31-3-2011	20,775	56,900	*Asst. Yr. 2018-19† 31-3-2018*	30,680	38,355
Asst. Yr. 2012-13 31-3-2012	28,040	56,290	*Asst. Yr. 2019-20† 31-3-2019*	31,640	37,245
Asst. Yr. 2013-14 31-3-2013	29,610	54,030			

Notes :

1. Value of gold contained in gold ornaments should be reduced by 14 to 20 per cent of ruling rates of standard gold, as per the practice prevalent in the bullion market and the amount of reduction has to be worked out in the following manner :

	Plain gold bangles and ornaments made of solid gold	*Other gold ornaments*
Difference in value between 24 carats of standard gold and 22 carats of gold ornaments (gold ornaments are generally made of 22 carats of gold)	8.33%	8.33%
Soldering made of copper, silver, etc., used in making ornaments	2.5% to 5%	8.33%
Shortage of gold in melting, mint charges payable to Government, expenditure on freight, insurance, etc., of sending gold ornaments to approved mint for conversion into standard gold bars	1.25%	1.25%
Margin of profit of the dealer when ornaments are sold in market	2%	2%
Total reduction	14.08% to 16.58%	19.91%

2. Silverwares, utensils, etc., is liable for wealth-tax.

3. Conversion table:

10 grams	=	0.857 tola	1 tola	=	11.664 grams
1 kilogram	–	85.734 tolas	10 tolas	=	116.638 grams

†Wealth-tax is not applicable from the assessment year 2016-17.

R-5

Tax saving schemes at a glance

Name of securities	*Rate of interest***	*Limits of investment*	*Exemption under the IT Act*	*Exemption under the WT Act*
(1)	*(2)*	*(3)*	*(4)*	*(5)*
1, 2, 3 and 5-year Time Deposit	Interest @ 6.9 per cent, 6.9 per cent, 6.9 per cent and 7.7 per cent p.a. (calculated at quarterly compounding basis)	No limit on deposits (Minimum : Rs. 200) ; account can be opened, in multiples of Rs. 50 in a single name or joint names; even a minor can open account	Interest chargeable to tax (no TDS). Deposit* in 5 years Time Deposit Scheme qualifies for deduction under section 80C from the assessment year 2008-09	Not chargeable to wealth-tax
5-year National Savings Certificates VIII Issue	Compound (yearly) interest @ 7.9 per cent p.a. payable on maturity	No limit on deposit	Investment and accrued interest (for first 4 years) qualify for deduction under section 80C. Interest chargeable to tax on accrual basis (no TDS).	Not chargeable
10-year National Savings Certificates IX Issue (now discontinued)	Compound (half-yearly) interest @ 8.8 per cent p.a. payable on maturity	No limit on deposit	Investment and accrued interest (for first 9 years) qualify for deduction under section 80C. Interest chargeable to tax on accrual basis (no TDS).	Not chargeable
5-year Post Office Recurring Deposit	Interest @ 7.2 per cent p.a. compounded quarterly but payable on maturity[3].	No limit on deposits. Deposits can be made in multiples of Rs. 5 p.m. (minimum : Rs. 10 per month)	Interest chargeable to tax (no TDS)	Investment not chargeable to wealth-tax
15-year Public Provident Fund[1]	Compound interest @ 7.9 per cent every year but payable at the time of maturity	Minimum : Rs. 500 and maximum : Rs. 1,50,000 in every financial year	Interest totally exempt under section 10(*11*); investment qualifies for deduction under section 80C*	Investment not chargeable to wealth-tax

1. Subscribers are allowed to continue their public provident fund accounts beyond 15 years. Non-Resident Indians (NRIs) are not eligible to open an account under the Public Provident Fund Scheme. If, however, a resident who subsequently becomes NRI during the currency of maturity period prescribed under Public Provident Fund Scheme, may continue to subscribe to the Fund till its maturity on a non-repatriation basis. An account opened on behalf of a Hindu Undivided Family prior to May 13, 2005, shall be closed after expiry of 15 years from the end of the year in which the initial subscription was made and the entire amount standing at the credit of the subscriber shall be refunded. In the case of accounts opened on behalf of Hindu Undivided Family, where 15 years from end of the year in which initial subscription was made, has already been completed, they shall also be closed on March 31, 2011 and the entire amount standing at the credit of the subscriber shall be refunded - Notification No. GSR 956(E), dated December 7, 2010.

2. 3 per cent p.a. on public accounts and security deposit account for purchase of motor vehicle or tractor and 3 per cent on other documents.

3. If the account is continued beyond the maturity period without fresh deposit, then interest is credited (compounded quarterly) @ 7.50 per cent (8 per cent with effect from December 1, 2011 and 8.4 per cent with effect from April 1, 2012).

*When a deposit is made in the Public Provident Fund account, Senior Citizen Saving Scheme, and Time Deposit Scheme in Post Office by means of cheque/draft, the date of encashment of the cheque is treated as date of deposit.

**These rates are applicable with effect from April 1, 2012.

(1)	(2)	(3)	(4)	(5)
Post Office Savings Bank Account	Interest @ 4 per cent p.a. credited annually[2]	Minimum : Rs. 20 and maximum : Rs. 1,00,000 for an individual and Rs. 2,00,000 for two or more adults jointly in one or more accounts. No limit on group/institutional or official capacity accounts	Interest exemption under section 10(*15*)(*i*) is as follows : Full exemption up to the assessment year 2011-12, Rs. 3,500 (in a single account)/ Rs. 7,000 (in a joint account) is exempt from the assessment year 2012-13.†	Investment not chargeable to wealth-tax
Post Office monthly income account [6 year (if account opened before December 1, 2011), 5 year (if account opened on or after December 1, 2011)]	Interest @ 7.6 per cent	One or more accounts can be opened but deposits cannot exceed Rs. 4,50,000 in single account and Rs. 9,00,000 in joint account. Only one deposit in the account in the multiple of Rs. 1,500 is permitted	Interest chargeable to tax (no TDS)	Investment not chargeable to wealth-tax
7.75% (7 year) Savings (Taxable) Bonds	7.75 per cent payable half-yearly or compounded with half-yearly rests	No maximum limit, amount can be invested in multiple of Rs. 1,000, open for investment by (resident) individual or by HUF	Interest chargeable to tax (tax to be deducted at source)	Investment not chargeable to wealth-tax
5 year Senior Citizen Savings Scheme, 2004 (Post office)	8.6 per cent per annum payable quarterly[4]	Maximum deposit Rs. 15 lakh (account can be opened by a resident individual who is 60 years of age; or by a resident individual who is 55-60 years of age and who is retired under VRS)	Interest chargeable to tax. Investment qualifies for deduction under section 80C from the assessment year 2008-09*	No wealth-tax
Sukanya Samriddhi Account	Compound (yearly) interest @ 8.4 per cent p.a.	Minimum Rs. 1,000, maximum Rs. 1,50,000 in a financial year (no limit on number of deposit in a month or in a financial year)	Interest totally exempt from tax under section 10(*11A*); investment qualifies for deduction under section 80C	Not chargeable

4. If the interest payable every quarter is not claimed by a depositor, such interest will not earn any additional interest. If account is continued after maturity [extension is possible for a further period of 3 years by making an application in Form B], it will be eligible for interest at the rate applicable to new account opened on the date of maturity.

*When a deposit is made in the Public Provident Fund account, Senior Citizen Saving Scheme, and Time Deposit Scheme in Post Office by means of cheque/draft, the date of encashment of the cheque is treated as date of deposit.

† Deduction is also available under section 80TTA or 80TTB [*see* paras 107.31 and 107.32].

R-6

Rates of depreciation (for income-tax)

AS APPLICABLE FROM THE ASSESSMENT YEAR 2006-07 ONWARDS

Block of assets [*see para 48.3-3*]	*Depreciation allowance as percentage of written down value*	
	AY 2006-07 to 2017-18	*AY 2018-19 onwards*
1	2	3
PART A		
TANGIBLE ASSETS		
I. BUILDING [*See* Notes 1 to 4 below the Table]		
(*1*) Buildings which are used mainly for residential purposes except hotels and boarding houses	5	5
(*2*) Buildings other than those used mainly for residential purposes and not covered by sub-items (1) above and (3) below	10	10
(*3*) Buildings acquired on or after the 1st day of September, 2002 for installing machinery and plant forming part of water supply project or water treatment system and which is put to use for the purpose of business of providing infrastructure facilities under clause (*i*) of sub-section (4) of section 80-IA	100	40
(*4*) Purely temporary erections such as wooden structures	100	40
II. FURNITURE AND FITTINGS		
Furniture and fittings including electrical fittings [*See* Note 5 below the Table]	10	10
III. MACHINERY AND PLANT		
(*1*) Machinery and plant other than those covered by sub-items (2), (3) and (8) below :	15[c]	15[c]
[a](*2*) Motor cars, other than those used in a business of running them on hire, acquired or put to use on or after the 1st day of April, 1990	15	15
(*3*) (*i*) Aeroplanes - Aeroengines	40	40
[b](*ii*) Motor buses, motor lorries and motor taxis used in a business of running them on hire	30	30
(*iii*) Commercial vehicle which is acquired by the assessee on or after the 1st day of October, 1998, but before the 1st day of April, 1999 and is put to use		

a. Jeeps are classifiable as motor cars — *Crompton Engg. Co. (Madras) Ltd.* v. *CIT* [1992] 193 ITR 483 (Mad.)/*CAIT* v. *Good Hope Enterprises* [1992] 197 ITR 236 (Ker.).

b. Trucks primarily used for assessee's own business and occasionally let out on hire will not fall under this entry unless assessee carries on a business of running them on hire—*CIT* v. *Manjeet Stone Co.* [1991] 190 ITR 183 (Raj.); Vehicles plying between fixed points for carriage of passengers fall under this entry—*ITO* v. *Sarojini Transports (P.) Ltd.* [1986] 17 ITD 1014 (Mad.); Mobile crane mounted on a lorry falls under this entry—*Gujco Carriers* v. *CIT* [2002] 122 Taxman 206 (Guj.); Rigs and Compressors mounted on a lorry do not fall under this item—*CIT* v. *Popular Borewell Service* [1992] 194 ITR 12 (Mad.); Motor vans are akin to motor lorries or motor buses—*Circular No. 609, dated 29-7-1991*/*CIT* v. *Kodak Ltd.* [1990] 181 ITR 275 (Bom.); Ambulance van falls under this entry—*CIT* v. *Dr. K.R. Jayachandran* [1995] 212 ITR 637 (Ker.); Air-conditioned vehicles fall under this entry—*CIT* v. *Urmila Goel* [1986] 52 CTR (Delhi) 276.

c. 40 per cent if conditions of rule 5(2) are satisfied. For rule 5(2), log on to *taxmann.com/readyreckoner.aspx*.

1	2	3
for any period before the 1st day of April, 1999 for the purposes of business or profession in accordance with the third proviso to clause (*ii*) of sub-section (1) of section 32 [*See* Note 6 below the Table]	40	40
(*iv*) New commercial vehicle which is acquired on or after the 1st day of October, 1998, but before the 1st day of April, 1999 in replacement of condemned vehicle of over 15 years of age and is put to use for any period before the 1st day of April, 1999 for the purposes of business or profession in accordance with the third proviso to clause (*ii*) of sub-section (1) of section 32 [*See* Note 6 below the Table]	60	40
(*v*) New commercial vehicle which is acquired on or after the 1st day of April, 1999 but before the 1st day of April, 2000 in replacement of condemned vehicle of over 15 years of age and is put to use before the 1st day of April, 2000 for the purposes of business or profession in accordance with the second proviso to clause (*ii*) of sub-section (1) of section 32 [*See* Note 6 below the Table]	60	40
(*vi*) New commercial vehicle which is acquired on or after the 1st day of April, 2001 but before the 1st day of April, 2002 and is put to use before the 1st day of April, 2002 for the purposes of business or profession [*See* Note 6 below the Table]	50	40
(*via*) New commercial vehicle which is acquired on or after the 1st day of January, 2009 but before the 1st day of October, 2009 and is put to use before the 1st day of October, 2009 for the purposes of business or profession [*See* paragraph 6 of the Notes below this Table]	50	40
[d](*vii*) Moulds used in rubber and plastic goods factories	30	30
(*viii*) Air pollution control equipment, being— (*a*) Electrostatic precipitation systems (*b*) Felt-filter systems (*c*) Dust collector systems (*d*) Scrubber-counter current/venturi/packed bed/cyclonic scrubbers (*e*) Ash handling system and evacuation system	100	40
(*ix*) Water pollution control equipment, being— (*a*) Mechanical screen systems (*b*) Aerated detritus chambers (including air compressor) (*c*) Mechanically skimmed oil and grease removal systems (*d*) Chemical feed systems and flash mixing equipment (*e*) Mechanical flocculators and mechanical reactors (*f*) Diffused air/mechanically aerated activated sludge systems (*g*) Aerated lagoon systems (*h*) Biofilters (*i*) Methane-recovery anaerobic digester systems (*j*) Air floatation systems (*k*) Air/steam stripping systems (*l*) Urea Hydrolysis systems (*m*) Marine outfall systems (*n*) Centrifuge for dewatering sludge (*o*) Rotating biological contractor or bio-disc (*p*) Ion exchange resin column (*q*) Activated carbon column	100	40
(*x*) (*a*) Solidwaste control equipments being - caustic/lime/chrome/mineral/cryolite recovery systems (*b*) Solidwaste recycling and resource recovery systems	100	40
(*xi*) Machinery and plant, used in semi-conductor industry covering all integrated circuits (ICs) (excluding hybrid integrated circuits) ranging from		

d. Company manufacturing insulated wires and cables is not covered under this entry—*CIT* v. *Falcon Wires (P.) Ltd.* [1980] 123 ITR 427 (Mad.).

1	2	3
small scale integration (SSI) to large scale integration/very large scale integration (LSI/VLSI) as also discrete semi-conductor devices such as diodes, transistors, thyristors, triacs, etc., other than those covered by entries (*viii*), (*ix*) and (*x*) of this sub-item and sub-item (8) below	30	30
(*xia*) Life saving medical equipment, being—		
(*a*) D.C. Defibrillators for internal use and pace makers (*b*) Haemodialysors (*c*) Heart lung machine (*d*) Cobalt Therapy Unit (*e*) Colour Doppler (*f*) SPECT Gamma Camera (*g*) Vascular Angiography System including Digital subtraction Angiography (*h*) Ventilator used with anaesthesia apparatus (*i*) Magnetic Resonance Imaging System (*j*) Surgical Laser (*k*) Ventilators other than those used with anaesthesia (*l*) Gamma knife (*m*) Bone Marrow Transplant Equipment including silastic long standing intravenous catheters for chemotherapy (*n*) Fibreoptic endoscopes including Paediatric resectoscope/audit resectoscope, Peritoneoscopes, Arthoscope, Microlaryngoscope, Fibreoptic Flexible Nasal Pharyngo Bronchoscope, Fibreoptic Flexible Laryngo Bronchoscope, Video Laryngo Bronchoscope and Video Oesophago Gastroscope, Stroboscope, Fibreoptic Flexible Oesophago Gastroscope (*o*) Laparoscope (single incision)	40†	40
(*4*) Containers made of glass or plastic used as re-fills	50	40
(*5*) Computers including computer software [*See* note 7 below the Table]	60	40
(*6*) Machinery and plant, used in weaving, processing and garment sector of textile industry, which is purchased under TUFS on or after the 1st day of April, 2001 but before the 1st day of April, 2004 and is put to use before the 1st day of April, 2004 [*See* Note 8 below the Table]	50	40
(*7*) Machinery and plant, acquired and installed on or after the 1st day of September, 2002 in a water supply project or a water treatment system and which is put to use for the purpose of business of providing infrastructure facility under clause (*i*) of sub-section (4) of section 80-IA [*See* Notes 4 and 9 below the Table]	100	40
(*8*) (*i*) Wooden parts used in artificial silk manufacturing machinery[e]	100	40
(*ii*) Cinematograph films - bulbs of studio lights	100	40
(*iii*) Match factories - Wooden match frames	100	40
(*iv*) Mines and quarries :		
(*a*) Tubs, winding ropes, haulage ropes and sand stowing pipes (*b*) Safety lamps	100	40
(*v*) Salt works - Salt pans, reservoirs and condensers, etc., made of earthy, sandy or clayey material or any other similar material	100	40
(*vi*) Flour mills - Rollers	80	40
(*vii*) Iron and steel industry - Rolling mill rolls	80	40
(*viii*) Sugar works - Rollers	80	40

e. Machinery used for dyeing, bleaching and printing of cloth manufactured by some other person will not fall under this item—*CIT* v. *Jaypee Dyeing House* [1999] 239 ITR 418 (Bom.).

†Applicable from the assessment year 2004-05.

1	2	3
(*ix*) Energy saving devices, being—		
A. Specialised boilers and furnaces:		
(*a*) Ignifluid/fluidized bed boilers (*b*) Flameless furnaces and continuous pusher type furnaces (*c*) Fluidized bed type heat treatment furnaces (*d*) High efficiency boilers (thermal efficiency higher than 75 per cent in case of coal fired and 80 per cent in case of oil/gas fired boilers)	80	40
B. Instrumentation and monitoring system for monitoring energy flows:		
(*a*) Automatic electrical load monitoring systems (*b*) Digital heat loss meters (*c*) Micro-processor based control systems (*d*) Infra-red thermography (*e*) Meters for measuring heat losses, furnace oil flow, steam flow, electric energy and power factor meters (*f*) Maximum demand indicator and clamp on power meters (*g*) Exhaust gases analyser (*h*) Fuel oil pump test bench	80	40
C. Waste heat recovery equipment:		
(*a*) Economisers and feed water heaters (*b*) Recuperators and air pre-heaters (*c*) Heat pumps (*d*) Thermal energy wheel for high and low temperature waste heat recovery	80	40
D. Co-generation systems:		
(*a*) Back pressure pass out, controlled extraction, extraction-*cum*-condensing turbines for co-generation along with pressure boilers (*b*) Vapour absorption refrigeration systems (*c*) Organic rankine cycle power systems (*d*) Low inlet pressure small steam turbines	80	40
E. Electrical equipment:		
(*a*) Shunt capacitors and synchronous condenser systems (*b*) Automatic power cut off devices (relays) mounted on individual motors (*c*) Automatic voltage controller (*d*) Power factor controller for AC motors (*e*) Solid state devices for controlling motor speeds (*f*) Thermally energy-efficient stenters (which require 800 or less kilocalories of heat to evaporate one kilogram of water) (*g*) Series compensation equipment (*h*) Flexible AC Transmission (FACT) devices - Thyristor controlled series compensation equipment (*i*) Time of Day (ToD) energy meters (*j*) Equipment to establish transmission highways for National Power Grid to facilitate transfer of surplus power of one region to the deficient region (*k*) Remote terminal units/intelligent electronic devices, computer hardware/software, router/bridges, other required equipment and associated communication systems for supervisory control and data acquisition systems, energy management systems and distribution management systems for power transmission systems (*l*) Special energy meters for Availability Based Tariff (ABT)	80	40

1	2	3
F. Burners:		
(*a*) 0 to 10 per cent excess air burners (*b*) Emulsion burners (*c*) Burners using air with high pre-heat temperature (above 300°C)	80	40
G. Other equipment:		
(*a*) Wet air oxidation equipment for recovery of chemicals and heat (*b*) Mechanical vapour recompressors (*c*) Thin film evaporators (*d*) Automatic micro-processor based load demand controllers (*e*) Coal based producer gas plants (*f*) Fluid drives and fluid couplings (*g*) Turbo charges/super-charges (*h*) Sealed radiation sources for radiation processing plants	80	40
[f](*x*) Gas cylinders including valves and regulators	60	40
(*xi*) Glass manufacturing concerns - Direct fire glass melting furnaces	60	40
[g](*xii*) Mineral oil concerns:		
(*a*) Plant used in field operations (above ground) distribution - Returnable packages (*b*) Plant used in field operations (below ground), but not including kerbside pumps including underground tanks and fittings used in field operations (distribution) by mineral oil concerns	60	40
(*c*) Oil wells not covered in clauses (*a*) and (*b*) (with effect from the assessment year 2016-17)	15	15
(*xiii*) Renewal energy devices being—		
(*a*) Flat plate solar collectors (*b*) Concentrating and pipe type solar collectors (*c*) Solar cookers (*d*) Solar water heaters and systems (*e*) Air/gas/fluid heating systems (*f*) Solar crop driers and systems (*g*) Solar refrigeration, cold storages and air-conditioning systems (*h*) Solar steels and desalination systems (*i*) Solar power generating systems (*j*) Solar pumps based on solar-thermal and solar-photovoltaic conversion (*k*) Solar-photovoltaic modules and panels for water pumping and other applications (*l*) Windmills and any specially designed devices which run on windmills installed on or before March 31, 2012 or installed on or after April 1, 2014 (*m*) Any special devices including electric generators and pumps running on wind energy installed on or before March 31, 2012 or installed on or after April 1, 2014 (*n*) Biogas plant and biogas engines (*o*) Electrically operated vehicles including battery powered or fuel-cell powered vehicles (*p*) Agricultural and municipal waste conversion devices producing energy (*q*) Equipment for utilising ocean waste and thermal energy (*r*) Machinery and plant used in the manufacture of any of the above sub-items	80	40

f. Mere fact that assessee sold some cylinders during the previous year will not convert the cylinders into stock-in-trade. The cylinders must be capable of containing gas, and there is no requirement that the cylinders must be filled with gas—*Chawla Architects & Consultants (P.) Ltd.* v. *Asstt. CIT* [1995] 54 ITD 330 (Bom.).

g. Petroleum company distributing gas for cooking purpose is a 'mineral oil concern'—*CIT* v. *Burmah Shell Oil Storage & Distribution Co. of India Ltd.* [1978] 115 ITR 891 (Cal.); Vegetable oil is not a 'mineral oil'—*CIT* v. *Distillers Trading Corporation Ltd.* [1982] 137 ITR 894 (Delhi).

1	*2*	*3*
(9) (*i*) Books owned by assessees carrying on a profession—		
(*a*) Books, being annual publications	100	40
(*b*) Books, other than those covered by entry (*a*) above	60	40
(*ii*) Books owned by assessees carrying on business in running lending libraries	100	40
IV. SHIPS		
(1) Ocean-going ships including dredgers, tugs, barges, survey launches and other similar ships used mainly for dredging purposes and fishing vessels with wooden hull	20	20
(2) Vessels ordinarily operating on inland waters, not covered by sub-item (3) below	20	20
(3) Vessels ordinarily operating on inland waters being speed boats [*See* Note 10 below the Table]	20	20
PART B		
INTANGIBLE ASSETS		
Know-how, patents, copyrights, trademarks, licences, franchises or any other business or commercial rights of similar nature	25	25

Notes:

1. "Buildings" include roads, bridges, culverts, wells and tubewells.

2. A building shall be deemed to be a building used mainly for residential purposes, if the built-up floor area thereof used for residential purposes is not less than sixty-six and two-third per cent of its total built-up floor area and shall include any such building in the factory premises.

3. In respect of any structure or work by way of renovation or improvement in or in relation to a building referred to in *Explanation 1* of clause (*ii*) of sub-section (1) of section 32, the percentage to be applied will be the percentage specified against sub-item (1) or (2) of item I as may be appropriate to the class of building in or in relation to which the renovation or improvement is effected. Where the structure is constructed or the work is done by way of extension of any such building, the percentage to be applied would be such percentage as would be appropriate, as if the structure or work constituted a separate building.

4. Water treatment system includes system for desalination, demineralisation and purification of water.

5. "Electrical fittings" include electrical wiring, switches, sockets, other fittings and fans, etc.

6. "Commercial vehicle" means "heavy goods vehicle", "heavy passenger motor vehicle", "light motor vehicle", "medium goods vehicle" and "medium passenger motor vehicle" but does not include "maxi-cab", "motor-cab", "tractor" and "road-roller". The expressions "heavy goods vehicle", "heavy passenger motor vehicle", "light motor vehicle", "medium goods vehicle", "medium passenger motor vehicle", "maxi-cab", "motor-cab", "tractor" and "road-roller" shall have the meanings respectively as assigned to them in section 2 of the Motor Vehicles Act, 1988 (59 of 1988).

7. "Computer software" means any computer programme recorded on any disc, tape, perforated media or other information storage device.

8. "TUFS" means Technology Upgradation Fund Scheme announced by the Government of India in the form of a Resolution of the Ministry of Textiles *vide* No. 28/1/99-CTI of 31-3-1999.

9. Machinery and plant includes pipes needed for delivery from the source of supply of raw water to the plant and from the plant to the storage facility.

10. "Speed boat" means a motor boat driven by a high speed internal combustion engine capable of propelling the boat at a speed exceeding 24 kilometers per hour in still water and so designed that when running at a speed, it will plane, *i.e.*, its bow will rise from the water.

Depreciation rates for power generating units (applicable from the assessment year 1998-99)

Class of assets	*Depreciation allowance as percentage of actual cost*
(*a*) Plant and Machinery in generating stations including plant foundations :—	
(*i*) Hydro-electric	3.4
(*ii*) Steam electric NHRS & Waste heat recovery Boilers/plants	7.84
(*iii*) Diesel electric and Gas plant	8.24
(*b*) Cooling towers and circulating water systems	7.84
(*c*) Hydraulic works forming part of Hydro-electric system including :—	
(*i*) Dams, spillways weirs, canals, reinforced concrete flumes and syphons	1.95
(*ii*) Reinforced concrete pipelines and surge tanks steel pipelines, sluice gates, steel surge (tanks), hydraulic control valves and other hydraulic works.	3.4
(*d*) Building and civil engineering works of permanent character, not mentioned above	
(*i*) Office & showrooms	3.02
(*ii*) Containing Thermo-electric generating plant	7.84
(*iii*) Containing Hydro-electric generating plant	3.4
(*iv*) Temporary erection such as wooden structures	33.4
(*v*) Roads other than Kutcha roads	3.02
(*vi*) Others	3.02
(*e*) Transformers, transformer (Kiosk) sub-station equipment & other fixed apparatus (including plant foundations)	
(*i*) Transformers (including foundations) having a rating of 100 kilo volt amperes and over	7.81
(*ii*) Others	7.84
(*f*) Switchgear including cable connections	7.84
(*g*) Lightning arrestor :	
(*i*) Station type	7.84
(*ii*) Pole type	12.77
(*iii*) Synchronous condenser	5.27
(*h*) Batteries	33.4
(*i*) Underground cable including joint boxes and disconnectioned boxes	5.27
(*ii*) Cable duct system	3.02
(*i*) Overhead lines including supports :	
(*i*) Lines on fabricated steel operating at nominal voltages higher than 66 kilo volts	5.27
(*ii*) Lines on steel supports operating at nominal voltages higher than 13.2 kilo volts but not exceeding 66 kilo volts	7.84
(*iii*) Lines on steel or reinforced concrete supports	7.84
(*iv*) Lines on treated wood supports	7.84
(*j*) Meters	12.77
(*k*) Self-propelled vehicles	33.40
(*l*) Air-conditioning plants :	
(*i*) Static	12.77
(*ii*) Portable	33.40
(*m*) (*i*) Office furniture and fittings	12.77
(*ii*) Office equipments	12.77
(*iii*) Internal wiring including fittings and apparatus	12.77
(*iv*) Street light fittings	12.77
(*n*) Apparatus let on hire	
(*i*) Other than motors	33.4
(*ii*) Motors	12.77
(*o*) Communication equipment :	
(*i*) Radio and high frequency carrier system	12.77
(*ii*) Telephone lines and telephones	12.77
(*p*) Any other assets not covered above	7.69

Depreciation under Companies Act, 2013

[1]*SCHEDULE II*[2]

(*See* section 123)

USEFUL LIVES TO COMPUTE DEPRECIATION

PART 'A'

1. Depreciation is the systematic allocation of the depreciable amount of an asset over its useful life. The depreciable amount of an asset is the cost of an asset or other amount substituted for cost, less its residual value. The useful life of an asset is the period over which an asset is expected to be available for use by an entity, or the number of production or similar units expected to be obtained from the asset by the entity.

2. For the purpose of this Schedule, the term depreciation includes amortisation.

3. Without prejudice to the foregoing provisions of paragraph 1,—

[3][*(i) The useful life of an asset shall not be longer than the useful life specified in Part 'C' and the residual value of an asset shall not be more than five per cent of the original cost of the asset:*

Provided *that where a company uses a useful life or residual value of the asset which is different from the above limits, justification for the difference shall be disclosed in its financial statement.*

[4][*(ii) For intangible assets, the relevant Indian Accounting Standards (Ind AS) shall apply. Where a company is not required to comply with the Indian Accounting Standards (Ind AS), it shall comply with relevant Accounting Standards under Companies (Accounting Standards) Rules, 2006], except in case of intangible assets (Toll Roads) created under 'Build, Operate and Transfer', 'Build, Own, Operate and Transfer' or any other form of public private partnership route in case of road projects. Amortisation in such cases may be done as follows:—*

(a) Mode of amortisation

$$\text{Amortisation Rate} = \frac{\text{Amortisation Amount}}{\text{Cost of Intangible Assets (A)}} \times 100$$

Amortisation Amount =

$$\text{Cost of Intangible Assets (A)} \times \frac{\text{Actual Revenue for the year (B)}}{\text{Projected Revenue from Intangible Asset (till the end of the concession period) (C)}}$$

(b) Meaning of particulars are as follows :—

Cost of Intangible Assets (A) = *Cost incurred by the company in accordance with the accounting standards.*

1. Corresponds to Schedule XIV of the 1956 Act.
2. Enforced with effect from April 1, 2014.
3. Substituted for clauses (*i*) to (*iii*) *vide* Notification No. GSR 237(E) [F. No. 17/60/2012-CL-V], dated 31-3-2014, w.e.f. April 1, 2014. Prior to their substitution, clauses (*i*) to (*iii*) read as under :

   "(*i*) In case of such class of companies, as may be prescribed and whose financial statements comply with the accounting standards prescribed for such class of companies under section 133 the useful life of an asset shall not normally be different from the useful life and the residual value shall not be different from that as indicated in Part C, provided that if such a company uses a useful life or residual value which is different from the useful life or residual value indicated therein, it shall disclose the justification for the same.

   (*ii*) In respect of other companies the useful life of an asset shall not be longer than the useful life and the residual value shall not be higher than that prescribed in Part C.

   (*iii*) For intangible assets, the provisions of the Accounting Standards mentioned under sub-para (*i*) or (*ii*), as applicable, shall apply."
4. Substituted for "(*ii*) For intangible assets, the provisions of the accounting standards applicable for the time being in force shall apply" by Notification No. GSR 1075(E), dated November 17, 2016 (as corrected by Notification No. GSR 1127(E) [F.No.17/60/2012-CL-V], dated December 9, 2016), w.e.f. accounting period commencing on or after April 1, 2016.

Actual Revenue for the year (B) = *Actual revenue (toll charges) received during the accounting year.*

Projected Revenue from Intangible Asset (C) = *Total projected revenue from the Intangible Assets as provided to the project lender at the time of financial closure/agreement.*

The amortisation amount or rate should ensure that the whole of the cost of the intangible asset is amortised over the concession period.

Revenue shall be reviewed at the end of each financial year and projected revenue shall be adjusted to reflect such changes, if any, in the estimates as will lead to the actual collection at the end of the concession period.

(c) *Example:—*

Cost of creation of Intangible Assets : *Rs. 500 Crores*

Total period of Agreement : *20 Years*

Time used for creation of Intangible Assets : *2 Years*

Intangible Assets to be amortised in : *18 Years*

Assuming that the Total revenue to be generated out of Intangible Assets over the period would be Rs. 600 crore, in the following manner:—

Year No.	Revenue (In Rs. Crores)	**Remarks**
Year 1	*5*	*Actual*
Year 2	*7.5*	*Estimate**
Year 3	*10*	*Estimate**
Year 4	*12.5*	*Estimate**
Year 5	*17.5*	*Estimate**
Year 6	*20*	*Estimate**
Year 7	*23*	*Estimate**
Year 8	*27*	*Estimate**
Year 9	*31*	*Estimate**
Year 10	*34*	*Estimate**
Year 11	*38*	*Estimate**
Year 12	*41*	*Estimate**
Year 13	*46*	*Estimate**
Year 14	*50*	*Estimate**
Year 15	*53*	*Estimate**
Year 16	*57*	*Estimate**
Year 17	*60*	*Estimate**
Year 18	*67.5*	*Estimate**
Total	*600*	

'' will be actual at the end of financial year.*

Based on this the charge for first year would be Rs. 4.16 Crore (approximately) (i.e. Rs. 5/Rs. 600 × Rs. 500 Crores) which would be charged to profit and loss and 0.83% (i.e. Rs. 4.16 Crore/Rs. 500 Crore × 100) is the amortisation rate for the first year.

Where a company arrives at the amortisation amount in respect of the said Intangible Assets in accordance with any method as per the applicable Accounting Standards, it shall disclose the same.]

PART 'B'

4. The useful life or residual value of any specific asset, as notified for accounting purposes by a Regulatory Authority constituted under an Act of Parliament or by the Central Government shall be applied in calculating the depreciation to be provided for such asset irrespective of the requirements of this Schedule.

PART 'C'

5. Subject to Parts A and B above, the following are the useful lives of various tangible assets:

Nature of assets	*Useful Life*
I. Buildings [NESD]	
(*a*) Buildings (other than factory buildings) RCC Frame Structure	60 Years
(*b*) Buildings (other than factory buildings) other than RCC Frame Structure	30 Years
(*c*) Factory buildings	-do-
(*d*) Fences, wells, tube wells	5 Years
(*e*) Others (including temporary structure, etc.)	3 Years
II. Bridges, culverts, bunders, etc. [NESD]	30 Years
III. Roads [NESD]	
(*a*) Carpeted roads	
(*i*) Carpeted Roads—RCC	10 Years
(*ii*) Carpeted Roads—other than RCC	5 Years
(*b*) Non-carpeted roads	3 Years
IV. Plant and Machinery	
(*i*) **General rate applicable to plant and machinery not covered under special plant and machinery**	
(*a*) Plant and Machinery other than continuous process plant not covered under specific industries	15 Years
[1][(b) *Continuous process plant for which no special rate has been prescribed under* (ii) *below [NESD]*	*25 Years*]
(*ii*) **Special Plant and Machinery**	
(*a*) Plant and Machinery related to production and exhibition of Motion Picture Films	
1. Cinematograph films—Machinery used in the production and exhibition of cinematograph films, recording and reproducing equipments, developing machines, printing machines, editing machines, synchronizers and studio lights except bulbs	13 Years
2. Projecting equipment for exhibition of films	-do-
(*b*) Plant and Machinery used in glass manufacturing	
1. Plant and Machinery except direct fire glass melting furnaces — Recuperative and regenerative glass melting furnaces	13 Years
2. Plant and Machinery except direct fire glass melting furnaces — Moulds [NESD]	8 Years
3. Float Glass Melting Furnaces [NESD]	10 Years
(*c*) Plant and Machinery used in mines and quarries—Portable underground machinery and earth moving machinery used in open cast mining [NESD]	8 Years
(*d*) Plant and Machinery used in Telecommunications [NESD]	
1. Towers	18 Years
2. Telecom trans-receivers, switching centres, transmission and other network equipment	13 Years
3. Telecom—Ducts, Cables and optical fibre	18 Years
4. Satellites	-do-

1. Substituted *vide* Notification No. GSR 237(E) [F. No. 17/60/2012-CL-V], dated March 31, 2014, w.e.f. April 1, 2014. Prior to its substitution, clause (*b*) read as under :

"(*b*) Continuous process plant for which no special rate has been prescribed under (*ii*) below [NESD] 8 Years"

Nature of assets	Useful Life
(e) Plant and Machinery used in exploration, production and refining oil and gas [NESD]	
1. Refineries	25 Years
2. Oil and gas assets (including wells), processing plant and facilities	-do-
3. Petrochemical Plant	-do-
4. Storage tanks and related equipment	-do-
5. Pipelines	30 Years
6. Drilling Rig	-do-
7. Field operations (above ground), Portable boilers, drilling tools, well-head tanks, etc.	8 Years
8. Loggers	-do-
(f) Plant and Machinery used in generation, transmission and distribution of power [NESD]	
1. Thermal/Gas/Combined Cycle Power Generation Plant	40 Years
2. Hydro Power Generation Plant	-do-
3. Nuclear Power Generation Plant	-do-
4. Transmission lines, cables and other network assets	-do-
5. Wind Power Generation Plant	22 Years
6. Electric Distribution Plant	35 Years
7. Gas Storage and Distribution Plant	30 Years
8. Water Distribution Plant including pipelines	-do-
(g) Plant and Machinery used in manufacture of steel	
1. Sinter Plant	20 Years
2. Blast Furnace	-do-
3. Coke ovens	-do-
4. Rolling mill in steel plant	-do-
5. Basic oxygen Furnace Converter	25 Years
(h) Plant and Machinery used in manufacture of non-ferrous metals	
1. Metal pot line [NESD]	40 Years
2. Bauxite crushing and grinding section [NESD]	-do-
3. Digester section [NESD]	-do-
4. Turbine [NESD]	-do-
5. Equipments for Calcination [NESD]	-do-
6. Copper Smelter [NESD]	-do-
7. Roll Grinder	40 Years
8. Soaking Pit	30 Years
9. Annealing Furnace	-do-
10. Rolling Mills	-do-
11. Equipments for Scalping, Slitting, etc. [NESD]	-do-
12. Surface Miner, Ripper Dozer, etc., used in mines	25 Years
13. Copper refining plant [NESD]	-do-
(i) Plant and Machinery used in medical and surgical operations [NESD]	
1. Electrical Machinery, X-ray and electrotherapeutic apparatus and accessories thereto, medical, diagnostic equipments, namely, Cat-Scan, Ultrasound Machines, ECG Monitors, etc.	13 Years
2. Other Equipments.	15 Years
(j) Plant and Machinery used in manufacture of pharmaceuticals and chemicals [NESD]	

Nature of assets	Useful Life
1. Reactors	20 Years
2. Distillation Columns	-do-
3. Drying equipments/Centrifuges and Decanters	-do-
4. Vessel/storage tanks	-do-
(k) Plant and Machinery used in civil construction	
1. Concreting, Crushing, Piling Equipments and Road Making Equipments	12 Years
2. Heavy Lift Equipments—	
Cranes with capacity of more than 100 tons	20 Years
Cranes with capacity of less than 100 tons	15 Years
3. Transmission line, Tunneling Equipments [NESD]	10 Years
4. Earth-moving equipments	9 Years
5. Others including Material Handling /Pipeline/Welding Equipments [NESD]	12 Years
(l) Plant and Machinery used in salt works [NESD]	15 Years
V. Furniture and fittings [NESD]	
(i) General furniture and fittings	10 Years
(ii) Furniture and fittings used in hotels, restaurants and boarding houses, schools, colleges and other educational institutions, libraries; welfare centres; meeting halls, cinema houses; theatres and circuses; and furniture and fittings let out on hire for use on the occasion of marriages and similar functions.	8 Years
VI. Motor Vehicles [NESD]	
1. Motor cycles, scooters and other mopeds	10 Years
2. Motor buses, motor lorries, motor cars and motor taxies used in a business of running them on hire	6 Years
3. Motor buses, motor lorries and motor cars other than those used in a business of running them on hire	8 Years
4. Motor tractors, harvesting combines and heavy vehicles	-do-
5. Electrically operated vehicles including battery powered or fuel cell powered vehicles	8 Years
VII. Ships [NESD]	
1. Ocean-going ships	
(i) Bulk Carriers and liner vessels	25 Years
(ii) Crude tankers, product carriers and easy chemical carriers with or without conventional tank coatings	20 Years
(iii) Chemicals and Acid Carriers :	
(a) With Stainless steel tanks	25 Years
(b) With other tanks	20 Years
(iv) Liquefied gas carriers	30 Years
(v) Conventional large passenger vessels which are used for cruise purpose also	-do-
(vi) Coastal service ships of all categories	-do-
(vii) Offshore supply and support vessels	20 Years
(viii) Catamarans and other high speed passenger for ships or boats	-do-
(ix) Drill ships	25 Years
(x) Hovercrafts	15 Years
(xi) Fishing vessels with wooden hull	10 Years
(xii) Dredgers, tugs, barges, survey launches and other similar ships used mainly for dredging purposes	14 Years
2. Vessels ordinarily operating on inland waters—	
(i) Speed boats	13 Years
(ii) Other vessels	28 Years

Nature of assets	*Useful Life*
VIII. Aircrafts or Helicopters [NESD]	20 Years
IX. Railway sidings, locomotives, rolling stocks, tramways and railways used by concerns, excluding railway concerns [NESD]	15 Years
X. Ropeway structures [NESD]	15 Years
XI. Office equipment [NESD]	5 Years
XII. Computers and data processing units [NESD]	
(*i*) Servers and networks	6 Years
(*ii*) End user devices, such as, desktops, laptops, etc.	3 Years
XIII. Laboratory equipment [NESD]	
(*i*) General laboratory equipment	10 Years
(*ii*) Laboratory equipments used in educational institutions	5 Years
XIV. Electrical Installations and Equipment [NESD]	10 years
XV. Hydraulic works, pipelines and sluices [NESD]	15 Years

Notes.—

1. "Factory buildings" does not include offices, godowns, staff quarters.

2. Where, during any financial year, any addition has been made to any asset, or where any asset has been sold, discarded, demolished or destroyed, the depreciation on such assets shall be calculated on a *pro rata* basis from the date of such addition or, as the case may be, up to the date on which such asset has been sold, discarded, demolished or destroyed.

3. The following information shall also be disclosed in the accounts, namely:—

(*i*) depreciation methods used; and

(*ii*) the useful lives of the assets for computing depreciation, if they are different from the life specified in the Schedule.

[1][4. (*a*) Useful life specified in Part C of the Schedule for whole of the asset and where cost of a part of the asset is significant to total cost of the asset and useful life of that part is different from the useful life of the remaining asset, useful life of that significant part shall be determined separately.

(*b*) The requirement under sub-paragraph (*a*) shall be voluntary in respect of the financial year commencing on or after the 1st April, 2014 and mandatory for financial statements in respect of financial years commencing on or after the 1st April, 2015.]

5. [2][***]

6. The useful lives of assets working on shift basis have been specified in the Schedule based on their single shift working. Except for assets in respect of which no extra shift depreciation is permitted (indicated by NESD in Part C above), if an asset is used for any time during the year for double shift, the depreciation will increase by 50% for that period and in case of the triple shift the depreciation shall be calculated on the basis of 100% for that period.

7. From the date this Schedule comes into effect, the carrying amount of the asset as on that date—

(*a*) shall be depreciated over the remaining useful life of the asset as per this Schedule;

(*b*) after retaining the residual value, [3][may be recognised] in the opening balance of retained earnings where the remaining useful life of an asset is *nil*.

8. "Continuous process plant" means a plant which is required and designed to operate for twenty-four hours a day.

---

1. Paragraph 4 substituted by Notification F.No.17/60/2012-CL-V, dated 29-8-2014, w.e.f. August 29, 2014. Prior to its substitution, said paragraph read as under :

"4. Useful life specified in Part C of the Schedule is for whole of the asset. Where cost of a part of the asset is significant to total cost of the asset and useful life of that part is different from the useful life of the remaining asset, useful life of that significant part shall be determined separately."

2. Omitted *vide* Notification No. GSR 237(E) [F. No. 17/60/2012-CL-V], dated March 31, 2014, w.e.f. April 1, 2014. Prior to its omission, Paragraph 5 read as under :

"5. Depreciable amount is the cost of an asset, or other amount substituted for cost, less its residual value. Ordinarily, the residual value of an asset is often insignificant but it should generally be not more than 5% of the original cost of the asset."

3. Substituted for "shall be recognized" by Notification F.No.17/60/2012-CL-V, dated August 29, 2014, w.e.f. August 29, 2014.

R-7

Deductions and allowances under the Income-tax Act

FOR THE ASSESSMENT YEARS 2019-20 AND 2020-21

Section	*Nature of deduction*	*Who can claim*	*Para No.*
	UNDER THE HEAD "SALARIES"		
16(*ia*)	Standard deduction (maximum : Rs. 40,000 for the assessment year 2019-20, **Rs. 50,000 from the assessment year 2020-21**).	Salaried employees	16.1
16(*ii*)	Entertainment allowance [subject to maximum of Rs. 5,000]	Government employees	13.2
16(*iii*)	Tax on employment within the meaning of article 276(2) of the Constitution, leviable by or under any law	Salaried employees	16.3
	UNDER THE HEAD "INCOME FROM HOUSE PROPERTY"		
23(1), proviso	Taxes levied by local authority and paid by the owner	All assessees	39.2
24(*a*)	Standard deduction [30 per cent of net annual value]	All assessees	39.3-1
24(*b*)	Interest on borrowed capital	All assessees	39.3-2 and 40.1-1a
	UNDER THE HEAD "PROFITS AND GAINS OF BUSINESS OR PROFESSION"		
30	Rent, rates, taxes, repairs and insurance for buildings	All assessees	48.1
31	Repairs and insurance of machinery, plant and furniture	All assessees	48.2
32	Depreciation [subject to certain conditions]	All assessees	48.3
32AC	Investment allowance	Companies	48.4
32AD	Additional investment allowance for setting up industrial undertakings in Andhra Pradesh, Bihar, Telangana and West Bengal	All assessees	48.5
33AB	Tea/Coffee/rubber development account	All assessees carrying on the business of growing and manufacturing tea or coffee or rubber in India	48.6
33ABA	Site restoration fund	All assessees engaged in the business of the prospecting for, or extraction or production of, petroleum or natural gas or both in India	48.7
35	Expenditure on scientific research [subject to certain conditions]	All assessees	48.9
35ABA	Expenditure for obtaining right to use spectrum for telecommunication services	Any assessee	48.11
35ABB	Expenditure for obtaining licence to operate telecommunication services	All assessees	48.12
35AC	Expenditure on eligible projects/schemes	All assessees	48.13

Section	*Nature of deduction*	*Who can claim*	*Para No.*
35AD	Expenditure on specified business	All assessees (only Indian companies in some cases)	48.14
35CCA	Expenditure by way of payment to associations and institutions for carrying out rural development programmes and contribution towards notified Rural Development Funds [subject to certain conditions]	All assessees	48.15
35CCC	Weighted deduction for expenditure incurred on agricultural extension project	All assessees	48.15A
35CCD	Weighted deduction for expenditure for skill development	Companies	48.15B
35D	Amortisation of preliminary expenses [deductible in five equal instalments]	Indian companies and resident non-corporate assessees	48.16
35DD	Amortisation of expenditure in case of amalgamation or demerger	Indian company	48.17
35DDA	Amortisation of expenditure incurred under voluntary retirement scheme	All assessees	48.18
35E	Expenditure on prospecting, etc., for certain minerals [deductible in ten equal instalments]	Indian companies and resident non-corporate assessees engaged in prospecting, etc., of any minerals	48.19
36(1)(*i*)	Premium paid in respect of insurance against risk of damage or destruction of stocks/stores	All assessees	48.20
36(1)(*ia*)	Premium paid for insurance on life of cattle owned by a member of a society engaged in supplying milk to the federal milk co-operative society	Federal milk co-operative societies	48.21
36(1)(*ib*)	Medical insurance paid by employers	All assessees	48.22
36(1)(*ii*)	Bonus or commission paid to employees	All assessees	48.23
36(1)(*iii*)	Interest on borrowed capital	All assessees	48.24
36(1)(*iiia*)	Discount on zero coupon bond	Infrastructure capital companies/ infrastructure capital funds/public sector funds/public sector banks	48.25
36(1)(*iv*)	Contributions to recognised provident fund and approved superannuation fund	All assessees	48.26
36(1)(*v*)	Contributions to approved gratuity fund	All assessees	48.27
36(1)(*va*)	Employees' contributions to staff welfare schemes	All assessees	48.28
36(1)(*vi*)	Write off allowance in respect of animals [subject to certain conditions]	All assessees	48.29
36(1)(*vii*)	Bad debts	All assessees	48.30
36(1)(*viia*)	Provisions for bad and doubtful debts in respect of advances made by rural branches of banks	Scheduled banks and non-scheduled banks	48.31
36(1)(*viii*)/ (*viiia*)	Amount transferred to special reserve	Approved Financial Corporations and public companies of specified nature/scheduled banks/National Housing Bank	48.32

Section	Nature of deduction	Who can claim	Para No.
36(1)(*ix*)	Expenditure for promoting family planning amongst employees [deductible in 5 equal annual instalments in the case of capital expenditure]	Companies	48.33
36(1)(*x*)	Contribution towards notified Exchange Risk Administration Fund	Public financial institutions	48.34
36(1)(*xii*)	Expenditure incurred by statutory entities	Statutory entities	48.36
36(1)(*xiii*)	Banking cash transaction tax	Any assessee	48.37
36(1)(*xv*)	Securities transaction tax	All assessees	48.37
36(1)(*xvi*)	Commodities transactions tax	All assessees	48.37
36(1)(*xvii*)	Expenditure incurred for purchase of sugarcane	Co-operative societies	48.39
36(1)(*xviii*)	**Marked to market loss**	All assessees	48.40
37(1)	Any other expenditure [not being personal or capital expenditure and expenditure mentioned in sections 30 to 36] laid out wholly and exclusively for business	All assessees	48.43
37(2B)	Expenditure on advertisement	All assessees	48.41
	UNDER THE HEAD "CAPITAL GAINS"		
48	Expenditure incurred wholly and exclusively in connection with transfer of capital asset	All assessees	65
48	Cost of acquisition of capital asset and of any improvement thereto*	All assessees	66 and 67
	UNDER THE HEAD "INCOME FROM OTHER SOURCES"		
57(*i*)	Any reasonable sum paid by way of commission or remuneration for the purpose of realising dividend/interest on securities	All assessees	78
57(*ii*)	Repairs, insurance and depreciation of buildings, plant and machinery and furniture	Assessees engaged in the business of letting out of machinery, plant and furniture on hire	78
57(*iii*)	Any other expenditure (not being capital expenditure) expended wholly and exclusively for earning such income	All assessees	78
	DEDUCTION UNDER CHAPTER VI-A IN RESPECT OF PAYMENTS		
80C**	Life insurance premia, provident fund contribution (maximum : Rs. 1,50,000)	Individuals and HUFs	107.1
80CCC**	Pension fund [maximum : Rs. 1,50,000]	Individuals	107.2A
80CCD(1)**	Contribution by an employee or any other individual towards National Pension System (NPS) (up to 10% of the salary of the employee or up to 20% of gross total income in the case of any other individual)	Individuals	107.2B
80CCD(1B)	Contribution by an individual towards NPS (maximum : Rs. 50,000)	Individuals	107.2B
80CCD(2)	Contribution by the employer towards NPS (up to 10% of salary of the employee)	Employees	107.2B
80D	Medical insurance premia [subject to maximum of Rs. 1,00,000]	Individuals and HUFs	107.3

*Indexed cost of acquisition and indexed cost of improvement in the case of long-term capital asset (other than debentures and bonds).

**The aggregate amount of deduction under sections 80C, 80CCC and 80CCD(1) [*i.e.*, contribution by an employee (or any other individual) towards NPS] cannot exceed Rs. 1,50,000.

Section	*Nature of deduction*	*Who can claim*	*Para No.*
80DD	Maintenance including medical treatment of a handicapped dependent who is a person with disability [maxi mum : Rs. 1,25,000]	Resident individuals or resident HUFs	107.4
80DDB	Medical treatment expenses [maximum : Rs. 1,00,000]	Resident individuals or resident HUFs	107.5
80E	Payment of interest of loan taken for higher studies	Individuals	107.6
80EE	Interest on loan taken for residential property	Individuals	107.6A
80G	Donations to certain funds, charitable institutions [subject to maximum of 50 per cent of qualifying donation (100 per cent in some cases)]	All assessees	107.7
80GG	Rent paid for furnished/unfurnished accommodation [subject to maximum of Rs. 24,000]	Individuals	107.8
80GGA	Certain donations for scientific research or rural development	All assessees not having any income chargeable under the head "Profits and gains of business or profession"	107.9
80GGB/ 80GGC	Contribution to political parties		107.10
	DEDUCTION UNDER CHAPTER VI-A IN RESPECT OF CERTAIN INCOMES		
80-IA	Profits and gains from enterprises engaged in infrastructure development	All assessees	107.17
80-IAB	Profits and gains by an undertaking engaged in development of SEZ	Developers	107.17A
80-IAC	Profits and gains from eligible start-up	Companies/LLPs	107.17B
80-IB	Profits and gains from industrial undertakings	All assessees	107.18
80-IBA	Profits and gains from housing projects	All assessees	107.18A
80-IC	Profits of certain undertakings or enterprises in certain special category States	All assessees	107.19
80-ID	Profits and gains from business of hotels/convention centres	All assessees	107.19A
80-IE	Understandings in North Eastern States	All assessees	107.19B
80JJA	Profits and gains from the business of collecting and processing of bio-degradable waste	All assessees	107.20
80JJAA	Employment of new workmen/employee	All assessees	107.21
80LA	Income of offshore Banking Units	Scheduled banks	107.22A
80P	Specified incomes [subject to amount specified in subsection (2)]	Co-operative societies	209.1
80PA	Profits and gains derived from eligible business (applicable from assessment year 2019-20)	Producer companies	107.25
80QQB	Royalty income of authors (maximum : Rs. 3 lakh)	Resident individuals	107.27
80RRB	Royalty on patents (maximum : Rs. 3 lakh)	Resident individuals	107.30
80TTA	Interest on deposits in savings account	Individuals/HUFs	107.31
80TTB	Interest on deposits with bank/co-operative bank/post office (maximum : Rs. 50,000) (applicable from the assessment year 2019-20)	Senior citizens	107.32
80U	Income of a person with disability [maximum : Rs. 1,25,000]	Resident individuals	107.33

R-8

Provisions of sections 44D, 44DA and 115A in brief

Royalty or fees for technical service received by a foreign company or a non-resident non-corporate assessee from Government or an Indian concern	*Deduction under sections 28 to 44D and 57*	*Deduction under sections 80CCC to 80U*	*Rate of tax on such royalty or fees for the assessment years 2019-20 and 2020-21 [on 1-2-3]*
(1)	(2)	(3)	(4)
A. Such royalty is received under an agreement made before April 1, 1961 or such technical fees is received under an agreement made before March 1, 1964			
A1. Where the agreement is approved by the Government	*Note 1*	Deduction is available	40 per cent†
A2. Where the agreement is not approved	*Note 1*	Deduction is available	40 per cent†
B. Such royalty is received under an agreement made after March 31, 1961 but before April 1, 1976 or such technical fees is received under an agreement made after February 29, 1964 but before April 1, 1976			
B1. Where agreement is approved by the Central Government	*Note 1*	Deduction is available	50 per cent†
B2. Where such agreement is not approved by the Central Government	*Note 1*	Deduction is available	40 per cent†
C. Such royalty or technical fees is received under an agreement made after March 31, 1976 but before April 1, 2003			
C1. Where such agreement is with the Government	No deduction	Deduction is available	10 per cent†
C2. Where such agreement is with an Indian concern, the agreement is approved by the Central Government	No deduction	Deduction is available	10 per cent†
C3. Where the agreement relates to a matter included in the industrial policy, for the time being in force, of the Government of India, the agreement is in accordance with that policy	No deduction	Deduction is available	10 per cent†
C4. Where such royalty is in consideration for the transfer of all or any rights (including the granting of a licence) in respect of copyright in any book on a subject referred to in the proviso to sub-section (1A) of section 115A to the Indian concern or in respect of computer software referred to in the second proviso to section 115A(1A) to a person resident in India	No deduction	Deduction is available	10 per cent†
C5. In any other case	No deduction if taxpayer is a foreign company (non-resident non-corporate assessee can claim deduction)	Deduction is available	40 per cent† in the case of foreign company (applicable normal rate in the case of non-resident non-corporate assessee)

† *Plus* surcharge and health and education cess.

(1)	*(2)*	*(3)*	*(4)*
D. Such royalty or technical fee is received under an agreement made after March 31, 2003			
D1. Where royalty and technical fees is effectively connected to Permanent Establishment (PE) in India	Deduction is available	Deduction is available	Applicable rate
D2. Where PE is absent but the case is covered by section 115A(1) [*i.e.*, C1 to C4 (*supra*)]	No deduction	Deduction is available	10 per cent†
D3. In any other case	Deduction is available [*see* Note 3]	Deduction is available	Applicable rate

Notes:

1. Deduction shall not exceed in the aggregate twenty per cent of the gross amount of such royalty or fees as reduced by so much of the gross amount of such royalty as consists of lump sum consideration for the transfer outside India of, or the imparting of information outside India in respect of, any data, documentation, drawing or specification relating to any patent, invention, model, design, secret formula or process or trademark or similar property.

2. The tax rates given in the column 4 of the table *supra* are not applicable where a lower rate is prescribed under an Avoidance of Double Taxation Agreement entered into by the Central Government under section 90 [*see* Referencer 10].

3. Neither section 44D (agreement is made after March 31, 2003) nor section 115A(3) (it is not agreement covered by C1 to C4) will apply in such a case. In other words the computation will be governed by the normal provisions of the Act.

† *Plus* surcharge and health and education cess.

R-9

Computation of income and tax under sections 115A, 115AB, 115AC, 115AD, 115BBA and 115D

Sections	*Nature of income*	*Deductions under sections 28 to 44C and 57*	*Whether the benefit of computing capital gain in foreign currency as provided by the first proviso to section 48 and the rule of indexation as provided by the second proviso to section 48 are applicable*	*Deduction under sections 80CCC to 80U*	*Tax rate [subject to Referencer 10]*	*Is it necessary to submit return of income*
(1)	*(2)*	*(3)*	*(4)*	*(5)*	*(6)*	*(7)*
115A(1)(*a*)	The following incomes in the case of a non-resident non-corporate assessee or a foreign company—					
	a. dividend*	Not available	—	Not available‡	20 per cent†	*Note 1*
	b. interest received from Government or an Indian concern on monies borrowed or debt incurred by Government or the Indian concern in foreign currency	Not available	—	Not available‡	20 per cent†	*Note 1*
	c. interest received from an infrastructure debt fund referred to in section 10(*47*)	Not available	—	Not available‡	5 per cent†	*Note 1*
	d. interest as referred to in section 194LC/194LD/194LBA(2)	Not available	—	Not available‡	5 per cent†	Note 1
	e. income received in respect of units, purchased in foreign currency of a Mutual Fund specified under clause (*23D*) of section 10 or of the Unit Trust of India	Not available	—	Not available‡	20 per cent†	*Note 1*

*It is not applicable in the case of dividend referred to in section 115-O [*see* para 207.2].

†*Plus* surcharge and health and education cess.

‡ **Deduction under section 80LA is available in the case of a unit of an International Financial Services Centre (applicable from the assessment year 2020-21).**

(1)	(2)	(3)	(4)	(5)	(6)	(7)
115A(1)(*b*)	Royalty or technical fees of a non-resident non-corporate assessee or a foreign company	*See* Refer-encer 8	—	*See* Refer-encer 8	*See* Refer-encer 8	*Yes*
115AB	The following incomes of an assessee, being an overseas financial organisation—					
	a. income received in respect of units purchased in foreign currency	Not available	—	Not available	10 per cent†	*Yes*
	b. income by way of long-term capital gains arising from the transfer of units pur-chased in foreign currency	—	First proviso is applicable but second proviso to section 48 is not applicable	Not available	10 per cent†	*Yes*
115AC	The following incomes* of a non-resident :					
	a. income by way of interest or dividends (not being dividend referred to in sec-tion 115-O), on bonds or Global Depository Receipts of an Indian company issued in accordance with the noti-fied scheme, *i.e.,* Foreign Currency Convertible Bonds and Ordinarily Glo-bal Depository Receipts (Through Depository Re-ceipt Mechanism) Scheme, 1993/Issue of Foreign Cur-rency Exchangeable Bonds Scheme, 2008 or on bonds/ Global Depository Receipts of a public sector company sold by the Government and purchased by him in foreign currency	Not available	—	Not available	10 per cent†	*Note 1*
	b. income by way of long-term capital gains arising from transfer of bonds or, as the case may be, shares referred above	—	First and second provisos to section 48 are not appli-cable	Not available	10 per cent†	*Yes*
115ACA	Income from Global Deposito-ry Receipts held by a resident individual who is an employee of an Indian company engaged in specified knowledge based industry or service** or an em-ployee of its subsidiary engaged in specified knowledge based industry or service					
	• Dividend [other than divi-dend referred to in section	Not available	—	Not available	10 per cent†	*Yes*

*Where an assessee acquires shares or bonds, as the case may be, in a resulting or amalgamated company by virtue of his holding shares in the amalgamating or demerged company in accordance with the provisions of section 115AC(1), the provisions of section 115AC(1) shall apply to such shares or bonds.

**Specified knowledge based industry or service means information technology software/services, entertainment service, pharma-ceutical industry, bio-technology industry or any other notified industry or service.

†*Plus* surcharge and health and education cess.

(1)	(2)	(3)	(4)	(5)	(6)	(7)
	115-O] on Global Depository Receipts of an Indian company engaged in specified knowledge based industry/ service issued under notified* employees stock option scheme and purchased in foreign currency					
	• Long-term capital gain on transfer of such receipts	—	First and second provisos to section 48 are not applicable	Not available	10 per cent†	*Yes*
115AD	The following income of a notified Foreign Institutional Investor*:					
	a. income (not being dividend referred to in section 115-O) received in respect of securities (other than units referred to in section 115AB)	Not available	—	Not available	20 per cent†	*Yes*
	b. income by way of short-term or long-term capital gains arising from the transfer of such securities	—	First and second provisos to section 48 are not applicable	Not available	Long-term : 10 per cent†, long-term u/s 112A in excess of Rs. 1 lakh : 10 per cent†, short-term u/s 111A: 15 per cent† any other short-term: 30 per cent†	*Yes*
	c. interest referred to in section 194LD (from the assessment year 2014-15)	Not available	—	Not available	5 per cent†	*Yes*
115BBA(1) (*a*)**	The following income of non-resident sportsman who is a foreign citizen					
	i. participation in India in any game (other than a game the winnings wherefrom are taxable under section 115BB) or sports; or	Not available	—	Not available	20 per cent†	*Note 1*
	ii. advertisement; or	Not available	—	Not available	20 per cent†	*Note 1*

*For notified institutions, *see Taxmann's Direct Taxes Circulars*, Vol. 2, 2009 edn.

†*Plus* surcharge and health and education cess.

**Payments made to the umpires of match referees do not come within the purview of section 115BBA because the umpires and match referees are neither sportsmen nor are they non-resident sports associations or institutions so as to attract the provisions contained in section 115BBA—*Indcom* v. *CIT* [2011] 200 Taxman 40 (Cal.).

(1)	(2)	(3)	(4)	(5)	(6)	(7)
	iii. Contribution of article relating to any game or sport in India in newspapers, magazines or journals	Not available	—	Not available	20 per cent†	*Note 1*
115BBA(1) (*b*)	Any amount guaranteed to be paid or payable to a non-resident sports association or institution in relation to any game (not being a game referred to in section 115BB) or sports played in India	Not available	—	Not available	20 per cent†	*Note 1*
115BBA(1) (*c*)	Income of a non-resident foreign citizen entertainer	Not available	—	Not available	20 per cent†	*Note 1*
115D	The following incomes of a non-resident Indian or a person of Indian origin :					
	a. investment income from foreign exchange assets	No deduction under any provision	—	Not available	20 per cent†	*Note 1*
	b. long-term capital gain on transfer of foreign exchange assets	—	First proviso to section 48 is applicable but not the second proviso	Not available	10 per cent†	*Note 1*

Note 1 : It is not necessary for an assessee referred to in section 115A(1), 115AC(1), 115BBA or 115D to furnish his return of income under section 139(1) if—

a. his income in respect of which he is assessable under the Act during the previous year consisted only of income referred to in section 115A(1)(*a*) or 115AC(1)(*a*) or 115BBA or section 115D; and

b. the tax deductible at source under the Act has been deducted from such income.

†*Plus* surcharge and health and education cess.

R-10

Withholding Tax Rates

[Tax rates applicable in India under ADT Agreement]

	Dividend [not being covered by section 115-O]		*Interest*		*Royalty*		*Fees for technical service*	
	Right of State to tax	*Tax rate*	*Right of State to tax*	*Tax rate*	*Right of State to tax*	*Tax rate*	*Right of State to tax*	*Tax rate*
Albania	Both	10%	Both	10%	Both	10%	Both	10%
Armenia	Both	10%	Both	10%	Both	10%	Both	10%
Australia	Both	15%	Both	15%	Both	[Note 3]	Both	[Note 3]
Austria	Both	10%	Both	10%	Both	10%	Both	10%
Bangladesh	Both	10% (if at least 10% of the capital of the company paying the dividend is held by the recipient)	Both	10% [Note 2]	Both	10%	No separate provision	
Belarus	Both	10% if paid to a company holding 25% shares; otherwise 15%	Both	10% [Note 2]	Both	15%	Both	15%
Belgium	Both	15%	Both	15% (10% if granted by a bank)	Both	10%	Both	10%
Bhutan	Both	10%	Both	10% [Note 2]	Both	10%	Both	10%
Botswana	Both	7.5% (if shareholder is a company and holds at least 25% shares in the investee-company); otherwise 10%	Both	10%	Both	10%	Both	10%
Brazil	Both	15%	Both	15% [Note 2]	Both	25% for use of trademark; 15% for others	No separate provision	
Bulgaria	Both	15%	Both	15% [Note 2]	Both	15% of royalty relating to literary, artistic, scientific works other than films or tapes used for radio or television broadcasting; 20% in other cases	Both	20%
Canada	Both	15% if at least 10% of the shares of the company paying the dividends is held by the recipient of dividend; 25% in other cases	Both	15% [Note 2]	Both	10%-20%	Both	10%-20%
China	Both	10%	Both	10% [Note 2]	Both	10%	Both	10%
Columbia	Both	5%	Both	10% [Note 2]	Both	10%	Both	10%

	Dividend [not being covered by section 115-O]		Interest		Royalty		Fees for technical service	
	Right of State to tax	Tax rate	Right of State to tax	Tax rate	Right of State to tax	Tax rate	Right of State to tax	Tax rate
Croatia	Both	15% (5% if shareholder is a company and holds at least 10% shares)	Both	10%	Both	10%	Both	10%
Cyprus	Both	10%	Both	10% [Note 2]	Both	10%	Both	10%
Czech Republic	Both	10%	Both	10% [Note 2]	Both	10%	Both	10%
Denmark	Both	15% if at least 25% of the shares of the company paying the dividend is held by the recipient; 25% in other cases	Both	10% if loan is granted by bank; 15% for others [Note 2]	Both	20%	Both	20%
Estonia	Both	10%	Both	10%	Both	10%	Both	10%
Ethiopia	Both	7.5%	Both	10%	Both	10%	Both	10%
Fiji	Both	10%	Both	10% [Note 2]	Both	10%	Both	10%
Finland	Both	10%	Both	10% [Note 2]	Both	10%	Both	10%
France	Both	10%	Both	10%	Both	10%	Both	10%
Georgia	Both	10%	Both	10%	Both	10%	Both	10%
Germany	Both	10%	Both	10% [Note 2]	Both	10%	Both	10%
Greece	Source	20%	Source	20%	Source	10%	No separate provision	
Hong Kong	Both	5%	Both	10% [Note 2]	Both	10%	Both	10%
Hungary	Both	10%	Both	10%	Both	10%	Both	10%
Indonesia	Both	10%	Both	10% [Note 2]	Both	10%	Both	10%
Iceland	Both	10%	Both	10%	Both	10%	Both	10%
Ireland	Both	10%-15%	Both	10% [Note 2]	Both	10%	Both	10%
Israel	Both	10%	Both	10% [Note 2]	Both	10%	Both	10%
Italy	Both	15% if at least 10% of the shares of the company paying dividend is beneficially owned by the recipient company; 25% in other cases	Both	15% [Note 2]	Both	20%	Both	20%
Japan	Both	10%	Both	10%	Both	10%	Both	10%
Jordan	Both	10%	Both	10% [Note 2]	Both	20%	Both	20%
Kazakhstan	Both	10%	Both	10% [Note 2]	Both	10%	Both	10%
Kenya	Both	10%	Both	10% [Note 2]	Both	10%	Both	10%
Korea	Both	15%	Both	10% [Note 2]	Both	10%	Both	10%
Kuwait	Both	10%	Both	10%	Both	10%	Both	10%
Kyrgyz Republic	Both	10%	Both	10%	Both	15%	Both	15%
Libyan Arab Jamahiriya	Source	20%	Source	20%	Source	30%	No separate provision	
Latvia	Both	10%	Both	10%	Both	10%	Both	10%

	Dividend [not being covered by section 115-O]		Interest		Royalty		Fees for technical service	
	Right of State to tax	Tax rate	Right of State to tax	Tax rate	Right of State to tax	Tax rate	Right of State to tax	Tax rate
Lithuania	Both	5%*, 15%	Both	10%	Both	10%	Both	10%
Luxembourg	Both	10%	Both	10%	Both	10%	Both	10%
Macedonia	Both	10%	Both	10%	Both	10%	Both	10%
Malaysia	Both	5%	Both	10%	Both	10%	Both	10%
Malta	Both	10%	Both	10% [Note 2]	Both	10%	Both	10%
Mangolia	Both	15%	Both	15% [Note 2]	Both	15%	Both	15%
Mauritius	Both	5% if at least 10% of the capital of the company paying the dividend is held by the recipient; 15% in other cases	Both	7.5%	Both	15%	Both	10%
Montenegro	Both	5% (in some cases 15%)	Both	10%	Both	10%	Both	10%
Myanmar	Both	5%	Both	10%	Both	10%	No separate provision	
Morocco	Both	10%	Both	10% [Note 2]	Both	10%	Both	10%
Mozambique	Both	7.5%	Both	10%	Both	10%	No separate provision	
Namibia	Both	10%	Both	10% [Note 2]	Both	10%	Both	10%
Nepal	Both	5%**, 10%	Both	10%	Both	15%	No separate provision	
Netherlands	Both	10%	Both	10% [Note 2]	Both	10%	Both	10%
New Zealand	Both	15%	Both	10% [Note 2]	Both	10%	Both	10%
Norway	Both	10%	Both	10%	Both	10%	Both	10%
Oman	Both	10% if at least 10% of shares are held by the recipient; 12.5% in other cases	Both	10% [Note 2]	Both	15%	Both	15%
Philippines	Both	15% if at least 10% of the shares of the company paying the dividend is held by the recipient; 20% in other cases	Both	10% if interest is received by a financial institution or insurance company; 15% in other cases	Both	15% if it is payable in pursuance of any collaboration agreement approved by the Government of India	—	—
Poland	Both	10%	Both	10%	Both	15%	Both	15%
Portuguese Republic	Both	10%-15%	Both	10%	Both	10%	Both	10%
Quatar	Both	5%-10%	Both	10% [Note 2]	Both	10%	Both	10%
Romania	Both	10%	Both	10%	Both	10%	Both	10%
Russian Federation	Both	10%	Both	10% [Note 2]	Both	10%	Both	10%
Saudi Arabia	Both	5%	Both	10%	Both	10%	No separate provision	

*If the beneficial owner is a company (other than a partnership) which holds directly at least 10 per cent of the capital of the company paying the dividends.

**5% if beneficial owner of shares is a company and it holds at least 10% shares.

	Dividend [not being covered by section 115-O]		Interest		Royalty		Fees for technical service	
	Right of State to tax	Tax rate	Right of State to tax	Tax rate	Right of State to tax	Tax rate	Right of State to tax	Tax rate
Serbia	Both	5% (if recipient is company and holds 25% shares) otherwise 15%	Both	10%	Both	10%	Both	10%
Singapore	Both	10% if at least 25% of the shares of the company paying the dividend is held by the recipient; 15% in other cases	Both	10% if loan is granted by a bank/similar institute including an insurance company; 15% for others	Both	10%	Both	10%
Slovenia	Both	5-15%	Both	10%	Both	10%	Both	10%
South Africa	Both	10%	Both	10% [Note 2]	Both	10%	Both	10%
Spain	Both	15%	Both	15% [Note 2]	Both	[Note 4]	Both	[Note 4]
Sri Lanka	Both	7.5%	Both	10%	Both	10%	Both	10%
Sudan	Both	10%	Both	10%	Both	10%	Both	10%
Sweden	Both	10%	Both	10% [Note 2]	Both	10%	Both	10%
Swiss	Both	10%	Both	10% [Note 5]	Both	10%	Both	10%
Syrian Arab Republic	Both	10% (5% if shareholder is a company holding at least 10% shares)	Both	10%	Both	10%	No separate provision	
Taipei	Both	12.5%	Both	10%	Both	10%	Both	10%
Tajikistan	Both	10% (5% if shareholder is a company and holds 25% shares)	Both	10%	Both	10%	No separate provision	
Tanzania	Both	5%*, 10%	Both	10%	Both	10%	No separate provision	
Thailand	Both	10%	Both	10% [*see* Note 2]	Both	10%	No separate provision	
Trinidad and Tobago	Both	10%	Both	10% [Note 2]	Both	10%	Both	10%
Turkey	Both	15%	Both	10% if recipient is bank, etc.; 15% in other cases [Note 2]	Both	15%	Both	15%
Turkmenistan	Both	10%	Both	10% [Note 2]	Both	10%	Both	10%
Uganda	Both	10%	Both	10%	Both	10%	Both	10%
Ukraine	Both	10%-15%	Both	10% [Note 2]	Both	10%	Both	10%
United Arab Emirates	Both	10%	Both	5% if loan is granted by a bank/similar financial institute; 12.5% for others	Both	10%	No separate provision	
United Arab Republic	Source	10%	Source	20%	Source	30%	No separate provision	

*5% if received by a company owning at least 25% share in the company paying.

	Dividend [not being covered by section 115-O]		Interest		Royalty		Fees for technical service	
	Right of State to tax	Tax rate	Right of State to tax	Tax rate	Right of State to tax	Tax rate	Right of State to tax	Tax rate
United Kingdom	Both	15%	Both	10% if interest is paid to a bank; 15% for others [Note 2]	Both	[Note 3]	Both	[Note 3]
United Mexican States	Both	10%	Both	10%	Both	10%	Both	10%
United States	Both	15% if at least 10% of the voting stock of the company paying the dividend is held by the recipient; 25% in other cases	Both	10% if loan is granted by a bank/similar institute including insurance company; 15% for others	Source	[Note 3]	Source	[Note 3]
Uruguay	Both	5%	Both	10%	Both	10%	Both	10%
Uzbekistan	Both	10%	Both	10% [Note 2]	Both	10%	Both	10%
Vietnam	Both	10%	Both	10% [Note 2]	Both	10%	Both	10%
Zambia	Both	5% if at least 25% of the shares of the company paying the dividend is held for a period of at least 6 months prior to the date of payment of the dividend; 15% in other cases	Both	10% [Note 2]	Both	10%	Both	10%

1. 10 per cent of the gross amount of the interest on loans made or guaranteed by a bank or other financial institution carrying on *bona fide* banking or financing business or by an enterprise which holds directly or indirectly at least 10 per cent of the capital of the company paying the interest.
2. Dividend/interest earned by the Government and certain institutions like the Reserve Bank of India is exempt from taxation in the country of source.
3. Royalties and fees for technical services would be taxable in the country of source at the following rates :
   a. 10 per cent in case of rental of equipment and services provided along with know-how and technical services ;
   b. any other case—
      i. during first five years of the agreement[6]—
         - 15 per cent if the payer is Government or specified organisation;
         - 20 per cent in other cases;
      ii. subsequent years, 15% in all cases.

   Income of Government and certain institutions will be exempt from taxation in the country of source.
4. Royalties and fees for technical services would be taxable in the country of source at the following rates :
   a. 10 per cent in case of royalties relating to the payments for the use of, or the right to use, industrial, commercial or scientific equipment;
   b. 20 per cent in case of fees for technical services and other royalties.
5. 10 per cent of the gross amount of the interest on loans made or guaranteed by a bank or other financial institution carrying on *bona fide* banking or financing business or by an enterprise which holds directly or indirectly at least 20 per cent of the capital of the company paying the interest.
6. As the five-year time-limit is now over, point (*i*) does not have any practical utility in the present context.

R-11

Period of limitation

Section	*Nature of compliance*	*Limitation of time*
(1)	*(2)*	*(3)*
2(*48*)	Filing application for getting zero coupon bonds notified	3 months before the date of issue of bonds (but not earlier than 24 months immediately before the first day of the financial year in which bonds are to be issued)
2(*48*)	Submission of chartered accountant's certificate in respect of zero coupon bonds specifying the amount invested in each year	Within 2 months from the end of each financial year
Section 9(1)(*i*), *Explanation 5*	Electronically submission of information in Form No. 49D pertaining to any transfer of the share of, or interest in, a foreign company/entity	Within 90 days from the end of the financial year in which any such transfer takes place (within 90 days of the transaction where the transaction has the effect of directly or indirectly transferring the rights of management in relation to Indian concern)
9A	Uploading a statement in Form No. 3CEK with digital signature pertaining to eligible investment trust	Within 90 days from the end of the previous year (applicable from the assessment year 2016-17)
9A	Submitting a report from a chartered accountant in Form No. 3CEJ relating to arm's length price in respect of the remuneration paid by an eligible investment fund to the fund manager	On or before the due date of submission of return of income under section 139(1)
10(*21*)	Furnishing (by a research association) a statement to accumulate/set apart income for future application by uploading Form No. 10	Before the expiry of time allowed for submission of return of income under section 139(1)
10A(8)	Furnishing declaration by industrial undertaking in any free trade zone for not availing tax holiday under section 10A	Before due date for furnishing return of income under section 139(1)
10B(8)	Furnishing declaration by assessee in respect of 100 per cent export-oriented undertaking for not availing tax holiday under section 10B	Before due date for furnishing return of income under section 139(1)
11(1), *Explanation*	Exercising option available under *Explanation* to section 11(1) by uploading Form No. 9A	Before the expiry of time allowed for submission of return of income under section 139(1) (applicable from the assessment year 2016-17)
11(2)	Furnishing a statement to accumulate/set apart income for future application by uploading Form No. 10	Before the expiry of time allowed for submission of return of income under section 139(1)
12A(1)(*ab*)	Filing application for re-registration in the case of a trust (registered under section 12A/12AA) which has adopted or undertaken modifications of the objects which do not conform to the conditions of registration	Within a period of 30 days from the date of such adoption or modifications of the objects (applicable from the assessment year 2018-19)
12AA	Passing order by Commissioner granting approval for registration of trust	Within 6 months from the end of the month in which application is received
35(1)(*iii*)	Notifying (or rejecting) a research association, etc., for the purpose of section 35(1)(*ii*)/(*iii*)	Within 12 months from the end of the month in which such application is received

(1)	(2)	(3)
35(2AA)	Filing annual audited accounts for each approved programme by the National Laboratory, etc.	October 31 each year
35(2AA)	Submitting copy of audited statement of accounts for approved programmes	Within 6 months of completion
35(2AA)	Passing order by the prescribed authority in Form 3CH	Within 2 months from receipt of application
35(2AB)	Electronically furnishing report by prescribed authority in relation to in-house research facility in Part A of Form No. 3CL	Within 120 days of grant of approval
35(2AB)	Submitting copy of audited accounts in Form No. 3CLA to the Secretary, Department of Scientific and Industrial Research	On or before due date of submission of return of income
35(2AB)	Electronically furnishing report by prescribed authority quantifying the expenditure incurred on in-house research and eligible for weighted deduction in Part B of Form No. 3CL	Within 120 days of submission of audit report
35ABA(3)	Withdrawing deduction claimed and granted to the assessee under section 35ABA, if subsequently there is a failure to comply with the provisions specified in said section	Within 4 years from the end of the previous year in which the failure to comply with the conditions referred to in section 35ABA takes place
44AB	Getting accounts audited by a chartered accountant and furnishing audit report to the Department	Due date of furnishing return of income under section 139(1)
90/90A/91	Submitting a statement in Form No. 67 and certificate/statement referred to in rule 128(8)(ii) pertaining to foreign tax credit	On or before the due date of submission of return of income under section 139(1)
92CA(3A)	Passing order by Transfer Pricing Officer under section 92CA(3)	At any time before 60 days prior to the date on which the period of limitation referred to in section 153/153B for passing assessment/reassessment/recomputation order, expires
92CD(1)	Submission of modified return in accordance with and limited to advance pricing agreement	Within 3 months from the end of the month in which advance price agreement was entered
92CD(5)(a)	Passing order under section 92CD(3) in respect of modified return (applicable from July 1, 2012)	Within 1 year from the end of the financial year in which modified return is furnished
115BA(4)	Exercising option under section 115BA(1) for lower tax rate by a domestic company	On or before the due date of submission of first return of income under section 139(1) (applicable from the assessment year 2017-18)
115BBF(3)	Exercising option[$] for taxation of royalty income in respect of patent developed and registered in India for any previous year in accordance with the provisions of section 115BBF(1)	On or before the due date of submission of return of income under section 139(1) (applicable from the assessment year 2017-18)
115JB(4)	Obtaining a certificate from a chartered accountant in Form No. 29B pertaining to computation of book profit in the case of a company	On or before the due date of submission of return of income under section 139(1)
115JC(3)	Obtaining a certificate from a chartered accountant in a prescribed form pertaining to computation of alternate minimum tax and adjusted total income in the case of a limited liability partnership	On or before the due date of submission of return of income under section 139(1)

[$]The assessee shall furnish Form No. 3CFA electronically under digital signature or through electronic verification code. For detailed discussion, log on to *taxmann.com/readyreckoner.aspx*.

(1)	*(2)*	*(3)*
115JG(3)(*iii*)	Recomputing income to withdraw the benefit, exemption or relief claimed under section 115JG(1) in case of failure to comply with the conditions of RBI scheme or notification of the Government (applicable from the assessment year 2013-14)	Within 4 years from the end of the previous year in which failure to comply with condition takes place
115-O(3)	Payment of dividend tax	Within 14 days from the date of (*a*) declaration (*b*) distribution, or (*c*) payment of any dividend (whichever is earlier).
115QA(3)	Payment of tax on distributed income for buy-back of unlisted shares (up to July 4, 2019) or **any shares** (on or after July 5, 2019).	Within 14 days from the date of payment of any consideration to shareholders on buy-back of unlisted shares (applicable from June 1, 2013)
115R(3)/115U	Payment of tax on distributed income	Within 14 days from the date of distribution or payment of such income, whichever is earlier.
115TA(2)	Payment of tax on distributed income by securitisation trusts	Within 14 days from the date of distribution or payment of income by securitisation trust to its investors.
115TA(3)	Furnishing statement of income distributed to investors by securitisation trust	September 15 immediately after the end of financial year (applicable only for the assessment year 2014-15)
115TCA(4)	Furnishing statement to PCIT/CIT of income paid or credited by a securitisation trust in Form No. 64E	November 30 immediately after the end of the financial year
115TCA(4)	Furnishing statement to investors of income distributed by a securitisation trust in Form No. 64F	June 30 immediately after the end of the financial year
115TD(1)	Transfer of all assets in case of dissolution of a charitable trust to another charitable trust to avoid tax on accreted income	Within 12 months from the end of the month in which dissolution takes place (applicable from June 1, 2016)
115TD(5)	Payment of tax on accreted income	Within 14 days from the date of merger or the date on which the order cancelling the registration is received or the date on which the order rejecting application for fresh registration is received, etc. (applicable from June 1, 2016)
115UA(4)	Furnishing statement by a business trust to the Principal Commissioner/Commissioner of income distributed	November 30 immediately after the end of the financial year
115UA(4)	Furnishing statement of income distributed by a business trust to unitholders	June 30 immediately after the end of the financial year
115UB(7)	Furnishing statement by an investment fund to the Principal Commissioner/Commissioner of income distributed by uploading Form No. 64D	November 30 immediately after the end of the financial year
115UB(7)	Furnishing statement in Form No. 64C of income distributed by an investment fund to its unitholders	June 30 immediately after the end of the financial year
115VP(2)	Making application for opting for tonnage tax scheme	Within initial period (*i.e.*, during October 1, 2004 and December 31, 2004) in the case of an existing company. Within 3 months in the case of newly incorporated company.
115VP(4)	Passing order granting or refusing the approval of the option of tonnage tax scheme	Within one month from the end of the month in which application is received
115VR	Renewal of tonnage tax scheme	Within one year from the end of the previous year in which the option ceases to have effect
115VY	Opting for tonnage tax scheme by amalgamated company	Within 3 months from the date of the approval of amalgamation
115WD*	Furnishing return of fringe benefits	September 30 of the assessment year in the case of a company and a person whose books are required to be audited and July 31 of the assessment year in other cases.

*Not applicable from the assessment year 2010-11 onwards.

(1)	(2)	(3)
115WE(1)*	Sending intimation under section 115WE	Within one year from the end of the financial year in which return is made.
115WE(2)*	Serving notice for hearing for regular assessment in the case of fringe benefits	Within 6 months from the end of the financial year in which return is submitted
115WH(3)*	Issuing notice where fringe benefits have escaped assessment	Within 6 years from the end of the assessment year
115WJ*	Payment of advance tax in respect of fringe benefit tax	Within the same time-limit as is given under section 211 in the case of advance payment of income-tax*
124(3)	Challenging Assessing Officer's jurisdiction	Where a return is made under section 139(1), before expiry of 1 month from the date on which a notice under section 142(1) or 143(2) is served or before the completion of assessment, whichever is earlier. Where no return is made before the expiry of time allowed by notice under section 142(1) or under section 148 for making the return or under section 144 for showing cause why best judgment assessment should not be made, whichever is earlier
131(3)	Retention of impounded books or documents by Assessing Officer/Assistant Director without obtaining approval of Chief Commissioner/Director General/ Commissioners/Director	Not more than 15 days (exclusive of holidays)
132(8)	Retaining books of account or other documents seized under section 132(1) or 132(1A) by authorised officer	Not more than 30 days from the date of assessment order under section 158BC(*c*)/153A
132(9A)	Handing over the seized assets by the Authorised Officer to the Assessing Officer having jurisdiction	Within a period of 60 days from the date on which the last authorisation for search was executed
132(9B)	Provisional attachment of property for protecting interest of revenue	Within 60 days from the date on which the last of the authorisations for search was executed (applicable from April 1, 2017)
132(9C)	Expiry of provisional attachment order made under section 132(9B)	After the expiry of 6 months from the date of such order (applicable from April 1, 2017)
132(9D)	Making a reference to valuation officer to estimate fair market value of property	Within 60 days from the date on which the last of the authorisations for search was executed (applicable from April 1, 2017)
132B(1)(*i*) first proviso	Making application for release of the seized asset	Within 30 days from the end of the month in which the asset was seized.
132B(1)(*i*), second proviso	Releasing seized asset after recovering existing tax liability	Within 120 days from the date on which last authorisation for search was executed
139(1)	Where the assessee is a company and it is required to furnish a report in Form No. 3CEB under section 92E pertaining to international transaction(s) [applicable for the assessment year 2011-12]	November 30 of the assessment year
139(1)	*A.* Where the assessee is required to furnish a report in Form No. 3CEB under section 92E pertaining to international transaction(s) [applicable from the assessment year 2012-13]	November 30 of the assessment year
	B. Where a report under section 92E is not required—	
	(*a*) Where the assessee is a company	September 30 of the assessment year

*Not applicable from the assessment year 2010-11 onwards.

(1)	(2)	(3)
	(b) Where the assessee is a non-corporate assessee—	
	(i) in the case where accounts are to be audited or where accounts of the firm in which assessee is a working partner are required to be audited	September 30 of the assessment year
	(ii) in the case of a co-operative society	September 30 of the assessment year
	(iii) in other cases	July 31 of the assessment year
139(3)	Filing of return of loss	Within the time allowed under section 139(1)
139(4)	Filing belated return of income	Within 1 year from the end of the relevant assessment year or before completion of assessment, whichever is earlier Before the end of the relevant assessment year or before the completion of assessment, whichever is earlier (applicable from the assessment year 2017-18)
139(4A)	Filing return by every person receiving of income in respect of which he is assessable as a representative assessee from property held under trust/legal obligation wholly or partly for charitable or religious purposes, etc., if total income exceeds maximum amount not chargeable to tax	Within the time allowed under section 139(1)
139(4B)	Filing of return by every political party, having taxable income, by its chief executive officer	Within the time allowed under section 139(1)
139(4C)	Filing of return by scientific research association; news agency; association, institution as is referred to in section 10(*23C*), etc.	Within the time allowed under section 139(1)
139(5)	Revising return submitted under section 139(1)/142(1)/(with effect from the assessment year 2017-18) 139(4)	Within 1 year from the end of the relevant assessment year or before the completion of assessment, whichever is earlier (applicable up to the assessment year 2017-18) Within the relevant assessment year or before the completion of assessment, whichever is earlier (applicable from the assessment year 2018-19)
139(9)	Rectifying defect in return of income	Within 15 days from date of intimation by Assessing Officer or extended time
139A	Filing application for allotment of permanent account number	On or before June 30 of the assessment year in some cases
139A(5)	Uploading half yearly statement in Form No. 61 containing particulars of declarations received in Form No. 60 during half year ending on September 30 and March 31	Within one month from the half year ending on September 30 and March 31
140A(1)	(i) Payment of income-tax on self-assessment	Before furnishing return of income
	(ii) Payment of interest on tax due for filing belated return or default or delay in payment of advance tax	
142A(6)	Sending report by the Valuation Officer to the Assessing Officer	Within 6 months from the end of the month in which a reference is made by the Assessing Officer under section 142A(1)
143(1)(a), second proviso	Sending objection in response to intimation for adjustments under section 143(1)(a)	Within 30 days of issue of such intimation (applicable from the assessment year 2017-18)
143(1)	Sending intimation under section 143(1)	Before expiry of 1 year from the end of the financial year in which the return is made
143(2)	Serving notice for hearing for regular assessment	6 months from the end of the financial year in which return is submitted

(1)	(2)	(3)
144BA(2)	Furnishing objection by an assessee to the notice of invoking GAAR provisions by the Commissioner (applicable from April 1, 2016)	Within such period (but not exceeding 60 days) as specified in the notice
144BA(13)	Issuing direction by Approving Penal under section 144BA(6) in respect of the declaration of an agreement as an impermissible avoidance arrangement under Chapter X-A (applicable from April 1, 2016)	Within 6 months from the end of the month in which the reference is received from the Commissioner
144C(2)	Filing acceptance of variation to the Assessing Officer or filing objection with Dispute Resolution Panel and the Assessing Officer	Within 30 days of the receipt of draft order
144C(4)	Passing assessment order under section 144C(3)	Within one month from the end of the month in which acceptance is received from the assessee or the period of filing objection expires
144C(12)	Issuing direction to the Assessing Officer by the Dispute Resolution Panel	Within 9 months from the end of the month in which the draft order is forwarded to the eligible assessee
144C(13)	Passing assessment order in conformity with the directions issued by the Dispute Resolution Panel	Within one month from the end of the month in which such direction is received
147	Reassessment where assessment has been made under section 143(3) or 147	Within 4 years from the end of relevant assessment year [unless escapement of income is because of assessee's failure to file return under section 139 or in pursuance of notice under section 142(1) or 148 or to disclose fully and truly all material facts or unless escapement of income is in relation to any asset located outside India]
149(1)	Issuing notice under section 148 if the escaped income—	
	(*i*) is less than Rs. 1,00,000	Within 4 years from end of the relevant assessment year
	(*ii*) is Rs. 1,00,000 or more	Within 6 years from end of the relevant assessment year
	(*iii*) is in relation to any asset (including financial interest in any entity) located outside India	Within 16 years from end of the relevant assessment year
149(3)	Issuing notice under section 148 to person who has been treated as agent of non-resident under section 163	Within 6 years from end of the relevant assessment year
150	Issuing notice under section 148 for assessment/reassessment/re-computation pursuant to any finding direction in an order passed (*i*) by any authority in any proceeding under Income-tax Act in appeal/reference/revision (*ii*) by a court in any proceeding under any other law	No time-limit [*see* also section 150(2)]
153(1)	Passing assessment order under section 143 or 144 or 115WE or 115WF	Within 2 years† from end of the assessment year in which income was first assessable (up to May 31, 2016)
153(2)	Making assessment/reassessment, etc., under section 147	Within 1 year‡ from the end of the financial year in which notice under section 148 is served (up to May 31, 2016)

†However, if a reference is made to Transfer Pricing Officer (TPO), the assessment can be completed by the Assessing Officer within 36 months from the end of the assessment year.

‡ If notice for reassessment under section 148 is served on or after April 1, 2010 and during the course of reassessment or proceedings for fresh assessment, a reference is made to TPO, the assessment can be completed by the Assessing Officer within 2 years from the end of the assessment year.

(1)	(2)	(3)	
153(2A)	Making assessment order in pursuance of order under section 250, 254, 263 or 264 setting aside or cancelling assessment	Within 1 year** from end of the financial year in which order under section 250/254 is received by Chief Commissioner/ Commissioner or an order under section 263/264 is passed by Chief Commissioner or Commissioner (up to May 31, 2016)	
153(4)	Making assessment/reassessment relating to any assessment year which has been revised under section 153A(2)	Within one year from the end of the month of revival or period given under section 153 or 153B(1), whichever is later (up to May 31, 2016)	
153(1)	Passing assessment order under section 143 or 144	*Time-limit applicable from June 1, 2016*	
		Assessment year	*Time-limit (to be determined from the end of the assessment year in which income was first assessable)*
		AY 2017-18 (or earlier)	21 months††
		AY 2018-19	18 months††
		AY 2019-20 (or later)	12 months††
153(2)	Making assessment/reassessment, etc., under section 147	*Time-limit applicable from June 1, 2016*	
		Date of issue of notice under section 148	*Time-limit (to be determined from the end of the financial year in which notice under section 148 is served)*
		Before April 1, 2019	9 months††
		On or after April 1, 2019	12 months††
153(3)	Making an order of fresh assessment in pursuance of an order under section 254/263/264, setting aside or cancelling an assessment	*Time-limit applicable from June 1, 2016*	
		Date when order under section 254 is received by Principal CCIT/ CCIT/Principal CIT/CIT or date when order under section 263/264 is passed by Principal CIT/CIT	*Time-limit (to be determined from the end of the financial year in which order under section 254 is received or order under section 263/264 is passed by the concerned authority mentioned in the earlier column)*
		Before April 1, 2019	9 months††
		On or after April 1, 2019	12 months††
153(5)	Giving effect to an order under section 250/254/260/262/263/264 by Assessing Officer, wholly or partly, otherwise than making a fresh assessment/re-assessment	Within a period of 3 months‡‡ from the end of the month in which order under section 250/254/260/262 is received by the Principal Chief CIT/Chief CIT/Principal CIT/CIT, as the case may be, the order under section 263/264 is passed by the Principal CIT/CIT (applicable from June 1, 2016)#	
153(5), second proviso	Where an order under section 250/ 254/260/262/263/264 requires verification of any issue by way of submission of any document by the assessee or any other person or where an opportunity of being heard is to be provided to the assessee	Time-limit of section 153(3) will apply (with effect from June 1, 2016)	

** If order under section 254 is received by the Commissioner on or after April 1, 2010 or where an order under section 263 or 264 is passed by the Commissioner on or after April 1, 2010 and during the course of reassessment or proceedings for fresh assessment, a reference is made to TPO, the assessment can be completed by the Assessing Officer within 2 years from the end of the assessment year.

‡‡ May be extended for an additional period of 6 months by Principal CIT/CIT on receipt of written request from Assessing Officer.

However, pending assessment as on June 1, 2016, the time limit for passing the relevant order is March 31, 2017.

††Where a reference is made under section 92CA(1) to TPO during assessment/reassessment proceedings, the period available for assessment/re-assessment shall be extended by 12 months.

<table>
<tr><th>(1)</th><th>(2)</th><th colspan="3">(3)</th></tr>
<tr><td>153(6)(i)</td><td>Making an order of assessment/reassessment/recomputation on assessee (or any person) in consequence of or to give effect to any finding/direction contained in an order under section 250/254/260/262/263/264 or an order of any court in a proceeding (not by way of appeal/reference under the Act)</td><td colspan="3">Within 12 months from the end of the month in which such order is received/passed by Principal CIT/CIT (applicable from June 1, 2016)#</td></tr>
<tr><td>153(6)(ii)</td><td>Making an order of on the partner of a firm in consequence of the assessment made on the firm under section 147</td><td colspan="3">Within 12 months from the end of the month in which the assessment order in the case of firm is passed (applicable from June 1, 2016)#</td></tr>
<tr><td>153B</td><td>Passing assessment order under section 153A</td><td colspan="3">Within a period of 2 years[£] from end of the financial year in which the last of the authorisations for search/requisition under section 132/132A was executed. This period cannot be less than 1 year from the end of the financial year in which books of account, etc., are handed over under section 153C to the concerned Assessing Officer (up to May 31, 2016)</td></tr>
<tr><td rowspan="5">153B</td><td rowspan="5">Passing assessment order under section 153A</td><td colspan="3">Time-limit applicable from June 1, 2016</td></tr>
<tr><td>Date when last of authorisations under section 132/ 132A was executed</td><td>Time-limit (to be determined from the end of the financial year in which last of the authorisations under section 132/132A was executed)</td><td>Alternate time-limit for action under section 153C (to be determined from the end of the financial year in which books of account, etc., are handed over under section 153C to the concerned AO)</td></tr>
<tr><td>Prior to April 1, 2018</td><td>21 months††</td><td>9 months††</td></tr>
<tr><td>During FY 2018-19</td><td>18 months††</td><td>12 months††</td></tr>
<tr><td>On or after April 1, 2019</td><td>12 months††</td><td>12 months††</td></tr>
<tr><td>154(1)/(7)</td><td>Rectifying any mistake apparent from record by income-tax authority referred to in section 116</td><td colspan="3">Within 4 years from end of the financial year in which order sought to be amended is passed or within 6 months from the end of the month in which rectification application is received by the income-tax authority, whichever is earlier</td></tr>
<tr><td>155(1)/(2)</td><td>Amending assessment order of partner of firm (for the assessment year 1992-93 or earlier years) or member of AOP/BOI for inclusion of correct share from firm/AOP/BOI</td><td colspan="3">Within 4 years from end of the financial year in which final order is passed in case of firm/AOP/BOI</td></tr>
<tr><td>155(1A)</td><td>Amending assessment order of a partner of firm</td><td colspan="3">Within 4 years from end of the financial year in which final order is passed in the case of the firm</td></tr>
<tr><td>155(4)</td><td>Recomputing total income for succeeding year(s) in respect of loss or depreciation recomputed under section 147</td><td colspan="3">Within 4 years from end of the financial year in which order under section 147 is passed</td></tr>
</table>

£ Where the last of the authorization for search under section 132/132A was executed on or after April 1, 2009 and during the course of assessment/reassessment proceedings (or proceeding referred to in section 153C), a reference is made to TPO, the assessment can be completed by the Assessing Officer within 3 years from the end of the assessment year or 24 months from the end of the financial year in which books of account or documents or assets seized or requisitioned are handed over under section 153C to the Assessing Officer having jurisdiction over such other person, whichever is later.

††Where a reference is made under section 92CA(1) to TPO during assessment/reassessment proceedings, the period available for assessment/re-assessment shall be extended by 12 months.

However, pending assessment as on June 1, 2016, the time limit for passing the relevant order is March 31, 2017.

(1)	(2)	(3)
155(4A)	Withdrawing investment allowance allowed under section 32A if—	
	(a) asset is sold within 8 years	Within 4 years from end of previous year in which sale took place
	(b) investment allowance reserve is not utilised for acquiring new asset within 10 years	Within 4 years from end of said 10 years
	(c) reserve is misutilised before expiry of 10 years	Within 4 years from end of previous year in which amount is so misutilised
155(5)	Withdrawing development rebate under section 33 if asset is sold within 8 years or reserve is misutilised	Within 4 years from end of previous year in which sale took place or reserve is so misutilised
155(5A)	Withdrawing development allowance under section 33A if land is sold within 8 years or reserve is misutilised	Within 4 years from end of previous year in which sale took place or reserve is so misutilised
155(7)	Recomputing distributable income and additional tax liability under section 104	Within 4 years from end of financial year in which final order was passed
155(7B)	Recomputing deemed capital gains under section 47A	Within 4 years from end of previous year in which capital asset is converted into stock-in-trade or in which parent company/holding company ceases to have 100 per cent shareholding in subsidiary company
155(10A)	Amending order of assessment so as to exclude unadjusted amount of capital gain on long-term capital asset not chargeable under section 54E(1)	Within 4 years from end of financial year in which original assessment is made
155(11)	Amending order of assessment so as to exclude unadjusted amount of capital gain not chargeable by virtue of extended period given under section 54H	Within 4 years from the end of the financial year in which compensation is received by the assessee
155(13)	Amending assessment order so as to allow deduction under section 80HHB, 80HHC, 80HHD, 80HHE, 80-O, 80R, 80RR or 80RRA	Within 4 years from the end of the previous year in which income is received in convertible foreign exchange in India
155(14)	Amending order of assessment so as to give tax credit in respect of tax deducted (or from the assessment year 2007-08 tax collected) at source	Within 2 years from the end of assessment year TDS or TCS certificate may be submitted, recomputation will be completed by the Assessing Officer within time-limit given by section 154
155(14A)	Amending assessment order or intimation or deemed intimation so as to give foreign tax credit under section 90/90A/91 (earlier it was not given because the quantum of foreign tax was disputed)	Within 6 months from the end of the month in which dispute is settled (applicable from the April 1, 2018)
155(15)	Amending order of assessment so as to compute capital gains by taking the full value of the consideration to be the value as is revised in appeal, revision or reference	Within 4 years from the end of the previous year in which order revising the value was passed in the appeal, revision or reference.
155(16)	Amending order of assessment so as to compute capital gain by taking into consideration compensation as ordered by the Court, Tribunal or authority	Within 4 years from the end of the previous year in which the order reducing compensation was passed by the Court/Tribunal/Other authority.
155(17)	Amending order of assessment so as to recalculate amount deductible under section 80RRB in case the name of the assessee has been excluded from patents register	Within 4 years from the end of the previous year in which the order of the Controller/High Court was passed
158AA(1)	Filing application by the Assessing Officer to Appellate Tribunal stating that an appeal on the question of law arising in the relevant case may be filed when the decision on the question of law becomes final in the other case	Within 60 days from the date of receipt of order of the Commissioner (Appeals) [applicable from June 1, 2015]

(1)	(2)	(3)
158AA(4)	Filing appeal to the Appellate Tribunal when order of Commissioner (Appeals) referred to in section 158AA(1) is not in conformity with the final decision of Supreme Court on the question of law in the other case	Within 60 days from the date on which the order of Supreme Court in the other case is communicated to the Commissioner/Principal Commissioner [applicable from June 1, 2015]
158BE(1)	Passing order under section 158BC	Within 1 year from the end of the month in which last of the authorisation for search was executed.
158BE(2)	Passing order of block assessment in the cases of other person	Within 1 year from the end of the month in which notice under Chapter XIV-B was served
160(1), *Explanation 1*	Filing declaration by trustee(s) for converting 'oral trust' into 'trust declared by a duly executed instrument in writing'	Within 3 months from date of declaration of 'oral trust'
172(3)	Return of full amount paid or payable to non-resident owner or charterer of ship towards passenger fares, freight, etc., to be furnished by master of ship to Assessing Officer	Before departure of ship from any port in India, or within 30 days thereafter if permitted by Assessing Officer
172(4A)	Passing assessment order under section 172(4) in the case of a non-resident engaged in shipping	Within 9 months from the end of the financial year in which return is furnished (up to December 31, 2008, in case return is furnished before April 1, 2007)
172(7)	Submission of claim by owner or charterers of ship that assessment be made and tax payable by him be determined in accordance with other provisions of the Act	Before expiry of assessment year relevant to previous year in which ship has departed from Indian port
176(3)	Giving notice of discontinuance of business/profession to Assessing Officer	Within 15 days of discontinuance
178(1)	Giving notice of appointment as liquidator to Assessing Officer	Within 30 days of appointment
178(2)	Notifying liquidator as to amount of tax payable by company	Within 3 months from date on which Assessing Officer receives notices of appointment of liquidator
197A(2)	Quarterly uploading of declarations received (in Form No. 15G/15H) by payer of income	Within 15 days from the end of first, second and third quarter and within 30 days from the end of fourth quarter†
200 (read with rule 30)	Paying tax deducted at source under sections 192 to 195	Within time-limit as prescribed under rule 30, *See* para 174
200(3)	Quarterly statement of TDS deposited	*See* para 174.3-1
200A(1)	Sending intimation to the deductor specifying the sum determined to be payable or the amount of refund due to him under section 200A(1)(*d*)	Within one year from the end of the financial year in which the statement under section 200 is filed (applicable from April 1, 2010)
201(3)	Passing an order deeming a person to be an assessee-in-default for failure to deduct the whole or any part of the tax from a person resident in India	• *In case statement is filed by the deductor under section 200* - Within 2 years* from the end of the financial year in which statement is filed under section 200 (applicable up to September 30, 2014) • *In case no such statement is filed* - Within 4 years* (6 years applicable from April 1, 2010) from the end of the financial year in which payment is made or credit is given (applicable from April 1, 2010 to September 30, 2014) • · *In case statement is filed or not filed* - Time-limit is as follows – - Within 7 years from the end of the financial year in which payment is made or credit is given (applicable during October 1, 2014 and August 31, 2019).

† Time-limit has been extended as follows – For the period October 1, 2015 to June 30, 2016 : October 31, 2016, for the period July 1, 2016 to September 30, 2016 : December 31, 2016.

*Order pertaining to the financial year 2007-08 (or earlier years) can be passed at any time up to March 31, 2011.

<table>
<tr><th>(1)</th><th colspan="2">(2)</th><th>(3)</th></tr>
<tr><td></td><td colspan="2"></td><td>- Within 7 years from the end of the financial year in which payment is made or credit is given or 2 years from the end of the financial year in which the correction statement is delivered [under proviso to section 200(3)], whichever is later (applicable with effect from September 1, 2019).</td></tr>
<tr><td>203(1)</td><td colspan="2">Certificate of tax deducted</td><td>• Salary TDS certificate in Form No. 16 along with Form No. 12BA - On or before May 31 after the end of financial year (to be issued annually).
• Non-salary TDS certificate in Form No. 16A - To be issued quarterly (for time-limit, see para 174.4-1).</td></tr>
<tr><td>203A</td><td colspan="2">Applying to Assessing Officer for allotment of Tax-deduction and collection Account Number</td><td>Within one month from end of month in which the tax was deducted or collected</td></tr>
<tr><td>206A</td><td colspan="2">Furnishing quarterly return in respect of payment of interest without TDS</td><td>July 31, October 31, January 31 and June 30 after the end of each quarter</td></tr>
<tr><td>206C(3)</td><td colspan="2">Payment of tax collected from the respective buyers of specified goods under section 206C(1) to the credit of Central Government or as the Board directs</td><td>See para 174.</td></tr>
<tr><td>206C(3)</td><td colspan="2">Submitting quarterly statement of TCS deposited</td><td>Within 15 days time after the end of each quarter on June 30, September 30, December 31 and within 45 days from the end of last quarter</td></tr>
<tr><td>206C(5)</td><td colspan="2">Person collecting tax under section 206C(1) from respective buyers to give them a certificate about the amount and rate of tax collected, etc.</td><td>On or before July 30 (first quarter), October 30 (second quarter), January 30 (third quarter) and May 30 (fourth quarter) (to be issued only quarterly)</td></tr>
<tr><td>206CB(1)</td><td colspan="2">Sending intimation to the collector specifying the sum determined to be payable or the amount of refund due to him under section 206CB(1)(d)</td><td>Within one year from the end of the financial year in which the statement under section 206C is filed (applicable from June 1, 2015)</td></tr>
<tr><td>211(1)</td><td colspan="2">Payment of advance tax in specified instalments (with effect from June 1, 2016) :</td><td></td></tr>
<tr><td></td><td>For any assessee (except an eligible assessee given in the next column)</td><td>An eligible assessee in respect of an eligible business or profession referred to in section 44AD or 44ADA</td><td></td></tr>
<tr><td></td><td>1. Up to 15 per cent</td><td>—</td><td>On or before June 15</td></tr>
<tr><td></td><td>2. Up to 45 per cent</td><td>—</td><td>On or before September 15</td></tr>
<tr><td></td><td>3. Up to 75 per cent</td><td>—</td><td>On or before December 15</td></tr>
<tr><td></td><td>4. Up to 100 per cent</td><td>1. Up to 100 per cent</td><td>On or before March 15</td></tr>
<tr><td>211(2)</td><td colspan="2">Payment of the appropriate part of whole amount of advance tax as demanded under section 210(3) and (4) after the due dates of instalments</td><td>On or before each date specified in section 211(1) falling after date of service of demand notice</td></tr>
<tr><td>220(1)</td><td colspan="2">Payment of amount other than advance tax in response to notice under section 156</td><td>Within 30 days of service of demand notice or within date extended on request or within shorter period specified in revenue's interest</td></tr>
<tr><td>220(2A)</td><td colspan="2">Order accepting/rejecting the application of assessee for waiver of interest payable under section 220(2)</td><td>Within 12 months from the end of the month in which the application is received (applicable from June 1, 2016)†</td></tr>
</table>

† Order pertaining to an application pending as on June 1, 2016 can be passed on or before May 31, 2017.

(1)	*(2)*	*(3)*
239(2)(*c*)/(*d*)	Making claim for refund	Within 1 year from last day of relevant assessment year‡ (applicable up to August 31, 2019)
245C(1)	Application for settlement of case to Settlement Commission	At any stage during the pendency of a case before the Assessing Officer
245C(1E)	Application for settlement before Settlement Commission under sub-section (1) where books of account, documents etc., have been seized	Not before 120 days of seizure
245D(1)	Rejecting/allowing the application for settlement	Within 7 days notice shall be issued to the applicant to justify admission of his application, within 14 days from the receipt of application the order pertaining to rejecting/allowing the application shall be made
245D(2B)	Calling report by the Settlement Commission from Commissioner	Within 30 days from the date of receipt of application
245D(2B)	Submission of report by the Commissioner to Settlement Commission	Within 30 days from the date of communication from the Settlement Commission
245D(2C)	Declaring application as invalid by the Settlement Commission	Within 15 days from the date of receipt of report from the Commissioner
245D(3)	Furnishing a report by the Commissioner to the Settlement Commission in the matters covered by the application	Within 90 days from the date of receipt of communication from the Settlement Commission
245D(4A)	Passing order of settlement	Within 12 months from the end of the month in which application was made (if an application is filed on or after June 1, 2007 but before June 1, 2010) or within 18 months from the end of the month in which application was made (if an application is filed on or after June 1, 2010)
245D(6B)	Amending any order passed by the Settlement Commission with a view to rectifying any mistake apparent from the record	Within 6 months from the date of passing order under section 245D(4) (applicable from June 1, 2011) or within the period of 6 months from the end of the month in which the application for rectification has been made by the Principal Commissioner or the Commissioner or the applicant, as the case may be (applicable from June 1, 2015)
245D(6B)	Application to Settlement Commission for rectification by Principal Commissioner, Commissioner or applicant	Within 6 months from the end of the month in which the order under section 245D(4) is passed by the Settlement Commission (applicable from June 1, 2015)
245D(7)	Completion of proceedings where settlement becomes void as provided in section 245D(6)	Within 2 years from the end of the financial year in which the settlement becomes void
245E, proviso	Reopening of completed proceedings by Settlement Commission if an application is made before June 1, 2007	Reopening of proceeding is not possible where period between end of assessment year to which proceeding relates and the date of application for settlement under section 245C exceeds 9 years
245Q(3)	Withdrawing an application for obtaining advance ruling	Within 30 days from the date of application
245R(6)	Giving advance ruling	Within 6 months from receipt of application
249(2)/(3)	Filing appeal to Commissioner (Appeals)—	
	(*a*) relating to tax deducted at source under section 195	Within 30 days from date of payment of tax or within extended time
	(*b*) relating to any assessment/penalty	Within 30 days from date of service of demand notice or within extended time.
	(*c*) in any other case	Within 30 days from date of communication of order or within extended time
253(3)/(3A)†	Filing appeal to Tribunal	Within 60 days [30 days in the case of an appeal against order under section 158BC(*c*)] from date on which order

† Section 253(3A) has been omitted with effect from June 1, 2016.

‡ For belated claim of refund, *see* Circular No. 9/2015[$], dated June 9, 2015.

[$]For Circular No. 9/2015, log on to *taxmann.com/readyreckoner.aspx*.

(1)	*(2)*	*(3)*
		sought to be appealed against is communicated or within extended time
253(4)/(5)	Filing memo of cross-objections to Tribunal	Within 30 days of receipt of notice of filing appeal or within extended time
254(2)	Rectification of apparent mistake by Tribunal	Within 4 years from the date of impugned order [or (with effect from June 1, 2016) 6 months from the end of the month in which the order was passed]
256(1)	(*i*) Filing application to Tribunal requiring it to refer to High Court any question of law	Within 60 days of service of Tribunal's order under section 254 or within extended period not exceeding 30 days
	(*ii*) Drawing up statement of case and referring it to High Court by Tribunal	Within 120 days of receipt of application
256(2)	Filing application to High Court if Tribunal refuses to state case	Within 6 months from date of service of notice of refusal to state case
256(3)	Application by assessee for claiming refund of fee after Tribunal's refusal to state case	Within 30 days from date of receipt of refusal notice
263(2)	Revising orders prejudicial to revenue by Commissioner	Within 2 years from end of financial year in which order sought to be revised was passed
263(3)	Revision by Commissioner of orders passed pursuant to any finding or direction by Tribunal, High Court or Supreme Court	No time-limit
264(2)	Revision of orders by Commissioner on his own motion (not prejudicial to assessee)	Within 1 year of order sought to be revised
264(3)	Filing revision petition to Commissioner (order not to be prejudicial to assessee)	Within 1 year from date of communication of order sought to be revised or date of his knowledge in respect thereof or within extended time
264(6)	Revision order by the Commissioner on an application made under section 264 after September 30, 1998	Within one year from the end of the financial year in which such application is made
270AA(2)	Application to the Assessing Officer to grant immunity for imposition of penalty under section 270A and initiation of proceedings under section 276C/276CC	Within one month from the end of the month in which such order is received (applicable from April 1, 2017)
270AA(4)	Passing an order by the Assessing Officer granting immunity from passing of penalty, etc., under section 270AA(3)	Within one month from the end of the month in which application under section 270AA(1) is received (applicable from April 1, 2017)
271GB(4)(*b*)	Failure to inform the prescribed authority and furnish correct report to avoid penalty under section 271GB(4)	Within 15 days of discovery of inaccuracy (applicable from the assessment year 2017-18)
273A(4A)	Passing order under section 273A(4) accepting/rejecting assessee's application (in full or part) to reduce or waive penalty	Within 12 months from the end of the month in which such application is received by Principal CIT/CIT (such order can be passed on or before May 31, 2017 in case of application pending as on June 1, 2016)
273AA(3A)	Passing order by Principal CIT/CIT accepting/rejecting assessee's application (in full or part) to grant immunity from penalty	Within 12 months from the end of the month in which such application is received by Principal CIT/CIT (such order can be passed on or before May 31, 2017 in case of application pending as on June 1, 2016)
275	Imposing penalties under Chapter XXI:	
	(*a*) in a case where appeal is filed to Commissioner (Appeals) [and Commissioner (Appeals) passes the order on or after June 1, 2003]	Before the expiry of financial year in which proceedings which give rise to penalty proceedings are completed, or within 12 months from end of the financial year in which the order of Commissioner (Appeals) is received by the Chief Commissioner/Commissioner, whichever period expires later

(1)	(2)	(3)
	(*b*) in a case where appeal is filed to Commissioner (Appeals) [and Commissioner (Appeals) passes the order before June 1, 2003] or in a case where appeal is filed to Tribunal	Before the expiry of financial year in which proceedings which give rise to penalty proceedings are completed, or within 6 months from the end of the month in which the order of Commissioner (Appeals)/Tribunal is received by the Chief Commissioner/Commissioner, whichever period expires later
	(*c*) in a case where relevant assessment or other order is subject-matter of revision under section 263 or 264	Within 6 months from the end of month in which revision order is passed.
	(*d*) in any other case	Before expiry of financial year in which proceedings (in course of which action for imposition of penalty has been initiated) are completed, or within 6 months from end of month in which penalty action is initiated, whichever is later
281B(4)	Submitting valuation report by the Valuation Officer estimating fair market value of property provisionally attached	Within 30 days from the date of receipt of such reference (applicable from June 1, 2016)
281B(5)	Revoking provisional attachment order under section 281B(3)	Within 45 days of receipt of guarantee [where reference is made to Valuation Officer under section 281B(4)] or within 15 days of receipt of guarantee [in any other case] (applicable from June 1, 2016)
281B(7)	Invoking bank guarantee if assessee fails to renew guarantee referred to in section 281B(3)	Within 15 days before the expiry of guarantee referred to in section 281B(3) (applicable from June 1, 2016)
285	Submission of a prescribed statement by a non-resident having liaison office in India in Form No. 49C	May 30 after the end of the financial year (applicable from June 1, 2011)
285B	Furnishing of statement by film producers	Within 30 days from end of financial year or within 30 days from date of completion of film, whichever is earlier
285BA	Furnishing annual information return (AIR)	After the end of each financial year but within the time given below - - August 31 (for transactions registered/recorded during the financial year 2015-16 or any earlier year) - May 31 (for transactions registered/recorded during the financial year 2016-17 or any subsequent year)
285BA(1)(*k*)	Annual statement of reportable account by reporting financial institution	On or before May 31 after the expiry of each calendar year (statement pertaining to calendar year 2014 may be furnished by the August 31, 2015)
286(2)	Furnishing a report for every reporting accounting year by a parent entity or the alternate reporting entity, resident in India, to prescribed authority in respect of the international group of which it is a constituent	Within 12 months from the end of said reporting accounting year (applicable from the assessment year 2017-18)
286(4)	Furnishing a report for a constituent entity of an international group (resident in India) [other than an entity covered under section 286(2)] for a reporting accounting year, if the parent entity is not obliged to file report under section 286(2) or the parent entity is resident of a country with which India does not have an agreement providing for exchange of the report, etc.	Within 12 months from the end of the reporting accounting year† [where, however, the parent entity of the constituent entity is resident of a country (where, there has been a "systematic failure" of the country), the period for submission of report shall be 6 months from the end of the month in which systematic failure has been intimated]

† Circular No. 9/2018[$] has extended the period for furnishing of the report till March 31, 2019 in respect of reporting accounting years ending up to February 28, 2018. Circular No. 7/2019[$] has extended the period till April 30, 2019 (in a few cases), in respect of reporting accounting years ending up to April 29, 2018.

[$] For Circular No. 9/2018 and Circular No. 7/2019, log on to taxmann.com/readyreckoner.aspx.

(1)	*(2)*	*(3)*
286(6)	Producing information/document to the prescribed authority for the purpose of determining accuracy of report furnished by any reporting entity	Within 30 days of receipt of notice (prescribed authority on an application made by reporting entity may extend the period of 30 days by further period not exceeding 30 days) (applicable from the assessment year 2017-18)
Schedule II Part I, Rule 3	Execution of certificate drawn up	Not before 15 days after date of service of notice under rule 2
Schedule II Part I, Rule 14	Filing of application by officer holding the sale relating to recovery from defaulting purchasers	Within 15 days from date of resale
Schedule II Part II, Rule 25(5)	Attachment of growing crop which does not admit of being stored	Not less than 20 days before it is likely to be fit to be cut or gathered
Schedule II Part II, Rule 40	Sale of movable property (other than property, subject to speedy and natural decay and property in relation to which expense of keeping it in custody is likely to exceed its value)	Not before 15 days from date on which copy of sale proclamation was affixed in TRO's office
Schedule II Part III, Rule 57	Payment of full amount of purchase money on sale of immovable property	Within 15 days from date of sale
Schedule II Part III, Rule 60	Application to set aside sale of immovable property on deposit of specified sum	Within 30 days from date of sale
Schedule II Part III, Rule 61	Application to set aside sale of immovable property on ground of non-service of notice or irregularity	Within 30 days from date of sale
Schedule II Part III, Rule 62	Application for setting aside sale on ground that defaulter had no saleable interest	Within 30 days from date of sale
Schedule II Part III, Rule 68B	Sale of attached immovable property	- *Up to August 31, 2019* - Within 3 years (4 years in some cases as specified in the first proviso) from the end of the financial year in which order giving rise to a demand becomes final - *From September 1, 2019* - Within 7 years (8 years in some cases as specified in the first proviso) from the end of the financial year in which order giving rise to a demand becomes final (Board may extend, for reasons to be recorded in writing, the aforesaid period of 7 years for a further period not exceeding 3 years)
Schedule IV Part A, Rule 13	Appeal by employer against order of Chief Commissioner or Commissioner refusing to recognise or withdrawing recognition from a provident fund	Within 60 days of such order
Schedule IV Part B, Rule 8	Appeal by employer against order of Chief Commissioner or Commissioner refusing to approve or withdrawing approval granted to a superannuation fund	Within 60 days of such order
Schedule IV Part C, Rule 8	Appeal by employer against order of Chief Commissioner or Commissioner refusing to approve or withdrawing approval granted to a gratuity fund	Within 60 days of such order

(1)	*(2)*	*(3)*
Securities Transaction Tax [Finance (No. 2) Act, 2004]		
101	Filing of return by recognised stock exchange or mutual fund	On or before June 30 after the end of financial year
102	Making assessment	Within 2 years from the end of relevant financial year
103	Rectification of mistake	Within one year from the end of the financial year in which the order sought to be amended was passed
110	Filing appeal to Commissioner (Appeals)	Within 30 days from the date of receipt of order of the AO
111	Filing appeal to Tribunal	Within 60 days from the date on which the order sought to be appealed is communicated.

R-12

Time-limit for issue of notice during 2019-20 under section 148

Assessment year[6]	*Minimum income which has been escaped from assessment*	
	If original assessment is completed under section 143(3) or 147 Rs.	*If original assessment is completed under any other section Rs.*
2003-04 to 2012-13[7]	—[2]	—[4]
2013-14[5]	1,00,000[2]	1,00,000[4]
2014-15	1,00,000[2]	1,00,000[4]
2015-16	Any[1]	Any[3]
2016-17	Any[1]	Any[3]
2017-18	Any[1]	Any[3]
2018-19	Any[1]	Any[3]

Notes :

1. Any Assessing Officer who is not below the rank of Assistant Commissioner or Deputy Commissioner can issue notice. An Assessing Officer who is below the rank of Assistant Commissioner or Deputy Commissioner can issue notice only if the Joint Commissioner (or Additional Commissioner) is satisfied on the reasons recorded by such Assessing Officer that it is a fit case for issue of such notice. From June 1, 2015, no notice shall be issued by an Assessing Officer (who is below the rank of Joint Commissioner) unless the Joint Commissioner is satisfied, on the reasons recorded by such Assessing Officer, that it is a fit case for the issue of such notice.

2. Notice mentioned in point (*1*) (*supra*) can be issued only if the Chief Commissioner/Commissioner is satisfied on the reasons recorded by the Assessing Officer that it is a fit case for issue of notice. From June 1, 2015, no notice shall be issued by an Assessing Officer unless the Principal Chief Commissioner or Chief Commissioner or Principal Commissioner or Commissioner is satisfied, on the reasons recorded by the Assessing Officer, that it is a fit case for the issue of such notice.

3. Notice can be issued by the Assessing Officer. From June 1, 2015, no notice shall be issued by an Assessing Officer (who is below the rank of Joint Commissioner) unless the Joint Commissioner is satisfied, on the reasons recorded by such Assessing Officer, that it is a fit case for the issue of such notice.

4. No notice can be issued by the Assessing Officer who is below the rank of Joint Commissioner (or Additional Commissioner) unless the Joint Commissioner (or Additional Commissioner) is satisfied that on the reason recorded by Assessing Officer that it is a fit case for issue of such notice. From June 1, 2015, no notice shall be issued by an Assessing Officer unless the Principal Chief Commissioner or Chief Commissioner or Principal Commissioner or Commissioner is satisfied, on the reasons recorded by the Assessing Officer, that it is a fit case for the issue of such notice.

5. If the person on whom notice under section 148 is to be served during the financial year 2019-20 is a person treated as an agent of a non-resident (under section 163), the notice shall not be issued for assessment years prior to the assessment year 2013-14.

6. During the financial year 2019-20, notice cannot be issued for any assessment year, prior to the assessment year 2013-14 unless escapement of income is in relation to any asset located outside India [*see* also two exceptions given by section 150 and the proviso to section 147].

7. During the financial year 2019-20, notice can be issued for assessment years 2003-04 to 2012-13, only if escapement of income is in relation to any asset located outside India.

R-13

Provisions of sections 54, 54B, 54D, 54EC, 54F, 54G, 54GA and 54H

Different questions	*Section 54*	*Section 54B*	*Section 54D*	*Section 54EC*	*Section 54F*	*Section 54G*	*Section 54GA*
1. Who can claim exemption under these sections	Individual/ Hindu undivided family	Individual/ Hindu undivided family	Any person	Any person	Individual/ Hindu undivided family	Any person	Any person
2. Which capital asset — short-term or long-term is eligible for exemption	Long-term	Short-term/ long-term	Short-term/ long-term	Long-term	Long-term	Short-term/ long-term	Short-term/ long-term
3. Which specific asset is eligible for exemption	A residential house property	Agricultural land if it was used by the individual or his parents for agricultural purposes for at least 2 years immediately prior to transfer	Land or building forming part of an industrial undertaking which is compulsorily acquired by the Government and which is used for 2 years for industrial purposes prior to its acquisition	Any long-term capital asset (being land or building or both)	Any long-term capital asset (other than a residential house property) provided on the date of transfer the taxpayer does not own more than one residential house property[1] (except the new house as stated in *4 infra*).	Land, building, plant or machinery in order to shift an industrial undertaking from urban area to rural area	Land, building, plant or machinery in order to shift an industrial undertaking from urban area to any special economic zone
4. Which asset the taxpayer should acquire to get the benefit of exemption	Only 1† residential house in India (prior to the assessment year 2015-16; a residential house property)	Agricultural land (may be in rural area or urban area)	Land or building for industrial purposes	Bonds of National Highways Authority of India or Rural Electrification Corpn. or notified bonds (investment cannot exceed Rs. 50 lakh in current year and next year)	Only 1 residential house in India (prior to the assessment year 2015-16 : A residential house property)	Land, building, plant or machinery in order to shift an undertaking to rural area.	Land, building, plant or machinery in order to shift an undertaking to any special economic zone
4.1 What is time-limit for acquiring the new asset	*Purchase* : 1 year backward or 2 years forward *Construction*: 3 years forward	2 years forward	3 years forward	6 months forward	*Purchase* : 1 year backward or 2 years forward *Construction:* 3 years forward	1 year backward or 3 years forward	1 year backward or 3 years forward

1. Any residential house other than the new house (up to the assessment year 2000-01).

† If the amount of capital gain does not exceed Rs. 2 crore, the assessee can purchase/construct two residential house properties (from the assessment year 2020-21). However, this concession is available only once in lifetime.

Different questions	*Section 54*	*Section 54B*	*Section 54D*	*Section 54EC*	*Section 54F*	*Section 54G*	*Section 54GA*
4.2 From which date the time-limit shall be determined	From the date of transfer of house property but in case of compulsory acquisition from the date of receipt of compensation	From the date of transfer of agricultural land	From the date of receipt of compensation	From the date of transfer of long-term capital asset but in the case of compulsory acquisition from the date of receipt of compensation	From the date of transfer of capital asset but in case of compulsory acquisition from the date of receipt of compensation	From the date of transfer	From the date of transfer
5. How much is exempt	Investment in the new asset or capital gain, whichever is lower	Investment in the new asset or capital gain, whichever is lower	Investment in the new asset or capital gain, whichever is lower	Investment in the new asset or capital gain, whichever is lower	Investment in the new asset/net sale consideration × capital gain	Investment in the new asset or capital gain, whichever is lower	Investment in the new asset or capital gain, whichever is lower
6. Is it possible to revoke the exemption in a subsequent year	If the new asset is transferred within 3 years of its acquisition	If the new asset is transferred within 3 years of its acquisition	If the new asset is transferred within 3 years of its acquisition	If the new asset is transferred or it is converted into money or a loan is taken on security of the new asset within 3 years† of its acquisition	(*a*) If the new asset is transferred within 3 years of its acquisition, (*b*) if another residential house is purchased within 2 years of transfer of original asset, or (*c*) if another residential house is constructed within 3 years of the transfer of original asset	If the new asset is transferred within 3 years of its acquisition	If the new asset is transferred within 3 years of its acquisition
6.1 When the exemption is revoked it is taxable in the year in which the default is committed. What will be status of the notional income	Short-term capital gain	Short-term capital gain	Short-term capital gain	Long-term capital gain	Long-term capital gain	Short-term capital gain	Short-term capital gain
7. Whether scheme of deposit is applicable	*Yes*	*Yes*	*Yes*	*No*	*Yes*	*Yes*	*Yes*
7.1 What is the scheme of deposit	*See* Note *infra*	*See* Note *infra*	*See* Note *infra*	—	*See* Note *infra*	*See* Note *infra*	*See* Note *infra*

Note - Scheme of deposit - If the new asset is not acquired up to the due date of submission of return of income, then the taxpayer will have to deposit the money in "Capital gain deposit account scheme" with a nationalised bank. The proof of

† 5 years of investment is made on or after April 1, 2018.

deposit should be submitted along with return of income. On the basis of actual investment and the amount deposited in the deposit account, exemption will be given to the taxpayer.

The taxpayer can acquire a new asset by withdrawing from the deposit account. But the new asset should be acquired within the time-limit mentioned in 4.1 *supra.* If the deposit account is not fully utilised for acquiring the new asset, the unutilised amount [but in case of section 54F it is unutilised amount/net sale consideration × capital gain] will become chargeable to tax in the previous year in which the specified time-limit [as mentioned in para 4.1 *supra*] expires [in case of sections 54 and 54F when the 3 year time limit expires]. It will be taxable as short-term/long-term capital gain depending upon the original capital gain. The unutilised amount can be withdrawn by the taxpayer after the expiry of the aforesaid time-limit.

R-14

Dates with direct taxes[1]

Date	*Obligation*	*Form number*
April 15, 2019	Upload quarterly statement under rule 37BB(7)[$] by an authorised dealer in respect of foreign remittances made during the quarter ending March 31, 2019	Form No. 15CC
April 30, 2019	• Upload declarations received from recipients in Form No. 15G/15H during the quarter ending March 31, 2019	
	• Upload statement containing particulars of declarations received in Form No. 60 during October 1, 2018 and March 31, 2019 to Director/Joint Director (Intelligence and Criminal Investigation)	Form No. 61
May 15, 2019	• Quarterly statement of TCS for the quarter ending March 31, 2019	Form No. 27EQ
May 30, 2019	• Quarterly TCS certificates in respect of tax collected during the quarter ending March 31, 2019	Form No. 27D
	• Electronic submission of a statement by non-resident (under section 285) having a liaison office in India for the financial year 2018-19	Form No. 49C
May 31, 2019	• Return of tax deduction from contributions paid by the trustees of an approved superannuation fund	
	• Annual statement of financial transaction under section 285BA(1) to be furnished electronically in respect of financial year 2018-19	Form No. 61A
	• Electronic submission of annual statement of reportable account required to be furnished under section 285BA(1)(*k*) by reporting financial institution pertaining to calendar year 2018	Form No. 61B
	• Quarterly statement of tax deducted for the quarter ending March 31, 2019	TDS salary : Form No. 24Q TDS other : Form No. 26Q TDS non-resident : Form No. 27Q
June 15, 2019	• First instalment of advance income-tax for the assessment year 2020-21 (for any assessee other than the person who is covered by section 44AD or 44ADA)	No statement/estimate is required to be submitted
	• Certificate of tax deducted at source to employees in respect of salary paid and tax deducted during 2018-19	Form Nos. 12BA and 16**
	• Quarterly TDS certificate (in respect of tax deducted for payments other than salary) for the quarter ending March 31, 2019	Form No. 16A*
June 29, 2019	• Electronically submission of information pertaining to any transfer of the share of, or interest in, a foreign company/entity as referred to	Form No. 49D†

1. Where the last day for filing return of income/loss or any other return under direct taxes is a day on which the office is closed, the assessee can file the return on the next day afterwards on which the office is open and, in such cases, the return will be considered to have been filed within the specified time-limit—Circular No. 639[$], dated November 13, 1992.

*TDS certificate in Form No. 16A shall be issued after downloading it from TRACES Portal by all deductors (including Government deductors who deposit TDS in the Central Government Account through book entry).

**Part A of TDS certificate in Form No. 16 shall be issued by downloading from TRACES Portal.

† Form No. 49D should be uploaded within 90 days of the transaction where the transaction has the effect of directly or indirectly transferring the rights of management in relation to the Indian concern.

$ For rule 37BB and Circular No. 639, log on to *taxmann.com/readyreckoner.aspx*.

Date	*Obligation*	*Form number*
June 29, 2019	in *Explanation 5* to section 9(1)(*i*) which takes place during the financial year 2018-19	
	• Upload statement of the financial year 2018-19 under section 9A(5) with digital signature pertaining to eligible investment fund	Form No. 3CEK
June 30, 2019	• Return in respect of securities transaction tax for the financial year 2018-19	Form No. 1 (for stock exchange), Form No. 2 (for mutual fund)
	• Quarterly return of non-deduction of tax at source by a banking company from interest on time deposit in respect of the quarter ending March 31, 2019	Form No. 26QAA
	• Report by an approved institution/public sector company under section 35AC(4)/(5) for the year ending March 31, 2019	Form No. 58C or 58D
	• Annual statement of income distributed by a business trust to unit-holders pertaining to the financial year 2018-19	Form No. 64B
	• Annual statement of income distributed by investment fund to unit-holders pertaining to the financial year 2018-19	Form No. 64C
	• Electronically submission of annual return of equalisation levy pertaining the financial year 2018-19	Form No. 1
	• Annual statement pertaining to income distribution during 2018-19 by a securitisation trust to be provided to investor under section 115TCA	Form No. 64F
July 15, 2019	• Upload declarations received from recipients in Form No. 15G/ 15H during the quarter ending June 30, 2019	
	• Quarterly statement of TCS for the quarter ending June 30, 2019	Form No. 27EQ
	• Upload quarterly statement under rule 37BB(7)[$] by an authorised dealer in respect of foreign remittances made during the quarter ending June 30, 2019	Form No. 15CC
July 30, 2019	• Quarterly TCS certificate for the quarter ending June 30, 2019	Form No. 27D
July 31, 2019	• Annual return of income for the assessment year 2019-20 if the assessee is not required to submit return of income on September 30, 2019 or November 30, 2019	Form No. ITR-1 to ITR-7
	• Upload option available under *Explanation* to section 11(1) to apply income of previous year in the next year or in future (if the assessee is required to submit return of income on July 31, 2019)	Form No. 9A
	• Upload statement to accumulate/set apart income for future application under section 10(*21*) or 11(2) (if the assessee is required to submit return of income on July 31, 2019)	Form No. 10
	• Upload (for claiming foreign tax credit) statement of foreign income offered for tax for the previous year 2018-19 and of foreign tax deducted or paid on such income, if due date of submission of return of income is July 31, 2019	Form No. 67
	• Submit a report under rule 10V(7) from a chartered accountant for the previous year 2018-19 relating to arm's length price in respect of the remuneration paid by an eligible investment fund to the fund manager (if the assessee is required to submit return of income on July 31, 2019)	Form No. 3CEJ
	• Quarterly return of non-deduction of tax at source by a banking company from interest on deposit in respect of the quarter ending June 30, 2019	Form No. 26QAA
	• Quarterly statement of tax deducted for the quarter ending June 30, 2019	TDS salary : Form No. 24Q

[$] For rule 37BB, log on to *taxmann.com/readyreckoner.aspx.*

Date	Obligation	Form number
July 31, 2019		TDS other : Form No. 26Q TDS non-resident : Form No. 27Q
	• Statement by scientific research association, university, college or other association or Indian scientific research company as required by rules 5D, 5E and 5F (if due date of submission of return of income is July 31, 2019)	—
August 15, 2019	• Quarterly TDS certificate (in respect of tax deducted for payments other than salary) for the quarter ending June 30, 2019	Form No. 16A*
September 15, 2019	• Second instalment of advance income-tax for the assessment year 2020-21 (for any assessee other than the person who is covered by section 44AD or 44ADA)	No statement/estimate is required to be submitted
September 30, 2019	• Annual return of income for the assessment year 2019-20 if the assessee (not having any international or specified domestic transaction) is (*a*) corporate-assessee or (*b*) non-corporate assessee (whose books of account are required to be audited) or (*c*) working partner (of a firm whose accounts are required to be audited)	Form No. ITR-1 to ITR-7
	• Audit report under section 44AB for the assessment year 2019-20 in the case of a corporate-assessee or non-corporate assessee (who is required to submit his/its return of income on September 30, 2019)	Form Nos. 3CA or 3CB and 3CD
	• Statement by scientific research association, university, college or other association or Indian scientific research company as required by rules 5D, 5E and 5F (if due date of submission of return of income is September 30, 2019)	—
	• Upload option available under *Explanation* to section 11(1) to apply income of previous year in the next year or in future (if the assessee is required to submit return of income on September 30, 2019)	Form No. 9A
	• Upload statement to accumulate/set apart income for future application under section 10(*21*) or 11(2) (if the assessee is required to submit return of income on September 30, 2019)	Form No. 10
	• Electronically submit copy of audit of accounts to the Secretary, Department of Scientific and Industrial Research in case company is eligible for weighted deduction under section 35(2AB) [if company does not have any international/specified domestic transaction]	Form No. 3CLA
	• Upload (for claiming foreign tax credit) statement of foreign income offered for tax for the previous year 2018-19 and of foreign tax deducted or paid on such income, if due date of submission of return of income is September 30, 2019	Form No. 67
	• Submit a report under rule 10V(7) from a chartered accountant for the previous year 2018-19 relating to arm's length price in respect of the remuneration paid by an eligible investment fund to the fund manager (if the assessee is required to submit return of income on September 30, 2019)	Form No. 3CEJ
October 15, 2019	• Quarterly statement of TCS for the quarter ending September 30, 2019	Form No. 27EQ
	• Upload quarterly statement under rule 37BB(7)[$] by an authorised dealer in respect of foreign remittances made during the quarter ending September 30, 2019	Form No. 15CC
	• Upload declarations received from recipients in Form No. 15G/15H during the quarter ending September 30, 2019	

*TDS certificate in Form No. 16A shall be issued after downloading it from TRACES Portal by all deductors (including Government deductors who deposit TDS in the Central Government Account through book entry).

[$] For rule 37BB, log on to *taxmann.com/readyreckoner.aspx*.

Date	*Obligation*	*Form number*
October 30, 2019	• Quarterly TCS certificate for the quarter ending September 30, 2019	Form No. 27D
October 31, 2019	• Annual audited accounts for each approved programmes under section 35(2AA)	—
	• Upload statement containing particulars of declarations received in Form No. 60 during April 1, 2019 to September 30, 2019 to Director/Joint Director (Intelligence and Criminal Investigation)	Form No. 61
	• Quarterly return of non-deduction of tax at source by a banking company from interest on time in respect of the quarter ending September 30, 2019	Form No. 26QAA
	• Quarterly statement of tax deducted for the quarter ending September 30, 2019	TDS salary : Form No. 24Q TDS other : Form No. 26Q TDS non-resident : Form No. 27Q
November 15, 2019	• Quarterly TDS certificate (in respect of tax deducted for payments other than salary) for the quarter ending September 30, 2019	Form No. 16A*
November 30, 2019	• Annual return of income for the assessment year 2019-20 in the case of an assessee if he/it is required to submit a report under section 92E pertaining to international or specified domestic transaction(s)	ITR-1 to ITR-7
	• Audit report under section 44AB for the assessment year 2019-20 in the case of an assessee who is also required to submit a report pertaining to international or specified domestic transactions under section 92E	Form Nos. 3CA or 3CB and 3CD
	• Electronically submit copy of audit of accounts to the Secretary, Department of Scientific and Industrial Research in case company is eligible for weighted deduction under section 35(2AB) [if company has international/specified domestic transactions]	Form No. 3CLA
	• Statement by scientific research association, university, college or other association or Indian scientific research company as required by rules 5D, 5E and 5F (if due date of submission of return of income is November 30, 2019)	-
	• Electronic submission of statement of income distribution by venture capital company or venture capital fund in respect of income distributed during 2018-19	Form No. 64
	• Annual statement (of income distributed during the financial year 2018-19) by a business trust to be electronically submitted to the Principal Commissioner/Commissioner	Form No. 64A
	• Annual statement of income distributed during the financial year 2018-19 by investment fund to be electronically submitted to the Principal Commissioner/Commissioner	Form No. 64D
	• Upload (for claiming foreign tax credit) statement of foreign income offered for tax for the previous year 2018-19 and of foreign tax deducted or paid on such income, if due date of submission of return of income is November 30, 2019	Form No. 67
	• Submit a report under rule 10V(7) from a chartered accountant for the previous year 2018-19 relating to arm's length price in respect of the remuneration paid by an eligible investment fund to the fund manager (if the assessee is required to submit return of income on November 30, 2019)	Form No. 3CEJ

*TDS certificate in Form No. 16A shall be issued after downloading it from TRACES Portal by all deductors (including Government deductors who deposit TDS in the Central Government Account through book entry).

Date	*Obligation*	*Form number*
November 30, 2019	• Upload option available under *Explanation* to section 11(1) to apply income of previous year in the next year or in future (if the assessee is required to submit return of income on November 30, 2019)	Form No. 9A
	• Upload statement to accumulate/set apart income for future application under section 10(*21*) or 11(2) (if the assessee is required to submit return of income on November 30, 2019)	Form No. 10
	• Annual statement of income distributed during 2018-19 by a securitisation trust to its investors to be furnished electronically with digital signature to the PCIT/CIT	Form No. 64E
December 15, 2019	• Third instalment of advance income-tax for the assessment year 2020-21 (for any assessee other than the person who is covered by section 44AD or 44ADA)	No statement/estimate is required to be submitted
January 15, 2020	• Quarterly statement of TCS for the quarter ending December 31, 2019	Form No. 27EQ
	• Upload declarations received from recipients in Form No. 15G/15H during the quarter ending December 31, 2019	
	• Upload quarterly statement under rule 37BB(7)[$] by an authorised dealer in respect of foreign remittances made during the quarter ending December 31, 2019	Form No. 15CC
January 30, 2020	• Quarterly TCS certificate for the quarter ending December 31, 2019	Form No. 27D
January 31, 2020	• Quarterly statement of tax deducted for the quarter ending December 31, 2019	TDS salary : Form No. 24Q TDS other : Form No. 26Q TDS non-resident : Form No. 27Q
	• Quarterly return of non-deduction at source by a banking company from interest on deposit in respect of the quarter ending December 31, 2019	Form No. 26QAA
February 15, 2020	• Quarterly TDS certificate (in respect of tax deducted for payments other than salary) for the quarter ending December 31, 2019	Form No. 16A[*]
March 15, 2020	• First instalment (in the case of an assessee covered by section 44AD/44ADA) or fourth instalment (in the case of any other person) of advance income-tax for the assessment year 2020-21	No estimate/statement is required to be submitted
April 15, 2020	• Upload quarterly statement under rule 37BB(7)[$] by an authorised dealer in respect of foreign remittances made during the quarter ending March 31, 2020	Form No. 15CC
April 30, 2020	• Upload declarations received from recipients in Form No. 15G/15H during the quarter ending March 31, 2020	
	• Upload statement containing particulars of declarations received in Form No. 60 during October 1, 2019 and March 31, 2020 to Director/Joint Director (Intelligence and Criminal Investigation)	Form No. 61
May 15, 2020	• Quarterly statement of TCS in respect of tax collected for the quarter ending March 31, 2020	Form No. 27EQ
May 30, 2020	• Quarterly TCS certificate in respect of tax collected during the quarter ending March 31, 2020	Form No. 27D
	• Electronic submission of statement by a non-resident (under section 285) having a liaison office in India for the financial year 2019-20	Form No. 49C
May 31, 2020	• Annual statement of financial transaction under section 285BA(1) to be furnished electronically in respect of financial year 2019-20	Form No. 61A

[*]TDS certificate in Form No. 16A shall be issued after downloading it from TRACES Portal by all deductors (including Government deductors who deposit TDS in the Central Government Account through book entry).

[$] For rule 37BB, log on to *taxmann.com/readyreckoner.aspx.*

Date	*Obligation*	*Form number*
May 31, 2020	• Electronic submission of annual statement of reportable account required to be furnished under section 285BA(1)(*k*) by reporting financial institution pertaining to calendar year 2019	Form No. 61B
	• Quarterly statement of tax deducted for the quarter ending March 31, 2020	TDS salary : Form No. 24Q TDS other : Form No. 26Q TDS non-resident : Form No. 27Q
	• Return of tax deduction from contributions paid by the trustees of an approved superannuation fund	

Notes—

1. Tax deducted/collected should be deposited within 7 days from the end of the month in which tax is deducted/collected. However, this rule is not applicable in the following cases—

- If tax is deducted/collected by an office of Government and tax is to be deposited without production of income-tax challan, tax deducted or collected should be deposited on the same day.
- Tax deducted under any section (except section 194-IA and section 194-IB) by a person (not being an office of Government) in the month of March should be deposited by April 30 after the end of the financial year.
- Tax deducted under section 194-IA or section 194-IB by any person should be deposited within 30 days from the end of the month in which tax is deducted.
- In some cases (*i.e.*, sections 192, 194A, 194D and 194H), the Assessing Officer may permit quarterly deposit of TDS, in such cases tax should be deposited within 7 days from the end of each quarter (30 days from the end of fourth quarter).

2. When tax is deducted/collected by a Government office and paid without production of a challan, the deductor/collector shall report tax so deducted/collected to the Pay and Accounts Officer or the Treasury Officer or the Cheque Drawing and Disbursing Officer or any other person (by whatever name called) who is responsible for crediting such sum to the credit of the Central Government. The person to whom tax deduction/collection is reported by the deductors/collectors, shall submit a statement in Form No. 24G. It should be submitted within the time-limit given below –

	Time-limit
Where statement relates to month of March	On or before 30 days*
Where statement relates to any other month	On or before 15 days*

*From the end of the month in respect of tax deducted/collected by the deductors/collectors and reported to him for that month.

It should be submitted to a notified agency [*i.e.*, an agency authorized by the Director General of Income-tax (Systems)].

PART A

Income-tax

Terminology

Income of previous year is chargeable to tax in the immediately following assessment year [paras 1 and 2]. Tax incidence, however, depends upon residential status of a taxpayer [paras 4 and 5]

Assessment year [Sec. 2(9)]

1. Assessment year may be defined as a year in which the income of the previous year is to be assessed. In some countries it is called "tax year". It always starts on April 1 and ends on March 31 of the next year. Thus, the assessment year 2019-20 starts on April 1, 2019 and ends on March 31, 2020.

Previous year [Sec. 3]

2. Income of the previous year is taxed in the immediately following assessment year. In some countries it is called "income year".

From the assessment year 1989-90 onwards all assessees are required to follow the financial year (*i.e.*, the year ending on March 31) as the previous year. This uniform previous year has to be followed for all sources of income.

Except in the case mentioned in para 2.1, previous year is the financial year immediately preceding the assessment year. For instance, for the assessment year 2019-20, the immediately preceding financial year (*i.e.*, 2018-19) is the previous year.

2.1 ***Previous year in the case of newly set up business/profession*** - In the case of a newly set up business or profession or a source of income newly coming into existence, the first previous year will be the period commencing from the date of setting up of the business/profession or, as the case may be, the date on which the source of income newly comes into existence and ending on the immediately following March 31.

2.2 ***When income of previous year is not taxable in the immediately following assessment year*** - The rule that the income of the previous year is assessable as the income of the immediately following assessment year has certain exceptions. These are : (*a*) income of a non-resident from shipping; (*b*) income of persons leaving India either permanently or for a long period of time; (*c*) income of bodies formed for short duration; (*d*) income of a person trying to alienate his assets with a view to avoiding payment of tax; and (*e*) income of a discontinued business. In these cases, income of the previous year may be taxed as the income of the assessment year immediately preceding the normal assessment year.

Assessee [Sec. 2(7)]

3. "Assessee" means a person by whom income-tax or any other sum of money is payable under the Act. It includes every person in respect of whom any proceeding under the Act has been taken for the assessment of his income or loss and the amount of refund due to him. It also includes a person who is assessable in respect of the income or loss of another or who is deemed to be an assessee or an assessee in default under any provision of the Act.

Under section 2(*31*), "person" includes (*a*) an individual, (*b*) a Hindu undivided family, (*c*) a company, (*d*) a firm, (*e*) an association of persons or a body of individuals, (*f*) a local authority, and (*g*) every artificial juridical person not falling within any of the preceding categories. These are the seven categories of persons chargeable to tax under the Act.

Residential status - General norms

4. Assessees are either (*a*) resident in India, or (*b*) non-resident in India. However, resident individuals and Hindu undivided families have to be (*a*) resident and ordinarily resident; or (*b*) resident but not ordinarily resident. The residential status of an assessee is to be determined for each previous year. If a person is resident in India in a previous year relevant to an assessment year in respect of any source of income, he shall be deemed to be resident in India in the previous year(s) relevant to the same assessment year in respect of each of his other sources of income.

Residential status of an individual [Sec. 6]

5. An individual may be (*a*) resident and ordinarily resident, (*b*) resident but not ordinarily resident, or (*c*) non-resident.

5.1 ***Resident and ordinarily resident [Sec. 6(1), 6(6)(a)]*** - To find out whether an individual is "resident and ordinarily resident" in India, one has to proceed as follows—

- *Step 1* - First find out whether such individual is "resident" in India [*see* para 5.1-1].
- *Step 2* - If such individual is "resident" in India, then find out whether he is "ordinarily resident" in India [*see* para 5.1-2].

5.1-1 *BASIC CONDITIONS TO TEST AS TO WHEN AN INDIVIDUAL IS RESIDENT IN INDIA* - Under section 6(*1*) an individual is said to be resident in India in any previous year, if he satisfies at least one of the following basic conditions—

a. he is in India in the previous year for a period of 182 days or more; or

b. he is in India for a period of 60 days or more during the previous year and 365 days or more during the four years immediately preceding the previous year.

5.1-1a EXCEPTIONS - The aforesaid rule of residence is subject to the following exceptions—

1. By virtue of *Explanation 1*(*a*) to section 6(*1*) the period of "60 days" referred to in (*b*) above has been extended as follows—

Assessment years	*Who can take the benefit of extended period*	*Extended period*
1990-91 onwards	An Indian citizen who leaves India during the previous year for the purpose of employment outside India or an Indian citizen who leaves India during the previous year as a member of the crew of an Indian ship	182 days[1]

For this purpose, the requirement is not leaving India for taking employment outside India but leaving India for the purposes of employment (the employment may be in India or may be outside India). To put it differently, the individual need not be an unemployed person—*British Gas India (P.) Ltd., In re* [2006] 155 Taxman 326 (AAR - New Delhi). He may be employed in India and leave India during the previous year on a foreign assignment of his employer company. Alternatively, he may be an unemployed person who goes outside India to take an employment outside India.

2. By virtue of *Explanation 1*(*b*), the period of "60 days" referred to in (*b*) above has been extended as follows in the case of a person who comes on a visit to India—

Assessment years	*Who can take the benefit of extended period*	*Extended period*
1995-96 onwards	Indian citizen or a person of Indian origin	182 days
1990-91 to 1994-95	Indian citizen or a person of Indian origin	150 days

A person is deemed to be of Indian origin if he, or either of his parents or any of his grand-parents, was born in undivided India.

5.1-2 *ADDITIONAL CONDITIONS TO TEST WHEN A RESIDENT INDIVIDUAL IS ORDINARILY RESIDENT IN INDIA* - Under section 6(*6*), a resident individual is treated as "resident and ordinarily resident" in India if he satisfies the following two additional conditions—

i. he has been *resident* in India in at least 2[2] out of 10 previous years immediately preceding the relevant previous year; and

ii. he has been in India for a period of 730 days or more during 7 years immediately preceding the relevant previous year.

---

1. In the case of an individual, being a citizen of India and a member of the crew of a foreign bound ship leaving India, the period or periods of stay in India shall not include the period given in rule 126. Under rule 126[$], the period beginning on the date entered into the Continuous Discharge Certificate in respect of joining the ship by the said individual for the eligible voyage and ending on the date entered into the Continuous Discharge Certificate in respect of signing off by that individual from the ship in respect of such voyage, shall not be included in the period of stay in India.

2. 9 years up to the assessment year 2003-04.

[$]For rule 126, log on to *taxmann.com/readyreckoner.aspx.*

5.2 ***Resident but not ordinarily resident*** - An individual who satisfies one or more of the basic conditions laid down in section 6(*1*), but does not satisfy the two additional conditions laid down in section 6(*6*) is treated as resident but not ordinarily resident in India.

5.3 ***Non-resident*** - An individual is a non-resident in India during the previous year if he satisfies none of the basic conditions laid down in section 6(*1*) [*see* para 5.1-1].

5.4 ***Rule of residence in brief*** - The table given below highlights the rule of residence in brief for the assessment year 2019-20 :

TABLE

• BASIC CONDITIONS AT A GLANCE		
In the case of an Indian citizen who leaves India during the previous year for the purpose of employment or, in the case of an Indian citizen who leaves India during the previous year as a member of the crew of an Indian ship	*In the case of an Indian citizen or a person of Indian origin (who is abroad) who comes to India on a visit during the previous year*	*In the case of an individual [other than an individual mentioned in columns (1) and (2)]*
(1)	*(2)*	*(3)*
a. Presence for at least 182 days in India during the previous year 2018-19 *b.* *Non-functional*	*a.* Presence for at least 182 days in India during the previous year 2018-19 *b.* *Non-functional*	*a.* Presence for at least 182 days in India during the previous year 2018-19 *b.* Presence in India for at least 60 days during the previous year 2018-19 and 365 days during April 1, 2014 to March 31, 2018.

• ADDITIONAL CONDITIONS AT A GLANCE
i. Resident in India in at least 2[3] years out of previous years 2008-09 to 2017-18 [or must satisfy at least one of the basic conditions, in 2[3] out of 10 immediately preceding previous years] (*i.e.*, during the previous years 2008-09 to 2017-18). *ii.* Presence of at least 730 days in India during April 1, 2011 and March 31, 2018.

• RULE OF RESIDENCE AT A GLANCE		
Resident and ordinarily resident	*Resident and not ordinarily resident*	*Non-resident*
Must satisfy at least one of the basic conditions and both of the additional conditions [*i.e.*, one of (*a*) or (*b*) and both of (*i*) and (*ii*)]	Must satisfy at least one of the basic conditions and one or none of the additional conditions [*i.e.*, one of (*a*) or (*b*) and one or none of (*i*) or (*ii*)]	Should not satisfy any of the basic conditions.

5-E1 X left India for the first time on November 25, 2016 for meeting his friends. During the calendar year 2017 he came to India on September 1 and stayed for a period of 10 days. During the calendar year 2018, he did not visit India at all but finally came to India on January 16, 2019. Determine the residential status of X for the assessment year 2019-20.

●

During the previous year 2018-19, the assessee was in India for 75 days and during the four years preceding the previous year, he was in India for 980 days (10 days during 2017-18, 239 days during 2016-17, 366 days during 2015-16 and 365 days during 2014-15). Thus, he satisfies one of the conditions laid down in section 6(*1*) for being treated as resident in India. In addition, the assessee also satisfies the two additional conditions laid down in section 6(*6*) as he was resident in India in 2 years out of 10 years immediately preceding the previous year 2018-19 (during the period 2008-2018 he was resident in India in all the years except 2017-18) and during 7 years immediately preceding the previous year 2018-19, he was in India for more than 730 days. He will, therefore, be treated as resident and ordinarily resident in India for the assessment year 2019-20.

5-E2 X, an Indian citizen, who is appointed as senior taxation officer by the Government of Libya, leaves India, for the first time on September 25, 2017 for joining his duties in Libya. During the previous year 2018-19, he comes to India on a visit of 175 days. Determine the residential status of X for the assessment years 2018-19 and 2019-20.

●

---

3. 9 years up to the assessment year 2003-04.

During the previous year 2017-18, X was in India for 178 days and during the four years immediately preceding the previous year 2017-18 he was in India for more than 365 days. Though he satisfies one of the conditions laid down in section 6(*1*), yet by virtue of *Explanation 1* to section 6(*1*), he will be non-resident for the assessment year 2018-19 (an Indian citizen leaving India for the purpose of employment, is treated as resident in India only if he has been in India in that year for at least 182 days).

During the previous year 2018-19 (for the assessment year 2019-20), X comes to India for 175 days. Therefore, X satisfies none of the conditions laid down by section 6(*1*) [read with *Explanation 1* to section 6(*1*)]. He will, accordingly, be treated as non-resident in India for the assessment year 2019-20.

Residential status in the case of other persons

6. In the case of other persons residential status is determined as under—

6.1 ***Residential status of a Hindu undivided family [Sec. 6(2)]*** - A Hindu undivided family is said to be resident in India if the control and management of its affairs are wholly or partly situated in India. Control and management means *de facto* control and management and not merely the right to control or manage—*CIT* v. *Nandlal Gandalal* [1960] 40 ITR 1 (SC).

A resident Hindu undivided family is "ordinarily resident" in India if the karta or manager of the family (including successive kartas) is resident in India in at least 2 years[4] out of 10 years immediately preceding the relevant previous year and is in India for 730 days or more during 7 years immediately preceding the relevant previous year. If the karta or manager of a resident family is not resident in India in at least 2[4] out of 10 immediately preceding previous years or is not present in India for at least 730 days in 7 immediately preceding previous years as aforesaid, the family will be regarded as resident but not ordinarily resident in India.

A Hindu undivided family will be non-resident in India if its control and management is situated wholly outside India.

6.2 ***Residential status of a firm or an association of persons [Sec. 6(4)]*** - A partnership firm or an association of persons is said to be resident in India if the control and management of its affairs are wholly or partly situated within India during the relevant previous year. It is however, treated as non-resident in India if the control and management of its affairs are situated wholly without India.

6.3 ***Residential status of a company [Sec. 6(3)]*** - Residential status of a company is determined as follows –

Section	*Company*	*Residential status*
6(3)(*i*)	Indian company	Always resident in India [Note 1]
6(3)(*ii*)	A foreign company (whose turnover/gross receipt in the previous year is more than Rs. 50 crore)	It will be resident in India if its place of effective management (POEM), during the relevant previous year, is in India [Note 2]
6(3)(*ii*)	A foreign company (whose turnover/gross receipt in the previous year is Rs. 50 crore or less)	Always non-resident in India [Note 3]

Notes –

1. An Indian company is always resident in India. Even if an Indian company is controlled from a place located outside India (or even if shareholders of an Indian company controlling more than 51 per cent voting power are non-resident and/or located outside India), the Indian company is resident in India. An Indian company can never be non-resident.

2. A foreign company (with effect from the assessment year 2017-18) is resident in India if its place of effective management (POEM), during the relevant previous year, is in India. For this purpose, the place of effective management means a place where key management and commercial decisions that are necessary for the conduct of the business of an entity as a whole are, in substance made. For this purpose, a set of guiding principles (to be followed in determination of POEM) have been issued by the Board in Circular No. 6/2017[$], dated January 24, 2017. In a case where a foreign company is said to be resident in India on account of its POEM being in India (and such foreign company has not been resident in India in any of the preceding years), then a few special provisions are applicable for the computation of total income, treatment of unabsorbed depreciation, set off or carry forward and set off of losses, collection and recovery, etc. Such modifications are given in section 115JH read with Notification No. SO 3039(E)[$], dated June 22, 2018.

3. Provisions of section 6(3)(*ii*) shall not apply to a foreign company having turnover or gross receipts of Rs. 50 crore or less in a financial year – Circular No. 8/2017[$], dated February 23, 2017. In other words, a foreign company (whose annual turnover/gross receipts is Rs. 50 crore or less) cannot be resident in India from the assessment year 2017-18 onwards.

---

4. 9 years up to the assessment year 2003-04.

[$] For Circular No. 6/2017, Circular No. 8/2017 and Notification No. SO 3039(E), log on to *taxmann.com/readyreckoner.aspx*.

Incidence of tax [Sec. 5]

7. Under the Act, incidence of tax on a taxpayer depends on his residential status and also on the place and the time of accrual or receipt of income.

7.1 ***Incidence of tax in the case of a resident and ordinarily resident-assessee [Sec. 5(1)]*** - A resident and ordinarily resident in India is assessable to tax in respect of—

a. income which is received (or deemed to be received) in India in the previous year by or on his behalf;

b. income which accrues or arises (or is deemed to accrue or arise) to him in India during the previous year; and

c. income which accrues or arises to him outside India during the relevant previous year.

7.2 ***Incidence of tax in the case of a resident but not ordinarily resident-assessee [Sec. 5(1)]*** - The liability to tax of a resident but not ordinarily resident is the same as in the case of a resident and ordinarily resident. However, in the case of a resident but not ordinarily resident, income is not liable to tax in India unless (*a*) income is received or deemed to be received in India, (*b*) income is accrued or deemed to be accrued in India, or (*c*) business is controlled from a place within India or profession is set up in India.

7.3 ***Incidence of tax in the case of a non-resident [Sec. 5(2)]*** - A non-resident is liable to tax in respect of income received (or deemed to be received) in India by or on his behalf and income that accrues or arises (or is deemed to accrue or arise) in India during the previous year.

7.4 ***Income deemed to accrue or arise in India [Sec. 9]*** - Certain incomes are deemed to accrue or arise in India under section 9 even though they may actually accrue or arise outside India. This section applies to all assessees irrespective of their residential status, nationality, domicile and place of business. The categories of income which are deemed to accrue or arise in India are as under :

Nature of income			*Whether income is deemed to accrue or arise in India*
Income from business connection in India [*see* para 7.4-1]			Yes
Income from any property, asset or source of income in India			Yes
Capital gain on transfer of a capital asset situated in India			Yes
Income from salary if service is rendered in India			Yes
Income from salary (not being perquisite/allowance) if service is rendered outside India (provided the employer is Government of India and the employee is a citizen of India)			Yes
Income from salary if service is rendered outside India (not being a case stated above)			No
Dividend paid by the Indian company			Yes
Income arising outside India [being **any sum of money referred to in section 2(24)(*xviia*)] paid on or after July 5, 2019, by a person resident in India to a non-resident/foreign company**			Yes
Nature of income [Sec. 9(1)(v)/(vi)/(vii)[5]]	*From whom income is received*	*Payer's source of income*	
Interest	Government of India	Any	Yes
Interest	A person resident in India	Borrowed capital is used by the payer for carrying on business/profession outside India or earning any income outside India	No
Interest	A person resident in India	Borrowed capital is used by the payer for any other purpose	Yes
Interest	A person non-resident in India	Borrowed capital is used by the payer for carrying on business/profession in India	Yes
Interest	A person non-resident in India	Borrowed capital is used by the payer for any other purpose	No

5. Income of a non-resident shall be deemed to accrue or arise in India under clause (*v*) or clause (*vi*) or clause (*vii*) of section 9(1) and shall be included in his total income, whether or not,—

a. the non-resident has a residence or place of business or business connection in India; or

b. the non-resident has rendered services in India.

Nature of income [Sec. 9(1)(v)/(vi)/(vii)[5]]	From whom income is received	Payer's source of income	
Royalty/fees for technical services	Government of India	Any	Yes
Royalty/fees for technical services	A person resident in India	Payment is relatable to a business or profession or any other source carried on by the payer outside India	No
Royalty/fees for technical services	A person resident in India	Payment is relatable to any other source of income	Yes
Royalty/fees for technical services	A person non-resident in India	Payment is relatable to a business or profession or any other source carried by the payer in India	Yes
Royalty/fees for technical services	A person non-resident in India	Payment is relatable to any other source of income	No

7.4-1 *INCOME FROM BUSINESS CONNECTION [SEC. 9(1)(i)]* - The following conditions should be satisfied —

- *Condition one* - The taxpayer has a "business connection" in India.
- *Condition two* - By virtue of "business connection" in India, income actually arises outside India.

If the above conditions are satisfied, income which arises outside India because of "business connection" in India, is deemed to accrue or arise in India.

7.4-1a WHAT IS BUSINESS CONNECTION - It includes a person acting on behalf of a non-resident and who performs any one or more of the following—

- *Activity one* - He exercises in India an authority to conclude contracts on behalf of the non-resident (it does not cover the activity of only the purchase of goods or merchandise for the non-resident).
- *Activity two* - He has no such authority but habitually maintains in India a stock of goods or merchandise from which he regularly delivers goods or merchandise on behalf of the non-resident.
- *Activity three* - He habitually secures order in India (mainly or wholly) for the non-resident or for non-residents under the same management.
- *Activity four (applicable from the assessment year 2019-20)* - He habitually plays the principal role leading to conclusion of contracts by the non-resident and the contracts are –

a. in the name of the non-resident; or

b. for the transfer of the ownership of (or for the granting of the right to use) property owned (or the non-resident has right to use) by the non-resident; or

c. for the provision of services by the non-resident.

Where a business is carried on in India through a person referred to in *Activity one, two, three* or *four* (*supra*) only so much of income as is attributable to the operations carried out in India shall be deemed to accrue or arise in India. Business connection includes a profession connection.

Moreover, from the assessment year 2019-20, significant economic presence of a non-resident in India shall constitute "business connection" in India. "Significant economic presence" for this purpose, shall mean—

a. transaction in respect of any goods, services or property carried out by a non-resident in India (including provision of download of data or software in India), if the aggregate of payments arising from such transactions during the previous year exceeds such amount as may be prescribed; or

b. systematic and continuous soliciting of business activities or engaging in interaction with such number of users as may be prescribed, in India through digital means.

Above activities shall constitute significant economic presence in India (whether or not the agreement for such transactions or activities is entered in India; or the non-resident has a residence or place of business in India; or the non-resident renders services in India). However, only so much of income as is attributable to the transactions referred to in (*a*) or (*b*) shall be deemed to accrue or arise in India.

7.4-1a[1] *Independent brokers/agents are excluded* - The "business connection", shall not include cases where the non-resident carries on business through a broker, general commission agent or any other agent of an independent status, provided that such a person is acting in the ordinary course of his business. Where a broker, general commission agent or any other agent works (mainly or wholly) on behalf of a non-resident or other non-residents under the same management, he shall not be deemed to be a broker, general commission agent or an agent of an independent status.

5. *See* page A-5.

7.4-1b TAXATION OF BUSINESS PROCESS OUTSOURCING (BPO) UNIT - A BPO unit is situated in India. Outsourcing of business processes by non-residents/foreign companies to BPO units in India is a common feature now-a-days. The activities performed by BPO units in India on behalf of non-residents/ foreign companies range from mere procurement of orders for sale of goods or provision of services and answering sales related queries, to the provision itself of services like software maintenance service, debt collection service, software development service, credit card/mobile telephone related service etc. In some cases the BPO unit in India performs the entire or major portion of the revenue generating activities of the non-resident enterprise.

Income deemed to be earned in India - As per Circular No. 5/2004[$], dated September 28, 2004 income will be determined as follows—

	Taxability of income in India	
Different situations	*Income of BPO unit in India*	*Income of non-residents/ foreign companies deemed to accrue or arise in India*
If there is no business connection between the BPO unit in India and non-resident entity and the BPO unit in India is not a Permanent Establishment (PE) of the non-resident entity	Income of BPO unit in India is taxable in India	Nothing will be taxable in the hands of non-resident/foreign companies because of business connection in India
If there is business connection between the BPO unit in India and non-resident entity and the BPO unit in India is a Permanent Establishment (PE) of the non-resident entity	Income of BPO unit in India is taxable in India	So much of the profit which is attributable to PE in India is taxable in hands of foreign entity in India

Permanent Establishment (PE) - A non-resident or a foreign company is treated as having a Permanent Establishment in India under Article 5 of the Double Taxation Avoidance Agreements entered into by India with different countries if the said non-resident entity carries on business in India through a branch, sales office, etc., or through an agent (other than an independent agent) who habitually exercises an authority to conclude contracts or regularly delivers goods or merchandise or habitually secures orders on behalf of the non-resident principal.

How to calculate income of PE - Profit of the PE will be calculated as if it were a distinct and separate enterprise engaged in the same or similar activities under the same or similar conditions and dealing wholly independently with the enterprise of which it is a PE. In determining the profits of a PE there shall be allowed as deductions expenses which are incurred for the purposes of the PE including executive and general administrative expenses so incurred, whether in India or elsewhere. What are the expenses that are deductible would have to be determined in accordance with the accepted principles of accountancy and the provisions of the Income-tax Act. In other words, the profits to be attributed to a PE are those, which that PE would have made if, instead of dealing with its Head Office, it had been dealing with an entirely separate enterprise under conditions and at prices prevailing in the ordinary market. This corresponds to the "arm's length principle". Hence, in determining the profits attributable to a PE, it will be necessary to determine the price of the services rendered by the PE to the Head Office or by the Head Office to the PE on the basis of arm's length principle.

7.4-1c OPERATIONS NOT TAKEN AS BUSINESS CONNECTION - The following operations do not amount to business connection by virtue of specific provisions in the Act—

• *Case 1 - Where all operations are not carried out in India* [Explanation 1(*a*) *to section 9(1)(i)*] - If all business operations are not carried out in India, the income of the business deemed to accrue or arise in India shall be only such part of income as is reasonably attributable to the operations carried out in India.

Apportionment of profits should be on a rational basis and should not be arbitrary—*Bikaner Textile Merchants Syndicate Ltd.* v. *CIT* [1965] 58 ITR 169 (Raj.). Where the only trading activity operation within India was the negotiation and conclusion of the contract and the contract was performed entirely outside India, it was held by the Madras High Court that only 10 per cent of the profits was deemed to accrue or arise in India—*Annamalais Timber Trust & Co.* v. *CIT* [1961] 41 ITR 781.

• *Case 2 - Purchase of goods for export* [Explanation 1(*b*) *to section 9(1)(i)*] - In the case of a non-resident no income shall be deemed to accrue or arise in India to him through or from operations which are confined to the purchase of goods in India for the purpose of export.

• *Case 3 - Collection of news and views* [Explanation 1(*c*) *to section 9(1)(i)*] - No income shall be deemed to accrue or arise in the case of a non-resident engaged in the business of running a news agency or of publishing

[$] For Circular No. 5/2004, log on to *taxmann.com/readyreckoner.aspx.*

newspapers, magazines or journals from activities confined to the collection of news and views in India for transmission out of India.

• *Case 4 - Shooting of cinematograph film in India* [Explanation 1(d) *to section 9(1)(i)*] - In the case of a non-resident no income shall be deemed to accrue or arise in India through or from operations which are confined to the shooting of any cinematograph film in India, if such a non-resident is either an individual who is not a citizen of India, or a firm which does not have any partner who is a citizen of India or who is a resident in India, or a company which does not have any shareholder who is a citizen of India or is a resident in India.

• *Case 5 - Display of uncut and unassorted diamond in a notified special zone* [Explanation 1(e) *to section 9(1)(i)*] - In the case of a foreign company engaged in the business of mining of diamonds, no income shall be deemed to accrue or arise in India through or from the activities which are confined to the display of uncut and unassorted diamond (without any sorting or sale) in any special zone notified by the Central Government in the Official Gazette in this behalf (applicable from the assessment year 2016-17).

• *Case 6* - In the case of an "eligible investment fund", the fund management activity carried out through an "eligible fund manager" acting on behalf of such fund shall not constitute business connection in India of the said fund [sec. 9A$, applicable from the assessment year 2016-17].

7.4-1d WITHDRAWAL OF CIRCULAR NO. 23 - The Central Board of Direct Taxes has withdrawn Circular No. 23, dated July 23, 1969, Circular No. 163, dated May 29, 1975 and Circular No. 786, dated February 7, 2000 *vide* Circular No. 7/2009, dated October 22, 2009.

7.4-1e WITHDRAWAL OF AFORESAID CIRCULAR AND ITS IMPACT ON TAXABILITY OF EXPORT COMMISSION IN INDIA - The Supreme Court in the case of *CIT* v. *Toshoku Ltd.* [1980] 125 ITR 525$ held that the commission earned by a non-residents for services rendered outside India could not be deemed to be the income in terms of section 9(1)(*i*) [which refers to income from 'business connection'], on the ground that no operations were carried out in India.

The Authority for Advance Rulings (AAR) in the case of *Spahi Projects (P.) Ltd., In re* [2009] 183 Taxman 92$, after considering the provisions of section 9(1)(*i*), held that commission paid to an agent in South Africa for distribution of the products of the applicant in South Africa could not be deemed to have accrued or arisen in India in the absence of 'business connection' in India.

Based on the aforesaid decisions, the undisputed legal position emerges that income earned by a non-resident foreign agent for procuring orders outside India cannot be deemed to be income to have accrued or arisen in India for the purposes of section 9(1)(*i*) – *CIT* v. *Capricorn Food Products India Ltd.* [2014] 61 SOT 196 (Chennai), *Gujarat Reclaim & Rubber Products Ltd.* v. *CIT* [2013] 60 SOT 22 (Mum.), *CIT* v. *Farida Shoes (P.) Ltd.* [2013] 143 ITD 400 (Chennai), *Allied Nippon Ltd.* v. *CIT* [2013] 145 ITD 81 (Delhi), *CIT* v. *Shiva Texyarn Ltd.* [2015] 53 taxmann.com 495 (Chennai), *Zanav Home Collection* v. *CIT* [2015] 55 taxmann.com 200 (Bang.).

The aforesaid Circulars were explanatory Circulars and not benevolent ones. These Circulars were issued to explain the legal position and did not extend any concession. The withdrawal of the aforesaid Circulars does not mean that export commission to overseas agents has become taxable in India. In other words, taxability of such commission will be determined with reference to the legal provisions given in the Act and the judicial rulings in this matter. The above quoted rulings of the Apex Court$ and the AAR$ will remain in operation in spite of withdrawal of the aforesaid Circulars.

7.4-2 *INCOME FROM ANY PROPERTY, ASSET OR SOURCE OF INCOME SITUATED IN INDIA [SEC. 9(1)(i)]* - Income through or from any property, asset or source of income in India is deemed to accrue or arise in India. The expression "through" means "by means of", "in consequence of" or "by reason of".

7.4-3 *INCOME THROUGH THE TRANSFER OF CAPITAL ASSET SITUATED IN INDIA [SEC. 9(1)(i)]* - Any capital gain through the transfer of a capital asset situated in India, is deemed to accrue or arise in India. The expression "through" means "by means of", "in consequence of" or "by reason of".

7.4-3a AMENDMENT MADE BY THE FINANCE ACT, 2012 - The Finance Act, 2012 inserted certain clarificatory amendments in the provisions of section 9. The amendments, *inter alia*, included insertion of *Explanation 5* in section 9(1)(*i*) with retrospective effect from the assessment year 1962-63[6]. The *Explanation 5* clarifies that an asset or capital asset, being any share[7] or interest in a company or entity registered or

6. *See* page A-9.

7. However, these provisions are not applicable in the case of any asset or capital asset being investment held by a non-resident, directly or indirectly, in –
   - a Foreign Institutional Investor [as referred to in the *Explanation (a)* to section 115AD (for the assessment years 2012-13 to 2014-15)];
   - Category-I or Category II Foreign Portfolio Investor under the SEBI (Foreign Portfolio Investors) Regulations, 2014 (for the assessment year 2015-16 onwards).

$For *CIT* v. *Toshoku Ltd.* [1980] 125 ITR 525 (SC), *Spahi Projects (P.) Ltd.*, In re [2009] 183 Taxman 92 (AAR) and section 9A, log on to *taxmann.com/readyreckoner.aspx*.

incorporated outside India shall be deemed to be situated in India if the share or interest derives, directly or indirectly, its value substantially from the assets located in India.

• *Meaning of the expression "substantially"* - The Delhi High Court in the case of *DIT* v. *Copal Research Ltd.* [2014] 49 taxmann.com 125 (Delhi) examined the meaning of expression "substantially" and held that gains arising from sale of a share of a company incorporated overseas, which derives less than 50 per cent of its value from assets situated in India would certainly not be taxable under section 9(1)(*i*) read with *Explanation 5* thereto.

7.4-3b FURTHER AMENDMENT APPLICABLE FROM THE ASSESSMENT YEAR 2016-17 - The following amendments have been made with effect from the assessment year 2016-17 –

• *"Substantial"* - The share or interest of a foreign company or entity shall be deemed to derive its value substantially from the assets (whether tangible or intangible) located in India, if on the specified date, the value of Indian assets, –

a. exceeds the amount of Rs. 10 crore; and

b. represents at least 50 per cent of the value of all the assets owned by the company or entity.

• *Taxation on proportionate basis* - The taxation of gains arising on transfer of a share or interest deriving, directly or indirectly, its value substantially from assets located in India will be on proportional basis. The method for determination of proportionality is given in rule 11UB$.

• *Exemption in case foreign entity that is transferred directly or indirectly owns Indian assets* - Exemption shall be available to the transferor of a share of, or interest in, a foreign entity if the transferor (along with its associated enterprises) –

a. neither holds the right of control or management;

b. nor holds voting power or share capital or interest exceeding 5 per cent of the total voting power or total share capital, in the foreign company or entity directly holding the Indian assets.

• *Exemption in the case of amalgamation/demerger*- The transfer of shares in a foreign company (deriving value of assets substantially from assets situated in India) on account of amalgamation/demerger of foreign companies will be exempt from tax subject to the satisfaction of the conditions given by section 47(*viab*)/(*vicc*).

7.4-3c DECLARATION OF DIVIDEND BY COMPANY HAVING SUBSTANTIAL ASSETS IN INDIA - If dividend is declared by a foreign company outside India, it cannot be deemed to accrue or arise in India, even if the foreign company declaring dividend have substantial assets (held by it directly or indirectly) located in India. This rule is applicable even if the foreign company satisfies the conditions given in above para - Circular No. 4/2015$, dated March 26, 2015.

7.4-4 *INCOME BY WAY OF INTEREST, ROYALTY AND TECHNICAL FEES [SEC. 9(1)(*v*)/(*vi*)/(*vii*)]* - These are deemed to accrue or arise in India in the following cases :

1. Interest, royalty or technical fees received from the Central Government/any State Government, is deemed to accrue or arise in India.

2. Interest, royalty or technical fees received from a resident person, is deemed to accrue or arise in India in the hands of recipient. However, this rule is not applicable (*a*) if borrowed money is utilised by the payer for carrying on a business/profession outside India or for earning any income outside India; or (*b*) payment of royalty/technical fees pertains to a business/profession carried on by the payer outside India or earning any income outside India.

3. Interest, royalty or technical fees received from a non-resident, is deemed to accrue or arise in India in the hands of recipient, if (*a*) borrowed money is utilised by the payer for carrying on a business/profession in India; or (*b*) payment of royalty/technical fees pertains to a business/profession carried on by the payer in India or earning any income in India.

• Royalty for this purpose includes consideration for the transfer of any right in respect of a patent, invention, model, design, secret formula, or process or trademark or similar property. This provision has been amended (with retrospective effect from June 1, 1976[8]). After the amendment, "royalty" also includes transfer of all or

---

8. *Vide* Letter [F.No. 500/111/2009-FTD-1(PT.)], dated May 29, 2012, the Board has pointed out that the amendment has been made with retrospective effect in order to clarify the legislative intent and state the position of law from the date of coming into effect of these sections in the Act. Further the Board has directed that where assessment proceedings have been completed under section 143(3) before April 1, 2012, and no notice for reassessment has been issued prior to that date, then such case shall not be reopened under section 147/148 on account of the abovementioned clarificatory amendments introduced by the Finance Act, 2012. However, assessment or any other order which stand validated due to the said clarificatory amendments in the Finance Act, 2012 would of course be enforced.

$For rule 11UB and Circular No. 4/2015, log on to *taxmann.com/readyreckoner.aspx*.

any right for use (or right to use) a computer software (including granting of a licence) irrespective of the medium through which such right is transferred. Further, royalty includes any consideration in respect of any right, property or information, whether or not—

a. the possession or control of such right, property or information is with the payer;
b. such right, property or information is used directly by the payer;
c. the location of such right, property or information is in India[8].

• Royalty also includes consideration for the use of any patent, invention, model, design, secret formula or process or trade mark or similar property. This provision has been amended (with retrospective effect from June 1, 1976[8]). After the amendment, the expression "process" includes transmission by satellite (including up-linking, amplification, conversion for down-linking of any signal), cable, optic fibre or by any other similar technology, whether or not such process is secret.

• Section 9(1)(*v*) has been amended with effect from the assessment year 2016-17 to provide that in the case of a non-resident, being a person engaged in the business of banking, any interest payable by the permanent establishment in India of such non-resident to the head office or any permanent establishment or any other part of such non-resident outside India shall be deemed to accrue or arise in India and shall be chargeable to tax in addition to any income attributable to the permanent establishment in India.

Hints for tax planning in respect of residential status

8. For the purpose of tax planning the following broad propositions should be borne in mind. However, these propositions would hold good only in the context in which they have been made—

• In order to enjoy non-resident status, individuals who are visiting India on a business trip or in some other connection, should not stay in India for more than 181 days during one previous year and their total stay in India during any four previous years preceding the relevant previous year should in no case exceed 364 days.

• If individuals having been in India for more than 365 days during the four years preceding the relevant previous year, wish to stay in India for more than 60 days, they should plan their visit to India in such a manner that their total stay in India falls under two previous years. To illustrate, such persons can come to India any time in the first week of February and stay up to May 29 without incurring any risk of losing their non-resident status.

• An Indian citizen or a person of Indian origin (whether rendering service outside India or not) can stay for a maximum of 181 days on a visit to India without losing his non-resident status. If, however, such persons wish to stay in India for more than 181 days, they should plan their visit in such a manner that their maximum stay of 362 days comes under two previous years, stay in each previous year being not more than 181 days.

• An Indian citizen, leaving India for the purpose of *employment*, will not be treated as a resident in India, unless he has been in India in that year for 182 days or more. In other words, Indian citizens going abroad for the purpose of *employment* can stay in India for 181 days without becoming resident in that year, even if they were in India for more than 365 days during the four preceding years. This concession is available only to those who want to leave the country for the purpose of *employment*. However, the term "employment" is not defined in the Act. One has, therefore, to depend upon judicial pronouncements. It would be useful to quote, Denman and Vaisey, JJ. in this context—

- Per Denman, J. - "I do not think that employment means only where one is set to work by others to earn money; a man may employ himself so as to earn profits in many ways"—*Partridge* v. *Mallandine* [1886] 18 QBD 276 (DC).
- Per Vaisey, J. - "The word 'employment' is one of very wide significance. But the words 'employer' and the 'employee' are much more restricted in their meanings. Thus, I may be said to 'employ' my time or my talents without being in any proper sense an employer, and I may also be said to be employed in some pursuit or activity without being an 'employee' "—*Westall Richardson Ltd.* v. *Roulson* [1954] 2 AER 448.

Applying the aforesaid ratios, there is no reason why a professional who expects to set up an independent practice in, or a businessman who wants to shift his activities to, a foreign country should be denied the benefit of this concession. A similar ruling is given by the Karnataka High Court in the case of *CIT* v. *O. Abdul Razak* [2011] 198 Taxman 1.

• A non-resident can escape tax liability in respect of income earned out of India if he first receives it out of India and then remits the whole or a part of it to India, even though the business is controlled from India.

• A person who is not ordinarily resident, earning income outside India from a business controlled outside India, can avoid tax liability if he first receives such income in a foreign country and then remits the whole or a part of it to India, either in the same year or in the following year(s).

• Not ordinarily resident persons can claim set off of losses sustained in a business controlled from outside India against their income taxable in India provided they shift the control of the business to India.

---

8. *See* page A-9.

Heads of income [Sec. 14]

9. As per section 14, income of a person is computed under the following five heads :

1. Salaries

2. Income from house property

3. Profits and gains of business or profession

4. Capital gains

5. Income from other sources.

• The aggregate income under these heads is termed as "gross total income". In other words, gross total income means total income computed in accordance with the provisions of the Act before making any deduction under sections 80C to 80U.

9.1 ***Expenditure incurred in relation to exempt income, not deductible [Sec. 14A]*** - Section 14A, inserted from the assessment year 1962-63, provides that no deduction shall be made in respect of expenditure incurred by the assessee in relation to income which does not form part of the total income under the Act. In the case of composite business, expenditure pertaining to income exempt from tax shall be determined as per prescribed method (*i.e.*, rule 8D).

9.1-1 *EXPENDITURE PERTAINING TO INCOME NOT CHARGEABLE TO TAX - PRESCRIBED MODE [Rule 8D]* - The expenditure in relation to income which does not form part of total income shall be the aggregate of the following—

1. Expenditure directly relating to such income.

2. An amount equal to 1 per cent of the annual average of the monthly average of the opening and closing balances of the value of investment (*i.e.*, investment, income from which is exempt from tax).

The amount referred to in (*1*) and (*2*) (*supra*) shall not exceed the total expenditure claimed by the assessee.

9.1-1E1 X is a commission agent of a manufacturing company. Besides, he has shares in a few Indian companies as investor. He gives the following information pertaining to previous year 2018-19 –

	Rs.
Income from commission agency business	10,00,000
Dividend income from shares in Indian companies	2,00,000
Fees for consultancy paid to an investment consultant (it pertains to investment in shares, dividend income is given above, it is deducted from commission agency business)	10,000
Common interest expenditure pertaining to taxable (*i.e.*, commission agency business) and non-taxable (*i.e.*, dividend income) (entire interest is deducted while computing commission agency business income given above)	40,000

Investment in shares as on first and last date of each month (in Rs.)		*Monthly average investment (in Rs.)*	
- April 1, 2018	14,00,000		
- April 30, 2018	16,00,000	April 2018	15,00,000
- May 31, 2018	18,00,000	May 2018	17,00,000
- June 30, 2018	7,50,000	June 2018	12,75,000
- July 31, 2018	8,50,000	July 2018	8,00,000
- August 31, 2018	19,00,000	August 2018	13,75,000
- September 30, 2018	27,00,000	September 2018	23,00,000
- October 31, 2018	11,00,000	October 2018	19,00,000
- November 30, 2018	11,50,000	November 2018	11,25,000
- December 31, 2018	13,50,000	December 2018	12,50,000
- January 31, 2019	12,00,000	January 2019	12,75,000
- February 28, 2019	14,00,000	February 2019	13,00,000
- March 31, 2019	13,00,000	March 2019	13,50,000
Total of monthly average			1,71,50,000
Annual average of monthly average			14,19,167

X claims that out of Rs. 40,000, expenditure pertaining to dividend income is zero. Likewise, he claims that fees paid to investment consultant pertains to commission agency business and nothing is spent for earning dividend income. Assessing Officer is not satisfied with the claim made by X.

•

	Rs.
Expenditure directly pertaining to exempt dividend income (*i.e.*, consultancy fee) (*a*)	10,000
Interest expenditure pertaining to dividend income [being 1% of annual average of monthly average of opening and closing balance of the value of investment in shares (*i.e.*, 1% of Rs. 14,19,167)] (*b*)	14,192
Expenditure pertaining to exempt income [*i.e.*, (*a*) + (*b*)]	24,192
Business income chargeable to tax (Rs. 10,00,000 + Rs. 24,192)	10,24,192

9.1-2 *OTHER POINTS* - One should also keep in view the following propositions –

• The above provisions of rule 8D shall be applied only if the Assessing Officer is not satisfied with the correctness of the claim of expenditure (pertaining to exempt income) made by the assessee. The Assessing Officer must record his dissatisfaction with the correctness of the claim of expenditure made by the assessee or with the correctness of the claim made by the assessee that no expenditure has been incurred. It is only when this condition precedent is satisfied that the Assessing Officer is required to determine the amount of expenditure in relation to income not includible in total income in the manner indicated in rule 8D as given above—*Cellica Developers (P.) Ltd.* v. *CIT* [2014] 63 SOT 255 (Kol.).

• Disallowance provisions of section 14A and rule 8D are applicable even where taxpayer in a particular year has not earned any exempt income – Circular No. 5/2014, dated February 11, 2014. However, judicial rulings are available to the effect that section 14A is not applicable if during the relevant previous year no exempt income is received or receivable – *see CIT* v. *State Bank of Patiala* [2018] 99 taxmann.com 285 (Punj. & Har.)[9], *CIT* v. *Oil Industries Development Board* [2019] 103 taxmann.com 325 (Delhi)[10].

• Section 14A applies to all heads of income and aims at disallowance of expenditure incurred in relation to incomes which do not form part of total income – *ITO* v. *Daga Capital Management (P.) Ltd.* [2009] 117 ITD 169 (Mum).

• Where the assessee has sufficient funds (*e.g.*, his own funds on which interest is not payable, partners current capital on which interest is not payable, shareholders fund consisting of share capital/reserves/surplus or any other interest-free funds) for making investments in shares and mutual funds, the Assessing Officer cannot invoke section 14A for disallowance of expenditure attributable to exempt income—*CIT* v. *Taikisha Engineering India Ltd.* [2015] 229 Taxman 143 (Delhi), *CIT* v. *NHPC Ltd.* [2015] 53 taxmann.com 301 (Delhi), *CIT* v. *Ercon Composites* [2014] 49 taxmann.com 489 (Jodh.), *CIT* v. *Gujarat Narmada Valley Fertilizers Co. Ltd.* [2015] 67 SOT 254 (Ahd.), *T And T Motors Ltd.* v. *CIT* [2015] 58 taxmann.com 295 (Delhi). Similarly, where interest-free funds available with assessee are far in excess of investments generating tax-free income, no part of interest expenditure will be disallowed—*CIT* v. *Gujarat Narmada Valley Fertilizers Co. Ltd.* [2014] 31 ITR 668 (Ahd.). One can conclude that if the assessee has made investment out of accumulated/surplus funds (and not out of borrowed funds), no interest can be disallowed under section 14A—*West Coast Paper Mills Ltd.* v. *CIT* [2014] 52 taxmann.com 268 (Mum.). Likewise, where investment in shares is fully financed out of sale proceeds of shares held as long term capital investment and income earned on sale of those shares is also offered as long term capital gains, there was no reason for disallowance of interest expenditure by invoking provisions of section 14A – *Sanjay Kumar J. Poddar* v. *CIT* [2015] 68 SOT 43 (Mum.).

• Where the actual expenditure to the exempt income is identifiable, the principle of apportionment of such expenditure by applying section 14A read with rule 8D is not possible – *Yatish Trading Co. (P.) Ltd.* v. *CIT* [2011] 129 ITD 237 (Mum.).

• Section 14A is applicable as per the methodology given in rule 8D. In respect of depreciation no part can be disallowed by applying section 14A—*Vishnu Anant Mahajan* v. *CIT* [2012] 137 ITD 189 (Ahd.).

• Amounts borrowed for investment in foreign subsidiaries will not attract section 14A for the reason that the dividend from foreign companies are chargeable to tax and being not an exempt income, the disallowance of interest on monies borrowed will not apply—*CIT* v. *Suzlon Energy Ltd.* [2013] 215 Taxman 272 (Guj.)

• Disallowance contained in section 14A cannot be applied in respect of incomes which are eligible for deduction under Chapter VI-A or eligible for deduction under any other provision—*CIT* v. *Kribhco* [2012] 209 Taxman 252 (Delhi).

• Where tax free investments were made much earlier out of own funds, the subsequent borrowings by way of bank loan will not lead to disallowance of any part of interest expenditure under section 14A—*CIT* v. *Indian Sugar Exim Corpn. Ltd.* [2012] 206 Taxman 242 (Delhi).

• In the case of an assessee eligible for claiming Tonnage Tax Scheme under Chapter XII-G, disallowance under section 14A cannot be made on such income taxed on presumptive basis—*CIT* v. *Four M. Maritime*

---

9. SLP, against the judgment, has been dismissed – *CIT* v. *State Bank of Patiala* [2018] 259 Taxman 314 (SC).

10. SLP, against the judgment, has been dismissed – *CIT* v. *Oil Industry Development Board* [2019] 103 taxmann.com 326 (SC).

(P.) Ltd. [2015] 152 ITD 557 (Chennai). In the same analogy, assessee offering income under presumptive provisions such as section 44AD or 44AE will not be subjected to disallowance under section 14A in respect of such presumptive incomes.

• Section 14A does not provide that if income is liable to tax at a lower rate, then also proportionate expenditure should not be allowed as deduction - *CIT* v. *American Express Bank Ltd.* [2012] 138 ITD 288 (Mum.).

• All expenses connected with exempt income have to be disallowed under section 14A regardless of whether they are direct or indirect, fixed or variable and managerial or financial in accordance with law—*Kalpataru Construction Overseas (P.) Ltd.* v. *CIT* [2007] 13 SOT 194 (Mum.). It is not open to Assessing Officer to make disallowance under section 14A according to his own discretion or on *ad hoc* basis and he is statutorily required to compute disallowance in manner provided by sub-sections (2) and (3) of section 14A—*CIT* v. *Citicorp Finance (India) Ltd.* [2007] 12 SOT 248 (Mum.).

• In variable *"A"* prescribed in the formula given in rule 8D(*2*)(*ii*) (to make disallowance in case of common interest expenditure), interest (attributable to exempt income as well as taxable income) shall be excluded —*PRI. CIT* v. *Bharti Overseas (P.) Ltd.* [2015] 64 taxmann.com 340 (Delhi).

Income from "Salaries"

Salary	*Para number*	*Example number*
PRE-COMPUTATION STEPS		
DETERMINE RESIDENTIAL STATUS OF SALARIED EMPLOYEE	5.1	5-E1 and 5-E2
FIND OUT WHETHER INCOME IS TAXABLE UNDER SECTION 15	10 and 11	—
COMPUTATION STEPS		
COMPUTE TAXABLE VALUE OF DIFFERENT PAYMENTS		
❑ Salary	12	–
❑ Allowances	13	–
❑ Perquisites	14	–

Meaning of "Salary" [Sec. 17(*1*)]

10. The term "salary" is defined to include the following :

a. wages;

b. any annuity or pension;

c. any gratuity;

d. any fees, commissions, perquisites or profits in lieu of or in addition to any salary or wages;

e. any advance of salary;

f. any payment received by an employee in respect of any period of leave not availed by him;

g. the portion of the annual accretion in any previous year to the balance at the credit of an employee participating in a recognised provident fund to the extent it is taxable;

h. transferred balance in a recognised provident fund to the extent it is taxable; and

i. contribution by the Central Government to the account of an employee under a pension scheme referred to in section 80CCD (*i.e.* NPS).

Basis of charge [Sec. 15]

11. For the purpose of chargeability to tax, salary consists of :

a. any salary *due*[11] from an employer (or a former employer) to an assessee in the previous year, whether actually paid or not ;

11. What is taxable under section 15 is "salary due" and not "salary accrued". For instance, X gets salary of Rs. 4.5 lakh (return is also submitted by including Rs. 4.5 lakh as salary) for the previous year 2011-12. Later on, it is discovered that Rs. 1.5 lakh is wrongly calculated and paid to him. The excess amount of Rs. 1.5 lakh is recovered from the current year's salary of Rs. 7 lakh. For the current year (*i.e.*, the financial year 2018-19), salary on accrual basis is Rs. 7 lakh. Actual amount due after adjusting excess payment of earlier year is Rs. 5.5 lakh. The amount which constitutes "salary due from an employer" is only the amount net of recovery of Rs. 5.5 lakh — *Vrajeshwari B. Parikh* v. *ITO* [2015] 61 taxmann.com 235 (Ahd.).

b. any salary *paid or allowed* to him in the previous year by or on behalf of an employer (or a former employer), though not due or before it became due ; and

c. any *arrears* of salary *paid or allowed* to him in the previous year by or on behalf of an employer (or a former employer), if not charged to income-tax for any earlier previous year.

Salary income is chargeable to tax either on due basis or on receipt basis. Once salary has accrued, its subsequent waiver is only an application of income and is liable to be taxed. Income is taxable as salary under section 15 only if an employer-employee relationship exists between the payer and the payee.

Salary

12. The term "salary" signifies a recompense or consideration given to any person for pains bestowed upon another person's business. Tax treatment of different receipts are given below :

Different items	*Tax treatment*
Basic salary	Taxable under section 15.
Dearness allowance/pay	Taxable under section 15.
Advance salary	Taxable in the year of receipt [*see* also para 22.1].
Arrears of salary	Taxable in the year of receipt, if not taxed on due basis [*see* para 22.1].
Leave encashment at the time of retirement	Exempt in some cases [*see* para 12.1].
Salary in lieu of notice	Taxable on receipt basis.
Salary to partner	Not chargeable under the head "Salaries" but taxable under the head "Profits and gains of business or profession".
Fees and commission	Taxable under section 15.
Bonus	Taxable under section 15.
Gratuity	Exempt in some cases [*see* para 12.2].
Pension	Exempt in some cases [*see* para 12.3].
Annuity from employer	Taxable as salary.
Annual accretion to the credit balance in a recognised provident fund	*1.* Excess of employer's contribution over 12% of salary is taxable. *2.* Excess of interest credited over the notified rate of interest (*i.e.*, 9.5 per cent per annum) is taxable [for details *see* para 17].
Contribution by Central Government or any other employer towards NPS	Taxable as salary [*see* also para 107.2B]
Retrenchment compensation	Exempt from tax to the extent of least of the following: *a.* amount calculated under section 25F(*b*) of the Industrial Disputes Act; or *b.* such amount (not being less than Rs. 50,000) as notified by the Central Government (amount notified by the Government is Rs. 5,00,000 if a worker is retrenched after December 31, 1996) [*see* also para 22].
Remuneration for extra work	Taxable.
Voluntary payments	Taxable if payment is made with reference to services rendered by virtue of employment. However, a lump sum payment made gratuitously or by way of compensation or otherwise to the widow or other legal heirs of an employee, who dies while still in active service, is not taxable—Circular No. 573$, dated August 21, 1990. If a person or his heir receives *ex gratia* payment from the Central Government/State Government/Local Authority/Public Sector Undertaking, consequent upon injury to the person/death of a family member, while on duty, such an *ex gratia* payment will not be liable to income-tax - Circular No. 776$, dated June 8, 1999.
Salary from a United Nations Organisation	Not taxable.
Salary to a foreign citizen	Exempt in some cases [*see* para 21].
Payment received at the time of voluntary retirement [in accordance with any scheme approved by the Central Government]	*See* para 12.4.

12.1 ***Leave salary*** - Leave salary is taxable on the following basis :

• In the case of an employee of the Central Government or a State Government[12], any amount received as cash equivalent of leave salary in respect of the period of earned leave at his credit at the time of retirement/superannuation is exempt from tax [Sec. 10(*10AA*)(*i*)].

12. A professor/teacher of a university established under an Act of Parliament/State legislature (as well as college affiliated to such university or constituent college of such university) is treated as Government employee for this purpose – *Ram Kanwar Rana* v. *ITO* [2016] 71 taxmann.com 54 (Delhi - Trib.).

$ For Circular Nos. 573 and 776, log on to *taxmann.com/readyreckoner.aspx.*

• In the case of a non-Government employee (*i.e.*, an employee other than an employee of the Central Government or a State Government) leave salary is exempt from tax under section 10(*10AA*)(*ii*) to the extent of the least of the following—

a. cash equivalent of the leave salary in respect of the period of earned leave to the credit of an employee only at the time of retirement whether on superannuation or otherwise (earned leave entitlements cannot exceed 30 days for every year of actual service rendered for the employer from whose service he has retired); or

b. 10 months' "average salary" ; or

c. the amount not chargeable to tax as specified by the Government [*see* para 12.1-1] ; or

d. leave encashment actually received at the time of retirement.

"Average salary", for the aforesaid purpose, is to be calculated on the basis of average salary drawn during the period of 10 months immediately preceding the retirement/superannuation [for meaning of "salary" for this purpose, *see* para 13.1-1].

Where the cash equivalent of unutilised earned leave is received by an employee from two or more employers in the same year, or different years, the maximum amount exempt from tax under section 10(*10AA*)(*ii*) shall not exceed the amount specified in para 12.1-1.

12.1-1 *MAXIMUM AMOUNT NOT CHARGEABLE TO TAX AS SPECIFIED BY THE GOVERNMENT* - The maximum amount not chargeable to tax as specified by the Government, is as follows :

Date of retirement (whether on superannuation or otherwise)	*Amount Rs.*
Before January 1, 1982	25,500
Between January 1, 1982 and June 30, 1986	30,000
Between July 1, 1986 and December 31, 1986	73,400
Between January 1, 1987 and June 30, 1987	75,600
Between July 1, 1987 and December 31, 1987	77,760
Between January 1, 1988 and March 31, 1995	79,920
Between April 1, 1995 and June 30, 1995	1,30,320
Between July 1, 1995 and July 1, 1997	1,35,360
Between July 2, 1997 and April 1, 1998	2,40,000
After April 2, 1998	3,00,000

12.1-2 *CLARIFICATION FROM THE BOARD* - The following clarifications are given by the Board in respect of leave salary—

• Relief under section 89 read with rule 21A [*see* para 22] would be admissible in respect of encashment of leave salary by an employee when in service—Circular No. 431[$], dated September 12, 1985.

• Salary paid to the legal heirs of the deceased employee in respect of privilege leave standing to the credit of such employee at the time of his/her death is not taxable as salary—Circular letter No.: F. 35/1/65-IT(B)[$], dated November 5, 1965.

• Sum equivalent of leave salary received by the family of a Government servant who died in harness, is not taxable in the hands of the recipient—Circular No. 309[$], dated July 3, 1981.

12.1-3 *SCOPE OF EXEMPTION UNDER SECTION 10(*10AA*)(ii)* - Exemption under section 10(*10AA*) is available in respect of cash equivalent of earned leave at the employee's credit only at the time of retirement, whether such retirement is on superannuation or otherwise.

The word "otherwise" covers the case of retirement which takes place not at the time of superannuation but any other time. According to the Madras High Court in *CIT* v. *R.V. Shahney* [1986] 159 ITR 160, voluntary retirement from service is one such case which comes within the four corners of the expression "otherwise than superannuation".

12.1-E1 Determine the amount of exemption under section 10(*10AA*) in the following cases :

Name of the employee retiring from a company in the private sector on February 28, 2019	*X*	*Y*	*Z*
Salary at the time of retirement	Rs. 22,600	Rs. 22,600	Rs. 22,600
Average salary received during the 10 months ending on February 28, 2019	Rs. 22,100	Rs. 22,100	Rs. 22,100
Duration of service	24 years	24 years	24 years
Leave entitlement for every year of service	1½ months	1½ months	1½ months
Leave availed while in service	—	19 months	26 months
Leave at the credit of the employee at retirement	36 months	17 months	10 months
Leave salary paid at retirement at the rate of Rs. 22,600 per month	Rs. 8,13,600	Rs. 3,84,200	Rs. 2,26,000

[$] For Circular No. 309, Circular No. 431 and Circular Letter No. F.35/1/65, log on to *taxmann.com/readyreckoner.aspx*.

•

The amount of exemption under section 10(*10AA*) will be computed as under :

	X Rs.	*Y* Rs.	*Z* Rs.
Leave entitlement at the rate of one month's leave for every year of service	24 months	24 months	24 months
Leave availed while in service	—	19 months	26 months
Leave to the credit of each employee at the time of retirement (*i.e.*, 24 months—leave availed while in service)	24 months	5 months	*Nil*
a. Cash equivalent of leave to the credit of each employee at the time of retirement (*i.e.*, at the rate of Rs. 22,100 per month)	5,30,400	1,10,500	*Nil*
b. 10 months' average salary (*i.e.*, Rs. 22,100 × 10)	2,21,000	2,21,000	2,21,000
c. Maximum amount not taxable	3,00,000	3,00,000	3,00,000
d. Amount received from the employer	8,13,600	3,84,200	2,26,000
Amount not taxable under section 10(*10AA*) [*i.e.*, the least of (*a*), (*b*), (*c*) or (*d*)]	2,21,000	1,10,500	*Nil*
Amount taxable	5,92,600	2,73,700	2,26,000

12.2 *Gratuity [Sec. 10(10)]*[13] - Gratuity is taxable on the following basis :

12.2-1 *IN THE CASE OF A GOVERNMENT EMPLOYEE [SEC. 10(10)(i)]* - Any death-*cum*-retirement gratuity received by an employee of the Central Government, State Government or local authority[14], is wholly exempt from tax.

• A professor/teacher of a university established under an Act of Parliament/State legislature (as well as college affiliated to such university or constituent college of such university) is treated as Government employee for this purpose – *Ram Kanwar Rana* v. *ITO* [2016] 71 taxmann.com 54 (Delhi - Trib.).

12.2-2 *IN THE CASE OF AN EMPLOYEE COVERED BY THE PAYMENT OF GRATUITY ACT [SEC. 10(10)(ii)]* - Any gratuity received by an employee covered by the Payment of Gratuity Act, 1972, is exempt from tax to the extent of (*i*) 15 days' salary (7 days in the case of employees of seasonal establishments) based on the salary last drawn for every completed year of service or part thereof in excess of 6 months; (*ii*) Rs. 20,00,000 (Rs. 10,00,000, before March 29, 2018, Rs. 3,50,000 from September 24,1997 to May 23, 2010), or (*iii*) gratuity actually received, whichever is less.

Gratuity in excess of the aforesaid limits is taxable in the hands of the assessee. However, the assessee can claim relief under section 89 [*see* para 22.2]. "Salary" for the purpose of the aforesaid limits means salary last drawn by the employee and includes dearness allowance but does not include any bonus, commission, house rent allowance, overtime wages or any other allowance. Salary of 15 days is calculated by dividing the salary last drawn by 26 and multiplying it by 15.

12.2-3 *IN THE CASE OF ANY OTHER EMPLOYEE [SEC. 10(10)(iii)]* - Any other gratuity [not covered by paras 12.2-1 and 12.2-2], received by an employee on retirement, death, termination, resignation or on his becoming incapacitated prior to retirement, is exempt from tax to the extent of the least of (*i*) Rs. 20,00,000[16]; (*ii*) half month's salary for each completed year of service[15]; or (*iii*) gratuity actually received.

Gratuity in excess of the aforesaid limits is taxable in the hands of the employee on *due* or *receipt* basis. The assessee can, however, claim relief under section 89 [*see* para 22.2].

While calculating completed years, any fraction of the year shall be ignored. For instance, if the service of a retiring employee is 20 years, 10 months and 25 days, 20 years shall be taken for this purpose, ignoring the balance of 10 months and 25 days.

Average monthly salary is calculated on the basis of the salary of 10 months immediately preceding the month in which the person retires, etc. Salary, for this purpose, means basic salary and includes dearness allowance[17], if the terms of employment so provide, but excludes all other allowances and perquisites. If,

13. Exemption under section 10(*10*) is available even in the case of resignation—*Manish Chhabra* v. *CIT* [2011] 46 SOT 189 (Mum.).
14. Employees of statutory corporation are not covered by it.
15. The words "each year of completed service" used in section 10(*10*) are not confined to completed years of service under one employer and have to be interpreted to mean an employee's total service under two different employers including employer other than one from whose service he has retired, provided he was not paid gratuity by the former employer—*CIT* v. *P.N. Mehra* [1993] 201 ITR 930 (Bom.).
16. Rs. 30,000 in relation to gratuity becoming payable before January 31, 1982, Rs. 36,000 in relation to gratuity becoming payable after January 30, 1982 but before March 31, 1985, Rs. 50,000 in relation to gratuity becoming payable after March 30, 1985, but before January 1, 1986, Rs. 1,00,000 in relation to gratuity becoming payable after December 31, 1985 but before April 1, 1995, Rs. 2,50,000 in relation to gratuity becoming payable after March 31, 1995 but before September 24, 1997, Rs. 3,50,000 in relation to gratuity becoming payable after September 23, 1997 but before May 24, 2010 and Rs. 10,00,000 in relation to gratuity becoming payable on or after May 24, 2010 but before March 29, 2018.
17. Dearness allowance/pay shall be considered only when it is part of salary for computing all retirement benefits (like pension, leave encashment, gratuity, provident fund, etc.). If dearness allowance/pay is part of salary for computing only some (not all) of the retirement benefits, then it is not taken into consideration for this purpose—*ITO* v. *Sr. Accounts Officer, Pay & Accounts, DHBVNL* [2009] 33 SOT 37 (Delhi).

however, under the terms of employment, commission is payable at a fixed percentage of turnover achieved by an employee, such commission would partake of the character of "salary"—*Gestetner Duplicators (P.) Ltd.* v. *CIT* [1979] 1 Taxman 1/117 ITR 1 (SC).

Where gratuities are received by an employee from more than one employer in the same previous year, or different years, the aggregate maximum amount of gratuity exempt from tax under section 10(*10*)(*iii*) cannot exceed Rs. 20,00,000[16].

Any gratuity paid to an employee while he continues to remain in service (whether or not after he has put in a minimum specified period of service) is not exempt from tax, though the assessee can claim relief under section 89.

12.2-E1 X, an employee of the Central Government of India, receives Rs. 11,05,000 as gratuity at the time of his retirement on September 13, 2018. Is the gratuity fully exempt from tax ?

•

Gratuity received by him will be fully exempt from tax under section 10(*10*)(*i*).

12.2-E2 X, an employee of PQ Co. Ltd. (and covered by the Payment of Gratuity Act, 1972) receives Rs. 9,25,000 as gratuity. He retires on December 26, 2018 after rendering service of 28 years and 7 months. At the time of retirement his monthly salary was Rs. 18,000. Is the entire amount of gratuity exempt from tax ?

•

In this case 29 years will be taken as completed years of service. 15 days' salary is Rs. 10,384.62 [*i.e.*, Rs. 18,000 (being salary last drawn) × 15÷26].

Out of Rs. 9,25,000 received as gratuity, the least of the following will be exempt from tax: (*i*) Rs. 3,01,153.85 (being 15 days' salary for each completed year of service, *i.e.*, Rs. 10,384.62 × 29); (*ii*) Rs. 20,00,000; or (*iii*) Rs. 9,25,000 (being gratuity actually received). Hence, Rs. 3,01,153.85 is exempt from tax and the balance of Rs. 6,23,846.15 is taxable for the assessment year 2019-20. X can, however, claim relief under section 89 [*see* para 22.2].

12.2-E3 X, who is not covered by the Payment of Gratuity Act, 1972, retires on September 30, 2018 from ABC Ltd. and receives Rs. 11,00,000 as gratuity after service of 38 years and 7 months. Average monthly salary of 10 months immediately preceding the retirement is Rs. 52,560. What amount of gratuity will be exempt from tax ?

•

Out of Rs. 11,00,000 received as gratuity, the least of the following is exempt from tax: (*i*) Rs. 20,00,000; (*ii*) Rs. 9,98,640 (being half month's average salary for each year of completed service, *i.e.*, Rs. 52,560 × ½ × 38); or (*iii*) Rs. 11,00,000 (being amount received as gratuity).

Rs. 9,98,640 (being the least) is exempt from tax and the balance of Rs. 1,01,360 is taxable for the assessment year 2019-20. X can, however, claim relief under section 89 [*see* para 22.2].

12.3 *Pension* - The tax treatment of pension in different cases is given below—

	Different situations	*Tax treatment*
Case 1	Pension is received from UNO by the employee or his family members	It is not chargeable to tax
Case 2	Family pension received by the family members of armed forces	It is exempt under section 10(*19*) in some cases.
Case 3	Family pension received by family members in other cases	It is taxable in the hands of recipients under section 56 under the head "Income from other sources". Standard deduction is available under section 57 which is $^1/_3$ of such pension or Rs. 15,000, whichever is lower.
Case 4	Pension in the case of an employee (received after retirement but during his life time) who has joined the Central Government (on or after January 1, 2004) or who has joined any other employer (on, before or after January 1, 2004)	*See* para 12.3-2.
Case 5	Pension (received by the employee after retirement but during his life time, in any other case) [sec. 17(*1*)(*ii*)]	*See* para 12.3-1.

12.3-1 *PENSION [SEC. 17(1)(ii)]* - Pension covered under *Case 5* above is chargeable to tax as follows—

• Uncommuted pension is taxable as salary under section 15 in the hands of a Government employee as well as a non-Government employee.

• Any commuted pension received by an employee of the Central Government, State Government, local authority or statutory corporation is wholly exempt from tax under section 10(*10A*)(*i*). Judges of the Supreme Court and High Courts are entitled to exemption of commuted pension under section 10(*10A*)(*i*)—Circular

16. *See* page A-16.

No. 623, dated January 6, 1992. Government employees absorbed in a public sector undertaking are entitled to exemption in respect of lump sum received on commutation of pension—*CK. Karunakaran* v. *Union of India* [1980] 4 Taxman 178 (Delhi).

• Payment in commutation of pension received by any other employee—

- in a case where the employee receives gratuity, the commuted value of one-third of the pension which he is normally entitled to receive,
- in any other case, the commuted value of one-half of such pension,

is exempt from tax.

If payment in commutation of pension received by the employee exceeds the aforesaid limits, such excess is liable to tax in the assessment year relevant to the previous year in which it is due or paid. The assessee can, however, claim relief in terms of section 89 read with rule 21A [*see* para 22].

12.3-2 *NATIONAL PENSION SYSTEM (NPS)* - NPS is applicable to new entrants to Government service or any other employer. As per the scheme, it is mandatory for persons entering the Government service on or after January 1, 2004, to contribute 10 per cent of salary every month towards NPS. A matching contribution is required to be made by the employer to the said account. The tax treatment under NPS is as follows—

1. Contribution by the employer to NPS is first included under the head "Salaries" in hands of the employee.

2. Such contribution is deductible to the extent of 10 per cent of the salary of the employee under section 80CCD(2). However, this deduction has been increased to **14 per cent** of salary in the case of a Central Government employee, with effect from the assessment year 2020-21.

3. Employee's contribution to NPS (to the extent of 10 per cent of the salary of the employee) is also deductible under section 80CCD(1)[17].

4. Pension received out of the aforesaid amount is chargeable to tax in the hands of the recipient. However, some exemption is available on partial withdrawal before retirement or withdrawal at the time of retirement [for detailed discussion, *see* para 107.2B].

5. "Salary" for the purpose of *points 1* and *2* (*supra*) includes dearness allowance, if the terms of employment so provide[18], but excludes all other allowances and perquisites. It also includes commission if commission is payable at a fixed percentage of turnover achieved by an employee.

6. The aggregate amount of deduction under sections 80C, 80CCC and 80CCD(1) [*i.e.*, contribution by employee (or any other individual) towards NPS] cannot exceed Rs. 1,50,000.

7. Moreover, from the assessment year 2016-17, the employee (or any other individual who has joined NPS) can claim in respect of his contribution an additional amount (up to Rs. 50,000) under section 80CCD(1B). Contribution under section 80CCD(1B) is not covered by cumulative ceiling which is given in point No. 6 (*infra*).

• *Provisions illustrated* - X is employed (since 2010) by the Central Government (or any other employer). During the previous year 2018-19, he gets Rs. 80,000 per month as salary and Rs. 10,000 per month as dearness allowance (60 per cent is considered for retirement benefits). Employer annually contributes Rs. 1,04,000 towards NPS. X, however, annually contributes Rs. 1,05,000. Income from other sources of X is Rs. 9,00,000. X deposits every year Rs. 90,000 in public provident fund, which is deductible under section 80C. Further, X is eligible for a deduction of Rs. 25,000 under section 80CCC. Income of X will be calculated as follows –

	Rs.	*Rs.*
Salary (Rs. 80,000 × 12)		9,60,000
Dearness allowance (Rs. 10,000 × 12)		1,20,000
Employer's contribution towards NPS		1,04,000
Gross salary		11,84,000
Less: Standard deduction		40,000
Salary income		11,44,000
Income from other sources		9,00,000
Gross total income		20,44,000
Less: Deductions –		
Under section 80CCD(1B) (assessee's contribution to NPS up to Rs. 50,000)		50,000
Under section 80CCD(2) [employer's contribution towards NPS : Rs. 1,04,000 but subject to a maximum of 10% of salary of Rs. 10,32,000 (*i.e.*, Rs. 9,60,000 + 60% of dearness allowance of Rs. 1,20,000]		1,03,200

17. However, for the assessment year 2015-16, it cannot exceed Rs. 1,00,000.

18. Dearness allowance/pay shall be considered only when it is part of salary for computing **all** retirement benefits (like provident fund, pension, leave encashment, gratuity, etc.). If dearness allowance/pay is part of salary for computing only some (not all) of the retirement benefits, then it is not taken into consideration for this purpose.

	Rs.	*Rs.*
Under section 80C (PPF contribution)	90,000	
Under section 80CCC	25,000	
Under section 80CCD(1) [X's contribution towards NPS : Rs. 55,000 (*i.e.*, Rs. 1,05,000 – Rs. 50,000 considered under section 80CCD(1B)) but subject to a maximum of 10% of salary of Rs. 10,32,000]	55,000	
Total	1,70,000	
Amount deductible under sections 80C, 80CCC and 80CCD(1) within overall limit of Rs. 1,50,000 (the aforesaid amount of Rs. 1,70,000 is deductible to the extent of Rs. 1,50,000)		1,50,000
Net income		17,40,800

12.4 ***Compensation received at the time of voluntary retirement or separation [Sec. 10(10C)]*** - Compensation received at the time of voluntary retirement or separation is exempt from tax if the following conditions are satisfied—

1. Compensation is received on voluntary retirement or separation

2. Compensation is received by an employee of the following undertakings—

a. an authority established under a Central, State or Provincial Act;

b. local authority;

c. university;

d. an Indian Institute of Technology;

e. the State Government;

f. the Central Government;

g. a notified institute having importance throughout India or any State (*i.e.*, International Crops Research Institute for Semi-Arid Tropics; Action for Food Production, New Delhi, Government Tool Room & Training Centre, Rajajinagar Industrial Estate, Bangalore);

h. notified institute of management (*i.e.*, Indian Institute of Management, Ahmedabad, Bangalore, Calcutta or Lucknow and the Indian Institute of Foreign Trade, New Delhi);

i. public sector company; or

j. any company or a co-operative society.

3. Compensation is received in accordance with the scheme of voluntary retirement/separation which is framed in accordance with prescribed guidelines—*see* para 12.4-1.

4. Maximum amount of exemption is Rs. 5,00,000.

5. Where exemption has been allowed to an employee under section 10(*10C*) for any assessment year, no exemption thereunder shall be allowed to him in relation to any other assessment year.

12.4-1 *PRESCRIBED GUIDELINES* - The guidelines for the purpose of section 10(*10C*) have been laid down in rule 2BA[$]. The scheme of voluntary retirement should be in accordance with the following requirements, namely—

a. it applies to an employee who has completed 10 years of service or completed 40 years of age (this condition is, however, not applicable if the amount is received at the time of voluntary separation from a public sector company);

b. it applies to all employees (by whatever name called), including workers and executives of a concern excepting directors of a company or a co-operative society;

c. the scheme of voluntary retirement or separation has been drawn to result in overall reduction in the existing strength of the employees ;

d. the vacancy caused by voluntary retirement or separation is not to be filled up[19], nor the retiring employee is to be employed in another company or concern belonging to the same management ; and

e. the amount receivable on account of voluntary retirement or separation of the employee, does not exceed the amount equivalent to 3 months' salary for each completed year of service or monthly emoluments at the time of retirement multiplied by the balance months of service left before the date of his retirement on superannuation, whichever is more.

---

19. Merely because the scheme for voluntary retirement does not expressly set out that vacant posts will not be filled up, it cannot result in a scheme not being a scheme falling under section 10(*10C*)—*CIT* v. *Koodathil Kallyatan Ambujakshan* [2008] 175 Taxman 113 (Bom.).

$ For rule 2BA, log on to *taxmann.com/readyreckoner.aspx*.

The following points should also be kept in view :

- Taxpayers can frame different schemes of voluntary retirement for different classes of their employees. However, these schemes have to conform to the aforesaid guidelines prescribed in rule 2BA of the Income-tax Rules.
- For meaning of 'salary', *see* para 13.1-1.
- It is the last salary drawn which is to form the basis for computing the amount of payment.
- One of the requirements in the guidelines prescribed for schemes of voluntary retirement is that the scheme should apply to an employee of a company who has completed 10 years of service or 40 years of age. Since the employee of a company (presuming that he is less than 40 years of age) which has been set up less than 10 years ago, cannot satisfy the aforesaid requirement, the amount receivable by him shall not be entitled to income-tax exemption under section 10(*10C*).
- The scheme of voluntary retirement should be drawn to result in overall reduction in the existing strength of the employees of a company. This requirement reflects the criterion of economic viability for framing the schemes of voluntary retirement. The scheme which does not result in overall reduction in the existing strength of the employees of a company will not be in accordance with the guidelines prescribed for the purpose of section 10(*10C*).
- The requirement in the guidelines which reflects the economic criterion is to the effect that the scheme of voluntary retirement has been drawn to result in overall reduction in the existing strength of the employees of the company. Therefore, schemes can be drawn even by profit-making companies.
- Section 10(*10C*) has been amended with effect from the assessment year 2010-11 to provide that the person who has availed a relief under section 89 in respect of compensation for voluntary retirement or separation or termination of service, will not be able to claim any exemption under section 10(*10C*) for the same assessment year or any other assessment year.

12.5 ***Salary received by a teacher/professor from SAARC Member States*** - As per avoidance of double taxation agreement among Government of SAARC Member States (*i.e.*, Bangladesh, Bhutan, India, Maldives, Nepal, Pakistan and Sri Lanka), a professor (or teacher or research scholar) is not chargeable to tax in respect of his salary (including allowances and perquisites) if a few conditions are satisfied. These conditions are given below—

1. The professor (or teacher or research scholar) is or was a resident of the Member State immediately before visiting the other Member State. For this purpose, an individual shall be deemed to be a resident of a Member State if he/she is resident in that Member State in the fiscal year in which he/she visits the other Member State or in the immediately preceding fiscal year.

2. The professor (or teacher or research scholar) visits the other Member State for the purpose of teaching or engaging in research, or both, at a university, college or other similar approved institution in that other Member State.

3. Remuneration (for teaching or research) of such teacher shall be exempt from tax in that other Member State for a period not exceeding 2 years from the date of his/her arrival in that other Member State.

12.6 ***Salary to non-resident seafarer*** - Salary accrued to a non-resident seafarer for services rendered outside India on a foreign going ship (with Indian flag or foreign flag) shall not be included in the total income merely because the said salary has been credited in the NRE account maintained with an Indian bank by the seafarer – Circular No. 13/2017, dated April 11, 2017.

Allowance

13. Allowance is generally defined as a fixed quantity of money or other substance given regularly in addition to salary for the purpose of meeting some particular requirements connected with the service rendered by the employee or as compensation for unusual conditions of that service—*Mutual Acceptance Co. Ltd.* v. *FCT* [1944] 69 CLR 389. Under the Act, it is taxable under section 15 on "due" or "accrual" basis, irrespective of the fact that it is paid in addition to or in lieu of salary.

Tax treatment of different allowances is given below :

Different allowances	*Tax treatment*
City compensatory allowance	Taxable
House rent allowance	Exempt in some cases, *see* para 13.1
Entertainment allowance	Exempt in some cases, *see* para 13.2
Special allowance	Notified special allowances are exempt, *see* para 13.3.
Foreign allowance	Exempt from tax if paid outside India by the Government to an Indian citizen for rendering service outside India [section 10(7)]

Different allowances	*Tax treatment*
Tiffin allowance, fixed medical allowance and servant allowance	Taxable under section 15
Allowance to High Court Judges	Not taxable, *see* para 13.4
Allowance from a United Nations Organisation	Not taxable
Allowance to other foreign citizen	*See* para 21
Compensatory allowance under article 222(2) of the Constitution	Not taxable—*Bishambar Dayal* v. *CIT* [1976] 103 ITR 813 (MP)
Allowance of teacher/researcher from SAARC Member States	Exempt up to 2 years, *see* para 12.5
Sumptuary allowance to serving Chairman/members of UPSC	Not chargeable to tax.
Allowance to retired Chairman and retired members of UPSC	An allowance (subject to a maximum of Rs. 14,000 per month) for defraying the service of an orderly and for meeting expenses incurred towards secretarial assistance on contract basis, is not chargeable to tax.
Any other allowance	Taxable

13.1 ***House rent allowance [Sec. 10(13A) and rule 2A]*** - Exemption in respect of house rent allowance is regulated by rule 2A. The least of the following is exempt from tax—

a. an amount equal to 50 per cent of salary, where the residential house is situated at Bombay, Calcutta, Delhi or Madras and an amount equal to 40 per cent of salary where the residential house is situated at any other place ;

b. house rent allowance received by the employee in respect of the period during which the rental accommodation is occupied by the employee during the previous year ; or

c. the excess of rent paid over 10 per cent of salary.

13.1-1 *OTHER POINTS* - The following points should also be kept in view—

• "Salary" for the purpose of computation of exemption means basic salary and includes dearness allowance[20] if terms of employment so provide. It also includes commission based on a fixed percentage of turnover achieved by an employee as per terms of contract of employment—*Gestetner Duplicators (P.) Ltd.* v. *CIT* [1979] 1 Taxman 1/117 ITR 1 (SC), but excludes all other allowances and perquisites.

• Exemption under section 10(*13A*) is not available if an employee resides in his own house or if the employee does not incur any expenditure on payment of rent. Conversely, if the house in which the employee resides is not owned by him and he pays rent for it, he can claim exemption within the parameters of section 10(*13A*). Exemption is available even if the house is owned by a close relative (maybe wife or husband or father or mother) and for which rent is regularly paid (there is no legal requirement but in such cases rent should be paid regularly on monthly basis through bank transfer entry)—*Bajrang Prasad Ramdharani* v. *CIT* [2013] 60 SOT 66 (Ahd.).

• To avail exemption under section 10(*13A*), there is no requirement that the employee should not own a house. If an employee resides in a rented property, he can claim exemption under section 10(*13A*) even if he owns a house[21] (in the same city or in a different city).

13.1-E1 X, who resides in Calcutta, gets Rs. 6,00,000 as basic salary. He receives Rs. 1,70,000 as house rent allowance. Rent paid by him is Rs. 1,80,000. Find out the amount of taxable house rent allowance for the assessment year 2019-20.

•

Out of Rs. 1,70,000 received as house rent allowance, the least of the following is exempt from tax: (*a*) Rs. 3,00,000 being 50% of salary, (*b*) Rs. 1,70,000, being house rent allowance, or (*c*) Rs. 1,20,000, being excess of rent paid over 10% of salary. In this case, Rs. 1,20,000 is exempt from tax.

---

20. Dearness allowance/pay shall be considered only when it is part of salary for computing all retirement benefits (like pension, leave encashment, gratuity, provident fund, etc.). If dearness allowance/pay is part of salary for computing only some (not all) of the retirement benefits, then it is not taken into consideration for this purpose—*ITO* v. *Sr. Accounts Officer, Pay & Accounts, DHBVNL* [2009] 33 SOT 37 (Delhi).

21. Income from house owned by the employee would be calculated within the parameters of sections 22 to 27. If the house owned by the employee is let out, the entire interest liability pertaining to the house is deductible under section 24(*b*). If the house is self-occupied (it is possible if the house owned by employee is used by his parents/children/other relatives or if the house could not be utilised because it is situated at some other place), interest liability is deductible under section 24(*b*) up to Rs. 2,00,000 (in some cases up to Rs. 30,000). In such cases, exemption under section 10(*13A*) and deduction under section 24(*b*) can be claimed simultaneously.

13.1-E2 X, a resident of Bengaluru, receives Rs. 20,00,000 as basic salary. In addition, he gets Rs. 6,00,000 as dearness allowance (forming part of basic salary), 3.5 per cent commission on sales made by him (sale made by X during the previous year 2018-19 is Rs. 80,00,000) and Rs. 2,40,000 as house rent allowance. He, however, pays Rs. 2,80,000 as house rent. Determine the quantum of house rent allowance exempt from tax for the assessment year 2019-20.

•

Out of Rs. 2,40,000, the least of the following is exempt: (*a*) Rs. 11,52,000 being 40% of salary (*i.e.*, basic salary, dearness pay and commission : Rs. 2,80,000), (*b*) Rs. 2,40,000, being house rent allowance, or (*c*) *Nil*, being the excess of rent paid (*i.e.*, Rs. 2,80,000) over 10% of salary (*i.e.*, Rs. 2,88,000). As the least of the three is *nil*, the entire house rent allowance is taxable.

13.2 ***Entertainment allowance [Sec. 16(ii)]*** - Entertainment allowance is first included in salary income under the head "Salaries" and thereafter a deduction is given on the basis enumerated in the following paragraphs—

• In the case of a Government employee, the least of (*i*) Rs. 5,000; (*ii*) 20 per cent of basic salary; or (*iii*) the actual amount of entertainment allowance, is eligible for deduction.

• In the case of a non-Government employee, no deduction is available from the assessment year 2002-03.

For this purpose "salary" excludes any allowance, benefit or other perquisites.

13.3 ***Special allowances prescribed as exempt [Sec. 10(14) read with rule 2BB]*** - The following special allowances are exempt under section 10(*14*), read with rule 2BB—

Name of allowance	*Place at which allowance is exempt*	*Maximum amount exempt from tax*
(*1*)	(*2*)	(*3*)
1. Any allowance (by whatever name called) granted to meet the cost of travel on tour or on transfer (including any sum paid in connection with transfer, packing and transportation of personal effects on such transfer)	Any place	To the extent the allowance is utilised for the purpose specified in column (*1*)
2. Conveyance allowance granted to meet the expenditure on conveyance in performance of duties of an office[22]	Any place	To the extent the allowance is utilised for the purpose specified in column (*1*)
3. Any allowance, whether granted period on tour or for the journey in connection with transfer, to meet the ordinary daily charges incurred by an employee on account of absence from his normal place of duty	Any place	To the extent the allowance is utilised for the purpose specified in column (*1*)

22. Expenditure for covering the journey between office and residence is not treated as expenditure in performance of official duty. *See* also "transport allowance" *infra.*

(1)	(2)	(3)
4. Any allowance (by whatever name called) to meet the expenditure on a helper where such helper is engaged for the performance of duties of an office	Any place	To the extent the allowance is utilised for the purpose specified in column (*1*)
5. Any allowance (by whatever name called) granted for encouraging the academic, research and other professional pursuits	Any place	To the extent the allowance is utilised for the purpose specified in column (*1*)
6. Any allowance (by whatever name called) to meet the expenditure on the purchase or maintenance of uniform[23] for wear during the performance of duties of an office	Any place	To the extent the allowance is utilised for the purpose specified in column (*1*)
7. Any special compensatory allowance in the nature of special compensatory (hilly area) allowance or high altitude allowance or uncongenial climate allowance or snow bound area allowance or avalanche allowance	**I.** (*a*) *Manipur:* Mollan/RH-2365 (*b*) *Arunachal Pradesh :* (*i*) Kameng, (*ii*) North Eastern Arunachal Pradesh where heights are 9,000 ft. and above, (*iii*) Areas east and west of Siang and Subansiri sectors. (*c*) *Sikkim :* (*i*) Area North-NE-East of line Chhaten LR 0105 Launchung LR 1902, pt. 4326 LW 1790, pt. 4349 LW 1479, pt. 3601 LW 1471 to mile 13 LW 1367 to Berluk LW 2253, (*ii*) All other areas at 9,000 ft. and above. (*d*) *Uttar Pradesh :* Areas of Harsil, Mana and Malari Sub-Divisions and other areas of heights at 9,000 ft. and above. (*e*) *Himachal Pradesh :* (*i*) All areas at 9,000 ft. and above ahead of line joining Puhkajakunzomla towards the bower, (*ii*) Area ahead of line joining Karchham and Shigrila towards the bower, (*iii*) All areas in Kalpa, Spiti, Lahaul and Tisa. (*f*) *Jammu & Kashmir:* (*i*) All areas from NR 396950 to NR 350850, NR 370790, NR 311776 North of Shaikhra Village, North of Pindi Village to NR 240800, (*ii*) Areas of Doda, Sank and other post located in areas at a height of 9,000 ft. and above, (*iii*) North of line Kud-Dudu and Basttgarh, Bilwar, Batote and Patnitop, (*iv*) All areas ahead of Zojila served by Road Srinagar-Zojila-Leh in Leh District, (*v*) Gulmarg - all areas forward of line joining Anita Linyan 3309 Kaunrali-2407, (*vi*) Uri South - all areas forward of Kaunrali-Kandi 1810 Kustam 1505 - Sebasantra 1006 Changez 0507-Jak 19904 Keekar 9704 Jamun 9607 Neeta 9508, (*vii*) BAAZ Kaiyan Bowl - all areas forward of Dulurj 9712 - BAAZ 0317 - Shamsher 0416 including New Shamsher 0615 -	Rs. 800[24] per month

23. Normal dress worn by employees is not uniform for purpose of exemption as uniform allowance under section 10(*14*)—*ONGC, Basin Baroda* v. *CIT* [2014] 63 SOT 105 (Ahd.), *Facets Polishing Works (P.) Ltd.* v. *ITO* [2015] 58 taxmann.com 373 (Ahd.).

24. Rs. 600 up to July 31, 1997 (*i.e.*, the assessment year 1997-98).

(1)	*(2)*	*(3)*
	Zoravar 1017 - Malaugan Base 1027 - Radha 0836 to Nastachun Pass 9847, (*viii*) Tangdhar - all areas west of Nastachun Pass Tangdhar Bowl and on Shamshabari Range and forward of it, (*ix*) Karan and Machhal sub-sectors - all areas along the line Pharkiangali 0869 to Z Gali 4376 and forward of Shamshabari Range, (*x*) Panzgam, Trehgam and Drugmul.	
	II. Siachen area of Jammu & Kashmir.	Rs. 7,000[25] per month
	III. All places located at a height of 1,000 metres or more above the sea level, other than places specified at (I) and (II) above.	Rs. 300[26] per month
8. Any Special Compensatory Allowance in the nature of Border Area Allowance, Remote Locality Allowance or Difficult Area Allowance or Disturbed Area Allowance (applicable from August 1, 1997, *i.e.*, the assessment year 1998-99)	**I.** (*a*) Little Andaman, Nicobar and Narcondum Islands; (*b*) North and Middle Andamans; (*c*) Throughout Lakshadweep and Minicoy Islands; (*d*) All places on or north of the following demarcation line: Point 14600 (2881) to Sala MS 2686-Matau MS 6777 - Sakong MT 1379-Bamong-Khonawa MO 2803 - Nyapin MO 7525 - River Khru to its junction with the river Kamla MP - 2226 - Taliha - Yapuik MK 7410 - Gshong MK 9749 - Yinki Yong NF 4324-Damoroh MF 6208 - Ahinkolin NF 8811 - Kronli MG 2407 - Hanli NM 4096 - Gurongon NM 4592-Loon NM 7579 - Mayuliang NM 0169-Chawah NM 9943 - Kamphu NM 1125 - Point 6490 (NM 1493) Vijayanagar NSA-486; (*e*) Following areas in Himachal Pradesh : (*i*) Pangi Tehsil of Chamba District; (*ii*) Following Panchayats and villages of Bharmour Tehsil of Chamba District; (*A*) Panchayat Badgaun, Bajol, Deol, Kugti, Nayagam and Tundah (*B*) Villages Gatu of Gram Panchayat Jagat Kanarsi of Gram Panchayat Cauhata; (*iii*) Lahul and Spiti District; (*iv*) Kinnaur district: (*A*) Asrang, Chitkul and Hango Kuno Charang Panchayats (*B*) 15/20 Area comprising the Gram Panchayats of Chhota Khamba, Nathpa and Rupi, (*C*) Pooh sub-Division excluding the Panchayat Areas specified above; (*v*) 15/20 Area of Rampur Tehsil comprising of Panchayats of Koot, Labana-Sadana, Sarpara and Chandi Branda of Shimla District; (*vi*) 15/20 Area of Nirmand Tehsil, comprising the Gram Panchayats of Kharga, Kushwar and Sarga of Kullu District. (*f*) Chimptuipui District of Mizoram and areas beyond 25 km. from Lunglei town in Lunglei District of Mizoram. (*g*) Following areas in Jammu and Kashmir: (*i*) Niabat Bani, Lohi, Malhar and Macchodi of Kathua District; (*ii*) Dudu, Basantgarh, Lander Thamag Illaqa, Thakrakote and Nagote of Udhampur District; (*iii*) All areas in Tehsil Mahore except those specified at III(*f*)(*i*) below in Udhampur District; (*iv*) Illaqas of Padder and Niabat Nowgaon in Kishtwar Tehsil of Doda District; (*v*) Leh District; (*vi*) Entire Gurez-Niabat, Tangdhar, Sub-Division and Keran Illaqa of Baramulla District. (*h*) Following areas of Uttar Pradesh : (*i*) Chamoli District; (*ii*) Pithoragarh District; (*iii*) Uttarkashi District; (*i*) Throughout Sikkim State.	Rs. 1,300 per month
	II. Installations in the Continental shelf of India and the Exclusive Economic Zone of India.	Rs. 1,100 per month
	III. (*a*) Throughout Arunachal Pradesh other than areas covered by those specified at I(*d*) above. (*b*) Throughout Nagaland State. (*c*) South Andaman (including Port Blair). (*d*) Throughout Lunglei District (excluding areas beyond 25 km. from Lunglei town) of Mizoram. (*e*) Dharmanagar, Kailasahar, Amarpur and Khowai in Tripura. (*f*) Following areas in Jammu and Kashmir : (*i*) Areas up to Goel from Kamban side and areas upto Arnas from Keasi side in Tehsil Mahore of Udhampur District; (*ii*) Matchill in Baramulla District.	Rs. 1,050 per month

25. Rs. 1,200 up to July 31, 1997 (*i.e.*, the assessment year 1997-98).

26. Rs. 150 up to July 31, 1997 (*i.e.*, the assessment year 1997-98).

(1)	(2)	(3)
	(*g*) Following areas in Himachal Pradesh — (*i*) Bharmour Tehsil, excluding Panchayats and villages covered by those specified at I(*e*)(*ii*) above of Chamba District; (*ii*) Chhota Bhangal and Bara Bhangal area of Kangra District; (*iii*) Kinnaur District other than areas specified at 1(*e*)(*iv*); (*iv*) Dodra - Kawar Tehsil, Gram Panchayats of Darkali in Rampur, Kashapath Tehsil and Munish, Ghori Chaibis of Pargana Sarahan of Shimla District.	
	IV. (*a*) Throughout Aizawal District of Mizoram	Rs. 750 per month
	(*b*) Throughout Tripura except areas those specified at III (*e*).	
	(*c*) Throughout Manipur.	
	(*d*) Following areas of Himachal Pradesh — (*i*) Jhandru Panchayat in Bhatiyat Tehsil, Churah Tehsil, Dalhousie Town (including Banikhet proper) of Chamba District. (*ii*) Cuter Seraj (excluding Village of Jakat-Khana and Burow in Nirmand Tehsil of Kullu District. (*iii*) Following areas of Mandi District :—(*A*) Chuhar Valley (Jogindernagar Tehsil) (*B*) Bagara, Chhatri, Chhotdhar, Garagushain, Gatoo, Gharyas, Janjehli, Jaryar, Johar Kalhani Kalwan, Kholanal, Loth, Silibagi, Somachan, Thachdhar, Tachi and Thana Panchayats of Thunag Tehsil; (*C*) Binga, Kamlah, Saklana, Tanyar and Tarakholah, Panchayats of Dharampur Block (*D*) Balidhar, Bagra, Gopalpur, Khajol, Mahog, Mehudi, Manj, Pekhi, Sainj, Sarahan and Teban, Panchayats of Karsog Tehsil. (*E*) Bohi, Batwara, Dhanyara, Paura-Kothi, Seri and Shoja, Panchayats of Sundernagar Tehsil. (*iv*) Following areas and offices of Kangra District : (*A*) Dharamsala town and Women's ITI. Dari, Mechanical Workshop, Ramnagar; Child Welfare and Town Country Planning Offices. Sakoh; CRSF Office at lower Sakoh; Kangra Milk Supply Scheme, Shamnagar; Tea Factory, Dari; Forest Corporation Office, Shamnagar; Tea Factory, Dari; Settlement Office, Shamnagar and Binwa Project, Shamnagar. Offices located outside the Municipal limit of Dharamsala town but included in Dharamsala town for purposes of eligibility to Special Compensatory (Remote Locality) Allowance; (*B*) Palampur town, including HPKVV Campus at Palampur and H.P. Krishi Vishvavidyalaya Campus; Cattle Development Office, Jersy Farm, Banuri; Sericulture Office/ Indo-German Agriculture Workshop/HPPWD Division, Bundla; Electrical Sub-Division, Lohna; D.P.O. Corporation, Bundla and Electrical HPSEE Division, Ghuggar offices located outside the municipal limits of Palampur town but included in Palampur town for the purpose of above allowance. (*v*) Chopal Tehsil; Ghoris, Panjgaon, Patsnu, Naubis and Teen Koti of Pargana Sarahan; Deothi Gram Panchayat of Taklesh Area; Pargana Barabis; Kasba Rampur and Ghori Nog of Pargana Rampur of Rampur Tehsil of Shimla District and Shimla Town and its suburbs (Dhalli, Jatog, Kasumpti, Mashobara, Taradevi and Tutu). (*vi*) Panchayats of Bani, Bakhali (Pachhad Tehsil), Bharog Bheneri (Paonata Tehsil), Birla (Nahan Tehsil), Dibber (Pachhad Tehsil) of Thanan Kasoga (Nahan Tehsil) in Sirmour District and Transgiri Tract of Sirmour District. (*vii*) Mangal Panchayat of Solan District;	
	(*e*) Following areas in Jammu and Kashmir :— (*i*) Areas in Poonch and Rajouri Districts excluding the towns of Poonch and Rajouri and Sunderbani and other Urban areas in the two districts;	
	(*f*) Following areas in Jammu and Kashmir :— Areas not included in I(*g*), III(*f*) and IV(*e*) above, but which are within a distance of 8 km. from the line of actual control or at places which may be declared as qualifying for Border Allowance from time to time by the State Government for their own staff.	
	V. Jog Falls in Shimoga District in Karnataka.	Rs. 300 per month
	VI. (*a*) Throughout the State of Himachal Pradesh other than areas covered by those specified in I(*e*), III(*g*) and IV(*d*)	Rs. 200 per month
	(*b*) Throughout the State of Assam and Meghalaya	

(1)	*(2)*	*(3)*
9. Special Compensatory (Tribal Areas/Schedule Areas/Agency Areas) Allowance	(*a*) Madhya Pradesh; (*b*) Tamil Nadu; (*c*) Uttar Pradesh; (*d*) Karnataka; (*e*) Tripura; (*f*) Assam; (*g*) West Bengal; (*h*) Bihar; (*i*) Orissa	Rs. 200[27] per month
10. Any allowance granted to an employee working in any transport system to meet his personal expenditure during his duty performed in the course of running of such transport from one place to another place provided that such employee is not in receipt of daily allowance	Whole of India	70 per cent of such allowance up to a maximum of Rs. 10,000[28] per month
11. Children education allowance (by whatever name called)	Whole of India	Rs. 100[29] per month per child up to a maximum of two children
12. Any allowance granted to an employee to meet the hostel expenditure on his child (by whatever name called)	Whole of India	Rs. 300[30] per month per child up to a maximum of two children
13. Compensatory Field Area Allowance[32]	(*a*) Following areas in Arunachal Pradesh—(*i*) Tirap and Changlang districts; (*ii*) all areas north of the line joining point 4448 in LZ 4179 - Nukme Dong MS 3272 - Sepla MT 2969 - Palin MO 9213 - Daporijo NR 5841 - Along NL 1273 - Hunli NM 3196 - Tidding Tuwi MT 6369 - Hayuliang NN 0170 - Tawaken MT 8136 - Champai Bun NM 8814, all inclusive (*b*) Throughout Manipur and Nagaland (*c*) Following areas in Sikkim—All areas north and north-east of line joining Phalut LV 4750 - Gezing LV 7059 - Mangkha LV 6160 - Penlang La; LW 0666 - Rangli LW 1448 - BP 1 in LW 2453 on Indo-Bhutan Border, all inclusive (*d*) Following areas in Himachal Pradesh,—all areas east of line joining Umasila NV 3951; Udaipur NY 8663 - Manikaran SB 2300 - Pir Parbati Pass TA 1459 - Taranda TA 2335 - Barasua Pass TA 8801, all inclusive (*e*) Following areas in Uttar Pradesh—all areas north and north-east of line joining Barasua Pass, Gangnani TG 1362 - Govind Ghat TG 0937 - Tapovan TH 1822 - Musiari TN 8982 - Relagad TO 2466, all inclusive	Rs. 2,600[31] per month

27. Rs. 100 up to July 31, 1997 (*i.e.*, assessment year 1997-98).

28. Rs. 3,000 up to July 31, 1997 (*i.e.*, assessment year 1997-98) and Rs. 6,000 up to August 31, 2008 (*i.e.*, assessment year 2008-09).

29. Rs. 50 up to July 31, 1997 (*i.e.*, assessment year 1997-98).

30. Rs. 150 up to July 31, 1997 (*i.e.*, assessment year 1997-98).

31. Rs. 975 for the assessment years 1995-96 to 1997-98 and Rs. 1,300 for the assessment years 1998-99 and 1999-2000.

32. Any assessee claiming exemption in respect of the allowance mentioned at serial number *13* shall not be entitled to the exemption in respect of the allowance referred to at serial number *8*.

(1)	(2)	(3)
	(*f*) Following areas in Jammu and Kashmir—(*i*) areas north and east of line joining Zojila MU 3036 - Baralachala NE 6672 along the Great Himalayan Range, all inclusive; (*ii*) all areas west of line joining Point 1556 in NR 5470 - Gulmarg MT 3105 - Naushara MY 3105 - Ringapat MT 2133 - Handwara MT 2043 - Laingyal MT 2339 - Point 8405 in 4565 - North of line joining point 8403 - Bunakut MT 5453 - Razan NN 2239 - Zojila, all inclusive; (*iii*) all areas west of line joining tip of Chicken Neck RD 7073 - Canal Junction RD 6364 - Mawa Brahmana RD 6183 - Chauki RD 6393 - Road junction RD 6499 - Baramgala MY 3854 - Point 1556 in NR 5470, all inclusive.	
14. Compensatory Modified field area Allowance[33]	(*a*) Following areas in Punjab and Rajasthan—areas west of line joining Jessai, Barmer, Jaisalmer, Pokharan, Udasar, Mahajan Ranges, Suratgarh, Lalgarh, Jattan, Abohar, Govindgarh, Fazilka, Jandiala Guru, Moga, Dholewal, Deas, Bir Sarangwal, Hussainiwalla, Dera Baba Nanak, Laisain Bulge up to the international border, all inclusive (*b*) Following areas in Haryana—Satrod (Hissar) (*c*) Following areas in Himachal Pradesh—areas North of line joining Narkanda, Keylong up to Field Area line/High Altitude line (*d*) Following areas in Arunachal Pradesh and Assam—(*i*) Cachar and North Cachar districts of Assam including Silchar; (*ii*) all areas of Arunachal Pradesh and Assam north of river Brahmaputra except Tejpur, Misamari and Field Areas (*e*) Throughout Mizoram and Tripura (*f*) Following areas in Sikkim and West Bengal—areas northwards of line joining Sevoke LV 9112 -Burdong LV 9850 - Sherwani LV 9453 - Bagrakot LW 0113 - Damdim LW 1109 - New Mal - Hasimara - QB 7894 Ganga Ram Tea Estate QA 1377 up to the High Altitude line/Field Area line/international border, all inclusive (*g*) Following areas in Uttar Pradesh—areas north of line joining Uttarkashi, Karan Prayag, Gauchar, Joshimath, Chamoli, Rudra Prayag, Askote, Charamgad, Dharchula, Kausani and Narendra Nagar up to international border, all inclusive (*h*) Following areas in Jammu and Kashmir—(*i*) areas west of line joining Pattan, Baramulla, Kupwara, Drugmula, Panges, Mankes, Buniyar, Pantha Chowk, Khanabal, Anantnag, Khundru and Khru up to the existing High Altitude line, all inclusive; (*ii*) Areas west of the line joining - BP 19, Brahmana-di-Bari, Jindra, Dhansal, Katra, Sanjhi Chatt, Batote, Patnitop, Ramban and Banihal upto the existing High Altitude line, all inclusive.	Rs. 1,000 per month[34]
15. Any special allowance in the nature of counter-insurgency allowance granted to the members of armed forces operating in areas away from their permanent locations[33]	Whole of India	Rs. 3,900 per month[35]

33. Any assessee claiming exemption in respect of the allowance mentioned at serial numbers *14* and *15* shall not be entitled to the exemption in respect of the allowance referred to at serial number *8*.

34. Rs. 375 per month for the assessment years 1995-96 to 1997-98 and Rs. 500 per month for the assessment years 1998-99 and 1999-2000.

35. Rs. 975 per month for the assessment years 1995-96 to 1997-98 and Rs. 1,300 per month for the assessment years 1998-99 and 1999-2000.

(1)	*(2)*	*(3)*
16. Transport allowance granted to an employee (other than an employee referred to in *17 infra*) to meet his expenditure for the purpose of commuting between place of his residence and the place of his duty	Whole of India	Rs. 1,600 per month (up to the assessment year 2018-19)[36, 37, 38]
17. Transport allowance granted to an employee, who is blind or deaf and dumb or orthopaedically handicapped with disability of lower extremities to meet his expenditure for the purpose of commuting between the place of his residence and the place of his duty	Whole of India	Rs. 3,200 per month[39]
18. Underground allowance granted to an employee who is working in uncongenial, unnatural climate in underground mines	Whole of India	Rs. 800 per month[40]
19. Any special allowance in the nature of high altitude (uncongenial climate) allowance granted to the member of the armed forces operating in high altitude areas	(*a*) For altitude of 9,000 to 15,000 feet (*b*) For altitude above 15,000 feet	Rs. 1,060 per month[40] Rs. 1,600 per month[40]
20. Any special allowance granted to the members of the armed forces in the nature of special	Whole of India	Rs. 4,200 per month[40]

36. In the case of Chairman/members of UPSC, transport allowance is not chargeable to tax (without any monetary ceiling) by virtue of section 10(*45*).

37. Increased from Rs. 800 to Rs. 1,600 with effect from April 1, 2015 *vide* Notification No. 39/2015, dated April 13, 2015. Technically it means that Rs. 1,600 is applicable from the assessment year 2015-16. However, Government tax experts are of the view that the enhanced exemption rate of Rs. 1,600 is applicable from the previous year 2015-16.

38. Withdrawn with effect from the assessment year 2019-20.

39. Increased from Rs. 1,600 to Rs. 3,200 with effect from April 1, 2015, *ibid.*

40. Applicable from the assessment year 2000-01.

(1)	(2)	(3)
compensatory highly active field area allowance		
21. Any special allowance granted to the member of the armed forces in the nature of island (duty) allowance	Andaman & Nicobar and Lakshadweep Group of Islands	Rs. 3,250 per month[41]

13.4 ***Allowance to High Court and Supreme Court Judges*** - The following allowances are not chargeable to tax :

- Any allowance paid to High Court Judges under section 22A(2) of the High Court Judges (Conditions of Service) Act, 1954 is not chargeable to tax.
- Sumptuary allowance given to High Court Judges under section 22C of the High Court Judges (Conditions of Service) Act, 1954 and to Supreme Court Judges under section 23B of the Supreme Court Judges (Conditions of Service) Act, 1958 is not chargeable to tax.

13.5 ***Allowances received by a teacher/professor from SAARC Member States*** - *See* para 12.5.

Perquisites [Sec. 17(2)]

14. "Perquisite" may be defined as any casual emolument or benefit attached to an office or position in addition to salary or wages. It also denotes something that benefits a man by *going into his own pocket*; it does not, however, cover mere reimbursement of necessary disbursements—*Owen* v. *Pook (Inspector of Taxes)* [1969] 2 WLR 775.

14.1 ***Perquisites chargeable/not chargeable to tax*** - The Table given below gives a list of perquisites chargeable (or not chargeable) to tax—

Different perquisites given under section 17(2) chargeable to tax (list of taxable perquisites)	*Para No. (for detailed discussion)*	*When these perquisites are not taxable (list of tax-free perquisites)*
(1)	*(2)*	*(3)*
1. Furnished/unfurnished house without rent or at concessional rent	15.1, 15.2, 15.3	*1.* Not chargeable to tax if provided in a "remote area". *2.* Hotel or guest house accommodation for 15 days (in aggregate in a previous year) can be provided immediately after transfer at the new location as a tax-free perquisite. *3.* If an employee is transferred and housing facility is provided to him at the new location (he has yet to vacate a house given at the old location), for a period of 90 days immediately after transfer only one house (at the option of the employee at the old location or new location) is chargeable to tax and the other one will be tax-free. *4.* Further, rent-free house is not taxable if it is provided to a High Court Judge, Supreme Court Judge, Union Minister, Leader of Opposition in Parliament, an Official in Parliament and serving Chairman and members of UPSC
2. Service of a sweeper, gardener, watchman or personal attendant	15.4	Not taxable if the employee is a non-specified employee [*see* para 14.1-1]
3. Supply of gas, electricity or water for household purposes	15.5	Not taxable if the employee is a non-specified employee [*see* para 14.1-1]
4. Education facility to employee's family members	15.6	Not taxable if the employee is a non-specified employee [*see* para 14.1-1]
5. Leave travel concession	15.7	*1.* Not taxable twice in a block of 4 years *2.* Not taxable if the employee is a non-specified employee [*see* para 14.1-1]

41. Applicable from the assessment year 2000-01.

Different perquisites given under section 17(2) chargeable to tax (list of taxable perquisites)	*Para No. (for detailed discussion)*	*When these perquisites are not taxable (list of tax-free perquisites)*
(1)	*(2)*	*(3)*
6. Amount paid by an employer in respect of any obligation which otherwise would have been payable by the employee	15.8	Tax borne by employer on non-monetary perquisites of employees
7. Amount payable by an employer directly or indirectly to effect an assurance on the life of employee or to effect a contract of an annuity	15.9	Contribution to recognized provident fund
8. Interest-free/concessional loan	15.10	*1.* If aggregate amount of original loan does not exceed Rs. 20,000, the perquisite is not taxable. *2.* Loan for medical treatment (given in rule 3A[$]) is not taxable subject to a few conditions
9. Providing use of movable asset	15.11	Providing use of computer/laptop in any case
10. Transfer of movable asset	15.12	
11. Medical facility	15.13	*1.* Medical facility provided in a hospital owned or maintained by the employer is not chargeable to tax. *2.* Medical facility provided by an employer in a Government hospital or approved hospital (if a few conditions are satisfied) or a private hospital (if such private hospital is recommended by the Government for the medial treatment of Government employees) is not chargeable to tax. *3.* Medical insurance premium paid or reimbursed by the employer is not chargeable to tax. *4.* Any other expenditure incurred or reimbursed by the employer for providing medical facility in India is chargeable to tax[42]. *5.* Expenditure on medical treatment outside India is not chargeable to tax, if a few conditions are satisfied. *6.* Further, the perquisite in respect of medical facility is not taxable if the employee is a non-specified employee [*see* para 14.4-1]
12. Car or any other automotive conveyance	15.14	*1.* Not taxable if the employee is a non-specified employee [*see* para 14.1-1]. *2.* Conveyance facility between office and residence is not taxable. *3.* Conveyance facility to High Court judges, Supreme Court judges and serving Chairman and members of UPSC, is not chargeable to tax
13. Transport facility by a transport undertaking	15.15	*1.* Not taxable if it is provided by an airline or the railways. *2.* Not taxable if the employee is a non-specified employee [*see* para 14.1-1]
14. Free food and beverage	15.16	*1.* Food and non-alcoholic beverages provided in working hours in remote area or in an offshore installation are exempt from tax. *2.* Tea, coffee or non-alcoholic beverages and snacks in working hours are tax-free perquisites. *3.* Meals (lunch and/or dinner) in office hours is not taxable if cost to the employer is Rs. 50 (or less) per meal
15. Travelling, touring accommodation	15.17	
16. Gift or gift voucher	15.18	Gift is in kind up to Rs. 5,000 is exempt
17. Credit card	15.19	Initial fees payable for obtaining corporate membership (if a few conditions are satisfied)
18. Club	15.20	Health club or Sports club facility if a few conditions are satisfied
19. Tax of employee paid by employer	15.21	Tax on non-monetary perquisite paid by employer is exempt

42. Rs. 15,000 is exempt up to the assessment year 2018-19.

[$] For rule 3A, log on to *taxmann.com/readyreckoner.aspx.*

Different perquisites given under section 17(2) chargeable to tax (list of taxable perquisites)	*Para No. (for detailed discussion)*	*When these perquisites are not taxable (list of tax-free perquisites)*
(1)	*(2)*	*(3)*
20. Value of any specified security/sweat equity shares allotted or transferred to an employee or former employee	15.22	
21. Employer's contribution towards superannuation fund in excess of Rs. 1.5 lakh[43] per year	15.23	Not chargeable to tax up to Rs. 1.5 lakh[43] per year
22. Perquisites received by a teacher/professor from SAARC Member States	12.5	Not taxable for 2 years
23. Any other benefit or amenity, service, right or privilege	15.24	Telephone/mobile is not chargeable to tax

14.1-1 *SPECIFIED/NON-SPECIFIED EMPLOYEES* - An employee is either a specified employee or a non-specified employee.

• *Classification - "Specified employee" and "Non-specified employee"* - Perquisites given under *2, 3, 4, 5, 11, 12* and *13* are taxable only when an employee is a specified employee. In other words, perquisites given under *2, 3, 4, 5, 11, 12* and *13* are not taxable in the hands of a non-specified employee.

• *Classification - Does not have much practical utility* - The classification between specified and non-specified employee is of limited application in the practical sense. This is because an employee is referred to as a non-specified employee only when he is drawing annual salary of Rs. 50,000 or less in a financial year. Since the exemption slab for all individuals is at least Rs. 2,50,000 (for the assessment year 2019-20), one can infer that largely all employees (who pay income-tax) are specified employees. The statement that perquisites given under *2, 3, 4, 5, 11, 12* and *13* are not taxable in the case of a non-specified employee, does not have much practical utility, as all employees paying tax are specified employees. However, the meaning of specified/non-specified employee is given in the following paras for theoretical purposes—

• *Non-specified employee* - Any employee, other than a specified employee, is a "non-specified employee".

• *Who is a specified employee* - The following employees are known as specified employees—

1. A director-employee - An employee who is a director in the employer-company at any time during the previous year, is a specified employee of the company in which he is a director.

2. An employee who has substantial interest in the employer-company - An employee who has a substantial interest in the employer-company at any time during the previous year is a specified employee of the company in which he has substantial interest. A person has substantial interest in the employer-company, if he is a beneficial owner of equity shares carrying 20 per cent or more voting power in the employer-company.

3. An employee drawing in excess of Rs. 50,000 - An employee (not covered by the above two categories), whose income chargeable for the previous year under the head "Salaries" (exclusive of the value of all benefits or amenities not provided by way of monetary payments) exceeds Rs. 50,000, is a specified employee. For computing the sum of Rs. 50,000, the following are excluded or deducted :

a. all non-monetary benefits;

b. monetary benefits which are not taxable under section 10 [for instance, house rent allowance to the extent exempt under section 10(*13A*) is excluded]; and

c. deduction on account of entertainment allowance and deduction on account of professional tax.

Where salary is received from more than one employer, the aggregate salary from these employers will have to be taken into account for the purpose of determining the aforesaid monetary ceiling.

Valuation of perquisites

15. Those perquisites which are taxable in the hands of employees, are valued in accordance with the provisions laid down under the Income-tax Rules and executive instructions—

1. Under the rules, perquisites provided by the employer (directly or indirectly) to the employee or any member of his household (by reason of his employment) shall be considered. "Member of household" shall include—

a. spouse (whether dependent or not);

b. children and their spouses (whether dependent or not);

43. Rs. 1 lakh up to the assessment year 2016-17.

c. parents (whether dependent or not); and

d. servants and dependants.

15.1 ***Valuation of rent-free unfurnished accommodation [Rule 3(1)]*** - "Accommodation" includes a house, flat, farm house (or part thereof), or accommodation in a hotel, motel, service apartment, guest-house, caravan, mobile home, ship or other floating structure. For the purpose of valuation of the perquisite in respect of unfurnished accommodation, employees are divided in the following two categories—

a. Central and State Government employees [*see* para 15.1-1].

b. Private sector employees or other employees [*see* para 15.1-2].

15.1-1 *CENTRAL AND STATE GOVERNMENT EMPLOYEES* - This category includes Central and State Government employees. The following conditions should be satisfied to come in this category—

a. the accommodation is provided by the Union or a State Government ; and

b. such accommodation is provided to their employees either holding office or post in connection with the affairs of Union or State or serving with any body or undertaking under the control of such Government on deputation.

Employees of a local authority or a foreign Government are, however, not covered by this category but in residual category mentioned in para 15.1-2.

• *Basis of valuation* - The value of perquisite in respect of accommodation provided to such employee is equal to the licence fee which would have been determined by the Central or State Government in accordance with the rules framed by the Government for allotment of houses to its officers.

• *Exception* - Rent-free official residence provided to a Judge of a High Court under section 22A(1) of the High Court Judges (Conditions of Service) Act, 1954, or to a Judge of the Supreme Court under section 23(1) of the Supreme Court Judges (Conditions of Service) Act, 1958 is exempt from tax. A similar exemption is extended to an official of Parliament, a Union Minister, a Leader of Opposition in Parliament and serving Chairman/members of UPSC.

15.1-2 *PRIVATE SECTOR OR OTHER EMPLOYEES* - Under this category are covered those employees who do not fall in the first category covered by para 15.1-1. In this category, value of the perquisite in respect of rent-free accommodation depends on salary of the employee and lease rent of the accommodation.

15.1-2a SALARY - HOW TO CALCULATE - For the purpose of valuation of perquisite in respect of rent-free accommodation, salary includes :

a. basic salary;

b. dearness allowance/pay, if terms of employment so provide[44];

c. bonus;

d. commission;

e. fees;

f. all other taxable allowances (excluding amount not taxable); and

g. any monetary payment (by whatever name called).

For this purpose salary does not include the following :

i. dearness allowance/pay, if not taken into account while calculating retirement benefits, like provident fund, gratuity, etc., or if term of employment does not so provide;

ii. employer's contribution to provident fund account of an employee;

iii. all allowances which are exempt from tax;

iv. value of perquisites [under section 17(*2*)]; and

v. lump-sum payments received at the time of termination of service or superannuation or voluntary retirement, like gratuity, severance pay, leave encashment, voluntary retrenchment benefits, commutation of pension and similar payments.

• One should note the following points—

1. "Salary" shall be determined on "due" basis - While computing salary for the purpose of valuation of perquisite in respect of rent-free accommodation, basic salary, bonus, commission, fees, allowances, etc., are

---

44. Dearness allowance/pay shall be considered only when it is part of salary for computing all retirement benefits (like pension, leave encashment, gratuity, provident fund, etc.). If dearness allowance/pay is part of salary for computing only some (not all) of the retirement benefits, then it is not taken into consideration for this purpose—*ITO* v. *Sr. Accounts Officer, Pay & Accounts, DHBVNL* [2009] 33 SOT 37 (Delhi).

included on "due" basis. For instance, advance salary of a period other than the previous year is not included even if the same is received in the previous year. Similarly, salary due in the previous year is included, even if it is received after the end of the previous year. In other words, salary due for the period during which rent-free accommodation is occupied by the employee will be considered, whether it is received during the previous year or not.

2. *Salary from two or more employers* - Salary from all employers in respect of the period during which accommodation is provided will be taken into consideration.

3. *Monetary payments* v. *Perquisites* - A combined reading of the above points suggests [*see* (*g*) and (*iv*) *supra*] that monetary payments which are in the nature of perquisites shall not be included.

4. *Gas, electricity, water bills, payment of income-tax* - Payment of gas, electricity, water and income-tax bill (being perquisite) is not taken into consideration.

15.1-2b BASIS OF VALUATION - The basis of valuation is given below—

Population of city as per 2001 census where accommodation is provided	*Where the accommodation is owned by the employer*	*Where the accommodation is taken on lease or rent by the employer*
Exceeding 25 lakh	15 per cent of salary in respect of period during which the accommodation is occupied by the employee	*a.* 15% of salary; or *b.* lease rent (paid or payable) by employer, whichever is less.
Exceeding 10 lakh but not exceeding 25 lakh	10 per cent of salary in respect of period during which the accommodation is occupied by the employee	
Any other	7.5 per cent of salary in respect of period during which the accommodation is occupied by the employee	

Notes :

1. The above rules are not applicable to any accommodation located in a 'remote area' (*i.e.*, an area located at least 40 kilometres away from a town having a population not exceeding 20,000) provided to an employee working at a mining site or an onshore oil exploration site, or a project execution site or a dam site or power generation site or an offshore site. A project site for this purpose means site of project up to the stage of its commissioning—Circular No. 15/2001, dated December 12, 2001.

2. Moreover, the perquisite in respect of accommodation of temporary nature (and having plinth area of 800 sq. ft. or less) which is located at least 8 km. away from the local limits of a municipality or cantonment board provided to an employee working at a mining site or an onshore oil exploration site, or a project execution site or a dam site or power generation site or an offshore site, is not chargeable to tax.

3. Where on account of the transfer of an employee from one place to another, he is provided with accommodation at the new place of posting while retaining the accommodation at the other place, the value of perquisite shall be determined with reference to only one such accommodation which has the lower value for a period not exceeding 90 days and thereafter the value of perquisite shall be charged for both such accommodations.

15.1-2E1 X, a purchase manager of a private sector company, gets the following emoluments during the previous year 2018-19 : Basic salary : Rs. 8,60,000 ; bonus : Rs. 60,000 ; project allowance : Rs. 5,000 ; commission on purchases made by him : Rs. 16,500 ; dearness pay (not forming part of salary) : Rs. 33,000 ; education allowance (including allowance for hostel expenditure) for two children of X who are medical students at Delhi : Rs. 12,600 and gas bills paid by the employer on behalf of X : Rs. 4,500. Besides, the employer provides a rent-free house owned by it in Bombay to X for his residential purposes. The house is provided on September 15, 2018, though it is occupied by X only from October 1, 2018. While municipal valuation of the house is Rs. 94,000 per annum, market rent of a similar property in the same locality is Rs. 1,76,000. The employer-company maintains the garden attached to the house (salary of gardener and other maintenance expenses : Rs. 12,000). Standard rent under the Bombay Rent Control Act is Rs. 90,000. Determine the taxable value of the perquisite in respect of rent-free house for the assessment year 2019-20.

•

Salary for the purpose of determining perquisite value of rent-free house works out to be Rs. 9,44,500 [*i.e.*, Rs. 8,60,000 + Rs. 60,000 + Rs. 5,000 + Rs. 16,500 + Rs. 12,600 — amount exempt from tax under section 10(*14*) in respect of education allowance (Rs. 100 per month per child for a maximum of two children) and hostel expenditure allowance (Rs. 300 per month per child for a maximum of two children) : Rs. 9,600]. Salary of the period during which the house is occupied (*i.e.*, October 1, 2018 to March 31, 2019) by X is Rs. 4,72,250 (*i.e.*, Rs. 9,44,500 × 6 ÷ 12). Rs. 70,838 (being 15% of salary is taxable value of the perquisite).

15.1-2E2 X is employed by A Ltd. in Delhi. His salary and allowances are as follows—Basic salary Rs. 35,000 per month (increased to Rs. 38,000 per month from October 1, 2018), dearness pay : 40 per cent of basic salary (60 per cent of which is considered for computing provident fund), commission : Rs. 10,000 per month (increased to Rs. 14,000 per month from December 1, 2018). Bonus : 25 per cent of basic salary (payable annually in the month of November). X is transferred to Bombay on September 1, 2018. He has been provided a rent-free unfurnished house (owned by the company) at Delhi which he has occupied up to December 31, 2018. The employer-company has provided a leased accommodation at Bombay with effect from September 1, 2018 (lease rent being Rs. 9,000 per month up to October 31, 2018, Rs. 18,000 per month from November 1, 2018). Find out the taxable value of the perquisite in respect of the rent-free accommodation for the assessment year 2019-20.

•

Taxable value of the perquisite shall be determined as follows : *(Rs. in '000)*

Different months of the previous year	*Basic salary*	*Dearness pay [40% of 60% of (1)]*	*Commission*	*Bonus [25% of (1)]*	*Salary for the purpose of valuation of house [(1)+(2)+(3)+(4)]*	*Value of Delhi house [15% of (5)]*	*Lease rent of Bombay house*	*Value of Bombay house [15% of (5) or (7) whichever is less]*	*Taxable value*
	(1)	*(2)*	*(3)*	*(4)*	*(5)*	*(6)*	*(7)*	*(8)*	*(9)*
April 2018	35	8.4	10	8.75	62.15	9.32	—	—	9.32
May 2018	35	8.4	10	8.75	62.15	9.32	—	—	9.32
June 2018	35	8.4	10	8.75	62.15	9.32	—	—	9.32
July 2018	35	8.4	10	8.75	62.15	9.32	—	—	9.32
August 2018	35	8.4	10	8.75	62.15	9.32	—	—	9.32
September 2018	35	8.4	10	8.75	62.15	9.32	9	9	9[45]
October 2018	38	9.12	10	9.5	66.62	9.99	9	9	9[45]
November 2018	38	9.12	10	9.5	66.62	9.99	18	9.99	9.99[45]
December 2018	38	9.12	14	9.5	70.62	10.59	18	10.59	10.59+ 10.59[45]
January 2019	38	9.12	14	9.5	70.62	—	18	10.59	10.59
February 2019	38	9.12	14	9.5	70.62	—	18	10.59	10.59
March 2019	38	9.12	14	9.5	70.62	—	18	10.59	10.59
Total									127.54

15.2 ***Valuation of rent-free furnished accommodation*** - In the case of furnished accommodation, first presume that the accommodation is unfurnished and then work out the valuation according to the method explained in para 15.1. To the figure, so arrived at, *add :*

a. 10 per cent (per annum) of the original cost of furniture, if furniture is owned by the employer ;

b. actual hire charges payable (whether paid or payable), if furniture is hired by the employer.

Meaning of "furniture" - "Furniture" here includes radio sets, television sets, refrigerators, air-conditioners and other household appliances.

• *Accommodation provided in a hotel*[46] - In case of accommodation provided in a hotel[46], the perquisite value shall be calculated at the rate of 24 per cent of salary paid or payable for the previous year or actual charges paid or payable to such hotel[46], whichever is lower, for the period during which such accommodation is provided. Where, however, accommodation is provided in hotel[46] and the following two conditions are satisfied, nothing is chargeable to tax :

a. the hotel[46] accommodation is provided for a period not exceeding in aggregate 15 days; and

b. such accommodation is provided on an employee's transfer from one place to another place.

15.2-E1 X received during the previous year ending March 31, 2019, emoluments consisting of basic pay : Rs. 1,62,000; special allowance : Rs. 9,000 ; entertainment allowance : Rs. 8,000 and reimbursement of medical expenditure : Rs. 20,000. His employer has also provided a rent-free furnished flat in Bombay. Lease rent of the unfurnished flat is Rs. 50,000. Some of the household appliances provided to X (with effect from June 1, 2018) are owned by the employer (cost price of which is Rs. 36,000, date of purchase is April 1, 1960 and written down value, as on April 1, 2018 is Rs. 620). Employer pays Rs. 10,000 annually as hire charges for three air-conditioners installed throughout the previous year in rent-free flat. Compute the value of the perquisite if : (*a*) X is a Secretary in the Ministry of Law and Rs. 4,000 is the licence fee

---

45. Up to August 31, 2018, X has been posted at Delhi. From September 1, 2018, X is transferred to Bombay. For 4 months, he has been provided houses both at Bombay and Delhi. Out of 4 months, for 3 months (September, October and November) one of the two houses whose taxable value is lower will be taxable. However, for the month of December, perquisite will be taxable at both the places.

46. For the purpose of rule 3, "hotel" includes licensed accommodation in the nature of motel, service apartment or guest house.

of unfurnished flat as per the Central Government rules ; (*b*) X is the Managing Director of ABC (P.) Ltd. Does it make any difference if X has been provided a hotel accommodation throughout the year (tariff being Rs. 1,20,000 per annum) ?

•

Valuation of unfurnished flat :

1. If X is a Secretary to the Central Government - Rs. 4,000 is the taxable value of the unfurnished flat.

2. If X is the Managing Director of ABC (P.) Ltd. - Salary for the purpose of calculating taxable value of the perquisite works out to be Rs. 1,79,000 (*i.e.*, Rs. 1,62,000 + Rs. 9,000 + Rs. 8,000). As lease rent of unfurnished flat (*i.e.*, Rs. 50,000) exceeds 15% of salary, Rs. 26,850 (being 15% of salary) is taxable value of the perquisite.

Valuation of furniture	*Rs.*
10% per annum of cost of furniture (*i.e.*, 10% of Rs. 36,000 × 10/12)	3,000
Add : Rent of air-conditioners	10,000
Valuation of furniture	13,000

Valuation of furnished flat :

	Valuation of		
	Unfurnished flat Rs.	*Furniture Rs.*	*Furnished flat Rs.*
If X is a Secretary to the Central Government	4,000	13,000	17,000
If X is a Managing Director of ABC (P.) Ltd.	26,850	13,000	39,850

Valuation of hotel accommodation - Rs. 42,960 (being 24% of salary or Rs. 1,20,000, whichever is lower) is chargeable to tax whether X is a Government employee or non-Government employee.

15.3 ***Valuation of accommodation provided at concessional rent*** - In the case of an accommodation provided to an employee at concessional rent, the valuation will be made as if the employee had been provided rent-free accommodation [*see* paras 15.1 and 15.2] and the amount so computed will be reduced by the rent payable by the employee. If the balancing amount is zero or negative, nothing is chargeable to tax.

15.4 ***Valuation of perquisite in respect of free domestic servants*** - The value of benefit to the employee (or any member of his household) resulting from the provision by the employer of services of a sweeper, a gardener, a watchman or a personal attendant, shall be the actual cost to the employer. The actual cost in such a case shall be the total amount of salary paid or payable by the employer or any other person on his behalf for such services as reduced by any amount paid by the employee for such services.

The following points should be noted—

1. If an employer provides a rent-free house (owned by employer) to his employee, expenses (inclusive of salary of a gardener) incurred by the employer on maintenance of garden and ground attached to the house, is not taxable separately — Circular No. 122, dated October 19, 1973.

2. Domestic servant allowance given to an employee is always chargeable to tax. It is taxable even if the allowance is used for engaging a domestic servant.

15.5 ***Valuation of perquisite in respect of gas, electricity or water supply provided free of cost*** - It is taxable on the following basis :

Mode of valuation	*Gas, electricity or water is purchased by the employer from an outside agency*	*Gas, electricity or water is supplied by the employer out of own sources*
Step 1 - Find out cost to the employer	Amount paid or payable by the employer to the outside agency	Manufacturing cost per unit incurred by the employer
Step 2 - *Less* : Amount recovered from the employee	Recovery from the employee	Recovery from the employee
Taxable value of the perquisite (*Step 1—Step 2*)	Balancing amount (if it is positive)	Balancing amount (if it is positive)

15.6 ***Valuation of perquisite in respect of free education*** - The basis of valuation is explained below :

• *Training of employees* - Amount spent for providing free education facilities to, and training of, the employee is not taxable.

• *Fixed education allowance for children* - Fixed education allowance given in cash by the employer to the employee to meet the cost of education of the family members of the employee is not taxable to the extent of Rs. 100 per month per child (for a maximum of 2 children). An additional exemption is available in respect of allowance granted to meet hostel expenditure at the rate of Rs. 300 per month per child for a maximum of two children. The remaining amount is taxable in all cases.

• *Payment of school fees of employee's children* - School fees of the family members of the employee paid by the employer directly to the school is taxable as a perquisite.

• *Reimbursement of school fees of employee's children* - Reimbursement of expenditure incurred for education of the family members of the employee is taxable as a perquisite. Any such reimbursement of tuition fees to the Central Government employee is, therefore, taxable—Circular Letter No. 35/7/65-IT(B), dated February 12, 1965.

• *Education facility in employer's institute* - The table given below highlights the provisions—

Different situations	*Amount chargeable to tax*
Where the educational institution is owned and maintained by the employer and educational facility is provided or where such educational facility is provided in any institute by reason of employee's employment with the employer—	
a. Where educational facility is provided to employee's children [proviso to rule 3(5)]—	
- Where cost of education or value of such benefit does not exceed Rs. 1,000 per month per child (no restriction on number of children)	*Nil*
- Where such amount exceeds Rs. 1,000 per month per child	Cost of such education in a similar institution[47] in or near the locality (–) Rs. 1,000 per month per child[2] (–) amount paid or recovered from the employee
b. Where educational facility is provided to a member of his household (other than children)	Cost of such education in a similar institution[47] in or near the locality (–) amount paid or recovered from the employee

Notes—

1. Grand children and other member of household are included in (*b*) *supra.*

2. The following judicial rulings are important—

- Proviso to rule 3(5) stands attracted only where the educational institution is itself maintained and owned by the employer and free educational facilities are provided to the children of the employee—*Birla Vidya Niketan* v. *ITO* [2008] 166 Taxman 492 (Delhi).
- A literal reading of rule 3(5) indicates that if the cost of education per child exceeds Rs. 1,000 per month, the entire cost will be the value of the perquisite. However, keeping in view the departmental instructions in respect of free meal *vide* Circular No. 29/2017[$], dated December 5, 2017, where the similar language is used, only the sum in excess of Rs. 1,000 per month per child alone should be treated as perquisite.

  The same view is taken by the Delhi Tribunal in the case of *ITO* v. *Bal Bharti Public School* [2007] 17 SOT 151. In the case of *CIT* v. *Director, Delhi Public School* [2011] 202 Taxman 318, the Punjab and Haryana High Court has taken a contrary view (*i.e.*, nothing is taxable only if cost of education in a similar institute after excluding amount recovered from the employee is equal to or less than Rs. 1,000 per month. In case, it exceeds Rs. 1,000 per month, the entire amount is chargeable to tax). It is respectfully submitted that the decision of *Delhi Public School* (*supra*) requires reconsideration.

• *Scholarship* - Amount of scholarship given by the employer-company to children of its employees solely at its discretion without reference to terms of employment is not assessable as perquisite in hands of employee—*CIT* v. *M.N. Nadkarni* [1986] 161 ITR 544 (Bom.).

15.6-E1 Find out the taxable value of the perquisite for the assessment year 2019-20 in the following cases—

1. X is an employee in the Accounts Department of A Ltd. On September 16, 2018, he attends a seminar on "Perquisite Valuation". Seminar fees of Rs. 7,500 is paid by A Ltd.

47. For this purpose, one cannot take cost of education (as in the case of other students) in the same school—*CIT* v. *Delhi Public School* [2008] 167 Taxman 134 (Delhi). For this purpose, both direct and indirect expenses incurred in running a school (excluding depreciation of building) shall be considered—*CIT* v. *Director, Delhi Public School* [2011] 202 Taxman 318 (Punj. & Har.).

[$] For Circular No. 29/2017, log on to *taxmann.com/readyreckoner.aspx.*

2. Y's son is a student of ninth class of DPS, Noida. Rs. 17,800 being tuition fees of Y's son is paid/reimbursed by B. Ltd. where Y is employed. There is no arrangement between B Ltd. and DPS, Noida.

3. Star Public School, Ajmer, is owned and maintained by C Ltd., a manufacturing company. Books of account of the school and C Ltd. are maintained separately. Z is an employee of C Ltd. The following family members of Z are students in Star Public School—

	Cost of education in a similar institution	*Amount charged from Z*
A, daughter of Z	Rs. 5,500 per month	Rs. 800 per month
B, dependent brother of Z	Rs. 6,000 per month	Rs. 1,600 per month

4. Suppose in (*3*) (*supra*) Star Public School is not owned/maintained by C Ltd. As per arrangement of C Ltd. with the school, family members of employees of C Ltd. can have educational facility in the school. 100 seats are reserved for this purpose for which the company annually pays Rs. 40 lakh to the school (no separate billing by the school to the employee of C Ltd.). Family members of Z are students of the school. Cost of education in a similar institute and amount charged from Z by C Ltd. are given in the table in (3) (*supra*).

•

1. Expenditure on training/education of an employee is not chargeable to tax. X is, therefore, not chargeable to tax.

2. Rs. 17,800, being tuition fees paid/reimbursed by B Ltd. is taxable in the hands of Y.

3. School is maintained by the employer. Amount taxable in the hands of Z will be as follow—

	Rs.
A (daughter of Z) [12 × (Rs. 5,500 – Rs. 1,000 – Rs. 800)]	44,400
B (brother of Z) [12 × (Rs. 6,000 – Rs. 1,600)]	52,800

4. The taxable amount will be the same as given in (3) (*supra*).

15.7 ***Valuation of leave travel concession in India [Sec. 10(5)]***[48] - Leave travel assistance, extended by an employer to an employee for going anywhere in India along with his family, is exempt on the basis of provisions given in the table below –

Different situations	*Amount of exemption if journey is performed on or after October 1, 1997*
• Where journey is performed by air	Amount of air economy class fare of the National Carrier by the shortest route or the amount spent, whichever is less
• Where journey is performed by rail	Amount of air-conditioned first class rail fare by the shortest route or the amount spent, whichever is less
• Where the places of origin of journey and destination are connected by rail and journey is performed by any other mode of transport	Amount of air-conditioned first class rail fare by the shortest route or the amount spent, whichever is less.
• Where the places of origin of journey and destination (or part thereof) are not connected by rail	
❑ Where a recognised public transport system exists	First class or deluxe class fare by the shortest route or the amount spent, whichever is less.
❑ Where no recognised public transport system exists	Air-conditioned first class rail fare by the shortest route (as if the journey had been performed by rail) or the amount actually spent, whichever is less.

15.7-1 *OTHER POINTS* - One should also keep in view the following points—

• *Meaning of "family"* - The aforesaid exemption is available in respect of fare for going anywhere in India along with "family". For this purpose, "family" includes spouse and children[49] of the employee. It also includes parents, brothers and sisters of the employee, who are wholly or mainly dependent upon the employee. However, family does not include more than two surviving children of an individual born on or after October 1, 1998 (in reckoning this limit of two children, children born out of multiple births after the first child will be treated as 'one child only').

• *Only 2 journeys in a block of 4 years is exempt* - Exemption on the aforesaid basis is available in respect of 2 journeys performed in a block of four calendar years commencing from 1986. The different blocks are :

48. The value of leave travel concession provided to a serving Chairman or member of the UPSC and members of his family, is not chargeable to tax by virtue of section 10(*45*).

49. Child includes step child and adopted child.

a. 2006-2009 (*i.e.*, January 1, 2006 to December 31, 2009);
b. 2010-2013 (*i.e.*, January 1, 2010 to December 31, 2013);
c. 2014-2017 (*i.e.*, January 1, 2014 to December 31, 2017);
d. 2018-2021 (*i.e.*, January 1, 2018 to December 31, 2021);

• *"Carry-over" concession* - If an assessee has not availed travel concession or assistance during any of the specified four-year block periods on one of the two permitted occasions (or on both occasions), exemption can be claimed in the first calendar year of the next block (but in respect of only one journey). This is known as "carry over concession". In such case, the exemption so availed will not be counted for the purposes of claiming the future exemptions allowable in respect of 2 journeys in the subsequent block.

Provision illustrated - For the block 2014-2017 X can claim exemption in respect of LTC under section 10(*5*) on two occasions. X has availed the exemption only on one occasion (or he has not availed the exemption at all) during 2014-2017, then he can take the benefit of "carry-over" concession. The benefit of carry over is available only in respect of one journey provided he avails LTC exemption under section 10(*5*) in the first calendar year of the next block (*i.e.*, during the calendar year 2018). In addition, he can avail exemption on two more occasions during 2018-2021.

• *Exemption is based upon actual expenditure* - The quantum of exemption is limited to the actual expenses incurred on the journey. In other words, without performing any journey and incurring expenses thereon, no exemption can be claimed.

• *Exemption is available in respect of fare* - The exemption is strictly limited to expenses on air fare, rail fare, bus fare only. No other expenses, like scooter or taxi charges at both ends, porterage expenses during the journey and lodging/boarding expenses will qualify for exemption.

• *Exemption is available in respect of shortest route* - Where the journey is performed by a circuitous route, the exemption is limited to what is admissible by the shortest route. Likewise, where the journey is performed in a circular form touching different places, the exemption will be limited to what is admissible for the journey from the place of origin to the farthest point reached, by the shortest route.

• *Fixed allowance is not subject to exemption* - Fixed sum paid to employees by way of leave travel allowance on basis of self-declaration made by employees would not be exempt under section 10(*5*)—*Dr. Reddy Laboratories Ltd.* v. *ITO* [1996] 58 ITD 104 (Hyd.).

15.7-E1 X is Head, Finance Department, A Ltd. According to the service rules, he is entitled for executive class air fare for domestic travelling (whether on business trip or on LTC). For the current block, he takes LTC for Mumbai-Delhi (travelling dates : May 10/15, 2019, Mrs. X and two children accompanied him, journey inbound/outbound by Jet Airways, executive class one way fare for one person charged by Jet Airways : Rs. 25,700). A Ltd. reimburses not only the entire expenditure on fare of Rs. 2,05,600 (*i.e.*, Rs. 25,700 × 4 × 2) but also boarding and lodging expenditure of Rs. 70,000. Points for consideration are (*a*) whether exemption is available under section 10(*5*) as X has not travelled by Air India, and (*b*) whether exemption would be available on the basis of economy class air fare of Air India (assume that economy class one way fare offered by Air India for Mumbai-Delhi route on May 10/15, 2019 is as follows – Web Special - Economy : Rs. 4,900, Super Value - Economy : Rs. 7,100, Flexible - Economy : Rs. 13,200, LTC - Economy : Rs. 13,300).

•

Exemption cannot be denied merely on the basis that the concerned employee has not travelled by Air India. However, the amount of exemption depends upon Air India economy class fare. For this purpose, Air India LTC (economy) fare may be adopted. Exemption would be limited to Rs. 1,06,400 (*i.e.*, Rs. 13,300 × 4 × 2). Amount chargeable to tax in the hands of X will be Rs. 1,69,200 (*i.e.*, Rs. 2,05,600 +Rs. 70,000 – Rs. 1,06,400).

15.8 ***Employee's obligation met by employer [Sec. 17(2)(iv)]*** - Amount paid by an employer in respect of any obligation which otherwise would have been payable by the employee is taxable in all cases.

15.9 ***Amount payable by employer to effect an assurance on the life of employee [Sec. 17(2)(v)]*** - Amount payable by an employer, directly or indirectly, to effect an assurance on the life of the assessee or to effect a contract for an annuity (other than payments made to recognised provident fund or approved superannuation fund or deposit-linked insurance fund established under the Coal Mines Provident Fund Act or Employees' Provident Fund Act) is taxable in the hands of all employees. It may, however, be noted that insurance premium paid by the employer under certain schemes, such as, Group Insurance Schemes, Employees' State Insurance Schemes and Fidelity Guarantee Scheme, is not regarded as perquisite in view of the fact that an employee has merely an expectancy of benefit in such schemes.

15.10 ***Valuation of perquisite in respect of interest-free loan or loan at concessional rate of interest*** - If a loan is given by an employer to the employee (or any member of his household), it is a perquisite chargeable to tax. It is taxable on the following basis—

Step 1	Find out the "maximum outstanding monthly balance" (*i.e.*, the aggregate outstanding balance for each loan as on the last day of each month).
Step 2	Find out rate of interest charged by the State Bank of India (SBI) as on the first day of the relevant previous year in respect of loan for the same purpose advanced by it [*see* para 15.10-1].
Step 3	Calculate interest for each month of the previous year on the outstanding amount mentioned in *Step 1* at the rate of interest given in *Step 2*.
Step 4	From the total interest calculated for the entire previous year under *Step 3*, deduct interest actually recovered, if any, from the employee during the previous year.
Step 5	The balance amount [*i.e. Step 3 minus Step 4*] is taxable value of the perquisite.

15.10-1 *SBI LENDING RATES* - SBI lending rates are as follows—

	As on April 1, 2018[50] for the assessment year 2019-20		*As on April 1, 2019[50] for the assessment year 2020-21*	
	For women borrowers	*For other borrowers*		
Home loan	8.35% – 8.70%	8.40% – 8.75%	8.7% – 9.1%	8.75% – 9.15%
Car loan	8.90% – 9.40%	8.90% – 9.40%	9.3% – 9.8%	9.3% – 9.8%
Certified pre-owned car	12.80%	12.80%	11.05% – 12.05%	11.05% – 12.05%
Super bike loan	11.80%	11.80%	11.8%	11.8%
Two-wheeler loan	17.40%	17.40%	17.6%	17.6%
Education loan (up to Rs. 7.5 lakh)	10.15%[51]	10.15%[51]	10.55%[51]	10.55%[51]
Education loan (above Rs. 7.5 lakh)	10.90%[51]	10.90%[51]	10.8%[51]	10.8%[51]

15.10-2 *WHEN PERQUISITE IS NOT CHARGEABLE TO TAX* - In the following cases, the perquisite is not chargeable to tax—

Exemption 1	If a loan is made available for medical treatment in respect of diseases specified in rule 3A$ (the exemption is, however, not applicable to so much of the loan as has been reimbursed to the employee under any medical insurance scheme).
Exemption 2	Where the amount of original loan (or loans) does not exceed in the aggregate Rs. 20,000.

Example 1 - X takes a loan of Rs. 2,00,000 from his employer on May 1, 2018 for medical treatment of Mrs. X (medical treatment is specified in rule 3A). Hospital bill is Rs. 2,00,000. The perquisite is not chargeable to tax. Suppose in this case insurance claim of Rs. 50,000 is received on October 15, 2018 which is retained by X. In such a situation, interest on Rs. 50,000 will be chargeable in hands of X with effect from October 15, 2018.[52]

Example 2 - X takes a loan of Rs. 15,000 from his employer on May 28, 2018 (no other loan is taken so far). As the amount of loan does not exceed Rs. 20,000, nothing is chargeable to tax. Suppose in this case another loan of Rs. 5,500 is taken from the employer on July 17, 2018. Now the aggregate amount of loan exceeds Rs. 20,000. Consequently, interest on Rs. 20,500 (*i.e.*, Rs. 15,000 + Rs. 5,500) will be chargeable to tax with effect from July 17, 2018.[52]

Example 3 - X takes a loan of Rs. 1,70,000 from his employer on October 1, 2010. It is repayable by way of quarterly instalments. On April 1, 2018, the outstanding amount is Rs. 20,000. The perquisite is not exempt from tax, as the amount of original loan is more than Rs. 20,000.

15.10-3 *OTHER POINTS* - The following points should be noted—

1. Interest will be calculated according to the method given above. No other method (*e.g.*, cost of capital/fund to employer) shall be taken into consideration.

50. As downloaded from https://www.sbi.co.in on September 18, 2018 at 4:34 pm and April 22, 2019 at 4:51 pm (for complete list, one can visit SBI website).

51. Concession in interest for girl students : 0.5%, 1% concession for full tenure of the loan, if interest is serviced promptly as and when applied during the moratorium period, including course duration.

52. The basis of calculation shall be the "maximum outstanding balance" on the last of each month.***The basis of calculation shall be the "maximum outstanding balance" on the last of each month.

2. If a closely held company gives a loan to an employee who holds at least 10 per cent voting power, such loan is deemed as dividend under section 2(*22*)(*e*), if a few conditions are satisfied. Even in such a case, the perquisite value of interest-free loan is chargeable to tax.

15.10-E1 Determine the taxable value of the perquisite in the following cases :—

1. X is employed by A Ltd. On June 1, 2018, the company gives an interest-free housing loan of Rs. 14,00,000. Loan is repayable after 10 years but before 12 years. Assume SBI lending rate is 8.70 per cent.

2. Y is employed by B Ltd. On April 1, 2018, he takes a festival loan of Rs. 25,000 from B Ltd. B Ltd. recovers interest @ 10 per cent per annum from Y. Assume SBI lending rate is 15.95 per cent.

3. C Ltd. gives the following interest-free loan to Z, an employee of the company—Rs. 15,000 for child's education and Rs. 5,000 for purchasing a refrigerator.

4. A purchases a Honda City 1.6 Lxi on March 1, 2018 from a loan of Rs. 8,00,000 taken at concessional rate of 5 per cent per annum from his employer XYZ Ltd. As per the agreed terms of repayment, A is supposed to repay in monthly instalments of Rs. 25,000 starting from January 1, 2019. Compute the taxable value of perquisite in respect of concessional loan for the previous year 2018-19 on the assumption that interest @ 5 per cent is actually paid by A to his employer and SBI lending rate for similar loan is 9.25 per cent.

5. B takes an interest-free loan of Rs. 7,00,000 from his employer PQR Ltd., on June 16, 2018 for medical treatment of his wife who is suffering from a disease specified in rule 3A. Mrs. B is also covered under a mediclaim insurance cover. Insurance company reimburses her of the hospitalization charges of Rs. 2,50,000 on January 1, 2019. According to terms of repayment of loan, B has to pay Rs. 12,000 per month on the seventh day of each month starting from November 2018. Ascertain the taxable value of perquisite in respect of interest-free loan for the previous year 2018-19. The amount paid by the insurance company is retained by B (assume that SBI lending rate is 18.5 per cent).

●

For the assessment year 2019-20, the taxable value of the perquisite will be as under—

1. The lending rate of SBI on April 1, 2018 for similar loan is 8.70% per annum. Rs. 1,01,500 (being interest @ 8.70% on Rs. 14,00,000 from June 1, 2018 to March 31, 2019) is taxable in the hands of X.

2. The SBI lending rate for a similar loan is 15.95%. Rs. 1,487.50 [being interest @ 5.95% (*i.e.*, 15.95% - 10%) on Rs. 25,000 for one year] is taxable in the hands of Y.

3. Nothing is taxable in the hands of Z as the amount of loan does not exceed Rs. 20,000.

4. The lending rate of SBI for a similar loan is 9.25%. Out of 9.25%, A, the assessee, actually pays interest @ 5% to the employer. The balance of 4.25% (*i.e.*, 9.25% – 5%) is taxable. Maximum monthly outstanding amount for the various months in the previous year 2018-19 is as follows :

Month	*Maximum monthly outstanding amount on last day of the month* Rs.	*Interest* Rs.
April 30, 2018	8,00,000	2,833.33 (*i.e.*, Rs. 8,00,000 × 4.25% × 1/12)
May 31, 2018	8,00,000	2,833.33
June 30, 2018	8,00,000	2,833.33
July 31, 2018	8,00,000	2,833.33
August 31, 2018	8,00,000	2,833.33
September 30, 2018	8,00,000	2,833.33
October 31, 2018	8,00,000	2,833.33
November 30, 2018	8,00,000	2,833.33
December 31, 2018	8,00,000	2,833.33
January 31, 2019	7,75,000	2,744.79 (*i.e.*, Rs. 7,75,000 × 4.25% × 1/12)
February 28, 2019	7,50,000	2,656.25 (*i.e.*, Rs. 7,50,000 × 4.25% × 1/12)
March 31, 2019	7,25,000	2,567.71 (*i.e.*, Rs. 7,25,000 × 4.25% × 1/12)
	Total	33,469

Taxable value of concessional loan is Rs. 33,469 for the previous year 2018-19.

5. The perquisite in respect of interest-free loan provided for medical treatment in respect of a disease specified in rule 3A is not taxable. However, it will not include that amount as has been reimbursed to the employee under any medical insurance scheme. Therefore, out of loan of Rs. 7,00,000 granted to B, Rs. 2,50,000 reimbursed by insurance company on January 1, 2019 will be taken into account for computing taxable value of perquisite. The SBI lending rate for a similar loan is 18.5% on April 1, 2018.

Month	*Maximum monthly outstanding amount on the last day of the month* Rs.	*Interest* Rs.
January 31, 2019	2,38,000	3,669.17 (*i.e.*, Rs. 2,38,000 × 18.5% × 1/12)
February 28, 2019	2,26,000	3,484.17 (*i.e.*, Rs. 2,26,000 × 18.5% × 1/12)
March 31, 2019	2,14,000	3,299.17 (*i.e.*, Rs. 2,14,000 × 18.5% × 1/12)
	Total	10,452.50

Taxable value of interest-free loan is Rs. 10,452.50 for the previous year 2018-19.

15.11 ***Perquisite in respect of use of movable assets*** - The value of benefit to the employee resulting from the use by the employee (or any member of his household) of any movable asset (other than assets already specified above) belonging to the employer or hired by him shall be taxable as follows :

Mode of valuation	*Perquisite in respect of use of movable assets*		
	Computer/ laptops or car	*Any other assets*	
		Owned by employer	*Taken on hire by employer*
Step 1 - Find out cost to the employer	*Nil*	10% per annum of actual cost	Amount of rent paid or payable
Step 2 - *Less* : Amount recovered from the employee	*Nil*	Recovery from the employee	Recovery from the employee
Taxable value of the perquisite (*Step 1 – Step 2*)	*Nil*	Balancing amount (if it is positive)	Balancing amount (if it is positive)

15.12 ***Valuation of the perquisite in respect of movable assets sold by an employer to its employees at a nominal price*** - The value of benefit to the employee arising from the transfer of any movable asset, belonging to the employer (directly or indirectly) to the employee (or any member of his household) shall be determined to be the amount representing the actual cost of such asset to the employer as reduced by the cost of normal wear and tear calculated at the rate given below for each completed year during which such asset was put to use by the employer. The amount so calculated shall be reduced by the amount, if any, paid or recovered from the employee being the consideration for such transfer.

Rate of normal wear and tear is as follows :

- Electronic items/computers — 50 per cent by reducing balance method
- Motor car — 20 per cent by reducing balance method
- Any other — 10 per cent of cost

Electronic gadgets in this case means data storage and handling devices like computer, digital diaries and printers. They do not include household appliances (*i.e.*, white goods) like washing machines, microwave ovens, mixers, hot plates, ovens etc.—Circular No. 29/2017[$], dated December 5, 2017.

15.12-E1 Find out the taxable value of the perquisite in the following cases—

1. X is given a laptop by the employer-company for using it for office and private purposes (ownership is not transferred). Cost of the laptop to the employer is Rs. 96,000.

2. On October 15, 2018, the company gives its music system to Y for domestic use. Ownership is not transferred. Cost of music system (in 2010) to the employer was Rs. 15,000.

3. The employer sells the following assets to the employees on January 1, 2019—

Name of employee	Z	A	B
Asset sold	*Car*	*Computer*	*Fridge*
Cost of the asset to employer	Rs. 6,96,000	Rs. 1,17,000	Rs. 40,000
Date of purchase (put to use on the same day)	May 15, 2016	May 15, 2016	May 15, 2016
Sale price	Rs. 2,10,000	Rs. 24,270	Rs. 1,000

Before the sale on January 1, 2019, these assets were used for business purpose by the employer.

•

[$] For Circular No. 29/2017, log on to *taxmann.com/readyreckoner.aspx.*

1. X is provided use of laptop by the employer. The perquisite is not chargeable to tax.

2. Y is provided a music system by the employer. The taxable value of the perquisite is determined @ 10% per annum of cost. Accordingly Rs. 690 (being Rs. 15,000 × 10/100 × 168 days ÷ 365 days) is chargeable to tax.

3. The taxable value of the perquisite in the hands of Z, A and B shall be determined as follows—

	Car Rs.	*Computer* Rs.	*Fridge* Rs.
Cost of the asset on May 15, 2016	6,96,000	1,17,000	40,000
Less : Normal wear and tear for the first year ending May 14, 2017 (20% of Rs. 6,96,000, 50% of Rs. 1,17,000, 10% of Rs. 40,000)	1,39,200	58,500	4,000
Balance on May 15, 2017	5,56,800	58,500	36,000
Less : Normal wear and tear for the second year ending May 14, 2018 (20% of Rs. 5,56,800, 50% of Rs. 58,500, 10% of Rs. 40,000)	1,11,360	29,250	4,000
Balance on May 15, 2018	4,45,440	29,250	32,000
Less : Sale consideration	2,10,000	24,270	1,000
Taxable value of the perquisite	2,35,440	4,980	31,000

Note - In the case of car and computer/electronic items, normal wear and tear is calculated @ 20% and 50% per annum respectively on the basis of written down value. In the case of any other asset, normal wear and tear is calculated at the rate of 10% per annum of cost of the asset to the employer. Normal wear and tear for a part of the year is not taken into consideration.

15.13 *Valuation of medical facilities* - The following shall not be treated as perquisite :

1. Medical facility provided in a hospital, clinic, dispensary or nursing home maintained by the employer.

2. Reimbursement, by the employer, of expenditure incurred by the employee on his medical treatment or treatment of any member of his family[53] in any hospital (including dispensary/clinic/nursing home) maintained by the Government, local authority, or in a hospital approved by the Government for its employees.

3. Payment made by the employer directly (or reimbursement of the expenditure to the employee) to a hospital (including dispensary/clinic/nursing home) which is approved by the Chief Commissioner having regard to the prescribed guidelines [*see* para 15.13-1] in connection with the medical treatment of the employee or any member of his family[53] for treatment of prescribed diseases or ailments [for prescribed diseases or ailments, *see* para 15.13-2] subject to the condition that the employee shall attach with his return of income a certificate[54] from the approved hospital specifying the prescribed disease or ailment for which hospitalisation was required and the receipt for the amount paid to the hospital.

4. Group medical insurance (*i.e.,* Mediclaim) obtained by the employer for his employees or reimbursement of insurance premium to the employee who takes such medical insurance on his life or on the life of his family members.

5. Reimbursement by the employer of amount spent by the employee in obtaining medical treatment for himself or any member of his family[53] from any doctor, not exceeding in the aggregate, Rs. 15,000 in a year (however, this exemption is not available from the assessment year 2019-20).

6. Any expenditure incurred by the employer (or reimbursement of expenditure incurred by the employee) on medical treatment of the employee or any member of the family[53] of such employee outside India is taxable subject to the conditions given below :—

---

53. For the purpose of valuation of perquisite in respect of medical facilities, "family", in relation to employee means (*a*) the spouse and children of the employee ; and (*b*) the parents, brothers and sisters of the employee or any of them wholly or mainly dependent on the employee.

54. Nothing can be annexed or attached along with return of income in new Forms ITR-1 to ITR-6. The certificate should be taken from the prescribed authority and it should be retained by the employee. It can be produced before the Assessing Officer when it is demanded by him.

Perquisite not chargeable to tax under clause (vi) of proviso to section 17(2)	*Condition to be satisfied*
• Medical treatment of employee or any member of family of such employee outside India	Expenditure shall be excluded from perquisite only to the extent permitted by the Reserve Bank of India
• Cost on travel of the employee/any member of his family and one attendant who accompanies the patient in connection with treatment outside India	Expenditure shall be excluded from perquisite only in the case of an employee whose gross total income, as computed before including therein the said expenditure, does not exceed Rs. 2,00,000
• Cost of stay abroad of the employee or any member of the family for medical treatment and cost of stay of one attendant who accompanies the patient in connection with such treatment	Expenditure shall be excluded from the perquisite only to the extent permitted by the Reserve Bank of India

15.13-1 *HOSPITAL APPROVED BY THE CHIEF COMMISSIONER* - In granting approval to any hospital for the purpose of sub-clause (*b*) of clause (*ii*) of the proviso to section 17(2), the Chief Commissioner shall satisfy himself that the hospital is registered with the local authority and fulfils the following requirements, namely :

• The building used for the hospital complies with the municipal bye-laws in force.

• The rooms are well ventilated, lighted and are kept in clean and hygienic condition.

• At least ten iron spring beds are provided for patients.

• At least one properly equipped operation theatre is provided with a minimum floor space of 180 square feet and with a separate sterilization room.

• At least one labour room is provided, with a minimum floor space of 180 square feet, in case the hospital provides medical service for maternity cases.

• Aseptic conditions are maintained in the operation theatre and the labour room.

• A duty room is provided for the nursing staff on duty.

• Adequate space for storage of medicines, food articles, equipments, etc., is provided.

• The water used in the hospital or nursing home is fit for drinking.

• Adequate arrangements are made for isolating septic and infectious patients.

• The hospital is provided with and maintains : (*a*) high pressure sterilizer and instrument sterilizer; (*b*) oxygen cylinders and necessary attachments for giving oxygen; (*c*) adequate surgical equipments, instruments and apparatus including intravenous apparatus; (*d*) a pathological laboratory for testing of blood, urine and stool; (*e*) electro-cardiogram monitoring system; (*f*) stand-by generator for use in case of power failure.

• There is at least one qualified doctor available on duty round the clock for every 20 beds or fraction thereof.

• In hospitals providing intensive care unit facilities, there are at least 2 qualified doctors available on duty round the clock exclusively for such intensive care unit.

• One nurse is on duty round the clock for every 5 beds or a fraction thereof.

• In hospitals providing intensive care unit facilities, there are at least 4 nurses provided exclusively for every 4 beds or fraction thereof for such intensive care unit.

• The hospital maintains record of health of every patient containing information about the patient's name, address, occupation, sex, age, date of admission, date of discharge, diagnosis of disease and treatment undertaken.

15.13-2 *PRESCRIBED DISEASES OR AILMENTS* - For the purpose of sub-clause (*b*) of clause (*ii*) of the proviso to clause (2) of section 17, the prescribed diseases or ailments shall be the following, namely : (*a*) cancer; (*b*) tuberculosis; (*c*) acquired immunity deficiency syndrome; (*d*) disease or ailment of the heart, blood, lymph glands, bone marrow, respiratory system, central nervous system, urinary system, liver, gall bladder, digestive system, endocrine glands or the skin, requiring surgical operation; (*e*) ailment or disease of the eye, ear, nose or throat, requiring surgical operation; (*f*) fracture in any part of the skeletal system or dislocation of vertebrae requiring surgical operation or orthopaedic treatment; (*g*) gynaecological or obstetric ailment or disease requiring surgical operation, cesarean operation or laparoscopic intervention; (*h*) ailment or disease of the organs mentioned at (*d*), requiring medical treatment in a hospital for at least three continuous days; (*i*) gynaecological or obstetric ailment or disease requiring medical treatment in a hospital for at least three continuous days; (*j*) burn injuries requiring medical treatment in a hospital for at least three continuous days; (*k*) mental disorder neurotic or psychotic requiring medical treatment in a hospital for at least three continuous days; (*l*) drug addiction requiring medical treatment in a hospital for at least seven continuous days; (*m*) anaphylactic shocks including insulin shocks, drug reactions and other allergic manifestations requiring medical treatment in a hospital for at least three continuous days.

15.14 ***Valuation of perquisite in respect of motor car*** - The table below gives the basis of valuation of perquisite in respect of motor car and other modes of conveyance provided to the employees.

Different situations	*Value of the perquisite*
(1)	*(2)*
I. WHERE CAR IS OWNED BY THE EMPLOYEE	
A. When car expenses are met by the employee	Not a perquisite, hence not taxable himself
B. When maintenance and running expenses are met or reimbursed by the employer	
a. if the car is used wholly for official purposes	No value provided a few conditions are satisfied [*see* para 15.14-1]
b. if the car is used wholly for private purposes	*Step 1* - Find out actual expenditure incurred by the employer *Step 2* - *Less*: Amount recovered from the employee Balancing amount (if it is positive) is taxable value of the perquisite
c. if the car is partly used for official purposes and partly for private purposes	*Step 1* - Find out actual expenditure incurred by the employer *Step 2* - *Less*: Amount used for official purposes (*i.e.*, a sum calculated at the rate of Rs. 1,800 per month where the cubic capacity of the engine does not exceed 1.6 litres[55] or Rs. 2,400 per month if such capacity exceeds 1.6 litres[55]; and Rs. 900 per month if chauffeur is provided or a higher sum for official purposes as per records of the employer as stated in para 15.14-1 and as certified by the employer) *Step 3* - *Less*: Amount recovered from employee Balancing amount (if it is positive) is taxable value of the perquisite
II. WHEN CAR IS OWNED OR HIRED BY EMPLOYER	
A. When maintenance and running expenses are met or reimbursed by employer	
a. if the car is wholly used for official purposes	No value provided a few conditions are satisfied [*see* para 15.14-1]
b. if the car is wholly used for private purposes of the employee or any member of his household	*Step 1* - Find out actual expenditure incurred by the employer [*i.e.*, expenditure on running and maintenance including remuneration of the chauffeur *plus* normal wear and tear of the car (at the rate of 10 per cent per annum of actual cost to the employer) or hire charges if car is taken on hire] *Step 2* - *Less*: Amount recovered from employee Balancing amount (if it is positive) is taxable value of the perquisite
c. if the car is used partly for official and partly for private purposes of the employee or any member of his household	A sum calculated at the rate of Rs. 1,800 per month where the cubic capacity of the engine does not exceed 1.6 litres[55] or Rs. 2,400 per month if such capacity exceeds 1.6 litres[55]; and Rs. 900 per month if chauffeur is provided *Nothing is deductible in respect of any amount recovered from the employee*

55. 1600cc.

(1)	*(2)*
B. When maintenance and running expenses are met by employee	
a. if the car is used wholly for official purposes	Not a perquisite, hence not taxable
b. if the car is used wholly for private purposes	*Step 1* - Find out expenditure incurred by the employer (*i.e.*, hire charges if car is taken on rent or normal wear and tear at the rate of 10 per cent of the actual cost of the car if car is owned by the employer *plus* salary of chauffeur, if any, paid or payable by employer) *Step 2* - *Less*: Amount recovered from employee Balancing amount (if it is positive) is taxable value of the perquisite
c. if the car is used partly for official and partly for private purposes and maintenance in respect of private use is borne by the employee	A sum calculated at the rate of Rs. 600 per month where the cubic capacity of the engine does not exceed 1.6 litres[55] or Rs. 900 per month if such capacity exceeds 1.6 litres[55]; and Rs. 900 per month if chauffeur is provided *Nothing is deductible in respect of any amount recovered from the employee*
III. WHEN EMPLOYEE OWNS ANY AUTOMOTIVE CONVEYANCE (OTHER THAN CAR) AND RUNNING AND MAINTENANCE CHARGES ARE MET OR REIMBURSED BY EMPLOYER	
A. If it is used wholly for official purposes	No value provided a few conditions are satisfied [*see* para 15.14-1]
B. If it is used partly for official and partly for private purposes	*Step 1* - Find out actual expenditure incurred by the employer *Step 2* - *Less*: Amount used for official purposes (*i.e.*, a sum calculated at the rate of Rs. 900 per month or a higher sum for official purposes as per records of the employer as stated in para 15.14-1 and as certified by the employer) *Step 3* - *Less*: Amount recovered from employee Balancing amount (if it is positive) is taxable value of the perquisite

15.14-1 *CONDITIONS TO BE SATISFIED IF CAR IS USED FOR OFFICIAL PURPOSES* - Where the employer or the employee claim that the motor-car is used wholly and exclusively in the performance of official duty, the following conditions should be satisfied—

Condition 1	The employer has maintained complete details of journey undertaken for official purpose which may include date of journey, destination, mileage, and the amount of expenditure incurred thereon.
Condition 2	The employer gives a certificate to the effect that the expenditure was incurred wholly and exclusively for the performance of official duties.

• The above conditions should also be satisfied if a car is owned by the employee, expenses are incurred or reimbursed by the employer and the employee claims that the expenses for official purposes is more than Rs. 1,800 per month (or Rs. 2,400 per month if cc rating of car exceeds 1,600cc).

15.14-2 *OTHER POINTS* - One should also keep in view the following points —

• *'Month' - Meaning of* - The word "month" in the table denotes completed month according to the English calendar and a part of the month is left out of consideration.

55. 1600cc.

• *When two (or more cars) are allowed* - The perquisite will be valued as follows —

1. Two or more cars are owned or hired by the employer.

2. The employee (or any member of his household) are allowed the use of such motor-cars (or all or any of such motor-cars) (otherwise than wholly and exclusively in the performance of his duties).

3. In respect of one of such cars (as selected by the employee), the value of perquisite shall be the amount calculated in accordance with II(A)(*c*) of the Table (*supra*) as if the employee had been provided one motor-car for use partly in the performance of his duties and partly for his private or personal purposes.

4. In respect of other remaining car or cars, the value of the perquisite shall be the amount calculated in accordance with item II(A)(*b*) of the Table (*supra*) as if he had been provided with such car or cars exclusively for his private or personal purposes.

• *Car at concessional rate* - If motor car is provided at a concessional rate, the valuation is made according to the basis stated above as if the employee has been provided a free motor car and the amount so computed is reduced by the amount charged by the employer for use of motor car. However, nothing is deductible in situation II(A)(*c*) and II(B)(*c*) in respect of amount recovered from employee.

• *Car facility between office and residence* - The use of motor car by an employee for the purposes of going from his residence to the place where the duties of employment are to be performed or from such place back to his residence, is not chargeable to tax.

• *Conveyance facility to judges* - Conveyance facility provided to High Court Judges under section 22B of the High Court Judges (Conditions of Service) Act, 1954 and to Supreme Court Judges under section 23A of the Supreme Court Judges (Conditions of Service) Act, 1958 is not chargeable to tax.

• *Conveyance facility to Chairman/members of UPSC* - Conveyance facility (including transport allowance) provided to serving Chairman/members of UPSC is not chargeable to tax.

15.15 ***Valuation of perquisite in respect of free transport provided by a transport undertaking to its employees*** - Taxable value of the perquisite shall be determined on the basis of value at which the employer offers such benefit to the public as reduced by any amount recovered from the employee. Nothing is, however, chargeable to tax in the hands of employees of railways/airlines.

15.16 ***Valuation of perquisite in respect of lunch/refreshment, etc.*** - If any lunch allowance, dinner allowance or refreshment allowance is given to an employee, it is chargeable to tax.

The value of free meals provided by the employer is taxable as follows—

Mode of valuation	*Food and non-alcoholic beverages is provided in working hours in remote area or in an offshore installation*	*Lunch/refreshment is provided in working hours or extended working hours at any other place*	
		Tea, snacks and non-alcoholic beverages in office premises	*Food in office premises or through non-transferable paid vouchers usable only at eating joints*
Step 1 - Find out cost to the employer	*Nil*	*Nil*	Cost to the employer in excess of Rs. 50 per meal
Step 2 - *Less*: Amount recovered from the employee	*Nil*	*Nil*	Recovery from the employee
Taxable value of the perquisite (*Step 1 – Step 2*)	*Nil*	*Nil*	Balancing amount (if it is positive)

• The following points should be noted —

1. Tea or similar non-alcoholic beverages and snacks (in the form of light refreshments) during working hours are not charged to tax as perquisite.

2. Expenditure on provision of free meals in excess of Rs. 50 per meal should be treated as perquisite—Circular No. 29/2017$, dated December 5, 2017.

3. Working hours include extended office hours (like working on holidays, over-time).

$ For Circular No. 29/2017, log on to *taxmann.com/readyreckoner.aspx*.

15.17 ***Valuation of perquisite in respect of travelling, touring, accommodation*** - The basis of valuation is as follows—

Mode of valuation	*Perquisite in respect of travelling, touring, accommodation and any other expenses paid by employer for any holiday availed by employee (or any member of household) other than leave travel concession referred to in para 15.7*	
	Where such facility is available uniformly to all employees	*Where such facility is not available uniformly to all employees*
Step 1 - Find out cost to the employer	Expenditure incurred by the employer	Value at which such facilities are offered by other agencies to the public
Step 2 - *Less*: Amount recovered from the employee	Recovery from the employee	Recovery from the employee
Taxable value of the perquisite (*Step 1 – Step 2*)	Balancing amount (if it is positive)	Balancing amount (if it is positive).

Notes:

1. Where the employee is on official tour and the expenses are incurred in respect of any member of his household accompanying him, the amount of expenditure so incurred shall also be a perquisite or amenity.

2. Where any official tour is extended as a vacation, the value of such perquisite will be limited to the expenses incurred in relation to such extended period of stay or vacation.

15.18 ***Valuation of perquisite in respect of gift, voucher or token*** - The value of any gift [or voucher, or token in lieu of which such gift may be received by the employee (or by the member of his household)] on ceremonial occasions or otherwise shall be determined as the sum equal to the amount of such gift. The perquisite is taxable. Where, however, the value of such gift, voucher or token, as the case may be, is below Rs. 5,000 in the aggregate during the previous year, the value of perquisite shall be taken as *nil*.

The following points should be noted—

1. Gifts made in cash or convertible into money (like gift cheques) are not exempt.

2. Gifts up to Rs. 5,000 in aggregate per annum would be exempt, beyond which it would be taxable—Circular No. 15/2001[$], dated December 12, 2001.

15.19 ***Valuation of perquisite in respect of credit card*** - The perquisite in respect of credit card is taxable as follows—

Step 1	Find out expenditure incurred by the employer in respect of credit card used by the employee or any member of his household [*see* para 15.19-1]
Step 2	*Less* : Expenditure on use for official purposes [*see* para 15.19-2]
Step 3	*Less* : Amount, if any, recovered from the employee

Note - The balance amount (if it is positive) is the taxable value of the perquisite.

15.19-1 *EXPENDITURE INCURRED BY EMPLOYER* - It includes the amount of expenses including membership fees and annual fees incurred by the employee or any member of his household, which is charged to a credit card (including any add-on-card), provided by the employer (or otherwise paid or reimbursed by the employer).

15.19-2 *EXPENDITURE FOR OFFICIAL USE* - Expenditure on use of credit card for official purposes is deductible. To claim deduction, the following conditions should be satisfied—

Condition 1	Complete details in respect of such expenditure is maintained by the employer which may, *inter alia*, include the date of expenditure and the nature of expenditure.
Condition 2	The employer gives a certificate for such expenditure to the effect that the same was incurred wholly and exclusively for the performance of official duties.

15.20 ***Valuation of perquisite in respect of club expenditure*** - The perquisite in respect of club facility is taxable as follows—

[$] For Circular No. 15/2001, log on to *taxmann.com/readyreckoner.aspx*.

Step 1	Find out expenditure incurred by the employer in respect of club facility used by the employee or any member of his household [*see* para 15.20-1]
Step 2	*Less :* Expenditure on use for official purposes [*see* para 15.20-2]
Step 3	*Less :* Amount, if any, recovered from the employee

Note - The balance amount (if it is positive) is the taxable value of the perquisite.

15.20-1 *EXPENDITURE INCURRED BY EMPLOYER* - The following points should be noted—

1. It includes any expenditure on club facility used by the employee or any member of his household which is paid or reimbursed by the employer.

2. It includes amount of annual or periodical fees paid or payable to a club.

3. Health club, sports facilities, etc., provided uniformly to all classes of employees by the employer at employer's premises are exempt. Consequently, expenditure on such facility is not included.

4. Initial one time deposits or fees for corporate or institutional membership, where benefit does not remain with a particular employee after cessation of employment are exempt—Circular No. 17/2014, dated December 10, 2014. Consequently, initial fees/deposits, in such case, is not included.

15.20-2 *EXPENDITURE FOR OFFICIAL USE* - Expenditure on use of club facility for official purposes is deductible. To claim deduction, the following conditions should be satisfied—

Condition 1	Complete details in respect of such expenditure is maintained by the employer which may, *inter alia,* include the date of expenditure, the nature of expenditure and its business expediency.
Condition 2	The employer gives a certificate for such expenditure to the effect that the same was incurred wholly and exclusively for the performance of official duties.

15.21 ***Tax on perquisite paid by employer [Sec. 10(10CC)]*** - If tax is paid by an employer on behalf of an employee, the same (being in the nature of an obligation which, but for such payment, would have been payable by the employee) is considered a perquisite, and is chargeable to tax.

With effect from the assessment year 2003-04, an employer has been given an option to pay tax on the whole (or part) value of perquisite (not provided for by way of monetary payments), on behalf of an employee. Clause (*10CC*) was inserted in section 10 with effect from the assessment year 2003-04 to exempt the amount of tax actually paid by an employer, at his option, on the income in the nature of a perquisite (not provided for by way of monetary payment) on behalf of an employee, from being included in perquisites. Such tax paid by the employer shall not be treated as an allowable expenditure in the hands of the employer under section 40. The aforesaid exemption is available only in respect of tax on non-monetary perquisite paid by employer. If tax on salary is paid by the employer on behalf of the assessee, it is a perquisite provided for by way of non-monetary payment and, therefore, the provisions of section 10(*10CC*) would be applicable—*RBF Rig Corpn. LIC (RBFRC)* v. *CIT* [2007] 165 Taxman 101 (Delhi)(SB).

Provisions illustrated - The following illustrations are given to have better understanding—

1. During the previous year 2018-19, A Ltd. pays Rs. 1,50,000 per month as salary to X (28 years) and provides a rent-free unfurnished house (lease rent being Rs. 40,000 per month). The tax on perquisite is paid by A Ltd. as follows—

	Rs.
Salary	18,00,000
Value of perquisite (15 per cent of salary)	2,70,000
Gross salary	20,70,000
Less: Standard deduction	40,000
Salary	20,30,000
Other income	*Nil*
Gross total income	20,30,000
Less: Deductions under section 80C	1,50,000
Net income	18,80,000
Tax on net income (including HEC)	3,91,560
Average rate of tax (Rs. 3,91,560 ÷ Rs. 18,80,000 × 100)	20.83%
Tax on non-monetary perquisite (20.83% of Rs. 2,70,000)	56,235

While calculating business income of A Ltd., Rs. 56,235 is not deductible by virtue of section 40(*a*)(*v*) [amount deductible being Rs. 18,00,000 + Rs. 4,80,000]. In the hands of X, Rs. 56,235 is not chargeable to tax. The same rule is applicable if tax on perquisite paid by A Ltd. is lower than Rs. 56,235. If, however, tax paid by A Ltd. is more than Rs. 56,235 then the "excess" amount is deductible in the hands of A Ltd. and the same is chargeable to tax in the hands of X.

2. X is a foreign citizen. He is employed by B Ltd. (an Indian company located at Mumbai) on annual salary of Rs. 9,00,000. Besides, he gets allowances (taxable amount : Rs. 1,08,000), non-monetary perquisites (taxable amount : Rs. 1,80,000) and monetary perquisites (taxable amount : Rs. 1,22,000). B Ltd. pays Rs. 3,40,000 as income-tax (out of its pocket) on behalf of X. X is eligible for deduction of Rs. 1,00,000 under sections 80C, 80D and 80G.

Out of Rs. 3,40,000, tax on non-monetary perquisites is exempt under section 10(*10CC*). Tax on non-monetary perquisites can be calculated with the help of quadratic equation (*see* any 10th standard school text book on mathematics). A similar example is given in Taxmann's *Direct Taxes Law and Practice, 2019* Professional Edition (*see* Problem 63-P6). The following calculations are given for ready reference for the assessment year 2019-20 —

	Rs.	*Rs.*
Salary		9,00,000
Allowances		1,08,000
Non-monetary perquisites		1,80,000
Monetary perquisites		1,22,000
Income-tax paid by employer	3,40,000	
Less: Exemption under section 10(*10CC*) [*see* computation given below]	77,767	2,62,233
Gross salary		15,72,233
Less: Standard deduction		40,000
Salary		15,32,233
Any other income		*Nil*
Gross total income		15,32,233
Less: Deduction under sections 80C, 80D and 80G		1,00,000
Net income (rounded off)		14,32,230
Tax liability on net income (including health and education cess) (rounded off)		2,51,860
Average rate of tax (Rs. 2,51,860 ÷ Rs. 14,32,230)		17.58%
Tax @ 17.58% on non-monetary perquisites of (Rs. 1,80,000 + Rs. 2,62,233)		77,767
Income exempt under section 10(*10CC*)		77,767
Amount not deductible under section 40(*a*)(*v*)		77,767

15.22 ***Sweat equity shares*** - If the following conditions are satisfied, value of sweat equity shares will be taxable in the hands of employees—

1. The security or shares involved are "specified security" or "sweat equity shares". For this purpose, specified security means "securities as defined in section 2(*h*) of the Securities Contracts (Regulation) Act and where employees stock option has been granted under any plan or scheme therefor, includes the securities offered under such plan or scheme". Section 2(*h*) of the Securities Contracts (Regulation) Act defines securities to include the following—

a. shares, scrips, stocks, bonds, debentures, debenture stock or other marketable securities of a like nature in or of any incorporated company or other body corporate;

b. derivative;

c. units or any other instrument issued by any collective investment scheme to the investors in such schemes;

d. security receipt as defined in clause (*zg*) of section 2 of the Securitisation and Reconstruction of Financial Assets and Enforcement of Security Interest Act, 2002;

e. units or any other such instrument issued to the investors under any mutual fund scheme;

f. Government securities;

g. such other instruments as may be declared by the Central Government to be securities; and

h. rights or interest in securities.

"Sweat equity shares" means "equity shares issued by a company to its employees or directors at a discount or for consideration other than cash for providing know-how or making available rights in the nature of intellectual property rights or value additions, by whatever name called".

2. Specified security or sweat equity shares are allotted or transferred on or after April 1, 2009. If these securities or shares are transferred during April 1, 2007 and March 31, 2009, then employer is liable to pay fringe benefit tax under section 115WB(1)(*d*).

3. Specified security or sweat equity shares are allotted by the employer or former employer to the employee.

4. Specified security or sweat equity shares may be transferred to the employee or former employee, directly or indirectly.

5. These securities or shares are transferred to the employee either free of cost or at a concessional rate.

• *Consequences when the above conditions are satisfied* - If the above conditions are satisfied, perquisite will be taxable in the hands of employee in the assessment year relevant to the previous year in which shares or securities are allotted or transferred to the employee. For this purpose, one has to find out fair market value of shares or securities according to the prescribed method. Fair market value of shares or securities will be calculated on the date on which the employee exercises the option. Amount actually paid or recovered from the employee in respect of such shares or securities shall be deducted.

• *Valuation of specified security or sweat equity share* - Rule 3 provides the following guidelines—

Quoted shares - In a case where, on the date of exercise of the option, the share in the company is listed on a recognized stock exchange in India, the fair market value shall be the average of the opening price and closing price of the share on that date on the said stock exchange. Where, however, on the date of exercise of the option, the share is listed on more than one recognized stock exchanges, the fair market value shall be the average of opening price and closing price of the share on the recognised stock exchange which records the highest volume of trading in the share. Where on the date of exercise of the option, there is no trading in the share on any recognized stock exchange in India, the fair market value shall be the closing price of the share on any recognised stock exchange on a date closest to the date of exercise of the option and immediately preceding such date.

For this purpose "closing price" of a share on a recognised stock exchange on a date shall be the price of the last settlement on such date on such stock exchange. Where the stock exchange quotes both "buy" and "sell" prices, the closing price shall be the "sell" price of the last settlement. "Opening price" of a share on a recognised stock exchange on a date shall be the price of the first settlement on such date on such stock exchange. Where the stock exchange quotes both "buy" and "sell" prices, the opening price shall be the "sell" price of the first settlement.

Unquoted shares - In a case where, on the date of exercise of the option, the share in the company is not listed on a recognized stock exchange in India, the fair market value shall be such value of the share in the company as determined by a merchant banker on the specified date. "Specified date" means the date of exercise of the option; or any date earlier than the date of exercise of the option, not being a date which is more than 180 days earlier than the date of exercise of the option.

15.22-E1 The following information is given by X, Y and Z—

	X	*Y*	*Z*
Date of joining	April 1, 1969	April 1, 1969	April 1, 1969
Date of grant of option	April 1, 2002	April 1, 2002	April 1, 2002
Grant period	April 1, 2002 to March 31, 2005	April 1, 2002 to March 31, 2005	April 1, 2002 to March 31, 2005
The period during which the option can be exercised to purchase 500 shares at a pre-determined price of Rs. 30 per share	April 1, 2005 to March 31, 2018	April 1, 2005 to March 31, 2018	April 1, 2005 to March 31, 2018
Date of vesting	April 1, 2005	April 1, 2005	April 1, 2005
Fair market value on the date of vesting	Rs. 100 per share	Rs. 100 per share	Rs. 100 per share
Date on which option is exercised by applying for 400 shares	March 20, 2009	March 20, 2009	March 20, 2018

	X	Y	Z
Fair market value on the date of exercise of option	Rs. 700 per share	Rs. 700 per share	Rs. 800 per share
Date of allotment	March 29, 2009	March 29, 2009	April 1, 2018
Fair market value on the date of allotment	Rs. 750 per share	Rs. 750 per share	Rs. 860 per share
Date when demat account of the employee is credited	March 30, 2009	April 1, 2009	April 2, 2018

•

In the case of X and Y, shares are allotted before April 1, 2009. Consequently, fringe benefit tax is applicable in the hands of employer. Value of fringe benefits will be Rs. 28,000 [*i.e.*, 400 shares × (Rs. 100 – Rs. 30)]. Cost of acquisition in the hands of X and Y for the purpose of determining capital gain at the time of transfer of these shares will be Rs. 100 per share (*i.e.*, the fair market value on the date of vesting of the option).

However, in the case of Z, fringe benefit tax is not applicable in the hands of employer. Perquisite will be taxable in the hands of Z, as shares are allotted on or after April 1, 2009. The value of the perquisite will be Rs. 3,08,000 [*i.e.*, 400 shares × (Rs. 800, being fair market value on the date of exercise of option – Rs. 30, being pre-determined price)]. The cost of acquisition in the hands of Z for the purpose of determining capital gain at the time of transfer of these shares will be Rs. 800 per share (*i.e.*, the fair market value on the date of exercise of the option). The following points should be noted—

1. Suppose in the above case, X is based in India only for a period of 3 months out of the grant period of 3 years (*i.e.*, April 1, 2002 to March 31, 2005). The value of fringe benefit chargeable to tax in the hands of employer will be proportionately reduced (taxable value of perquisite will be Rs. 2,333, *i.e.*, 3 months ÷ 36 months × Rs. 28,000). This was clarified by the Board *vide* Circular No. 9/2007$, dated December 20, 2007.

2. Suppose in the above case, Z is based in India only for a period of 3 months out of the grant period of 3 years. In such a case, it is debatable whether (or not) the taxable value of perquisite in the hands of Z should be proportionately reduced[56]. The Central Board of Direct Taxes should give a clarification on this point (maybe similar to the clarification given in Circular No. 9/2007, dated December 20, 2007).

15.22-E2 A joins B Ltd. on May 1, 2018 (salary being Rs. 1,20,000 per month). A owns a building which is transferred by him to his employer-company on December 1, 2018 for a consideration of Rs. 49,20,000. The sale consideration will be paid by C Ltd. which is holding company of B Ltd. A will be allotted 2,000 shares in C Ltd. at his option at any time during January 1, 2019 and March 31, 2019 at a pre-determined price of Rs. 40 per share (market value is Rs. 2,500 per share on December 1, 2018).

•

This will not be taxable as perquisite under section 17(*2*)(*vi*) as shares are not allotted for providing know-how or making available rights in the nature of intellectual property. However, capital gain on transfer of building will be chargeable to tax according to the provisions of section 45.

15.22-E3 Z is a scientist having special knowledge in the field of bio-technology. He was in the USA till 2008 before joining A Ltd., an Indian company, on January 1, 2008 (salary being Rs. 2,50,000 per month). Besides, A Ltd. has given an option to Z to get shares in A Ltd. (as given below) in consideration for providing technical knowledge which Z has gained while working with an overseas multinational company in the USA—

Date of granting the option	January 2, 2008
Date of vesting of the option	December 31, 2008
What is the option	To purchase 1,000 shares in A Ltd. at pre-determined price of Re. 1 per share at any time during December 31, 2008 and December 31, 2019
Date of exercise of option (lot one)	January 1, 2009 (to purchase 600 shares)
Date of allotment (lot one)	January 1, 2009
Fair market value on December 31, 2008	Rs. 7,000 per share
Fair market value on January 1, 2009	Rs. 7,500 per share
Date of exercise of option (lot two)	March 25, 2018 (to purchase 400 shares)
Date of allotment (lot two)	April 1, 2018
Fair market value on March 25, 2018	Rs. 7,500 per share
Market value of the technical knowledge provided by Z to A Ltd.	Rs. 58,00,000

•

56. The Delhi Tribunal has given a favourable ruling on this point in the case of *CIT* v. *Robert Arthur Keltz* [2013] 35 taxmann.com 424.

$ For Circular No. 9/2007, log on to *taxmann.com/readyreckoner.aspx.*

Tax consequences of allotment of 600 shares (i.e., lot one) - Fringe benefit tax is applicable in the case of lot one as shares are transferred to Z in consideration of employment before April 1, 2009. Value of fringe benefit taxable in the hands of A Ltd. for the assessment year 2009-10 is Rs. 41,99,400 [*i.e.*, 600 shares × (Rs. 7,000 – Re. 1)]. Cost of acquisition of 600 shares in the hands of Z is Rs. 7,000 per share.

Tax consequences of allotment of 400 shares (i.e., lot two) - The option is exercised on March 25, 2018. 400 shares are allotted to Z on April 1, 2018. The perquisite is taxable under section 17(*2*)(*vi*) as shares are allotted for making available right in the nature of intellectual property to the employer-company. The value of perquisite chargeable to tax for the assessment year 2019-20 is Rs. 29,99,600 [*i.e.*, 400 shares × (Rs. 7,500 – Re. 1)]. Cost of acquisition of 400 shares in the hands of Z will be Rs. 7,500 per share.

15.23 ***Employer's contribution towards approved superannuation fund*** - Employer's contribution towards an approved superannuation fund is chargeable to tax in the hands of employees to the extent such contribution exceeds Rs. 1.5 lakh[57] per assessment year. It is taxable in the year in which contribution is made.

15.24 ***Perquisites received by a teacher/professor from SAARC Member States*** - *See* para 12.5.

15.25 ***Any other benefit, amenity, etc.*** - This is a residual head. It covers any other benefit or amenity, service, right or privilege provided by any employer. However, it does not cover the following—

1. Perquisite already included in preceding paras - Any perquisite, which is included in preceding paras [*i.e.*, paras 15.1 to 15.24], is not taxable under this head.

2. Telephone/mobile phone - The perquisite in respect of telephone/mobile phone is not taxable in the case of any employee of any organization. Moreover, in the case of retired Chairman and retired members of UPSC, the value of a residential telephone free of cost and the number of free calls to the extent of 1,500 per month (over and above the number of free calls per month allowed by the telephone authorities), is not chargeable to tax.

• *Mode of valuation* - The value of benefit, amenity, service, right or privilege which come under this residual head, shall be determined on the basis of cost to the employer under an arm's length transaction as reduced by the employee's contribution, if any.

15.25-E1 X is employed by A Ltd., a garment manufacturing company (salary being Rs. 30,000 per month). Besides, he has been provided the following perquisites—

1. Fixed and mobile telephone (expenditure of the employer: Rs. 18,000 per annum approximately).

2. X can purchase every year up to 10 shirts manufactured by the company at a concessional price of Rs. 50 per shirt (manufacturing cost to the employer: Rs. 200 per shirt, MRP: Rs. 1,100 per shirt, discount given to whole sellers: 42 per cent on MRP). During the previous year, X has purchased 6 shirts.

3. Rent-free house owned by the employer in Mumbai.

Find out the value of perquisites chargeable to tax in the hands of X.

•

Value of perquisites given in the problem will be determined as follows—

1. Telephone including mobile phone - It is not covered by any of preceding paras. However, it is not chargeable to tax.

2. Sale of garments at concessional rate - It is not covered by any of the preceding paras. Consequently, it would be taxable in the hands of X [value of the perquisite being Rs. 900, *i.e.*, (Rs. 200 – Rs. 50) × 6].

3. Residential house - It will be taxable in the hands of X (value being Rs. 54,000, *i.e.*, 15% of the salary).

Deductions from salary income [Sec. 16]

16. Income chargeable under the head "Salaries" is computed after making the following deductions :

a. standard deduction up to the assessment year 2005-06 [sec. 16(*i*)—*see* para 16.1];

b. standard deduction from the assessment year 2019-20 [sec. 16(*ia*) – *see* para 16.1];

c. entertainment allowance [sec. 16(*ii*)—*see* paras 16.2 and 13.2]; and

d. professional tax [sec. 16(*iii*)—*see* para 16.3].

16.1 ***Standard deduction*** - Standard deduction is available as follows –

• *From the assessment year 2020-21* - Standard deduction is **Rs. 50,000 or the amount of salary, whichever is lower.**

---

57. Rs. 1 lakh up to the assessment year 2016-17.

• *For the assessment year 2019-20* - Standard deduction is Rs. 40,000 or the amount of salary, whichever is lower.

• *For the assessment years 2006-07 to 2018-19* - Standard deduction is not available.

• *From the assessment years 2002-03 to 2005-06* - Standard deduction under section 16(*i*), for the assessment years 2002-03 to 2005-06 was as under—

Salary income before giving standard deduction (i.e., after giving deduction in respect of entertainment allowance and professional tax)	*Amount of standard deduction for the assessment years 2002-03 and 2003-04*	*Amount of standard deduction for the assessment years 2004-05 and 2005-06*
Rs. 1.50 lakh or less	One-third of gross salary or Rs. 30,000, whichever is less	40 per cent of gross salary or Rs. 30,000 whichever is lower
More than Rs. 1.50 lakh but not more than Rs. 3 lakh	Rs. 25,000	Rs. 30,000
More than Rs. 3 lakh but not more than Rs. 5 lakh	Rs. 20,000	Rs. 30,000
More than Rs. 5 lakh	*Nil*	Rs. 20,000

16.2 ***Entertainment allowance [Sec. 16(ii)]*** - As explained earlier, entertainment allowance is first included in salary and thereafter a deduction is allowed in accordance with the rules mentioned in para 13.2.

16.3 ***Professional tax or tax on employment [Sec. 16(iii)]*** - Professional tax or tax on employment levied by a State under article 276(2) of the Constitution is allowed as a deduction from the assessment year 1990-91.

Employees' provident fund

17. The following table explains the treatment of provident funds in the assessment of salaried employees :

	Statutory provident fund	*Recognised provident fund*	*Unrecognised provident fund*
Employer's contribution to provident fund	Exempt from tax	Exempt up to 12[58] per cent of salary[1]; excess of employer's contribution over 12[58] per cent of salary[1] is taxable	Exempt from tax
Deduction under section 80C on employee's contribution	Available	Available	Not available
Interest credited to provident fund	Exempt from tax	Exempt from tax if rate of interest does not exceed the notified rate (*i.e.*, 9.5 per cent); otherwise, excess of interest over the notified rate is taxable[2]	Exempt from tax
Lump sum payment at the time of retirement or termination of service.	Exempt from tax	Exempt from tax in some cases[3], otherwise provident fund will be treated as an unrecognised fund from the beginning[4]	Payment received in respect of employee's own contribution is exempt from tax, Interest on employee's contribution is taxable under the head "Income from other sources"—*CIT* v. *G. Hyatt* [1971] 80 ITR 177 (SC). Balance is taxable under the head "Salaries". However, relief can be claimed under section 89 [*see* para 22]

58. 10 per cent up to the assessment year 1997-98.

Notes :

1. "Salary" here means basic salary. It includes dearness allowance and dearness pay[59] if terms of employment so provide, and excludes all other allowances and perquisites. If, however, as per contract of employment, commission is determined at a fixed percentage of turnover achieved by an employee, then such commission would partake of the character of salary—*Gestetner Duplicators (P.) Ltd.* v. *CIT* [1979] 1 Taxman 1/117 ITR 1 (SC).

2. Interest credited to a recognised provident fund is exempt from tax if the rate of interest does not exceed the notified rate given below :

Date of credit of interest (both days inclusive)	*Notified rate of interest (per cent)*
Between April 1, 1974 and March 24, 1975	6.5
Between March 25, 1975 and July 20, 1977	7.5
Between July 21, 1977 and October 26, 1978	8
Between October 27, 1978 and August 31, 1981	8.25
Between September 1, 1981 and June 1, 1983	9
Between June 2, 1983 and August 22, 1984	9.5
Between August 23, 1984 and June 17, 1985	10
Between June 18, 1985 and March 31, 1986	10.5
Between April 1, 1986 and March 31, 2001	12
On or after April 1, 2001	9.5

3. Accumulated balance payable to an employee participating in a recognized provident fund shall be exempt in the hands of employee in the following situations :

- If the employee has rendered continue service with his employer for a period of 5 years or more. For the purpose of calculating 5 year time-limit, service rendered with the previous employer shall be included, if the previous employer also maintained recognized provident fund and the provident fund balance of the employee was transferred by him to the current employer.
- If the employee has been terminated because of certain reasons which are beyond his control (*e.g.*, ill health of the employee, discontinuation of business by employer, completion of project for which the employee was employed, etc.).
- If the employee has resigned before completion of 5 years but he joins another employer (who maintains recognized provident fund and provident fund money with the current employer is transferred to the new employer).
- If the entire balance standing to the credit of the employee is transferred to his account under a pension scheme referred to in section 80CCD and notified by the Central Government (*i.e.*, NPS).

4. Lump sum payment received from unrecognized provident fund at the time of retirement/termination shall be taxable as follows :

- Payment received in respect of employer's contribution and interest thereon is taxable under the head "Salaries".
- Payment received in respect of interest on employee's contribution is taxable under the head "Income from other sources".
- Payment received in respect of employee's contribution is not chargeable to tax.

17-E1 X (40 yrs.), posted at Bombay, gets salary of Rs. 70,000 per month during 2018-19 from XYZ Ltd. He contributes Rs. 1,20,000 to the provident fund. His employer contributes Rs. 1,05,000. His other allowances are : project allowance : Rs. 30,000 and medical allowance : Rs. 3,000 and 0.5 per cent commission on sales achieved by him. During the year, turnover achieved by X is Rs. 4,80,000. Employer provides a Maruti 800 car with a chauffeur for his private and official purposes. The amount of interest credited to the provident fund on May 10, 2018 @ 12 per cent per annum comes to Rs. 3,49,000. He pays Rs. 4,000 as premium on a life insurance policy taken in 2005 of Rs. 15,000 taken on his own life. He pays tuition fees of Rs. 40,000 for his daughter. Income of X from other sources is Rs. 3,13,000. Determine the taxable income and tax liability of X for the assessment year 2019-20 on the assumption that the provident fund is a (*a*) statutory provident fund (SPF), (*b*) recognised provident fund (RPF), or (*c*) unrecognised provident fund (UPF).

•

Taxable income of X will be computed as under :	*SPF* *Rs.*	*RPF* *Rs.*	*UPF* *Rs.*
Salary (*i.e.*, Rs. 70,000 × 12)	8,40,000	8,40,000	8,40,000
Project allowance	30,000	30,000	30,000
Medical allowance	3,000	3,000	3,000

59. Dearness allowance/pay shall be considered only when it is part of salary for computing all retirement benefits (like pension, leave encashment, gratuity, provident fund, etc.). If dearness allowance/pay is part of salary for computing only some (not all) of the retirement benefits, then it is not taken into consideration for this purpose—*ITO* v. *Sr. Accounts Officer, Pay & Accounts, DHBVNL* [2009] 33 SOT 37 (Delhi).

	SPF Rs.	RPF Rs.	UPF Rs.
Commission (½% of Rs. 4,80,000)	2,400	2,400	2,400
Free motor car (Rs. 1,800 × 12)	21,600	21,600	21,600
Free chauffeur (Rs. 900 × 12)	10,800	10,800	10,800
Employer's contribution towards provident fund in excess of 12% of salary [*i.e.,* Rs. 1,05,000 – 12% of (Rs. 8,40,000 + Rs. 2,400)]	—	3,912	—
Interest credited in provident fund in excess of 9.5% per annum (*i.e.,* Rs. 3,49,000 × 2.5 ÷ 12)	—	72,708	—
Gross salary	9,07,800	9,84,420	9,07,800
Less : Standard deduction	40,000	40,000	40,000
Salary income	8,67,800	9,44,420	8,67,800
Other income	3,13,000	3,13,000	3,13,000
Gross total income	11,80,800	12,57,420	11,80,800
Less : Deduction under section 80C	1,50,000	1,50,000	43,000
Net income (rounded off)	10,30,800	11,07,420	11,37,800
Tax	1,21,740	1,44,726	1,53,840
Add : Surcharge	*Nil*	*Nil*	*Nil*
Total	1,21,740	1,44,726	1,53,840
Add : Health and education cess	4,870	5,789	6,154
Tax liability	1,26,610	1,50,520	1,59,990

Notes :

1. If commission is based upon a fixed percentage of turnover achieved by an employee, it is included in basic pay for this purpose [*see* para 17].

2. Deduction under section 80C is calculated as under :

Qualifying amount :			
- Provident fund contribution	1,20,000	1,20,000	*Nil*
- LIC payment (maximum 20% of sum assured)	3,000	3,000	3,000
- Tuition fees	40,000	40,000	40,000
Total	1,63,000	1,63,000	43,000
Amount deductible	1,50,000	1,50,000	43,000

3. Rebate under section 87A is not available, as net income of X is more than Rs. 3,50,000.

Approved superannuation fund

18. It means a superannuation fund which has been and continues to be approved by the Commissioner in accordance with the rules contained in Part B of the Fourth Schedule. The tax treatment of contribution to and payment from the fund is as under—

- Employer's contribution is exempt from tax.[60]
- Employee's contribution qualifies for deduction under section 80C.
- Interest on the accumulated balance is exempt from tax.
- Section 10(*13*) grants exemption in respect of payment from the fund :

a. to the legal heirs on the death of the beneficiary (*e.g.,* payment to widow of the beneficiary) ; or

b. to an employee in lieu of or in commutation of an annuity on his retirement at or after the specified age or on his becoming incapacitated prior to such retirement ; or

c. by way of refund of contribution on the death of the beneficiary ; or

60. However, employer's contribution towards an approved superannuation fund is chargeable to tax to the extent it exceeds the following -
- Rs. 1 lakh per annum (for the assessment years 2010-11 to 2016-17),
- Rs. 1.5 lakh per annum (from the assessment year 2017-18 onwards).

d. by way of refund of contribution to an employee on his leaving otherwise than in the circumstances mentioned in (*b*), to the extent to which such payment does not exceed the contribution made prior to April 1, 1962 (for instance, where the amount received by an employee does not include any contribution made prior to April 1, 1962, the whole amount is taxable).

Approved gratuity fund

19. It means a gratuity fund which has been and continues to be approved by the Commissioner in accordance with the rules contained in Part C of the Fourth Schedule. Tax treatment of contribution to and payment from the fund is as under :

- Employer's contribution is exempt from tax.
- Actual payment received by the employee is exempt within the limits specified in section 10(*10*) [*see* para 12.2].

Tax on salary of non-resident technicians [Sec. 10(*5B*)]

20. Exemption under section 10(*5B*) is not available from the assessment year 2003-04.

Salary of foreign citizens [Sec. 10(*6*)]

21. The remuneration received by foreign nationals as diplomatic personnel, consular personnel, trade Commissioners, staff of a foreign mission, is exempt from tax.

Relief under section 89

22. If an individual receives any portion of his salary[61] in arrears or in advance, or receives profit in lieu of salary, he can claim relief in terms of section 89[62] read with rule 21A. The relief is also available in respect of family pension received in arrears.

22.1 ***Computation of relief when salary or family pension has been received in arrears or in advance [Rule 21A(2)]*** - The relief on salary received in arrears or in advance (hereinafter to be referred as "the additional salary") is computed in the manner laid down in rule 21A(2) as under :

1. Calculate the tax payable on the total income, including the additional salary of the relevant previous year in which the same is received.

2. Calculate the tax payable on the total income, excluding the additional salary of the relevant previous year in which the same is received.

3. Find out the difference between the tax at (*1*) and (*2*).

4. Compute the tax on the total income after excluding the additional salary in the previous year to which such salary relates.

5. Compute the tax on the total income after including the additional salary in the previous year to which such salary relates.

6. Find out the difference between the tax at (*4*) and (*5*).

7. The excess of tax computed at (*3*) over the tax computed at (*6*) is the amount of relief admissible under section 89(1). No relief is, however, admissible if the tax computed at (*3*) is less than the tax computed at (*6*). In such a case, the assessee-employee need not apply for relief.

22.1-E1 During the previous year ending March 31, 2019, X, a salaried employee (age : 40 years), received Rs. 10,67,000 as basic salary and Rs. 20,000 as arrears of bonus of the financial year 1992-93. During the previous year 1992-93, X has received Rs. 50,000 as salary. X deposits Rs. 1,500 (during 1992-93) and Rs. 10,000 (during 2018-19) in public provident fund.

•

The admissible relief under section 89 in respect of bonus paid in the assessment year 2019-20 will be computed as under :

61. Relief under section 89 is available in respect of salary and so, it is, by virtue of section 17(1)(*iv*), as a natural corollary thereof, available *qua* perquisites – *Rajesh Kumar* v. *CIT* [2018] 97 taxmann.com 618 (Agra.).

62. The department insists that the concerned employee should submit electronically Form No. 10E along with his return of income to claim rebate under section 89 (however, there is no such legal requirement under the Income-tax Act or Income-tax Rules).

	Taxable income and tax liability on "receipt" basis		*Taxable income and tax liability on "accrual" basis*	
	2019-20	*1993-94*	*2019-20*	*1993-94*
	Rs.	*Rs.*	*Rs.*	*Rs.*
Salary	10,67,000	50,000	10,67,000	50,000
Arrears of salary	20,000	—	—	20,000
Gross salary	10,87,000	50,000	10,67,000	70,000
Less : Standard deduction	40,000	12,000	40,000	12,000
Gross total income	10,47,000	38,000	10,27,000	58,000
Less : Deduction under section 80C	10,000	*Nil*	10,000	*Nil*
Net income	10,37,000	38,000	10,17,000	58,000
Tax on net income	1,23,600	2,000	1,17,600	6,800
Less : Rebate under section 88	*Nil*	300	*Nil*	300
Tax	1,23,600	1,700	1,17,600	6,500
Add : Surcharge	*Nil*	—	*Nil*	—
Tax and surcharge	1,23,600	1,700	1,17,600	6,500
Add: Health and education cess	4,944	—	4,704	—
Tax liability	1,28,544	1,700	1,22,304	6,500

	Rs.
Tax liability of the two assessment years on receipt basis	1,30,244
Tax liability of the two assessment years on accrual basis	1,28,804
Tax relief under section 89 for the assessment year 2019-20 (*i.e.,* Rs. 1,30,244 – Rs. 1,28,804)	1,440
Tax payable for the assessment year 2019-20 (*i.e.,* Rs. 1,28,544 – Rs. 1,440)	1,27,100

22.2 ***Computation of relief in respect of gratuity [Rule 21A(3)]*** - Under section 89, a relief can be claimed if gratuity is received in excess of the limits specified in para 12.2. However, no relief is admissible if taxable gratuity is in respect of services rendered for less than five years. Cases in which the relief is admissible may be divided into two categories, namely, (*i*) where the gratuity payable is in respect of past service of 15 years or more; and (*ii*) where such period is 5 years or more but less than 15 years. Relief in a case belonging to the first category is worked out as under :

1. Compute the average rate of tax on the total income including the gratuity in the year of receipt.

2. Find out the tax on gratuity at the average rate of tax computed at (*1*) above.

3. Compute the average rate of tax by adding one-third of the gratuity to the other income of each of the three preceding years.

4. Find out the average of the three average rates computed in the manner specified in (*3*) above and compute the tax on gratuity at that rate.

5. The difference between the tax on gratuity computed at (*2*) and that at (*4*) will be the relief admissible under section 89(1).

In cases covered under the second category, the relief is computed on similar lines as above with the only difference that instead of average of the average rates of the preceding three years, the average of the rates of the preceding two years is computed by adding one-half of the gratuity to the other income of each of the preceding two years.

22.2-E1 X (age : 58 years) received from his employer Rs. 3,45,417 as death-*cum*-retirement gratuity on March 31, 2019, after rendering service of 23 years out of which Rs. 3,36,417 is exempt under section 10(*10*). In addition, he received during the year Rs. 15,08,000 as salary and Rs. 1,23,100 as bank interest on fixed deposits. For the assessment years 2018-19, 2017-18 and 2016-17 his income was Rs. 7,20,000 (salary: Rs. 6,40,000 *plus* bank interest on fixed deposits: Rs. 80,000), Rs. 3,40,000 (salary: Rs. 2,37,000 *plus* bank interest on fixed deposits: Rs. 1,03,000) and Rs. 3,22,850 (*i.e.,* salary Rs. 2,33,000 *plus* bank interest on fixed deposits Rs. 89,850 respectively. He pays Rs. 40,000 per annum as premium on an endowment insurance policy on the life of his wife.

•

Relief under section 89 will be worked out as under:

	Assessment years			
	2016-17 Rs.	*2017-18* Rs.	*2018-19* Rs.	*2019-20* Rs.
Salary income	2,33,000	2,37,000	6,40,000	15,08,000
Add : One-third (*i.e.*, Rs. 9,000 × ⅓) of taxable gratuity (Rs. 9,000) in income of each of the three assessment years 2016-17, 2017-18 and 2018-19; and the entire taxable gratuity in the year 2019-20	3,000	3,000	3,000	9,000
Gross salary	2,36,000	2,40,000	6,43,000	15,17,000
Less : Standard deduction	*Nil*	*Nil*	*Nil*	40,000
Taxable salary	2,36,000	2,40,000	6,43,000	14,77,000
Bank interest on fixed deposits	89,850	1,03,000	80,000	1,23,100
Gross total income	3,25,850	3,43,000	7,23,000	16,00,100
Less : Deduction under section 80C	40,000	40,000	40,000	40,000
Net income (rounded off)	2,85,850	3,03,000	6,83,000	15,60,100
Income-tax[63]	1,585	300	49,100	2,80,530
Add : Surcharge	—	—	—	—
Tax and surcharge	1,585	300	49,100	2,80,530
Add: Education cess	32	6	982	—
Add: Secondary and higher education cess	16	3	491	—
Add: Health and education cess	—	—	—	11,221
Tax payable on total income (rounded off)	1,630	310	50,570	2,91,751
Average rates of tax	0.57%	0.10%	7.40%	18.70%
Average of the average rates of tax for assessment years 2016-17, 2017-18 and 2018-19	2.69%	2.69%	2.69%	—
Tax on Rs. 9,000 @ 2.69%				242
Tax on Rs. 9,000 @ 18.70%				1,683
Refund under section 89				1,441

Tax for the assessment year 2019-20 (*i.e.*, Rs. 2,91,751 – Rs. 1,441) : Rs. 2,90,310.

22.3 ***Computation of relief in respect of compensation on termination of employment [Rule 21A(4)]*** - If compensation is received by the assessee from his employer or former employer at or in connection with termination of his employment after continuous service for not less than 3 years and where the unexpired portion of his term of employment is also not less than 3 years, the relief is calculated in the same manner as if gratuity was paid to the employee in respect of service rendered for a period of 15 years or more [*see* para 22.2].

22.4 ***Computation of relief in respect of payment in commutation of pension [Rule 21A(5)]*** - A relief can be claimed in respect of payment in commutation of pension received in excess of the limits mentioned in para 12.3. Such relief is computed in the same manner as if gratuity was paid to the employee in respect of service rendered for a period of 15 years or more [*see* para 22.2].

22.5 ***Computation of relief in respect of other payments [Rule 21A(6)]*** - In respect of payment received by an employee other than those mentioned in paras 22.1 to 22.4 above, the relief under section 89(1) will be granted by the Board after examining the circumstances of each individual case.

22.6 ***Procedure for claiming the tax relief*** - In order to claim tax relief under the aforesaid circumstances, the assessee should give the relevant information in his return of income.

63. Rebate under section 87A is not available, as net income exceeds Rs. 3,50,000. Surcharge is not applicable, as net income does not exceed Rs. 1 crore/Rs. 50 lakh.

Basically, the relief under section 89 is arithmetical. It involves finding out of two rates of tax. The first is the rate of tax applicable to the total income including the extra amount in the year of receipt. The second is finding out the rate by adding the arrears to the total income of the years to which they relate. For this purpose, the Assessing Officer should ask for a true and authentic statement of the total income of the earlier years to which the arrears pertain. There is, therefore, no warrant for issuing a notice under section 148 or calling for returns of income of earlier years—Circular No. 331, dated March 22, 1982.

Hints for tax planning

23. For the purpose of tax planning under the head "Salaries" the following propositions should be borne in mind. However, these propositions would hold good only in the context in which they have been made :

• It should be ensured that, under the terms of employment, dearness allowance and dearness pay form a part of basic salary. This will minimise tax incidence on house rent allowance, gratuity and commuted pension. Likewise, incidence of tax on the employer's contribution to a recognised provident fund will be lesser if dearness allowance forms a part of basic salary.

• The Supreme Court has held in *Gestetner Duplicators (P.) Ltd.* v. *CIT* [1979] 1 Taxman 1/117 ITR 1 that commission, payable as per terms of contract of employment at a fixed percentage of turnover achieved by an employee, falls within the expression "salary" as defined in rule 2(*h*) of Part A of the Fourth Schedule. Consequently, tax incidence on house rent allowance, gratuity and commuted pension will be lesser if commission is paid at a percentage of turnover achieved by the employee.

• As uncommuted pension is always taxable, employees should get their pension commuted. Commuted pension is fully exempt from tax in the case of Government employees and partly exempt from tax in the case of non-Government employees who can claim relief under section 89.

• An employee, being a member of a recognised provident fund, who resigns before completing five years of continuous service, should ensure that he joins a concern which maintains a recognised provident fund for the simple reason that the accumulated balance of the provident fund with the former employer will be exempt from tax, provided the same is transferred to the new employer, who also maintains a recognised provident fund.

• Since the employer's contribution towards a recognised provident fund is exempt from tax up to 12 per cent of salary, employers may give extra benefit to their employees by raising their contribution to 12 per cent of salary without increasing any tax liability.

• While medical allowance payable in cash is taxable, provision of medical facilities (in certain hospitals) is not taxable if some conditions are satisfied. Therefore, employees should go in for free medical facilities instead of a fixed medical allowance.

• Since incidence of tax on retirement benefits like gratuity, commuted pension, accumulated balance of an unrecognised provident fund is lower if they are paid in the beginning of the financial year, employers and employees should mutually plan their affairs in such a way that retirement, termination or resignation, as the case may be, takes place in the beginning of a financial year.

• An employee should take the benefit of relief available under section 89 [*see* para 22] wherever possible. Relief can be claimed even in the case of a sum received from an unrecognised provident fund so far as it is attributable to the employer's contribution and interest thereon. Although gratuity received during employment is not exempt from tax under section 10(*10*), relief under section 89 can be claimed. It should, however, be ensured that the relief is claimed only when it is beneficial.

• Pension received in India by a non-resident assessee from abroad is taxable in India. If, however, such pension is first received by or on behalf of the employee in a foreign country and later on remitted to India, it will be exempt from tax.

• As the perquisite in respect of leave travel concession is not taxable in the hands of employees if certain conditions are satisfied, it should be ensured that the travel concession should be claimed to the maximum possible extent without attracting any incidence of tax.

• As the perquisite in respect of residential telephone, providing use of computer/laptops, gift of movable assets (other than computer, electronic items, car) by employer after using for 10 years or more, and free refreshments during office hours, are not taxable, employees can claim these benefits without adding to their tax bill.

• Since the term "salary" includes basic salary, bonus, commission, fees and all other taxable allowances for the purposes of valuation of perquisite in respect of rent-free house, it would be advantageous if an employee goes in for perquisites rather than for taxable allowances. This will reduce valuation of rent-free house.

• If a rent-free furnished or unfurnished accommodation is provided by the employer at concessional rent, deduction under section 80GG can be claimed if certain conditions are satisfied.

Example on computation of salary income

24-E1 X, an employee of ABC Ltd., receives the following emoluments during the previous year ending March 31, 2019 : salary : Rs. 8,67,800 ; bonus : Rs. 2,200 ; salary in lieu of leave : Rs. 2,000 ; and entertainment allowance Rs. 3,000. Besides the aforesaid emoluments, his employer provided free gas and water for his domestic use (cost Rs. 4,000), a domestic servant (salary paid by employer : Rs. 18,000), concessional education facility for his two sons in a school maintained by it (cost of education : Rs. 16,800, amount paid by X : Rs. 2,000), free meals in office (Rs. 117 per meal for 250 days) and free holiday home facility at Simla (cost Rs. 8,000). Salary of a cook (Rs. 9,000) engaged by X is paid by his employer during the year. On March 31, 2019, the employer-company sells an air-conditioner for Rs. 1,000 (cost of air-conditioner to the company : Rs. 45,000, date of purchase : June 30, 2014). X contributes Rs. 92,000 towards recognised provident fund ; his employer contributes Rs. 90,000. Further, during the previous year X has purchased for Rs. 10,000 shares in a notified infrastructure company for the purpose of section 80C. He deposits Rs. 11,000 in approved annuity plan of LIC for the purpose of section 80CCC. Determine the taxable income and tax liability for the assessment year 2019-20. Income from other sources is Rs. 1,09,000.

•

	Rs.
Salary	8,67,800
Bonus	2,200
Salary in lieu of leave	2,000
Entertainment allowance	3,000
Free gas and water	4,000
Free domestic servant	18,000
Concessional education facility (as the cost of education does not exceed Rs. 1,000 per month per child, it is not chargeable to tax)	—
Free meal facility [(Rs. 117 – Rs. 50) × 250]	16,750
Free holiday home facility	8,000
Salary of cook	9,000
Sale of air-conditioner [Rs. 45,000 – Rs. 18,000 (being normal wear and tear for 4 years @ 10% p.a.) — Rs. 1,000, being amount paid by X]	26,000
Gross salary	9,56,750
Less : Standard deduction	40,000
Taxable salary	9,16,750
Income from other sources	1,09,000
Gross total income	10,25,750
Less : Deduction	
Under section 80C [Rs. 92,000 + Rs. 10,000, subject to the maximum of Rs. 1,50,000] : Rs. 1,02,000	
Under section 80CCC [Maximum : Rs. 1,00,000] : Rs. 11,000	
Aggregate deduction under sections 80C, 80CCC and 80CCD	1,13,000
Net income	9,12,750
Tax liability	
Income-tax[64] [*see* Part B of the Reckoner]	95,050
Add : Surcharge	*Nil*
Total	95,050
Add : Health and education cess	3,802
Tax liability (rounded off)	98,850

64. Rebate under section 87A is not available as income of the assessee is more than Rs. 3,50,000.

Income from house property

	Para number	Example number
PRE-COMPUTATION STEPS		
❑ Find out whether rental income is taxable under section 22	38	—
COMPUTATION STEPS—LET OUT PROPERTIES		
❑ Determine gross annual value	39.1	39.1-4a-E1, 39.1-4a-E2, 39.1-4b-E1, 39.1-4c-E1, 39.1-4c-E2, 39.1-4d-E1
❑ Deduct municipal tax (actually paid)	39.2	—
❑ Make deductions available under section 24	39.3	39.3-1E1, 39.3-2E1
COMPUTATION STEPS—ONE SELF-OCCUPIED RESIDENTIAL PROPERTY (UP TO ASSESSMENT YEAR 2019-20)/**TWO SELF-OCCUPIED PROPERTIES** (FROM THE ASSESSMENT YEAR 2020-21)		
❑ If the property is self-occupied (it is neither let out nor any other benefit is derived)	40.1-1	40.1-1E1
❑ If the property is not actually occupied by reason of the fact that owing to his employment, business or profession carried on at any other place, he has to reside at that place in a rented property	40.1-2	—
❑ If a part of property is self-occupied and a part is let out	40.1-3	40.1-3E1
❑ If a property in self-occupied for a part of the year and let out for other part	40.1-4	40.1-4E1
COMPUTATION STEPS—OTHER SELF-OCCUPIED RESIDENTIAL PROPERTY OR PROPERTIES		
❑ Deemed as let out property	39.1	—
COMPUTATION STEPS—SELF-OCCUPIED COMMERCIAL PROPERTIES		
❑ Income not taxable under section 22 under the head "Income from house property"	38	—

Chargeability [Sec. 22]

38. Under the Income-tax Act, the owner of a house property (consisting of any building or land appurtenant thereto) is taxed on the income in the form of its annual value under the head "Income from house property".

While income from building or land appurtenant thereto (*i.e.,* land attached or situated in the vicinity of building) is taxable as property income under this head, rental income from vacant land or plot is taxable under the head "Income from other sources". In case composite rent is received for property as well as services and amenities, the annual value of such property is assessable under section 22 and the profit arising from services and amenities is chargeable to tax under section 28 or 56.

A club owns a house property and it provides recreational and refreshment facilities exclusively to its members and their guests. Its facilities are not available to non-members. The club is run on 'no profit no loss' basis in that the members pay for all their expenses and are not entitled to any share in the profit. Surplus, if any, is used for maintenance and development of the club. The business of trust is governed by principle of mutuality. It is not only the surplus from the activities of the business of the club that is excluded from the levy of income-tax, even the annual value of the club house as contemplated in section 22 will be outside the purview of the levy of income-tax—*Chelmsford Club* v. *CIT* [2000] 109 Taxman 215 (SC).

38.1 ***Who is owner*** - It is the legal owner of a house property who is chargeable to tax in respect of property income. In the following cases enumerated by section 27[65] persons are deemed to be owners of the house property for the purpose of computing income from house property —

1. An individual, who transfers house property otherwise than for adequate consideration to his or her spouse (not being a transfer in connection with an agreement to live apart) or to his minor child (not being a married daughter), is treated as deemed owner of the house property.

2. The holder of an impartible estate is treated as deemed owner of the house property.

3. A member of a co-operative society, company or other association of persons, to whom a building or a part thereof is allotted or leased under a house building scheme of the society, company or association of persons, is treated as deemed owner of such property.

4. A person who comes to have control over the property in part performance of a contract of the nature referred to in section 53A of the Transfer of Property Act (*i.e.*, acquiring a property under a power of attorney transaction) or by virtue of such transactions as are referred to in clause (*f*) of section 269UA (*i.e.*, taking a property on lease for not less than 12 years) is deemed as owner of such property.

Basis of computing income from a let out house property

39. Income from a let out house property is determined as under :

	Rs.
Gross annual value [*see* para 39.1]	xxxxxxxxx
Less : Municipal taxes [*see* para 39.2]	xxxxxxxxx
Net annual value	xxxxxxxxx
Less : Deduction under section 24 [*see* para 39.3]	
- Standard deduction [*see* para 39.3-1]	xxxxxxxxx
- Interest on borrowed capital [*see* para 39.3-2]	xxxxxxxxx
Income from house property	xxxxxxxxx

39.1 ***Gross annual value [Sec. 23(1)]*** - Though the tax under the head "Income from house property" is a tax on income, yet it is not a tax upon rent but upon inherent capacity of a building to yield income[66]. The standard selected as a measure of the income to be taxed is annual value.

Gross annual value is determined as follows—

Step I	Find out reasonable expected rent of the property [*see* para 39.1-1]
Step II	Find out rent actually received or receivable after excluding unrealized rent but before deducting loss due to vacancy [*see* para 39.1-2]
Step III	Find out which one is higher : amount computed in *Step I* or *Step II.*
Step IV	Find out loss because of vacancy[67]
Step V	*Step III minus Step IV* is gross annual value [*see* para 39.1-3]

39.1-1 *STEP I - FIND OUT REASONABLE EXPECTED RENT [SEC. 23(1)(*a*)]* - Reasonable expected rent is deemed to be the sum for which the property might reasonably be expected to be let out from year to year.

In determining reasonable rent, several factors have to be taken into consideration, such as, location of the property, annual ratable value of the property fixed by municipalities, rents of similar properties in neighbourhood, rent which the property is likely to fetch having regard to demand and supply, cost of construction of the property and nature and history of the property. These factors play a vital role in

65. Section 27 has limited application. It is applicable only for the purpose of sections 22 to 26. It has no application for the purpose of computation of capital gains – *ITO* v. *Pradeep Steel Re-Rolling Mills (P.) Ltd.* [2014] 61 SOT 104 (Mum.).

66. Where the house property (consisting of any building and land appurtenant thereto) is held as stock-in-trade and the property (or any part of the property) is not let during the whole or any part of the previous year, the annual value of such property (or part thereof) shall be taken as *nil* (with effect from the assessment year 2018-19). However, this concession is available only for a limited period given below –

- period up to 1 year from the end of the financial year in which the certificate of completion of construction of the property is obtained from the competent authority (applicable for the assessment years 2018-19 and 2019-20),
- period up to **2 years from the end of the financial year** (as stated above) (applicable for the assessment year 2020-21).

67. Loss due to vacancy is deductible in the case of let out property. It is deductible even if the property remains vacant for the entire previous year–*Vikas Keshav Garud* v. *ITO* [2016] 71 taxmann.com 214 (Pune - Trib.). It is respectfully submitted that the ruling of Andhra Pradesh High Court in the case of *Vivek Jain* v. *CIT* [2011] 202 Taxman 499, requires reconsideration.

determining reasonable expected rent of a house property. In a majority of cases, however, expected rent can be determined by taking into consideration the following factors :

a. municipal valuation of the property [*see* para 39.1-1a]; or

b. fair rent of the property [*see* para 39.1-1b],

The higher of (*a*) or (*b*) is generally taken as expected rent. If, however, a property is covered by a Rent Control Act, then the amount so computed cannot exceed the 'standard rent' [*see* para 39.1-1c] determinable under the Rent Control Act.

39.1-1a MUNICIPAL VALUATION - For collecting municipal taxes, the local authority makes a periodical survey of all buildings in its jurisdiction. Such valuation may be taken as a strong evidence representing the earning capacity of a building. It cannot, however, be considered to be a conclusive evidence. In some big cities (like Delhi, Bombay, Madras and Calcutta) municipal authorities determine net rateable value after deducting 10 per cent of the gross rateable value on account of repairs and an allowance for service taxes (such as sewerage tax and water tax). The net municipal valuation, therefore, requires an adjustment for determining expected rent for income-tax purposes.

39.1-1b FAIR RENT OF THE PROPERTY - Fair rent of the property can be determined on the basis of a rent fetched by a similar property in the same or similar locality. Though two properties cannot be alike in every respect, the evidence afforded by transactions of other parties in the matter of other properties in the neighbourhood, more or less comparable with the property in question, is relevant in arriving at reasonable expected rent.

39.1-1c STANDARD RENT UNDER RENT CONTROL ACTS - The Supreme Court has observed in the cases of *Sheila Kaushish* v. *CIT* [1981] 7 Taxman 1 and *Amolak Ram Khosla* v. *CIT* [1981] 7 Taxman 51 that a landlord cannot reasonably expect to receive from a hypothetical tenant anything more than the standard rent[68] under a Rent Control Act and this would be equally applicable to a tenant who has lost his right to apply for fixation of the standard rent or to the owner himself. These judgments make it clear that if a property is covered under a Rent Control Act, its reasonable expected rent cannot exceed the standard rent (fixed or determinable) under the Rent Control Act.

39.1-1d PROVISION ILLUSTRATED - As mentioned earlier, the reasonable expected rent under *Step I* will be computed on the basis of three factors, namely—

a. municipal valuation (*MV*),

b. fair rent of the property (*FR*); and

c. standard rent of the property (*SR*).

The higher of (*MV*) and (*FR*), subject to maximum of (*SR*) is reasonable expected rent under *Step I.*

The example given below illustrates the aforesaid propositions—

(*Rs. in thousand*)

	A	*B*	*C*	*D*	*E*
Municipal value (MV)	40	40	40	40	40
Fair rent (FR)	46	46	46	48	51
Standard rent (SR)	NA	45	35	45	63
Reasonable expected rent under *Step I* [(MV) or (FR), whichever is higher, subject to maximum of (SR)]	46	45	35	45	51*

*Reasonable expected rent cannot exceed the amount of standard rent. Reasonable expected rent can, however, be lower than standard rent—*see Dr. Balbir Singh* v. *MCD* [1985] 152 ITR 388 (SC). In other words, standard rent is the maximum amount of reasonable expected rent. In the case of E, Rs. 51,000 (being higher of municipal valuation and fair rent) is the reasonable expected rent. Since this amount is lower than the maximum ceiling (*i.e.*, standard rent : Rs. 63,000), it is taken as reasonable expected rent.

39.1-2 *STEP II - FIND OUT RENT ACTUALLY RECEIVED OR RECEIVABLE* - It may be calculated as under—

Rent of the previous year (or that part of the previous year) for which the property is available for letting out	XXXX
Less : Unrealised rent if a few conditions are satisfied	XXXX
Rent received/receivable	XXXX

68. Standard rent is the maximum rent which a person can legally recover from his tenant under a Rent Control Act.

The following points should be noted—

1. Loss due to vacancy shall not be deducted from the aforesaid computation. It shall be deducted under *Step IV.*

2. Sometimes a tenant pays a composite rent of property as well as certain benefits provided by the landlord. To determine rent received/receivable, composite rent must be disintegrated and it is only that part of it attributable to the let out of property which would form the basis for the aforesaid calculation.

3. Occupier's (*i.e.,* tenant's) share of municipal tax realised from the tenant cannot be added to actual rent received/receivable as it is the occupier's duty to pay municipal tax—*CIT* v. *Gillanders Arbuthnot & Co. Ltd.* [1983] 142 ITR 598 (Cal.).

4. If the tenant has undertaken to bear the cost of repairs, the amount spent by the tenant cannot be added to rent received or receivable—*CIT* v. *Parbutty Churn Law* [1965] 57 ITR 609 (Cal.).

5. No addition can be made to rent received or receivable with respect to any notional interest on deposit made by a tenant with landlord—*CIT* v. *Satya Co. Ltd.* [1994] 75 Taxman 193 (Cal.).

39.1-2a WHEN UNREALISED RENT SHALL BE EXCLUDED [EXPLN. TO SEC. 23(1)] - Unrealised rent (which the owner could not realise) shall be excluded from rent received/receivable only if the following conditions are satisfied—

1. The tenancy is *bona fide.*

2. The defaulting tenant has vacated, or steps have been taken to compel him to vacate the property.

3. The defaulting tenant is not in occupation of any other property of the assessee.

4. The assessee has taken all reasonable steps to institute legal proceedings for the recovery of the unpaid rent or satisfies the Assessing Officer that legal proceedings would be useless.

39.1-3 *COMPUTATION WITH THE HELP OF ILLUSTRATIONS* - To have better understanding, the following problems are given—

39.1-3E1 X, Y, Z, A and B separately own the following properties—

(Rs. in thousand)

	H1 X	*H2* Y	*H3* Z	*H4* A	*H5* B
Municipal value (MV)	105	105	105	105	105
Fair rent (FR)	107	107	107	107	107
Standard rent under the Rent Control Act (SR)	*NA*	88	88	135	135
Actual rent	103	112	86	114	97
Unrealized rent (conditions mentioned in para 39.1-2a are satisfied)	1	2	1	2	1
Period of the previous year (in months)	12	12	12	12	12
Period during which the property remains vacant	*Nil*	*Nil*	*Nil*	*Nil*	*Nil*

Find out the gross annual value for the assessment year 2019-20.

•

In this case gross annual value shall be determined as follows—

(Rs. in thousand)

Computation of gross annual value	X	Y	Z	A	B
Step I - Reasonable expected rent of the property [MV or FR, whichever is higher, but subject to maximum of SR]	107	88	88	107	107
Step II - Rent received/receivable after deducting unrealized rent but before adjusting loss due to vacancy	102	110	85	112	96
Step III - Amount computed in *Step I* or *Step II,* whichever is higher	107	110	88	112	107
Step IV - Loss due to vacancy	*Nil*	*Nil*	*Nil*	*Nil*	*Nil*
Step V - Gross annual value is *Step III minus Step IV*	107	110	88	112	107

39.1-3E2 X owns a house property (municipal valuation: Rs. 1,45,000, fair rent: Rs. 1,36,000, standard rent: Rs. 1,24,000). It is let out throughout the previous year (rent being Rs. 8,000 per month up to November 15, 2018 and Rs. 14,000 per month thereafter). X transfers the property to Y on January 31, 2019. Find out the gross annual value of the property in the hands of X for the assessment year 2019-20.

•

Computation of gross annual value	*Rs.*
Municipal value from April 1, 2018 to January 31, 2019 (Rs. 1,45,000 ÷ 12 × 10) (MV)	1,20,833
Fair rent from April 1, 2018 to January 31, 2019 (Rs. 1,36,000 ÷ 12 × 10) (FR)	1,13,333
Standard rent from April 1, 2018 to January 31, 2019 (Rs. 1,24,000 ÷ 12 × 10) (SR)	1,03,333
Step I - Reasonable expected rent of the property [MV or FR, whichever is higher, but subject to maximum of SR]	1,03,333
Step II - Rent received/receivable after deducting unrealized rent but before adjusting loss due to vacancy (Rs. 8,000 × 7.5 + Rs. 14,000 × 2.5)	95,000
Step III - Amount computed in *Step I* or *Step II*, whichever is higher	1,03,333
Step IV - Loss due to vacancy	*Nil*
Step V - Gross annual value is *Step III minus Step IV*	1,03,333

39.1-3E3 Find out the gross annual value in respect of the following properties for the assessment year 2019-20—

(Rs. in thousand)

	X	*Y*	*Z*	*A*	*B*
Municipal value (MV)	140	180	180	140	231
Fair rent (FR)	145	185	185	145	262
Standard rent (SR)	142	175	175	142	241
Actual rent if property is let out throughout the previous year 2018-19	168	168	168	168	252
Unrealised rent of the previous year 2018-19	14	42	1	70	42
Unrealised rent of the previous year 2017-18	3	4	5	6	7
Period when the property remains vacant (in number of months)	(1/2)	(1)	(1)	(3)	(5)
Loss due to vacancy	7	14	14	42	105

•

Computation of gross annual value					
Step I - Reasonable expected rent of the property [MV or FR, whichever is higher, but subject to maximum of SR]	142	175	175	142	241
Step II - Rent received/receivable after deducting unrealized rent of the current previous year but before adjusting loss due to vacancy (unrealized of earlier years is not considered)	154	126	167	98	210
Step III - Amount computed in *Step I* or *Step II*, whichever is higher	154	175	175	142	241
Step IV - Loss due to vacancy	7	14	14	42	105
Step V - Gross annual value is *Step III minus Step IV*	147	161	161	100	136

39.2 ***Deduct municipal taxes*** - From the gross annual value computed above, deduct municipal taxes (including service taxes) levied by any local authority in respect of the house property. Municipal taxes are deductible only if (*a*) these taxes are borne by the owner, and (*b*) are actually paid by him during the previous year.

Municipal taxes, levied by local authority but not paid by the assessee during the previous year, are not deductible. If property is situated in a foreign country, municipal taxes levied by foreign local authority are deductible (if such taxes are paid by the owner).

The remaining amount left after deduction of municipal taxes is net annual value.

39.3 ***Deduction under section 24*** - The following two deductions are available under section 24—

a. standard deduction [*see* para 39.3-1] ; and

b. interest on borrowed capital [*see* para 39.3-2].

The list of allowance of section 24 is exhaustive—*Indian City Properties* v. *CIT* [1965] 55 ITR 262 (Cal.) and *CIT* v. *H.G. Gupta & Sons* [1984] 149 ITR 253 (Delhi). In other words, no deduction can be claimed in respect of that expenditure which is not specified in section 24. For instance, no deduction can be claimed in respect of expenses on insurance, ground rent, land revenue, repairs, collection charges, electricity, water supply, salary of liftman, etc.

39.3-1 *STANDARD DEDUCTION [SEC. 24(*a*)]* - 30 per cent of net annual value is deductible irrespective of any expenditure incurred by the taxpayer.

39.3-2 *INTEREST ON BORROWED CAPITAL [SEC. 24(*b*)]* - Interest on borrowed capital is allowable as deduction on accrual basis (even if books of account are kept on cash basis), if capital is borrowed for the purpose of purchase, construction, repair, renewal or reconstruction of the house property.

The following points should also be kept in view :

- As the deduction is available on "accrual" basis, it should be claimed as deduction on yearly basis, even if the interest is not actually paid during the year.
- Deduction is available even if neither the principal nor the interest is a charge on property.
- Interest on unpaid interest is not deductible—*Shew Kissen Bhatter* v. *CIT* [1973] 89 ITR 61 (SC).
- No deduction is allowed for any brokerage or commission for arranging the loan.
- Interest on a fresh loan, taken to repay the original loan raised for the aforesaid purposes, is allowable as deduction—Circular No. 28, dated August 20, 1969.
- Any interest chargeable under the Act, in the hands of recipient and payable out of India, on which tax has not been paid or deducted at source, and in respect of which there is no person who may be treated as an agent, is not deductible, by virtue of section 25, in computing income chargeable under the head "Income from house property".

39.3-2a INTEREST OF PRE-CONSTRUCTION PERIOD - Interest payable by an assessee in respect of funds borrowed for the acquisition or construction of a house property and pertaining to a period prior to the previous year in which such property has been acquired or constructed, to the extent it is not allowed as a deduction under any other provision of the Act, is deductible in five equal annual instalments, commencing from the previous year in which the house is acquired or constructed.

- *What is pre-construction period* - Interest of pre-construction period is deductible in five equal instalments. The first instalment is deductible in the year in which construction of property is completed or in which property is acquired. For this purpose "pre-construction period" means the period commencing on the date of borrowing and ending March 31 immediately prior to the date of completion of construction/date of acquisition or date of repayment of loan, whichever is earlier.

39.3-2E1 X takes a loan of Rs. 40,000 @ 15 per cent per annum for constructing a house on June 10, 2013. Construction of the house is completed on January 20, 2019.

Date of repayment of loan is (a) January 16, 2024, or (b) June 30, 2020, or (c) October 31, 2016.

•

If date of repayment of loan is January 16, 2024 or June 30, 2020, then pre-construction period ends on March 31, 2018 (being March 31 immediately prior to the date of completion of construction/acquisition). Interest on Rs. 40,000 @ 15 per cent per annum from June 10, 2013 to March 31, 2018 is Rs. 28,849. Amount of instalment deductible in first 5 years is Rs. 5,770 (*i.e.*, Rs. 28,849/5).

If date of repayment of loan is October 31, 2016, then pre-construction period ends on October 31, 2016 (being March 31, immediately prior to completion of construction or date of repayment of loan, whichever is earlier). Interest on Rs. 40,000 @ 15 per cent per annum from June 10, 2013 to October 31, 2016 comes to Rs. 20,351 (instalment deductible in first 5 previous years being Rs. 4,070). The table given below highlights the interest deductible in different previous years :

	Previous years						
	Ending on March 31, 2019	*2019-20*	*2020-21*	*2021-22*	*2022-23*	*2023-24*	*2024-25*
	Rs.	*Rs.*	*Rs.*	*Rs.*	*Rs.*	*Rs.*	*Rs.*
If date of repayment of loan is January 16, 2024 :							
Current year's interest	6,000[69]	6,000	6,000	6,000	6,000	4,767	*Nil*
Pre-construction period's interest	5,770	5,770	5,770	5,770	5,770	*Nil*	*Nil*
Total deduction	11,770	11,770	11,770	11,770	11,770	4,767	*Nil*
If date of repayment of loan is June 30, 2020							
Current year's interest	6,000[69]	6,000	1,479	*Nil*	*Nil*	*Nil*	*Nil*
Pre-construction period's interest	5,770	5,770	5,770	5,770	5,770	*Nil*	*Nil*
Total deduction	11,770	11,770	7,249	5,770	5,770	*Nil*	*Nil*

69. Although the construction of the property is completed on January 20, 2019 (*i.e.*, during 2018-19), the interest of the entire financial year 2018-19 is treated as current year's interest. Interest prior to the year 2018-19 (*i.e.*, the year in which construction is completed) is pre-construction period's interest. The same rule is applicable if the construction is completed on March 31, 2019.

	Previous years						
	Ending on March 31, 2019 Rs.	2019-20 Rs.	2020-21 Rs.	2021-22 Rs.	2022-23 Rs.	2023-24 Rs.	2024-25 Rs.
If date of repayment of loan is October 31, 2016 :							
Current year's interest	Nil	Nil	Nil	Nil	Nil	Nil	Nil
Pre-construction period's interest	4,070	4,070	4,070	4,070	4,070	Nil	Nil
Total	4,070	4,070	4,070	4,070	4,070	Nil	Nil

Note - Interest is calculated on the basis of number of days. While the day of borrowing is included, the day of repayment of loan is excluded.

How to compute taxable income from self-occupied property or properties

40. Before steps for computation are explained, it would be advisable to highlight the following features which regulate tax incidence on self-occupied properties :

• *Own property used for business/profession* - Where an assessee uses his property for carrying on any business or profession, no income is chargeable to tax under the head "Income from house property". The assessee, in such a case, is not entitled to claim any deduction on account of rent in respect of such house property in computing taxable profits of the business or profession.

• *Property given to employees* - When the letting out of residential quarters to employees is subservient and incidental to the main business, the property is considered as occupied by the owner for the purpose of his own business—*CIT* v. *Delhi Cloth & General Mills Co. Ltd.* [1966] 59 ITR 152 (Punj.). Where, however, the employer charges rent from his employees for the property in question, such rent is chargeable under the head "Profits and gains of business or profession".

• *Own property used for own residential purposes* - Where an assessee has occupied his property for own residential purposes, tax treatment is as follows –

	Up to the assessment year 2019-20	*From the assessment year 2020-21*
If only one property is used for own residential purposes	It is treated as self-occupied property	It is treated as self-occupied property
If two properties are used for own residential purposes	Only one house (according to the choice of the taxpayer) is treated as self-occupied property and the other house will be "deemed to be let out"	**Two residential properties are treated as self-occupied properties**
If more than two properties are used for own residential purposes	Only one house (according to the choice of the taxpayer) is treated as self-occupied property and other houses will be treated as "deemed to be let out"	**Only two houses (according to the choice of the taxpayer) are treated as self-occupied** properties and other house/houses will be treated as "deemed to be let out"

In the case of "deemed to be let out" property/properties, taxable income will be calculated in the manner explained in para 39. Gross annual value shall be determined under *Step I* [*see* para 39.1-1].

In the case of one self-occupied property (or two self-occupied properties with effect from assessment year 2020-21), treated as such, the procedure for determining taxable income is as follows :

40.1 ***Computation of annual value of one self-occupied property***[70] - In the case of a self-occupied property[71], treated as such, the procedure for determining taxable income is as follows :

40.1-1 *HOUSE PROPERTY FULLY UTILISED THROUGHOUT THE PREVIOUS YEAR FOR SELF-RESIDENTIAL PURPOSES [SEC. 23(2)(a)]* - Where the property consists of one house‡ in the occupation of the owner for his own residence, the annual value of such house shall be taken to be *nil*, under section 23(2)(*a*), if the following conditions are satisfied :

70. **Two** self-occupied properties (applicable from the assessment year 2020-21).
71. **Two** houses (applicable from the assessment year 2020-21).

a. the property (or part thereof) is not actually let during whole (or any part) of the previous year ; and

b. no other benefit is derived therefrom.

The following are some of the examples where the above conditions are satisfied—

1. X owns a property. Throughout the previous year 2018-19, it is used by him (and his family members) for own residence purposes. No part of the property is let out or put to some other use.

2. Y owns a property. It is transferred on December 1, 2018. Between April 1, 2018 and December 1, 2018 it is used by Y and his family for residential purpose. It is neither let out nor put to any other use.

3. Z purchased a property on June 1, 2018. Since then it is occupied by Z for his residential purposes. Neither it is let out nor it is put to some other use.

In the case of one house[72] (which is not let out nor put to any other use) used throughout the previous year by the owner for his residential purpose, income shall be determined as follows—

Gross annual value	*Nil*
Less: Municipal tax	*Nil*
Net annual value	*Nil*
Less: Deduction under section 24	
Standard deduction	*Nil*
Interest on borrowed capital	Deductible [*see* para 40.1-1a]
Income from self-occupied property/properties	xxxxxxxxxxx

40.1-1a INTEREST ON BORROWED CAPITAL [SEC. 24(*b*)] - Interest on borrowed capital [of the current year and pre-construction period] is deductible as explained in para 39.3-2. However, it is deductible in the case of one self-occupied property **(two self-occupied properties** from the assessment year 2020-21) subject to a maximum ceiling given below –

• *Maximum ceiling if capital is borrowed on or after April 1, 1999* - If the following three conditions are satisfied, interest on borrowed capital is deductible up to Rs. 2,00,000[73]—

a. capital is borrowed on or after April 1, 1999 for acquiring or constructing a property;

b. the acquisition or construction should be completed within 5 years (3 years, applicable up to the assessment year 2016-17) from the end of financial year in which the capital was borrowed; and

c. the person extending the loan certifies that such interest is payable in respect of the amount advanced for acquisition or construction of the house or as re-finance of the principal amount outstanding under an earlier loan taken for such acquisition or construction.

The following points should be noted—

1. If capital is borrowed for any other purpose (*e.g.*, if capital is borrowed for reconstruction, repairs or renewals of a house property), then the maximum amount of deduction on account of interest is Rs. 30,000.

2. There is no stipulation regarding the date of commencement of construction. Consequently, the construction of the residential unit could have commenced before April 1, 1999 but, if the aforesaid three conditions are satisfied, the higher deduction of Rs. 2,00,000[73] would be available. Also there is no stipulation regarding the construction/acquisition of the residential unit being entirely financed by the loan taken on or after April 1, 1999. It may be so in part. However, the higher deduction of Rs. 2,00,000[73] towards interest can be claimed only in relation to that part of the loan which has been taken and utilised for construction/acquisition after April 1, 1999. The loan taken prior to April 1, 1999 will carry deduction of interest up to Rs. 30,000 only (as stated in para given below)—Circular No. 8/2007, dated December 5, 2007.

• *Maximum ceiling in any other case* - If the above three conditions [(*a*), (*b*) and (*c*) (*supra*)] are not satisfied, then interest on borrowed capital is deductible up to a maximum of Rs. 30,000[74]. In other words in the following cases, interest on borrowed capital is deductible up to Rs. 30,000[74]—

a. if capital is borrowed before April 1, 1999 for purchase, construction, reconstruction, repairs or renewals of a house property ;

72. **Two houses** (applicable from the assessment year 2020-21).

73. Rs. 75,000 for the assessment year 2000-01, Rs. 1,00,000 for the assessment year 2001-02 and Rs. 1,50,000 for the assessment years 2002-03 to 2014-15.

74. Rs. 5,000 for the assessment years 1987-88 to 1994-95, Rs. 10,000 for the assessment years 1995-96 and 1996-97 and Rs. 15,000 for the assessment years 1997-98 and 1998-99.

b. if capital is borrowed on or after April 1, 1999 for reconstruction, repairs or renewals of a house property.

40.1-1E1 X owns a house property. It is used by him throughout the previous year 2018-19 for his (and his family members) residence. Municipal value of the property is Rs. 1,66,000, whereas fair rent is Rs. 1,76,000 and standard rent is Rs. 1,50,000. The following expenses are incurred by X : repairs : Rs. 20,000, municipal tax : Rs. 16,000, insurance : Rs. 2,000; interest on capital borrowed to construct the property : Rs. 2,56,000; interest on capital borrowed by mortgaging the property for daughter's marriage : Rs. 20,000 (in either case capital is borrowed after April 1, 1999). Income of X from business is Rs. 7,10,000. Find out the net income of X for the assessment year 2019-20.

•

	Rs.
Gross annual value	*Nil*
Less: Municipal tax	*Nil*
Net annual value	*Nil*
Less: Interest on borrowed capital	– 2,00,000
Property income	(-) 2,00,000
Business income	7,10,000
Net income	5,10,000

40.1-2 *A HOUSE PROPERTY, WHICH IS NOT ACTUALLY OCCUPIED BY THE OWNER OWING TO EMPLOYMENT OR BUSINESS/PROFESSION, CARRIED ON AT ANY OTHER PLACE [SEC. 23(2)(*b*)]* - Section 23(2)(*b*) is applicable if the following conditions are satisfied—

a. the taxpayer owns a house property, which cannot actually be occupied by him by reason of the fact that owing to his employment, business or profession, carried on at any other place;

b. he has to reside at that other place in a building not owned by him;

c. the property mentioned at (*a*) (or part thereof) is not actually let out during whole (or any part of the previous year); and

d. no other benefit is derived from the above property by the owner.

If the above conditions are satisfied, income from the property shall be determined according to the method given in para 40.1-1.

40.1-2a OTHER POINTS - The following points should also be kept in view—

• Some nexus between the fact of residing in a building not belonging to the assessee and his employment, business or profession must be shown before the benefit of section 23(2)(*b*) can be availed in respect of residential house which is not occupied by the assessee. In *Shikharchand Jain* v. *CIT* [1982] 11 Taxman 124 (MP), the assessee did not occupy his own residential house but resided with his father in the same town in a house two miles away. The assessee was a bachelor and, therefore, for his own convenience resided with his father. It was held by the High Court that since the assessee had not left his house vacant on account of business compulsion but on account of personal convenience, he was not entitled to the benefit of section 23(2)(*b*).

• Section 23(2)(*b*) would apply in all those cases where officials and dignitaries, under the Constitution of India and even otherwise had to reside in official residences instead of their own residences by reason of their office — *CIT* v. *Justice Avadh Behari Rohtagi* [1985] 21 Taxman 409 (Delhi).

40.1-3 *WHEN A PART OF PROPERTY IS SELF-OCCUPIED AND A PART IS LET OUT* - If a house property consists of two or more independent residential units, one of which is self-occupied for own residential purposes and other unit(s) are let out, income is computed as follows—

1. Unit self-occupied for residential purpose throughout the previous year (which is not let out nor put to any other use)	*See* para 40.1-1
2. Let out units	*See* para 39
3. Unit self-occupied for residential purpose for a part of year and lying vacant for remaining part because of business or profession is situated at some other place	*See* para 40.1-2

40.1-3E1 X owns a residential house property. It has two equal residential units—Unit 1 and Unit 2. While Unit 1 is self-occupied by X for his residential purpose, Unit 2 is let out (rent being Rs. 6,000 per month, rent of 2 months could not be recovered). Municipal value of the property is Rs. 1,30,000, standard rent is Rs. 1,25,000 and fair rent is Rs. 1,40,000.

Municipal tax is imposed @ 12 per cent which is paid by X. Other expenses for the previous year 2018-19 being repairs: Rs. 250, insurance: Rs. 600, interest on capital (borrowed during 1997) for constructing the property: Rs. 63,000.

Find the income of X for the assessment year 2019-20 on the assumption that income of X from other sources is Rs. 1,80,000.

●

	Rs.
Unit 1 - Self-occupied	
Gross annual value	*Nil*
Less: Municipal tax	*Nil*
Net annual value	*Nil*
Less: Interest on borrowed capital [1/2 of Rs. 63,000 or Rs. 30,000 whichever is lower]	30,000
Income of Unit 1	(-) 30,000
Unit 2 - Let out	
Municipal value (50% of Rs. 1,30,000) (MV)	65,000
Fair rent (50% of Rs. 1,40,000) (FR)	70,000
Standard rent (50% of Rs. 1,25,000) (SR)	62,500
Annual rent (Rs. 6,000 × 12)	72,000
Unrealised rent	12,000
Gross annual value	Rs.
Step I - Reasonable expected rent of the property [MV or FR, whichever is higher, but subject to maximum of SR]	62,500
Step II - Rent received/receivable after deducting unrealized rent but before adjusting loss due to vacancy	60,000
Step III - Amount computed in *Step I or Step II*, whichever is higher	62,500
Step IV - Loss due to vacancy	*Nil*
Step V - Gross annual value is *Step III minus Step IV*	62,500
Gross annual value	62,500
Less: Municipal tax (50% of 12% of Rs. 1,30,000)	7,800
Net annual value	54,700
Less: Deductions under section 24	
Standard deduction (30% of Rs. 54,700)	16,410
Interest on borrowed capital (50% of Rs. 63,000)	31,500
Income of Unit 2	6,790
Computation of income of X	
Income from house property	
Unit 1: Rs. (-) 30,000	
Unit 2: Rs, 6,790	(-) 23,210
Other income	1,80,000
Net income	1,56,790

40.1-4 *WHERE A HOUSE IS SELF-OCCUPIED FOR A PART OF THE YEAR AND LET OUT FOR REMAINING PART OF THE YEAR* - In this case, the benefit of section 23(2)(*a*) [*see* para 40.1-1] is not available and income will be computed as if the property is let out.

40.1-4E1 X owns a property at Delhi (municipal value: Rs. 1,64,000, fair rent: Rs. 2,16,000, standard rent: Rs. 1, 80,000). The house is let out up to January 31, 2019 (monthly rent being Rs. 14,000). From February 1, 2019, the property is self-occupied for own residential purposes. Expenses incurred by X are: municipal tax: Rs. 6,000 (actually paid), repairs: Rs. 2,100, insurance: Rs. 1,100, interest on capital borrowed (date of borrowing being June 10, 1991) for acquiring the property: Rs. 1,23,000. Assuming that the income of X from other sources is Rs. 11,86,000, find out the net income of X for the assessment year 2019-20. Does it make any difference if the property is let out up to January 31, 2019 @ Rs. 19,000 per month. There is no unrealised rent.

●

	If rent is Rs. 14,000 per month Rs.	*If rent is Rs. 19,000 per month Rs.*
Municipal valuation (MV)	1,64,000	1,64,000
Fair rent (FR)	2,16,000	2,16,000
Standard rent (SR)	1,80,000	1,80,000
Actual rent	1,40,000	1,90,000
Gross annual value		
Step I - Reasonable expected rent of the property [MV or FR, whichever is higher, but subject to maximum of SR]	1,80,000	1,80,000
Step II - Rent received/receivable after deducting unrealized rent but before adjusting loss due to vacancy	1,40,000	1,90,000
Step III - Amount computed in *Step I or Step II*, whichever is higher	1,80,000	1,90,000
Step IV - Loss due to vacancy	*Nil*	*Nil*
Step V - Gross annual value is *Step III minus Step IV*	1,80,000	1,90,000
Less: Municipal tax	6,000	6,000
Net annual value	1,74,000	1,84,000
Less : Deductions under section 24		
Standard deduction (30% of Rs. 1,74,000 or Rs. 1,84,000)	52,200	55,200
Interest on borrowed capital	1,23,000	1,23,000
Income from property	(–)1,200	5,800
Other income	11,86,000	11,86,000
Net income	11,84,800	11,91,800

40.2 ***Provisions in brief*** - The provisions governing tax incidence on self-occupied house property/ properties may be summarized as follows —

Self-occupied property/properties	*Tax treatment*
1. If such property is used by the owner for the purpose of carrying on his business or profession	Income is not taxable under the head "Income from house property". Any income and expenditure in respect of such property will be considered while calculating income from business or profession under section 28
2. If such property is used for the residence of the owner and his family members—	
2.1 If only one property is used for such purpose—	
2.1-1 If such property is used throughout the previous year for own residential purposes, it is not let out or put to any other use	Nothing is taxable. Only interest on borrowed capital is deductible subject to a maximum of Rs. 30,000/2,00,000 [*see* para 40.1-1]
2.1-2 If such property could not be occupied throughout the previous year because employment, business or profession of the owner is situated at some other place	Same as above [*see* para 40.1-2]
2.1-3 When a part of the property (being independent residential unit) is self-occupied and the other part is let out	Income from the independent unit, which is self-occupied, will not be taxable. Interest on borrowed capital is deductible up to Rs. 30,000/Rs. 2,00,000. Income from the unit which is let out is to be computed as if the unit is let out [*see* para 39]
2.1-4 When such property is let out for a part of the year and let out for the other part of the year	No concession is available. The house will be taken as let out property [*see* para 40.1-4]
2.2 If two properties are used for own residential purposes	- *Up to assessment year 2019-20* - Only one property selected by the taxpayer will be treated as self-occupied [*see* paras 40.1-1 to 40.1-4]. Other property will be deemed as let out [*see* para 39]. - *From the assessment year 2020-21* - **Two residential properties are treated as self-occupied properties** [*see* paras 40.1-1 to 40.1-4].

Self-occupied property/properties	*Tax treatment*
2.3 If more than two properties are used for own residential purposes	- *Up to assessment year 2019-20* - Only one property selected by the taxpayer will be treated as self-occupied [*see* paras 40.1-1 to 40.1-4]. Other properties will be deemed as let out [*see* para 39]. - *From the assessment year 2020-21* - **Only two houses (according to the choice of the taxpayer) are treated as self-occupied** properties [*see* paras 40.1-1 to 40.1-4]. Other remaining property/properties will be treated as "deemed to be let out" [*see* para 39].

40.3 ***Other points for consideration*** - The aforesaid rules (*i.e.,* provision mentioned in paras 40.1-1, 40.1-2 and 40.1-3) are applicable only in the case of natural persons. In other words, limited liability companies, firms, associations and clubs cannot claim the benefit of steps mentioned above as they cannot occupy a house for residential purposes. The karta of a Hindu undivided family (being a natural person) is, however, entitled to the aforesaid benefit.

• *When owner occupies a house in some other capacity* - The aforesaid provisions cannot be applied to cases where the owner of the house is not occupying his own house in his capacity as "owner" for residential purposes. If the assessee lets out his house to his employer-company which, in turn, allots the same to him as rent-free quarter, the assessee is not entitled to the aforesaid benefits, as he occupies the house not as owner but only in his capacity as sub-tenant of the employer-company—*D.R. Sunder Raj* v. *CIT* [1979] 2 Taxman 458 (AP).

Special provisions when unrealised rent is realised subsequently [Sec. 25A][75]

41. The amount of rent received in arrears or the amount of unrealised rent realised subsequently by an assessee shall be charged to income-tax in the previous year in which such rent is received or realized. The following points should be noted –

1. The recipient of arrears of rent (or the recipient of unrealised rent) is chargeable to tax in the year in which such rent is received, regardless of the fact whether in the year of receipt the house property is owned by him or not.

2. The recipient can claim 30 per cent of the arrears of rent (or the unrealised rent realised subsequently) as deduction.

41-E1 X owns a residential property in Chennai. It is let out to A Ltd. (rent being Rs. 40,000 per month). Municipal value of the property is Rs. 2,20,000, fair rent is Rs. 4,80,000. A Ltd. pays municipal tax. On April 7, 2018, rent is increased from Rs. 40,000 per month to Rs. 45,000 per month with retrospective effect from April 1, 2017. X gets Rs. 60,000 (being arrears of rent for the financial year 2017-18) on April 20, 2018. Find out the net income of X for the assessment year 2019-20 on the assumption that his income from other sources is Rs. 5,00,000.

•

	Rs.
Municipal value (MV)	2,20,000
Fair rent (FR)	4,80,000
Standard rent (SR)	*NA*
Step I - Reasonable expected rent of the property [MV or FR, whichever is higher, subject to maximum of SR]	4,80,000
Step II - Rent received/receivable after deducting unrealized rent but before adjusting loss due to vacancy (Rs. 45,000 × 12)	5,40,000
Step III - Amount computed in *Step I or Step II,* whichever is higher	5,40,000
Step IV - Loss due to vacancy	*Nil*
Step V - Gross annual value is *Step III minus Step IV*	5,40,000
Less: Municipal tax (paid by tenant, not deductible)	*Nil*
Net annual value	5,40,000

75. From the assessment year 2017-18, provisions of sections 25A, 25AA and 25B have been simplified (for these sections, *see* Taxmann's Direct Taxes Ready Reckoner, 39th Edition). These sections have been merged under a single new section 25A.

	Rs.
Less: Standard deduction under section 24(*a*) (*i.e.*, 30% of net annual value)	1,62,000
Income from property	3,78,000
Arrears of rent (pertaining to earlier year) received in the previous year 2018-19	
Arrears received (Rs. 5,000 × 12)	60,000
Less: Standard deduction under section 25A(2) [*i.e.*, 30% of Rs. 60,000]	18,000
Arrears of rent chargeable to tax	42,000
Income under the head "Income from house property" (*i.e.*, Rs. 3,78,000 + Rs. 42,000)	4,20,000
Income from other sources	5,00,000
Net income	9,20,000

Mode of taxation of arrears of rent in the year of receipt [Sec. 25A][76]

42. *See* para 41.

Hints for tax planning

43. For the purpose of tax planning, the following broad propositions should be borne in mind. However, these propositions would hold good in the context in which they have been made.

• If a person has occupied more than one house[77] for his own residence, only one house[77] of his own choice is treated as self-occupied and all the other houses are deemed to be let out. The tax exemption applies only in the case of one self-occupied house[77] and not in the case of deemed to be let out properties. Care should, therefore, be taken while selecting the house[77] to be treated as self-occupied, in order to minimise the tax liability.

• As interest payable out of India is not deductible if tax is not deducted at source (and in respect of which there is no person who may be treated as an agent under section 163) care should be taken to deduct tax at source in order to avail exemption under section 24(*b*).

• As amount of municipal tax is deductible on "payment" basis and not on "due" or "accrual" basis, it should be ensured that municipal tax is actually paid during the previous year if the assessee wants to claim deduction.

• As a member of a co-operative society to whom a building or part thereof is allotted or leased under a house building scheme is the deemed owner of the property, it should be ensured that interest *payable* (even if not paid) by the assessee, on outstanding instalments of the cost of the building, is claimed as a deduction under section 24(*b*).

• If an individual makes a cash gift to his wife who purchases a house property with the gifted money, the individual will not be deemed as deemed owner of the property under section 27(*i*)—*K.D. Thakar* v. *CIT* [1979] 120 ITR 190 (Guj.). Taxable income of the wife from the property is, however, includible in the income of individual in terms of section 64(1)(*iv*). Such income is to be computed under section 23(2) if she uses the house property for her own residential purposes. It can, therefore, be advised that if an individual transfers an asset, other than house property, even without adequate consideration, he can escape the deeming provision of section 27(*i*) and the consequent hardship.

• Under section 27(*i*), if a person transfers a house property without consideration to his/her spouse (not being a transfer in connection with an agreement to live apart), or to his minor child (not being a married daughter), the transferor is deemed to be the owner of the house property. This deeming provision was found necessary in order to bring this situation in line with the provision of section 64. But when the scope of section 64 was extended to cover transfer of assets without adequate consideration to son's wife or minor grandchild by the Taxation Laws (Amendment) Act, 1975, with effect from the assessment year 1976-77 onwards, the scope of section 27(*i*) was not similarly extended. Consequently, if a person transfers house property to his son's wife without adequate consideration, he will not be deemed to be the owner of the property under section 27(*i*), but income earned from the property by the transferee will be included in the income of the transferor under section 64(1)(*vi*) [*see* para 84]—*see* *CIT* v. *H.L. Gulati* [1982] 11 Taxman 167 (All.). For the purpose of sections 22 to 27, the transferee will, thus, be treated as the owner of the house property and

76. From the assessment year 2017-18, provisions of sections 25A, 25AA and 25B have been simplified (for these sections, *see* Taxmann's Direct Taxes Ready Reckoner, 39th Edition). These sections have been merged under a single new section 25A.

77. **Two houses**, from the assessment year 2020-21.

income computed in her hands is included in the income of the transferor under section 64(1)(*vi*). Such income is to be computed under section 23(2) if the transferee uses that property for self-occupation. Therefore, in some cases it is beneficial to transfer the house property without adequate consideration to son's wife.

Profits and gains of business or profession

	Para number	*Example number*
PRE-COMPUTATION STEPS		
❑ Find out whether business/profession income is taxable under section 28	47	—
COMPUTATION STEPS		
❑ Find out net profit as per P & L a/c	—	—
❑ Deduct those expenditures which are not claimed but are allowable as deduction under sections 30 to 37	48	—
❑ *Add* those expenses which have been debited to P & L a/c but are not allowable as deduction under sections 40, 40A and 43B	49	—
❑ Deduct those incomes which have been credited to P & L a/c but are not taxable under section 28	—	—
❑ *Add* those incomes which are not credited to P & L a/c but which are taxable as business income	—	—

Chargeability [Sec. 28]

47. The following incomes are chargeable to tax under the head "Profits and gains of business or profession":

• Profits and gains of any business[78] or profession carried on by the assessee at any time during the previous year. Income earned from the exercise of any "profession" or "vocation", which involves the idea of occupation requiring either purely intellectual skill or any manual skill, is taxable under this head.

• Any compensation or other payment due to or received by any person specified by section 28(*ii*)[79].

• Income derived by a trade, profession or similar association from specific services performed for its members.

• Profit on sale of a licence granted under the Imports (Control) Order, 1955 made under the Imports & Exports (Control) Act, 1947.

• Cash assistance (by whatever name called) received/receivable by any person against exports under any scheme of the Government.

• Any duty of customs/excise repaid or repayable as drawback to any person against exports under the Customs and Central Excise Duties Drawback Rules, 1971.

• Value of any benefits or perquisites[80] arising from a business or the exercise of a profession.

• Interest, salary, bonus, commission or remuneration due to or received by a partner of a firm from such firm.

• Any sum received for not carrying out any activity in relation to any business [or (with effect from the assessment year 2017-18) profession] or not to share any know-how, patent, copyright, trademark, etc.

---

78. Where the assessee itself, irrespective of the period of holding the listed shares and securities, opts to treat them as stock-in-trade, the income arising from transfer of such shares/securities would be treated as its business income—Circular No. 6/2016[$], dated February 29, 2016.

79. It includes (from the assessment year 2019-20) compensation in connection with termination (or modification) of terms and conditions of any contract relating to the business of recipient.

80. Payment received by a partner in realization of his share in net value of assets upon his retirement from a firm does not fall under this point—*Prashant S. Joshi* v. *ITO* [2010] 189 Taxman 1 (Bom.).

[$] For Circular No. 6/2016, log on to *taxmann.com/readyreckoner.aspx.*

• The fair market value of inventory as on the date on which it is converted into, or treated as, a capital asset determined in the prescribed manner (applicable from the assessment year 2019-20).

• Any sums received under a Keyman Insurance Policy including the sum by way of bonus on such policy.

• Any sum received (or receivable) in cash or kind, on account of any capital asset (other than land or goodwill or financial instrument) being demolished, destroyed, discarded or transferred, if the whole of the expenditure on such capital asset has been allowed as a deduction under section 35AD (applicable from the assessment year 2010-11 onwards).

Expenses expressly allowed as deduction

48. Deduction in respect of the following has been expressly allowed against profits and gains of business or profession :

48.1 ***Rent, rates, taxes, repairs and insurance for building [Sec. 30]*** - In respect of premises taken on rent, the actual rent paid by the assessee and, if he has undertaken to bear cost of repairs, the expenditure on repairs (not being capital expenditure from the assessment year 2004-05) are permissible deductions. In respect of premises owned by the assessee, no deduction is allowable on account of notional rent; amount spent on current repairs (not being capital expenditure from the assessment year 2004-05) is, however, allowed as deduction. Besides, the amount paid on account of land revenue, local rates and insurance premium against the risk of damage or destruction of the business premises are also allowable as business deduction under this section.

48.2 ***Repairs and insurance of machinery, plant and furniture [Sec. 31]*** - The expenditure incurred on current repairs (not being capital expenditure from the assessment year 2004-05), in respect of the plant, machinery and furniture used for business purposes is allowable as deduction under this section. If, however, expenditure is incurred to bring into existence an advantage of an enduring nature or a new capital asset, it cannot be regarded as an expenditure on current repairs. Similarly, the premium paid in respect of insurance against risk of damage or destruction of such assets is an allowable deduction.

The Supreme Court in *CIT* v. *Sri Mangayarkarasi Mills (P.) Ltd.* [2009] 182 Taxman 141 held that integrated process of manufacture of yarn in textile mill or for that matter inter-connection among the various machines does not take away the independent identity and distinct function of each machine. It held that each machine in a textile mill should be treated independently as such and not as mere part of an entire composite machinery of the spinning mill. On expenditure on replacement of one of the machines, the Apex Court ruled out deduction either as current repairs or under the residuary head as it termed it as a capital expenditure.

48.3 ***Depreciation [Sec. 32]*** - In order to claim depreciation, an assessee has to fulfil the following conditions :

• The asset should be owned[81] by the assessee. Where, however, an assessee carries on business or profession in a building not owned by him but taken on lease, he is entitled to depreciation in respect of the capital expenditure incurred by him after March 31, 1970 on the construction of any structure or any work in relation to the building by way of improvement, renovation or extension.

• The asset, in respect of which depreciation is claimed, must have been used[82] for the purpose of business. Where, however, the asset is partly used for business or profession and partly used for private and personal purposes, a reasonable proportion of the depreciation attributable to the business user of the asset is allowed [sec. 38].

• Under the Income-tax Act, one can claim depreciation in respect of the following assets—

Tangible assets	Building, machinery, plant or furniture
Intangible assets acquired after March 31, 1998	Know-how, patents, copyrights, trademarks, licences, franchises or any other business or commercial rights of similar nature.

The following points should be noted—

1. Depreciation is available even in respect of a fractional ownership of an asset.

81. The extended meaning of words "deemed owner" given by section 27(*iii*) can be imported to interpret word 'owner' for the purpose of claiming depreciation—*Century Galaxy Developers Ltd.* v. *CIT* [2009] 27 SOT 163 (Bang.).

82. Once an asset is part of a block of assets and depreciation is granted on that block, it cannot be denied in its subsequent year on the ground that one of the assets is not used by the assessee in some of years. The concept "user" of assets has to apply upon block as a whole instead of an individual asset—*Unitex Products Ltd.* v. *ITO* [2008] 22 SOT 430 (Mum.), *CIT* v. *Bharat Aluminium Co. Ltd.* [2010] 187 Taxman 111 (Delhi), *CIT* v. *Oswal Agro Mills Ltd.* [2011] 197 Taxman 25 (Delhi), *Swati Synthetics Ltd.* v. *ITO* [2010] 38 SOT 208 (Mum.).

2. Accounting Standard on 'Leases' issued by the Institute of Chartered Accountants of India requires capitalization of the asset by the lessees in financial lease transaction. By itself, the accounting standard will have no implication on the allowance of depreciation on assets under the provisions of the Income-tax Act—Circular No. 2 of 2001, dated February 9, 2001. However, it cannot be concluded that after Circular 2/2001, lessee cannot claim depreciation in the case of financial lease. If lessee (in the case of financial lease) can exercise the rights of the owner not on behalf of lessor but in his own right, depreciation is available to the lessee.

3. From the assessment year 2002-03, depreciation under section 32(1) will be available whether (or not) the assessee has claimed, the deduction for depreciation while computing his total income.

4. In cases of *CIT* v. *General Industries Corpn.* [1985] 155 ITR 430 as well as *CIT* v. *Nagpur Golden Transport Co.* [1998] 233 ITR 389, the Delhi High Court had held that in a hire purchase scheme, the hirer would be entitled to claim depreciation. These judgments clearly go against the contention that until the last instalment is paid the ownership vests in the seller and not in the hirer—*VLS Finance Ltd.* v. *Dy. CIT* [2006] 5 SOT 363 (Delhi).

Consequently, if the following conditions are satisfied, depreciation can be claimed by hirer—

a. the hire purchase agreement must show that as long as hirer discharges his obligation, he has an uninterrupted right over the asset for all practical purposes; and

b. the seller will eventually lose all rights, title and interest in asset if the hirer discharges his obligation (*i.e.*, payment of all instalments)

If the above conditions are satisfied, depreciation will be available to the hirer (and not seller). It is incorrect to state that in such a case depreciation is available to the seller until the last instalment is paid.

5. "Building" means the superstructure only and does not include site—*CIT* v. *Alps Theatre* [1967] 65 ITR 377 (SC). "Plant" includes ships, vehicles, books (including technical know-how report), scientific apparatus and surgical equipments used for the purpose of business or profession but does not include tea bushes or livestock or (from the assessment year 2004-05) building, furniture and fittings.

48.3-1 *DISALLOWANCE OF DEPRECIATION* - Depreciation is disallowed in the following cases -

• For the assessment years 1971-72 to 1997-98, no depreciation is allowed under section 37(4)(*ii*) in respect of a building used as a guest house. Any asset used therein also does not qualify for depreciation allowance.

• Where a car is used otherwise than in a business of running it on hire for tourists :

a. depreciation is not allowed on the excess of the actual cost over Rs. 25,000 if the car is acquired, after March 31, 1967 but before March 1, 1975; and

b. depreciation (including terminal depreciation) is wholly disallowed if the car is a foreign car and has been acquired after February 28, 1975 but before April 1, 2001 (depreciation is available if a foreign made car is acquired after March 31, 2001).

Where a foreign motor car is used outside India in a business or profession carried on by the assessee in another country, depreciation will be allowed on the same even if the foreign made car is acquired after February 28, 1975 but before April 1, 2001.

• Where an assessee incurs any expenditure for acquisition of a depreciable asset in respect of which a payment (or aggregate of payments made to a person in a day), otherwise than by an account payee cheque/draft or use of electronic clearing system through a bank account (**or through prescribed electronic mode**), exceeds Rs. 10,000, such payment shall not be eligible for normal/additional depreciation (applicable from the assessment year 2018-19).

48.3-2 *BASIC CONCEPTS FOR COMPUTATION OF DEPRECIATION ALLOWANCE* - To understand the method of computation of depreciation, one must know the following :

Terms	*Section/rule*	*Reference*
• Method of depreciation	32	Written down value method[83]
• Rates of depreciation	Appendix to the Income-tax Rules	*See* Referencer 6
• Block of assets	2(*11*)	*See* para 48.3-3
• Written down value	43(*6*)	*See* para 48.3-4
• Actual cost	43(*1*)	*See* para 48.3-8

83. From the assessment year 1998-99, depreciation is available according to "straight-line" method at the option of the assessee in the case of an undertaking engaged in generation or generation and distribution of power [*see* para 48.3-10].

48.3-3 *BLOCK OF ASSETS [SEC. 2(11)]* - The term "block of assets" has been defined by section 2(*11*) to mean a group of assets falling within a class of assets, comprising—

a. tangible assets, being buildings, machinery, plant or furniture;

b. intangible assets, being know-how, patents, copyrights, trademarks, licences, franchises or any other business or commercial rights of similar nature,

in respect of which the same percentage of depreciation is prescribed. A "block of assets" includes assets of all units of the assessee having the same rate of depreciation and not assets of only one unit. The user of the asset is important for the purpose of actual allowability of depreciation, but not for determining whether the asset falls within the block of assets or not.

There were 13 different blocks of assets (up to the assessment year 2017-18). From the assessment year 2018-19, the maximum rate of depreciation has been reduced to 40 per cent. Consequently, from the assessment year 2018-19, number of blocks of assets are reduced to 9 as given below –

Number	*Nature of asset*	*Rate of depreciation*
Block 1	*Buildings* - Residential buildings other than hotels and boarding houses	5%
Block 2	*Buildings* - Office, factory, godowns or buildings[84] which are not mainly used for residential purpose [it covers hotels and boarding houses but does not cover those which are covered under Blocks 1 and 3]	10%
Block 3	*Buildings* - The following buildings : *a.* buildings acquired on or after September 1, 2002 for installing machinery and plant forming part of water supply project or water treatment system and which is put to use for the purpose of business of providing infrastructure facilities under clause (*i*) of sub-section (4) of section 80-IA; *b.* temporary erections such as wooden structures	40%
Block 4	*Furniture* - Any furniture/fittings including electrical fittings	10%
Block 5	*Plant and machinery* - Any plant or machinery (not covered by Block 6, 7, 8, 9, 10, 11 or 12) and motor cars (other than those used in a business of running them on hire) acquired or put to use on or after April 1, 1990	15%
Block 6	Ocean-going ships, vessels ordinarily operating on inland waters including speed boats	20%
Block 7	*Plant and machinery* - Buses, lorries and taxies used in the business of running them on hire[85], machinery used in semi-conductor industry, moulds used in rubber and plastic goods factories.	30%
Block 8	*Plant and machinery* - Block includes the following – • Aeroplanes, aeroengines. It also includes commercial vehicle acquired after September 30, 1998 but before April 1, 1999 and put to use before April 1, 1999 and life saving medical equipment and plant and machinery which satisfy conditions of rule 5(2)[$]. • Containers made of glass or plastic used as refills and the following— *a.* new commercial vehicle acquired during 2001-02 and put to use before March 31, 2002 for the purpose of business or profession, *b.* machinery/plant used in weaving, processing and garment sector of textile industry which is purchased under Technology Upgradation Fund Scheme during April 1, 2001 and March 31, 2004 and put to use up to March 31, 2004; and *c.* new commercial vehicle which is acquired during January 1, 2009 and September 30, 2009 and is put to use before October 1, 2009 for the purposes of business or profession.	

84. Toll roads and bridges can be considered as building for this purpose—*CIT* v. *Noida Toll Bridge Co. Ltd.* [2014] 220 Taxman 6 (All.). However, the Central Board of Direct Taxes (*vide* Circular No. 9/2014[$], dated April 23, 2014) has clarified that the cost of construction on development of infrastructure facility of roads/highways under BOT projects may be amortized and claimed as allowable business expenditure. The amortization allowable may be computed at the rate which ensures that the whole of the cost incurred in creation of infrastructural facility of road/highway is amortized evenly over the period of concessionaire agreement after excluding the time taken for creation of such facility.

85. This block is applicable only when the assessee is in the business of hiring out its/his buses, lorries or taxies. If a timber merchant, for delivery of goods to his customers, uses lorries, this block is not applicable, even if transportation income is included in business income. Higher rate of depreciation is admissible on motor trucks used in a business of running them on hire. Therefore, user of the same in the business of transportation is the test—*CIT* v. *Gupta Global Exim (P.) Ltd.* [2008] 171 Taxman 474/305 ITR 132 (SC).

[$] For Rule 5(2) and Circular No. 9/2014, log on to *taxmann.com/readyreckoner.aspx.*

Number	*Nature of asset*	*Rate of depreciation*
	• Computers[86] including computer software and new commercial vehicle acquired in replacement of condemned vehicle of 15 years of age which is put to use before April 1, 1999 (if acquired during October 1, 1998 and March 31, 1999) or before April 1, 2000 (if acquired during 1999-2000). It also includes books (other than annual publications) owned by a professional. It also includes gas cylinders; plant used in field operations by mineral oil concerns; direct fire glass melting furnaces. • Energy saving devices; renewal energy devices; rollers in flour mills, sugar works and steel industry (however, it does not include windmills or any special device, which run on windmills installed after March 31, 2012 but before April 1, 2014). • Air pollution control equipments; water pollution control equipments; solid waste control equipments, recycling and resource recovery systems; machinery acquired and installed on or after September 1, 2002 in a water supply project or water treatment system or for the purpose of providing infrastructure facility; wooden parts used in artificial silk manufacturing machinery; cinematograph films, bulbs of studio lights; wooden match frames; some plants used in mines, quarries and salt works; and books (being annual publications) owned by assessees carrying on a profession or books (may or may not be annual publications) owned by a person carrying on business in running lending libraries	40%
Block 9	*Intangible assets (acquired after March 31, 1998)* - Know-how, patents, copyrights, trademarks, licences, franchises and any other business or commercial rights of similar nature[87].	25%

48.3-4 *WRITTEN DOWN VALUE [SEC. 43(6)]* - Written down value for the assessment year 2019-20 will be determined as under :

Step 1 - Find out depreciated value of the block of assets on April 1, 2018.

Step 2 - To this value, add "actual cost" [*see* para 48.3-8] of the asset [falling in the block] acquired during the previous year ending March 31, 2019 relevant for the assessment year 2019-20.

Step 3 - From the resultant figure, deduct moneys received, receivable (together with scrap value) in respect of that asset (falling within the block of assets) which is sold, discarded, demolished or destroyed during the previous year ending March 31, 2019 relevant for the assessment year 2019-20. However, the amount of deduction cannot exceed the value of block of assets computed up to *Step 2 supra*.

The resulting amount is the written down value of the block of assets on March 31, 2019 relevant for the assessment year 2019-20.

One may determine the written down value for other assessment years on the similar basis.

• *Slump sale* - In the case of a slump sale, the following shall be reduced from the value determined after *Step 2*—

Actual cost of assets falling in the block transferred by "slump sale".

---

86. It includes computer peripherals which are an integral part of computer, routers and switches—*CIT* v. *Datacraft India Ltd.* [2010] 40 SOT 295 (Mum.)(SB), *Climate Systems India Ltd.* v. *CIT* [2010] 2 ITR (Trib.) 168 (Delhi).

87. The expression 'any other business or commercial rights of similar nature' would include such rights which can be used as a tool to carry on the business—*Skyline Caterers (P.) Ltd.* v. *ITO* [2008] 20 SOT 269 (Mum.). The following assets are held as "any other business or commercial rights of similar nature" and are entitled for depreciation—

- Goodwill—*Kotak Forex Brokerage Ltd.* v. *CIT* [2009] 33 SOT 237 (Mum.), *Hindustan Coca Cola Beverages (P.) Ltd.* v. *CIT* [2009] 34 SOT 171 (Delhi), *B. Raveendran Pillai* v. *CIT* [2010] 194 Taxman 477 (Ker.).
- Goodwill arising on amalgamation—*CIT* v. *Smifs Securities Ltd.* [2012] 24 taxmann.com 222 (SC).
- Licence granted by a State Government to collect toll—*Ashoka Info (P.) Ltd.* v. *CIT* [2010] 35 SOT 50 (Pune).
- Licences/approvals/registrations acquired for operating hotels—*Piem Hotels Ltd.* v. *CIT* [2011] 128 ITD 275 (Mum.).
- Non-compete right acquired by payment of non-compete fee — *ITO* v. *Medicorp Technologies India Ltd.* [2009] 30 SOT 506 (Chennai). However, the Mumbai Tribunal in the case of *P.D. Warehousing Corpn.* v. *CIT* [2011] 132 ITD 157 held that the payment made to a retiring partner so that he cannot claim any right, title or interest in on-going firm, did not give rise to any tangible or intangible asset.
- Stock exchange membership card—*Techno Shares & Stocks Ltd.* v. *CIT* [2010] 193 Taxman 248 (SC).
- Website - *Makemytrip (India) (P.) Ltd.* v. *CIT* [2012] 51 SOT 19 (Delhi).
- Specified intangible assets (such as business claims, business information, business records, contracts, know-how) acquired under slump sale agreement—*Areva T & D India Ltd.* v. *CIT* [2012] 208 Taxman 252 (Delhi).
- Compensation paid by a firm to its retiring partner can be treated as goodwill and, since, goodwill is an asset under *Explanation* 3(*b*) to section 32(1), depreciation on such payment is available - *CIT* v. *Swastik Industries* [2016] 240 Taxman 510 (Guj.).

Less :

a. depreciation actually allowed in respect of that asset in respect of any previous year relevant to the assessment year commencing before 1988-89; and

b. depreciation that would have been allowable from the assessment year 1988-89 onwards as if that asset was the only asset in the relevant block of assets.

It may be noted that the amount of reduction under *Step 3* cannot exceed the value of assets computed up to *Step 2.*

• *Written down value in respect of assets acquired during the period when income was exempt - Explanation 6* was inserted in section 43(*6*) with retrospective effect from the assessment year 2003-04. It is applicable if the following conditions are satisfied—

1. The assessee was not required to compute his total income for the purposes of the Income-tax Act for any previous year or years preceding the previous year (hereinafter referred to as "preceding previous year") relevant to the assessment year under consideration.

2. The assessee maintains books of account in respect of such preceding previous year(s).

3. The assessee provides depreciation in the books of account pertaining to such preceding previous year(s).

If the above three conditions are satisfied, then—

1. Actual cost of an asset shall be adjusted by the amount attributable to the revaluation of such asset, if any, in the books of account.

2. The total amount of depreciation on such asset provided in the books of account of the assessee in respect of such preceding previous year(s) shall be deemed to be the depreciation actually allowed under the Income-tax Act for the purposes of section 43(*6*).

3. The depreciation actually allowed as above shall be adjusted by the amount of depreciation attributable to such revaluation.

48.3-4E1 A plant was purchased by X & Co. (a partnership firm) on September 1, 2016 for Rs. 20 lakh. The income of the firm was exempt up to March 31, 2018. The firm maintains books of account but does not provide depreciation in respect of the plant purchased on September 1, 2016.

•

In the previous year 2018-19 (when the income of the firm becomes chargeable to tax), depreciation will be available on the actual cost of Rs. 20 lakh. The notional depreciation from September 1, 2016 to March 31, 2018 shall not be deducted from the actual cost even under the amended provisions, as the firm has not claimed any depreciation in respect of the plant in its books of account.

48.3-4E2 Income of X Ltd. is exempt up to March 31, 2018. The following information is taken from the books of account of the company in respect of a plant purchased by it on June 10, 2015 –

Date	*Transaction*	*Amount Rs.*
June 10, 2015	Cost of plant	1,00,000
March 31, 2016	Depreciation for the year ending March 31, 2016 @ 15.33%	15,330
April 1, 2016	Written down value	84,670
April 1, 2016	Revaluation of the asset (amount transferred to revaluation reserve account)	20,000
March 31, 2017	Written down value before depreciation	1,04,670
March 31, 2017	Depreciation for the year ending March 31, 2017 @ 15.33%	16,045
April 1, 2017	Written down value	88,625
March 31, 2018	Depreciation for the year ending March 31, 2018 @ 15.33%	13,586
April 1, 2018	Written down value	75,039

•

In the above case, depreciation would be available for the previous year 2018-19 (*i.e.,* assessment year 2019-20) as follows –

Date	*Transaction*	*Amount Rs.*
June 10, 2015	Cost of plant	1,00,000
March 31, 2016	*Less:* Notional depreciation for the year ending March 31, 2016 @ 15.33% as provided in the books of account	15,330
April 1, 2016	Written down value	84,670
April 1, 2016	Revaluation of the asset (ignore it)	*Nil*
March 31, 2017	Written down value before depreciation	84,670
March 31, 2017	*Less:* Notional depreciation for the year ending March 31, 2017 @ 15.33% as provided in the books of account but after ignoring the effect of revaluation	12,980
April 1, 2017	Written down value	71,690
March 31, 2018	*Less:* Notional depreciation for the year ending March 31, 2018 @ 15.33% as provided in the books of account but after ignoring the effect of revaluation	10,990
April 1, 2018	Written down value for the purpose of section 43(*6*)	60,700
March 31, 2019	Depreciation under section 32 for the previous year 2018-19 on the assumption that rate of depreciation is 15% and there is no other asset in the block of assets (15% of Rs. 60,700, no additional depreciation)	9,105

48.3-5 *COMPUTATION OF DEPRECIATION ALLOWANCE* - From the assessment year 1988-89, depreciation is admissible on the basis of block of assets. To ascertain the amount of depreciation, one should find out the following :

- Written down value of block of assets[88] [*see* para 48.3-4].
- Rate of depreciation [*see* Referencer 6].

48.3-5a RULE OF COMPUTATION - The product of the aforesaid two is the amount of depreciation. For instance, if written down value of a block of assets [*i.e.*, buildings, rate of depreciation : 10 per cent] is Rs. 3,19,400 for the previous year 2018-19, depreciation will be Rs. 31,940 [being 10 per cent of Rs. 3,19,400] for the said previous year and the depreciated value of the block on April 1, 2019 will be Rs. 2,87,460 (*i.e.*, Rs. 3,19,400 – Rs. 31,940).

The aforesaid rule is, however, not applicable in the cases mentioned in para 48.3-5b.

- Where an assessee incurs any expenditure for acquisition of a depreciable asset in respect of which a payment (or aggregate of payments made to a person in a day), otherwise than by an account payee cheque/ draft or use of electronic clearing system through a bank account (**or through prescribed electronic mode**), exceeds Rs. 10,000, such payment shall not be eligible for normal/additional depreciation (applicable from the assessment year 2018-19).

48.3-5b EXCEPTIONS TO THE RULE - In the cases given below, the above-mentioned rule is not applicable :

1. If the written down value of a block of assets is reduced to zero though the block is not empty [*see* para 48.3-5b[1]].

2. If the block of assets is empty or ceases to exist on the last day of the previous year (though the written down value is not zero) [*see* para 48.3-5b[2]].

3. In the case of imported cars [*see* para 48.3-5b[3]].

4. In the case of succession or amalgamation or business re-organisation [*see* para 48.3-5b[4]].

5. If in the first year in which an asset is acquired and it is put to use for less than 180 days [*see* para 48.3-5b[5]].

48.3-5b[1] *When the written down value of a block of assets is reduced to zero* - No depreciation is admissible where the written down value has been reduced to zero, though the block of assets does not cease to exist on the last day of the previous year.

For instance, on April 1, 2018, depreciated value of a block of assets (rate of depreciation : 15 per cent) is Rs. 80,000. It consists of Plants A and B. The assessee purchases an old Plant C (rate of depreciation : 15 per cent) during the previous year 2018-19 for Rs. 30,000 and sells Plant A on May 3, 2018 for Rs. 1,80,000. In this case on March 31, 2019, the assessee has Plant B and Plant C in the block of assets, though the written down value of the block is zero. No depreciation will be admissible for the previous year 2018-19 (*i.e.*, the assessment year 2019-20) as is evident from the computations given below —

88. Actual cost in some cases—*See* para 48.3-9.

	Rs.
Depreciated value of the block consisting of Plants A and B	80,000
Add: Actual cost of Plant C	30,000
Total	1,10,000
Less: Sale consideration of Plant A [though the plant is sold for Rs. 1,80,000, the amount of reduction cannot exceed Rs. 1,10,000 ; the difference of Rs. 70,000 is short-term capital gain under section 50(1) —*see* para 66.1-3 for detailed discussion]	1,10,000
Written down value of the block consisting of Plants B and C	*Nil*
Less: Depreciation for the previous year 2018-19	*Nil*
Depreciated value of the block consisting of Plants B and C on April 1, 2019	*Nil*

48.3-5b² *If block of assets ceases to exist* - If a block of assets ceases to exist or if all assets of the block have been transferred and the block of assets is empty on the last day of the previous year, no depreciation is admissible in such case.

For instance, X Ltd. owns two plants — Plant A and Plant B — on April 1, 2018 (rate of depreciation : 15 per cent, depreciated value on April 1, 2018 : Rs. 2,37,000). The company purchases Plant C on May 31, 2018 for Rs. 20,000 and sells Plant A (on April 10, 2018), Plant B (on December 12, 2018) and Plant C (on March 1, 2019) for Rs. 10,000, Rs. 15,000 and Rs. 24,000, respectively.

Written down value of the block of assets will be determined as under :

	Rs.
Depreciated value of the block consisting of Plants A and B	2,37,000
Add: Cost of Plant C	20,000
Total	2,57,000
Less: Sale proceeds of Plants A, B and C	49,000
Written down value of the block (which is empty)	2,08,000

In the aforesaid case, no depreciation is admissible, as the block of assets ceases to exist on the last day of the previous year. Rs. 2,08,000 will be treated as short-term capital loss on sale of Plants A, B and C [*see* para 66.1-3 for detailed discussion]. Depreciated value of the block on the first day of the next previous year (*i.e.*, on April 1, 2019) will be taken as *nil* (*i.e.*, written down value on March 31, 2019 : Rs. 2,08,000 *minus* short-term capital loss : Rs. 2,08,000).

48.3-5b³ *Imported cars* - No depreciation is admissible in respect of any motor car, manufactured out of India, where such car was acquired by the assessee after February 28, 1975 but before April 1, 2001. If, however, an imported car (acquired during March 1, 1975 and March 31, 2001) is used in the business of running it on hire for tourists or for the purpose of business or profession outside India, then depreciation is admissible at the usual rate. However, if a foreign made car is acquired after March 31, 2001, depreciation is available at the usual rate.

48.3-5b⁴ *Depreciation in case of succession, amalgamation, business re-organisation or demerger* - In the cases of succession in business and amalgamation of companies, the predecessor and the successor or the amalgamating company and the amalgamated company, as the case may be, are entitled to depreciation allowance on the same assets, which in aggregate, exceeds the depreciation allowance admissible for a previous year at the prescribed rates. Fifth proviso was inserted in section 32 with effect from the assessment year 1997-98 to restrict the aggregate deduction for this allowance in a year to the deduction computed at the prescribed rates and apportion the allowance in the ratio of the number of days for which the assets were used by them.

• The above provisions are also applicable from the assessment year 1999-2000 in the case of business re-organisation covered by section 47(*xiii*)/(*xiv*) [*i.e.*, where a firm/proprietary concern is succeeded by a company and certain conditions are satisfied].

• A similar provision has been made with effect from the assessment year 2000-01 in the case of demerged company and resulting company.

• The above provision has been extended with effect from the assessment year 2011-12 to the case of conversion of private company or unlisted public company into limited liability partnership if such conversion satisfies the requirement of section 47(*xiiib*).

48.3-5b⁴E1 X owns a block of assets (consisting of plants A and B, depreciation rate 15 per cent) on April 1, 2018. Depreciated value of the block is Rs. 10,40,000. On July 7, 2018, the block of assets is transferred by X to Y for Rs. 30,70,000. Find out the tax consequences under the following situations—

1. X is amalgamating company and Y, being an Indian company, is the amalgamated company and the block of assets is transferred by X to Y in a scheme of amalgamation. Y does not own any other asset.

2. Suppose in (*1*)(*supra*) Y is a foreign company.

3. Suppose in (*1*) Y owns a block of assets (consisting of plants C and D, depreciation rate 15 per cent) on April 1, 2018. Depreciated value of the block of assets being Rs. 6,40,000. Y purchases plant E (rate of depreciation 15 per cent) on March 10, 2019 for Rs. 2,90,000. Plant E is not eligible for additional depreciation. It is put to use on the same day.

4. X is a partnership firm. It is converted into Y company. The conversion satisfies the conditions of section 47(*xiii*). Y does not own any other asset.

5. X is a firm. The business of X is taken over by Y, a partner in the firm. On April 1, 2018, Y owns plants C and D (depreciation rate 15 per cent, depreciated value of the block Rs. 60,78,000). Y purchases plant E on December 5, 2018 (depreciation rate 15 per cent, actual cost Rs. 36,000). Plant E is not eligible for additional depreciation. It is put to use on the same day. On March 13, 2019, Y sells plant C for Rs. 26,40,000.

•

Computation of depreciation allowance on Plants A and B

	Rs.
Depreciated value of the block on April 1, 2018	10,40,000
Depreciation @ 15%	1,56,000
Apportionment between X and Y	
Number of days when the assets are held by X (from April 1, 2018 to July 6, 2018)	97 days
Number of days when assets are held by Y (365 days – 97 days)	268 days
Depreciation available to X (Rs. 1,56,000 × 97 ÷ 365)	41,458
Depreciation available to Y (Rs. 1,56,000 × 268 ÷ 365)	1,14,542

Tax consequences in the hands of X and Y

	Situation 1 Rs.	*Situation 2* Rs.	*Situation 3* Rs.	*Situation 4* Rs.	*Situation 5* Rs.
Tax consequences in the hands of X					
Depreciation	41,458	41,458	41,458	41,458	41,458
Short term capital gain under section 48 read with section 45	*Nil*[1]	20,30,000[2]	*Nil*[1]	*Nil*[3]	20,30,000
Depreciation in the hands of Y					
Depreciated value of the block on April 1, 2018	*Nil*	*Nil*	6,40,000	*Nil*	60,78,000
Add : "Actual cost" of assets acquired from X	10,40,000	30,70,000	10,40,000	30,70,000	30,70,000
Add : Actual cost of plant E acquired by Y	-	-	2,90,000	-	36,000
Less: Assets sold during the year	-	-	-	-	26,40,000
Written down value of the block	10,40,000	30,70,000	19,70,000	30,70,000	65,44,000
Depreciation					
❑ On assets acquired from X	1,14,542	1,14,542	1,14,542	1,14,542	1,14,542
❑ On Plant E	-	-	21,750[4]	-	2,700[6]
❑ On other assets	-	-	96,000[5]	-	5,15,700[7]
Total depreciation	1,14,542	1,14,542	2,32,292	1,14,542	6,32,942
Written down value of the block on April 1, 2019	9,25,458	29,55,458	17,37,708	29,55,458	59,11,058

Notes :

1. It is exempt under section 47(*vi*).

2. As the amalgamated company is not an Indian company, the provisions of section 47(*vi*) are not applicable.

3. It is exempt under section 47(*xiii*).

4. It is 15% of 1/2 of Rs. 2,90,000 as Plant E is put to use for less than 180 days during the previous year.

5. It is 15% of (Rs. 19,70,000 – Rs. 10,40,000 – Rs. 2,90,000).

6. It is 15% of 1/2 of Rs. 36,000.

7. It is 15% of (Rs. 65,44,000 – Rs. 30,70,000 – Rs. 36,000).

8. In the above example, situation *4* covers the case if a firm is converted into company by satisfying conditions of section 47(*xiii*). The tax treatment will be same in the following cases [except exemption under section 47(*xiii*)]—

a. if X is a firm and the business is taken over by Y a partner in the firm;

b. if X is HUF and the business is taken over by Y a member of the family;

c. if X is a sole proprietor and business is taken over by Y, a firm in which X is one of the partners.

d. if X is a sole proprietor and business is taken over by satisfying conditions of section 47(*xiv*) by a company in which X is one of the shareholders.

e. if X is a private company or unlisted public company and the business is taken over by a LLP by satisfying conditions of section 47(*xiiib*).

In (*d*) if conditions of section 47(*xiv*) are satisfied or in (*e*) if conditions of section 47(*xiiib*) are satisfied, exemption will be available to X under that section.

9. In situations *2, 4* and *5* if the Assessing Officer is satisfied that fair market value of Plants A and B is less than Rs. 30,70,000 (being the consideration paid by Y), then he can take action under *Explanation 3* to section 43(*1*).

48.3-5b[5] *When an asset is put to use for less than 180 days in the year of acquisition* - If any asset falling within a block of assets is acquired by the assessee during the previous year and it is put to use for the purpose of business or profession for a period of less than 180 days in that previous year, the deduction in respect of such asset shall be restricted to 50 per cent of the amount calculated at the percentage prescribed in the case of block of assets comprising such asset. The aforesaid provision is applicable if the following conditions are satisfied :

1. If the asset is "acquired" during the previous year.

2. It is put to use for a period of less than 180 days.

When the two conditions are satisfied, depreciation shall be restricted to 50 per cent of the amount calculated at the percentage prescribed.

For instance, X Ltd. owns two buildings A and B on April 1, 2018 (rate of depreciation : 10 per cent, depreciated value : Rs. 14,15,700). It purchases on December 1, 2018 building C for Rs. 3,10,000 (rate of depreciation : 10 per cent) and sells building A during the previous year 2018-19 (say on January 10, 2019) for Rs. 8,70,000, then depreciation for the previous year 2018-19 shall be determined as under :

	Rs.
Depreciated value of the block (*i.e.*, buildings A and B) on April 1, 2018	14,15,700
Add: Cost of building C (purchased on December 1, 2018)	3,10,000
Total	17,25,700
Less : Sale proceeds of building A	8,70,000
Written down value of the block	8,55,700
Depreciation [as building C is purchased in the year 2018-19 and it is put to use for less than 180 days, depreciation on Rs. 3,10,000 will be 50% of 10% of Rs. 3,10,000 and on the remaining amount depreciation will be 10% of (Rs. 8,55,700–Rs. 3,10,000)]	70,070
Depreciated value of the block on April 1, 2019	7,85,630

If, in the aforesaid case, building A is sold for Rs. 15,87,000, depreciation will be determined as under :

Depreciated value on April 1, 2018	14,15,700
Add: Cost of building C	3,10,000
Total	17,25,700
Less: Sale proceeds of building A	15,87,000
Written down value	1,38,700
Depreciation [as the written down value is lower than cost of building C which is put to use for less than 180 days, depreciation shall be 50% of 10% of Rs. 1,38,700]	6,935
Depreciated value of the block on April 1, 2019	1,31,765

The following observations one should keep in mind—

• The aforesaid restriction is applicable only in the year in which an asset is acquired and not in subsequent years.

• Since in the case of partition of a joint Hindu family, dissolution of a firm, conversion of a firm into a company, no asset is "acquired" by the successor, the aforesaid provision is not applicable.

• If an asset is kept ready for use for more than 180 days before the end of the previous year but actually used for less than 180 days, the aforesaid restriction would not apply. This view is in line with the interpretation of the courts that "use" includes "ready for use". In other words, the word "used" in this section may be given a wider meaning and embrace passive as well as active user—*Vishwanath Bhaskar Sathe* v. *CIT* 10 ITC 386 (Bom.).

48.3-6 *PROVISIONS ILLUSTRATED* - To have better understanding of the aforesaid provisions, the following illustrations are given :

48.3-6E1 X Ltd. owns the following assets on April 1, 2017 :

Asset	*Actual cost* Rs.	*Written down value on April 1, 2017* Rs.	*Rate of depreciation (per cent)*
Building			
A	20,00,000	12,50,000	10
B	5,00,000	1,25,000	10
C	2,00,000	40,000	5
Plant			
A	70,000	35,100	15
B	1,10,000	78,000	15
C	20,000	7,000	30
D	40,000	31,000	30

The company acquires the following assets (additional depreciation is not available) after April 1, 2017 :

Asset	*Cost* Rs.	*Date of acquisition*	*Date when it is put to use*	*Rate of depreciation (per cent)*
Building D	8,00,000	May 30, 2017	June 3, 2017	10
Building E	3,00,000	June 10, 2017	March 7, 2018	5
Plant E	5,00,000	August 2, 2017	December 7, 2017	15
Plant F	2,10,000	March 10, 2018	December 1, 2018	15
Plant G	90,000	May 9, 2018	November 1, 2018	30

The company sells the following assets after April 1, 2017 :

Asset	*Date of sale*	*Sale consideration* Rs.
Building A	May 10, 2017	14,00,000
Plant B	May 15, 2017	1,20,000
Plant D	December 19, 2017	1,15,000
Plant C	December 9, 2018	32,000

•

The written down value and amount of depreciation for the assessment years 2018-19 and 2019-20 will be as follows :

❑ *First block : Building (rate of depreciation : 10%)*

	Rs.
Aggregate amount of written down value of buildings A and B on April 1, 2017 (*i.e.*, Rs. 12,50,000 + Rs. 1,25,000)	13,75,000
Add : Cost of Building D acquired during the previous year 2017-18	(+) 8,00,000
Less: Sale consideration of building A sold during the previous year 2017-18 (this amount cannot, however, exceed Rs. 13,75,000 + Rs. 8,00,000)	(–) 14,00,000
Written down value for the previous year 2017-18	7,75,000
Less : Depreciation for the previous year 2017-18 (assessment year 2018-19) [*i.e.*, 10% of Rs. 7,75,000]	77,500
Remaining amount	6,97,500
Add : Cost of building acquired during the previous year 2018-19	*Nil*
Less : Selling price of building sold during the previous year 2018-19	*Nil*

	Rs.
Written down value for the previous year 2018-19	6,97,500
Less : Depreciation for the previous year 2018-19 (assessment year 2019-20)	69,750
Balance	6,27,750
❑ *Second block : Building (rate of depreciation : 5%)*	
Written down value of Building C	40,000
Add: Cost of Building E acquired during the previous year 2017-18	(+) 3,00,000
Written down value for the previous year 2017-18	3,40,000
Less: Depreciation for the previous year 2017-18 (assessment year 2018-19) [5% of Rs. 40,000 and 2.5% of Rs. 3,00,000]	9,500
Written down value for the previous year 2018-19	3,30,500
Less: Depreciation for the previous year 2018-19 (assessment year 2019-20)	16,525
Balance	3,13,975
❑ *Third block : Plant (rate of depreciation : 15%)*	
Aggregate amount of written down value of Plants A and B on April 1, 2017 (*i.e.,* Rs. 35,100 + Rs. 78,000)	1,13,100
Add: Cost of Plant E acquired during the previous year 2017-18	(+) 5,00,000
Less: Sale consideration of Plant B sold during the previous year 2017-18	(-) 1,20,000
Written down value for the previous year 2017-18	4,93,100
Less: Depreciation for the previous year 2017-18 (assessment year 2018-19) [*i.e.,* 50% of 15% of Rs. 4,93,100]	36,983
Balance	4,56,117
Add: Cost of Plant F put to use during the previous year 2018-19	(+) 2,10,000
Written down value for the previous year 2018-19	6,66,117
Less: Depreciation for the previous year 2018-19 (assessment year 2019-20)	99,918
Balance	5,66,200

Note : During the previous year 2018-19, Plant F is put to use for the first time and is used for less than 180 days. It is qualified for normal depreciation, as it is not acquired during the previous year 2018-19.

❑ *Fourth block : Plant (rate of depreciation : 30%)*	
Aggregate amount of written down value of Plants C and D on April, 1, 2017 (*i.e.,* Rs. 7,000 + Rs. 31,000)	38,000
Add: Cost of plant acquired during the previous year 2017-18	*Nil*
Less: Sale consideration of Plant D sold during the previous year 2017-18 [though the plant is sold for Rs. 1,15,000, the amount of reduction cannot exceed Rs. 38,000 + (*Nil*)] [*see* para 66.1-3, for computation of capital gains]	38,000
Written down value for the previous year 2017-18	*Nil*
Less: Depreciation for the previous year 2017-18	*Nil*
Balance	*Nil*
Add: Cost of Plant G put to use during the previous year 2018-19	90,000
Less: Sale consideration of Plant C sold during the previous year 2018-19	32,000
Written down value for the previous year 2018-19	58,000
Less: Depreciation for the previous year 2018-19 (assessment year 2019-20) [*i.e.,* 50% of 30% of Rs. 58,000, as plant G is put to use for less than 180 days during 2018-19]	8,700
Balance	49,300

48.3-7 *COMPUTATION OF ADDITIONAL DEPRECIATION [Sec. 32(1)(*iia*)]* - These provisions are given below—

48.3-7a CONDITIONS - To claim additional depreciation the following conditions should be satisfied—

1. Manufacture/production of any article - The assessee should be engaged in the manufacture or production[89] of any article or thing (may be priority sector item or even non-priority sector item given in the Eleventh Schedule).

---

89. A few example of manufacture or production : mining of coal – *Integrated Coal Mining Ltd.* v. *CIT* [2016] 67 taxmann.com 260 (Kol.), production of radio programme – *CIT* v. *Radio Today Broadcasting Ltd.* [2016] 237 Taxman 126 (Delhi), embroidery work on synthetic fabrics – *CIT* v. *Vijay Pataka Synthetics* [2015] 63 taxmann.com 214 (Guj.), business of printing or printing and publishing – Circular No.15/2016[$], dated May 19, 2016.

[$] For Circular No. 15/2016, log on to *taxmann.com/readyreckoner.aspx.*

2. New plant and machinery installed and acquired after March 31, 2005 - Additional depreciation is available only in respect of new plant and machinery acquired and installed after March 31, 2005. The following points should be noted—

• Additional depreciation is not available in respect of building or furniture even if the other conditions are satisfied.

• Additional depreciation is not available in respect of old plant and machinery.

3. Eligible plant and machinery - Any new plant and machinery which has been acquired and installed after March 31, 2005 by an assessee is qualified for additional depreciation. However, the following assets are not eligible for additional depreciation—

a. ships and aircrafts; or

b. any machinery or plant which, before its installation by the assessee, was used either within or outside India by any other person; or

c. any machinery or plant which is installed in any office premises or any residential accommodation, including accommodation in the nature of a guest house; or

d. any office appliances[90] or road transport vehicles; or

e. any machinery or plant, the whole of the actual cost of which is allowed as a deduction (whether by way of depreciation or otherwise) in computing the income chargeable under the head "Profits and gains of business or profession" of any one previous year.

48.3-7b RATE OF ADDITIONAL DEPRECIATION - Additional depreciation is available @ 20 per cent of the actual cost of new plant and machinery acquired and installed after March 31, 2005. If, however, the asset is put to use for less than 180 days in the year in which it is acquired, the rate of additional depreciation is 10 per cent (the remaining 10 per cent shall be allowed as deduction in the next year[91]).

• Where an assessee incurs any expenditure for acquisition of a depreciable asset in respect of which a payment (or aggregate of payments made to a person in a day), otherwise than by an account payee cheque/ draft or use of electronic clearing system through a bank account (**or through prescribed electronic mode**), exceeds Rs. 10,000, such payment shall not be eligible for normal/additional depreciation (applicable from the assessment year 2018-19).

48.3-7c ADDITIONAL DEPRECIATION IN THE CASE OF GENERATION OR GENERATION AND DISTRIBUTION OF POWER[92] - Section 32(1)(*iia*) was amended by the Finance Act, 2012 with effect from the assessment year 2013-14. After the amendment an assessee engaged in the business of generation or generation and distribution of power[92] shall also be allowed additional depreciation. The legal position (before and after amendment) is highlighted in the table given below—

Different situations	*Whether cost of new plant and machinery for generation/distribution of power† is eligible for additional depreciation under section 32(1)(iia)*	
	Before amendment (i.e., up to the assessment year 2012-13)	*After amendment (i.e., from the assessment year 2013-14 onwards)*
1. An assessee who is engaged in the business of generation or generation and distribution of power[92]–		
1.1 If normal depreciation is claimed on straight-line basis under section 32(1)(*i*)	*No*	*No* [*see* Note 1]
1.2 If normal depreciation is claimed on the basis of written down value of the block of assets under section 32(1)(*ii*)	*No*	*Yes*

90. Computer (installed in supervisory offices in factory compound) for supervision of manufacturing activity and which constitutes integral part of a factory, is eligible for additional depreciation—*Hero Moto Corp Ltd.* v. *CIT* [2013] 60 SOT 25 (Delhi).

91. Section 32 has been amended to provide that if the asset is put to use for less than 180 days in the year of acquisition, then additional depreciation would be 10 per cent of the cost of acquisition in the first year and the balance 10 per cent would be available in the immediately succeeding previous year. The amended provisions are applicable from the assessment year 2016-17. For earlier assessment years, one can take the shelter of the judicial rulings given in cases of *Apollo Tyres Ltd.* v. *ACIT* [2014] 45 taxmann.com 337 (Cochin-Trib.), *CIT* v. *Cosmo Films Ltd.* [2012] 24 taxmann.com 189 (Delhi), *CIT* v. *SIL Investment Ltd.* [2012] 26 taxmann.com 78 (Delhi).

92. Extended to generation, transmission or distribution of power (with effect from the assessment year 2017-18).

Different situations	*Whether cost of new plant and machinery for generation/distribution of power is eligible for additional depreciation under section 32(1)(iia)*	
	Before amendment (i.e., up to the assessment year 2012-13)	*After amendment (i.e., from the assessment year 2013-14 onwards)*
2. An assessee (who is engaged in manufacture/production of any article/goods) owns power generating unit for captive consumption –		
2.1 If normal depreciation in respect of power generating unit is claimed on straight-line basis under section 32(1)(*i*)	*No*	*No* [*see* Note 1]
2.2 If normal depreciation is claimed on the basis of written down value of the block of assets under section 32(1)(*ii*)	*Yes* [*see* Note 2]	*Yes*

Notes –

1. Even after the amendment, a power generating unit which claims depreciation on straight-line basis under section 32(1)(*i*) cannot claim any additional depreciation in respect of investment in new plant and machinery. This is because of the fact that the additional depreciation under section 32(1)(*iia*) is available only in those cases where normal depreciation is claimed under section 32(1)(*ii*) on the basis of written down value of block of assets.

2. Manufacturing companies (owning power generation units for captive consumption) were eligible for additional depreciation even before the amendment—*CIT* v. *Texmo Precision Castings* [2010] 321 ITR 481 (Mad.), *CIT* v. *VTM Ltd.* [2010] 187 Taxman 319 (Mad.) and *CIT* v. *Hi Tech Arai Ltd.* [2010] 321 ITR 477 (Mad.).

48.3-7d ADDITIONAL DEPRECIATION AT THE RATE OF 35 PER CENT IN ANDHRA PRADESH, BIHAR, TELANGANA OR WEST BENGAL - In order to incentivise acquisition and installation of plant and machinery for setting up of manufacturing units in the notified backward area in Andhra Pradesh, Bihar, Telangana or West Bengal, the existing scheme of additional depreciation has been modified as follows –

1. Investment in new plant and machinery in notified backward area in Andhra Pradesh, Bihar, Telangana or West Bengal will be qualified for additional depreciation at the rate of 35 per cent (instead of 20 per cent). If, however, the new plant and machinery is put to use for less than 180 days in the year of acquisition, then additional depreciation will be limited to 17.5 per cent of actual cost in that year. The balance 17.5 per cent will be allowed in the immediately succeeding previous year.

2. The new plant and machinery should be acquired on or after April 1, 2015.

3. The new plant and machinery should be acquired for the purpose of setting up an undertaking/enterprise in the above noted backward area during the period beginning on April 1, 2015 and ending before April 1, 2020.

4. The eligible machinery or plant for this purpose shall not include the machinery or plant which are currently not eligible for additional depreciation as per the existing proviso to section 32(1)(*iia*).

48.3-7E1 X Ltd. is engaged in the business of manufacture of computer hardware since 1996. During the previous year 2018-19, the following assets are acquired and put to use—

(Rs. in thousand)

	Block 1	Block 2	Block 3
Rate of depreciation	15%	30%	40%
Number of assets in the block	11	12	17
Depreciated value of the block on April 1, 2018	18,00	25,00	5,00
Additions of plants (new) during the previous year 2018-19			
Plant A	57,00	—	—
Plant B	—	4,00	—
Plant C	—	—	17,00
Sale of old plants (one plant in each block)	8	28,70	42,00

Plants A, B and C are acquired during May 2018 and put to use during September 2018. However, Plant B is put to use in the last week of March 2019. Find out the amount of depreciation, additional depreciation and capital gains.

•

Computation of additional depreciation

	Plant A	*Plant B*	*Plant C*
Whether additional depreciation is available	Yes	Yes	Yes
Rate of additional depreciation	20%	10%	20%
	Rs.	*Rs.*	*Rs.*
Actual cost	57,00,000	4,00,000	17,00,000
Additional depreciation (total Rs. 15,20,000)	11,40,000	40,000	3,40,000
Computation of normal depreciation—			
	Block 1	*Block 2*	*Block 3*
Rate of depreciation	15%	30%	40%
	Rs.	*Rs.*	*Rs.*
Depreciated value of the block on April 1, 2018	18,00,000	25,00,000	5,00,000
Add: Actual cost of Plants A, B and C acquired during the previous year	57,00,000	4,00,000	17,00,000
Total (*a*)	75,00,000	29,00,000	22,00,000
Less : Sale proceeds of old plants	(-) 8,000	(-) 28,70,000	(-) 42,00,000
Written down value of the block on March 31, 2019	74,92,000	30,000	*Nil*
Less : Normal depreciation	11,23,800	4,500	*Nil*
Less : Additional depreciation as computed earlier	11,40,000	40,000	3,40,000
Depreciated value of the block on April 1, 2019	52,28,200	*Nil*	*Nil*
Computation of capital gains			
Sale proceeds of old plants	8,000	28,70,000	42,00,000
Whether capital gain is taxable [*the block does not cease to exist, sale proceeds do not exceed the opening balance *plus* new addition, *i.e.*, (*a*)]	No*	No*	Yes
Less : Cost of acquisition [*i.e.*, (*a*)]	-	-	22,00,000
Short-term capital gain	*Nil*	*Nil*	20,00,000

Note - X Ltd. can claim normal depreciation of Rs. 11,28,300 [*i.e.*, Rs. 11,23,800 + Rs. 4,500]. It is also eligible for additional depreciation of Rs. 15,20,000 as computed above. Besides, X Ltd. can claim investment allowance under section 32AC.

48.3-8 *MEANING OF "ACTUAL COST" [SEC. 43(1)]* - It means the actual cost to the assessee as reduced by that proportion of the cost thereof, if any, as has been met, directly or indirectly, by any other person or authority. Interest paid or payable on capital borrowed for the acquisition and installation of plant and machinery is treated as a part of actual cost and, consequently, the assessee is entitled to claim depreciation on such interest also. However, amount payable as interest in connection with acquisition of asset and relatable to a period after the asset is first put to use does not form part of actual cost. Likewise, commission paid to the banker for giving guarantee to the supplier of the asset is deemed as part of actual cost.

• In order to discourage cash transactions even for capital expenditure, section 43(*1*) has been amended with effect from the assessment year 2018-19. The amended version provides that where an assessee incurs any expenditure for acquisition of any asset in respect of which a payment (or aggregate of payments made to a person in a day), otherwise than by an account payee cheque/draft or use of electronic clearing system through a bank account (**or through prescribed electronic mode**), exceeds Rs. 10,000, such payment shall be ignored for the purposes of determination of actual cost of such asset. Consequently, normal depreciation/additional depreciation under section 32 and investment allowance under section 32AD will not be available pertaining to a payment (exceeding Rs. 10,000) which is made otherwise than by an account payee cheque/draft or use of electronic clearing system, etc.

• Section 43(*1*) enumerates the cases where actual cost of an asset is taken at a notional figure. This is determined as follows :

Different circumstances	*Notional cost under section 43(1)*
1. Asset is used in business after it ceases to be used for scientific research related to that business	Actual cost of the asset to assessee [*less* deduction allowed under section 35] [*Explanation 1*]. In other words, it is taken as zero.
2. When inventory is converted into, or treated as, capital asset	Fair market value on the date of conversion which is taken into consideration for the purpose of section 28(*via*) [*Explanation 1A*, applicable from the assessment year 2019-20]
3. Asset acquired by way of gift or inheritance	Actual cost to the previous owner [*less* (*a*) depreciation actually allowed up to the assessment year 1987-88 and (*b*) depreciation allowable for assess-

Different circumstances	*Notional cost under section 43(1)*
	ment year 1988-89 onwards as if that asset is the only asset in the block] [*Explanation 2*]
4. If the assets were used previously by any other person for the purpose of his business and the Assessing Officer is satisfied that the main purpose of the transfer to the assessee was the reduction of tax liability	Actual cost as determined by Assessing Officer with prior approval of Joint Commissioner having regard to the circumstances of the case [*Explanation 3*]
5. Assets earlier transferred by assessee to another person is subsequently reacquired by him	Lower of (*a*) actual cost of asset as initially acquired by assessee [*less* depreciation actually allowed to him up to assessment year 1987-88 and depreciation allowable for assessment year 1988-89 onwards as if that asset is the only asset in the block] or (*b*) actual price for which asset is reacquired [*Explanation 4*]
6. Asset previously used by first person (let's say F) and on which depreciation has been allowed to him, acquired by second person (let's say S) but leased back to the first person (*i.e.*, F)	Actual cost in the hands of the second person (*i.e.*, S) shall be the written down value of such asset to the first person (*i.e.*, F) at the time of transfer [*Explanation 4A*]
7. Building acquired by assessee is subsequently brought into use for business purposes	Actual cost of the building [*less* total depreciation that would have been allowable had the building been used for the purpose of business since its acquisition]. For this purpose, depreciation shall be calculated at the rate in force on the date when the building is brought into use for business purpose [*Explanation 5*]
8. Assets transferred by parent company to its 100% subsidiary (or *vice versa*) if transferee-company is an Indian company	Actual cost to transferee company will be the same as it would have been if the transferor-company had continued to hold the asset for the purpose of its business [*Explanation 6*]
9. Assets transferred under a scheme of amalgamation to an Indian company	Actual cost to the amalgamated company will be same as it would have been if the amalgamating company had continued to hold the asset for the purpose of its business [*Explanation 7*]
10. Asset transferred to an Indian resulting company in case of demerger	Actual cost to the resulting company will be same as it would have been if the demerged company had continued to hold the asset for the purpose of its business [*Explanation 7A*]
11. If duty of excise or additional duty under section 3 of Customs Tariff Act is leviable on asset acquired	Actual cost [*less* duty of excise/customs for which Cenvat credit has been claimed and allowed under Central Excise Rules, 1944 in respect of such asset] [*Explanation 9*]
12. Asset acquired where portion of cost is met by Government or any other person in form of subsidy, grant or reimbursement, etc.	Actual cost [*less* cost met by Government or any other person in the form of subsidy, grant or reimbursement][93]. If such subsidy, etc., is not directly relatable to any particular asset, then the amount received shall be apportioned in an appropriate manner [*Explanation 10*]
13. Asset acquired by a non-resident outside India and brought by him to India for the purpose of business and profession	Actual cost [*less* depreciation that would have been allowable in India had the asset been used for the purpose of business or profession since the date of its acquisition] [*Explanation 11*]
14. Assets acquired by a company under a scheme for corporatisation of a recognised stock exchange in India	Actual cost of the asset had there been no such corporatisation [*Explanation 12*]
15. Assets in respect of which deduction is claimed and allowed under section 35AD	• *Nil*[94] in the hands of an assessee who has claimed deduction under section 35AD (applicable from the assessment year 2010-11) • *Nil* in the hands of a person who has acquired an asset from a person (who has availed deduction under section 35AD) by any mode given below (applicable from the assessment year 2010-11) — *a.* by way of gift or will or an irrevocable trust;

93. Waiver of loan would not fall in the category of "grant, subsidy or reimbursement" and on waiver of loan, the *Explanation 10* to section 43(*1*) is not attracted—*Steelco Gujarat Ltd.* v. *CIT* [2009] 33 SOT 437 (Ahd.).

94. Where any capital asset in respect of which deduction allowed under section 35AD is deemed to be the income of the assessee in accordance with the provisions of sub-section (7B) of the said section, the actual cost to the assessee shall be the actual cost to the assessee, as reduced by an amount equal to the amount of depreciation calculated at the rate in force that would have been allowable had the asset been used for the purposes of business since the date of its acquisition (applicable from the assessment year 2018-19).

Different circumstances	*Notional cost under section 43(1)*
	b. on any distribution on liquidation of the company; *c.* by such mode of transfer as is referred to in section 47(*i*)/(*iv*)/(*v*)/(*vi*)/(*vib*)/(*xiii*) and (*xiv*); and *d.* (applicable from the assessment year 2011-12) by such mode of transfer as is referred to in section 47(*xiiib*) [*Explanation 13*].

48.3-9 *UNABSORBED DEPRECIATION*[95] - While dealing with unabsorbed depreciation[96] one should keep in mind the following points :

- Depreciation allowance[96] of the previous year is first deductible from the income chargeable under the head "Profits and gains of business or profession".
- If depreciation allowance[96] is not fully deductible under the head "Profits and gains of business or profession" because of absence or inadequacy of profits, it is deductible from income (other than income chargeable under the head "Salaries"[97]) chargeable under other heads of income for the same assessment year.
- If depreciation allowance[96] is still unabsorbed, it can be carried forward to the subsequent assessment year(s). No time-limit is fixed for the purpose of carrying forward of unabsorbed depreciation; it can be carried forward for indefinite period, if necessary. In the subsequent year(s), unabsorbed depreciation[96] can be set off against any income whether chargeable under the head "Profits and gains of business or profession" or under any other head (not being income chargeable under the head "Salaries"[97]). In the matter of set off, the following order of priority is followed in the subsequent year(s) :—

a. Current depreciation[96].

b. Brought forward business loss.

c. Unabsorbed depreciation[96].

It may be said that if in the subsequent year(s), there is no brought forward business loss, unabsorbed depreciation[96] can be added to current depreciation for the purpose of claiming deduction.

48.3-9E1 X submits the following particulars :

	Previous years	
	2018-19 Rs.	*2019-20* Rs.
Income from salary (after standard deduction)	1,00,000	2,00,000
Business profits (before depreciation)	16,000	18,000
Current depreciation	1,34,000	1,32,000
Income from other sources	10,000	80,000

Determine the taxable income of X for the assessment years 2019-20 and 2020-21.

●

ASSESSMENT YEAR 2019-20 (PREVIOUS YEAR 2018-19)

Profits and gains of business or profession :		
Business profits	16,000	
Less : Depreciation	1,34,000	*Nil*
Depreciation not deductible against business profits	1,18,000	
Income from salary		1,00,000
Income from other sources	10,000	
Less: Depreciation	10,000	—
Net income		1,00,000

Note: Unabsorbed depreciation of Rs. 1,08,000 will be carried forward.

ASSESSMENT YEAR 2020-21 (PREVIOUS YEAR 2019-20)

Profits and gains of business or profession :	
Business income	18,000

95. These provisions are applicable from the assessment year 2002-03. For provisions applicable up to the assessment year 2001-02, *see Taxmann's Direct Taxes Ready Reckoner*, 2001 edition.

96. These provisions are also applicable in the case of carry forward of unabsorbed capital expenditure on scientific research/family planning.

97. Applicable from the assessment year 2005-06.

	Rs.	Rs.
Less : Depreciation (*i.e.*, current depreciation : Rs. 1,32,000 + unabsorbed depreciation of the previous year 2018-19 : Rs. 1,08,000)	2,40,000	*Nil*
Depreciation not deductible against business income	2,22,000	
Income from salary		2,00,000
Income from other sources :	80,000	
Less : Depreciation	2,22,000	*Nil*
Net income		2,00,000

Note: As per section 71(2A) from the assessment year 2005-06, an assessee shall not be entitled to set-off of any loss under the head "Profits and gains of business or profession" against income under the head "Salaries". Consequently, unabsorbed depreciation of Rs. 80,000 is set-off against income from other sources and remaining unabsorbed depreciation of Rs. 1,42,000 will be carried forward.

48.3-10 *DEPRECIATION ON STRAIGHT-LINE BASIS IN THE CASE OF POWER UNITS* - An undertaking engaged in generation or generation and distribution of power can claim depreciation (in respect of assets acquired after March 31, 1997) according to any one of the following methods —

Straight-line basis	Depreciation can be claimed according to straight-line basis in the case of tangible assets at the percentage specified in Appendix IA to the Income-tax Rules [*see* Referencer 6] on the actual cost of individual asset. The aggregate depreciation cannot exceed the "actual cost".
Written down value basis	Alternately, such undertaking can claim depreciation, at its option, according to written down value method like any other assessee [*see* para 48.3-5]. The option for this purpose shall be exercised[98] before the due date of furnishing return of income. Once the option is exercised, it shall be final and shall apply to all the subsequent years.

48.3-10a TERMINAL DEPRECIATION (*i.e.*, LOSS ON TRANSFER) OR BALANCING CHARGE (*i.e.*, GAIN ON TRANSFER) IN THE CASE OF POWER UNITS - When a depreciable asset (on which depreciation is claimed on straight-line basis) of a power generating unit is sold, discarded, demolished or destroyed in a previous year, then terminal depreciation (in case of loss) is deductible or balancing charge (in case of gain) is taxable.

Terminal depreciation or balancing charge is calculated as follows—

Step one	Find out the written down value of the depreciable asset on the first day of the previous year in which such asset is sold, discarded, demolished or destroyed.
Step two	Find out the sale consideration (*i.e.*, money payable to the taxpayer in respect of such depreciable asset *plus* scrap value if any). It is the actual money (received or receivable in cash or by cheque or draft) and it does not include any other thing or benefit which can be converted in terms of money—*CIT* v. *Kasturi & Sons Ltd.* [1999] 103 Taxman 342 (SC).

48.3-10a[1] *Terminal depreciation* - If the amount calculated under *Step two* is less than the amount of *Step one*, then the deficiency is deductible as terminal depreciation. The following points should be noted—

1. When the asset is sold, discarded, etc., in the previous year in which it is first put to use, any loss arising therefrom is not allowed as terminal depreciation but is treated as capital loss.

2. Terminal depreciation allowance cannot be claimed if the asset is not used for the purpose of business or profession of the assessee at least for sometime during the previous year in which the sale takes place.

3. Terminal depreciation is allowed only if it is actually written off in the books of the assessee.

48.3-10a[2] *Balancing charge under section 41(2) and capital gain under section 50A* - If the amount calculated under *Step two* is more than the amount of *Step one*, then tax treatment of such surplus is as follows—

1. So much of the surplus which is equal to the amount of depreciation already claimed, is taxable as balancing charge under section 41(2) as business income.

2. The remaining surplus (if any) is taxable under the head "Capital gains".

---

98. There is no specific form or method prescribed for exercising the option. The claim can be made in the return of income and should reflect in audit report—*K.K.S.K. Leather Processors (P.) Ltd.* v. *ITO* [2010] 126 ITD 215 (Chennai). Once the assessee exercises his option (maybe belatedly), there is no requirement for further exercising option in the subsequent year—*K. Ravi* v. *CIT* [2010] 2 ITR (Trib.) 752 (Chennai).

• *Other points* - The following points should be noted—

1. Where an asset is sold, discarded, etc., in the previous year in which it is first put to use, any profit arising therefrom will not be chargeable to tax as balancing charge but will be treated as capital gains and chargeable to tax under section 45 under the head "Capital gains".

2. Balancing charge is taxable under section 41(2) in the previous year in which sale price, insurances, salvage or compensation money becoming due (whether the business is in existence in that year or not). In case of compulsory acquisition, it is taxable in the year of receipt of compensation. In case of additional compensation, it is taxable in the year of receipt of additional compensation—*CIT* v. *United Provinces Electric Supply Co.* [2000] 110 Taxman 134 (SC).

• *Provisions illustrated* - X Ltd. is a power generating unit. On December 20, 2017, it purchases a plant for Rs. 20 lakh which is eligible for depreciation @ 12.77 per cent on straight-line basis. The plant is sold for *(a)* Rs. 30,000 or *(b)* Rs. 18,72,300 or *(c)* Rs. 19,00,000 or *(d)* Rs. 21,50,000 on May 20, 2018.

	Rs.
Actual cost	20,00,000
Less : Depreciation for the previous year 2017-18 [½ of 12.77 per cent of Rs. 20 lakh, as it is put to use for less than 180 days]	1,27,700
Written down value on April 1, 2018 (*i.e.*, the first day of the previous year in which the plant is sold)	18,72,300

Terminal depreciation/balancing charge or capital gain

	Situation (a)	Situation (b)	Situation (c)	Situation (d)
Sale proceeds	30,000	18,72,300	19,00,000	21,50,000
Less : Written down value	18,72,300	18,72,300	18,72,300	18,72,300
Surplus	(-)18,42,300	*Nil*	27,700	2,77,700
Terminal depreciation deductible for the previous year 2018-19	18,42,300	*Nil*		
Balancing charge under section 41(2) taxable for the previous year 2018-19 [not to exceed the depreciation claimed]	*Nil*	*Nil*	27,700	1,27,700
Capital gain under section 50A for the previous year 2018-19				
Sale proceeds	30,000	18,72,300	19,00,000	21,50,000
Less : Cost of acquisition as per section 50A [*i.e.*, written down value - terminal depreciation + balancing charge]	30,000	18,72,300	19,00,000	20,00,000
Short-term capital gain	*Nil*	*Nil*	*Nil*	1,50,000

Note : Section 50A does not define the expression "as adjusted" used therein. It is assumed that—
"As adjusted", in relation to written down value, means diminished by any loss deducted or increased by any profit assessed, under the provisions of clause (*iii*) of sub-section (1) of section 32 or sub-section (2) of section 41.

48.4 ***Investment allowance for investment in new plant and machinery [Sec. 32AC applicable for the assessment years 2014-15 and 2017-18]*** - Section 32AC has been inserted to provide for investment allowance in order to encourage substantial investment in new plant and machinery. Investment allowance is in addition to depreciation.

48.4-1 *CONDITIONS* - Investment allowance is available if the following conditions are satisfied –

• The assessee is a company.

• It is engaged in the business of manufacture or production of any article or thing.

• It has acquired and installed a "new asset". "New asset" for this purpose is a new plant or machinery. But it does not include the following –

a. any plant or machinery which before its installation by the assessee was used either within or outside India by any other person;

b. any plant or machinery installed in any office premises or any residential accommodation, including accommodation in the nature of a guest house;

c. any office appliances including computers or computer software;

d. any vehicle;

e. ship or aircraft; or

f. any plant or machinery, the whole of the actual cost of which is allowed as deduction (whether by way of depreciation or otherwise) in computing the income chargeable under the head "Profits and gains of business or profession" of any previous year.

48.4-2 *AMOUNT OF INVESTMENT ALLOWANCE UNDER SECTION 32AC(1)* - A company which satisfies the above conditions can claim investment allowance under section 32AC(1), if the aggregate amount of actual cost of "new asset" acquired and installed by the company after March 31, 2013 but before April 1, 2015 exceeds Rs. 100 crore. Both 'acquisition' and 'installation' of the new asset (*i.e.*, new plant and machinery) are required to be made after March 31, 2013 but before April 1, 2015. If the new asset is acquired on or before March 31, 2013 but installed after March 31, 2013, it does not qualify for investment allowance.

The amount of investment allowance under section 32AC(1) for the assessment years 2014-15 and 2015-16 shall be determined as follows –

• *Assessment year 2014-15* - If the aggregate amount of actual cost of new asset (which is acquired and installed during the financial year 2013-14) exceeds Rs. 100 crore, investment allowance is available for the assessment year 2014-15. The amount of allowance is 15 per cent of actual cost of new asset acquired and installed during the previous year 2013-14.

• *Assessment year 2015-16* - Amount of investment allowance shall be calculated as follows –

		Rs.
Actual cost of new asset acquired and installed during April 1, 2013 and March 31, 2015	(*a*)*	*xxx*
15% of (*a*)	(*b*)	*xxx*
Less: Investment allowance allowed as deduction for the assessment year 2014-15	(*c*)	*xxx*
Investment allowance for the assessment year 2015-16 [(*b*) – (*c*)]		*xxx*

*If (*a*) is Rs. 100 crore or less, no deduction will be available under section 32AC(1).

48.4-3 *AMOUNT OF INVESTMENT ALLOWANCE UNDER SECTION 32AC(1A)* - A company which satisfies conditions given in para 48.4-1 can claim investment allowance under section 32AC(1A). Under section 32AC(1A), investment allowance is available if the aggregate amount of actual cost of "new asset" acquired and installed by the company during any previous year exceeds Rs. 25 crore. The amount of investment allowance is 15 per cent of actual cost of new asset acquired and installed during the previous year. This deduction is available for the assessment years 2015-16 to 2017-18. However, no deduction is available for the assessment year 2015-16 under section 32AC(1A) to a company which is eligible for deduction under section 32AC(1).

• *Modification applicable for the assessment years 2016-17 and 2017-18* - The dual condition of acquisition and installation causes genuine hardship when after acquiring an asset, the company could not install it in the same previous year. To avoid hardship in such cases, section 32AC(1A) has been amended. Under the modified version, new asset (of an amount exceeding Rs. 25 crore) has to be acquired in the previous year. However, installation may be made on or before March 31, 2017 in order to avail the benefit of investment allowance. Where the installation of the new asset is in a year other than the year of acquisition, the deduction under section 32AC(1A) shall be allowed in the year in which the new asset is installed.

48.4-4 *WITHDRAWAL OF INVESTMENT ALLOWANCE* - The new asset should not be sold or otherwise transferred within a period of 5 years from the date of its installation. If the new asset is sold or transferred within 5 years from its installation, the amount of investment allowance allowed to the assessee shall be deemed to be the income of assessee of the previous year in which such asset is sold or otherwise transferred. Such deemed income will be taxable under the head "Profit and gains of business or profession". Such deemed income shall be taxable in addition to taxability of capital gain which arises under section 45, read with section 50.

• *Above restriction not to apply in case of amalgamation/demerger* - The above restriction does not apply in a case of amalgamation or demerger. In other words, if the undertaking of the assessee-company is amalgamated or demerged within 5 years from the date of installation of new asset, investment allowance allowed to the amalgamating company or demerged company will not be taken back. However, the amalgamated company or the resulting company should not transfer the new asset within 5 years (from its installation by the amalgamating company or demerged company). If it is sold or otherwise transferred within 5 years by the amalgamated company/resulting company, the notional income stated above will be taxable in the hands of amalgamated company or resulting company.

48.5 ***Investment allowance in notified backward area in Andhra Pradesh, Bihar, Telangana or West Bengal [Sec. 32AD, applicable from the assessment year 2016-17]*** - Additional investment allowance is available under section 32AD. This deduction is over and above the deduction available under section 32AC. Accordingly, if an undertaking is set up in the notified backward areas in Andhra Pradesh, Bihar, Telangana or West Bengal by a company, it shall be eligible to claim deduction under the provisions of section 32AC as well as under section 32AD if it fulfils the conditions (such as investment above a specified threshold) specified in the said section 32AC and conditions specified under section 32AD.

• *Conditions for claiming deduction under section 32AD* - The following conditions should be satisfied in order to avail tax incentive of additional investment allowance under section 32AD –

1. The assessee may be a company or any other person.

2. He/it sets up an undertaking/enterprise for manufacture or production of any article or thing on or after April 1, 2015.

3. Such undertaking must be set up in any backward area (notified by the Central Government) in Andhra Pradesh, Bihar, Telangana or West Bengal.

4. He/it acquires and installs (for the purposes said undertaking) a "new asset". "New asset" for this purpose is a new plant or machinery. But it does not include the following –

a. any plant or machinery which before its installation by the assessee was used either within or outside India by any other person;

b. any plant or machinery installed in any office premises or any residential accommodation, including accommodation in the nature of a guest house;

c. any office appliances including computers or computer software;

d. any vehicle;

e. ship or aircraft; or

f. any plant or machinery, the whole of the actual cost of which is allowed as deduction (whether by way of depreciation or otherwise) in computing the income chargeable under the head "Profits and gains of business or profession" of any previous year.

5. The new asset should be acquired and installed after March 31, 2015 but before April 1, 2020. Both 'acquisition' and 'installation' of the new asset (*i.e.*, new plant and machinery) are required to be made after March 31, 2015 but before April 1, 2020.

• *Quantum of investment allowance* - If the above conditions are satisfied, investment allowance is 15 per cent of actual cost[99] of "new asset". It will be available in the year in which the new asset is installed.

48.6 ***Tea/Coffee/Rubber Development Account [Sec. 33AB]*** - An assessee can claim deduction under section 33AB if certain conditions are satisfied :

1. It must be engaged in the business of growing and manufacturing tea in India (or coffee or rubber from the assessment year 2004-05).

2. It must make the following deposit (hereinafter referred to as "special account")—

a. deposit with National Bank for Agriculture and Rural Development (hereinafter referred to as "NABARD") any amount (or amounts) in an account maintained by the assessee with that bank in accordance with and for the purpose specified in a scheme approved by the Tea Board or Coffee Board or Rubber Board; or

b. deposit any amount in the Deposit Account opened by the assessee in accordance with, and for the purposes specified in, a scheme framed by the Tea Board or Coffee Board or Rubber Board with the previous approval of the Central Government.

3. The aforesaid amount shall be deposited within 6 months from the end of the previous year or before the due date of furnishing the return of income, whichever is earlier.

4. The accounts of the taxpayer should be audited by a chartered accountant and the report of the auditor in Form No. 3AC is to be filed[1] along with the return of the relevant assessment year. In cases where the accounts of the taxpayer are required to be audited under any other law, *e.g.*, under the Companies Act, it would be sufficient if the accounts are audited under that law and the audit report as per that law is furnished[99] with the return along with a further report in Form No. 3AC for the purposes of this provision.

48.6-1 *AMOUNT OF DEDUCTION* - Amount of deduction is :

a. a sum equal to amounts deposited as mentioned in para 48.6 ; or

b. 40 per cent of the profit of such business computed under the head "Profits and gains of business or profession" before making any deduction under section 33AB and before adjusting brought forward business loss under section 72,

whichever is less.

99. Where an assessee incurs any expenditure for acquisition of any asset in respect of which a payment (or aggregate of payments made to a person in a day), otherwise than by an account payee cheque/draft or use of electronic clearing system through a bank account, exceeds Rs. 10,000, such payment shall not be eligible for investment allowance under section 32AD (applicable from the assessment year 2018-19).

1. Form No. 3AC is to be submitted electronically.

The following points should also be kept in mind :

1. Where any deduction is claimed under this section, no deduction shall be allowed in respect of such amount in any other previous year.

2. Where a deduction is claimed and allowed under this section to an association of persons or body of individuals, no deduction shall be allowed to any member of the association or body in respect of the same deposit.

3. Any excess deposit made during a previous year is not treated as deposit made in the next year or any other year.

48.6-2 *AMOUNT CAN BE WITHDRAWN FOR THE PURPOSE OF THE SCHEME* - The amount standing to the credit of the "special account" may be withdrawn only for the purpose specified in such scheme. Except in the circumstances mentioned in para 48.6-3, if the amount released from the "special account" in a year is not utilised in the same previous year for the purpose for which it is released, the amount not so utilised will be treated as taxable profits of that year and taxed accordingly.

48.6-3 *CONSEQUENCES IN THE CASE OF CLOSURE OF BUSINESS* - Apart from the purposes specified in the scheme, the amount standing to the credit of the "special account" may be allowed to be withdrawn in the following circumstances :

When the amount can be withdrawn and it is treated as taxable profit	*When the amount can be withdrawn and it is not treated as income*
1. Closure of business *2.* Dissolution of firm	*1.* Death of the taxpayer *2.* Partition of Hindu undivided family *3.* Liquidation of company

Where an amount is withdrawn because of closure of business or because of dissolution of firm, the amount withdrawn will be treated as taxable profit and taxed accordingly on the basis as if the business was continuing or the firm had not been dissolved. In all other cases, *viz.*, death of the taxpayer, partition of the Hindu undivided family and liquidation of the company, the amounts withdrawn on closure of account because of the occurrence of any of these events will not be included in the taxable income even though the amounts have not been utilized for any of the purposes specified in scheme.

48.6-4 *AMOUNT WITHDRAWN FROM THE SPECIAL ACCOUNT CANNOT BE UTILISED FOR CERTAIN PURPOSES* - There is an overriding condition that the deduction under this provision cannot be claimed in relation to amounts utilized for the purpose of any machinery or plant to be installed in any office premises or residential accommodation including guest houses ; any office appliance (other than computers) ; any other plant or machinery which either is installed in an undertaking producing low priority items specified in the Eleventh Schedule in the Income-tax Act or is an item of plant or machinery entitled to 100 per cent write off by way of depreciation or for any other reason in any one year.

48.6-5 *CONSEQUENCE IF THE NEW ASSET IS TRANSFERRED IN 8 YEARS* - The deduction allowed under this section shall be withdrawn if the asset acquired out of the money withdrawn from the special account is sold or otherwise transferred. These provisions are given below—

To whom it is transferred	*Transfer within 8 years from the end of the previous year in which the asset is acquired*	*Transfer after 8 years*
• Transfer to the Central Government, a State Government, a local authority, a statutory corporation or a Government company	Deduction will not be withdrawn	Deduction will not be withdrawn
• Transfer in a scheme of succession of a firm by company [*see* Note]	Deduction will not be withdrawn	Deduction will not be withdrawn
• Transfer in any other case	Deduction will be withdrawn	Deduction will not be withdrawn

Note: Transfer in a scheme of succession of a firm by company should satisfy the following points—

a. the scheme continues to apply to the company in the manner applicable to the firm;

b. the successor company takes over all the properties and liabilities of the firm; and

c. all the shareholders of the company are partners of the firm before the succession.

48.7 ***Site restoration fund [Sec. 33ABA]*** - An assessee can claim deduction under section 33ABA, if certain conditions are satisfied :

48.7-1 *CONDITIONS* - The assessee must satisfy the following conditions :

1. The taxpayer is engaged in the business of the prospecting for, or extraction or production of petroleum or natural gas or both in India.

2. The Central Government has entered into an agreement with the taxpayer for such business.

3. It must—

a. deposit with SBI any amount in an account (hereinafter referred to as special account) maintained by the assessee with that bank in accordance with and for the purpose specified in, a scheme approved by the Government of India in the Ministry of Petroleum and Natural Gas ; or

b. deposit any amount in an account (hereinafter referred to as site restoration account) opened by the assessee in accordance with, and for the purposes specified in, a scheme framed by the Ministry of Petroleum and Natural Gas (hereinafter referred to deposit scheme).

4. The aforesaid amount shall be deposited before the end of the previous year.

5. The accounts of the taxpayer should be audited by a chartered accountant and the report of the auditor [Form No. 3AD] is filed[2] along with the return of the relevant assessment year. In cases where the accounts of the taxpayer are required to be audited under any other law, *e.g.*, under the Companies Act, it would be sufficient if the accounts are audited under that law and the audit report as per that law is furnished with the return along with a further report in the form prescribed for the purposes of this provision.

48.7-2 *AMOUNT OF DEDUCTION* - Amount of deduction is :

a. a sum equal to amounts deposited as mentioned in para 48.7-1; or

b. 20 per cent of the profit of such business computed under the head "Profits and gains of business or profession" before making any deduction under section 33ABA and before adjusting brought forward business loss under section 72,

whichever is less.

The following points should also be kept in mind :

1. Where any deduction is claimed under this section, no deduction shall be allowed in respect of such amount in any other previous year.

2. Where a deduction is claimed and allowed under this section, to a firm, association of persons or body of individuals, no deduction shall be allowed to any partner of the firm or the member of the association or body in respect of the same deposit.

48.7-3 *AMOUNT CAN BE WITHDRAWN FOR THE PURPOSE OF THE SCHEME* - The amount standing to the credit of such special account or site restoration account may be withdrawn only for the purpose specified in the scheme or deposit scheme. If the amount released by SBI or the amount withdrawn from site restoration account in a year is not utilized in the same previous year for the purpose for which it is released, the amount not so utilized will be treated as taxable profits of that year and taxed accordingly.

48.7-4 *CONSEQUENCES IN CASE OF CLOSURE OF BUSINESS* - Where any amount standing to the credit of the assessee in the special account or in the Site Restoration Account is withdrawn on closure of the account during any previous year by the assessee, the amount so withdrawn from the account, as reduced by the amount, if any, payable to the Central Government by way of profit or production share as provided in the agreement referred to in section 42, shall be deemed to be the profits and gains of business or profession of that previous year and shall accordingly be chargeable to income-tax as the income of that previous year. Where any amount is withdrawn on closure of the account in a previous year in which the business carried on by the assessee is no longer in existence, the above provisions shall apply as if the business is in existence in that previous year.

48.7-5 *AMOUNT CANNOT BE UTILISED FOR CERTAIN PURPOSES* - There is an overriding condition that the deduction under this provision cannot be claimed in relation to amounts utilized for the purpose of any machinery or plant to be installed in any office premises or residential accommodation including guest house; any office appliance, other than computers; any other plant or machinery which either is installed in

2. Form No. 3AD is to be submitted electronically.

an undertaking producing low priority items specified in the Eleventh Schedule in the Act or is an item of plant or machinery entitled to 100 per cent write off by way of depreciation or for any other reason in any one year.

48.7-6 *CONSEQUENCES IF THE NEW ASSET IS TRANSFERRED WITHIN 8 YEARS* - The deduction allowed under this provision will be withdrawn if the asset acquired in accordance with the scheme is sold or otherwise transferred within 8 years of the end of the previous year. These provisions are the same as given in para 48.6-5.

48.8 ***Reserve for shipping business [Sec. 33AC]*** - An Indian public limited company (engaged in the business of operation of ship) can claim deduction under section 33AC. However, deduction under section 33AC is not available from the assessment year 2005-06.

48.9 ***Expenditure on scientific research [Sec. 35]*** - The deduction in respect of expenditure on scientific research may be grouped as under :

48.9-1 *REVENUE EXPENDITURE INCURRED BY AN ASSESSEE WHO HIMSELF CARRIES ON SCIENTIFIC RESEARCH [SEC. 35(1)(i)]* - Where the assessee himself carries on scientific research and incurs revenue expenditure, deduction is allowed for such expenditure only if such research relates to his business. Further, where salary has been paid to an employee engaged in scientific research or any expenditure has been incurred on purchase of materials used in scientific research, such salary or expenditure, paid or incurred after March 31, 1973, but within three years immediately preceding the commencement of the business, is deemed to have been paid or incurred in the previous year in which the business is commenced to the extent it is certified by the authority prescribed for this purpose under rule 6 [prescribed authority is Director-General (Income-tax Exemptions) in concurrence with the Secretary, Department of Scientific and Industrial Research, Government of India].

48.9-2 *CONTRIBUTION TO OUTSIDERS [SEC. 35(1)(ii)/(iii)]* - Where the assessee does not himself carry on research but makes contributions to the following institutions for this purpose, a deduction is allowed as follows—

To whom contribution can be given	*Deduction (as a percentage of actual expenditure)*			
	Up to AY 2010-11	*For the AYs 2011-12 to 2017-18*	*For the AYs 2018-19 to 2020-21*	*From the AY 2021-22 onwards*
An approved[3] scientific association which has, as its object, undertaking of scientific research related or unrelated to the business of assessee [sec. 35(1)(*ii*)]	125%	175%	150%	100%
An approved[3] university, college or other institution for the use of scientific research related or unrelated to the business of assessee [sec. 35(1)(*ii*)]	125%	175%	150%	100%
An approved* university, college or other institution for the use of research in social sciences or statistical research related or unrelated to the business of the assessee [sec. 35(1)(*iii*)]	125%	125%	100%	100%

Notes :

❑ The above-mentioned research association, university, college or other institution shall make an online application in the prescribed form [*i.e.*, Form No. 3CF-I or 3CF-II] to the CIT or Director of Income-tax having jurisdiction over the applicant, for approval. A copy of application in Form No. 3CF-I or 3CF-II shall be sent to the Member (IT), Central Board of Direct Taxes.

❑ The prescribed authority may, before granting approval, call for such documents (including audited annual accounts) or information from the scientific research association, etc., in order to satisfy itself about the genuineness of the activities of the research association, etc.

❑ In the cases mentioned above, order granting the approval or rejecting the application shall be passed within 12 months from the end of the month in which such application is received by the Member (IT), CBDT.

3. For list of approved associations/institutions, *see Taxmann's Direct Taxes Circulars,* 2014 edn., Vol. 1. If notification under section 10(*23C*)(*iv*) or 35(1)(*ii*) is issued after the completion of assessment of the taxpayer for the relevant assessment year, exemption/deduction can be given by rectification of mistake under section 154—Circular No. 725, dated October 16, 1995.

❑ Notification issued by the prescribed authority shall at one time have effect for not more than three assessment years, including an assessment year or assessment years commencing before the date on which such notification is issued (as may be specified in the notification). The three-year time-limit is not applicable on or after July 13, 2006.

❑ If the Assessing Officer is satisfied that the activities of the aforesaid university/college/institution [referred to in section 35(1)(*ii*)/(*iii*)] are not being carried out in accordance with all or any of the conditions subject to which approval was given to such institution by the Central Government, he may recommend the Central Government to withdraw the approval given under section 35 [second proviso to section 143(3)].

❑ Deduction in respect of contribution made by an assessee to the aforesaid institutions shall not be denied (from the assessment year 2006-07) merely on the ground that after the contribution made by the assessee to these institutions, the approval granted to these institutions have been withdrawn. In other words, contribution to these institutions will be qualified for deduction even if after the date of making contribution, the approval granted to these institutions have been withdrawn.

48.9-3 *AMOUNT PAID TO AN APPROVED SCIENTIFIC RESEARCH COMPANY [SEC. 35(1)(*iia*)]* - Section 35(1)(*iia*) is applicable if the following conditions are satisfied—

1. The taxpayer is any person (maybe an individual, HUF, firm, company or any other person).

2. The taxpayer has paid any sum to an Indian company (hereinafter referred as "payee-company") to be used by the payee for scientific research.

3. The scientific research may or may not be related to the business of the taxpayer.

4. The payee-company has as its main object the scientific research and development.

5. The payee-company is for the time being approved by the prescribed authority (*i.e.*, the Chief Commissioner of Income-tax having jurisdiction over the applicant). An application shall be submitted online for this purpose in Form No. 3CF-III.

6. The payee-company fulfils such other conditions as may be prescribed. These conditions are given in rule 5F[$].

• *Amount of deduction* - If the above conditions are satisfied, the taxpayer can claim a deduction under section 35(1)(*iia*). The amount of deduction is -

- for the assessment years 2009-10 to 2017-18 : 125 per cent of the amount paid;
- from the assessment year 2018-19 onwards : 100 per cent of the amount paid.

• *Payee-company cannot claim deduction under section 35(2AB)* - With a view to avoid multiple claims for deduction, it has been provided that the payee-company approved under the provisions of section 35(2)(*iia*) is not entitled to claim deduction under section 35(2AB). However, deduction to the extent of 100 per cent of the sum spent as revenue expenditure or capital expenditure on scientific research which is available under section 35(1) will continue to be allowed.

48.9-4 *CAPITAL EXPENDITURE INCURRED BY AN ASSESSEE WHO HIMSELF CARRIES ON SCIENTIFIC RESEARCH [SEC. 35(2)]* - Where the assessee incurs any expenditure of a capital nature on scientific research related to his business, the whole of such expenditure incurred in any previous year is allowable as deduction for that previous year. The following points should also be kept in view :

1. The assessee should incur expenditure of a capital nature on scientific research and there is no requirement that such an expenditure should be capitalized in its books of account - *CIT* v. *Hindustan Construction Co. Ltd.* [2015] 60 taxmann.com 421 (Bom.).

2. Where any capital expenditure has been incurred before the commencement of the business, the aggregate of such expenditure, incurred within three years immediately preceding the commencement of the business, is deemed to have been incurred in the previous year in which the business is commenced [*Explanation* to section 35(2)(*ia*)].

3. The aforesaid deduction is not available in respect of capital expenditure incurred on the acquisition of any land after February 29, 1984.

4. If the asset is sold *without having been used* for other purposes, surplus or deduction allowed, whichever is less, is chargeable to tax as business income of the previous year in which the sale took place [sec. 41(3)]. The excess of surplus over deduction allowed is, however, chargeable to tax as capital gains.

5. Deduction by way of depreciation is not admissible in respect of an asset used in scientific research, either in the year in which the capital expenditure is incurred or in a subsequent year.

[$] For Rule 5F, log on to *taxmann.com/readyreckoner.aspx.*

48.9-5 *CONTRIBUTION TO NATIONAL LABORATORY [SEC. 35(2AA)]* - The provisions of section 35(2AA) are given below—

48.9-5a CONDITIONS - The following conditions should be satisfied—

1. The payment is made to—

a. National Laboratory; or

b. University; or

c. Indian Institute of Technology; or

d. Specified person as approved by the prescribed authority.

2. The above payment is made under a specific direction that it should be used by the aforesaid person for undertaking scientific research programme approved by the prescribed authority.

48.9-5b AMOUNT OF DEDUCTION - If the aforesaid conditions are satisfied, the taxpayer is eligible for deduction as follows—

	Deduction
For the assessment years 1994-95 to 2010-11	125% of actual payment
For the assessment year 2011-12	175% of actual payment
For the assessment years 2012-13 to 2017-18	200% of actual payment
For the assessment years 2018-19 to 2020-21	150% of actual payment
From the assessment year 2021-22 onwards	100% of actual payment

Such contribution which is eligible for deduction under the aforesaid provisions is not eligible for any other deduction under the Act.

The aforesaid deduction will not be denied (with effect from the assessment year 2006-07) merely on the ground that after the payment made by the assessee to these institutions, the approval granted to National Laboratory/specified person has been withdrawn or approval granted to scientific research programme of National Laboratory/University/IIT/specified person have been withdrawn.

48.9-5c MEANING OF DIFFERENT TERMS - The meaning of different terms is as follows—

- "National Laboratory" for this purpose means a scientific laboratory functioning at national level under the aegis of the Indian Council of Agricultural Research, the Indian Council of Medical Research or the Council of Scientific and Industrial Research, the Defence Research and Development Organisation, the Department of Electronics, the Department of Bio-Technology or the Department of Atomic Energy.
- The prescribed authority is the head of a National Laboratory or a University or an Indian Institute of Technology, as the case may be. In the case of "specified person" the prescribed authority is the Principal, Scientific Adviser to the Government of India. Such authority shall before granting approval satisfy itself about the feasibility of carrying out the scientific research. The aforesaid authority shall submit its report to the Principal Director General or Director General or (with effect from April 1, 2016) Principal Chief Commissioner or Chief Commissioner in such form as may be prescribed.

48.9-6 *EXPENSES ON IN-HOUSE RESEARCH AND DEVELOPMENT [SEC. 35(2AB)]* - From the assessment year 1998-99, sub-section (2AB) has been inserted in section 35. It provides for a deduction in respect of expenditure on in-house research and development expenses subject to the following—

- *Conditions* - One has to satisfy the following conditions—

1. The taxpayer is a company.

2. The company should be engaged in the business of bio-technology or in any business of manufacture or production of any article or thing except those specified in the Eleventh Schedule.[4]

3. It incurs any expenditure on scientific research and such expenditure is of capital nature or revenue nature[6] (not being expenditure in the nature of cost of any land and building[5]). The expenditure on scientific research in relation to drugs and pharmaceuticals shall include expenditure incurred on clinical drug trial, regulatory approval and filing an application for a patent.

4. Up to the assessment year 2009-10, the company shall be engaged in the business of bio-technology or in the business of manufacture or production of any drugs, pharmaceuticals, electronic equipments, computers, telecommunication equipments, chemicals or any other article or thing notified by the Board (*i.e.*, manufacture or production of an aircraft or helicopter or computer software or automobile including automobile components).

5. Cost of building (excluding cost of land) is eligible for 100 per cent deduction under section 35(2).

6. Both capital and revenue expenses are eligible for weighted deduction under section 35(2AB) – *CIT* v. *Eicher Motors Ltd.* [2018] 98 taxmann.com 412 (SC).

4. The taxpayer has entered into an agreement with the prescribed authority for co-operation in such research and development facility and for audit of the accounts maintained for that facility or (with effect from the assessment year 2016-17) fulfils such conditions with regard to maintenance of accounts and audit thereof and furnishing of reports in such manner as may be prescribed.

5. On the application of the company in Form No. 3CK, the research and development facility is approved by the prescribed authority (*i.e.*, Secretary, Department of Scientific and Industrial Research) in Form No. 3CM[7]. The prescribed authority shall submit its report in relation to the approval of the said facility in Part A of Form No. 3CL to the Principal CIT/Chief CIT/Principal Director General/Director General having jurisdiction over such company within 120 days of grant of approval. However, an assessee cannot be denied deduction under section 35(2AB) merely on the ground that the prescribed authority has not submitted Form No. 3CL in time to income-tax department—*CIT* v. *Famy Care Ltd.* [2015] 67 SOT 85 (Mum.).

6. The company shall maintain a separate account for each approved facility, which shall be audited annually. A report of audit in Form No. 3CLA shall be electronically furnished to the prescribed authority (*i.e.*, Secretary, Department of Scientific and Industrial Research) on or before the due date of submission of return of income. The prescribed authority shall furnish electronically its report quantifying the expenditure incurred on in-house research and development facility by the company during the previous year and eligible for weighted deduction under section 35(2AB). This report shall be furnished by the prescribed authority in Part B of Form No. 3CL to the Principal CIT/Chief CIT/Principal Director General/Director General having jurisdiction over such company within 120 days of submission of audit report.

• *Amount of deduction* - If all the above conditions are satisfied, the quantum of deduction is as follows—

For the assessment years 1998-99 to 2000-01	125% of the expenditure incurred
For the assessment years 2001-02 to 2010-11	150% of the expenditure incurred
For the assessment years 2011-12 to 2017-18	200% of actual payment
For the assessment years 2018-19 to 2020-21	150% of actual payment
From the assessment year 2021-22 onwards	100% of actual payment

A company approved under the provisions of section 35(1)(*iia*) is not eligible to claim weighted deduction under section 35(2AB). However, deduction under section 35(1)(*i*)/(2) can be claimed to the extent of 100 per cent of the sum spent as revenue expenditure or capital expenditure on scientific research.

Other points - In respect of the aforesaid expenditure, no deduction shall be allowed under any other provisions of the Act. The prescribed authority shall furnish electronically its report, –

a. in relation to approval of in-house research facility in Part A of form No. 3CL;

b. quantifying the expenditure incurred on in-house research and development facility by the company during the previous year and eligible for weighted deduction under section 35(2AB) in Part B of Form No. 3CL.

The above report shall be furnished electronically by the prescribed authority to the Principal CIT/Chief CIT/Principal Director General/Director General having jurisdiction over such company within 120 days of grant of approval or submission of audit report.

48.9-E1 XYZ Ltd., a paper manufacturing concern, purchases a machine on March 1, 2016 for Rs. 6,10,000 for its laboratory with a view to improving the quality of art paper manufactured by it. X Ltd. is not approved under section 35(2AB).

1. What will be the amount of deduction under section 35 on account of capital expenditure of Rs. 6,10,000 for the assessment year 2016-17 ?

2. If the research activity for which the aforesaid machine is purchased ceases in 2017 and the machinery is brought into business proper on November 1, 2017 (market value of the machine : Rs. 2,30,000); depreciation is admissible at the rate of 15 per cent; depreciated value of the relevant block of assets on April 1, 2017 is Rs. 14,07,860 and sold for Rs. 1,90,000 on April 4, 2018, what will be the amount of depreciation and amount of chargeable profit under section 41(3) ?

3. If the research activity for which the machine was purchased ceases on November 1, 2017 (market value of the machine : Rs. 2,30,000) and the machine is sold on April 4, 2018 without using it for another purpose, sale price being Rs. 1,90,000 or Rs. 15,00,000.

•

1. As the scientific research is related to the business of assessee, the whole of capital expenditure of Rs. 6,10,000 is allowable as deduction under section 35 for the assessment year 2016-17.

2. The machine is brought into business proper on November 1, 2017.

---

7. Non-receipt of Form No. 3CM is at best a procedural lapse and is not fatal for denial of claim of deduction under section 35(2AB) – *Minilec India (P.) Ltd.* v. *CIT* [2018] 93 taxmann.com 213 (Pune - Trib.).

Tax treatment of depreciation will be as under :

	Rs.
Depreciated value of the block of assets on April 1, 2017	14,07,860
Add : Cost of machine transferred from laboratory on November 1, 2017 [*i.e.*, Rs. 6,10,000—deduction of Rs. 6,10,000 claimed under section 35]	*Nil*
Written down value	14,07,860
Less : Depreciation for the previous year 2017-18 [15% of Rs. 14,07,860]	2,11,179
Depreciated value of the block on April 1, 2018	11,96,681
Less : Sale proceeds of machine sold on April 4, 2018	1,90,000
Written down value	10,06,681
Less : Depreciation for the previous year 2018-19 (15% of Rs. 10,06,681)	1,51,002
Depreciated value of the block on April 1, 2019	8,55,679

There will be no capital gain or loss in this case

3. Tax treatment for the assessment year 2018-19 will be as under :

	If the sale price is	
	Rs. 1.90 lakh *Rs.*	*Rs. 15 lakh* *Rs.*
Amount chargeable under section 41(3) (*i.e.*, sale proceeds but subject to maximum of deduction claimed under section 35 for the assessment year 2016-17)	1,90,000	6,10,000
Capital gain under section 45		
Sale proceeds	1,90,000	15,00,000
Less : Cost of acquisition	6,10,000	6,10,000
Short-term capital gain	(-) 4,20,000	8,90,000

Note - It can be seen from the above computation that when the capital asset is transferred for Rs. 1.90 lakh without putting it to some other use, the taxpayer can claim short-term capital loss of Rs. 4.20 lakh, apart from claiming deduction under section 35—*Pharmson Pharmaceuticals Ltd.* v. *CIT* [2003] 87 ITD 868 (Ahd.). To avoid double deduction, it is suggested to the Government that a suitable amendment should be made in section 35 incorporating the following—

"Where deduction is allowed in respect of a capital expenditure under section 35(1)(*iv*), no deduction shall be allowed in respect of the said expenditure under any other provision of the Act in any year".

48.10 ***Expenditure on acquisition of patent rights, copyrights, know-how [Secs. 35A and 35AB]*** - Deduction under sections 35A and 35AB is not available in respect of expenditure incurred after March 31, 1998.

48.11 ***Expenditure for obtaining right to use spectrum for telecommunication services [Sec. 35ABA, applicable from the assessment year 2017-18]*** - Section 35ABA provides tax treatment of spectrum fees on the following lines—

1. Any capital expenditure incurred and actually paid by an assessee on the acquisition of any right to use spectrum for telecommunication services by paying spectrum fee will be allowed as a deduction in equal instalments over the period for which the right to use spectrum remains in force. Deduction will be available starting from the year in which actual payment is made (or the year of commencement of business, whichever is later) and ending with the year when spectrum comes to an end, irrespective of the previous year in which the liability for the expenditure was incurred according to the method of accounting regularly employed by the assessee or payable in such manner as may be prescribed.

2. Where the spectrum is transferred and proceeds of the transfer are less than the expenditure remaining unallowed, a deduction equal to the expenditure remaining unallowed as reduced by the proceeds of transfer, shall be allowed in the previous year in which the spectrum has been transferred.

3. If the spectrum is transferred and proceeds of the transfer exceed the amount of expenditure remaining unallowed, the excess amount shall be chargeable to tax as profits and gains of business in the previous year in which the spectrum has been transferred.

4. Unallowed expenses in a case where a part of the spectrum is transferred would be amortised.

5. Where any deduction has been claimed and granted to the assessee in accordance with the above provisions and, subsequently, there is failure to comply with any of the provisions of this section, then the deduction shall be deemed to have been wrongly allowed. In such a case, the Assessing Officer can re-compute the total income of the assessee for the previous year (in which deduction was claimed) and make the necessary rectification. Such rectification can be done within 4 years from the end of the previous year in which the failure takes place.

6. Under the scheme of amalgamation, if the amalgamating company sells or transfer the spectrum to an amalgamated company, being an Indian company, then the provisions of this section will apply to amalgamated company as they would have applied to amalgamating company if later has not transferred the spectrum. Similar rules will be applicable in the case of demerger.

48.12 ***Amortisation of telecom licence fees [Sec. 35ABB]*** - Section 35ABB was inserted with effect from the assessment year 1996-97.

48.12-1 *CONDITIONS* - Deduction under section 35ABB is available if the following conditions are satisfied—

1. The expenditure is capital in nature[8].

2. It is incurred for acquiring any right to operate telecommunication services.

3. The expenditure may be incurred either before the commencement of business or at any time thereafter.

4. The payment for which has actually been made to obtain licence.

If all the above conditions are satisfied, then one can claim deduction under section 35ABB. If, however, these conditions are not satisfied, then deduction under section 35ABB is not available [one may claim deduction under section 37(1)].

48.12-2 *AMOUNT OF DEDUCTION* - The payment will be allowed as deduction in equal instalments over the period starting from the year in which such payment has been made (if payment is made before the commencement of business, deduction is available from the year in which business is commenced) and ending in the year in which the licence comes to an end. It may be noted that the deduction starts from the year in which actual payment of expenditure is made irrespective of the previous year in which the liability for the expenditure is incurred according to the method of accounting regularly employed by the assessee.

48.12-3 *PROFIT OR LOSS ON SALE OF TELECOM LICENCE* - Any profit or loss on sale of telecom licence is taken into consideration while computing business income. The relevant rules are given below. In the table given below, WDV is the written down value (*i.e.*, the expenditure incurred remaining unallowed) on the first day of the previous year in which telecom licence is transferred—

Different situations	*Tax treatment*
1. Entire telecom licence is transferred	
1.1 When sale consideration is less than WDV	WDV *minus* sale consideration is allowed as deduction under section 35ABB in the year of sale.
1.2 When sale consideration is more than WDV	The excess of sale consideration over WDV is taxable as business income in the year of sale (subject to rules given in Notes 1, 2 and 3 below).
2. When a part of telecom licence is transferred	
2.1 When sale consideration is less than WDV	WDV *minus* sale consideration will be allowed as deduction over the unexpired period.
2.2 When sale consideration is more than WDV	Same tax treatment as is given in 1.2 (*supra*)

Notes

1. In situations 1.2 and 2.2, the amount taxable as business income cannot exceed deduction allowed under section 35ABB in the earlier years.

2. The aforesaid amount is taxable whether (or not) business is in existence.

3. In respect of the same expenditure no further deduction will be allowed under section 35ABB.

48.12-4 *CONSEQUENCES IN CASE OF AMALGAMATION OR DEMERGER* - Where, under the scheme of amalgamation, a telecom licence is transferred by the amalgamating company to the amalgamated company (being an Indian company), then deduction will not be available under section 35ABB to the amalgamating company. However, the provisions of section 35ABB continue to apply to the amalgamated company as these would have applied to the amalgamating company if the latter had not transferred the licence.

• A similar rule is applicable from the assessment year 2000-01 in the case of demerger. For this purpose, sub-section (7) provides that the aforesaid provisions relating to transfer of licence shall not be applicable in the case of demerged company and the provisions of the section allowing deduction of expenditure incurred for obtaining the licence shall be applicable to the resulting company as it would have applied to demerged company.

8. Interest payable on overdue payment of licence fee cannot be said to be capital expenditure and it is qualified for deduction under section 37(1) and not under section 35ABB—*Fascel Ltd.* v. *CIT* [2009] 34 SOT 8 (Delhi). Royalty payable by an assessee-telecommunication-company to the Wireless Planning Commission (being different from license fee paid to operate telecommunication services) in terms of license agreement, is not covered by section 35ABB and, hence, allowable as deduction under section 37(1)—*CIT* v. *Fascel Ltd.* (*supra*).

48.12-5 *DEPRECIATION UNDER SECTION 32 NOT AVAILABLE* - Where a deduction for any previous year is claimed and allowed under section 35ABB, then no deduction shall be allowed under section 32 for the same previous year or any subsequent previous year in respect of the same expenditure.

48.12-E1 X Ltd., a company providing telecommunication service, obtains a telecom licence on April 20, 2018 for a period of 10 years which ends on March 31, 2028 (licence fee being Rs.18 lakh). Find out the amount of deduction under section 35ABB if—

a. the entire amount is paid on May 6, 2018; or

b. the entire amount is paid on April 1, 2019;

c. the entire amount is paid in three equal instalments on April 30, 2018, April 30, 2019 and April 30, 2020.

●

Situation (a) - The payment of Rs. 18 lakh is deductible in 10 instalments over a period of 10 years during the previous years 2018-19 to 2027-28 (the amount deductible each year being Rs. 1.8 lakh).

Situation (b) - The payment is deductible in 9 years starting from the year of payment, *i.e.*, the previous year 2019-20 and ending with the previous year 2027-28 (the amount deductible each year being Rs. 2 lakh).

Situation (c) - The entire payment is made in three instalments. Deduction under section 35ABB is available as under :—

	First instalment	*Second instalment*	*Third instalment*	*Total*
Date of payment	April 30, 2018	April 30, 2019	April 30, 2020	
Period during which deduction is available	10 years (2018-19 to 2027-28)	9 years (2019-20 to 2027-28)	8 years (2020-21 to 2027-28)	
Amount of payment	Rs. 6 lakh	Rs. 6 lakh	Rs. 6 lakh	
	Rs.	*Rs.*	*Rs.*	*Rs.*
Amount deductible in previous year				
2018-19	60,000	—	—	60,000
2019-20	60,000	66,667	—	1,26,667
2020-21 onwards	60,000	66,667	75,000	2,01,667

48.12-E2 X Ltd., a company which provides telecom services, acquires a telecom licence on April 5, 2018 for a period of 15 years which ends on March 31, 2033 (licence fees being Rs.15 lakh paid on May 6, 2018). The licence is transferred by X Ltd. on December 20, 2020 for *(a)* Rs. 6,92,000, *(b)* Rs.13,70,000 or *(c)* Rs.15,60,000. Compute the amount chargeable to tax.

●

	Rs.
Cost of licence which is paid on May 6, 2018	15,00,000
Less : Amount written off during the previous years 2018-19 and 2019-20	2,00,000
Written down value on April 1, 2020	13,00,000

Tax treatment when telecom licence is transferred on December 20, 2020

	Sale consideration		
	Rs. 6.92 lakh *Rs.*	*Rs. 13.70 lakh* *Rs.*	*Rs. 15.60 lakh* *Rs.*
Sale proceeds	6,92,000	13,70,000	15,60,000
Less : Written down value on April 1, 2020	13,00,000	13,00,000	13,00,000
Surplus	(-)6,08,000	70,000	2,60,000
Amount deductible during the previous year 2020-21 under section 35ABB(2)	6,08,000	—	—
Amount chargeable to tax during the previous year 2020-21 as notional business income, it cannot exceed the amount of deduction claimed in earlier years under section 35ABB	—	70,000	2,00,000
Short-term capital gains			
Sale proceeds	6,92,000	13,70,000	15,60,000
Less : Cost of acquisition	15,00,000	15,00,000	15,00,000
Short-term capital gain/loss	(-)8,08,000	(-)1,30,000	(+)60,000

Note - It can be seen from the above data that when the telecom licence is transferred for Rs. 6.92 lakh, the taxpayer can claim short-term capital loss of Rs. 8.08 lakh, apart from claiming deduction under section 35ABB. To avoid double deduction, it is suggested to the Government that a suitable amendment should be made in section 35ABB incorporating the following—

"Where a deduction is allowed in respect of a capital expenditure under section 35ABB, no deduction shall be allowed in respect of the said expenditure under any other provision of the Act in any year".

48.13 ***Expenditure on eligible projects or scheme [Sec. 35AC]*** - Deduction is available under section 35AC (up to the assessment year 2017-18)[9] for promoting social and economic welfare or uplift of the public.

48.13-1 *WHO CAN CLAIM DEDUCTION* - Any taxpayer can claim deduction under section 35AC as follows—

Assessee	*To whom the payment should be made*	*Direct expenditure on eligible project*
A company	Deduction is available if the taxpayer incurs any expenditure by way of payment of any sum to a public sector company or a local authority or to an association or institution approved by the National Committee for carrying out any eligible project or scheme	A company can also directly incur expenditure in respect of eligible project and claim the same as deduction.
A person other than a company	Same as above	Direct expenditure is not permitted

In computing profits of business or profession chargeable to tax, a deduction is allowed in respect of the expenditure incurred for an eligible project or scheme for promoting social and economic welfare or upliftment of the public as may be specified by the Central Government on the recommendations of the National Committee. Companies shall, however, be allowed the deduction also in cases where the expenditure is incurred by them directly on an eligible project or scheme.

48.13-2 *CERTIFICATE FROM THE RECIPIENT/CHARTERED ACCOUNTANT* - The claim for deduction should be supported by an audit certificate obtained from the public sector company, local authority or approved association or institution to whom the payment is made in Form No. 58A, or from the chartered accountant in cases where the claim is in respect of expenditure directly incurred by a company on an eligible project or scheme in Form No. 58B.

48.13-3 *ELIGIBLE PROJECT/SCHEME* - "Eligible project or scheme" means such project or scheme for promoting the social and economic welfare of, or the upliftment of, the public as the Central Government may, by notification in the Official Gazette, specify in this behalf on the recommendations of the National Committee.

48.14 ***Deduction in respect of expenditure on specified business [Sec. 35AD]*** - Section 35AD was inserted (with effect from the assessment year 2010-11) to provide for investment-linked tax incentive.

48.14-1 *CONDITIONS* - The following conditions should be satisfied to avail of the benefit of deduction under section 35AD—

• *Condition 1 - Specified business* - Deduction under section 35AD is available only in the case of a "specified business" given below—

No.	*Specified business*	*Who should own the business*	*Approval (if any)*	*Date of commencement of business*
1.	Setting up and operating a cold chain facility [*see* Note 1][10]	Any person	Not required	On or after April 1, 2009
2.	Setting up and operating a warehousing facility for storage of agricultural produce[10]	Any person	Not required	On or after April 1, 2009
3.	Laying and operating a cross-country natural gas or crude or petroleum oil pipeline network for distribution, including storage facilities being an integral part of such network	An Indian company or a consortium of Indian companies or an authority/ Board/corporation established under any Central or State Act	Should be approved by Petroleum and Natural Gas Regulatory Board and notified by the Central Government [*see* Note 2]	• On or after April 1, 2007, in the case of laying and operating a cross-country natural gas pipeline network for distribution or storage. • In other cases, on or after April 1, 2009.
4.	Building and operating anywhere in India a hotel of 2 star or above category (applicable from the assessment year 2011-12, *see* also Note 3)	Any person	No approval required; however, hotel should be classified by the Central Government as 2 star hotel or above category	On or after April 1, 2010
5.	Building and operating, anywhere in India, any hospital with at least 100 beds for patients (applicable from the assessment year 2011-12)[10]	Any person	No approval required	On or after April 1, 2010

9. No deduction under section 35AC will be available from the assessment year 2018-19 onwards. In view of this amendment, any request received after December 31, 2016 for the grant/modification/extension of approval beyond March 31, 2017 under section 35AC shall not be considered/entertained by the National Committee – Press release, dated August 19, 2016.

10. If the specified business is of the nature referred to in Point Nos. *1, 2, 5, 7, 8* (*supra*) and has commenced its operation on or after April 1, 2012, it is eligible for weighted deduction at the rate of 150 per cent of the qualifying expenditure. However, weighted deduction is not available from the assessment year 2018-19 onwards.

No.	Specified business	Who should own the business	Approval (if any)	Date of commencement of business
6.	Developing and building a housing project (applicable from the assessment year 2011-12)	Any person	Developing and building housing project should be under a scheme for slum re-development or rehabilitation framed by the Central Government/State Government and notified by the Board in accordance with prescribed guidelines	On or after April 1, 2010
7.	Developing and building a housing project (applicable from the assessment year 2012-13)[10]	Any person	Developing and building the housing project should be under a scheme for affordable housing framed by the Central Government or a State Government and notified by the Board [*see* Rule 11-OA[$]]	On or after April 1, 2011
8.	Production of fertilizer in India (applicable from the assessment year 2012-13)[10]	Any person	Not required	On or after April 1, 2011
9.	Setting up and operating an inland container depot or a container freight station	Any person	As notified or approved under the Customs Act	On or after April 1, 2012
10.	Bee-keeping and production of honey and beeswax	Any person	No approval	On or after April 1, 2012
11.	Setting up and operating a warehousing facility for storage of sugar	Any person	No approval	On or after April 1, 2012
12.	Laying and operating a slurry pipeline for the transportation of iron ore	Any person	No approval	On or after April 1, 2014
13.	Setting up and operating a semiconductor wafer fabrication manufacturing unit	Any person	As notified by the Board in accordance with such guidelines as may be prescribed [*see* rule 11-OB[$]]	On or after April 1, 2014
14.	Developing or maintaining and operating or developing, maintaining and operating a new infrastructure facility (applicable from the assessment year 2018-19)	An Indian company or a consortium of Indian companies or an authority/board/corporation/any other body established or constituted under any Central or State Act	The eligible entity has entered into an agreement with Central/State Government/local authority/any other statutory body for developing, maintaining, etc., of new infrastructure facility	On or after April 1, 2017

Note 1 - "Cold chain facility" means a chain of facilities for storage or transportation of agricultural and forest produce, meat and meat products, poultry, marine and dairy products, products of horticulture, floriculture and apiculture and processed food items under scientifically controlled conditions including refrigeration and other facilities necessary for the preservation of such produce. In this definition, the words 'storage' and 'transportation' are separated by the conjunction 'or'. 'Storage' and 'transportation' are complementary to each other and the absence of one will not make the chain complete. However, separation is specified by use of the word 'or'. Consequently, an assessee is eligible for deduction under section 35AD even if it has operated only cold storage plant and does not operate transportation facility—*ITO* v. *Ambika Sheet Grah (P.) Ltd.* [2009] 119 ITD 235 (Agra).

Note 2 - This business should make not less than one-third (for a natural gas pipeline network) or one-fourth (for petroleum product pipeline network) of its total pipeline capacity available for use on common carrier basis by any person other than the assessee or an associated person. Associated person is a person who participates in the management of the assessee; holds at least 26 per cent voting power in the assessee; appoints more than half of the board of directors or who guarantees not less than 10 per cent of the total borrowing of the assessee.

---

10. If the specified business is of the nature referred to in Point Nos. *1, 2, 5, 7, 8* (*supra*) and has commenced its operation on or after April 1, 2012, it is eligible for weighted deduction at the rate of 150 per cent of the qualifying expenditure. However, weighted deduction is not available from the assessment year 2018-19 onwards.

[$]For Rules 11-OA and 11-OB, log on to *taxmann.com/readyreckoner.aspx.*

Note 3 - Where an assessee builds a two-star (or above category) hotel and, subsequently, while continuing to own the hotel, transfers the operation thereof to another person, the assessee shall be deemed to be carrying on the specified business of building and operating hotel for the purpose of section 35AD (applicable from the assessment year 2011-12).

Note 4 - Infrastructure facility means—

a. a road including toll road, a bridge or a rail system;

b. a highway project including housing or other activities being an integral part of the highway project;

c. a water supply project, water treatment system, irrigation project, sanitation and sewerage system or solid waste management system;

d. a port, airport, inland waterway, inland port or navigational channel in the sea.

• *Condition 2 - Specified business should be new business* - The specified business should not be set up by splitting up, or the reconstruction, of a business already in existence. Moreover, it should not be set up by the transfer of old plant and machinery.

20 per cent old machinery is permitted - If the value of the transferred assets does not exceed 20 per cent of the total value of the machinery or plant used in the business, this condition is deemed to have been satisfied.

Second-hand imported machinery is treated as new - Any machinery or plant which was used outside India by any person (other than the assessee) shall not be regarded as machinery or plant previously used for any purpose, if the following conditions are fulfilled—

1. Such machinery or plant was not, at any time previous to the date of the installation by the assessee, used in India.

2. Such machinery or plant is imported into India from any country outside India.

3. No deduction on account of depreciation in respect of such machinery or plant has been allowed or is allowable under the Act in computing the total income of any person for any period prior to the date of the installation of the machinery or plant by the assessee.

• *Condition 3 - Audit of books of account* - Books of account of the assessee should be audited.

48.14-2 *AMOUNT OF DEDUCTION* - 100 per cent of capital expenditure incurred wholly and exclusively for the purpose of specified business carried on by an assessee is deductible in the previous year in which the expenditure is incurred. Specified business *1, 2, 5, 7* and *8* (as mentioned in para 48.14-1) is eligible for weighted deduction at the rate of 150 per cent of qualifying expenditure for the assessment years 2013-14 to 2017-18, if operation is commenced on or after April 1, 2012. Moreover, deduction under section 35AD is subject to the following propositions—

1. Any expenditure of capital nature shall not include any expenditure incurred on the acquisition of any land or goodwill or financial instrument. Deduction under section 35AD is not available in respect of any such expenditure. Moreover, deduction under section 35AD is not available (with effect from the assessment year 2018-19) pertaining to any expenditure in respect of which payment (or aggregate of payments) made to a person in a day [otherwise than by an account payee cheque/draft/use of electronic clearing system through a bank account (**or through prescribed electronic mode**)] exceeds Rs. 10,000.

2. Expenditure incurred prior to the commencement of operation, wholly and exclusively, for the purpose of any specified business, shall be allowed as deduction during the previous year in which the assessee commences the operation of his specified business, if the amount is capitalized in the books of account of the assessee on the date of commencement of operation.

3. If operation of the business of laying and operating a cross-country natural gas distribution network is commenced during April 1, 2007 and March 31, 2009, the capital expenditure (not being for acquiring land or goodwill or financial instrument) incurred before April 1, 2009 (to the extent not allowed as deduction under any section earlier) will be allowed as additional deduction under section 35AD for the assessment year 2010-11.

48.14-3 *CONSEQUENCES OF CLAIMING DEDUCTION UNDER SECTION 35AD* - The following consequences should be noted—

1. If deduction is claimed and allowed under section 35AD, the assessee shall not be allowed any deduction in respect of the specified business under the provisions of Chapter VIA under sections 80HH to 80RRB for the same or any other assessment year. Moreover, no deduction shall be allowed (with effect from the assessment year 2015-16) under the provisions of section 10AA in respect of a specified business when deduction is claimed under section 35AD.

2. No deduction in respect of the expenditure in respect of which deduction has been claimed shall be allowed to the assessee under any other provisions of the Income-tax Act.

3. Any sum received or receivable on account of any capital asset, in respect of which deduction has been allowed under section 35AD, being demolished, destroyed, discarded or transferred shall be treated as income of the assessee and chargeable to income-tax under the head "Profits and gains of business or profession".

4. Any loss computed in respect of the specified business shall not be set off except against profits and gains, if any, of any other specified business. To the extent the loss is unabsorbed, the same will be carried forward for set off against profits and gains from any specified business in the following assessment year and so on.

5. If the assessee owns two units one of them qualifies for deduction under section 35AD and the other one is not eligible for the same and there is inter-unit transfer of goods or services between the two units, then for the purpose of section 35AD calculation will be made as if such transactions are made at the market value.

6. Any asset in respect of which a deduction is claimed and allowed under section 35AD, shall be used only for the specified business for a period of 8 years beginning with the previous year in which such asset is acquired or constructed. If such asset is used for any purpose other than the specified business, the total amount of deduction so claimed and allowed in any previous year in respect of such asset, as reduced by the amount of depreciation allowable in accordance with the provisions of section 32 as if no deduction had been allowed under section 35AD, shall be deemed to be business income of the assessee of the previous year in which the asset is so used (applicable from the assessment year 2015-16).

48-14-E1 On April 1, 2018, X Ltd. commences the operation of a warehousing facility in Andhra Pradesh for storage of agricultural produce. The following information is available from the records of company—

Expenses incurred prior to April 1, 2018

	Rs.
Purchase of land for warehouse	50,00,000
Construction cost of warehouse	8,00,000
Purchase of know-how for warehouse	10,00,000
Salary to staff	78,000

These expenses are capitalized on March 31, 2018.

Expenses incurred during 2018-19

Construction cost of warehouse	60,00,000
Purchase of old plant and machinery (from domestic market)	2,00,000
Purchase of old plant and machinery (from Germany)	4,00,000
Purchase of new plant and machinery	9,00,000
Purchase of goodwill	3,50,000

Profit and loss account for the year 2018-19

	Rs.		*Rs.*
Depreciation of building (@ 5%)	3,40,000	Amount collected from persons using warehouse	78,00,000
Depreciation of machinery (@ 23.333%)	3,50,000		
Cost of know-how (amount written off)	10,00,000		
Other operating expenses	7,51,000		
Donation to a political party	10,000		
Net profit	53,49,000		
	78,00,000		78,00,000

Out of other operating expenses, a payment of Rs. 40,000 is made in cash. Other operating expenses are deductible under section 37. Find out the taxable income of X Ltd. for the assessment year 2019-20 on the assumption that X Ltd. has the following income from other sources – income from the business of commission agency: Rs. 20,15,000 (computed under the provisions of the Income-tax Act) and dividend from a foreign company: Rs. 50,000.

•

Amount deductible under section 35AD	*Rs.*
Expenditure incurred prior to the commencement of operation (to the extent these are capitalized)	
Purchase of land (not qualified for deduction)	*Nil*
Construction cost of warehouse	8,00,000
Purchase of know-how	10,00,000
Salary to staff	78,000

		Rs.
Expenditure incurred during the previous year		
Construction cost of warehouse		60,00,000
Purchase of machinery (Rs. 2,00,000 + Rs. 4,00,000 + Rs. 9,00,000)		15,00,000
Total		93,78,000
Amount deductible under section 35AD		93,78,000
Computation of income from warehouse		
Net profit as per profit and loss account		53,49,000
Add: Depreciation of building (not deductible as cost of building is eligible for deduction under section 35AD)		3,40,000
Add: Depreciation of machinery (not deductible as cost of machinery is qualified for deduction under section 35AD)		3,50,000
Add: Cost of know-how (not deductible as deduction is available under section 35AD)		10,00,000
Add: Amount paid in cash (operating expenses)		40,000
Add: Donation to political party		10,000
Less: Deduction under section 35AD		(-) 93,78,000
Loss from warehouse		(-) 22,89,000
Computation of income		
	Rs.	
Commission agency business	20,15,000	
Warehouse	(-) 22,89,000	
Business income (loss from operating warehouse, being a specified business under section 35AD, cannot be set off against any other income except income from a specified business)		20,15,000
Income from other sources (dividend from foreign company)		50,000
Gross total income		20,65,000
Less: Deduction under section 80GGB (donation to a political party)		10,000
Net income		20,55,000

Notes :

1. Second hand imported machinery is taken as new machinery. The business of operating warehouse is formed by using new machinery of Rs. 13,00,000 and old machinery of Rs. 2,00,000. Value of old plant and machinery does not exceed 20 per cent of the total value of plant and machinery. Other conditions of section 35AD are satisfied. X Ltd. is, therefore, eligible for deduction under section 35AD.

2. Loss from operating warehouse (by virtue of section 73A) can be set off only against profit and gains, if any, of any other business specified under section 35AD. In this case, X Ltd. does not have any other specified business. Loss will be carried forward (without any time-limit) for being set off against income from operating warehouse or any other specified business under section 35AD.

3. Minimum alternate tax provisions will be applicable. Tax liability will be 30.9% of Rs. 20,55,000 or 19.055% of book profit (*i.e.*, Rs. 53,49,000 + Rs. 20,15,000 + Rs. 50,000), whichever is more.

48.15 ***Payment to associations and institutions for carrying out rural development programmes [Sec. 35CCA]*** - Section 35CCA provides deduction of sums paid by an assessee to :

a. any association or institution to be used for carrying out any programme of rural development [sec. 35CCA(1)(*a*), for conditions *see* para 48.15-1];

b. an association or institution which has as its object the training of persons for implementation of a rural development programme [sec. 35CCA(1)(*b*), for conditions *see* para 48.15-2];

c. the National Fund for Rural Development set up by the Government [sec. 35CCA(1)(*c*), *see* para 48.15-3]; and

d. the National Urban Poverty Eradication Fund.

48.15-1 *CONDITIONS FOR AVAILING DEDUCTION UNDER SECTION 35CCA(1)(a)* - The deduction under section 35CCA(1)(*a*) will not be allowed unless :

a. the association or institution has as its object the undertaking of programmes of rural development;

b. the association or institution is for the time being approved by the prescribed authority;

c. the programme of rural development, for which sums are paid, has been approved by the prescribed authority before March 1, 1983;

d. where such payment is made after February 28, 1983, such programme involves work by way of construction of any building or other structure (whether for use as a dispensary, school, training or welfare centre, workshop or for any other purpose) or the laying of any road or the construction or boring of a well/tube-well or the installation of any plant and machinery and such work commenced before March 1, 1983.

48.15-2 *CONDITIONS FOR AVAILING DEDUCTION UNDER SECTION 35CCA(1)(b)* - The deduction in respect of expenditure by way of payment of any sum to any association or institution which has as its objective the training of persons for implementing programmes of rural development will not be allowed unless the taxpayer furnishes a certificate from such association or institution to the effect that :

a. the prescribed authority had approved the association or institution before March 1, 1983; and

b. the training of persons for implementing any programme of rural development had been started by the association or institution before March 1, 1983.

The certificates required to be furnished will not be issued by any institution or association unless it has obtained from the prescribed authority an authorisation in writing to issue certificates of such nature.

48.15-3 *NATIONAL FUNDS FOR RURAL DEVELOPMENT - GUIDELINES* - Taxpayers interested in joining the national effort of eradicating poverty, increasing agricultural production, creating employment and bringing about improvement in rural life can make contributions in the name of the National Fund for Rural Development. The contributions can be sent to the Secretary, National Fund for Rural Development, Prime Minister's Office, South Block, New Delhi. The donors to the said Fund can also indicate their preference for the area or the locality and the rural development programme for which the donation is to be used as also the voluntary agency through which the programme may be implemented.

48.15A ***Expenditure on agricultural extension project [Sec. 35CCC, applicable from the assessment year 2013-14]*** - An assessee who incurs any expenditure on a notified agricultural extension project is qualified for weighted deduction of 150 per cent of such expenditure for the assessment years 2013-14 to 2020-21 [from the assessment year 2021-22, an assessee can claim 100 per cent of expenditure as deduction (but not weighted deduction)]. If a deduction is allowed under this section, no deduction will be available for the same expenditure under any other provision of the Act in the same year or in a subsequent year.

48.15B ***Expenditure on skill development project [Sec. 35CCD, applicable from the assessment year 2013-14]*** - A company which incurs any expenditure on any notified skill development project is qualified for weighted deduction of 150 per cent of such expenditure for the assessment year 2013-14 to 2020-21 [from the assessment year 2021-22, an assessee can claim 100 per cent of expenditure as deduction (but not weighted deduction)]. The following points should be noted :

- Cost of any land or building is not eligible for any deduction under section 35CCD. However, cost of building is eligible for depreciation under section 32.
- If a deduction is allowed under this section, no deduction will be available for the same expenditure under any other provision of the Act in the same year or in a subsequent year.

48.16 ***Amortisation of preliminary expenses [Sec. 35D]*** - Certain preliminary expenses [sec. 35D(2)] incurred by an Indian company or a resident non-corporate assessee before the commencement of business qualify for amortisation. The benefit of amortisation is also available if preliminary expenses are incurred after the commencement of business in connection with extension of an industrial undertaking (or any undertaking with effect from the assessment year 2009-10) or setting up a new industrial unit (or any unit with effect from the assessment year 2009-10). The aggregate amount of the expenditure cannot exceed 5[11] per cent of the cost of the project [as defined in clause (*a*) of the *Explanation* to section 35D(3)]. While the ceiling limit of 5[11] per cent of the cost of the project applies to all assessees, an Indian company is given an option to elect an alternative limit of 5[11] per cent of capital employed [as defined in clause (*b*) of the *Explanation* to section 35D(3)]. One-fifth[12] of the qualifying expenditure is allowable as deduction in each of the five[13] successive years beginning with the year in which the business commences or, as the case may

---

11. 2.5 per cent if expenditure is incurred up to March 31, 1998.

12. One-tenth if expenditure is incurred up to March 31, 1998.

13. 10 if expenditure is incurred up to March 31, 1998.

be, the previous year in which extension of the industrial undertaking is completed or the new industrial unit commences production or operation.

48.16-1 *AUDIT REPORT* - In the case of a non-corporate assessee, the amortisation is admissible, subject to the condition that the accounts of assessee for the relevant year in which the qualifying expenditure is incurred, have been audited by a chartered accountant. In such cases, the assessee is required to furnish online, along with the return of income for the first year, in which the deduction is claimed, the audit report in Form No. 3AE.

48.16-2 *CONSEQUENCES IN THE CASE OF AMALGAMATION OR DEMERGER* - The benefit of amortisation of preliminary expenses under section 35D are ordinarily available only to the assessee who incurred the expenditure. The benefit will not, however, be lost in a case where the undertaking of an Indian company which is entitled to the amortisation is transferred to another Indian company in a scheme of amalgamation within the 5-year[13] period of amortisation. In that event, the deduction in respect of previous year in which the amalgamation takes place and the following previous year within the 5-year[13] period, will be allowed to the amalgamated company and not to the amalgamating company.

• A similar provision has been made with effect from the assessment year 2000-01 in the case of demerger where the resulting company will be able to claim amortisation of preliminary expenses as if demerger had not taken place.

48.16-3 *EXPENSES ON ISSUE OF SHARES/DEBENTURES* - The table given below highlights whether expenditure for raising capital/loan is deductible under section 35D or 37(1)—

Different expenses	*Incurred by a new concern before commencement of business*	*Incurred by an existing concern after commencement of business in connection with extension of an undertaking or setting up a new unit*
Expenditure on issue of bonus shares	Sec. 35D	Sec. 37(1)[14]
Expenditure on issue of shares (not being bonus shares)	Sec. 35D	Sec. 35D[15]
Expenditure on issue of debentures	Sec. 35D	Sec. 37(1)

48.17 *Amortisation of expenditure in case of amalgamation/demerger [Sec. 35DD]* - If an Indian company incurs any expenditure for the purpose of amalgamation or demerger, it is allowed as deduction in five successive years in five equal instalments. The first instalment is deductible in the previous year in which amalgamation or demerger takes place.

A similar provision is applicable in the case of amalgamation or demerger of co-operative banks.

48.18 *Amortisation of expenditure under voluntary retirement scheme [Sec. 35DDA]* - Expenditure by way of payment of any sum to an employee in connection with his voluntary retirement (under any scheme of voluntary retirement), is deductible in 5 successive years in 5 equal instalments. The first instalment is deductible in the year in which such amount is actually paid (deduction is available on payment basis and not on accrual basis). Each part of the payment in connection with voluntary retirement is deductible in 5 years in 5 equal instalments.

• The following points should be noted—

1. The above rule is applicable even if the scheme of voluntary retirement has not been framed in accordance with guidelines prescribed under section 10(*10C*).

---

13. 10 if expenditure is incurred up to March 31, 1998.

14. In *CIT* v. *General Insurance Corpn.* [2006] 156 Taxman 96, the Supreme Court has said that the issue of bonus shares by capitalization of reserves is merely a reallocation of company's funds. There is no inflow of fresh funds or increase in the capital employed, which remains the same. If that be so, then it cannot be held that the company has acquired a benefit or advantage of enduring nature. The total funds available with the company will remain the same and the issue of bonus shares will not result in any change in the capital structure of the company. Issue of bonus shares does not result in the expansion of capital base of the company. Thus, the expenditure on issuance of bonus shares is revenue expenditure.

15. Applicable only if shares are issued in connection with extension of the existing unit or in connection with setting up a new unit.

2. Where voluntary retirement payment is made by predecessor and before completion of 5 years it is succeeded in a scheme of business reorganization (like amalgamation/merger of Indian companies or co-operative banks, conversion of firm/proprietary concern/private or unlisted company into company/LLP), the deduction for the remaining years will be available to the successor from the year in which the conversion takes place.

48.19 ***Amortisation of expenditure on prospecting, etc., for development of certain minerals [Sec. 35E read with the Seventh Schedule]*** - The expenses incurred after March 31, 1970 on any operation relating to prospecting for and on development of the specified minerals (Seventh Schedule), qualify for amortisation in the hands of Indian companies and non-corporate resident assessees. The expenses qualified for amortisation are those incurred under the specified heads [excluding certain expenses specified in sub-section (3)] during the five-year period ending with the year of commercial production. The amortisation of the qualifying expenditure is allowed in equal instalments over a period of ten years against the profits from the commercial exploitation of any mine of the specified minerals.

48.19-1 *AUDIT REPORT* - The amortisation is subject to the requirement that the accounts of the non-corporate assessees are audited by a chartered accountant and the assessee online furnishes, along with his return of income for the first year in which amortisation is claimed, the audit report in Form No. 3AE.

48.19-2 *CONSEQUENCES IN THE CASE OF AMALGAMATION OR DEMERGER* - The amortisation under section 35E is available only to the assessee who incurs the expenditure. However, in the case of an Indian company, the benefit of amortisation is preserved where the undertaking of the company is transferred to another Indian company under a scheme of amalgamation within the 10-year period. In such an event, the amortisation of outstanding instalments in respect of the previous year in which the amalgamation takes place and the remaining previous years of the 10-year period will be allowed to the amalgamated company and not the amalgamating company.

• Sub-section (7A) was inserted, with effect from the assessment year 2000-01, to provide for similar provisions to cases of demerger where such deduction can be availed of by the resulting company as if the demerger had not taken place.

48.20 ***Insurance premium [Sec. 36(1)(i)]*** - The amount of any premium paid in respect of insurance against risk of damage, or destruction of stocks or stores, used for the purpose of business or profession, is allowable as deduction.

48.21 ***Insurance premium paid by a federal milk co-operative society [Sec. 36(1)(ia)]*** - Insurance premium paid by a federal milk co-operative society on the lives of cattle, owned by the members of a primary milk co-operative society affiliated to it, is allowed as deduction.

48.22 ***Insurance premium on health of employees [Sec. 36(1)(ib)]*** - Under section 36(1)(*ib*) a deduction can be claimed by a taxpayer if the following conditions are satisfied :

• The taxpayer pays premium to keep in force an insurance on the health of employees.

• The premium is paid by cheque. However, from the previous year 2007-08, such premium can be paid by any mode other than cash.

• Premium is paid under a scheme framed in this behalf by the General Insurance Corporation of India and approved by the Central Government [or with effect from the assessment year 2007-08, under a scheme approved by IRDA].

48.23 ***Bonus or commission to employees [Sec. 36(1)(ii)]*** - Bonus or commission to an employee is allowable as deduction provided it is not payable to him as profit or dividend if it had not been payable as bonus or commission. The deduction is available in the year of payment [*see* also para 49.7].

48.24 ***Interest on borrowed capital [Sec. 36(1)(iii)]*** - Interest paid on capital borrowed for the purposes of business or profession is allowable as deduction. If capital is borrowed for acquiring a capital asset, then interest liability pertaining to the period till the asset is put to use cannot be allowed as deduction under section 36(1)(*iii*) from the assessment year 2004-05.

48.25 ***Discount on zero coupon bonds*** - Discount on zero coupon bond is deductible on *pro rata* basis.

48.25-1 *MEANING OF ZERO COUPON BOND* - Clause (*48*) was inserted in section 2 with effect from the assessment year 2006-07. According to this clause, zero coupon bond must satisfy the following three conditions—

1. It is a bond issued by any infrastructure capital company or infrastructure capital fund or public sector company or scheduled bank on or after June 1, 2005.

2. In respect of such bond, no payment/benefit is received (or receivable) before maturity/redemption from infrastructure capital company or infrastructure capital fund or public sector company.

3. Such bond is specified by the Central Government by notification in the Official Gazette.

48.25-1a GUIDELINES FOR NOTIFICATION - Zero coupon bonds are notified by the Central Government subject to the following guidelines—

- Application should be made in Form No. 5B.
- The application should be made at least 3 months before the date of issue of zero coupon bonds. However, such application cannot be made in respect of such bonds, which are to be issued after two financial years immediately following the financial year in which such application is made. For instance, if the proposed date of issue of bonds is June 14, 2019, the application can be made on or after April 1, 2017 but on or before March 13, 2019.
- The application should be accompanied by a copy of certificate of incorporation/a copy of registered trust deed/a copy of relevant Act under which the applicant has been incorporated.
- The life of bond should not be less than 10 years and more than 20 years.
- The applicant should have an investment grade rating from at least two registered credit rating agencies.
- The applicant should have made necessary arrangements for listing the zero coupon bonds.
- An undertaking should be furnished by the applicant to invest the money realized on issue of zero coupon bonds in the following manner—

If the applicant is infrastructure capital company/fund	*If the applicant is public sector company*
25 per cent or more of the money realized shall be invested before the end of the next financial year (*i.e.*, the financial year immediately following the financial year in which the bonds are issued).	15 per cent or more of the money realized shall be invested before the end of the next financial year (*i.e.*, the financial year immediately following the financial year in which the bonds are issued).
The balance should be utilized within a period of 4 financial years immediately following the financial year in which the bonds are issued.	The balance should be utilized within a period of 6 financial years immediately following the financial year in which the bonds are issued.

- A certificate from a chartered accountant shall be submitted within 2 months from the end of each financial year specifying the amount invested in each financial year.

48.25-2 *TAX TREATMENT IN THE HANDS OF COMPANY ISSUING SUCH BONDS* - The following points should be noted—

1. Discount (being the difference between amount received and the amount payable on redemption/maturity by the issuing company) is allowed as deduction on *pro rata* basis. The *pro rata* deduction is available under section 36(1)(*iiia*) having regard to the period of life of such bond as may be prescribed. "Period of life of the bond" means the period commencing from the date of issue of the bond and ending on the date of the maturity or redemption of such bond.

2. Tax is not deductible at source under section 194A by the payer company.

48.25-3 *TAX TREATMENT IN THE HANDS OF INVESTOR* - The following points should be noted—

1. Maturity/redemption of zero coupon bonds amounts to "transfer" under section 2(*47*)(*iva*).

2. If period of holding is more than 12 months, such bonds is long-term capital asset under section 2(*42A*).

3. Long-term capital gains is taxable at the rate of 10 per cent [+ SC + HEC] without indexation under section 112.

48.25-E1 Zero coupon bonds are issued by X Ltd. (infrastructure capital company) on October 4, 2018 (issue price : Rs. 85, face value as well as amount payable at the time of redemption : Rs. 100, redemption date : July 10, 2029, number of bonds subscribed by public : 1,00,000). These bonds are notified by the Government as zero coupon bonds for the purpose of section 2(*48*).

•

Pro rata *deduction available to X Ltd.*—
Amount of discount offered by X Ltd. [(Rs. 100 – Rs. 85) × 1,00,000] : Rs. 15,00,000 (*a*)
Date of issue : October 4, 2018
Date of issue (rounded off) : October 1, 2018 (if fraction is 15 days or more, it is taken as one month)
Date of redemption : July 10, 2029
Date of redemption (rounded off) : June 30, 2029 (if fraction is less than 15 days, it shall be ignored)
Period of life of the bond (June 30, 2029 *minus* October 1, 2018) : 129 months (*b*)
Pro rata deduction for 1 month : Rs. 11,628 [(*a*) ÷ (*b*)] (*c*)
Amount deductible for the previous year 2018-19 : Rs. 69,767 [(*c*) × 6]
Amount deductible for the previous years 2019-20 to 2028-29 : Rs. 1,39,535 [(*c*) × 12] per year
Amount deductible for the previous year 2029-30 : Rs. 34,883 [(*c*) × 3]

48.26 ***Employer's contribution to recognised provident fund and approved superannuation fund [Sec. 36(1)(iv)]*** - Employer's contribution towards a recognised provident fund or an approved superannuation fund is allowable as deduction subject to the limits laid down for the purpose of recognising the provident fund or approving superannuation fund [Fourth Schedule and rules 87 and 88]. However, such contribution is allowed as deduction to the extent it is actually paid [sec. 43B—*see* para 49.7].

48.26A ***Employer's contribution to National Pension System (NPS) [Sec. 36(1)(*iva*), applicable from the assessment year 2012-13]*** - Employer's contribution towards NPS (as referred to in section 80CCD) on account of an employee is deductible from the assessment year 2012-13[16]. However, deduction is limited to 10 per cent of salary of the employee [for meaning of salary, *see* para 13.1-1].

48.27 ***Contribution towards approved gratuity fund [Sec. 36(1)(v)]*** - Employer's contribution towards an approved gratuity fund created by him exclusively for the benefit of his employees under an irrevocable trust is allowable as deduction. However, by virtue of section 43B, such contribution is allowed as deduction subject to a few conditions [*see* para 49.7].

48.28 ***Employees' contribution to staff welfare schemes [Sec. 36(1)(va)]*** - Deductions in respect of any sum received by the taxpayer as contribution from his employees towards any welfare fund of such employees is allowed as deduction only if such sum is credited by the taxpayer to the employee's account in the relevant fund on or before the due date. For the purposes of this section, "due date" means the date by which the assessee is required as an employer to credit such contribution to the employee's account in the relevant fund under the provisions of any law or term of contract of service or otherwise.

• *Applicability of section 43B in case of employees' contribution towards provident fund* - Section 43B is not applicable in the case of employees' contribution towards staff welfare schemes. Such contribution is governed by section 36(1)(*va*). In other words, if employees' contribution towards provident fund or any other staff welfare scheme is credited by the employer after due date and grace period (under provident fund regulations) it is not deductible under section 36(1)(*va*), even it is credited/paid on or before due date of submission of return of income under section 139(1) – *CIT* v. *South India Corporation Ltd.* [2015] 232 Taxman 241 (Ker.), *CIT* v. *Merchem Ltd.* [2015] 61 taxmann.com 119 (Ker.), *Unifac Management Services (India) (P.) Ltd.* v. *CIT* [2019] 260 Taxman 60 (Mad.). However, many contrary rulings (favourable to taxpayers) are available—*see CIT* v. *Kichha Sugar Co. Ltd.* [2013] 216 Taxman 90 (Uttarakhand), *CIT* v. *Hemla Embroidery Mills (P.) Ltd.* [2013] 217 Taxman 207 (Punj. & Har.), *Spectrum Consultants India (P.) Ltd.* v. *CIT* [2013] 215 Taxman 597 (Kar.), *CIT* v. *AIMIL Ltd.* [2010] 188 Taxman 265 (Delhi), *CIT* v. *Ozer Merchant Co-operative Bank Ltd.* [2014] 62 SOT 14 (Pune), *CIT* v. *State Bank of Bikaner & Jaipur* [2014] 225 Taxman 6 (Raj.), *CIT* v. *Jaipur Vidyut Vitran Nigam Ltd.* [2015] 228 Taxman 214 (Raj.), *CIT* v. *Magus Customers Dialog (P.) Ltd.* [2015] 231 Taxman 379 (Kar.), *CIT* v. *Rajasthan State Beverages Corpn. Ltd.* [2017] 84 taxmann.com 173 (Raj.)[17].

48.29 ***Write off allowance for animals [Sec. 36(1)(vi)]*** - In respect of animals which are used for the purpose of business or profession (not as stock-in-trade) and have died or become permanently useless, the difference between the actual cost of the animals to the assessee and the amount realised (if any) in respect of carcasses or sale of animals is allowable as deduction.

48.30 ***Bad debts [Sec. 36(1)(vii)]*** - Amount of any debt or part thereof is allowable as deduction subject to the following conditions :

a. the debt has been taken into account in computing the income of the assessee of that previous year or of an earlier previous year, or represents money lent in the ordinary course of business of banking or money-lending which is carried on by the assessee; and

---

16. Prior to the assessment year 2012-13, it was deductible under section 37(1) without any upper limit.

17. SLP against the judgment of the Rajasthan High Court has been rejected—*CIT* v. *Rajasthan State Beverages Corporation Ltd.* [2017] 250 Taxman 16 (SC).

b. it has been written off[18] as irrecoverable in the accounts of the assessee for that previous year (transfer to provision for bad and doubtful debts account is not taken as bad debts written off).

In a case where the debt ultimately recovered is less than the difference between the debt and amount so deducted, such deficiency is deductible in the previous year in which ultimate recovery is made. Conversely, where the debt ultimately recovered is more than the difference between the debt and amount so deducted, such excess amount is chargeable to tax in the assessment year relevant to the previous year of recovery [sec. 41(4)].

• *When debts become irrecoverable but not recorded in books of account* - If a debt becomes irrecoverable on the basis of Income Computation and Disclosure Standards [notified under section 145(2)] without recording the same in the accounts, it shall be allowed as deduction in the previous year in which such debt becomes irrecoverable and it shall be deemed that such debt has been written off as irrecoverable in the accounts for the purposes of section 36(1)(*iii*) (applicable from the assessment year 2016-17).

• *Deduction in the case of a bank which is eligible for deduction under section 36(1)*(viia) - Deduction relating to a bad debt (or part thereof) in the case of a bank to which section 36(1)(*viia*) applies is limited to the amount by which such debt exceeds the credit balance in the provision for bad and doubtful debts account made under that section [*see* para 48.30]. The Supreme Court in the case of *Catholic Syrian Bank Ltd.* v. *CIT* [2012] 206 Taxman 182, explained the mode of computation of deduction pertaining to bad debts when one is also entitled for deduction for provision for bad and doubtful debts under section 36(1)(*viia*). However, the law has been amended to supersede the Supreme Court's ruling with effect from the assessment year 2014-15. The scope of Supreme Court's ruling and subsequent amendment has been explained in Examples 0.23-E1 to 0.23-E4 in Taxmann's *Direct Taxes Ready Reckoner, 36th edition.*

48.31 ***Provision for bad and doubtful debts relating to rural branches of commercial banks [Sec. 36(1)(viia)]*** - The amount of deduction is given below :

	Amount deductible in respect of provision for bad and doubtful debts				
	Scheduled bank [other than a foreign bank] and a non-scheduled bank[19] *[see Note 1]*		*Public financial institution, State financial corporation, State Industrial investment corporation [see Note 2]*	*Foreign bank*	*Non-banking financial company*
	Up to the assessment year 2002-03	*From the assessment year 2003-04*			*From the assessment year 2017-18*
• Total income (computed before this deduction and amount deductible under sections 80C to 80U)	5 per cent of such income	7.5 per cent of such income (8.5 per cent with effect from the assessment year 2018-19)	5 per cent of such income	5 per cent of such income	5 per cent of such income
• Aggregate average advances made by rural branches	10 per cent of such advances	10 per cent of such advances	—	—	—

Notes—

1. In order to strengthen the financial position of the banks, an option has been given to a scheduled bank/unscheduled bank (but other than foreign banks) for a period of five years from the assessment year 2000-01 to the assessment year 2004-05. Under the option, such banks can claim a deduction for any provision made by it in respect of doubtful or loss assets in accordance with the guidelines issued by the Reserve Bank of India for an amount not exceeding 5 per cent (for the assessment years 2000-01 to 2002-03) or 10 per cent (for the assessment years 2003-04 and 2004-05) of the amount of such loss assets or doubtful assets as shown in the books of account of the bank on the last day of the previous year.

18. After April 1, 1989, it is not necessary for an assessee to establish that debt, in fact, has become irrecoverable; it is enough if bad debt is written off as irrecoverable in accounts of assessee — *T.R.F. Ltd.* v. *CIT* [2010] 190 Taxman 391 (SC).

19. From the assessment year 2007-08 onwards, this benefit will also be available in the case of a co-operative bank but other than a primary agricultural credit society or a primary co-operative agricultural and rural development bank.

2. An option has been given to Public Financial Institution, State Financial Corporation or State Industrial Investment Corporation for a period of 2 years (*i.e.*, the assessment years 2003-04 and 2004-05) to claim a deduction for any provision made by it in respect of doubtful or loss assets in accordance with the guidelines issued by the Reserve Bank of India for an amount not exceeding 10 per cent of the amount of such loss assets or doubtful assets as shown in the books of account of the bank on the last day of the previous year.

3. A scheduled bank (other than a foreign bank) or a non-scheduled bank shall, at its option, be allowed a further deduction (with effect from the assessment year 2004-05) in excess of the limits specified in the foregoing provisions, for an amount not exceeding the income derived from redemption of securities in accordance with a scheme framed by the Central Government. No deduction shall, however, be allowed unless such income has been disclosed in the return of income under the head "Profits and gains of business or profession".

4. "Non-banking financial company" means -

a. a financial institution which is a company;

b. a non-banking institution which is a company and which has as its principal business the receiving of deposits, under any scheme or arrangement or in any other manner, or lending in any manner;

c. such other non-banking institution or class of such institutions, as RBI may, with the previous approval of the Central Government and by notification in the Official Gazette, specify.

48.32 *Transfer to special reserve [Sec. 36(1)(viii)]* - The scheme of section 36(1)(*viii*) is given below—

48.32-1 *WHO CAN CLAIM DEDUCTION* - The following are eligible for deduction under the section :—

Who can claim deduction in respect of amount transferred to the special reserve account	*What is eligible business for the purpose of calculating deduction*
ICICI, IFCI, IDBI, LIC, UTI, Infrastructure Development Finance Company Limited, or a public financial institution notified by the Central Government under section 4A of the Companies Act, 1956, a financial corporation, banking company, co-operative bank (other than a primary agricultural credit society or a primary co-operative agricultural and rural development bank).	The business of providing long-term finance in India for industrial or agricultural development or development of infrastructure facility in India or (up to the assessment year 2009-10) construction or purchase of residential houses in India or (from the assessment year 2010-11 onwards) development of housing in India.
A housing finance company (*i.e.*, a public company formed in India with the main object of carrying on the business of providing long-term finance for purchase or construction of residential house in India).	The business of providing long-term finance for construction or purchase of residential houses in India.
Any other financial corporation including the public company.	The business of providing long-term finance for development of infrastructure facility.

• *Infrastructure facility* - For this purpose "infrastructure facility" means—

a. infrastructure facility as given in *Explanation* to section 80-IA(4)(*i*) or any other public facility of a similar nature as may be notified by the Board[20],

b. an undertaking referred to in section 80-IA(4)(*ii*)/(*iii*)/(*iv*)/(*vi*),

c. an undertaking referred to in section 80-IB(10).

• *Long-term finance* - The expression "long-term finance" has been defined to mean any loan or advance, where the terms under which money is loaned or advanced provide for repayment along with interest thereof during a period of not less than 5 years.

48.32-2 *AMOUNT OF DEDUCTION* - The amount of deduction under section 36(1)(*viii*) is as follows —

a. the amount transferred during the previous year to the special reserve account created for the purpose of section 36(1)(*viii*) ; or

b. 20 per cent[21] of the profits derived from the business activities mentioned in para 48.32-1 *supra* which is computed under section 28 but before claiming deduction under section 36(1)(*viii*) ; or

20. The following are notified for this purpose—

(*1*) Inland Container Depot and Container Freight Station notified under the Customs Act, 1962 (52 of 1962), (*2*) Mass Rapid Transit System, (*3*) Light Rail Transit System, (*4*) Expressways, (*5*) Intra-urban or semi-urban roads like ring roads of urban by-passes or flyovers, (*6*) Bus and truck terminals, (*7*) Subways, (*8*) Road dividers, (*9*) Bulk Handling terminals which are developed or maintained or operated for development of rail system, (*10*) Multilevel Computerized Car Parking.

21. 40 per cent up to the assessment year 2007-08.

c. 200 per cent of (paid-up share capital and general reserve as on the last day of the previous year) *minus* the balance of the special reserve account on the first day of the previous year,

whichever is lower.

48.33 ***Family planning expenditure [Sec. 36(1)(ix)]*** - Any *bona fide* expenditure incurred by a company for the purpose of promoting family planning among its employees is allowable as deduction. If, however, such expenditure is of a capital nature, one-fifth of such expenditure is allowable as deduction for the previous year in which it was incurred and the balance is deductible in equal instalments in the next four years.

48.34 ***Contribution towards Exchange Risk Administration Fund [Sec. 36(1)(x)]*** - Contribution made by a public financial institution towards Exchange Risk Administration Fund is allowed as deduction for the assessment years 1989-90 to 2007-08.

48.35 ***Deduction of Y2K expenses [Sec. 36(1)(xi)]*** - Section 36(1)(*xi*) is applicable only if expenditure is incurred by an assessee during 1999-2000 (*i.e.*, on or after April 1, 1999 but on or before March 31, 2000).

48.36 ***Expenditure incurred by entities established under statutory Act [Sec. 36(1)(xii)]*** - Any expenditure (not being in the nature of capital expenditure) incurred by a corporation or a body corporate (by whatever name called) constituted or established by a Central, State or Provincial Act for the objects and purposes authorised by the Act under which such corporation or body corporate was constituted or established shall be allowed as a deduction from the assessment year 2002-03 in computing the income under the head "Profits and gains of business or profession". From the assessment year 2008-09, the above deduction shall be allowed only if such corporation or body corporate is notified[22] by the Central Government, having regard to the objects and purposes of the corresponding Central, State or Provincial Act.

48.37 ***Banking transaction tax, securities transaction tax and commodities transaction tax*** - These taxes are deductible as follows—

	Deduction under section 36	*Rebate under section 88E*
Banking transaction tax	Deductible	No
Securities transaction tax	Deductible under section 36 from the assessment year 2009-10 onwards	For the assessment years 2005-06 to 2008-09, rebate is available under section 88E. No rebate under section 88E from the assessment year 2009-10
Commodities transaction tax	Deductible from the assessment year 2014-15	–

48.38 ***Contribution to credit guarantee trust fund [Sec. 36(1)(xiv)]*** - From the assessment year 2008-09, a public financial institution can claim deduction in respect of its contribution to a notified credit guarantee trust fund for small industries (*i.e.*, Credit Guarantee Fund Trust for micro and small enterprises).

48.39 ***Expenditure by co-operative society for purchase of sugarcane [Sec. 36(1)(xvii), applicable from the assessment year 2016-17]*** - Under this clause, deduction is allowed in respect of expenditure incurred by a co-operative society (engaged in the business of manufacture of sugar) for purchase of sugarcane at a price which is equal to (or less than) the price fixed or approved by the Government.

48.39-E1 XYZ Co-operative Sugar Ltd. is a registered co-operative society under the Tamil Nadu Coop. Societies Act. It is in the business of manufacture and sale of sugar along with byproducts to the best advantage of its shareholding members (who are farmers and engaged in cultivation of sugarcane). The following data is noted from the accounts of the co-operative society –

	Rs.
Gross turnover of sale of sugar and by products	2,87,86,000
Less:	
- Cost of sugarcane (quantum of sugarcane utilised during the year to manufacture sugar : 8,700 tonne × Rs. 3,200 per tonne paid to the members for procurement of sugarcane)	2,78,40,000
- Other expenses (including depreciation)	9,10,000
Net profit as per profit and loss account	36,000

22. Notified institutions are National Dairy Development Board and Hyderabad Urban Development Authority.

Other information - Sugarcane procurement price fixed by Tamil Nadu Government is Rs. 2,800 per tonne [*i.e.,* Fair Remunerative Price (FRP) fixed by the Central Government : Rs. 2,400 per tonne + State Advisory price : Rs. 400 per tonne]. However, higher amount is paid (as given above) by the assessee co-operative society for procuring sugarcane from its members. Determine the taxable income of co-operative society if the assessment year is 2019-20.

•

By paying higher amount for procurement of sugarcane, the accounting profit of the society has been reduced and income of its members has increased. This will result in lower tax liability for co-operative society. However, tax liability of its members will not increase as income in the hands of members is agricultural income which is not chargeable to tax. To check this practice, clause (*xvii*) has been inserted in section 36(1) with effect from the assessment year 2016-17. Under the amended provisions, co-operative societies (engaged in manufacture of sugar) will get deduction pertaining to purchase of sugarcane at a price which is equal to (or less than) the price fixed or approved by the Government. The excess amount (if any) will not be deductible under section 36 or under section 37 (or under any provisions of the Act).

Taxable income of XYZ Co-operative Sugar Ltd. will be calculated as follows –

	Rs.
Net profit as per profit and loss account	36,000
Add: Cost of sugarcane debited to profit and loss account	2,78,40,000
Less: Cost of sugarcane as per section 36(1)(*xviii*) (*i.e.,* 8,700 tonne × Rs. 2,800 per tonne)	2,43,60,000
Taxable income	35,16,000

48.40 ***Marked to market loss [Sec. 36(1)(xviii), application from the assessment year 2017-18]*** - Marked to market loss or other **expected loss as computed in the manner provided in ICDS, shall be allowed as deduction** with effect from the assessment year 2017-18.

48.41 ***Advertisement expenditure [Sec. 37(2B)]*** - No allowance is available in respect of expenditure incurred by an assessee on advertisement in any souvenir, brochure, tract, pamphlet or the like published by a political party. Other remaining expenses on advertisement are deductible according to the provisions given under section 37(1).

• *Disallowance under section 37(2B) and deduction under section 80GGB* - Contribution to a political party is deductible under section 80GGB (if a contribution is made by an Indian company) or under section 80GGC (if a contribution is made by a person other than an Indian company). Expenditure by way of advertisement to a magazine owned by a political party, is treated as "contribution" to a political party for the purpose of section 80GGB, but not for the purpose of section 80GGC. In other words, advertisement expenditure (in a magazine owned by a political party) is deductible under section 80GGB if the taxpayer is an Indian company but the same is not deductible under section 80GGC if the taxpayer is a person other than an Indian company.

48.42 ***Expenses deductible from commission earned by life insurance agents, UTI agents, post office/ Government securities agents and agents of notified mutual funds*** - By Circular Nos. 594 (dated May 15, 1991), 648 (dated March 30, 1993) and 677 (dated January 28, 1994), the Board have specified conditions for giving *ad hoc* deductions from commission earned by insurance agents, UTI's agents, post office/ Government securities agents and agents of mutual funds.

These agents may be broadly divided into the following two groups :

48.42-1 *WHERE COMMISSION EARNED IS LESS THAN RS. 60,000* - The benefit of *ad hoc* deduction is available to agents who do not maintain detailed accounts for expenses incurred by them and have gross aggregate commission (from all sources specified in column *1* of the Table *infra*) of less than Rs. 60,000 during the previous year. In such cases, the amount of *ad hoc* deduction shall be determined as given in columns *2* and *3* below :

Commission	Ad hoc *deduction*	*Maximum deduction*
(1)	*(2)*	*(3)*
1. Agents of Life Insurance Corporation of India :		
1.1 First year's commission	50 per cent of first year's commission	
1.2 Renewal commission	15 per cent of renewal commission	Rs. 20,000 in respect of *1.1* and *1.2* or *1.3*
1.3 First year's commission and renewal commission where separate figures are not available	$33^1/_3$ per cent of first year's commission and renewal commission	
1.4 Bonus commission	No deduction	Zero

Commission	Ad hoc *deduction*	*Maximum deduction*
(1)	*(2)*	*(3)*
2. Agents of Unit Trust of India :		
2.1 Commission received by authorised agents	50 per cent of such commission	Not specified
3. Agents of specified securities (*see* Note) :		
3.1 Commission received by authorised agents	50 per cent of such commission	Not specified
4. Agents of notified mutual fund under section 10(*23D*) :		
4.1 Commission received by authorised agents	50 per cent of such commission	Not specified

Note : For the purpose of 3 *supra*, specified securities are :

National Savings Certificates VIII Issue, Social Securities Certificates, Post Office Time Deposit Accounts, Post Office Recurring Deposit Accounts, National Savings Scheme, 1987, Post Office Monthly Income Account Scheme, Kisan Vikas Patra, Public Provident Fund Accounts, and Deposit Scheme for Retiring Government Employees, 1989.

48.42-2 *WHERE COMMISSION EARNED IS MORE THAN RS. 60,000* - The benefit of *ad hoc* deduction is not available to agents who have earned gross aggregate commission (from all sources specified in column *1* of Table *supra*) of more than Rs. 60,000 in the previous year. The admissibility of expenditure claimed by such agents will be decided according to the provisions of sections 30 to 43B.

48.43 ***General deductions [Sec. 37]*** - Any expenditure not specifically covered by sections 30 to 36 is deductible under section 37, provided the following conditions are satisfied—

a. it should be in respect of a business carried on by the assessee;

b. it should have been laid out or expended wholly and exclusively for the purpose of the business;

c. it must have been incurred during the previous year ;

d. it should not be in the nature of capital expenditure or personal expenditure of the assessee; and

e. the expenditure should not have been incurred for any purpose which is an offence or is prohibited by any law[23].

A few instances of such expenditure are :

- Recurring expenses incurred on imparting basic training to Apprentices under the Apprentices Act, 1961 —Circular No. 192, dated March 10, 1976.
- Expenses incurred on the occasion of Diwali and *mahurat* subject to the ITO being satisfied that the expenses are not of personal, social or religious nature—Circular Letter No. 13A/20/68$ - IT(A-II), dated October 3, 1968.
- Initial expenditure on the first installation of fluorescent tube lights is treated as capital expenditure and all subsequent expenditure for replacement of tubes is treated as revenue expenditure—Circular No. 69, dated November 27, 1951.
- Loss through embezzlement by an employee—Circular No. 35, dated November 24, 1965.
- Professional tax paid by a person carrying on business or trade—Circular No. 16, dated September 18, 1969.
- Rebate or bonus passed on by the consumer co-operative stores to their members on the value of the purchases made by them during a year—Circular No. 117, dated August 22, 1973.
- Premium paid by a firm on keyman insurance policy of its partner - Circular No. 38/2016$, dated November 22, 2016.

23. The Medical Council of India (with prior sanction of the Central Government) has amended "Indian Medical Council (Professional Conduct, Etiquette and Ethics) Regulations, 2002", on December 10, 2009. As per the amended regulations, a medical practitioner shall not receive any gift from any pharmaceutical or allied health care industry and their sales people or representatives. Similarly, a medical practitioner shall not accept any travel facility (or hospitality of any kind) inside the country or outside from any pharmaceutical or allied healthcare industry for vacation or for attending conferences, seminars, workshops. If these expenses are debited as sales promotion or sponsorship expenditure (or otherwise), these expenses would be an inadmissible expenditure *vide Explanation* to section 37(1)– Circular No. 5/2012$, dated August 1, 2012. Further, the Board clarified in the Circular that the sum equivalent to value of freebees enjoyed by the aforesaid medical practitioner or professional associations is also taxable as business income (or income from other sources) in the hands of recipient. It may be noted that the expenditure incurred by a pharma or healthcare company through distribution of free samples to doctors, is not covered by the aforesaid circular. The object of distribution of the samples of the drugs to the doctors is to make them aware that such drugs are available in the market in relation to the cure of a particular affliction and, therefore, to persuade them to prescribe the same in appropriate cases. Consequently, expenditure on pre-distribution of drugs to doctors is deductible – *Eskayef (Now known as SmithKline Beecham) Pharmaceuticals (India) Ltd.* v. *CIT* [2000] 111 Taxman 561 (SC).

$ For Circular Letter No. 13A/20/68, Circular No. 5/2012 and Circular No. 38/2016, log on to *taxmann.com/readyreckoner.aspx.*

• All expenditure on maintenance of a tea garden including expenditure on the maintenance of an area that has not reached maturity—Income-tax Circular published by Directorate of Inspection (RS & P), 1968 edition, page 192.

• Deposit made under "own your telephone" scheme [is allowable as deduction in the year of payment and in case the telephone is not installed and the money is returned, it is chargeable to tax under section 41(1)]—Circular Letter F. No. 204/70/75 -IT(A-II), dated May 10, 1976.

• Annual listing fee paid to the stock exchange—Circular Letter F. No. 10/67/65 - IT(A-I), dated August 26, 1965.

• Expenses incurred on civil defence measures as specified by the Board, even when there is no emergency—Circular No. 316, dated September 30, 1981.

• Litigation expenses for defending monopoly rights.

• Litigation expenses incurred in restraining another company from using assessee's trade mark.

• Brokerage paid for raising loan to finance business.

• Stamp and registration charges for the purpose of entering into agreement for obtaining overdraft facilities.

• Amount spent towards stamps, registration fees, lawyer's fees, etc., for obtaining loan or raising money by issue of debentures (not share).

48.43-1 *INTEREST ON DELAYED PAYMENTS TO MICRO, SMALL AND MEDIUM UNDERTAKING - NOT DEDUCTIBLE* - The Micro, Small and Medium Enterprises Development Act, 2006 (MSMEDA, 2006) which provides for facilitating the promotion and development and enhancing the competitiveness of micro, small and medium enterprises has come into force from October 2, 2006. The provisions of sections 22 and 23 of the said Act have a bearing on the assessment of 'buyers' under the Income-tax Act, 1961. Here, the term 'buyer' means a person who buys any goods or receives any services from a 'supplier' for a consideration. Section 23 of MSMEDA, 2006 lays down that the amount of interest payable or paid by any buyer under or in accordance with the provisions of this Act (*i.e.*, three times of bank rate) shall not be allowed as deduction in the computation of income. Section 22 of the MSMEDA, 2006, *inter alia*, requires disclosure of the principal and interest due thereon separately in the annual statement of accounts. This enables the Assessing Officers to ascertain correct amount of disallowance on account of interest payable or paid by the buyer—Instruction No. 12/2006, dated December 14, 2006.

48.43-2 *CORPORATE SOCIAL RESPONSIBILITY EXPENDITURE [EXPLN. 2 TO SEC. 37(1)]* - Any expenditure incurred by an assessee on the activities relating to corporate social responsibility (CSR) referred to in section 135 of the Companies Act, 2013 shall not be deemed to have been incurred for the purpose of business and hence shall not be allowed as deduction under section 37. However, the CSR expenditure which is of the nature described in sections 30 to 36 or section 80G shall be allowed as deduction under those sections subject to fulfilment of conditions, if any, specified therein.

Amounts expressly disallowed under the Act

49. The following expenses are expressly disallowed by the Act while computing income chargeable under the head "Profits and gains of business or profession". Besides these provisions, no deduction is permissible in respect of any expenditure or allowance under sections 28 to 44C in respect of income referred to in sections 115A, 115AB, 115AC, 115AD, 115BBA and 115D [*see* Referencer 9].

49.1 ***Amounts not deductible under section 40*** - In the case of *any assessee*, the following expenses are expressly disallowed under section 40(*a*)[24] :

49.1-1 *TDS DEFAULT PERTAINING ANY SUM (OTHER THAN SALARY) PAYABLE OUTSIDE INDIA OR PAYABLE TO NON-RESIDENT/FOREIGN COMPANY [SEC. 40(a)(i)]* - The provisions of disallowance of section 40(*a*)(*i*) from the assessment year 2015-16[25] are given below –

If the following conditions are satisfied, the payer is supposed to deduct tax at source –

a. the amount payable is interest, royalty, technical fees or any other sum (but not salary);

b. in the hands of the recipient, it is chargeable to tax in India; and

c. the aforesaid sum is payable outside India or to a non-resident/foreign company.

If these conditions are satisfied, tax is deductible under the Act.

• *Disallowance of expenditure under section 40*(a)(i) - If TDS default is committed in respect of payment/credit given to a foreign company/non-resident, the expenditure is disallowed in the hands of payer under section 40(*a*)(*i*). These provisions are given below –

24. Depreciation is not an outgoing expenditure and, therefore, provisions of section 40(*a*)(*i*) are not attracted on such deduction—*SAB Miller India Ltd.* v. *CIT* [2015] 63 taxmann.com 341 (Mum.).

25. For provisions applicable up to the assessment year 2014-15, *see Taxmann's Direct Taxes Ready Reckoner*, 2014-15 editions.

TDS default	*Is such expenditure deductible in the current previous year*	*Is such expenditure deductible in any subsequent previous year*
Case 1 - Tax is deductible but not deducted	100 per cent of such expenditure is disallowed in the current year	If tax is deducted in any subsequent year, the expenditure (which is disallowed in the current year) will be deducted in the year in which TDS will be deposited by the assessee with the Government
Case 2 - Tax is deductible (and is so deducted) during the current financial year but it is not deposited on or before the due date of submission of return of income under section 139(1)	100 per cent of such expenditure is disallowed in the current year	If tax is deposited with the Government after the due date of submission of return of income, the expenditure (which is disallowed in the current year) will be deductible in that year in which tax will be deposited

Note - If recipient is a non-resident or foreign company and TDS default is committed by the payer, 100 per cent of the expenditure is disallowed in the hands of payer, as given above. Similar rule is applicable if recipient is a resident and TDS default is committed (however, not 100 per cent but 30 per cent expenditure is disallowed). The rule pertaining to TDS default (in case recipient is resident) is given by section 40(*a*)(*ia*) and explained in para 49.1-2.

49.1-1a WHEN RECIPIENT HAS PAID TAX - The above provisions have been amended with effect from the assessment year 2020-21[26]. Under the amended provisions, a relief is given in *Case 1* (and not in *Case 2*) of para 49.1-1. This relief is available if the following conditions are satisfied –

1. Tax is deductible on the aforesaid payments but it is not deducted (wholly or partly) by the payer (*i.e.*, *Case 1*).

2. **The payer is not deemed to be an assessee-in-default under the first proviso to section 201(1).** Under the first proviso to section 201(1), the payer is not deemed to be an assessee-in-default if –

a. the recipient has furnished his return of income under section 139;

b. the recipient has taken into account the above income in such return of income;

c. the recipient has paid the tax due on the income declared in such return of income, and

d. the payer uploads a certificate to this effect from a chartered accountant in Form No. 26A.

If the above conditions are satisfied, then for the purpose of section 40(*a*)(*i*) it shall be deemed that the payer has deducted and paid the tax on such amount on the date of the furnishing of return of income by the recipient [*see* para 49.1-2a for illustrations].

49.1-1E1 X Ltd. is an Indian company. Profit and loss account of X Ltd. for the year ending March 31, 2019 is given below –

	Rs.		*Rs.*
Commission	2,00,000	Gross profit	1,05,50,000
Interest	3,00,000		
Rent	8,00,000		
License fees of software	17,50,000		
Salary	18,00,000		
Other expenses	27,00,000		
Net profit	30,00,000		
	1,05,50,000		1,05,50,000

The due date of filing of return of income of the assessment year 2019-20 for X Ltd. is September 30, 2019. Recipients of commission, interest, rent, license fees and salary (given in the profit and loss account) are non-residents or foreign companies. In the hands of recipients, these payments/credits are chargeable to tax in India. Consequently, tax is deductible by X Ltd. Tax deduction (TDS) details of these payments are given in the table below –

Nature of expenditure	*Date on which tax is required to be deducted by X Ltd.*	*Actual date of tax deduction by X Ltd.*	*Date of deposit of TDS by X Ltd.*
Commission : Rs. 2,00,000	July 13, 2018	July 13, 2018	July 30, 2019
Interest : Rs. 3,00,000	December 24, 2018	December 24, 2018	November 8, 2019
Rent : Rs. 8,00,000	June 6, 2018	Not deducted	–
License fees of software : Rs. 17,50,000	October 20, 2018	May 10, 2019	June 3, 2019
Salary : Rs. 18,00,000	January 1, 2019	January 1, 2019	December 17, 2019

26. *See* footnote 29 to para 49.1-2a.

In the case of rent, tax is not deducted during the financial year 2018-19 (and till date it is not deducted). In the case of license fees of software, tax is not deducted during the financial year 2018-19 (but it is deducted and deposited in the next financial year, *i.e.*, 2019-20 as given above). Find out the net income of X Ltd. for the assessment year 2019-20.

•

Payment/credit of commission, interest, rent and fees to a non-resident/foreign company are covered by section 40(*a*)(*i*). Salary to a non-resident is, however, covered by section 40(*a*)(*iii*) and discussed in para 49.1-7. These payments are deductible as follows –

Nature of expenditure	*Which TDS default is applicable - Case 1 or Case 2*	*In which year expenditure is deductible in the hands of X Ltd.*
Commission : Rs. 2,00,000	None	Tax is deducted in the current previous year (*i.e.*, 2018-19). It is deposited with Government on or before the due date of submission of return of income for the current year (*i.e.*, September 30, 2019). Consequently, commission of Rs. 2,00,000 is deductible in the previous year 2018-19.
Interest : Rs. 3,00,000	*Case 2*	Tax is deducted in the current previous year (*i.e.*, 2018-19). However, tax is not deposited with the Government till the due date of submission of return of income for the previous year 2018-19 (*i.e.*, September 30, 2019). Consequently, interest of Rs. 3,00,000 is not deductible for computing income of the previous year 2018-19. However, it is deductible in the year of deposit of TDS. If TDS is deposited on November 8, 2019, the interest of Rs. 3,00,000 will be deductible in the previous year 2019-20.
Rent : Rs. 8,00,000	*Case 1*	Tax is deductible but not deducted. Consequently, the entire rent of Rs. 8,00,000 is not deductible for computing income of the previous year 2018-19. If X Ltd. deducts and deposits TDS in any subsequent year, it will be allowed as deduction in the year in which TDS is deposited by X Ltd.
License fees of software : Rs. 17,50,000	*Case 1*	Tax is deductible during the previous year 2018-19 but it is not deducted during the previous year 2018-19. Consequently, the entire license fees of Rs. 17,50,000 becomes a non-deductible business expenditure of X Ltd. for the previous year 2018-19. However, license fees will be allowed as deduction in the previous year in which TDS is deposited. If TDS is deposited on June 3, 2019, license fees of Rs. 17,50,000 will become deductible in the previous year 2019-20.
Salary : Rs. 18,00,000	–	Salary to non-resident is covered by section 40(*a*)(*iii*) which is explained in para 49.1-7. Under section 40(*a*)(*iii*) disallowance is applicable only if tax is neither deposited nor deducted. Date of deduction and deposit of tax is not relevant if recipient of salary is a non-resident. Consequently, there is no disallowance in this case and the entire salary is deductible for the previous year 2018-19.

Computation of income of X Ltd. –

	Rs.
Net profit as per profit and loss account	30,00,000
Adjustments –	
Add: Interest	3,00,000
Add: Rent	8,00,000
Add: Fees	17,50,000
Net income	58,50,000

49.1-2 *TDS DEFAULT PERTAINING TO ANY SUM PAYABLE TO A RESIDENT [SEC. 40(*a*)(*ia*)]* - In respect of the following payments/credit to a resident, tax is deductible under Chapter XVII-B[27] of the Income-tax Act (*i.e.*, sections 192 to 206AA)–

1. Salary	*8.* Payment in respect of life insurance policy
2. Interest	*9.* Payment in respect of deposits under NSS
3. Dividends	*10.* Payment on account of certain units
4. Winnings from lottery or crossword puzzles	*11.* Rent
5. Winnings from horse races	*12.* Payment on purchase of immovable property
6. Payments to contractors	*13.* Technical/professional fees, royalty, fees to a part time director
7. Commission or brokerage (including insurance commission)	*14.* Payment of compensation on acquisition of immovable property

27. Up to the assessment year 2014-15, section 40(*a*)(*ia*) covers TDS defaults under sections 193, 194A, 194C, 194H, 194-I and 194J. Disallowance is 100 per cent of expenditure.

• *Disallowance of above expenditure from the assessment year 2015-16 under section 40(a)(ia)* - If TDS default is committed in respect of the above payment/credit given to a resident, 30 per cent[27] of such expenditure is disallowed in the hands of payer under section 40(*a*)(*ia*). These provisions are given below –

TDS default	*Is such expenditure deductible in the current previous year*	*Is such expenditure deductible in any subsequent previous year*
Case 1 - Tax is deductible but not deducted	30 per cent of such expenditure is disallowed in the current year	If tax is deducted in any subsequent year, the expenditure (which is disallowed in the current year) will be deducted in the year in which TDS will be deposited by the assessee with the Government
Case 2 - Tax is deductible (and is so deducted) during the current financial year but it is not deposited on or before the due date of submission of return of income under section 139(1)	30 per cent of such expenditure is disallowed in the current year	If tax is deposited with the Government after the due date of submission of return of income, the expenditure (which is disallowed in the current year) will be deductible in that year in which tax will be deposited

The following points should be noted –

1. If TDS default (*Case 1* or *Case 2*) pertaining to payment/credit given to a resident is committed, 30 per cent of such expenditure becomes a non-deductible expenditure under section 40(*a*)(*ia*) with effect from the assessment year 2015-16. Up to the assessment year 2014-15, 100 per cent of such expenditure was not deductible.

2. If TDS default pertaining to salary payment to a resident in India is committed, disallowance provisions of section 40(*a*)(*ia*) are applicable only with effect from the assessment year 2015-16. Salary TDS default were not covered by provisions of section 40(*a*)(*ia*) up to the assessment year 2014-15.

49.1-2E1 Calculate the income of X Ltd. in Example 49.1-1E1 on the assumption that recipients of commission, interest, rent, license fees of software and salary are persons resident in India. Dates of deduction of tax and deposit of TDS are the same as given in the example.

•

Payment/credit of commission, interest, rent, fees and salary to a resident are covered by section 40(*a*)(*ia*). These payments are deductible as follows –

Nature of expenditure	*Which TDS default is applicable - Case 1 or Case 2*	*In which year expenditure is deductible in the hands of X Ltd.*
Commission : Rs. 2,00,000	None	Tax is deducted in the current previous year (*i.e.*, 2018-19). It is deposited with Government on or before the due date of submission of return of income for the current year (*i.e.*, September 30, 2019). Consequently, commission of Rs. 2,00,000 is deductible in the previous year 2018-19.
Interest : Rs. 3,00,000	*Case 2*	Tax is deducted in the current previous year (*i.e.*, 2018-19). However, tax is not deposited with the Government till the due date of submission of return of income for the previous year 2018-19 (*i.e.*, September 30, 2019). Consequently, 30% of interest of Rs. 3,00,000 (*i.e.*, Rs. 90,000) is not deductible for computing income of the previous year 2018-19 (however, balance of Rs. 2,10,000 is deductible for the previous year 2018-19). Rs. 90,000 will be deductible in the year of deposit of TDS. If TDS is deposited on November 8, 2019, Rs. 90,000 (being the amount disallowed earlier) will be deductible in the previous year 2019-20.
Rent : Rs. 8,00,000	*Case 1*	Tax is deductible but not deducted. Consequently, 30% of rent of Rs. 8,00,000 (*i.e.*, Rs. 2,40,000) is not deductible for computing income of the previous year 2018-19 (however, the balance of Rs. 5,60,000 is deductible for the previous year 2018-19). If X Ltd. deducts and deposits TDS in any subsequent year, Rs. 2,40,000 (being the amount disallowed earlier) will be allowed as deduction in the year in which TDS is deposited by X Ltd.
License fees of software : Rs. 17,50,000	*Case 1*	Tax is deductible during the previous year 2018-19 but it is not deducted during the previous year 2018-19. Consequently, 30% of license fees of Rs. 17,50,000 (*i.e.*, Rs. 5,25,000) becomes a non-deductible business expenditure of X Ltd. for the previous year 2018-19 (the balance of Rs. 12,25,000 is deductible for the

27. Up to the assessment year 2014-15, section 40(*a*)(*ia*) covers TDS defaults under sections 193, 194A, 194C, 194H, 194-I and 194J. Disallowance is 100 per cent of expenditure.

Nature of expenditure	*Which TDS default is applicable - Case 1 or Case 2*	*In which year expenditure is deductible in the hands of X Ltd.*
		previous year 2018-19). If TDS is deposited on June 3, 2019, Rs. 5,25,000 (being the amount disallowed earlier) will become deductible in the previous year 2019-20.
Salary : Rs. 18,00,000	*Case 2*	TDS default pertaining to salary payments to resident employees are covered by disallowance provisions of section 40(*a*)(*ia*). Since TDS is not deposited till the due date of submission of return of income, 30% of salary (*i.e.*, Rs. 5,40,000) is not deductible for computing income of the previous year 2018-19 (however, the balance of Rs. 12,60,000 is deductible for the previous year 2018-19). TDS pertaining to this payment is deposited on December 17, 2019. Rs. 5,40,000 (being the amount disallowed earlier) will be deductible in the previous year 2019-20.

Computation of income of X Ltd. –

	Rs.
Net profit as per profit and loss account	30,00,000
Adjustments –	
Add: 30% of interest (*i.e.*, 30% of Rs. 3,00,000)	90,000
Add: 30% of rent (*i.e.*, 30% of Rs. 8,00,000)	2,40,000
Add: 30% of fees (*i.e.*, 30% of Rs. 17,50,000)	5,25,000
Add: 30% of salary (*i.e.*, 30% of Rs. 18,00,000)	5,40,000
Net income	43,95,000

• *Tax not deducted up to the assessment year 2014-15 (100 per cent expenditure disallowed) but TDS deposited in the next year – Amount deductible in the next year (100 per cent or 30 per cent)* - On expenditure pertaining to royalty of Rs. 1,00,000, tax is not deducted by X Ltd. during the financial year 2013-14 (assessment year 2014-15). The entire expenditure of Rs. 1,00,000 is disallowed while calculating income of X Ltd. for the assessment year 2014-15. In the financial year 2018-19, tax is deducted and deposited by X Ltd. Now a question arises whether for the previous year 2018-19 (assessment year 2019-20) amount deductible in the hands of X Ltd. will be Rs. 1,00,000 or Rs. 30,000. The first proviso to section 40(*a*)(*ia*) [as amended by the Finance (No. 2) Act, 2014] provides that "30 per cent of such sum shall be allowed as a deduction in computing the income of the previous year in which such tax has been paid". A plain reading of this proviso gives the impression that X Ltd. will get a deduction of Rs. 30,000 for the assessment year 2019-20.

However, CBDT has clarified that in such a case (*i.e.*, when before amendment 100 per cent expenditure was disallowed up to the assessment year 2014-15), the whole of the amount disallowed under section 40(*a*)(*ia*) shall be allowed under the first proviso to section 40(*a*)(*ia*) in the previous year in which tax deducted at source has been paid – Circular No. 1/2015[$], dated January 21, 2015. Consequently, in the above case, Rs. 1,00,000 will be deductible while computing business income of X Ltd. for the previous year 2018-19 (assessment year 2019-20).

• *Whether section 40(*a*)(*ia*) is applicable only in respect of expenses actually "paid" without TDS* - Tax is deductible under sections 193, 194A, 194C, 194H, 194-I and 194J either at the time of payment or at the time of giving credit to the recipient. Section 40(*a*)(*ia*) is applicable in respect of TDS defaults whether amount is paid or payable. This observation has now been upheld by the Apex Court in the case of *Palam Gas Service* v. *CIT* [2017] 81 taxmann.com 43 (SC).

• *Short deduction is not subject to disallowance* - If tax is deducted at source but there is only some shortfall due to difference of opinion about provisions applicable, the assessee can be declared to be an assessee-in-default under section 201 but no disallowance can be made invoking section 40(*a*)(*ia*)—*CIT* v. *S.K. Tekriwal* [2011] 15 taxmann.com 289 (Kolkata - Trib.), *CIT* v. *Chandabhoy & Jassobhoy* [2012] 49 SOT 448 (Mum.).

• *Disallowance under section 40(*a*)(*ia*) can increase business income eligible for deduction under section 80-IB* - In *S.B. Builders & Developers* v. *ITO* [2011] 45 SOT 335 (Mum.), the business mentioned in section 80-IB(10) was the only business of the assessee and the business income was increased because of disallowance under section 40(*a*)(*ia*), the Tribunal held that the business income so computed [after disallowance under section 40(*a*)] would be eligible for deduction under section 80-IB.

[$]For Circular No. 1/2015, log on to *taxmann.com/readyreckoner.aspx.*

• *Disallowance under section 40*(a)*(*ia*) cannot be avoided even if TDS is not deposited because of excess tax paid during last year* - Irrespective of the fact that an assessee is entitled to claim refund of excess tax paid or get it adjusted against tax liability under other provisions of the Act, he cannot withhold tax deducted by him so as to adjust the same against excess taxes paid earlier. Non-deposit of TDS even in such a case will attract disallowance provisions of section 40(*a*)—*HCC Pati Joint Venture* v. *CIT* [2011] 46 SOT 263 (Mum.).

• *Whether disallowance applicable in case of capital expenditure* - If loan is taken to finance the purchase of a capital asset, interest liability (pertaining to the period till the asset is put to use) can be capitalised. If there is a TDS default under section 194A for such interest, depreciation on the interest component (which is part of "actual cost") cannot be denied by invoking the provisions of section 40(*a*)(*ia*)—*Sonic Biochem Extractions (P.) Ltd.* v. *ITO* [2013] 59 SOT 4 (Mum.).

• *Whether section 40(*a*)(*ia*) can be invoked when TDS default pertains to procedures* - Under section 194C, tax is not deductible if the recipient transport contractor intimates his PAN to the payer. In such a case, the payer will have to submit PAN details of the recipient in Form No. 26Q. If the payer fails to give PAN details in Form No. 26Q, section 40(*a*)(*ia*) cannot be invoked to disallow amount payable to transport contractor—*CIT* v. *Valibhai Khanbhai Mankad* [2013] 216 Taxman 18 (Guj.). Similarly, if Form No. 15G/15H is not submitted within the stipulated period to the Commissioner, disallowance provisions under section 40(*a*)(*ia*) cannot be invoked – *Vijaya Bank* v. *ITO* [2014] 66 SOT 20 (Delhi).

• *Whether reimbursement to an agent/associate enterprise (without TDS) can be disallowed under section 40(*a*)(*ia*) when tax was properly deducted by the agent/associate enterprise* - Technical fees (or any other expenditure like rent, commission, royalty, professional fees, etc.) is paid by an agent or associate enterprise on behalf of the assessee. Tax is deducted properly within the legal parameters by the agent/associate enterprise. Later on the assessee reimburses the expenditure to the agent/associate enterprise. Tax is not deductible on such reimbursement to the agent/associate enterprise – *see Metro Railway, Kolkata* v. *ITO* (TDS) [2013] 32 taxmann.com 232 (Kol.), *Temasek Holdings Advisors (I) (P.) Ltd.* v. *CIT* [2013] 60 SOT 134 (Mum.), *CIT* v. *Harbanslal Malhotra & Sons (P.) Ltd.* [2013] 217 Taxman 112 (Cal.), *CIT* v. *Gujarat Narmada Valley Fertilizers Co. Ltd.* [2013] 217 Taxman 114 (Guj.), *CIT* v. *Vector Shipping Services (P.) Ltd.* [2013] 218 Taxman 93 (All.)[28]. The same proposition is given by Circular No. 5/2002[$], dated July 30, 2002. Consequently, reimbursement of expenditure cannot be disallowed in the hands of the assessee by invoking section 40(*a*)(*ia*) in such cases.

49.1-2a WHEN RECIPIENT HAS PAID TAX - The above provisions have been amended by the Finance Act, 2012 with effect from the assessment year 2013-14[29]. Under the amended provisions, a relief is given in *Case 1* (and not in *Case 2*) of para 49.1-2. This relief is available if the following conditions are satisfied –

1. Tax is deductible on the aforesaid payments but it is not deducted (wholly or partly) by the payer (*i.e., Case 1*).

2. The payer is not deemed to be an assessee-in-default under the first proviso to section 201(1). Under the first proviso to section 201(1), the payer is not deemed to be an assessee-in-default if –

a. the resident recipient[29a] has furnished his return of income under section 139;

b. the resident recipient[29a] has taken into account the above income in such return of income;

c. the resident recipient[29a] has paid the tax due on the income declared in such return of income, and

d. the payer uploads a certificate to this effect from a chartered accountant in Form No. 26A.

If the above conditions are satisfied, then for the purpose of section 40(*a*)(*ia*) it shall be deemed that the payer has deducted and paid the tax on such amount on the date of the furnishing of return of income by the resident recipient.[29a]

---

28. SLP against the Allahabad High Court ruling has been rejected by the Supreme Court on July 2, 2014.

29. The Courts have been unanimous in holding that amendments, which are intended to remove unintended hardships, are declaratory in nature and, therefore, will operate retrospectively. The Delhi High Court in *CIT* v. *Ansal Land Mark Township (P.) Ltd.* [2015] 61 taxmann.com 45 had occasion to decide about retrospectivity of this amendment. Even though this amendment is made effective from the assessment year 2013-14, yet the Court held that it to be declaratory and curative in nature and, therefore, applicable retrospectively from the assessment year 2005-06.

29a. **Resident/non-resident recipient** (applicable from September 1, 2019), as an identical relief is available in the case of TDS default under section 40(a)(*i*).

[$]For Circular No. 5/2002, log on to *taxmann.com/readyreckoner.aspx.*

• *Provisions illustrated* - Consider the following cases -

1. X Ltd. credits a sum of Rs. 45,000 as commission to Y Ltd. (an Indian company) on April 20, 2018 without deducting tax at source. Y Ltd. pays advance tax on the due dates on its income (including Rs. 45,000).

Entire tax liability is paid by Y Ltd. by advance payment of tax during the financial year 2018-19 and/or by payment of self-assessment tax at the time of submission of return of income. Return of income of Y Ltd. for the assessment year 2019-20 is submitted on July 10, 2019. X Ltd. has a certificate in Form No. 26A to this effect from a chartered accountant.

Tax treatment of non-deduction of tax by X Ltd. and subsequent payment by the recipient is as follows -

Assessment year 2019-20 - Tax is not deducted by X Ltd. during the financial year 2018-19. Consequently, 30 per cent of commission of Rs. 45,000 (*i.e.*, Rs. 13,500) will be disallowed in the hands of X Ltd. for the assessment year 2019-20.

Assessment year 2020-21 - After payment of tax by Y Ltd., the recipient of commission, X Ltd. cannot be treated as an assessee-in-default under the provisions of first proviso to section 201(1), as the following conditions are satisfied -

a. Y Ltd., the recipient of commission, has furnished its return of income under section 139 (late submission does not affect on this point);

b. Y Ltd. has taken into account the above income in such return of income;

c. Y Ltd. has paid the tax due on the income declared in such return of income; and

d. X Ltd. has a certificate to this effect from a chartered accountant in Form No. 26A[$].

Under the provisions as amended by the Finance Act, 2012, it will be assumed that X Ltd. has deducted and deposited tax on July 10, 2019. As a consequence, Rs. 13,500 will be allowed as deduction in the hands of X Ltd. for the previous year 2019-20.

2. On July 10, 2018, X Ltd. credits Rs. 10,80,000 as rent to B (a resident individual) after deducting tax at the rate of 10 per cent under section 194-I. The tax so deducted by X Ltd. is not deposited till March 31, 2019. However, B submits his return of income on July 15, 2019 after including Rs. 10,80,000 in his income. As per his return of income a refund of Rs. 4,00,000 is due to him.

In this case, the amended provisions are not applicable (the amended provisions are applicable only when the payer fails to deduct the whole or any part of tax). If tax is deducted but not paid, the amended provisions [as well as the first proviso to section 201(1)] are not applicable. X Ltd. cannot claim any deduction for the previous year 2018-19 or 2019-20 in respect of 30 per cent of rent payment of Rs. 10,80,000.

49.1-3 *DEFAULT PERTAINING TO NON-DEDUCTION/NON-DEPOSIT OF EQUALISATION LEVY [SEC. 40(*a*)(*ib*), APPLICABLE FROM THE ASSESSMENT YEAR 2017-18]* - Any consideration paid or payable (to a non-resident for a specified service on which equalisation levy is applicable) will be disallowed from the assessment year 2017-18 in the following cases—

1. Equalisation levy is deductible and such levy has not been deducted.

2. Equalisation levy is deductible (and it is so deducted) but it is not deposited [on or before the due date of submission of return of income under section 139(1)].

If, however, equalisation levy is deducted/deposited in a subsequent year, the aforesaid consideration shall be allowed as a deduction in computing the income of the previous year in which such levy has been paid.

49.1-3A *SECURITIES TRANSACTION TAX [SEC. 40(*a*)(*ib*)]* - The provisions are given below—

	Disallowance of securities transaction tax under section 40(a)(ib)	*Rebate under section 88E*
For the assessment years 2005-06 to 2008-09	Securities transaction tax is not deductible	Rebate under section 88E is available
From the assessment year 2009-10 onwards	Disallowance under section 40(*a*)(*ib*) has been omitted and securities transaction tax will be deductible as business expenditure under section 36(1)(*xv*)	No rebate

49.1-4 *FRINGE BENEFITS TAX* - Any sum paid on account of fringe benefits tax is not deductible.

49.1-5 *INCOME-TAX [SEC. 40(*a*)(*ii*)]* - Any sum paid on account of income-tax (*i.e.*, any rate or tax levied on the profits or gains of any business or profession) is not deductible. Similarly, any interest/penalty/fine for non-payment or late payment of income-tax is not deductible. This rule is applicable whether income-tax is payable in India or outside India.

• Tax of a non-resident professional borne by the Indian payer is nothing but part of professional fees for the payer. It is deemed as income of non-resident professional. It cannot be disallowed in the hands of the payer as payment of "income-tax" — *Karan Johar* v. *CIT* [2011] 46 SOT 21 (Mum.).

[$]Electronic submission of Form No. 26A is required. For detailed procedure, log on to *taxmann.com/readyreckoner.aspx*.

49.1-6 *WEALTH-TAX [SEC. 40(*a*)(*iia*)]* - Any sum paid on account of wealth-tax under the Wealth-tax Act, 1957, or tax of a similar nature chargeable under any law outside India is not deductible.

49.1-6A *CERTAIN FEE, CHARGE, ETC. PAID BY A STATE GOVERNMENT UNDERTAKING TO THE STATE GOVERNMENT [SEC. 40(*a*)(*iib*), APPLICABLE FROM THE ASSESSMENT YEAR 2014-15*[30]*]* - Any amount –

a. paid by way of royalty, licence fee, service fee, privilege fee, service charge or any other fee or charge, by whatever name called, which is levied exclusively on; or

b. which is appropriated, directly or indirectly, from,

a State Government undertaking by the State Government, is not allowed as deduction from the assessment year 2014-15.

• For this purpose, a State Government undertaking includes—

a. a corporation established by or under any Act of the State Government;

b. a company in which more than 50 per cent of the paid-up equity share capital is held by the State Government;

c. a company in which more than 50 per cent of the paid-up equity share capital is held by the entity referred to in (*a*) or (*b*) (whether singly or taken together);

d. a company or corporation in which the State Government has the right to appoint the majority of the directors or to control the management or policy decisions, directly or indirectly, including by virtue of its shareholding or management rights or shareholders agreements or voting agreements or in any other manner;

e. an authority, a board or an institution or a body established or constituted by or under any Act of the State Government or owned or controlled by the State Government.

49.1-7 *SALARY PAYABLE OUTSIDE INDIA WITHOUT TAX DEDUCTION [SEC. 40(*a*)(*iii*)]* - Section 40(*a*)(*iii*) is applicable if the following conditions are satisfied—

1. The payment is chargeable under the head "Salary" in the hands of the recipient.

2. It is payable—

a. outside India (to any person resident or non-resident); or

b. in India to a non-resident.

3. Tax has not been paid to the Government nor deducted at source under the Income-tax Act.

If the aforesaid conditions are satisfied, then the payment is not allowed as deduction.

• *Provisions illustrated* - The following illustration is given in respect of salary payable for the previous year 2018-19 by a company to (*a*) any person outside India or (*b*) non-resident in India —

Amount Rs.	*Date on which tax is supposed to be deducted (i.e., the date of salary payment)*	*Actual date of tax deduction*	*When tax should be deposited under section 200(1)*	*Actual date of tax deposit*	*Previous year in which salary payment is deductible*
40,000	July 31, 2018	July 31, 2018	August 7, 2018	November 10, 2018	2018-19
90,000	March 31, 2019	March 31, 2019	April 30, 2019	April 7, 2019	2018-19
1,60,000	March 31, 2019	March 31, 2019	April 30, 2019	May 12, 2019	2018-19
70,000	March 31, 2019	Not deducted	April 30, 2019	May 12, 2019	2018-19
75,000	March 31, 2019	March 31, 2019	April 30, 2019	Not deposited	2018-19
95,000	March 31, 2019	Not deducted	April 30, 2019	Not deposited	Not deductible

49.1-8 *PROVIDENT FUND PAYMENT WITHOUT TAX DEDUCTION AT SOURCE [SEC. 40(*a*)(*iv*)]* - Any payment to a provident fund (or other fund established for the benefit of employees of the assessee) is not deductible if the assessee has not made effective arrangements to secure that tax shall be deducted at source from any payments made from the fund which are chargeable to tax under the head "Salaries".

49.1-9 *TAX ON PERQUISITE PAID BY THE EMPLOYER [SEC. 40(*a*)(*v*)]* - The provisions of section 40(*a*)(*v*) are given below—

1. The employer provides non-monetary perquisites to employees.

2. Tax on non-monetary perquisites is paid by the employer.

3. The tax so paid by the employer is not taxable in the hands of employees by virtue of section 10(*10CC*).

4. While calculating income of the employer, the tax paid by the employer on non-monetary perquisites is not deductible under section 40(*a*)(*v*). For detailed discussion, *see* para 15.21.

---

30. Section 40(*a*)(*iib*) is applicable from the assessment year 2014-15 and not with retrospective effect – *Karnataka State Beverages Corpn. Ltd.* v. *CIT* [2016] 67 taxmann.com 316 (Kar.).

49.2 ***Amounts not deductible in respect of payment to relatives [Sec. 40A(2)]*** - Any expenditure incurred by an assessee in respect of which payment has been made to the persons mentioned in para 49.2-3 is liable to be disallowed in computing business profit to the extent such expenditure is considered to be excessive or unreasonable, having regard to the fair market value of goods or services or facilities, etc. Before, understanding the implication of section 40A(2), it is imperative to understand the meaning of terms "relative" and "persons having substantial interest"—

49.2-1 *WHO IS RELATIVE [SEC. 2(41)]* -The term "relative" in relation to an individual, means the husband, wife, brother or sister or any lineal ascendant or descendant of that individual [sec. 2(*41*)].

49.2-2 *"SUBSTANTIAL INTEREST" - MEANING OF* - A person is deemed to have substantial interest in the business or profession if such person is the beneficial owner of at least 20 per cent of equity capital (in the case of a company) or if such person is entitled to 20 per cent profits of a concern (in any other case) at any time during the previous year.

49.2-3 *PAYMENT TO PERSONS COVERED BY SECTION 40A(2)* - If a payment is made by a taxpayer in respect of an expenditure to the persons mentioned in column (*2*) of the table given below, section 40A(2) is applicable and, consequently, to the extent such expenditure is considered to be excessive or unreasonable having regard to the fair market value of goods, services, facilities, etc., it shall be disallowed.[31] In other words, if the following conditions are satisfied, then to the extent the payment is excessive, it will be disallowed—

Condition 1 - Expenditure is incurred for goods, services or facilities.

Condition 2 - For the above expenditure, payment is made to a person mentioned in column 2 of the table infra.

Condition 3 - Such expenditure is considered as excessive or unreasonable having regard to the following—

i. fair market value of the commodity or service or facility; or

ii. legitimate business needs of the business of the assessee; or

iii. benefit derived by or accruing to assessees as a result of the expenditure.

For *Condition 3*, the Assessing Officer is required to record a finding as to whether expenditure is excessive or unreasonable in relation to any one of the three requirements [*i.e.*, (*i*) or (*ii*) or (*iii*), given above], which are independent and alternative to each other. All the three requirements need not to exist simultaneously. In a given case, if any one of the requirements [*i.e.*, (*i*) or (*ii*) or (*iii*), given above] along with *Condition 1* and *Condition 2* is satisfied, the provisions of section 40A(2) can be invoked and applied. If the Assessing Officer finds (cogent reasons should be assigned by the Assessing Officer) that a part of the expenditure (payment made to a relative or inter-connected person, given in the Table *infra*) is excessive having regard to the legitimate needs of the business, the disallowance provisions of section 40A(2) will be applicable, even if, the amount paid is not more than the fair market value of goods supplied, or services rendered, by the recipient — *Coronation Flour Mills* v. *CIT* [2010] 188 Taxman 257 (Guj.).

If the payer and recipient are in the same tax bracket and pays tax at the same rate, there is no question of diversion of funds to avoid tax and disallowance under section 40A(2) may not be attracted — *CIT* v. *V.S. Dempo & Co. (P.) Ltd.* [2011] 196 Taxman 193 (Bom.).

Who has incurred the expenditure (i.e., the taxpayer)	*To whom the payment is made*	*Example*
1. An individual	To a relative	X purchases goods from his brother.
2. A company	To a director of the company or any relative of the director	A, B and C are three directors of X Ltd., X Ltd. employs Mrs. A or Mrs. B is paid for her tax advise by X Ltd.
3. A firm	To a partner of the firm or a relative of the partners[32]	A and B are two partners of AB and Co., a firm. The firm purchases raw material from the sister of B.

31. For the assessment years 2013-14 to 2016-17, the aforesaid disallowance shall not be made in respect of a specified domestic transaction referred to in section 92BA, if such transaction is at arm's length price [as defined in section 92F(*ii*)].

32. If remuneration payable to partners is within the ceiling limit prescribed under section 40(*b*), section 40A(2) is not attracted—*CIT* v. *Great City Manufacturing Co.* [2009] 33 SOT 31 (Delhi).

Who has incurred the expenditure (i.e., the taxpayer)	*To whom the payment is made*	*Example*
4. An association of persons	To a member of the association or a relative of the member	XY, an association of persons, has X and Y as its two members. The association purchases goods manufactured by the son of X.
5. A Hindu undivided family`	To a member of the family or relative of such person	X is the karta of the X (HUF) with other members being Y, Z and A. The family appoints Mrs. A as selling agent.
6. Any taxpayer	To an individual who has a substantial interest in the business of the taxpayer or a relative of such individual.	X holds 20 per cent equity share capital in X Ltd. which hires trucks owned by the brother of X and pays rent.
7. Any taxpayer	To a company who has a substantial interest in the business of the taxpayer, any director of such company or a relative of such director (or from the assessment year 2013-14, any other company carrying on business/profession in which the first mentioned company has a substantial interest).	Y Ltd. holds 20 per cent equity shares in X Ltd. A and B are directors of Y Ltd. X Ltd. pays salary to Mrs. B. Suppose, Y Ltd. holds 20 per cent equity shares in Z Ltd. and X Ltd. purchases raw material from Z Ltd. (applicable from the assessment year 2013-14).
8. Any taxpayer	To a firm/association of persons/Hindu undivided family who has a substantial interest in the business of the taxpayer or partner/member of such person or a relative of partner/member.	A and B are two partners of AB and Co., a partnership firm. AB and Co. holds 20 per cent equity share capital in X Ltd. which appoints Mrs. B as a software consultant.
9. Any taxpayer	To a company, one of whose directors has a substantial interest in the business of the taxpayer or payment is made to any director of such company or any relative of such director.	A and B are directors of Y Ltd. A holds 20 per cent equity share capital in X Ltd. which purchases material for packaging from Mrs. B.
10. Any taxpayer	To a firm/association of persons/HUF, one of whose partners/members has a substantial interest in business of the taxpayer or payment is made to any other partner/member of such firm/association/HUF or any relative of such person.	A and B are two partners of Y and Co., a firm. B is 20 per cent partner in X and Co., another firm. X and Co. appoints Mrs. A as its legal advisor and pays fees.
11. An individual	To a person in whose business the taxpayer or any of his relative has a substantial interest.	Mrs. X holds 20 per cent equity share capital in Y Ltd. X purchases goods from Y Ltd.
12. A company	To a person in whose business the taxpayer/any director of taxpayer/any relative of such director has a substantial interest.	Mrs. A owns 20 per cent equity capital in Y Ltd. A is a director in X Ltd., X Ltd. purchases raw material from Y Ltd.
13. A firm/association of persons/HUF	To a person in whose business the taxpayer/any partner/member of the taxpayer or any relative of such partner/member has a substantial interest.	A's brother B is a 30 per cent partner in Y Co., a firm. A is a partner in X Co., another firm. X Co. purchases goods from Y Co.

Note : In the examples mentioned in column 3, if the payment is excessive or unreasonable, then the Assessing Officer may disallow the excess payment. For instance, in example 1, X purchases goods (1000 kg.) from his brother at the rate of Rs. 100 per kg., whereas the market rate is Rs. 90 per kg., then the Assessing Officer shall disallow Rs. 10,000 (*i.e.*, Rs. 10 × 1000). Similarly, in example 2, X Ltd. employs Mrs. A on salary of Rs. 15,000 per month, whereas Mrs. A will not get more than Rs. 6,000 per month from any other employer, then Rs. 9,000 per month shall be disallowed in the hands of X Ltd.

49.3 ***Amounts not deductible in respect of expenditure exceeding Rs. 10,000[33] [Sec. 40A(3)]*** - If an assessee incurs any expenditure in respect of which payment in excess of Rs. 10,000[33] is made otherwise

33. Rs. 20,000 up to the assessment year 2017-18. To avoid disallowance under section 40A(3) from the assessment year 2018-19, payment exceeding Rs. 10,000 should be made by an account payee cheque/draft or use of electronic clearing system through a bank account (**or through prescribed electronic mode**). However, the monetary limit of Rs. 35,000 (which was inserted with effect from October 1, 2009) for payment made for plying, hiring or leasing goods carriages, will continue.

than by an account payee cheque[34] or an account payee bank draft, 100 per cent[35] of such expenditure will not be allowable as deduction. Rule 6DD, however, prescribes the cases and circumstances in which payment in excess of Rs. 10,000[33] may be made otherwise than by an account payee cheque or an account payee bank draft without attracting the disallowance. Even payment made for purchase of goods falls within the expression "expenditure" occurring in this section.

49.3-1 *EXCEPTIONS* - Rule 6DD prescribes the following circumstances under which no disallowance will be made of the expenditure even if the payment exceeding Rs. 10,000[33] is made otherwise than by an account payee cheque or demand draft—

- Payment made to banking and other credit institutions[36], such as the Reserve Bank of India, commercial banks in the public and private sectors, co-operative banks or land mortgage banks, primary credit/ agricultural credit societies, Life Insurance Corporation of India, [rule 6DD(*a*)].
- Payment made to Government (both Central and State Governments), if under the rules framed by it, such payment is required to be made in legal tender, such as a payment of direct taxes, GST, customs duty, excise, railway freight, sales tax, etc. [rule 6DD(*b*)]. It covers any payment to the Government (not merely taxes). For instance, if scrap is purchased from Indian Railways in cash, section 40A(3) is not applicable, as it is payment to the Government – *Devendrappa M. Kalal* v. *ITO* [2012] 53 SOT 23 (Bang.).
- Payment through the banking system, *e.g.*, letters of credit, mail or telegraphic transfer, book adjustment in the same bank or between one bank and another and bills of exchange payable to a bank, use of electronic clearing system through a bank account, credit card and debit card [rule 6DD(*c*)].
- Payment made by book adjustment by an assessee in the account of the payee against money due to the assessee for any goods supplied or services rendered by him to the payee [rule 6DD(*d*)].
- Payment to a cultivator, grower or producer in respect of the purchase of agricultural[37] or forest produce or product of animal husbandry (including live stock, meat, hides and skins) or dairy or poultry farming or fish or fish products or products of horticulture or apiculture (even if these products have been subjected to some processing provided the processing has been done by the cultivator, grower or the producer of the product) [rule 6DD(*e*)].

Product of animal husbandry - If payment exceeding Rs. 10,000[33] is made to a producer of the products of animal husbandry (including livestock, meat, hides and skins) otherwise than by an account payee cheque or draft for the purchase of such produce, no disallowance should be attracted under section 40A(3). This exception is, however, not be available on the payment for the purchase of livestock, meat, hides and skins from a person who is not proved to be the producer of these goods and is only a trader, broker or any other middleman by whatever name called—Circular No. 4/2006[$], dated March 29, 2006.

Purchase of animals - Any person, by whatever name called, who buys animals from the farmers, slaughters them and then sells the raw meat carcasses to the meat processing factories or to the traders/retail outlets would be considered as producer of livestock and meat. The exemption is subject to the following conditions—

1. A declaration from the person receiving the payment that he is a producer of meat;

2. A confirmation that the payment, otherwise than by an account payee cheque or account payee bank draft, was made on his insistence; and

3. A further confirmation from a veterinary doctor certifying that the person specified in the certificate is a producer of meat and that slaughtering was done under his supervision—Circular No. 8/2006[$], dated October 6, 2006.

- Payment made to a producer in respect of purchase of products manufactured or processed without the aid of power in a cottage industry [rule 6DD(*f*)].

---

33. Rs. 20,000 up to the assessment year 2017-18. To avoid disallowance under section 40A(3) from the assessment year 2018-19, payment exceeding Rs. 10,000 should be made by an account payee cheque/draft or use of electronic clearing system through a bank account (**or through prescribed electronic mode**). However, the monetary limit of Rs. 35,000 (which was inserted with effect from October 1, 2009) for payment made for plying, hiring or leasing goods carriages, will continue.

34. If payment is made through banker's cheque/pay order/call deposit receipt issued by a bank in favour of the recipient, section 40A(3) is not attracted — *CIT* v. *Vijay Kumar Goel* [2010] 324 ITR 376 (Chhattisgarh).

35. 20 per cent up to the assessment year 2007-08.

36. This exception applies only to payments to RBI, commercial banks in public/private sector, co-operative banks, LIC, etc., and not to payments made in any party's account maintained by these institutions.

37. Cash payment for farmers for purchase of paddy, is not subject to disallowance under section 40A(3) – *CIT* v. *Keerthi Agro Mills (P.) Ltd.* [2017] 87 taxmann.com 31 (Ker.). SLP against High Court ruling has been dismissed – *CIT* v. *Keerthi Agro Mills (P.) Ltd.* [2018] 257 Taxman 1 (SC).

[$] For Circular No. 4/2006 and Circular No. 8/2006, log on to *taxmann.com/readyreckoner.aspx.*

• Payment made to a person who ordinarily resides or carries on business in a village not served by any bank [rule 6DD(*g*)][38].

• Payment of terminal benefits, such as gratuity, retrenchment compensation, etc., payable to an employee or his legal heirs and if such sum does not exceed Rs. 50,000 in aggregate [rule 6DD(*h*)].

• Payment made by an assessee by way of salary to his employee after deducting tax from salary in accordance with the provisions of section 192 and when such employee—

a. is temporarily posted for a continuous period of 15 days or more in a place other than his normal place of duty or on a ship ; and

b. does not maintain any account in any bank at such place or ship [rule 6DD(*i*)].

• Payment required to be made on a day on which the banks were closed either on account of holiday or strike [rule 6DD(*j*)].

• Payment made by any person to his agent who is required to make payment in cash for goods or services on behalf of such person [rule 6DD(*k*)]. For instance, if cash payment (in excess of Rs. 10,000[33]) is made by an assessee to his agent for procuring raw material, it cannot be disallowed under section 40A(3) read with rule 6DD(*k*) - *CIT* v. *Sri Shanmuga Ginning Factory* [2013] 218 Taxman 76 (Mad.). However, an employee cannot be considered as an agent for this purpose—*CIT* v. *Vijaykumar Rameshchand & Co.* [2007] 108 ITD 626 (Pune).

• Payment made by an authorised dealer or a money changer against purchase of foreign currency or travellers cheques in the normal course of his business [rule 6DD(*l*)].

49.3-2 *SCOPE OF SECTION 40A(3)* - The following points should be considered to understand the scope of section 40A(3)—

1. If the aggregate payment (otherwise than by an account payee cheque/draft) to the same person during a day exceeds Rs. 10,000[33], the provisions of section 40A(3) will apply and the entire amount of such payment will be disallowed.

2. If an assessee makes payment of two different bills (none of them exceeds Rs. 10,000[33]) at the same time in cash or by bearer cheque or crossed cheque/draft, section 40A(3) is not applicable even if the aggregate payment is more than Rs. 10,000[33]. This is because of the fact that section 40A(3) is applicable only in respect of an "expenditure" which is excess of Rs. 10,000[33]. In other words, unless the amount of the bill and the amount payment exceed Rs. 10,000[33], section 40A(3) is not applicable.

3. Where the assessee makes payment over Rs. 10,000[33] at a time, partly by an account payee cheque and partly in cash to some parties but the payment in cash alone at one time does not exceed Rs. 10,000[33], section 40A(3) is not attracted.

4. Provision of section 40A(3) does not apply in respect of an expenditure which is not to be claimed as deduction under sections 30 to 37.

49.3-3 *WHERE DEDUCTION HAS BEEN CLAIMED EARLIER ON DUE BASIS AND PAYMENT IS MADE IN THE CURRENT YEAR* - A special provision has been made in respect of those cases where deduction was claimed earlier on due basis. These provisions are given below—

1. The taxpayer had claimed a deduction in respect of an expenditure in any of the earlier years.

2. The amount of deduction exceeded Rs. 10,000[33].

3. In the current year, payment is made in respect of the aforesaid liability.

4. The payment exceeds Rs. 10,000[33].

5. The payment is made otherwise than by an account payee cheque or draft.

If the above conditions are satisfied, the payment so made shall be deemed to be the business income of the taxpayer of the previous year in which the payment is made. No specific provision has been made that the payment so made shall be taxable as business income even if the business has been discontinued.

---

33. Rs. 20,000 up to the assessment year 2017-18. To avoid disallowance under section 40A(3) from the assessment year 2018-19, payment exceeding Rs. 10,000 should be made by an account payee cheque/draft or use of electronic clearing system through a bank account (**or through prescribed electronic mode**). However, the monetary limit of Rs. 35,000 (which was inserted with effect from October 1, 2009) for payment made for plying, hiring or leasing goods carriages, will continue.

38. If the payment is made in a town having banking facilities to a villager whose village has no bank, this exemption is not available—Press Note dated May 8, 1969. If the place where recipient resides or carries on business is having banking facility, this exemption is not available merely because recipient has not opened his bank account—*ITO* v. *Kenaram Saha & Subhash Saha* [2008] 116 TTJ (Kol.)(SB) 289.

Provisions illustrated - Consider the following cases—

1. X Ltd. is a manufacturing company. On March 31, 1998, the company makes a provision for an outstanding bill of Rs. 80,000 for purchase of raw material. This provision appears on the liability side of the balance sheet as well as on the debit side of profit and loss account. It is allowed as deduction for computing the income of the company for the assessment year 1998-99. On April 4, 2006, out of Rs. 80,000, Rs. 27,000 is paid in cash. In this case, 20 per cent of Rs. 27,000 is disallowed under section 40A(3). This disallowance is applicable while re-computing income for the assessment year 1998-99. The Assessing Officer, in this case, can recompute the tax liability of the company for the assessment year 1998-99 by disallowing Rs. 5,400. This recomputation can be done under section 154 by the Assessing Officer at any time up to March 31, 2012.

2. Suppose in the above case, out of the outstanding balance, Rs. 30,000 is paid (otherwise than by account payee cheque or draft) on September 1, 2018, Rs. 30,000 will be taken as business income of the company for the assessment year 2019-20 by virtue of section 40A(3A) and it will be taxable.

49.3-E1 Determine the amount of disallowance in the cases given below—

1. Generally X pays salary to his employees by account payee cheques. Salary of December 2018 is, however, paid to three employees A, B and C in cash (payment being Rs. 6,000, Rs. 10,000 and Rs. 10,500, respectively).

2. X Ltd. purchases goods on credit from Y Ltd. on May 6, 2018 for Rs. 86,000 which is paid as follows—

a. Rs. 5,000 in cash on May 11, 2018;

b. Rs. 40,000 by a crossed cheque on May 31, 2018;

c. Rs. 41,000 by an account payee cheque.

3. Z Ltd. purchases goods on credit from A Ltd. on May 10, 2018 for Rs. 6,000 and on May 30, 2018 for Rs. 5,000. The total payment of Rs. 11,000 is made by a bearer cheque on June 1, 2018.

4. A Ltd. purchases goods on credit from a relative of a director on June 20, 2018 for Rs. 50,000 (market value : Rs. 42,000). The amount is paid in cash on June 25, 2018.

5. B Ltd. purchases raw material on credit from A who holds 20 per cent equity share capital in B Ltd. (the amount of bill being Rs. 36,000, market price being Rs. 9,000). It is paid in cash on July 26, 2018.

●

1. Rs. 10,500, being 100% of salary paid in cash to C will be disallowed.

2. Nothing will be disallowed out of the payment of Rs. 5,000 in cash on May 11, 2018, as the payment does not exceed Rs. 10,000. 100% of Rs. 40,000 will be disallowed. Nothing will be disallowed out of Rs. 41,000.

3. Though the amount of payment exceeds Rs. 10,000, nothing shall be disallowed. To attract disallowance, the amount of bill as well as the amount of payment should be more than Rs. 10,000—*Raja & Co.* v. *CIT* [2014] 64 SOT 12 (Cochin).

4. Out of the payment of Rs. 50,000, Rs. 8,000 (being the excess payment to a relative) shall be disallowed under section 40A(2). As the payment is made in cash and the remaining amount exceeds Rs. 10,000, 100% of the balance (*i.e.*, Rs. 42,000) shall be disallowed under section 40A(3).

5. Out of the payment of Rs. 36,000, Rs. 27,000 (being the excess payment to a person holding a substantial interest) shall be disallowed under section 40A(2). The remaining amount (*i.e.*, Rs. 9,000) does not exceed Rs. 10,000. Nothing shall be disallowed under section 40A(3) even if the payment is made in cash.

49.4 ***Provision for payment of gratuity under section 40A(7)*** - No deduction is allowed in computing business income in respect of a mere provision made by the assessee in his books of account for the payment of gratuity to his employees on retirement or termination of employment or for any other reason. The provision made for the purpose of payment of sums by way of contribution towards an approved gratuity fund or for the purpose of making any payment on account of gratuity that has become payable during the previous year is, however, eligible for deduction.

49.5 ***Contribution to non-statutory funds under section 40A(9)*** - No deduction is allowed in the computation of taxable profits in respect of any sum paid by the assessee as an employer towards the setting up or formation of, or as contribution to any fund, trust, company, association of persons, body of individuals, society registered under the Societies Registration Act, or other institution, for any purpose except where such sum is paid or contributed (within the limits laid down under the relevant provisions) to a recognised provident fund or an approved gratuity fund or an approved superannuation fund or (with effect from the assessment year 2012-13) National Pension System (NPS) or for the purposes and to the extent required by or under any other law.

49.6 ***Marked to market loss under section 40A(13)*** - No deduction or allowance shall be allowed (with effect from the assessment year 2017-18) in respect of any marked to market loss or other expected loss [except as allowable under section 36(1)(*xviii*)].

49.7 ***Unpaid statutory liability under section 43B*** - Section 43B is applicable only if the taxpayer maintains books of account on the basis of mercantile system of accounting. The provisions of section 43B are given below—

49.7-1 *GENERAL RULE - CERTAIN EXPENSES ARE DEDUCTIBLE ON PAYMENT BASIS* - The following expenses (which are otherwise deductible under the other provisions of the Income-tax Act) are deductible on payment basis—

a. any sum payable by way of tax, duty, cess or fee (by whatever name called under any law for the time being in force);

b. any sum payable by an employer by way of contribution to provident fund or superannuation fund or any other fund for the welfare of employees;

c. any sum payable as bonus or commission to employees for service rendered;

d. any sum payable as interest on any loan or borrowing from a public financial institution (*i.e.*, ICICI, IFCI, IDBI, LIC and UTI) or a state financial corporation or a state industrial investment corporation[39];

e. **any sum payable as interest on any loan or borrowing from a deposit-taking non-banking finance company (NBFC) and systematically important non deposit-taking NBFC (applicable from the assessment year 2020-21);**

f. interest on any term loan or advance taken from a scheduled bank [or (with effect from the assessment year 2018-19) a co-operative bank other than a primary agricultural credit society or a primary co-operative agricultural and rural development bank];

g. any sum payable by an employer in lieu of leave at the credit of his employee; and

h. (with effect from the assessment year 2017-18) any sum payable to the Indian Railways for the use of railway assets.

The above expenses are deductible in the year in which payment is actually made.
There is, however, one exception which is given in para 49.7-2 below :

49.7-2 *EXCEPTION - WHEN DEDUCTIBLE ON ACCRUAL BASIS* - The exception is applicable if the following two conditions are satisfied -

1. Payment in respect of the aforesaid expenses is actually made on or before the due date of submission of return of income.

2. The evidence of such payment is submitted along with the return of income[40].

If the above two conditions are satisfied and if the assessee maintains books of account on mercantile basis, then the expenditure is deductible on "accrual" basis in the year in which the liability is incurred.

49.7-3 *PROVISIONS ILLUSTRATED* - X Ltd. (not having any international or specified domestic transaction) maintains books of account on mercantile basis. For the previous year 2018-19 (*i.e.*, the assessment year 2019-20), interest on term loan taken from Punjab National Bank (or any other sum given in para 49.7-1) is Rs. 1,95,000. The amount is paid as follows—

Date of payment	*Amount Rs.*
May 2, 2018	25,000
November 20, 2018	20,000
August 16, 2019	25,000
December 5, 2019	30,000
June 12, 2020	35,000
November 20, 2020	40,000
Not paid so far	20,000

As the expenditure is covered by section 43B, it is deductible on payment basis in the year in which payment is made. However, if payment is made on or before the due date of submission of return of income for the assessment year 2019-20 (*i.e.*, on or before September 30, 2019) then such payment is deductible on accrual basis for the previous year 2018-19. Consequently, these payments are deductible as follows :

Date of payment	*Amount Rs.*	*Previous year in which deductible*	*Reasons*
May 2, 2018	25,000	2018-19	Payment made during the relevant year is deductible in that year
November 20, 2018	20,000	2018-19	Payment made during the relevant year is deductible in that year

39. HSBC and ICICI Banks are not state financial corporation or state industrial investment corporation for purpose of disallowance under section 43B—*Rabo India Finance Ltd.* v. *CIT* [2011] 14 taxmann.com 83 (Mum. - Trib.).

40. However, no annexure is possible with the new Income-tax Return Forms, *i.e.*, ITR-1 to ITR-7; such evidence should be kept by the taxpayer himself and it can be produced before the Assessing Officer whenever he is required to produce it.

Date of payment	*Amount Rs.*	*Previous year in which deductible*	*Reasons*
August 16, 2019	25,000	2018-19	Payment made after the end of the relevant year but on or before the due date of submission of return of income (*i.e.*, September 30, 2019) is deductible in the year in which the liability is incurred
December 5, 2019	30,000	2019-20	Payment made after the due date of submission of return of income (*i.e.*, made after September 30, 2019) is deductible in the year in which the payment is made
June 12, 2020	35,000	2020-21	Payment made after the due date of submission of return of income (*i.e.*, made after September 30, 2019) is deductible in the year in which the payment is made
November 20, 2020	40,000	2020-21	Payment made after the due date of submission of return of income (*i.e.*, made after September 30, 2019) is deductible in the year in which the payment is made
Not paid	20,000	Not deductible	Not deductible as the payment is not made

49.7-4 *CONVERSION OF UNPAID SALES TAX INTO LOAN*- Several State Governments have introduced sales tax deferred schemes as a part of the incentives offered to entrepreneurs for setting up industries in backward areas. Under these schemes, eligible units are permitted to collect sales tax and retain such tax for a prescribed period. After this period, the sales tax is to be paid to the Government either in lump sum or in instalments.

In such a case a problem arises, whether sales tax is treated as "paid" for the purpose of section 43B. The following broad conclusions may be drawn on the basis of judicial rulings and Board's Circulars—

1. If under the sales tax legislation, sales tax so deferred is treated as actually paid then statutory liability shall be treated to have been discharged for the purpose of section 43B—Circular No. 496[$], dated September 25, 1987.

2. For this purpose, a State Government may amend its Sales Tax Act to provide that the sales tax (deferred under an incentive scheme framed by it) will be treated as actually paid so as to meet the requirements of section 43B—*CIT* v. *Gujarat Polycrete Pvt. Ltd.* [2000] 246 ITR 463 (SC).

3. Some State Governments, instead of amending the Sales Tax Act, have issued Government Orders notifying schemes under which sales tax is deemed to have been actually collected and disbursed as loans. The amount of sales tax liability converted into loans may be allowed as deduction in the assessment for the previous year in which such conversion has been permitted by or under Government Orders—Circular No. 674[$], dated December 29, 1993.

In other words, where sales tax due to the Government is converted as loan to be repaid by the assessee subsequently by instalments, it would amount to actual payment of sales-tax—*CIT* v. *Goodluck Silicate Industries (P.) Ltd.* [2002] 178 CTR (Guj.) 92.

49.7-5 *CONVERSION OF OUTSTANDING INTEREST INTO LOAN*[41] - Conversion of unpaid interest into loan[41] is not taken as payment of interest. The converted interest, by whatever name called, in the wake of its conversion into a loan or borrowing or advance, will be eligible for deduction in the computation of income of the previous year in which the converted interest is 'actually paid'. In other words, nomenclature of the sum of converted interest will make no difference as the sum of converted interest whenever is actually paid will not represent repayment of the principal—Circular No. 7/2006[$], dated July 17, 2006.

Provisions illustrated - The following illustrations are given to have better understanding—

1. Loan taken from a bank on March 31, 2013 is Rs. 20,00,000. Interest unpaid up to March 31, 2018 is Rs. 2,00,000. In the restructuring arrangement entered into in this case, the unpaid interest has been converted into a Funded Interest Term Loan (FITL) which has been shown separately from the original loan and no interest is chargeable on FITL. This converted interest (*i.e.*, FITL) is to be paid in 4 annual instalments from April 1, 2022 (each instalment being Rs. 50,000). In this case, deduction to the extent of the amount actually paid against the payment of instalment of FITL of Rs. 2,00,000 under section

41. Conversion of outstanding interest liability into share capital is not hit by this provision — *JSW Steels Ltd.* v. *CIT*[2011] 9 taxmann.com 77 (Bang. - ITAT).

[$]For Circular Nos. 496, 674 and 7/2006, log on to *taxmann.com/readyreckoner.aspx.*

43B shall be allowed in the relevant assessment year when it is actually paid. Interest on the original principal of Rs. 20,00,000, if any, actually paid will be independently allowable under section 43B.

2. Suppose in the above case, interest is payable on FITL. In such a situation the following shall be deductible on actual payment basis according to the provisions of section 43B—

a. interest on original loan of Rs. 20,00,000;

b. re-payment of FITL; and

c. interest on FITL

3. Loan taken by the assessee from a term lending institution in May, 2014 is Rs. 14 crore. Interest not paid up to April 1, 2018 is Rs. 2 crore. In a restructuring arrangement unpaid interest of Rs. 2 crore is merged with the principal amount of Rs. 14 crore. After merger the amount of loan becomes Rs. 16 crore which is payable by the taxpayer in 5 equal annual instalments from April 1, 2018. In the previous year 2018-19, the first instalment of Rs. 3.2 crore is paid by the taxpayer. The amount of deduction in the computation of income on account of actual payment of interest will be worked out in the following manner :

Rs. 3.2 crore × Rs. 2 crore ÷ Rs. 16 crore = Rs. 40 lakh.

Out of the repayment of Rs. 3.2 crore in the first year, deduction of Rs. 40 lakh will be admissible in terms of the provisions of section 43B as deduction, as Rs. 40 lakh out of Rs. 3.2 crore actually paid represents interest component. Balance Rs. 2.80 crore representing repayment of the principal shall not be admissible as deduction in the computation of income.

49.7-6 *JUDICIAL RULINGS* - One must keep in view the following—

1. Royalty payable to the Government in respect of mineral rights is a 'tax' within meaning of section 43B—*Grasim Industries Ltd.* v. *CIT* [1999] 64 TTJ (Mum.) 357.

2. Interest payable to the Government of Haryana on arrears of purchase tax is not "tax" within the meaning of section 43B—*CIT* v. *Padmavati Raje Cotton Mills Ltd.* [1999] 239 ITR 355 (Cal.).

3. X Ltd. purchases machinery from A Ltd. and draws a promissory note in favour of A Ltd. duly accepted by its bankers. A Ltd. discounts the promissory notes from Punjab National Bank and Punjab National Bank rediscounts the promissory note from IDBI. X Ltd. is required to make payment to IDBI through its banker with interest. Interest payable to IDBI is not covered by section 43B, as there is no direct financial arrangement with IDBI.

4. A 'kist' is neither duty nor tax and, therefore, would not come within the purview of section 43B—*CIT* v. *Shiva & Co.* [2001] 119 Taxman 597 (Kar.).

5. Audit fee payable to Government, by a co-operative society, is not covered by section 43B as it is not tax or fee—*CIT* v. *Shree Warma Sahakari Sakhar Karkhana* [2001] 119 Taxman 422 (Bom.).

6. Interest on municipal tax is not covered by section 43B as it is not an adjunct to municipal tax—*CIT* v. *Orient Beverages Ltd.* [2001] 117 Taxman 106 (Cal.).

7. Electricity tax collected by an Electricity Board on behalf of the Government is not subject to the provisions of section 43B—*Kerala State Electricity Board* v. *CIT* [2010] 329 ITR 91 (Ker.).

8. Mandi tax is not a tax as it is paid by a trader because some services are provided by the mandi—*CIT* v. *Mohansingh & Sons* [1995] 216 ITR 432 (MP).

9. Electricity charges are neither tax, nor duty nor cess and, hence, they cannot be tagged in the provisions of section 43B.

10. Furnishing bank guarantee cannot be equated with actual payment. Actual payment requires that money must flow from the assessee to the public exchequer as such as specified in section 43—*CIT* v. *McDowell & Co. Ltd.* [2009] 180 Taxman 514 (SC).

11. Bottling fee payable under excise law for acquiring a right of bottling of IMFL does not fall within purview of section 43B—*CIT* v. *McDowell & Co. Ltd.* [2009] 180 Taxman 514 (SC).

12. SEBI turnover fees is subject to section 43B—*I. Kay Holding Co. (P.) Ltd.* v. *CIT* [2009] 32 SOT 586 (Delhi).

13. Advance custom duty is allowable as an expenditure under section 43B—*CIT* v. *Samtel Color Ltd.* [2009] 184 Taxman 120 (Delhi).

14. Duty paid on sale of electricity is covered by section 43B — *CIT* v. *Gujarat Urja Vikas Nigam Ltd.* [2010] 322 ITR 539 (Guj.).

15. Payment to gratuity fund operated by LIC is covered by section 43B — *CIT* v. *Popular Vehicles & Services Ltd.* [2010] 189 Taxman 14 (Ker.).

16. A car manufacturer deposits certain amount on regular basis in Excise Personal Ledger Account in terms of rule 173G of Central Excise Rules, 1944, in order to clear goods. The amount so deposited cannot be disallowed under section 43B – *CIT* v. *Maruti Suzuki India Ltd.* [2013] 212 Taxman 603 (Delhi).

17. Service tax is not covered within the purview of section 43B – *CIT* v. *Real Image Media Technologies (P.) Ltd.* [2008] 114 ITD 573 (Chennai). However, a contrary ruling is given by the Hyderabad Bench of the Tribunal in the case of *Bartronics India Ltd.* v. *CIT* [2012] 52 SOT 188.

18. "Actual payment" means "actual payment" and not actual receipt and delivery of currency by two transacting parties when they are creditor and debtor both. When interest is paid out of fund lying in any another account of the assessee with such creditor, then that is "actual payment"—*CIT* v. *Shakti Spring Industries (P.) Ltd.* [2013] 219 Taxman 124 (Jharkhand).

19. In *Hero Moto Corp Ltd.* v. *CIT* [2013] 60 SOT 25 (Delhi), the assessee-company entered into a master policy with LIC, whereby assessee paid annual premium to LIC, which in turn, paid leave salary directly to employees. The Tribunal held that there was no direct payment of leave encashment by the assessee, same could not be disallowed under section 43B(*f*), and was to be allowed as business expenditure under section 37(1).

20. Section 43B is not applicable to interest on Government loans and for dearness allowance arrears of employees—*CIT* v. *U.P. Rajya Vidyut Utpadan Nigam Ltd.* [2013] 218 Taxman 153 (All.).

21. Vend fee collected by a State Government from a sugar manufacturer for giving special benefit to repair or replace old machinery is a "fee" and attracts disallowance provisions of section 43B—*CIT* v. *Travancore Sugars & Chemicals Ltd.* [2015] 58 taxmann.com 86 (SC).

49.7-E1 X Ltd. is a manufacturing company. It does not have any international or specified domestic transaction. The profit and loss account of X Ltd. for the year ending March 31, 2019 is given below :

	Rs.		*Rs.*
Opening stock	15,600	Sales	88,10,000
Manufacturing expenses	78,96,100	Closing stock	18,700
Salary to employees	90,000		
Employer's contribution to provident fund	9,000		
Other expenses	32,000		
Net profit	7,86,000		
	88,28,700		88,28,700

Notes :

1. Out of the salary of Rs. 90,000, contribution of employees towards provident fund is Rs. 9,000 which is credited by X Ltd. in the provident fund account of employees. However, Rs. 3,200 is credited in these accounts after the "due date" (under provident fund rules) of making payment.

2. Employer's contribution towards provident fund is paid by cheques as follows :

	Rs.
Paid during the previous year 2018-19	8,000
Paid during April 1, 2019 and September 30, 2019	800
Paid after September 30, 2019	200

Determine the taxable income of X Ltd. for the assessment year 2019-20 on the assumption that (*a*) the provident fund is recognised, and (*b*) the provident fund is unrecognised.

•

	If the provident fund is recognised Rs.	*If the provident fund is unrecognised Rs.*
Net profit as per profit and loss account	7,86,000	7,86,000
Add: Sum received by the assessee from his employees as their contributions to the provident fund [Sec. 2(*24*)(*x*)]	9,000	9,000
Total	7,95,000	7,95,000
Less : Amount deductible under section 36(1)(*va*) on account of employees' contribution towards provident fund to the extent such contributions are credited by X Ltd. to the employees' account before "due date" under the provident fund regulations (Rs. 9,000 — Rs. 3,200)	5,800	5,800
Balance	7,89,200	7,89,200
Add: Disallowance		
Under section 40A(9) in respect of employer's contribution towards unrecognised provident fund [*see* para 49.5]	—	9,000
Under section 43B in respect of employer's contribution towards provident fund which is paid after September 30, 2019	200	—
Income under the head "Profits and gains of business or profession"	7,89,400	7,98,200

Deemed profits chargeable to tax as business income [Secs. 41 and 176(3A) & (4)]

50. By virtue of section 41, the following receipts are chargeable to tax as business income notwithstanding that the business or profession to which the receipts relate ceased to be in existence in the year in which they are received :

50.1 ***Recovery against any deduction [Sec. 41(1)]*** - Section 41(1) is applicable if the following conditions are satisfied—

1. In any of the earlier years a deduction was allowed to the taxpayer in respect of loss, expenditure or trading liability incurred by the assessee.

2. During the current previous year, the taxpayer—

a. has obtained a refund of such loss or expenditure (it may be in cash or any other manner); or

b. has obtained some benefit in respect of such trading liability by way of remission or cessation[42] thereof ("remission or cessation" for this purpose includes unilateral act of the assessee by way of writing off of such liability in his books of account).

If the above two conditions are satisfied the amount obtained by such person (or the value of benefit accruing to him) shall be deemed to be profits and gains of business or profession and accordingly chargeable to tax as the income of that previous year.

The following points should be noted—

- For the purpose of condition 2(*a*) (*supra*) there may (or may not) be any remission or cessation of trading liability.
- Where the assessee to whom any allowance or deduction has been allowed in respect of loss, expenditure or trading liability, is succeeded in his business either because of amalgamation or demerger of two companies or on account of the constitution of new firm or the business is continued by some other person when the assessee ceases to carry on the business, then the person succeeding will be chargeable to tax on any amount received in relation to which deduction or allowance has been made.
- Provisions of section 41(1) can be invoked to tax excise duty refunds received in the relevant assessment year even when the part of excise duty was not claimed as expenditure in the profit and loss account of earlier years and the assessee had kept a separate account in respect of collection and payment of excise duty—*Mysore Thermo Electric (P.) Ltd.* v. *CIT* [1996] 221 ITR 504 (Kar.).
- The aforesaid rule is applicable even if the business is not in existence in the year of recovery.

50.2 ***Balancing charge [Sec. 41(2)]*** - *See* para 48.3-10a[2].

42. Waiver of loan does not amount to cessation of trading liability – *CIT* v. *Mahindra & Mahindra Ltd.* [2018] 93 taxmann.com 32 (SC).

50.3 ***Sale of assets used for scientific research [Sec. 41(3)]*** - Where any capital asset used in scientific research is sold *without having been used* for other purposes and the sale proceeds, together with the amount of deduction allowed under section 35, exceeds the amount of the capital expenditure, such surplus or the amount of deduction allowed, whichever is less, is chargeable to tax as business income in the year in which the sale took place.

50.4 ***Recovery of bad debts [Sec. 41(4)]*** - Where any bad debt has been allowed as deduction under section 36(1)(*vii*) and the amount subsequently recovered on such debt is greater than the difference between the debt and the deduction so allowed, the excess realisation is chargeable to tax as business income of the year in which the debt is recovered.

50.5 ***Amount withdrawn from special reserve [Sec. 41(4A)]*** - Where any amount is withdrawn from any reserve created under section 36(1)(*viii*), it will be chargeable to tax in the year in which the amount is withdrawn, regardless of the fact whether the business is in existence in that year or not.

50.6 ***Recovery after discontinuance of business or profession [Sec. 176(3A), (4)]*** - Section 176(4) is applicable where any profession is discontinued in any year on account of cessation of the profession by, or the retirement or death of, the person carrying on the profession. Section 176(3A) is applicable where any business is discontinued in any year. By virtue of these sub-sections of section 176, any sum received after the discontinuance of the business or profession is deemed to be the income of the recipient and charged to tax in the year of receipt.

Maintenance of accounts by persons [Sec. 44AA]

51. To understand the provisions of compulsory maintenance of books of account by certain persons, one must know the meaning of the terms "specified professions" and "non-specified professions".

51.1 ***"Specified profession"*** - For the purpose of section 44AA and rule 6F legal, medical, engineering, architectural, accountancy, technical consultancy, or interior decoration or any other notified profession [*i.e.*, authorised representative, film artist, company secretary and (from the assessment year 2002-03) information technology] are specified professions. For this purpose "authorised representative" means a person, who represents any other person, on payment of any fee or remuneration, before any Tribunal or authority constituted or appointed by or under any law for the time being in force, but does not include an employee of the person so represented or a person carrying on legal profession or a person carrying on the profession of accountancy.

"Film artist", for the aforesaid purpose, means any person engaged in his professional capacity in the production of a cinematograph film, whether produced by him or by any other person as an actor, a cameraman, a director, a music director, an art director, a dance director, an editor, a singer, a lyricist, a story writer, a screen play writer, a dialogue writer and a dress designer.

51.2 ***"Non-specified profession"*** - A non-specified profession is a profession other than a "specified profession" mentioned above.

51.3 ***Requirement of compulsory maintenance of books of account*** - The requirement of section 44AA and rule 6F for compulsory maintenance of books of account may be summarised by grouping different taxpayers in the following categories :

• *Category A* - Persons carrying on a "specified profession" whose gross receipts in the profession *do not exceed Rs. 1,50,000*[43] in any (one or more) of the three years immediately preceding the previous year (or where the profession has been newly set up in the previous year, his gross total receipts in the profession for that year are not likely to exceed the said amount).

Persons coming under this category are required to maintain such "books of account and other documents" as may enable the Assessing Officer to compute their taxable income under the Income-tax Act. It may be noted that the Board has not prescribed books of account to be maintained for persons falling under this category.

• *Category B* - Persons carrying on a "specified profession" whose gross receipts in the profession *exceed Rs. 1,50,000*[43] in all the three years immediately preceding the previous year (or where the profession has been newly set up in the previous year, his gross total receipts in the profession for that year are likely to exceed the said amount).

Persons coming in this category are required to maintain such books of account as are prescribed by rule 6F [*see* para 51.4 *infra*].

---

43. Rs. 60,000 (Rs. 80,000 in the case of a person who in the course of medical profession dispenses drugs and medicines) up to April 5, 2000.

• *Category C*- Persons carrying on a "non-specified profession". It also includes a business whose income from such business or profession does not exceed Rs. 1,20,000[44], or the total sales, turnover or gross receipts thereof are not in excess of Rs. 10,00,000[45], in all the three years immediately preceding the previous year (or when the business or profession is newly set up, income/total sales, turnover or gross receipts are not likely to exceed the said amount).

Persons coming under this category are *not required* to maintain any books of account.

• *Category D*- Persons carrying on a "non-specified profession". It also includes a business whose income from such business or profession exceeds Rs. 1,20,000[44] or the total sales, turnover, or gross receipts thereof are in excess of Rs. 10,00,000[45] in any of the three years immediately preceding the previous year (or when the business or profession is newly set up, income/total sales, etc., are likely to exceed the said amount). Moreover, this category also includes the following assessees -

1. An assessee covered under section 44AD[46] or section 44AE or section 44AF[46], or (with effect from the assessment year 2004-05) section 44BB or 44BBB, if it is claimed that the profits and gains from the business are lower than the profits and gains computed in accordance with the provisions of these sections.

2. (From the assessment year 2011-12) an assessee who is covered by section 44AD and claims that the profits and gains from the business are lower than the profits and gains computed in accordance with the provisions of section 44AD(1) and if his income exceeds the maximum amount which is not chargeable to tax.

3. (From the assessment year 2017-18) an assessee who is covered by section 44AD(4) and his income exceeds the maximum amount which is not chargeable to income-tax.

Persons falling under this category are required to maintain such "books of account and other documents" as may enable the Assessing Officer to compute their taxable income under the Income-tax Act. However, the Board has not prescribed the account books to be maintained by persons falling under this category.

51.4 ***Specified books of account*** - The Board has specified certain books of account under rule 6F for persons falling under category B (*supra*). The prescribed books are as follows :

a. a cash book (*i.e.*, a record of all cash receipts and payments kept and maintained from day to day and giving the cash balance in hand of each day or at the end of a specified period not exceeding a month);

b. a journal, if the accounts are maintained according to the mercantile system of accounting;

c. a ledger;

d. carbon copies of bills (whether machine numbered or, otherwise serially numbered) exceeding Rs. 25, issued by the person and carbon copies or counterfoils of machine numbered or otherwise serially numbered receipts issued by the person;

e. original bills wherever issued to the person and receipts in respect of expenditure incurred by the person or, where such bills and receipts are not issued and the expenditure incurred does not exceed fifty rupees, payment vouchers prepared and signed by the person (preparation of vouchers is not necessary where cash book contains adequate particulars of expenditure).

Apart from the aforesaid books of account and documents, a person carrying on medical profession (*i.e.*, a practitioner of any system of medicine—physicians, surgeons, dentists, pathologists, radiologists, vaids, hakims, etc.) is required to keep the following additional books/documents :

a. a daily case register in Form No. 3C showing the date, patient's name, nature of professional services rendered (*i.e.*, general consultation, surgery, injection, visit, etc.), fees received and date of receipt; and

b. an inventory under broad heads, as on the first and the last days of the previous year, of the stock of drugs, medicines, and other consumable accessories used for the purpose of his profession.

The following points also need consideration :

• The aforesaid books of account and documents (other than those relating to a previous year which has come to an end) should be kept and maintained by the person at the place where he is carrying on the profession or, where the profession is carried on in more places than one, at the principal place of his profession. If, however, the person keeps and maintains separate books of account in respect of each place where the profession is carried on, such books of account and other documents may be kept and maintained at the respective places at which the profession is carried on.

• The aforesaid books of account and documents should be kept and maintained for a period of 6 years from the end of the relevant assessment year.

---

44. Rs. 2,50,000 (from the assessment year 2018-19) in the case of an individual/HUF.

45. Rs. 25,00,000 (from the assessment year 2018-19) in the case of an individual/HUF.

46. Up to the assessment year 2010-11.

• Where, however, the assessment in relation to any assessment year has been reopened under section 147, all the books of account and other documents which were kept and maintained at the time of reopening of the assessment should continue to be so kept and maintained till the assessment so reopened has been completed.

Audit of accounts by certain persons [Sec. 44AB]

52. The provisions of section 44AB are given below :

52.1 ***Who has to get his accounts audited on compulsory basis*** - The following persons are required to get their accounts compulsorily audited by a chartered accountant—

Different taxpayers	*When they are covered by the provisions of compulsory audit under section 44AB*
A person carrying on business	If the total sales, turnover or gross receipt in business for the previous year(s) relevant to the assessment year exceed or exceeds Rs. 1 crore[47 48]
A person carrying on profession	If his gross receipts in profession for the previous year(s) relevant to the assessment year exceeds Rs. 50 lakh[49]
A person covered under section 44AD[50], 44AE, 44AF[50], 44BB or 44BBB	If such person claims that the profits and gains from the business are lower than the profits and gains computed under these sections (irrespective of his turnover)
A person covered under section 44AD	If such person claims that the profits and gains from the business are lower than the profits and gains computed in accordance with the provisions of section 44AD(1) and if his income exceeds the maximum amount which is not chargeable to tax (applicable for the assessment years 2011-12 to 2016-17)
A person covered under section 44ADA	If such person claims that the profits and gains from the profession are lower than the profits and gains computed in accordance with the provisions of section 44ADA and if his income exceeds the maximum amount which is not chargeable to tax (applicable from the assessment year 2017-18)
A person covered under section 44AD(4)	If a person carrying on business is covered by the provisions of section 44AD(4) and his income exceeds the maximum amount which is not chargeable to income-tax in the previous year (applicable from the assessment year 2017-18).

Note : Section 44AB is not applicable in the case of assessees who come within the purview of section 44B or 44BBA.

52.2 ***Due date for getting books audited/submission of audit report and Form No.*** - These provisions are given in the table below—

Different taxpayers	*Audit Form No.*	*Statement particulars*	*Due date for getting books audited*	*Due date for submission of audit report*
In the case of a person who carries on business or profession and who is required by or under any law to get his accounts audited	Form No. 3CA	Form No. 3CD	Due date of furnishing return of income under section 139(1)[51]	Due date of furnishing return of income under section 139(1)[51]
In the case of a person who carries on business or profession but not being a person referred to above	Form No. 3CB	Form No. 3CD	Due date of furnishing return of income under section 139(1)[51]	Due date of furnishing return of income under section 139(1)[51]

Notes :

1. In cases where accounts are required to be audited by or under any other law (as in the case of companies and co-operative societies), it is sufficient if accounts are audited under such other law before September 30† of the assessment

47. Rs. 2 crore in the case of a person, who declares business profit in accordance with the provisions of section 44AD(1) (applicable from the assessment year 2017-18).

48. For the assessment years 2011-12 and 2012-13, it was Rs. 60 lakh. Rs. 1 crore[47] is applicable from the assessment year 2013-14.

49. For the assessment years 2011-12 and 2012-13, it was Rs. 15 lakh. Rs. 25 lakh was applicable for the assessment years 2013-14 to 2016-17.

50. Omitted from the assessment year 2011-12.

51. September 30 of the assessment year (in case of assessees having international or specified domestic transaction(s) : November 30 of the assessment year).

year and the assessee obtains before the said date, a report of the audit as required under such law and also a report of audit from a chartered accountant in the forms given above.

2. From April 1, 2013, audit report should be submitted electronically. Provisions pertaining to electronic submission of audit report were not applicable prior to April 1, 2013 (for period prior to April 1, 2013, audit report may be retained by the assessee and it may be furnished in original whenever the Assessing Officer wants to examine it in assessment proceedings or otherwise).

3. In the case of an assessee carrying on a business/profession, it is necessary to comply with the provisions of section 44AB only in respect of his business/profession income. It would not be necessary to comply with the provisions of section 44AB in respect of his other income—*Ghai Constructions* v. *State of Maharashtra* [2009] 184 Taxman 52 (Bom.).

Computation of income on estimated basis under section 44AD

53. Section 44AD provides special provisions for computing business profit on presumptive basis from the assessment year 2011-12.

• *Conditions* - The provisions of section 44AD are applicable only if the following conditions are satisfied—

1. Eligible assessee - The assessee should be an eligible assessee. Eligible assessee for this purpose is a person resident in India who is an individual, a Hindu undivided family or a partnership firm (not being a limited liability firm).

2. Has not claimed some deductions - The assessee has not claimed any deduction under sections 10A, 10AA, 10B, 10BA, 80HH to 80RRB in the relevant assessment year.

3. Eligible business - The assessee should be engaged in any business (whether it is retail trading or wholesale trading or civil construction or any other business). However, the following persons are not eligible to avail any benefit under section 44AD –

a. a person carrying on profession as referred to in section 44AA(1);

b. a person earning income in the nature of commission or brokerage;

c. a person carrying on any agency business; or

d. a person who is in the business of plying, hiring or leasing goods carriages.

4. Turnover - Total turnover/gross receipt in the previous year of the business should not exceed Rs. 2 crore (this limit was Rs. 1 crore for the assessment years 2013-14 to 2016-17, and Rs. 60 lakh for the assessment years 2011-12 and 2012-13)

• *Consequences if the above conditions are satisfied* - If the above conditions are satisfied, the income from the eligible business is estimated at 8 per cent[52] of the gross receipt or total turnover. The following points should be noted—

1. The assessee can voluntarily declare a higher income in his return.

2. All deductions under sections 30 to 38, including depreciation and unabsorbed depreciation, are deemed to have been already allowed and no further deduction is allowed under these sections (subject to an exception given below).

3. However, in the case of a firm (up to the assessment year 2016-17), the normal deduction in respect of salary and interest to partners under section 40(*b*) shall be allowed (this deduction is not available from the assessment year 2017-18).

4. The written down value is calculated, where necessary, as if depreciation as applicable has been allowed.

5. Further, it will be assumed that disallowance, if any, under sections 40, 40A and 43B has been considered while calculating the estimated income @ 8 per cent[52].

6. An assessee, who opts for the above scheme, is exempted (up to the assessment year 2016-17) from payment of advance tax related to such business. From the assessment year 2017-18, an assessee (who opts from the above scheme) is required to pay advance tax related to such business. However, advance tax can be paid during the financial year (immediately prior to the assessment year) on or before March 15 (no need to pay advance tax related to such business on or before June 15, September 15 or December 15).

7. An assessee opting for the above scheme shall be exempted from maintenance of books of account related to such business as required under section 44AA.

---

52. 6 per cent in respect of total turnover or gross receipts received by an account payee cheque/draft or use of electronic clearing system through a bank account (**or through prescribed electronic mode**) during the previous year or before the due date of submission of return of income under section 139(1) (applicable from the assessment year 2017-18).

• *Is it possible to declare lower income (up to assessment year 2016-17)* - A taxpayer can declare his income to be lower than the deemed profits and gains as stated above. The following consequences are applicable if the taxpayer declares his income which is lower than the deemed profits and gains as stated above—

1. The taxpayer will have to maintain the books of account as per section 44AA (irrespective of income or turnover) if his total income exceeds the exemption limit.

2. The taxpayer will have to get his books of account audited under section 44AB (irrespective of turnover) if his total income exceeds the exemption limit.

• *Is it possible to declare lower income (from the assessment year 2017-18) [Sec. 44AD(4)]* - Where an eligible assessee declares profit for any previous year at the rate of 8 per cent[52] of turnover under section 44AD and he declares profit for any of the 5 consecutive subsequent assessment years at lower than 8 per cent[52], he shall not be eligible to claim the benefit of the provisions of section 44AD for 5 subsequent assessment years [i.e., subsequent to the assessment year relevant to the previous year in which the profit has not been declared at the rate of 8 per cent[52]]. For example, an eligible assessee claims to be taxed on presumptive basis of 8 per cent[52] of turnover under section 44AD for assessment year 2018-19. He offers income of Rs. 8 lakh on the turnover of Rs. 1 crore. For assessment year 2019-20 and assessment year 2020-21 also he offers income in accordance with the provisions of section 44AD. However, for assessment year 2021-22, he offers income of Rs. 5 lakh on turnover of Rs. 1 crore. In this case since he has not offered income in accordance with the provisions of section 44AD for 5 consecutive assessment years, after assessment year 2018-19, he will not be eligible to claim the benefit of section 44AD for next five assessment years (i.e., for assessment years 2022-23 to 2026-27). Consequently, for the assessment years 2021-22 to 2026-27,—

a. he will have to maintain the books of account as per section 44AA (irrespective of income or turnover) if his total income exceeds the exemption limit; and

b. he will have to get his books of account audited under section 44AB (irrespective of turnover) if his total income exceeds the exemption limit.

The above consequences will be applicable even if for the assessment years 2022-23 to 2026-27, he wants to declare 8 per cent[52] (or higher) of turnover as his business income.

• *Other points* - The following points should be kept in view—

1. While computing income of assessee under section 44AD, the Assessing Officer does not have the power to assess anything in excess of returned income if returned income is more than 8 per cent[52] of total receipt/sale consideration—*Abhi Developers* v. *ITO* [2007] 12 SOT 444 (Ahd.). Even disallowance provisions of sections 40, 40A and 43B are not applicable—*ITO* v. *Mark Construction* [2012] 53 SOT 22 (Kol.). Moreover, no addition can be made on the ground that assessee was not able to explain discrepancies in account books—*CIT* v. *Nitin Soni* [2012] 207 Taxman 332 (All.). The concerned assessee is not under any obligation to explain individual entry of cash deposit in his bank, unless such entry has no nexus with the gross receipts—*CIT* v. *Surinder Pal Anand* [2010] 192 Taxman 264 (Punj. & Har.).

2. Section 44AD would not apply where gross receipts of an assessee are more than Rs. 2 crore (as given above), even if the said figure includes undisclosed income—*CIT* v. *Sobti Construction (India)* [2008] 174 Taxman 39 (Delhi).

Computation of professional income of estimated basis under section 44ADA

53A. Section 44ADA is applicable from the assessment year 2017-18. The provisions of section 44ADA are given below -

1. The assessee is resident and engaged in a profession referred to in section 44AA(1) (*i.e.*, such as legal, medical, engineering or architectural profession or the profession of accountancy or technical consultancy or interior decoration or any other profession as is notified by the Board).

2. Gross receipts of the assessee from the profession does not exceed Rs. 50 lakh.

3. If the above two conditions are satisfied, income of the assessee shall be calculated on estimated basis at a sum equal to 50 per cent of the total gross receipts.

4. The assessee can voluntarily declare a higher income in his return.

5. All deductions under sections 30 to 38, including depreciation and unabsorbed depreciation, are deemed to have been already allowed and no further deduction is allowed under these sections. Even salary/interest to partners is not deductible.

---

52. 6 per cent in some cases as given above (applicable from the assessment year 2017-18).

6. The written down value is calculated, where necessary, as if depreciation as applicable has been allowed. Moreover, it will be assumed that disallowance, if any, under sections 40, 40A and 43B has been considered while calculating the estimated income @ 50 per cent.

7. An assessee can declare his income to be lower than the deemed profits and gains as stated above. The following consequences are applicable if the taxpayer declares his income which is lower than the deemed profits and gains as stated above -

- The assessee will have to maintain the books of account as per section 44AA, if his total income exceeds the exemption limit.
- The assessee will have to get his books of account audited under section 44AB (irrespective of turnover), if his total income exceeds the exemption limit.

Computation of income on estimated basis in the case of taxpayers engaged in the business of plying, leasing or hiring trucks

54. The salient features of the scheme are given below :

• *Not more than 10 goods carriages* - The scheme applies to a person owning not more than 10 goods carriages at any time during the previous year. For this purpose, an assessee who is in possession of a goods carriage, whether taken on hire purchase or on instalments and for which the whole or part of the amount payable is still due, shall be deemed to be the owner of such goods carriages.

• *Mode of estimation of income (applicable from the assessment year 2019-20)* - The mode of estimation of income, as revised with effect from the assessment year 2019-20, is as follows –

Heavy goods vehicle (more than 12,000 kg. gross vehicle weight) - For a heavy goods vehicle, the profits and gains shall be an amount equal to Rs. 1,000 per ton of gross vehicle weight (or unladen weight) for every month (or part of a month) during which the heavy goods vehicle is owned by the assessee in the previous year or an amount claimed to have been actually earned from such vehicle, whichever is higher.

Other than heavy goods vehicle - In the case of a goods carriage (other than heavy vehicle), the profits and gains shall be an amount equal to Rs. 7,500 for every month (or part of a month) during which the goods carriage is owned by the assessee in the previous year or an amount claimed to have been actually earned from such goods carriage, whichever is higher.

• *Mode of estimation of income (applicable up to the assessment year 2018-19)* - The income from each goods carriage[53] being a "heavy goods vehicle" shall be estimated at Rs. 7,500[53a] for every month (or part of a month) during which the goods carriage is owned by the assessee. The income from each goods carriage, other than a heavy goods vehicle shall be estimated at Rs. 7,500[54] for every month (or part of a month) during which the goods carriage is owned by the assessee. In either case, the taxpayer can declare his income from trucks at a higher amount than that specified above.

For this purpose "goods carriage" means any motor vehicle constructed or adapted for use solely for the carriage of goods, or any motor vehicle not so constructed or adapted when used for the carriage of goods; and "heavy goods vehicle" means any goods carriage the gross vehicle weight of which, or a tractor or a road-roller the unladen weight of either of which exceeds 12,000 kilograms.

For instance, an assessee owns a commercial vehicle for 8 months and 3 days, a medium goods vehicle for 11 months and a medium goods vehicle for 12 months during the previous year. His profits and gains from three trucks shall be deemed to be (Rs. 7,500 × 9) + (Rs. 7,500 × 11) + (Rs. 7,500 × 12), *i.e.*, Rs. 2,40,000.

• *No further deduction* - The estimated income is comprehensive. All deductions under sections 30 to 38 including depreciation and unabsorbed depreciation shall be deemed to have been already allowed and no further deduction will be allowed under these sections. However, in the case of a firm, the normal deduction under section 40(*b*) shall be allowed. The written down value will be calculated, where necessary, as if depreciation as applicable has been allowed.

• *Accounts/audit not required* - The assessee is neither required to maintain books of account under the provisions of section 44AA, nor required to get his accounts audited under the provisions of section 44AB,

---

53. JCB, which is an earth moving machinery used for excavation of earth, lifting of heavy materials, etc., in process of construction, cannot be termed as a 'goods carriage' and income from hiring of JCB cannot be computed by applying provisions of section 44AE—*Gaylord Constructions* v. *ITO* [2008] 175 Taxman 99 (Coch.).

53a. Rs. 2,000 up to the assessment year 2002-03. Rs. 3,500 for the assessment years 2003-04 to 2010-11 and Rs. 5,000 for the assessment years 2011-12 to 2014-15.

54. Rs. 1,800 up to the assessment year 2002-03. Rs. 3,150 for the assessment years 2003-04 to 2010-11 and Rs. 4,500 for the assessment years 2011-12 to 2014-15.

in respect of his income from truck business. However, even such an assessee should comply with the requirements of both sections 44AA and 44AB in respect of his businesses which are not covered by this scheme.

• *Normal provisions applicable for other incomes* - Income from the truck business, estimated in accordance with this provision, is aggregated with other incomes of the assessee, from any other business or under other heads of income, in accordance with the normal provisions of the Act. Accordingly, all deductions under sections 80C to 80U will be available to the assessee, if the conditions therein are fulfilled.

• *Consequences if lower income is declared* - An assessee may claim his income to be lower than the deemed profits and gains, subject to the condition that the books of account and other documents are kept and maintained as required under section 44AA and the assessee gets his accounts audited irrespective of turnover and furnishes a report of such audit as prescribed under section 44AB.

Computation of profits and gains of retail business [Sec. 44AF, applicable up to the assessment year 2010-11[55]]

55. The salient features of section 44AF (as applicable up to the assessment year 2010-11) are as follows—

1. The scheme is applicable in the case of an assessee who is engaged in retail trade in any goods or merchandise. He may be an individual, HUF, firm, company or any other taxpayer.

2. The turnover of the assessee does not exceed Rs. 40 lakh.

3. If the above two conditions are satisfied, then profits and gains of such business shall be presumptively computed at 5 per cent of the gross receipt, or, as the case may be, a sum higher than the aforesaid sum as may be declared by the assessee in his return of income.

4. Under this scheme, the assessee is deemed to have been allowed the deductions under sections 30 to 38 including depreciation and unabsorbed depreciation. Deduction under section 40(*b*) shall be available. Accordingly, the written down value of any asset used for the purpose of the business of the assessee will be deemed to have been calculated as if the assessee had claimed and had actually been allowed the deduction in respect of depreciation for each of the relevant assessment year.

5. The assessee is not required to maintain books of account under section 44AA and get the accounts audited under section 44AB in respect of such income unless the assessee claims that the profits and gains from the aforesaid business are lower than the profits and gains deemed to be his income under section 44AF.

6. An assessee may claim his income to be lower than the deemed profits and gains, subject to the condition that the books of account and other documents are kept and maintained as required under section 44AA and the assessee gets his accounts audited irrespective of turnover and furnishes a report of such audit as prescribed under section 44AB.

Special provision for computing deductions in the case of business reorganization of co-operative banks [Sec. 44DB]

56. Section 44DB was inserted with effect from the assessment year 2008-09. It is applicable in the case of business reorganization of co-operative banks. It provides method and quantum of claiming deduction under sections 32, 35D, 35DD and 35DDA in the hands of amalgamating/demerged co-operative bank and amalgamated/resulting co-operative bank.

56.1 ***In the year in which amalgamation or demerger takes place*** - In the year in which change of ownership takes place because of the aforesaid reasons, deduction under sections 32, 35D, 35DD and 35DDA shall be calculated as under—

1. Find out the amount of deduction under the aforesaid sections of the previous year in which ownership of assets changes because of the aforesaid reasons on the assumption that the amalgamation or demerger has not taken place.

2. The amount of deduction so determined shall be apportioned between the (*a*) amalgamating co-operative bank and amalgamated co-operative bank, or (*b*) demerged co-operative bank and resulting co-operative bank, as the case may be, in the ratio of number of days for which the assets are used by them during the previous year in which ownership changes.

56.2 ***In subsequent years*** - The provisions of sections 35D, 35DD and 35DDA shall, in a case where an undertaking of the amalgamating/demerged co-operative bank entitled to the deduction under that section is transferred before the expiry of the period specified in that section to amalgamated/resulting co-operative bank, apply to the successor in the financial years subsequent to the year of business

55. In view of the substitution of section 44AD [*see* para 53.1], section 44AF is not applicable from the assessment year 2011-12.

reorganization as they would have applied to the predecessor, if the business reorganization had not taken place.

Special provisions for full value of consideration for transfer of land or building [Sec. 43CA, applicable from the assessment year 2014-15]

57. Where the consideration for the transfer of an asset (other than capital asset), being land or building or both, is less than the stamp duty value, the value so adopted or assessed or assessable shall be deemed to be the full value of the consideration for the purposes of computing income under the head "Profits and gains of business or profession". For this purpose, section 43CA has been inserted from the assessment year 2014-15.

• Where the date of an agreement fixing the value of consideration for the transfer of the asset and the date of registration of the transfer of the asset are not same, the stamp duty value may be taken as on the date of the agreement for transfer and not as on the date of registration for such transfer. However, this exception shall apply only in those cases where amount of consideration or a part thereof for the transfer has been received by any mode other than cash on or before the date of the agreement.
• Other provisions of section 50C will be applicable for the operation of section 43CA [see para 69.17].

57.1 ***Modifications applicable from the assessment year 2019-20*** - The following amendments have been made with effect from the assessment year 2019-20 –

• Where the value adopted or assessed or assessable by the stamp valuation authority does not exceed 105 per cent of the consideration received or accruing as a result of the transfer, the consideration so received as a result of the transfer, shall be deemed to be the full value of the consideration.

• Where the date of agreement fixing the value of consideration for transfer of the asset and the date of registration of such transfer of asset are not the same, stamp duty value on the date of the agreement shall be taken as full value of consideration where the amount of consideration (or a part thereof) has been received by way of an account payee cheque/draft or by use of electronic clearing system through a bank account (**or through prescribed electronic mode**) on or before the date of agreement for transfer of the asset.

Special provisions in relation to ICDS

58. The following special provisions have been incorporated with effect from the assessment year 2017-18 –

• *Taxation of foreign exchange fluctuation [Sec. 43AA]* - Section 43AA has been inserted with effect from the assessment year 2017-18. It provides that any gain or loss arising on account of any change in foreign exchange rates shall be treated as income or loss and such gain or loss shall be computed in accordance with ICDS. This rule will be applicable in respect of all foreign currency transactions including those relating to monetary items and non-monetary items or translation of financial statements of foreign operations or forward exchange contracts or foreign currency translation reserves.

• *Income from construction and service contracts [Sec. 43CB]* - Section 43CB has been inserted with effect from the assessment year 2017-18. It provides that profits and gains of a construction contract or a contract for providing services shall be determined on the basis of percentage of completion method in accordance with ICDS. However, the following points should be noted –

1. in the case of a contract for providing services with duration less than 90 days, the profits and gains shall be determined on the basis of project completion method.

2. In the case of a contract for provision of services involving indeterminate number of acts over a specific period of time, the profits and gains arising from such contract shall be determined on the basis of a straight line method.

3. For the aforesaid purpose, the contract revenue shall include retention money and the contract costs shall not be reduced by any incidental income in the nature of interest, dividends or capital gains.

Capital gains

	Para number	Example number
PRE-COMPUTATION STEPS		
❑ Find out whether the asset sold is a "capital asset" under section 2(*14*)	60	—
❑ Find out whether the asset is "transferred" during the previous year	62	—
COMPUTATION STEPS		
❑ Find out sale consideration	64	—
❑ Deduct cost of acquisition (or indexed cost of acquisition in the case of long-term capital asset) and cost of improvement (or indexed cost of improvement in the case of long-term capital asset) and expenditure incurred in connection with transfer	66 to 68	66.1-3E1, 68.2-1E1, 68.2-2E1, 68.2-3E1, 68.2-4E1, 68.2-5E1.
❑ Deduct amount of exemption under section 54 [if capital asset is a residential house property (long-term)]	71.1	71.1-E1-2
❑ Deduct amount of exemption under section 54B [if capital asset is agricultural land (short-term or long-term)]	71.2	71.2-E1
❑ Deduct amount of exemption under section 54D [if land and building forming part of an industrial undertaking is acquired by the Government (short-term or long-term)]	71.3	71.3-E1
❑ Deduct amount of exemption under sections 54EC and 54ED [if the asset transferred is a capital asset]	71.4	71.4-1E1 and 71.4-2E1
❑ Deduct amount of exemption under section 54F [if the asset transferred is any long-term capital asset but other than a residential house]	71.5	71.5-E1-2
❑ Deduct amount of exemption under section 54G [if the capital asset is transferred in connection with shifting of an industrial undertaking]	71.6	71.6-E1
❑ Deduct amount of exemption under section 54GA [if capital gain arises in case of shifting of industrial undertaking from urban area to SEZ]	71.7	—
❑ Deduct amount of exemption under section 54GB [if capital asset is residential property]	71.8	71.8-E1 to 71.8-E3
COMPUTATION OF TAX LIABILITY	72	72-E1-3

Chargeability [Sec. 45]

59. Any profit or gain arising from the sale or transfer of a capital asset is chargeable to tax under the head "Capital gains". It is deemed to be the income of the previous year in which the transfer of the capital asset takes place. Capital gains arising from the transfer of immovable property are chargeable to tax in the previous year, in which the effective transfer of title is conveyed and registered [in the case of transfer of property under section 53A of the Transfer of Property Act when agreement to sell is made and possession is transferred].

Meaning of capital asset [Sec. 2(*14*)]

60. "Capital asset" is defined to include property of any kind, whether fixed or circulating, movable or immovable, tangible or intangible.

60.1 ***Positive list*** - It includes the following –

1. "Property" includes any rights in or in relation to an Indian company, including rights of management or control or any other rights whatsoever.

2. Property of any kind held by an assessee (whether or not connected with his business or profession).

3. Any securities held by a Foreign Institutional Investor which has invested in such securities in accordance with the regulations made under the SEBI Act (applicable with effect from assessment year 2015-16).

60.2 ***Negative list*** - The following assets are excluded from the definition of "capital assets"—

a. any stock-in-trade [other than securities mentioned in 3 (*supra*)], consumable stores or raw material held for the purpose of business or profession;

b. personal effects of the assessee, that is to say, movable property including wearing apparel and furniture held for his personal use or for the use of any member of his family dependent upon him (jewellery, archaeological collections, drawings, paintings, sculptures; or any work of art are treated as a capital asset even though it is meant for personal use of the assessee);

c. agricultural land in rural area in India;

d. 6½ per cent Gold Bonds, 1977 or 7 per cent Gold Bonds, 1980 or National Defence Gold Bonds, 1980 issued by the Central Government;

e. Special Bearer Bonds, 1991; and

f. Gold Deposit Bonds issued under the Gold Deposit Scheme, 1999 or (with effect from the assessment year 2016-17) deposit certificates issued under the Gold Monetisation Scheme, 2015.

• *Rural area* - Rural area for the above purpose is as follows –

From the assessment year 2014-15 - Any area which is outside the jurisdiction of a municipality or cantonment board having a population of 10,000 or more and also which does not fall within distance (to be measured aerially) given below –

2 kilometres from the local limits of municipality/cantonment board	If the population of the municipality/cantonment board is more than 10,000 but not more than 1 lakh
6 kilometres from the local limits of municipality/cantonment board	If the population of the municipality/cantonment board is more than 1 lakh but not more than 10 lakh
8 kilometres from the local limits of municipality/cantonment board	If the population of the municipality/cantonment board is more than 10 lakh

For the above purpose, "population" means the population according to the last preceding census of which the relevant figures have been published before the first day of the previous year.

Up to the assessment year 2013-14 - Any area which is outside the jurisdiction of a municipality or cantonment board having a population of 10,000 or more and also which does not fall within such notified[56] distance [up to 8 kilometres - *see* Notification No. SO 10(E), dated January 6, 1994] from the local limits of such municipality or cantonment board.

• *Shares* - In respect of listed shares and securities held for a period of more than 12 months immediately preceding the date of its transfer, if the assessee desires to treat the income arising from the transfer thereof as capital gain, the same shall not be put to dispute by the Assessing Officer. The taxpayers shall not be allowed to adopt a different/contrary stand in this regard in subsequent years. However, these principles shall not apply in cases where genuineness of transaction itself is questionable (such as bogus claims of long-term capital gain/short-term capital loss or any other sham transactions) – Circular No. 6/2016[$], dated February 29, 2016. Similarly, CBDT has decided that the income arising from transfer of unlisted shares would be considered under the head "Capital gains", irrespective of period of holding, with a view to avoid disputes/litigation and to maintain uniform approach – Letter F.No. 225/12/2016[$]/ITA.II, dated May 2, 2016.

Types of capital asset

61. "Short-term capital asset" means a capital asset held by an assessee for not more than 36 months immediately prior to its date of transfer. An asset other than a short-term capital asset is regarded as a long-term capital asset.

• *Exceptions* - Generally, holding period should be more than 36 months to become long-term capital asset. However, in the following cases, the period of holding should be more than the period given below to become long-term capital asset –

	If transfer takes place –			
	On or after April 1, 2017	*During the previous year 2016-17*	*After July 10, 2014 but before April 1, 2016*	*On or before July 10, 2014*
Equity or preference shares in a company (listed)	12 months +	12 months +	12 months +	12 months +
Equity or preference shares in a company (unlisted)	24 months +	24 months +	36 months +	12 months +
Immovable property (being land or building or both)	24 months +	36 months +	36 months +	36 months +
Securities (like debentures, bonds, government securities, derivatives, etc.) (listed)	12 months +	12 months +	12 months +	12 months +
Units of UTI (listed or unlisted)	12 months +	12 months +	12 months +	12 months +
Units of equity oriented mutual fund[57] (listed or unlisted)	12 months +	12 months +	12 months +	12 months +
Units of debt oriented mutual fund (listed or unlisted)	36 months +	36 months +	36 months +	12 months +
Zero coupon bonds (listed or unlisted)	12 months +	12 months +	12 months +	12 months +

56. If the Central Government has not issued any notification for the above purpose under section 2(*14*)(*iii*)(*b*) for a particular municipality, agricultural land situated outside the local limits of such municipality (even within 8 kilometres) cannot be treated as agricultural land situated in urban area – *CIT* v. *Madhukumar N. (HUF)* [2012] 208 Taxman 394 (Kar.).

57. From the assessment year 2019-20, "equity oriented mutual fund" will have the same meaning assigned to it in section 112A [*see* para 72.2].

[$] For Circular No. 6/2016 and Letter F.No. 225/12/2016, log on to *taxmann.com/readyreckoner.aspx.*

61.1 ***How to determine period of holding***[58] - In determining the period for which any capital asset is held by the assessee :

Different situations	*How to calculate the period of holding*
• Shares held in a company-in-liquidation	The period subsequent to the date on which the company goes into liquidation shall be excluded
• Capital asset which becomes the property of the assessee in the circumstances mentioned in section 49(1) read with section 2(*42A*)/47 [*i.e.,* when an asset is acquired by gift, will, succession, inheritance or the asset is acquired at the time of partition of family or under a revocable or irrevocable trust or under amalgamation, etc.]	The period for which the asset was held by the previous owner should be included.
• Conversion of inventory into a capital asset	The period shall be reckoned from the date of its conversion into capital asset (applicable from the assessment year 2019-20)
• Allotment of shares in amalgamated Indian company in lieu of shares held in amalgamating company	The period of holding shall be counted from the date of acquisition of shares in the amalgamating company
• Right shares	The period of holding shall be counted from the date of allotment of right shares.
• Right entitlement	The period of holding will be considered from the date of offer to subscribe to shares to the date when such right entitlement is renounced by the person.
• Bonus shares	The period of holding shall be counted from the date of allotment of bonus shares
• Issue of shares by the resulting company in a scheme of demerger to the shareholders of the demerged company	The period of holding shall be counted from the date of acquisition of shares in the demerged company [*see* example 1 (*infra*)]
• Membership right held by a member of recognised stock exchange	The period of holding shall be considered from the date of becoming member of stock exchange [*see* example 2 (*infra*)]
• Sweat equity shares allotted by employer	The period of holding shall be reckoned from the date of allotment or transfer of such equity shares (applicable from the assessment year 2008-09)
• Unit of a business trust [allotted pursuant to transfer of shares as referred to in section 47(*xvii*)]	The period of holding shall include the period for which shares were held by the assessee (applicable from the assessment year 2015-16)
• Units which become the property of the assessee in consideration of transfer referred to in section 47(*xviii*)	The period of holding shall include the period for which the unit or units in the consolidating scheme of the mutual fund were held by the assessee (applicable from the assessment year 2016-17)
• Shares in a company [acquired by the non-resident assessee on redemption of Global Depository Receipts referred to in section 115AC(1)(*b*) held by such assessee]	The period shall be reckoned from the date on which a request for such redemption was made (applicable from the assessment year 2016-17)
• Conversion of bonds or debentures, debenture-stock or deposit certificates in any form of a company into shares or debentures of that company	The period of holding shall be considered from the date of acquisition of bond, debenture, debenture-stock or deposit certificate (applicable from the assessment year 2016-17)
• Asset disclosed under Income Declaration Scheme, 2016	- Immovable property (evidenced by a deed registered with a State Government) : Period of holding shall be considered from the date of acquisition - Any other asset : Period of holding shall be reckoned from June 1, 2016
• Conversion of a branch of a foreign company into Indian subsidiary company of the foreign bank within the parameters of section 115JG	In the case of a capital asset which became the property of the Indian subsidiary company, there shall be included the period for which the asset was held by the said branch of the foreign company [and by the previ-

58. In the case of allotment of a flat/plot by a housing board (like, DDA, HUDA) the period of holding will be determined from the date of allotment (not from the date when possession is given or when conveyance deed is signed) – *Madhu Kaul* v. *CIT* [2014] 225 Taxman 86 (Punj. &Har.), *Jitendra Mohan* v. *ITO* [2007] 11 SOT 594 (Delhi), *CIT* v. *K. Ramakrishnan* [2014] 224 Taxman 139 (Delhi). Contrary ruling – *Gulshan Malik* v. *CIT* [2014] 223 Taxman 243 (Delhi).

Different situations	*How to calculate the period of holding*
	ous owner, if any, who has acquired the capital asset by a mode of acquisition referred to in section 49(1)(*i*)/(*ii*)/(*iii*)/(*iv*)]
• Capital asset which becomes the property of an Indian subsidiary company in consequence to conversion of a branch of foreign company into Indian subsidiary company [section 115JG(1)]	The period for which the asset was held by the said branch of the foreign company [and by the previous owner who has acquired the capital asset by a mode of acquisition referred to in section 49(1)(*i*)/(*ii*)/(*iii*)/(*iv*) or section 115JG(1)].
• Conversion of preference shares into equity shares	The period of holding shall be considered from the date of acquisition of preference shares (applicable from the assessment year 2018-19)
• Units held by an assessee in the consolidating plan of a mutual fund scheme, made in consideration of the allotment to him of units, in the consolidated plan of that scheme of the mutual fund	Period of holding shall also include the period for which the units in the consolidating plan of the mutual fund scheme were held by him (applicable from the assessment year 2017-18)
• Transactions in shares and securities not given above -	
1. Date of purchase (through stock exchanges) of shares/securities	Date of purchase by broker on behalf of investor.
2. Date of transfer (through stock exchanges) of shares and securities	Date of broker's note provided such transactions are followed up by delivery of shares and also the transfer deeds.
3. Date of purchase/transfer of shares/securities (transaction taken place directly between parties and not through stock exchanges)	Date of contract of sale as declared by parties provided it is followed up by actual delivery of shares and the transfer deeds.
4. Date of purchase/sale of shares/securities purchased in several lots at different points of time but delivery taken of in one lot and subsequently sold in parts	The first-in-first-out (FIFO) method shall be adopted to reckon the period of the holding of the security, in cases where the dates of purchase and sale cannot be correlated through specific number of the scrips. In other words, the assets acquired last will be taken to be remaining with the assessee while assets acquired first will be treated as sold.
5. Transfer of a security by a depository (*i.e.*, demat account)	The period of holding shall be determined on the basis of the first-in-first-out method.

Transfer of capital asset

62. Transfer, in relation to a capital asset, includes sale, exchange or relinquishment of the asset or the extinguishment of any rights therein or the compulsory acquisition thereof under any law [sec. 2(*47*)].

• Reduction of share capital by company by reducing face value of its shares and paying off balance to shareholder would result in extinguishment of proportionate right in shares held by shareholder so that amount paid by company to shareholder on reduction of share capital would be exigible to capital gains tax in hands of shareholder —*Kartikeya V. Sarabhai* v. *CIT* [1997] 94 Taxman 164/228 ITR 163 (SC).

• Where assessee had purchased preference shares at less than face value and on redemption of shares by company, assessee received more than what she had paid for shares, redemption of preference shares amounts to "sale, exchange or relinquishment of asset" within the meaning of section 2(*47*)(*i*)—*Anarkali Sarabhai* v. *CIT* [1997] 90 Taxman 509/224 ITR 422 (SC).

• The transaction of lending shares of some distinctive numbers and receiving back shares of some other numbers is not "exchange" of assets within the meaning of "transfer" as defined in section 2(*47*). The meaning of the word "exchange" necessarily involves exchange of two different assets. The asset received back in the aforesaid type of transaction is not different from what was lent so long as it represents the same fraction of the ownership of the company. Hence, the transaction of lending of shares or any other security under the securities lending scheme would not result in "transfer" for the purpose of invoking the provisions relating to capital gains—Circular No. 751, dated February 10, 1997.

• Fixed Maturity Plans (FMPs) are closed ended mutual funds having a fixed maturity date wherein the duration of investment is decided upfront. To enable the FMPs to qualify as a long-term capital asset, some Asset Management Companies (AMCs) administering mutual funds have offered extension of the duration of the FMPs to a date beyond 36 months from the date of the original investment by providing to the investor an option of roll-over of FMPs in accordance with the provisions of Regulation 33(4) of the SEBI (Mutual Funds) Regulations, 1996. The Board has clarified that the roll over in accordance with the aforesaid regulation will not amount to transfer as the scheme remains the same. No capital gains will arise at the time of exercise of the option by the investor to continue in the same scheme. The capital gains will, however, arise at the time of redemption of the units or opting out of the scheme, as the case may be – Circular No. 6/2015, dated April 9, 2015.

62.1 ***Certain transactions included in definition of transfer*** - The following transactions are also included in "transfer" :

• By an amendment made by the Taxation Laws (Amendment) Act, 1984, the definition of "transfer" was enlarged, with effect from the assessment year 1985-86, to provide that, in a case where a capital asset is converted by the owner thereof into (or is treated by him as) stock-in-trade of a business carried on by him, such conversion (or treatment of) the capital asset shall also be regarded as a "transfer" of the asset [*see* para 69.1].

• The definition of transfer of capital asset under section 2(*47*) was extended with effect from the assessment year 1988-89 to include the following transactions :

a. any transaction involving the allowing of the possession of any immovable property to be taken or retained in part performance of a contract of the nature referred to in section 53A of the Transfer of Property Act, 1882; and

b. any transaction (whether by way of becoming a member of, or acquiring shares in a co-operative society, company or other association of persons or by way of agreement or any arrangement or in any other manner whatsoever) which has the effect of transferring or enabling the enjoyment of, any immovable property.

For the aforesaid purposes, "immovable property" shall have the same meaning as in clause (*d*) of section 269UA.

• With effect from the assessment year 2006-07, maturity/redemption of zero coupon bonds is treated as "transfer".

• "Transfer" includes disposing of, or parting with, an asset (or any interest therein) or creating any interest in any asset in any manner whatsoever (directly or indirectly, absolutely or conditionally, voluntarily or involuntarily), by way of an agreement (whether entered into in India or outside India) or otherwise. This rule is applicable even if such transfer of rights has been characterised as being effected or dependent upon or flowing from the transfer of a share (or shares) in a company registered or incorporated outside India (applicable with retrospective effect from the assessment year 1962-63[59] onwards).

62.2 ***Certain transactions not included in transfer*** - For the purpose of section 45, the following transactions are not regarded as transfers :

a. distribution of assets in kind by a company to its shareholders on its liquidation [sec. 46(1)];

b. any distribution of capital assets in kind by a Hindu undivided family to its members at the time of total or partial partition [sec. 47(*i*)];

c. any transfer of capital asset under a gift[60] or a will or an irrevocable trust [sec. 47(*iii*)] [transfer under a gift or an irrevocable trust of a capital asset being shares, debentures or warrants allotted by a company, directly or indirectly, to its employees under the Employees' Stock Option Plan or Scheme framed in accordance with guidelines issued by the Central Government shall be deemed as "transfer", from the assessment year 2001-02[61]];

d. any transfer of a capital asset by a company to its wholly-owned Indian subsidiary company [sec. 47(*iv*)[62]—*see* also para 69.2];

e. any transfer of a capital asset by a wholly-owned subsidiary company to its Indian holding company [sec. 47(*v*)[62]—*see* also para 69.2];

f. any transfer, in a scheme of amalgamation, of a capital asset by the amalgamating company to the amalgamated company, if the latter company is an Indian company [sec. 47(*vi*)];

---

59. *Vide* Letter [F.No.500/111/2009-FTD-1(PT.)], dated May 29, 2012, the Board has pointed out that the amendment has been made with retrospective effect in order to clarify the legislative intent and state the position of law from the date of coming into effect of these sections in Act. Further the Board has directed that where assessment proceedings have been completed under section 143(3) before April 1, 2012, and no notice for reassessment has been issued prior to that date, then such case shall not be reopened under section 147/148 on account of the abovementioned clarificatory amendments introduced by the Finance Act, 2012. However, assessment or any other order which stand validated due to the said clarificatory amendments in the Finance Act, 2012 would of course be enforced.

60. The definition of "deemed gift" in section 2(*xii*) or in section 4(1) of Gift-tax Act cannot be imported for purpose of construing word 'gift' occurring in sections 47(*iii*) and 49(1)(*ii*) — *M. Suseela* v. *ITO*[2010] 125 ITD 253/2 ITR (Trib.) 760 (Vishakhapatnam).

61. Market value on the date of gift shall be taken as full value of consideration for this purpose.

62. Provisions of section 47(*iv*)/(*v*) are not applicable in the case of transfer of capital asset made after February 29, 1988 as stock-in-trade.

g. any transfer of shares in Indian company held by a foreign company to another foreign company in pursuance of a scheme of amalgamation between the two foreign companies, if at least 25 per cent of the shareholders of the amalgamating foreign company continue to remain shareholders of the amalgamated foreign company and such transfer does not attract tax on capital gains in the country, in which the amalgamating company is incorporated; [sec. 47(*via*)];

h. any transfer in a scheme of amalgamation of a banking company with a banking institution [sec. 47(*viaa*), applicable from the assessment year 2006-07];

i. any transfer, in a scheme of amalgamation, of a capital asset, being a share of a foreign company, referred to in *Explanation 5* to section 9(1)(*i*), which derives, directly or indirectly, its value substantially from the share or shares of an Indian company, held by the amalgamating foreign company to the amalgamated foreign company, if—

   a. at least 25 per cent of the shareholders of the amalgamating foreign company continue to remain shareholders of the amalgamated foreign company; and

   b. such transfer does not attract tax on capital gains in the country in which the amalgamating company is incorporated [sec. 47(*viab*)] (applicable from the assessment year 2016-17);

j. any transfer in a demerger of a capital asset by the demerged company to resulting company provided that resulting company is an Indian company [sec. 47(*vib*), applicable from the assessment year 2000-01];

k. any transfer of shares held in an Indian company by a demerged foreign company to the resulting foreign company if the following conditions are satisfied:—

   i. the shareholders holding not less than three fourths in value of the shares of the demerged foreign company continue to remain shareholders of the resulting foreign company; and

   ii. such transfer does not attract tax on capital gains in the country, in which the demerged foreign company is incorporated [sec. 47(*vic*), applicable from the assessment year 2000-01];

l. any transfer in a business reorganization of co-operative banks, of a capital asset by the predecessor to the successor [sec. 47(*vica*), applicable from the assessment year 2008-09];

m. any transfer by a shareholder, in a business reorganization of co-operative banks, of a capital asset being a share or shares held by him in predecessor if the transfer is made in consideration of the allotment to him of any share or shares in successor [sec. 47(*vicb*), applicable from the assessment year 2008-09];

n. any transfer in a demerger, of a capital asset, being a share of a foreign company, referred to in *Explanation 5* to section 9(1)(*i*), which derives, directly or indirectly, its value substantially from the share or shares of an Indian company, held by the demerged foreign company to the resulting foreign company, if,—

   a. the shareholders, holding not less than 75 per cent in value of the shares of the demerged foreign company, continue to remain shareholders of the resulting foreign company;

   b. such transfer does not attract tax on capital gains in the country in which the demerged foreign company is incorporated; and

   c. the provisions of sections 391 to 394 of the Companies Act, 1956 shall not apply in case of demerger given above [sec. 47(*vicc*)] (applicable from the assessment year 2016-17);

o. any transfer or issue of shares by the resulting company in a scheme of demerger to the shareholders of the demerged company if the transfer or issue is made in consideration of demerger of the undertaking [sec. 47(*vid*), applicable from the assessment year 2000-01];

p. any transfer by a shareholder, in a scheme of amalgamation of share(s) held by him in the amalgamating company, if the transfer is made in consideration of the allotment to him of any share(s) in the amalgamated company[63] and the amalgamated company is an Indian company [sec. 47(*vii*)];

q. the transfer of a capital asset by a non-resident of such foreign currency convertible bonds or Global Depository Receipts as are referred to in sub-section (1) of section 115AC held by him to another non-resident where the transfer is made outside India [sec. 47(*viia*)];

r. any transfer, made outside India, of a capital asset being rupee denominated bond of an Indian company issued outside India, by a non-resident to another non-resident [sec. 47(*viiaa*)] (applicable from the assessment year 2018-19);

s. any transfer of capital asset [being bonds/GDR referred to in section 115AC(1) or rupee denominated bond of an Indian company or derivative **or (with effect from the assessment year 2020-21) securities notified by the Central Government**] made by a non-resident on a recognised stock exchange located in

63. Except where the shareholder itself is the amalgamated company (applicable from the assessment year 2013-14).

any international financial services centre and where the consideration is paid/payable in foreign currency [sec. 47(*viiab*)];

t. any transfer of a capital asset, being a Government Security carrying a periodic payment of interest, made outside India through an intermediary dealing in settlement of securities, by a non-resident to another non-resident [sec. 47(*viib*)] (applicable from the assessment year 2015-16);

u. any transfer by an individual of Sovereign Gold Bond issued by RBI under the Sovereign Gold Bond Scheme, 2015, by way of redemption [sec. 47(*viic*)] (applicable from the assessment year 2017-18);

v. any transfer of agricultural land in India effected before March 1, 1970 [sec. 47(*viii*)];

w. any transfer of a capital asset, being any work of art, archaeological, scientific or art collection, book, manuscript, drawing, painting, photograph or print, to the Government or a University or the National Museum, National Art Gallery, National Archives or any other such public museum or institution as may be notified by the Central Government [sec. 47(*ix*)];

x. any transfer by way of conversion of bonds or debentures, debenture-stock or deposit certificate in any form, of a company into shares or debentures of that company [sec. 47(*x*)];

y. any transfer by way of conversion of bonds referred to in section 115AC(1)(*a*) into shares or debentures of any company [sec. 47(*xa*) applicable from the assessment year 2008-09];

z. any transfer by way of conversion of preference shares of a company into equity shares of that company [sec. 47(*xb*)] (applicable from the assessment year 2018-19);

za. any transfer by way of exchange of a capital asset being membership of a recognised stock exchange for shares of a company to which such membership is transferred if such exchange is effected on or before December 31, 1998 and such shares are reflected by the transferor for a period of not less than three years from the date of transfer [sec. 47(*xi*)];

zb. transfer of land under a scheme prepared and sanctioned under section 18 of the Sick Industrial Companies (Special Provisions) Act, 1985 by a sick industrial company which is managed by its workers' co-operative if such transfer is made during the period commencing from the previous year in which it has become a sick industrial company under section 17(1) of that Act and ending with the previous year during which the entire net worth (*i.e.*, paid-up capital and free reserve) of such company becomes equal to or exceeds the accumulated losses. "Free reserves" for this purpose means all reserves credited out of the profits and share premium account but does not include reserves credited out of re-valuation of assets, write back of depreciation provisions and amalgamation [sec. 47(*xii*)];

zc. transfer of a capital asset to the company where a firm is succeeded by a company in the business carried on by it (from the assessment year 2002-03 it also includes transfer of a capital asset in the course of corporatisation[64] of a recognised stock exchange in India as a result of which an association of persons or body of individuals is succeeded by a company) subject to following conditions—

- *i.* all the assets and liabilities of the firm relating to the business immediately before the succession shall become the assets and liabilities of the company;
- *ii.* all the partners of the firm immediately before the succession, become the shareholders of the company in the same proportion in which their capital accounts stood in the books of the firm on the date of succession;
- *iii.* the partners of the firm do not receive any consideration or benefit directly or indirectly, in any form or manner other than by way of allotment of shares in the company; and
- *iv.* the aggregate of the shareholding in the company of the partners of the firm is not less than 50 per cent of the total voting power in the company and their shareholding continues to be as such for a period of five years from the date of succession [sec. 47(*xiii*)][65];

zd. (with effect from the assessment year 2011-12), transfer of a capital asset by a private company/unlisted public company to a limited liability partnership (LLP), or any transfer of a share or shares held in the company by a shareholder, as a result of conversion of the company into LLP in accordance with sections 56 and 57 of the Limited Liability Partnership Act, subject to the following conditions —

- *i.* all assets and liabilities of the company immediately before conversion should become the assets and liabilities of the LLP at the time of conversion;
- *ii.* all the shareholders of the company immediately before the conversion should become the partners of the LLP and their capital contribution and profit sharing ratio in the LLP are in the same proportion as their shareholding in the company on the date of conversion;

---

64. Demutualisation or corporatisation with effect from the assessment year 2004-05.

65. *See* also para 69.9.

   iii. no consideration would be paid by LLP to the company, the shareholders of the company should not receive any consideration or benefit (directly or indirectly) other than by way of share in profit and capital contribution in the LLP;
   iv. the aggregate of the profit sharing ratio of the shareholders of the predecessor company in the LLP shall not be less than 50 per cent immediately after conversion and at the time during the period of five years from the date of conversion;
   v. the total sales, turnover or gross receipts in business of the company in any of the three previous years preceding the previous year in which the conversion takes place should not be more than Rs. 60 lakh;
   vi. the total value of the assets (as appearing in the books of account of the company) in any of the three previous years preceding the previous year in which the conversion takes place does not exceed Rs. 5 crore (applicable from the assessment year 2017-18); and
   vii. no amount is paid, either directly or indirectly, to any partner out of balance of accumulated profit standing in the accounts of the company on the date of conversion for a period of three years from the date of conversion [sec. 47(*xiiib*)];

ze. transfer of membership right in a stock exchange [sec. 47(*xiiia*)];

zf. transfer of a capital asset to the company where a proprietary concern is succeeded by a company in the business carried on by it subject to following conditions—
   i. all assets and liabilities of the sole proprietary concern relating to the business immediately before the succession shall become the assets and liabilities of the company;
   ii. the shareholding of the sole proprietor in the company is not less than 50 per cent of the total voting power in the company and shareholding shall continue to so remain for a period of five years from the date of the succession;
   iii. the sole proprietor does not receive any consideration or benefit directly or indirectly, in any form or manner other than by way of allotment of shares in the company [sec. 47(*xiv*)[65]];

zg. any transfer involved in a scheme for lending of any securities under an agreement or arrangement subject to the guidelines issued by the Securities and Exchange Board of India, or the Reserve Bank of India in this regard, which the assessee has entered into with the borrower of such securities [sec. 47(*xv*)];

zh. any transfer of capital asset in a reverse mortgage under a scheme notified by the Central Government [sec. 47(*xvi*) applicable from the assessment year 2008-09];

zi. any transfer of a capital asset, being share of a special purpose vehicle to a business trust in exchange of units allotted by that trust to the transferor [sec. 47(*xvii*)] (applicable from the assessment year 2015-16);

zj. any transfer by a unit holder of a capital asset, being a unit or units, held by him in the consolidating scheme of a mutual fund, made in consideration of the allotment to him of a capital asset, being a unit or units, in the consolidated scheme of the mutual fund, if the consolidation is of two or more schemes of equity oriented fund or of two or more schemes of a fund other than equity oriented fund [sec. 47(*xviii*)] (applicable from the assessment year 2016-17); and

zk. any transfer by a unit holder of units held by him in the consolidating plan of a mutual fund scheme, made in consideration of the allotment to him of units, in the consolidated plan of that scheme of the mutual fund [sec. 47(*xix*)] (applicable from the assessment year 2017-18).

The aforesaid transactions are not recognised as "transfer" for the purpose of section 45. Therefore, any profit or gain arising on the above-noted transactions is not chargeable to tax under section 45; conversely, any loss arising therefrom is not liable to be set off against other incomes of the assessee.

Capital gains - How computed [Sec. 48]

63. Computation of capital gain depends upon the nature of capital asset transferred, *viz.*, short-term capital asset or long-term capital asset. Capital gain arising on transfer of a short-term capital asset is short-term capital gain, whereas transfer of a long-term capital asset generates long-term capital gain. The tax incidence is higher in the case of short-term capital gain as compared to long-term capital gain.

Method of computation of short-term and long-term capital gains (as applicable from the assessment year 1993-94 onwards) is as follows :

65. *See* also para 69.9.

Computation of short-term capital gain	*Computation of long-term capital gain*
1. Find out full value of consideration [*see* para 64]	*1.* Find out full value of consideration [*see* para 64]
2. Deduct the following :	*2. Deduct* the following :
a. expenditure incurred wholly and exclusively in connection with such transfer [*see* para 65];	*a.* expenditure incurred wholly and exclusively in connection with such transfer [*see* para 65];
b. cost of acquisition [*see* para 66]; and	*b.* indexed cost of acquisition [*see* para 68]; and
c. cost of improvement [*see* para 67].	*c.* indexed cost of improvement [*see* para 68].
3. From the resulting sum deduct the exemption provided by sections 54B, 54D, 54G and 54GA [*see* para 71]	*3.* From the resulting sum deduct the exemption provided by sections 54, 54B, 54D, 54EC, 54ED, 54EE, 54F, 54G, 54GA and 54GB [*see* para 71]
4. The balancing amount is short-term capital gain.	*4.* The balancing amount is long-term capital gain.

Note : Securities transaction tax is not deductible while computing income under the head "Capital gains".

63.1 ***When the benefit of indexation is not available in the case of long-term capital asset*** - In the following cases, the benefit of indexation is not available even if such asset is a long-term capital asset -

Capital assets	*Who is the transferor*
Bonds or debentures[66] [other than (*a*) capital indexed bonds issued by the Government or (*b*) Sovereign Gold Bond issued by RBI under the Sovereign Gold Bond Scheme, 2015]	Any person
Shares in or debentures of an Indian company acquired by utilizing convertible foreign exchange as mentioned in first proviso to section 48	Non-resident
Equity share in a company or a unit of equity oriented mutual fund or a unit of a business trust referred to in section 112A [*see* para 72.2]	Any person
Depreciable asset (other than an asset used by a power generating unit eligible for depreciation on straight line basis)	Any person
Undertaking/division transferred by way of slump sale as covered by section 50B	Any person
Equity share in a company or units of equity oriented fund or unit of a business trust referred to in section 112A (applicable from the assessment year 2019-20)	Any person
Units purchased in foreign currency as given in section 115AB	Offshore fund
Global depository receipts (GDR) purchased in foreign currency as given in section 115AC	Non-resident
Global depository receipts (GDR) purchased in foreign currency as given in section 115ACA	Resident individual
Securities as given in section 115AD	Foreign Institutional Investors [FII]

Note : In the above cases, the provisions relating to indexed cost of acquisition and indexed cost of improvement are not applicable.

63.2 ***Capital gains exempt from tax under sections 10 and 115JG*** - In the cases given below, capital gains are not chargeable to tax. Conversely, in the cases given below if assets are transferred at a loss, such capital loss is not taken into consideration—*see CIT* v. *S.S. Thiagarajan* [1981] 129 ITR 115 (Mad.), *Ramjilal Rais* v. *CIT* [1965] 58 ITR 181 (All.).

63.2-1 *CAPITAL GAIN ON TRANSFER OF US 64 [SEC. 10(33)]* - Any income arising from the transfer of a capital asset being a unit of US 64 is not chargeable to tax where the transfer of such assets takes place on or after April 1, 2002. This rule is applicable whether the capital asset (US 64) is long-term capital asset or short-term capital asset.

63.2-2 *LONG-TERM CAPITAL GAIN ON TRANSFER OF BSE-500 EQUITY SHARES [Sec. 10(36)]* - This exemption is available if the following conditions are satisfied –

1. Capital gain arises on transfer of long-term equity shares (being shares in a BSE-500 Index of the Bombay Stock Exchange, as on March 1, 2003).

2. These shares were purchased on or after March 1, 2003 but before March 1, 2004.

3. Capital gain arises on transfer of these shares in a recognized stock exchange.

63.2-3 *CAPITAL GAIN ON COMPULSORY ACQUISITION OF URBAN AGRICULTURE LAND [SEC. 10(37)]* - Section 10(*37*) is applicable if the following conditions are satisfied—

1. The assessee is an individual or a Hindu undivided family.

2. He or it owns an agriculture land situated in urban area mentioned in section 2(*14*)(*iii*)(*a*)/(*b*).

66. Preference shares (redeemable or non-redeemable) are not bonds or debentures and indexation benefit is available.

3. There is transfer of the agriculture land by way of compulsory acquisition or the consideration for transfer is approved or determined by the Central Government (not by a State Government) or RBI.

4. The agriculture land was used by the assessee (and/or his parents if the land was owned by an individual) for agricultural purposes during 2 years immediately prior to the date of transfer.

5. The asset may be long-term capital asset or short-term capital asset.

6. Capital gain arises from compensation (and/or additional compensation) or consideration which is received by the assessee after March 31, 2004.

• If the above conditions are satisfied, capital gain (short-term or long-term) is exempt from tax from the assessment year 2005-06.

63.2-4 *LONG-TERM CAPITAL GAIN ON TRANSFER OF SECURITIES NOT CHARGEABLE TO TAX IN CASES COVERED BY TRANSACTION TAX [SEC. 10(38)]* - Exemption under section 10(*38*) is not available from the assessment year 2019-20. Long-term capital gain is taxable according to the provisions of section 112A [*see* para 72.2].

• *Provisions illustrated* - Consider the following cases—

1. X purchases equity shares on August 16, 2016 (cost : Rs. 85,000 + securities transaction tax paid : Rs. 85). These shares are transferred on August 20, 2017 in the Bombay Stock Exchange (sale consideration Rs. 2,00,000, securities transaction tax paid Rs. 200). Since shares are long-term capital assets and securities transaction tax is applicable, capital gain is exempt from tax (no tax liability). However, from the assessment year 2019-20, such gain is chargeable to tax under section 112A [for detailed discussion, *see* para 72.2].

2. Suppose in the above case, shares are transferred on August 10, 2017. In such a case, shares are short-term capital assets, the above exemption is not available. However, short-term capital gain of Rs. 1,15,000 (*i.e.*, Rs. 2,00,000 — Rs. 85,000) is taxable under section 111A at the rate of 15 per cent [+ SC + (EC + SHEC) or HEC] [securities transaction tax is not taken into consideration to calculate short-term capital gain].

3. Suppose in the above case, the transferor is a dealer in share. In such a case, shares are not capital asset. The surplus of Rs. 1,14,715 (*i.e.*, Rs. 2,00,000 — Rs. 200 — Rs. 85,000 — Rs. 85) will be treated as business income and taxable under the head "Profits and gains of business or profession" [securities transaction tax is taken into consideration to calculate business income].

63.2-5 *CAPITAL GAIN EXEMPTION UNDER SECTION 115JG(1)* - Section 115JG was inserted by the Finance Act, 2012 with effect from the assessment year 2013-14. Under this section capital gains which arise on conversion of an Indian branch of a foreign bank into an Indian subsidiary, is not chargeable to tax. These provisions are given below –

1. The Reserve Bank of India will frame a scheme for the purpose of conversion of an Indian branch of a foreign bank into an Indian subsidiary company of the foreign company.

2. If the conversion takes place in accordance with the scheme framed by RBI and subject to the conditions notified by the Central Government[67], the capital gain arising on such conversion shall not be chargeable to tax.

3. In the above case, the provisions of the Act relating to treatment of unabsorbed depreciation, set off or carry forward of losses, tax credit in respect of tax paid on deemed income relating to certain companies and the computation of income in the case of the foreign company and the Indian subsidiary company shall apply with such exceptions, modifications and adaptations as may be specified in that notification.

4. If there is a failure to comply with any condition specified in the RBI schemes or notification of the Government, normal provisions of the Act will apply without giving effect to the aforesaid exemption.

5. Where such default is committed after claiming capital gain exemption, the benefit of exemption will be taken back by recomputing the income of the assessee under section 154 of the previous year in which conversion took place. The time-limit of 4-year under section 154(7) shall be determined from the end of the year in which the default is committed.

63.2-6 *COMPENSATION UNDER SECTION 96 OF RFCTLARR ACT, 2013* - Capital gain arising out of any award/agreement under Right to Fair Compensation and Transparency in Land Acquisition, Rehabilitation and Resettlement Act, 2013, is exempt from tax.

63.2-7 *CAPITAL GAIN ARISING UNDER LAND POOLING SCHEME OF ANDHRA PRADESH GOVERNMENT [SEC. 10(37A)]* - In Land pooling scheme (of Andhra Pradesh Government), the compensation in the form of reconstituted plot or land is provided to landowners. For this scheme, capital gain exemption is available (from the assessment year 2015-16) under section 10(*37A*), if a few conditions are satisfied [*see* para 69.21]

---

67. The Central Government has notified a few conditions *vide* Notification No. SO 6053(E)[\$], dated December 6, 2018.

[\$] For Notification No. SO 6053(E), log on to *taxmann.com/readyreckoner.aspx.*

Full value of consideration [Sec. 48]

64. The dictionary meaning of the word "full" is "whole or entire, or complete". The word "full" has been used in this section in contrast to "a part of the price". The expression "full value" means the whole price without any deduction whatsoever and it cannot refer to the adequacy or inadequacy of the price bargained for. Nor has it any reference to the market value of the capital asset which is the subject-matter of the transfer. The consideration for the transfer of the capital asset is what the transferor receives in lieu of the asset he parts with, namely, money or money's worth.

64.1 ***Cases when "full value of consideration" is determined on notional basis*** - In the cases given below "full value of consideration" is determined on notional basis according to the different provisions given in the Income-tax Act—

Different situations	*The amount which is taken as full value of consideration*	*Section*	*Para No.*
Capital gain generated by a non-resident at the time of redemption of rupee denominated bonds of an Indian company held by him	The following shall be excluded from full value of consideration— Amount equivalent to appreciation of rupee between the date of issue and the date of redemption against the foreign currency in which the investment is made (applicable from the assessment year 2017-18)	Fourth proviso to section 48	
Shares/debentures/warrants/allotted by an employer to an employee under notified Employees Stock Option Plan/Scheme and such shares, etc., are gifted by the concerned employee to any person	Market value at the time of gift	Fifth proviso to section 48	
In case of transfer of land/building, if – - stamp duty value exceeds sale consideration (applicable up to the assessment year 2018-19) - stamp duty value exceeds 105 per cent of sale consideration (applicable from the assessment year 2019-20)	The value adopted by the Stamp Valuation Authority of the State Government	50C	69.17
Transfer of unlisted shares in a company at less than fair market value	Fair market value of such shares (to be determined as prescribed) (applicable from the assessment year 2018-19)	50CA	69.19
Money or other asset received under any insurance from an insurer due to damage or destruction of a capital asset.	Value of money or the fair market value of the asset (on the date of receipt)	45(1A)	69.16
Conversion of capital asset into stock in trade	Fair market value of the capital asset on the date of conversion	45(2)	69.1
Transfer of capital asset by a partner/member to firm/association of persons/body of individuals as his capital contribution	Amount recorded in the books of account of the firm/association of persons/body of individuals as the value of the capital asset	45(3)	69.3
Distribution of capital asset by firm/association of persons/body of individuals to its partners/members on its dissolution	Fair market value of such asset on the date of transfer	45(4)	69.3
Transfer by an individual/HUF (*i.e.*, owner) of land/building under a "specified agreement" (*i.e.*, a joint development agreement) to a developer	Stamp duty value (on the date of issue of completion certificate) of share of the owner in the developed property as increased by cash consideration, if any (applicable from the assessment year 2018-19)	45(5A)	69.18
Money or other assets received by shareholders at the time of liquidation of the company	Total of money *plus* market value of assets received on the date of distribution *less* amount assessed	46(2)	69.10

Different situations	*The amount which is taken as full value of consideration*	*Section*	*Para No.*
	as deemed dividend under section 2(22)(*c*)		
Where the consideration received or accruing as a result of the transfer is not ascertainable or cannot be determined	Fair market value of the said asset on the date of transfer (applicable from the assessment year 2013-14)	50D	

Expenditure on transfer

65. Expenditure incurred wholly and exclusively in connection with the transfer of a capital asset is deductible from full value of consideration. The expression "expenditure incurred wholly and exclusively in connection with such transfer" means expenditure incurred which is necessary to effect the transfer. Examples of such expenses are : brokerage or commission paid for securing a purchaser, cost of stamp, registration fees borne by the vendor, travelling expenses incurred in connection with transfer, litigation expenditure for claiming enhancement of compensation awarded in the case of compulsory acquisition of assets.

One should also keep in view the following propositions :

- Vague claim for expenses is not allowable—*B.N. Pinto* v. *CIT* [1974] 96 ITR 306 (Mys.).
- Expenditure in connection with transfer need not necessarily have been incurred prior to passing of title—*CIT* v. *P. Rajendran* [1981] 127 ITR 810 (Kar.).
- If a sum has already been subject-matter of deduction under other heads, the same cannot be allowed as deduction under section 48—*CIT* v. *Maithreyi Pai* [1985] 152 ITR 247 (Kar.).

Cost of acquisition

66. Cost of acquisition of an asset is the value for which it was acquired by the assessee. Expenses of capital nature for completing or acquiring the title to the property are includible in the cost of acquisition.

One should keep in mind the following propositions taken from judicial rulings :

- Ground rent cannot be said to be expenditure incurred by the assessee for the acquisition of the capital asset and it cannot, therefore, be included in computing the actual cost to the assessee of the capital asset—*CIT* v. *Mithlesh Kumari* [1973] 92 ITR 9 (Delhi).
- Interest on moneys borrowed to purchase asset is part of actual cost of asset.
- Expenses on suits for amending articles of association are of a capital nature and are a part of the cost of shares—*CIT* v. *Bengal Assam Investors Ltd.* [1969] 72 ITR 319 (Cal.).
- Litigation expenses incurred for compelling the company to register the shares in the name of the assessee would be of capital nature, forming a part of the cost of acquisition of the shares—*Bengal Assam Investors Ltd.* (*supra*).
- Estate duty paid in respect of inherited property can neither be treated as a part of the cost of acquisition of property nor as cost of improvement—*S. Valliammai* v. *CIT* [1981] 127 ITR 713 (Mad.).

66.1 ***Notional cost of acquisition*** - In the cases given below, the cost of acquisition is taken at notional figure :

Different situations	*Notional cost of acquisition*	*For detailed discussion, refer to para given below*
1. Additional compensation in the case of compulsory acquisition	*Nil*	69.4-3
2. Assets received by a member on liquidation of the company	Fair market value of such asset on the date of distribution	69.10
3. Stock or shares becoming property of the assessee on consolidation, conversion, etc.	Cost of acquisition of such stock or shares from which such asset is derived	

Different situations	*Notional cost of acquisition*	*For detailed discussion, refer to para given below*
4. Allotment of shares in an amalgamated Indian company[68] to the shareholders of amalgamating company[69] in a scheme of amalgamation of the two companies	Cost of acquisition of shares in the amalgamating company[69]	
5. Conversion of shares into debentures	That part of the cost of debentures in relation to which asset is acquired by the assessee	
6. Conversion of preference shares into equity shares	Cost of acquisition of preference shares (applicable from the assessment year 2018-19)	
7. Units held by an assessee in the consolidating plan of a mutual fund scheme, made in consideration of the allotment to him of units, in the consolidated plan of that scheme of the mutual fund [sec. 47(*xix*)]	Cost of acquisition of the units in the consolidating plan of the mutual fund scheme (applicable from the assessment year 2017-18)	
8. Allotment of shares/securities by a company to its employees under Employees' Stock Option Plan/Scheme approved by Central Government	• If the option is exercised by the employee during the previous year 1999-2000 or on or after April 1, 2009 : Fair market value on the date of exercise of option • If the option is exercised in any other year but up to March 31, 2007 : Amount actually paid by the employee • If option is exercised on or after April 1, 2007 but before April 1, 2009 : Fair market value of shares/securities on the date on which the option vests with the employee.	69.13
9. Property covered by section 56(2)(*vii*)/(*viia*)/(*x*)	The value which has been considered for the purpose of section 56(2)(*vii*)/(*viia*)/(*x*)	
10. Asset disclosed under Income Declaration Scheme, 2016	Fair market value of the asset declared under the scheme on June 1, 2016 (on the basis of which tax, surcharge and penalty is paid under the scheme)	–
11. Allotment of shares in Indian resulting company[70] to the shareholders of demerged[71] company	Cost of acquisition of shares in demerged company[71] × Net book value of assets transferred in demerger ÷ Net worth of the demerged[71] company immediately before demerger	69.14
12. Cost of acquisition of original shares in demerged company[71] after demerger	Cost of acquisition of such shares *minus* amount calculated above	69.14
13. Cost of acquisition of assets acquired by successor LLP from a predecessor private company/unlisted public company at the time of conversion of the company into LLP by satisfying the requirement of section 47(*xiiib*)	Cost of acquisition of the assets to the previous owner (*i.e.*, predecessor private company / unlisted public company) (applicable from the assessment year 2011-12)	
14. Cost of acquisition of capital asset (being rights of a partner in a limited liability partnership) which became the property of the assessee at the time of conversion of a private company/unlisted public company into the LLP	Cost of acquisition to the assessee of the share or shares in the company immediately before conversion (applicable from the assessment year 2011-12)	
15. Depreciable assets covered by section 50	The opening balance of the block of assets on the first day of the previous year *plus* actual cost of the assets acquired during the year and which fall within the same block of assets	66.1-3
16. Depreciable assets of a power generating unit as covered by section 50A	The written down value of the asset *minus* terminal depreciation *plus* balancing charge	48.3-10

68. Or amalgamated co-operative bank from the assessment year 2008-09.
69. Or amalgamating co-operative bank from the assessment year 2008-09.
70. Or resulting co-operative bank from the assessment year 2008-09.
71. Or demerged co-operative bank from the assessment year 2008-09.

Different situations	*Notional cost of acquisition*	*For detailed discussion, refer to para given below*
17. Undertaking/division acquired by way of slump sale as covered under section 50B	Net worth of such undertaking	69.15
18. New asset acquired for claiming exemption under section 54, 54B, 54D, 54G or 54GA if it is transferred within three years	Actual cost of acquisition *minus* exemption claimed under these sections	71.1, 71.2, 71.3, 71.6
19. Goodwill of business or trade mark or brand name associated with business or right to manufacture, produce or process any article or thing or right to carry on any business [or (with effect from assessment year 2017-18) profession], tenancy right, stage permits or loom hours	• If these assets were acquired by gift, will, etc., under section 49(1) and the previous owner had purchased these assets: Cost of acquisition to the previous owner • If the owner has purchased these assets: Actual cost of acquisition is taken • If these assets are self generated: Zero	69.6-1
20. Right shares	Amount actually paid by assessee	69.8
21. Right to subscribe to shares (*i.e.*, right entitlement)	*Nil*	69.8
22. Bonus shares	• If allotted to the assessee before April 1, 2001† : Fair market value on that date • In any other case: *Nil*	69.7
23. Allotment of equity shares and right to trade in stock exchange, allotted to members of stock exchange under a scheme of demutualisation or corporatisation of stock exchanges in India as approved by SEBI	• Cost of acquisition of shares: Cost of acquisition of original membership of the stock exchange • Cost of acquisition of trading or clearing rights of the stock exchange: *Nil*	
24. Capital asset, being a unit of business trust, acquired in consideration of a transfer referred to in section 47(*xvii*)	Cost of acquisition of shares referred to in section 47(*xvii*) [applicable from the assessment year 2015-16]	
25. Units in a consolidating scheme of a mutual fund which become the property of the assessee in consideration of transfer referred to in section 47(*xviii*)	Cost of acquisition shall be the cost of acquisition of units in the consolidating scheme of the mutual fund (applicable from the assessment year 2016-17)	
26. Shares in a company acquired by a non-resident assessee on redemption of Global Depository Receipts [referred to in section 115AC(1)(*b*) held by such assessee]	Cost of acquisition of such shares shall be calculated on the basis of the price prevailing on any recognised stock exchange on the date on which a request for such redemption was made (applicable from the assessment year 2016-17)	
27. Specified asset referred to in section 10(*37A*) (*i.e.*, reconstituted plot or land given to an assessee under Land Pooling Scheme of Andhra Pradesh) which is transferred after the expiry of 2 years from the end of the financial year in which possession of such specified asset is handed over to the assessee	Stamp duty value of the specified asset on the last day of the second financial year after the end of the financial year in which the possession of the said specified asset is handed over to the assessee (applicable from the assessment year 2018-19)	
28. Capital asset (being share in developed property received by owner from a developer under joint development agreement)	Stamp duty value (on the date of issue of completion certificate) of share of the owner in the developed property as increased by cash consideration, if any (applicable from the assessment year 2018-19)	
29. Capital asset (being held by a trust/institution in respect of which accreted income has been computed and the tax has been paid thereon in accordance with the provisions of Chapter XII-EB)	The fair market value of the asset which has been taken into account for computation of accreted income as on the specified date referred to in section 115TD(*2*) (applicable from the assessment year 2017-18)	

Different situations	*Notional cost of acquisition*	*For detailed discussion, refer to para given below*
30. Conversion of stock-in-trade into capital asset	Fair market value on the date of conversion shall be taken as cost of acquisition (applicable from the assessment year 2019-20)	
31. Long-term capital asset (being equity share or unit of an equity oriented mutual fund or unit of a business trust) referred to in section 112A and acquired before February 1, 2018	It is higher of – *a.* the actual cost of acquisition; and *b.* lower of (*A*) fair market value of such asset on January 31, 2018; or (*B*) full value of consideration as a result of transfer	72.2
32. Any other capital asset		
- if it became the property of the assessee before April 1, 2001[72] by gift, will, etc., in modes specified in section 49(1)	Cost of acquisition to the previous owner or fair market value as on April 1, 2001[72], whichever is higher	66.1-2
- if it became the property of the assessee before April 1, 2001[72]	Cost of acquisition or fair market value as on April 1, 2001[72] whichever is more	66.1-2
- if it became the property of the assessee after April 1, 2001[72] by gift, will, etc., in modes specified in section 49(1)	Cost of acquisition to the previous owner	66.1-1
- if it became the property of the assessee after April 1, 2001[72]	Actual cost of acquisition	

66.1-1 *COST TO THE PREVIOUS OWNER [SEC. 49(1)]* - The cost to the previous owner is deemed to be the cost of acquisition to the assessee in cases where a capital asset becomes the property of the assessee under any mode of transfer described below [sec. 49(1)]—

a. acquisition of property on any distribution of assets on the total or partial partition of a Hindu undivided family;

b. acquisition of property under a gift or will;

c. acquisition of property—

i. by succession, inheritance or devolution, or

ii. on any distribution of assets on the dissolution of a firm, body of individuals or other association of persons where such dissolution had taken place before April 1, 1987, or

iii. on any distribution of assets on the liquidation of a company, or

iv. under a transfer to a revocable or an irrevocable trust, or

v. on any transfer by a wholly-owned Indian subsidiary company from its holding company, or

vi. on any transfer, by an Indian holding company from its wholly-owned subsidiary company, or

vii. on any transfer, in a scheme of amalgamation, by the amalgamated company from the amalgamating company which comes under section 47(*vi*)/(*via*)/(*viaa*)/(*viab*), or

viii. on any transfer, in a demerger, by the resulting company from demerged company which comes under section 47(*vib*)/(*vicc*) (applicable from the assessment year 2016-17), or

ix. on any transfer, in a demerger, of a capital asset, being shares held in an Indian company, by the demerged foreign company to the resulting foreign company and which comes under section 47(*vic*) (applicable from the assessment year 2018-19), or

x. on any transfer in a scheme of business re-organisation of a co-operative bank which comes under section 47(*vica*)/(*vicb*), or

xi. any transfer in a scheme of conversion of private company/unlisted public company into LLP which comes under section 47(*xiiib*) (applicable from the assessment year 2011-12), or

72. April 1, 1981 (applicable up to the assessment year 2017-18).

xii. on any transfer in the case of conversion of firm/sole-proprietary concern into company which comes under section 47(*xiii*)/(*xiv*) [applicable from the assessment year 1999-2000]; or

d. acquisition of property, by a Hindu undivided family where one of its members has converted his self-acquired property into joint family property after December 31, 1969.

In the aforesaid circumstances, cost to the previous owner would be taken as cost to the assessee and indexation benefit is available from the year in which the previous owner acquired the asset.

Where the previous owner has acquired the property in the aforesaid manner, the previous owner of the property means the last previous owner who acquired the property by means other than those discussed above. Cost of any improvement of the asset borne by the previous owner, or the assessee, will be added to such cost. For instance, if X acquires a house property in 1985 from his father under a will, the cost of property to the father will be taken as the cost of acquisition at the time of sale of property by X. If, however, the father of X has acquired the property from a partnership firm on its dissolution, cost to the partnership firm will be taken as the cost of acquisition at the time of its sale by X.

66.1-1E1 X (HUF) is a Hindu undivided family. The family acquires a residential house at Delhi for Rs. 2,10,000 on April 1, 2017. The family undergoes complete partition on November 1, 2017 and the residential house is allotted to Y, a member of the family. Y sells the house on March 15, 2019 for Rs. 6,90,000. Determine the amount of chargeable capital gains in the case of X (HUF) and Y.

•

X (HUF) : X (HUF) has transferred a house property to Y at the time of partition. Since the transaction is not treated as *transfer* under section 47(*i*), surplus arising thereon is not taxable.

Y: Since Y has transferred a house property, he is chargeable to tax as follows :

	Rs.
Sale consideration	6,90,000
Less : Cost of acquisition [since capital asset was acquired in one of the circumstances mentioned in section 49(1), cost of the previous owner is taken as cost of acquisition]	2,10,000
Capital gain	4,80,000

66.1-2 *COST OF ACQUISITION BEING THE FAIR MARKET VALUE AS ON APRIL 1, 2001*[72] *[SEC. 55(2)]* - In the following cases, the assessee may take at his option, either the actual cost or the fair market value of the asset[73] (other than a depreciable asset), as on April 1, 2001[72] as cost of acquisition :

a. where the capital asset became the property of the assessee before April 1, 2001[72]; or

b. where the capital asset became the property of the assessee by any mode referred to in section 49(1) [*see* para 66.1-1] and the capital asset became the property of the previous owner before April 1, 2001[72].

66.1-3 *COST OF ACQUISITION IN THE CASE OF DEPRECIABLE ASSETS [SEC. 50]* - Under the system of providing depreciation on block of assets, written down value of any block of assets may be reduced to *nil* for any of the following two reasons—

1. Situation one [Sec. 50(1)]- The moneys receivable by the assessee in regard to the assets sold or otherwise transferred during the previous year together with the amount of scrap value may exceed the written down value at the beginning of the year as increased by the actual cost of assets acquired‡ during the previous year.

2. Situation two [Sec. 50(2)] - All the assets in the relevant block may be transferred during the year.

Capital gains in the aforesaid two cases will be determined as under—

• *Situation one [Sec. 50(1)]* - In a case where any block of assets does not cease to exist but full value of the consideration received or accruing as a result of transfer of the depreciable asset by the assessee during the previous year exceeds the following amounts, namely—

a. expenditure incurred wholly or exclusively in connection with such transfer or transfers ;

b. the written down value of the block of assets at the beginning of the previous year ; and

---

72. April 1, 1981 (applicable up to the assessment year 2017-18).

73. A reference under section 50C to the Valuation Officer can be made only in respect of valuation of an asset at time of its transfer which has given rise to occasion for levy of capital gains tax. Such reference cannot be made for purpose of evaluating asset as on April 1, 1981 or April 1, 2001—*Neville De Noranha* v. *CIT* [2008] 26 SOT 35 (Kol.)(URO).

c. the actual cost[74] of any asset falling within the block of assets acquired[75] during the previous year, such excess shall be deemed to be short-term capital gain [*see* example 66.1-3E1].

• *Situation two [Sec. 50(2)]* - Sub-section (2) of section 50 is applicable only where any block of assets ceases to exist because all assets in that block are sold during the previous year. The cost of acquisition in such a case shall be the aggregate of the following—

a. written down value of block of assets at the beginning of the previous year ; and

b. actual cost[74] of any asset falling within that block of assets acquired[75] by the assessee during the previous year.

If the consideration received falls short of the cost of acquisition (as computed *supra*) and expenditure incurred wholly and exclusively in connection with such transfer by virtue of section 48(*i*), the shortfall will be short-term capital loss. On the other hand, if consideration so received exceeds the cost of acquisition and expenditure incurred wholly and exclusively in connection with the transfer, the excess will be chargeable to tax as short-term capital gain [*see* example 66.1-3E2].

• *Other points* - The following points should be noted —

1. If a depreciable asset in respect of which depreciation was allowed in past (not being the case of power unit as stated above) is transferred and the case does not fall under any of the above two situations, then capital gain is not chargeable to tax.

2. In the case of plant and machinery (cost being Rs. 5,000 or less) acquired up to March 31, 1995, the entire cost was allowed as deduction under proviso to section 32(1)(*ii*). Such plant and machinery does not form part of any block of assets and, consequently, profit on sale of such asset is not taxable either as a balancing charge under section 41(2) or as capital gain under section 50. Proviso to section 32(1)(*ii*), which permitted 100 per cent deduction in the case of plant and machinery (costing up to Rs. 5,000), was omitted by the Finance Act, 1995 with effect from the assessment year 1996-97 (or previous year 1995-96) onwards. If a depreciable asset (being plant and machinery, cost of acquisition Rs. 5,000 or less) is acquired on or after March 31, 1995, it is qualified for depreciation like any other depreciable asset and on its transfer, short-term capital gain will arise within the parameters of section 50—*Nectar Beverages (P.) Ltd.* v. *DIT* [2009] 182 Taxman 319 (SC).

3. Section 50 is not applicable in the case of transfer of a capital asset, if depreciation thereon was never allowed to the assessee. For instance, if a plant (purchased earlier but no depreciation allowed as it was not put to use) is transferred, section 50 is not applicable and capital gain in such a case will be calculated by applying other provisions of the Act—*CIT* v. *Santosh Structural & Alloys Ltd.* [2012] 20 taxmann.com 501 (Punj. & Har.).

66.1-3E1 X owns the following assets on April 1, 2018 (rate of depreciation : 15 per cent) :

Assets	*Written down value on April 1, 2018*	*Date of acquisition*
	Rs.	
Plant A	3,00,000	April 1, 1975
Plant B	2,00,000	May 10, 1974
Plant C	5,00,000	March 13, 1986

During the previous year 2018-19, the following plants are purchased/sold by X :

Assets	*Rate of depreciation*	*Date of purchase/ sale*	*Selling price*	*Cost price*
			Rs.	*Rs.*
Plant D (old)	15%	March 10, 2019	—	4,08,000
Plant E (old)	15%	March 1, 2019	—	20,000
Plant A	15%	April 1, 2018	6,00,000	—

74. Where an assessee incurs any expenditure for acquisition of any depreciable asset in respect of which a payment (or aggregate of payments made to a person in a day), otherwise than by an account payee cheque/draft or use of electronic clearing system through a bank account (**or through prescribed electronic mode**), exceeds Rs. 10,000, such payment shall not be eligible for this purpose (applicable from the assessment year 2018-19).

75. For the purpose of section 50, it is not necessary that the asset should be put to use—*Fluroscent Fixtures (P.) Ltd.* v. *ITO* [2009] 34 SOT 48 (Mum.), *Artic* v. *CIT* [1999] 68 ITD 462 (Mum.).

Assets	*Rate of depreciation*	*Date of purchase/ sale*	*Selling price*	*Cost price*
			Rs.	*Rs.*
Building A	10%	June 10, 2018	—	2,00,000
Plant C	15%	May 10, 2018	12,50,000	—
Plant F (old)	30%	March 10, 2019	—	15,00,000

Determine the amount of depreciation and capital gain/loss for the assessment year 2019-20 (expenditure incurred on sale of plants A and C is Rs. 10,000).

•

First block : Plant (rate of depreciation : 15%)		*Rs.*
Depreciated value of the block on April 1, 2018 (Rs. 3,00,000 + Rs. 2,00,000 + Rs. 5,00,000)		10,00,000
Add : Cost of plant (falling in this block) acquired during the previous year 2018-19 (*i.e.*, Plant D : Rs. 4,08,000 + Plant E : Rs. 20,000)		4,28,000
		14,28,000
Less : Sale consideration of Plants A and C sold during the previous year 2018-19 (*i.e.*, Rs. 6,00,000 + Rs. 12,50,000 ; subject to maximum of Rs. 14,28,000)		14,28,000
Written down value		*Nil*
Depreciation on first block		*Nil*
Capital gain on sale of Plants A and C		
Sale consideration		18,50,000
Less :		
Expenses on transfer		10,000
Cost of acquisition :	*Rs.*	
❑ Depreciated value of the block on April 1, 2018	10,00,000	
❑ Cost of assets falling in the block acquired during the previous year	4,28,000	14,28,000
Short-term capital gain		4,12,000

Depreciation on other assets will be determined as under :

	Second block	*Third block*
Name of asset	Plant	Building
Rate of depreciation	30%	10%
	Rs.	*Rs.*
Depreciated value on April 1, 2018	*Nil*	*Nil*
Add : Cost of assets purchased during 2018-19	15,00,000	2,00,000
Less : Sale consideration of assets transferred during the year	—	—
Written down value	15,00,000	2,00,000
Depreciation [*30% of 50% of Rs. 15,00,000, as Plant F is purchased during the previous year and put to use for less than 180 days]	2,25,000*	20,000

66.1-3E2 X Ltd. owns the following assets on April 1, 2018:

Assets	*Rate of depreciation*	*Depreciated value on April 1, 2018*
		Rs.
Plant A	15%	4,05,000
Plant B	15%	1,95,000
Plant C	15%	7,05,700

On June 10, 2018, it acquires Plant D for Rs. 20,000 (rate of depreciation : 15%). The company sells the following assets during the year 2018-19—

Assets	*Sale consideration* Rs.	*Expenses on transfer* Rs.
Plant A	2,12,000	12,000
Plant B	6,17,500	—
Plant C	4,30,000	—
Plant D	95,000	200

Determine the amount of depreciation and capital gain for the assessment year 2019-20. Is it possible to avoid tax on capital gain ?

•

First block : Plant (rate of depreciation 15%)

		Rs.
Depreciation		
Depreciated value of plants A, B and C (Rs. 4,05,000 + Rs. 1,95,000 + Rs. 7,05,700)		13,05,700
Add: Cost of Plant D acquired during the year		20,000
		13,25,700
Less: Sale consideration of Plants A, B, C and D (*i.e.*, Rs. 2,12,000 + Rs. 6,17,500 + Rs. 4,30,000 + Rs. 95,000, but subject to maximum of Rs. 13,25,700)		13,25,700
Written down value		*Nil*
Depreciation		*Nil*
Capital gains		
Sale consideration of Plants A, B, C and D (Rs. 2,12,000 + Rs. 6,17,500 + Rs. 4,30,000 + Rs. 95,000)		13,54,500
Less: Cost of acquisition	Rs.	
- Depreciated value of the block on April 1, 2018	13,05,700	
- Cost of assets acquired during the year 2018-19	20,000	13,25,700
Balance		28,800
Less: Expenses on transfer		12,200
Short-term capital gain		16,600

Notes:

1. Tax on short-term capital gain can be avoided if the company purchases another plant (eligible for depreciation at the rate of 15%) during the previous year 2018-19 of Rs. 16,600 or more.

Assuming X Ltd. acquires a plant (rate of depreciation : 15 per cent) of Rs. 15,000 during the previous year 2018-19, the amount of chargeable short-term capital gains will be reduced to Rs. 1,600, though the amount of depreciation will remain *nil.* If, however, cost of such plant is Rs. 40,000, short-term capital gain will be reduced to *nil.* In such case depreciation can be claimed on Rs. 11,200.

2. In the aforesaid case, if Plants A, B, C and D are transferred for less than Rs. 13,25,700, the deficiency would be treated as short-term capital loss.

66.1-4 *COST OF ACQUISITION IN THE CASE OF BONUS SHARES* - *See* para 69.7.

66.1-5 *COST OF ACQUISITION IN THE CASE OF RIGHT SHARES AND RIGHT RENOUNCEMENTS* - *See* para 69.8.

66.1-6 *COST OF ACQUISITION IN THE CASE OF ADVANCE MONEY RECEIVED [SEC. 51]* - In the course of negotiations for transfer of a capital asset, the assessee (*i.e.*, transferor) received advance money. Later on the prospective purchaser could not pay the balance consideration and the advance money is retained or forfeited by the assessee or advance money is forfeited by the assessee because of some other reason. The tax treatment of advance money so forfeited or retained by the assessee is as follows –

1. If advance money is forfeited during the previous year 2013-14 (or any earlier previous year) - It is not taxable in the hands of recipient till the capital asset (in respect of which advance money was received and forfeited) is transferred. If capital asset is not transferred during his lifetime, advance money forfeited by him will not be chargeable to tax. Conversely, if the capital asset is transferred during his lifetime, the advance money will be deducted from the cost for which the asset was acquired or the written down value or the fair market value, as the case may be, in computing the cost of acquisition.

2. If advance money is forfeited during the previous year 2014-15 (or any subsequent previous year) - It is taxable in the hands of recipient under section 56(2)(*ix*) under the head "Income from other sources" in the year in which advance money is forfeited. Consequently, it will not be deducted from cost of acquisition when the capital asset is ultimately transferred.

66.1-7 *COST OF ACQUISITION WHEN DEBENTURES ARE CONVERTED INTO SHARES [SEC. 49(2A)]* - Any transfer by way of conversion of debentures, debenture-stock, or deposit certificates in any form, of a company into shares or debentures of that company will not be regarded as a transfer giving rise to any capital gains. Further, it is also provided that on the sale of shares or debentures received on such conversion, the capital gain shall be computed by taking the cost of acquisition as that part of the cost of debentures, debenture-stock or deposit certificates which has been appropriated towards the shares or debentures.

Cost of improvement

67. The provisions regarding cost of improvement are given below—

67.1 ***General meaning*** - Cost of improvement is capital expenditure incurred by an assessee in making any additions/improvement to the capital asset. It also includes any expenditure incurred to protect or complete the title to the capital assets or to cure such title. To put it differently, any expenditure incurred to increase the value of the capital asset is treated as cost of improvement.

67.2 ***Special provisions under the Income-tax Act*** - The following special provisions given under section 55 in respect of cost of improvement should be noted—

1. Expenditure incurred before April 1, 2001[76] *not considered* - Any cost of improvement incurred before April 1, 2001[76] is not taken into consideration for calculating capital gain chargeable to tax. This rule does not have any exception. In other words, cost of improvement includes only expenditure on improvement incurred on or after April 1, 2001[76]. Expenditure incurred on improvement of a capital asset before April 1, 2001[76] is always taken as equal to zero.

2. Double deduction not permitted - Cost of improvement does not include any expenditure which is deductible in computing the income chargeable under the heads "Interest on securities", "Income from house property", "Profits and gains of business or profession" and "Income from other sources".

67.2-1 *COST OF IMPROVEMENT IN DIFFERENT SITUATIONS* - Keeping in view the above provisions, cost of improvement shall be determined in the different situations as follows—

Different situations	*When the capital asset was acquired by gift, will, etc., under the provisions of section 49(1)*	*In any other case*
• Cost of improvement in relation to goodwill of a business or a right to manufacture, produce or process any article/thing or right to carry on any business [or (with effect from assessment year 2017-18) profession],—		
a. when these assets are self-generated	*Nil*	*Nil*
b. when these assets are purchased and later on transferred	*Nil*	*Nil*
• Cost of improvement in relation to any other asset acquired—		
a. before April 1, 2001[76]	Cost of improvement incurred by the assessee and the previous owner (ignoring the expenditure incurred before April 1, 2001[76])	Cost of improvement incurred by the assessee (ignoring the expenditure incurred before April 1, 2001[76])
b. on or after April 1, 2001[76]	Cost of improvement incurred by the assessee and the previous owner	Cost of improvement incurred by the assessee

Indexed cost of acquisition and indexed cost of improvement

68. *Explanation (iii)* to section 48 defines the term "indexed cost of acquisition" as the amount which bears to the cost of acquisition [for meaning, *see* para 66], the same proportion as the cost inflation index for the year in which the asset is transferred bears to the cost inflation index for the first year in which the asset was held by the assessee or for the year beginning on April 1, 2001[76], whichever is later.

76. April 1, 1981 (applicable up to the assessment year 2017-18).

Similarly, indexed cost of improvement is defined as an amount which bears to the cost of improvement [for meaning of cost of improvement, *see* para 67], the same proportion as the cost inflation index for the year in which the asset is transferred bears to the cost inflation index for the year in which the improvement to the asset took place.

68.1 ***Cost inflation index*** - "Cost inflation index" for any year means such index as the Central Government may, having regard to seventy-five per cent of the average rise in the consumer price index for urban non-manual employees[77] for the immediately preceding previous year to such previous year, by notification in the Official Gazette, specify in this behalf.

The Central Government has notified the cost inflation index for the purpose of long-term capital gain as follows :

Previous year	*CII*	*Previous year*	*CII*	*Previous year*	*CII*	*Previous year*	*CII*
2001-02	100	2006-07	122	2011-12	184	2016-17	264
2002-03	105	2007-08	129	2012-13	200	2017-18	272
2003-04	109	2008-09	137	2013-14	220	2018-19	280
2004-05	113	2009-10	148	2014-15	240	2019-20	NA
2005-06	117	2010-11	167	2015-16	254	2020-21	NA

68.2 ***How to convert cost of acquisition/improvement into indexed cost of acquisition/improvement*** - Indexed cost of acquisition is calculated as follows –

68.2-1 *INDEXED COST OF ACQUISITION* - Indexed cost of acquisition shall be calculated as follows –

• *General rule* - Generally, indexed cost of acquisition is calculated as follows -

$$\text{Cost of acquisition} \times \frac{\text{Cost inflation index (CII) for the year in which the asset is transferred}}{\text{CII for the year in which asset was first held by the assessee or 2001-02}^{78}\text{, whichever is later}}$$

• *When the asset was acquired under the circumstances given by section 49(1)* - If an asset was acquired by gift or Will [or under any circumstances given by section 49(1)], indexed cost of acquisition at the time of its transfer shall be calculated as follows –

$$\text{Cost of acquisition} \times \frac{\text{Cost inflation index (CII) for the year in which the asset is transferred}}{\text{CII for the year in which asset was first held by the previous owner or 2001-02}^{78}\text{, whichever is later}}$$

The Bombay High Court in the case of *CIT* v. *Manjula J. Shah* [2012] 204 Taxman 691 has held that indexed cost of acquisition has to be computed with reference to year in which previous owner first held asset (and not year in which the assessee became owner of asset). A similar ruling is given by the Delhi High Court in the case of *Arun Shungloo Trust* v. *CIT* [2012] 205 Taxman 456. Practical examples are solved in the Reckoner on the basis of these High Court rulings.

68.2-2 *INDEXED COST OF IMPROVEMENT* - Indexed cost of improvement shall be calculated as follows –

$$\text{Cost of improvement} \times \frac{\text{CII for the year in which the asset is transferred}}{\text{CII for the year in which improvement took place}}$$

68.2-E1 X purchases a house property for Rs. 26,000 on May 10, 1992. He gets the first floor of the house constructed in 1994-95 by spending Rs. 40,000. He dies on September 12, 1998. The property is transferred to Mrs. X by his will. Mrs. X spends Rs. 30,000 and Rs. 36,000 during 1999-2000 and 2004-05 respectively for renewal/reconstruction of the property. Mrs. X sells the house property for Rs. 48,50,000 on March 15, 2019 (brokerage paid by Mrs. X is Rs. 34,500). The fair market value of the house on April 1, 2001 is Rs. 2,70,000.

•

77. Consumer Price Index (Urban) [applicable from the assessment year 2016-17].

78. 1981-82, up to the assessment year 2017-18.

Computation of capital gain	*Rs.*	*Rs.*
Sale consideration		48,50,000
Less : Expenditure on transfer	34,500	
Indexed cost of acquisition (*see* Note 1)	7,56,000	
Indexed cost of improvement (*see* Note 2)	89,204	8,79,704
Long-term capital gain		39,70,296

Notes :

1. Indexed cost of acquisition

Cost to the previous owner	26,000
Fair market value on April 1, 2001	2,70,000
Cost inflation index for 2001-02	100
Cost inflation index for 2018-19	280
Indexed cost of acquisition (*i.e.*, Rs. 2,70,000 × 280 ÷ 100)	7,56,000

2. Indexed cost of improvement

Cost of improvement incurred prior to April 1, 2001 (not considered)	—
Cost of improvement incurred in 2004-05	36,000
Cost inflation index for 2004-05	113
Cost inflation index for 2018-19	280
Indexed cost of improvement (*i.e.*, Rs. 36,000 × 280 ÷ 113)	89,204

68.2-E2 X purchases a property on April 1, 1986 for Rs. 95,000. He enters into agreement for sale of the property to A on November 1, 2002 and receives Rs. 10,000 as advance. A could not, however, keep his promise and the advance of Rs. 10,000 given by him is forfeited by X. Later on he gifts the property to his friend Y on May 15, 2004. The following expenses are incurred by X and Y for renewals of the property :

	Rs.
Addition of two rooms by X during 1988-89	35,000
Addition of first floor by X during 2002-03	45,000
Addition of second floor by Y during 2009-10	1,25,000

Fair market value of the property on April 1, 2001 is Rs. 2,45,000.

Y enters into an agreement to sell the property for Rs. 8,50,000 to B on April 1, 2008 after receiving an advance of Rs. 50,000. B could not pay the balance within the stipulated time of two months and Y forfeits the advance of Rs. 50,000 as per agreement with B. Y ultimately finds a buyer in C to whom property is transferred for Rs. 35,00,000 on December 1, 2018. Stamp duty value is Rs. 40,00,000. Compute the capital gain chargeable to tax in the hands of Y for the assessment year 2019-20.

•

Computation of capital gain in the case of Y	*Rs.*
Sale consideration (being stamp duty value, as it exceeds 105% of sale consideration)	40,00,000
Less : Indexed cost of acquisition (Note 1)	5,46,000
Indexed cost of improvement (Note 2)	3,56,486
Long-term capital gain	30,97,514

Notes :

1. Indexed cost of acquisition is determined as under :

Cost of acquisition to the previous owner (*a*)	95,000
Fair market value on April 1, 2001 (*b*)	2,45,000
Cost to the previous owner or fair market value on April 1, 2001 [(*a*) or (*b*), whichever is more]	2,45,000
Less : Advance money forfeited by Y (amount forfeited by the previous owner shall not be considered)	50,000
Amount to be considered for indexation	1,95,000
Cost inflation index for 2001-02 (*i.e.*, cost inflation index of 1986-87 or 2001-02, whichever is later)	100
Cost inflation index for 2018-19	280
Indexed cost of acquisition (*i.e.*, Rs. 1,95,000 × 280 ÷ 100)	5,46,000

	Rs.
2. Indexed cost of improvement is determined as under :	
Expenditure incurred prior to April 1, 2001 (it shall be ignored)	Nil
Expenditure incurred on or after April 1, 2001 :	
- during 2002-03 (indexed cost of improvement : Rs. 45,000 × 280 ÷ 105)	1,20,000
- during 2009-10 (indexed cost of improvement : Rs. 1,25,000 × 280 ÷ 148)	2,36,486
	3,56,486

Capital gain in certain special cases - How to compute

69. In the following cases the method of computation is different from what is discussed in the above paras.

69.1 ***Computation of capital gain in the case of conversion of capital asset into stock-in-trade [Sec. 45(2)]*** - The provisions of section 45(2) are given below—

69.1-1 *SUPREME COURT RULING RESPONSIBLE FOR THIS RULE* - The Supreme Court in *CIT* v. *Bai Shirinbai K. Kooka* [1962] 46 ITR 86 had held that where the assessee, holding by way of investment shares in companies, commenced a business in shares converting the shares into stock-in-trade of the business and subsequently sold these shares at profit, the assessable profit was the difference between the sale price of the shares and market price of the shares prevailing on the date when shares were converted into stock-in-trade of the business in shares. In other words, the appreciation in the value of the capital asset between the date of purchase of shares and the date of its conversion into stock is not chargeable to tax.

69.1-2 *RULE OF SECTION 45(2)* - The effect of this judgment has been nullified by the Taxation Laws (Amendment) Act, 1984 by amending sections 2(*47*) and 45 on the following lines—

- With effect from the assessment year 1985-86, conversion of investment into stock-in-trade of a business[79] is treated as transfer under section 2(*47*). It is treated as transfer in the year in which capital asset is converted into stock-in-trade[80].
- The notional capital gain arising from transfer by way of conversion of a capital asset into stock-in-trade is chargeable to tax in the year in which the stock-in-trade is sold [sec. 45(2) inserted with effect from the assessment year 1985-86].
- For the purpose of computing the capital gain in such cases, the fair market value of the capital asset on the date on which it was converted[81] or treated as stock-in-trade shall be deemed to be the full value of the consideration received or occurring as a result of the transfer of the capital asset.

69.1-E1 X converts his capital asset (acquired on June 10,1967 for Rs. 70,000, fair market value on April 1, 1981 : Rs. 1,80,000) into stock-in-trade on March 10, 1984 (fair market value : Rs. 4,80,000) and, subsequently, sells the stock-in-trade so converted for Rs. 7,30,000 on June 10, 2018. Determine the amount of assessable profits.

•

Since the capital asset in this case is converted into stock-in-trade during the previous year relevant for the assessment year 1984-85, it will not be treated as transfer under section 2(*47*) (the amended definition is applicable from the assessment year 1985-86). Nothing is, therefore, chargeable to tax under section 45. Business profits, as per the ruling of the Supreme Court in *CIT* v. *Bai Shirinbai K. Kooka* [1962] 46 ITR 86, chargeable to tax for the assessment year 2019-20 is Rs. 2,50,000 (*i.e.*, Rs. 7,30,000 – Rs. 4,80,000).

69.1-E2 In example 69.1-E1, assume, that the capital asset is converted into stock-in-trade during the previous year relevant to the assessment year 1985-86 (say on April 1, 1984), other things remaining the same, find out assessable profits.

•

Since the capital asset is converted into stock-in-trade during the previous year relevant to the assessment year 1985-86, it will be treated as "transfer" under section 2(*47*) for the assessment year 1985-86.

Capital gain shall be computed on the assumption that the capital asset is transferred on April 1, 1984. However, by virtue of section 45(2) such capital gain will be taxable for the assessment year 2019-20 (*i.e.*, relevant to the previous year in which stock-in-trade is transferred).

---

79. It may be a new business or an existing business.

80. The period of 6 months for making investments in specified assets for the purpose of sections 54EA, 54EB and 54EC should be taken from the date such stock-in-trade is sold or otherwise transferred, in terms of section 45(2)—Circular No. 791, dated June 2, 2000.

81. For purpose of section 45(*2*), date of conversion of capital asset into stock-in-trade has to be determined either on basis of entry passed in the books of account of the assessee or intention of the assessee to exploit capital asset as stock-in-trade for its business purpose – *Puran Ratilal Mehta* v. *CIT* [2019] 102 taxmann.com 187 (Mum.).

	Rs.
Full value of consideration (*i.e.*, fair market value on the date of conversion)	4,80,000
Less : Indexed cost of acquisition (*i.e.*, Rs. 1,80,000 × 125*/100)	
*Cost inflation index for the year in which the asset is converted into stock-in-trade	2,25,000
Long-term capital gain	2,55,000

Business profits chargeable to tax for the assessment year 2019-20 will, however, be Rs. 2,50,000, as computed earlier.

69.2 ***Withdrawal of exemption given by section 47(iv)/(v) [Secs. 47A and 49(3)]*** - Any transfer of capital asset by a company to its wholly owned Indian subsidiary company or by a wholly owned subsidiary company to its Indian holding company, is not treated as transfer by virtue of section 47(*iv*)/(*v*).

69.2-1 *CASES WHEN EXEMPTION IS TAKEN BACK* - In the following two cases, the above exemption shall be withdrawn —

1. If at any time before the expiry of 8 years from the date of transfer of a capital asset between holding company and its wholly owned subsidiary company, such capital asset is converted by the transferee-company into (or is treated by it as) stock-in-trade of its business.

2. The holding company ceases to hold the whole of the share capital of the subsidiary company before the expiry of the period of 8 years aforesaid.

69.2-2 *CONSEQUENCES* - In any of the above noted two cases, transfer of capital asset between holding and subsidiary company is chargeable to tax by virtue of section 47A. In such a case, cost of acquisition in the hands of the transferee-company will be the cost for which the asset was acquired by it.

69.2-E1 S Ltd. is a wholly-owned subsidiary of A Ltd. (both are Indian companies). On April 10, 1984 (relevant to the assessment year 1985-86), S Ltd. transfers a capital asset to A Ltd. (acquired on April 6, 1981 for Rs. 50,000) for Rs. 1,50,000. Fair market value on April 1, 2001 is Rs. 36,000. A Ltd. sells the asset on May 10, 2018 for Rs. 3,40,000. The following situations are considered :

1. Before the sale of asset, A Ltd. has not converted it into stock-in-trade and it does not cease to hold entire share capital of S Ltd.

2. A Ltd. has converted the capital asset into stock-in-trade before its sale on May 10, 2018 (date of conversion : June 10, 1987, fair market value : Rs. 3,10,000).

3. Though A Ltd. does not convert capital asset into stock-in-trade, it ceases to hold the entire share capital of S Ltd. on June 10, 1988 when 5 per cent shareholding in S Ltd. is transferred by way of sale to the public.

●

1. Under situation (1), transfer between A Ltd. and S Ltd. will not be treated as transfer by virtue of section 47(*v*). Consequently, nothing will be taxable in the hands of S Ltd. A Ltd. will, however, be taxable in respect of capital gain computed as under :

	Rs.
Sale consideration	3,40,000
Less : Indexed cost of acquisition (*i.e.*, Rs. 50,000 × 280 ÷ 100[82])	1,40,000
	2,00,000

2. *Under situation (2),* the chargeable profit will be determined as under :

❑ *S Ltd.* : Since A Ltd. has converted the capital asset into stock-in-trade within 8 years from April 10, 1984, exemption granted by section 47(*v*) will not be available and, consequently, Rs. 1,00,000 (*i.e.*, Rs. 1,50,000 — Rs. 50,000) will be treated as long-term capital gain (by virtue of section 47A) of S Ltd. for the assessment year 1985-86.

If the assessment of S Ltd. is completed, the Assessing Officer has power to reopen the assessment for this purpose under section 155(7B) at any time before 4 years from the end of the previous year in which the capital asset is converted into stock-in-trade (*i.e.*, up to March 31, 1992).

❑ *A Ltd.* : Rs. 30,000 (*i.e.*, Rs. 3,40,000 — Rs. 3,10,000) will be chargeable to tax under section 28(*i*) as business profits for the assessment year 2019-20. Besides, capital gain will be determined as under :

	Rs.
Full value of consideration received [fair market value on the date of conversion of capital stock into stock-in-trade under section 45(2)]	3,10,000
Less : Indexed cost of acquisition (*i.e.*, Rs. 1,50,000 × 150[83] ÷ 125[84])	1,80,000
Long-term capital gain	1,30,000

82. Cost inflation index for 2001-02.

83. Cost inflation index of 1987-88, *i.e.*, the year in which capital asset is transferred by converting it into stock-in-trade, by virtue of section 45(2) capital gain shall be taxable for the assessment year 2019-20.

84. Cost inflation index for 1984-85.

3. *Under situation (3)*, the chargeable profit will be determined as under :

❑ *S Ltd.* : Since A Ltd. has transferred shareholding in S Ltd. before the expiry of 8 years from April 10, 1984, the exemption granted by section 47(*v*) will not be available and, consequently, Rs. 1,00,000 (*i.e.*, Rs. 1,50,000 *minus* Rs. 50,000) will be treated as long-term capital gain by virtue of section 47A for the assessment year 1985-86. If assessment of S Ltd. is completed, the Assessing Officer has power to reopen the assessment under section 155(7B) at any time up to March 31, 1993 (*i.e.*, up to 4 years from the end of the previous year in which shareholding is transferred).

❑ *A Ltd.* : Capital gain will be determined as under :

	Rs.
Sale consideration	3,40,000
Less : Indexed cost of acquisition (*i.e.*, Rs. 1,50,000 × 280 ÷ 100)	4,20,000
Long-term capital gain	(–)80,000

69.3 *Computation of capital gains on transfer of firm's assets to partners and* vice versa *[Sec. 45(3)/(4)]* - Section 45(3)/(4) provides for charging to tax profits or gains arising from the transfer of a capital asset by a partner to a firm or by a member to an association of persons or body of individuals, or *vice versa*. In the case of transfer of a capital asset by a partner to a firm, or by a member to an association of persons or body of individuals, the amount recorded in the books of account of the firm, association or body as the value of the capital asset, shall be deemed to be the full value of the consideration. In the case of transfer by way of distribution of capital assets by a firm, an association of persons or a body of individuals, the fair market value of the asset as on the date of transfer shall be deemed to be the full value of the consideration.

• Section 45(4) is not applicable at the time of retirement of one of the partners and the business is continued as a going concern by the remaining partners—*Purayannur Industries* v. *CIT* [2009] 317 ITR (AT) 56 (Cochin), *Prashant S. Joshi* v. *ITO* [2010] 189 Taxman 1 (Bom.), *CIT* v. *Goyal Dresses* [2010] 126 ITD 131 (Chennai).

• Section 45(4) is not applicable when assets are transferred to a company at the time of conversion of the firm into company—*Aum Chemicals* v. *CIT* [2009] 119 ITD 21 (Mum.).

• Period of holding of property in hands of partner (which was acquired by such partner on dissolution of firm) is to be construed from date of dissolution of firm (and not date on which such property was acquired by the firm) – *Amar Kanayalal Nagpal* v. *ITO* [2018] 94 taxmann.com 51 (Mum.).

• The assessee-firm (having 3 partners) has purchased property under a registered sale deed. Later on, it is reconstituted and 5 new partners bring share contribution by cheque. Nearly a year thereafter, erstwhile 3 partners take their share in partnership asset by cheque and go out of partnership. Even if this device is adopted merely to transfer immovable property, capital gain is not chargeable to tax. Section 45(4) cannot be invoked (there being no distribution of capital asset to partners) – *CIT* v. *Dynamic Enterprises* [2014] 63 SOT 91(Chennai).

69.3-E1 X and Y form a partnership firm. Soon after formation of the firm X brings on July 10, 2018, the following assets as his capital contribution :

	Gold Rs.	*Silver Rs.*
Fair market value on the date of transfer by X to firm	5,40,000	72,000
Amount recorded in books of account	6,00,000	50,000
Actual cost	30,000	12,000
Year of acquisition	2005-06	2016-17

Rs. 6,50,000 is credited in the capital account of X in the firm. Is X chargeable to tax in this case ?

•

Surplus arising on transfer of assets by a partner to the firm is chargeable to tax. Amount recorded in the books is treated as full value of consideration for this purpose :

	Gold Rs.	*Silver Rs.*
Value of consideration received as a result of transfer (*i.e.*, amount recorded in books of account, fair market value on the date of transfer is not relevant)	6,00,000	50,000
Less : Cost of acquisition (indexed cost of acquisition in case of gold, *i.e.*, Rs. 30,000 × 280 ÷ 117)	71,795	12,000
Long-term capital gain	5,28,205	—
Short-term capital gain	—	38,000

69.3-E2 X, Y and Z are three partners of a firm. On March 10, 2019, the firm is dissolved. The following assets are distributed to the partners :

	Residential house (taken by X) Rs.	*Shares (taken by Y)* Rs.	*Land (taken by Z)* Rs.
Fair market value on March 10, 2019	26,20,000	90,000	80,000
Agreed value as per dissolution deed	11,70,000	46,000	82,000
Stamp duty value	15,30,000	—	39,000
Cost of acquisition	40,000	5,000	8,000
Year of acquisition	1989-90	2008-09	2003-04
Fair market value on April 1, 2001	1,00,000	N.A.	N.A.

Determine the amount of chargeable capital gains of the firm for the assessment year 2019-20.

•

	Residential house Rs.	*Shares* Rs.	*Land* Rs.
Sale proceeds (being fair market value on the date of transfer; agreed value or stamp duty value not relevant)	26,20,000	90,000	80,000
Less : Indexed cost of acquisition. (*Rs. 1,00,000 × 280 ÷ 100 ; **Rs. 5,000 × 280 ÷ 137 ; ***Rs. 8,000 × 280 ÷ 109)	2,80,000*	10,219**	20,550***
Long-term capital gain	23,40,000	79,781	59,450

69.4 ***Computation of capital gains in the case of compulsory acquisition of an asset [Sec. 45(5)]*** - The provisions of section 45(5) are given below—

69.4-1 *WHEN SECTION 45(5) IS APPLICABLE* - In any of the following cases section 45(5) is applicable—

1. When the transfer of a capital asset is by way of compulsory acquisition under any law.

2. When a capital asset is transferred (not by way of compulsory acquisition) and the consideration is approved or determined by the Central Government (not by a State Government) or the Reserve Bank of India.

69.4-2 *WHEN INITIAL COMPENSATION IS RECEIVED - TAX TREATMENT* - In any of the two cases mentioned in para 69.4-1, the initial compensation is taken as sale consideration and, accordingly, capital gain is computed. It is chargeable to tax in the previous year in which such compensation (or part thereof) is first received. It may be noted that capital gain is not taxable in the year in which the capital asset is transferred but it is taxable in the first year in which the initial compensation (or part thereof) is received.

• However, the amount of compensation received in pursuance of an interim order of the court, Tribunal or other authority shall be chargeable to tax in the previous year in which the final order of such court, Tribunal or other authority is made (applicable from the assessment year 2015-16).

69.4-3 *WHEN ENHANCED COMPENSATION RECEIVED* - In any of the two cases given in para 69.4-1, if any compensation is enhanced by a court, Tribunal or any authority, then it is taxable as follows—

1. It shall be taxable in the previous year in which enhanced compensation is received by the assessee.

2. In this case, cost of acquisition and the cost of improvement shall be taken as *nil.*

3. Litigation expenses for getting the compensation enhanced are deductible as expenses on transfer.

4. If the enhanced compensation is received by any other person (because of the death of the transferor or for any other reason), it is taxable as income of the recipient.

The aforesaid rules are applicable whether the compensation is enhanced by the court/Tribunal/authority on an appeal of the taxpayer or because of any other reason.

69.4-3a WHEN ENHANCED COMPENSATION IS PAID BUT IT IS SUBJECT-MATTER OF DISPUTE - The provisions are given below—

1. If compensation or additional compensation is received from the Government, it will be considered while calculating capital gains of the year in which such compensation is received, even if such compensation is subject-matter of dispute by the Government.

2. Where such compensation or consideration is subsequently reduced by any court, Tribunal or other authority, the capital gain of that year, in which the compensation received was taxed, shall be recomputed accordingly.

3. The Assessing Officer shall amend the order of assessment to revise the computation of said capital gain of that year by taking the compensation so reduced by the court, Tribunal or any other authority to be the full value of consideration. The Assessing Officer has power to recompute capital gain within 4 years from the end of the previous year in which the order reducing the compensation was passed by the court, Tribunal or other authority [*see* Example 69.4-E2].

69.4-E1 The Central Government acquired a house property owned by X on October 17, 2014. This property was purchased on April 10, 1986, for Rs. 16,000 (cost of improvement incurred during 2005-06 : Rs. 40,000 and fair market value of the property on April 1, 2001 was Rs. 32,000). The Government awards Rs. 5,67,000 as compensation which is received as follows— Rs. 10,000 on May 13, 2018 and Rs. 5,57,000 on April 11, 2019. Being aggrieved against the award, X files an appeal. The Court, as per order dated August 1, 2019, enhanced the compensation from Rs. 5,67,000 to Rs. 8,50,000. X receives on April 15, 2020, Rs. 3,29,300 [*i.e.*, additional compensation of Rs. 2,83,000 and interest of Rs. 46,300 (interest of the period : October 2014 to August 2019)]. Expenditure on litigation is Rs. 15,000. Compute the income chargeable to tax.

●

Assessment year 2019-20 (*i.e.*, relevant to the previous year 2018-19 in which initial compensation or part thereof is first received) :

	Rs.
Initial compensation	5,67,000
Less : Indexed cost of acquisition (Note 1)	76,800
Indexed cost of improvement (Note 2)	82,051
Long-term capital gain	4,08,149

Notes

1. Indexed cost of acquisition is computed as follows : Rs. 32,000* × 240** ÷ 100*** = Rs. 76,800.

*Fair market value on April 1, 2001.

**Cost inflation index for 2014-15 (*i.e.*, the year in which property is acquired).

***Cost inflation index for 2001-02.

2. Index cost of improvement is computed as follows : Rs. 40,000* × 240** ÷ 117*** = Rs. 82,051.

*Cost of improvement.

**Cost inflation index of the year in which property is acquired (*i.e.*, 2014-15).

***Cost inflation index of the year in which improvement took place.

Assessment year 2021-22 (*i.e.*, relevant to the previous year 2020-21 in which additional compensation and interest are received) :

	Rs.
Additional compensation	2,83,000
Less :	
Cost of acquisition	*Nil*
Cost of improvement	*Nil*
Expenditure (*i.e.*, Rs. 15,000 × Rs. 2,83,000 ÷ Rs. 3,29,300)	12,891
Long-term capital gain	2,70,109
Income from other sources [Rs. 46,300 — 50% deduction under section 57(*iv*)]	23,150

69.4-E2 X purchases a house property in 2002. It is compulsorily acquired by the Central Government on April 20, 2012 (indexed cost of acquisition is Rs. 40,000). Compensation paid by the Government on May 6, 2018 : Rs. 6,00,000. The Delhi High Court increases the compensation from Rs. 6,00,000 to Rs. 9,30,000 on the appeal filed by X (legal expenditure incurred by X : Rs. 10,000). The Government on June 10, 2020 pays the additional compensation of Rs. 3,30,000 but it files an appeal in the Supreme Court against the judgment of the Delhi High Court. The Supreme Court reduces the quantum of compensation from Rs. 9,30,000 to Rs. 7,50,000 by its judgment dated March 20, 2022. X repays Rs. 1,80,000 to the Government on April 6, 2022. Legal expenditure incurred by X in Supreme Court is Rs. 25,000.

●

Assessment year 2019-20	*Rs.*
Sale consideration (being the original compensation)	6,00,000
Less : Indexed cost of acquisition	40,000
Long-term capital gains	5,60,000

	Rs.
Assessment year 2021-22	
Sale consideration (being the additional compensation awarded by Delhi High Court)	3,30,000
Less : Indexed cost of acquisition	*Nil*
Less : Expenses on transfer	10,000
Long-term capital gains	3,20,000
Recomputation of income of the assessment year 2021-22 after the verdict of Supreme Court	
Sale consideration (Rs. 7,50,000 *minus* Rs. 6,00,000 being the original compensation)	1,50,000
Less : Indexed cost of acquisition	*Nil*
Less : Expenses on transfer (Rs. 10,000 + Rs. 25,000)	35,000
Long-term capital gains	1,15,000

Note : The Assessing Officer can re-compute the income of the assessment year 2021-22 within 4 years from the end of the year in which order of the Supreme Court, reducing the compensation, is passed (*i.e.*, March 31, 2026, being 4 years from last date of the year in which March 20, 2022 falls).

69.5 ***Computation of capital gains in the case of non-resident [First proviso to sec. 48]*** - First proviso to section 48 is applicable only in the case of a non-resident. Under this provision, capital gain is calculated in foreign currency in some cases.

• *Conditions* - To avail the benefit of this provision, the following conditions should be satisfied—

1. The taxpayer is a non-resident (maybe an Indian or foreign citizen, or a corporate-assessee or a non-corporate assessee but not being an assessee covered by sections 115AC and 115AD).

2. He acquires shares in (or debentures of) an Indian company (maybe public limited or private limited) by utilising foreign currency.

3. The asset may be short-term or long-term.

• *Rule of computation* - If the aforesaid conditions are satisfied, then the following procedure shall be adopted to determine capital gain (it may be noted that the procedure given below is applicable without any exception whenever the above conditions are satisfied)—

1. Capital gain shall be computed in the same foreign currency which was initially utilised in acquiring shares or debentures.

2. Capital gain so calculated in the foreign currency shall be reconverted into Indian currency.

3. The benefit of indexation shall not be available.

4. The aforesaid manner of computation of capital gain shall be applicable in respect of capital gain accruing or arising from every re-investment thereafter in (and sale of) shares in (or debentures of) an Indian company.

5. The aforesaid mode of computation is applicable only when the above-mentioned conditions are satisfied. In no other case, the above procedure is applicable.

6. The aforesaid mode of computation is not applicable when capital gain is covered by section 112A [*see* para 72.2].

▷ *How to determine capital gain* - In order to understand the method of computation of capital gain, it is imperative to know the meaning of (*a*) average exchange rate, and (*b*) buying rate.

▷ *Average exchange rate* - It is the average of the telegraphic transfer buying rate and telegraphic transfer selling rate of the foreign currency initially utilised in the purchase of the said asset.

For this purpose, telegraphic transfer buying/selling rate in relation to a foreign currency is rate of exchange adopted by the State Bank of India for purchasing or selling such currency where such currency is made available by that bank through telegraphic transfer.

▷ *Buying rate* - It is telegraphic transfer buying rate of such currency.

• Capital gain shall be determined as under—

	Conversion rate	*Conversion rate of which date is applicable*	*Computation*
1. Sale consideration	Average exchange rate	Date of transfer	Find out sale consideration in Indian currency and convert it into foreign currency at "average exchange rate" on the date of transfer (suppose it is *x*)

	Conversion rate	*Conversion rate of which date is applicable*	*Computation*
2. Cost of acquisition	Average exchange rate	Date of acquisition	Find out the cost of acquisition in Indian currency and convert it into foreign currency at "average exchange rate" on the date of acquisition (suppose it is *y*)
3. Expenditure on sale	Average exchange rate	Date of transfer	Find out the expenditure on transfer in Indian currency and convert it into foreign currency at "average exchange rate" on the date of transfer (not on the date when expenditure is incurred (suppose it is *z*)
4. Capital gain	Buying rate	Date of transfer	(*x—y—z*) will be reconverted into Indian currency at "buying rate" on the date of transfer

• The following points should be noted —

1. Even if the aforesaid provisions are applicable, the option of adopting fair market value on April 1, 2001 is available—*Alcan Inc.* v. *DIT* [2007] 16 SOT 8 (Mum.).

2. If the capital gain is short-term capital gain and securities transaction tax is applicable, the capital gain is taxable at the rate of 15 per cent[85]. If the capital gain is long-term capital gain and securities transaction tax is applicable, capital gain is exempt from tax under section 10(*38*) [however, this exemption is not available from the assessment year 2019-20 and long-term capital gain is taxable under section 112A—*see* para 72.2]. If the capital gain is long-term capital gain and securities transaction tax is not applicable, such gain would be taxable at the rate of 20 per cent[85] [in some cases at the option of taxpayer at the rate of 10 per cent[85] under proviso to section 112(1)—*see* para 72.1-3].

69.5-E1 X, a non-resident foreign citizen, remits US $ 60,000 to India on August 10, 2001. The amount is partly utilised on August 17, 2001 for purchasing 50,000 preference shares in Lotus Ltd., an Indian company, at the rate of Rs. 12 per share (brokerage paid : Re. 1 per share). These shares are sold for Rs. 28 per share on April 10, 2015 (brokerage paid on April 16, 2015 @ Rs. 1.50). The sale consideration is utilised on April 25, 2015 for purchasing 40,000 preference shares in Indian Sugars and Chemicals Ltd. at the rate of Rs. 34 per share (brokerage paid : Re. 1 per share). Shares in Indian Sugars and Chemicals Ltd. are transferred on April 20, 2018 @ Rs. 90 per share (brokerage paid @ Rs. 1.55 per share on June 30, 2018).

Find out the capital gains chargeable to tax for the assessment years 2016-17 and 2019-20 on the assumption that the telegraphic transfer, buying and selling rates of US dollars adopted by the State Bank of India are as follows :

	Buying (1 US $) Rs.	*Selling (1 US $)* Rs.
August 10, 2001	18.30	19.10
August 17, 2001	18.40	19.30
April 10, 2015	25.90	26.40
April 16, 2015	26.10	26.60
April 25, 2015	26.10	26.60
April 20, 2018	48.30	49.10
June 30, 2018	48.40	49.20

•

For computing capital gains one has to find out the average of the telegraphic transfer buying rate and the telegraphic transfer selling rate on the date of purchase and sale of shares. Date of making expenditure in connection with transfer is not relevant.

These rates are as follows :

Average rate on	*(1 US $)* Rs.
August 17, 2001	18.85
April 10, 2015	26.15
April 25, 2015	26.35
April 20, 2018	48.70

85. [+ SC + HEC]

Assessment year 2016-17	*Rs.*	*US $*
Sale consideration	14,00,000*	—
(* 50,000 × Rs. 28) ; ** Rs. 14,00,000 ÷ Rs. 26.15	—	53,537.28 **
Less : Cost of acquisition (* 50,000 × Rs. 13 ; ** Rs. 6,50,000 ÷ Rs. 18.85)	6,50,000*	34,482.76**
Expenditure on transfer (* Rs. 75,000 ÷ Rs. 26.15)	75,000	2,868.07*
Long-term capital gain	N.A.	16,186.46
Long-term capital gain in Indian currency ($ 16,186.46 × Rs. 25.90)	4,19,229.26	—

Assessment year 2019-20		
Sale consideration *Rs. 90 × 40,000, ** Rs. 36,00,000 ÷ Rs. 48.70	36,00,000*	73,921.97**
Less :		
Cost of acquisition (*Rs. 35 × 40,000, ** Rs. 14,00,000 ÷ Rs. 26.35)	14,00,000*	53,130.93**
Expenditure on transfer (*Rs. 1.55 × 40,000,** Rs. 62,000 ÷ Rs. 48.70)	62,000*	1,273.10**
Balance	N.A.	19,517.94
Long-term capital gain (*i.e.*, $ 19,517.94 × Rs. 48.30)	9,42,716.54	—

Notes :

1. The benefit of deduction of indexed cost of acquisition is not available in the aforesaid case.

2. The aforesaid procedure is applicable even in the case of short-term capital gain.

69.5-1 *SPECIAL PROVISIONS IN THE CASE OF A NON-RESIDENT INDIAN [SEC. 115F]* - If the following conditions are satisfied, one can take the benefit of section 115F :

- The taxpayer is a non-resident Indian (*i.e.*, an individual being a citizen of India or a person of Indian origin who is non-resident; a person shall be deemed to be of Indian origin if he, or either of his parents or any of his grand-parents, was born in undivided India).
- He has transferred a specified asset [*i.e.*, shares in an Indian company, debentures of an Indian public limited company, deposits with an Indian public limited company or Central Government securities (hereinafter referred to as "original asset")] which has been acquired or purchased with, or subscribed to in, convertible foreign exchange.
- Such asset is a long-term capital asset.
- Within 6 months of the transfer of the original asset, the taxpayer has invested the whole or any part of net consideration (*i.e.*, consideration *less* expenses on transfer) in any of the following assets (hereinafter referred to as "new asset") —

a. shares in an Indian company ;

b. debentures of an Indian public limited company ;

c. deposit with an Indian public limited company (including a banking company) ;

d. Central Government securities ; or

e. National Savings Certificates VI and VII Issues.

69.5-1a AMOUNT OF EXEMPTION - If all the above conditions are satisfied, exemption is available as follows :

- If the cost of the new asset is not less than the net consideration in respect of the original asset transferred, the entire capital gain arising from the transfer is exempt from tax.
- If the cost of the new asset is less than the net consideration in respect of the original asset transferred, the exemption from long-term capital gain is granted proportionately on the basis of investment of net consideration in the new asset, *i.e.*, amount invested in the new asset × long-term capital gain/amount of net consideration as a result of transfer of the original asset.

69.5-1b CONSEQUENCES IF THE NEW ASSET IS TRANSFERRED WITHIN 3 YEARS - In case the new asset acquired by the assessee is transferred or converted into money within a period of three years from the date of its acquisition, the capital gain exempted by virtue of the provisions given above is deemed to be income by way of long-term capital gain of the previous year in which such new asset is so transferred or converted into money.

69.5-1c OPTION TO AVAIL OR NOT TO AVAIL THE BENEFIT OF SECTION 115F - A non-resident Indian may elect (by virtue of section 115-I) not to be governed by the provisions of section 115F for any assessment year by giving a declaration in the return of income to this effect.

69.5-1E1 In example 69.5-E1, assume that X is a non-resident Indian and he wants to avail the benefit of section 115F.

•

Assessment year 2016-17

Since X has invested the entire net consideration received on the sale of 50,000 shares in Lotus Ltd. (*i.e.*, Rs. 14,00,000 – Rs. 75,000) in acquiring a new asset (*i.e.*, shares in Indian Sugars and Chemical Ltd.) within 6 months from the transfer, the resulting long-term capital gain of Rs. 4,19,229 is not chargeable to tax for the assessment year 2016-17.

Assessment year 2019-20

Shares in Indian Sugars and Chemical Ltd. have been transferred within 3 years from the date of acquisition. Consequently, the exemption given for the assessment year 2016-17 will be revoked and income under the head "Capital gains" for the assessment year 2019-20 will be as follows :

	Rs.
Long-term capital gain on transfer of shares in Indian Sugars & Chemical Ltd. [as computed earlier]	9,42,716.54
Deemed long-term capital gain	4,19,229.26
Income under the head "Capital gains"	13,61,945.80

69.6 ***Computation of capital gain in the case of self-generated assets*** - Before discussing the tax incidence on transfer of a self generated asset, it is better to define first the term "self-generated asset".

Self-generated asset - An asset which does not cost anything to the assessee in terms of money in its creation or acquisition, is a self generated asset.

69.6-1 *WHEN TRANSFER OF A SELF-GENERATED ASSET IS CHARGEABLE TO TAX* - By virtue of specific provisions under the Act, transfer of the following self-generated assets is chargeable to tax under the head "Capital gains"—

Self-generated assets	*Sale considera-tion*	*Cost of acquisi-tion*	*Cost of improve-ment*	*Expenses on transfer*	*Capital gain*
1. Goodwill of a business, right to manufacture, produce or process any article or right to carry on any business [or (with effect from assessment year 2017-18) profession]	Actual	*Nil*	*Nil*	Actual	Sale consideration *minus* expenses on transfer
2. Tenancy rights, route permits and loom hours, trade mark or brand name associated with a business	Actual	*Nil*	Actual	Actual	Sale consideration *minus* cost (or indexed cost) of improvement *minus* expenses on transfer

1. The above rules are applicable only in the case of "self-generated assets". If an asset is purchased and later on sold, then the actual purchase price and improvement cost are taken as cost of acquisition and cost of improvement.

2. If goodwill is purchased and later on transferred, the purchase price will be taken as cost of acquisition and cost of improvement is taken as *nil.* A similar rule is applicable when a right to manufacture, produce or process any article/thing is purchased and later on transferred.

3. Even if the aforesaid assets were acquired before April 1, 2001, the option of adopting the fair market value on the said date is not available.

69.6-2 *WHEN TRANSFER OF A SELF-GENERATED ASSET IS NOT CHARGEABLE TO TAX* - Transfer of any other self-generated asset [like self-generated goodwill of a profession (up to the assessment year 2016-17), a new formula patented by the inventor to grow seedless oranges] is not chargeable to tax. It is based upon the Supreme Court's ruling in *CIT* v. *B.C. Srinivasa Setty* [1981] 5 Taxman 1, wherein it was pointed out that the income chargeable to capital gains tax is to be computed by deducting from the full value of the consideration "the cost of acquisition of the capital asset and the cost of any improvement thereto". If it is not possible to ascertain cost of acquisition and/or cost of improvement, then transfer of such asset is not taxable under the Act.

The above ruling of the Supreme Court is not applicable in the case of self-generated assets mentioned in para 69.6-1 because of the modifications made in the Act after the above verdict of the court.

69.6-E1 X transfers the following assets on May 15, 2018—

	Cost Rs.	*Fair market value on April 1, 2001* Rs.	*Sale consideration* Rs.
Land (acquired in 1988)	20,000	45,000	8,55,000
Goodwill	—*	10,000	1,75,000
Tenancy rights	—*	30,000	2,00,000

*Self-generated

Determine the amount of capital gains chargeable to tax for the assessment year 2019-20.

•

	Land Rs.	*Goodwill* Rs.	*Tenancy right* Rs.
Sale consideration	8,55,000	1,75,000	2,00,000
Less : Indexed cost of acquisition in the case of land (*i.e.*, Rs. 45,000 × 28 ÷ 100)	1,26,000	*Nil*	*Nil*
Long-term capital gain	7,29,000	1,75,000	2,00,000

69.7 ***Cost of acquisition of bonus shares*** - Relevant provisions are summarised as follows —

	Cost of acquisition if original and bonus shares are transferred after March 31, 1995
• If original shares and bonus shares are acquired before April 1, 2001[86]	*Original shares* - Actual cost or fair market value on April 1, 2001[86], whichever is more *Bonus shares* - Fair market value on April 1, 2001[86]
• If original shares are acquired before April 1, 2001[86] but bonus shares are allotted after April 1, 2001[86]	*Original shares* - Actual cost or fair market value on April 1, 2001[86], whichever is more *Bonus shares - Nil*
• If original and bonus shares are acquired after April 1, 2001[86]	*Original shares* - Actual cost *Bonus shares - Nil*

Moreover, in the case of a capital asset being a share, security or unit which is allotted without any payment on the basis of holding of any other financial asset, the period for treating such share, security or unit as a short-term capital asset shall be calculated from the date of allotment of such share, security or unit as the case may be.

69.8 ***Capital gain on transfer of right shares and right entitlement*** - Cost of acquisition in different situations will be as follows :

Different situations	*Cost of acquisition*
Original shares (on basis of which the taxpayer becomes entitled to right shares)	Amount actually paid for acquiring shares
Rights entitlement (which is renounced by the assessee in favour of a person)	*Nil*

86. April 1, 1981 (applicable up to the assessment year 2017-18).

Different situations	*Cost of acquisition*
Rights shares acquired by the taxpayer by exercising his rights entitlement	Amount actually paid by the taxpayer for acquiring asset
Rights shares purchased by the person in whose favour the rights entitlement has been renounced	Purchase price paid to renouncer of rights entitlement *plus* amount paid to the company which has allotted the rights shares.

69.8-E1 X holds 1,000 (non-listed) equity shares in A Ltd. since 1988 (cost of acquisition : Rs. 10,000, fair market value on April 1, 2001 : Rs. 16,000). A Ltd. offers 2,000 right shares of Rs. 10 each to X on May 1, 2018 at a premium of Rs. 50. X subscribes for 800 rights shares and renounces 1,200 shares in favour of C by transferring the right entitlement for a consideration of Rs. 4,800. X sells 1,800 shares in A Ltd. on March 30, 2019 @ Rs. 200 per share. C also transfers his 1,200 shares @ Rs. 201 per share on March 31, 2019.

•

Assessment of X for the assessment year 2019-20	Rs.
Sale proceeds of 1,000 original shares	2,00,000
Less : Indexed cost of acquisition (Rs. 16,000 × 280 ÷ 100)	44,800
Long-term capital gain	1,55,200
Sale proceeds of 800 right shares (Rs. 200 × 800)	1,60,000
Less : Cost of acquisition (*i.e.*, Rs. 60 × 800)	48,000
Short-term capital gain	1,12,000
Sale proceeds of right entitlement of 1,200 shares	4,800
Less : Cost of acquisition	*Nil*
Short-term capital gain	4,800
Assessment of C for the assessment year 2019-20	
Sale proceeds of 1,200 shares	2,41,200
Less : Cost of acquisition [*i.e.* (Rs. 60 × 1,200) + Rs. 4,800]	76,800
Short-term capital gain	1,64,400

69.9 ***Withdrawal of exemption given under section 47(xiii)/47(xiv) [Sec. 47A(3)]*** - The following conditions should be satisfied—

1. A firm or proprietary concern is converted into company by satisfying conditions of section 47(*xiii*)/(*xiv*).

2. As conditions of section 47(*xiii*)/(*xiv*) are satisfied, capital gain is not chargeable to tax in the hands of firm/ sole proprietary concern.

3. If after conversion, any of the conditions of section 47(*xiii*)/(*xiv*) are not satisfied, then capital gain (which was not taxed earlier) will become chargeable to tax in the hands of company.

• *Provisions illustrated* - X & Co. is a firm of X and Y (1 : 2) whose balance sheet as on April 1, 2018 is as follows :—

Balance Sheet of X & Co. as on April 1, 2018

	Rs.		Rs.
Capital		Plant and machinery	80,000
X	1,00,000	House property (acquired in 2005-06)	2,00,000
Y	2,00,000	Stock-in-trade	40,000
Sundry creditors	1,00,000	Debtors	70,000
		Bank and cash balances	10,000
	4,00,000		4,00,000

A Ltd. is incorporated on April 1, 2018 which takes over the assets and liabilities of X & Co. as follows :—

	Agreed valuation Rs.	*Cost of acquisition for the purpose of income-tax* Rs.
Plant and machinery	2,80,000	80,000
House property	10,00,000	2,00,000
Stock in trade	60,000	—
Debtors	70,000	—
Bank and cash balances	10,000	—
Total	14,20,000	
Less : Sundry creditors	1,00,000	
Net consideration	13,20,000	
Equity shares (44,000 equity shares of Rs. 10) allotted to X by A Ltd.	4,40,000	—
Equity shares (88,000 equity shares of Rs. 10) allotted to Y by A Ltd.	8,80,000	—

Capital gain and business income of X & Co.

	Plant and machinery Rs.	*House property* Rs.	*Stock-in-trade* Rs.
Sale consideration	2,80,000	10,00,000	60,000
Less : Cost of acquisition or indexed cost of acquisition [Rs. 2,00,000 × 280 ÷ 117]	80,000	4,78,632	40,000
Business income	—	—	20,000
Short-term capital gain	2,00,000	—	—
Long-term capital gain	—	5,21,368	—

In this case the firm will pay tax in respect of business income of Rs. 20,000 and the capital gain of Rs. 7,21,368 will not be taxable in the hands of the firm as conversion of the firm into company is not treated as "transfer" by virtue of section 47(*xiii*).

One of the conditions of section 47(*xiii*) is that the aggregate shareholding in the company of the partners of the firm should not be less than 50 per cent of the total voting power in the company and their shareholding continues to be as such for a period of five years from the date of the succession.

In other words, the aggregate of the shareholding of X and Y in A Ltd. should not be less than 50 per cent uptil April 1, 2023. If suppose Y transfers all of his shares on April 6, 2020 to Z, then A Ltd. will be chargeable to tax in respect of Rs. 7,35,043 as profits and gains. It is not clear from the language of section 47A(3) as to the head under which the company would be taxed. However, having regard to the placement of section 47A(3) in the provisions relating to taxation of capital gains, it appears that it would be treated as capital gains. Consequently, A Ltd. will be chargeable to tax in respect of long-term capital gains of Rs. 5,21,368 and short-term capital gain of Rs. 2,00,000 and this will be deemed as income of the previous year 2020-21 (*i.e.*, the assessment year 2021-22).

69.9A *Withdrawal of exemption given under section 47(xiiib) [Sec. 47A(4), applicable from the assessment year 2011-12 onwards]* - Under section 47(*xiiib*) if capital assets are transferred by a private company/unlisted public company to a limited liability partnership (LLP) at the time of conversion of the company into LLP, then the conversion is not treated as "transfer" and, consequently, capital gain is not chargeable to tax in the hands of predecessor company and its shareholders. However, exemption under section 47(*xiiib*) is available only if 6 conditions given therein are satisfied [for these conditions, *see* para 62.2(*za*)]. These conditions should be satisfied at the time of conversion. One of the conditions requires that aggregate of the profit sharing ratio in the LLP of the shareholders of the predecessor company should not be lower than 50 per cent at any time during the period of 5 years commencing from the date of conversion. Similarly, another condition requires that accumulated profit of the company should not be distributed to the partners in next three years.

Suppose, a company and its shareholders take the benefit of exemption under section 47(*xiiib*) by satisfying the 6 conditions at the time of conversion into LLP and later on in a subsequent year, the LLP fails to comply with the two conditions stated above. In such a situation,—

a. the amount of capital gain exemption given to the predecessor company will become income by way of capital gain of the LLP of the year in which non-compliance takes place; and

b. the amount of capital gain exemption given to the shareholders of the predecessor company will become income by way of capital gain of the shareholders of the predecessor company of the year in which non-compliance takes place.

69.10 ***Capital gain on distribution of assets by companies in liquidation [Sec. 46]*** - The provisions of section 46 are given below—

69.10-1 *TAX TREATMENT IN THE HANDS OF THE COMPANY [SEC. 46(1)]* - Section 46(1) is applicable if the following three conditions are satisfied—

a. assets are distributed by a company ;

b. the assets are distributed at the time of liquidation ; and

c. the assets are distributed to the shareholders.

If all the three conditions are satisfied, there is no "transfer" in such distribution and capital gain is not chargeable in the hands of the company.

69.10-2 *TAX TREATMENT IN THE HANDS OF THE SHAREHOLDERS [SEC. 46(2)]* - When a shareholder receives money or other assets at the time of liquidation of the company (in which he is a shareholder), section 46(2) is applicable. Capital gain under section 46(2) shall be determined as follows—

1. Find out the money received and the market value of other assets on the date of distribution.

2. Find out the amount treated as dividend under section 2(*22*)(*c*) [any distribution by a company at the time of liquidation is treated as dividend to the extent of accumulated profit of the company and the company will have to pay dividend distribution tax, dividend will be exempt in the hands of shareholders].

3. The excess of (*1*) over (*2*) is treated as full value of consideration received on transfer of shares.

4. From the consideration [as calculated at *3 supra*], deduct cost of acquisition/indexed cost of acquisition, expenditure on sale, etc., to find out capital gain.

69.10-E1 X purchases 4,000 equity shares in Y Ltd. on April 16, 2003 at the rate of Rs. 2 per share. Y Ltd. goes into liquidation on November 30, 2018. The balance sheet of the company as on November 30, 2018 is as follows—

	Rs.		*Rs.*
40,000 equity shares	4,00,000	10,000 Debentures of Z Ltd. (cost : Rs. 9,00,000, acquired in May 2007)	28,00,000
Accumulated profit	30,00,000	Cash in hand	12,16,659
Provision for dividend tax	6,16,659		
	40,16,659		40,16,659

The assets are distributed to the shareholders. Consequently, X gets 1,000 debentures of Z Ltd. (market value Rs. 2,80,000) and Rs. 60,000 in cash on November 30, 2018. He transfers 1,000 debentures on April 6, 2019 for Rs. 3,10,000. Find out the tax consequences of these transactions.

●

Y Ltd. - During the previous year 2018-19, the company has distributed assets (being debentures of Z Ltd.) to its shareholders at the time of liquidation. Even if the cost of debentures is Rs. 9 lakh and the market value is Rs. 28 lakh, the surplus is not taxable, as by virtue of section 46(1) distribution of capital assets in kind to shareholders at the time of liquidation is not treated as "transfer". It may be noted that the difference of Rs. 19 lakh is tax-free income.

	Rs.
Total distribution to shareholders [*i.e.*, debentures in Z Ltd. of Rs. 28 lakh + Rs. 6 lakh]	34,00,000
Out of which treated as dividend under section 2(*22*)(*c*) to the extent of accumulated profit	30,00,000
Tax on dividend [15/85 of Rs. 30,00,000 + SC + HEC]	6,16,659
Income of X at the time of liquidation of the company [*assessment year 2019-20*]—	
Amount received by X on November 30, 2018 (*i.e.*, market value of 1,000 debentures + Rs. 60,000)	3,40,000
Less: Dividend on which Y Ltd. has paid dividend tax	3,00,000
Balance which is treated as full value of consideration on transfer of 4,000 shares in Y Ltd.	40,000
Less: Indexed cost of acquisition [Rs. 4,000 × 2 × 280 ÷ 109]	20,550
Long-term capital gain	19,450

	Rs.
Income of X for the assessment year 2020-21—	
Sale consideration of 1,000 debentures of Z Ltd. on April 6, 2019	3,10,000
Less: Cost of acquisition (being the market value on November 30, 2018)[87]	2,80,000
Short-term capital gain	30,000

69.11 ***Transfer of security in demat form [Sec. 45(2A)]*** - The provisions of section 45(2A) are given below—

1. Section 45(2A) is applicable if shares/securities are transferred in "demat" form.

2. If shares/securities are transferred in "demat" form, beneficial owner of shares/securities is chargeable to tax.

3. For computing capital gain chargeable to tax, the cost of acquisition and period of holding of any security shall be determined on the basis of first-in-first-out (FIFO) method.

69.11-1 *BOARD'S CLARIFICATION ON FIFO SYSTEM* - The Board has issued the following clarification *vide* Circular No. 768$, dated June 24, 1998—

1. FIFO method will be applied only in respect of the dematerialised holdings because in case of sale of dematerialised securities, the securities held in physical form cannot be construed to have been sold as they continue to remain in possession of the investor and are identified separately.

2. In the depository system, the investor can open and hold multiple accounts. In such a case, where an investor has more than one security account, FIFO method will be applied account-wise. This is because in case where a particular account of an investor is debited for sale of securities, the securities lying in his other account cannot be construed to have been sold as they continue to remain in that account.

3. If in an existing account of dematerialised stock, old physical stock is dematerialised and entered at a later date, under the FIFO method, the basis for determining the movement out of the account is the date of entry into the account. This is illustrated by the following examples :

Date of credit	*Particulars*	*Quantity*
June 1, 2018	Purchased directly in dematerialised form on May 25, 2018	2,000
June 5, 2018	Dematerialised share originally purchased in November 2003	5,000
June 10, 2018	Purchased directly in dematerialised form of June 10, 2018	4,000
June 15, 2018	Dematerialised shares originally purchased in May, 1979	3,000

If say, 2,500 shares were sold from out of this account, then the period of holding and the cost of acquisition of the first 2,000 shares should be as from May 25, 2018 and the cost thereof, whereas the balance 500 shares will be treated as having been acquired in November 2003, at the relevant cost. This is the effect of the FIFO method.

69.12 ***Capital gain on purchase by a company of its own shares/securities [Sec. 46A]*** - Section 46A was inserted with effect from the assessment year 2000-01. It provides that any consideration received by a shareholder (or a holder of other specified securities) from any company on purchase of its own shares (or other specified securities) held by such shareholder (or holder of other specified securities) shall be chargeable to tax on the difference between the cost of acquisition and the value of consideration received by the shareholder (or by the holder of securities), as capital gains. The computation of capital gains shall be made in accordance with the provisions of section 48.

"Specified securities" includes employees' stock option or other securities as may be notified by the Central Government.

• *Tax payable on distributed income by company under section 115QA and tax exemption to shareholders under section 10(34A)* - In the cases given below, the company (buying its own shares) is required to pay tax on distributed income[88] under section 115QA with effect from June 1, 2013[89]. In these cases, when tax is payable by the company, income (or capital gain) is exempt in the hands of shareholders under section 10(*34A*)–

87. When the shareholder sells the asset (which was received at the time of liquidation of the company) he would be assessable under section 45 on the excess of sale price over market value of asset on the date of distribution by liquidator if he has been assessed to tax on the basis of such market value under section 46(2) [sec. 55(2)(*b*)(*iii*)]. If, however, he was not charged to tax under section 46(2) on the basis of market value of assets received at the time of liquidation, then cost to previous owner will be taken to compute capital gain chargeable to tax [sec. 49(1)(*iii*)(*c*)].

88. Quantum of distributed income shall be determined in accordance with rule 40BB$.

89. CBDT has clarified that consideration received on buy-back of shares between the period April 1, 2000 till May 31, 2013 would be taxed as capital gains in the hands of the recipient in accordance with section 46A and no such amount shall be treated as dividend in view of provisions of section 2(*22*)(*iv*) – Circular No. 3/2016, dated February 26, 2016.

$For rule 40BB and Circular No. 768, log on to *taxmann.com/readyreckoner.aspx.*

- Buy-back of unlisted shares (during June 1, 2013 and July 4, 2019,
- Buy-back of **listed/unlisted shares (on or after July 5, 2019).**

69.12-E1 On May 10, 2018, X Ltd. purchases its own shares (face value : Rs. 10, amount offered to shareholders : Rs. 90 per share). Total amount distributed by X Ltd. on buy-back of 20,000 shares is Rs. 18,00,000. These shares were issued in 2008-09 at a premium of Rs. 15. A is one of the shareholders. He holds 2,000 shares (cost of acquisition : Rs. 27 per share, year of acquisition : 2011-12). He gets Rs. 1,80,000. Find out the tax consequences in the hands of A and X Ltd. in the following different situations. Assume that net income of A is not more than Rs. 50 lakh.

Situation 1 - Shares in X Ltd. are not listed in any recognised stock exchange in India.

Situation 2 - Shares in X Ltd. are listed in the National Stock Exchange. At the time of buy-back, securities transaction tax is applicable. However, when A acquired 2000 shares, securities transaction tax was not applicable (as shares were acquired from a friend outside recognised stock exchange).

Situation 3 - Shares in X Ltd. are listed in the National Stock Exchange and Bombay Stock Exchange. At the time of buy-back, securities transaction tax is applicable. Moreover, securities transaction tax was paid by A at the time of acquisition of 2000 shares (as shares were acquired through a transaction in Bombay Stock Exchange). Fair market value of shares in X Ltd. on January 31, 2018 (as per highest stock exchange quotation) is Rs. 30 per share.

Situation 4 - Shares in X Ltd. are listed (or unlisted) in a recognised stock exchange in India and buy-back takes place on or after July 5, 2019.

•

Situation 1 (buy-back of unlisted shares on or before July 4, 2019) and Situation 4 (buy-back of listed or unlisted shares on or after July 5, 2019) - In these situations, A is not chargeable to tax. His capital gain is exempt under section 10(*34A*). However, X Ltd. will have to pay tax on distributed income under section 115QA as follows –

	Rs.
Amount paid to shareholders at the time of buy-back (Rs. 90 × 20,000)	18,00,000
Less: Amount received at the time of issue of shares in 2008-09 (Rs. 25 × 20,000)	5,00,000
Distributed income	13,00,000
Tax on distributed income @ 20%	2,60,000
Add: Surcharge @ 12%	31,200
Add: Health and education cess [4% of (Rs. 2,60,000 + Rs. 31,200)]	11,648
Tax liability of X Ltd. under section 115QA	3,02,848

Situation 2 (buy-back of listed shares prior to July 5, 2019, STT is paid at the time of buy-back but not at the time of acquisition of shares by A) - As shares are listed (buy-back takes place prior to July 5, 2019), X Ltd. is not liable to pay tax under section 115QA. However, A will have to pay tax [exemption under section 10(*34A*) is not available]. In this situation, capital gain in the hands of A will be calculated under section 46A read with section 112 as follows (section 112A is not applicable, as STT is not paid by A at the time of acquisition of shares) –

	Rs.
Full value of consideration received by A (Rs. 90 × 2,000)	1,80,000
Less: Indexed cost of acquisition [(Rs. 27 × 2,000) × 280 ÷ 184]	82,174
Long-term capital gain	97,826
Tax @ 20.8% (if indexation benefit is taken) [20.8% of Rs. 97,826] (*a*)	20,348
Tax @ 10.4% (if indexation benefit is not taken) [10.4% of 2,000 shares × (Rs. 90 – Rs. 27)] (*b*)	13,104
Tax liability of A [(*a*) or (*b*), whichever is lower]	13,104

Situation 3 (buy-back of listed shares prior to July 5, 2019, STT is paid at the time of acquisition as well as at the time of buyback) - X Ltd. is not liable to pay tax under section 115QA. Capital gain will be chargeable to tax in the hands of A [exemption under section 10(*34A*) is not available]. Conditions of section 112A are satisfied [*see* para 72.2]. Consequently, tax liability of A will be calculated under section 112A as follows –

	Rs.
Full value of consideration received by A (Rs. 90 × 2,000)	1,80,000
Less: Cost of acquisition [actual cost of acquisition : Rs. 27 per share, fair market value on January 31, 2018 : Rs. 30 per share (Rs. 30 × 2,000)]	60,000
Long-term capital gain	1,20,000
Tax liability as per section 112A [10.4% of (Rs. 1,20,000 – Rs. 1,00,000)]	2,080

69.13 *Capital gain on transfer of shares/security by an employee received as stock option/sweat equity plan [Sec. 49]* - The provisions of section 49 and other related issues are given below—

Different situations	*Allotment of shares/securities by the employer-company to its employees without charging anything or at concessional rate*
Tax on perquisite in respect of allotment of shares/securities by the employer in the employer-company without charging anything or at concessional rate	If the option is exercised by the concerned employee during 1999-2000 or after March 31, 2009, then the perquisite is chargeable to tax (the value being fair market value on the date of exercise of option *minus* acquisition cost paid by the employee).
Transfer of these shares/securities by the employees	Capital gains is taxable in the year in which shares/securities are transferred. Cost of acquisition will be as follows— - if shares are allotted during 1999-2000 or after March 31, 2009, fair market value on the date of exercise of option - if shares are allotted before April 1, 2007 (not being during 1999-2000), the amount actually paid to acquire shares - if shares are allotted on or after April 1, 2007 but before April 1, 2009, fair market value on the date of vesting of option (purchase price paid to the employer or FBT paid to employer shall not be considered).
Transfer of these shares/securities by the employees by gift or under an irrevocable transfer	Capital gains is taxable in the hands of transferor (*i.e.*, donor) in the year in which these shares/securities are gifted [fair market value of shares on the date of gift is taken as full value of consideration]. Cost of acquisition in the hands of transferor (*i.e.*, donor) would be taken as given above. Transferee (*i.e.*, the donee) will be subject to the provisions of section 56(2)(*vii*)/(*x*) — *see* para 77.5-1.

69.14 *Computation of capital gain on transfer of shares allotted in the scheme of demerger* - Sub-section (2C)[90] was inserted in section 49 with effect from the assessment year 2000-01 so as to provide that the cost of acquisition of the shares in the resulting company shall be the amount which bears to the cost of acquisition of shares held by the assessee in the demerged company the same proportion as the net book value of the assets transferred in a demerger bears to the net worth of the demerged company immediately before such demerger. For this purpose "net worth" shall mean the aggregate of the paid-up share capital and general reserves as appearing in the books of account of the demerged company immediately before the demerger.

• The following points should be noted—

1. The cost of acquisition of the original shares held by the shareholder in the demerged company shall be deemed to have been reduced by the amount as so arrived under sub-section (2C) (as mentioned above).

2. To find out whether or not shares in the resulting company are long-term capital asset, the period of holding shall be determined from date of acquisition of shares in the demerged company.

3. The indexation will start from the date of allotment of shares in the demerged company.

69.14-E1 X Ltd. (demerged company) has two Units—A and B. The following is the balance sheet of X Ltd.—

(Rs. in thousand)

Paid-up share capital (15,000 shares of Rs. 10)	150	Unit A	80
		Unit B	70
	150		150

Unit A is transferred in a scheme of demerger to Y Ltd., an Indian company (*i.e.*, resulting company) for a consideration of Rs. 80,000 on March 31, 2018. Y Ltd. will not make any payment to X Ltd. The sale consideration will be paid by Y Ltd. by allotment of shares in Y Ltd. to the shareholders of X Ltd.

---

90. From the assessment year 2008-09, provisions of section 49(2C) will also be applicable in the case of demerger of co-operative banks.

Z holds 1,500 shares in X Ltd. (purchased by him on June 11, 2002 for Rs. 6 per share). He has been allotted 800 shares in Y Ltd. on March 31, 2018. Now Z holds shares in X Ltd. (1,500) and Y Ltd. (800). These shares are transferred on April 10, 2018 for Rs. 15 and Rs. 13 per share respectively (shares are transferred outside a recognised stock exchange). Find out the capital gain chargeable to tax in the hands of Z on the assumption that securities transaction tax is not applicable.

•

Computation of capital gain

	Y Ltd.	*X Ltd.*
Period of holding	June 11, 2002 to April 10, 2018	June 11, 2002 to April 10, 2018
Cost inflation index of		
- year in which the asset was first held	105	105
- the year of transfer	280	280
Sale consideration [*Rs. 13 × 800; **Rs. 15 × 1,500]	10,400*	22,500**
Less : Indexed cost of acquisition[91] [*Rs. 6 × 800 × 280 ÷ 105; **Rs. 2.80 × 1,500 × 280 ÷ 105]	12,800*	11,200**
Long-term capital gain	(-) 2,400	11,300

69.15 ***Special provision for computation of capital gains in the case of slump sale [Sec. 50B]*** - Provisions of section 50B, applicable for computation of capital gains in the case of slump sale, are given below —

1. Any profits or gains arising from the slump sale effected in the previous year shall be chargeable as long-term capital gains and shall be deemed to be the income of the previous year in which the transfer took place. Where, however, any capital asset being one or more undertakings owned and held by the assessee for not more than 36 months is transferred under the slump sale, then capital gain shall be deemed to be short-term capital gain.

2. In the case of slump sale of the capital asset being one or more undertaking, the "net worth" of the undertaking shall be taken as cost of acquisition and cost of improvement. "Net worth" for this purpose is the aggregate value of total assets of the undertaking or division as reduced by the value of liabilities of such undertaking or division as appearing in the books of account. Any change in the value of assets on account of revaluation of assets shall be ignored for the purpose of computing the net worth. The aggregate value of total assets of such undertaking or division shall be the written down value of block of assets determined in accordance with the provisions contained in sub-item (*C*) of section 43(*6*)(*c*)(*i*) in the case of depreciable assets, *nil* in the case of capital assets in respect of which the whole of the expenditure has been allowed or is allowable as a deduction under section 35AD and the book value for all other assets.

3. The benefit of indexation will not be available.

4. Every assessee, in the case of slump sale, shall furnish along with the return of income, a report of a chartered accountant in Form No. 3CEA[92] indicating the computation of the net worth of the undertaking or division, as the case may be, and certifying that the net worth of the undertaking or division, as the case may be, has been correctly arrived at.

69.16 ***Computation of capital gain when insurance claim is received [Sec. 45(1A)]*** - In *Vania Silk Mills (P.) Ltd.* v. *CIT* [1991] 59 Taxman 3, the Supreme Court *held* that insurance claim received on account of destruction of asset is not chargeable to tax as "destruction" does not amount to transfer. The effect of the judgment has been nullified to some extent by inserting sub-section (1A) in section 45 with effect from the assessment year 2000-01.

91. Cost of acquisition is calculated as follows — Total investment in 2002 by Z : Rs. 9,000 (*i.e.*, Rs. 1,500 shares in X Ltd. × Rs. 6). After demerger this investment will be divided in the ratio of 70:80 for finding cost of acquisition of Rs. 1,500 shares in X Ltd. and 800 shares in Y Ltd. Cost of acquisition of shares in X Ltd. will be Rs. 2.80 (*i.e.*, Rs. 9,000 × 70 ÷ 150 ÷ 1,500). Likewise, cost of acquisition of shares in Y Ltd. will be Rs. 6 (*i.e.*, Rs. 9,000 × 80 ÷ 150 ÷ 800).

92. From April 1, 2014, audit report should be submitted electronically. Provisions pertaining to electronic submission of audit report were not applicable prior to April 1, 2014 (for period prior to April 1, 2014, audit report may be retained by the assessee and it may be furnished in original whenever the Assessing Officer wants to examine it in assessment proceedings or otherwise).

69.16-1 *WHEN SECTION 45(1A) IS ATTRACTED* - The following two conditions should be satisfied—

• *Condition one* - Compensation is received because of 'damage to' or 'destruction of' any capital asset.

• *Condition two* - The damage or destruction is a result of four categories of circumstances, *viz.*, (*i*) flood, typhoon, hurricane, cyclone, earthquake or other convulsion of nature; or (*ii*) riot or civil disturbance; or (*iii*) accidental fire or explosion; or (*iv*) action by an enemy or action taken in combating an enemy (whether with or without a declaration of war).

If the aforesaid two conditions are satisfied, then section 45(1A) is attracted.

69.16-1a CONSEQUENCES WHERE SECTION 45(1A) IS APPLICABLE - Where a person receives at any time during the previous year any money or other assets under any insurance from an insurer and the above two conditions are satisfied, then the following three consequences, one should note—

1. Any profits or gains arising from receipt of such money or other assets shall be chargeable to income-tax under the head "Capital gains".

2. It shall be deemed to be the income of such person for the previous year in which such money or other asset is received.

3. For this purpose, the value of any money or the fair market value of other asset (on the date of receipt) shall be deemed to be the full value of the consideration received or accruing as a result of transfer of such asset.

69.16-2 *WHEN SECTION 45(1A) IS NOT APPLICABLE* - The provisions are given below—

• *If insurance compensation is a capital receipt* - If the two conditions mentioned in para 69.16-1 are not satisfied, then section 45(1A) is not applicable and, consequently, insurance compensation (if it is a capital receipt) will not be chargeable to tax as per ruling given by the Supreme Court in *Vania Silk Mills (P.) Ltd.* v. *CIT* [1991] 59 Taxman 3. Consider a case where a road accident takes place in which vehicles and machinery or furniture being carried are destroyed. A ship, being overweight, is sunk and assets are lost. The receipt of insurance compensation in such circumstances is not chargeable to tax under section 45(1A). The reasons for destruction being other than those mentioned in one of the conditions mentioned in para 69.16-1. The compensation received will have to be dealt with as per the Supreme Court's judgments in the case of *Vania Silk Mills (P.) Ltd.* v. *CIT* [1991] 191 ITR 647/59 Taxman 3.

• *If insurance compensation is a revenue receipt* - If the two conditions mentioned in para 69.16-1 are not satisfied and insurance compensation is a revenue receipt, then section 45(1A) is not applicable but the receipt may be taxable as trading receipt under section 28 or 56. For instance, insurance compensation for theft of stock-in-trade is not taxable under section 45(1A) but it will be taxable under section 28.

69.17 ***Computation of capital gains in the case of land and building [Sec. 50C]*** - The provisions of section 50C are given below—

69.17-1 *CONDITIONS* - Section 50C is applicable if the following conditions are satisfied -

Condition 1	There is a transfer of land or building or both. The asset may be long-term capital asset or short-term capital asset. It may be depreciable or non-depreciable asset.
Condition 2	• *Up to the assessment year 2018-19* - Stamp duty value [*i.e.*, value adopted/assessed/assessable[93] by any authority of a State Government for the purpose of payment of stamp duty (hereinafter referred as "Stamp duty Authority")] in respect of such transfer exceeds sale consideration. • *From the assessment year 2019-20* - Stamp duty value (as stated above) exceeds 105 per cent of sale consideration.

69.17-2 *CONSEQUENCES IF THE ABOVE CONDITIONS ARE SATISFIED* - If the above conditions are satisfied, the value adopted (or assessable[93]) by the Stamp duty Authority shall be taken as full value of consideration for the purpose of computation of capital gains [it is illustrated in Example 69.17-E1].

93. The word "assessable" was inserted with effect from October 1, 2009. It means the price which the stamp valuation authority would have (notwithstanding anything to the contrary contained in any other law for the time being in force) adopted or assessed, if it were referred to such authority for the purposes of the payment of stamp duty.

• *If the stamp duty value on the date of agreement and on the date of registration is different* - It is quite possible that stamp duty on the date of agreement (fixing the value of consideration) is different from stamp duty on the date of registration. In such a case, the stamp duty on the date of agreement may be taken (and not as on the date of registration). This was inserted with effect from the assessment year 2017-18. However, this rule shall apply only in those cases where amount of consideration (or a part thereof) has been received by way of an account payee cheque/draft [or by use of electronic clearing system through a bank account (**or through prescribed electronic mode**)] before the date of the agreement [it is illustrated in Example 69.17-E2].

• *When assessee disputes value adopted by stamp duty authority* - Stamp duty value may be determined as follows –

Different situations	*Stamp duty value [see Example 69.17-E3]*
Where the assessee accepts the value adopted by Stamp duty authority	Value adopted by Stamp duty authority.
Where the assessee has disputed value adopted by Stamp duty authority under the Stamp Act (*i.e.*, stamp duty proceedings)	The stamp duty valuation as finally accepted for stamp duty purpose
Where the assessee claims before Income-tax authorities that value adopted by Stamp duty authority is more than the fair market value (but he has not disputed such valuation in stamp duty proceedings)	The Assessing Officer will have to refer the matter to the Valuation Officer and the fair market value determined by him will be substituted for stamp duty value (if value so determined is more than original stamp duty value, the original stamp duty value will be taken).

• *Other points* - The following points should be noted —

1. Where an assessee objects to stamp duty valuation, the Assessing Officer is duty bound to refer the matter to the Valuation Officer—*Ajmal Fragrances & Fashions (P.) Ltd.* v. *CIT* [2009] 34 SOT 57 (Mum.).

2. No tolerance band is prescribed in section 50C (up to the assessment year 2018-19). Consequently (up to the assessment year 2018-19) stamp duty value is taken as full value of consideration, even if difference in stamp duty value and stated sale consideration is marginal—*Heilgers Development & Construction Co. (P.) Ltd.* v. *CIT* [2013] 32 taxmann.com 147 (Kol.). However, tolerance band of 5 per cent is applicable (as stated above) from the assessment year 2019-20.

3. Where the date of an agreement fixing the value of consideration and the date of registration are not same, the stamp duty value may be taken as on the date of the agreement for transfer (and not as on the date of registration) for such transfer. However, this exception shall apply only in those cases where amount of consideration (or a part thereof) has been received by way of an account payee cheque/draft or by use of electronic clearing system through a bank account (**or through prescribed electronic mode**) before the date of the agreement. This rule is applicable from the assessment year 2017-18 (for earlier years one can take the shelter of different available judicial rulings, one of them is given below).

4. On June 1, 2015, X enters into an agreement to transfer a property to B. B pays the consideration on the same day and the possession is handed over to him. However, the conveyance deed is registered on October 5, 2015. In this case, stamp duty value on June 1, 2015 is applicable for the purpose of section 50C—*CIT* v. *S. Venkat Reddy* [2013] 57 SOT 117 (Hyd.).

69.17-E1 X transfers a house property on February 15, 2019 (sale consideration given below in different situations). Indexed cost of acquisition is Rs. 8,00,000 (in all situations). Find out long-term capital gain chargeable to tax for the assessment year 2019-20.

Different situations	*Stamp duty value at the time of transfer Rs.*	*Sale consideration as per agreement Rs.*
Situation 1	65,00,000	60,00,000
Situation 2	63,00,000	60,00,000
Situation 3	61,00,000	60,00,000

•

Different situations	*Sale consideration*	*105% of sale consideration*	*Stamp duty value*	*Full value of consideration [see Note]*	*Indexed cost of acquisition*	*Long-term capital gain [Column 5 – Column 6]*
	Rs.	*Rs.*	*Rs.*	*Rs.*	*Rs.*	*Rs.*
(1)	*(2)*	*(3)*	*(4)*	*(5)*	*(6)*	*(7)*
Situation 1	60,00,000	63,00,000	65,00,000	65,00,000	8,00,000	57,00,000
Situation 2	60,00,000	63,00,000	63,00,000	60,00,000	8,00,000	52,00,000
Situation 3	60,00,000	63,00,000	61,00,000	60,00,000	8,00,000	52,00,000

Note - Stamp duty value at the time of transfer is taken as full value of consideration, if it exceeds 105% of actual sale consideration. In other words, if *Column 4* is more than *Column 3, Column 4* value will be taken, otherwise section 50C is not applicable and value of *Column 2* will be taken.

69.17-E2 On April 6, 2018, X enters into an agreement to transfer a commercial plot for an agreed consideration of Rs. 65,00,000 (advance payment of Rs. 1,00,000 is received by an account payee cheque on the same day). Stamp duty value on April 6, 2018 is Rs. 68,00,000. Sale deed is registered on December 27, 2018 (stamp duty value on the date of registration is Rs. 71,00,000). Indexed cost of acquisition of the commercial plot is Rs. 34,00,000. Find out the amount of long-term capital gain chargeable to tax for the assessment year 2019-20.

•

Section 50C provides that where stamp duty value on the date of agreement and on the date of registration are not the same, the stamp duty value on the date of the agreement shall be taken [if the amount of consideration or a part thereof has been received on or before the date of agreement by an account payee cheque/draft or by use of electronic clearing system through a bank account (or through prescribed electronic mode)]. In this case, a part of consideration is received by an account payee cheque on the date of agreement. Stamp duty value on the date of agreement shall be taken (*i.e.*, Rs. 68,00,000). 105% of agreed consideration is Rs. 68,25,000 (*i.e.*, 105% of Rs. 65,00,000). Capital gain shall be calculated as follows –

	Rs.
Full value of consideration (stamp duty value of Rs. 68,00,000 does not exceed 105% of actual sale consideration, section 50C is not applicable and actual sale consideration is taken as full value of consideration)	65,00,000
Less: Indexed cost of acquisition	34,00,000
Long-term capital gain	31,00,000

69.17-E3 X owns a piece of land situated in Noida (date of acquisition: March 1, 2004, cost of acquisition: Rs. 73,382, value adopted by Stamp duty authority at the time of purchase: Rs. 85,000). On March 30, 2019, the piece of land is transferred for Rs. 4 lakh. Find out the capital gains chargeable to tax in the following situations—

1. The value adopted by Stamp duty authority is Rs. 5.5 lakh. X does not dispute it.

2. The value adopted by the Stamp duty authority is Rs. 5.75 lakh. X files an appeal under the Stamp Act and Stamp duty valuation has been reduced to Rs. 4.90 lakh by the Allahabad High Court.

3. The value adopted by the Stamp duty authority is Rs. 5.60 lakh. X does not challenge it under the Stamp Act. However, he claims before the Assessing Officer that Rs. 5.60 lakh is more than the fair market value of the land. The Assessing Officer refers it to the Valuation Officer who determines Rs. 5.25 lakh as fair market value.

4. In Situation (3), suppose the value adopted by the Valuation Officer is Rs. 6.10 lakh.

•

	Situations			
	(1) *Rs.*	*(2)* *Rs.*	*(3)* *Rs.*	*(4)* *Rs.*
Full value of consideration [*see* Note 1]	5,50,000	4,90,000	5,25,000	5,60,000
Less: Indexed cost of acquisition [Rs. 73,382 × 280 ÷ 109]	1,88,504	1,88,504	1,88,504	1,88,504
Long-term capital gains	3,61,496	3,01,496	3,36,496	3,71,496

Notes –

1. Stamp duty value at the time of transfer is taken as full value of consideration, if it exceeds 105% of actual sale consideration. In this case, actual sale consideration is Rs. 4,00,000. Stamp duty value (in *Situations 1, 2, 3* and *4*) exceeds Rs. 4,20,000 (*i.e.*, 105% of Rs. 4,00,000). Consequently, stamp duty value is taken as full value of consideration by virtue of section 50C.

2. Value adopted by the Stamp duty authority at the time of acquisition cannot be taken as cost of acquisition.

69.18 *Computation of capital gain in the case of joint development agreement [Secs. 45(5A) and 49(7)]* - The following special provisions have been made with effect from the assessment year 2018-19 for computation of capital gains in the case of joint development agreement.

• *Conditions* - These provisions are applicable when the following conditions are satisfied –

1. The assessee (*i.e.*, land/building owner) is an individual or a Hindu undivided family.

2. The assessee has entered into a "specified agreement" with a builder/joint developer for development of housing project. "Specified agreement" means a registered agreement in which a person owning land or building or both, agrees to allow another person to develop a real estate project on such land or building or both, in consideration of a share, being land or building or both in such project, whether with or without payment of part of the consideration in cash.

• *Capital gain computation* - If the above two conditions are satisfied, capital gain shall be taxable in the hands of owner of land/building as income of the previous year in which the certificate of completion for the whole or part of the project is issued by the competent authority. The stamp duty value of the share of owner of land/building in the developed property on the date of issuing of said certificate of completion (as increased by any monetary consideration received, if any), shall be deemed to be the full value of the consideration received or accruing as a result of the transfer of the capital asset. However, if the owner of land/building transfers his share in the project to any other person on or before the date of issue of said certificate of completion, the capital gains (as determined under general provisions of the Act) shall be deemed to be the income of the previous year in which such transfer took place and shall be computed as per provisions of the Act without taking into account the above special provisions of section 45(5A).

69.18-E1 Find out the tax consequences in the case given below –

- X purchased a plot of land in Cochin during 1986-87 (1,000 sq. mtr., cost of acquisition : Rs. 2 lakh).
- Fair market value of the plot on April 1, 2001 : Rs. 6.80 lakh.
- He enters into a "specified agreement" with A Ltd. (a developer) on April 20, 2017 (cash consideration paid immediately : Rs. 20 lakh, total area to be developed : 30,000 sq. ft., share of X in the constructed area : 60 per cent, share of A Ltd. : 40 per cent).
- Construction of the project is completed on March 1, 2018. Completion certificate of first 5 floors is issued by the appropriate authority on May 20, 2018. For the remaining 6 floors, the certificate is issued on March 5, 2019.
- Stamp duty value of 60 per cent of the developed area given to X is as follows –

	60% given to X	*40% retained by A Ltd.*
Floor 1 to floor 5 (stamp duty value on May 20, 2018)	Rs. 21 crore	Rs. 14 crore
Floor 6 to floor 11 (stamp duty value on March 5, 2019)	Rs. 27 crore	Rs. 18 crore

•

Size of the plot of land is 1,000 sq. mtr. Under the joint development (*i.e.*, "specified agreement"), 40% of the plot is transferred to A Ltd. A Ltd. will pay consideration in the form of 60% of the developed area. Capital gain on transfer of 40% plot will be taxable in the previous year 2018-19 (assessment year 2019-20) (*i.e.*, the previous year in which completion certificate is issued by the appropriate authority) as follows –

	Rs.
Full value of consideration pertaining to transfer of 40% plot to A Ltd. (Rs. 21 crore + Rs. 27 crore + cash consideration of Rs. 20 lakh)	48,20,00,000
Less: Cost of acquisition [higher of actual cost or fair market value on April 1, 2001 : Rs. 6,80,000 × 40% × CII of 2018-19 : 280 ÷ CII of 2001-02 : 100]	7,61,600
Long-term capital gain	48,12,38,400

The following points should be noted –

1. If the property constructed on 60% plot (*i.e.*, share of X) is residential building and X owns not more than one residential house property, he can claim exemption under section 54F. For this purpose, investment in new residential house will be Rs. 48 crore (*i.e.*, Rs. 21 crore + Rs. 27 crore). Quantum of exemption will be Rs. 47,92,41,560 (*i.e.*, Rs. 48 crore ÷ Rs. 48.2 crore × Rs. 48,12,38,400).

2. If X transfers his share in the developed project before the issue of completion certificate, the above computation will not be applicable. Capital gain on account of transfer of 40% plot to A Ltd. will be taxable in the year in which X transfers his share in the developed project. Quantum of capital gain in such a case shall be determined on the basis of other provisions of the Act [ignoring section 45(5A)].

3. Indexed cost of acquisition is deductible. For this purpose, cost of acquisition is multiplied by a fraction. Numerator of the fraction is CII (cost inflation index) of the year in which transfer takes place. For the above computation, it is assumed that the year of transfer of 40% plot is the year in which completion certificate is issued by the appropriate authority [nowhere section 45(5A) specifies that the year of issue of completion certificate is the year of transfer].

4. If the completion certificate for floor 6 to floor 11 is issued in the financial year 2019-20 (not in 2018-19 itself), then capital gain will be taxable in 2 previous years. For such a situation, mode of computation is not given in section 45(5A).

5. If X transfers his share in the developed project (*i.e.*, 60% of the developed area given to him by A Ltd.), the cost of acquisition for computation of capital gain will be Rs. 48,20,00,000.

69.19 ***Computation of capital gain in the case of transfer of unlisted shares in a company [Sec. 50CA, applicable from the assessment year 2018-19]*** - Section 50CA is applicable if an assessee transfers shares in a company (other than quoted shares) at less than the fair market value (FMV) of such share determined in accordance with the prescribed manner [*see* para 77.5-1b]. In such a case, the FMV of such shares shall be deemed to be the full value of consideration for the purposes of computation of capital gain.

• *Exceptions* - **With effect from the assessment year 2020-21, the provisions of section 50CA will not be applicable** in the case of any consideration received or accruing as a result of transfer by such **class of persons** and subject to such **conditions** as may be **prescribed by the Board**.

69.20 ***Computation of capital gain in relation to a long-term capital asset referred to in section 112A*** - In the case of long-term capital asset (being an equity share in a company or unit of an equity oriented fund or a unit of a business trust) referred to in section 112A, the mode of computation of capital gain is subject to the following special provisions –

1. Indexation benefit is not available.

2. Cost of acquisition of such asset shall be computed in the manner provided by section 55(2)(*ac*).

These provisions are discussed in para 72.2.

69.21 ***Tax incentive for the development of capital of Andhra Pradesh [Secs. 10(37A) and 49]*** - As per section 96 of the Right to Fair Compensation and Transparency in Land Acquisition, Rehabilitation and Resettlement Act, 2014, the specified compensation received by the landowner in lieu of acquisition of land, is exempt from income-tax. The Land Pooling Scheme is an alternative form of arrangement made by the Government of Andhra Pradesh for formation of new capital city of Amaravati to avoid land acquisition disputes and lessen the financial burden associated with payment of compensation under that Act. In the Land Pooling Scheme of the Andhra Pradesh Government, an owner of the plot gets a Land Pooling Ownership Certificate (LPOC) at the time of handing over of possession of his land to the Government. He may retain LPOC or he can transfer it to anybody. If he retains it, he will get a reconstituted plot of land (commercial and/or residential) in the developed city in lieu of LPOC. He may retain the plot of land or transfer it.

With a view to provide tax exemption, clause (*37A*) has been inserted in section 10 and section 49 has been amended.

• *Section 10(*37A) - Clause (*37A*) has been inserted in section 10 with effect from the assessment year 2015-16. Exemption under section 10(*37A*) is applicable if the following conditions are satisfied –

1. The taxpayer (land owner) is an individual/HUF.

2. He owns land or building or both on June 2, 2014.

3. Such land is transferred under the land pooling scheme covered under the Andhra Pradesh Capital City Land Pooling Scheme (Formulation and Implementation) Rules, 2015 made under the provisions of the Andhra Pradesh Capital Region Development Authority Act, 2014 and the rules, regulations and Schemes made under the said Act.

Exemption - If the above conditions are satisfied, capital gains arising from the following transfer shall not be chargeable to tax by virtue of section 10(*37A*) –

1. Capital gain on transfer of land or building or both, under land pooling scheme.

2. Capital gain on transfer of LPOC (which is received in lieu of land transferred under the scheme).

3. Capital gain on transfer of reconstituted plot or land by said taxpayer within 2 years from the end of the financial year in which the possession of such plot or land was handed over to him.

• *Section 49* - Section 49 has been amended (with effect from the assessment year 2018-19) so as to provide that where reconstituted plot or land, received under land pooling scheme, is transferred after the expiry of

2 years from the end of the financial year in which the possession of such plot or land was handed over to the said assessee, the cost of acquisition of such plot or land shall be deemed to be its stamp duty value on the last day of the second financial year after the end of financial year in which the possession of such asset was handed over to the assessee.

69.21-E1 X owns a plot of land which is situated near Vijayawada on June 2, 2014 (cost of acquisition : Rs. 20,000, year of acquisition : 2001-02). This plot of land is transferred under land pooling scheme of the Andhra Pradesh Government on July 6, 2015. The appropriate authority issues Land Pooling Ownership Certificate (LPOC). Find out the tax consequences under the following situations –

1. Capital gain which arises on transfer of land under Land Pooling Scheme during the previous year 2015-16.

2. Suppose, X transfers LPOC on November 1, 2015 for Rs. 20,00,000.

3. Suppose, X does not transfer LPOC. Andhra Pradesh Government gives a reconstituted plot of land of 200 square meter. Letter of possession is given on March 3, 2018. Actual possession of reconstituted plot is handed over to X on April 20, 2018. X transfers plot of land on March 27, 2021 for Rs. 97,00,000. Stamp duty value of the plot is Rs. 98,00,000 on March 27, 2021 and Rs. 98,50,000 on March 31, 2021.

4. X does not transfer plot of land up to March 31, 2021. Plot of land is transferred on April 5, 2021 for Rs. 99,00,000.

●

1. Capital gain arising on transfer of land under Land Pooling Scheme is exempt under section 10(*37A*).

2. Capital gain which arises on transfer of LPOC is exempt under section 10(*37A*).

3. X takes possession of reconstitution plot of land on April 20, 2018 (*i.e.*, during the financial year 2018-19). If the plot of land is transferred at any time before the expiry of 2 years from the end of the financial year 2018-19, full capital gain exemption will be available under section 10(*37A*). The 2 year time-limit expires on March 31, 2021. In this case, plot of land is transferred on or before March 31, 2021. Consequently, capital gain exemption is available under section 10(*37A*) for the previous year 2020-21.

4. If the plot of land is transferred on April 5, 2021, exemption under section 10(*37A*) is not available. Capital gain will be calculated as follows –

- Full value of consideration : Rs. 99,00,000 (assuming that stamp duty value on the date of transfer is lesser).
- Cost of acquisition : Rs. 98,50,000 (being stamp duty value on March 31, 2021).
- Period of holding : April 20, 2018 to April 5, 2021 (no special provision is made to determine period of holding from March 31, 2021).
- Status of capital asset : Long-term.
- Indexation benefit : It will be available from the previous year 2018-19 (no special provision is made to give indexation benefit from the previous year 2020-21 in which the 2 year time-limit expires).

Valuation of capital asset - When can be referred to Valuation Officer

70. With a view to ascertaining the fair market value of a capital asset, the concerned Assessing Officer may refer the valuation of the capital asset to the Valuation Officer appointed by the Income-tax Department in the following cases:

a. where the value of the assets as claimed by the assessee is in accordance with the estimate made by a registered valuer (who works in a private capacity under a licence issued by the Central Board of Direct Taxes and his valuation is not binding on the Income-tax Department), but the Assessing Officer is of the opinion that the value so claimed is less than its fair market value (or, where with effect from July 1, 2012, is at variance with its fair market value);

b. where the Assessing Officer is of the opinion that the fair market value of the asset exceeds the value of the asset by more than Rs. 25,000 or 15 per cent of the value claimed by the assessee, whichever is less [rule 111AA] ; or

c. where the Assessing Officer is of the opinion that having regard to the nature of an asset and relevant circumstances, it is necessary to do so.

Capital gains - When and to what extent exempt from tax

71. The Income-tax Act grants total/partial exemption of capital gains under sections 54, 54B, 54D, 54EC, 54F, 54G, 54GA, 54GB and 54H.

71.1 ***Capital gains arising from the transfer of residential house property [Sec. 54]*** - The provisions of section 54 are given below—

71.1-1 *CONDITIONS* - The following conditions should be satisfied—

• The house property is a residential house[94] whose income is taxable under the head "Income from house property"[95] and transferred by an individual or a Hindu undivided family.

• The house property (maybe self-occupied or let out) is a long-term capital asset (*i.e.*, it must be held for a period of more than 24 months[96] before sale or transfer)[97].

• To avail exemption under section 54, the assessee will have to purchase or construct a residential house (from the assessment year 2015-16 only one residential house[98] can be purchased or constructed). For this purpose, house can be purchased within a period of one year before the transfer (or within 2 years after the date of transfer). Alternatively, house can be constructed within 3 years from the date of transfer. In the case of compulsory acquisition, the above time-limit of 1-year, 2-year and 3-year is applicable from the date of receipt of compensation (whether original or additional).

• The new house property which is purchased or constructed within the time-limit specified above should be situated in India (applicable from the assessment year 2015-16).

The following points should also be kept in view :

❑ Construction of the house should be completed within 3 years from the date of transfer. Date of commencement of construction is irrelevant. Construction may be commenced even before the transfer of the house—*CIT* v. *J.R. Subramanya Bhat* [1986] 28 Taxman 578 (Kar.).

❑ Case of allotment of a flat under the self-financing scheme of DDA (or similar schemes of co-operative societies and other institutions) is treated as construction of house for this purpose—Circular No. 471, dated October 15, 1986, and Circular No. 672, dated December 16, 1993.

❑ If the whole of the consideration is paid and possession of the house is obtained, the exemption contemplated under section 54 is clearly attracted—*CIT* v. *Laxmichand Narpal Nagda* [1995] 78 Taxman 219 (Bom.). If the substantial amount is paid in terms of purchase agreement within the stipulated period, the exemption under section 54 is available even if the possession is handed over after the stipulated period—*CIT* v. *R.L. Sood* [2000] 108 Taxman 227 (Delhi).

❑ Nowhere it has been mentioned in section 54 that the same funds must be utilized for the purchase of another residential house; requirement of law is that the assessee should purchase a residential house within the specified period and the source of funds is quite irrelevant — *Ishar Singh Chawla* v. *CIT* [2010] 130 TTJ (Mum.)(UO) 108, *Muneer Khan* v. *ITO* [2010] 41 SOT 504 (Hyd.).

• The house property so purchased or constructed has not been transferred within a period of 3 years from the date of purchase or construction.

71.1-2 *AMOUNT OF EXEMPTION* - If the amount of the capital gain is less than the cost of the new house property[99], the entire amount of capital gains is exempt from tax. On the other hand, if the amount of the capital gains is greater than the cost of the new house property[99], the difference between the amount of capital gains and the cost of the new house is chargeable to tax as capital gains.

There is no requirement for claiming exemption under section 54 that the assessee should file his return of income before the due date prescribed under section 139(1)— *Esther Christopher Mascarenhas* v. *ITO* [2011] 9 taxmann.com 99 (Mum. - ITAT).

---

94. It is not necessary that only one property is transferred.

95. The Board has clarified *vide* Circular No. 538, dated July 13, 1989 that exemption is available under section 54, in respect of self-occupied residential house property, even if income from such house may be computed at *nil* or at a negative figure by virtue of section 23(2)(*a*).

96. 36 months, if transfer takes place before April 1, 2017.

97. An assessee purchase land in 2005. Building was constructed thereon in 2014. Building as well as land is transferred in 2015. The Court held that the assessee is entitled to claim benefit of exemption under section 54 in respect of capital gain arising on transfer of land as well as building— *C.N. Anantharam* v. *ACIT* [2015] 230 Taxman 34 (Kar.).

98. **If the amount of capital gain does not exceed Rs. 2 crore, the assessee can purchase/construct two residential house properties (from the assessment year 2020-21). However, this concession is available only once in lifetime.**

99. Including cost of land— Circular No. 667, dated October 18, 1993. If an assessee chooses to purchase a house and incurs *bona fide* expenditure on improvement for making it habitable, it would be eligible as investment in new asset for purpose of section 54 - *Meher R. Surti* v. *ITO* [2014] 61 SOT 5 (Mum.).

71.1-3 *CONSEQUENCES IF THE NEW HOUSE IS TRANSFERRED WITHIN 3 YEARS* - If the new house property is transferred, within a period of 3 years from the date of its purchase or construction, the amount of capital gains arising therefrom, together with the amount of capital gains exempted earlier, will be chargeable to tax in the year of sale of the new house property.

To attain this, it has been provided that if the new house is transferred within 3 years from the date of its acquisition or date of completion of construction, the amount of exemption under section 54 shall be reduced from the cost of acquisition of the new house, while calculating short-term capital gain on the transfer of the new asset.

71.1-4 *SCHEME OF DEPOSIT IN RESPECT OF EXEMPTION UNDER SECTION 54* - Where the amount of capital gain is not appropriated or utilised by the assessee for purchase or construction of the new residential house before the due date of furnishing the return of income, it shall be deposited by him on or before the due date of furnishing the return of income, in the Deposit Account in any branch (except rural branch) of a public sector bank or IDBI Bank in accordance with the Capital Gains Accounts Scheme, 1988. The amount already utilised for the purchase or construction of the new house together with the amount so deposited shall be deemed to be the amount utilised for the purchase of a new house under section 54. If the amount deposited is not utilised fully for purchase or construction of the new house within the stipulated period, then the amount not so utilised shall be treated as long-term capital gain of the previous year in which the period of three years from the date of transfer of the original asset expires[1]. In such case the assessee shall be entitled to withdraw such amount in accordance with the aforesaid scheme.

71.1-E1 Determine the amount of exemption under section 54 and capital gains chargeable to tax in respect of the following transactions—

1. X sells a residential house property in Agra for Rs. 28,00,000 on April 23, 2018 which was purchased by him on April 20, 2004 for Rs. 9,70,000. Value adopted for stamp duty is Rs. 29,45,000. On June 16, 2018, he purchases a house in Delhi for Rs. 62,00,000 for the purpose of residence of his daughter.

2. On July 18, 2020, X sells the house property in Delhi for Rs. 66,90,000 (stamp duty value is Rs. 78,00,000). Can he also claim exemption under section 54 in respect of transaction (2) ?

●

CAPITAL GAINS IN TRANSACTION (1)	*Rs.*
Sale proceeds (*i.e.*, stamp duty value, as it exceeds 105% of sale consideration)	29,45,000
Less : Indexed cost of acquisition [Rs. 9,70,000 × 280 ÷ 113]	24,03,540
Capital gains	5,41,460
Less : Exemption under section 54	5,41,460*
Capital gains chargeable to tax for the assessment year 2019-20	*Nil*

*As X has invested more than Rs. 5,41,460 in purchase of a house in Delhi within 2 years from the transfer of house in Agra, the entire amount of capital gains will be exempt.

CAPITAL GAINS IN TRANSACTION (2)	*Rs.*
Sale proceeds (*i.e.*, stamp duty value, as it exceeds 105% of sale consideration)	78,00,000
Less: Cost of acquisition [Rs. 62,00,000 being the actual cost *minus* Rs. 5,41,460, being the exemption granted under section 54 in transaction (*1*) as the new house in Delhi is sold within three years from the date of purchase] × CII of 2020-21 : 300 (assumed figure) ÷ CII of 2018-19 : 280]	60,62,721
Long-term capital gains	17,37,279*

*Delhi property is transferred after 24 months. It is a long-term capital asset. Exemption can be claimed under section 54, if another residential house property is purchased/acquired within the stipulated period.

71.1-E2 X owns a residential house at Delhi since 1988 (income is taxable under section 22). The house is sold by him on May 10, 2018 for Rs. 85,00,000. The stamp duty value is Rs. 1,25,00,000 (cost of acquisition : Rs. 4,32,400, fair market value on April 1, 2001 : Rs. 4,10,000). On July 16, 2019 he deposits Rs. 62,00,000 in a bank account specified for the purpose of section 54.

By withdrawing from the deposit account he purchases a house property at Kota on May 5, 2020 for Rs. 43,00,000. Construction of an additional floor in the Kota house is completed by May 9, 2021; entire cost of construction of Rs. 17,50,000 is financed by withdrawing from the deposit account. The unutilised amount in the deposit account is withdrawn by him after May 10, 2021.

---

1. Regarding the taxability of the unutilised deposit amount in the case of an individual who dies before the expiry of the stipulated period, the Board has clarified that in such cases the said amount cannot be taxed in the hands of the deceased. This amount is not taxable in the hands of legal heirs also as the unutilised portion of the deposit does not partake of the character of income in their hands but is only a part of the estate devolving upon them—Circular No. 743[$], dated May 6, 1996.

[$] For Circular No. 743, log on to *taxmann.com/readyreckoner.aspx*.

Determine the amount of capital gains chargeable to tax.

•

Assessment year 2019-20	*Rs.*
Sale proceeds (stamp duty value, as it exceeds 105% of sale consideration)	1,25,00,000
Less : Indexed cost of acquisition [Rs. 4,32,400 × 280 ÷ 100]	12,10,720
Balance	1,12,89,280
Less : Exemption under section 54 (amount deposited in deposit account : Rs. 62,00,000)	62,00,000
Long-term capital gain	50,89,280

Assessment year 2022-23 [i.e., *relevant to the previous year in which 3-year time limit from the date of sale of house (May 10, 2018) expires*]

	Rs.
Amount of deposit in the bank account on July 16, 2019	62,00,000
Less :	
Cost of house purchased on May 5, 2020 in Kota	43,00,000
Cost of construction in Kota property	17,50,000
Long-term capital gain	1,50,000

71.2 *Capital gains arising from the transfer of land used for agricultural purpose [Sec. 54B]* - Exemption under section 54B is available to an individual. From the assessment year 2013-14, it is also available to a Hindu undivided family.

Capital gains arising from the transfer of land, being used by an individual or his parents or Hindu undivided family for agricultural purposes[2] for a period of 2 years, immediately preceding the date of transfer, are exempt from tax if the assessee has purchased another land for agricultural purpose within a period of 2 years from the date of such transfer.

71.2-1 *AMOUNT OF EXEMPTION* - If the amount of capital gains is less than the cost of the new agricultural land, the entire amount of capital gains is exempt. On the other hand if the amount of capital gains is greater than the cost of the new agricultural land, the difference between the amount of capital gains and the cost of new land is chargeable to tax as capital gains.

71.2-2 *CONSEQUENCES IF THE NEW AGRICULTURAL LAND IS TRANSFERRED WITHIN 3 YEARS* - If the new agricultural land is transferred within a period of 3 years from the date of its purchase, the amount of capital gains arising therefrom, together with the amount of capital gains exempted earlier, will be chargeable to tax as capital gains in the year of sale of the new agricultural land. To attain this, it has been provided that if the new agricultural land is transferred within 3 years from the date of its acquisition, the amount of exemption under section 54B shall be reduced from the cost of acquisition of the new agricultural land, while computing short-term capital gains on the transfer of the new agricultural land. It may be noted that if the new agricultural land is situated in a rural area in India, the gain arising on its transfer is not chargeable to tax, as an agricultural land situated in a rural area is not a "capital asset" under section 2(*14*).

71.2-3 *SCHEME OF DEPOSIT IN RESPECT OF EXEMPTION UNDER SECTION 54B* - Where the amount of capital gain is not appropriated or utilised by the assessee for purchase of the agricultural land before the date for furnishing the return of income, it shall be deposited by him on or before the due date of furnishing the return of income in the deposit account in any branch (except rural branch) of a public sector bank or IDBI Bank in accordance with Capital Gains Accounts Scheme, 1988. The amount already utilised for purchase of the agricultural land together with the amount so deposited shall be deemed to be the amount utilised for the purchase of agricultural land.

If the amount deposited is not utilised fully for purchase of the agricultural land within the stipulated period, then the amount not so utilised shall be treated as the capital gain of the previous year in which the period of 2 years from the date of transfer of the original asset expires[3]. In such case the assessee shall be entitled to withdraw such amount in accordance with the aforesaid scheme.

2. If an assessee is unable to cultivate an agricultural land due to vagaries of nature and non-availability of resources, exemption under section 54B cannot be denied on its sale—*CIT* v. *N. Raghu Varma* [2013] 32 taxmann.com 383 (Hyd.).
3. *See* also footnote 1, para 71.1-4.

71.2-E1 X sells agricultural land situated within the municipal limits of Calcutta on July 1, 2018 for Rs. 34,00,000 (stamp duty value : Rs. 40,07,000) which was purchased by him in June 2006 for Rs. 3,00,000. On June 1, 2019 he purchases agricultural land for Rs. 4,10,000 and deposits Rs. 10,30,000 in a deposit account for availing exemption under section 54B. He purchases another agricultural land on June 30, 2020 for Rs. 8,47,000 by withdrawing from the deposit account. Amount left in the deposit account is withdrawn by the end of July 10, 2020. Determine the amount of capital gains.

•

Assessment year 2019-20	*Rs.*
Sale proceeds	40,07,000
Less: Indexed cost of acquisition [Rs. 3,00,000 × 280 ÷ 122]	6,88,525
Balance	33,18,475
Less : Exemption under section 54B	
- Cost of agricultural land purchased on June 1, 2019	4,10,000
- Amount deposited in the deposit account	10,30,000
Long-term capital gains	18,78,475
Assessment year 2021-22 (i.e., *relevant to the previous year in which 2 years from the date of sale of agricultural land expires)*	
Amount deposited in the deposit account	10,30,000
Less : Amount utilised in purchasing agricultural land up to June 30, 2020	8,47,000
Long-term capital gains	1,83,000

71.3 *Capital gains on compulsory acquisition of land and building, forming part of industrial undertaking [Sec. 54D]* - The provisions of section 54D are given below—

71.3-1 *CONDITIONS* - Capital gains arising on compulsory acquisition of any land or building forming a part of an industrial undertaking is exempt from tax if the following conditions are satisfied—

• Such land or building was used by the assessee for the purpose of the industrial undertaking for at least 2 years preceding the date of compulsory acquisition.

• The assessee has purchased any other land or building within a period of 3 years from the date of receipt of compensation or constructed a building within such period.

• Newly acquired land or building should be used for the purpose of shifting or re-establishing the said undertaking or setting up another industrial undertaking.

71.3-2 *AMOUNT OF EXEMPTION* - If the amount of capital gains is less than the cost of the new land or building, the entire amount of capital gains is exempt from tax. On the other hand, if the amount of capital gains is greater than the cost of the new land or building, the difference between the amount of capital gains and the cost of new land or building is chargeable to tax as capital gains.

71.3-3 *CONSEQUENCES IF NEW LAND OR BUILDING IS TRANSFERRED WITHIN 3 YEARS* - If the new land or building is transferred within a period of 3 years from the date of its purchase or construction, the amount of capital gains arising therefrom, together with the amount of capital gains exempted earlier, will be chargeable to tax in the year of sale of the new land and building.

To attain this, it has been provided that if the new asset is transferred within 3 years from the date of its acquisition, the amount of exemption under section 54D shall be reduced from the cost of acquisition of the new asset while calculating short-term capital gain on the transfer of the new asset.

71.3-4 *SCHEME OF DEPOSIT* - Where the amount of capital gain is not appropriated or utilised by the assessee for purchase or construction of the new asset before the date for furnishing the return of income, it shall be deposited by him on or before the due date of furnishing the return of income, in the deposit account in any branch (except rural branch) of a public sector bank or IDBI Bank in accordance with Capital Gains Accounts Scheme, 1988. The amount already utilised for the purchase or construction of the new asset together with the amount so deposited shall be deemed to be the amount utilised for the purchase or construction of the new asset. If the amount deposited is not utilised fully for the purchase or construction of the new asset within the stipulated period, then the amount not so utilised shall be treated as the capital gain of the previous year in which the period of 3 years from the date of transfer of the original asset expires[3]. In such case the assessee shall be entitled to withdraw such amount in accordance with the aforesaid scheme.

3. *See* also footnote 1, para 71.1-4.

71.3-E1 XYZ Ltd. has an industrial undertaking in Tamil Nadu. An industrial plot owned by the company (cost of acquisition in 2002-03 : Rs. 70,000) is compulsorily acquired by the Government of Tamil Nadu on May 15, 2014. The State Government pays Rs. 19,10,000 on June 23, 2018 as compensation under an award. The company purchases a land for the purpose of industrial undertaking for Rs. 15,00,000 on May 13, 2019. The company, however, sells the land for Rs. 15,95,000 on September 14, 2020. Determine the amount of exemption under section 54D and amount of capital gains chargeable to tax.

•

	Rs.
Compensation from the Government	19,10,000
Less : Indexed cost of acquisition [Rs. 70,000 × 240 ÷ 105]	1,60,000
Capital gains	17,50,000
Less : Exemption under section 54D (*as the company has invested Rs. 15,00,000 in purchasing land for the purpose of industrial undertaking, exemption is available to the extent of Rs. 15,00,000)	15,00,000*
Long-term capital gains chargeable to tax for the assessment year 2019-20	2,50,000
Sale proceeds of land sold on September 14, 2020	15,95,000
Less : Cost of acquisition (Rs. 15,00,000, being actual cost *minus* Rs. 15,00,000 being the amount of exemption granted in the assessment year 2019-20 as the land is sold within 3 years from the date of its purchase)	*Nil*
Short-term capital gains chargeable to tax for the assessment year 2021-22	15,95,000

71.4 ***Capital gain not to be charged on investment in certain bonds [Sec. 54EC]*** - The salient features of section 54EC are given below —

71.4-1 *CONDITIONS* - The following conditions should be satisfied :

1. Long-term capital asset - A long-term capital asset[4] is transferred by an assessee (who may be an individual, firm, company, or any other person) during the previous year. From the assessment year 2019-20, section 54EC is applicable only if long-term capital asset (being land or building or both) is transferred.

2. Investment in "specified asset" - Within 6 months[5] from the date of transfer of the asset, the assessee should invest[6] the whole (or any part of) capital gain in long-term specified assets. "Long-term specified assets" means any bond redeemable after 3 years (5 years, if such bond is issued on or after April 1, 2018) issued—

a. by the National Highways Authority of India (NHAI); or

b. by the Rural Electrification Corporation Ltd. (REC); or

c. by any other authority but bonds are notified by the Central Government for this purpose (applicable from the assessment year 2018-19).

The investment made on or after April 1, 2007 in the long-term specified assets noted above by an assessee during any one financial year cannot exceed Rs. 50 lakh. Moreover, from the assessment year 2015-16, investment made by an assessee in the specified asset, out of capital gains arising from transfer of one or more original assets, during the financial year in which the original asset or assets are transferred and in the subsequent financial year should not exceed Rs. 50 lakh.

71.4-2 *AMOUNT OF EXEMPTION* - The amount of exemption under section 54EC is as follows —

a. the amount of capital gains generated on transfer of capital asset; or

b. the amount invested in specified asset as stated above,

whichever is lower.

The cost of specified assets which is considered for the purpose of section 54EC shall not be eligible for deduction under section 80C.

---

4. An assessee is entitled to exemption under section 54E in respect of capital gains arising on transfer of a capital asset (period of holding more than 36 months) on which depreciation has been allowed – *CIT* v. *V.S. Dempo Company Ltd.* [2016] 242 Taxman 434 (SC).

5. Due to non-availability of these bonds, some persons could not avail of benefit under section 54EC, and for some other persons the effective time available for making the investment is less than six months. With a view to removing the hardship caused to taxpayers, the Central Board of Direct Taxes has issued an order under section 119(2)(*c*) on June 30, 2006 extending the time limitation for making the investments under section 54EC as under—
   (*a*) up to September 30, 2006 in case of persons where the long-term capital asset was transferred between September 29, 2005 and December 31, 2005 (both dates inclusive);
   (*b*) up to December 31, 2006 in case of persons where the long-term capital asset was transferred between January 1, 2006 and June 30, 2006 (both dates inclusive) — Order F. No. 142/09/2006-TPL, dated June 30, 2006.

6. The date of investment by the assessee must be regarded as the date on which payment is made — *Hindustan Unilever Ltd.* v. *CIT* [2010] 191 Taxman 119 (Bom.).

71.4-3 *CONSEQUENCES IF THE NEW ASSET IS TRANSFERRED WITHIN FIVE YEARS*[7] - If the specified assets are transferred (or converted into money or any loan/advance is taken on the security of specified assets) within 5 years[7] from the date of their acquisition, the amount of capital gains arising from the transfer of original asset which was not charged to tax, will be deemed to be the income by way of long-term capital gains of the previous year in which specified assets are transferred, etc.

71.4-4 *JUDICIAL RULINGS* - The following judicial rulings may be considered for understanding the provisions of section 54EC–

1. The Pune Bench of Tribunal in the case of *Mahesh Nemichandra Ganeshwade* v. *ITO* [2012] 51 SOT 155 held that where the assessee received sale consideration of a property in instalments, and he invested amount in specified bonds within a period of 6 months from date of receipts, he was entitled to deduction under section 54EC. The Bombay High Court in the case of *CIT* v. *Cello Plast* [2012] 209 Taxman 617, further extended this principle. If the assessee wants to invest in bonds of REC which are not available throughout the period of 6 - month, the time-limit of 6 - month should be extended even if bonds of NHAI are available.

2. If investment in bonds is closed for subscription, investment made immediately after reopening of subscription is qualified for exemption under section 54EC even if it is beyond 6 - month time-limit – *Aspi Ginwala, Shree Ram Engg. & Mfg. Industries* v. *CIT* [2012] 52 SOT 16 (Ahd).

3. If income of minor child or spouse is clubbed in the hands of an individual, minor child and spouse can separately invest up to Rs. 50 lakh for the purpose of claiming exemption under section 54EC. Capital gain (after claiming exemption under sections 54 to 54GB) will be clubbed in the hands of individual – *CIT* v. *Rajeev Goyal* [2012] 22 taxmann.com 34 (Kol.).

4. Where assessee purchased specified bonds prior to date of sale of property, exemption under section 54EC is not available –*Dakshaben R. Patel* v. *CIT* [2012] 22 taxmann.com 237 (Ahd.).

5. Section 50 does not have an overriding effect over section 54EC. Consequently, depreciable asset (transfer after 36 months) would be eligible for exemption under section 54EC—*CIT* v. *Aditya Medisales Ltd.* [2013] 218 Taxman 477 (Guj.).

71.4-E1 On March 10, 2019, X sells a plot for Rs. 97,86,000 (cost of acquisition on March 8, 2007: Rs. 8,10,000). Expenses on purchase and transfer are Rs. 10,000 and Rs. 20,000 respectively. On March 15, 2019, he acquires bonds of National Highways Authority of India (investment being Rs. 45,00,000). Further, he purchases Rs. 35,00,000 REC Bonds on April 20, 2019. These bonds are redeemable after 62 months. Find out the amount of exemption under section 54EC.

●

	Rs.
Sale consideration	97,86,000
Less : Expenses on transfer	20,000
Net sale consideration	97,66,000
Less : Indexed cost of acquisition [*i.e.*, Rs. 8,20,000 × 280 ÷ 122]	18,81,967
Long-term capital gain	78,84,033
Less : Exemption under section 54EC (*i.e.*, Rs. 45,00,000 + Rs. 35,00,000[8])	50,00,000
Capital gain chargeable to tax	28,84,033

Note : X should not transfer the bonds of NHAI/REC or take a loan on the security of these bonds or otherwise convert these bonds into money, within 5 years[7] from the date of acquisition (*i.e.* March 15, 2019 or April 20, 2019). If X transfers these bonds (or X takes any loan or advance on security of these bonds) within 5 years[7] from the date of acquisition, then the amount of exemption will be deemed as income by way of long-term capital gain of the previous year in which he transfers these bonds. Suppose X transfers NHAI bonds on January 25, 2021 (but he keeps REC bonds till maturity), then Rs. 15,00,000 will be chargeable to tax as long-term capital gains for the previous year 2020-21.

71.4A ***Capital gain not to be charged on investment in units of a specified fund [Sec. 54EE, applicable from the assessment year 2017-18]*** -The provisions of section 54EE, applicable from the assessment year 2017-18, are given below -

1. The assessee has transferred a long-term capital asset.

2. He has invested the whole (or any part) of capital gains in long-term specified assets (to be notified by the Central Government to finance start-ups). Such investment can be made at any time within 6 months from the date of transfer of original asset. The amount of such investment (made on or after April 1, 2016) by an assessee during any financial year cannot exceed Rs. 50 lakh. Moreover, investment made by an assessee in long-term specified assets, out of capital gains arising from transfer of one or more original

7. 3 years, if the investment in specified asset is made before April 1, 2018.

8. Investment in these bonds in one financial year cannot be more than Rs. 50 lakh. In this case, bonds of Rs. 45,00,000 are purchased in the financial year 2018-19 and bonds of Rs. 35,00,000 are purchased in the financial year 2019-20 (in either of the two cases, investment is made within the time-limit of 6 months). However, law has been amended on this point with effect from the assessment year 2015-16. Investment in the year of transfer and in the next financial year cannot exceed Rs. 50,00,000.

assets, during the financial year in which the original asset or assets are transferred and in the subsequent financial year should not exceed Rs. 50 lakh.

Amount of exemption -Amount of exemption under section 54EE is the amount of capital gain or amount invested in long-term specified assets, whichever is lower.

Revocation of exemption -The long-term specified assets should not be transferred (not even loan or advance is taken on security of such assets) within 3 years from the date of acquisition. If long-term specified assets are transferred (or loan or advance is taken on security of such assets) within 3 years, the amount of exemption given earlier will be revoked and it shall be chargeable to tax as long-term capital gain in the year in which such specified assets are transferred (or loan or advance is taken).

71.4A-E1 X transfers a residential house property (being a long-term capital asset) on December 17, 2018 for Rs. 5,20,00,000 (indexed cost of acquisition : Rs. 90,00,000, expenditure on transfer : Rs. 5,20,000). To get the benefit of exemption under different sections, he acquires the following assets –

a. a residential house property on May 20, 2019 : Rs. 3,33,86,000;
b. long-term specified assets notified for the purpose of section 54EE –
   - on March 10, 2019 : Rs. 40,00,000;
   - on June 1, 2019 : Rs. 30,00,000;
c. REC capital gain bonds –
   - on March 11, 2019 : Rs. 41,00,000;
   - on August 1, 2019 : Rs. 31,00,000.

Would it make any difference if transferor is X Ltd.?

•

Computation of capital gain for the assessment year 2019-20 –

	X *Rs.*	*X Ltd.* *Rs.*
Full value of consideration	5,20,00,000	5,20,00,000
Less: Expenditure on transfer and indexed cost of acquisition	95,20,000	95,20,000
Balance	4,24,80,000	4,24,80,000
Less: Exemptions –		
Under section 54	3,33,86,000	–
Under section 54EC	41,00,000	41,00,000
Under section 54EE (Rs. 40,00,000 + Rs. 30,00,000, subject to maximum of Rs. 50,00,000)	50,00,000	50,00,000
Long-term capital gain chargeable to tax	*Nil*	3,33,80,000

71.4A-E2 In the above example, X or X Ltd. takes a loan on security of specified assets (notified for the purpose of section 54EE) which were purchased on March 10, 2019. Loan is taken on May 20, 2020.

•

If the specified assets (acquired under section 54EE) are transferred (or converted into money or any loan/advance is taken on security of specified assets) within 3 years from the date of acquisition, the exemption claimed earlier under these sections, will be deemed as long-term capital gain of the previous year in which specified assets are transferred (or loan or advance is taken). In this case, specified assets are purchased on March 10, 2019. Loan is taken on security of specified assets on May 20, 2020. Consequently, the exemption given (in the assessment year 2019-20) will be revoked. Long-term capital gain taxable for the previous year 2020-21 (assessment year 2021-22) will be Rs. 19,94,000 in the hands of X or Rs. 20,00,000 in the case of X Ltd.

71.5 *Capital gains on transfer of a long-term capital asset other than a house property [Sec. 54F]* - The provisions of section 54F are as follows :

71.5-1 CONDITIONS - Exemption under section 54F is available if the following conditions are satisfied :

• The assessee is an individual or a Hindu undivided family.

• The asset transferred is any long-term capital asset but other than a residential house.

• The assessee has purchased, within one year before the date of transfer or 2 years after the date of transfer or constructed within 3 years after the date of transfer (or from the date of receipt of compensation in the case of compulsory acquisition), one residential house (hereinafter referred to as "new house"[9]).

9. Whose income is taxable under the head "Income from house property".

The following points should also be kept in view :

- Date of commencement of construction is not relevant.
- Allotment of flat under self-financing scheme of the Delhi Development Authority (or under similar schemes of co-operative societies or other institutions) is treated as construction of house for this purpose—Circular No. 471, dated October 15, 1986 and Circular No. 672, dated December 16, 1993.

• The new house property which is purchased or constructed within the time-limit specified above should be situated in India (applicable from the assessment year 2015-16).

• The assessee should not sell or transfer the new house within 3 years of its purchase or construction.

• The assessee should not own[10] on the date of transfer of the original asset more than one residential house[11] (other than the new house). He should also not purchase within a period of 2 years after such date or construct within a period of 3 years after such date any residential house[9] (other than the new house).

71.5-2 *AMOUNT OF DEDUCTION* - If the above conditions are satisfied, the capital gain will be treated in a concessional manner as under :

1. If the cost of the new house[12] is not less than the net consideration in respect of the capital asset transferred, the entire capital gain arising from the transfer will be exempt from tax.

2. If the cost of the new house[12] is less than the net consideration in respect of the asset transferred, the exemption from long-term capital gain will be granted proportionately on the basis of investment of net consideration either for purchase or construction of the residential house (*i.e.*, cost of new house × capital gains ÷ net consideration). Net consideration in respect of the transfer of a capital asset means the full value of the consideration received or accruing as a result of the transfer of the capital asset after deduction of any expenditure incurred, wholly and exclusively, in connection with the transfer.

71.5-3 *CIRCUMSTANCES WHEN EXEMPTION GRANTED UNDER SECTION 54F MAY BE WITHDRAWN* - In the following cases, exemption granted under section 54F can be withdrawn—

a. if the individual sells or transfers the new house within 3 years of its purchase or construction; or

b. if the individual purchases, within a period of 2 years of the transfer of original asset, or constructs within a period of 3 years of transfer of such asset, a residential house[9] other than the new house.

In the aforesaid two cases, the amount of capital gains arising from the transfer of the original asset, which was not charged to tax, will be deemed to be the income by way of long-term capital gains of the year in which new house is transferred or another residential house[9] (other than the new house) is purchased or constructed, as the case may be.

71.5-4 *SCHEME OF DEPOSIT* - Where the amount of net consideration is not appropriated or utilised by the assessee for purchase or construction of the new house before the date of furnishing of return of income, it shall be deposited by him on or before the due date of furnishing the return of income, in the deposit account in any branch (except rural branch) of a public sector bank or IDBI Bank in accordance with the Capital Gains Accounts Scheme, 1988. The amount already utilised for the purchase/construction of the new house together with the amount so deposited shall be deemed to be the amount utilised for the purchase/construction of the new house. If the amount so deposited is not utilised fully for the purchase/construction of the new house within the stipulated period, the proportionate amount shall be treated as long-term capital gain of the previous year in which the period of 3 years from the date of transfer of the original asset expires[13]. In such case, the assessee shall be entitled to withdraw the unutilised amount in accordance with the scheme.

71.5-5 *OTHER POINTS* - One should also keep in view the following—

1. If by applying section 54F, there is no income in hands of a minor child to be added under section 64(1A), the benefit under section 54F cannot be denied to minor child on the ground that father of minor child had two residential houses at the time of transfer of the capital asset—*CIT* v. *Madan Lal Bassi* [2004] 88 ITD 557 (Chd.).

---

9. Whose income is taxable under the head "Income from house property".

10. For this purpose "ownership" does not mean only registered ownership. Even beneficial ownership would be sufficient to debar the benefit - *Gopal D. Shetty* v. *ITO* [2008] 25 SOT 53 (Pune).

11. Any residential house (up to the assessment year 2000-01).

12. Including cost of land—Circular No. 667, dated October 18, 1993. Cost of vacant land appurtenant to and forming part of a residential unit is to be considered for claim of exemption under section 54F, even if no construction has been done on appurtenant land—*CIT* v. *Narendra Mohan Uniyal* [2009] 34 SOT 152 (Delhi).

13. *See* also footnote 1, para 71.1-4.

2. Where an assessee purchases ground floor of a house and later, when vendor builds first floor, the assessee purchases first floor by a separate sale deed, the assessing authority is not justified in disallowing the assessee's claim for exemption of capital gains on ground that ground floor and first floor constitute two residential houses and, therefore, provisions of section 54F(2) are attracted—*Hansa Bai Sanghi* v. *ITO* [2004] 89 ITD 239 (Hyd.).

3. Once it is demonstrated that consideration received on transfer of a capital asset has been invested either in purchase or in construction of a residential house, even though these transactions are not complete in all respects as required under law, the same would not disentitle assessee from benefit of exemption under section 54F – *CIT* v. *Sambandam Udaykumar* [2012] 206 Taxman 150 (Kar.), *V. A. Tharabai* v. *CIT* [2012] 50 SOT 537 (Chennai), *Usha Vaid* v. *ITO* [2012] 25 taxmann.com 188 (Asr.).

4. If house properties are owned by assessee's wife then the same cannot be treated as owned by the assessee for disallowing exemption under section 54F to the assessee nonetheless income from such properties are clubbed in the assessee's hands under section 22, read with sections 27 and 64 – *S. Krishna Kumar* v. *CIT* [2012] 22 taxmann.com 200 (Chennai).

5. Only requirement for claiming exemption under section 54F is construction of residential house and it does not matter that house constructed is on agricultural land or on other land – *CIT* v. *Om Prakash Goyal* [2012] 53 SOT 158 (Jaipur).

6. Exemption under section 54F will be admissible even where the assessee has registered residential house property in the name of his minor daughter – *N. Ram Kumar* v. *CIT* [2012] 25 taxmann.com 337 (Hyd.).

7. Amount spent towards making additions or improvements in habitable house property would also be eligible for section 54F exemption—*Rahana Siraj* v. *CIT* [2015] 58 taxmann.com 333 (Kar.).

8. Where an assessee owns more than one residential house even jointly with another person, the benefit of exemption under section 54F is not available—*M.J. Siwani* v. *CIT* [2015] 232 Taxman 335 (SC).

71.5-E1 X sells non-listed shares in a private sector company on July 10, 2018 for Rs. 88,05,000 (cost of acquisition on June 15, 2006 : Rs. 30,000, expenses on sale : Rs. 5,000). On July 10, 2018, he owns one residential house property. To get the benefit of exemption under section 54F, X deposits on July 30, 2019 Rs. 60,00,000 in Capital Gains Deposit Account Scheme. By withdrawing from the Deposit Account, he purchases a residential house property at Delhi on July 6, 2020 for Rs. 48,00,000. Ascertain —

a. the amount of capital gain chargeable to tax for the assessment year 2019-20;

b. tax treatment of the unutilised amount ;

c. when can he withdraw the unutilised amount ; and

d. what X has to do to ensure that exemption under section 54F is never taken back.

•

Assessment year 2019-20

	Rs.
Sale consideration	88,05,000
Less :	
Expenses	5,000
Indexed cost of acquisition [Rs. 30,000 × 280 ÷ 122]	68,852
Balance	87,31,148
Less : Exemption under section 54F [Rs. 60,00,000 being the amount deposited in Deposit Account÷ Rs. 88,00,000 being net sale consideration × Rs. 87,31,148 being the amount of capital gain]	59,53,055
Long-term capital gain	27,78,092

Notes —

1. In this case, X has not fully utilised the deposit account for acquiring a residential house property. Out of Rs. 60 lakh deposited for acquiring the house, it is utilised to the extent of Rs. 48 lakh. Tax treatment of Rs. 12 lakh, being the unutilised amount, will be as follows —

	Rs.
Unutilised amount (*a*)	12,00,000
Net sale consideration (*b*)	88,00,000
Original capital gain (*c*)	87,31,148
Notional long-term capital gain [*i.e., (a)/(b)* × *(c)*]	11,90,611
Effective exemption under section 54F [*i.e.,* Rs. 59,53,055 — Rs. 11,90,611]	47,62,444

Rs. 11,90,611 will be chargeable to tax as long-term capital gain after the expiry of 3 years from date of transfer of shares (*i.e.,* July 9, 2021). Consequently, it will be taxable for the assessment year 2022-23.

2. The unutilised amount of Rs. 12 lakh can be withdrawn by X at any time after July 9, 2021.

3. If X sells the new house at Delhi before July 6, 2023, then Rs. 47,62,444 (exemption under section 54F) will be taken as long-term capital gains of the year in which the house is sold.

4. If X purchases any other residential house before July 10, 2020 or constructs any other residential house (income of which is taxable under section 22) before July 10, 2021, then Rs. 47,62,444 (exemption under section 54F) will be deemed as long-term capital gain of the year in which another house is purchased or constructed.

71.5-E2 X purchases 1,000 non-listed shares in Y Ltd. on August 16, 2001 for Rs. 18,180. On May 17, 2002, he gets 500 bonus shares and on October 20, 2009 acquires 1,500 right shares for Rs. 25,223. He sells 3,000 shares in Y Ltd. on February 12, 2019 at the rate of Rs.110 per share (brokerage on sale : 1 per cent). He owns one residential house property. He purchases another residential house on July 29, 2019 for Rs. 2,90,000. Ascertain the amount of capital gains chargeable to tax for the assessment year 2019-20.

●

	1000 original shares Rs.	*500 bonus shares Rs.*	*1500 right shares Rs.*
Sale consideration	1,10,000	55,000	1,65,000
Less : Expenses on transfer	1,100	550	1,650
Net sale consideration	1,08,900	54,450	1,63,350
Less : Indexed cost of acquisition [Rs. 18,180 × 280/100; Rs. 25,223 × 280/148]	50,904	*Nil*	47,719
Long-term capital gain	57,996	54,450	1,15,631
Long-term capital gain as percentage of net sale consideration	53.26%	100%	70.79%
Order of preference for claiming exemption under section 54F	3	1	2
Exemption under section 54F [*see* Note]	38,351	54,450	1,15,631
Capital gain	19,645	*Nil*	*Nil*

Note - The amount of exemption is determined as under—

	Investment utilised for claiming exemption Rs.	*Exemption Rs.*
Bonus shares [Rs. 54,450/Rs. 54,450 × Rs. 54,450]	54,450	54,450
Right shares [Rs. 1,63,350/1,63,350 × Rs. 1,15,631]	1,63,350	1,15,631
Original shares [Rs. 72,200/1,08,900 × Rs. 57,996]	72,200	38,451
Total [any other order of preference will give lower exemption]	2,90,000	2,08,532

71.6 ***Capital gain arising on transfer of assets in cases of shifting of industrial undertaking from urban area [Sec. 54G]*** - Section 54G provides exemption on transfer of assets in the case of shifting of industrial undertaking from an urban area.

71.6-1 *CONDITIONS* - Exemption can be availed if the following conditions are satisfied :

- A capital asset (being plant, machinery, land or building or any right in land or building) used for the purpose of an industrial undertaking situated in an urban area is transferred. For this purpose "urban area" means any such area within the limits of a municipal corporation or municipality as the Central Government may, having regard to the population, concentration of industries, need for proper planning of the area and other relevant factors, by general or special order, declare to be an urban area for the purpose of this section.
- The transfer is effected in the course of, or in consequence of, the shifting of such industrial undertaking (hereinafter referred to as the original asset) to any area other than an urban area.
- The assessee has within a period of 1 year before or 3 years after the date on which the transfer took place:
  a. purchased a new machinery or plant for the purpose of business of the industrial undertaking in the area to which the said undertaking is shifted ;
  b. acquired building or land or constructed building for the purpose of his business in the said area ;
  c. shifted the original asset and transferred the establishment of such undertaking to such area ; and
  d. incurred expenses on such other purpose as may be specified in a scheme framed by the Central Government for the purpose of this section.

71.6-2 *AMOUNT OF EXEMPTION* - If the aforesaid conditions are satisfied, the capital gains will be dealt as follows :

- If the amount of the capital gain is greater than the cost and expense incurred in relation to all or any of the purposes mentioned in (*a*) to (*d*) *supra* (such cost and expenses being hereinafter referred to as the new asset), the difference between the amount of the capital gain and the cost of the new asset shall be charged under section 45 as the income of the previous year and for the purpose of computing in respect of the new asset any capital gain arising from its transfer within a period of 3 years of its being purchased, acquired, constructed or transferred, as the case may be, the cost shall be *nil.*
- If the amount of the capital gain is equal to, or less than the cost of the new asset, the capital gain shall not be charged under section 45; and for the purpose of computing in respect of the new asset any capital gain arising from its transfer within a period of 3 years of its being purchased acquired, constructed or transferred, as the case may be, the cost shall be reduced by the amount of the capital gain.

71.6-3 *SCHEME OF DEPOSIT* - Where the amount of capital gain is not appropriated or utilised by the assessee towards the new asset before the date for furnishing the return of income, it shall be deposited by him on or before the due date of furnishing the return of income, in the deposit account in any branch (except rural branch) of a public sector bank or IDBI Bank in accordance with the Capital Gains Accounts Scheme, 1988. The amount already utilised for the new asset together with the amount so deposited shall be deemed to be the amount utilised for the new asset. If the amount deposited is not utilised fully for the new asset within the stipulated period, then the amount not so utilised shall be treated as the capital gain of the previous year in which the period of 3 years from the date of transfer of the original asset expires.[14] In such case the assessee shall be entitled to withdraw such amount in accordance with the aforesaid scheme.

71.6-E1 X Ltd. owns an industrial undertaking at Nagpur. The undertaking is situated in an urban area. As per policy of the State Government, the industrial undertaking is shifted to a rural area. In the process of shifting, the company sells the following assets :

	Plant and machinery	*Building*	*Furniture*
	Rs.	*Rs.*	*Rs.*
Year of acquisition	1977	1978	1976
Cost of acquisition (as per section 50)	9,50,000	10,75,000	25,000
Sale proceeds (date of sale : March 25, 2019)	17,92,000	38,90,000	32,000
Cost of assets acquired during April-May 2019 for the purpose of shifting the undertaking to a rural area	30,50,000	4,00,000	3,70,000

Assuming the industrial undertaking is transferred to rural area by June 25, 2019, find out the capital gains chargeable to tax for the assessment year 2019-20.

●

Computation of capital gain

	Plant and machinery	*Building*	*Furniture*
	Rs.	*Rs.*	*Rs.*
Sale proceeds	17,92,000	38,90,000	32,000
Less : Cost of acquisition	9,50,000	10,75,000	25,000
Short-term capital gain (by virtue of section 50, it will be treated as short-term capital gain)	8,42,000	28,15,000	7,000
Short-term capital gain which is qualified for the purpose of section 54G (*i.e.*, Rs. 8,42,000 + Rs. 28,15,000)			36,57,000
Less : Amount invested in plant, machinery and building (*i.e.*, Rs. 30,50,000 + 4,00,000)			34,50,000
Short-term capital gain on plant, machinery and building			2,07,000
Short-term capital gain on sale of furniture (on sale of furniture, exemption is not available under section 54G)			7,000
Short-term capital gain chargeable to tax			2,14,000

71.7 ***Capital gains on transfer of assets in cases of shifting of industrial undertaking from urban area to any Special Economic Zone [Sec. 54GA]*** - Section 54GA gives exemption in case of shifting of an industrial undertaking from urban area to a special economic zone.

14. *See* also footnote 1, para 71.1-4.

71.7-1 *CONDITIONS* - Exemption can be availed if the following conditions are satisfied—

1. A capital asset (being plant, machinery, land or building or any right in land or building) used for the purpose of an industrial undertaking situated in an urban area is transferred.

2. The transfer is effected in the course of, or in consequence of, the shifting of such industrial undertaking (hereinafter referred to as the "original asset") to any Special Economic Zone. Such Special Economic Zone may be situated in urban area or any other area.

3. The assessee has within a period of 1 year before or 3 years after the date on which the transfer took place—

a. purchased machinery or plant for the purposes of business of the industrial undertaking in the Special Economic Zone to which the said undertaking is shifted;

b. acquired building or land or constructed building for the purposes of his business in the Special Economic Zone;

c. shifted the original asset and transferred the establishment to Special Economic Zone; and

d. incurred expenses on such other purpose as may be specified in a scheme framed by the Central Government for the purposes of this section.

71.7-2 *AMOUNT OF EXEMPTION* - If the above conditions are satisfied, then the amount of exemption is equal to—

a. the amount of capital gain generated on transfer of capital assets in the case of shifting of an industrial undertaking as stated above; or

b. the cost and expenses incurred in relation to all or any of the purposes mentioned in (*a*) to (*d*) *supra* (such cost and expenses being hereinafter referred to as the new asset),

whichever is lower.

71.7-3 *CONSEQUENCES IF THE NEW ASSET IS TRANSFERRED WITHIN 3 YEARS* - If the new asset is transferred within a period of 3 years from the date of its purchase/construction/acquisition, the amount of exemption given earlier under section 54G would be taken back.

71.7-4 *SCHEME OF DEPOSIT IN RESPECT OF EXEMPTION UNDER SECTION 54GA* - These provisions have been framed on similar lines as given in sections 54, 54B, etc.

71.8 ***Capital gain on transfer of residential property [Sec. 54GB, applicable from the assessment year 2013-14]*** - Section 54GB has been inserted from the assessment year 2013-14. The provisions of section 54GB are given below –

• *Who can claim exemption* - Under section 54GB, exemption is available to an individual or a Hindu undivided family.

• *Which asset is qualified for exemption* - Exemption under section 54GB is available if the assessee transfers a long-term capital asset, being a residential property (a house or a plot of land). The transfer should take place during April 1, 2012 and March 31, 2017 (in case of an investment in eligible start-up, the residential property can be transferred up to March 31, **2021**).

• *Which new asset the taxpayer should acquire* - Before the due date of furnishing of return of income under section 139(1), the assessee shall utilize the net sale consideration for subscription in equity shares in an "eligible company". The "eligible company" should utilize this amount for the purchase of a "new asset" within 1 year from the date of subscription in equity shares. If, however, the company does not utilize this amount for the purchase of a "new asset" before the due date of furnishing of return of income by the assessee (*i.e.*, transferor of residential property), it shall be deposited by the company in capital gain deposit account. In such a case, exemption would be available on the basis of amount deposited in the deposit account.

• *How much is exempt* - Amount of exemption is as follows (it cannot, however, exceed the amount of capital gain) –

Investment in "new asset" by the eligible company ÷ Net sale consideration × Capital gain

Net sale consideration is sale consideration *minus* expenditure on transfer incurred by the transferor.

• *Is it possible to revoke the exemption* - In the following cases, exemption will be taken back and the amount of exemption (or proportionate exemption) given earlier under section 54GB will become long-term capital gain of the assessee (*i.e.*, transferor of residential property). It shall be taxable in the year in which the assessee or the eligible company commits the following defaults –

1. If the equity shares in the eligible company are sold or otherwise transferred by the assessee within 5 years from the date of acquisition.

2. If the "new asset" is sold or otherwise transferred by the eligible company within the period given below –

- In the case of a "new asset" being **computer or computer software** acquired by an eligible start-up: Within **3 years** from the date of acquisition (applicable from the assessment year 2020-21).
- In the case of any other "new asset" : Within 5 years from the date of acquisition.

3. If the deposit account is not utilized fully or partly by the eligible company for purchasing the new asset within 1 year from the date of subscription in equity shares (by the assessee).

● *What is "eligible company"* - It means a company which satisfies the following conditions –

1. It is incorporated on or after April 1 (of the previous year in which residential property is transferred) but on or before the due date of submission of return of income under section 139(1) by the assessee (*i.e.*, transferor of residential property).

2. It is engaged in the business of manufacture of any article or thing [or (with effect from the assessment year 2017-18) in an eligible business].

3. The assessee (*i.e.*, transferor of residential property) has more than 50 per cent (**30 per cent**, applicable from the assessment year 2020-21) share capital (or voting right) after subscription in shares by the assessee.

4. The company qualifies to be a SME (*i.e.*, small or medium enterprise under the Micro, Small and Medium Enterprises Act, 2006) (*i.e.*, where the investment in plant and machinery is more than Rs. 25 lakh but not more than Rs. 10 crore). Alternatively, the company is an eligible start-up (applicable from the assessment year 2017-18).

● *What is new asset* - It means new plant and machinery but does not include the following –

1. Any plant or machinery which is used in India or outside India by any person before its installation by the eligible company.

2. Any plant or machinery which is installed in office premises/residential accommodation/guest house.

3. Any office appliance.

4. Computers or computer software [however (from the assessment year 2017-18), in the case of an eligible start-up, being a technology driven start-up so certified by the Inter-Ministerial Board of Certification notified by the Central Government, the new asset shall include computers or computer software].

5. Any vehicle.

6. Any plant or machinery which is allowed 100 per cent deduction (by depreciation or otherwise) in any previous year.

● *What is "eligible start-up" or "eligible business"* - "Eligible business" means a business which involves innovation, development, deployment or commercialisation of new products, processes or services driven by technology or intellectual property. "Eligible start-up" means a company engaged in eligible business and satisfies the following conditions -

1. It is incorporated during April 1, 2016 and March 31, 2019.

2. The total turnover of its business does not exceed Rs. 25 crore in any of the previous years during April 1, 2016 and March 31, 2021.

3. It holds a certificate of eligible business from the Inter-Ministerial Board of Certification as notified by the Central Government.

71.8-E1 X, an individual, has income from salary and house property. Besides, he owns a business whose annual turnover is not more than Rs. 25 lakh. On May 14, 2016, he transfers a residential house property (or a residential plot of land) for Rs. 1,15,00,000 (expenses on transfer incurred by X : Rs. 3,00,000, indexed cost of acquisition : Rs. 14,60,000, year of acquisition : 1992-93, indexed cost of improvement : Rs. 8,15,000). Stamp duty value is Rs. 1,24,00,000 on which the purchaser pays stamp duty.

X Ltd. is incorporated on December 1, 2016 for manufacture or production of chemicals in Andhra Pradesh. There are 10 shareholders in X Ltd. X is one of the shareholders. He holds 51 per cent shares (date of subscription of shares in X Ltd.: December 10, 2016, total investment by X in shares in X Ltd. : Rs. 85,00,000). Out of Rs. 85,00,000, the company makes the following investments –

Date	*Investment*	*Amount Rs.*
March 1, 2017	New plant and machinery	40,00,000
July 1, 2017	New plant and machinery	6,00,000

Date	*Investment*	*Amount* Rs.
July 10, 2017	Old plant and machinery	10,00,000
July 31, 2017	Amount deposited in capital gain deposit account (CGDA 1)	25,00,000
August 1, 2017	Amount deposited in capital gain deposit account (CGDA 2)	4,00,000
December 8, 2017	New plant and machinery (purchased by withdrawing from CGDA 1)	22,50,000
December 12, 2017	New plant and machinery (purchased by withdrawing from CGDA 1)	2,50,000

Find out the amount of exemption under section 54GB.

•

Amount of capital gain before giving exemption under section 54GB –

	Rs.
Full value of consideration (being stamp duty value as per section 50C)	1,24,00,000
Less: Expenses on transfer borne by X	3,00,000
Net sale consideration	1,21,00,000
Less: Indexed cost of acquisition	14,60,000
Less: Indexed cost of improvement	8,15,000
Capital gain	98,25,000

Whether exemption is available in this case under section 54GB - Exemption under section 54GB is available, as the following conditions are satisfied –

1. X is an individual.

2. He has transferred a residential house (being a long-term capital asset) on May 14, 2016.

3. The due date of submission of return of income for the assessment year 2017-18 is July 31, 2017. After transfer of residential house but on or before July 31, 2017, X has acquired shares in X Ltd. (date of acquisition being December 10, 2016, investment by X in shares of X Ltd. is Rs. 85,00,000). X Ltd. is an eligible company (it is engaged in manufacture or production of goods and investment in plant and machinery is more than Rs. 25,00,000 but not more than Rs. 10 crore).

4. X Ltd. has utilized Rs. 85,00,000 in purchase of new plant and machinery (except office appliances, computers, computer software, vehicles, machinery for residential accommodation, machinery which is qualified for 100% deduction). This investment is made within 1 year from December 10, 2016. If X Ltd. does not utilize this amount (wholly or partly) till the due date of submission of return of income by X (*i.e.*, July 31, 2017), the unutilized amount should be deposited in capital gain deposit scheme. In this case, between December 10, 2016 and July 31, 2017, X Ltd. has purchased new plant and machinery for Rs. 46,00,000 (Rs. 40,00,000 + Rs. 6,00,000, old plant and machinery of Rs. 10,00,000 cannot be considered for exemption under section 54GB). Besides, it deposits Rs. 25,00,000 in capital gain deposit account scheme on July 31, 2017 (deposit of Rs. 4,00,000 after July 31, 2017 will not be considered). The total qualifying investment made by X Ltd. till July 31, 2017 is Rs. 71,00,000 (Rs. 46,00,000 + Rs. 25,00,000).

5. On the basis of investment of Rs. 71,00,000 by X Ltd., X can claim exemption under section 54GB as follows –

	Rs.
Capital gain	98,25,000
Less: Exemption under section 54GB (Rs. 71,00,000 ÷ Rs. 1,21,00,000 × Rs. 98,25,000)	57,65,083
Capital gain on transfer of residential house property taxable in the hands of X for the assessment year 2017-18	40,59,917

Consequences of not utilising capital gain deposit account fully - X Ltd. has deposited Rs. 25,00,000 on July 31, 2017. X has claimed the aforesaid exemption on the basis of investment by X Ltd. in new plant and machinery and deposit made up to July 31, 2017. Rs. 25,00,000 should be utilized by X Ltd. in purchasing new plant and machinery at any time within 1 year from the date of subscription of shares by X in X Ltd. (*i.e.*, before December 10, 2017). In this case, before December 10, 2017, X Ltd. has purchased new plant and machinery of Rs. 22,50,000 (any investment in plant and machinery on or after December 10, 2017 is not eligible). In other words, Rs. 2,50,000 not utilised before December 10, 2017 will be considered for calculating revocation of exemption in the hands of X for the previous year 2017-18 (*i.e.*, assessment year 2018-19) as follows –

	Rs.
Exemption claimed originally in the assessment year 2017-18	57,65,083
Less: Exemption under section 54GB on the basis of utilization of Rs. 22,50,000 out of Rs. 25,00,000 in the deposit account (qualifying investment Rs. 40,00,000 + Rs. 6,00,000 + Rs. 22,50,000 : Rs. 68,50,000) (Rs. 68,50,000 ÷ Rs. 1,21,00,000 × Rs. 98,25,000)	55,62,087
Long-term capital gain in the hands of X for the assessment year 2018-19	2,02,996

71.8-E2 X transfers (in example 71.8-E1) shares in X Ltd. on January 15, 2020 for Rs. 90,00,000.

•

X should not transfer shares in X Ltd. within 5 years from December 10, 2016 (*i.e.*, before December 10, 2021). In this case, X has transferred these shares within 5 years. Consequently, X will be chargeable to tax for the previous year 2019-20 (*i.e.*, assessment year 2020-21) as follows –

	Rs.
Full value of consideration	90,00,000
Less: Indexed cost of acquisition (cost of acquisition is Rs. 85,00,000, it is assumed that indexed cost of acquisition is Rs. 89,10,000)	89,10,000
Long-term capital gain	90,000
Add: Notional long-term capital gain (exemption given under section 54GB will be taken back)	55,62,087
Capital gain taxable for the assessment year 2020-21	56,52,087

71.8-E3 X does not transfer (in the above case) shares in X Ltd. However, X Ltd. transfers plant and machinery (purchased on July 1, 2017) on June 17, 2021 for Rs. 94,000.

•

X Ltd. should not transfer new plant and machinery within 5 years from the date of acquisition. In this case, the plant and machinery purchased on July 1, 2017 is transferred on June 17, 2021 for Rs. 94,000. Capital gain in the hands of X Ltd. will be calculated within the parameters of section 50. However, the capital gain exemption claimed by X under section 54GB will be revoked. From the language of section 54GB, it is not clear whether the entire exemption or proportionate exemption would be revoked. On logical interpretation, proportionate exemption should be revoked for the previous year 2021-22 (assessment year 2022-23) as follows –

	Rs.
Exemption under section 54GB	55,62,087
Less: Quantum of exemption if the new plant and machinery purchased on July 1, 2017 is not considered (qualifying investment Rs. 40,00,000 + Rs. 22,50,000 : Rs. 62,50,000) (Rs. 62,50,000 ÷ Rs. 1,21,00,000 × Rs. 98,25,000)	50,74,897
Long-term capital gain in the hands of X for the assessment year 2022-23	4,87,190

71.9 ***Extension of time limit for acquiring new asset [Sec. 54H]*** - Section 54H provides that where the transfer of the original asset is by way of compulsory acquisition under any law and the amount of compensation awarded for such acquisition is not received by the assessee on the date of such transfer, the period of acquiring the new asset under sections 54, 54B, 54D, 54EC and 54F by the assessee or the period for depositing or investing the amount of capital gain shall be extended in relation to such amount of compensation as is not received on the date of transfer. The extended period shall be reckoned from the date of receipt of the amount of compensation.

Short-term/long-term capital gains - How charged to tax

72. Tax on short-term and long-term capital gains is computed as follows –

Long-term capital gain (if securities transaction tax is not applicable)	Taxable under section 112 [*see* para 72.1]
Long-term capital gain (if securities transaction tax is applicable)	Taxable under section 112A, if a few conditions specified therein are satisfied [*see* para 72.2]. If these conditions are not satisfied, such gain will be taxable under section 112.
Short-term capital gain (if securities transaction tax is not applicable)	Taxable like any other income (no special rate)
Short-term capital gain (if securities transaction tax is applicable)	Taxable under section 111A [*see* para 72.4]

72.1 ***Tax on long-term capital gain*** - Long-term capital gain is taxable at a flat rate of 20 per cent [+ SC + HEC][16]. However, in some cases [*see* para 72.1-3] the tax rate is 10 per cent [+ SC + HEC][16].

72.1-1 *DEDUCTIONS UNDER SECTIONS 80C TO 80U ARE NOT AVAILABLE* - Deductions under sections 80C to 80U are not available in respect of long-term capital gain.

72.1-2 *EXEMPTION LIMIT IN SOME CASES [PROVISO TO SEC. 112(1)(*a*)]* - Long-term capital gain is taxable at the rate of 20 per cent (in some cases 10 per cent). The entire amount is taxable at these rates (no exemption limit). However, in the case of a resident individual/HUF, the benefit of exemption limit[15] is available, if taxable income (*minus* long-term capital gain) is less than exemption limit[15]. In such a case, the following shall be deducted from the long-term capital gain –

15. *See* Foot Note on page A205.
16. *See* Foot Note on page A-205.

Exemption limit[15]—(Net income or taxable income—Long-term capital gain)

After deducting the aforesaid amount, the balance amount of long-term capital gain is chargeable to tax at the rate of 20 per cent or 10 per cent [+ SC + HEC][16].

• *Provisions illustrated* - X (28 years) is a resident individual. For the assessment year 2019-20, he has the following incomes—

	Rs.
Long-term capital gain (LT)	33,000
Salary income (after standard deduction)	2,00,000
Bank interest (fixed deposits)	47,000
Net income (NI)	2,80,000

In this case, X is a resident individual. Exemption limit is Rs. 2,50,000. Taxable income (*minus* long-term capital gain) is Rs. 2,47,000. It is less than exemption limit. Consequently, from the long-term capital gain the following shall be deducted—

Rs. 2,50,000 (exemption limit)—[Rs. 2,80,000 (NI)—Rs. 33,000 (LT)] = Rs. 3,000

In this case, the long-term capital gain chargeable to tax will be Rs. 30,000 (*i.e.*, Rs. 33,000 – Rs. 3,000).

72.1-3 *10 PER CENT TAX RATE IN SOME CASES* - Long-term capital gain in the hands of non-residents under section 115AB, 115AC, 115AD or 115E is taxable at the rate of 10 per cent [+ SC + HEC][16]. Besides, in the following cases long-term capital gain is taxable at the rate of 10 per cent.

72.1-3a UNLISTED SECURITIES - Long-term capital gain in the hands of a non-resident/foreign company is taxable at the rate of 10 per cent [+ SC + HEC][16], if such gain arises on transfer of unlisted securities or unlisted shares in a company in which the public are not substantially interested. However, this rule is applicable only if the indexation benefit is not claimed and capital gain is calculated without giving effect to the first proviso to section 48 (under this proviso capital gain is calculated in foreign currency if a few conditions are satisfied).

72.1-3b LONG-TERM CAPITAL GAINS IN RESPECT OF SHARES, SECURITIES AND UNITS [SEC. 112] - If the following conditions are satisfied, then tax on long-term capital gain will be computed under *Option One* or *Option Two* as given below —

• *Conditions* - The following conditions should be satisfied —

Condition 1	The taxpayer is an individual, HUF, company or any other person (maybe resident or non-resident).
Condition 2	The asset is a long-term capital asset.

15. Exemption limit for the assessment year 2019-20 is Rs. 2,50,000 [higher exemption limit (*a*) in the case of a resident senior citizen born on or after April 2, 1939 but on or before April 1, 1959: Rs. 3,00,000; and (*b*) in the case of a resident super senior citizen born on or before April 1, 1939: Rs. 5,00,000].
Exemption limit for the assessment year 2020-21 is Rs. 2,50,000 [higher exemption limit (*a*) in the case of a resident senior citizen born on or after April 2, 1940 but on or before April 1, 1960: Rs. 3,00,000; and (*b*) in the case of a resident super senior citizen born on or before April 1, 1940: Rs. 5,00,000].

16. Surcharge (as a percentage of income-tax) is applicable as follows—

	Net income range	*Assessment year 2019-20*	*Assessment year 2020-21*
Individuals/HUF/AOP/BOI/ artificial juridical person	0 – Rs. 50 lakh Rs. 50 lakh – Rs. 1 crore Rs. 1 crore – Rs. 2 crore Rs. 2 crore – Rs. 5 crore Above Rs. 5 crore	*Nil* 10% 15% 15% 15%	*Nil* 10% 15% **25%** **37%**
Firm/co-operative society/ local authority	0 – Rs. 1 crore Above Rs. 1 crore	*Nil* 12%	*Nil* 12%
Domestic company	0 – Rs. 1 crore Rs. 1 crore – Rs. 10 crore Above Rs. 10 crore	*Nil* 7% 12%	*Nil* 7% 12%
Foreign company	0 – Rs. 1 crore Rs. 1 crore – Rs. 10 crore Above Rs. 10 crore	*Nil* 2% 5%	*Nil* 2% 5%

Health and education cess is 4% of tax and surcharge

Condition 3	The long-term capital asset is— *a.* a security listed in any recognised stock exchange in India; or *b.* (up to the assessment year 2014-15) a unit of UTI or mutual fund (whether listed or not), or *c.* zero coupon bonds.

Note : As per section 2(*h*), "securities" include—(*i*) shares, scrips, stocks, bonds, debentures, debenture stock or other marketable securities of a like nature in or of any incorporated company or other body corporate ; (*ii*) Government securities ; (*iii*) such other instruments as may be declared by the Central Government to be securities ; and (*iv*) rights or interest in securities.

In other words, shares, debentures, Government securities or bonds are "securities" for this purpose.

• *Tax computation* - If the conditions given in box are satisfied, tax shall be computed as follows (*i.e.*, under *Option 1* or *Option 2*, whichever is lower) —

Option 1	*Option 2*
1. Find out sale consideration	*1.* Find out sale consideration
2. Deduct : Indexed cost of acquisition/improvement[17] and expenses on transfer	*2. Deduct* : Cost of acquisition/improvement and expenses on transfer
3. The balancing amount [*i.e.*, (*1*) — (*2*)] is long-term capital gain	*3.* The balancing amount [*i.e.*, (*1*) - (*2*)] is long-term capital gain
4. Tax liability is 20 per cent [+ SC + HEC][16] of (*3*).	*4.* Tax liability is 10 per cent [+ SC + HEC][16] of (*3*).

The taxpayer has an option in respect of each transaction to pay tax under *Option 1* or *Option 2*, whichever is lower. It is difficult to state when *Option 2* is better. However, in the case of transfer of listed bonus shares, listed debentures, listed bonds and zero coupon bonds, *Option 2* will be better as compared to *Option 1*.

• *Other points* - The following points should be noted—

1. Capital loss computed from a source with indexation can be set off against capital gain computed without indexation from another source—*Mohanlal N. Shah (HUF)* v. *CIT* [2008] 26 SOT 381 (Mum.), *CIT* v. *Anuj A. Sheth* [2010] 190 Taxman 330 (Bom.).

2. If several transactions have taken by way of sale of shares, etc., the assessee can avail the benefit of indexation in a few transactions and avail the 10 per cent tax rate on the remaining transactions—*Devinder Prakash Kalra* v. *CIT* [2005] 97 TTJ (Delhi) 372.

3. In the case of a non-resident, capital gain is computed without indexation in foreign currency if a few conditions are satisfied [*see* para 69.5]. Even in such a case, one can avail the benefit of 10 per cent tax rate—*McLeod Russel India Ltd., In re* [2008] 168 Taxman 175 (AAR - New Delhi), *Fujitsu Services Ltd.*, In re [2009] 182 Taxman 263 (AAR - New Delhi), *Cairn U.K. Holdings Ltd.* v. *DIT* [2013] 38 taxmann.com 179 (Delhi).

72.1-E1 During the previous year 2018-19, X (33 years) sells the following assets :

	Non-listed bonds	*Gold*	*Shares (non-listed)*	*Debentures (non-listed)*
Date of sale	*March 31, 2019*	*April 10, 2018*	*May 17, 2018*	*March 5, 2019*
Date of acquisition	*April 10, 2018*	*June 3, 1998*	*April 10, 2002*	*April 10, 1982*
	Rs.	*Rs.*	*Rs.*	*Rs.*
Sale consideration	50,000	8,15,000	3,60,000	70,000
Cost of acquisition	44,000	1,60,000	1,20,000	40,000
Fair market value on April 1, 2001	—	2,85,000	—	34,000

Income from other sources is Rs. 14,18,000. Donation to an approved charitable trust is Rs. 10,000. The assessee deposits Rs. 1,50,000 in public provident fund.

Find out the tax liability.

•

16. See Foot Note, para 72.

17. Cost of acquisition/cost of improvement, in cases where indexation benefit is blocked [*see* para 63.1].

Capital gain will be computed as under :

	Bonds Rs.	Gold Rs.	Shares Rs.	Debentures Rs.
Sale consideration	50,000	8,15,000	3,60,000	70,000
Cost of acquisition (in the case of bonds and debentures the benefit of indexation is not available)	44,000	—	—	40,000
Indexed cost of acquisition	—	7,98,000[18]	3,20,000[19]	—
Capital gain	6,000	17,000	40,000	30,000

	Rs.
Long-term capital gain (*i.e.*, Rs. 17,000 + Rs. 40,000 + Rs. 30,000)	87,000
Short-term capital gain	6,000
Income from other sources	14,18,000
Gross total income	15,11,000
Less : Deduction under section 80C	1,50,000
Less : Deduction under section 80G (50% of Rs. 10,000)	5,000
Net income (rounded off)	13,56,000
Tax on net income will be determined as under :	
Net income (excluding long-term capital gain)	12,69,000
Income-tax on the aforesaid income	1,93,200
Long-term capital gain	87,000
Tax on long-term capital gain (@ 20%)	17,400
Tax on net income[20] (Rs. 1,93,200 + Rs. 17,400)	2,10,600
Add : Surcharge (applicable if net income exceeds Rs. 50 lakh)	*Nil*
Tax and surcharge	2,10,600
Add: Health and education cess	8,424
Tax on net income	2,19,020

Note : The benefit of option mentioned under para 72.1-3b is not available as bonds, shares and debentures are non-listed.

72.1-E2 From the following data, find out tax liability for the assessment year 2019-20 :

	X (a resident individual) (age : 32 years) Rs.	AB (HUF) (a resident Hindu undivided family) Rs.
Income from house property	2,65,000	2,72,000
Capital gain		
- Short-term	12,000	12,000
- Long-term on sale of silver	35,000	60,000
Deductions under sections 80CCC, 80D, and 80G	7,000	8,000
Payment of life insurance premium, contribution to public provident fund	28,000	30,000

•

	X Rs.	AB (HUF) Rs.
Computation of net income		
Income from house property	2,65,000	2,72,000
Capital gain	47,000	72,000
Gross total income	3,12,000	3,44,000
Less : Deduction under section 80C	28,000	30,000
Less : Deduction under sections 80CCC, 80D and 80G	7,000	8,000
Net income	2,77,000	3,06,000
Computation of tax		
Net income (excluding long-term capital gain) (*a*)	2,42,000	2,46,000
Income-tax on (*a*)	*Nil*	*Nil*

18. Rs. 2,85,000 × 280 ÷ 100.

19. Rs. 1,20,000 × 280 ÷ 105.

20. Rebate under section 87A is available only in the case of a resident individual if his/her taxable income is Rs. 3,50,000 or less.

	X (a resident individual) (age : 32 years) Rs.	AB (HUF) (a resident Hindu undivided family) Rs.
Income-tax on long-term capital gain		
*20% of [Rs. 35,000—(Rs. 2,50,000—Rs. 2,42,000)] :		
**20% of [Rs. 60,000—(Rs. 2,50,000—Rs. 2,46,000)] :	5,400*	11,200**
Less: Rebate under section 87A (100% of tax or Rs. 2,500, whichever is lower) (not applicable in the case of HUF)	2,500	*Nil*
Balance	2,900	11,200
Add: Surcharge (applicable if net income exceeds Rs. 50 lakh)	—	—
Tax and surcharge	2,900	11,200
Add: Health and education cess	116	448
Tax payable (rounded off)	3,020	11,650

72.1-E3 X, a resident Hindu undivided family, has the following income for the previous year 2018-19 :

	Rs.
Business income	(—)15,000
Short-term capital gain on transfer of silver	63,000
Long-term capital gain on sale of land	8,21,000

Find out the tax liability for the assessment year 2019-20, assuming that the family pays life insurance premium of Rs. 65,000 (sum assured : Rs. 8,00,000) (policy taken in May 2018).

•

	Long-term Capital gain Rs.	Short-term Capital gain Rs.
Capital gain	8,21,000	63,000
Less: Business loss	(-) 15,000	—
Gross total income	8,06,000	63,000
Less: Deduction under section 80C	—	65,000
Net income	8,06,000	*Nil*
Tax [*i.e.*, 20% of (Rs. 8,06,000 – Rs. 2,50,000)]		1,11,200
Add: Health and education Cess		4,448
Tax liability [rounded off]		1,15,650

Note : If the net income (other than long-term capital gain) is below the amount of first slab which is not taxable (*i.e.*, Rs. 2,50,000), then the long-term capital gain shall be reduced by the amount by which the total income (other than long-term capital gain) falls short of the maximum amount which is not chargeable to tax.

In this case, net income (other than long-term capital gain) is *nil*. Therefore, long-term capital gain shall be reduced by Rs. 2,50,000.

72.1-E4 On July 30, 2018, X (31 years) sells the following assets —

	Preference shares in A Ltd. (listed) Rs.	Preference shares in B Ltd. (listed) Rs.	Shares in C Ltd. (non-listed) Rs.
Sale consideration	5,00,000	11,25,000	6,89,000
Cost of acquisition	1,04,000	4,27,000	80,000
Date of acquisition	May 10, 2002	June 6, 2003	April 6, 2006

Income of X from other sources is Rs. 8,86,000. X deposits Rs. 1,50,000 in public provident fund. Find out the net income and tax liability for the assessment year 2019-20.

•

	Preference shares in A Ltd. Rs.	Preference shares in B Ltd. Rs.	Shares in C Ltd. Rs.
Sale consideration	5,00,000	11,25,000	6,89,000
Less : Indexed cost of acquisition	2,77,333[21]	10,96,881[22]	1,83,607[23]
Long-term capital gain	2,22,667	28,119	5,05,393

Computation of net income	Rs.
Long-term capital gain	7,56,179
Income from other sources	8,86,000
Gross total income	16,42,179
Less : Deduction under section 80C	1,50,000
Net income (rounded off)	14,92,180
Computation of tax	
Tax on income other than long-term capital gain (*i.e.*, tax on Rs. 7,36,000)	59,700
Add : Tax on long-term capital gain (*see* Note)	1,46,303
Tax[24]	2,06,003
Add : Surcharge	*Nil*
Tax	2,06,003
Add : Health and education cess	8,240
Tax payable (rounded off)	2,14,240

Note : Computation of tax on long-term capital gain

	Shares in A Ltd. Rs.	Shares in B Ltd. Rs.	Shares in C Ltd. Rs.
Tax on long-term capital gain as computed (after deducting indexed cost of acquisition) @ 20% (*a*)	44,533	5,624	1,01,079
Whether option mentioned in para 72.1-3b is available [*shares in C Ltd. are non-listed]	*Yes*	*Yes*	*No**
Sale consideration	5,00,000	11,25,000	—
Less : Cost of acquisition	1,04,000	4,27,000	—
Balance (*b*)	3,96,000	6,98,000	—
Tax on (*b*) @ 10% (*c*)	39,600	69,800	—
Effective tax [(*a*) or (*c*), whichever is lower]	39,600	5,624	1,01,079

72.2 ***Tax on long-term capital gains in certain cases [Sec. 112A]*** - Section 112A is applicable (with effect from the assessment year 2019-20) only if the following conditions are satisfied –

Condition 1	The total income includes any income chargeable under the head "Capital gains".
Condition 2	The capital gains arise from the transfer of a long-term capital asset being an equity share in a company or a unit of an equity oriented fund or a unit of a business trust.
Condition 3	At the time of transfer of equity share/equity oriented mutual fund unit/unit of business trust, securities transaction tax (STT) has been paid.
Condition 4	In case capital gain arises on transfer of equity shares, securities transaction tax (STT) was paid also at the time of acquisition of shares. However, the Board has clarified that the requirement of STT payment at the time of acquisition is applicable only when shares were acquired after October 1, 2004.

• *Transactions in any International Financial Service Centre not subject to* Condition 3 - *Condition 3* given above is not applicable in the case of a transfer undertaken on a recognised stock exchange located in any

21. Rs. 1,04,000 × 280 ÷ 105.
22. Rs. 4,27,000 × 280 ÷ 109.
23. Rs. 80,000 × 280 ÷ 122.
24. Rebate under section 87A is available only in the case of a resident individual if his/her taxable income does not exceed Rs. 3,50,000 (for the assessment year 2019-20) or Rs. 5,00,000 (for the assessment year 2020-21).

International Financial Service Centre. However, this concession is available only when the consideration for such transfer is received or receivable in foreign currency.

• *Condition 4 not applicable in a few notified cases - Condition 4 is* not applicable in a few notified cases given below (in these cases the requirement of payment of STT at the time of acquisition of equity shares is not applicable) –

- Acquisition which has been approved by the Supreme Court, High Court, National Company Law Tribunal, SEBI or RBI.
- Acquisition by any non-resident in accordance with FDI guidelines of the Indian Government.
- Acquisition by an investment fund [referred to in sec. 115UB].
- Acquisition through preferential issue to which Chapter VII of SEBI (Issue of Capital and Disclosure) Regulations does not apply.
- Acquisition through an issue of share by a company.
- Acquisition by scheduled banks, reconstruction or securitisation companies or public financial institutions during their ordinary course of business.
- Acquisition under ESOP.
- Acquisition under SEBI (Substantial Acquisition of Shares and Takeovers) Regulations.
- Acquisition from the Government.
- Acquisition by mode of transfer [as per sections 45(3)/(4), 47, 50B] if previous owner has acquired shares by any of the modes given in this list.

• *Equity oriented fund* - For the above purpose, equity oriented fund means a fund set-up under a scheme of a mutual fund specified under section 10(*23D*) and, —

a. in a case where the fund invests in the units of another fund which is traded on a recognised stock exchange, —
   - a minimum of 90 per cent of the total proceeds of such fund is invested in the units of such other fund; and
   - such other fund also invests a minimum of 90 per cent of its total proceeds in the equity shares of domestic companies listed on a recognised stock exchange; and

b. in any other case, a minimum of 65 per cent of the total proceeds of such fund is invested in the equity shares of domestic companies listed on a recognised stock exchange.

The percentage of equity shareholding or unit held in respect of the fund, as the case may be, shall be computed with reference to the annual average of the monthly averages of the opening and closing figures.

72.2-1 *TAX COMPUTATION UNDER SECTION 112A* - If 4 conditions given above are satisfied, tax on long-term capital gain (mentioned in *Condition 2*) will be calculated on the basis of parameters given below –

• *Long-term capital gain in excess of Rs. 1 lakh taxable at 10 per cent* - If long-term capital gain (mentioned in *Condition 2*) does not exceed Rs. 1 lakh, it is not chargeable to tax. If such gain exceeds Rs. 1 lakh, the amount in excess of Rs. 1 lakh is taxable at the rate of 10 per cent (+ SC + 4 per cent HEC). The rate of 10 per cent is applicable whether the assessee is a corporate-assessee or a non-corporate assessee.

• *Benefit of exemption limit in some cases* - Proviso to section 112A(2) gives exemption limit benefit. This benefit is available only in the case of a resident individual or a resident HUF (maybe ordinarily resident or not ordinarily resident). Moreover, this benefit is available only if the total income (as reduced by long-term capital gain mentioned in *Condition 2*) is less than the exemption limit.

• *Provisions illustrated* - Consider the following cases

Case 1 - Y (64 years) is a resident individual. For the assessment year 2019-20, he has following income –

	Rs.
Long-term capital gain on transfer of equity shares (four conditions given above are satisfied) (capital gain is computed within the parameters given under section 112A)	1,80,000
Other income	2,75,000
Net income (or taxable income or total income)	4,55,000

In this case, net income (as reduced by long-term capital gain) is Rs. 2,75,000. Exemption limit is Rs. 3,00,000. Y is unable to fully utilise his exemption limit. Unutilised exemption limit is Rs. 25,000 which will be deducted from capital gain of Rs.

1,80,000. In other words, out of long-term capital gain of Rs. 1,80,000, amount chargeable to tax under section 112A is Rs. 1,55,000. Tax will be calculated as follows –

	Rs.
Tax on long-term capital gain under section 112A [10% of (long-term capital gain exceeding Rs. 1,00,000)]	5,500
Add: Health and education cess @ 4%	220
Tax liability	5,720

Case 2 - Z (50 years) is a resident individual. For the assessment year 2019-20, he has following income –

	Rs.
Long-term capital gain on transfer of equity shares (four conditions given above are satisfied) (capital gain is computed within the parameters given under section 112A)	1,25,00,000
Other income	60,000
Net income (or taxable income or total income)	1,25,60,000

In this case, net income (as reduced by long-term capital gain) is Rs. 60,000. Exemption limit is Rs. 2,50,000. Z is unable to fully utilise his exemption limit. Unutilised exemption limit is Rs. 1,90,000 which will be deducted from capital gain of Rs. 1,25,00,000. In other words, out of long-term capital gain of Rs. 1,25,00,000, amount chargeable to tax under section 112A is Rs. 1,23,10,000. Tax will be calculated as follows –

	Rs.
Tax on long-term capital gain under section 112A [10% of (long-term capital gain exceeding Rs. 1,00,000)]	12,21,000
Tax on other income	*Nil*
Tax	12,21,000
Add: Surcharge @ 15%	1,83,150
Tax and surcharge	14,04,150
Add: Health and education cess @ 4%	56,166
Tax liability (rounded off)	14,60,320

72.2-2 *MODE OF COMPUTATION OF COST OF ACQUISITION* - If tax is payable under section 112A, cost of acquisition of equity shares/units shall be calculated according to the provisions given under section 55(2)(*ac*)[25]. This provision is applicable only in respect of equity shares/units acquired by the assessee before February 1, 2018. Cost of acquisition shall be calculated as follows[25] –

Step 1 - Find out actual cost of acquisition of equity shares/units. *Step 2* - Find out fair market value of equity shares/units on January 31, 2018 (but it cannot be more than sale consideration of equity shares/units).
Cost of acquisition shall be deemed to be amount computed in *Step 1* or *Step 2,* whichever is higher.

• *Fair market value on January 31, 2018* - Fair market value on January 31, 2018 shall be calculated as follows –

1. Shares/units which are quoted on January 31, 2018 - In a case where equity share/unit is listed on any recognised stock exchange, the highest price of share/unit quoted on such exchange on January 31, 2018 is taken as fair market value. Where, however, there is no trading in such share/unit on such exchange on January 31, 2018, the highest price of such share/unit on such exchange on a date immediately preceding January 31, 2018 when such share/unit was traded on such exchange, shall be the fair market value.

2. Units not listed - In a case where a unit is not listed on a recognised stock exchange, the net asset value (NAV) of such unit as on January 31, 2018 is taken as fair market value.

---

25. Long-term capital gain on transfer of equity shares/units of equity oriented mutual funds (which was subject to securities transaction tax) was exempt from tax under section 10(*38*). The Finance Act, 2018 (Finance Bill was presented in Lok Sabha on February 1, 2018) made significant amendments to tax such capital gain with effect from the assessment year 2019-20. However, any surplus which arises after the purchase of equity shares/units but before the presentation of the Finance Bill, is not taxable. To make it workable, definition of "cost of acquisition" has been outlined in such a way that nothing will be taxable in respect of any appreciation in the value of equity shares/units till January 31, 2018 (*i.e.,* before the presentation of Finance Bill, 2018 in Lok Sabha).

3. Shares (not listed on January 31, 2018) but listed on the date of transfer - In a case, where equity share is listed on a recognised stock exchange at the time of transfer (but not listed on January 31, 2018), fair market value on January 31, 2018 will be calculated (after giving indexation benefit in a limited mode up to the previous year 2017-18) as follows –

$$\text{Cost of acquisition} \times \frac{\text{Cost inflation index (CII) of 2017-18 (i.e., 272)}}{\text{CII for the year in which the shares were first held by the assessee (or previous owner in a few cases) or 2001-02, whichever is later}}$$

• *Provisions illustrated* - Consider the following cases

Case 1 - Consider the following situations (1,000 shares are transacted at Bombay Stock Exchange but value of 1 equity share is given below) –

		Situation 1 Rs.	*Situation 2* Rs.	*Situation 3* Rs.	*Situation 4* Rs.	*Situation 5* Rs.
Cost of acquisition on September 20, 2017	(*a*)	410	710	900	800	30
Fair market value as per highest quotation on January 31, 2018	(*b*)	730	780	300	1,000	100
Sale consideration on March 15, 2019	(*c*)	760	650	910	825	400

Fair market value for the purpose of calculating tax liability under section 112A shall be calculated as follows –

Step 1 - Cost of acquisition on September 20, 2017	(*a*)	410	710	900	800	30
Step 2 - Fair market value on January 31, 2018 but it cannot be more than sale consideration [lower of (*b*) or (*c*)]	(*d*)	730	650	300	825	100
Cost of acquisition for the purpose of section 112A [(*a*) or (*d*), whichever is higher]	(*e*)	730	710	900	825	100
Long-term capital gain per share under section 112A [(*c*) – (*e*)]		30	(–) 60	10	*Nil*	300

Case 2 - The above mode of determining cost of acquisition is applicable only if shares/units are acquired prior to February 1, 2018. Suppose in *Situation 1*, the date of acquisition is February 10, 2018 (no other change). "Cost of acquisition" will be taken as Rs. 410 (above rules are not applicable).

Case 3 - In the following cases, shares are listed after January 31, 2018 (assume that shares are listed for the first time in March 2018 or April 2018) –

	Situation 1 Rs.	*Situation 2* Rs.
Date of acquisition of 1,000 shares	July 1, 2003	June 1, 1995
Cost of acquisition of 1,000 shares (shares are not listed, STT not paid)	60,000	38,000
Fair market value on April 1, 2001	–	40,000
Sale consideration of 1,000 shares on June 7, 2018 (transacted at BSE and STT @ 0.1% which comes to Rs. 3,000 is paid)	30,00,000	30,00,000

Cost of acquisition and capital gain will be calculated as follows –

Step 1 - Cost of acquisition (actual cost or fair market value on April 1, 2001, whichever is higher in *Situation 2*)	(*a*)	60,000	40,000
Step 2 - Fair market value on January 31, 2018 but it cannot be more than sale consideration	(*b*)	1,49,725[26]	1,08,800[27]
Cost of acquisition for the purpose of section 112A [(*a*) or (*b*), whichever is higher]	(*c*)	1,49,725	1,08,800
Long-term capital gain under section 112A [*i.e.*, sale consideration – (*c*)]		28,50,275	28,91,200

26. Rs. 60,000 × CII of 2017-18 : 272 ÷ CII of 2003-04 : 109.

27. Rs. 40,000 × CII of 2017-18 : 272 ÷ CII of 2001-02 : 100.

72.2-3 *OTHER POINTS* - For computation of tax under section 112A, the following points should be kept in view –

1. Indexation benefit (barring the case given above) is not available when tax is payable under section 112A.

2. Mode of computation of capital gain in foreign currency in the case of a non-resident (specified by first proviso to section 48) is not applicable when tax is payable under section 112A.

3. Deductions under sections 80C to 80U are not available from long-term capital gain (mentioned in *Condition 2*).

4. Rebate under section 87A is not available from income-tax on long-term capital gain mentioned in *Condition 2.* However, the rebate under section 87A shall be allowed from the income-tax on the total income as reduced by tax payable on such capital gains.

72.2-E1 The following information is given by X (32 years) –

	Rs.
Cost of acquisition of 500 equity shares in A Ltd. on March 25, 2014 (securities transaction tax is paid)	55,000
Fair market value on January 31, 2018 (highest quotation in Bombay Stock Exchange and National Stock Exchange on January 31, 2018 : Rs. 180) (Rs. 180 × 500)	90,000
Date of transfer of 500 equity shares in A Ltd.	April 20, 2018
Full value of consideration [*(Rs. 490 × 500), (securities transaction tax is paid)]	2,45,000*
Income other than capital gains	12,00,000

Find out the tax liability of X for the assessment year 2019-20.

•

Conditions of section 112A are satisfied. Consequently, tax on capital gain will be calculated within the parameters of section 112A as follows –

	Rs.
Cost of acquisition for the purpose of section 112A –	
- Actual cost of acquisition	55,000
- Fair market value on January 31, 2018 or sale consideration, whichever is lower	90,000
Cost of acquisition (higher of the above figures)	90,000
Computation of income –	
Long-term capital gain (Rs. 2,45,000 – Rs. 90,000)	1,55,000
Other incomes	12,00,000
Net income	13,55,000
Computation of tax –	
Income-tax on long-term capital gain (10% of capital gain in excess of Rs. 1,00,000)	5,500
Income-tax on other incomes	1,72,500
Income-tax	1,78,000
Add: Health and education cess	7,120
Tax liability	1,85,120

72.2-E2 X (49 years) purchases 1,000 shares in C Ltd. on January 20, 2014 from a friend at the rate of Rs. 350 per share (though shares in C Ltd. are quoted in Bombay Stock Exchange, securities transaction tax is not paid as transaction is made outside the stock exchange). Highest market quotation on January 31, 2018 is Rs. 440 per share. He transfers 900 shares in C Ltd. on December 15, 2018 at the rate of Rs. 470 per share (securities transaction tax is paid at the time of transfer). Income of X from other sources for the previous year 2018-19 is Rs. 20,00,000.

•

Tax is computed under section 112A only if 4 conditions are satisfied [*see* para 72.2]. In this case, *Condition 4* is not satisfied (securities transaction tax is not paid at the time of acquisition of shares). Consequently, section 112A is not applicable. Tax will be computed under section 112 as follows –

	Rs.
Full value of consideration (Rs. 470 × 900)	4,23,000
Less: Indexed cost of acquisition [Rs. 350 × 900 × CII of 2018-19 : 280 ÷ CII of 2013-14 : 220)	4,00,909
Long-term capital gain	22,091
Other income	20,00,000
Net income	22,22,090

	Rs.
Computation of tax –	
Income-tax on long-term capital gain under section 112 [20% of Rs. 22,091 or 10% of capital gain without indexation of Rs. 1,08,000, whichever is lower]	4,418
Tax on other income	4,12,500
Income-tax	4,16,918
Add: Health and education cess	16,677
Tax liability (rounded off)	4,33,600

72.2-E3 X (61 years) acquires 10,000 equity shares in B Ltd. on March 16, 2006. He gets 8,000 bonus shares on March 11, 2013. X transfers original shares in the previous year 2014-15. He transfers 5,000 bonus shares on November 2, 2018 at the rate of Rs. 900 per share (securities transaction tax is paid at the time of transfer). Fair market value of shares in B Ltd. as per Bombay Stock Exchange quotation is Rs. 300 on January 31, 2018. Income of X for the previous year 2018-19 from other sources is Rs. 26,40,000. He has a brought forward short-term capital loss of Rs. 2,90,000 pertaining to the assessment year 2015-16.

•

Section 112A is applicable only if 4 conditions are satisfied [*see* para 72.2]. First 3 conditions are satisfied. *Condition 4* is not applicable in a few notified cases (securities transaction tax is not paid at the time of acquisition of bonus shares, these shares are issued by the company, this transaction is covered by the notification issued by CBDT). Consequently, tax is calculated under section 112A as follows –

	Rs.
Full value of consideration (Rs. 900 × 5,000)	45,00,000
Less: Cost of acquisition [*Step 1* - Actual cost : *Nil*, *Step 2* - Fair market value on January 31, 2018 : Rs. 300, whichever is more] (Rs. 300 × 5,000)	15,00,000
Long-term capital gain	30,00,000
Less: Brought forward capital loss	2,90,000
Long-term capital gain	27,10,000
Other income	26,40,000
Net income	53,50,000
Computation of tax –	
Income-tax on long-term capital gain under section 112A [10% of (Rs. 27,10,000 – Rs. 1,00,000)]	2,61,000
Income-tax on other income of Rs. 26,40,000	6,02,000
Income-tax	8,63,000
Add: Surcharge	86,300
Income-tax and surcharge	9,49,300
Add: Health and education cess	37,972
Tax liability (rounded off)	9,87,270

72.2-E4 X (61 years) acquires 10,000 unlisted equity shares in B Ltd. on March 16, 1986. He gets 5,000 bonus shares –
- **on July 15, 1999 (fair market value on April 1, 2001 : Rs. 20 per share, on the basis of net asset value) [*Situation 1*]; or**
- **on July 15, 2001 (fair market value on April 1, 2001 : Rs. 20 per share, on the basis of net asset value) [*Situation 2*].**

X transfers original shares in the previous year 2002-03. He transfers 5,000 bonus shares on December 20, 2018 at the rate of Rs. 600 per share (transfer transacted at NSE and STT paid). Find out the amount of long-term capital gain on transfer of bonus shares. Shares in B Ltd. are quoted for the first time on August 31, 2018.

•

			Situation 1 *Rs.*	*Situation 2* *Rs.*
Step 1	- Cost of acquisition of bonus shares	(*a*)	20	*Nil*
Step 2	- Fair market value on January 31, 2018	(*b*)	54.40[28]	*Nil*[29]
	- Selling price on December 20, 2018	(*c*)	600	600
	- [lower of (*b*) or (*c*)]	(*d*)	54.40	*Nil*
Cost of acquisition for the purpose of section 112A [(*a*) or (*d*), whichever is higher]		(*e*)	54.40	*Nil*
Long-term capital gain under section 112A [(*c*) – (*e*)] [5,000 × (Rs. 600 – Rs. 54.40 in *Situation 1* and 0 in *Situation 2*)]			27,28,000	30,00,000

28. Rs. 20 × CII of 2017-18 : 272 ÷ CII of 2001-02 : 100.
29. Rs. 0 × CII of 2017-18 : 272 ÷ CII of 2001-02 : 100.

72.2-E5 X (38 years) transfers the following capital assets during the previous year 2018-19 –

	Equity shares (A Ltd.) Rs.	*Equity shares (B Ltd.) Rs.*	*Equity shares (C Ltd.) Rs*	*House property Rs.*
Full value of consideration	6,70,000	8,000	98,000	80,00,000
Cost of acquisition (all assets were acquired in 1997-98)	40,000	51,000	90,000	8,00,000
Fair market value on April 1, 2001	42,000	54,000	92,000	10,50,000
Fair market value on January 31, 2018 (as per Bombay Stock Exchange market quotation)	4,80,000	68,000	30,000	–

Securities transaction tax is paid at the time of transfer (as well as at the time of acquisition) of these shares. X has a brought forward long-term capital loss pertaining to transfer of unlisted shares during the previous year 2011-12 (amount of loss being Rs. 47,94,000). Income of X from other sources for the previous year 2018-19 is Rs. 67,90,000.

•

Computation of cost of acquisition for the purpose of section 112A –

		A Ltd. Rs.	*B Ltd. Rs.*	*C Ltd. Rs*
Step 1 - Cost of acquisition (actual cost of acquisition or fair market value on April 1, 2001, whichever is higher)	(*a*)	42,000	54,000	92,000
Step 2 - Fair market value as per highest quotation on January 31, 2018	(*b*)	4,80,000	68,000	30,000
- Selling price during the previous year 2018-19	(*c*)	6,70,000	8,000	98,000
- [lower of (*b*) or (*c*)]	(*d*)	4,80,000	8,000	30,000
Cost of acquisition for the purpose of section 112A [(*a*) or (*d*), whichever is higher]	(*e*)	4,80,000	54,000	92,000

Computation of capital gain –

	Equity shares (A Ltd.) Rs.	*Equity shares (B Ltd.) Rs.*	*Equity shares (C Ltd.) Rs*	*House property Rs.*
Full value of consideration	6,70,000	8,000	98,000	80,00,000
Less: Cost of acquisition	4,80,000	54,000	92,000	–
Less: Indexed cost of acquisition [Rs. 10,50,000 × 280 (assumed figure) ÷ 100]	–	–	–	29,40,000
Capital gains	1,90,000	(–) 46,000	6,000	50,60,000
Less: Long-term capital loss on transfer of shares in B Ltd.	–	(+) 46,000	–	(–) 46,000
Less: Brought forward loss pertaining to transfer of unlisted shares	–	–	–	(–) 47,94,000
Long-term capital gain	1,90,000	*Nil*	6,000	2,20,000

Computation of total income and tax liability –

	Rs.
Long-term capital gain –	
- Taxable under section 112A	1,96,000
- Taxable under section 112	2,20,000
Other income	67,90,000
Net income	72,06,000

Computation of tax	*Rs.*
Income-tax on long-term capital gain under section 112A (10% of Rs. 96,000)	9,600
Income-tax on long-term capital gain under section 112 (20% of Rs. 2,20,000)	44,000
Income-tax on other income of Rs. 67,90,000	18,49,500
Income-tax	19,03,100
Add: Surcharge	1,90,310
Income-tax and surcharge	20,93,410
Add: Health and education cess	83,736
Tax liability (rounded off)	21,77,150

72.2-E6 X (48 years) transfers the following assets during the previous year 2018-19 –

	Gold *Rs.*	*Equity oriented mutual fund units* *Rs.*	*House property* *Rs.*
Full value of consideration	7,00,000	10,00,000	80,00,000
Stamp duty value	–	–	84,00,000
Cost of acquisition (all assets were acquired during 2002-03)	2,04,286	3,00,000	20,42,857
Market quotation on January 31, 2018 in stock exchange	–	Not available	–
NAV on January 31, 2018	–	5,00,000	–

Securities transaction tax is paid at the time of transfer of mutual fund units. X purchases a residential house property for Rs. 32,00,000 on April 10, 2019 (he does not own any house property). Income of X from other sources is Rs. 27,00,000.

•

	Gold *Rs.*	*Equity oriented mutual fund units* *Rs.*	*House property* *Rs.*
Full value of consideration	7,00,000	10,00,000	80,00,000
Less: Cost of acquisition (being NAV on January 31, 2018 in the absence of market quotation)	–	5,00,000	–
Less: Indexed cost of acquisition [Rs. 2,04,286 × 280 ÷ 105, Rs. 20,42,857 × 280 ÷ 105]	5,44,763		54,47,619
Capital gain before exemption	1,55,237	5,00,000	25,52,381
Less: Exemption under section 54	–	–	25,52,381
Less: Exemption under section 54F [investment in house property : Rs. 6,47,619 (*i.e.,* Rs. 32,00,000 – Rs. 25,52,387) ÷ Rs. 7,00,000 × Rs. 1,55,237]	1,43,621	–	–
Long-term capital gain	11,616	5,00,000	*Nil*

Computation of income and tax –

	Rs.
Long-term capital gain taxable under section 112	11,616
Long-term capital gain taxable under section 112A	5,00,000
Other income	27,00,000
Net income	32,11,620

Computation of tax	*Rs.*
Income-tax on long-term capital gain under section 112A (10% of Rs. 4,00,000)	40,000
Income-tax on long-term capital gain under section 112 (20% of Rs. 11,616)	2,323
Income-tax on other income of Rs. 27,00,000	6,22,500
Income-tax	6,64,823
Add: Health and education cess	26,593
Tax liability (rounded off)	6,91,420

Note - In the above calculations, exemption under section 54F is taken against capital gain which arises on transfer of gold. Alternatively, it can be taken against capital gain which arises on transfer of mutual fund units (if it is otherwise beneficial to the taxpayer). One can make alternative calculations as follows –

	Gold Rs.	*Equity oriented mutual fund units* Rs.	*House property* Rs.
Capital gain before exemption	1,55,237	5,00,000	25,52,381
Less: Exemption under section 54	–	–	25,52,381
Less: Exemption under section 54F [investment in house property : Rs. 6,47,619 (*i.e.*, Rs. 32,00,000 – Rs. 25,52,381) ÷ Rs. 10,00,000 × Rs. 5,00,000]	–	3,23,810	–
Long-term capital gain	1,55,238	1,76,190	*Nil*

Computation of income and tax –

	Rs.
Long-term capital gain taxable under section 112	1,55,238
Long-term capital gain taxable under section 112A	1,76,190
Other income	27,00,000
Net income	30,31,430
Computation of tax	
Income-tax on long-term capital gain under section 112A (10% of Rs. 76,190)	7,619
Income-tax on long-term capital gain under section 112 (20% of Rs. 1,55,238)	31,048
Income-tax on other income of Rs. 27,00,000	6,22,500
Income-tax	6,61,167
Add: Health and education cess	26,447
Tax liability (rounded off)	6,87,610

Consequently, it is beneficial for the taxpayer to avail of exemption under section 54F against capital gain which arises on transfer of units of equity oriented mutual funds.

72.2-E7 X (25 years) acquires 800 shares in A Ltd. in 1996-97 for Rs. 2,00,000 (shares in A Ltd. are not quoted). Fair market value of these shares on first of April 2001 is Rs. 2,10,000. A Ltd. is amalgamated with B Ltd. on December 1, 2017. X is allotted 400 shares in B Ltd. in lieu of shares in A Ltd. X transfers 400 shares in B Ltd. on May 6, 2018 for Rs. 45,00,000 (transacted at NSE, STT paid). Income of X from other sources for the previous year 2018-19 is Rs. 16,00,000. On December 1, 2018, X transfers a short-term capital asset and incurs a loss of Rs. 24,10,000. Find out tax liability for the assessment year 2019-20 under the following different situations –

Situation 1 - Shares in B Ltd. are listed in NSE and market quotation on January 31, 2018 is Rs. 5,000 per share.

Situation 2 - Shares in B Ltd. are listed only with effect from February 25, 2018.

•

	Situation 1 Rs.	*Situation 2* Rs.
Full value of consideration	45,00,000	45,00,000
Less:		
Securities transaction tax	–	–
Cost of acquisition [being Rs. 5,000 (market quotation on January 31, 2018) × 400]	20,00,000	–
Cost of acquisition [Rs. 2,10,000 × CII of 2017-18 : 272 ÷ CII of 2001-02 : 100]	–	5,71,200
Long-term capital gain	25,00,000	39,28,800
Less: Short-term capital loss	24,10,000	24,10,000
Balance long-term capital gain	90,000	15,18,800
Other income	16,00,000	16,00,000
Net income	16,90,000	31,18,800

	Situation 1 Rs.	Situation 2 Rs.
Computation of tax		
Income-tax on long-term capital gain under section 112A (10% of Rs. 14,18,000)	*Nil*	1,41,800
Income-tax on other income of Rs. 16,00,000	2,92,500	2,92,500
Income-tax	2,92,500	4,34,300
Add: Health and education cess	11,700	17,372
Tax liability (rounded off)	3,04,200	4,51,670

72.3 ***Tax on short-term capital gain if securities transaction tax is not applicable*** - If securities transaction tax is not applicable, short-term capital gain is taxable like any other income (no special rate).

72.4 ***Tax on short-term capital gain if securities transaction tax is applicable*** - Short-term capital gain is taxable at the rate of 15 per cent [+ SC + HEC][30] under section 111A. This rule is applicable in the case of short-term capital gain which arises on transfer of a capital asset [being equity shares in a company or a unit of equity oriented fund (**as defined for the purpose of section 112A**) or a unit of business trust] and transaction is chargeable to securities transaction tax at the time of transfer. This concessional tax treatment is also applicable if transaction is undertaken in foreign currency on a recognised stock exchange located in an International Financial Services Centre[31].

72.4-1 *DEDUCTIONS UNDER SECTIONS 80C TO 80U ARE NOT AVAILABLE* - Deductions under sections 80C to 80U are not available in respect of short-term capital gain, if securities transaction tax is applicable.

72.4-2 *EXEMPTION LIMIT IN SOME CASES [PROVISO TO SEC. 111A]* - Short-term capital gain (where securities transaction tax is applicable) is taxable at the rate of 15 per cent. The entire amount is taxable at 15 per cent (no exemption limit). However, in the case of a resident individual/HUF, the benefit of exemption limit[32] is available if taxable income (*minus* short-term capital gain, which is subject to securities transaction tax) is less than exemption limit. In such a case, the following shall be deducted from the short-term capital gain –

> Exemption limit—(Net income or taxable income–Short-term capital gain, where securities transaction tax is applicable)

After deducting the aforesaid amount, the balance amount of short-term capital gain is chargeable to tax at the rate of 15 per cent [+ SC + HEC].

Provisions illustrated - Mrs. X (58 years) is a resident individual. For the assessment year 2018-19, she has the following incomes—

	Rs.
Short-term capital gain on transfer of shares (securities transaction tax is applicable) (ST)	24,000
Short-term capital gain on transfer of gold	45,000
Bank interest	36,000
Salary income (after standard deduction)	1,62,000
Net income (NI)	2,67,000

30. *See* para 72.1.

31. "International Financial Services Centre" means an International Financial Services Centre which is set-up in a special economic zone and approved by the Central Government under section 18(1) of Special Economic Zone Act, 2005.

32. Exemption limit for the assessment year 2019-20 is Rs. 2,50,000 [higher exemption limit (*a*) in the case of a resident senior citizen born on or after April 2, 1939 but on or before April 1, 1959: Rs. 3,00,000; and (*b*) in the case of a resident super senior citizen born on or before April 1, 1939: Rs. 5,00,000].
Exemption limit for the assessment year 2020-21 is Rs. 2,50,000 [higher exemption limit (*a*) in the case of a resident senior citizen born on or after April 2, 1940 but on or before April 1, 1960: Rs. 3,00,000; and (*b*) in the case of a resident super senior citizen born on or before April 1, 1940: Rs. 5,00,000].

In this case, Mrs. X is a resident individual. Her exemption limit is Rs. 2,50,000. Taxable income (*minus* short-term capital gain subject to securities transaction tax) is Rs. 2,43,000. It is less than exemption limit. Consequently, from the short-term capital gain the following shall be deducted—

Rs. 2,50,000 (exemption limit)—[Rs. 2,67,000 (NI)—Rs. 24,000 (ST)] = Rs. 7,000

In this case, the short-term capital gain chargeable to tax will be Rs. 17,000 (*i.e.*, Rs. 24,000 – Rs. 7,000).

Hints for tax planning

73. For the purpose of tax planning the following propositions should be borne in mind. However, these propositions would hold good in the context in which they have been made :

• Since long-term capital gains bear lower tax, taxpayer should so plan as to transfer their capital assets normally only 36[33] months after acquisition. It is pertinent to note that if capital asset is one which becomes the property of the taxpayer in any of the manner specified in para 66.1-1 the period for which they were held by the previous owner is also to be counted in computing 36[33] months.

• If a property is transferred by an individual to his minor son without adequate consideration, it should be sold only after the son attains majority in order to avoid clubbing of income under section 64.

• The assessee should take advantage of the exemption under section 54 by investing the capital gain arising from the sale of a residential house property in the purchase of another house within the specified period. It may be noted that for claiming exemption for the assessment year 2015-16 (or any subsequent year), the new house property should be situated in India.

• In order to claim advantage of the exemptions under sections 54B, 54D and 54EC it should be ensured that the investment in the new asset is made only after effecting transfer of capital assets.

• In order to take the advantage of exemption under sections 54, 54B, 54D, 54EC, 54F, 54G, 54GA and 54GB, the taxpayer should ensure that the newly acquired asset is not transferred within the specified period from the date of acquisition. In this context, it is interesting to note that the transfer of newly acquired asset according to the modes mentioned in para 62.2 is not regarded as "transfer" even for this purpose. Consequently, newly acquired assets may be transferred even within the specified period of their acquisition according to the modes mentioned in para 62.2 without attracting capital gains tax liability. Alternatively, it will be advisable that instead of selling or converting assets acquired under sections 54, 54B, 54D, 54F, 54G, 54GA and 54GB, into money, the taxpayer should obtain loan against the security of such asset (even by pledge) to meet the exigency.

• In two cases, surplus arising on sale or transfer of capital assets is chargeable to tax as short-term capital gain by virtue of section 50. These cases are : (*a*) when the written down value of a block of assets is reduced to *nil*, though all the assets falling in that block are not transferred, (*b*) when a block of assets ceases to exist. Tax on short-term capital gain can be avoided if :

a. another capital asset, falling in that block of asset, is acquired at any time during the previous year; or

b. benefit of section 54G is availed.

Taxpayers desiring to avoid tax on short-term capital gains under section 50 on sale or transfer of a capital asset, can acquire another capital asset, falling in that block of assets, at any time during the previous year. A major part of the investment can be financed out of tax saving.

33. 12 month/24 months in a few cases [*see* para 61].

Income from other sources

	Para number
PRE-COMPUTATION STEPS	
❑ Check whether income is taxable under section 56	76 and 77
COMPUTATION STEPS	
❑ Determine income taxable as income from other sources	77
❑ Make deductions provided by section 57	78

Basis of charge [Sec. 56(1)]

76. This is the last and residual head of charge of income. A *source* of income which does not specifically fall under any one of the other four heads of income (*viz.*, "Salaries", "Income from house property", "Profits and gains of business or profession" or "Capital gains") is to be computed and brought to charge under section 56 under the head "Income from other sources". In other words, it can be said that the residuary head of income can be resorted to only if none of the specific heads is applicable to the income in question, and that it comes into operation only if the preceding heads are excluded.

Some incomes taxable under section 56(1) under the head "Income from other sources" are : Income from subletting, interest on bank deposits and loans, income from royalty, director's fees, ground rent, agricultural income from outside India, director's commission for standing as a guarantor to bankers, director's commission for underwriting shares of a new company, examination fees received by a teacher, rent of a plot of land, insurance commission, mining rent and royalties, interest on foreign Government securities, casual income, annuity payable under a will, and salaries payable to a Member of Parliament.

Chargeable income [Sec. 56(2)]

77. By virtue of section 56(2), the following incomes are chargeable to tax under this head, namely, dividends, winnings from lotteries, crossword puzzles, horse races, card games, etc., income from machinery, plant or furniture let on hire and interest on securities (if the same is not taxable as business income under section 28). In some cases, gift is taxable under this head [*see* para 77.5]. Besides, interest received on compensation or enhanced compensation is taxable under the head "Income from other sources" in the year in which it is received (applicable from the assessment year 2010-11).

77.1 ***Dividend [Sec. 56(2)(i)]*** - Under section 2(*22*), the following payments or distributions by a company to its shareholders are deemed as dividends to the extent of accumulated profits[34] of the company—

a. any distribution entailing the release of the company's assets [sec. 2(*22*)(*a*)];

b. any distribution of debentures, debenture-stock, deposit certificates and bonus to preference shareholders [sec. 2(*22*)(*b*)];

c. distribution on liquidation of the company [sec. 2(*22*)(*c*)];

d. distribution on reduction of capital [sec. 2(*22*)(*d*)]; and

e. any payment by way of advance or loan to the following :

   i. a shareholder (being a person who is beneficial owner of equity shares) holding not less than 10 per cent of the voting power; or

   ii. any concern in which such shareholder is a member or a partner and in which he has substantial interest [sec. 2(*22*)(*e*)].

34. Accumulated profits include all profits of a company up to the date of distribution or payment. However, in the case of a company in liquidation it includes all profits of the company up to the date of liquidation. Where, the liquidation is consequent on the compulsory acquisition of a company's undertaking by the Government or a Government company, accumulated profits do not include any profits of the company prior to the three successive years immediately preceding the previous year in which such acquisition took place. With effect from the assessment year 2018-19, *Explanation 2A* has been inserted in section 2(*22*) to widen the scope of the term 'accumulated profits' so as to provide that in the case of an amalgamated company, accumulated profits (whether capitalised or not) or losses, shall be increased by the accumulated profits of the amalgamating company (whether capitalized or not) on the date of amalgamation.

• The following points should be noted—

1. Under section 2(*22*)(*e*), the amount advanced for business transaction would not fall within the definition of 'deemed dividend'. In other words, if the amount advanced does not bear the characteristics of loans and advances, section 2(*22*)(*e*) is not applicable—*CIT* v. *Creative Dyeing & Printing (P.) Ltd.* [2009] 184 Taxman 483 (Delhi).

2. Where money-lending (giving loan) is a substantial part of the business of the company, the provisions of section 2(*22*)(*e*) are not applicable. For this purpose, the factual position as it stands during relevant previous year alone is supposed to be taken into consideration to decide the issue whether lending of money is substantial part of business of concerned company—*Rekha Modi* v. *ITO* [2007] 13 SOT 512 (Delhi). In *CIT* v. *Parle Plastic Ltd.* [2011] 196 Taxman 62, the Bombay High Court explained the expression "substantial part of the business". It pointed out that the term 'substantial' does not mean major and there is nothing in law that suggests that in order to show that a part of the whole to be treated as "substantial part", the part must exceed 50 per cent of the whole.

3. Any subsequent dividend to the extent it is set off against any loan or advance [deemed as dividend under section 2(*22*)(*e*)] is not treated as "dividend".

4. The expression "concern" for the purpose of this provision, means a Hindu undivided family or a firm or an association of persons or a body of individuals or a company. Further, a person shall be deemed to have a substantial interest in a concern, other than a company, if such person is at any time during the previous year beneficially entitled to not less than 20 per cent of the income of such concern. In relation to a company, the provisions of section 2(*32*) will apply.

5. The following shall not be treated as "dividend"—

a. any payment made by a company on purchase of its own shares in accordance with the provisions contained in section 77A of the Companies Act; or

b. any distribution of shares made in accordance with the scheme of demerger by the resulting company to the shareholders of the demerged company whether or not there is a reduction of capital in the demerged company.

77.1-1 *TAX TREATMENT IN THE HANDS OF SHAREHOLDERS* - Tax treatment is given below —

Status of the company which declares dividend	*Taxability in the hands of shareholders*	*Dividend distribution tax payable by company which declares dividend*
A : Non-domestic company	It is taxable in the hands of a shareholder (if it is received in India or if the shareholder is resident and ordinarily resident in India)	No dividend distribution tax
B: Domestic company [not being dividend under section 2(*22*)(*e*)]	*General rule* - In the hands of shareholder, such dividend is exempt under section 10(*34*). *Exception* - From the assessment year 2017-18, dividend income is taxable in the hands of shareholders under section 115BBDA, if a few conditions are satisfied (provisions of section 115BBDA are given below)	The company (which declares dividend) is required to pay dividend distribution tax under section 115-O. It is applicable even if the shareholder is subject to tax under section 115BBDA
C: Domestic company [being loan or advance deemed as dividend under section 2(*22*)(*e*)]		
❑ Deemed dividend distribution up to March 31, 2018	Taxable in the hands of recipient under section 56 under the head "Income from other sources"	No dividend distribution tax under section 115-O
❑ Deemed dividend distribution on or after April 1, 2018	Not taxable in the hands of recipient by virtue of exemption given by section 10(*34*)	The company (which distributes deemed dividend as loan or advance) is liable for dividend distribution tax under section 115-O at the rate of 30 per cent (+ SC + HEC, effective rate is 34.944 per cent).

77.1-1a *DIVIDEND TAXABLE UNDER SECTION 115BBDA* - Section 115BBDA is applicable if the following two conditions are satisfied –

1. The assessee (*i.e.*, shareholder who gets dividend from domestic company/companies) is resident in India. He is any resident person [but not being a domestic company, or a fund/institution/trust/university/educational institution/hospital/other medical institution referred to in section 10(*23C*)(*iv*)/(*v*)/(*vi*)/(*via*), or a trust/institution registered under section 12A/12AA].

2. Total income of the assessee includes any income in aggregate exceeding Rs. 10 lakh by way of dividend [not being deemed dividend under section 2(*22*)(*e*)] declared/distributed or paid by a domestic company or companies.

If the above two conditions are satisfied, dividend income from domestic companies in excess of Rs. 10 lakh is chargeable to tax at the rate of 10 per cent [+ SC + HEC]. Taxation of dividend income in excess of Rs. 10 lakh shall be on gross basis. However, tax under section 115BBDA is not applicable in the case of deemed dividend under section 2(*22*)(*e*).

77.1-1E1 Find out the tax liability for the assessment year 2019-20 in the following cases (B is non-resident, all other taxpayers are resident) –

	X (40 years)	*Y (45 years)*	*Z (firm)*	*A Ltd.*	*B (61 years)*
	Rs.	*Rs.*	*Rs.*	*Rs.*	*Rs.*
Business income of the previous year 2018-19	3,00,000	40,00,000	40,00,000	40,00,000	23,00,000
Dividend [not being deemed dividend under section 2(*22*)(*e*)] from different domestic companies (dividend tax is paid by these companies) –					
- from D Ltd.	40,00,000	9,60,000	15,000	11,00,000	40,00,000
- from E Ltd.	10,000	*Nil*	3,000	18,00,000	10,000
- from F Ltd.	8,90,000	*Nil*	29,82,000	21,00,000	8,90,000
Expenditure for earning above dividend income	2,60,000	90,000	80,000	12,00,000	2,60,000
Deemed dividend [under section 2(*22*)(*e*)] received from G Ltd. (dividend tax is paid by G Ltd.)	7,00,000	17,00,000	80,000	11,85,000	20,10,000
Deduction under sections 80C to 80U	4,10,000	2,15,000	7,00,000	8,18,000	4,10,000

•

Aggregate dividend [not being deemed dividend under section 2(*22*)(*e*)] from all domestic companies	49,00,000	9,60,000	30,00,000	50,00,000	49,00,000
Less: Expenses (not deductible)	*Nil*	*Nil*	*Nil*	*Nil*	*Nil*
Balance	49,00,000	9,60,000	30,00,000	50,00,000	49,00,000
Less: Dividend income exempt under section 10(*34*)	10,00,000	9,60,000	10,00,000	50,00,000	49,00,000
Dividend (taxable under section 115BBDA) (no deduction is allowed) (*a*)	39,00,000	*Nil*	20,00,000	*Nil*	*Nil*
Other incomes –					
Deemed dividend under section 2(*22*)(*e*) [exempt under section 10(*34*)]	*Nil*	*Nil*	*Nil*	*Nil*	*Nil*
Business income	3,00,000	40,00,000	40,00,000	40,00,000	23,00,000
Total of other incomes	3,00,000	40,00,000	40,00,000	40,00,000	23,00,000
Less: Deduction under sections 80C to 80U	4,10,000	2,15,000	7,00,000	8,18,000	4,10,000
Income (other than dividend income taxable under section 115BBDA) (*b*)	*Nil*	37,85,000	33,00,000	31,82,000	18,90,000
Net income/total income [(*a*) + (*b*)]	39,00,000	37,85,000	53,00,000	31,82,000	18,90,000
Tax on net income					
Tax on dividend income under section 115BBDA [*i.e.*, 10% of (*a*)]	3,90,000	*Nil*	2,00,000	*Nil*	*Nil*
Tax on balance	*Nil*	9,48,000	9,90,000	9,54,600	3,79,500
Total	3,90,000	9,48,000	11,90,000	9,54,600	3,79,500
Add : Health and education cess	15,600	37,920	47,600	38,184	15,180
Tax liability (rounded off)	4,05,600	9,85,920	12,37,600	9,92,780	3,94,680

77.2 ***Winnings from lotteries, crossword puzzles, horse races and card games, etc.*** - Gross winnings from lotteries, crossword puzzles, races including horse races (other than income from the activity of owning and maintaining race horses), card games and other games of any sort or from gambling or betting of any nature whatsoever shall be chargeable to income-tax under section 115BB[35] at a flat rate of 30 per cent (without claiming any allowance or expenditure).

Meaning of "lottery" and "card games" - From the assessment year 2002-03, the expression "lottery" includes winnings from prizes awarded to any person by draw of lots or by chance or in any other manner whatsoever, under any scheme or arrangement by whatever name called and "card game and other game of any sort" includes any game show, an entertainment programme on television or electronic mode, in which people compete to win prizes or any other similar game.

77.3 ***Interest on securities*** - Interest on securities is taxable under the head "Income from other sources" if the same is not taxable as business income under section 28. If books of account in respect of such income are maintained on "cash basis", then the interest is taxable on "receipt basis". If, however, books of account are not maintained or are maintained on the basis of mercantile system of accounting, then interest on securities is taxable on "accrual" basis.

77.3-1 *INTEREST EXEMPT UNDER SECTION 10(15)*[36] - Interest on the following is exempt from tax :

• Interest on notified securities, bonds and certificates. The notified securities/bonds, etc., are : 12 - years National Savings Annuity Certificates; National Defence Gold Bonds, 1980; Special Bearer Bonds, 1991; Treasury Savings Deposit Certificates; Post Office Cash Certificates (5 years); National Plan Certificates (10 years); National Plan Savings Certificates (12 years); Post Office National Savings Certificates (12 years/7 years); Public Account of Post Office Savings Account Rules (interest up to Rs. 5,000); Post Office Saving Rules; Post Office CTD; Fixed Deposit [Government Savings Certificates (Fixed Deposit) Rules, 1968 or Post Office (Fixed Deposit) Rules, 1968]; Special Deposit Scheme, 1981 and Non-Resident (Non-Repatriable) Rupee Deposit Scheme.

• Interest to an individual and Hindu undivided family on 7 per cent Capital Investment Bonds.

• Interest on notified bonds arising to non-resident Indians [*i.e.*, NRI Bonds, and NRI Bonds (Second Series), issued by the State Bank of India].

• Interest on securities held by the Issue Department of the Central Bank of Ceylon.

• Interest payable to any foreign bank performing central banking functions outside India in respect of deposits made by such bank with any scheduled bank in India.

• Interest on 9 per cent Relief Bonds, 1987 in the case of an individual or a Hindu undivided family.

• Interest on notified debentures of public sector companies—*see Taxmann's Direct Taxes Circulars.*

• Interest on deposits made in a notified scheme by a retired Government employee and an employee of a public sector company out of the money due to him on account of retirement. No tax liability under the Income-tax Act will arise on the amount payable to the nominee on the death of the depositor. Interest income of a spouse nominee after employee's death is exempt if the nominee opts to continue the account. If the nominee is not the spouse of the depositor, the amount lying to the credit of the depositor will devolve upon the nominee as a capital receipt on which no income-tax shall be payable at the time of devolution.

77.4 ***Income from machinery, plant or furniture let on hire [Sec. 56(2)(ii)/(iii)]*** - Income from machinery, plant or furniture belonging to the assessee and let on hire is taxable as income from other sources if the same is not chargeable to tax under the head "Profits and gains of business or profession". When an assessee lets on hire machinery, plant or furniture and also building and letting of building is inseparable from the letting of machinery, plant or furniture, the income from the letting of building is taxable as income from other sources if the same is not chargeable to tax under the head "Profits and gains of business or profession".

77.5 ***Money/property is received without consideration or for inadequate consideration [Sec. 56(2)]*** - These provisions are regulated by different clauses of section 56(2) as follows –

---

35. Section 115BB is applicable and winnings from lotteries, crossword puzzles, horse races, etc., are taxable at the rate of 30 per cent irrespective of the fact whether such income is taxable as business income or income from other sources — *CIT* v. *Manjoo & Co.* [2010] 195 Taxman 39 (Ker.).

36. From the assessment year 2012-13, Post Office Savings Bank Account interest will be exempt only to the extent of Rs. 3,500 in the case of an individual account and Rs. 7,000 in the case of joint account. Moreover, one can claim deduction under section 80TTA [*See* para 107.31].

Section	*Recipient of property (who is chargeable to tax)*	*Property covered*	*Period during which property is received*	*Para No.*
56(2)(*v*)	Individual/HUF	Sum of money exceeding Rs. 25,000	On or after September 1, 2004 but before April 1, 2006	77.5-3
56(2)(*vi*)	Individual/HUF	Sum of money exceeding Rs. 50,000	On or after April 1, 2006 but before October 1, 2009	77.5-2
56(2)(*vii*)	Individual/HUF	Money/property[37] under 5 different categories	On or after October 1, 2009 but before April 1, 2017	77.5-1
56(2)(*viia*)	Firm/closely held company	Shares of a closely held company	On or after June 1, 2010 but before April 1, 2017	77.6
56(2)(*x*)	Any person	Money/property[37] under 5 different categories	On or after April 1, 2017	77.5-1

77.5-1 *MONEY/PROPERTY[37] RECEIVED WITHOUT CONSIDERATION OR INADEQUATE CONSIDERATION [SEC. 56(2)(vii)/(x)]* - Section 56(2)(*vii*) is applicable when sum of money/property[37] is received by an individual/HUF on or after October 1, 2009 and money/property[37] falls in any of the following 5 categories. The scope of this provision has been extended by section 56(2)(*x*). The extended version is applicable when a sum of money/property[37] is received by any person on or after April 1, 2017 and money/property[37] falls in any of the following 5 categories.

• *Five categories* - Receipt of sum of money/property should fall in any of the following five categories—

Different categories	*Tax treatment*	*For the ceiling of Rs. 50,000 whether a single transaction would be examined or all transactions of the previous year will be considered*
Category 1 - Any sum of money (gift in cash or by cheque or draft)	If aggregate amount of sum of money received without any consideration from one or more persons during a previous year exceeds Rs. 50,000, the whole of such aggregate value is chargeable to tax	All transactions
Category 2 - Immovable property without consideration	If any immovable property (without any consideration) is received and the stamp duty value of which exceeds Rs. 50,000, stamp duty value is chargeable to tax.	Single transaction
Category 3 - Immovable property for a consideration (applicable from the assessment year 2014-15)	• *From the assessment year 2019-20* - An immovable property is received for a consideration. The transaction satisfies the following conditions – *a.* stamp duty value exceeds 105 per cent of consideration; and *b.* the difference between stamp duty value and consideration is more than Rs. 50,000. If the above two conditions are satisfied, the difference between stamp duty value and consideration is chargeable to tax. • *Up to the assessment year 2018-19* - An immovable property is received for a consideration. The transaction satisfies the following conditions – *a.* stamp duty value exceeds consideration; and *b.* the difference between stamp duty value and consideration is more than Rs. 50,000. If the above two conditions are satisfied, the difference between stamp duty value and consideration is chargeable to tax.	Single transaction

37. "Property" for this purpose means the following capital asset of the assessee (*i.e.*, recipient) : (*i*) immovable property being land or building or both; (*ii*) shares and securities; (*iii*) jewellery; (*iv*) archaeological collection; (*v*) drawings; (*vi*) paintings; (*vii*) sculptures; (*viii*) any work of art, or (*ix*) (with effect from June 1, 2010) bullion.

38. "Movable property" for this purpose means the following capital asset of the assessee (*i.e.*, recipient) : shares and securities; jewellery; archaeological collections; drawings; painting; sculptures; any work of art, or (with effect from June 1, 2010) bullion.

Different categories	*Tax treatment*	*For the ceiling of Rs. 50,000 whether a single transaction would be examined or all transactions of the previous year will be considered*
Category 4 - Movable property[38] without consideration	If aggregate fair market value of movable properties received without consideration during a previous year exceeds Rs. 50,000, the whole of aggregate fair market value of movable property[38] or properties is chargeable to tax.	All transactions
Category 5 - Movable property[38] for a consideration which is less than fair market value	If movable property[38] is received for a consideration which is less than the aggregate fair market value of the property[38] by an amount exceeding Rs. 50,000, then the difference between aggregate fair market value and the consideration is chargeable to tax.	All transactions

• *Exempted categories* - While calculating the above monetary limit of Rs. 50,000 in any of the five categories, any sum of money or property* received from the following shall not be considered—

1. Money/property[37] received from a relative.

2. Money/property[37] received on the occasion of the marriage of the individual.

3. Money/property[37] received by way of will/inheritance.

4. Money/property[37] received in contemplation of death of the payer.

5. Money/property[37] received from a local authority.

6. Money/property[37] received from any fund, foundation, university, other educational institution, hospital, medical institution, any trust or institution referred to in section 10(*23C*).

7. Money/property[37] received from a charitable institute registered under section 12A/12AA.

8. Money/property received by any fund/trust/university/other educational institutions/hospital/other medical institution referred to in section 10(*23C*)(*iv*)/(*v*)/(*vi*)/(*via*) (applicable if money/property is received on or after April 1, 2017).

9. Money/property received by way of the following transactions which are not regarded as transfer under section 47 –

Received on or after April 1, 2016 –
- Shares received at the time of business re-organisation of a co-operative bank [sec. 47(*vicb*)] - Shares received at the time of demerger [sec. 47(*vid*)] - Shares received at the time of amalgamation [sec. 47(*vii*)]
Received on or after April 1, 2017 –
- Property received by way of distribution at the time of total or partial partition of HUF [sec. 47(*i*)] - Property received by an Indian holding company from its 100 per cent subsidiary company or property received by an Indian subsidiary company from its 100 per cent holding company [sec. 47(*iv*)/(*v*)] - Property received in a scheme of amalgamation/demerger [sec. 47(*vi*)/(*vib*)] - Shares received at the time of amalgamation/demerger of foreign companies [sec. 47(*via*)/(*vic*)] - Property received in a scheme of amalgamation of banking company [sec. 47(*viaa*)] - Property received at the time of business re-organisation of co-operative bank [sec. 47(*vica*)].

10. Money/property[37] received from an individual by a trust created or established solely for the benefit of relative of the individual (applicable if money/property is received on or after April 1, 2017).

11. Money or property[37] **received from such class of persons and subject to such conditions, as may be prescribed** (applicable from the assessment year 2020-21).

77.5-1a OTHER RELEVANT POINTS - The following points should be noted—

1. The value of movable property[38] shall be the fair market value as on the date of receipt in accordance with the method given in rules 11U and 11UA[$] [*see* para 77.5-1b]. In the case of immovable property, the value of the property shall be the stamp duty value of the property.

---

37. See previous page.

38. See previous page.

[$]For rules 11U and 11UA, log on to *taxmann.com/readyreckoner.aspx.*

2. For the aforesaid purpose, the term "relative" means–

	If taxpayer is X
1. Spouse of the individual	Mrs. X
2. Brother or sister of the individual	Brothers/sisters of X
3. Brother or sister of the spouse of the individual	Brothers/sisters of Mrs. X
4. Brother or sister of either of the parents of the individual	Brothers/sisters of father/mother of X
5. Any lineal ascendant or descendant of the individual	Lineal ascendant or descendant of X
6. Any lineal ascendant or descendant of the spouse of the individual	Lineal ascendant or descendant of Mrs. X
7. Spouse of the person referred to in (2) to (6)	Spouse of the aforesaid persons

Note - If the taxpayer is X and he receives gifts from any of his relatives (given in column 2 of the table), such gifts is not be chargeable to tax. The Rajkot Bench of the Tribunal has held that even gifts received by an individual from a group of relatives (like HUF) is exempt from tax—*Vineetkumar Raghavjibhai Bhalodia* v. *ITO* [2011] 46 SOT 97. Moreover, with effect from October 1, 2009, gift received by a Hindu undivided family from its members is treated as gift received from a "relative".

3. The above provisions cover –

- a receipt of money/property by an individual/HUF (if it is received up to March 31, 2017);
- a receipt of money/property by any person (if it is received on or after April 1, 2017).

4. Gift on the occasion of marriage of the recipient is not chargeable to tax. Gifts on other occasions (*e.g.*, gifts on birthday, etc.) are, however, chargeable to tax. Further, marriage gift may be received from relatives, friends or any other person.

5. The above provision is applicable whether the recipient is a resident or non-resident. Even a gift received by a non-resident in India is chargeable to tax.

6. The above provision is applicable whether the donor is a resident or a non-resident.

7. "Property" for the aforesaid purpose means the following capital asset of the assessee (*i.e.*, recipient): (*i*) immovable property being land or building or both; (*ii*) shares and securities; (*iii*) jewellery; (*iv*) archaeological collections; (*v*) drawings; (*vi*) paintings; (*vii*) sculptures; (*viii*) any work of art, or (*ix*) (with effect from June 1, 2010) bullion. It may be noted that the above provisions are applicable to the 'property' which is in the nature of a capital asset of the recipient. In other words, the above provisions do not apply to stock-in-trade, raw material and consumable stores of any business of such recipient. Further, if an assessee gets a gift of agricultural land situated in a rural area in India, it is not chargeable to tax in the hands of recipient, as rural agricultural land is not treated as a "capital asset" under section 2(*14*).

8. "Jewellery" for this purpose means—

a. ornaments made of gold, silver, platinum or any other precious metal or any alloy containing one or more of such precious metals, whether or not containing any precious or semi-precious stone, and whether or not worked or sewn into any wearing apparel;

b. precious or semi-precious stones, whether or not set in any furniture, utensil or other article or worked or sewn into any wearing apparel.

77.5-1b VALUATION RULES - Movable and immovable properties for the above purpose shall be valued as follows—

Different properties	*Valuation of property*
1. Immovable property	Stamp duty value of the property [*see* Note 4]
2. Jewellery, archaeological collections, drawings, paintings, sculptures or any work of art	• *If purchased from a registered dealer* - If jewellery, archaeological collections, etc., are received by the way of purchase on the valuation date, from a registered dealer (under sales tax), the invoice value of these properties shall be the fair market value • *In any other case* - The price which such jewellery, archaeological collections, etc., would fetch if sold in the open market on the valuation date [*see* Note 1]
3. Quoted shares and securities (received by way of a transaction carried out through a recognized stock exchange in India)	The transaction value as recorded in such stock exchange

Different properties	*Valuation of property*
4. Quoted shares and securities (not being received by way of a transaction carried out through a recognized stock exchange in India)	The lowest price of such shares and securities quoted on any recognized stock exchange in India on the valuation date. If, however, on the valuation date such shares and securities are not traded on any recognized stock exchange, the lowest price of such shares and securities on a date immediately preceding the valuation date (when such shares/securities are traded) shall be the fair market value
5. Unquoted equity shares (*Option 1*)	Assets [*Note 2*] xxxx *Less*: Liabilities [*Note 3*] xxxx Net worth xxxx Value of one share = Net worth × Paid up value of one share ÷ Total amount of paid up equity share capital as shown in balance sheet
5. Unquoted equity shares (*Option 2*) [applicable only in the case of section 56(2)(*viib*)]	The fair market value of the unquoted equity shares shall be determined (at the option of the assessee) by a merchant banker[39] as per the Discounted Free Cash Flow method.
6. Other unquoted shares and securities	The fair market value shall be estimated to be the price it would fetch if sold in the open market on the valuation date and the assessee may obtain a report from a Category I merchant banker (registered with SEBI) or a chartered accountant in respect of such valuation

Notes—

1. If jewellery, archaeological collections, etc., are received by the way of a purchase on the valuation date, from a registered dealer (under sales tax), the invoice value of these properties shall be the fair market value. In case these properties are received by any other mode and the value of the properties exceeds Rs. 50,000, then the assessee may obtain the report of registered valuer in respect of the price it would fetch if sold in the open market on the valuation date.

2. Amount of asset[40] shall be calculated as follows –

- *Jewellery and artistic work* - The price which these assets would fetch if sold in the open market based on the valuation report obtained from a registered valuer.
- *Shares and securities* - Fair market value of shares and securities as determined in the manner provided in *Points 3, 4* and *5* above.
- *Immovable property* - Stamp duty value adopted/assessed/assessable.
- *Any other asset* - Book value in the balance sheet.

The amount calculated above shall be reduced by any amount of tax paid as TDS/TCS/advance tax (excluding refund claimed) and any amount shown in the balance sheet as asset (including the unamortised amount of deferred expenditure) which does not represent the value of any asset.

3. Book value of liabilities shown in the balance sheet, but not including the following amounts, namely—

a. the paid-up capital in respect of equity shares;

b. the amount set apart for payment of dividends on preference shares and equity shares where such dividends have not been declared before the date of transfer at a general body meeting of the company;

c. reserves and surplus, by whatever name called, even if the resulting figure is negative, other than those set apart towards depreciation;

d. any amount representing provision for taxation, other than amount of tax paid as deduction or collection at source or as advance tax payment as reduced by the amount of tax claimed as refund under the Income-tax Act, to the extent of the excess over the tax payable with reference to the book profits in accordance with the law applicable thereto;

e. any amount representing provisions made for meeting liabilities, other than ascertained liabilities;

f. any amount representing contingent liabilities other than arrears of dividends payable in respect of cumulative preference shares.

---

39. Or by a chartered accountant (up to May 23, 2018).

40. For the purpose of section 56(2)(*viib*), amount of the asset shall be calculated on the basis of book value of the assets in the balance sheet.

4. Where the date of an agreement fixing the value of consideration for the transfer of immovable property and the date of registration are not same, the stamp duty value may be taken as on the date of the agreement for transfer and not as on the date of registration for such transfer. However, this exception shall apply only in those cases where the amount of consideration (or a part thereof) has been received by way of an account payee cheque/draft or by use of electronic clearing system through a bank account (**or through prescribed electronic mode**), on or before the date of agreement for transfer of such immovable property.

77.5-1c PROVISIONS ILLUSTRATED - Consider the following cases—

1. Property received by gift before October 1, 2009 - X gets a gift of a house property from his friend A on September 30, 2009. Stamp duty value of the property on the date of gift is Rs. 40,00,000. In the hands of X, nothing is chargeable to tax, as gift of property is received before October 1, 2009. The same rule is applicable if a movable property is received by way of gift before October 1, 2009. The provisions of section 56(2)(*vii*) are applicable only with effect from October 1, 2009.

In the hands of transferor A, it is not treated as transfer because of section 47(*iii*) and the transferor will not be chargeable to tax under section 45. Section 50C will not have any role to play.

If X transfers this property, cost of acquisition will be the cost to the previous owner A.

2. Immovable property received by gift on or after October 1, 2009 but stamp duty value is up to Rs. 50,000 - X gets a gift of a house property from his friend A on April 10, 2018. Stamp duty value of the property on the date of gift is Rs. 50,000. In the hands of X, nothing is chargeable of tax, as stamp duty value of the immovable property does not exceed Rs. 50,000.

In the hands of transferor A, it is not treated as transfer [transfer of an asset by gift is not treated as "transfer" under section 47(*iii*)] and the transferor will not be chargeable to tax under section 45. Section 50C will not have any role to play.

If X transfers this property, the cost to the previous owner A will be taken as cost of acquisition of this property in the hands of X.

3. Immovable property received as capital asset by gift and the stamp duty value is more than Rs. 50,000 - X gets a gift of a house property from his friend A on May 20, 2018. X is not a dealer in properties and the house property is received as a capital asset. Stamp duty value of the property on the date of gift is Rs. 45,00,000. In the hands of X, Rs. 45,00,000 will be taxable as income under section 56(2)(*x*) under the head "Income from other sources" for the assessment year 2019-20.

In the hands of transferor A, it is not treated as transfer [transfer of an asset by gift is not treated as "transfer" under section 47(*iii*)] and the transferor will not be chargeable to tax under section 45. Section 50C will not have any role to play.

If X transfers this property, Rs. 45,00,000 will be taken as the cost of acquisition of this property in the hands of X.

4. Immovable properties received as capital asset by gift - X is a salaried employee (or X is a businessman, but not a dealer in properties, or recipient is X Ltd., not a property dealer). On June 1, 2018, he gets a gift of house property situated in Delhi (stamp duty value : Rs. 70,00,000) from A. On July 1, 2018, he gets gift of a property in Pune (stamp duty value : Rs. 50,000) from B. In the hands of X, stamp duty value of Delhi property of Rs. 70,00,000 will be taxable as income under the head "Income from other sources". However, nothing is taxable in respect of Pune property, as the stamp duty value does not exceed Rs. 50,000.

In the hands of transferors (*i.e.*, A and B), nothing will be taxable under the head "Capital gains", as gift is not treated as transfer. Section 50C will not have any role to play.

If X transfers Delhi property, Rs. 70,00,000 will be taken as cost of acquisition. In the case of transfer of Pune property by X, the cost of acquisition will be cost to the previous owner B.

5. Purchase of immovable property (or properties) for a consideration which is lower than stamp duty value - X purchases a house property situated in Nagpur from A on March 31, 2019 for a consideration which is less than stamp duty value. The difference between stamp duty value and actual consideration will be taxable in the hands of X under section 56(2)(*x*), if the following two conditions are satisfied –

a. stamp duty value exceeds 105 per cent of consideration; and

b. different between stamp duty value and consideration is more than Rs. 50,000.

The data pertaining to stamp duty and actual purchase consideration paid by X is given below –

	Situation 1 *Rs.*	*Situation 2* *Rs.*	*Situation 3* *Rs.*	*Situation 4* *Rs.*
Stamp duty value	32,00,000	8,80,000	1,39,000	30,90,000
Purchase consideration	30,00,000	8,30,000	1,30,000	30,00,000
105% of purchase consideration	31,50,000	8,71,500	1,36,500	31,50,000
Whether stamp duty value exceeds 105% of purchase consideration	*Yes*	*Yes*	*Yes*	*No*
Stamp duty value *minus* purchase consideration	2,00,000	50,000	9,000	90,000
Amount taxable in the hands of X under section 56(2)(*x*)	2,00,000	*Nil*	*Nil*	*Nil*
Cost of acquisition in the hands of X for calculating capital gain (in future)	32,00,000	8,30,000	1,30,000	30,00,000
Full value of consideration in the hands of transferor A under section 50C	32,00,000	8,80,000	1,39,000	30,00,000

6. *Immovable property received as stock-in-trade by gift* - X or X Ltd. is a dealer in properties. On June 20, 2018, he/it gets a house property by gift for business purposes from A. Stamp duty value of the property is Rs. 83,00,000.

Section 56(2)(*x*) is applicable only when a property is received as a capital asset. Since house property in the hands of X or X Ltd. is stock-in-trade, nothing will be taxable under section 56(2)(*x*) under the head "Income from other sources".

In the hands of transferor A, it is not treated as transfer [transfer of an asset by gift is not treated as "transfer" under section 47(*iii*)] and the transferor will not be chargeable to tax under section 45. Section 50C will not have any role to play.

If X or X Ltd. transfers this property as stock-in-trade, the cost to the previous owner A will be taken as cost of acquisition of stock-in-trade.

7. *Rural agricultural land* - X gets a gift of a plot of land (being agricultural land) situated in a rural area in India from A on September 1, 2018. Stamp duty value is Rs. 6,70,000. Agricultural land situated in a rural area in India, is not a "capital asset" under section 2(*14*). Section 56(2)(*x*) is applicable only if a "capital asset" is received by gift. Consequently, nothing will be taxable in the hands of X under the head "Income from other sources".

There will be no capital gain in the hands of A at the time of gift. If X transfers the agricultural land, he will not be subject to tax under the head "Capital gains".

8. *Motor car is received by gift* - On September 2, 2018, X gets a gift of motor car from A. Fair market value of the car is Rs. 2,10,000. Nothing is taxable in the hands of X under section 56(2)(*x*). This section is applicable if gift is received of land or building. This section is also applicable if movable property (being shares and securities, jewellery, archaeological collections, drawings, paintings, sculptures, any work of art or bullion) is received by gift or purchased for a consideration which is lesser than fair market value. If a car is received by gift or purchased for a consideration which is lower than fair market value, section 56(2)(*x*) is not applicable.

9. *Purchase of painting from a registered dealer* - On July 25, 2018, X purchases a Tagore painting from Shyam Art Gallery, Andheri West, Mumbai *vide* Bill No. 426/2018. Painting is purchased at the invoice price of Rs. 5,25,000. Shyam Art Gallery is a registered dealer under GST. This painting can be easily sold in market for Rs. 9,00,000.

In the case of purchase of a movable property from a registered dealer (under sales tax/VAT/GST), the "invoice value" is taken as fair market value of the property for the purpose of section 56(2)(*x*). If such property is purchased at the "invoice value" from a registered dealer, nothing will be taxable under section 56(2)(*x*). In the above case, invoice value is Rs. 5,25,000. X has purchased the painting for Rs. 5,25,000. He will not be chargeable to tax under section 56(2)(*x*), even if it is possible to sell the same property in market for Rs. 9,00,000. The same rule is applicable if other properties (like jewellery, archaeological collections, drawings, sculptures, etc.) are purchased from a registered dealer at the "invoice value".

10. Purchase of painting from a person other than registered dealer - On September 20, 2018, X purchases a Tagore painting (as a capital asset) for Rs. 8,00,000 from A (A is not a dealer in paintings). The fair market value of the painting is Rs. 11,00,000 (it can be easily sold in market for Rs. 11,00,000). The difference of Rs. 3,00,000 is taxable in the hands of X under section 56(2)(*x*) under the head "Income from other sources". If X transfers this painting, the cost of acquisition for the purpose of calculating capital gain will be Rs. 11,00,000.

In the hands of A for the purpose of calculating capital gains, the full value of consideration will be Rs. 8,00,000 (section 50C is not applicable in the case of movable properties).

11. Painting/jewellery received by gift or purchased for inadequate consideration - X gives the following information about movable properties (being capital assets)—

Movable properties (1)	*Fair market value (2)*	*Purchase price (3)*	*Difference (4) [i.e., the excess of (2) over (3)]*
	Rs.	*Rs.*	*Rs.*
Received by gift—			
Gold chain from A	32,000	*Nil*	32,000
Painting from B	18,000	*Nil*	18,000
Total	50,000	*Nil*	50,000
Purchase for inadequate consideration—			
Work of art from C1,00,000	90,000	10,000	
Gold ring from D	85,000	45,000	40,000
Total	1,85,000	1,35,000	50,000

In this case, the aggregate fair market value of movable properties received by gift is not more than Rs. 50,000. Consequently, nothing is taxable in respect of movable properties received by gift.

The aggregate fair market value of movable properties purchased is Rs. 1,85,000 and the aggregate purchase price is Rs. 1,35,000. The difference is not more than Rs. 50,000. Nothing is taxable under section 56(2)(*x*) on account of purchase of movable properties for inadequate consideration.

If, however, the fair market value of gold chain is Rs. 32,001 and gold ring is Rs. 85,001, Rs. 1,00,002 will be taxable under the head "Income from other sources" in the hands of X.

77.5-E1 X receives the following gifts during the previous year 2018-19—

1. On the occasion of marriage of X, he gets Rs. 2,90,000 as gift on April 2, 2018 (out of which Rs. 2,00,000 is received from friends of X and Mrs. X and remaining amount is received from close relatives of X and Mrs. X).

2. On June 22, 2018, he gets a gift of Rs. 23,000 from C, who is cousin of his father.

3. On August 18, 2018, he gets a gift of Rs. 15,000 from D, who is elder brother of his grandfather.

4. On September 20, 2018, he gets a gift of Rs. 7,00,000 from his grandmother.

5. A computer received from his employer (it was purchased for Rs. 65,000 by the employer on May 1, 2018 and given as gift to X on October 20, 2018).

6. On November 2, 2018, X purchases a house property from his friend D for Rs. 65,000 (stamp duty value of the property is Rs. 10,00,000).

7. On November 30, 2018, X gets a gift of a plot of land from his grandfather (stamp duty value is Rs. 15,00,000).

8. On December 30, 2018, X gets by gift a commercial flat from the elder brother of his father-in-law (stamp duty value is Rs. 25,00,000).

9. On January 6, 2019, he gets a gift of Rs. 2,00,000 (cash gift of Rs. 25,000 and gift of a work of art whose market value is Rs. 1,75,000) from a notified public charitable institution.

10. X receives on January 11, 2019 a house property under will of a person known to him. The stamp duty value is Rs. 15,40,000.

11. On January 20, 2019, he gets a wrist watch by gift (fair market value : Rs. 40,000) from his friend B.

12. On January 25, 2019, he purchases a work of art for Rs. 16,00,000 from an exhibition in New York (the fair market value of the work of art on the date of purchase is Rs. 17,00,000).

13. On February 1, 2019, he purchases a commercial property for Rs. 16,00,000 (stamp duty value is Rs. 16,75,000).

14. On February 5, 2019, he gets a birthday gift of a gold chain (fair market value : Rs. 11,000) from his friend.

15. On February 10, 2019, X gets by way of gift a plot of land in Pune from a partnership firm. The partnership firm has only two partners—father of X and Mrs. X. The stamp duty value of the plot of land is Rs. 19,00,000.

16. On February 16, 2019, X purchases 500 shares in Tata Chemicals from his friend D at Rs. 90 per share (outside stock exchange). The lowest market quotation in the Bombay Stock Exchange and the National Stock Exchange on the date of purchase is Rs. 300 and 310 respectively.

17. On March 1, 2019, X gets a gift of gold ring from a cousin of his mother-in-law. The fair market value is Rs. 20,000.

18. On March 20, 2019, X gets a painting by way of gift from C Ltd. Mrs. X holds 70 per cent shares in C Ltd. The fair market value of painting is Rs. 19,000.

19. On March 25, 2019, X gets a small plot of land by way of gift from a cousin of Mrs. X (stamp duty value is Rs. 44,000).

20. On March 31, 2019, X receives a shop (situated in Jammu) by way of gift from a friend (stamp duty value is Rs. 50,000).

Compute the amount chargeable to tax in the hands of X under the head "Income from other sources" for the assessment year 2019-20.

•

	Cash gift	*Gift of immovable property*	*Gift of movable property*	*Purchase of movable property for inadequate consideration*	*Purchase of immovable property for inadequate consideration*
	Rs.	*Rs.*	*Rs.*	*Rs.*	
1. Gift on occasion of marriage of X (not taxable)	*Nil*	—	—	—	—
2. Cash gift from C (C is not "relative")	23,000	—	—	—	—
3. Cash gift from D (elder brother of grandfather is not "relative")	15,000	—	—	—	—
4. Cash gift from grandmother (gift from a "relative" is not taxable)	*Nil*	—	—	—	—
5. Gift from employer (it is taxable under the head "Salaries")	—	—	—	—	—
6. Purchase of immovable property for inadequate consideration	—	—	—	—	9,35,000
7. Gift of immovable property from grandfather (gift from "relative" is not taxable)	—	*Nil*	—	—	—
8. Gift of commercial property (elder brother of father-in-law is not "relative")	—	25,00,000	—	—	—
9. Gift from notified public charitable institute (not taxable)	*Nil*	—	*Nil*	—	—
10. Gift under a will (not taxable even if received from a non-relative)	—	*Nil*	—	—	—
11. Gift of a wrist watch [wrist watch is not "property" for the purpose of section 56(2)(*x*) and not taxable]	—	—	—	—	—
12. Purchase of a work of art for inadequate consideration	—	—	—	1,00,000	—
13. Purchase of immovable property for inadequate consideration (as the difference between stamp duty value and purchase price exceeds Rs. 50,000 but stamp duty value does not exceed 105% of purchase price, nothing is chargeable to tax)	—	—	—	—	—
14. Gift of gold chain	—	—	11,000	—	—
15. Gift from a partnership firm (partnership firm is not "relative" even if relatives of X are partners)	—	19,00,000	—	—	—
16. Purchase of shares for inadequate consideration [(Rs. 300 - Rs. 90) x 500]	—	—	—	1,05,000	—
17. Gift of gold ring (cousin of mother-in-law is not "relative" of X)	—	—	20,000	—	—
18. Gift from a company (company is not a "relative" even if Mrs. X is a major shareholder)	—	—	19,000	—	—
19. Gift of plot of land (not taxable as stamp duty value does not exceed Rs. 50,000)	—	*Nil*	—	—	—
20. Gift of shop (not taxable as stamp duty value does not exceed Rs. 50,000)	—	*Nil*	—	—	—
Total	38,000	44,00,000	50,000	2,05,000	9,35,000

Amount taxable under section 56(2)(*x*) under the head "Income from other sources" will be calculated as follows—

	Rs.
Cash gift (not taxable as the aggregate amount of cash gift does not exceed Rs. 50,000)	*Nil*
Gift of immovable properties	44,00,000
Gift of movable properties (not taxable as the aggregate amount does not exceed Rs. 50,000)	*Nil*
Purchase of immovable property for inadequate consideration	9,35,000
Purchase of movable properties for inadequate consideration	2,05,000
Amount taxable	55,40,000

77.5-2 *WHEN A SUM OF MONEY IS RECEIVED WITH CONSIDERATION AFTER MARCH 31, 2006 BUT BEFORE OCTOBER 1, 2009 [SEC. 56(2)(vi)]* - The provisions in respect of gift received on or after April 1, 2006 but before October 1, 2009 are briefly given below—

• *Conditions* - The following conditions should be satisfied—

a. the recipient is an individual or a Hindu undivided family;

b. any sum of money is received without consideration on or after April 1, 2006;

c. the aggregate amount of such money received by an individual/Hindu undivided family during a financial year from any person/persons exceeds Rs. 50,000.

If these conditions are satisfied the entire amount is chargeable to tax in the hands of recipient. In other words, if aggregate amount of such money received by an individual/Hindu undivided family during a financial year from any person/persons is Rs. 50,000 or less, nothing would be chargeable to tax. Conversely, if such amount is Rs. 50,000 or more, the entire amount is chargeable to tax.

• *Provisions not applicable in few cases* - While calculating the above monetary limit of Rs. 50,000, any sum of money received from the following shall not be considered—

1. Money received from a relative [*see* para 77.5-1a].

2. Money received on the occasion of the marriage of the individual.

3. Money received by way of will/inheritance.

4. Money received in contemplation of death of the payer.

5. Money received from a local authority.

6. Money received from any fund, foundation, university, other educational institution, hospital, medical institution, any trust or institution referred to in section 10(*23C*).

7. Money received from a charitable institute registered under section 12AA.

77.5-3 *GIFT RECEIVED ON OR AFTER SEPTEMBER 1, 2004 BUT BEFORE APRIL 1, 2006* - Section 56(2)(*v*) is applicable.

77.5-3a CONDITIONS - Section 56(2)(*v*) is applicable if the following conditions are satisfied—

1. The taxpayer is an individual or a Hindu undivided family.

2. During the previous year he or it has received any sum of money exceeding Rs. 25,000 without consideration.

3. Such sum of money is received on or after September 1, 2004 but before April 1, 2006.

4. The sum so received does not come in the exception list [*see* para 77.5-3c].

77.5-3b CONSEQUENCES WHEN THESE CONDITIONS ARE SATISFIED - If the above conditions are satisfied, the whole of such sum received by the individual/HUF will be taxable under section 56(2)(*v*) under the head "Income from other sources".

77.5-3c EXCEPTIONS - Section 56(2)(*v*) does not cover the following—

1. Any sum of money which is received before September 1, 2004.

2. Any sum of money which is received by way of consideration.

3. Any sum of money which is received from any relative [*see* para 77.5-1a].

4. Any sum of money which is received on the occasion of the marriage of the individual.

5. Any sum of money which is received under a will or by way of inheritance.

6. Any sum of money which is received in contemplation of death of the payer.

7. Any sum of money not exceeding Rs. 25,000 (no restriction on number of transactions).

77.6 ***Receipt of shares (in a closely held company) by a firm or a closely held company [Sec. 56(2)(viia)]*** - Clause (*viia*) was inserted in section 56(2) with effect from June 1, 2010. This clause is applicable if the following conditions are satisfied—

1. Recipient is a firm or a closely held company (*i.e.*, a company in which the public are not substantially interested).

2. The asset (which is received) is in the form of shares in a closely held company (*i.e.*, a company in which the public are not substantially interested).

3. These shares are received from any person.

4. Such shares are received on or after June 1, 2010 but before April 1, 2017[41].

5. Such shares are received without consideration or for an inadequate consideration.

6. Such shares are not received by way of a transaction referred to in section 47(*via*)/(*vic*)/(*vicb*)/(*vid*)/(*vii*) [*i.e.*, receipt of shares by a shareholder in a scheme of amalgamation, demerger, etc.].

- *Consequences if these conditions are satisfied* - If these conditions are satisfied, then value of such shares is taxable in the hands of recipient (*i.e.*, a firm or a closely held company) as follows—

Different situations	*Taxability in the hands of recipient (i.e., a firm or closely held company)*
Situation 1 - Shares are received without consideration and aggregate fair market value[42] of these shares received during the previous year does not exceed Rs. 50,000	Nothing is taxable in the hands of recipient
Situation 2 - Shares are received without consideration and aggregate fair market value[42] of these shares received during the previous year exceeds Rs. 50,000	Aggregate fair market value will be taxable in the hands of recipient
Situation 3 - Shares are received for a consideration which is less than fair market value[42] and the aggregate difference does not exceed Rs. 50,000	Nothing is taxable in the hands of recipient
Situation 4 - Shares are received for a consideration which is less than fair market value[42] and the aggregate difference exceeds Rs. 50,000	Aggregate fair market value *minus* aggregate consideration, will be taxable in the hands of recipient.

Note - Situation Nos. 2 and 4 cannot be combined.

77.7 ***Share premium in excess of fair market value [Sec. 56(2)(viib), applicable from the assessment year 2013-14]*** - Section 56(2)(*viib*) has been inserted with effect from the assessment year 2013-14. It is applicable as follows—

1. Recipient is a company (not being a company in which the public are substantially interested).

2. It receives consideration for issue of shares (preference shares or equity shares) from a resident person.

3. The consideration received for issue of shares exceeds the face value of such shares. In other words, shares are issued at a premium.

If the above conditions are satisfied, the aggregate consideration received for such shares as exceeds the fair market value of the shares, shall be chargeable to income-tax in the hands of recipient-company under section 56(2)(*viib*) under the head "Income from other sources".

- The above provisions are not applicable in the following two cases—

a. where the consideration for issue of shares is received by a venture capital undertaking from a venture capital company or a venture capital fund [or (with effect from the assessment year 2020-21) a **specified fund having Category I or Category II Alternative Investment Fund Certificate**]; or

b. where the consideration for issue of shares is received by a company from a class or classes of person as notified by the Central Government [for this purpose, the Central Government has specified that the above provisions of section 56(2)(*viib*) are not applicable when consideration is received by a company from a resident for issue of shares of a "startup" company – *see* para 77.7-1].

- The fair market value of the shares shall be the higher of the value—

a. as may be determined in accordance with the method given in rule 11UA[$] [*see* para 77.5-1b]; or

b. as may be substantiated by the company to the satisfaction of the Assessing Officer, based on the value of its assets, including intangible assets, being goodwill, know-how, patents, copyrights, trademarks, licences, franchises or any other business or commercial rights of similar nature.

41. Share received on or after April 1, 2017 are covered by section 56(2)(*x*) [*see* para 77.5-1].

42. For fair market value, *see* para 77.5-1b.

[$]For rule 11UA, log on to *taxmann.com/readyreckoner.aspx*.

Provisions illustrated - X Ltd. is a public limited company but its shares are not listed in any stock exchange in India on April 6, 2018. On April 6, 2018, 5,000 shares are issued to A, 10,000 shares are issued to B and 20,000 shares are issued to C. These shares are issued in one of the following situations—

	Different situations			
	1	*2*	*3*	*4*
Face value per share (in Rs.)	10	10	10	10
Issue price per share (in Rs.)	10	9	40	40
Fair market value of each share determined under section 56(2)(*viib*) (in Rs.)	3	4	42	31

The following points should be noted—

1. In *Situation 1,* shares are issued at par. In *Situation 2* shares are issued at a discount. The provisions of section 56(2)(*viib*) are applicable only when shares are issued at premium. Consequently, nothing is taxable under the head "Income from other sources" under section 56(2)(*viib*) in *Situations 1* and *2.*

2. In *Situation 3,* shares are issued at premium. The total consideration per share (*i.e.,* face value *plus* premium) is Rs. 40. Fair market value of shares as determined under section 56(2)(*viib*) is Rs. 42. As fair market value is more than the consideration received, nothing is taxable under the above provisions.

3. In *Situation 4,* fair market value per share is Rs. 31. Consideration received from shareholders is Rs. 40 per share. The excess consideration of Rs. 9 per share is taxable if the following two conditions are satisfied—

a. X Ltd. is a company in which the public are not substantially interested under section 2(*18*) for the previous year 2018-19; and

b. shareholders are resident in India for the previous year 2018-19.

Suppose, shares in X Ltd. are not listed in any recognized stock exchange in India up to March 31, 2019 and during the previous year 2018-19 A and B are resident in India (C is non-resident), the amount taxable under section 56(2)(*viib*) will be Rs. 1,35,000 in the hands of X Ltd. [*i.e.,* Rs. 9 × (5,000 shares to A + 10,000 shares to B)].

4. Suppose, C was never in India up to April 6, 2018, but he comes to India on September 3, 2018 (*i.e.,* after issue of shares to him) for 182 days. He will be resident in India. Amount taxable in the hands of X Ltd. under section 56(2)(*viib*) will be increased to Rs. 3,15,000.

5. In *Situations 1, 2* and *3,* section 56(2)(*viib*) is not applicable. In these situations (and also in *Situation 4*), it is quite possible that the amount received from shareholder becomes chargeable to tax in the hands of X Ltd. under the provisions of section 68.

6. Suppose, shares of X Ltd. are listed in the Bombay Stock Exchange with effect from March 7, 2019. X Ltd. will be a company in which the public are substantially interested within the parameters of section 2(*18*) for the previous year 2018-19. Consequently, nothing will be taxable under section 56(2)(*viib*) even in *Situation 4.* Even section 68 will not be applicable.

77.7-1 *EXEMPTION AVAILABLE TO A "STARTUP" FOR THE PURPOSE OF SECTION 56(2)(*viib*)* - For the purpose of section 56(2)(*viib*), exemption is available to a "startup" if a few conditions, given by Notification No. GSR 127(E)$, dated February 19, 2019, are satisfied.

77.7-1a WHAT IS STARTUP - An entity shall be considered as a startup which satisfies the following parameters –

- It is incorporated as a private limited company or registered as a partnership firm/limited liability partnership (LLP) in India.
- The entity is not formed by splitting up or reconstruction of an existing business.
- Turnover of the entity for any of the financial years since incorporation/registration has not exceeded Rs. 100 crore.
- Entity is working towards innovation, development or improvement of products or processes or services, or if it is a scalable business model with a high potential of employment generation or wealth creation.
- An entity (which satisfies the above conditions) is considered as a "startup" up to a period of 10 years from the date of incorporation/registration.

A startup shall make an online application over the mobile app or portal set up by the Department for Promotion of Industry and Internal Trade (DPIIT). The DPIIT may, after calling for such documents or information and making such enquires, as it may deem fit, –

a. recognise the eligible entity as Startup; or

b. reject the application by providing reasons.

77.7-1b CONDITIONS FOR EXEMPTION UNDER SECTION 56(2)(*viib*) - If an entity is recognised as "startup" under the above provisions, it is eligible for exemption under section 56(2)(*viib*) if the following conditions are satisfied –

$ For Notification No. GSR 127(E), log on to *taxmann.com/readyreckoner.aspx.*

• *Aggregate share capital* - Aggregate amount of paid up share capital and share premium of the startup after issue (or proposed issue) of share, if any, does not exceed Rs. 25 crore. However, for the purpose of computation of Rs. 25 crore, shares issued to the following persons shall not be included –

a. a non-resident;

b. a venture capital company or a venture capital fund;

c. a "specified company" (meaning given below).

• *Shares issued to a "specified company"* - Share issued by a "startup" to a specified company is exempt for the purpose of section 56(2)(*viib*). Further, such shares shall not be included for the purpose of computation of the aforesaid ceiling of Rs. 25 crore. For this purpose, "specified company" means –

- a company whose shares are frequently traded within the meaning of SEBI (Substantial Acquisition of Shares and Takeovers) Regulations, and
- on the last date of financial year (preceding the year in which shares are issued), net worth of the company exceeds Rs. 100 crore (or turnover exceeds Rs. 250 crore).

• *Startup has not invested in a few assets* - The startup has not invested in any of the following assets at the time of issue or proposed issue of shares at premium (moreover, startup shall not invest in any of these assets for the period of 7 years from the end of the latest financial year in which shares are issued at premium) –

Investment cannot be made in these assets	*Exceptions (investment can be made in these assets)*
1. Residential building (or land appurtenant thereto)	If such building is used by the startup for the purposes of renting or held by it as stock-in-trade, in the ordinary course of business
2. Land or non-residential building, or both	If such asset is occupied by the startup for its business or used by it for purposes of renting or held by it as stock-in trade, in the ordinary course of business
3. Loans and advances	Loans or advances extended in the ordinary course of business by the startup where the lending of money is substantial part of its business
4. Capital contribution made to any other entity	–
5. Shares and securities	–
6. Motor vehicle , aircraft, yacht or any other mode of transport, the actual cost of which exceeds Rs. 10 lakh	If such vehicle, aircraft, etc., is held by the startup for the purpose of plying, hiring, leasing or as stock-in-trade, in the ordinary course of business
7. Jewellery	If jewellery is held by the startup as stock-in-trade in the ordinary course of business
8. Archaeological collections, drawings, paintings, sculptures, any work of art, or bullion (whether in the nature of capital asset or otherwise)	–

• *Declaration* - If the above conditions are satisfied and the entity wants to avail exemption from the operation of section 56(2(*viib*), it shall file a duly signed declaration in Form 2 [given in Notification No. GSR 127(E), dated February 19, 2019] to DPIIT. On receipt of such declaration, the DPIIT shall forward the same to the CBDT.

• *Revocation* - In case the startup (which has furnished the aforesaid declaration in Form 2) invests in any of the assets [given in *Column 1* of the table (*infra*)] before the end of 7 years from the end of the latest financial year in which the shares are issued at premium, the exemption provided under section 56(2)(*viib*) shall be revoked with retrospective effect.

Second proviso to section 56(2)(*viib*) (inserted with effect from the assessment year 2020-21) provides that in case of **failure to comply with the aforesaid conditions, the consideration received for issue of shares (which exceeds the fair market value of such shares), shall be deemed to be the income of the company chargeable to tax** for the previous year in which the failure to comply with any of the aforesaid conditions has taken place. Further, it shall be deemed that the company has under-reported the said income in consequence of the misreporting referred to in section 270A(8)/(9) for the said previous year.

77.8 ***Interest on compensation [Sec. 56(2)(viii), applicable from the assessment year 2010-11 onwards]*** - Income by way of interest received on compensation or on enhanced compensation, shall be assessed under the head "Income from other sources" in the year in which it is received. Under section 57(*iv*), 50 per cent of such interest is deductible. However, no other deduction is permitted.

77.9 ***Advance money [Sec. 56(2)(ix), applicable from the assessment year 2015-16 onwards]*** - Where any sum of money, received as an advance or otherwise in the course of the negotiations for transfer of a capital asset, is forfeited and the negotiations do not result in transfer of such capital asset, then, such sum shall be chargeable to income-tax under the head "Income from other sources".

77.10 ***Compensation on termination of employment [Sec. 56(2)(xi), applicable from the assessment year]*** - Any compensation or other payment due to or received by any person, by whatever name called, in connection with the termination of his employment (or the modification of the terms and conditions relating thereto) shall be chargeable to income-tax under the head "Income from other sources" from the assessment year 2019-20.

77.11 ***Interest on Kisan Vikas Patras*** - The amount of interest accrued on investment in Kisan Vikas Patras by an assessee is to be calculated on the basis of following Table received from the Department of Economic Affairs wherein rate of interest and maturity amount for Rs. 1,000 denomination of Kisan Vikas Patras are given :

Period from the date of certificate to the date of its encashment	*Purchased from 1-3-2003 to 30-11-2011*		*Purchased from 18-11-2014 to 31-3-2016*		*Purchased from 1-4-2016 to 30-9-2016*		*Purchased from 1-10-2016 to 31-3-2017*	
	Rate of interest %	*Maturity value Rs.*	*Rate of interest %*	*Maturity value Rs.*	*Rate of interest %*	*Maturity value Rs.*	*Rate of interest %*	*Maturity value Rs.*
1 year	6.40	1065.02	7.46	1076	6.73	1068	6.59	1067
2 years	6.40	1134.28	7.46	1158	6.73	1142	6.59	1138
2 years and 6 months	6.40	1170.51	7.46	1201	6.73	1180	6.59	1176
3 years	6.40	1207.95	7.47	1246	6.74	1220	6.6	1215
3 years and 6 months	6.88	1267.19	7.48	1293	6.74	1261	6.6	1255
4 years	6.88	1310.80	7.47	1341	6.73	1303	6.59	1296
4 years and 6 months	6.88	1355.90	7.47	1391	6.73	1347	6.59	1339
5 years	7.36	1435.63	7.47	1443	6.73	1392	6.59	1383
5 years and 6 months	7.36	1488.49	7.47	1497	6.74	1439	6.6	1429
6 years	7.36	1543.30	7.47	1553	6.73	1487	6.6	1476
6 years and 6 months	7.85	1649.13	7.47	1611	6.73	1537	6.59	1524
7 years	7.85	1713.82	7.47	1671	6.73	1589	6.6	1575
7 years and 6 months	7.85	1781.06	7.47	1733	6.73	1643	6.59	1626
8 years	7.85	1850.93	7.47	1798	6.73	1698	6.59	1680
8 years and 4 months	NA	NA	–	2000	NA	NA	NA	NA
8 years and 6 months	NA	NA	NA	NA	6.73	1755	6.59	1735
8 years and 7 months	–	2000.00	NA	NA	NA	NA	NA	NA
9 years	NA	NA	NA	NA	6.73	1814	6.59	1793
9 years and 2 months	NA	NA	NA	NA	–	2000	NA	NA
9 years and 4 months	NA	NA	NA	NA	NA	NA	–	2000

Note : Maturity values cited are calculated on half-yearly compounding basis based on the rate of interest cited— Circular No. 687, dated August 19, 1994. Deduction under section 80L is not available.

77.12 ***Interest on Indira Vikas Patras*** - Interest at the rates given below shall be deemed to accrue on Indira Vikas Patras at the end of each year calculated from the date of initial purchase of certificate:

Date of purchase	*Compound rate of interest*	*Amount of taxable interest on certificate of Rs. 1,000*					
		At the end of first year Rs.	*At the end of second year* Rs.	*At the end of third year* Rs.	*At the end of fourth year* Rs.	*At the end of fifth year* Rs.	*At the end of 5 years and six months* Rs.
• Certificates purchased after March 31, 1987 but before March 1, 1988	13.43 per cent	134.30	152.34	172.80	196.00	222.32	122.24
• Certificates purchased after February 29, 1988 but before September 2, 1993	14.97 per cent	149.70	172.11	197.87	227.50	252.82	—

Date of purchase	Compound rate of interest	Amount of taxable interest on certificate of Rs. 1,000					
		At the end of first year	At the end of second year	At the end of third year	At the end of fourth year	At the end of fifth year	At the end of 5 years and six months
		Rs.	Rs.	Rs.	Rs.	Rs.	Rs.
• Certificates purchased after September 1, 1993 but before January 1,1999	13.43 per cent	134.30	152.34	172.80	196.00	222.32	122.24
• Certificates purchased after December 31, 1998	12.25 per cent	122.50	137.51	154.35	173.26	194.48	217.90*

*At the end of sixth year.

Note : Deduction under section 80L is not available.

77.13 *Interest on National Savings Certificates* - *See* para 107.1-2c.

77.14 *Deep discount bonds* - *Vide* Circular No. 2/2002, dated February 15, 2002, the Board has issued certain clarifications.

77.14-1 POSITION BEFORE ISSUE OF CIRCULAR NO. 2/2002[43] - The Board had earlier clarified by way of certain letters issued to the Reserve Bank of India and others that the difference between the bid price (subscription price) and the redemption price (face value) of such bonds will be treated as interest income assessable under the Income-tax Act. On transfer of the bonds before maturity, the difference between the sale consideration and the cost of acquisition would be taxed as income from capital gains where the bonds were held as investment, and as business income where the bonds were held as trading assets. On final redemption, however, no capital gains will arise. It was further clarified that tax would be deducted at source on the difference between the bid price and the redemption price at the time of maturity.

77.14-2 POSITION AFTER ISSUE OF CIRCULAR NO. 2/2002 - Substantial changes has been made *vide* Circular No. 2/2002 which are given below—

77.14-2a GENERAL TREATMENT - Every person holding a Deep Discount Bond will make a market valuation of the bond as on March 31 of each financial year (hereafter referred to as the valuation date) and mark such bond to such market value in accordance with the guidelines issued by the Reserve Bank of India for valuation of investments. For this purpose, market values of different instruments declared by the Reserve Bank of India or by the Primary Dealers Association of India jointly with the Fixed Income Money Market and Derivatives Association of India may be referred to.

• The difference between the market valuations as on two successive valuation dates will represent the accretion to the value of the bond during the relevant financial year and will be taxable as interest income (where the bonds are held as investments) or business income (where the bonds are held as trading assets).

• In a case where the bond is acquired during the year by an intermediate purchaser (a person who has acquired the bond by purchase during the term of the bond and not as original subscription) the difference between the market value as on the valuation date and the cost for which he acquired the bond, will be taxed as interest income or business income, as the case may be, and no capital gains will arise as there would be no transfer of the bond on the valuation date.

77.14-2b TRANSFER BEFORE MATURITY - Where the bond is transferred at any time before the maturity date, the difference between the sale price and the cost of the bond will be taxable as capital gains in the hands of an investor or as business income in the hands of a trader. For computing such gains, the cost of the bond will be taken to be the aggregate of the cost for which the bond was acquired by the transferor and the income, if any, already offered to tax by such transferor (in accordance with para 77.14-2a above) up to the date of transfer.

• Since the income chargeable in this case is only the accretion to the value of the bond over a specific period, for the purposes of computing capital gains, the period of holding in such cases will be reckoned from the

43. The tax treatment of income as prescribed in Circular No. 2/2002 cannot be extended to 8 per cent RBI bonds—*K. Nagendrasa* v. *CIT* [2011] 12 taxmann.com 438 (Bang. - ITAT).

date of purchase/subscription, or the last valuation date in respect of which the transferor has offered income to tax, whichever is later. Since such period would always be less than one year, the capital gains will be chargeable to tax as short-term capital gains.

77.14-2c REDEMPTION - Where the bond is redeemed by the original subscriber, the difference between the redemption price and the value as on the last valuation date immediately preceding the maturity date will be taxed as interest income in the case of investors, or business income in the case of traders.

• Where the bond is redeemed by an intermediate purchaser, the difference between the redemption price and the cost of the bond to such purchaser will be taxable as interest or business income; as the case may be. For this purpose, again, the cost of the bond will mean the aggregate of the cost at which the bonds were acquired and the income arising from the bond which has already been offered to tax by the person redeeming the bond.

77.14-2d STRIPS - Apart from original issue of Deep Discount Bonds, such bonds can also be created by 'stripping', *i.e.*, the process of detaching the interest coupons from a normal coupon bearing bond and treating the different coupons and the stripped bond as separate instruments or securities ('strips') capable of being traded in independently. Such a mechanism, referred to as STRIPS (Separate Trading of Registered Interest and Principal of Securities) creates instruments which are in the nature of Deep Discount or Zero Coupon Bonds from out of the normal interest - bearing bonds. Accordingly, the tax treatment of the different components of principal and interest created by such stripping will be on the same lines as clarified in the preceding paragraphs in respect of Deep Discount Bonds.

• The process of stripping of a normal interest-bearing bond into its various components will not amount to a transfer within the meaning of the Income-tax Act as it merely involves the conversion of the unstripped bond into the corresponding series of STRIPS. Similarly, the reconstitution of STRIPS to form a coupon bearing bond will not amount to a transfer.

77.14-2e TAX DEDUCTION AT SOURCE - The difference between the bid price of a Deep Discount Bond and its redemption price, which is actually paid at the time of maturity, will continue to be subject to tax deduction at source under section 193. Under the existing provisions of that section, no tax is deductible at source on interest payable on Government securities. Further, the Central Government is empowered to specify any such bonds issued by an institution, authority, public sector company or co-operative society by way of notification, exempting them from the requirement of tax deduction at source.

77.14-2f OPTION TO INVESTORS - Considering the difficulties which might be faced by small non-corporate investors in determining market values under the RBI guidelines and computing income taxable in each year of holding, such investors holding Deep Discount Bonds upto an aggregate face value of Rs. 1,00,000 may, at their option, continue to offer income for tax in accordance with the earlier clarifications issued by the Board referred to in para 77.14-1 above.

77.14-2g CLARIFICATIONS - The following clarifications are issued by press note dated March 20, 2002—

1. It is an established principle that a circular issued by CBDT cannot have a retrospective tax effect. Circular 2/2002 on deep discount bonds specifies the tax treatment in respect of bonds which are issued after the issue of the circular, and does not seek to impose the modified treatment on existing bond-holders. Further, non-corporate persons who invest small amounts in new issues (face value up to Rs. 1 lakh) can still opt for the old system.

2. Valuing the bonds every year on the basis of RBI guidelines will not pose any problem as such values can be obtained from the issuers themselves, who will invariably be the RBI or a public financial institution.

3. The amount received on redemption would always be liable to tax deduction at source as per normal provisions of the Act. However, no TDS is required on interest payable on Government securities. Bonds issued by an institution, authority, public sector company or co-operative society can also be exempted from the requirement of TDS by notification.

Deduction [Section 57]

78. The income chargeable to tax under this head is computed after making the following deductions :

1. In the case of dividend income[44] (and interest on securities : any reasonable sum paid by way of remuneration or commission for the purpose of realising dividend or interest.

---

44. Not being dividends under section 115-O or section 115BBDA.

2. In the case of income in the nature of family pension : Rs. 15,000 or 33$^1/_3$ per cent of such income, whichever is lower.

3. In the case of income from machinery, plant or furniture let on hire :

a. repairs to building [section 30(*a*)(*ii*)];

b. current repairs to machinery, plant or furniture and insurance premium [section 31];

c. depreciation on building, machinery, plant or furniture [section 32]; and

d. unabsorbed depreciation [section 32(2)].

4. Any other expenditure (not being a capital expenditure) expended wholly and exclusively for the purpose of earning of such income.

5. In the case of interest on compensation or enhanced compensation : 50 per cent of such interest (applicable from the assessment year 2010-11).

Other points

79. The following points should be noted—

79.1 ***Amount not deductible under section 58*** - The following are not deductible by virtue of section 58 :

79.1-1 *PERSONAL EXPENSES* [*SEC. 58(1)*(a)(i)] - Any personal expenditure of the assessee is not deductible.

79.1-2 *INTEREST* [*SEC. 58(1)*(a)(ii)] - Any interest chargeable under the Act which is payable outside India on which tax has not been paid or deducted at source is not deductible.

79.1-3 *SALARY* [*SEC. 58(1)*(a)(iii)] - Any payment chargeable under the head "Salaries" and payable outside India is not deductible if tax has not been paid or deducted therefrom [*see* para 49.1-7].

79.1-4 *WEALTH-TAX* [*SEC. 58(1A)*] - Any sum paid on account of wealth-tax is not deductible.

79.1-5 *TDS DEFAULT* [*SEC. 58(1A)*] - Disallowance provisions pertaining to TDS defaults covered by section 40(*a*)(*ia*) will be applicable with effect from the assessment year 2018-19 [*see* para 49.1-2].

79.1-6 *AMOUNT SPECIFIED BY SECTION 40A* [*SEC. 58(2)*] - Any amount specified by section 40A is not deductible while calculating income under the head "Income from other sources" [*see* paras 49.2, 49.3, 49.4 and 49.5].

79.1-7 *EXPENDITURE IN RESPECT OF ROYALTY AND TECHNICAL FEES RECEIVED BY A FOREIGN COMPANY* [*SEC. 58(3)*] - In the case of foreign companies expenditure in respect of royalties and technical service fees as specified by section 44D is not deductible.

79.1-8 *EXPENDITURE IN RESPECT OF WINNINGS FROM LOTTERY* [*SEC. 58(4)*] - No deduction shall be allowed under any provision of the Act in computing the income by way of any winnings from lotteries, crossword puzzles, races including horse races[45], card games and other games of any sort or from gambling or betting of any form or nature. Consequently, while computing the aforesaid income the following are not deductible—

1. No deduction is permissible under section 57.

2. Losses cannot be set off under sections 70, 71 and 72 against the aforesaid incomes. Under section 58(4) an allowance in connection with income under the head "Income from other sources" is not deductible under any provision of the Act including sections 70, 71 and 72 in computing income by way of winnings from lotteries, crossword puzzles, etc.; an allowance is appropriation for any purpose—*De Roche* v. *De Roche* 94 NW 767, 770.

3. No deduction is permissible under sections 80C to 80U.

Where, however, a certain percentage has to be foregone by the winner to the Government/agency conducting the lotteries, it is deductible (as it amounts to diversion by overriding title)— Circular No. 461, dated July 9, 1986.

79.2 ***Amounts not deductible by virtue of sections 115A, 115AB, 115AC, 115AD, 115BBA and 115D*** - No deduction is available under section 57 in the case of income referred to in sections 115A, 115AB, 115AC, 115AD, 115BBA and 115D.

79.3 ***Deemed profit chargeable to tax*** - The provisions of section 41(1) is applicable for computing income under the head "Income from other sources".

---

45. It covers winnings from races, etc. This provision is not applicable in the case of income from the activity of owning and maintaining race horses.

Clubbing of income

Generally, an assessee is taxed in respect of his own income. In some cases, however, the Income-tax Act deviates from this principle and the assessee may be taxed, under sections 60 to 64, in respect of incomes which legally belong to some other person

Transfer of income without transfer of assets [Sec. 60]

80. If any person transfers income without transferring the ownership of the asset, such income is taxable in the hands of the transferor. It will not make any difference whether the transfer is revocable or irrevocable or it was effected before or after the commencement of the Act.

Revocable transfer of assets [Sec. 61]

81. Any income arising to any person by virtue of a revocable transfer of assets is chargeable to tax as the income of the transferor. This is subject to the following two exceptions laid down by section 62 :

- Where the income arises to any person by virtue of a transfer by way of trust which is not revocable during the lifetime of the beneficiary and, in the case of any other transfer, which is not revocable during the lifetime of the transferee.
- Where the income arises to any person by virtue of a transfer made before April 1, 1961, which is not revocable for a period of six years or more.

Remuneration of spouse [Sec. 64(1)(ii)]

82. An individual is chargeable to tax in respect of any remuneration received by the spouse from a concern in which the individual has substantial interest.

82.1 ***When clubbing is not attracted*** - Remuneration solely attributable to the application of technical or professional knowledge and experience of the spouse is not clubbed, irrespective of the fact whether such remuneration is received from a firm or any other person.

82.2 ***When both husband and wife have a substantial interest in a concern*** - Where both husband and wife have a substantial interest in a concern and both are in receipt of remuneration from such concern, remuneration will be included in the total income of husband or wife whose total income excluding such remuneration is greater.

82.3 ***Substantial interest*** - An individual is deemed to have substantial interest, if he (individually or along with his relatives) beneficially holds equity shares carrying not less than 20 per cent voting power in the case of a company or is entitled to not less than 20 per cent of the profits in the case of a concern other than a company at any time during the previous year. "Relative", in relation to an individual, means the husband, wife, brother or sister or any lineal ascendant or descendant of that individual [section 2(*41*)].

82.4 ***Income eligible for clubbing*** - Income to be clubbed in the hands of individual is limited to salary, commission, fees or any other remuneration received by the spouse, directly or indirectly, whether in cash or in kind. Any other income, not covered by the aforesaid categories is, however, outside the scope of this section even if it accrues to the spouse from a concern in which the individual has a substantial interest.

Income from assets transferred to spouse [Sec. 64(1)(*iv*)]

83. Where an asset (other than house property) is transferred by an individual to his spouse (directly or indirectly), otherwise than for adequate consideration or in connection with an agreement to live apart, any income from such asset is deemed to be the income of the transferor.

Income from assets transferred to son's wife [Sec. 64(1)(*vi*)]

84. If an individual, directly or indirectly, transfers assets after May 31, 1973, without adequate consideration to son's wife, income arising from such assets is included in the total income of the transferor.

Income from assets transferred to a person for the benefit of spouse [Sec. 64(1)(*vii*)]

85. Where an asset is transferred by an individual, directly or indirectly, without adequate consideration, to a person or an association of persons for the immediate or deferred benefit of his or her spouse, income arising from the transferred asset is included in the total income of the transferor to the extent of such benefit.

Income from assets transferred to a person for the benefit of son's wife [Sec. 64(1)(*viii*)]

86. Where an asset is transferred by an individual, directly or indirectly, on or after June 1, 1973, without adequate consideration, to a person or an association of persons for the immediate or deferred benefit of son's wife, income arising, directly or indirectly, from the transferred assets is included in the total income of the transferor to the extent of such benefit.

Income of minor child [Sec. 64(1A)]

87. All income which arises or accrues to the minor shall be clubbed (with effect from the assessment year 1993-94) in the income of his parent. However, the income derived by the minor from manual work or from any activity involving his talent or specialised knowledge and experience and income of minor child suffering from any disability of the nature specified in section 80U will not be included in the income of his parent.

The income of minor will be included in the income of that parent whose total income [excluding the income includible under section 64(1A)] is greater and where the marriage of the parents does not subsist, the income of minor will be includible in the income of that parent who maintains the minor child in the relevant previous year. Where any such income is once included in the total income of either parent, any such income arising in any succeeding year shall not be included in the total income of the other parent, unless the Assessing Officer is satisfied (after giving that parent an opportunity of being heard) that it is necessary so to do.

In case the income of an individual includes the income of his minor child in terms of section 64(1A), such individual shall be entitled to an exemption of Rs. 1,500 in respect of each minor child if the income of such minor includible under section 64(1A) exceeds that amount. Where, however, the income of any minor so includible is less than Rs. 1,500, the aforesaid exemption shall be restricted to the income so included in the total income of the individual.

Conversion of self-acquired property into joint family property and subsequent partition [Sec. 64(2)]

88. Where a member of a Hindu undivided family has converted his self-acquired property into joint family property after December 31, 1969 (or where a member transfers his property without consideration to his Hindu undivided family), income arising from the converted or transferred property will be dealt with as follows—

- The entire income from the converted property or transferred property is taxable as the income of the transferor.
- If the converted property or transferred property is subsequently partitioned amongst the members of the family, the income derived from such converted property or transferred property as is received by the spouse of the transferor will be taxable in his hands.

88-E1 X transfers his self-acquired property being debentures of face value of Rs. 22,00,000 (yielding annual interest income at the rate of 15 per cent, interest accrues on March 31, every year) to his HUF without any consideration on April 1, 1981. On April 1, 1985, the HUF undergoes complete partition whereby the converted property is divided amongst the members of the family as follows :

	Share in the converted property Rs.	*Annual income from such property Rs.*
X	50,000	7,500
Mrs. X	60,000	9,000
Y (major son of X)	5,00,000	75,000
Mrs. Y	8,00,000	1,20,000
A (son of Y, date of birth : August 17, 1976)	2,50,000	37,500
B (son of X, date of birth : June 10, 1969)	5,40,000	81,000

•

Income from the transferred property shall be taxable in the hands of the family members as follows :

(*Rs. in thousand*)

	Assessment years				
	1982-83 to 1985-86	*1986-87 and 1987-88*	*1988-89 to 1992-93*	*1993-94 and 1994-95*	*1995-96 onwards*
X	3,30	7.5 + 9[46] + 81[46]	7.5 + 9[46]	7.5 + 9[46]	7.5 + 9[46]
Mrs. X	—	—	—	—	—
Y	—	75	75	75 + 36[47]	75
Mrs. Y	—	1,20	1,20	1,20	1,20
A	—	37.5	37.5	—	37.5
B	—	—	81	81	81
Total	3,30	3,30	3,30	3,28.5	3,30

Income from the accretion to assets

89. In the aforesaid cases, income arising to the transferee from the property transferred is taxable in the hands of the transferor. However, income arising to the transferee from the accretion of such property or from accumulated income of such property is not includible in the total income of the transferor. For instance, where X transfers Rs. 1,00,000 to his wife without any consideration and Mrs. X deposits the money in a bank, interest received from the bank on such deposits is taxable in the hands of X. If, however, Mrs. X purchases debentures of a company from the accumulated interest income, interest received by Mrs. X on debentures is taxable in her hands and is not to be clubbed with the income of X.

Clubbing of negative income

90. Under section 64, the income of specified persons is liable to be included in the total income of the individual in the circumstances mentioned in paras 80 to 89. For the purposes of including the income of specified persons in the income of the individual, the word "income" will include a loss.

Set off of losses

The process of setting off of losses and their carry forward may be covered in the following steps :

****Step 1 - Inter-source adjustment under the same head of income [para 96]***

****Step 2 - Inter-head adjustment in the same assessment year [para 97]***

(step 2 is applied only if a loss cannot be set off, fully or partly under step 1)

****Step 3 - Carry forward of loss [para 98] (step 3 is applied only if a loss cannot be set off, fully or partly under steps 1 and 2)***

---

46. By virtue of section 64(2).

47. By virtue of section 64(1A) on the assumption that income of Y is greater than that of Mrs. Y, amount included in the table is after claiming exemption of Rs. 1,500.

Set off of loss under the same head of income [Sec. 70]

96. If the net result for any assessment year in respect of any source under any head of income is a loss, the assessee is entitled to have the amount of such loss set off against the income from any other source under the same head of income. To the aforesaid rule, the following are the exceptions—

• *Loss from speculation business* - Loss in a speculation business [section 43(5) and *Explanation* to section 28 and section 73] can be set off only against the profit in a speculation business.

• *Loss from a specified business* - Any loss, computed in respect of any specified business referred to in section 35AD [*see* para 48.14] shall not be set off except against profits and gains, if any, of any specified business under section 35AD (applicable from the assessment year 2010-11 onwards).

• *Long-term capital loss* - From the assessment year 2003-04, long-term capital loss can be set off only against long-term capital gain.

• *Loss from the activity of owning and maintaining race horses* - Loss incurred in the business of owning and maintaining race horses cannot be set off against income, if any, from any other source except income from such business.

• *Loss cannot be set off against winnings from lotteries, crossword puzzles, etc.* - By virtue of section 58(4) a loss cannot be set off against winnings from lotteries, crossword puzzles, races including horse races, card games and other games of any sort or from gambling or betting of any form or nature.

Barring the aforesaid five cases, any other loss can be set off against any other income within the same head of income. For instance,—

a. loss from a house property can be set off against income from any other house property ;

b. loss from a non-speculation business can be set off against income from speculation or non-speculation business ;

c. short-term capital loss can be set off against any capital gain (whether long-term or short-term) ;

d. loss from an activity (other than the activity of owning and maintaining race horses) can be set off against any income but other than income from winnings from lotteries, crossword puzzles, etc.

Set off of loss from one head against income from another head [Sec. 71]

97. Where the net result of computation made for any assessment year in respect of any head of income is a loss, the same can be set off against the income from other heads. To the aforesaid rule, the following are the exceptions and propositions—

- Loss in a speculation business cannot be set off against any other income.
- Loss, computed in respect of any specified business referred to in section 35AD [*see* para 48.14] cannot be set off against any other income (applicable from the assessment year 2010-11 onwards).
- Losses under the head "Capital gains" cannot be set off against income under other heads of income.
- Loss from the business of owning and maintaining race horses cannot be set off against any other income.
- Loss from business/profession cannot be set off against income under the head "Salaries" [applicable from the assessment year 2005-06 onwards].
- Section 71(3A) has been inserted with effect from the assessment year 2018-19. It provides that set-off of loss under the head "Income from house property" against any other head of income shall be restricted to Rs. 2 lakh for any assessment year[48].
- By virtue of section 58(4) [*see* para 79.1-8] a loss cannot be set off against winnings from lotteries, crossword puzzles, races (including horse races), card games and other games of any sort or from gambling or betting of any form or nature.
- Where income from a particular source is exempt from tax, (*e.g.*, incomes exempt under section 10) loss from such a source cannot be set off against income chargeable to tax. For the purpose of section 71, loss of profits must be a loss of taxable profits—*Ramjilal Rais* v. *CIT* [1965] 58 ITR 181 (All.). No specific provision is required to be incorporated in the Act for denying the set off of such a loss against an assessee's taxable income.

97-E1 The following information is given by X for the assessment year 2019-20 –

		Expenditure incurred to earn income in Rs.		
	Income in Rs.	*Municipal tax*	*Interest on borrowed capital*	*Other expenses*
Salary (after standard deduction)	50,00,000	–	–	4,000
Bank interest	4,00,000	–	–	Nil

48. However, the unabsorbed loss shall be allowed to be carried forward (for next 8 years) for set-off in subsequent years (against income under the head "Income from house property").

	Income in Rs.	*Expenditure incurred to earn income in Rs.*		
		Municipal tax	*Interest on borrowed capital*	*Other expenses*
Property 1 (let out)	11,46,000	1,000	2,05,000	–
Property 2 (self-occupied)	Nil	4,000	3,65,000	–
Property 3 (let out)	1,00,000	2,000	7,00,000	–

Determine the amount of net income for the assessment year 2019-20. He is eligible for deduction of Rs. 1,30,000 under section 80C.

•

Computation of house property income –

	Property 1 Rs.	Property 2 Rs.	Property 3 Rs.
Gross annual value	11,46,000	*Nil*	1,00,000
Less: Municipal tax	1,000	*Nil*	2,000
Net annual value	11,45,000	*Nil*	98,000
Less: Standard deduction	3,43,500	*Nil*	29,400
Less: Interest on borrowed capital (in the case of self-occupied property, it cannot exceed Rs. 2,00,000)	2,05,000	2,00,000	7,00,000
Income from property [total : (–) Rs. 2,34,900]	5,96,500	(–) 2,00,000	(–) 6,31,400

Computation of net income –

	Rs.
Salary	50,00,000
Bank interest	4,00,000
Total	54,00,000
Less: House property loss (house property loss is Rs. 2,34,900, amount deductible is limited to Rs. 2,00,000)	2,00,000
Gross total income	52,00,000
Deduction under section 80C	1,30,000
Net income	50,70,000

Note - Unadjusted house property loss of Rs. 34,900 will be carried forward.

Carry forward of loss

98. If a loss cannot be set off either under the same head or under the different heads because of absence or inadequacy of income of the same year, it may be carried forward and set off against the income of the subsequent year. Under the Act, the following losses can be carried forward—

a. loss under the head "Income from house property" (applicable from the assessment year 1999-2000, *see* para 98.3);

b. loss under the head "Profits and gains of business or profession" (*i.e.,* loss from speculative or non-speculative business) [*see* para 98.1];

c. loss under the head "Capital gains" (*i.e.,* short-term or long-term capital loss) [*see* para 98.2];

d. loss under the head "Income from other sources" only from the activity of owning and maintaining race horses [*see* para 98.4].

Other remaining losses cannot be carried forward.

98.1 ***Carry forward and set off of business loss other than speculation loss [Sec. 72]*** - The right of carry forward and set off of loss arising in a business or profession is subject to the following restrictions—

• The loss can be carried forward and set off against the profits of any business or profession in a subsequent year (not necessarily the same business in which the loss has been incurred).

For this purpose, business profits would also include profits derived from a business activity but assessable under a head other than "Profits and gains of business or profession". For instance, where shares in a foreign company are held by an assessee as a part of his trading asset, dividends on such shares would form a part of business income and, consequently, he will be entitled to claim set off of business loss brought forward from earlier years against dividend of the current year. Similarly, profit on transfer of a business depreciable asset is not taxable under section 28 under the heads "Profits and gains of business or profession" but taxable as short-term capital gains. Such income can be used for adjusting brought forward business losses—*Digital Electronics Ltd.* v. *CIT* [2011] 16 taxmann.com 316 (Mum.-Trib.).

- From the assessment year 2000-01, business/profession loss can be carried forward even if the business/profession in which the loss was incurred is not continued during the year in which he wants to set off the loss.
- Loss can be carried forward and set off against the profits of the assessee who incurred the loss. However, this rule has some exceptions [*see* for instance, para 99].
- Loss cannot be carried forward for more than 8 assessment years. The time-limit of 8 year is not applicable in the case of unabsorbed depreciation allowance, unabsorbed capital expenditure on scientific research and unabsorbed capital expenditure on family planning [*see* para 48.3-8].
- Loss cannot be carried forward unless it is determined in pursuance of a return filed by the assessee under section 139. If the return of loss is submitted after the due date, the delay may be condoned if a few conditions are satisfied—- Circular No. 9/2015$, dated June 9, 2015[49]. Application for condonation of delay shall not be entertained beyond the period of 6 years from the end of the assessment year for which such application is made. Such application should be disposed of within 6 months from the end of the month in which application is received by the department.
- Brought forward loss of a business referred to in section 35AD can be set off in a subsequent year only against income from the business referred to in section 35AD (applicable from the assessment year 2010-11 onwards). There is no time-limit for this purpose.

98.2 ***Carry forward and set-off of capital loss [Sec. 74]*** - Where the net result of computation under the head "Capital gains" is a loss, such loss shall be carried forward to the following assessment year and it can be set off against any income under the head "Capital gains" as follows—

1. From the assessment year 2003-04, long-term capital loss can be set off only against long-term capital gain[50].

2. Short-term capital loss can be set off against any capital gains (*i.e.*, short-term or long-term capital gains).

3. Short-term/long-term capital loss can be carried forward for 8 assessment years immediately succeeding the assessment year in which the loss was first computed.

4. Such loss cannot be carried forward unless the return is filed within the time-limit of section 139(1). If the return of loss is submitted after the due date, the delay may be condoned if a few conditions are satisfied—Circular No. 9/2015$, dated June 9, 2015[49].

98.3 ***Carry forward and set off of loss from house property [Sec. 71B]*** - Section 71B was inserted with effect from the assessment year 1999-2000. It provides that where the assessee incurs any loss under the head "Income from house property" and such loss is not fully adjusted under other heads of income in the same assessment year, then from the assessment year 1999-2000 the balance loss shall be allowed to be carried forward and set off in subsequent years subject to a limit of 8 assessment years against income from house property.

---

49. CBDT has power under section 119(2) to condone delay in case of a return which is filed late and where a claim for carry forward of losses is made—*Lodhi Property Co. Ltd.* v. *Department of Revenue* [2010] 191 Taxman 74 (Delhi). Moreover, disentitlement for carry forward of loss under section 80 comes into play only when the original income-tax return disclosing loss sought to be carried forward is not filed within time prescribed under section 139(1); date of filing of revised return is not to be considered for this purpose—*CIT* v. *Ashok Walia* [2013] 60 SOT 72 (URO) (Kol.).

50. Though transfer of depreciable asset, held for more than 36 months, gives rise to short term capital gain for the purpose of computation of income under section 50, it shall be considered as long term capital gain for setting off losses under section 74—*CIT* v. *Parrys (Eastern) (P.) Ltd.* [2016] 238 Taxman 14 (Bom.).

$ For Circular No. 9/2015, log on to *taxmann.com/readyreckoner.aspx.*

98.4 ***Rule of carry forward of loss in brief*** - The Table given below highlights the rule of carry forward of loss in brief :

Type of loss to be carried forward to next year(s)	*Profit against which carried forward loss can be set off in next year(s)*	*For how many years loss can be carried forward*	*Should the business be continued*	*Is it necessary to submit return of loss in time*
1. House property loss	Income under the head "Income from house property"	8 years	NA	No
2. Speculation loss	Speculation profits	4 years[51]	Not necessary	Yes[53]
3. Non-speculation business loss				
3.1 On account of unabsorbed depreciation, capital expenditure on scientific research and family planning	Any income (not being salary income from the assessment year 2005-06)	No time-limit	Not necessary	No
3.2 Loss from a specified business under section 35AD [*see* para 48.14]	Income from a specified business under section 35AD	No time-limit	Not necessary	Yes (No, up to AY 2015-16)[53]
3.3 Other remaining business loss	Any business profit (whether from speculation or otherwise)	8 years	Not necessary[52]	Yes[53]
4. Capital loss				
4.1 Short-term capital loss	Any income under the head "Capital gains"	8 years	Not necessary	Yes[53]
4.2 Long-term capital loss	Long-term capital gains (up to the assessment year 2002-03 any income under the head "Capital gains")	8 years	Not necessary	Yes[53]
5. Loss from the activity of owning and maintaining race horses	Income from the activity of owning and maintaining race horses	4 years	Yes	Yes[53]

98.5 ***Loss on sale of shares, securities or units [Sec. 94(7)]*** - Sub-section (7) was inserted in section 94 from the assessment year 2002-03.

• *Record date* - Record date is the date to be fixed by a company/mutual fund/UTI for the purposes of entitlement of the holder of the securities/shares/units to receive dividend (or income).

• *Conditions* - Section 94(7) is applicable if the following conditions are satisfied—

1. Any person buys or acquires any securities/shares/units within a period of 3 months before the record date.

2. Such a person sells or transfers such securities/shares/units within a period of 3 months (9 months in the case of units, from the assessment year 2005-06) after the record date.

3. The dividend or income on such securities/shares/units received (or receivable) by such person is exempt from tax.

• *Consequences if the above conditions are satisfied* - If the above conditions are satisfied, then loss arising to the taxpayer on account of purchase and sale of securities/shares/units, to the extent such loss does not exceed the amount of dividend income received (or receivable) on such securities/shares/units, shall be ignored for the purpose of computing the income chargeable to tax.

98.5-E1 X purchases on May 10, 2018, 1000 equity shares (non-listed) of Rs. 10 each in A Ltd. @ Rs. 55.55. On October 20, 2018, he transfers 800 equity shares @ Rs. 37 per share and remaining 200 shares are transferred on December 20, 2018 @ Rs. 20 per share. A Ltd. declares 50 per cent dividend (record date : August 3, 2018). During the previous year 2018-19, he has generated long-term capital gain of Rs. 76,000 on sale of gold.

•

51. 8 years up to the assessment year 2005-06.

52. From the assessment year 2000-01 the loss can be carried forward even if the business/profession is discontinued.

53. If return of income is submitted after the due date, the delay may be condoned if a few conditions are satisfied—Circular No. 9/2015[$], dated June 9, 2015.

[$] For Circular No. 9/2015, log on to *taxmann.com/readyreckoner.aspx*.

	800 shares Rs.	200 shares Rs.
Sale consideration	29,600	4,000
Less : Cost of acquisition	44,440	11,110
Short-term capital gain	(–) 14,840	(–) 7,110
Dividend	4,000	1,000
Whether section 94(7) is applicable	*Yes*	*No*

Computation of income

Long-term capital gain on sale of gold	76,000
Less :	
Short-term capital loss on sale of 800 shares [Rs. 14,840 – Rs. 4,000]	(–) 10,840
Short-term capital loss on sale of 200 shares	(–) 7,110
Long-term capital gain	58,050

98.6 ***Loss arising in the case of bonus stripping [Sec. 94(8)]*** - To prevent the practice of bonus stripping, section 94(8) has been inserted.

98.6-1 *CONDITIONS* - Section 94(8) is applicable if the following conditions are satisfied—

1. The taxpayer buys or acquires any unit (hereinafter referred to as "original unit") within a period of 3 months prior to the record date.

2. Such person is allotted additional units without any payment on the basis of holding of such units (hereinafter referred to as "bonus units") on such record date.

3. Such person sells or transfers all (or any) of the original units within a period of 9 months after such record date.

4. But he continues to hold all (or any) of the bonus units.

98.6-2 *CONSEQUENCES IF THE ABOVE CONDITIONS ARE SATISFIED* - Section 94(8) imposes the following restrictions if the above conditions are satisfied—

1. The loss (if any) arising to the taxpayer on account of purchase and sale of all (or any) of the aforesaid original units shall be ignored for the purposes of computing his income chargeable to tax.

2. The amount of loss so ignored shall be deemed to be the cost of purchase or acquisition of bonus units as are held by him on the date of such sale or transfer.

98.6-E1 The following information is given—

Name of the units - Units of ITD Mutual Fund (debt based) (face value : Rs. 10).

Record date for allotment of bonus unit - November 3, 2018 (a person holding 3 units will get 1 bonus unit).

X purchases 6,000 above-mentioned units on August 26, 2018 at the rate of Rs. 70 per unit. On November 3, 2018, he gets 2,000 bonus units. After November 3, 2018, the following transactions take place—

- *Transaction 1 - On January 10, 2019, he transfers 500 original units at the rate of Rs. 75 per unit.* The resulting short-term capital gain of Rs. 2,500 is chargeable to tax. Since there is no loss in this transaction, section 94(8) is not applicable and the transaction does not have any consequence in respect of future transactions.

Transaction 2 - On February 12, 2019, X transfers 1,000 original units at the rate of Rs. 55 per unit. The resulting short-term capital loss of Rs. 15,000 shall be ignored. Rs. 15,000 will become cost of acquisition of 2,000 bonus units (*i.e.*, Rs. 7.5 per unit).

Transaction 3 - On February 26, 2019, he transfers 800 bonus units at the rate of Rs. 45 per unit. Cost of acquisition is taken as Rs. 7.5 per unit. The resulting short-term capital gain of Rs. 30,000 shall be chargeable to tax.

Transaction 4 - On February 28, 2019, he transfers 700 original units at the rate of Rs. 46 per unit. The resulting short-term capital loss of Rs. 16,800 shall be ignored. Rs. 16,800 will become cost of acquisition of remaining 1,200 bonus units (*i.e.*, Rs. 14 per unit *plus* Rs. 7.5 calculated after Transaction 2).

Transaction 5 - On March 3, 2019, he transfers 600 bonus units at the rate of Rs. 30 per unit. Cost of acquisition is taken as Rs. 21.5 per unit. The resulting short-term capital gain of Rs. 5,100 shall be chargeable to tax.

Carry forward and set off of business loss and depreciation - When permissible in the hands of amalgamated/ resulting company or co-operative bank [Secs. 72A, 72AA and 72AB]

99. Generally, depreciation and business loss can be carried forward by a person who has incurred the loss. Sections 72A, 72AA and 72AB provide a few exceptions to this rule. These provisions are as follows—

a. amalgamation of companies [*see* para 99.1];

b. demerger [*see* para 99.2];

c. conversion of a proprietary concern/firm into company [*see* para 99.3];

d. conversion of private company/unlisted public company into limited liability partnership [*see* para 99.4];

e. amalgamation of banking company with banking institution [*see* para 99.5]; and

f. merger/demerger of co-operative banks [*see* para 99.6].

99.1 ***Amalgamation*** - If the following conditions are satisfied, then the accumulated business loss and the unabsorbed depreciation[54] of the amalgamating company shall be deemed to be loss business/ depreciation of the amalgamated company for the previous year in which the amalgamation is effected—

a. there has been (*a*) an amalgamation of a company owning an industrial undertaking[55] or a ship or a hotel with another company or (*b*) an amalgamation of a banking company referred to in section 5(*c*) of the Banking Regulation Act, 1949 with a specified bank; or (*c*) (from the assessment year 2008-09) an amalgamation of a public sector airlines with another public sector airlines;

b. the amalgamating company has been engaged in the business[56] in which the accumulated business loss occurred or depreciation remains unabsorbed for 3 years or more years;

c. the amalgamating company has held continuously as on the date of the amalgamation at least three-fourths of the book value of fixed assets held by it 2 years prior to the date of amalgamation;

d. the amalgamated company continues to hold at least three-fourths in the book value of fixed assets of the amalgamating company which it has acquired as a result of amalgamation for 5 years from the effective date of amalgamation;

e. the amalgamated company continues the business of the amalgamating company for a minimum period of 5 years; and

f. the amalgamated company fulfils such other conditions [*see* para 99.1-1] as may be prescribed to ensure the revival of the business of the amalgamating company or to ensure that the amalgamation is for genuine business purpose.

In case the above specified conditions are not fulfilled, then that part of brought forward business loss and unabsorbed depreciation which has been set off by the amalgamated company shall be treated as the income of the amalgamated company for the year in which the failure to fulfil the conditions occurs.

For the aforesaid purpose, an "industrial undertaking" means an undertaking engaged in the manufacture or processing of goods, or the manufacture of computer software or the business of generation or distribution of electricity or any other form of power or mining or the construction of ships, aircrafts or rail systems or the business of providing telecommunication services whether basic or cellular, including radio paging, domestic satellite service, network of trunking, broadband network and internet services. The "specified bank" means the State Bank of India or a subsidiary bank as defined in the State Bank of India (Subsidiary Bank) Act, 1959, or a nationalised bank.

99.1-1 *PRESCRIBED CONDITIONS [RULE 9C]* - *Vide* rule 9C the following conditions are prescribed—

1. The amalgamated company, owning an industrial undertaking of the amalgamating company by way of amalgamation, shall achieve the level of production of at least 50 per cent of the installed capacity of the said undertaking before the end of 4 years from the date of amalgamation and continue to maintain the said minimum level of production till the end of 5 years from the date of amalgamation.

---

54. Unabsorbed depreciation includes unabsorbed capital expenditure on scientific research/family planning—*ITO* v. *Mahyco Vegetable Seeds Ltd.* [2008] 24 SOT 46 (Mum.).

55. Hospital is not an industrial undertaking—*CIT* v. *Apollo Hospitals Enterprises Ltd.* [2008] 171 Taxman 397 (Mad.).

56. Section 72A(2)(*i*) clearly uses the words 'engaged in business' and there is no requirement of starting of production to be eligible for deduction—*CIT* v. *Gujarat Nre Coke Ltd.* [2008] 25 SOT 47 (Kol.).

However, the Central Government, on an application made by the amalgamated company, may relax the condition of achieving the level of production or the period during which the same is to be achieved or both in suitable cases having regard to the genuine efforts made by the amalgamated company to attain the prescribed level of production and the circumstances preventing such efforts from achieving the same.

2. The amalgamated company shall furnish to the Assessing Officer a certificate in Form No. 62[57], duly verified by an accountant, with reference to the books of account and other documents showing particulars of production, along with the return of income for the assessment year relevant to the previous year during which the prescribed level of production is achieved and for subsequent assessment years relevant to the previous years falling within 5 years from the date of amalgamation.

99.2 ***Demerger*** - In the case of demerger, the accumulated business loss and unabsorbed depreciation of the demerged company will be allowed to be carried forward and set off in the hands of the resulting company.

The Central Government may, for this purpose, by notification in the Official Gazette, specify such conditions as it considers necessary to ensure that the demerger is for genuine business purposes.

How to compute the business loss/depreciation allowance which will be carried forward by the resulting company - If the business loss/depreciation is directly relatable to the undertakings transferred to the resulting company, then such business loss/depreciation shall be allowed to be carried forward in the hands of the resulting company.

Where, however, such business loss or unabsorbed depreciation is not directly relatable to the undertakings transferred to the resulting company, it will be apportioned between the demerged company and the resulting company in the same proportion in which the assets of the undertakings have been retained by the demerged company and transferred to the resulting company, and it will be allowed to be carried forward and set off in the hands of the demerged company or the resulting company, as the case may be.

99.3 ***Business loss of a firm or a proprietary concern/firm [Sec. 72A(4)]*** - Sub-section (4) of section 72A provides that in cases of succession of business, whereby a firm is succeeded by a company fulfilling the conditions laid down in section 47(*xiii*) or a proprietary concern is succeeded by a company fulfilling the conditions laid down in section 47(*xiv*), the accumulated business loss and the unabsorbed depreciation of the predecessor firm or proprietary concern, as the case may be, shall be deemed to be the business loss or as the case may be, allowance for depreciation of the successor company for the previous year in which business reorganisation was effected and the other provisions of the Act relating to set off and carry forward of business loss and allowance for depreciation shall apply accordingly.

• *When after claiming set off, condition of section 47*(xiii)/(xiv) *are not complied* - When conditions of section 47(*xiii*)/(*xiv*) are not complied with, the set off of business loss or allowance of depreciation made in the previous year in the hands of the successor company shall be deemed to be the income of the company chargeable to tax in the year in which such conditions are not complied with.

• *Meaning of "unabsorbed depreciation" and "accumulated loss"* - "Accumulated loss" and "unabsorbed depreciation" means so much of the loss/depreciation of the predecessor firm/proprietary concern under the head "Profits and gains of business or profession" (not being speculative business loss) which such firm/concern would have been entitled to carry forward and set off if the business re-organisation had not taken place.

• *Provisions illustrated* - X and Y (1:3) are two partners of X & Co. on March 31, 2018. It has brought forward business loss of Rs. 10 crore which remains due to be set off at the end of seventh year which falls on March 31, 2018. As per section 72, a loss cannot be allowed to be carried forward for more than 8 years. Thus X & Co. has one more year after which the unadjusted accumulated loss will lapse. Now the firm is converted into a company with effect from April 1, 2018. All the assets and liabilities of the firm are taken over by the company. Shares have been allotted to X and Y (1:3) in consideration of transfer of the business of the firm. The brought forward loss of the firm can be set off by the company. The unadjusted loss will get a new lease of life for another 8 years. For this purpose, the brought forward loss shall be treated as loss of the previous year 2018-19 of the company and it can be set off against the income of the previous year 2018-19 and if it is not possible to set off, it can be carried forward up to the previous year 2026-27.

One of the conditions for carry forward of the loss of the firm is that the aggregate of the shareholding in the company of the partners of the firm should not less than 50 per cent of the total voting power in the company and their shareholding continues to be as such for a period of 5 years from the date of the succession.

Suppose the loss of Rs. 10 crore is set off by the company during the previous years 2018-19 and 2019-20 and Y transfers his entire shareholding on May 6, 2020, then Rs. 10 crore will become income of the previous year 2020-21 of the company.

99.4 ***Conversion of private company/unlisted public company into LLP [Sec. 72A(6A), applicable from the assessment year 2011-12]*** - In the case of succession of business, whereby a company (*i.e.*, a private

57. Form No. 62 is to be submitted electronically.

limited company or unlisted public limited company) is succeeded by a limited liability partnership fulfilling the conditions laid down in section 47(*xiiib*), the accumulated business loss and the unabsorbed depreciation (including unadjusted capital expenditure on scientific research) of the predecessor company, shall be deemed to be the business loss or as the case may be, allowance for depreciation of the successor limited liability partnership for the previous year in which business reorganisation was effected and the other provisions of the Act relating to set off and carry forward of business loss and allowance for depreciation shall apply accordingly.

• *When conditions of section 47(*xiiib*) are not complied* - When after adjusting loss, the successor limited liability partnership fails to comply with the conditions of section 47(*xiiib*), the amount of loss for depreciation adjusted by the limited liability partnership shall be deemed to be the income of the limited liability partnership chargeable to tax in the year in which such conditions are not complied with.

• *Meaning of "unabsorbed depreciation" and "accumulated loss"* - "Accumulated loss" and "unabsorbed depreciation" mean so much of the loss/depreciation of the predecessor company under the head "Profits and gains of business or profession" (not being speculative business loss) which such company would have been entitled to carry forward and set off if the business re-organisation had not taken place.

99.5 ***Amalgamation of banking company with banking institution*** [***Sec. 72AA***] - Section 72AA was inserted with effect from the assessment year 2005-06 with a view to providing carry forward and set-off of accumulated loss and unabsorbed depreciation allowance of a banking company against the profits of a banking institution under a scheme of amalgamation sanctioned by the Central Government.

99.6 ***Accumulated loss and unabsorbed depreciation allowance in business reorganization of co-operative banks [Sec. 72AB, applicable from the assessment year 2008-09]*** - The successor co-operative bank can set off and carry forward loss and depreciation allowance of the predecessor co-operative bank if a few conditions are satisfied.

Exemptions and deductions

Exemption available under sections 10, 10A, 10AA, 10B, 10BA, 10C, 13A, 80C to 80U are of special nature and are allowed to certain specified categories of taxpayers [Referencer 7]. While sections 10, 10A, 10AA, 10B, 10BA and 13A specify tax-free incomes [paras 104 to 106], sections 80C to 80U provide deductions from gross total income [para 107] in order to arrive at taxable income

Exemptions and deductions

102. Exemptions and deductions available under the Act may broadly be grouped as under :

a. Tax-free income [secs. 10, 10A, 10B, 10BA and 13A].

b. Deductions from gross total income [secs. 80C to 80U].

c. Income forming a part of total income on which no income-tax is payable.

Tax-free incomes [Secs. 10 and 13A]

103. The incomes enumerated below are exempt from tax under sections 10 and 13A :

• Agricultural income [clause (*1*)].

• Payments received from family income by a member of a Hindu undivided family [clause (*2*)].

• Share of profit from a firm [clause (*2A*)].

• Interest received by a non-resident from prescribed securities [clause (*4*)].

• Interest received by a person[58] who is resident outside India on amounts credited in the "Non-resident (External) Account"[59] [clause (*4*)].

• In the case of an Indian citizen or a person of Indian origin who is a non-resident, the interest from notified Central Government securities [*i.e.*, National Savings Certificates, VI and VII Issues] if such certificates are issued before June 1, 2002 and subscribed in foreign currency or other foreign exchange remitted from outside through official channels [clause (*4B*)].

• **Interest** payable **to a non-resident/foreign company** by an **Indian company/business trust** pertaining to money borrowed from a source outside India by way of issue of **rupee denominated bond [as referred to in section 194LC(2)(*ia*)] during September 17, 2018 and March 31, 2019** [clause (*4C*)].

• Any income accrued or arisen to, or received by, a specified fund as a result of **transfer of capital asset [referred to in section 47(*viiab*)], on a recognised stock exchange located in any International Financial Services Centre (and where the consideration for such transaction is paid or payable in convertible foreign exchange), to the extent such income accrued or arisen to, or is received in respect of units held by a non-resident** [clause (*4D*), applicable from the assessment year 2020-21].

• Leave travel concession provided by an employer to his Indian citizen employee [clause (*5*)—*see* para 15.17].

• Remuneration received by foreign diplomats of all categories [clause (*6*)].

• Salary received by a foreign citizen in India as an employee of a foreign enterprise provided his stay in India does not exceed 90 days [clause (*6*)(*vi*)].

• Salary received by a non-resident foreign citizen as a member of ship's crew provided his total stay in India does not exceed 90 days [clause (*6*)(*viii*)].

• Remuneration received by an employee, being a foreign national, of a foreign Government deputed in India for training in a Government establishment or public sector undertaking [clause (*6*)(*xi*)].

• Tax paid on behalf of foreign companies [clause (*6A*)].

• Tax paid by Government or an Indian concern in the case of a non-resident/foreign company [clause (*6B*)].

• Income arising to notified foreign companies from services provided in or outside India in projects connected with the security of India [clause (*6C*)].

• Any income arising to a non-resident/foreign company by way of royalty from (or fees for technical services rendered in or outside India to) the National Technical Research Organisation [clause (*6D*), applicable from the assessment year 2018-19].

• Foreign allowance granted by the Government of India to its employees posted abroad [clause (*7*)].

• Remuneration received from a foreign Government by an individual who is in India in connection with any sponsored co-operative technical assistance programme with a foreign Government and the income of the family members of such employee [clauses (*8*) and (*9*)].

• Remuneration/fees received by non-resident consultants and their foreign employers [clauses (*8A*) and (*8B*)].

• Death-*cum*-retirement gratuity subject to the limits specified in para 12.2 [clause (*10*)].

• Commuted value of pension subject to the limits specified in para 12.3 [clause (*10A*)].

• Leave salary [clause (*10AA*)—*see* para 12.1].

• Retrenchment compensation [clause (*10B*)—*see* para 12].

• Compensation received by victims of Bhopal gas leak disaster [clause (*10BB*)].

• Compensation from the Central Government or a State Government or a local authority received by an individual or his legal heir on account of any disaster [clause (*10BC*)—applicable from the assessment year 2005-06].

• Compensation received from a public sector company at the time of voluntary retirement or separation [clause (*10C*), *see* para 12.4].

• Tax on non-monetary perquisite paid by employer [clause (*10CC*)][60].

---

58. Joint holders of account are qualified for exemption—Circular No. 592, dated February 4, 1991.

59. Taking into account the circumstances under which the NRIs have returned to India and in view of the decision of the Reserve Bank of India to allow them to maintain their NRE/FCNR Accounts up to March 31, 1991, the Central Board of Direct Taxes have clarified that individuals normally resident in Kuwait and returning to India after August 2, 1990 would be eligible for the exemption under section 10(*4*)(*ii*) in respect of such accounts maintained up to June 30, 1991—Circular No. 604.

60. Exemption under section 10(*10C*) is available only in respect of tax on non-monetary perquisite paid by employer. The exemption is available whether an employer pays Indian income-tax or foreign income-tax pertaining to non-monetary perquisites of his employee — *Pramod Bhasin* v. *CIT* [2012] 53 SOT 175 (Delhi). If tax on salary is paid by the employer on behalf of his/its employee, it is a perquisite provided for by way of non-monetary payment and, therefore, the provisions of section 10(*10CC*) would be applicable—*RBF Rig Corpn. LIC (RBFRC)* v. *CIT* [2007] 165 Taxman 101 (Delhi)(SB).

• Any sum (including bonus) on life insurance policy (not being a Keyman insurance policy) [clause (*10D*)].
• Any amount from statutory provident fund or public provident fund [clause (*11*)].
• Any payment from Sukanya Samriddhi Account [clause (*11A*), applicable from the assessment year 2015-16].
• Accumulated balance due and becoming payable to an employee from a recognized provident fund to the extent it is provided in rule 8 of Part A of the Fourth Schedule [clause (*12*)—*see* para 17].
• Any payment from NPS to an employee [or a non-employee (applicable from the assessment year 2019-20)] on closure of his account or his opting out of NPS (to the extent it does not exceed 40 per cent (**60 per cent**, applicable from the assessment year 2020-21) of total amount payable to him at the time of closure) [clause (*12A*)].
• Partial withdrawal (to the extent of 25 per cent of contribution made by an employee) from NPS [clause (*12B*), applicable from the assessment year 2018-19].
• Amount from an approved superannuation fund to legal heirs of the employee [clause (*13*)—*see* para 18].
• House rent allowance subject to certain limits [clause (*13A*)—*see* para 13.1].
• Special allowance granted to an employee [clause (*14*)—*see* para 13.3].
• Income received by a public financial institution as exchange risk premium in certain cases [clause (*14A*)].
• Interest from certain exempted securities [clause (*15*)—*see* para 77.3-1].
• Payment made by an Indian company, engaged in the business of operation of an aircraft, to acquire an aircraft on lease from a foreign Government or foreign enterprise [clause *15A*].
• Scholarship granted to meet the cost of education [clause (*16*)].
• Daily allowance of a Member of Parliament or State Legislature (entire amount is exempt), and any other allowance subject to certain conditions [clause (*17*)].
• Rewards given by the Central or State Government for literary, scientific or artistic work or attainment or for service for alleviating the distress of the poor, the weak and the ailing, or for proficiency in sports and games or gallantry awards approved by the Government [clause (*17A*)].[61]
• Pension and family pension of gallantry award winners [clause (*18*)].
• Family pension received by family members of armed forces [clause (*19*)].
• Notional property income of any one place occupied by a former ruler [clause (*19A*)].
• Income of local authorities [clause (*20*)].
• Any income of housing boards constituted in India for planning, development or improvement of cities, towns or villages [clause (*20A*)].
• Any income of an approved research association [clause (*21*)].
• Income of a notified news agency [clause (*22B*)].
• Any income (other than interest on securities, income from property, income received for rendering any specific services and income by way of interest or dividends) of approved professional bodies [clause (*23A*)].
• Any income received by any person on behalf of any Regimental Fund or non-public fund established by the armed forces of the Union for the welfare of the past and present members of such forces or their dependants [clause (*23AA*)].
• Income of funds established for the welfare of employees [clause (*23AAA*)].
• Any income of the pension fund set up by LIC or any other insurer approved by the Controller of Insurance or Insurance Regulatory and Development Authority [clause (*23AAB*)].
• Any income (other than business income) of a trust or a society approved by Khadi and Village Industries Commission [clause (*23B*)].
• Income of an authority whether known as Khadi and Village Industries Board or by any other name for the development of khadi and village industries [clause (*23BB*)].
• Income arising to any body or authority established, constituted or appointed under any enactment for the administration of public, religious or charitable trusts or endowments or societies for religious or charitable purposes [clause (*23BBA*)].
• Income of the European Economic Community derived in India by way of interest, dividends or capital gains in certain cases under the European Community International Institutional Partners Scheme, 1993 [clause (*23BBB*)].

---

61. Any payment made, whether in cash or in kind, as a reward by the Central Government or a State Government to the medal winners of the Olympic Games or Commonwealth Games or Asian Games - Order [F. No. 199/03/2013-ITA.1], dated January 28, 2014.

- Any income of SAARC Fund for Regional Projects [clause (*23BBC*)].
- Any income of Secretariat of Asian Organisation of Supreme Audit Institutions [clause (*23BBD*)]
- Any income of IRDA [clause (*23BBE*)]
- Income of the Central Electricity Regulatory Commission [clause (*23BBG*)].
- Income of the Prasar Bharati (Broadcasting Corpn. of India) [clause (*23BBH*), applicable from the assessment year 2013-14].
- Income received by any person on behalf of specified national funds, approved public charitable institutions, educational institute and hospital [clause (*23C*)][62].
- Income of a Mutual Fund set up by a public sector bank or public financial institution [clause (*23D*)].
- Any income of a securitisation trust from the activity of securitisation [clause (*23DA*)].
- Income of investor protection fund [clause (*23EA*)].
- Income of Credit Guarantee Fund Trust [clause (*23EB*)].
- Income of Investor Protection Fund by way of contributions from commodity exchange and the members thereof [clause (*23EC*)].
- Any income of Investor Protection Fund by way of contributions received from a depository [clause (*23ED*)].
- Specified income of Core Settlement Guarantee Fund [clause (23EE), applicable from the assessment year 2016-17].
- Income by way of dividend or long-term capital gain of venture capital fund/undertaking [clause (*23FA*)].
- Income of venture capital fund/venture capital company [clause (*23FB*)].
- Any income of an investment fund other than the income chargeable under the head "Profits and gains of business or profession" [clause (*23FBA*), applicable from the assessment year 2016-17].
- Any income referred to in section 115UB, accruing or arising to, or received by, a unitholder of an investment fund, being that proportion of income which is of the same nature as income chargeable under the head "Profits and gains of business or profession" [clause (*23FBB*), applicable from the assessment year 2016-17].
- Any income of a business trust by way of interest received or receivable from a special purpose vehicle [clause (*23FC*)].
- Any income of a business trust, being a real estate investment trust, by way of renting or leasing or letting out any real estate asset owned directly by such business trust [clause (*23FCA*), applicable from the assessment year 2016-17].
- Any distributed income (referred to in section 115UA), received by a unitholder from the business trust, not being that proportion of the income which is of the same nature as the income referred to in clause (*23FC*) or clause (*23FCA*) [clause (*23FD*)].
- Income by way of interest on securities, property income and income from other sources of a registered trade union or an association of registered trade unions [clause (*24*)].
- Any income received by a person on behalf of statutory provident fund, recognised provident fund, approved superannuation fund, approved gratuity fund and approved coal-mines provident fund [clause (*25*)].
- Income of Employees' State Insurance Fund [clause (*25A*)].
- Income of a member of a scheduled tribe, residing in Nagaland, Manipur, Tripura, Arunachal Pradesh, Mizoram and Ladakh which accrues/arises to him from any source in the said area or any income by way of dividend and interest on securities [clause (*26*)].
- Any income of an individual, being a Sikkimese, which accrues or arises from any source in the State of Sikkim or by way of dividend or interest on securities [clause (*26AAA*)].
- Any income of an agricultural produce marketing committee/board constituted under any law for the purpose of the marketing of agricultural produce [clause (*26AAB*)].
- Any income of a statutory corporation or of a body/institution, financed by the Government formed for promoting the interest of scheduled castes/tribes [clause (*26B*)].
- Income of National Minorities Development and Finance Corporation [clause (*26BB*)].
- Income of ex-serviceman corporations [clause (*26BBB*)].
- Income of a co-operative society formed for promoting interest of members of scheduled castes/tribes [clause (*27*)].
- Income of certain Commodity Boards/Authorities [clause (*29A*)].

62. *See* Circular No. 14/2015, dated August 17, 2015.

• Subsidy from the Tea Board for replanting or replacement of tea bushes or for rejuvenation or consolidation of areas used for cultivation of tea in India [clause (*30*)].

• Subsidy received by planters [clause (*31*)].

• Income of a minor child up to Rs. 1,500 in respect of each minor child whose income is includible under section 64(1A) [clause (*32*)].

• Capital gains on transfer of US64 [clause (*33*), *see* para 63.2-1].

• Dividend from domestic companies [not being dividend (from the assessment year 2017-18) in excess of Rs. 10 lakh which is covered by section 115BBDA] [clause (*34*) – *see* para 77.1-1a].

• Any income arising to a shareholder on account of buy-back of (*a*) unlisted shares (during June 1, 2013 and July 4, 2019, or (*b*) **listed/unlisted shares (on or after July 5, 2019)** by the company as referred to in section 115QA [clause (*34A*)].

• Interest on units of a Mutual Fund on or after April 1, 2003 [clause (*35*)].

• Any income (received on or before May 31, 2016) by way of distributed income referred to in section 115TA received from a securitisation trust by any person being an investor of the said trust [clause (*35A*)].

• Capital gains on transfer of listed equity shares [clause (*36*)].

• Capital gain on compensation received on compulsory acquisition of urban agriculture land [clause (*37*)—*see* para 63.2-3].

• Capital gain arising to an individual/HUF under Andhra Pradesh Capital City Land Pooling Scheme, 2015 [clause (*37A*), applicable from the assessment year 2015-16].

• Long-term capital gain in some cases, if transfer takes place before April 1, 2018 [clause (*38*), *see* para 63.2-4].

• Income from any international sporting event [clause (*39*)][63].

• Grant received by subsidiary company from holding company in the case of revival of an existing business of power generation [clause (*40*)].

• Capital gain in the above case [clause (*41*)].

• Income of a body under an agreement [clause (*42*)].

• Any income received by an individual as a loan, either in lump sum or in instalment in a transaction of reverse mortgage [clause (*43*)].

• Any income received by any person for, or on behalf of, the New Pension System Trust [clause (*44*)].

• Notified allowances/perquisites given to the Chairman, a retired Chairman or any other member or retired member of the Union Public Service Commission [clause (*45*)].

• Any specified income arising to a notified body/authority/board/trust/commission with the object of regulating/administrating any activity for the benefit of general public [clause (*46*)].

• Any income of an infrastructure debt fund set up in accordance with notified guidelines [clause (*47*)].

• Any income received in India in Indian currency by a foreign company on account of sale of crude oil (or with effect from the assessment year 2014-15, any other notified goods or notified service) to any person in India [clause (*48*)].

• Any income accruing or arising to a foreign company on account of storage of crude oil in a facility in India and sale of crude oil therefrom to any person resident in India [clause (*48A*), applicable from the assessment year 2016-17].

• Any income accruing or arising to a foreign company on account of sale of leftover stock of crude oil, if any, from the facility in India after the expiry of the agreement or the arrangement referred to in section 10(*48A*) [or on termination of such agreement/arrangement in accordance with the terms mentioned therein, applicable from the assessment year 2019-20], if a few conditions (as notified by the Central Government) are satisfied [clause (*48B*)].

• Any income of the National Financial Holdings Company Ltd. [clause (*49*)].

• Any income arising from any specified service provided on or after the date on which the provisions of Chapter VIII of the Finance Act, 2016 comes into force and chargeable to equalisation levy under that Chapter [clause (*50*)].

• Any income of a political party by way of interest on securities, property income, income from other sources or income by way of political contributions [sec. 13A].

• Voluntary contribution received by an electoral trust if a few conditions are satisfied [sec. 13B].

63. *See* Notification No. 91/2009, dated December 8, 2009.

Special provisions in respect of newly established undertakings in free trade zone, etc. [Sec. 10A]

104. Section 10A makes special provision in respect of newly established undertakings in free trade zone, etc. The provisions given below are applicable from the assessment year 2001-02.

104.1 ***Conditions to be satisfied*** - In order to get deduction, an undertaking must satisfy the following conditions :

104.1-1 *MUST BEGIN MANUFACTURE OR PRODUCTION IN FREE TRADE ZONE* - It has begun or begins to manufacture/produce[64] articles or things or computer software during the following years—

Location	*Year*
Free Trade Zone	During the previous year relevant to the assessment year 1981-82 or any subsequent year.
Electronic hardware technology park or software technology park	During the previous year relevant to the assessment year 1994-95 or any subsequent year.
Special economic zone	From April 1, 2000 to March 31, 2005[65]

104.1-2 *SHOULD NOT BE FORMED BY SPLITTING/RECONSTRUCTION OF BUSINESS* - The industrial undertaking should not have been formed by the splitting up or reconstruction of a business already in existence. However, where an industrial undertaking is formed as a result of re-establishment, reconstruction or revival by the assessee of the business of any such industrial undertaking as is referred to in section 33B, in the circumstances and within the period specified in that section the same will qualify for the tax concession.

104.1-3 *SHOULD NOT BE FORMED BY TRANSFER OF OLD MACHINERY* - The industrial undertaking should not have been formed by the transfer of a new business of machinery or plant previously used for any purpose. For this purpose, any machinery or plant which was used outside India by any person other than the assessee is not regarded as machinery or plant previously used for any purpose if the following conditions are fulfilled, namely:

a. such machinery or plant was not previously used in India;

b. such machinery or plant is imported into India from a foreign country; and

c. no deduction on account of depreciation in respect of such machinery or plant has been allowed or is allowable in computing the total income of any person for any period prior to the installation of the machinery or plant by the assessee.

Further, this tax concession is not denied in a case where the total value of used machinery or plant transferred to the new business does not exceed 20 per cent of the total value of the machinery or plant used in that business.

104.1-4 *THERE MUST BE REPATRIATION OF SALE PROCEEDS INTO INDIA* - Sale proceeds of articles or things or computer software exported out of India must be received in, or brought into India by the assessee in convertible foreign exchange during the previous year or within a period of six months from the end of the relevant previous year. For instance, for the assessment year 2011-12, the repatriation of the sale proceeds into India must be completed on or before September 30, 2011. The sale proceeds shall be deemed to have been received in India where such sale proceeds are credited to a separate account maintained for the purpose by the assessee with any bank outside India with the approval of the Reserve Bank of India.

• *Extension of time-limit* - The aforesaid limit of six months can be extended by the Reserve Bank of India or such other competent authority as is authorised under any law for the time being in force for regulating payments and dealings in foreign exchange.

• *Remittance after the expiry of time-limit* - If foreign exchange is not remitted within six months from the end of the previous year (or within the extended time-limit as approved by RBI[66]), then deduction under sections 10A, 10B and 10BA is not available. In such a case—

a. if the foreign currency is remitted after the expiry of time-limit of 6 months (or after the expiry of extended time-limit);

b. the Assessing Officer shall amend the order of assessment so as to allow deduction under sections 10A, 10B and 10BA;

c. the order shall be amended within a period of 4 years from the end of the previous year in which the foreign currency is remitted.

104.1-5 *AUDIT* - Deduction under section 10A shall not be admissible with effect from April 1, 2001, unless the assessee furnishes in the prescribed form [Form No. 56F] along with the return[67] of income, the report of a

64. It will also include polishing of precious stones with effect from the assessment year 2004-05.

65. In the case of unit which begins to manufacture or produce an article or thing or computer software on or after April 1, 2005 in a special economic zone, deduction will not be available under section 10A. Such unit can claim deduction under section 10AA.

66. Extension of time for realization of export proceeds by the competent authority under FEMA can be said to be approval granted by the competent authority under section 10A(3)—*CIT* v. *Morgan Stanley Advantage Services (P.) Ltd.* [2011] 202 Taxman 40 (Bom.).

67. From April 1, 2014, audit report should be submitted electronically. Provisions pertaining to electronic submission of audit report were not applicable prior to April 1, 2014 (for period prior to April 1, 2014, audit report may be retained by the assessee and it may be furnished in original whenever the Assessing Officer wants to examine it in assessment proceedings or otherwise).

chartered accountant certifying that the deduction has been correctly claimed in accordance with the provisions of section 10A.

104.1-6 *DEDUCTION SHOULD BE CLAIMED IN THE RETURN OF INCOME* - Deduction under section 10A is not available unless it is claimed in the return of income. In other words, if the assessee fails to make a claim in his return of income of this deduction, the same will not be allowed (applicable from the assessment year 2003-04 onwards).

104.2 ***Amount of deduction - General provision*** - If the aforesaid conditions are satisfied, the deduction under section 10A may, be computed as under :

Profits of the business of the undertaking × Export turnover ÷ Total turnover of the business carried on by the undertaking[68]

• The following points should be considered—

1. Export turnover - For this purpose, 'export turnover' means the consideration in respect of export by the undertaking of articles or things or computer software received in (or brought into) India by the assessee in convertible foreign exchange within the prescribed period but does not include the following :

a. freight;

b. telecommunication charges;

c. insurance attributable to the delivery of the articles or things or computer software outside India;

d. expenses, if any, incurred in foreign exchange in providing the technical services outside India.

Freight, telecommunication charges and insurance are deductible only if the assessee from the importers recovers these in addition to sale price of goods. If nothing is recovered from the importers but these expenses are incurred by the assessee, then no adjustment is required. In cases where such expenses are separately charged, the expenses are required to be reduced from the consideration received for the purpose of arriving the export turnover—*Patni Telecom (P.) Ltd.* v. *ITO* [2008] 22 SOT 38 (Hyd.). When these expenses are excluded for the purposes of 'export turnover' then on the same assumption, reason and analogy it should be excluded from 'total turnover'.

Sale of software by one STP to another STP within the country cannot be treated as deemed export for the purposes of exemption under section 10A—*Tata Elxsi Ltd.* v. *CIT* [2008] 115 TTJ (Bang.) 423.

2. Site development - On site development of computer software (including services for development of software) outside India, shall be deemed to be export of computer software outside India.

3. Foreign exchange fluctuation - Deduction under section 10A has to be allowed in respect of profit on account of foreign exchange gain—*Renaissance Jewellery (P.) Ltd.* v. *ITO* [2005] 4 SOT 50 (Mum.).

4. Royalty - Royalty earned from export of software is entitled to relief under section 10A—*Wipro Limited* v. *CIT* [2005] 96 TTJ (Bang.) 211.

5. Losses of other undertakings - Profit for the business of undertaking shall be calculated without adjusting losses and unabsorbed depreciation of other undertakings (eligible or non-eligible unit under section 10A)—*CIT* v. *Yokogawa India Ltd.* [2007] 13 SOT 470 (Bang.), *FCI Technology Services Ltd.* v. *CIT* [2011] 9 taxmann.com 47 (Coch. - ITAT).

6. Brought forward losses - Brought forward losses (incurred after April 1, 2001) cannot be deducted from profit of the business of the undertaking. In other words, deduction under section 10A will be available in respect of profit of an eligible undertaking without setting off of brought forward losses.

7. Section 80AB - Deduction under section 10A is not controlled by section 80AB as deduction under section 10A is not a deduction under Chapter VI-A—*Enercon Wind Farms (Krishna) Ltd.* v. *CIT* [2008] 21 SOT 29 (Mum.).

8. Arm's Length price - As per proviso to section 92C(4), no deduction under section 10A or 10AA or 10B or under Chapter VI-A is to be allowed in respect of amount of income by which the total income of the assessee is enhanced as a result of computation of arm's length price—*I Gate Global Solutions Ltd.* v. *CIT* [2008] 24 SOT 3 (Bang.).

104.2-1 *PERIOD OF DEDUCTION* - If the aforesaid conditions are satisfied, the assessee can claim deduction under section 10A from his total income, for a period of ten consecutive assessment years beginning with the assessment year relevant to the previous year in which the undertaking begins to manufacture or produce such articles or things or computer software.

• For the undertakings which have claimed exemption up to assessment year 2000-01 under the old section 10A, the deduction shall be available for the unexpired period of the 10 consecutive assessment years under the new section 10A.

• For an undertaking which was initially located in free trade zone or export processing zone and is subsequently located in a special economic zone by reason of conversion of such zones into a special economic zone, the deduction shall be available for 10 years from the previous year in which the undertaking was first set up in such free trade zone or export processing zone.

• 'Relevant assessment year' means any assessment year falling within a period of ten consecutive assessment years referred to in section 10A.

• No deduction under section 10A shall be allowed to any undertaking from the assessment year 2012-13.

---

68. For the assessment year 2003-04, 90 per cent of it is deductible.

104.3 ***Amount of deduction - Special provision*** - The deduction under section 10A in the case of an undertaking which begins to manufacture or produce articles or things or computer software during April 1, 2002 and March 31, 2005[69] in any special economic zone, shall be as follows[70] (this deduction is available even beyond the assessment year 2011-12)—

• *First 5 years* - 100 per cent of profits and gains derived from the export of such articles or things or computer software is deductible for a period of 5 consecutive assessment years (beginning with the assessment year relevant to the previous year in which the undertaking begins to manufacture or produce such articles or things or computer software, as the case may be).

• *Sixth and seventh year* - 50 per cent of such profits and gains is deductible for further 2 assessment years.

• *Eighth, ninth and tenth year* - For the next three years, a further deduction would be available to the extent of 50 per cent of the profit provided an equivalent amount is debited to the profit and loss account of the previous year and credited to Special Economic Zone Re-investment Allowance Reserve Account (hereinafter referred to as Special Reserve Account). The following conditions should be satisfied—

1. The Special Reserve Account should be utilised for the purpose of acquiring new plant and machinery.

2. The new plant and machinery should be first put to use before the expiry of 3 years from the end of the year in which the Special Reserve Account was created.

3. Until the acquisition of new plant and machinery the Special Reserve Account can be utilised for the business purposes of the undertaking but it cannot be utilised for distribution of dividends/profits or for remittance outside India as profits or for creating an asset outside India.

4. Prescribed particulars [Form No. 56FF][71] should be submitted in respect of new plant and machinery along with the return of income for the previous year in which such plant and machinery was first put to use.

5. If the Special Reserve Account is misutilised then the deduction would be taken back in the year in which the Special Reserve Account is misutilised. If the Special Reserve Account is not utilised for acquiring new plant and machinery within three years as stated above then the deduction would be taken back in the year immediately following the period of three years.

Special provisions in respect of newly established units in Special Economic Zone [Section 10AA]

104A. Section 10AA was inserted to give income-tax concession to newly established units in Special Economic Zone.

104A.1 ***Conditions*** - The following conditions should be satisfied to claim deduction under section 10AA—

• *Condition 1* - The assessee is an entrepreneur as defined in section 2(*j*) of SEZ Act, 2005. Entrepreneur is a person who has been granted a letter of approval by the Development Commissioner to set up a unit in a Special Economic Zone.

• *Condition 2* - The unit in Special Economic Zone begins to manufacture or produce articles or things or provide services on or after April 1, 2005 but before April 1, 2020 (the benefit under section 10AA will not be available to units commencing activities on or after April 1, 2020). Manufacture for this purpose means to make, produce, fabricate, assemble, process or bring into existence, by hand or by machine, a new product having a distinctive name, character or use and shall include processes such as refrigeration, cutting, polishing, blending, repair, remaking, re-engineering and includes agriculture, aquaculture, animal husbandry, floriculture, horticulture, pisciculture, poultry, sericulture, viticulture and mining.

• *Condition 3* - It is not formed by the splitting up, or reconstruction, of a business already in existence [for a few exceptions, *see* para 107.18-1a[1]].

o *Development of software or providing IT enabled services in SEZ units* - The transfer or redeployment of technical manpower from existing unit(s) to a new unit located in SEZ, in the first year of commencement of business, shall not be construed as splitting up or reconstruction of an existing business, provided the assessee satisfies any one of the following two tests given below –

Test 1 - The number of technical manpower so transferred as at the end of the first financial year does not exceed 50 per cent of the total technical manpower actually engaged in development of software or IT enabled products in the new unit.

Test 2 - The net addition of the new technical manpower in all units of the assessee (enterprise) is at least equal to the number that represents 50 per cent of the total technical manpower of the new SEZ unit during such previous year.

---

69. If these activities are commenced after March 31, 2005, one can claim deduction under section 10AA.

70. Deduction will not be available from the assessment year 2006-07 if return of income is not submitted on or before the due date given in section 139(1) [*see* para 118.3].

71. Form No. 56FF is to be submitted electronically.

The assessee has a choice of complying with any one of the two alternatives tests (*i.e.*, *Test 1* or *Test 2*) given above. Moreover, the above criteria is applicable only in the case of an assessee engaged in the development of software or in providing IT Enabled Services in SEZ units eligible for deduction under section 10A or under section 10AA – Circular No. 14/2014, dated October 8, 2014.

• *Condition 4* - It is not formed by a transfer to a new business of machinery and plant previously used for any purpose. [for two exceptions, *see* para 104.1-3]

• *Condition 5* - The assessee has income from export of articles or thing or from services from such unit. In other words, the assessee has exported goods or provided services out of India from the Special Economic Zone by land, sea, air or by any other mode, whether physical or otherwise.

• *Condition 6* - Books of the account of the taxpayer should be audited. The taxpayer should submit[72] audit report in Form No. 56F along with the return of income.

• *Condition 7* - Deduction under section 10AA is not available unless it is claimed in the return of income. In other words, if the assessee fails to make a claim in his return of income of this deduction, the same will not be allowed (applicable from the assessment year 2003-04 onwards).

104A.2 ***Amount of deduction*** - If the above conditions are satisfied, one can claim deduction[73] under section 10AA. Deduction depends upon quantum of profit derived from export of articles or things or services (including computer software). It is calculated as under—

Profits of the business of the undertaking × Export turnover of the undertaking ÷ Total turnover of the business carried on by the "undertaking"[74]

• *What is "export turnover"* - For this purpose, 'export turnover' means the consideration in respect of export by the undertaking of articles or things or services received in, or brought into India by the assessee, but does not include the following :

a. freight;

b. telecommunication charges;

c. insurance attributable to the delivery of the articles or things or computer software outside India;

d. expenses, if any, incurred in foreign exchange in providing the technical services (including computer software) outside India.

Freight, telecommunication charges and insurance are deductible only if the assessee from the importers recovers these in addition to sale price of goods. If nothing is recovered from the importers but these expenses are incurred by the assessee, then no adjustment is required. What is to be excluded is out of what is received. If the consideration received is only against the goods then there is no need to deduct such expenses from the consideration received in convertible foreign exchange. In cases where such expenses are separately charged, the expenses are required to be reduced from the consideration received for the purpose of arriving the export turnover—*Patni Telecom (P.) Ltd.* v. *ITO* [2008] 22 SOT 38 (Hyd.). When these expenses are excluded for the purposes of 'export turnover' then on the same assumption, reason and analogy it should be excluded from 'total turnover'.

• *Site development of computer software* - Profits and gains derived from on site development of computer software (including services for development of software) outside India shall be deemed to be the profits and gains derived from the export of computer software outside India.

• *Losses of other undertakings* - Losses of other undertakings (eligible or non-eligible under section 10AA) shall not be adjusted against profit of a unit which is eligible for deduction under section 10AA—*FCI Technology Services Ltd.* v. *CIT* [2011] 9 taxmann.com 47 (Coch. - ITAT).

• *Brought forward losses* - Brought forward losses (incurred after April 1, 2001) cannot be deducted from profit of the business of the undertaking. In other words, deduction under section 10AA will be available in respect of profit of an eligible undertaking without setting off of brought forward losses.

72. From April 1, 2014, audit report should be submitted electronically. Provisions pertaining to electronic submission of audit report were not applicable prior to April 1, 2014 (for period prior to April 1, 2014, audit report may be retained by the assessee and it may be furnished in original whenever the Assessing Officer wants to examine it in assessment proceedings or otherwise).

73. The amount of deduction under section 10AA shall be allowed from the total income of the assessee computed in accordance with the provisions of the Act (before giving effect to the provisions of section 10AA) and the deduction under this section shall not exceed such total income of the assessee (applicable from the assessment year 2018-19).

74. Applicable from the assessment year 2006-07 onwards.

• *Section 80AB* - Deduction under section 10AA is not controlled by section 80AB as deduction under section 10AA is not a deduction under Chapter VI-A—*Enercon Wind Farms (Krishna) Ltd.* v. *CIT* [2008] 21 SOT 29 (Mum.).

• *Proviso to section 92C(4)* - As per proviso to section 92C(4), no deduction under section 10A or 10AA or 10B or under Chapter VI-A is to be allowed in respect of amount of income by which the total income of the assessee is enhanced after computation of arm's length price.

• *Double deduction under sections 10AA and 35AD not possible* - If deduction is claimed in respect of a specified business [as referred to in section 35AD(8)(*c*)] under section 10AA, no deduction in respect of that business will be available under section 35AD (applicable from the assessment year 2015-16).

104A.2-1 *DEDUCTION FOR FIRST FIVE ASSESSMENT YEARS* - 100 per cent of the profit and gains derived from export of articles or things or from services is deductible for a period of 5 consecutive assessment years. Deduction for the first year is available in the assessment year relevant to the previous year in which the unit begins to manufacture or produce articles or things or provide services.

104A.2-2 *DEDUCTION FOR SIXTH ASSESSMENT YEAR TO TENTH ASSESSMENT YEAR* - 50 per cent of the profit and gains derived from export of articles or things or from services is deductible for the next 5 years.

104A.2-3 *DEDUCTION FOR ELEVENTH ASSESSMENT YEAR TO FIFTEENTH ASSESSMENT YEAR* - For the next 5 years, a further deduction would be available to the extent of 50 per cent of the profit provided an equivalent amount is debited to the profit and loss account of the previous year and credited to Special Economic Zone Re-investment Allowance Reserve Account (hereinafter referred to as Special Reserve Account). The following conditions should be satisfied—

1. The Special Reserve Account should be utilised for the purpose of acquiring new plant and machinery.

2. The new plant and machinery should be first put to use before the expiry of 3 years from the end of the year in which the Special Reserve Account was created. For instance, if the reserve account was created during the previous year ending March 31, 2013, it should be utilized for acquiring machinery or plant on or before March 31, 2016.

3. Until the acquisition of new plant and machinery the Special Reserve Account can be utilised for the business purposes of the undertaking but it cannot be utilised for distribution of dividends/profits or for remittance outside India as profits or for creating an asset outside India.

4. Prescribed particulars [Form No. 56FF] should be submitted online in respect of new plant and machinery along with the return of income for the previous year in which such plant and machinery was first put to use.

5. If the Special Reserve Account is misutilised, then the deduction would be taken back in the year in which the Special Reserve Account is misutilised. If the Special Reserve Account is not utilised for acquiring new plant and machinery within three years as stated above, then the deduction would be taken back in the year immediately following the period of three years. For instance, if Rs. 1,50,000 is transferred to the reserve account for the year ending March 31, 2013 and out of which only Rs. 96,000 is utilized for acquiring plant and machinery up to March 31, 2016, then Rs. 54,000 would be taxable for the previous year 2016-17.

104A.3 ***Consequences for merger and demerger***[75] - Where an undertaking is transferred to another company under a scheme of amalgamation or demerger, the deduction under section 10AA shall be allowable in the hands of the amalgamated or the resulting company. However, no deduction shall be admissible under this section to the amalgamating company or the demerged company for the previous year in which amalgamation or demerger takes place.

104A.4 ***Consequences of claiming deduction under section 10AA*** - One should note the following consequences—

• Unabsorbed depreciation allowances or unabsorbed capital expenditure on scientific research or family planning (pertaining to the assessment year 2005-06 or earlier years) are not allowed to be carried forward and set off against the income of assessment years following the period of deduction. However, this restriction is not applicable to losses in respect of other businesses—*Lason India (P.) Ltd.* v. *ITO* [2008] 301 ITR (AT) 306 (Chennai).

• The losses under section 72(1) or 74(1) or 74(3) (pertaining to the assessment year 2005-06 or earlier years) are not allowed to be carried forward in assessment years succeeding[76] the period of deduction. The

75. A similar benefit is available in the case of sections 10A, 10B, 80-IA, 80-IAB, 80-IB, 80-IC and 80-IE, if transferor and transferee companies are Indian companies. However, under section 80-IA the benefit is available only when amalgamation/demerger takes place before April 1, 2007.

76. This restriction will apply only to post-tax holiday period and not to previous years within tax holiday period - *Enercon Wind Farms (Krishna) Ltd.* v. *CIT* [2008] 21 SOT 29 (Mum.).

deductions under section 80-IA or 80-IB shall also not be available to such undertakings after the expiry of tax holiday period.

• However, there is no bar to adjust losses under sections 70 and 71. In other words, if loss is incurred by an undertaking which is otherwise eligible for deduction under section 10AA, it can be set off under the provisions of sections 70 and 71 against other incomes of the taxpayer—*Sovika Infotek Ltd.* v. *ITO* [2008] 23 SOT 273 (Mum.).

• In the assessment year following period of deduction, the depreciation will be computed on the written down value of the asset as if the depreciation has actually been allowed in respect of each assessment year falling in the period of exemption.

104A.5 ***Power of Assessing Officer to recompute profit*** - The Assessing Officer has power to recompute profit in some cases. These cases are given by section 80-IA(8)/(10) [*see* para 107.17-1c[4]].

104A.6 ***Clarifications from Board*** - *Vide* Circular No. 1/2013[$], dated January 17, 2013, the Board has given the following clarifications pertaining to sections 10A, 10AA and 10B –

1. Profits and gains derived from "services for development of software" outside India would also be deemed as profits derived from export. Consequently, profits earned as a result of deployment of technical manpower at the client's place abroad specifically for software development work pursuant to a contract between the client and the eligible unit should not be denied benefits under sections 10A, 10AA and 10B provided such deputation of manpower is for the development of such software and all the prescribed conditions are fulfilled.

2. Tax benefits under sections 10A, 10AA and 10B would not be denied merely on the ground that a separate and specific Master Services Agreement (MSA) does not exist for each Statement of Works (SOW). The SOW would normally prevail over the MSA in determining the eligibility for tax benefits unless the Assessing Officer is able to establish that there has been splitting up or reconstruction of an existing business or non-fulfilment of any other prescribed condition.

3. On the sole ground of change in ownership of an undertaking, the claim of exemption cannot be denied to an otherwise eligible undertaking and the tax holiday can be availed of for the unexpired period at the rates as applicable for the remaining years, subject to fulfilment of prescribed conditions.

4. No requirement in law to maintain separate books of account, the same cannot be insisted upon. However, since the deductions under these sections are available only to the eligible units, the Assessing Officer may call for such details or information pertaining to different units to verify the claim and quantum of exemption, if so required.

5. Tax holiday should not be denied merely on the ground of physical relocation of an eligible SEZ unit from one SEZ to another in accordance with Instruction No. 59 of Department of Commerce and if all the prescribed conditions are satisfied under the Income-tax Act. The unit so relocated will be eligible to avail of the tax benefit for the unexpired period at the rates applicable to such years.

6. Whether setting up of new unit/undertaking in a location (covered by section 10A, 10AA or 10B), where an eligible unit is already existing, would amount to expansion of such already existing unit is a matter of fact requiring examination and verification. However, setting up of such a fresh unit in itself would not make the unit ineligible for tax benefits, as long as the unit is set up after obtaining necessary approvals from the competent authorities; has not been formed by splitting or reconstruction of an existing business; and fulfils all other conditions prescribed in the relevant provisions of law.

7. The software developed abroad at a client's place would be eligible for benefits under the respective provisions, because these would amount to 'deemed export' and tax benefits would not be denied merely on this ground. However, since the benefits under these provisions can be availed of only by the units or undertakings set up under specified schemes in India, it is necessary that there must exist a direct and intimate nexus or connection of development of software done abroad with the eligible units set up in India and such development of software should be pursuant to a contract between the client and the eligible unit.

Special provisions in respect of newly established hundred per cent export-oriented undertakings [Sec. 10B]

105. Section 10B was inserted with a view to providing incentive (similar to tax holiday available under section 10A) to hundred per cent export-oriented units.

The provisions applicable from the assessment year 2001-02 are given below :

105.1 ***Conditions to be satisfied*** - An undertaking must satisfy the following conditions in order to avail the deduction under section 10B.

[$] For Circular No. 1/2013, log on to *taxmann.com/readyreckoner.aspx*.

105.1-1 *IT MUST BE AN APPROVED HUNDRED PER CENT EXPORT-ORIENTED UNDERTAKING* - The expression "hundred per cent export-oriented undertaking" means an undertaking which has been approved as a hundred per cent export-oriented undertaking by the Board appointed in this behalf by the Central Government in exercise of the powers conferred by section 14 of the Industries (Development and Regulation) Act, 1951, and the rules made under that Act[$].

105.1-2 *IT MUST PRODUCE OR MANUFACTURE ARTICLES OR THINGS OR COMPUTER SOFTWARE* - It must manufacture or produce any article or thing or computer software. The expression computer software means—

a. any computer programme recorded on any disc, tape, perforated media or other information storage device; or

b. any customized electronic data or any product or service of similar nature as may be notified by the Board,

which is transmitted or exported from India to any place outside India by any means.

The Central Board of Direct Taxes has specified the following Information Technology enabled products or services, as the case may be, for this purpose : (*i*) Back-office Operations; (*ii*) Call Centres; (*iii*) Content Development or Animation; (*iv*) Data Processing; (*v*) Engineering and Design; (*vi*) Geographic Information System Services; (*vii*) Human Resource Services; (*viii*) Insurance Claim Processing; (*ix*) Legal Databases; (*x*) Medical Transcription; (*xi*) Payroll; (*xii*) Remote Maintenance; (*xiii*) Revenue Accounting; (*xiv*) Support Centres; and (*xv*) Website Services.

• It is not the requirement of section 10B that the assessee-company should itself own plant, machinery or equipment and manufacture or produce computer software on the same in order to be eligible for the exemption—*ITO* v. *Techdrive (India) (P.) Ltd.* [2008] 24 SOT 1 (Mum.).

105.1-3 *IT SHOULD NOT BE FORMED BY SPLITTING/RECONSTRUCTION OF BUSINESS* - *See* para 104.1-2.

105.1-4 *IT SHOULD NOT BE FORMED BY TRANSFER OF OLD MACHINERY* - *See* para 104.1-3.

105.1-5 *THERE MUST BE REPATRIATION OF SALE PROCEEDS INTO INDIA* - *See* para 104.1-4.

105.1-6 *AUDIT REPORT SHOULD BE SUBMITTED*[77] *IN FORM NO. 56G* - *See* para 104.1-5.

105.1-7 *RETURN OF INCOME* - It should be submitted on or before due date[78].

105.1-8 *DEDUCTION SHOULD BE CLAIMED IN THE RETURN OF INCOME* - Deduction under section 10B is not available unless it is claimed in the return of income. In other words, if the assessee fails to make a claim in his return of income of this deduction, the same will not be allowed (applicable from the assessment year 2003-04 onwards).

105.2 ***Amount of deduction*** - If the aforesaid conditions are satisfied, the deduction under section 10B may be computed as under :

Profits of the business of the undertaking × Export turnover ÷ Total turnover of the business carried on by the undertaking[79]

• *Export turnover* - For this purpose, 'export turnover' means the consideration in respect of export by the undertaking of articles or things or computer software received in, or brought into India by the assessee in convertible foreign exchange within the prescribed period, but does not include the following :

a. freight;

b. telecommunication charges;

c. insurance attributable to the delivery of the articles or things or computer software outside India;

d. expenses, if any, incurred in foreign exchange in providing the technical services outside India.

• *On site development of software* - Profits and gains derived from on site development of computer software (including services for development of software) outside India shall be deemed to be the profits and gains derived from the export of computer software outside India.

105.3 ***Period of deduction*** - If the aforesaid conditions are satisfied, the assessee can claim deduction under section 10B, from his total income for a period of ten consecutive assessment years beginning with the assessment year relevant to the previous year in which the undertaking begins to manufacture or produce such articles or things or computer software.

• For the undertakings which have claimed exemption up to assessment year 2000-01 under the old section 10B, the deduction shall be available for the unexpired period of the 10 consecutive assessment years under the new section 10B.

• 'Relevant assessment year' means any assessment year falling within a period of ten consecutive assessment years referred to in section 10B.

• No deduction under section 10B shall be allowed to any undertaking from the assessment year 2012-13.

---

77. It is not possible to attach any report with new income-tax return forms. The assessee should himself retain the report. It may be furnished in original whenever the Assessing Officer wants to examine it in assessment proceedings or otherwise.

78. In case of genuine hardship, relief can be granted to assessee under section 10B even if return is not furnished on or before due date specified under section 139(1)—*Asstt. CIT* v. *Dhir Global Industries (P.) Ltd.* [2011] 43 SOT 640 (Delhi).

79. 90 per cent for the assessment year 2003-04.

[$]In actual practice, however, such approvals are granted by the Development Commissioners, which are later on ratified by the Board of Approvals.

Deduction in respect of export of artistic hand-made wooden articles [Sec. 10BA]

106. Section 10BA is applicable for the assessment years 2004-05 to 2009-10. Deduction under section 10BA is not available from the assessment year 2010-11 onwards.

Deductions from total income [Secs. 80C to 80U]

107. The deductions specified in sections 80C to 80U are allowed from the gross total income in order to arrive at the net income. The aggregate amount of the deductions under these sections cannot, however, exceed the gross total income (after excluding short-term capital gain taxable under section 111A, any long-term capital gain and incomes referred to in sections 115A, 115AB, 115AC, 115AD and 115D) of the assessee. Moreover, in view of section 80AB, deduction under sections 80HH to 80U is admissible in respect of net income computed under the provisions of the Act (*i.e.*, income arrived at after deducting permissible deductions and adjusting current or brought forward losses).

• Deductions under the following sections is not available, if return of income is not submitted on or before due date under section 139(1) –

- sections 80-IA, 80-IAB, 80-IB, 80-IC, 80-ID, 80-IE (for the assessment years 2006-07 to 2017-18);
- sections 80HH to 80RRB (from the assessment year 2018-19 onwards).

• Deduction in respect of profits and gains shall not be allowed under any provisions of section 10A or section 10AA or section 10B or section 10BA or under sections 80H to 80RRB, if a deduction in respect of same amount under any of the aforesaid sections has been allowed in the same assessment year. The aggregate deductions under these provisions shall not exceed the profits and gains of the undertaking or unit or enterprise or eligible business, as the case may be. No deductions under the above provisions shall be allowed if the deduction has not been claimed in the return of income[80] (applicable from the assessment year 2003-04).

• For the purpose of claiming deduction under section 35AD or under Chapter VI-A (*i.e.*, sections 80C to 80U), the transfer price of goods and services between the undertaking (*i.e.*, unit or enterprise eligible for these deductions) and any other undertaking or unit or enterprise or business of the assessee shall be determined at the market value (or arm's length price, with effect from the assessment year 2013-14) of such goods or services as on the date of transfer. This provision is applicable with effect from April 1, 2009 and accordingly, applicable to all cases where the proceedings are pending before any authority on or after such date.

• Where a deduction under any provision of sections 80HH to 80RRB is claimed and allowed in respect of profits of any of the specified business referred to in section 35AD(8)(*c*) for any assessment year, no deduction shall be allowed under the provisions of section 35AD in relation to such specified business for the same or any other assessment year (applicable from the assessment year 2011-12).

• Revenue subsidies (*e.g.*, transport subsidy, power subsidy, interest subsidy, etc.) received from the Government towards reimbursement of cost of production/manufacture or for sale of the manufactured goods, are part of profits and gains of business derived from an industrial undertaking/eligible business, and are admissible for applicable deduction under Chapter VI-A—Circular No. 39/2016[$], dated November 29, 2016.

• Disallowances under sections 32, 40(*a*)(*ia*), 40A(3), 43B, etc. (and other specific disallowances) related to the business activity against which the Chapter VI-A deduction has been claimed, result in enhancement of the profits of the eligible business, and deduction under Chapter VI-A is admissible on the profits so enhanced by the disallowance—Circular No. 37/2016[$], dated November 2, 2016.

107.1 ***Deduction in respect of life insurance premia, deferred annuity, contributions to provident fund, subscription to certain equity shares or debentures, etc. [Sec. 80C, applicable from the assessment year 2006-07]*** - Section 80C provides deduction in respect of specified qualifying amounts paid or deposited by the assessee in the previous year.

107.1-1 *SALIENT FEATURES OF SECTION 80C* - The following are the main provisions of section 80C—

• Under section 80C, deduction is available from gross total income.

• Deduction under section 80C is available only to an individual or a Hindu undivided family.

• Deduction is available on the basis of specified qualifying investments/contributions/deposits/payments (hereinafter referred to as "gross qualifying amount") made by the taxpayer during the previous year.

---

80. An assessee claims deduction under section 80-ID in the first year in his return of income which is uploaded in ITR-5. In the second year, he forgets to claim the same deduction in the return of income and deduction is not allowed by the Assessing Officer on the ground of not claiming the same in the return of income. On appeal, the Tribunal held that in view of the fact that in ITR-5, the assessee had claimed deduction under section 80-ID for first year, there did exist a mistake apparent from record which was liable to be rectified by allowing assessee's application for rectification – *Hotel Crystal Inn* v. *ITO* [2018] 91 taxmann.com 106 (Agra).

$ For Circular Nos. 37/2016 and 39/2016, log on to *taxmann.com/readyreckoner.aspx.*

• The gross qualifying amount would be allowed as deduction irrespective of the fact whether (or not) such amount is paid or deposited by the taxpayer out of his income chargeable to tax.

• The maximum amount deductible under section 80C is Rs. 1,50,000[81]. Moreover, the aggregate amount of deduction—

a. under sections 80C, 80CCC, 80CCD(1) [*i.e.*, contribution by an employee (or any other individual) towards NPS] and 80CCD(2) [*i.e.*, employer's contribution towards NPS] cannot exceed Rs. 1,00,000 (applicable for the assessment years 2006-07 to 2011-12); and

b. under sections 80C, 80CCC and 80CCD(1)[82] [*i.e.*, contribution by an employee (or any other individual) towards National Pension System (NPS)] cannot exceed Rs. 1,00,000 (for the assessment years 2012-13 to 2014-15) or Rs. 1,50,000 (from the assessment year 2015-16).

107.1-2 *COMPUTATION OF DEDUCTION UNDER SECTION 80C* - The deduction is calculated as per the following steps—

Step 1 - Gross qualifying amount [*see* para 107.1-2a]

Step 2 - Amount of deduction [*see* para 107.1-2b]

107.1-2a STEP 1 - GROSS QUALIFYING AMOUNT - Gross qualifying amount is the aggregate of the following :

Nature of payment
1. *Life insurance premium* (including payment made by Government employees to the Central Government Employees' insurance scheme and payment made by a person under children's deferred endowment assurance policy) [*see* Note 1]
2. Payment in respect of *non-commutable deferred annuity* [*see* Note 2]
3. Any sum deducted from salary payable to a Government employee for the purpose of securing him a *deferred annuity* (subject to a maximum of 20 per cent of salary) [*see* Note 3]
4. Contribution (not being repayment of loan) towards *statutory provident fund and recognized provident fund*
5. Contribution (not being repayment of loan) towards 15 year public provident fund [*see* Notes 4, 6 and 11]
6. Contribution towards an approved *superannuation fund*
7. Subscription to *National Savings Certificates* (VIII Issue and IX Issue) [*see* Note 7] and deposit in Sukanya Samriddhi Account [*see* Note 12]
8. Contribution for participating in the unit-linked insurance plan (*ULIP*) of Unit Trust of India [*see* Note 5]
9. Contribution for participating in the unit-linked insurance plan (*ULIP*) of LIC Mutual Fund (*i.e.*, formerly known as Dhanraksha plan of LIC Mutual Fund) [*see* Note 5]
10. Payment for *notified annuity plan* of LIC (*i.e.*, Jeevan Dhara and Jeevan Akshay) or any other insurer (*i.e.*, Immediate Annuity Plan of ICICI Prudential Life Insurance Company, Tata AIG Easy Retire Annuity Plan of Tata AIG Life Insurance Company)
11. Subscription towards *notified units of Mutual Fund* or UTI
12. Contribution to *notified pension fund* set up by Mutual Fund or UTI (*i.e.*, Retirement Benefit Unit Scheme of UTI, Kothari Pioneer Pension Plan of Kothari Mutual Fund and Reliance Retirement Fund)
13. Any sum paid (including accrued interest) as subscription to *Home Loan Account Scheme* of the National Housing Bank or contribution to any notified deposit scheme pension fund set up by the National Housing Bank[83].
14. Any sum paid as subscription *to any scheme of*— *a.* public sector company engaged in providing long-term finance for purchase/construction of residential houses in India (*i.e.*, public deposit scheme of HUDCO); *b.* housing board constituted in India for the purpose of planning, development or improvement of cities/towns
15. Any sum paid as *tuition fees* (not including any payment towards development fees/donation/payment of similar nature) whether at the time of admission or otherwise to any university/college/educational institution in India for full time education of any two children of an individual [*see* Note 10]
16. Any instalment or part payment towards the cost of purchase/construction of a residential property to a housing board or co-operative society (or repayment of housing loan taken from Government, bank, co-operative bank, LIC, National Housing Bank, assessee's employer where such employer is public company/public sector company/university/co-operative society) [*see* Note 9]

81. Rs. 1,00,000 up to the assessment year 2014-15.

82. From the assessment year 2012-13, employer's contribution towards NPS is outside the monetary ceiling of Rs. 1,00,000 or Rs. 1,50,000.

83. Notified scheme for this purpose is the National Housing Bank (Tax Saving) Term Deposit Scheme, 2008.

17. Amount invested in *approved debentures* of, and *equity shares* in, a public company engaged in infrastructure including power sector or units of a mutual fund proceeds of which are utilised for the developing, maintaining, etc., of a new infrastructure facility

18. Amount deposited in a fixed deposit for 5 years or more with a scheduled bank in accordance with a scheme framed and notified by the Central Government (applicable from the assessment year 2007-08) (it shall be a minimum of Rs. 100 or multiples thereof).

19. Subscription to any notified bonds of National Bank for Agriculture and Rural Development (*i.e.*, the NABARD Rural Development Bonds of NABARD) (applicable from the assessment year 2008-09).

20. Amount deposited under Senior Citizens Saving Scheme (applicable from the assessment year 2008-09) [Note 11].

21. Amount deposited in Five Year Time Deposit Scheme in post office (applicable from the assessment year 2008-09) [Note 11].

22. Amount **contributed (for a fixed period of not less than 3 years) by a Central Government employee to his NPS (Tier-II) account** (applicable from the assessment year 2020-21).

Notes:

1. In the case of an individual, policy should be taken on his own life, life of the spouse or any child (child may be dependent/independent, male/female, minor/major or married/unmarried). In the case of a Hindu undivided family, policy may be taken on the life of any member of the family. Insurance premium cannot exceed the maximum ceiling given below—

	Policy on the life of a person with disability or severe disability or on the life of a person suffering from disease or ailment as given in section 80DDB	*Policy on the life of any other person*
- If policy is issued before April 1, 2012	20% of sum assured[84]	20% of sum assured[84]
- If policy is issued during 2012-13	10% of sum assured[85]	10% of sum assured[85]
- If policy is issued on or after April 1, 2013	15% of sum assured[85]	10% of sum assured[85]

2. Annuity plan should be taken in the name of the individual, his wife/her husband or any child of such individual.

3. It should be for the benefit of the individual, his wife or children.

4. According to the Public Provident Fund Scheme, an individual can open public provident fund account in his own name or in the name of minor of whom he is guardian. However, according to the Income-tax Act, to get the benefit of deduction under section 80C, amount deposited by an individual in his own account or in the account of his/her spouse or in the account of any child (in the case of HUF-assessee in the account of any member of the family) is eligible for deduction.

5. In the case of an individual, ULIP should be taken on his own life, life of the spouse or any child (child may be dependent/independent, male/female, minor/major or married/unmarried). In the case of a Hindu undivided family, ULIP may be taken on the life of any member of the family.

6. There is no maximum ceiling under the Income-tax Act. However, under the public provident fund scheme, the maximum contribution is Rs. 1,50,000.

7. Accrued interest (which is deemed as reinvested) is also qualified for deduction for any year (except for the last year).

8. While an individual can make payment in any of the above referred investments, an HUF cannot invest in points 2, 3, 4, 5, 6, 7, 12 and 14 mentioned above.

9. The following payment made towards the *cost of purchase/construction of a new residential house property* is qualified for the purpose of section 80C :

a. any instalment or part payment of the amount due under any self-financing or other scheme of any development authority, housing board or other authority engaged in the construction and sale of house property on ownership basis ; or

b. any instalment or part payment of the amount due to any company or co-operative society of which the assessee is a shareholder or member[86] towards the cost of the house property allotted to him (it is not applicable if the assessee is not a shareholder or member of the company/co-operative society which provides house to the assessee); or

c. repayment of the amount borrowed by the assessee from —

i. the Central Government or any State Government, or

ii. any bank, including a co-operative bank, or

iii. the Life Insurance Corporation of India, or

---

84. Sum assured does not include any premium agreed to be returned and/or any benefit by way of bonus.

85. Sum assured means minimum amount assured under the policy without including any premium agreed to be returned and/or any benefit by way of bonus.

86. To claim benefit under section 80C of instalment paid or part-payment made towards cost of house property allotted to assessee, he must be a member/shareholder of company or co-operative society when instalment or part-payment is made—*Sandeep S. Shah* v. *ITO* [2002] 123 Taxman 696 (Mad.).

iv. the National Housing Bank, or

v. any public company formed and registered in India with the main object of carrying on the business of providing long-term finance for construction or purchase of houses in India for residential purposes which is eligible for deduction under section 36(1)(*viii*), or

vi. any company in which the public are substantially interested or any co-operative society, where such company or co-operative society is engaged in the business of financing the construction of houses, or

vii. the assessee's employer where such employer is an authority or a board or a corporation or any other body established or constituted under a Central or State Act, or

viii. the assessee's employer where such employer is a public company or public sector company, or a university established by law or a college affiliated to such university or local authority or co-operative society ;

d. stamp duty, registration fee and other expenses for the purpose of transfer of such house property to the assessee.

The following payments are not qualified for the purpose of section 80C :

a. the admission fee, cost of the share and initial deposit which a shareholder of a company or a member of a co-operative society has to pay for becoming such shareholder or member ; or

b. the cost of any addition or alteration to, or renovation or repair of, the house property which is carried out after the issue of the completion certificate in respect of the house property by the authority competent to issue such certificate or after the house property (or any part thereof) has either been occupied by the assessee or any other person on his behalf or been let out ; or

c. any expenditure in respect of which deduction is allowable under the provisions of section 24.

10. Full-time education includes any educational course offered by any university, college, school or other educational institution to a student who is enrolled full-time for the said course. Full-time education includes even play-school activities, pre-nursery and nursery classes. The amount allowable as tuition fees shall include any payment of fee to any university, college, school or other educational institution in India except the amount representing payment in the nature of development fees or donation or capitation fees or payment of similar nature—Circular No. 17/2014, dated December 10, 2014.

11. When a deposit is made in the Public Provident Fund account, Senior Citizen Saving Scheme and Time Deposit Scheme in Post Office by means of a cheque/draft, the date of encashment of the cheque is treated as date of deposit.

12. In the case of an individual, deposit in Sukanya Samriddhi Account can be made in the name of individual, or any girl child of that individual or any girl child for whom such person is the legal guardian, if the scheme so specifies.

107.1-2a[1] *Other points regarding computation of gross qualifying amount* - The following points are also relevant while calculating the gross qualifying amount :

• *Investment/deposits are qualified on payment basis* - The aforesaid sums qualify, for the purpose of section 80C, on "payment" basis. Payments made under the aforesaid heads during the previous year are qualified for the purpose of this section, regardless of the fact whether the payments relate to the previous year or years preceding or ensuing the previous year.

• *Minimum period of holding in some cases* - In respect of the investments/deposits/contributions eligible for deduction under section 80C, in some cases the law provides a minimum period of holding. Such cases are given below—

Nature of investments/deposits	*Number of item as per table given in para 107.2-1a*	*Minimum period of holding*
Unit-linked insurance plan (ULIP)	8 and 9	5 years
Life insurance premium	1	2 years
Cost of purchase/construction of a residential house property including repayment of loan	16	5 years
Deposit under Senior Citizen Saving Scheme	20	5 years
Time deposit in Post Office	21	5 years

Where a member participating in Unit-linked insurance plan, terminates his participation before making contribution for 5 years, then following consequences should be noted—

Whether any deduction would be available in respect of any contribution towards the above plan in the previous year in which the taxpayer terminates participation in the above plan before completing 5 years	Any contribution made towards the above plan in the said previous year will not be qualified for deduction under section 80C.
What will be the tax treatment in respect of deduction already taken in the preceding years	The quantum of deduction already taken in the preceding years would be deemed as income of the taxpayer in the year in which contribution to the plan is terminated.

A similar rule is applicable in respect of termination of life insurance policy before 2 years and transfer of residential house property before 5 years. In the case of withdrawal before 5 years by the depositor during his lifetime from amount deposited under Senior Citizen Saving Scheme or time deposit in Post Office, the amount withdrawn (excluding interest which has already been taxed in earlier years) will be taxable in the year of withdrawal.

107.1-2b AMOUNT OF DEDUCTION - Gross qualifying amount is the figure derived in para 107.1-2. However, amount deduction under section 80C is computed as under:

- Gross qualifying amount; or
- Rs. 1,50,000[87],

whichever is lower. It may be noted that the aggregate amount of deduction under sections 80C, 80CCC and 80CCD(1) cannot exceed Rs. 1,50,000[87].

107.1-2c FURTHER DEDUCTION ON ACCRUED INTEREST IN RESPECT OF INVESTMENT IN NATIONAL SAVING CERTIFICATES (VIII ISSUE AND IX ISSUE) - HOW TO CLAIM - The interest as specified in the Table below shall accrue to the holder or holders of the certificate at the end of each year and the interest so accruing at the end of each year (except for the last year) shall be deemed to have been re-invested on behalf of the holder and aggregated with the amount of face value of the certificate.

NSC VIII Issue

Amount of interest (Rs.) accruing on certificates of Rs. 100 denomination

When NSC was purchased ➡ / The year for which interest accrues	*On or after March 1, 2003 but before December 1, 2011*	*On or after December 1, 2011 but before April 1, 2012*	*During 2012-13*	*During 2013-14 to 2015-16*	*During April 1, 2016 and September 30, 2016*	*During October 1, 2016 and March 31, 2017*	*During April 1, 2017 and June 30, 2017*	*During July 1, 2017 and December 31, 2017*	*During January 1, 2018 and September 30, 2018*	*During October 1, 2018 and June 30, 2019*	*During July 1, 2019 and September 30, 2019*
First year	8.16	8.58	8.78	8.68	8.10	8.00	7.90	7.80	7.60	8.00	7.90
Second year	8.83	9.31	9.56	9.43	8.76	8.64	8.52	8.41	8.18	8.64	8.52
Third year	9.55	10.11	10.40	10.25	9.46	9.33	9.20	9.06	8.80	9.33	9.20
Fourth year	10.33	10.98	11.31	11.14	10.23	10.08	9.92	9.77	9.47	10.08	9.92
Fifth year	11.17	11.92	12.30	12.11	11.06	10.88	10.71	10.53	10.19	10.88	10.71
Sixth year	12.08	*NA*	*NA*	*NA*	*NA*	*NA*	*NA*	*NA*	*NA*	*NA*	*NA*

NSC IX Issue

Amount of interest (Rs.) accruing on certificate of Rs. 100 denomination

Year for which interest accrues	*When investment is made*			*Year for which interest accrues*	*When investment is made*		
	Before April 1, 2012	*During 2012-13*	*During 2013-14 to 2015-16*[88]		*Before April 1, 2012*	*During 2012-13*	*During 2013-14 to 2015-16*[88]
First year	8.89	9.10	8.99	Sixth year	13.61	14.06	13.83
Second year	9.68	9.93	9.80	Seventh year	14.82	15.34	15.08
Third year	10.54	10.83	10.68	Eighth year	16.13	16.74	16.43
Fourth year	11.48	11.81	11.64	Ninth year	17.57	18.26	17.91
Fifth year	12.50	12.89	12.69	Tenth year	19.13	19.92	19.52

Note : The amount of interest accruing on a certificate of any other denomination shall be proportionate to the amount specified in the Table above.

Interest is chargeable to tax on the basis of annual accrual specified above. Further, the amount of interest re-invested (for all years except last year) satisfies the test of having been paid out of income chargeable to tax and the same is entitled for deduction under section 80C.

107.1-E1 X, whose annual salary (before standard deduction) salary is Rs. 5,45,000, purchased Rs. 30,000 National Savings Certificates (VIII Issue) on December 10, 2012. He annually deposits Rs. 10,000 in National Children's Fund. Determine the amount of tax payable for the assessment years 2013-14 to 2019-20, on assumption that he does not intend to make any other investment up to the financial year 2018-19.

•

87. Rs. 1,00,000 up to the assessment year 2014-15.
88. Discontinued with effect from December 20, 2015.

ASSESSMENT YEARS

	2013-14 Rs.	2014-15 Rs.	2015-16 Rs.	2016-17 Rs.	2017-18 Rs.	2018-19 Rs.	2019-20 Rs.
Salary (after standard deduction)	5,45,000	5,45,000	5,45,000	5,45,000	5,45,000	5,45,000	5,05,000
Interest accrued on NSC Issue	—	2,634	2,868	3,120	3,393	3,690	*Nil*
Gross total income	5,45,000	5,47,634	5,47,868	5,48,120	5,48,393	5,48,690	5,05,000
Less: Deductions							
Under section 80C	30,000[1]	2,634[2]	2,868[3]	3,120[4]	3,393[5]	*Nil*[6]	*Nil*
Under section 80G	5,000	10,000	10,000	10,000	10,000	10,000	10,000
Net income	5,10,000	5,35,000	5,35,000	5,35,000	5,35,000	5,38,690	4,95,000
Tax	32,000	37,000	32,000	32,000	32,000	20,238	12,250
Add: Surcharge							
Tax and surcharge	32,000	37,000	32,000	32,000	32,000	20,238	12,250
Add: Education cess	640	740	640	640	640	405	-
Add: Secondary and higher education cess	320	370	320	320	320	202	-
Add: Health and education cess	-	-	-	-	-	-	490
Tax payable	32,960	38,110	32,960	32,960	32,960	20,850	12,740

1. Rs. 30,000 is deductible under section 80C.
2. Rs. 2,634 is deductible under section 80C.
3. Rs. 2,868 is deductible under section 80C.
4. Rs. 3,120 is deductible under section 80C.
5. Rs. 3,393 is allowable as deduction under section 80C.
6. Since interest of fifth year (due on December 10, 2017) is paid at the time of maturity of bonds (*i.e.*, on December 10, 2017) and is not reinvested in NSC VIII Issue, the same is not eligible for deduction under section 80C.

107.1-E2 Income of a resident is Rs. 13,20,000 (inclusive of interest on Government securities of Rs. 15,000). He invests Rs. 1,40,000 in schemes and deposits qualified for deduction under section 80C. He is eligible for deduction of Rs. 30,000 under section 80CCC. He pays Rs. 40,000 on account of mediclaim insurance premium on his own life and life of Mrs. X. Besides, he pays Rs. 27,000 as mediclaim insurance premium on the life of his mother (88 years) who is not dependent on him. Find out the tax liability for the assessment year 2019-20 if the taxpayer is (*a*) a senior citizen (64 years), (*b*) a resident woman (58 years) or (*c*) any other individual.

•

	Case (a) Rs.	*Case (b)* Rs.	*Case (c)* Rs.
Gross total income	13,20,000	13,20,000	13,20,000
Less: Deductions			
Under section 80C	1,40,000	1,40,000	1,40,000
Under section 80CCC	10,000	10,000	10,000
Under section 80D	67,000	52,000	52,000
Net income	11,03,000	11,18,000	11,18,000
Income-tax[89]	1,40,900	1,47,900	1,47,900
Add: Surcharge (applicable only if net income exceeds Rs. 50 lakh)	-	-	-
Income-tax and surcharge	1,40,900	1,47,900	1,47,900
Add: Health and education cess	5,636	5,916	5,916
Tax liability (rounded off)	1,46,540	1,53,820	1,53,820

89. Rebate under section 87A is not available as net income exceeds Rs. 3,50,000.

107.1-E3 X (62 yrs.) is a salaried employee. His basic salary is Rs. 40,000 per month. He gets one month salary as bonus. He has been provided a rent-free unfurnished house which is owned by the employer-company at the place of his posting, *i.e.*, Chennai. He gets company deposit interest of Rs. 17,70,000. He makes the following investments/deposits every year—

	Rs.
Life insurance premium on his own life taken on April 6, 2012 (sum assured: Rs. 80,000)	9,000
Notified equity linked saving scheme of UTI	12,000
Repayment of loan taken on July 1, 2001 for purchasing a house property (which is self-occupied by his family at Pune)	77,000
Payment of interest on the above loan	2,60,000
Tuition fees of two children (Rs. 14,000 + Rs. 26,000)	40,000
Notified bonds of infrastructure company (for the purpose of section 80C)	3,000
Deposit in home loan account scheme of NHB	9,000
Mediclaim insurance premium	36,000
Pension fund of LIC qualified for deduction under section 80CCC	14,000

On March 10, 2017, he purchases Rs. 10,000 National Saving Certificate VIII issue. No other investment is made by X. Find out the net income and tax liability for the assessment year 2019-20.

•

	Rs.
Basic salary	4,80,000
Bonus	40,000
Rent-free unfurnished house	78,000
Gross salary	5,98,000
Less: Standard deduction	40,000
Income from salary	5,58,000
Income from house property	(-)2,00,000
Interest	17,70,000
Interest on NSC (VIII issue) purchased on March 10, 2017	864
Gross total income	21,28,864
Less : Deductions	
Under section 80C [*see* Note]	1,49,864
Under section 80CCC	136
Under section 80D	36,000
Net income	19,42,860
Tax on net income[89]	3,92,858
Add: Health and education cess	15,714
Tax liability	4,08,570

Note - Gross qualifying amount for the purpose of section 80C is calculated as follows—

Life insurance premium (maximum 10% of Rs. 80,000)	8,000
Notified equity linked saving scheme of UTI	12,000
Repayment of loan taken for purchasing a house property	77,000
Tuition fees of two children (Rs. 14,000 + Rs. 26,000)	40,000
Home loan account scheme	9,000
Interest accrued on NSC (VIII issue) (8.64% of Rs. 10,000)	864
Notified bonds of infrastructure company	3,000
Gross qualifying amount	1,49,864
Amount deductible under section 80C (100% of gross qualifying amount subject to maximum of Rs. 1,50,000)	1,49,864

107.1A ***Deduction in respect of National Savings Scheme [Sec. 80CCA, applicable for the assessment years 1988-89 to 1992-93]*** - Deduction shall be allowed in the case of a taxpayer being an individual, a Hindu undivided family in relation to the deposits made under a notified scheme (*i.e.*, the National Savings Scheme) or notified annuity scheme of LIC (*i.e.*, Jeewan Dhara and Jeevan Akshay). The deduction is available in respect of the whole of the amount deposited as does not exceed—

89. Rebate under section 87A is not available as net income exceeds Rs. 3,50,000.

- Rs. 40,000 for the assessment years 1991-92 and 1992-93.
- Rs. 30,000 for the assessment years 1989-90 and 1990-91.
- Rs. 20,000 for the assessment year 1988-89.

• Consequence of the above provisions and other related issues as applicable to the assessment year 2019-20 are explained with the help of 107.1A-E1 and 107.1A-E2 given below—

107.1A-E1 On May 6, 2018, X withdraws Rs. 20,000 from the National Savings Scheme, 1987 which includes Rs. 6,000 as interest. Find out the amount chargeable to tax.

•

Rs. 20,000, being the amount withdrawn from the National Savings Scheme, 1987 is taxable under the head "Income from other sources" for the assessment year 2019-20.

107.1A-E2 During 2018-19, X gets the following payments—

	Date	*Principal Rs.*	*Interest Rs.*	*Bonus Rs.*	*Total Rs.*
National Savings Scheme, 1987	July 1, 2018	30,000	5,000	-	35,000
National Savings Scheme, 1992	May 1, 2018	65,000	15,000	-	80,000
Jeevan Dhara	March 1, 2019	10,000	-	2,000	12,000

Ascertain the amount chargeable to tax for the assessment year 2019-20, assuming that on transfer of a short-term capital asset on April 1, 2018 he gets an income of Rs. 6,00,000.

•

	Rs.	*Rs.*
Short-term capital gain		6,00,000
Income from other sources		
- National Savings Scheme, 1987	35,000	
- Interest on National Savings Scheme, 1992	15,000	
- Jeevan Dhara	12,000	62,000
Gross total income		6,62,000
Less: Deduction		*Nil*
Net income		6,62,000

Notes—

1. Contribution to the National Savings Scheme, 1992 was not deductible under section 80CCA. Out of the amount withdrawn from the National Savings Scheme, 1992, only interest is chargeable to tax.

2. Contribution to National Savings Scheme, 1987 was deductible under section 80CCA. If the amount is withdrawn from National Savings Scheme, 1987, then the entire amount (including interest) is taxable without any deduction.

107.2 ***Deduction in respect of investment made under Equity Linked Savings Scheme [Sec. 80CCB applicable for the assessment years 1991-92 and 1992-93]*** - Section 80CCB relating to deduction in respect of investment made in accordance with the notified Equity Linked Savings Scheme was applicable for the assessment years 1991-92 and 1992-93.

• Consequences of the above provisions and other related issues as applicable to the assessment year 2019-20 are explained with the help of 107.2-E1 given below—

107.2-E1 On March 10, 1992, X purchased 1,500 MEP92 units of Rs. 10 of UTI (being a notified Equity Linked Savings Scheme for section 80CCB) and claimed a deduction of Rs.10,000 under section 80CCB for the assessment year 1992-93.

On March 3, 1994, X purchased 1,700 units of MEP94 units of Rs.10 of UTI (being a notified Equity Linked Savings Scheme for section 88) and claimed a tax rebate of Rs. 2,000 (*i.e.*, 20 per cent of Rs.10,000) under section 88 for the assessment year 1994-95.

On June 6, 2018, X transfers MEP92 and MEP94 at the rate of Rs. 70 and Rs. 60 respectively through a broker of the Bombay Stock Exchange (securities transaction tax is applicable). Find out the net income of X for the assessment year 2019-20 assuming that the business income of X is Rs. 7,86,000. Further, assume that fair market value on April 1, 2001 of MEP 92 and MEP 94 is Rs. 12 and Rs. 14 and NAV on January 31, 2018 is Rs. 65 and Rs. 52.

•

	Rs.	*Rs.*
Business income		7,86,000
Capital gains		
Sale proceeds of MEP 92 (Rs. 70 × Rs. 1,500)	1,05,000	
Less: Cost of acquisition (Rs. 65 × 1,500)	97,500	
Capital gain (*a*)	7,500	

	Rs.	Rs.
Sale proceeds of MEP94 (Rs. 60 × 1,700)	1,02,000	
Less: Cost of acquisition (Rs. 52 × 1,700)	88,400	
Capital gain (*b*)	13,600	
Long-term capital gain [(*a*) + (*b*)]		21,100
Income from other sources [Rs.10,000, being the amount of deduction under section 80CCB, will be taxable when units MEP92 are transferred]		10,000
Gross total income		8,17,100
Less: Deductions under sections 80CCC to 80U		*Nil*
Net income (rounded off)		8,17,100
Tax on net income		
Tax on Rs. 21,100 under section 112A		*Nil*
Tax on balance		71,700
Total		71,700
Add: Health and education cess		2,868
Tax liability		74,570

107.2A ***Deduction in respect of contribution to pension fund [Sec. 80CCC]*** - Section 80CCC was inserted with effect from the assessment year 1997-98. This section provides a deduction to an individual for any amount paid or deposited by him in any annuity plan of the Life Insurance Corporation of India or any other insurer for receiving pension from a fund referred to in section 10(*23AAB*). The deduction shall be restricted to Rs. 1,50,000[90].

One should keep in view the following points :

1. Where after claiming deduction, the assessee or his nominee surrenders the annuity before the maturity date of such annuity, the surrender value shall be taxable in the hands of the assessee or his nominee, as the case may be, in the year of the receipt.

2. If deduction is claimed under section 80CCC, pension received will be taxable in the hands of the assessee or the nominee, as the case may be, in the year of the receipt.

3. The maximum amount deductible under section 80CCC is Rs. 1,50,000[90]. Moreover, the aggregate amount of deduction—

a. under sections 80C, 80CCC, 80CCD(1) [*i.e.*, contribution by an employee (or any other individual) towards NPS] and 80CCD(2) [*i.e.*, employer's contribution towards NPS] cannot exceed Rs. 1,00,000 (applicable for the assessment years 2006-07 to 2011-12); and

b. under sections 80C, 80CCC and 80CCD(1)[91] [*i.e.*, contribution by an employee (or any other individual) towards NPS] cannot exceed Rs. 1,00,000 (for the assessment years 2012-13 to 2014-15) or Rs. 1,50,000 (from the assessment year 2015-16).

107.2B ***Deduction in respect of contribution to National Pension System (NPS) - notified by Central Government [Sec. 80CCD]*** - These provisions are given below—

• *Conditions* - Section 80CCD is applicable if the following conditions are satisfied—

1. The taxpayer is an individual.

2. He is employed by the Central Government (on or after January 1, 2004), or employed by any other person. He may be even a self-employed person.

3. He has in the previous year paid or deposited any amount in his account under NPS. NPS covers New Pension Scheme (notified under Notification No. F. No. 5/7/2003-ECB & PR, dated December 22, 2003) and Atal Pension Yojna (as per Notification No. SO 529(E), dated February 19, 2016).

• *Consequences if the above conditions are satisfied* - If the above conditions are satisfied, then the following consequences given by section 80CCD should be noted—

1. Contribution towards NPS by employee (or any other individual assessee) [Sec. 80CCD(1)] - Assessee's contribution to NPS is deductible under section 80CCD(1) in the year in which contribution is made. No deduction is available in respect of employee's contribution which is in excess of 10 per cent of the salary of the employee. Likewise, if contribution by a taxpayer (not being an employee) exceeds 20 per cent[92] of his gross total income, the excess shall not be taken into consideration for the purpose of section 80CCD(1). For the assessment year 2015-16, amount deductible under section 80CCD(1) cannot exceed Rs. 1,00,000[93].

90. Rs. 1,00,000 for the assessment years 2007-08 to 2015-16, Rs. 10,000 up to the assessment year 2006-07.

91. From the assessment year 2012-13, employer's contribution towards NPS is outside the monetary ceiling of Rs. 1,00,000 or Rs. 1,50,000.

92. 10% up to the assessment year 2017-18.

93. The limit of Rs. 1,00,000 is not applicable from the assessment year 2016-17 onwards.

2. Contribution towards NPS by employer [Sec. 80CCD(2)] - Contribution by the employer to NPS is deductible under section 80CCD(2) in the hands of the concerned employee in the year in which contribution is made. However, no deduction is available in respect of employer's contribution which is in excess of 10 per cent [or (with effect from the assessment year 2020-21) **14 per cent, if employer is the Central Government**] of the salary of the employee.

3. Cumulative monetary ceiling -By virtue of section 80CCE, the aggregate amount of deduction under sections 80C, 80CCC and 80CCD(1) [*i.e.*, contribution by an employee (or any other individual) towards NPS] cannot exceed Rs. 1,50,000 (Rs. 1,00,000 for the assessment years 2012-13 to 2014-15). The ceiling limit is not applicable (from the assessment year 2012-13) in respect of employer's contribution towards NPS. Moreover, the ceiling limit will not be applicable in respect of an assessee's contribution towards NPS under section 80CCD(1B) from the assessment year 2016-17 which is given below.

4. Additional contribution up to Rs. 50,000 towards NPS under section 80CCD(1B)- Sub-section (1B) has been inserted in section 80CCD (with effect from the assessment year 2016-17) so as to provide for an additional deduction in respect of any amount paid (up to Rs. 50,000) for contributions made by any individual assessee under the NPS. On this contribution, the ceiling of Rs. 1,50,000 under section 80CCE will not be applicable. The additional deduction of Rs. 50,000 is available whether (or not) any claim under section 80CCD(1) has been made—Circular No. 19/2015, dated November 27, 2015. For instance, X (who is covered by NPS) gets salary of Rs. 8,00,000 per annum. He annually contributes 10 per cent of salary towards NPS and Rs. 1,21,000 towards PPF/LIP since 2014. For the assessment year 2019-20, he can claim deduction as follows -

- Rs. 50,000 under section 80CCD(1B).
- Rs. 30,000 under section 80CCD(1).
- Rs. 1,20,000 under section 80C.

X has not made any additional investment over and above the minimum requirement of 10 per cent contribution towards NPS. But he can claim deduction of Rs. 50,000 under section 80CCD(1B).

5. Tax at the time of withdrawal - The amount standing to the credit of an assessee in NPS, for which a deduction has already been claimed by him, and accretions to such account, shall be taxed as follows –

	Provisions applicable –			
	From the AY 2020-21	*For the AYs 2018-19 and 2019-20*	*For the AY 2017-18*	*Up to the AY 2016-17*
1. Partial withdrawal from NPS (to the extent it does not exceed 25% of an employee's contribution)	Exempt	Exempt	Taxable	Taxable
2. Amount received by an employee [or a non-employee (applicable from the assessment year 2019-20)] on closure of his account or on his opting out of the NPS	**60% exempt**	40% exempt	40% exempt	Taxable
3. In *(2)*, amount is received by a nominee on the death of the assessee	Exempt	Exempt	Exempt	Taxable
4. Pension received out of NPS	Taxable	Taxable	Taxable	Taxable
5. Amount received in *(2)*, *(3)*, *(4)* is utilized for purchasing an annuity plan in the same previous year	Exempt	Exempt	Exempt	Exempt
6. Pension received out of annuity plan purchased in *(5)*	Taxable	Taxable	Taxable	Taxable

6. Meaning of "salary" - "Salary" for the purpose of points *1* and *2* (*supra*) includes dearness allowance, (if the terms of employment so provide) and commission (if is payable at a percentage of turnover achieved by the employee), but excludes all other allowances and perquisites.

107.2B-E1 Find out net income in the following cases for the assessment year 2019-20 (age of the taxpayer in each case is 55 years) –

Situation 1 - X is employed by the Central Government since 2009. For the previous year 2018-19, his basic salary is Rs. 5,00,000 per annum. Besides, he gets dearness allowance of Rs. 50,000 per annum and telephone allowance of Rs. 60,000 per annum. His income of other sources is Rs. 2,40,000. The Central Government contributes 13 per cent of salary (including dearness allowance) towards NPS. The contribution of X towards NPS is Rs. 1,04,000. Besides, X deposits Rs. 96,000 in public provident fund, Rs. 5,000 in notified (section 80CCC) annuity plan of LIC, and pays mediclaim insurance premium of Rs. 35,000 (policy covers medical benefits for X and Mrs. X).

Situation 2 - X in the aforesaid case is employed by a private sector company and the employer has opted for NPS.

Situation 3 - X in the aforesaid case is employed by a private sector company and the employer has recognized provident fund. Contributions given in Situation 1 are towards recognized provident fund. Besides, X contributes an additional sum of Rs. 40,000 towards NPS.

Situation 4 - X is a self-employed person. His business income is Rs. 8,10,000 and income from other sources is Rs. 2,00,000. He annually contributes Rs. 2,60,000 towards NPS. Besides, X deposits Rs. 30,000 in public provident fund, deposits Rs. 5,000 in notified (section 80CCC) annuity plan of LIC, and pays mediclaim insurance premium of Rs. 35,000 (policy covers medical benefits for X and Mrs. X).

		Situations 1 and 2 Rs.	Situation 3 Rs.	Situation 4 Rs.
Basic salary and dearness allowance		5,50,000	5,50,000	*Nil*
Telephone allowance		60,000	60,000	*Nil*
Employer's contribution towards NPS (13% of Rs. 5,50,000)		71,500	*Nil*	*Nil*
Employer's contribution towards RPF (in excess of 12% of salary)		*Nil*	5,500	*Nil*
Gross salary		6,81,500	6,15,500	*Nil*
Less : Standard deduction		40,000	40,000	-
Salary income		6,41,500	5,75,500	*Nil*
Business income		*Nil*	*Nil*	8,10,000
Income from other sources		2,40,000	2,40,000	2,00,000
Gross total income (GTI)		8,81,500	8,15,500	10,10,000
Less: Deductions				
DEDUCTIONS NOT COVERED BY CUMULATIVE CEILING –				
Under section 80CCD(1B) (contribution by the assessee towards NPS up to Rs. 50,000)	(*a*)	50,000	40,000	50,000
Under section 80CCD(2) [contribution by employer towards NPS, subject to a maximum of 10% of salary]	(*b*)	55,000	*Nil*	*Nil*
Under section 80D (mediclaim insurance premium) (limited to Rs. 25,000 in the case of a person who is not a senior citizen)	(*c*)	25,000	25,000	25,000
DEDUCTIONS NOT COVERED BY CUMULATIVE CEILING OF RS. 1,50,000 –				
Under section 80C (PPF and contribution towards recognized provident fund)	(*d*)	(96,000)	(2,00,000)	(30,000)
Under section 80CCC (annuity plan of LIC)	(*e*)	(5,000)	(5,000)	(5,000)
Under section 80CCD(1) [contribution of X towards NPS (excluding the contribution considered above in section 80CCD(1B)), subject to a maximum of 10% of salary in the case of an employee or 20% of GTI in the case of a person other than employee]	(*f*)	(54,000)	*Nil*	(2,02,000)
Maximum deductible amount [*i.e.,* (*d*) + (*e*) + (*f*), subject to a maximum of Rs. 1,50,000]	(*g*)	1,50,000	1,50,000	1,50,000
Net income [GTI – (*a*) – (*b*) – (*c*) – (*g*)]		6,01,500	6,00,500	7,85,000

107.2C ***Deduction in respect of subscription to long-term infrastructure bonds [Sec. 80CCF, applicable for the assessment years 2011-12 and 2012-13]*** - Under section 80CCF, an individual or a Hindu undivided family can claim a deduction of the whole of the amount paid or deposited (up to a maximum of Rs. 20,000) during the previous year as subscription to notified long-term infrastructure bonds. Deduction under this section is available only for the assessment years 2011-12 and 2012-13. This deduction is over and above the existing overall limit of deduction on savings of up to Rs. 1,00,000 under sections 80C, 80CCC and 80CCD. No deduction under this section is available from the assessment year 2013-14.

107.2D ***Deduction in respect of investment made under Rajiv Gandhi Equity Saving Scheme [Sec. 80CCG, applicable from the assessment year 2013-14]*** - Section 80CCG has been inserted with effect from the assessment year 2013-14. Deduction under this section is available to a resident individual, if his gross total income does not exceed Rs. 10 lakh. (Rs. 12 lakh from the assessment year 2014-15).

• *Eligible investment to claim deduction* - Deduction under this section is available, if the assessee is a new retail investor as specified in the notified scheme and has acquired listed shares (or listed units from the assessment year 2014-15) in accordance with the notified scheme. The investment is locked-in for a period of 3 years from the date of acquisition in accordance with the above scheme. The assessee should also satisfy any other condition as may be prescribed.

• *Amount of deduction* - If the above conditions are satisfied, a deduction (up to the assessment year 2017-18[94]) is allowed under section 80CCG. The amount of deduction is 50 per cent of amount invested in

94. However, an assessee who has claimed deduction under this section for assessment year 2017-18 and earlier assessment years shall be allowed deduction under this section till the assessment year 2019-20, if he is otherwise eligible to claim the deduction as per the provisions of this section.

equity shares (or listed units from the assessment year 2014-15). However, the amount of deduction under this section cannot be more than Rs. 25,000. If the assessee, after claiming the aforesaid deduction, fails to satisfy the above conditions, the deduction originally allowed shall be deemed to be the income of the assessee of the year in which default is committed.

• *Period of deduction* - If any deduction is claimed by a resident individual under section 80CCG for the assessment year 2013-14, he shall not be entitled for any deduction under this section for any subsequent year. In other words, for the assessment year 2013-14 deduction under section 80CCG is one time deduction and is available only in one assessment year to the extent of 50 per cent of amount invested during the previous year 2012-13 or Rs. 25,000 whichever is less. However, this provision has been amended from the assessment year 2014-15. The modified provision permits deduction for 3 consecutive assessment years, beginning with the assessment year relevant to the previous year in which the listed equity shares or listed units of equity oriented fund are first acquired.

• *Salient features of scheme* - Scheme is open to new retail investors. It is also open to those who have opened the demat account but have not made any transaction in stocks and/or in derivatives till the date of notification of this scheme.

Under the Scheme, those stocks listed under the BSE 100 or CNX 100, or those of Public Sector Undertakings which are Navratnas, Maharatnas and Mini-ratnas would be eligible. Follow-on Public Offers (FPOs) of the above companies would also be eligible under the scheme. IPOs of PSUs (annual turnover being not less than Rs. 4,000 crore for each of the immediate past three years) which are listed in the relevant financial year are also eligible. In addition, Exchange Traded Funds (ETFs) and Mutual Funds (MFs) that have above eligible securities as their underlyings and are listed and traded in the Stock Exchanges and settled through a depository mechanism have also been brought under the scheme.

The total lock-in period for investments under the scheme is 3 years. Out of 3 years, the first year is blanket lock-in period, commencing from the date of last purchase of securities under the scheme. The general principle under which trading is allowed from second year onwards is that whatever is the value of stocks/units sold by the investor from the scheme portfolio, securities of the above nature of at least the same value are credited back into the account subsequently. However, the investor is allowed to take benefits of the appreciation of his portfolio, provided its value, as on the previous day of trading, remains above the investment for which they have claimed income-tax benefit.

107.3 *Deduction in respect of medical insurance premia [Sec. 80D]* - Deduction under section 80D is available if the following conditions are satisfied –

1. The taxpayer is an individual (maybe resident/non-resident or Indian citizen/foreign citizen) or a Hindu undivided family (maybe resident or non-resident).

2. Payment should be made out of income chargeable to tax.

3. Payment should be made by any mode other than cash. However, payment on account of preventive health check-up can be made by any mode (including cash).

107.3-1 *MAXIMUM DEDUCTIBLE AMOUNT* - The maximum deductible amount and other relevant points are given below –

		Deduction in the case of individual		*Deduction in the case of HUF*
For whose benefit payment can be made		Family	Parents	Any member of HUF
A.	*a.* Medi-claim insurance premium	Eligible	Eligible	Eligible
	b. Contribution to CGHS/notified scheme	Eligible	–	–
	c. Preventive health check-up payment	Eligible	Eligible	–
	Maximum deduction –			
	- General deduction [applicable in respect of (*a*), (*b*) and (*c*)]	Rs. 25,000	Rs. 25,000	Rs. 25,000
	- Additional deduction [applicable only in case of (*a*) when medi-claim policy is taken on the life of a senior citizen] –			
	❑ For the assessment years 2016-17 to 2018-19	Rs. 5,000	Rs. 5,000	Rs. 5,000
	❑ From the assessment year 2019-20	Rs. 25,000	Rs. 25,000	Rs. 25,000
B.	Medical expenditure on the health of a person who is a super senior citizen (senior citizen from the assessment year 2019-20) if medi-claim insurance is not paid on the health of such person	Eligible	Eligible	Eligible

		Deduction in the case of individual		*Deduction in the case of HUF*
	Maximum deduction in respect of (*B*) –			
	❑ For the assessment years 2016-17 to 2018-19	Rs. 30,000	Rs. 30,000	Rs. 30,000
	❑ From the assessment year 2019-20	Rs. 50,000	Rs. 50,000	Rs. 50,000
C.	Maximum deduction in respect of (*A*) and (*B*) –			
	❑ For the assessment years 2016-17 to 2018-19	Rs. 30,000	Rs. 30,000	Rs. 30,000
	❑ From the assessment year 2019-20	Rs. 50,000	Rs. 50,000	Rs. 50,000

Notes –

1. Family includes individual, spouse of the individual and dependent children of the individual.

2. Parents include father and mother (dependent or otherwise). Father-in-law and mother-in-law are not included.

3. The aggregate payment on account of preventive health check-up of self, spouse, dependent children, father and mother cannot exceed Rs. 5,000.

4. The above payments [given under (*A*) and (*B*)] should be made by any mode other than cash. However, payment on account of preventive health check-up can be made by any mode (including cash).

5. "Senior citizen" is a resident individual who is at least 60 years of age at any time during the previous year.

6. "Super senior citizen" is a resident individual who is at least 80 years of age at any time during the previous year.

7. In case of single premium health insurance policies having cover of more than one year, the aforesaid deduction shall be allowed (from the assessment year 2019-20) on proportionate basis for the number of years for which health insurance cover is provided.

107.3-E1 X (58 years) is the assessee. Other members of his family are Mrs. X (55 years) and dependent children Y and Z. Parents of X are resident in India but they have annual income of more than Rs. 25 lakh from business, rent and interest. The following expenditure is incurred by X during the previous year 2018-19 for the purpose of claiming deduction under section 80D –

	For X, Mrs. X, Y and Z	*For parents of X*
Mediclaim insurance premium payment by cheque	A = Rs. 2,000	D = Rs. 46,000
Contribution by cheque to Central Govt. Health Scheme	B = Rs. 6,000	E = 0
Cash payment for preventive health check-up	C = Rs. 8,000	F = Rs. 7,000

Find out the amount deductible under section 80D for the assessment year 2019-20.

●

The aggregate of C and F cannot exceed Rs. 5,000. To get maximum deduction, it is better in this case if C is taken as equal to Rs. 5,000 and F is taken as *zero*. Now total of A, B and C is Rs. 13,000 which is not more than Rs. 25,000. The amount deductible for X, Mrs. X and children will be Rs. 13,000. For parents (being senior citizens) the amount deductible will be Rs. 46,000. The aggregate deduction under section 80D will be Rs. 59,000.

107.3-E2 Suppose in above Example, A = Rs. 23,000, B = 0, C = Rs. 20,000, D = Rs. 24,000, E = 0 and F = Rs. 40,000.

●

The aggregate of C and F cannot exceed Rs. 5,000. To maximize deduction, C is taken as equal to Rs. 2,000 and F is taken as equal to Rs. 3,000.

Total of A, B and C is Rs. 25,000 which is deductible.

The total of D, E and F is Rs. 27,000 (*i.e.*, Rs. 24,000 + Rs. 3,000). Out of Rs. 27,000 mediclaim insurance premium is more than Rs. 5,000. Therefore, Rs. 27,000 is deductible for parents.

The aggregate deduction under section 80D will be Rs. 52,000.

107.3-E3 Suppose in Example 107.3-E1, A = 0, B = 0, C = Rs. 17,000, D = 0, E = 0 and F = Rs. 2,000.

●

The aggregate of C and F cannot exceed Rs. 5,000. In this case, mediclaim insurance premium (*i.e.*, A and D) and contribution to Central Government Health Scheme (*i.e.*, B and E) is *zero*. Therefore, only Rs. 5,000 is deductible under section 80D.

107.3-E4 Suppose in Example 107.3-E1, A = Rs. 18,000, B = Rs. 1,000, C = Rs. 500, D = Rs. 18,000, E = 0 and F = Rs. 41,000.

●

The aggregate of C and F cannot exceed Rs. 5,000. To maximize deduction, C is taken as equal to Rs. 500 and F is taken as equal to Rs. 4,500. The total of A, B and C is Rs. 19,500 which is deductible. The total of D, E and F is Rs. 22,500. The aggregate deductible amount under section 80D will be Rs. 42,000 (Rs. 19,500 + Rs. 22,500).

107.3-E5 Suppose in Example 107.3-E1, A = Rs. 600, B = Rs. 23,000, C = Rs. 7,000, D = Rs. 42,000, E = 0 and F = Rs. 26,000.

●

The aggregate of C and F cannot exceed Rs. 5,000. C is taken as equal to Rs. 1,400 and F is taken as equal to Rs. 3,600. The total of A, B and C is Rs. 25,000 which is deductible. The total of D, E and F is Rs. 45,600. Therefore, Rs. 45,600 is deductible for parents. The aggregate deduction is Rs. 70,600.

107.3-E6 X (39 years) incurs the following expenses for the benefit of his family (i.e., X, Mrs. X and dependent children) and parents [father (61 years), mother (56 years)] during the previous year 2018-19 –

	Medi-claim insurance premium (by cheque)	*Preventive health check-up expenditure (in cash)*	*Medical expenditure*
For the benefit of X, Mrs. X and children	A = Rs. 22,000	D = 0	G = Rs. 2,000
For the benefit of father	B = 0	E = Rs. 7,000	H = Rs. 48,000
For the benefit of mother	C = Rs. 6,000	F = 0	J = Rs. 1,000

The above medical expenditure is paid by cheque.

●

Medical expenditure will be deductible only if it is incurred on the health of a senior citizen. Consequently, the expenses G and J are not deductible. Preventive health check-up expenditure cannot be more than Rs. 5,000. Consequently, amount deductible pertaining to E will be limited to Rs. 5,000. Amount of deduction under section 80D will be as follows –

	Medi-claim insurance premium (including preventive health check-up expenditure) Rs.	*Medical expenditure* Rs.	*Total* Rs.
X, Mrs. X and children	22,000	*Nil*	22,000
Parents	11,000	48,000	50,000
Total			72,000

107.3-E7 Suppose in Example 107.3-E6, medical expenditure is incurred in cash.

●

Medical expenditure is not deductible if it is paid in cash. Consequently, Rs. 48,000 will not be deductible in the above case. Amount of deduction under section 80D will be Rs. 33,000.

107.3-E8 Suppose in Example 107.3-E6, B = Rs. 1,000 (no other change in data).

●

Medical expenditure is deductible only if the following conditions are satisfied –

1. It is paid by any mode other than cash.

2. It is incurred on the health of a senior citizen.

3. Medi-claim insurance premium is not paid on the health of such person during the previous year.

X has paid medi-claim insurance premium of Rs. 1,000 on the health of his father. As a consequence, medical expenditure of Rs. 48,000 will not be deductible. Amount deductible under section 80D will be Rs. 34,000 (*i.e.*, A : Rs. 22,000, B : Rs. 1,000, E : Rs. 5,000 and C : Rs. 6,000).

107.3-E9 Suppose in Example 107.3-E6, A = Rs. 19,000, B = 0, C = Rs. 27,000, D = Rs. 11,000, E = 0, F = 0 and H = Rs. 28,000.

●

Preventive health check-up expenditure (*i.e.*, total of D, E and F) cannot be more than Rs. 5,000. Therefore, D in this case will be limited to Rs. 5,000. Amount deductible under section 80D is as follows –

	Medi-claim insurance premium (including preventive health check-up expenditure) Rs.	*Medical expenditure* Rs.	*Total* Rs.
X, Mrs. X and children	24,000	*Nil*	24,000
Parents	27,000	28,000	50,000[94a]
Total			74,000

94a. Maximum.

107.4 ***Deduction in respect of maintenance including medical treatment of a handicapped dependent who is a person with disability [Sec. 80DD, applicable from the assessment year 1999-2000 onwards]*** - The provisions of section 80DD as applicable from the assessment year 2004-05 are given below—

107.4-1 *CONDITIONS* - The following conditions should be satisfied—

1. The taxpayer is resident in India (maybe ordinarily resident or not ordinarily resident).

2. The resident taxpayer is an individual (maybe an Indian citizen or foreign citizen) or a Hindu undivided family.

3. The taxpayer has opted for any (or both) of the following options—

Option 1	*Option 2*
The taxpayer has incurred an expenditure for the medical treatment (including nursing), training and rehabilitation of a dependent (being a person with disability)[97]	The taxpayer has paid or deposited under any scheme framed in this behalf by the Life Insurance Corporation or any other insurer, or the administrator[95] or specified company[96] and approved by the Board in this behalf, for maintenance of dependent (being a person with disability[97])

4. For the above purpose, a "dependent being a person with disability[97]" is a person who satisfies the following points—

a. in the case of an individual, dependent means the spouse, children, parents, brothers and sisters of the individual or any of them;

b. in the case of a Hindu undivided family, "dependent" means a member of a Hindu undivided family;

c. such person is wholly or mainly dependent upon such individual or Hindu undivided family for support and maintenance;

d. such person has not claimed any deduction under section 80U in computing his total income for the assessment year relating to the previous year;

e. "disability"[97] shall have the meaning assigned to it in section 2(*i*) of the Persons with Disabilities (Equal Opportunities, Protection of Rights and Full Participation) Act, 1995 [*see* para 107.33];

f. "person with disability" means a person having any "disability" stated above of not less than 40 per cent.

5. Under *option 2,* the scheme provides for payment of an annuity or a lump sum amount for the benefit of dependent, being a person with disability in the event of the death of the individual or the member of the Hindu undivided family in whose name subscription to the scheme has been made.

6. Under *option 2,* the assessee nominates either the dependent being a person with disability or any other person or a trust to receive the payment on his behalf, for the benefit of such dependent.

7. For claiming the deduction, the assessee shall have to furnish a copy of the certificate issued by the medical authority [*see* para 107.33] along with the return of income. Where the condition of disability requires reassessment, a fresh certificate from the medical authority shall have to be obtained after the expiry of the period mentioned on the original certificate in order to continue to claim the deduction.

107.4-2 *AMOUNT OF DEDUCTION* - The amount deductible is a fixed deduction of Rs. 75,000 (Rs. 50,000 up to the assessment year 2015-16) whenever the conditions specified above are satisfied, irrespective of the amount incurred or deposited under *Option 1* and/or *Option 2.* A higher deduction of Rs. 1,25,000 (Rs. 1,00,000 for the assessment years 2010-11 to 2015-16, Rs. 75,000 up to the assessment year 2009-10) shall be allowed, where such dependent is a person with severe disability having any disability of 80 per cent or above.

107.4-3 *IF DEPENDENT PREDECEASES THE TAXPAYER* - If the dependent with disability predeceases the individual or the member of the Hindu undivided family referred to above, an amount equal to the amount paid or deposited as stated above shall be deemed to be the income of the assessee of the previous year in which such amount is received by the assessee and shall accordingly be chargeable to tax as the income of that previous year.

107.4-E1 X is a resident individual. He annually deposits a sum of Rs. 15,000 with LIC for the maintenance of his handicapped grandfather who is wholly dependent upon him. The disability is one which is specified in Rule 11A.

---

95. "Administrator" means the Administrator as referred to in clause (*a*) of section 2 of the Unit Trust of India (Transfer of Undertaking and Repeal) Act, 2002.

96. "Specified company" means a company as referred to in clause (*h*) of section 2 of the Unit Trust of India (Transfer of Undertaking and Repeal) Act, 2002.

97. Meaning of "disability" has been extended from the assessment year 2005-06 to include "autism", "cerebral palsy" and "multiple disability" referred to in clauses (*a*), (*c*) and (*h*) of section 2 of the National Trust for Welfare of Persons with Autism, Cerebral Palsy, Mental Retardation and Multiple Disabilities Act, 1999.

It also comes under section 2(*i*) of the Persons with Disabilities (Equal Opportunities, Protection of Rights and Full Participation) Act, 1995. A copy of certificate from medical authority is submitted.

•

As grandfather does not come within the definition of "dependent" in section 80DD, nothing shall be deducted under section 80DD.

107.4-E2 Suppose in Example 107.4-E1, the person with disability is dependent brother.

•

As brother comes in the definition of "dependent", Rs. 75,000 is deductible. If, however, the dependent brother is a person with severe disability over 80%, then Rs. 1,25,000 is deductible.

107.5 ***Deduction in respect of medical treatment [Sec. 80DDB]*** - The provisions of section 80DDB as applicable from the assessment year 2004-05 are given below—

107.5-1 *CONDITIONS* - One has to satisfy the following conditions—

1. The taxpayer is resident in India (maybe ordinarily resident or not ordinarily resident).

2. The taxpayer is an individual (maybe an Indian citizen or a foreign citizen) or a Hindu undivided family.

3. The taxpayer has actually paid any amount for the medical treatment of a specified disease or ailment as prescribed by the Board under rule 11DD [*see* para 107.5-3].

4. The expenditure is actually incurred for medical treatment of the assessee himself or wholly/mainly dependent husband/wife, children, parents, brothers and sisters of the taxpayer. If the taxpayer is a Hindu undivided family, the expenditure is actually incurred for the medical treatment of any member of the family who is wholly/mainly dependent upon the family.

5. The assessee shall have to submit a doctor's prescription[98] [*see* para 107.5-3]

107.5-2 *AMOUNT OF DEDUCTION* - If the above conditions are satisfied, actual expenditure on medical treatment is deductible under section 80DDB. However, deduction cannot exceed the maximum amount given below –

	Maximum limit Rs.	*Maximum limit in the case of senior citizen Rs.*	*Maximum limit in the case of super senior citizen Rs.*
Up to the assessment year 2015-16	40,000	60,000	–
For the assessment years 2016-17 to 2018-19	40,000	60,000	80,000
From the assessment year 2019-20	40,000	1,00,000	–

Notes –

1. "Senior citizen" is a resident individual who is at least 60 years (65 years, up to the assessment year 2012-13) of age at any time during the previous year.

2. "Super senior citizen" is a resident individual who is at least 80 years of age at any time during the previous year.

• Deduction under this section shall be reduced by the amount received, if any, under an insurance from an insurer, or reimbursed by an employer, for the medical treatment of the person referred to above.

107.5-3 *PRESCRIBED DISEASES AND CERTIFICATE FROM A DOCTOR* - For the purpose of section 80DDB, the following diseases have been specified under rule 11DD (*Column 1* of the Table given below). To get the benefit of deduction, prescription in respect of these diseases/ailments shall be issued by the following specialists given in *Column 2* of the Table –

Specified diseases	*Prescription in respect of the diseases or ailments specified in* Column 1 *to be issued by the following specialists –*
Neurological diseases where the disability level has been certified to be of 40% and above,—(*a*) Dementia; (*b*) Dystonia Musculorum Deformans; (*c*) Motor Neuron Disease; (*d*) Ataxia; (*e*) Chorea; (*f*) Hemiballismus; (*g*) Aphasia; (*h*) Parkinsons Disease	A Neurologist having a Doctorate of Medicine (DM) degree in Neurology or any equivalent recognised degree
Malignant cancers	An Oncologist having a Doctorate of Medicine (DM) degree in Oncology or any equivalent recognised degree

98. It is not possible to attach any prescription with new income-tax return forms. The assessee should himself retain the prescription. It may be furnished in original whenever the Assessing Officer wants to examine it in assessment proceedings or otherwise.

Specified diseases	*Prescription in respect of the diseases or ailments specified in* Column 1 *to be issued by the following specialists –*
Full Blown Acquired Immuno-Deficiency Syndrome (AIDS)	Any specialist having a post-graduate degree in General or Internal Medicine, or any equivalent recognised degree
Chronic Renal failure	A Nephrologist having a Doctorate of Medicine(DM) degree in Nephrology or a Urologist having a Master of Chirurgiae (MCh) degree in Urology or any equivalent recognised degree
Hematological disorders : (*a*) Hemophilia; (*b*) Thalassaemia	A specialist having a Doctorate of Medicine (DM) degree in Hematology or any equivalent recognised degree

Notes –

1. Where in respect of any diseases or ailments specified above, the patient is receiving the treatment in a Government hospital, the prescription may be issued by any specialist working full-time in that hospital and having a postgraduate degree in General or Internal Medicine or any equivalent recognised degree.

2. For the prescription referred to above, no format or form has been issued. The prescription shall contain the name and age of the patient, name of the disease or ailment along with the name, address, registration number and the qualification of the specialist issuing the prescription. Where, however, the patient is receiving the treatment in a Government hospital, such prescription shall also contain the name and address of the Government hospital.

107.5-E1 Find out the amount of deduction under section 80DDB in the following cases for the assessment year 2019-20—

Name of the taxpayer	*X*	*Y*	*Z*	*A*	*B*
Residential status of the taxpayer	Resident	Resident	Resident	Resident	Non-resident
Expenditure incurred on medical treatment of dependent mother in a hospital recognised by the Chief Commissioner (amount in rupees)	50,000	96,000	1,60,000	1,00,000	54,000
Age of mother	59 years	69 years	73 years	63 years	64 years
Residential status of dependent mother	Resident	Non-resident	Resident	Non-resident	Resident
Whether the disease is specified under rule 11DD made by the Board	Yes	Yes	Yes	Yes	Yes
Amount received from insurance company (amount in rupees)	4,000	14,000	90,000	15,000	7,000
Amount received from the employer of the taxpayer (amount in rupees)	2,000	3,000	14,000	20,000	16,000

•

Amount of deduction under section 80DDB	*X* *Rs.*	*Y* *Rs.*	*Z* *Rs.*	*A* *Rs.*	*B* *Rs.*
Deduction under section 80DDB if no money is recovered from insurance company and employer	40,000	40,000	1,00,000	40,000	*Nil*
Less : Amount received from insurance company and employer	6,000	17,000	1,04,000	35,000	23,000
Amount of deduction under section 80DDB	34,000	23,000	*Nil*	5,000	*Nil*

Note - The perquisite in respect of reimbursement of medical expenditure by employer is not chargeable to tax in this case.

107.6 ***Deduction in respect of interest on loan taken for higher education [Sec. 80E]*** - Deduction under section 80E is available from the assessment year 1995-96 if the following conditions are satisfied :

1. The assessee is an individual.

2. He had taken a loan from any financial institution [*i.e.*, a banking company or notified financial institution[99]] or an approved charitable institution [*i.e.*, an institution approved for the purpose of section 10(*23C*) or 80G(2)(*a*)].

99. HDFC Ltd., Credila Financial Services Private Ltd.

3. The loan was taken for the purpose of pursuing higher education [*i.e.,* all fields of studies (including vocational studies) pursued after passing the Senior Secondary Examination or its equivalent from any school, board or university recognised by the Central Government or State Government or local authority or by any other authority authorized by the Central Government or State Government or local authority to do so]. There is no condition that higher education should be in India only—*Nitin Shantilal Muthiyan* v. *CIT* [2015] 59 taxmann.com 416 (Pune).

4. The loan is taken by the taxpayer for the purpose of pursuing his own higher education (or from the assessment year 2008-09, for the purpose of his higher education or higher education of relatives, *i.e.,* spouse/ any child). With effect from the assessment year 2010-11, the scope of the expression "relative" has been extended to cover the student for whom the taxpayer is the legal guardian.

5. Amount is paid by the individual during the previous year by way of interest on such loan (up to the assessment year 2005-06, deduction was also available in respect of repayment of loan subject to limit given below).

6. Such amount is paid out of his income chargeable to tax.

107.6-1 *AMOUNT OF DEDUCTION* - The following amount is deductible when all the aforesaid conditions are satisfied :

• *From the assessment year 2006-07* - Entire payment of interest is deductible. The deduction is available for a maximum of 8 years or till the interest is paid, whichever is earlier. This deduction is allowed in computing the taxable income of the initial assessment year (*i.e.,* the assessment year relevant to the previous year in which the assessee starts paying the interest on the loan) and seven immediately succeeding assessment years (or until the above interest is paid in full, whichever is earlier).

• *Up to the assessment year 2005-06* - The amount deductible is—

a. amount paid during the year by way of repayment of loan and/or interest thereon ; or

b. Rs. 40,000 (Rs. 25,000 up to the assessment year 2000-01);

whichever is lower.

The first year in which the deduction is available is the year in which the person starts repaying the loan. The deduction is available for a maximum period of 8 years or till the principal amount of such loan together with interest is liquidated, whichever is earlier.

107.6A ***Deduction in respect of interest on loan taken for residential house property [Sec. 80EE, applicable from the assessment year 2017-18[1] onwards]*** - The provisions of section 80EE are given below.

• *Conditions* - The following conditions should be satisfied in order to claim deduction under section 80EE—

1. The assessee is an individual. He may be resident or non-resident.

2. He has taken a loan.

3. Loan is taken for acquisition of residential house property.

4. Loan is taken from a bank or a housing finance company. Bank for this purpose means a banking company to which the Banking Regulation Act, 1949 applies including any bank or banking institution referred to in section 51 of that Act. A housing finance company means a public company formed or registered in India with the main object of carrying on the business of providing long-term finance for construction or purchase of residential houses in India.

5. Loan has been sanctioned by the bank/housing finance company during April 1, 2016 and March 31, 2017.

6. The amount of loan sanctioned for residential house property does not exceed Rs. 35 lakh.

7. The value of residential house property does not exceed Rs. 50 lakh.

8. The assessee does not own any residential house property on the date of sanction of loan.

• *Amount of deduction* - If the above conditions are satisfied, the assessee can claim deduction under section 80EE. Deduction is available in respect of interest payable on the above loan or Rs. 50,000, whichever is less. Deduction is available for the assessment year 2017-18 and subsequent assessment years.

• *Same interest is not deductible twice* - If interest is claimed as deduction under section 80EE, such interest (or such portion of interest) is not again deductible under section 24(*b*) or under any other provision of the Act for the same or any other assessment year.

107.6A-E1 Find out the amount of deduction under section 80EE for the assessment year 2017-18 in the following cases (in all cases taxpayers are individuals, loan is taken from State Bank of India for acquisition of residential property) –

---

1. Under old section 80EE, a similar deduction was available for the assessment year 2014-15 (quantum of deduction was up to Rs. 1 lakh in respect of loan sanctioned during the financial year 2013-14, amount of sanctioned loan : not exceeding Rs. 25 lakh, value of residential house property : not exceeding Rs. 40 lakh).

Name of assessee (Case No.)	*Date of making application*	*Date on which loan sanctioned*	*Amount of loan sanctioned*	*Value of residential house property*	*Whether assessee owns any residential house property on date of loan sanctioned*	*Interest payable for the previous year 2016-17*
			Rs.	*Rs.*		*Rs.*
X (Case 1)	March 11, 2016	May 10, 2016	35 lakh	50 lakh	No	78,750
Y (Case 2)	March 11, 2016	May 10, 2016	35 lakh	50 lakh	No	50,000
Z (Case 3)	March 11, 2016	May 10, 2016	35 lakh	50 lakh	No	70,000
A (Case 4)	March 11, 2016	May 10, 2016	35 lakh	50 lakh	No	10,000
B (Case 5)	March 20, 2017	May 10, 2017	35 lakh	50 lakh	No	50,000
C (Case 6)	March 11, 2016	May 10, 2016	36 lakh	50 lakh	No	50,000
D (Case 7)	March 11, 2016	May 10, 2016	35 lakh	51 lakh	No	50,000
E (Case 8)	March 11, 2016	May 10, 2016	35 lakh	50 lakh	Yes	50,000

•

Case 1 - X satisfies all conditions of section 80EE. Rs. 50,000 is deductible under section 80EE. In respect of this interest, deduction under section 24 or any other section is not available. Date of making loan application is irrelevant. Date on which residential property is acquired is not considered for the purpose of deduction under section 80EE. Suppose, in this case, rate of interest is 9 per cent and loan of Rs. 35 lakh is released on January 1, 2017 but the property is acquired (or construction of property is completed) on June 1, 2018. Interest liability of the previous year 2016-17 is Rs. 77,671 out of which Rs. 50,000 is deductible under section 80EE. Interest liability of the previous year 2017-18 is Rs. 3,15,000, out of which Rs. 50,000 is deductible under section 80EE.

Pre-construction period for the purpose of section 24(*b*) will be January 1, 2017 to March 31, 2018. Interest liability of pre-construction period comes to Rs. 3,92,671. Out of which Rs. 1 lakh is claimed as deduction under section 80EE for the previous years 2016-17 and 2017-18. The balance of Rs. 2,92,671 is deductible as pre-construction period's interest in 5 years in 5 equal instalments. The first instalment of Rs. 58,534 will be deductible in the previous year 2018-19 along with current year's interest of the previous year 2018-19 (*i.e.*, Rs. 3,15,000) as follows –

Deduction pertaining to interest available under different sections	*If property of X is –*	
	Self-occupied *Rs.*	*Let out* *Rs.*
Deduction under section 24(*b*)	2,00,000	3,73,534
Deduction under section 80EE	50,000	*Nil*

Case 2 - Y can claim deduction of Rs. 50,000 under section 80EE.

Case 3 - Z can claim deduction of Rs. 50,000 under section 80EE. The balance of Rs. 20,000 can be claimed as deduction under section 24, if the relevant conditions are satisfied.

Case 4 - A can claim deduction of Rs. 10,000 under section 80EE.

Case 5 - Loan is not sanctioned during the previous year 2016-17. Date of application is irrelevant. Deduction under section 80EE is not available. However, deduction can be claimed under section 24.

Case 6 - As the amount of sanctioned loan is more than Rs. 35 lakh, deduction under section 80EE is not available. This rule is applicable even if amount of loan actually released during the previous year 2016-17 is Rs. 35 lakh or less. However, C can claim deduction under section 24.

Case 7 - As the value of residential property is more than Rs. 50 lakh, deduction under section 80EE is not available. There is no notional definition for "value" of residential property for this purpose. Consequently, stamp duty value is not considered for the purpose of section 80EE.

Case 8 - Deduction under section 80EE is not available as E owns a residential property on the date of sanction of loan. E can, however, claim deduction under section 24.

107.6B ***Deduction in respect of interest on loan taken for certain house property [Sec. 80EEA, applicable from the assessment year 2020-21 onwards]*** - Deduction under section 80EEA is available if the following conditions are satisfied –

1. The assessee is an individual.

2. He is not eligible to claim any deduction under section 80EE.

3. He has taken a loan for the purpose of acquisition of residential house property.

4. The loan is sanctioned by a financial institution (*i.e.*, a bank or banking institution or a housing finance company) during April 1, 2019 and March 31, 2020.

5. The stamp duty value of the residential house property does not exceed Rs. 45 lakh.

6. The assessee does not own any residential house property on the date of sanction of loan.

• *Amount of deduction* - If the above conditions are satisfied, the assessee can claim deduction under section 80EEA. **Deduction is available in respect of interest payable on the above loan or Rs. 1,50,000, whichever is less.** Deduction is available for the assessment year 2020-21 and subsequent assessment years.

• *Same interest is not deductible twice* - If interest is claimed as deduction under section 80EEA, such interest (or such portion of interest) is not again deductible under section 24(*b*) or under any other provision of the Act for the same or any other assessment year.

107.6C ***Deduction in respect of interest on loan taken for purchase of electric vehicle [Sec. 80EEB, applicable from the assessment year 2020-21 onwards]*** - Deduction under section 80EEB is available if the following conditions are satisfied –

1. The assessee is an individual.

2. He has taken a loan for the purpose of purchase of an electric vehicle.

3. Loan is taken from a financial institution (*i.e.*, a bank or any deposit taking NBFC or a systematically important non-deposit taking NBFC).

4. Loan is sanctioned during April 1, 2019 and March 31, 2023.

• *Amount of deduction* - If the above conditions are satisfied, the assessee can claim deduction under section 80EEB. **Deduction is available in respect of interest payable on the above loan or Rs. 1,50,000, whichever is less.** Deduction is available for the assessment year 2020-21 and subsequent assessment years.

• *Same interest is not deductible twice* - If interest is claimed as deduction under section 80EEB, such interest (or such portion of interest) is not again deductible under any other provision of the Act for the same or any other assessment year.

107.7 ***Deduction in respect of donations to certain funds, charitable institutions, etc. [Sec. 80G]*** - The deduction under section 80G is available to any taxpayer (maybe individual, company, firm or any other person, maybe resident or non-resident[2]) and calculated under the following three steps :

Step 1 : Gross qualifying amount [*see* para 107.7-1]

Step 2 : Net qualifying amount [*see* para 107.7-2]

Step 3 : Amount deductible [*see* para 107.7-3]

107.7-1 *STEP 1 - GROSS QUALIFYING AMOUNT* - Gross qualifying amount is the aggregate of the donations made to any of the institutions/fund given in column *1* of the table given in para 107.7-3. Donation made in kind shall not be included.

107.7-2 *STEP 2 - NET QUALIFYING AMOUNT* - Net qualifying amount is limited to 10 per cent of gross total income of the assessee as reduced by the following :

a. amount deductible under sections 80CCC to 80U (but not section 80G);

b. such incomes on which income-tax is not payable;

c. long-term capital gains;

d. short-term capital gains taxable @ 10 per cent under section 111A; and

e. incomes referred to in section 115A, 115AB, 115AC or 115AD.

The aforesaid ceiling does not apply in relation to donations made to funds specified in (*a*), (*b*), (*c*), (*d*), (*e*), (*f*), (*g*), (*h*), (*i*), (*j*), (*k*), (*l*), (*m*), (*n*), (*o*), (*p*), (*q*), (*r*), (*s*), (*t*), (*u*), (*zc*), (*zd*), (*ze*), (*zf*) and (*zg*) of *Step 1*.

107.7-3 *AMOUNT DEDUCTIBLE* - Net qualifying amount is eligible for deduction on the basis given below in column (*3*) of table *infra*—

2. Donation to Clean Ganga Fund by a non-resident is not eligible for deduction under section 80G.

Donee	Maximum limit	Deduction (as a percentage of net qualifying amount)
a. National Defence Fund set up by the Central Government	Not applicable	100 per cent[3]
b. Jawaharlal Nehru Memorial Fund	Not applicable	50 per cent
c. Prime Minister's Drought Relief Fund	Not applicable	50 per cent
d. Prime Minister's National Relief Fund	Not applicable	100 per cent
e. Prime Minister's Armenia Earthquake Relief Fund	Not applicable	100 per cent
f. Africa (Public Contributions - India) Fund	Not applicable	100 per cent
g. National Children's Fund	Not applicable	100 per cent[4]
h. Indira Gandhi Memorial Trust	Not applicable	50 per cent
i. Rajiv Gandhi Foundation	Not applicable	50 per cent
j. National Foundation for Communal Harmony	Not applicable	100 per cent
k. An approved university/educational institution[5]	Not applicable	100 per cent
l. The Maharashtra Chief Minister's Relief Fund during October 1, 1993 and October 6, 1993 and the Chief Minister's Earthquake Relief Fund	Not applicable	100 per cent
m. Any fund set up by the State Government of Gujarat for providing relief to the victims of earthquake in Gujarat	Not applicable	100 per cent
n. Zila Saksharta Samiti	Not applicable	100 per cent
o. National Blood Transfusion Council and State Council for Blood Transfusion	Not applicable	100 per cent
p. Fund set up by a State Government for the medical relief to the poor	Not applicable	100 per cent
q. Central Welfare Fund of the Army and Air Force and the Indian Naval Benevolent Fund	Not applicable	100 per cent
r. Andhra Pradesh Chief Minister's Cyclone Relief Fund	Not applicable	100 per cent
s. National Illness Assistance Fund	Not applicable	100 per cent
t. Chief Minister's Relief Fund or Lieutenant Governor's Relief Fund	Not applicable	100 per cent
u. National Sports Fund or National Cultural Fund or Fund for Technology Development and Application	Not applicable	100 per cent
v. Any other fund or any institution which satisfies conditions mentioned in section 80G(5)[6]	As given in para 107.7-2	50 per cent

3. 50 per cent up to the assessment year 1999-2000.
4. 50 per cent up to the assessment year 2013-14.
5. For the purposes of section 80G(2)(*a*)(*iiif*), the prescribed authority,—
   a. in relation to a University or any non-technical institution of national eminence shall be the Director General (Income-tax Exemptions) who shall grant approval with the concurrence of the Secretary, University Grants Commission ;
   b. in relation to any technical institution of national eminence shall be the Director General (Income-tax Exemptions) who shall grant approval with the concurrence of the Secretary, All India Council of Technical Education.
6. The application for approval of any institution or fund shall be submitted online in Form No. 10G$. The application shall be accompanied by the following documents, namely :
   a. copy of registration granted under section 12A or copy of notification issued under section 10(*23*) or 10(*23C*) ;
   b. notes on activities of institution of fund since its inception or during the last year, whichever is less ;
   c. copies of accounts of the institution or fund since its inception or during the last three years, whichever is less.

   • The Commissioner may call for such further documents or information from the institution or fund or cause such inquiries to be made as he may deem necessary in order to satisfy himself about the genuineness of the activities of such institution or fund.

   • Where the Commissioner is satisfied that all conditions laid down in section 80G(5)(*i*) to (*iv*) are fulfilled by the institution or fund, he shall record such satisfaction in writing and grant approval to the institution or fund specifying the assessment year or years for which the approval is valid.

   • Where the Commissioner is satisfied that one or more of such conditions are not fulfilled, he shall reject the application for approval, after recording the reasons for such rejection in writing. However, no order or rejection of an application shall be passed without giving the institution or fund an opportunity of being heard.

(Contd. on next page)

Donee	*Maximum limit*	*Deduction (as a percentage of net qualifying amount)*
w. Government or any local authority to be utilised for any charitable purpose other than the purpose of promoting family planning	As given in para 107.7-2	50 per cent
x. Any authority referred to in section 10(*20A*) [*i.e.*, an authority constituted in India for the purpose of dealing with and satisfying the need for housing accommodation or for the purpose of planning/development of towns, villages, etc.]	As given in para 107.7-2	50 per cent
y. Any corporation specified in section 10(*26BB*) for promoting interest of minority community	As given in para 107.7-2	50 per cent
z. Government or any approved local authority, institution or association to be utilised for the purpose of promoting family planning	As given in para 107.7-2	100 per cent
za. Any notified temple, mosque, gurdwara, church or other place (for renovation or repair)	As given in para 107.7-2	50 per cent
zb. Donation by a company to the Indian Olympic Association or to any other association or institution notified for the development of infrastructure for sports and games in India or the sponsorship of sports and games in India (applicable from the assessment year 2001-02)	As given in para 107.7-2	100 per cent
zc. Any trust, institution or fund to which section 80G(5C) applies for providing relief to the victims of earthquake in Gujarat (contribution can be made during January 26, 2001 and September 30, 2001)	Not applicable	100 per cent
zd. National Trust for Welfare of Persons with Autism, Cerebral Palsy, Mental Retardation and Multiple Disabilities (applicable for the assessment year 2002-03)	Not applicable	100 per cent
ze. Swachh Bharat Kosh[7] (from the assessment year 2015-16)	Not applicable	100 per cent
zf. Clean Ganga Fund[7] (amount donated by residents only) (from the assessment year 2015-16)	Not applicable	100 per cent
zg. National Fund for Control of Drug Abuse (from the assessment year 2016-17)	Not applicable	100 per cent

Maximum amount - Where the aggregate of the sums mentioned in (*v*), (*w*), (*x*), (*y*), (*z*) *(za) or (zb) supra* exceeds 10 per cent of the adjusted gross total income, then the amount in excess of 10 per cent of the adjusted gross total income will be ignored while computing the aggregate of the sums in respect of which deduction is to be allowed.

(Contd. from pre-page)

• The time limit, within which the Commissioner shall pass an order either granting the approval or rejecting the application shall not exceed six months from the end of the month in which the application is made. However, in computing the period of six months, any time taken by the applicant in not complying with the directions of the Commissioner shall be excluded— Notification No. 9099, dated September 21, 1992.

• Where an institution or fund has been approved under clause (*vi*) of section 80G(5) for the previous year 2007-08, such institution or fund shall be deemed to have been established for charitable purposes and approved [for the purpose of section 80G(5)(*vi*)] for the previous year 2008-09.

• Approval of the Commissioner under section 80G(5)(*vi*) has effect for such assessment year or years, not exceeding five assessment years, as may be specified in the approval. However, the time-limit of 5 years has been omitted with effect from October 1, 2009 by the Finance (No. 2) Act, 2009. After this amendment, the approval once granted shall continue to be valid in perpetuity. Accordingly, existing approvals expiring on or after October 1, 2009 shall be deemed to have been extended in perpetuity, unless specifically withdrawn. However, in case of approvals expiring before October 1, 2009, these will have to be renewed and once renewed these shall continue to be valid in perpetuity, unless specifically withdrawn—Circular No. 7/2010, dated October 27, 2010. Further, the Commissioner will also have the power to withdraw the approval if the Commissioner is satisfied that the activities of such an institution or fund are not genuine or are not being carried out in accordance with the objects of the institution or fund.

$ For requirement of Form No. 10G, log on to *taxmann.com/readyreckoner.aspx.*

7. Donations to Swachh Bharat Kosh and Clean Ganga Fund is eligible for deduction under section 80G only if the amount is not spent by the assessee in pursuance of Corporate Social Responsibility (CSR) under section 135(5) of the Companies Act, 2013.

107.7-4 *MODE OF PAYMENT* - Donation can be given in cash or by cheque or draft. However, no deduction shall be allowed under section 80G in respect of donation in cash of an amount exceeding Rs. 10,000 (for the assessment years 2013-14 to 2017-18) or Rs. 2,000 (from the assessment year 2018-19 onwards).

107.7-5 *PROOF OF PAYMENT* - Proper proof of payment must be submitted to claim deduction—*Golecha Properties (P.) Ltd.* v. *CIT* [1988] 171 ITR 47 (Raj.). However, simply because a receipt which is produced before the Assessing Officer is defective (not affixed with revenue stamps) it does not automatically invalidate the donation itself.

A receipt issued by the donee-institute should be submitted to get the benefit of deduction. If, however, donations are made to the National Defence Fund, the Army Central Welfare Fund, Indian Naval Benevolent Fund, Air Force Central Welfare Fund, National Relief Fund, the Chief Minister's Relief Fund or the Lieutenant Governor's Relief Fund, through the employer by a consolidated cheque, deduction will be available on the basis of certificate issued by DDO/employer in this behalf — Circular No. 777, dated July 1, 1999, Circular No. 782, dated November 13, 1999, Circular No. 7/2001, dated March 21, 2001 and Circular No. 2/2005, dated January 12, 2005.

107.7-E1 X (32 years), an Indian citizen, gives the following particulars of his income and expenditure for the previous year 2018-19:

	Rs.
Business income	3,00,000
Long-term capital gain on sale of gold	1,00,000
Short-term capital gain on sale of debentures	20,000
Short-term capital gain taxable @ 15 per cent under section 111A	30,000
Income from other sources (including bank interest : Rs. 19,000)	25,700
Donation[8] to the Jawahar Lal Nehru Memorial Fund	24,000
Donation[8] to the Government of India for promotion of family planning	27,700
Donation[8] to Prime Minister's National Relief Fund	18,000
Donation[8] to Africa (Public, Contributions—India) Fund	5,000
Donation[8] to National Foundation for Communal Harmony	7,000
Donation[8] to an approved charitable trust	22,000
Donation in kind to an approved charitable trust	3,000
Donation[8] to an approved university	7,500
Payment[8] of mediclaim insurance premium	16,000
Deposit in public provident fund	7,000

Determine the net income of X for the assessment year 2019-20.

•

Business income	3,00,000
Capital gains	1,50,000
Income from other sources	25,700
Gross total income	4,75,700
Less : Deductions	
Under section 80C	7,000
Under section 80D	15,000
Under section 80G (*see* Note 1)	79,535
Net income (rounded off)	3,74,170

Notes :

1. Computation of deduction under section 80G :

	Gross qualifying amount *Rs.*	*Net qualifying amount* *Rs.*	*Rate of deduction*	*Amount of deduction* *Rs.*
Jawahar Lal Nehru Memorial Fund	24,000	24,000	50%	12,000
Prime Minister's National Relief Fund	18,000	18,000	100%	18,000
Africa (Public Contributions—India) Fund	5,000	5,000	100%	5,000

8. Payment by cheque.

	Gross qualifying amount Rs.	Net qualifying amount Rs.	Rate of deduction	Amount of deduction Rs.
National Foundation for Communal Harmony	7,000	7,000	100%	7,000
Approved university	7,500	7,500	100%	7,500
Charitable trust (given in kind)	*Nil*	*Nil*	*NA*	*Nil*
Charitable trust (in cash)	22,000	4,670 (*see* Note 2)	50%	2,335
Government of India for promoting family planning	27,700	27,700 (*see* Note 2)	100%	27,700
Total	1,11,200	93,870	—	79,535

2. In respect of donation for family planning and approved charitable trust, amount to be included in net qualifying amount is the lower of (*a*) Rs. 49,700 (being amount of donation) or (*b*) Rs. 32,370 (being 10% of adjusted gross total income computed under Note 3). Rs. 32,370 (being the lower sum), is to be included. As the amount of Rs. 32,370, represents aggregate amount of net qualifying donations in respect of family planning and to charitable trust, separate amounts in respect of these will be as under :

	Rs.
Donation to the Government for promoting family planning	27,700
Donation to approved charitable institution (*i.e.*, Rs. 32,370—Rs. 27,700)	4,670
	32,370

3. *Adjusted gross total income*

Gross total income	4,75,700
Less : Long-term capital gain and short-term capital gain under section 111A	1,30,000
Balance	3,45,700
Less : Amount of deduction under sections 80C to 80U (except section 80G)	22,000
Adjusted gross total income	3,23,700

107.8 ***Deduction in respect of rent paid [Sec. 80GG]*** - In computing total income, an assessee is allowed a deduction in respect of expenditure towards payment of rent for any furnished or unfurnished accommodation occupied by him for the purpose of his own residence provided the following conditions are satisfied:

- He should be a self-employed person and/or a salaried employee who is not in receipt of house rent allowance at any time during the previous year.
- He or his spouse or minor child (including step child and adopted child) or the Hindu undivided family of which he is a member, should not own any residential accommodation in India or abroad. Deduction under section 80GG is denied where the taxpayer, his spouse or minor child or the Hindu undivided family of which he is a member, owns any residential accommodation at the place where the taxpayer resides, performs the duties of his office, or employment or carries on his business or profession. Where, however, the taxpayer owns any residential accommodation at any other place and the concession in respect of self-occupied house property under section 23(2)(*a*) or 23(4)(*a*) is claimed by him in respect of such accommodation, no deduction is allowed in respect of the rent paid under section 80GG even if he does not own any residential accommodation at the place where he ordinarily resides, performs the duties of his office or employment or carries on his business or profession.
- The assessee should file online declaration in Form No. 10BA regarding the expenditure incurred by him towards payment of rent.

Amount of deduction - The amount deductible under this section is *the least of* the following amounts:

a. Rs. 5,000 per month (Rs. 2,000 per month, up to the assessment year 2016-17);

b. 25 per cent of total income (total income is calculated after excluding long-term capital gain, short-term capital gain under section 111A, and income referred to in section 115A or 115D and amount deductible under sections 80C to 80U but before making any deduction under this section); or *c.* the excess of actual rent paid over 10 per cent of total income (total income is calculated after excluding long-term capital gain, short-term capital gain under section 111A, and income referred to in section 115A or 115D and amount deductible under sections 80C to 80U but before making any deduction under this section).

107.8-E1 X, a salaried employee, receives Rs. 6,48,000 as salary and Rs. 42,000 as project allowance. His employer provides an unfurnished house at concessional rent of Rs. 1,00,000. The house is situated in Delhi and rent of the house paid by the employer is Rs. 1,92,000. His income from other sources is Rs. 67,860. He pays Rs. 20,000 as medical insurance premium and deposits Rs. 5,500 in public provident fund. Can he claim deduction under section 80GG ? Also determine the net income of X for the assessment year 2019-20.

•

An assessee can claim deduction under section 80GG if he satisfies all the conditions mentioned in para 107.8. Since X satisfies all the conditions, he can claim deduction under section 80GG. For the purpose of this section, it is immaterial whether rent is paid to landlord or to employer.

Net income of X will be computed as under :	*Rs.*
Salary	6,48,000
Project allowance	42,000
Perquisite in respect of house. Rent of the house, *i.e.*, Rs. 1,92,000, or 15% of salary, (*i.e.*, Rs. 6,48,000 + Rs. 42,000), whichever is lower, is taxable value of the tax-free perquisite; since the employer charges Rs. 1,00,000 as rent, valuation of the concession is Rs. 3,500 (*i.e.*, Rs. 1,03,500 – Rs. 1,00,000)	3,500
Gross salary	6,93,500
Less : Standard deduction	40,000
Income from salary	6,53,500
Income from other sources	67,860
Gross total income	7,21,360
Less : Deductions under sections 80C to 80U	
Under section 80C in respect of public provident fund	5,500
Under section 80D in respect of medical insurance premium	20,000
Under section 80GG in respect of rent paid, being the least of the following : *a.* Rs. 60,000 (being Rs. 5,000 × 12); or *b.* Rs. 1,73,965 (being 25% of total income, *i.e.*, 25% of Rs. 6,95,860); *c.* Rs. 30,414 (being excess of rent paid over 10% of total income, *i.e.*, Rs. 1,00,000 – 10% of Rs. 6,95,860). Rs. 30,414, being the least, is therefore deductible	30,414
Net income (rounded off)	6,65,450

Note - "Total income" for the purpose of section 80GG is Rs. 6,95,860, *i.e.*, Rs. 7,21,360 - Rs. 5,500 - Rs. 20,000.

107.9 ***Deduction in respect of certain donations for scientific research or rural development [Sec. 80GGA]*** - An assessee (other than an assessee whose gross total income includes income[9] chargeable under the head "Profits and gains of business or profession") is entitled to deduction in the computation of his total income in respect of the following payments/donations—

• Sums paid to a research association which has as its object the undertaking of scientific research, or to a university, college or other institution to be used for scientific research where such association, university, college or institution has been approved by the prescribed authority for the purpose of section 35(1)(*ii*).

• Sums paid to a university or a research association which has as its object the undertaking of research in social science or statistical research, college or other institution to be used for research in social science or statistical research provided such university, association, college or institution is approved for the purpose of section 35(1)(*iii*).

• Sums paid to an approved association or institution which has as its object the undertaking of any programme of rural development to be used for carrying out any such programme approved under section 35CCA.

• Sums paid to an approved association or institution which has as its object the training of persons for implementing programmes of rural development.

---

9. Even a person who has business loss under the head "Profits and gains of business or profession" cannot claim deduction under section 80GGA—*K. Anji Reddy* v. *CIT* [2013] 59 SOT 92 (Hyd.).

• Sums paid to a public sector company, local authority or an approved association or institution for carrying out any eligible project or scheme, referred to in section 35AC [applicable from the assessment year 1992-93 onwards].

• Sum paid (before April 1, 2002) to an approved association or institution, which has as its object the undertaking of any programme of conservation of natural resources or of afforestation, to be used for carrying out any programme approved under section 35CCB.

• Any sum paid towards notified rural development fund [*i.e.*, National Fund for Rural Development notified *vide* Notification No. GSR 84(E), dated February 28, 1984].

• Sum paid (before April 1, 2002) to notified fund for afforestation.

• Sums paid to notified National Poverty Eradication Fund.

Other points - Where deduction under this section is claimed and allowed, deduction will not be allowed in respect of the same payment under any other provision of the Act for the same or any other assessment year. Deduction available under section 80GGA shall not be denied merely on the ground that after the contribution made by the assessee to above institutions, the approval granted to these institutions has been withdrawn. In other words, contribution to these institutions will be qualified for deduction even if after the date of making contribution, the approval granted to these institutions has been withdrawn.

107.9-1 *MODE OF PAYMENT* - Donation can be given in cash or by cheque or draft. However, no deduction shall be allowed under section 80GGA in respect of a cash contribution (exceeding Rs. 10,000) from the assessment year 2013-14.

107.10 ***Deduction in respect of contributions given by companies to political parties [Sec. 80GGB]*** - In computing the total income of an Indian company, any sum contributed by it (in the previous year) to any political party or (from the assessment year 2010-11) an electoral trust, is deductible. From the assessment year 2014-15, no deduction shall be allowed in respect of any sum contributed by way of cash.

• The word "contribute" has the meaning assigned to it under section 293A of the Companies Act, 1956. Political party means any political party registered under section 29A of the Representation of the People Act, 1951.

• For advertisement expenditure in a souvenir/brochure owned by a political party, *see* para 48.41.

107.10A ***Deduction in respect of contributions given by any person to political parties [Sec. 80GGC]*** - In computing the total income of an assessee (not being local authority and every artificial juridical person wholly or partly funded by the Government), any amount of contribution made by him (in the previous year), to a political party or (from the assessment year 2010-11) an electoral trust, is deductible. From the assessment year 2014-15, no deduction shall be allowed in respect of any sum contributed by way of cash.

• "Political party" means a political party registered under section 29A of the Representation of the People Act, 1951.

• For advertisement expenditure in a souvenir/brochure owned by a political party, *see* para 48.41.

107.11 ***Deduction in respect of profits and gains from projects outside India [Sec. 80HHB]*** - Deduction under section 80HHB is not available from the assessment year 2005-06.

107.12 ***Deduction in respect of profits and gains from housing projects aided by World Bank [Sec. 80HHBA]*** - Section 80HHBA was inserted with effect from the assessment year 1999-2000. No deduction under section 80HHBA is available from the assessment year 2005-06.

107.13 ***Deduction in respect of export turnover [Sec. 80HHC]*** - Deduction under section 80HHC is not available from the assessment year 2005-06.

107.14 ***Deduction under section 80HHD in respect of earning in convertible foreign exchange*** - Deduction under section 80HHD is not available from the assessment year 2005-06.

107.15 ***Deduction under section 80HHE in respect of profits from export of computer software*** - Deduction under section 80HHE is not available from the assessment year 2005-06.

107.16 ***Deduction in respect of profits and gains from export or transfer of film software [Sec. 80HHF]*** - Deduction under section 80HHF is not available from the assessment year 2005-06.

107.17 *Deduction under section 80-IA*[10] *in respect of profits and gains from industrial undertaking or enterprises engaged in infrastructure development etc. - How to find out* - Deduction under section 80-IA is available only to the following businesses carried on by an undertaking (however, deduction under section 80-IA is not available to a person who executes a works contract[11] entered into with the undertakings or enterprises given below) :

a. provision of infrastructure facility [*see* para 107.17-1];

b. telecommunication services [*see* para 107.17-2];

c. industrial parks or special economic zone [*see* para 107.17-3] ;

d. power generation, transmission and distribution [*see* para 107.17-4];

e. undertaking set up for reconstruction of a power unit [*see* para 107.17-5]; and

f. (for the assessment years 2008-09 and 2009-10), a cross-country natural gas distribution network [*see* para 107.17-6].

107.17-1 *INFRASTRUCTURE FACILITY* - The provisions of section 80-IA as applicable to an undertaking providing infrastructure facility are given below —

107.17-1a CONDITIONS - An undertaking providing infrastructure facility must satisfy the following conditions —

107.17-1a[1] *It should provide infrastructure facility* - The enterprise must carry on the business of (*a*) developing, or (*b*) maintaining and operating, or (*c*) developing, maintaining and operating any infrastructure facility.

• *Meaning of "Infrastructure facility"* - "Infrastructure facility" means[12] —

a. a road including toll road, a bridge or a rail system;

b. a highway project including housing or other activities being an integral part of the highway project;

c. a water supply project, water treatment system, irrigation project, sanitation and sewerage system or solid waste management system; and

d. a port, airport, inland waterway or inland port[13] or (from the assessment year 2008-09) navigational channel in the sea.

• *Build-Own-Lease-Transfer (BOLT) scheme of Indian railways* - It has been clarified by the Board, *vide* Circular No. 733, dated January 3, 1996, that the BOLT Scheme of the Indian railways shall be eligible for the benefit of section 80-IA since it is not legally possible for any enterprise other than the Indian railways to maintain and operate a railway system. However, this concession shall be applicable only to an infrastructure facility meant for development of rail system and not to any other infrastructure facility including rolling stocks.

• *Structures at ports* - Structures at ports for storage, loading and unloading, etc., will fall under the definition of "port" for the purposes of sections 10(*23G*) and 80-IA, if the following conditions were fulfilled:

a. the concerned port authority has issued a certificate that the said structures form part of the port; and

---

10. For provision of section 80-IA as applicable to the assessment year 1999-2000. *See Taxmann's Direct Taxes Ready Reckoner, 1999 edition.*

11. Further, with a view to preventing the misuse of the tax holiday under section 80-IA, it has been provided to clarify (with retrospective effect from 2000-01) that the tax holiday benefit under section 80-IA(4) will not be available in the case of a works contract awarded by any person (including the Central or State Government) and executed by an undertaking or enterprise referred to in section 80-IA(1).

12. The definition of 'infrastructure facility', introduced with effect from April 1, 2002 excludes 'any other public facility of a similar nature as may be notified by the Board in this behalf in the Official Gazette'. Under the earlier provisions, several public facilities have already been notified by the Board as 'infrastructure facilities'. In this connection, a need has been felt to clarify doubts as to whether such notified "infrastructure facilities" would continue to be eligible for such benefit on or after April 1, 2002. The Board has clarified that such projects, for which agreements have been entered into on or after April 1, 1995 but on or before March 31, 2001 and which have been notified by the Board on or before March 31, 2001, would continue to be exempt, subject to the fulfilment of the conditions prescribed in section 80-IA(4)(*i*)(*b*), as it existed prior to its substitution by the Finance Act, 2001—Circular No. 7/2002, dated August 26, 2002.

13. Inland Container Depots (ICDs) are inland ports for this purpose – *Container Corporation of India Ltd.* v. *CIT* [2012] 208 Taxman 62 (Delhi).

b. such structures have been built under BOT or BOLT schemes and there is an agreement that the same would be transferred to the said authority on the expiry of the time stipulated in the agreement—Circular No. 793, dated June 23, 2000.

• Under the treatment of effluents and its conveyance system, the effluents emanating from chemical industries are to be conveyed inside the sea through onshore pipeline and before discharging effluent through pipeline, entire load of effluent is to be treated to marine standards. Therefore, it is a part of 'water treatment system' and would accordingly, qualify as an infrastructure facility for the purposes of tax benefit under section 80-IA—Circular No. 1/2006, dated January 12, 2006.

• For and from assessment year 2002-03 onwards, structures at the ports for storage, loading and unloading etc. will be included in the definition of "port" for the purpose of sections 10(*23G*) and 80-IA, if the concerned port authority has issued a certificate that the said structures form part of the port—Circular No. 10/2005, dated December 16, 2005.

• *Widening of an existing road* - Widening of an existing road by constructing additional lanes as a part of a highway project by an undertaking would be regarded as a new "infrastructure facility". However, simply relaying of an existing road would not be classifiable as a new infrastructure facility for this purpose—Circular No. 4/2010[$], dated May 18, 2010.

107.17-1a² *Owned by an Indian company* - The enterprise is owned by a company registered in India or by a consortium of such companies or (from the assessment year 2006-07) by any statutory authority/board/corporation.

107.17-1a³ *Agreement* - The enterprise has entered into an agreement with the Central Government or a State Government or a local authority or any other statutory body for developing, maintaining and operating a new infrastructure facility subject to the condition that such infrastructure facility shall be transferred to the Central Government, State Government, local authority or such other statutory body, as the case may be, within the period stipulated in the agreement. From the assessment year 2002-03, the mandatory requirement that infrastructure facility shall be transferred to the Central Government, State Government, local authority or any other statutory authority, will not be applicable.

107.17-1a⁴ *Commencement* - The enterprise starts operating and maintaining the infrastructure facility on or after April 1, 1995. However, no deduction under this section will be available to any enterprise which starts the development or operation and maintenance of the infrastructure facility on or after April 1, 2017.

107.17-1a⁵ *Return of income* - From the assessment year 2006-07, return of income should be submitted on or before the due date of submission of return of income given by section 139(1). If return is not submitted or return is submitted belatedly, deduction under this section is not available.

107.17-1a⁶ *Deduction should be claimed in the return of income* - Deduction under section 80-IA is not available unless it is claimed in the return of income. In other words, if the assessee fails to make a claim in his return of income of this deduction, the same will not be allowed (applicable from the assessment year 2003-04 onwards).

107.17-1b AMOUNT OF DEDUCTION - If all the aforesaid conditions are satisfied, then 100 per cent of the profit is deductible for 10 years. The deduction commences from the initial assessment year [*see* also paras 107.17-1b¹ and 107.17-1b²].

107.17-1b¹ *What is initial assessment year* - Initial assessment year, for this purpose, means the assessment year specified by the assessee at his option to be the initial year, not falling beyond the fifteenth[14] assessment year starting from the previous year in which the enterprise begins operating and maintaining the infrastructure facility. The Board has explained this provision in its Circular No.1/2016[$], dated February 15, 2016.

However, the benefit of deduction is available only for 10 consecutive assessment years falling within a period of fifteenth[14] assessment years beginning with the assessment year in which an assessee begins operating and maintaining infrastructure facility.

---

14. "Twentieth" if the "infrastructure facility" is a highway project including housing or other activities being an integral part of the highway project and road including toll road, a bridge or a rail system, a water supply project, water treatment system, irrigation project, sanitation and sewerage system or solid waste management system.

$ For Circular No. 4/2010, log on to *taxmann.com/readyreckoner.aspx.*

$ For Circular No. 1/2016, log on to *taxmann.com/readyreckoner.aspx.*

• *Provisions illustrated* - A company which begins operating and maintaining an infrastructure facility (being inland port) during the previous year 2018-19 may choose the initial assessment year as follows—

Initial assessment year as selected by the assessee	*Assessment years for which 100 per cent deduction is available under section 80-IA*
1	2
Option 1 : 2019-20	2019-20 to 2028-29
Option 2 : 2020-21	2020-21 to 2029-30
Option 3 : 2021-22	2021-22 to 2030-31
Option 4 : 2022-23	2022-23 to 2031-32
Option 5 : 2023-24	2023-24 to 2032-33
Option 6 : 2024-25	2024-25 to 2033-34
Option 7 : 2025-26	2025-26 to 2033-34
Option 8 : 2026-27	2026-27 to 2033-34
Option 9 : 2027-28	2027-28 to 2033-34
Option 10 : 2028-29	2028-29 to 2033-34
Option 11 : 2029-30	2029-30 to 2033-34
Option 12 : 2030-31	2030-31 to 2033-34
Option 13 : 2031-32	2031-32 to 2033-34
Option 14 : 2032-33	2032-33 and 2033-34
Option 15 : 2033-34	2033-34

A taxpayer may select any one of the aforesaid options. However, *options 7 to 15* should be avoided as deduction under these options will be lower than that of *option 6.*

107.17-1b[2] *Housing and other development activities which are integral part of highway project* - By virtue of section 80-IA(6), the amount of deduction available in the case of an undertaking which is engaged in providing housing and other development activities is different. Under section 80-IA(6), the following conditions should be satisfied—

1. Housing or other activities are an integral part of the highway project.

2. Profits are computed on such basis and manner as may be prescribed.

3. Such profit is not liable to tax where the profit has been transferred to a special reserve account and the same is actually utilised for highway project excluding housing and other activities before the expiry of 3 years following the previous year in which such amount was transferred.

4. The amount remaining unutilised shall be chargeable to tax as income of the year in which transfer to reserve account took place.

How to compute profit of housing and other activities which are integral part of highway project - The profits of housing or other activities, which are integral part of a highway project, shall be computed on the basis and manner specified below :

a. in a case where the annual profits of the housing or other activities which are integral part of a highway project can be arrived at in accordance with the regular method of accounting followed, the profits so arrived at as computed under the provisions of the Act; or

b. in any other case, the amount of profits arrived at based on the percentage of completion of the activities referred to above during the relevant previous year.

Every assessee shall maintain separate accounts for the above activities and shall submit a certificate in Form No. 10CCC[15] from a chartered accountant.

• *Provision illustrated* - X Ltd. has constructed a hotel on Delhi Agra highway. Profit from the hotel construction for the previous year 2015-16 is Rs. 80 lakh which is transferred to a special reserve account and, consequently, it is not chargeable to tax. The special reserve account shall be utilised up to March 31, 2019 for highway projects but excluding housing and other activities. If suppose only Rs. 70 lakh is utilised for highway projects up to March 31, 2019, then the unutilised amount of Rs. 10 lakh will become taxable for the previous year 2015-16 (*i.e.*, the assessment year 2016-17).

107.17-1c OTHER POINTS - One should also keep in view the following points —

107.17-1c¹ *Audit report* - The deduction under section 80-IA is admissible only if the accounts of the eligible undertaking have been audited by a chartered accountant, and the audit report duly signed and verified by such accountant is furnished along with the return of income (Form No. 10CCB)[15].

• A separate report is to be furnished[15] by each undertaking or enterprise of the assessee claiming deduction under section 80-IA or 80-IB and shall be accompanied by the Profit and Loss Account and Balance Sheet of the undertaking or enterprise as if the undertaking or the enterprise were a distinct entity.

• In the case of an enterprise carrying on the business of developing or operating and maintaining or developing, operating and maintaining an infrastructure facility, the audit report in Form 10CCB shall be accompanied[15] by a copy of the agreement of the enterprise with the Central Government or the State Government or the local authority for carrying on the business of developing or operating and maintaining or developing, operating and maintaining the infrastructure facility.

• In any other case, the audit report in Form 10CCB shall be accompanied[15] by a copy of the agreement, approval or permission, as the case may be, to carry on the activity signed or issued by the Central Government or the State Government or the local authority for carrying on the eligible business—Notification No. 240/2002, dated September 6, 2002.

107.17-1c² *Double deduction not possible* - Section 80-IA provides that where deduction is claimed and allowed under section 80-IA, the profits to that extent shall not qualify for deduction for any assessment year under any other provision of Chapter VIA and in no case shall exceed the eligible profit of the industrial undertaking, as the case may be.

107.17-1c³ *Adjustment of losses* - Section 80-IA(5) provides that for the purpose of determining the quantum of deduction under section 80-IA for the assessment year immediately succeeding the initial assessment year or any subsequent assessment year, the profits and gains from the eligible business shall be computed as if such eligible business were the only source of income of the assessee during the previous year relevant to the initial assessment year and to every subsequent assessment year up to and including the assessment year for which the determination is to be made.

For instance, X Ltd. owns two undertakings : A (eligible for the purpose of section 80-IB) and B (not eligible for the purpose of section 80-IB). Date of commencement of production in the two cases is December 10, 2008.

Profit made by the two units is as follows :

(Rs. in lakh)

	Unit A	*Unit B*	*Income from other sources*	*Gross total income*	*Carried forward of loss to the next year*
Asst. year 2010-11	(-) 5	(-) 2	–	*Nil*	(-) 7
Asst. year 2011-12	(-) 12	1	–	*Nil*	(-) 18
Asst. year 2012-13	(-) 8	5	–	*Nil*	(-) 21
Asst. year 2013-14	(-) 3	17	–	*Nil*	(-) 7
Asst. year 2014-15	(-) 1	21	–	13	*Nil*
Asst. year 2015-16	4	6	–	10	*Nil*
Asst. year 2016-17	19	12	–	31	*Nil*
Asst. year 2017-18	14	13	2	29	*Nil*
Asst. year 2018-19	16	18	–	34	*Nil*
Asst. year 2019-20	19	(-) 7	6	18	*Nil*

15. From April 1, 2014, audit report should be submitted electronically. Provisions pertaining to electronic submission of audit report were not applicable prior to April 1, 2014 (for period prior to April 1, 2014, audit report and other statements/agreement/approval may be retained by the assessee and these may be furnished in original whenever the Assessing Officer wants in assessment proceedings or otherwise).

In the aforesaid case, the "initial previous year" is the previous year 2009-10 (*i.e.*, the year in which production was started). However, no deduction is available under section 80-IB till the assessment year 2014-15 as income from Unit A is negative. The entire loss of Unit A has been set off under sections 70 and 72 till the assessment year 2014-15. There is no loss brought forward from earlier years for the assessment year 2015-16 (or subsequent year).

However, to compute profit eligible for tax holiday under section 80-IA, it is assumed that Unit A is the only unit owned by X Ltd. Consequently, deduction will be available as under :

(Rs. in lakh)

	Asst. year 2015-16	*Asst. year 2016-17*	*Asst. year 2017-18*	*Asst. year 2018-19*	*Asst. year 2019-20*
Profit of Unit A	4	19	14	16	19
Profit of Unit B	6	12	13	18	(-) 7
Business income	10	31	27	34	12
Income from other sources	–	–	2	–	6
Gross total income *(a)*	10	31	29	34	18
Less : Deduction under section 80-IB in respect of Unit A					
Current year profit of Unit A	4	19	14	16	19
Less : Notionally brought forward loss from earlier years	–29	–25	–6	*Nil*	*Nil*
Balance	–25	–6	8	16	19
Deduction under section 80-IB (it is assumed that deduction is available @ 100%) (*total deduction under sections 80C to 80U cannot exceed gross total income) *(b)*	*Nil*	*Nil*	8	16	18*
Net income [*(a)* — *(b)*]	10	31	21	18	*Nil*

It may be noted that for the assessment year 2019-20 profit of Unit A for the purpose of deduction under section 80-IB will not be reduced by the loss incurred in Unit B.

The aforesaid example explains the provisions regarding deduction available under section 80-IB in cases where in the initial assessment year (and in a few subsequent years) the eligible unit incurs loss. Under section 80-IB (and also under sections 80-IC, 80-ID and 80-IE), the first year in which production is started, is taken as initial previous year. The concept explained with the help of above example is, therefore, equally applicable in sections 80-IC, 80-ID and 80-IE.

Under sections 80-IA and 80-IAB, however, initial assessment year may be selected by the assessee (it may be the first year of commencement of activity or a subsequent year as selected by the assessee for the purpose of claiming deduction under section 80-IA or 80-IAB). Deduction under sections 80-IA and 80-IAB is available from the initial assessment year (selected by the assessee) and not from the first year in which the business is commenced. In such cases, the concept of adjustment of losses discussed above requires some modifications which is explained with the help of another example as follows—

Y Ltd. owns a power generating unit (eligible for deduction under section 80-IA). The business of power generating was started during the financial year 2008-09. However, the company is in the business of manufacturing of chemicals since 1970. The following data is available from income-tax records of the company—

Previous years	*Income from power generating unit Rs. (in lakh)*	*Income from chemical manufacturing Rs. (in lakh)*	*Interest income taxable under section 56 Rs. (in lakh)*
2008-09	(-) 4010	2870	-
2009-10	(-) 4120	9580	-
2010-11	(-) 3570	3740	-
2011-12	(-) 2730	2500	-
2012-13	(-) 102	1800	-
2013-14	(-) 92	3700	-
2014-15	70	3810	-
2015-16	(-) 400	4020	-
2016-17	300	5310	800
2017-18	6080	(-)210	800
2018-19	7010	7600	800

Y Ltd. is entitled for deduction under section 80-IA at the rate of 100 per cent profit from the activity of power generation. This tax holiday will be available for 10 years. Section 80-IA(2) permits deduction, at the option of assessee, for any ten consecutive assessment years out of fifteen years beginning from the year in which the activity of power generation was commenced. As there is no profit before March 31, 2014, the company has opted for the previous year 2014-15 as the initial previous year for the purpose of claiming the benefit of deduction under section 80-IA.

Since in this case, the initial previous year is the previous year 2014-15, the provisions of section 80-IA will be applicable only from the previous year 2014-15. In other words, from the previous year 2014-15, it will be assumed that only source of income of Y Ltd. is income from generation of power for the purpose of computing the quantum of deduction available under section 80-IA. To put it differently, losses pertaining to the previous year prior to 2014-15 will not be taken into consideration for calculating the amount of deduction under section 80-IA which is available from the previous year 2014-15 onwards—*Mohan Breweries & Distilleries Ltd.* v. *CIT* [2008] 23 SOT 32 (Chennai)(URO), *Velayudhaswamy Spinning Mills (P.) Ltd.* v. *CIT* [2012] 21 taxmann.com 95 (Mad.)[16], *CIT* v. *Leo Fasteners* [2017] 84 taxmann.com 6 (Mad.)[17], *CIT* v. *Defree Engineering (P.) Ltd.* [2017] 77 taxmann.com 11 (Mad.)[18], *CIT* v. *Eastman Spinning Mills (P.) Ltd.* [2015] 231 Taxman 801 (Mad.), *Rangamma Steels & Malleables* v. *CIT* [2010] 132 TTJ (Chennai) 365, *Shevie Exports* v. *CIT* [2013] 33 taxmann.com 446 (Mum.), *Jivraj Tea & Industries Ltd.* v. *CIT* [2014] 62 SOT 74 (Ahd.), *Advik Hi tech (P.) Ltd.* v. *CIT* [2015] 67 SOT 158 (Pune). The taxable income of the Y Ltd. for different assessment years will be as follows—

Previous years	*Assessment years*	*Income from power generating unit* Rs. (in lakh)	*Income from chemical manufacturing* Rs. (in lakh)	*Adjustment of brought forward losses under section 72* Rs. (in lakh)	*Gross total income* Rs. (in lakh)	*Deduction under section 80-IA* Rs. (in lakh)	*Total income* Rs. (in lakh)
2008-09	2009-10	(-) 4010	2870	-	-	-	*Nil*
2009-10	2010-11	(-) 4120	9580	(-) 1140	4320	-	4320
2010-11	2011-12	(-) 3570	3740	-	170	-	170
2011-12	2012-13	(-) 2730	2500	-	-	-	*Nil*
2012-13	2013-14	(-) 102	1800	(-) 230	1468	-	1468
2013-14	2014-15	(-) 92	3700	-	3608	-	3608
2014-15	2015-16[22]	70	3810	-	3880	70	3810
2015-16	2016-17	(-) 400	4020	-	3620	-	3620
2016-17	2017-18	300	5310	-	6410[19]	*Nil*[20]	6410
2017-18	2018-19	6080	(-) 210	-	6670[19]	5980[21]	690
2018-19	2019-20	7010	7600	-	15410[19]	7010	8400

107.17-1c[4] *Power of the Income-tax Department to recompute profits* - In the following circumstances, the Assessing Officer has power to ignore the declared profit and to make necessary adjustments so as to arrive at the profits for the purpose of deduction under section 80-IA.

• If any goods held for the purpose of the eligible business is transferred to any other business carried on by the assessee, and *vice versa,* and in either case, the consideration if any for such transfer as recorded in the accounts of the eligible business does not correspond to the market value of such goods as on the date of transfer, profits of the eligible business will be computed as if the transfer in either case had been made at the market value of the goods as on that date. If such a manner of computation is found, in the opinion of the Assessing Officer, to present exceptional difficulties, the Assessing Officer is authorised to compute the profits on such reasonable basis as he may deem fit. This power has been granted to the Assessing Officer with a view to curbing any attempt to under-invoice or over-invoice of goods by the assessee in order to inflate

---

16. SLP dismissed against the High Court's ruling—*CIT* v. *Velayudhaswamy Spinning Mills (P.) Ltd.* [2016] 76 taxmann.com 176 (SC).

17. SLP dismissed against the High Court's ruling – *CIT* v. *Leo Fasteners* [2018] 95 taxmann.com 18 (SC).

18. SLP dismissed against the High Court's ruling—*CIT* v. *Defree Engineering (P.) Ltd.* [2017] 77 taxmann.com 27 (SC).

19. Includes interest income of Rs. 800 lakh taxable under section 56

20. It is after adjusting (notionally) the loss of Rs. 400 lakh pertaining to the earlier year.

21. It is after adjusting (notionally) the balance loss of Rs. 100 lakh out of Rs. 400 lakh pertaining to the earlier year. Notional brought forward of loss under section 80-IA(5) is operative only during the ten year period of deduction commencing from the initial assessment year and not for the period prior to the commencement of initial assessment year. Suppose this sub-section is not present, then the deduction for the assessment year 2017-18 would be Rs. 300 lakh. It is *nil* only because of operation of section 80-IA(5). Similarly, for assessment year 2018-19 deduction under section 80-IA is not Rs. 6080 lakh but it is restricted to Rs. 5980 lakh by reducing balance unabsorbed loss of Rs. 100 lakh.

22. Initial assessment year.

the profits of the eligible business. For this purpose, the expression "market value"[23] is defined to mean the price that such goods would ordinarily fetch on sale in the open market.

• If it appears to the Assessing Officer that business between the assessee (engaged in eligible business) and any other person is so arranged that the business transacted between them produces to the assessee more than the ordinary profits that might be expected to arise in such eligible business, either due to the close connection between the assessee and that other person or due to any other reason, then the Assessing Officer shall take the amount of profit as may be reasonably deemed to have been derived therefrom.[23]

107.17-1c[5] *Consequences of demerger/amalgamation* - If a company which is entitled for deduction under section 80-IA is amalgamated/demerged with another company (before claiming tax holiday for 10 years), the amalgamated company/resulting company can avail the benefit under section 80-IA for the unexpired period of tax holiday (including the previous year in which amalgamation/demerger takes place). However, this facility is available only when transferor-company and transferee-company are Indian companies.

• The aforesaid benefit in the case of section 80-IA is available only when amalgamation/demerger takes place before April 1, 2007.

• The aforesaid benefit in the case of sections 10A, 10AA, 10B, 80-IAB, 80-IB, 80-IC and 80-IE is available irrespective of date of amalgamation or demerger (or even if date of amalgamation/demerger is on or after April 1, 2007).[24]

107.17-1c[6] *Consequences of transfer of undertaking* - Where an infrastructure facility is transferred on or after April 1, 1999 by an enterprise which developed such infrastructure facility (*i.e.*, transferor enterprise) to another enterprise (*i.e.*, transferee enterprise) for the purpose of operating and maintaining the infrastructure facility on its behalf in accordance with the agreement with the Central Government, State Government, local authority or statutory body, section 80-IA shall apply to the transferee enterprise as if it were the enterprise to which such section applies and the deduction from profits and gains would be available to such transferee enterprise for the unexpired period during which the transferor enterprise would have been entitled to the deduction, if the transfer had not taken place. For example, if the transferor has availed of the deduction for development of an infrastructure facility for 6 years and thereafter transfers it to the transferee for operation and maintenance; such transferee will be eligible for deduction for remaining 4 years – Circular No. 10/2014[$], dated May 6, 2014.

107.17-2 *TELECOMMUNICATION SERVICES* - The following conditions should be satisfied—

1. It should be a new undertaking [*see* para 107.18-1a[1]]. However, this condition introduced by the Finance (No. 2) Act, 2004 will not apply to undertakings, which have started providing telecommunication services prior to April 1, 2004. Therefore, if an undertaking is formed by the transfer of old plant and machinery or splitting up or reconstruction of business already in existence but has started providing telecommunication services prior to April 1, 2004, it will continue to get the tax benefit available under section 80-IA of the Income-tax Act—Circular No. 5/2005, dated July 15, 2005.

2. It should not be formed by transfer of old plant and machinery [*see* para 107.18-1a[2]][25].

3. An undertaking engaged in providing telecommunication services starts providing telecommunication services whether basic or cellular including radio paging, domestic satellite service or network of turnking broadband network and internet services and electronic data inter-change service at any time after March 31, 1995 but before March 31, 2005. "Domestic satellite" for this purpose means a satellite owned and operated by an Indian company for providing telecommunication service.

4. From the assessment year 2006-07, return of income should be submitted on or before the due date of submission of return of income given by section 139(1). If return is not submitted or return is submitted belatedly, deduction under this section is not available.

---

23. Market value or the transaction value for the aforesaid purposes in the case of specified domestic transactions referred to in section 92BA (if aggregate value of such domestic transactions exceed Rs. 5 crore) shall be arm's length price [as defined in section 92F(*ii*)] from the assessment year 2013-14.

24. In the case of conversion of firm/sole proprietary concern into firm, the benefit of tax holiday can be availed by the transferee for the unexpired period—*ITO* v. *Advance Valves Global* [2011] 15 taxmann.com 342 (Delhi - Trib.), *CIT* v. *Mega Packages* [2011] 15 taxmann.com 80 (Punj. & Har.).

25. Applicable only in respect of an undertaking set up after March 31, 2004.

$ For Circular No. 10/2014, log on to *taxmann.com/readyreckoner.aspx*.

5. Deduction under section 80-IA is not available unless it is claimed in the return of income. In other words, if the assessee fails to make a claim in his return of income of this deduction, the same will not be allowed (applicable from the assessment year 2003-04 onwards).

107.17-2a AMOUNT OF DEDUCTION - If all the aforesaid conditions are satisfied, then deduction is available under section 80-IA as follows —

Assessee-enterprises	*% of profit deductible*	*Period of deduction commencing from the initial assessment year*
❑ Owned by a company or any other person	100	First 5 years
	30	Next 5 years

• *Initial assessment year* - Initial assessment year means the assessment year specified by the assessee at his option to be the initial year not falling beyond the fifteenth assessment year starting from the previous year in which the undertaking begins providing telecommunication services [*see* para 107.17-1b[1] for a detailed study].

107.17-2b OTHER POINTS - One should also keep in view the following points—

1. Audit report [*see* para 107.17-1c[1]].

2. Double deduction is not available [*see* para 107.17-1c[2]].

3. Computation of profit [*see* para 107.17-1c[3]].

4. Recomputation of profit by the Assessing Officer [*see* para 107.17-1c[4]].

5. Consequences of demerger/amalgamation [*see* para 107.17-1c[5]].

107.17-3 *INDUSTRIAL PARKS OR SPECIAL ECONOMIC ZONE* - An undertaking which develops and operates industrial park or develops a special economic zone must satisfy the following conditions in order to avail the benefit of section 80-IA —

1. It develops and operates or maintains and operates an industrial park or from the assessment year 2002-03 a special economic zone notified for this purpose in accordance with any scheme framed and notified by the Central Government.

2. The industrial park must start operating during April 1, 2006 and March 31, 2011 and it should be notified by the Central Government[26] under the Industrial Park Scheme, 2008 or the special economic zone must start operating during April 1, 1997 and March 31, 2005.

3. From the assessment year 2006-07, return of income should be submitted on or before the due date of submission of return of income given by section 139(1). If return is not submitted or return is submitted belatedly, deduction under this section is not available.

4. Deduction under section 80-IA is not available unless it is claimed in the return of income. In other words, if the assessee fails to make a claim in his return of income of this deduction, the same will not be allowed (applicable from the assessment year 2003-04 onwards).

107.17-3a AMOUNT OF DEDUCTION - If all the aforesaid conditions are satisfied, 100 per cent of profit is deductible for 10 years commencing from the initial assessment year.

• *Initial assessment year* - Initial assessment year means the assessment year specified by the assessee at his option to be the initial year not falling beyond the fifteenth assessment year starting from the previous year in which the undertaking begins operating developing industrial park [*see* para 107.17-1b[1] for a detailed study].

107.17-3b OTHER POINTS - One should also keep in view the following points —

1. Audit report [*see* para 107.17-1c[1]].

2. Double deduction is not available [*see* para 107.17-1c[2]].

3. Computation of profit [*see* para 107.17-1c[3]].

4. Recomputation of profit by the Assessing Officer [*see* para 107.17-1c[4]].

5. Where an undertaking develops an industrial park on or after April 1, 1999 or develops a special economic zone on or after April 1, 2001 and transfers the operation and maintenance of such industrial parks or special

26. For procedure for approval, *see* Notification No. 3/2008, dated January 8, 2008.

economic zone to another undertaking (*i.e.*, transferee undertaking), the deduction shall be allowed to such transferee undertaking for the remaining period in the ten consecutive assessment years in a manner as if the operation and maintenance were not so transferred to the transferee undertaking.

107.17-4 *POWER GENERATION/DISTRIBUTION* - The following conditions should be satisfied—

1. New undertaking - See para 107.18-1a[1].

2. Not to be formed by old plant and machinery - See para 107.18-1a[2]. For the assessment year 2005-06, this condition will not apply in the case of splitting up or reconstruction or reorganisation of State Electricity Boards.

3. Commencement - The undertaking must be set up in any part of India for the generation or generation and distribution of power[27] and it begins the operation at any time during April 1, 1993 and March 31, 2017. Alternately, it starts transmission or distribution by laying a network of new transmission or distribution lines at any time between April 1, 1999 and March 31, 2017.

Alternatively, it undertakes substantial renovation and modernisation of the existing transmission or distribution lines at any time during the period commencing on April 1, 2004 and ending on March 31, 2017. The term "substantial renovation and modernisation" has been defined to mean an increase in the book value of plant and machinery by 50 per cent as compared to book value of such plant and machinery on April 1, 2004.

4. Return of income - From the assessment year 2006-07, return of income should be submitted on or before the due date of submission of return of income given by section 139(1). If return is not submitted or return is submitted belatedly, deduction under this section is not available.

5. Deduction should be claimed in the return of income - Deduction under section 80-IA is not available unless it is claimed in the return of income. In other words, if the assessee fails to make a claim in his return of income of this deduction, the same will not be allowed (applicable from the assessment year 2003-04 onwards).

107.17-4a AMOUNT OF DEDUCTION - If all the aforesaid conditions are satisfied, 100 per cent of the profit is deductible for 10 years commencing from the initial assessment year.

• *Eligible profit* - Profit[28] which is eligible for deduction under section 80-IA is as follows —

Activity	*Profit available for deduction*
❑ Only generation of power	Profit from generation of power
❑ Generation and distribution of power	Profit from generation and distribution of power
❑ Laying a network of new transmission or distribution lines for starting transmission/distribution of power	Profit derived from laying of such network of new lines for transmission or distribution

• *Initial assessment year* - Initial assessment year means the assessment year specified by the assessee at his option to be the initial year not falling beyond the fifteenth assessment year starting from the previous year in which the undertaking generates power or commences transmission or distribution of power [*see* para 107.17-1b[1] for a detailed study].

107.17-4b OTHER POINTS - One should also keep in view the following points —

1. Audit report [*see* para 107.17-1c[1]].

2. Double deduction is not available [*see* para 107.17-1c[2]].

3. Computation of profit [*see* para 107.17-1c[3]].

4. Recomputation of profit by the Assessing Officer [*see* para 107.17-1c[4]].

5. Consequences of demerger/amalgamation [*see* para 107.17-1c[5]].

107.17-5 *RECONSTRUCTION OF POWER UNIT* - The provisions are given below :—

• *Conditions* - The following conditions should be satisfied—

1. It should be owned by an Indian company and set up for reconstruction or revival of a power generating plant.

2. It should be formed before November 30, 2005 with majority equity participation by public sector companies for the purposes of enforcing the security interest of the lenders to the company owning the power generating plant and such Indian company is notified before December 31, 2005 by the Central Government.

---

27. 'Power' and 'energy' are synonymous, which can be in several types and forms, be it heat, which is steam or mechanical or electrical, wind or be it thermal - *CIT* v. *Maharaja Shree Umaid Mills Ltd.* [2009] 29 SOT 278 (Jp.).

28. Where an assessee has set up a captive power generating unit, valuation of electricity for computing profit shall be at the rate at which electricity distribution companies are allowed to supply electricity to consumers – *CIT* v. *Reliance Industries Ltd.* [2019] 261 Taxman 358 (Bom.), *Gujarat Flurochemicals Ltd.* v. *CIT* [2018] 97 taxmann.com 10 (Ahd.).

3. Such undertaking begins to generate or transmit or distribute power before March 31, 2011.

4. Return of income - From the assessment year 2006-07, return of income should be submitted on or before the due date of submission of return of income given by section 139(1). If return is not submitted or return is submitted belatedly, deduction under this section is not available.

5. Deduction should be claimed in the return of income - Deduction under section 80-IA is not available unless it is claimed in the return of income. In other words, if the assessee fails to make a claim in his return of income of this deduction, the same will not be allowed (applicable from the assessment year 2003-04 onwards).

- *Amount of deduction* - *See* para 107.17-1b.
- *Other points* - *See* para 107.17-1c.

107.17-6 *CROSS-COUNTRY NATURAL GAS DISTRIBUTION* - For the assessment years 2008-09 and 2009-10[29] deduction under section 80-IA will be available to any undertaking carrying on the business of laying and operating a cross-country natural gas distribution network, including pipelines and storage facilities being an integral part of such network, if the following conditions are satisfied—

1. It is owned by a company registered in India or by a consortium of such companies or by an authority or a board or a corporation established or constituted under any Central or State Act.

2. It has been approved by the Petroleum and Natural Gas Regulatory Board and notified by the Central Government.

3. One-third of its total pipeline capacity is available for use on common carrier basis by any person other than the assessee or an associated person.

4. It starts functioning on or after April 1, 2007.

5. It fulfils such other conditions as may be prescribed.

6. The undertaking should not be formed by way of reconstruction or splitting up or by transfer to a new business of old plant and machinery (subject to certain exceptions).

7. Return of income should be submitted on or before the due date of submission of return of income.

8. Deduction under section 80-IA is not available unless it is claimed in the return of income. In other words, if the assessee fails to make a claim in his return of income of this deduction, the same will not be allowed.

- *Deduction* - If the above conditions are satisfied, 100 per cent deduction will be available for 10 consecutive assessment years out of 15 years beginning from the year in which an undertaking lays and begins to operate the cross-country natural gas distribution network.
- *Associated person* - For this purpose "associated person" in relation to the assessee means—

1. A person who participates directly or indirectly or through one or more intermediaries in the management or control or capital of the assessee.

2. A person who holds, directly or indirectly, shares carrying not less than 26 per cent of the voting power in the assessee.

3. A person who appoints more than half of the Board of directors or members of the governing board, or one or more executive directors or executive members of the governing board of the assessee.

4. A person who guarantees not less than 10 per cent of the total borrowings of the assessee.

107.17A ***Deductions in respect of profits and gains by an undertaking or enterprise engaged in development of Special Economic Zone [Sec. 80-IAB]*** - Section 80-IAB was inserted to give deduction to the developers of special economic zone from the assessment year 2006-07.

107.17A-1 *CONDITIONS* - The following conditions should be satisfied—

1. The taxpayer is a developer of a special economic zone.

2. The gross total income of the taxpayer includes profits and gains derived by an undertaking from any business of developing a special economic zone.

3. Such special economic zone is notified on or after April 1, 2005 and the development of special economic zone should begin on or before March 31, 2017.

4. The books of account of the taxpayer are audited.

5. From the assessment year 2006-07, return of income should be submitted on or before the due date of submission of return of income given by section 139(1). If return is not submitted or return is submitted belatedly, deduction under this section is not available.

---

29. The benefit of deduction under section 80-IA will not be available to the business of laying and operating a cross-country natural gas distribution network from the assessment year 2010-11. Any person availing this incentive can claim the benefit of deduction under section 35AD [*see* para 48.14].

6. Deduction under section 80-IAB is not available unless it is claimed in the return of income. In other words, if the assessee fails to make a claim in his return of income of this deduction, the same will not be allowed.

107.17A-2 *AMOUNT OF DEDUCTION* - If the above conditions are satisfied, the taxpayer can claim 100 per cent deduction in respect of the aforesaid profit. However, no deduction under this section will be available to a developer where the development of the special economic zone begins on or after April 1, 2017.

• *Period of deduction* - The aforesaid deduction is available for 10 consecutive assessment years. The deduction may be claimed, at the option of the taxpayer, for any 10 consecutive assessment years out of 15 years beginning from the year in which the special economic zone has been notified by the Central Government.

• *Transfer of undertaking* - If a taxpayer who develops a special economic zone on or after April 1, 2005 ("transferor") transfers the operation/maintenance of such zone to another developer ("transferee"), then deduction shall be allowed to the transferee for the remaining period of 10 years as if the operation and maintenance were not so transferred. Similar rule will be applicable in the case of amalgamation of an Indian company which has developed a special economic zone with another Indian company.

107.17A-3 *OTHER POINTS* - One should also keep in view the following points—

1. The profits and gains from the eligible business shall be computed as if such eligible business were the only source of income of the assessee during the relevant assessment year.

2. The Assessing Officer has power to recompute profit in some cases. These cases are given by section 80-IA(8)/(10).

3. Where any amount of profits and gains is claimed and allowed as deduction under section 80-IAB for any assessment year, deduction to the extent of such profits and gains shall not be allowed under sections 80HH to 80RRB and shall in no case exceeds profits and gains of such eligible business.

107.17B ***Deduction in respect of eligible start-up [Sec. 80-IAC, applicable from the assessment year 2017-18]*** - The provisions of section 80-IAC, applicable from the assessment year 2017-18, are given below -

• *Conditions* - The following conditions should be satisfied –

1. The assessee is a company or a limited liability partnership (LLP).

2. It is engaged in an eligible business. "Eligible business" means –

- *For the assessment year 2017-18* - A business which involves innovation, development, deployment or commercialisation of new products, processes or services driven by technology or intellectual property.
- *From the assessment year 2018-19* - A business carried out by an eligible start up engaged in innovation, development or improvement of products or processes or services or a scalable business model with a high potential of employment generation or wealth creation.

3. The above company or LLP is incorporated after March 31, 2016 but before April 1, **2021**.

4. Annual business turnover of the company or LLP does not exceed Rs. 25 crore in the previous year relevant to the assessment year for which deduction is claimed under section 80-IAC.

5. It holds a certificate of eligible business from the Inter-Ministerial Board of Certification as notified in the Official Gazette by the Central Government.

6. The above company or LLP is not formed by splitting up, or the reconstruction, of a business already in existence. However, this condition is not applicable in respect of a start-up which is formed as a result of the re-establishment, reconstruction or revival by the assessee of the business of any such undertaking as referred to in section 33B.

7. It is not formed by the transfer to a new business of machinery or plant previously used for any purpose [it is subject to a few exceptions, *see* para 107.18-1a[2]].

• *Amount of deduction* - If the above conditions are satisfied, 100 per cent of the profits and gains derived from such business is deductible for 3 consecutive assessment years. However, this deduction may, at the option of the assessee, be claimed by it for any 3 consecutive assessment years out of 5 years (7 years, from the assessment year 2018-19) beginning from the year in which the eligible start-up is incorporated. Books of account should be audited and audit report should be submitted along with the return of income. If the assessee fails to make a claim of deduction available under this section in its return of income, the same will not be allowed as deduction.

107.18 ***Deduction under section 80-IB in respect of profits and gains from certain industrial undertakings other than infrastructure development undertakings*** - Deduction under section 80-IB is available to different industrial undertakings as follows —

a. business of an industrial undertaking [*see* para 107.18-1];
b. operation of ship [*see* para 107.18-2];
c. hotels [*see* para 107.18-3];
d. industrial research [*see* para 107.18-4];
e. production of mineral oil [*see* para 107.18-5];
f. developing and building housing projects [*see* para 107.18-6];
g. integrated handling, storage and transportation of food grains units [*see* para 107.18-7];
h. multiplex theatres [*see* para 107.18-8];
i. convention centre [*see* para 107.18-9];
j. operating and maintaining hospital in rural area [*see* para 107.18-10]; and
k. hospital located in certain areas [*see* para 107.18-11].

107.18-1 *INDUSTRIAL UNDERTAKING* - The provisions of section 80-IB as (applicable to an industrial undertaking) are given below —

107.18-1a CONDITIONS - To claim deduction under section 80-IB, an industrial undertaking (*i.e.*, an undertaking which is mainly engaged in the business of the construction of ships or in the manufacture or processing of goods or in mining) must satisfy the following conditions :

107.18-1a¹ *It should be a new undertaking* - The industrial undertaking is not formed by splitting up, or the reconstruction, of a business already in existence. However, if a new industrial undertaking is set up in an old building, deduction shall be admissible as this section provides for new undertaking and does not provide for new building.

• *Exception* - The aforesaid condition of "new undertaking" is not applicable where the business is re-established, reconstructed or revived by the same assessee after the business of any industrial undertaking carried on by him in India is discontinued due to extensive damage to, or destruction of, any building, machinery, plant or furniture owned by the assessee (and used for the purpose of such business) as a direct result of (*i*) flood, typhoon, hurricane, cyclone, earthquake or other convulsion of nature, or (*ii*) riot or civil disturbance, or (*iii*) accidental fire or explosion, or (*iv*) action by any enemy or action taken in combating an enemy (whether with or without a declaration of war).

107.18-1a² *It should not be formed by transfer of machinery or plant previously used for any purpose* - It is not formed by a transfer to a new business of machinery and plant previously used for any purpose.

• *Two exceptions* - In the two cases given below, the aforesaid rule is not applicable—

❑ *20 per cent old machinery is permitted* - If the value of the transferred assets does not exceed 20 per cent of the total value of the machinery or plant used in the business, this condition is deemed to have been satisfied.

❑ *Second-hand imported machinery is treated as new* - Any machinery or plant which was used outside India by any person other than the assessee shall not be regarded as machinery or plant previously used for any purpose, if the following conditions are fulfilled :

1. Such machinery or plant was not, at any time prior to the date of the installation by the assessee, used in India.

2. Such machinery or plant is imported into India from any country outside India.

3. No deduction on account of depreciation in respect of such machinery or plant has been allowed or is allowable under the Act in computing the total income of any person for any period prior to the date of the installation of the machinery or plant by the assessee.

107.18-1a³ *It should not manufacture or produce articles specified in the Eleventh Schedule* - It manufactures or produces any article or thing (not being an article or thing specified in the list in the Eleventh Schedule) or operates cold storage plant, in any part of India.

• *Exception 1* - From the assessment year 2005-06, an industrial unit in Jammu and Kashmir should not manufacture or produce articles specified in Part C of the Thirteenth Schedule.

• *Exception 2* - Small-scale undertakings or an undertaking in a backward State can manufacture any goods/ article. Deduction is admissible to all small-scale industrial undertakings and those undertakings which are specified in para 107.18-1b *infra* even if they are engaged in the production of articles listed in the Eleventh Schedule.

Small scale industrial undertaking - An industrial undertaking in which the investment in fixed assets in plant and machinery whether held on ownership terms or on lease, or by hire purchase does not exceed Rs. 1 crore[30] (on the last day of the previous year) is a small-scale industrial undertaking.

- No small-scale or ancillary industrial undertaking referred to above shall be subsidiary of, or owned or controlled by other industrial undertaking.
- In calculating the value of plant and machinery the following shall be excluded namely : (*i*) the cost of equipment such as tools, jigs, dies, moulds and spare parts for maintenance and the cost of consumable stores; (*ii*) the cost of installation of plant and machinery ; (*iii*) the cost of research and development equipment and pollution control equipment ; (*iv*) the cost of generating sets, extra transformer, etc., installed by the undertaking as per the regulations of the State Electricity Board ; (*v*) the bank charges and service paid to the National Small Industries Corporation or the State Small Industries Corporation ; (*vi*) the cost involved in procurement or installation of cables, wiring, bus bars, electrical control panels (not those mounted or individual machines), oil circuit breakers/miniature circuit breakers, etc., which are necessarily to be used for providing electrical power to the plant and machinery/safety measures ; (*vii*) the cost of gas producer plant ; (*viii*) transportation charges (excluding of taxes, *i.e.*, sales tax, excise, etc.) for indigenous machinery from the place of manufacturing to the site of the factory ; (*ix*) charges paid for technical know-how for erection of plant and machinery; (*x*) cost of such storage tanks which store raw materials finished products only and are linked with the manufacturing process ; and (*xi*) cost of fire fighting equipments.

In the case of imported machinery, the following shall be included in calculating the value, namely : (*i*) import duty (excluding miscellaneous expenses as transportation from the port to the site of the factory, demurrage paid at the port ; (*ii*) the shipping charges ; (*iii*) customs clearance charges ; and (*iv*) sales tax.

107.18-1a[4] *It must start manufacturing between a specified period* - *See* para 107.18-1b.

107.18-1a[5] *It should employ 10/20 workers* - In a case where the industrial undertaking manufactures or produces articles or things, the undertaking employs 10 or more workers in a manufacturing process carried on with the aid of power, or employs 20 or more workers in a manufacturing process without the aid of power. This condition is applicable only for "industrial undertaking" and not for cold storage plant, ship or hotel.

107.18-1a[6] *Return of income* - From the assessment year 2006-07, return of income should be submitted on or before the due date of submission of return of income given by section 139(1). If return is not submitted or return is submitted belatedly, deduction under this section is not available.

107.18-1a[7] *Deduction should be claimed in the return of income* - Deduction under section 80-IB is not available unless it is claimed in the return of income. In other words, if the assessee fails to make a claim in his return of income of this deduction, the same will not be allowed (applicable from the assessment year 2003-04 onwards). However, section 80-IB does not require that the claim should be filed only in the original return. Such claim can be made even in the revised return—*Parmeshwar Cold Storage (P.) Ltd.* v. *CIT* [2011] 16 taxmann.com 88 (Ahd. - Trib.).

107.18-1b AMOUNT OF DEDUCTION - An industrial undertaking can claim deduction at the rates given in the table *infra*. The table also highlights conditions already mentioned in paras 107.18-1a[3] and 107.18-1a[4]. However, no deduction under these provisions will be applicable in cases covered by section 80-IC from the assessment year 2004-05.

---

30. Rs. 5 crore in some cases.

	Small scale industrial undertaking	*Industrial undertaking (including cold storage) set up in an industrial backward State [Eighth Schedule]*	*Industrial undertaking (including cold storage) set up in Category A notified backward district*	*Industrial undertaking (including cold storage) set up in Category B notified backward district*	*Cold chain facility for agricultural produce*	*Any other*
1. Nature of articles to be produced	Any	Any [*see* Note 2]	Other than those given in Eleventh Schedule	Other than those given in Eleventh Schedule	Cold chain facility for agricultural produce	Other than those given in Eleventh Schedule
2. Time-limit for commencement of production or operation	Between April 1, 1991 and March 31, 2002	Between April 1, 1993 and March 31, 2004 (March 31, 2012 in the case of Jammu and Kashmir)	Between October 1, 1994 and March 31, 2004	Between October 1, 1994 and March 31, 2004	Between April 1, 1999 and March 31, 2004	Between April 1, 1991 and March 31, 1995
3. Amount of deduction (period of deduction commences from initial assessment year)						
3.1 Owned by a company	30% for first 10 years	100% for first 5 years and 30% for next 5 years [*see* Note 1 *infra*]	100% for first 5 years and 30% for next 5 years	100% for first 3 years and 30% for next 5 years	100% for first 5 years and 30% for next 5 years	30% for first 10 years
3.2 Owned by a co-operative society	25% for first 12 years	100% for first 5 years and 25% for next 7 years [*see* Note 1 *infra*]	100% for first 5 years and 25% for next 7 years	100% for first 3 years and 25% for next 9 years	100% for first 5 years and 25% for next 7 years	25% for first 12 years
3.3 Owned by any other person	25% for first 10 years	100% for first 5 years and 25% for next 5 years [*see* Note 1 *infra*]	100% for first 5 years and 25% for next 5 years	100% for first 3 years and 25% for next 5 years	100% for first 5 years and 25% for next 5 years	25% for first 10 years

Notes—

1. In the case of an industrial undertaking operating in the North-Eastern Region (*i.e.*, the region comprising of the States of Arunachal Pradesh, Assam, Manipur, Meghalaya, Mizoram, Nagaland and Tripura), the amount of deduction is 100 per cent of the profit and deduction is available for the first 10 years commencing from the initial assessment year. This deduction is, however, available only in the case of such industries in the North-Eastern Region as are notified by the Central Government up to the assessment year 2003-04. No deduction will be available from the assessment year 2004-05 in respect of undertaking eligible for deduction under section 80-IC.

2. From the assessment year 2005-06, an industrial undertaking in the State of Jammu and Kashmir should not manufacture or produce cigarettes/cigars, distilled and brewed alcoholic drinks, aerated branded beverages and their concentrates.

• *What is initial assessment year* - "Initial assessment year" means the assessment year relevant to the previous year in which the industrial undertaking begins to manufacture or produce articles or things, or to operate its cold storage plant or plants.

The "article" in this context is the final or end-product for which the undertaking is set up to manufacture.

For instance, if a small-scale industrial undertaking starts manufacture/production on December 19, 2001, the initial assessment year will be 2002-03, and it will be eligible for deduction (subject to the satisfaction of the prescribed conditions in every year) for the assessment years 2002-03 to 2011-12 (in the case of co-operative society for the assessment years 2002-03 to 2013-14).

107.18-1c OTHER POINTS - One should keep in view the following points —

1. Audit report [*see* para 107.17-1c[1]].

2. Double deduction is not available [*see* para 107.17-1c[2]].

3. Computation of profit [*see* para 107.17-1c[3]].

4. Recomputation of profit by the Assessing Officer [*see* para 107.17-1c[4]].

5. Consequences of demerger/amalgamation [*see* para 107.17-1c[5]].

107.18-2 *OPERATION OF SHIP* - Now-a-days, this deduction is not available.

107.18-3 *HOTEL INDUSTRY* - Now-a-days, this deduction is not available.

107.18-4 *COMPANIES ENGAGED IN INDUSTRIAL RESEARCH* - Section 80-IB is applicable if the following conditions are satisfied—

1. The taxpayer is a company registered in India.

2. Such company has its main object the scientific and industrial research and development.

3. It is for the time being approved by the prescribed authority (*i.e.,* Secretary, Department of Scientific and Industrial Research).

4. From the assessment year 2006-07, return of income should be submitted on or before the due date of submission of return of income given by section 139(1). If return is not submitted or return is submitted belatedly, deduction under this section is not available.

5. Deduction under section 80-IB is not available unless it is claimed in the return of income. In other words, if the assessee fails to make a claim in his return of income of this deduction, the same will not be allowed.

107.18-4a AMOUNT OF DEDUCTION - If all the aforesaid conditions are satisfied, the following is deductible—

	If the company is approved by the prescribed authority at any time before April 1, 1999	*If the company is approved by the prescribed authority after March 31, 2000 but before April 1, 2007*
Amount of deduction	100 per cent of profit from such business	100 per cent of profit from such business
Period of deduction	5 years beginning with the initial[31] assessment year	10 years beginning with the initial[31] assessment year

107.18-4b OTHER POINTS - One should also keep in view the following points—

1. Double deduction is not available [*see* para 107.17-1c[2]].

2. Computation of profit [*see* para 107.17-1c[3]].

3. Recomputation of profit by the Assessing Officer [*see* para 107.17-1c[4]].

4. Consequences of demerger/amalgamation [*see* para 107.17-1c[5]].

107.18-5 *MINERAL OILS* - One should satisfy the following conditions —

1. It should be a new undertaking [*see* para 107.18-1a[1]]. An *Explanation* has been inserted so as to clarify (with retrospective effect from the assessment year 2000-01) that for this purpose, all blocks licensed under a single contract, which has been awarded under the New Exploration Licencing Policy announced by the Government of India *vide* Resolution No. O-19018/22/95-ONG.DO.VL, dated February 10, 1999 or has been awarded in pursuance of any law for the time being in force or has been awarded by Central or a State Government in any other manner, shall be treated as a single "undertaking".

2. It should not be formed by transfer of machinery or plant previously used for any purpose [*see* para 107.18-1a[2]].

3. It should commence commercial production as follows —

	*Commencing production of mineral oil***	*Commencing refining of mineral oil*	*Commencing production of natural gas**
Undertaking located in North-Eastern Region**	Before April 1, 1997	—	—
Undertaking located anywhere in India	After March 31, 1997*** but before April 1, 2017	After September 30, 1998 but before April 1, 2012	On or after April 1, 2009 but before April 1, 2017

31. Initial assessment year means the assessment year relevant to the previous year in which the company is approved by the prescribed authority.

*In blocks licensed under the VIII Round of bidding for award of exploration contracts under the New Exploration Licencing Policy announced by the Government of India *vide* Resolution No. 0-19018/22/95-ON.GD.OVL, dated February 10, 1999 or in blocks licensed under the IV Round of bidding for award of exploration contracts for Coal Bed Methane blocks.

**North-Eastern Region comprises of the States of Arunachal Pradesh, Assam, Manipur, Meghalaya, Mizoram, Nagaland, Sikkim and Tripura.

***However, it will not apply to blocks licensed under a contract awarded after March 31, 2011 under the New Exploration Licencing Policy announced by the Central Government (*vide* Resolution No. O-19018/22/95-ONG.DO.VL, dated February 10, 1999) or in pursuance of any law for the time being in force or by the Central or a State Government in any other manner.

****Mineral oil in its natural, commercial and technical sense includes petroleum products and natural gas—*Niko Resources Ltd.* v. *Union of India* [2015] 231 Taxman 100 (Guj.).

4. It should employ 10/20 workers [*see* para 107.18-1a[5]].

5. From the assessment year 2006-07, return of income should be submitted on or before the due date of submission of return of income given by section 139(1). If return is not submitted or return is submitted belatedly, deduction under this section is not available.

6. Deduction under section 80-IB is not available unless it is claimed in the return of income. In other words, if the assessee fails to make a claim in his return of income of this deduction, the same will not be allowed (applicable from the assessment year 2003-04 onwards).

107.18-5a AMOUNT OF DEDUCTION - 100 per cent of the profit is deductible for the first 7 years commencing with the year in which the undertaking commences commercial production of mineral oil or refining of mineral oil.

107.18-5b OTHER POINTS - One should also keep in view the following points —

1. Audit report [*see* para 107.17-1c[1]].

2. Double deduction is not available [*see* para 107.17-1c[2]].

3. Computation of profit [*see* para 107.17-1c[3]].

4. Recomputation of profit by the Assessing Officer [*see* para 107.17-1c[4]].

5. Consequences of demerger/amalgamation [*see* para 107.17-1c[5]].

107.18-6 *DEVELOPING AND BUILDING HOUSING PROJECTS* - An undertaking engaged in developing and building housing projects shall be eligible to claim deduction under section 80-IB. By virtue of *Explanation 10* to this section, any undertaking which executes the housing project as a works contract awarded by any other person (including Central or State Government) is not eligible for deduction under section 80-IB(10)[32]. To claim deduction, one should satisfy the following conditions—

Condition 1	The project should be approved by a local authority before March 31, 2008.		
Condition 2	The size of the plot of land is a minimum of one acre.		
Condition 3	The undertaking commences development and construction of the housing project after September 30, 1998 and it should complete construction[33]—		
	a. where housing project has been approved by local authority before April 1, 2004	:	On or before March 31, 2008

32. Explanation to section 80-IB(10) is applicable only in the case of a works contractor. It does not have any role to play in the case of a developer of a housing project under a development agreement. Generally, in the case of such development agreement, developer does not own land. But certainly such developer is not a works contractor. Consequently, a developer of a housing project can claim the benefit of section 80-IB(10) even if land is not owned by him - *CIT* v. *Shreeji Developers* [2013] 218 Taxman 100 (Guj.), *CIT* v. *Sanghvi & Doshi Enterprise* [2013] 214 Taxman 463 (Mad.), *CIT* v. *Mahadev Developers* [2013] 214 Taxman 130 (Guj.), *CIT* v. *Prathama Developers* [2013] 214 Taxman 131 (Guj.), *CIT* v. *Vishal Construction Co.* [2013] 217 Taxman 96 (Guj.), *CIT* v. *Shree Ram Construction* [2013] 215 Taxman 17 (Guj.).

33. There is no further condition that such construction and development of the housing project should also be on a land owned by an assessee undertaking.

<table>
<tr><td></td><td colspan="2">b. where housing project has been approved during 2004-05 : Within 4 years from the end of the financial year in which the housing project is approved by the local authority
c. where housing project has been approved on or after April 1, 2005 : Within 5 years from the end of the financial year in which the housing project is approved by the local authority</td></tr>
<tr><td>Condition 4</td><td colspan="2">The built-up area of the shops and other commercial establishments included in the housing project shall not exceed 5 per cent of the aggregate built-up area of the housing project or 2,000 sq. ft., whichever is less. With effect from the assessment year 2010-11, the built-up area of the shops and other commercial establishments included in the housing project should not exceed 3 per cent of the total built-up area of the housing project or 5,000 sq. ft., whichever is more.</td></tr>
<tr><td>Condition 5</td><td colspan="2">The built-up area of each residential unit should be subject to the following maximum limit -</td></tr>
<tr><td></td><td>Place where residential unit is situated</td><td>Minimum size of the plot of land should be one acre and the maximum built-up area of each residential unit should be as given below—</td></tr>
<tr><td></td><td>• Within the cities of Delhi and Mumbai</td><td>1,000 sq. ft.</td></tr>
<tr><td></td><td>• Within 25 kilometres from the local limits of Delhi and Mumbai</td><td>1,000 sq. ft.</td></tr>
<tr><td></td><td>• At any other place</td><td>1,500 sq. ft.</td></tr>
<tr><td>Condition 6</td><td colspan="2">If the allottee is a person other than individual, not more than one residential unit will be allotted to the same allottee. If the allottee is an individual, no other unit in the housing project should be allotted to the same individual and/or any of the following persons—(a) spouse or minor children of such individual; (b) the Hindu undivided family in which such individual is the karta; and (c) any person representing such individual, the spouse or minor children of such individual or the Hindu undivided family in which such individual is the karta (applicable from the assessment year 2010-11).</td></tr>
<tr><td>Condition 7</td><td colspan="2">From the assessment year 2006-07, return of income should be submitted on or before the due date of submission of return of income given by section 139(1). If return is not submitted or return is submitted belatedly, deduction under this section is not available.</td></tr>
<tr><td>Condition 8</td><td colspan="2">Deduction should be claimed in the return of income.</td></tr>
</table>

Notes:

1. Conditions two and *three* are not applicable in the case of a housing project, carried out in accordance with a scheme framed by the Central Government or a State Government for reconstruction or redevelopment of existing buildings in areas declared as slum areas under any law and such scheme is notified by the Board in this behalf.

2. The expression "built-up area" has been defined to mean the inner measurements of the residential unit at the floor level, including the projections and balconies, as increased by the thickness of the walls but not including the common areas shared with other residential units.

3. The date of issue of completion certificate is taken as date of completion of construction.

4. It is beneficial to obtain approval for each residential block separately—*CIT* v. *Brigade Enterprises (P.) Ltd.* [2009] 28 SOT 7 (Bang.).

5. On perusal of provisions of section 80-IB(10), one finds that it is not a mandatory requirement to fully utilize permissible FSI—*Radhe Developers* v. *ITO* [2008] 23 SOT 420 (Ahd.).

6. Merely because some flats are larger than the specified limit given above, an assessee will not lose benefit in its entirety. In other words, only with reference to flats which are more than prescribed area, the assessee would lose benefit, whereas he or it would be entitled to claim deduction in respect of residential units which are within the specified limit—*SJR Builders* v. *CIT* [2010] 3 ITR (Trib.) 569 (Bang.).

7. In order to allow assessee's claim for deduction under section 80-IB(10)(*b*), area of one acre available for development of housing project includes area required to be set apart for amenities as per norms of local body—*Bunty Builders* v. *ITO* [2010] 127 ITD 286 (Pune).

8. Independent residential units have to be treated as separate housing projects for the purpose of deduction under section 80-IB(10), if other conditions are satisfied. The housing project does not necessarily have to be various group of buildings constructed on a particular land but it can also be a particular building or any building which is a part of the large project for purpose of section 80-IB(10)—*Mudhit Madanlal Gupta* v. *CIT* [2011] 9 taxmann.com 235 (Mum. - ITAT).

9. Commercial use of residential units by purchaser would not disentitle the developer to benefit of section 80-IB(10)—*Manju Gupta* v. *CIT* [2011] 15 taxmann.com 287 (Mum. - Trib.).

10. Area of parking space should not be combined with area of residential unit so as to work out total area for purpose of finding out whether it exceeds specified limit mentioned in section 80-IB(10)—*Nikhil Associates* v. *ITO* [2011] 46 SOT 301 (Ahd.).

11. Where the assessee has completed housing project well before final date but local authority, for technical reasons, grants business use permission after such date, the assessee would be entitled for the benefit of deduction under section 80-IB – *CIT* v. *Tarnetar Corporation* [2012] 26 taxmann.com 180 (Guj.).

12. If a developer is ineligible for deduction under section 80-IB(10) because of size of plot being less than prescribed size and makes good deficiency later on, he is eligible for deduction under section 80-IB(10) -- *Baba Promoters & Developers* v. *ITO* [2012] 54 SOT 89 (Pune).

13. Open land and garden area cannot be included while computing total area of dwelling unit, which should be less than 1500 square feet area – *Baba Promoters & Developers* v. *ITO* [2012] 54 SOT 89 (Pune).

14. If profits of an eligible project can be clearly ascertained from audited books of account maintained by the developer, the Assessing Officer cannot refuse to give deduction under section 80-IB merely on the plea that the assessee has not maintained separate books of account – *CIT* v. *SMR Builders (P.) Ltd.* [2012] 54 SOT 105 (Hyd.).

15. An assessee cannot claim full deduction in respect of development of a housing project where utilization of FSI is way short of permissible limits and there does not exist any special ground for under utilization of FSI – *CIT* v. *Moon Star Developers* [2014] 225 Taxman 156 (Guj.).

107.18-6a AMOUNT OF DEDUCTION - If all the aforesaid conditions are satisfied, 100 per cent of the profit derived in any previous year relevant to any assessment year from such housing project is deductible.

107.18-6b OTHER POINTS - One should also keep in view the following points—

1. Audit report [*see* para 107.17-1c[1]].

2. Double deduction is not available [*see* para 107.17-1c[2]].

3. Computation of profit [*see* para 107.17-1c[3]].

4. Recomputation of profit by the Assessing Officer [*see* para 107.17-1c[4]].

5. Consequences of demerger/amalgamation [*see* para 107.17-1c[5]].

6. Even if some of the units in housing complex exceeded the area limit given above, relief under section 80-IB must be given on pro rata basis—*CIT* v. *Sheth Developers (P.) Ltd.* [2009] 33 SOT 277 (Mum.). In other words, if an assessee has developed a housing project wherein majority of residential units have a built-up area of less than 1,500 sq. ft., *i.e.*, limit prescribed by section 80-IB(10), and only a few residential units are exceeding built-up area of 1,500 sq. ft., there would be no justification to disallow entire deduction under section 80-IB(10)—*ITO* v. *Air Developers* [2009] 123 TTJ (Nag.) 959.

7. Deduction under section 80-IB(10) is available in respect of profits of a housing project as a whole, and, as such, it is not relevant as to what is portion of profits which can be said to be attributable to residential units (if the area used for shops and establishment does not exceed the limit given above)—*Brahma Associates* v. *CIT* [2009] 30 SOT 155 (Pune)(SB).

8. There is no merit in the view that deduction under section 80-IB(10) is not available to incomplete projects. A taxpayer having housing project and fulfilling all other requirements of section 80-IB(10) can adopt 'project-percentage method' to arrive at eligible profits for claim of prescribed deduction subject to preliminary satisfaction of the Assessing Officer about year of completion of project—*B. K. Pate Enterprises* v. *CIT* [2009] 125 TTJ (Pune) 974. Even the Board has clarified that the deduction can be claimed on a year-to-year basis where the assessee is showing profit from partial completion of the project in every year. In case the project is not completed within the specified time-limit of 4 or 5 years as started above, the deduction granted to the assessee in the earlier years should be withdrawn—Instruction No. 4/2009, dated June 30, 2009.

107.18-7 *UNDERTAKING ENGAGED IN THE BUSINESS OF PROCESSING, PRESERVATION AND PACKAGING OF FRUITS AND VEGETABLES OR INTEGRATED HANDLING, STORAGE AND TRANSPORTATION OF FOOD GRAINS [SEC. 80-IB(11A)]* - An undertaking deriving profit from the integrated business of handling, storage and transportation of food grains is eligible for tax holiday. From the assessment year 2005-06, it has been extended to the business of processing, preservation and packaging of fruits or vegetables. From the assessment year 2010-11, the tax holiday benefit has been extended to the business of processing, preservation and packaging of meat and meat products or poultry or marine or dairy products, if it begins to operate such business on or after April 1, 2009.

• From the assessment year 2006-07, return of income should be submitted on or before the due date of submission of return of income given by section 139(1).

• Deduction should be claimed in the return of income.

107.18-7a AMOUNT OF DEDUCTION - The amount of deduction available under section 80-IB is as follows—

Enterprises	*% of profit deductible*	*Period of deduction commencing from the initial assessment year*
❑ Owned by a company	100	First 5 years
	30	Next 5 years
❑ Owned by any other person	100	First 5 years
	25	Next 5 years

107.18-7b OTHER POINTS - One should also keep in view the following points—

1. Audit report [*see* para 107.17-1c[1]].

2. Double deduction is not available [*see* para 107.17-1c[2]].

3. Computation of profit [*see* para 107.17-1c[3]].

4. Recomputation of profit by the Assessing Officer [*see* para 107.17-1c[4]].

5. Consequences of demerger/amalgamation [*see* para 107.17-1c[5]].

107.18-8 *MULTIPLEX THEATRES* - "Multiplex theatres" means a building of a prescribed area, comprising of two or more cinema theatres and commercial shops of such size and number and having such other facilities and amenities as may be prescribed [*see* Rule 18DB[$] for prescribed facilities, etc.]. The following conditions should be satisfied in the case of multiplex theatre—

1. Such multiplex theatre is constructed at any time during April 1, 2002 and March 31, 2005.

2. The business of the multiplex is not formed by the splitting up, or the reconstruction, of a business already in existence or by the transfer to a new business of any building or of any machinery or of plant previously used for any purpose.

3. The assessee furnishes alongwith the return of income, the report of an audit in prescribed form from a chartered accountant, certifying that the deduction has been correctly claimed.

4. Such multiplex theatre is not located at a place within the municipal jurisdiction of Kolkata, Chennai, Delhi or Mumbai.

5. From the assessment year 2006-07, return of income should be submitted on or before the due date of submission of return of income given by section 139(1). If return is not submitted or return is submitted belatedly, deduction under this section is not available.

6. Deduction should be claimed in the return of income.

107.18-8a AMOUNT OF DEDUCTION - If the aforesaid conditions are satisfied, 50 per cent of the profits and gains derived from the business of building, owning and operating a multiplex theatre is deductible from the assessment year 2003-04 for a period of 5 consecutive years beginning from the initial assessment year.

Initial assessment year, for this purpose, is the assessment year relevant to the previous year in which a cinema hall, being a part of the said multiplex theatre, starts operating on a commercial basis.

107.18-8b OTHER POINTS - One should also keep in view the following points—

1. Audit report [*see* para 107.17-1c[1], Form No. 10CCBA].

2. Double deduction is not available [*see* para 107.17-1c[2]].

3. Computation of profit [*see* para 107.17-1c[3]].

4. Recomputation of profit by the Assessing Officer [*see* para 107.17-1c[4]].

5. Consequences of demerger/amalgamation [*see* para 107.17-1c[5]].

107.18-9 *CONVENTION CENTRE* - "Convention centre" means a building of a prescribed area comprising of convention halls to be used for the purpose of holding conferences and seminars, being of such size and number and having such other facilities and amenities, as may be prescribed.

[$] For rule 18DB, log on to *taxmann.com/readyreckoner.aspx.*

The following conditions should be satisfied in order to avail deduction under section 80-IB—

1. Such convention centre is constructed at any time during April 1, 2002 and March 31, 2005.

2. The business of the convention centre is not formed by the splitting up, or the reconstruction, of a business already in existence or by the transfer to a new business of any building or of any machinery or plant previously used for any purpose.

3. The assessee furnishes alongwith the return of income, the report of an audit in prescribed form from a chartered accountant, certifying that the deduction has been correctly claimed.

4. From the assessment year 2006-07, return of income should be submitted on or before the due date of submission of return of income given by section 139(1). If return is not submitted or return is submitted belatedly, deduction under this section is not available.

5. Deduction should be claimed in the return of income.

107.18-9a AMOUNT OF DEDUCTION - If the aforesaid conditions are satisfied, 50 per cent of the profits and gains derived by the assessee from the business of building, owning and operating a convention centre is deductible from the assessment year 2003-04 for a period of 5 consecutive years beginning from the initial assessment year.

Initial assessment year means the assessment year relevant to the previous year in which the convention centre starts operating on a commercial basis.

107.18-9b OTHER POINTS - One should keep in view the following points —

1. Audit report [*see* para 107.17-1c[1], Form No. 10CCBB].

2. Double deduction is not available [*see* para 107.17-1c[2]].

3. Computation of profit [*see* para 107.17-1c[3]].

4. Recomputation of profit by the Assessing Officer [*see* para 107.17-1c[4]].

5. Consequences of demerger/amalgamation [*see* para 107.17-1c[5]].

107.18-10 *OPERATING AND MAINTAINING A HOSPITAL IN RURAL AREA* - In order to claim deduction, the following conditions should be satisfied—

1. The assessee owns an undertaking deriving profits from the business of operating and maintaining a hospital in a rural area.

2. Such hospital is constructed at any time during October 1, 2004 and ending on March 31, 2008. For this purpose a hospital shall be deemed to have been constructed on the date on which a completion certificate in respect of such construction is issued by the concerned local authority.

3. The hospital has at least 100 beds for patients.

4. The construction of the hospital is in accordance with the regulations, for the time being in force, of the local authority.

5. From the assessment year 2006-07, return of income should be submitted on or before the due date of submission of return of income given by section 139(1). If return is not submitted or return is submitted belatedly, deduction under this section is not available.

6. Deduction should be claimed in the return of income.

107.18-10a AMOUNT OF DEDUCTION - If the above conditions are satisfied, 100 per cent of the profits and gains of such business is deductible from the assessment year 2005-06 for a period of 5 consecutive assessment years, beginning with the initial assessment year (*i.e.*, the assessment year relevant to the previous year in which the undertaking begins to provide medical services).

107.18-10b OTHER POINTS - One should also keep in view the following points—

1. Audit report online in Form No. 10CCBC [*see* para 107.17-1c[1]].

2. Double deduction is not available [*see* para 107.17-1c[2]].

3. Computation of profit [*see* para 107.17-1c[3]].

4. Recomputation of profit by the Assessing Officer [*see* para 107.17-1c[4]].

5. Consequences of demerger/amalgamation [*see* para 107.17-1c[5]].

107.18-11 *OPERATING AND MAINTAINING HOSPITAL IN CERTAIN AREAS* - With a view to encouraging investment in hospitals in non-metro cities, sub-section (11C) has been inserted in section 80-IB with effect from the assessment year 2009-10.

107.18-11a *CONDITIONS* - The benefit of deduction is available, if the following conditions are satisfied—

1. Location	The hospital is located anywhere in India, other than excluded area. The excluded area shall mean (or in other words, the hospital should not be located in) an area comprising the urban agglomerations of Greater Mumbai, Delhi, Kolkata, Chennai, Hyderabad, Bangalore and Ahmedabad, the districts of Faridabad, Gurgaon, Ghaziabad, Gautam Budh Nagar and Gandhinagar and the city of Secunderabad. The area comprising an urban agglomeration shall be the area included in such urban agglomeration on the basis of the 2001 census.
2. Construction	The hospital is constructed at any time during April 1, 2008 and March 31, 2013. For this purpose, a hospital shall be deemed to have been constructed on the date on which a completion certificate in respect of such construction is issued by the local authority concerned.
3. Commencement	The hospital should start functioning at any time during April 1, 2008 and March 31, 2013.
4. Number of beds	The hospital has at least 100 beds for patients.
5. Municipal bye-laws	The construction of the hospital is in accordance with the regulation or bye-laws of the local authority.
6. Audit report	The taxpayer should submit an audit report in Form No. 10CCBD certifying that deduction has been correctly claimed[34].
7. Return of income	Return of income should be submitted on or before the due date of submission of return of income given by section 139(1). If return is not submitted or return is submitted belatedly, deduction under this section is not available.
8. Deduction should be claimed in the return of income	Deduction should be claimed in the return of income. If the assessee fails to make a claim in his return of income of this deduction, the same will not be allowed.

107.18-11b *DEDUCTION* - If the above conditions are satisfied, 100 per cent of the profits and gains derived from the business of hospital shall be deductible for a period of 5 assessment years, beginning with the initial assessment year (*i.e.*, the assessment year relevant to the previous year in which the business of hospital starts functioning).

107.18-11c *OTHER POINTS* - One should keep in view the following points —

1. Double deduction is not available [*see* para 107.17-1c[1]].

2. Computation of profit [*see* para 107.17-1c[3]].

3. Recomputation of profit by the Assessing Officer [*see* para 107.17-1c[4]].

4. Consequences of demerger/amalgamation [*see* para 107.17-1c[5]].

107.18A ***Deduction in respect of profits from housing projects [Sec. 80-IBA, applicable from the assessment year 2017-18]*** - The provisions of section 80-IBA, applicable from the assessment year 2017-18, are given below -

• *Conditions* - Deduction under this section is available to an assessee (maybe an individual, HUF, AOP, BOI, company, firm or any other person), if the following conditions are satisfied -

1. The assessee has profits derived from the business of developing and building a housing project (*i.e.*, a project consisting predominantly of residential units with such other facilities and amenities as the competent authority may specify).

2. The project is approved by the competent authority after June 1, 2016, but on or before March 31, **2020**.

34. From April 1, 2014, audit report should be submitted electronically. Provisions pertaining to electronic submission of audit report were not applicable prior to April 1, 2014 (for a period prior to April 1, 2014, audit report may be retained by the assessee and it may be furnished in original whenever the Assessing Officer wants to examine it in assessment proceedings or otherwise).

3. The project is completed within a period of 3 years (5 years, applicable from the assessment year 2018-19) from the date of first approval by the competent authority. The project shall be deemed to have been completed when a certificate of completion of project as a whole is obtained in writing from the competent authority.

4. The built-up area[35] of the shops and other commercial establishments included in the housing project does not exceed 3 per cent of the aggregate built-up area[35].

5. Size of the plot, area of residential units and minimum utilization of FAR (floor area ratio) should satisfy the criteria given below.

6. The project is the only housing project on such plot of land as specified in *Column 2* of the table *infra.*

7. Where a residential unit in the housing project is allotted to an individual, no other residential unit in the housing project shall be allotted to the individual or the spouse or the minor children of such individual.

8. The **stamp duty value** of a residential unit in the housing project **does not exceed Rs. 45 lakh** (this condition is applicable if only if the housing project is **approved on or after September 1, 2019**).

9. The assessee should maintain separate books of account in respect of the housing project.

• *Condition pertaining to plot size, area of residential unit, etc.* - Apart from condition given above, the size of the plot, area of residential unit and utilization of FAR should not exceed the following –

A - IF THE PROJECT IS APPROVED PRIOR TO SEPTEMBER 1, 2019

Location of project	*Area of plot of land on which project is situated*	*Built-up area[35] of residential units comprised in the housing project*	*Utilisation of permissible FAR*
Project is located within the cities of Chennai, Delhi, Kolkata or Mumbai[36]	Not less than 1,000 square metres	Not to exceed 30 square metres	Not less than 90%
Project is located in any other place	Not less than 2,000 square metres	Not to exceed 60 square metres	Not less than 80%

B - IF THE PROJECT IS APPROVED ON OR AFTER SEPTEMBER 1, 2019

Location of project	*Area of plot of land on which project is situated*	*Carpet area[35] of residential units comprised in the housing project*	*Utilisation of permissible FAR*
Project is located within the metropolitan cities given in Note (*infra*)	**Not less than 1,000 square metres**	**Not to exceed 60 square metres**	**Not less than 90%**
Project is located in any other place	**Not less than 2,000 square metres**	**Not to exceed 90 square metres**	**Not less than 80%**

Note - It covers the metropolitan cities of Bengaluru, Chennai, Delhi NCR (limited to Delhi, Noida, Greater Noida, Ghaziabad, Gurugram, Faridabad), Hyderabad, Kolkata and Mumbai (whole of Mumbai Metropolitan Region).

• *Amount of deduction* - If the above conditions are satisfied, 100 per cent of the profit derived from the aforesaid business is deductible under section 80-IBA. However, deduction is not available to any assessee who executes the housing project as a works contract awarded by any person (including the Central/State Government). When deduction is allowed under this section, deduction to the extent of such profit is not available under any provision of the Act. Deduction should be claimed in the return of income (otherwise deduction is not available).

107.18A-E1 X Ltd. is in the business of construction of residential and commercial properties in Kolkata. In April 2018, it acquires a plot of land of 2,800 square metre in Rajpur Sonarpur (which is situated at a distance of 30 kilometres from Kolkata). It wants to construct residential units on the plot of land for which approval is taken from the local authority on June 15, 2018. Area of each residential unit will be 40 square metre. X Ltd. maintains separate books of account for this project. Income of X Ltd. from different sources before deduction under Chapter VI-A is as follows –

---

35. Carpet area from the assessment year 2018-19. "Carpet area" means the net usable floor area of an apartment [excluding (*a*) the area covered by the external walls, (*b*) areas under services shafts/exclusive balcony or verandah area/exclusive open terrace area, but including the area covered by the internal partition walls of the apartment].

36. It also includes project located within the distance (measured aerially) of 25 kilometres from the municipal limits of Chennai, Delhi, Kolkata or Mumbai (applicable only for the assessment year 2017-18).

Rs. in lakh

Previous year	*Housing project in Rajpur Sonarpur*	*Other housing project*	*Total*
2018-19	(–)90	980	890
2019-20	400	1000	1400
2020-21	500	1100	1600
2021-22	520	(–)20	500

Rajpur Sonarpur project is completed on April 20, 2021. Completion certificate is issued by the local authority on May 1, 2021. Other conditions of section 80-IBA are satisfied. Determine the amount of deduction available under section 80-IBA.

•

Housing project is situated out of municipal limits of Kolkata. Deduction under section 80-IBA is available if area of plot of land is not less than 2,000 square metre. In this case area of plot of land is 2,800 square metres and other conditions of section 80-IBA are satisfied. X Ltd. is, therefore, eligible to claim deduction under section 80-IBA as follows –

Rs. in lakh

Previous year	*Assessment year*	*Income from eligible housing project*	*Deduction under section 80-IBA*
2018-19	2019-20	(–)90	*Nil*
2019-20	2020-21	400	400
2020-21	2021-22	500	500
2021-22	2022-23	520	500[36a]

107.19 ***Deduction in respect of certain undertakings in Himachal Pradesh, Sikkim, Uttaranchal and North-Eastern States [Sec. 80-IC]*** - Section 80-IC was inserted from the assessment year 2004-05.

107.19-1 *CONDITIONS* - One has to satisfy the following conditions to claim deduction under section 80-IC—

107.19-1a NOT FORMED BY SPLITTING UP OR RECONSTRUCTION OF EXISTING BUSINESS - The industrial undertaking is not formed by splitting up, or the reconstruction, of a business already in existence.

The aforesaid condition of "new undertaking" is not applicable where the business is re-established, reconstructed or revived by the same assessee after the business of any industrial undertaking carried on by him in India is discontinued due to extensive damage to, or destruction of, any building, machinery, plant or furniture owned by the assessee (and used for the purpose of such business) as a direct result of (*i*) flood, typhoon, hurricane, cyclone, earthquake or other convulsion of nature, or (*ii*) riot or civil disturbance, or (*iii*) accidental fire or explosion, or (*iv*) action by any enemy or action taken in combating an enemy (whether with or without a declaration of war).

107.19-1b NOT FORMED BY TRANSFER OF OLD PLANT AND MACHINES - *See* para 107.18-1a[2].

107.19-1c INDUSTRIAL UNDERTAKING SHOULD BE SET UP IN CERTAIN SPECIAL CATEGORY OF STATES - The industrial undertaking should be set up in states given in *column 1* of the table given in para 107.19-2. Moreover, it should be in a specified area [*see column 3* of the table]

107.19-1d MANUFACTURE/PRODUCTION OF SPECIFIED GOODS - The industrial undertaking should manufacture/produce specified goods/articles [*see* columns (*3*) and (*4*) of the table given in para 107.19-2]

107.19-1e COMMENCEMENT - The industrial undertaking must begin to manufacture or produce article or thing within the time limit given in column (*2*) of the table given in para 107.19-2. In the case of an existing unit, substantial expansion should take place during the time-limit given in column (*2*) of the table.

107.19-1f AUDIT - The books of account the taxpayer should be audited and the audit report should be submitted[37] along with the return of income.

36a. Not to exceed gross total income of Rs. 500 lakh.

37. From April 1, 2014, audit report should be submitted electronically. Provisions pertaining to electronic submission of audit report were not applicable prior to April 1, 2014 (for period prior to April 1, 2014, audit report may be retained by the assessee and it may be furnished in original whenever the Assessing Officer wants to examine it in assessment proceedings or otherwise).

107.19-1g RETURN OF INCOME - From the assessment year 2006-07, return of income should be submitted on or before the due date of submission of return of income given by section 139(1). If return is not submitted or return is submitted belatedly, deduction under this section is not available.

107.19-1h DEDUCTION SHOULD BE CLAIMED IN THE RETURN OF INCOME - Deduction under section 80-IC is not available unless it is claimed in the return of income.

107.19-2 *AMOUNT OF DEDUCTION* - If the aforesaid conditions are satisfied, then deduction is available under section 80-IC as follows—

State in which the industrial undertaking is set up	*Time limit for commencement of production or substantial expansion [see para 107.19-2a]*	*Nature of articles to be produced if industrial undertaking is set up (or completes substantial expansion) in the industrial zone of the relevant State given in section 80-IC(2)(a) [see para 107.19-2b]*	*Nature of article to be produced if industrial undertaking is set up (or completes substantial expansion) in any area of the relevant State*	*Amount deductible [see also paras 107.19-2c and 107.19-2d]*
(1)	*(2)*	*(3)*	*(4)*	*(5)*
Sikkim	December 23, 2002 to March 31, 2007[38]	Any article but other than those given in the Thirteenth Schedule [Part A]	Any article given in Fourteenth Schedule [Part B]	100% of profit and gains of the industrial undertaking for 10 years commencing from the initial asset
Himachal Pradesh or Uttaranchal	January 7, 2003 to March 31, 2012	Any article but other than those given in the Thirteenth Schedule [Part B]	Any article given in Fourteenth Schedule [Part C]	100% of the profit and gains of the industrial undertaking for the first 5 years commencing with the initial assessment year and 25% (30% in the case of a company) for the next 5 years
North-Eastern State [*i.e.*, Arunachal Pradesh, Assam, Manipur, Meghalaya, Mizoram, Nagaland and Tripura]	December 24, 1997 to March 31, 2007[38]	Any article but other than those given in the Thirteenth Schedule[39]	Any article given in Fourteenth Schedule [Part A]	100% of profit and gain of industrial undertaking for 10 years commencing from the initial assessment year

107.19-2a WHAT IS SUBSTANTIAL EXPANSION - For the aforesaid purpose, substantial expansion is calculated as under—

1. Find out the book value of plant and machinery (before depreciation) as on the first day of the previous year in which substantial expansion is taken.

2. Find out the amount of investment in plant and machinery for expansion purposes.

3. Find out (2) ÷ (1)

If the proportion computed under (*3*)(*supra*) is 50 per cent or more, then it is taken as substantial expansion.

7. An assessee owns a manufacturing unit in Himachal Pradesh. He completes substantial expansion in the previous year 2003-04. Consequently, he is entitled for 100 per cent deduction for the first 5 years (*i.e.*, 2003-04 to 2007-08) and 50 per cent deduction for the next 5 years (*i.e.*, 2008-09 to 2012-13). He completes second substantial expansion during the previous year 2010-11. Consequently, from the previous year 2010-11 the rate of deduction will be increased to 100 per cent. As deduction is available only for 10 years, he will not get any deduction after the previous year 2012-13—*Tirupati LPG Industries Ltd.* v. *CIT* [2014] 151 ITD 1 (Delhi), *CIT* v. *Aarham Softronics* [2019] 261 Taxman 529 (SC).

---

38. *See* also para 107.19B.

39. Any article can be produced as Thirteenth Schedule has not provided negative list for North-Eastern States.

107.19-2b INDUSTRIAL ZONES GIVEN UNDER SECTION 80-IC(2) - If an industrial undertaking has begun or begins to manufacture or produce any article or thing (not being any article or thing specified in the Thirteenth Schedule), or manufactures or produces any article or thing (not being any article or thing specified in the Thirteenth Schedule) and undertakes substantial expansion during the period given in column 2 of the table (*supra*), then such industrial undertaking should be in the following industrial zones notified by the Board for the relevant State—

a. Export Processing Zone; or
b. Integrated Infrastructure Development Centre; or
c. Industrial Growth Centre; or
d. Industrial Estate; or
e. Industrial Park; or
f. Software Technology Park; or
g. Industrial Area; or
h. Theme Park

These areas shall be notified by the Board in accordance with the notified scheme of the Central Government.

107.19-2c PERIOD OF DEDUCTION NOT TO EXCEED 10 YEARS - No deduction shall be allowed to any undertaking or enterprise under section 80-IC, where the total period of deduction inclusive of the period of deduction under this section or under second proviso to section 80-IB(4) or under section 10C, as the case may be, exceeds 10 assessment years.

107.19-2d INITIAL ASSESSMENT YEAR - "Initial assessment year" means the assessment year relevant to the previous year, in which the undertaking or the enterprise begins to manufacture or produce articles or things, or commences operation or completes substantial expansion.

107.19-3 *OTHER POINTS* - One should also keep in view the following points—

1. Double deduction not allowed - In computing the total income of the assessee, no deduction shall be allowed under sections 80C to 80U or section 10A or 10B, in relation to the profits and gains of the undertaking or enterprise.

2. Adjustment of loss - *See* para 107.17-1c[3].

3. Computation of profit - *See* para 107.17-1c[4].

4. Consequences of merger/demerger - *See* para 107.17-1c[5].

107.19-E1 The following data is given in respect of X Ltd. (owning industrial Unit A), Y Ltd. (owning industrial unit B) and Z Ltd. (owning industrial unit C). These units are in operation since 1986 and are engaged in production of articles given in the Fourteenth Schedule. To increase the installed capacity, the three units are expanded as follows—

	Unit A	*Unit B*	*Unit C*
Expansion 1			
Date of commencement	April 10, 2011	April 10, 2010	June 10, 2010
Date of completion	January 7, 2012	March 12, 2011	March 24, 2012
Expansion 2			
Date of commencement	—	May 5, 2011	—
Date of completion	—	January 31, 2012	—

The amount of investment is given below :

	X Ltd. (Unit A) Rs. in lakh	*Y Ltd. (Unit B) Rs. in lakh*	*Z Ltd. (Unit C) Rs. in lakh*
Book value of plant and machinery (before depreciation) on April 1, 2010 (*a*)	84	84	84
Investment in plant and machinery during February 2011 (*b*)	Nil	20	20
[(*b*) as % of (*a*)]	[0%]	[23.81%]	[23.81%]
Book value of plant and machinery on April 1, 2011 (*c*)	84	1,04	1,04
Investment in plant and machinery during June 2011 (*d*)	42	22	22
[(*d*) as % of (*c*)]	[50%]	[21.15%]	[21.15%]
Book value on April 1, 2012 (*e*)	1,26	1,26	1,26

- In the three cases given above, book value of plant and machinery on April 1, 2010 is Rs. 84 lakh. During April 1, 2010 and March 31, 2012, additional investment of Rs. 42 lakh (which is 50% of Rs. 84 lakh) is made in plant and machinery. In the case of X Ltd., the entire expansion is completed in the previous year 2011-12. However, in the case of Y Ltd., the same investment is made for the purpose of 2 different expansions during 2 different years. In the case of Z Ltd. one expansion is completed in 2 years.

Consequently, investment made by X Ltd. during 2011-12 will be termed as substantial expansion and profit of Unit A will be qualified for deduction. Y Ltd. cannot claim any deduction under section 80-IC, as investments made by it during one year for one expansion is less than 50% of the book value of plant and machinery.

Z Ltd. can claim the benefit of deduction, as one expansion is completed in 2 different years and total investment of Rs. 42 lakh in plant and machinery is not less than 50 per cent of the investment in plant and machinery (before depreciation) on the first day of the previous year in which expansion work is started.

Amount of deduction in the case of X Ltd. or Z Ltd. is as follows —

	Percentage of profits of Unit A or Unit C deductible if Unit A or Unit C is situated in		
	Himachal Pradesh or Uttaranchal [deduction under section 80-IC]	*North-Eastern State [deduction under section 80-IE]*	*Rest of India*
If no deduction is claimed in respect of Unit A or Unit C under section 80-IB (2nd proviso) or 10C			
For the assessment years 2012-13 to 2016-17	100%	100%	*Nil*
For the assessment years 2017-18 to 2021-22	30%[1]	100%	*Nil*
From the assessment year 2022-23 onwards	*Nil*	*Nil*	*Nil*

Notes—

1. It is 25% if Unit A is owned by a non-corporate entity.

2. No other deduction will be allowed to X Ltd. and Z Ltd. under sections 10A, 10B and 80C to 80U if deduction is claimed under section 80-IC or section 80-IE.

107.19A *Deduction in respect of profits and gains from business of hotels/convention centres in NCR area [Sec. 80-ID, applicable from the assessment year 2008-09 onwards]* - Section 80-ID was inserted with effect from the assessment year 2008-09.

- *Conditions* - Section 80-ID is applicable, if the following conditions are satisfied—

1. The taxpayer engaged in the business of hotel located in a specified area given below. Alternatively, the taxpayer is engaged in the business of building, owning and operating a convention centre located in specified area given below—

Source of income	*Construction*	*Specified area*	*Applicable from assessment year*
2/3/4 star hotel	Constructed and started functioning during April 1, 2007 and July 31, 2010	National capital territory of Delhi and Faridabad, Gurgaon, Gautam Budh Nagar and Ghaziabad	Assessment year 2008-09 onwards
2/3/4 star hotel at a World heritage site	Constructed and started functioning during April 1, 2008 and March 31, 2013	Districts of Agra, Jalgaon, Aurangabad, Kancheepuram, Puri, Bharatpur, Chhatarpur, Thanjavur, Bellary, South 24 Parganas (excluding areas falling within the Kolkata Urban Agglomeration), Chamoli, Raisen, Gaya, Bhopal, Panchmahal, Kamrup, Goalpara, Nagaon, North Goa, South Goa, Darjeeling and Nilgiri	Assessment year 2009-10 onwards
Convention centre	Constructed during April 1, 2007 and July 31, 2010	National capital territory of Delhi and Faridabad, Gurgaon, Gautam Budh Nagar and Ghaziabad	Assessment year 2008-09 onwards

2. The aforesaid business is not formed by the splitting up, or the reconstruction, of a business already in existence [subject to a few exceptions - *see* para 107.18-1a[1]].

3. The aforesaid business is not formed by the transfer to a new business of machinery or plant previously used for any purpose [subject to a few exceptions - *see* para 107.18-1a[2]].

4. Audit report should be submitted[40] along with the return of income.

5. Return of income is submitted on or before the due date of submission of return of income given under section 139(1) [*see* para 118.3].

6. Deduction under section 80-ID is not available unless it is claimed in the return of income.

• *Amount of deduction* - If the above conditions are satisfied, 100 per cent of the profit and gains derived from the aforesaid business is deductible for five consecutive assessment years beginning from the initial assessment year. Initial assessment year for this purpose means the assessment year relevant to the previous year in which the business of the hotel starts functioning or the previous year in which the convention centre starts operating on a commercial basis.

107.19B ***Deduction in respect of certain undertakings in North-Eastern States [Sec. 80-IE]*** - Section 80-IE is applicable from the assessment year 2008-09.

• *Conditions* - The following conditions should be satisfied—

1. The taxpayer begins manufacture or production of goods or undertakes substantial expansion during April 1, 2007 and March 31, 2017. Alternatively, the taxpayer has begun to provide eligible services during April 1, 2007 and March 31, 2017. However, deduction under this section is not available in respect of manufacture or production of tobacco, pan masala, plastic carry bags of less than 20 microns or goods produced by petroleum oil and gas refineries. Eligible services for this purpose are hotel (2-star or above), nursing home (25 beds or more), old age homes, vocational training institutes for hotel management, catering and food crafts, entrepreneurship development, nursing and paramedical, civil aviation related training, fashion designing and industrial training, IT related training centres, IT hardware manufacture units and bio-technology.

2. The aforesaid activity takes place in any North-Eastern States (*i.e.*, Arunachal Pradesh, Assam, Manipur, Meghalaya, Mizoram, Nagaland, Sikkim and Tripura).

3. The aforesaid business is not formed by the splitting up, or the reconstruction, of a business already in existence [subject to a few exceptions - *see* para 107.18-1a[1]].

4. The aforesaid business is not formed by the transfer to a new business of machinery or plant previously used for any purpose [subject to a few exceptions - *see* para 107.18-1a[2]].

5. Audit report should be submitted[40] along with the return of income.

6. Return of income is submitted on or before the due date of submission of return of income given under section 139(1).

7. Deduction under section 80-IE is not available unless it is claimed in the return of income.

• *Amount of deduction* - If the aforesaid conditions are satisfied, 100 per cent of profit from the aforesaid business/services shall be deductible for 10 years beginning with the assessment year relevant to the previous year in which the undertaking begins to manufacture/produce article or things or complete substantial expansion. Substantial expansion for this purpose means increase in the investment in the plant and machinery by at least 25 per cent of the book value of plant and machinery (before taking depreciation in any year), as on the first day of the previous year in which the substantial expansion is undertaken.

• *Other points* - If deduction is claimed and allowed under the aforesaid provisions, the taxpayer will not be able to avail any deduction under sections 10A, 10AA, 10B, 10BA, 80C to 80U in relation to profits and gains of the above noted undertaking. Moreover, no deduction shall be allowed to an undertaking under section 80-IE where the total period of deduction under section 10C, second proviso to section 80-IB(4), section 80-IC and section 80-IE exceeds 10 assessment years.

107.20 ***Deduction in respect of profits and gains from the business of collecting and processing of bio-degradable waste [Sec. 80JJA, applicable from the assessment year 1999-2000]*** - Section 80JJA

40. From April 1, 2014, audit report should be submitted electronically. Provisions pertaining to electronic submission of audit report were not applicable prior to April 1, 2014 (for a period prior to April 1, 2014, audit report may be retained by the assessee and it may be furnished in original whenever the Assessing Officer wants to examine it in assessment proceedings or otherwise).

was inserted with effect from the assessment year 1999-2000. Deduction under section 80JJA is available where the gross total income of an assessee includes any profits and gains derived from the business of collecting[41], processing and treating of bio-degradable waste for generating power or producing bio-fertilizers, bio-pesticides or other biological agents or for producing bio-gas or making pellets or briquettes for fuel or organic manure. Deduction under section 80JJA is not available unless it is claimed in the return of income (applicable from the assessment year 2003-04 onwards).

• *Amount of deduction* - The amount of deduction for different assessment years is as follows—

From the assessment year 2000-01 onwards - The whole of the profits and gains of the above activities shall be deductible for a period of five consecutive assessment years beginning with the assessment year relevant to the previous year in which such business commences.

For the assessment year 1999-2000 - The whole of the profits and gains from the above activities or Rs. 5 lakh, whichever is less, is deductible.

• *Other points* - The following points should be noted—

1. For the purpose of claiming deduction under section 80JJA, business of collecting of biodegradable waste should be done by an assessee as a part of his business activities. If such activity is done by job work customers, the assessee would not be entitled to deduction—*CIT* v. *Padma S. Bora* [2010] 133 TTJ (Pune) 108.

2. Benefits of section 80JJA are available in respect of profits and gains derived from the manufacturing of fuel briquettes from bagasse generated by sugar factories—*CIT* v. *Smt. Padma S. Bora* [2010] 133 TTJ (Pune) 108.

107.21 ***Deduction in respect of employment of new employees [Sec. 80JJAA, applicable from the assessment year 2017-18]*** - Deduction under section 80JJAA (as applicable from the assessment year 2017-18) is available, if the following conditions are satisfied -

1. The assessee has income from business and he is subject to tax audit under section 44AB.

2. The business of the assessee is not formed by splitting up, or the reconstruction, of an existing business. However, this condition is not applicable in respect of a business which is formed as a result of the re-establishment, reconstruction or revival by the assessee of the business of any such undertaking as referred to in section 33B.

3. Business is not acquired by the assessee by way of transfer from any other person or as a result of any business reorganisation.

• *Amount of deduction* - If the above conditions are satisfied, an amount equivalent to 30 per cent of additional employee cost (incurred in the course of such business in the previous year) is deductible under section 80JJAA for 3 assessment years including the assessment year relevant to the previous year in which such employment is provided. Books of account should be audited and report of audit [Form No. 10DA] should be submitted electronically along with the return of income. Deduction should be claimed in the return of income (otherwise deduction is not available). The following points should be noted -

1. "Additional employee cost" means total emoluments paid or payable to additional employees employed during the previous year.

2. In the case of an existing business, the additional employee cost shall be *nil*, if—

a. there is no increase in the number of employees from the total number of employees employed as on the last day of the preceding year;

b. emoluments are paid otherwise than by an account payee cheque or account payee bank draft or by use of electronic clearing system through a bank account (**or through prescribed electronic mode**).

3. In the first year of a new business, emoluments paid or payable to employees employed during that previous year shall be deemed to be the additional employee cost.

4. "Additional employee" means an employee who has been employed during the previous year and whose employment has the effect of increasing the total number of employees employed by the employer as on the last day of the preceding year, but does not include,—

a. an employee whose total emoluments are more than Rs. 25,000 per month; or

41. It is incorrect to state that "collection" means collecting free of charge and not by purchasing the same. The word 'collecting' means to gather; to fetch. It is a neutral word and does not mean collection for consideration or collection without consideration. If an assessee collects bagasse from sugar factories (bagasse is a waste of a sugar factory and it is bio-degradable waste) after having made payment for the same, he is qualified to claim deduction under section 80JJA—*CIT* v. *Padma S. Bora* [2013] 214 Taxman 505/29 taxmann.com 230 (Bom.).

b. an employee for whom the entire contribution is paid by the Government under the Employees' Pension Scheme notified in accordance with the provisions of the Employees' Provident Funds and Miscellaneous Provisions Act, 1952;

c. an employee employed for a period of less than 240 days [150 days, if the assessee is engaged in the business of manufacturing of apparel (or footwear or leather products from the assessment year 2019-20)] during the previous year; or

d. an employee who does not participate in the recognised provident fund.

5. "Emoluments" means any sum paid or payable to an employee *in lieu* of his employment by whatever name called, but does not include employer's contribution to pension fund/provident fund/any other fund for the benefit of employee under any law. Further, it does not include lump sum payment at the time of termination of service, or superannuation or voluntary retirement, such as gratuity, severance pay, leave encashment, voluntary retrenchment benefits, commutation of pension and the like.

6. If a new employee is employed during the previous year for a period of less than 240 days or 150 days but is employed for a period of 240 days or 150 days, as the case may be, in the immediately succeeding year, he shall be deemed to have been employed in the succeeding year and the benefit of section 80JJAA will apply accordingly (applicable from the assessment year 2019-20).

107.21-E1 X & Co. is a limited liability partnership (date of commencement of business June 1, 2018). It owns and operates retail outlets in different parts of North India. During the previous year 2018-19, it appoints the following persons –

Date of appointment	*No. of employees*	*Designation*	*Salary (in Rs. per person)*
May 1, 2018	8	Storekeeper	18,000
June 1, 2018	12	Salesperson	25,000
July 1, 2018	4	Supervisor	28,000
October 1, 2018	25	Helper	11,000
Total	49		

Salary to storekeepers is paid in cash up to December 31, 2018. In other cases, salary is transferred by use of electronic clearing system through SBI, Noida. Determine the amount of deduction available under section 80JJAA for the assessment year 2019-20 under the following two situations –

Situation 1 - Turnover of X & Co. for the previous year 2018-19 is Rs. 6 crore and tax audit under section 44AB is applicable.

Situation 2 - Turnover of X & Co. for the previous year 2018-19 is Rs. 90 lakh and tax audit under section 44AB is not applicable.

•

Deduction under section 80JJAA is not available in *Situation 2* (as tax audit under section 44AB is not applicable). However, in *Situation 1* deduction under section 80JJAA shall be determined as follows –

	Salary [deductible under section 37(1)]	*Deduction under section 80JJAA*
	Rs.	*Rs.*
Storekeepers appointed on May 1, 2018 (Rs. 18,000 × 8 × 11 months)	15,84,000	4,75,200[42]
Salespersons appointed on June 1, 2018 (Rs. 25,000 × 12 × 10 months)	30,00,000	9,00,000[42]
Supervisors appointed on July 1, 2018 (Rs. 28,000 × 4 × 9 months)	10,08,000	*Nil*[43]
Helpers appointed on October 1, 2018 (Rs. 11,000 × 25 × 6 months)	16,50,000	*Nil*[44]
Total	72,42,000	13,75,200

42. It is 30% of salary. Deduction under section 80JJAA is in addition to deduction available under section 37(1). If salary is not paid by account payee cheque/draft (or not transferred by electronic clearing system through bank), deduction under section 80JJAA is not available. However, this rule is applicable in the case of an existing business (and not in the first year of a new business).

43. Deduction under section 80JJAA is not available in respect of employees whose total emoluments are more than Rs. 25,000 per month.

44. Helpers are employed for less than 240 days during the previous year 2018-19. No deduction is available under section 80JJAA. If these helpers are employed for at least 240 days in the previous year 2019-20, deduction can be claimed for the assessment year 2020-21.

107.21-E2 Taking into consideration the following information pertaining to the previous year 2019-20 in the above example, find out the amount deductible under section 80JJAA for the assessment year 2020-21 (tax audit is required for the previous year 2019-20, as turnover is more than Rs. 5 crore) –

	Situation 1	*Situation 2*
No. of employees as on March 31, 2019	49	49
Salespersons resigned during April 2019	6	*Nil*
No. of employees as on April 30, 2019	43	49
8 deputy managers appointed on May 1, 2019 (salary : Rs. 24,000 per month, increased to Rs. 28,000 with effect from February 1, 2020)	8	8
No. of employees as on May 31, 2019	51	57
General manager appointed on August 1, 2019 (on part time basis) (salary : Rs. 20,000 per month)	1	1
No. of employees as on March 31, 2020	52	58

Assume that helpers (who were appointed on October 1, 2018) are in employment with X and Co. on March 31, 2020.

•

	Situation 1	*Situation 2*
No. of employees as on March 31, 2019	49	49
No. of employees immediately after appointment of 8 deputy managers	51	57
Increase in total number of employees as compared to number of employees as on last day of preceding previous year (*a*)	2	8
No. of deputy managers qualified for deduction under section 80JJAA	2	8
	Rs.	*Rs.*
Salary payable to these deputy managers from May 1, 2019 to February 1, 2020 (from February 1, 2020 salary is more than Rs. 25,000, deduction under section 80JJAA is not available) [(*a*) × Rs. 24,000 × 9 months]	4,32,000	17,28,000
Salary to part-time general manager (Rs. 20,000 × 8 months)	1,60,000	1,60,000
Salary to helpers (who were appointed during 2018-19, employed for less than 240 days and could not get any deduction under section 80JJAA for the previous year 2018-19) (Rs. 11,000 × 25 × 12 months)	33,00,000	33,00,000
Total	38,92,000	51,88,000
Amount deductible under section 80JJAA (30% of total)	11,67,600	15,56,400

107.22 ***Deduction in respect of interest on certain securities, dividends, etc. [Sec. 80L]*** - No deduction under section 80L is available from the assessment year 2006-07.

107.22A ***Deduction in respect of certain income of Offshore Banking Units and International Financial Services Centre [Section 80LA]*** - The existing section 80LA has been substituted by a new section from the assessment year 2006-07.

• *Conditions* - The following conditions should be satisfied—

1. The assessee is—

a. a scheduled bank and having an offshore banking unit in a special economic zone; or

b. a foreign bank and having an offshore banking unit in a special economic zone; or

c. a unit of International Financial Services Centre.

2. The gross total income of the assessee includes (*a*) any income from the offshore banking unit in a Special Economic Zone; (*b*) from the business referred to in section 6(1) of the Banking Regulation Act, with an undertaking located in Special Economic Zone or any other undertaking which develops, develops and operates or operates and maintains a Special Economic Zone; (*c*) from any unit of the International Financial Services Centre from its business for which it has been approved for setting up in such a centre in a Special Economic Zone.

3. The report from a Chartered Accountant in Form No. 10CCF[45] certifying that the deduction has been correctly claimed in accordance with the provisions of this section should be submitted along with the return of income.

4. A copy of permission obtained under section 23(1)(*a*) of Banking Regulation Act should be submitted along with the return of income.

5. Deduction under section 80LA is not available unless it is claimed in the return of income.

45. From April 1, 2014, audit report should be submitted electronically. Provisions pertaining to electronic submission of audit report were not applicable prior to April 1, 2014 (for a period prior to April 1, 2014, audit report may be retained by the assessee and it may be furnished in original whenever the Assessing Officer wants to examine it in assessment proceedings or otherwise).

• *Amount of deduction* - If the above conditions are satisfied, deduction is available under section 80LA as follows –

Deduction available to scheduled bank/foreign bank having offshore banking unit in SEZ - 100 per cent of the aforesaid income is deductible for 5 consecutive assessment years beginning with the assessment year relevant to the previous year in which the permission as stated in point No. 4 (*supra*) or permission of SEBI or under any other law, is obtained. For the next 5 years, 50 per cent of such income would be deductible.

Deduction available to a unit of International Financial Services Centre - Such unit can avail the aforesaid deduction up to the assessment year 2019-20. **From the assessment year 2020-21, deduction shall be increased to 100 per cent for any 10 consecutive years**. The assessee, at his option, may claim the said deduction for any 10 consecutive assessment years out of 15 years beginning with the year in which the necessary permission is obtained.

107.23 ***Deduction in respect of inter-corporate dividends [Sec. 80M]*** - No deduction is available under section 80M for the assessment years 1998-99 to 2002-03 and from the assessment year 2004-05 onwards.

107.24 ***Deduction in respect of income of co-operative society [Sec. 80P]*** - *See* para 209.1.

107.25 ***Deduction in respect of certain income of producer companies [Sec. 80PA, applicable from the assessment year 2019-20]*** - Deduction under section 80PA is available if the following conditions are satisfied –

1. Assessee is a producer company [as defined in section 581A(*i*) of the Companies Act, 1956].

2. Total turnover of the company is less than 100 crore in any previous year.

3. Income of the company includes any profit and gains derived from the eligible business. Eligible business for this purpose is –

a. the marketing of agricultural produce grown by the members; or

b. the purchase of agricultural implements, seeds, livestock or other articles intended for agriculture for the purpose of supplying them to the members; or

c. the processing of the agricultural produce of the members.

• *Amount of deduction* - If the above conditions are satisfied, the producer company can claim 100 per cent deduction in respect of profits and gains of eligible business. This deduction is available for the assessment years 2019-20 to 2024-25.

107.26 ***Deduction in respect of professional income of authors of text books in Indian languages [Sec. 80QQA, applicable for the assessment years 1980-81 to 1989-90 and 1992-93 to 1996-97]*** - In computing the total income of an author, an amount equal to 25 per cent of the income from books is allowed as deduction for the assessment years 1980-81 to 1989-90 and 1992-93 to 1996-97 (no deduction under section 80QQA is available from the assessment year 1997-98 onwards).

107.27 ***Deduction in respect of royalty income of authors [Sec. 80QQB]*** - The provisions of section 80QQB, inserted from the assessment year 2004-05, are given below—

107.27-1 *CONDITIONS* - The following conditions should be satisfied—

1. The taxpayer is an individual resident in India (he may be an Indian citizen or foreign citizen or he may be resident and ordinarily resident or resident but not ordinarily resident in India. But he should not be a non-resident in India).

2. He is an author or joint author.

3. The book authored by him is work of literary, artistic or scientific nature[46]. However, the "books" shall not include brochures, commentaries, diaries, guides, journals, magazines, newspapers, pamphlets, text-books for schools, tracts and other publications of similar nature, by whatever name called.

4. The gross total income of the taxpayer includes any income, derived by him in the exercise of his profession, on account of any lump sum consideration for the assignment (or grant) of any of his interests in the copyright of the book, or of royalty or copyright fees (whether receivable in lump sum or otherwise) in respect of such

---

46. The words "literary work" has not defined under the Act but has been defined by section 2(*o*) of the Copyright Act, 1957. The expression literary work covers which are expressed in printing or writing irrespective of the question whether the quality or style is high or whether there is any literary merit or not. The expression literary work means not only such work which deals with any particular aspect of literature in poetry but also indicates a work which is literature, *i.e.*, anything in writing which could be said to come within the ambit of literary work – *Dilip Loyalka* v. *CIT* [2015] 64 taxmann.com 121 (Kol.). Computer programme forming part of the software falls within the description of literary or scientific work—*Dassault Systems K.K., In re* [2010] 188 Taxman 223 (AAR - New Delhi).

book. Consideration includes an advance payment on account of such royalties or copyright fees, which is not returnable.

5. The taxpayer shall have to furnish a certificate in Form No. 10CCD from the person responsible for paying the income.

6. Deduction under section 80QQB is not available unless it is claimed in the return of income.

107.27-2 *AMOUNT OF DEDUCTION* - If the aforesaid conditions are satisfied, then the amount of deduction is—

a. Rs. 3,00,000; or

b. income stated in (*4*) (*supra*),

whichever is lower.

107.27-3 *OTHER POINTS* - One should also keep in view the following points—

1. Where the eligible income is earned outside India, the deduction shall be allowed on so much of the income earned in foreign exchange, which is brought in India within six months from the end of previous year or within such further period as the competent authority may allow in this behalf. For this purpose, competent authority shall mean the Reserve Bank of India or such other authority as is authorised under any law for the time being in force for regulating payments and dealings in foreign exchange. Moreover, deduction will not be allowed unless the taxpayer furnishes online a certificate in Form 10H from the prescribed authority.

2. Where the income by way of royalty or the copyright fee, is not a lump sum consideration (in lieu of all rights of the assessee in the book) so much of the income (before allowing expenses attributable to such income) as is in excess of 15 per cent of the value of such books sold during the previous year, shall be ignored.

3. Where a deduction under section 80QQB for any previous year has been claimed and allowed, no deduction in respect of such income shall be allowed under any other provision of the Act in any assessment year.

107.27-E1 Determine the amount deductible under section 80QQB in the following cases pertaining to the assessment year 2019-20—

	X	*Y*	*Z*	*A*
	Rs.	*Rs.*	*Rs.*	*Rs.*
Royalty on books covered by section 80QQB	90,000	3,00,000	6,00,000	8,00,000
Is it lump sum payment for assignment of interest in copyright	*No*	*No*	*No*	*Yes*
Rate of royalty as % of value of books	18%	17.5%	12.5%	NA
Expenditure for earning royalty	10,000	1,10,000	1,80,000	2,40,000
Is royalty received from abroad	*Yes*	*Yes*	*No*	*Yes*
Amount remitted to India in convertible foreign exchange till September 30, 2019	70,000	2,80,000	*NA*	7,00,000

•

Amount of deduction				
a. Amount remitted to India in convertible foreign exchange within 6 months from the end of the previous year or within the extended time	70,000	2,80,000	—	7,00,000
b. Lump sum consideration	—	—	—	8,00,000
c. Royalty not exceeding 15%	75,000	2,57,143	6,00,000	—
d. The lowest of (*a*), (*b*) or (*c*)	70,000	2,57,143	6,00,000	7,00,000
e. Expenditure incurred	10,000	1,10,000	1,80,000	2,40,000
f. Amount deductible under section 80QQB [*i.e.*, (*d*) – (*e*) but subject to maximum of Rs. 3,00,000]	60,000	1,47,143	3,00,000	3,00,000

107.28 ***Deduction in respect of remuneration from certain foreign sources in the case of professors, teachers, etc. [Sec. 80R]*** - Deduction under section 80R is not available from the assessment year 2005-06.

107.29 ***Deduction in respect of professional income from foreign sources [Secs. 80RR, 80RRA]*** - Deduction under section 80RR is not available from the assessment year 2005-06.

107.30 ***Deduction in respect of royalty on patents [Sec. 80RRB applicable from the assessment year 2004-05]*** - Section 80RRB was inserted from the assessment year 2004-05.

107.30-1 *CONDITIONS* - The following conditions should be satisfied in order to claim deduction under section 80RRB —

1. The taxpayer is an individual (maybe an Indian citizen or foreign citizen).

2. He is resident in India (he may be ordinarily resident or not ordinarily resident but deduction under section 80RRB is not available if he is non-resident).

3. He is a patentee (he may be a co-owner of patent). Patentee means the person (being the true and first inventor of the invention), whose name is entered on the patent register as the patentee, in accordance with the Patents Act, 1970. It includes every such person (being the true and first inventor of the invention) where more than one person is registered as patentee under that Act in respect of that patent.

4. He is in receipt of any income by way of royalty in respect of patent, which is registered under the Patent Act after March 31, 2003. It includes any royalty income from working of or use of the patent. Further, it includes lump sum consideration for the transfer of all or any rights (including the granting of a license) in a patent, or for imparting of any information concerning the working or use thereof in India, or for rendering of any services in connection with the above. Lump sum consideration includes advance royalty which is not returnable. However, it does not include any consideration for sale of product manufactured with the use of patented process or of the patented article *per se* for commercial use. Further, any consideration, which is chargeable under the head "Capital gains" is not royalty. Where a compulsory licence is granted in respect of any patent under the Patents Act, 1970, the income eligible for the purposes of this section shall not exceed the amount of royalty under the terms and conditions of a licence settled by the Controller under that Act.

5. The assessee shall have to furnish a certificate in Form No. 10CCE[47], duly signed by the prescribed authority along [*i.e.*, the Controller under section 1(*b*) of Patents Act] with the return of income.

6. Deduction under section 80RRB is not available unless it is claimed in the return of income.

107.30-2 *AMOUNT OF DEDUCTION* - If the aforesaid conditions are satisfied, then the amount of deduction is -

a. Rs. 3,00,000; or

b. income stated in (*4*) (*supra*),

whichever is lower.

107.30-3 *OTHER POINTS* - One should also keep in view the following points—

1. Where any income is earned from sources outside India on which the deduction under the section is claimed, only so much of the income shall be considered, as is brought into India by, or on behalf of the assessee in convertible foreign exchange within a period of 6 months from the end of the previous year or within such further period as the competent authority may allow in this behalf. For this purpose, competent authority shall mean the Reserve Bank of India or such other authority as is authorised under any law for the time being in force for regulating payments and dealings in foreign exchange.

Where any income is earned from sources outside India, a certificate certifying that the deduction has been correctly claimed in accordance with the provision of this section (in Form No. 10H[47]), is required.

2. In case the patent is subsequently revoked by the Controller or the High Court or the name of the assessee is subsequently excluded from the patents register as patentee in respect of that patent, the deduction relatable to royalty income in respect of the period for which the patentee's claim was not valid, shall be withdrawn and the assessment may be rectified within a period of 4 years from the end of the previous year in which such order is passed by the High Court or Controller.

3. Where a deduction for any previous year has been claimed and allowed under section 80RRB in respect of any income referred to above, no deduction in respect of such income shall be allowed, under any other provision of the Act in any assessment year.

107.31 ***Deduction in respect of interest on deposits in savings accounts [Sec. 80TTA]*** - Section 80TTA has been inserted with effect from the assessment year 2013-14. It provides a deduction up to Rs. 10,000 in aggregate to an assessee (being an individual or a Hindu undivided family) in respect of any income by way of interest on deposits (not being time deposits) in a savings account with —

a. a banking company;

b. a co-operative society engaged in carrying on the business of banking (including a co-operative land mortgage bank or a co-operative land development bank); or

c. a post office.

• The following points should be noted –

1. From the assessment year 2019-20, the above deduction is not available in the case of a senior citizen who is eligible to claim deduction under section 80TTB.

2. Where the aforesaid income is derived from any deposit in a savings account held by, or on behalf of a firm, an association of persons or a body of individuals, no deduction shall be allowed in respect of such income in computing the total income of any partner of the firm or any member of the association or body.

---

47. Form Nos. 10CCE and 10H are to be submitted electronically.

107.31-1 *POST OFFICE SAVINGS BANK INTEREST EXEMPTION UNDER SECTION 10(15)(i)* - Post office savings bank interest is exempt up to Rs. 3,500 (in an individual account) and Rs. 7,000 (in a joint account) under section 10(*15*)(*i*) by virtue of Notification No. 32/2011, dated June 3, 2011, read with Notification No. GSR 607, dated June 9, 1989. The cumulative impact of sections 10(*15*)(*i*) and 80TTA is as follows—

	Up to the assessment year 2011-12 *Rs.*	*For the assessment year 2012-13* *Rs.*	*From the assessment year 2013-14* *Rs.*
Interest on Post Office Savings Bank [exemption under section 10(*15*)(*i*)]	Full exemption, nothing is taxable	Exemption up to Rs. 3,500 in a single account and Rs. 7,000 in a joint account	Exemption up to Rs. 3,500 in a single account and Rs. 7,000 in a joint account
Interest on savings account with a bank, co-operative bank and Post Office (deduction under section 80TTA)	No deduction	No deduction	Deduction up to Rs. 10,000

107.32 ***Deduction in respect of interest on deposits in case of senior citizens [Sec. 80TTB, applicable from the assessment year 2019-20]*** - Deduction under section 80TTB is available from the assessment year 2019-20), if the following conditions are satisfied –

1. The assessee is a senior citizen (*i.e.*, a resident individual who is at least 60 years of age at any time during the previous year).

2. His income includes interest on deposits with a bank/co-operative bank/post office (it may be interest on fixed deposits, interest on savings account or any other interest).

• *Amount of deduction* - If these conditions are satisfied, the assessee can claim deduction under section 80TTB which is equal to Rs. 50,000 or the amount of aforesaid interest, whichever is lower.

Where the aforesaid income is derived from any deposit in an account held by, or on behalf of a firm, an association of persons or a body of individuals, no deduction shall be allowed in respect of such income in computing the total income of any partner of the firm or any member of the association or body.

107.32-1 *POST OFFICE SAVINGS BANK INTEREST EXEMPTION UNDER SECTION 10(15)(i)* - *See* para 107.31-1.

107.33 ***Deduction in case of a person with disability [Sec. 80U]*** - The provisions of section 80U are given below—

107.33-1 *CONDITIONS* - Deduction is available if the following conditions are satisfied—

107.33-1a INDIVIDUAL - The taxpayer is an individual (maybe a citizen of India or foreign country).

107.33-1b RESIDENT IN INDIA - He is resident in India (maybe ordinarily resident or not ordinarily resident). Deduction under this section is not available if he is non-resident in India for the relevant assessment year.

107.33-1c PERSON WITH DISABILITY[48] - It means a person suffering from not less than 40 per cent of any disability given below—

i. blindness;
ii. low vision;
iii. leprosy-cured;
iv. hearing impairment;
v. locomotor disability;
vi. mental retardation;
vii. mental illness.

Blindness - "Blindness" refers to a condition where a person suffers from any of the following conditions, namely :—

i. total absence of sight; or
ii. visual acuity not exceeding 6/60 or 20/200 (snellen) in the better eye with correcting lenses; or
iii. limitation of the field of vision subtending an angle of 20 degree or worse.

48. The meaning of disability has been extended from the assessment year 2005-06 to include "autism", "cerebral palsy" and "multiple disability" referred to in clauses (*a*), (*c*) and (*h*) of section 2 of the National Trust for Welfare of Persons with Autism, Cerebral Palsy, Mental Retardation and Multiple Disabilities Act, 1999.

Low vision - "Person with low vision" means a person with impairment of visual functioning even after treatment or standard refractive correction but who uses or is potentially capable of using vision for the planning or execution of a task with appropriate assistive device.

Leprosy cured person - "Leprosy cured person" means any person who has been cured of leprosy but is suffering from—

i. loss of sensation in hands or feet as well as loss of sensation and paresis in the eye and eye-lid but with no manifest deformity;

ii. manifest deformity and paresis but having sufficient mobility in their hands and feet to enable them to engage in normal economic activity;

iii. extreme physical deformity as well as advanced age which prevents him from undertaking any gainful occupation.

Hearing impairment - "Hearing impairment" means loss of sixty decibels or more in the better ear in the conversational range of frequencies.

Locomotor disability - "Locomotor disability" means disability of the bones, joints or muscles leading to substantial restriction of the movement of the limbs or any form of cerebral palsy.

Mental retardation - "Mental retardation" means a condition of arrested or incomplete development of mind of a person, which is specially characterised by subnormality of intelligence.

Mental illness - "Mental illness" means any mental disorder other than mental retardation.

107.33-1d CERTIFIED BY MEDICAL AUTHORITY - The taxpayer shall have to furnish[49] a copy of the certificate issued by the medical authority (format of certificate is given below)[50] along with the return of income. Where the condition of disability requires reassessment, a fresh certificate from the medical authority shall have to be obtained after the expiry of the period mentioned on the original certificate in order to continue to claim the deduction.

"Medical authority" for this purpose means any hospital or institution specified by notification by the appropriate Government for the purpose of the Persons with Disabilities (Equal Opportunities, Protection of Rights and Full Participation) Act, 1995.

FORM

STANDARD FORMAT OF THE CERTIFICATE

NAME & ADDRESS OF THE INSTITUTE/HOSPITAL issuing the certificate

Certificate No. .... Date......................

CERTIFICATE FOR THE PERSONS WITH DISABILITIES

This is to certify that Shri/Smt./Kum.. son/ wife/daughter of Shri.. Age .... old male/female, Registration No.............................. is a case of .... He/She is physically disabled/ visual disabled/speech & hearing disabled and has ....% (...................... per cent) permanent (physical impairment/visual impairment/speech & hearing impairment) in relation to his/her ....

Notes:—

1. This condition is progressive/non-progressive/likely to improve/not likely to improve.

2. Re-assessment is not recommended/is recommended after a period of .... months/years.

*Strike out whichever is not applicable.

Sd/- (Doctor) Seal   Sd/- (Doctor) Seal   Sd/- (Doctor) Seal

Signature/Thumb impression of the patient.

Countersigned by the Medical Superintendent/CMO/Head of Hospital (with seal)

Recent attested photograph showing the disability affixed here.

CERTIFICATE OF MENTAL RETARDATION FOR GOVERNMENT BENEFITS

This is to certify that Shri/Kum..
son/daughter of.. of Village/Town/City .... with particulars given below :—

(*a*) Age

(*b*) Sex

(*c*) Signature/Thumb impression

CATEGORISATION OF MENTAL RETARDATION

Mild/Moderate/Severe/Profound

Validity of the Certificate : Permanent

Signature of Government Doctor/Hospital with seal
Chairperson Mental Retardation Certification Board

Recent Attested Photograph showing the disability affixed here.

Dated :

Place :

107.33-2 *AMOUNT OF DEDUCTION* - If the aforesaid conditions are satisfied, then a fixed deduction of Rs. 75,000 (Rs. 50,000 up to the assessment year 2015-16) is available. A higher deduction of

49. It is not possible to attach any certificate with new income-tax return forms. The assessee should himself retain the certificate. It may be furnished in original whenever the Assessing Officer wants to examine it in assessment proceedings or otherwise.

50. Form No. 10-IA if the person is suffering from autism, cerebral palsy, etc.

Rs. 1,25,000 (Rs. 1,00,000 up to the assessment year 2015-16) is allowed in respect of a person with severe disability (*i.e.*, having any disability of 80 per cent or above).

Deductions from tax liability

A taxpayer can claim tax rebate under section 86, 87A, 89, 90, 90A or 91

Deductions from tax liability

110. First determine net income and tax payable thereon at the rates mentioned in Referencer 1. From the sum of tax so determined, deduct the following tax reliefs/tax rebates :

- Rebate under section 86 in respect of share of profit from an association of persons [*see* para 197].
- Rebate under section 87A in the case of a resident individual.
- Relief under section 89 in respect of salary paid in advance or in arrears [*see* para 22].
- Relief for doubly taxed income under section 90, 90A or 91.

The mode of computation of the tax payable is as follows—

1. Tax on net income
2. Less: Rebate under section 87A
3. Find out (*1*) – (*2*).
4. Add : Surcharge
5. (*3*) + (*4*).
6. Add: Health and education cess [4% of (*5*)].
7. (*5*) + (*6*)
8. Less : Rebate under section 86, 89, 90, 90A or 91 [(*8*) cannot exceed (*7*)].
9. (*7*) — (*8*) is tax payable.

Rebate for resident individuals having total income up to Rs. 5 lakh (applicable for the assessment years 2014-15 to 2017-18 and 2020-21 onwards) or Rs. 3.5 lakh (applicable from the assessment years 2018-19 and 2019-20) [Sec. 87A]

111. With a view to providing tax relief to the individual taxpayers who are in lower income bracket, a rebate is provided for under section 87A.

• *Conditions* - This rebate is available if the following two conditions are satisfied –

1. Taxpayer is a resident individual (he may be ordinarily resident or not ordinarily resident).

2. His total income or net income or taxable income (*i.e.*, gross total income *minus* deduction under sections 80C to 80U) does not exceed Rs. 5 lakh/Rs. 3.5 lakh as given in table below.

• *Amount of rebate* - If the above two conditions are satisfied, the resident individual can claim rebate under section 87A. The amount of rebate is as follows –

Different years	*Total income should not exceed the amount given below*	*Amount of rebate under section 87A*
Assessment years 2014-15 to 2016-17	Rs. 5,00,000	100% of income-tax or Rs. 2,000, whichever is less
Assessment year 2017-18	Rs. 5,00,000	100% of income-tax or Rs. 5,000, whichever is less
Assessment years 2018-19 and 2019-20	Rs. 3,50,000	100% of income-tax or Rs. 2,500, whichever is less
Assessment year 2020-21 onwards	**Rs. 5,00,000**	**100% of income-tax or Rs. 12,500, whichever is less**

Rebate under section 87A is not available in the case of a non-resident individual, resident or non-resident HUF/AOP/BOI or any taxpayer other than resident individual.

111-E1 Find out tax liability for the assessment year 2019-20 in the case of X (who is resident individual and born on April 2, 1959 or any day after April 2, 1959) in the following situations –

Situation 1 - Net income : Rs. 2,60,000, *Situation 2* - Net income : Rs. 3,50,000, *Situation 3* - Net income : Rs. 5,00,000, *Situation 4* - Net income : Rs. 6,00,000.

•

	Situation 1 *Rs.*	*Situation 2* *Rs.*	*Situation 3* *Rs.*	*Situation 4* *Rs.*
Net income	2,60,000	3,50,000	5,00,000	6,00,000
Income-tax on net income	500	5,000	12,500	32,500
Less: Rebate under section 87A	500	2,500	*Nil*	*Nil*
Balance	*Nil*	2,500	12,500	32,500
Add: Surcharge	*Nil*	*Nil*	*Nil*	*Nil*
Total	*Nil*	2,500	12,500	32,500
Add: Health and education cess @ 4%	*Nil*	100	500	1,300
Tax liability	*Nil*	2,600	13,000	33,800

111-E2 Find out tax liability for the assessment year 2019-20 in the case of Y (who is resident individual and born on April 1, 1959) in the following situations –

Situation 1 - Net income : Rs. 3,10,000, *Situation 2* - Net income : Rs. 3,50,000, *Situation 3* - Net income : Rs. 5,00,000, *Situation 4* - Net income : Rs. 6,00,000.

•

X is a senior citizen. Tax liability will be calculated as follows –

	Situation 1 *Rs.*	*Situation 2* *Rs.*	*Situation 3* *Rs.*	*Situation 4* *Rs.*
Net income	3,10,000	3,50,000	5,00,000	6,00,000
Income-tax on net income	500	2,500	10,000	30,000
Less: Rebate under section 87A	500	2,500	*Nil*	*Nil*
Balance	*Nil*	*Nil*	10,000	30,000
Add: Surcharge	*Nil*	*Nil*	*Nil*	*Nil*
Total	*Nil*	*Nil*	10,000	30,000
Add: Education cess @ 3%	*Nil*	*Nil*	400	1,200
Tax liability	*Nil*	*Nil*	10,400	31,200

Agricultural income

Section 10(1) exempts agricultural income. In some cases, however, agricultural income is taken into account to determine tax on non-agricultural income

Definition [Sec. 2(*1A*)]

113. By virtue of section 2*(1A)*, the expression "agricultural income" means :

a. any rent or revenue derived from land which is situated in India and is used for agricultural purposes [sec. 2*(1A)(a)*] ;

b. any income derived from such land by agricultural operations including processing of the agricultural produce, raised or received as rent-in-kind so as to render it fit for the market, or sale of such produce [sec. 2*(1A)(b)*]; and

c. income attributable to a farm house[51] subject to the condition that the building is situated on or in the immediate vicinity of the land and is used as a dwelling house, storehouse, or other out-building and the land is assessed to land revenue or a local rate or, alternatively, the building is situated on or in the immediate vicinity of land which (though not assessed to land revenue or local rate) is situated in a rural area [sec. 2(*1A*)(*c*)].

---

51. With effect from the assessment year 2001-02, an *Explanation* was inserted to clarify that any income from such building or land arising from the use of the building or land for any purpose other than agriculture, shall not be included in the definition of "agricultural income".

• Section 10*(1)* exempts agricultural income from tax. The reason for exemption for agricultural income from Central taxation is that the Constitution gives exclusive power to make laws with respect to taxes on agricultural income to the State Legislature. However, in some cases agricultural income is taken into consideration to determine tax on non-agricultural income.

• From the assessment year 2009-10, any income derived from saplings or seedings grown in a nursery shall be deemed to be agricultural income.

• *Rural area* - Rural area for the above purpose is as follows –

From the assessment year 2014-15 - Any area which is outside the jurisdiction of a municipality or cantonment board having a population of 10,000 or more and also which does not fall within distance (to be measured aerially) given below –

2 kilometres from the local limits of municipality/ cantonment board	If the population of the municipality/cantonment board is more than 10,000 but not more than 1 lakh
6 kilometres from the local limits of municipality/ cantonment board	If the population of the municipality/cantonment board is more than 1 lakh but not more than 10 lakh
8 kilometres from the local limits of municipality/ cantonment board	If the population of the municipality/cantonment board is more than 10 lakh

For the above purpose, "population" means the population according to the last preceding census of which the relevant figures have been published before the first day of the previous year.

Up to the assessment year 2013-14 - Any area which is outside the jurisdiction of a municipality or cantonment board having a population of 10,000 or more and also which does not fall within such notified distance [up to 8 kilometres - *see* Notification No. SO 10(E), dated January 6, 1994] from the local limits of such municipality or cantonment board.

Income which is partly agricultural and partly from business [Rules 7, 7A, 7B and 8][52]

114. For disintegrating a composite business income which is partly agricultural and partly non-agricultural, the following rules are applicable—

Income[53]	*Non-agricultural income*	*Agricultural income*	*Income-tax Rules*
• Growing and manufacturing tea in India[54]	40%	60%	Rule 8
• Sale of centrifuged latex or cenex or latex based crepes (such as pale latex crepe) or brown crepes (such as estate brown crepe, remilled crepe, smoked blanket crepe or flat bark crepe) or technically specified block rubbers manufactured or processed from field latex or coagulum obtained from rubber plants grown by the seller in India	35%	65%	Rule 7A
• Sale of coffee grown and cured by seller	25%	75%	Rule 7B(1)
• Sale of coffee grown, cured, roasted and grounded by seller in India with or without mixing chicory or other flavouring ingredients	40%	60%	Rule 7B(1A)

114.1 ***Any other case [Rule 7]*** - For disintegrating a composite business income which is partly agricultural and partly non-agricultural, the *market value* of any agricultural produce, raised by the assessee or

52. These rules are applicable whether income is positive or negative. For instance, loss from the activity of growing and manufacturing tea in India to the extent of 40 per cent is treated as business (non-agricultural) loss which can be set off against any normal business income under section 70 and 60 per cent is taken as agricultural loss—*Hindustan Unilever Ltd.* v. *CIT* [2010] 191 Taxman 119 (Bom.).

53. Income in respect of the business given above is, in the first instance, computed under the Act as if it were derived from business after making permissible deduction. 40 or 35 or 25 per cent of the income so arrived at is treated as business income and the balance is treated as agricultural income. Salary and interest received by a partner from a firm (growing leaves and manufacturing tea or any other activity mentioned in the table) is taxable only to the extent of 40 or 35 or 25 per cent and the balance is treated as agricultural income.

54. If a person directly sells green tea leaves, income therefrom is 100 per cent agricultural income—*Union of India* v. *Belgachi Tea Co. Ltd.* [2008] 170 Taxman 209/304 ITR 1 (SC).

received by him as rent-in-kind and utilised as raw material in his business, is deducted. No further deduction is permissible in respect of any expenditure incurred by the assessee as a cultivator or receiver of rent-in-kind.

114.2 ***Position prior to the assessment year 2002-03*** - No proceedings under section 147 or under section 263 should be initiated for the assessment year(s) prior to the assessment year 2002-03 in the cases of assessees earning income from manufacture of rubber and/or coffee, for determining the income liable to income-tax, if the assessees had already paid agricultural income-tax on the whole of such income—Circular No. 5/2003, dated May 22, 2003.

Scheme of partial integration of tax on non-agricultural income with income derived from agriculture

115. The scheme of partial integration of tax on non-agricultural income with income derived from agriculture is applicable only in the case of individuals, Hindu undivided families, associations of persons, bodies of individuals or artificial juridical persons. It applies only when the aforesaid assessees have net agricultural income of an amount exceeding Rs. 5,000[55] [*see* para 116] in addition to non-agricultural income and non-agricultural income exceeds the maximum amount not chargeable to tax[56]. To put it differently, the scheme is applicable, if an individual, a Hindu undivided family, an association of persons or a body of individuals, etc., has non-agricultural income of more than the exemption limit[56] and agricultural income exceeds Rs. 5,000[55].

115.1 ***Computation of tax in cases covered by the scheme*** - In cases covered by the scheme, income-tax will be computed for the assessment years 2019-20 and 2020-21 in the following manner :

1. Net agricultural income is to be computed as if it were income chargeable to income-tax.

2. Agricultural and non-agricultural income of the assessee will then be aggregated and income-tax is calculated on the aggregate income as if such aggregate income were the total income.

3. The net agricultural income is then increased by the first slab of income on which tax is charged at *nil* rate and income-tax is calculated on net agricultural income, so increased, as if such income were the total income of the assessee.

4. The amount of income-tax determined at (*2*) will be reduced by the amount of income-tax determined under (*3*).

5. The amount so arrived at will be income-tax payable by the assessee. Rebate under section 87A shall be deducted. Surcharge and health and education cess shall be added.

Computation of net agricultural income

116. For the purpose of computing tax in the case of individuals, Hindu undivided families, etc., having net agricultural income in addition to the non-agricultural income, the net agricultural income for the assessment year 2019-20 will be computed as follows :

• *Rule 1* - Agricultural income of the nature referred in section 2*(1A)(a)* will be computed on the same basis as is adopted for the computation of income chargeable under the head "Income from other sources" under sections 57 to 59.

• *Rule 2* - Agricultural income of the nature referred in section 2*(1A)(b)* will broadly be computed as if it were income chargeable to tax under the head "Profits and gains of business or profession" and the provisions of sections 30 to 32, 36, 37, 40, 40A [other than sub-sections (3) and (4)], 41, 43, 43A, 43B and 43C will apply accordingly.

• *Rule 3* - Agricultural income of the nature referred in section 2*(1A)(c)* will be computed as if it were income chargeable under the head "Income from house property" under sections 23 to 27.

• *Rule 4* - Where an assessee derives income from sale of tea grown and manufactured by him in India, 60 per cent of the total income from such business, as computed in accordance with rule 8 of the Income-tax Rules, will be regarded as agricultural income [*see* also paras 114 and 114.1].

• *Rule 5* - Where the assessee is a member of an association of persons or a body of individuals (other than a Hindu undivided family, a company or a firm) which, in the previous year, has either no income chargeable to tax or has non-agricultural income not exceeding the maximum amount not chargeable to tax in the case

---

55. Rs. 600 up to assessment year 2001-02.

56. Exemption limit for the assessment year 2019-20 is Rs. 2,50,000 [higher exemption limit (*a*) in the case of a resident senior citizen born on or after April 2, 1939 but on or before April 1, 1959: Rs. 3,00,000; and (*b*) in the case of a resident super senior citizen born on or before April 1, 1939: Rs. 5,00,000].

Exemption limit for the assessment year 2020-21 is Rs. 2,50,000 [higher exemption limit (*a*) in the case of a resident senior citizen born on or after April 2, 1940 but on or before April 1, 1960: Rs. 3,00,000; and (*b*) in the case of a resident super senior citizen born on or before April 1, 1940: Rs. 5,00,000].

of an association of persons or a body of individuals, but has agricultural income, then the agricultural income or loss of the association or body is to be computed in accordance with these rules and the share of the assessee in the agricultural income or loss so computed will be regarded as agricultural income or loss of the assessee.

- *Rule 6* - Loss incurred in agriculture will be allowed to be set off against gains from agriculture. No set off will, however, be allowed in respect of assessee's share in agricultural loss of an association of persons or a body of individuals.
- *Rule 7* - Any tax levied by a State Government on agricultural income will be allowed as deduction.
- *Rule 8* - The unabsorbed loss from agricultural activities during the previous years relevant to the assessment years 2011-12 to 2018-19 will be set off against the agricultural income of assessment year 2019-20 in chronological order. Likewise, an unabsorbed loss from agriculture during the previous year relevant to the assessment years 2012-13 to 2019-20 will be taken into account in determining the net agricultural income for the purpose of payment of advance tax during the financial year 2019-20. The set off of loss will, in either case, be allowed only if such loss has already been determined. Where a person is succeeded by another person (otherwise than by inheritance), the person (other than the person who has incurred the loss) cannot claim the set off as discussed above.
- *Rule 9* - Where the net result of computation of agricultural income from various sources is a loss, the loss will be disregarded and the net agricultural income of the assessee shall be taken as *nil.*
- *Rule 10* - The net agricultural income of the assessee will be rounded off to the nearest multiple of Rs. 10.

Example

117-E1 For the assessment year 2019-20, the net agricultural income of an assessee is Rs. 7,86,000 and the non-agricultural income is Rs. 6,40,000. The taxpayer contributes Rs. 1,50,000 towards public provident fund. Find out the tax if the taxpayer is (*a*) X, an individual (age : 46 years), (*b*) Y, a HUF, (*c*) Z, a firm, (*d*) A Ltd., an Indian company.

•

Computation of tax in the cases of X and Y

Non-agricultural income is Rs. 4,90,000 (*i.e.*, Rs. 6,40,000 *minus* Rs. 1,50,000)

	X, Rs.	*Y, HUF Rs.*
1. Income-tax on Rs. 12,76,000 (*i.e.*, agricultural income : Rs. 7,86,000 + non-agricultural income : Rs. 4,90,000)	1,95,300	1,95,300
2. Income-tax on agricultural income : Rs. 7,86,000 + exempted slab of income Rs. 2,50,000	1,23,300	1,23,300
3. Income-tax computed at (*1*) *minus* income-tax computed at (2)	72,000	72,000
4. *Less* : Rebate under section 87A (applicable only in the case of a resident individual if non-agricultural income does not exceed Rs. 3,50,000)	—	—
5. Total	72,000	72,000
6. *Add* : Health and education cess @ 4%	2,880	2,880
7. Tax payable (rounded off)	74,880	74,880

In the case of Z (a firm) and A Ltd. tax liability will be as follows :

	Z Rs.	*A Ltd. Rs.*
Tax on non-agricultural income of Rs. 6,40,000 @ 30% [agricultural income is not considered in the case of firms and companies]	1,92,000	1,92,000
Add : Surcharge	*Nil*	*Nil*
Total	1,92,000	1,92,000
Add : Health and education cess	7,680	7,680
Tax liability	1,99,680	1,99,680

Return of income

Section 139 specifies different provisions for return of income. Every taxpayer is required to file voluntary return [para 118] within the specified time-limit [para 118.3]

Voluntary return

118. The following persons are under statutory obligation to file return of income by virtue of section 139—

Section	*Different situations*
139(1)(*a*)	A company/firm is required to submit its return of income (regardless of the quantum of income or loss).
139(1)(*b*)	A person (other than an individual/HUF/AOP/BOI/artificial juridical person/company/firm) is required to submit his/its return of income, if income exceeds exemption limit[58].
139(1)(*b*), read with sixth proviso	Individual/HUF/AOP/BOI/artificial juridical person is required to submit his/its return of income, if income [without claiming deduction under sections 10A, 10B, 10BA, 80C to 80U, (for the assessment years 2017-18 and 2018-19) under section 10(*38*) **and (from the assessment year 2020-21) under section 54/54B/54D/54EC/54F/54G/54GA/54GB**] exceeds the amount of exemption limit[57].
139(1)(*b*), read with seventh proviso (applicable with effect from the assessment year 2020-21)	**Any person (other than a company or a firm) who is not required to furnish the return of income under any other provision of section 139(1) and who during the previous year –** ***a.*** **has deposited an amount (or aggregate of the amounts) exceeding Rs. 1 crore in one (or more) current account(s) in a bank/co-operative bank; or** ***b.*** **has incurred expenditure of an amount (or aggregate of the amounts) exceeding Rs. 2 lakh for himself (or any other person) for travel to a foreign country; or** ***c.*** **has incurred expenditure of an amount (or aggregate of the amounts) exceeding Rs. 1 lakh towards consumption of electricity; or** ***d.*** **fulfils such other conditions as may be prescribed.**
139(4A)	A person in receipt of income derived from property held under a trust for charitable or religious purposes is required to submit return of income if its income (without giving exemption under section 11 or 12) exceeds exemption limit[58].
139(4B)	Chief executive officer of every political party is required to submit income-tax return if income of the political party (without giving exemption under section 13A) exceeds exemption limit[58].
139(4C)	If total income (without claiming any exemption given below) of the assessee (who is qualified to claim exemption under the following sections) exceeds the exemption limit[58] – - Section 10(*21*) - Section 10(*22B*) - Section 10(*23A*) - Section 10(*23AAA*) - Section 10(*23B*) - Section 10(*23C*)(*iiiab*)/(*iiiac*)/(*iiiad*)/(*iiiae*)/(*iv*)/(*v*)/(*vi*)/(*via*) - Section 10(*23D*) - Section 10(*23DA*) - Section 10(*23EC*) - Section 10(*23ED*) - Section 10(*23EE*) - Section 10(*23FB*) - Section 10(*24*)(*a*)/(*b*) - Section 10(*29A*) - Section 10(*46*) - Section 10(*47*)
139(4D)	Any university/college/other institution referred to in section 35(1)(*ii*)/(*iii*) is required to submit return of income (return has to be submitted whether there is income or loss. Such return has to be submitted even if it is not required by any other provision).
139(4E)/(4F)	These sub-sections cover submission of return by business trust/investment fund.

57. Exemption limit for the assessment year 2019-20 is Rs. 2,50,000 [higher exemption limit (a) in the case of a resident senior citizen born on or after April 2, 1939 but on or before April 1, 1959: Rs. 3,00,000; and (b) in the case of a resident super senior citizen born on or before April 1, 1939: Rs. 5,00,000].
Exemption limit for the assessment year 2020-21 is Rs. 2,50,000 [higher exemption limit (*a*) in the case of a resident senior citizen born on or after April 2, 1940 but on or before April 1, 1960: Rs. 3,00,000; and (*b*) in the case of a resident super senior citizen born on or before April 1, 1940: Rs. 5,00,000].

58. Exemption limit for the assessment years 2019-20 and 2020-21 is Rs. 2,50,000.

• *Non-resident* - The above provisions are applicable even if the concerned person is a non-resident.

• *Compulsory filing of income-tax return in relation to assets located outside India* - In the case of a resident person (but other than not ordinarily resident), it is mandatory to furnish return of income (from the assessment year 2016-17) if he/it at any time during the previous year, –

a. holds (as a beneficial owner or otherwise) any asset (including financial interest in any entity) located outside India or has signing authority in any account located outside India, or

b. is a beneficiary in any asset (including any financial interest in any entity) located outside India.

For any person (maybe individual or a person other than individual) who satisfies the above conditions, furnishing of return has become mandatory, irrespective of the fact whether the person has taxable income or not.

Exception - The above provisions shall not apply to an individual, being a beneficiary of any asset (including any financial interest in any entity) located outside India where, income, if any, arising from such asset is includible in the income of the person referred to in (*a*) (*supra*).

Beneficial owner - In respect of an asset means an individual who has provided, directly or indirectly, consideration for the asset for the immediate or future benefit, direct or indirect, of himself or any other person.

Beneficiary - In respect of an asset means an individual who derives benefit from the asset during the previous year and the consideration for such asset has been provided by any person other than such beneficiary.

118.1 ***Exemption provided by the Government when taxable income of an individual is up to Rs. 5,00,000*** - This exemption is available only for the assessment year 2012-13.

118.2 ***Return form*** - These forms are given below—

ITR Forms	*Subject*
ITR-1 (i.e., SAHAJ)	For a resident and ordinarily resident individual who has income from salary/family pension/one house property (not being brought forward loss or loss to be carried forward)/income from other sources (not being loss and not being winning from lottery/income from race horses) and who has not claimed any deduction under section 57 (except standard deduction pertaining to family pension) [*see* Note 1]
ITR-2	For an individual/HUF where the total income does not include income under the head business or profession
ITR-3	For an individual/HUF having income under the head business or profession
ITR-4 (i.e., Sugam)	For an individual or a resident and ordinarily resident HUF or a resident firm (non being LLP) deriving business income and such income is computed in accordance with special provisions referred to in section 44AD, 44ADA or 44AE [*see* Note 2]
ITR-5	For firms, AOPs and BOIs or any other person (not being individual or HUF or company or to whom ITR-7 is applicable)
ITR-6	For companies other than companies claiming exemption under section 11
ITR-7	For persons including companies required to furnish return under section 139(4A)/(4B)/(4C)/(4D)
ITR-V	Where the data of the return of income in Forms ITR-1, ITR-2, ITR-3, ITR-4 and ITR-5 transmitted electronically without digital signature

Note 1 - ITR-1 is not applicable in the case of a person who, –

- has assets (including financial interest in any entity) located outside India;
- has signing authority in any account located outside India;
- has income from any source outside India;
- has income to be apportioned in accordance with provisions of section 5A;
- is a director in any company;
- has held any unlisted equity share at any time during the previous year;
- is assessable for the whole (or any part) of the income on which tax has been deducted at source in the hands of a person other than the assessee;
- has claimed any relief of tax under section 90/90A/91;
- has agricultural income, exceeding Rs. 5,000;
- has total income, exceeding Rs. 50 lakh;
- has income taxable under section 115BBDA; or
- has income of the nature referred to in section 115BBE.

Note 2 - ITR-4 is not applicable in the case of a person mentioned in *Note 1* given above. Besides, ITR-4 is not applicable in the case of a person who, –

- owns more than one house property, the income of which is chargeable under the head "Income from house property";
- has any brought forward loss or loss to be carried forward under any head of income.

118.2-1 *MODE OF SUBMISSION* - Mode of submission of income-tax return for the assessment year 2019-20 is as follows–

Person	*Conditions*	*Mode of furnishing return*
Individual/ HUF	• *Case 1* - Accounts are required to be audited under section 44AB	Electronically with digital signature
	• *Case 2* - Return submitted by an individual (who was born before April 2, 1939) in ITR-1 or ITR-4	- Electronic mode given in *Case 3*; or - Paper format
	• *Case 3* - Any other case	Return can be submitted by using any one of the following electronic modes – *A.* Electronically under digital signature; or *B.* Transmitting the data in the return electronically under electronic verification code; or *C.* Transmitting the data in the return electronically and thereafter submitting the verification of the return in Form ITR-V[59].
Company	• *Case 4* - Any company	Electronically with digital signature
Person required to furnish return in ITR-7	• *Case 5* - Political party	Electronically with digital signature
	• *Case 6* - Any other case	Electronic mode given in *Case 3*
Firm, LLP or any person (not mentioned above) required to furnish return in ITR-5	• *Case 7* - Accounts are required to be audited under section 44AB	Electronically with digital signature
	• *Case 8* - Any other case	Electronic mode given in *Case 3*

Note - For the aforesaid table "electronic verification code" means a code generated for the purpose of electronic verification of the person furnishing the return of income as per the data structure and standards specified by Principal Director General (Systems) or Director General (Systems).

118.2-2 *MODE OF SUBMISSION OF AUDIT REPORT* - No document, audit report, statement, accounts, etc., can be attached with return forms. However, where an assessee is required to furnish a report of audit specified under section 10(*23C*)(*iv*)/(*v*)/(*vi*)/(*via*), section 10A, section 10AA, section 12A(1)(*b*), section 44AB, section 44DA, section 50B, section 80-IA, section 80-IB, section 80-IC, section 80-ID, section 80JJAA, section 80LA, section 92E, section 115JB or section 115VW or to give a notice under section 11(2)(*a*), he shall furnish the same electronically.

118.3 ***Time for filing return of income [Sec. 139(1)]*** - The due dates for filing returns of income are given below :

---

59. ITR-V should be sent within "specified period" by ordinary post (or speed post) to "Income-tax Department-CPC, Post Box No. 1, Electronic City Post Office, Bengaluru - 560100, Karnataka". "Specified period" for this purpose is 120 days from the date of uploading the electronic return. However, this period has been extended from time to time in past. If ITR-V is not furnished within the "specified period", then it will be deemed that the assessee has not submitted his return of income. In such a case, the assessee will have to re-submit the return.

Different situations	*Due date of submission of return [see also Note]*
1. Where the assessee is required to furnish a report under section 92E pertaining to international/specified domestic transaction(s)	November 30
2. Where the assessee is a company [not having international or specified domestic transaction(s)]	September 30
3. Where the assessee is a person [not having international or specified domestic transaction(s)] other than a company—	
3.1 In case where accounts of the assessee are required to be audited under any law	September 30
3.2 Where the assessee is a "working partner" in a firm whose accounts are required to be audited under any law	September 30
3.3 In any other case	July 31

Note : Where the last day for filing return/loss is a day on which the office is closed, the assessee can file the return on the next day afterwards on which the office is open and, in such cases, the return will be considered to have been filed within the specified time limit—Circular No. 639$, dated November 13, 1992.

Return of loss [Sec. 139]

119. Any person who has sustained a loss, should file a return of loss by the due dates mentioned in para 118.3 *supra.*

Extension of time not permissible

120. With effect from April 1, 1989, extension of time is not permissible.

Belated return [Sec. 139(4)]

121. If return is not furnished within the time allowed under section 139(1) or within the time allowed under notice issued under section 142(1), the person may furnish the return of any previous year at any time before—

a. the expiry of one year from the end of relevant assessment year or the completion of assessment[60], whichever is earlier (applicable up to the assessment year 2016-17);

b the end of relevant assessment year or the completion of assessment[60], whichever is earlier (applicable from the assessment year 2017-18).

• *Consequences of late submission* - If return is submitted after the due date of submission of return of income, the following consequences will be applicable. These rules are applicable even if a belated return is submitted within the time-limit given above—

1. The assessee will be liable for penal interest under section 234A.

2. The assessee shall be liable for late filing fee under section 234F from the assessment year 2018-19 onwards. Late filing fee under section 234F is Rs. 5,000 (if the return is furnished after the due date but on or before December 31 of the assessment year) or Rs. 10,000 (if return is furnished after December 31 of the assessment year). However, in a case where the total income does not exceed Rs. 5 lakh, the late filing fee amount shall not exceed Rs. 1,000.

3. A penalty of Rs. 5,000 may be imposed under section 271F if belated return is submitted after the end of assessment year (this penalty is not applicable if the return pertains to the assessment year 2018-19 or any subsequent year. Such case is covered by late filing fee under section 234F which is given above).

4. If return of loss is submitted after the due date[61], a few losses cannot be carried forward [*see* para 98].

5. If return is submitted belatedly[61], deduction under the following sections will not be available –

- sections 10A, 10B, 80-IA, 80-IAB, 80-IB, 80-IC, 80-ID and 80-IE (up to the assessment year 2017-18);
- sections 10A, 10B, 80-IA, 80-IAB, 80-IAC, 80-IB, 80-IBA, 80-IC, 80-ID, 80-IE, 80JJA, 80JJAA, 80LA, 80P, 80PA, 80QQB and 80RRB (from the assessment year 2018-19).

Revised return [Sec. 139(5)]

122. The provisions of section 139(5) are given below -

60. Assessment refers to assessment made under section 143(3) or 144. An intimation under section 143(1) is not assessment.

61. However, CBDT has power under section 119(2) to condone delay in case of a return which is filed late and where a claim for carry forward of losses is made—*Lodhi Property Co. Ltd.* v. *Department of Revenue* [2010] 191 Taxman 74 (Delhi), *Bombay Mercantile Co-op. Bank Ltd.* v. *CBDT* [2010] 195 Taxman 106 (Bom.). Delay may be condoned, if a few conditions are satisfied—Circular No. 9/2015$, dated June 9, 2015.

$ For Circular Nos. 639 and 9/2015, log on to *taxmann.com/readyreckoner.aspx.*

• *Up to the assessment year 2016-17* - If any person, having furnished a return under section 139(1) or in pursuance of a notice issued under section 142(1), discovers any omission or any wrong statement therein, he may furnish a revised return within one year from the end of the relevant assessment year or before the assessment‡ is made, whichever is earlier. A return filed under section 139(4) [see para 121] cannot be revised - *Kumar Jagdish Chandra Sinha* v. *CIT* [1996] 86 ITR 122 (SC).

• *For the assessment year 2017-18* - If any person, having furnished a return under section 139(1)/(4), discovers any omission or any wrong statement therein, he may furnish a revised return within one year from the end of the relevant assessment year or before the assessment[60] is made, whichever is earlier. From the assessment year 2017-18, even a belated return submitted under section 139(4) can be revised.

• *From the assessment year 2018-19* - If any person, having furnished a return under section 139(1)/(4), discovers any omission or any wrong statement therein, he may furnish a revised return at any time before the end of the relevant assessment year or before the assessment[60] is made, whichever is earlier.

Defective or incomplete return [Sec. 139(9)]

123. Section 139(9) is applicable as follows —

1. Defective return - The Assessing Officer considers that the return of income furnished by the assessee is defective [when a return becomes defective—*see* para 123.1].

2. Intimation of defect - The Assessing Officer may intimate the defect to the assessee.

3. Time-limit for rectification of defect - The Assessing Officer may give the assessee an opportunity to rectify the defect within a period of 15 days from the date of such intimation. This time-limit may be extended by the Assessing Officer on an application by the assessee.

If, however, an application filed by an assessee for extension time is not disposed of (*i.e.*, no action is taken and the Assessing Officer remains silent), then only conclusion is that time asked for by the assessee has been granted by the Assessing Officer - *Indus Motor Co. Ltd.* v. *CIT* [2009] 116 ITD 207 (Cochin).

4. If the defect is not rectified within the given time - If the defect is not rectified by the assessee within the period of 15 days or such further extended period, then the Assessing Officer shall treat the return as an invalid return and other provisions of the Income-tax Act would apply as if the assessee had failed to furnish the return.

5. If defect is rectified after the given time but before the completion of assessment - Where the assessee rectifies the defect after the expiry of the period of 15 days (or the further extended period), *but before assessment is made,* the Assessing Officer may condone the delay and treat the return as a valid return.

123.1 ***When a return is defective*** - A return of income is regarded as defective in the following cases—

123.1-1 *RETURN FORM HAS NOT BEEN DULY FILLED* - All items in income-tax return form (*i.e.*, ITR-1 to ITR-8) must be filled in the manner indicated in the return form. If any schedule of the relevant form is not applicable in the case of an assessee, it should be scored across as "——NA——". If any item is inapplicable, one should write "NA" against it. One should write "NIL" to denote *nil* figure. No column or row should be left blank. Otherwise the return may be liable to be held defective or even invalid.

123.1-2 *ANNEXURES, STATEMENTS, ACCOUNTS, ETC.* - Under section 139(9), a few statements, reports, proof of pre-paid taxes, accounts[62], etc., should accompany the return of income, otherwise the return will become defective. However, it is not possible to attach any certificate or report or computation or final accounts with new income-tax return forms. Likewise, it is not possible to attach proof of pre-paid taxes (like tax deducted/collected at source, advance payment of tax, self-assessment tax). The assessee should, therefore, retain these certificates, report, computation, final accounts, proof of pre-paid taxes with him.

---

60. Assessment refers to assessment made under section 143(3) or 144. An intimation under section 143(1) is not assessment.

62. These are as follows—

a. a statement showing the computation of tax payable on the basis of the return ;

b. the report of audit obtained under section 44AB (or where the report has been submitted prior to furnishing of return, a copy of audit report together with proof of furnishing the report) ;

c. the proof of pre-paid taxes (*i.e.*, tax deducted/collected at source, advance tax, self-assessment tax);

d. where regular books of account are maintained by an assessee :

i. copies of manufacturing account, trading account, profit and loss account or income and expenditure account, or any other similar account and balance sheet ;

ii. in the case of a proprietary business or profession, the personal account of the proprietor; in the case of a firm, association of persons or body of individuals, personal accounts of the partners or members; and in the case of a partner or member of a firm, association of persons or body of individuals, his personal account in the firm, association of persons or body of individuals ;

e. where the accounts of the assessee have been audited, copies of the audited profit and loss account and balance sheet and a copy of the auditor's report and cost audit report under section 233B of the Companies Act ;

f. where regular books of account are not maintained by the assessee, a statement indicating the amount of turnover or gross receipts, gross profit, expenses and net profit of the business or profession and the basis on which such amount have been computed, as also of the amount of total sundry debtors, sundry creditors, stock-in-trade and cash balance as at the end of the previous year.

These may be furnished whenever the Assessing Officer wants to examine them in assessment proceedings or otherwise. Return of income will not become defective because of non-fulfilment of this requirement.

123.2 ***Clarification from the Board*** - The following points (*vide* Circular No. 281, dated September 22, 1980) may be carefully noted in regard to the aforesaid provision in section 139(9) :

• *Defects other than the specified defects* - The provisions in section 139(9) are not applicable in the case of returns which do not contain any defect specified above. However, the Calcutta High Court in *CIT* v. *Rai Bahadur Bissesswarlal Motilal Malwasie Trust* [1992] 195 ITR 825 has held that the defects specified in section 139(9) are only illustrative and not exhaustive. The Assessing Officer cannot ignore the specified defects and must get them rectified but to contend that only the defects specified can be got rectified and no other defects would be putting unnecessary restrictions on the power of the Assessing Officer, leading to inconvenient consequences and absurd results not intended by the Legislature. The Assessing Officer has the power to ask the assessee to remove all defects in the return other than the defects making the return invalid.

• *Invalid return* - The provision makes a distinction between a defective return and an invalid return. A defective return is not always regarded as an invalid return. When a return contains any of the defects given by section 139(9), it is treated as defective return. If the assessee fails to rectify the same within the specified period, the return will be treated as an invalid return. In this connection, a reference may be made to section 292B which, *inter alia,* provides that no return of income will be invalid merely by reason of mistake, defect or omission in such return of income. The provision in section 139(9), however, overrides other provisions of the Income-tax Act (including section 292B) in this regard and in a case where any of the specified defects are not removed within the time allowed, the return will be treated as invalid return and the provisions of the Income-tax Act will apply as if the assessee had failed to furnish the return.

Permanent account number (PAN) [Sec. 139A]

124. Section 139A has been substituted with effect from July 1, 1995 to provide the following :

124.1 ***Allotment of permanent account number*** - The provisions regarding allotment of permanent account number.

124.1-1 *WHO HAS TO APPLY FOR PERMANENT ACCOUNT NUMBER* - The following persons should apply for allotment of permanent account number in Form No. 49A[63] (in the case of foreign citizen: Form No. 49AA)—

• Every person, if his total income assessable during the previous year exceeds the maximum amount which is not chargeable to tax or any person carrying on business or profession whose total sales, turnover or gross receipts are or is likely to exceed Rs. 5,00,000 in any previous year and who has not been allotted any permanent account number, is obliged to obtain permanent account number. Application should be submitted before May 31 of the assessment year for which the income exceeds the maximum amount not chargeable to tax or before the end of the accounting year for which gross receipt/turnover exceeds Rs. 5,00,000.

• A person who is required to furnish return of income under sub-section (4A) of section 139 (*i.e.,* charitable trust) is also required to obtain permanent account number before the end of the accounting year.

• In the case of a person who is entitled to receive any sum or income or amount, on which tax is deductible in any financial year, shall apply for allotment of permanent account number before the end of such financial year.

• Any resident person (not being an individual), which enters into a financial transaction of an amount aggregating to Rs. 2,50,000 (or more) in a financial year and which has not been allotted any permanent account number, is required to obtain permanent account number on or before May 31 immediately following such financial year.

Likewise, in the case of a person, who is the managing director, director, partner, trustee, author, founder, karta, chief executive officer, principal officer or office bearer of the aforesaid person or any person competent to act on behalf of the aforesaid person and who has not been allotted any permanent account number, is required to obtain permanent account number on or before May 31 immediately following the financial year in which the aforesaid person enters into financial transaction specified above.

• **Any person who intends to enter into such transaction as may be prescribed by the Board in the interest of revenue (applicable with effect from September 1, 2019).**

• The Central Government has specified the following persons who shall apply to the Assessing Officer for allotment of permanent account number—

63. A company (which is not registered under the Companies Act, 2013) can apply for Permanent Account Number in Form No. INC-7 specified under section 7(1) of the Companies Act.

	Time limit for application
Exporters and importers who are required to obtain an importer-exporter code under section 7 of Foreign Trade (Development and Regulations) Act,1992	Before making any export or import
Assessees as defined in rule 2(3) of the Central Excise Rules	Before making any application for registration under the Central Excise Rules
Persons who issue invoice under rule 57E requiring registration under the Central Excise Rules	As given above
Assessees as defined in section 65(6) of the Finance Act, 1994 relating to service tax	Before making an application for registration under the Service Tax Rules, 1994
Any person who wants registration under CST Act/general sales tax law of any State/Union Territory	Before making registration application under CST/general sales tax law

• From June 1, 2006, the Central Government has power to notify (for collection of any information) any person to apply for PAN.

124.1-2 *WHEN CAN ASSESSING OFFICER ALLOT PERMANENT ACCOUNT NUMBER SUO MOTU* - Besides above cases, the Assessing Officer may also allot a permanent account number to any other person by whom tax is payable (or with effect from June 1, 2006 tax not payable). Any other person may also apply for a permanent account number.

124.2 ***Intimation of permanent account number to be given to the person deducting or collecting tax at source [Sec. 139A(5A), (5C)]*** - The following provisions have been made with effect from June 1, 2001—

1. Intimate permanent account number to the person deducting tax at source [Sec. 139A(5A)] - Every person receiving any sum or income from which tax has been deducted shall intimate his permanent account number (or GIR number if permanent account number is not allotted) to the person responsible for deducting tax.

The above provisions shall not apply in case of a person whose total income is not chargeable to income-tax or who is not required to obtain permanent account number if such person furnishes to the person responsible for deducting tax a declaration referred to in section 197A to the effect that the tax on his estimated total income of the previous year to which such income relates will be *nil.*

2. Intimate permanent account to the person collecting tax at source [Sec. 139A(5C)] - Every "buyer", licensee or lessee under section 206C shall intimate his permanent account number to the "seller".

124.3 ***Where the permanent account number should be quoted*** - The permanent account number should be quoted as follows—

124.3-1 *QUOTE OWN PERMANENT ACCOUNT NUMBER IN RETURNS, CERTIFICATES, CORRESPONDENCE* - Every person shall quote his permanent account number (PAN) in all his returns/challans/correspondence with any income-tax authority. Besides, every person shall quote his PAN[63a] in all documents pertaining to the transactions specified in rule 114B and given in the Table (*infra*) -

	Transactions specified in rule 114B	*Value of transaction*
1.	Sale or purchase of a motor vehicle (other than two wheeler)	All such transactions
2.	Opening an account [other than a time-deposit referred to at Sl. No.12 and a Basic Savings Bank Deposit Account] with a bank/co-operative bank	All such transactions
3.	Making an application to a bank/co-operative bank/any other company or institution, for issue of a credit or debit card	All such transactions
4.	Opening of a demat account	All such transactions
5.	Payment to a hotel or restaurant against a bill or bills at any one time	Payment in cash of an amount exceeding Rs. 50,000
6.	Payment in connection with travel to any foreign country or payment for purchase of any foreign currency at any one time	Payment in cash of an amount exceeding Rs. 50,000
7.	Payment to a Mutual Fund for purchase of its units	Amount exceeding Rs. 50,000
8.	Payment to a company or an institution for acquiring debentures/bonds issued by it	Amount exceeding Rs. 50,000

63a. **With effect from September 1, 2019, every person who is required to furnish/intimate/quote his PAN and who, has not been allotted a PAN but possesses the Aadhaar number, may furnish his Aadhaar number in lieu of PAN. Further, every person receiving such documents shall also ensure that the PAN (or the Aadhaar number) has been duly quoted and authenticated.**

	Transactions specified in rule 114B	*Value of transaction*
9.	Payment to the RBI for acquiring bonds issued by it	Amount exceeding Rs. 50,000
10.	Deposit with a bank/co-operative bank	Deposits in cash exceeding Rs. 50,000 during any one day or exceeding Rs. 2,50,000 during November 9, 2016 and December 30, 2016
11.	Purchase of bank drafts/pay orders/banker's cheques from a bank/co-operative bank	Payment in cash for an amount exceeding Rs. 50,000 during any one day
12.	A time deposit with bank/co-operative bank/post office/Nidhi/ non-banking financial company	Amount exceeding Rs. 50,000 or aggregating to more than Rs. 5,00,000 during a financial year
13.	Payment for one or more pre-paid payment instruments to a bank/co-operative bank/any other company or institution	Payment in cash or by way of a bank draft/pay order/ banker's cheque of an amount aggregating to more than Rs. 50,000 in a financial year
14.	Payment as life insurance premium to an insurer	Amount aggregating to more than Rs. 50,000 in a financial year
15.	A contract for sale or purchase of securities (other than shares)	Amount exceeding Rs. 1,00,000 per transaction
16.	Sale or purchase, by any person, of shares in a company not listed in a recognised stock exchange	Amount exceeding Rs. 1,00,000 per transaction
17.	Sale or purchase of any immovable property	Amount exceeding Rs. 10,00,000 or valued by stamp valuation authority referred to in section 50C at an amount exceeding Rs. 10,00,000
18.	Sale or purchase, by any person, of goods or services of any nature other than those specified at Sl. Nos. *1* to *17* above	Amount exceeding Rs. 2,00,000 per transaction

• The following points should be noted -

1. Where a person, entering into any transaction referred to in the Table (*supra*), is a minor and who does not have any income chargeable to income-tax, he shall quote PAN of his father or mother or guardian, as the case may be, in the relevant document.

2. Any person who does not have PAN and who enters into any transactions given above, he shall make a declaration in Form No. 60 giving therein the particulars of such transaction. The declaration in Form No. 60 can be made either in paper form or electronically under the electronic verification code.

3. The above provisions of quoting PAN is not applicable in the case of following persons—

a. Central Government, the State Governments and the Consular Offices;

b. non-resident in respect of transactions other than a transaction referred to at Sl. Nos. *1, 2, 4, 7, 8, 10, 12, 14, 15, 16, 17* of the Table (*supra*).

4. "Payment in connection with travel" includes payment towards fare, or to a travel agent or a tour operator, or to an authorised person.

5. "Travel agent or tour operator" includes a person who makes arrangements for air, surface or maritime travel or provides services relating to accommodation, tours, entertainment, passport, visa, foreign exchange, travel related insurance or other travel related services either severally or in package.

6. "Time deposit" means any deposit which is repayable on the expiry of a fixed period.

124.3-2 *QUOTE PERMANENT ACCOUNT NUMBER OF RECIPIENT/PURCHASER IN TAX DEDUCTION/COLLECTION AT SOURCE* - The following provisions have been made with effect from June 1, 2001—

1. Tax deduction at source [sec. 139A(5B)] - Where any sum or income has been paid after deducting tax, every person deducting tax shall quote the permanent account number of the recipient, in a statement furnished in accordance with the provisions of section 192(2C), in all certificates furnished in accordance with the provision of section 203 (Form Nos. 16, 16A) and in all returns annual/quarterly (*i.e.*, Form Nos. 24, 26, 24Q, 26Q and 27Q, etc.).

2. Tax collection at source [Sec. 139A(5C)] - Every seller collecting tax under section 206C shall quote the permanent account number of every buyer, in all certificates furnished in accordance with the provisions of section 206C(5) and in all returns to an income-tax authority.

124.4 ***Verification of PAN in transactions specified in rule 114B [Rule 114C]*** - Mode of verification, as given in rule 114C, is summarized below —

• *Category A* - Any person being,—

a. a registering officer or an Inspector-General appointed under the Registration Act;

b. a person who sells the immovable property or motor vehicle;

c. a manager or officer of a bank/co-operative bank (referred to at Sl. Nos. *2, 3, 10, 11, 12, 13* of the Table given above);

d. post master;

e. stock broker/sub-broker/share transfer agent/banker to an issue/trustee of a trust deed/registrar to issue/merchant banker/underwriter/portfolio manager/investment adviser and such other intermediaries;

f. a depository, participant, custodian of securities or any other person (referred to at Sl. No. 4 of the Table given above);

g. the principal officer of a company (referred to at Sl. Nos. *3, 4, 8, 12, 13, 15, 16* of the Table given above);

h. the principal officer of an institution (referred to at Sl. Nos. *2, 3, 8, 10, 11, 12, 13* of the Table given above);

i. any trustee or authorised person of a Mutual Fund (referred to at Sl. No. *7* of the Table given above);

j. an officer of the RBI or of any agency bank authorised by the RBI;

k. a manager or officer of an insurer (referred to at Sl. No. *14* of the Table given above),

who, in relation to a transaction specified in the Table above, has received any document shall ensure after verification that PAN has been duly and correctly mentioned therein (or as the case may be, a declaration in Form 60 has been duly furnished with complete particulars).

• *Category B* - Any person (being a person raising bills referred to at Sl. Nos. *5, 6, 18* of the Table given above), who, in relation to the relevant transaction, has issued any document shall ensure after verification that PAN has been correctly furnished and the same shall be mentioned in such document (or a declaration in Form 60 has been duly furnished with complete particulars).

124.5 ***Time and manner in which persons referred to in rule 114C shall furnish a statement containing particulars of Form No. 60 [Rule 114D]*** - Rule 114D is applicable in the case of following person (who has received a declaration in Form No. 60 on or after January 1, 2016) —

1. Any person (other than a registering officer/Inspector-General appointed under the Registration Act) given under *Category A* [para 124.4].

2. Any person given under *Category B* [para 124.4] and who is required to get his accounts audited under section 44AB.

• The above person shall furnish electronically a statement in Form No. 61 containing particulars of such declaration to the Director of Income-tax (Intelligence and Criminal Investigation) or the Joint Director of Income-tax (Intelligence and Criminal Investigation) through online transmission of electronic data and obtain an acknowledgement number. Such a person is required to retain Form No. 60 for a period of 6 years from the end of the financial year in which the transaction is undertaken.

• Form No. 61 shall be uploaded half yearly as follows—

Declarations in Form No. 60 received during April 1 and September 30	Form No. 61 shall be uploaded by October 31
Declarations in Form No. 60 received during October 1 and March 31	Form No. 61 shall be uploaded by April 30

Quoting of Aadhaar number [Sec. 139AA]

124A. Section 139AA[64] has been inserted with effect from April 1, 2017. Provisions of this section are given below –

• *Category A* - Every person who is eligible to obtain Aadhaar number shall (on or after July 1, 2017) quote Aadhaar number –

a. in the application for the allotment of PAN;

b. in the income-tax return.

Where, however, the person does not possess the Aadhaar number, the Enrolment ID (of Aadhaar application form issued to him at the time of enrolment) shall be quoted in the application for PAN or in the return of income.

---

64. Provisions of section 139AA pass the 'test of proportionality' (right to privacy v. legitimate State interest) and is, therefore, not unconstitutional – *Justice K.S. Puttaswamy (Retd.)* v. *Union of India* [2018] 97 taxmann.com 585 (SC).

• *Category B* -Every person who has been allotted PAN as on the July 1, 2017, and who is eligible to obtain Aadhaar number, shall intimate his Aadhaar number to the prescribed authority in prescribed form on or before a date to be notified by the Central Government (*i.e.*, September 30, 2019)[65].

• *Consequences of non-intimation of Aadhaar* - In case of failure to intimate Aadhaar number –

- the PAN allotted to the person shall be deemed to be invalid and the other provisions of the Act shall apply (as if the concerned person had not been applied for allotment of PAN) (applicable up to August 31, 2019).
- **the PAN allotted to such person shall be made inoperative (in the prescribed manner)** (applicable with effect from September 1, 2019).

• *When provisions of section 139AA not applicable* -The provisions of section 139AA shall not apply to such person or class of classes of persons or any State or part of any State, as may be notified by the Central Government.

The Central Government has notified that the provisions of section 139AA shall not apply to an individual who does not possess the Aadhaar number or the Enrolment ID and is –

a. residing in Assam, Jammu and Kashmir and Meghalaya;
b. a non-resident as per the Income-tax Act;
c. of the age of 80 years or more at any time during the previous year (*i.e.*, super-senior citizen);
d. not a citizen of India.

It is not mandatory for an individual (as notified above) to quote his/her Aadhaar Number in return of income.

Self-assessment [Sec. 140A]

125. Where any tax is payable on the basis of any return furnished under section 115WD or 115WH or 139 or 142 or 148 or 153A or 158BC (after deducting advance payment of tax, tax deducted at source, or collected at source, double taxation relief, **relief under section 89**, tax credit under section 115JAA or 115JD), the assessee is required to pay the tax[66] before the filing of the return. It is mandatory for a person to pay (*a*) interest payable up to the date of filing the return along with the self-assessment tax, and (*b*) (from the assessment year 2018-19) late filing fee payable under section 234F. Interest is to be paid under sections 115WK, 234A, 234B and 234C[67]. The return of income is to be accompanied by proof of payment of tax, interest and fee. Where the amount paid by the assessee falls short of the aggregate of tax, interest and fee, the amount so paid shall first be adjusted towards fee payable and thereafter towards interest payable and the balance, if any, shall be adjusted towards tax payable.

Summary assessment without calling the assessee [Sec. 143(1)]

126. Under section 143(1), an Assessing Officer can complete the assessment without passing a regular assessment order. These provisions are explained in the paras given below :

126.1 ***Intimation*** - The total income of an assessee shall be computed under section 143(1) after making the following adjustments[68] to the total income in the return—

a. any arithmetical error in the return;
b. an incorrect claim, if such incorrect claim is apparent from any information in the return;
c. disallowance of loss claimed, if return of the previous year for which set off of loss is claimed was furnished beyond the due date specified under section 139(1) (applicable from the assessment year 2017-18);
d. disallowance of expenditure indicated in the audit report but not taken into account in computing the total income in the return (applicable from the assessment year 2017-18);

65. However, notwithstanding the last date of linking of Aadhaar number with PAN being extended to September 30, 2019, with effect from April 1, 2019, it is mandatory to quote Aadhaar number while filing the return of income as required under section 139AA(1)(*ii*) unless specifically exempted from the operation of section 139AA. Returns (whether submitted electronically or manually) cannot be filed without quoting the Aadhaar number - Notification No. 31/2019, dated March 31, 2019.

66. After March 31, 2008, all corporate assessees and other assessees (who are subject to compulsory audit under section 44AB) will have to make electronic payment of tax through internet banking facility offered by authorized banks. Alternatively, these taxpayers can make electronic payment of tax through internet by way of credit or debit cards. It is not necessary for the assessee to make payment of taxes from his own account in an authorized bank. An assessee can make electronic payment of taxes also from the account of any other person. However, the challan for making such payment must clearly indicate the Permanent Account Number (PAN) of the assessee on whose behalf the payment is made. - Circular No. 5/2008, dated July 17, 2008.

67. Interest under sections 234A, 234B, 234C and 115WK, for this purpose, shall be calculated on the basis of income as declared in the return of income.

68. These adjustments are not possible in the case of debatable issues—*CIT* v. *Haryana Telecom Ltd.* [2011] 14 taxmann.com 122 (Delhi - Trib.).

e. disallowance of deduction claimed under sections 10AA, 80-IA, 80-IAB, 80-IB, 80-IC, 80-ID or 80-IE, if the return is furnished beyond the due date specified under section 139(1) (applicable from the assessment year 2017-18); or

f. addition of income appearing in Form 26AS or Form 16A or Form 16 which has not been included in computing the total income in the return (applicable **only** for the assessment year 2017-18).

• *Other points* - The following points should be noted -

1. For the aforesaid purpose, the term "an incorrect claim apparent from any information in the return" shall mean such claim on the basis of an entry, in the return—

a. of an item, which is inconsistent with another entry of the same or some other item in such return;

b. in respect of which, information required to be furnished to substantiate such entry, has not been furnished under this Act; or

c. in respect of a deduction, where such deduction exceeds specified statutory limit which may have been expressed as monetary amount or percentage or ratio or fraction.

Further, these adjustments will be made only in the course of computerized processing without any human interface.

2. An opportunity (either in writing or in electronic mode) shall be provided to the assessee before making aforesaid adjustments to explain and rectify the same within 30 days of such intimation. The response received from the assessee, if any, shall be considered before making any adjustment. Where, however, no response is received within 30 days of the issue of such intimation, such adjustments shall be made (applicable from the assessment year 2017-18).

126.2 ***Time limit for intimation under section 143(1)*** - An intimation for tax or interest due under section 143(1) should not be sent after the expiry of one year from the end of the financial year in which return of income is made[69]. For instance, for the assessment year 2018-19, return is submitted by a taxpayer on July 27, 2018. An intimation may be sent up to March 31, 2020 (even if it is received by the assessee after March 31, 2020).

126.3 ***Other points*** - Processing of return of income under section 143(1) is mandatory even if scrutiny notice is issued under section 143(2). However, to address the concern of recovery of revenue in doubtful cases, section 241A provides that, for the returns furnished for assessment year 2017-18 (or any subsequent year), where refund of any amount becomes due to the assessee under section 143(1) and the Assessing Officer is of the opinion that grant of refund may adversely affect the recovery of revenue, he may, for the reasons recorded in writing and with the previous approval of the Principal Commissioner or Commissioner, withhold the refund up to the date on which the assessment is made.

Assessment in response to notice under section 143(2) [Sec. 143(3)]

127. Assessment under section 143(3) may be broadly grouped under the following categories—

127.1 ***Scrutiny under section 143*** - The scheme of scrutiny is applicable as follows—

1. A return of income (or loss) has been made under section 139 or in response to notice under section 142(1). If such return has not been furnished, notice under section 143(2) cannot be issued.

2. The Assessing Officer [or (with effect from June 1, 2016) the prescribed income-tax authority] considers it necessary or expedient to ensure that the assessee has not understated the income or has not computed excessive loss or has not under-paid the tax in any manner.

3. A notice[70] shall be served on the assessee under section 143(2)[71]. The notice requires the assessee to produce any evidence which the assessee may rely in support of the return (without pinpointing any specific allowance, claim, etc., made in the return).

4. Such notice shall be served on the assessee within a period of 6 months from the end of the financial year in which return is furnished. For instance, if return is submitted on November 2, 2018, notice under section

69. For the assessment years 2012-13, 2013-14 and 2014-15, such intimation may be sent up to March 31, 2017 (in the case of a valid return of income having claim of refund) – Order [F.No. 225/220/2016-ITA.II], dated October 25, 2016.

70. Scrutiny notice not valid if it's not issued as per CBDT's instruction for selection of a case for assessment—*Crystal Phosphates Ltd.* v. *CIT* [2013] 33 taxmann.com 116 (Delhi).

71. Where an assessee, being an owner of power-looms, files income-tax return for the first time for assessment year 2004-05, the same shall not be selected for scrutiny, provided the assessee makes a true disclosure of his stock of yarn and finished goods not exceeding Rs. 20,000 per power-loom, and furnishes along with the return of income evidence in support of ownership of power-looms in his name—Circular No. 4/2003, dated May 14, 2003. If an assessee has shown a sum equal to or higher than 6 per cent of his total turnover from the business of manufacturing and/or trading of diamonds as his income under the head 'Profits and gains of business or profession' for a particular assessment year, the Assessing Officer shall accept his trading results - Instruction No. 2/2008, dated February 22, 2008.

143(2) can be served on the assessee up to September 30, 2019. If such notice is issued on September 29, 2019, but is received by the assessee after September 30, 2019, it is not a valid notice.

5. After hearing such evidence as the assessee may produce in response to the notice under section 143(2) and such other evidence as the Assessing Officer may require on specified points and after taking into account all relevant materials which the Assessing Officer has gathered, he shall pass an assessment order in writing determining the total income or loss of the assessee and the sum payable by the assessee (or with effect from October 1, 1998, refund of any amount due to him) on the basis of such assessment order.

• *Clarification from the Board* - Now-a-days, scrutiny notices are issued in three different formats– limited scrutiny, complete scrutiny, manual scrutiny. In limited scrutiny cases, notices will contain the issue(s) identified for examination. The scope of enquiry shall be restricted to the limited scrutiny issues. These cases shall be completed expeditiously in a limited number of hearings. During the course of assessment proceedings in limited scrutiny cases, if it comes to the notice of the Assessing Officer that there is potential escapement of income exceeding Rs. 5 lakh (Rs. 10 lakh for Delhi, Mumbai, Chennai, Kolkata, Bengaluru, Hyderabad and Ahmedabad) requiring substantial verification on any other issue(s), then, the case may be taken up for complete scrutiny with the approval of the Pr. CIT/CIT concerned. E-scrutiny, which allows the assessee to reply to scrutiny questions over email, has also been started in the above-noted seven cities. Notice under section 143(2) includes a brief note regarding the benefits and procedure of assessment through e-mail based communication. However, the assessee has an option to opt out of this scheme after informing the Assessing Officer in writing in the beginning or subsequently during the course of assessment proceedings - Letter [F.No. 225/162/2016/ITA.II], dated July 11, 2016.

• *New scheme for scrutiny assessment* - A new scheme for the purpose of making assessments will be notified by the Central Government under section 143(3A) so as to impart greater transparency and accountability, by eliminating the interface between the Assessing Officer and the assessee, optimal utilization of the resources, and introduction of team-based assessment. Under this scheme, the Central Government will direct, by notification in the Official Gazette, that any of the provisions of the Act relating to assessment shall not apply, or shall apply with such exceptions, modifications and adaptations as may be specified therein. However, no such direction shall be issued after March 31, 2020. Each notification under this scheme shall be laid before each House of Parliament (applicable from April 1, 2018).

127.2 *Special procedure for assessment in the case of scientific research association, news agency, notified trust, etc.* - Under the provisions applicable before the amendment made by the Finance Act, 2002, the entities mentioned in clauses (*21*), (*22B*), (*23A*), (*23B*) and (*23C*)(*iv*), (*v*), (*vi*) and (*via*) of section 10 were not obliged to file their return of income as their income was exempt from tax under section 10. Consequently, it was not possible to ascertain as to whether these entities were complying with the conditions, subject to which their income was exempt under section 10.

These entities are either approved or notified and would now be required to file return of their income from the assessment year 2003-04.

A proviso was inserted in section 143(3) with effect from the assessment year 2003-04. The proviso is applicable as follows—

1. The proviso to section 143(3) is applicable in the case of following taxpayers who are required to submit return of income under section 139(4C)[72] or 139(4D)—

a. scientific research association referred to in section 10(*21*);

b. news agency referred to in section 10(*22B*);

c. association or institution referred to in section 10(*23A*);

d. institution referred to in section 10(*23B*);

e. fund or institution referred to in sub-clause (*iv*) or trust or institution referred to in sub-clause (*v*) or any university or other educational institution referred to in sub-clause (*vi*) or any hospital or other medical institution referred to in sub-clause (*via*) of section 10(*23C*);

f. university, college, etc., mentioned in section 35(1)(*ii*)/(*iii*).

2. In the aforesaid cases, assessment order can be passed after giving exemption under section 10. If, however, the Assessing Officer wants to assess these taxpayers without giving effect to provisions of section 10, then he has to follow the following steps—

a. the Assessing Officer should intimate the Central Government or the prescribed authority the contravention of the provisions of clause (*21*) or clause (*22B*) or clause (*23A*) or clause (*23B*) or clause (*23C*)(*iv*), (*v*),

72. Though section 139(4C) is applicable in the case of a trade union referred to in section 10(*24*), proviso to section 143(3) does not include the same.

(*vi*), (*via*) of section 10, as the case may be, by such scientific research association, news agency, association or institution or fund or trust or university or other educational institution or any hospital or other medical institution, where in his view such contravention has taken place; and

b. the approval granted to such scientific research association or other association or fund or trust institution or university or other educational institution or hospital or other medical institution should be withdrawn or notification issued in respect of such news agency or fund or trust or institution should be rescinded.

3. Since there would be a time-lag in the process of sending the intimation to the Central Government and receipt of the order rescinding the notification or withdrawing the approval, section 153 has been amended so as to provide that the period commencing from the date on which the Assessing Officer intimates to the Central Government or the prescribed authority the contravention, of the provisions of section 10 [as mentioned in 2(*a*) *supra*] and ending with the date on which the copy of the order withdrawing the approval or rescinding the notification, as the case may be, under those clauses is received by the Assessing Officer [as mentioned in 2(*b*) *supra*], shall be excluded in computing the period of limitation under section 153.

Best judgment assessment [Sec. 144]

128. The Assessing Officer, after considering all relevant material which he has gathered, is under an obligation to make an assessment of the total income or loss to the best of his judgment in the following cases :

a. if the person fails to make the return as required under section 139(1) and has not made a return or a revised return under sub-section (4) or (5) of that section ;

b. if any person fails to comply with all the terms of a notice under section 142(1) or fails to comply with the direction requiring him to get his accounts audited in terms of section 142(2A) ;

c. if any person, after having filed a return, fails to comply with the terms of a notice under section 143(2) requiring his presence or production of evidence and documents ; or

d. if the Assessing Officer is not satisfied about the correctness or the completeness of the accounts of the assessee or if no method of accounting has been regularly employed by the assessee.

In the case of best judgment assessment, an assessee has a right to file an appeal under section 246 or to make an application for revision under section 264 to the Commissioner.

One should also keep in view the following points :

1. The best judgment assessment can only be made after giving the assessee an opportunity of being heard. Such opportunity shall be given by issue of a notice to the assessee to show cause why the assessment should not be completed to the best of judgment and that opportunity for hearing will not be necessary where notice under section 142(1) has already been issued.

2. A refund cannot be granted under section 144.

Reference to Dispute Resolution Panel [Sec. 144C]

128A. The normal dispute resolution mechanism is time consuming and finality to high demand cases is attained only after a long drawn litigation till the Supreme Court. An alternate dispute resolution mechanism has been provided by the Finance (No. 2) Act, 2009. The salient features of the alternate dispute resolution mechanism are as under:—

1. The Assessing Officer shall forward a draft of the proposed order of assessment (hereinafter referred to as the draft order) to the eligible assessee if he proposes to make, on or after October 1, 2009, any variation in the income or loss returned which is prejudicial to the interest of such an assessee. For this purpose, an "eligible assessee" means—

a. any person in whose case the variation arises as a consequence of the order of the Transfer Pricing Officer passed under section 92CA(3); and

b. any foreign company.

2. On receipt of the draft order, the eligible assessee shall, within 30 days of the receipt by him of the draft order, file his acceptance of the variations to the Assessing Officer. Alternatively, within the said period of 30 days, the assessee can file his objections, if any, to such variation with the Dispute Resolution Panel and to the Assessing Officer.

3. The Assessing Officer shall complete the assessment on the basis of the draft order, if —

a. the assessee shall intimate to the Assessing Officer the acceptance of the variation; or

b. no objections are received within the period of 30 days as stated above.

4. The Assessing Officer shall (notwithstanding anything contained in section 153 or 153B), pass the assessment order within one month from the end of the month in which,—

a. the acceptance is received; or

b. the period of 30 days for filing of objections expires.

5. The Dispute Resolution Panel shall, in a case where any objections are received from the assessee, issue such directions, as it thinks fit, for the guidance of the Assessing Officer to enable him to complete the assessment.

6. The Dispute Resolution Panel shall issue the directions referred to above after considering the following, namely:—

a. draft order;

b. objections filed by the assessee;

c. evidence furnished by the assessee;

d. report, if any, of the Assessing Officer, Valuation Officer or Transfer Pricing Officer or any other authority;

e. records relating to the draft order;

f. evidence collected by, or caused to be collected by it; and

g. result of any enquiry made by, or caused to be made by it.

7. The Dispute Resolution Panel may, before issuing any directions referred to above —

a. make such further enquiry, as it thinks fit; or

b. cause any further enquiry to be made by any income-tax authority and report the result of the same to it.

8. The Dispute Resolution Panel may confirm, reduce or enhance the variations proposed in the draft order. Moreover, the Dispute Resolution Panel has power to consider any matter arising out of the assessment proceedings relating to the draft order, even if such matter was raised (or not) by the eligible assessee. However, it shall not issue any direction to set aside any proposed variation or issue any direction for further enquiry and for passing of the assessment order.

9. If the members of the Dispute Resolution Panel differ in opinion on any point, the point shall be decided according to the opinion of the majority of the members.

10. Every direction issued by the Dispute Resolution Panel shall be binding on the Assessing Officer.

11. No direction under the above provisions can be issued unless an opportunity of being heard is given to the assessee and the Assessing Officer on such directions which are prejudicial to the interest of the assessee or the interest of the revenue, respectively.

12. No direction under the above provisions shall be issued after 9 months from the end of the month in which the draft order is forwarded to the eligible assessee.

13. Upon receipt of the directions issued by Dispute Resolution Panel, the Assessing Officer shall, in conformity with the directions, complete (notwithstanding anything to the contrary contained in section 153 or 153B), the assessment within one month from the end of the month in which the direction is received. For this purpose, no further opportunity of being heard will be provided to the assessee.

- Further, the following consequential amendments have been made—

1. Section 131(1) has been amended so as to provide that "Dispute Resolution Panel" shall have the same powers as are vested in a Court under the Code of Civil Procedure, 1908.

2. Order passed by the Assessing Officer under section 143(3) or under section 154 in conformity with the directions of the Dispute Resolution Panel shall be appealable to the Tribunal and not to the Commissioner (Appeals).

3. Provisions of section 144C will not be applicable in the case of any order passed by the Assessing Officer with the prior approval of the Commissioner under section 144BA(12).

Reassessment [Secs. 147 to 151]

129. If the Assessing Officer has reason to believe that any income chargeable to tax has escaped assessment for any assessment year, he may assess or reassess such income. Once an assessment has been reopened, any other income which has escaped assessment and which comes to the notice of the Assessing Officer subsequently in the course of the proceeding under section 147 can also be included in the assessment, even if the reason for such issue has not been included in the reasons recorded under section 148(2).

• The Assessing Officer may assess or reassess such income, other than the income involving matters which are the subject matter of any appeal, reference or revision, which is chargeable to tax and has escaped assessment.

• If an assessment has been made for the relevant assessment year under section 143(3) or under section 147 no action shall be taken under section 147 after the expiry of four years from the end of the relevant assessment year, unless the income has escaped assessment due to the failure on the part of the assessee to file a return under section 139 or in response to a notice under section 142(1) or 148 or to disclose fully and truly all material facts necessary for his assessment. For this purpose production before the Assessing Officer of account books or other evidence from which material evidence could with due diligence have been discovered by the Assessing Officer will not necessarily amount to disclosure. However, the rules stated in this para will not be applicable where any income in relation to any asset (including financial interest in any entity) located outside India, chargeable to tax, has escaped assessment for any assessment year (applicable from July 1, 2012 and also for any assessment year beginning on or before April 1, 2012).

• *Cases of income escaping assessment*[73] - *Explanation 2* to section 147 clarifies that the following shall also be deemed to be cases of income escaping assessment—

a. where no return of income has been furnished by an assessee, although his total income is above the taxable limit;

b. where a return of income has been furnished, but no assessment has been made, and the assessee is found to have understated his income or claimed excessive loss, deduction, etc., in the return;

c. where the assessee has failed to furnish a report in respect of any international transaction which he was so required under section 92E[74];

d. where an assessment has been made, but income chargeable to tax has been under-assessed or has been assessed at too low a rate or any excessive loss or relief or depreciation allowance or any other allowance under the Act has been allowed;

e. where on the basis of information or document received from the prescribed income-tax authority under section 133C(2), it is noticed by the Assessing Officer that the income of the assessee exceeds the maximum amount not chargeable to tax (and the assessee has not furnished his return of income) or the assessee has understated the income or has claimed excessive loss, deduction, allowance or relief in the return furnished by him (applicable from June 1, 2016);

f. where a person is found to have any asset (including financial interest in any entity) located outside India[74].

129.1 ***Issue of notice [Sec. 148]*** - Before making the assessment, reassessment or recomputation under section 147, the Assessing Officer should serve on the assessee a notice requiring him to furnish a return of income. Before issuing a notice, the Assessing Officer is required to record reasons for doing so.

129.2 ***Time-limit and other conditions for issue of notice [Secs. 149 and 151]*** - Time-limit[75] and other conditions for issue of a notice under section 148 are given below :

TIME-LIMIT

	Up to 4 years from the end of the relevant assessment year	*Beyond 4 years but up to 6 years from the end of the relevant assessment year*	*Beyond 4 years but up to 16 years from the end of the relevant assessment year*
In cases subjected to scrutiny by way of assessment under section 143(3) or 147	If the escaped income is of any amount [Note 1]	If the escaped income is Rs. 1,00,000 or more [Note 2]	If income in relation to any asset (including financial interest in any entity) located outside India, chargeable to tax, has escaped assessment[74]
In other cases	If the escaped income is of any amount [Note 3]	If the escaped income is Rs. 1,00,000 or more [Note 4]	

73. Where a stamp valuation authority has adopted higher valuation of a property for the payment of stamp duty, the same cannot be a basis to conclude escapement of income in the hands of purchaser—*ITO* v. *Shiv Shakti Build Home (P.) Ltd.* [2011] 15 taxmann.com 293 (Jodhpur - Trib.).

74. Applicable from July 1, 2012 and also for any assessment year beginning on or before April 1, 2012.

75. Merely signing of a notice on the last date of the financial year, cannot be equated with the issuance of notice within the time as contemplated under section 149. The date of issue of a notice will be the date on which the same is handed over for service to the proper officer—*Kanubhai M. Patel (HUF)* v. *Hiren Bhatt or his Successors to Office* [2011] 202 Taxman 99 (Guj.).

Notes :

1. Any Assessing Officer who is not below the rank of Assistant Commissioner or Deputy Commissioner can issue notice. An Assessing Officer who is below the rank of Assistant Commissioner or Deputy Commissioner can issue notice only if the Joint Commissioner is satisfied on the reasons recorded by such Assessing Officer that it is a fit case for issue of such notice. From June 1, 2015, no notice shall be issued by an Assessing Officer (who is below the rank of Joint Commissioner) unless the Joint Commissioner is satisfied, on the reasons recorded by such Assessing Officer, that it is a fit case for the issue of such notice.

2. Notice mentioned in point *1 supra* can be issued only if the Chief Commissioner/Commissioner is satisfied on the reasons recorded by the Assessing Officer that it is a fit case for issue of notice. From June 1, 2015, no notice shall be issued by an Assessing Officer unless the Principal Chief Commissioner or Chief Commissioner or Principal Commissioner or Commissioner is satisfied, on the reasons recorded by the Assessing Officer, that it is a fit case for the issue of such notice.

3. Notice can be issued by the Assessing Officer. From June 1, 2015, no notice shall be issued by an Assessing Officer (who is below the rank of Joint Commissioner) unless the Joint Commissioner is satisfied, on the reasons recorded by such Assessing Officer, that it is a fit case for the issue of such notice.

4. No notice can be issued by an Assessing Officer who is below the rank of Joint Commissioner unless the Joint Commissioner is satisfied that on the reason recorded by Assessing Officer that it is a fit case for issue of such notice. From June 1, 2015, no notice shall be issued by an Assessing Officer unless the Principal Chief Commissioner or Chief Commissioner or Principal Commissioner or Commissioner is satisfied, on the reasons recorded by the Assessing Officer, that it is a fit case for the issue of such notice.

5. For determining income chargeable to tax which has escaped assessment, *see* para 129.

129.2-1 *EXCEPTIONS* - The following exceptions are applicable to the time limits given above :

1. Notice under section 148 may be issued at any time for the purpose of making an assessment, reassessment or recomputation in consequence of (or giving effect to) any finding or direction contained in an order passed by any authority, in any proceeding by way of appeal, reference or revision or by a Court.

2. If the person on whom notice under section 148 is to be served is a person treated as an agent of a non-resident (under section 163), then notice shall not be issued after the expiry of 6 years from the end of the relevant assessment year.

3. If an assessment has been made for the relevant assessment year under section 143(3) or under section 147, no action shall be taken under section 147 after the expiry of four years from the end of the relevant assessment year[76], unless the income has escaped assessment due to the failure on the part of the assessee to file a return under section 139 or in response to a notice under section 142(1) or 148 or to disclose fully and truly all material facts necessary for this assessment.

When can mistakes be rectified [Sec. 154]

130. The provisions of section 154 are given below—

130.1 ***Which order can be rectified [Sec. 154(1)]*** - To rectify any mistake apparent from record, an income-tax authority may amend the following orders—

a. an order passed under any provision of the Act;

b. an intimation or deemed intimation under section 143(1); or

c. amend any intimation under section 200A(1).

130.1-1 *IF THE ABOVE ORDER IS SUBJECT TO AN APPEAL [SEC. 154(1A)]* - If any of the above-mentioned order has been subject-matter of an appeal/revision, then it cannot be amended by the Assessing Officer under section 154. However, the Assessing Officer can amend the order in respect of any matter other than the matter considered and decided in appeal/revision.

130.2 ***Meaning of "mistake"*** - A mistake which can be rectified under section 154 is one which is patent, which is obvious and whose discovery is not dependent on argument or elaboration.

130.2-1 *MISTAKE WHICH CAN BE RECTIFIED* - The following are some of the examples of mistakes which can be rectified under this section : an error of law[77] or fact, a clerical or arithmetical mistake, error in

---

76. However, this rule will not be applicable where any income in relation to any asset (including financial interest in any entity) located outside India, chargeable to tax, has escaped assessment for any assessment year (applicable from July 1, 2012 and also for any assessment year beginning on or before April 1, 2012).

77. Where the sums referred to in the first proviso under section 43B had in fact been paid on or before the due dates mentioned therein, but the evidence therefor had been omitted to be furnished along with the return, the Assessing Officers can entertain applications under section 154 for rectification of the intimations under section 143(1)(*a*) or orders under section 143(3), as the case may be, and decide the same on merits—Circular No. 669, dated October 25, 1993.

determining written down value, overlooking the obligatory provisions of the Legislature, and mistake arising as a result of subsequent retrospective amendment of law.

Where the sums referred to section 43B had in fact been paid after the end of the previous year but on or before the due date of submission of refund of income, but the evidence therefore had been omitted to be furnished along with the return, the Assessing Officers can entertain applications under section 154 for rectification of the intimation - Circular No. 669, dated October 25, 1993.

130.2-2 *MISTAKE WHICH CANNOT BE RECTIFIED* - Where controversy can be resolved only by way of a complicated process of investigation, recourse cannot be taken to section 154. If on a question of construction on a point of law, two views are possible, no rectification can be done by invoking section 154. A question on which there is difference of opinion among two judges of High Court cannot be rectified by invoking provisions of section 154.

130.3 ***Who can point out the mistake to be rectified [Sec. 154(2)]*** - The provisions of section 154(2) are given below—

• An income-tax authority can rectify the mistake apparent from records on its own.

• An income-tax authority can rectify any mistake apparent from record if it has been brought to his notice by the assessee or deductor or (from June 1, 2015) collector.

• If there is mistake apparent from record in an order passed by the Commissioner (Appeals), the Commissioner (Appeals) can rectify the mistake if it has been brought to his notice by the assessee or deductor or (from June 1, 2015) collector or the Assessing Officer.

130.4 ***Time-limit*** - An order to rectify mistake can be made within the time-limit given below—

• No amendment under section 154 can be made after the expiry of 4 years from the end of the financial year in which the order sought to be amended was passed. The point at which the period of limitation commences is 4 years from the date of order sought to be amended (and not the date of original order).

• Where an application for amendment under section 154 is made by the assessee on or after June 1, 2001 to an income-tax authority, the authority shall pass an order within 6 months from the end of the month in which the application is received by it, either making the amendment or refusing to allow the claim.

CBDT has directed that all rectification applications must be disposed of after passing an order in writing, to be duly served upon the taxpayer concerned and not merely by making necessary rectification on the AST System— Instruction No. 2/2016, dated February 15, 2016.

130.4-1 *WHEN ORDER CAN BE PASSED AFTER THE TIME-LIMIT* - The authorities making rectification are authorised by the Board to dispose of an application even after the expiry of time-limit if a valid application had been filed by the assessee within the statutory time-limit but was not disposed of by the concerned authority within the aforesaid time-limit *vide* Circular No. 73, dated January 7, 1972.

130.5 ***Technical formalities*** - The following points should be noted—

• The order of rectification should be in writing.

• Where the rectification has the effect of enhancing tax liability or reducing refund, then the concerned income-tax authority should follow the following steps—

1. Before rectifying the mistake, a notice should be given to the assessee or deductor or (from June 1, 2015) collector and a reasonable opportunity of being heard should be provided.

2. After passing the rectification order, the Assessing Officer shall serve a notice of demand on the assessee or deductor or (from June 1, 2015) collector.

Obligation to furnish annual information return pertaining to financial transactions [Sec. 285BA]

131. The provisions of section 285BA are given below—

131.1 ***Financial transactions*** - These provisions are given below–

• *Transactions covered*[$] - Statement of financial transactions shall be furnished by every person mentioned in the Table (*infra*) in respect of all transactions of the nature/value specified in the Table (*infra*) which are recorded or registered by him during the financial year 2016-17 (or any subsequent year) -

[$] For Government's clarifications, log on to *taxmann.com/readyreckoner.aspx.*

	Nature and value of transaction	*Class of person (reporting person)*
1.	(*a*) Payment made in cash for purchase of bank drafts/pay orders/banker's cheque of an amount aggregating to Rs. 10 lakh or more in a financial year (*b*) Payments made in cash aggregating to Rs. 10 lakh or more during the financial year for purchase of pre-paid instruments issued by RBI (*c*) Cash deposits/cash withdrawals (including through bearer's cheque) aggregating to Rs. 50 lakh or more in a financial year, in or from one or more current account of a person	A bank/co-operative bank
2.	Cash deposits aggregating to Rs. 10 lakh or more in a financial year, in one or more accounts (other than a current account and time deposit) of a person	A bank/co-operative bank/Post Master General
3.	One or more time deposits (other than a time deposit made through renewal of another time deposit) of a person aggregating to Rs. 10 lakh or more in a financial year of a person	A bank/co-operative bank/Post Master General/Nidhi/non-banking financial company
4	Payments made by any person of an amount aggregating to— (*i*) Rs. 1 lakh or more in cash; or (*ii*) Rs. 10 lakh or more by any other mode, against bills raised in respect of one or more credit cards issued to that person, in a financial year	A bank/co-operative bank/any other company or institution issuing credit card
5.	Receipt from any person of an amount aggregating to Rs. 10 lakh or more in a financial year for acquiring bonds/debentures issued by the company or institution (other than the amount received on account of renewal of the bond or debenture issued by that company)	A company or institution issuing bonds or debentures
6.	Receipt from any person of an amount aggregating to Rs. 10 lakh or more in a financial year for acquiring shares (including share application money) issued by the company	A company issuing shares
7.	Buy back of shares from any person (other than the shares bought in the open market) for an amount or value aggregating to Rs. 10 lakh or more in a financial year.	A company listed on a recognised stock exchange purchasing its own securities under section 68 of the Companies Act, 2013
8.	Receipt from any person of an amount aggregating to Rs. 10 lakh or more in a financial year for acquiring units of one or more schemes of a Mutual Fund (other than the amount received on account of transfer from one scheme to another scheme of that Mutual Fund)	A trustee of a Mutual Fund or such other person managing the affairs of the Mutual Fund
9.	Receipt from any person for sale of foreign currency including any credit of such currency to foreign exchange card or expense in such currency through a debit or credit card or through issue of travellers cheque or draft or any other instrument of an amount aggregating to Rs. 10 lakh or more during a financial year	Authorised person under FEMA
10.	Purchase or sale by any person of immovable property for an amount of Rs. 30 lakh or more or valued by the stamp valuation authority referred to in section 50C at Rs. 30 lakh or more	Inspector-General/Registrar/Sub-Registrar under the Registration Act, 1908
11.	Receipt of cash payment exceeding Rs. 2 lakh for sale, by any person, of goods or services of any nature (other than those specified above)	Any person who is liable for audit under section 44AB
12.	Cash deposits$ during November 9, 2016 and December 30, 2016 aggregating to— - Rs. 12,50,000 or more, in one or more current account of a person - Rs. 2,50,000 or more, in one or more accounts (other than a current account) of a person.	A bank/Post Master General
13.	Cash deposits$ during April 1, 2016 to November 9, 2016 in respect of accounts that are reportable under Sl. No.12.	A bank/Post Master General

- *How to calculate threshold limit given above* - The reporting person mentioned in *Column 3* of the Table (*supra*) (other than the person at Sl. No. *10 or 11*) shall, while aggregating the amounts for determining the threshold amount for reporting in respect of any person,—

a. take into account all the accounts of the same nature as specified in *Column 2* of the Table (*supra*) maintained in respect of that person during the financial year;

b. aggregate all the transactions of the same nature as specified in *Column 2* of the Table (*supra*) recorded in respect of that person during the financial year;

c. attribute the entire value of the transaction or the aggregated value of all the transactions to all the persons, in a case where the account is maintained or transaction is recorded in the name of more than one person;

d. apply the threshold limit separately to deposits and withdrawals in respect of transaction specified in item 1(*c*) under *Column 2*, of the Table (*supra*).

• *Form No.* - Statement of financial transactions return shall be furnished in Form No. 61A to the Director of Income-tax (Intelligence and Criminal Investigation) or the Joint Director of Income-tax (Intelligence and Criminal Investigation) through online transmission of electronic data to a server designated for this purpose under the digital signature. However, a Post Master General or a Registrar or an Inspector General can furnish the return in Form No. 61A in a computer readable media (*i.e.*, CD/DVD), alongwith the verification in Form-V on paper.

• *Time-limit* - Statement of financial transactions return shall be furnished on or before May 31, immediately following the financial year in which the transaction is registered or recorded. However, the statement of financial transaction in respect of the transactions listed at serial numbers (*12*) and (*13*) in the Table (*supra*) shall be furnished on or before January 31, 2017.

• *Registration* - Every reporting person mentioned in *Column 3* of the Table (*supra*) shall communicate to the Principal Director General of Income-tax (Systems) the name, designation, address and telephone number of the Designated Director and the Principal Officer and obtain a registration number. "Designated Director" means a person designated by the reporting person to ensure overall compliance with the obligations imposed under section 285BA and rules 114B to 114E and includes—

a. the Managing Director/whole-time Director duly authorised by the Board of Directors, if the reporting person is a company;

b. the managing partner, if the reporting person is a partnership firm;

c. the proprietor, if the reporting person is a proprietorship concern;

d. the managing trustee, if the reporting person is a trust;

e. a person/individual, who controls and manages the affairs of the reporting entity, if the reporting person is AOP/BOI/any other.

131.2 ***Report by a reporting financial institution in respect of reportable account*** - With a view to facilitate effective exchange of information in respect of residents and non-residents, the scheme of section 285BA has been amended as to also provide for furnishing of statement by a prescribed reporting financial institution in respect of a specified financial transaction or reportable account to the prescribed income-tax authority. The statement of information shall be electronically furnished for each calendar year in Form No. 61B on or before May 31 of the next year [*see* rules 114F, 114G and 114H].

Where any person, who has furnished a statement of information comes to know or discovers any inaccuracy in the information provided in the statement, then, he shall, within a period of 10 days, inform the income-tax authority or other authority or agency referred to in section 285BA(1) the inaccuracy in such statement and furnish the correct information in the manner as may be prescribed.

Submission of statement by a non-resident having liaison office in India [Sec. 285]

132. Foreign companies or firms or associations of individuals operate in India through a branch or a liaison office after approval by the RBI. The branch constitutes a permanent establishment of the foreign entity and is, therefore, required to file a return of income along with requisite details. A non-resident does not file a return of income with regard to its liaison office on the ground that no business activity is allowed to be carried out in India.

To seek regular information from non-residents regarding the activities of their liaison offices in India, section 285 has been inserted with effect from June 1, 2011. Under this section, every person having a liaison office in India will have to file a statement online in Form No. 49C pertaining to the liaison office within 60 days from the end of the financial year (*i.e.*, on or before May 30 after the end of the financial year).

Furnishing of information or document by an Indian concern [Sec. 285A]

133. Section 285A has been inserted with effect from the assessment year 2016-17. It provides that where any share or interest in a company or entity registered or incorporated outside India derives, directly or indirectly, its value substantially from the assets located in India as referred to in the *Explanation 5* to section 9(1)(*i*), and such company or, as the case may be, entity holds such assets in India through or in an Indian concern, then, any such Indian concern shall, for the purposes of determination of income accruing or arising in India, under section 9(1)(*i*), furnish Form No. 49D. Form No. 49D shall be furnished electronically under digital signature to the Assessing Officer having jurisdiction over the Indian concern within a period of 90 days from the end of the financial year in which any transfer of the share of, or interest in, a company or entity incorporated outside India referred to in *Explanation 5* to section 9(1)(*i*) has taken place. Where, however, the transaction in respect of the share or the interest has the effect of directly or indirectly transferring the rights of management or control in relation to the Indian concern, the information shall be furnished in Form No. 49D within 90 days of the transaction.

The transferor of the share of, or interest in, a company or an entity that derives its value substantially from assets located in India, shall obtain and furnish along with the return of income a report from a chartered accountant in Form No. 3CT providing the basis of the apportionment in accordance with the formula and certifying that the income attributable to assets located in India has been correctly computed.

Penalty

Failure to comply with statutory provisions usually attracts some kind of penalty. For nature of different defaults and penalties related thereto, see para 137

Penalties for defaults

137. An assessee has been made liable to penalty for the different defaults committed by him under the different provisions of the Act. The provisions, applicable from April 1, 1989, are highlighted in the Table given below :

Section	*Nature of default*	*Minimum penalty*	*Maximum penalty*
(1)	*(2)*	*(3)*	*(4)*
140A(3)	Failure to pay whole or any part of income-tax or interest or both in accordance with the provisions of section 140A(1)	Such amount as the Assessing Officer may impose [Sec. 221(1)]	Tax in arrears
158BFA	Failure to furnish in time return of total income including undisclosed income in respect of search initiated under section 132/132A after December 31, 1997	Amount of tax leviable	300 per cent of the amount of tax leviable
221(1)	Default in making payment of tax within prescribed time	Such amount as the Assessing Officer may impose	Tax in arrears
270A	Penalty for under-reporting and misreporting of income (applicable from the assessment year 2017-18)	50 per cent of tax payable on under-reported income (200 per cent of such tax in the case of misreporting of income	—
271(1)(*b*)	Failure to comply with a notice under sections 115WD(2), 115WE(2), 142(1), 143(2) or with a direction issued under section 142(2A) (applicable up to the assessment year 2016-17)	Rs. 10,000[78] for each failure	Rs. 10,000[79] for each failure
271(1)(*c*)	Concealment of particulars of income or fringe benefits or furnishing of inaccurate particulars of income or fringe benefits (applicable up to the assessment year 2016-17)	100% of tax sought to be evaded	300% of amount of tax sought to be evaded

78. Rs. 1,000 up to May 31, 2001.

79. Rs. 25,000 up to May 31, 2001.

(1)	(2)	(3)	(4)
271(4)	Distribution of profit by registered firm otherwise than in accordance with partnership deed and as a result of which partner has returned income below the real income (applicable up to the assessment year 2016-17)	Up to 150 per cent of the difference between tax on partner's income assessed and tax as income returned	150 per cent of such difference
271A	Failure to keep or maintain books of account, documents, etc., as required under section 44AA	Rs. 25,000[80]	Rs. 25,000[81]
271AA(1)	Failure to keep and maintain information and document in respect of international transaction or (with effect from July 1, 2012) failure to report international transaction or furnishing of incorrect information [with effect from April 1, 2013, these provisions are also applicable in the case of specified domestic transactions]	2 per cent of the value of each international transaction	—
271AA(2)	Failure to furnish information document as required under section 92D(4) (applicable from the assessment year 2017-18)	Rs. 5,00,000	—
271AAA	Undisclosed income in the case of search (applicable if search is initiated on or after June 1, 2007 but before July 1, 2012)	*See* para 138.2-2	—
271AAB	Undisclosed income in the case of search (applicable if search is initiated on or after July 1, 2012)	*See* para 138.2-3	—
271AAC	Income determined by Assessing Officer includes any income referred to in sections 68 to 69D (if such income is not included by the assessee in his return of income or tax in accordance with section 115BBE has not been paid)	10% of tax payable under section 115BBE	—
271B	Failure to get accounts audited under section 44AB or furnish said report as required under section 44AB	½% of the total sales, turnover, or gross receipts	Rs. 1,00,000 (Rs. 1,50,000 with effect from April 1, 2011)
271BA	Failure to furnish report under section 92E (applicable from April 1, 2002)	Rs. 1,00,000	—
271C	Failure to deduct the whole or any part of tax as required under sections 192 to 196C or (with effect from June 1, 1997) if any person fails to pay tax on dividends under section 115-O [*see* para 207.2] or under second proviso to section 194B	Amount of tax which such person has failed to deduct or pay	—
271CA	Penalty for failure to collect tax at source (from April 1, 2007)	Amount of tax which a person has failed to collect	—
271D	Taking or accepting any loan or deposit or (with effect from June 1, 2015) specified sum[82] in contravention of the provisions of section 269SS	Amount of loan/deposit so taken or accepted	—

80. Rs. 2,000 up to May 31, 2001.

81. Rs. 1,00,000 up to May 31, 2001.

82. "Specified advance" means any sum of money in the nature of an advance, by whatever name called, in relation to transfer of an immovable property whether or not the transfer takes place.

(1)	(2)	(3)	(4)
271DA	Receiving an amount of Rs. 2 lakh or more otherwise than by an account payee cheque/draft/use of electronic clearing system through a bank account **(or through prescribed electronic mode)** in contravention of the provisions of section 269ST (applicable from April 1, 2017)	100% of the amount of such receipt	—
271DB	**Failure to provide facility for accepting payment through the prescribed electronic modes of payment referred to in section 269SU**	**Rs. 5,000** for every day during which such failure continues (applicable with effect from November 1, 2019)	—
271E	Repaying any loan or deposit or (with effect from June 1, 2015) specified advance[83] referred to in section 269T otherwise than in accordance with the provisions of section 269T	Amount of deposit so repaid	—
271F	Failure to furnish return of income as required by section 139 before the end of the relevant assessment year (applicable up to the assessment year 2017-18)	Rs. 5,000 (Rs. 1,000 up to May 31, 2001)	—
271FA	Failure to furnish annual information return (or statement of financial transaction or reportable account) under section 285BA(1)	Rs. 100 (Rs. 500 with effect from April 1, 2018) for each day of default[84]	—
271FA, proviso	Failure to furnish annual information return (or statement of financial transaction or reportable account) within period specified in notice under section 285BA(5) (applicable from April 1, 2014)	Rs. 500 (Rs. 1,000 with effect from April 1, 2018) for each day of default commencing from the day immediately following the day on which the time specified in notice for furnishing the return expires	—
271FAA	Failure to furnish accurate statement of financial transaction or reportable account – - under section 285BA(1)(*k*) [applicable during April 1, 2015 and August 31, 2019]; - under **section 285BA(1)** [applicable with effect from September 1, 2019];	Rs. 50,000	—
271FAB	Failure to furnish statement or information or document by an eligible investment fund as required by section 9A(5) (applicable from the assessment year 2016-17)	Rs. 5,00,000	—
271FB	Failure to furnish return of fringe benefits	Rs. 100 for each day of default	—
271G	Failure to furnish information or document pertaining to international transactions or (with effect from April 1, 2013) specified domestic transactions under section 92D	2 per cent of the value of international transaction for each failure	—

83. "Specified advance" means any sum of money in the nature of an advance, by whatever name called, in relation to transfer of an immovable property whether or not the transfer takes place.

84. CBDT has decided not to levy penalty under section 271FA in cases where Annual Information Return (AIR) under section 285BA in respect of specified financial transactions registered or recorded during the financial year 2004-05 is furnished on or before November 30, 2005—Press Release dated September 30, 2005.

(1)	(2)	(3)	(4)
271GA	Failure to furnish information or document under section 285A (applicable from the assessment year 2016-17)	*In the case of transferring right of management or control in relation to the Indian concern*: 2 per cent of value of transaction *In any other case* : Rs. 5,00,000	—
271GB(1)	Failure to furnish report under section 286(2) in respect of international group (applicable from the assessment year 2017-18)	Rs. 5,000 per day (if period of default does not exceed 1 month). Rs. 15,000 per day (for the period of default beyond 1 month)	—
271GB(2)	Failure to produce information/document to the prescribed authority under section 286(6) (applicable from the assessment year 2017-18)	Rs. 5,000 per day (beginning immediately following the day on which the period for furnishing the information expires)	—
271GB(3)	Continuity of failure referred to in section 271GB(1)/(2) after the order directing to pay penalty under section 271GB(1)/(2) has been served	Rs. 50,000 per day from the date of service of penalty order	—
271GB(4)	Furnishing inaccurate report under section 286(2) in respect of international group (applicable from the assessment year 2017-18)	Rs. 5,00,000	—
271H	Failure to submit (or furnishing incorrect statements in) quarterly TDS/TCS returns (applicable from July 1, 2012)	Rs. 10,000	Rs. 1,00,000
271-I	Failure to furnish information or furnishing inaccurate information under section 195(6) (applicable from June 1, 2015)	Rs. 1,00,000	—
271J	Furnishing incorrect information in reports or certificates by chartered accountant, merchant banker or registered valuer (applicable from April 1, 2017)	Rs. 10,000 for each report/ certificate	—
272A(1)(*a*)	Failure to answer any question put to a person (who is legally bound to state the truth of any matter touching the subject of his assessment) by an income-tax authority	Rs. 10,000[85] for each default	—
272A(1)(*b*)	Failure to sign any statement made by a person in course of income-tax proceeding	Rs. 10,000[85] for each default	—
272A(1)(*c*)	Failure to comply with summons issued under section 131(1) to attend office to give evidence and produce books of account or other documents	Rs. 10,000[85] for each default	—
272A(1)(*d*)	Failure to comply with a notice under sections 142(1), 143(2) or failure to comply a direction issued under section 142(2A) (applicable from the assessment year 2017-18)	Rs. 10,000 for each default	—
272A(2)	Failure to comply with a notice issued under section 94; to give notice of discontinuance of business/profession under section 176(3); to furnish returns/	Rs. 100 for every day during which default continues	Rs. 100 (Rs. 200 up to May 31, 1999) for every day during which default continues (the amount of pen-

85. Rs. 500 up to May 31, 2001.

(1)	(2)	(3)	(4)
	statement mentioned in section 133, 206, 206C or 285B; to allow inspection of register referred to in section 134 (or of any entry in such register or to allow copies of such register to be taken); to furnish return of income under section 139(4A) or 139(4C) or to deliver in due time a declaration mentioned in section 197A; to furnish a certificate as required in section 203 or 206C; to deduct and pay tax under section 226; to furnish a statement under section 192(2C); to deliver a copy of declaration referred to in section 206C(1A); to deliver within time a statement referred to in section 200(3)[86] or 206C(3)[86] or to deliver quarterly return under section 206A(1) or to deliver a statement in section 200(2A) or section 206C(3A)		alty in relation to declaration under section 197A, certificate in Form No. 16/16A as required under section 203, for failures in relation to return under sections 206 and 206C and for failure in relation to section 200(2A)/206C(3A), penalty not to exceed the amount of tax deductible or collectible)
272AA	Failure to comply with the provisions of section 133B	Any amount up to Rs. 1,000	Rs. 1,000
272B[87]	Failure to comply with provisions of section 139A	Rs. 10,000 **(with effect from September 1, 2019, Rs. 10,000 for each such default)**	—
272BB(1)	Failure to comply with the provisions of section 230A	Up to Rs. 10,000 (Rs. 5,000 up to May 31, 2001)	Rs. 10,000 (Rs. 5,000 up to May 31, 2001)
272BB(1A)	Failure to quote tax deduction or collection number	Rs. 10,000	—
272BBB	Failure to comply with provisions of section 206CA (applicable from June 1, 2002 to September 30, 2004)	Rs. 10,000	—

Notes :

• Penalty is not leviable under section 271, 271A, 271AA, 271B, 271BA, 271BB, 271C, 271CA, 271D, 271DA, **271DB**, 271E, 271F, 271FA, 271FAB, 271FB, 271G, 271GA, 271GB, 271H, 271-I, 271J, 272A(1)(*c*)/(*d*), 272A(2), 272AA(1), 272B, 272BB or 272BBB(1) if the assessee proves that there was reasonable cause for failure.

• The order imposing penalty must be passed before the expiry of the financial year in which the proceedings, which gave rise to penalty proceedings, are completed; or within 12 months from the end of the financial year in which the order of the first appellate authority is received by the Chief Commissioner or Commissioner, whichever period expires later. Where the assessment order, etc., is the subject-matter of revision by the Chief Commissioner or Commissioner under section 263 or 264, the limitation for passing penalty order is extended up to six months from the end of the month in which the order is passed.

• In the following cases, penalty can be imposed only with the prior approval of the Joint Commissioner:

1. Penalty by the Income-tax Officer where the penalty exceeds Rs. 10,000.

2. Penalty by the Assistant Commissioner or Deputy Commissioner where the penalty exceeds Rs. 20,000.

• While determining the amount of penalty, the law to be applied would be the law operative on the date when the default is committed. In the case of late filing of return, the default is said to be committed on the date when the return is to be filed and in the case of non-compliance of notice, default is taken to be committed on the day when the date given in the notice expires. In the case of concealment of income or furnishing of inaccurate particulars, the date of default is the date on which the return is filed and not the date on which income is earned.

---

86. Failure to submit quarterly TDS/TCS returns will not be governed by section 272A(2) with effect from July 1, 2012.

87. Penalty under section 272B is linked to a person (*i.e.*, a deductor who has committed the default of giving incorrect information of PAN of deductees). Maximum penalty is Rs. 10,000. It is not Rs. 10,000 per default. For instance, if it is found that in 30706 cases PAN is missing or incorrectly stated by the deductor, penalty of Rs. 30,70,60,000 (*i.e.*, Rs. 10,000 × 30706) cannot be imposed – *CIT* v. *DHTC Logistics Ltd.* [2014] 221 Taxman 83 (Delhi).

Penalty for concealment/under-reporting of income

138. Penalty in concealment/under-reporting of income is applicable as follows –

Section	*Nature*	*Applicability*	*Para No.*
A. ***Penalty where search has not been initiated***			
• Section 271(1)(*c*)	Concealment of income	Applicable up to the assessment year 2016-17	–[$]
• Section 270A	Under-reported income/ misreporting of income (not being covered by sections 68 to 69D)	Applicable from the assessment year 2017-18	138.1
• Section 271AAC	Unexplained cash credit/ unexplained investment/ undisclosed investment/ unexplained expenditure taxable under sections 68 to 69D	Applicable from the assessment year 2017-18 (amount of penalty is 6 per cent of unexplained cash credit/ unexplained investment, etc. Penalty can be avoided, if the assessee pays advance tax during the previous year and submits return of income after including unexplained cash credit, etc.)	–
B. ***Penalty where search has been initiated***			
• *Expln. 5* to section 271(1)	Undisclosed income/ asset found in search	Search is initiated before June 1, 2007	138.2-1
• *Expln. 5A* to section 271(1) and section 271AAA	Undisclosed income/ asset found in search	Search is initiated on or after June 1, 2007 but before July 1, 2012	138.2-2
• Section 271AAB(1)	Undisclosed income/ asset found in search	Search is initiated on or after July 1, 2012 but before December 15, 2016	138.2-3
• Section 271AAB(1A)	Undisclosed income/ asset found in search	Search is initiated on or after December 15, 2016	138.2-3

138.1 ***Penalty on the basis of misreporting of income applicable from the assessment year 2017-18 [Sec. 270A]*** - Section 270A has been inserted from the assessment year 2017-18. Under this section, the Assessing Officer, CIT (Appeals) or Principal CIT or CIT may, during the course of any proceedings under the Act, levy penalty if a person has under-reported his income.

138.1-1 *CASES OF UNDER-REPORTED INCOME* - A person shall be considered to have under-reported his income if, —

a. the income assessed is greater than the maximum amount not chargeable to tax, where no return of income is filed or **where return has been furnished for the first time under section 148**;

b. the assessed income is greater than the income determined upon processing under section 143(1)(*a*), where return is filed;

c. the income assessed is greater than the income assessed or reassessed immediately before such reassessment;

d. the income assessed or reassessed has the effect of reducing the loss or converting such loss into income;

e. the amount of deemed total income assessed or reassessed under section 115JB/115JC is greater than the deemed total income determined in the return processed under section 143(1)(*a*);

f. the amount of deemed total income assessed as per the provisions of section 115JB/115JC is greater than the maximum amount not chargeable to tax, where no return of income has been filed or **where return has been furnished for the first time under section 148**;

g. the amount of deemed total income reassessed as per the provisions of section 115JB/115JC is greater than the deemed total income assessed or reassessed immediately before such reassessment.

[$]For law applicable up to the assessment year 2016-17, log on to *taxmann.com/readyreckoner.aspx.*

138.1-2 *QUANTUM OF UNDER-REPORTED INCOME* - The amount of under-reported income shall be determined as follows –

Different situations	*Quantum of under-reported income*
Return has been furnished and income has been assessed for the first time	The difference between the amount of income assessed and the income determined under section 143(1)(*a*)
Return has not been furnished (or **where return has been furnished for the first time under section 148**) and income has been assessed for the first time	• *In the case of company/firm/local authority* - Income assessed • *In any other case* - The difference between the amount of income assessed and the maximum amount not chargeable to tax
Where income is not assessed for the first time	The difference between the amount of income assessed/reassessed/recomputed and the amount of income assessed/reassessed/recomputed in a preceding order
Where an assessment/reassessment has the effect of reducing the loss declared in the return or converting that loss into income	The difference between the loss claimed and the income (or loss) as assessed/reassessed
Where under-reported income arises out of determination of deemed income in accordance with the provisions of section 115JB/115JC	$(A - B) + (C - D)$

• *Calculation of under-reported income in case of applicability of provisions of section 115JB/115JC* - It shall be determined on the basis of the following formula –

Under-reported income = $(A - B) + (C - D)$		
A	=	The total income assessed as per the provisions other than the provisions contained in section 115JB or section 115JC (herein called general provisions).
B	=	The total income that would have been chargeable had the total income assessed as per the general provisions been reduced by the amount of under-reported income.
C	=	The total income assessed as per the provisions contained in section 115JB or section 115JC.
D	=	The total income that would have been chargeable had the total income assessed as per the provisions contained in section 115JB or section 115JC been reduced by the amount of under-reported income.

Note - Where the amount of under-reported income on any issue is considered both under the provisions contained in section 115JB or section 115JC and under general provisions, such amount shall not be reduced from total income assessed while determining the amount under item D.

• *Negative list* - Under-reported income shall not include the following –

a. where the assessee offers an explanation and the income-tax authority is satisfied that the explanation is *bona fide* and all the material facts have been disclosed;

b. where such under-reported income is determined on the basis of an estimate, if the accounts are correct and complete but the method employed is such that the income cannot properly be deducted therefrom;

c. where the assessee has, on his own, estimated a lower amount of addition or disallowance on the issue and has included such amount in the computation of his income and disclosed all the facts material to the addition or disallowance;

d. where the assessee had maintained information and documents as prescribed under section 92D, declared the international transaction and disclosed all the material facts relating to the transaction;

e. where the undisclosed income is on account of a search operation and penalty is leviable under section 271AAB.

138.1-3 *RATE OF PENALTY* - The rate of penalty shall be 50 per cent of the tax payable on under-reported income. However, in cases of under-reported income falling under misreporting of income, penalty shall be 200 per cent of the tax payable on such misreporting of income.

• *Misreporting of income [Sec. 270A(9)]* - Cases of misreporting of income shall be the following –

a. misrepresentation or suppression of facts;
b. failure to record investments in the books of account;
c. claim of expenditure not substantiated by any evidence;
d. recording of any false entry in the books of account;
e. failure to record any receipt in the books of account having a bearing on total income; and
f. failure to report any international transaction or any transaction deemed to be an international transaction or any specified domestic transaction, to which the provisions of Chapter X apply.

Income of the nature covered by **second proviso to section 56(2)(*viib*) shall be deemed to be misreporting of income** for the purpose of section 270A(9) (applicable from the assessment year 2020-21).

• *How to calculate tax on under-reported income* - The tax payable on under-reported income shall be calculated as follows –

Different situations	*Mode of computation of tax on under-reported income*
Case 1 - Where no return has been furnished (or **where return has been furnished for the first time under section 148**) and the income has been assessed for the first time	Amount of tax computed on (under-reported income + exemption limit)
Case 2 - Where total income determined under section 143(1)(*a*) or assessed/re-assessed/recomputed in a preceding order is a loss	Amount of tax computed on under-reported income, as if it were total income
Case 3 - In any other case	Tax on under-reported income is (*x* – *y*) *x* = Amount of tax computed on [under-reported income + total income determined under section 143(1)(*a*) or total income assessed/reassessed/recomputed in a preceding order] *y* = Amount of tax computed on total income determined under section 143(1)(*a*) or total income assessed/reassessed/recomputed in a preceding order

• *Double penalty not possible* - No addition or disallowance of an amount shall form the basis for imposition of penalty, if such addition or disallowance has formed the basis of imposition of penalty in the case of the person for the same or any other assessment year.

138.1-3E1 X (61 years) does not furnish his return of income for the assessment year 2019-20. The Assessing Officer completes assessment under section 144. Income assessed by the Assessing Officer is Rs. 1,14,00,000. It includes Rs. 40,00,000, being misreporting of income on account of misrepresentation or suppression of facts. Income of Rs. 1,14,00,000 includes a short-term capital gain of Rs. 18,00,000 on transfer of shares in the National Stock Exchange (as per documents made available by the assessee). Determine the amount of penalty under section 270A.

•

	Rs.
Income as per section 144	1,14,00,000
Less: Exemption limit	3,00,000
Under-reported income (out of which Rs. 40,00,000 is misreporting of income)	1,11,00,000

Computation of tax on under-reported income - In this case, return is not furnished and income is assessed for the first time. Mode of computation of tax on under-reported income as per *Case 1* (*supra*) is as follows –

	Rs.
Under-reported income	1,11,00,000
Add: Exemption limit	3,00,000
Total	1,14,00,000

	Rs.
Tax on Rs. 1,14,00,000 –	
Income-tax (15% of Rs. 18,00,000 and normal tax on balance of Rs. 96,00,000)	29,60,000
Add: Surcharge @ 15%	4,44,000
Add: Health and education cess	1,36,160
Tax on under-reported income	35,40,160

Computation of penalty –

	Under-reported income Rs.	*Misreporting of income Rs.*	*Total Rs.*
Under-reported income/misreporting of income	71,00,000	40,00,000	1,11,00,000
Tax on under-reported income/misreporting of income	22,64,427*	12,75,733**	35,40,160
Penalty leviable under section 270A (50% of tax on under-reported income, 200% of tax on misreporting income)	11,32,214	25,51,466	36,83,680

*71/111 of Rs. 35,40,160, **40/111 of Rs. 35,40,160.

138.1-3E2 X Ltd. is a domestic company. Its turnover for the previous year 2016-17 is Rs. 240 crore. For the assessment year 2019-20, tax is payable at the rate of 25 per cent on the income which is determined as follows –

	Income as per assessment order under section–		
	143(1) Rs.	*143(3) Rs.*	*147 Rs.*
Income	(–) 1,10,00,000	(–) 90,00,000	(–) 72,50,000
Add: Arithmetical error corrected while processing u/s 143(1)	20,00,000	–	–
Total	(–) 90,00,000	(–) 90,00,000	(–) 72,50,000
Add: Adjustment at the time of assessment/reassessment –			
- Addition because of misrepresentation or suppression of facts (a)	–	13,00,000	43,00,000
- Addition on estimation basis (accounts are correct and complete but method employed is such that income cannot be properly deduced therefrom) (b)	–	50,000	7,60,000
- Addition on account of under-reported income (c)	–	4,00,000	26,00,000
Assessed income	–	(–) 72,50,000	4,10,000

Determine the amount of penalty under section 270A.

•

In this case, addition (*a*) is on account of misreporting of income as per section 270A(9). Addition (*b*) is not treated as under-reported income. Addition (*c*) is treated as under-reported income. Tax on under-reported income/misreporting of income will be calculated as per *Case 2* given above. Penalty under section 270A may be calculated as follows –

	Order under section 143(3)		*Order under section 147*	
	Under-reported income Rs.	*Misreporting of income Rs.*	*Under-reported income Rs.*	*Misreporting of income Rs.*
Under-reported income/misreporting of income	4,00,000	13,00,000	26,00,000	43,00,000
Tax payable on the above income @ 25% (applicable rate) + HEC	1,04,000	3,38,000	6,76,000	11,18,000
Penalty leviable under section 270A				
- 50% of tax payable (under-reported income) [*see* Note]	52,000	–	3,38,000	–
- 200% of tax payable (misreporting of income)	–	6,76,000	–	22,36,000

Note - X Ltd. may apply under section 270AA for grant of immunity from imposition of penalty.

138.1-3E3 Recompute penalty under section 270A in the above example after making the following two alterations –
1. Under-reported income includes Rs. 50,000 on account of short-term capital gain chargeable under section 111A.
2. The assessee is X (born on August 31, 1976).

●

Penalty under section 270A may be calculated as follows –

	Order under section 143(3)		*Order under section 147*		*Total*
	Under-reported income Rs.	*Misre-porting of income Rs.*	*Under-reported income Rs.*	*Misre-porting of income Rs.*	*Rs.*
Under-reported income/misreporting of income	4,00,000	13,00,000	26,00,000	43,00,000	86,00,000
Tax payable on Rs. 86,00,000 (15% of Rs. 50,000 + normal tax on balance) + SC + SHEC	1,26,904[a]	4,12,439[b]	8,24,877[c]	13,64,220[d]	27,28,440
Penalty leviable under section 270A - 50% of tax payable (under-reported income) [*see* Note]	63,452	–	4,12,439	–	
- 200% of tax payable (misreporting of income)	–	8,24,878	–	27,28,440	

a. 4/86 of Rs. 27,28,440, *b.* 13/86 of Rs. 27,28,440, *c.* 26/86 of Rs. 27,28,440, *d.* 43/86 of Rs. 27,28,440

Note - X may apply under section 270AA for grant of immunity from imposition of penalty.

138.1-3E4 X (42 years) is a sole trader of a business. His income for the assessment year 2019-20 is determined as follows –

	Income as per assessment order under section –		
	143(1) Rs.	*143(3) Rs.*	*147 Rs.*
Income	4,90,000	8,66,000	81,58,000
Add: Arithmetical error corrected while processing u/s 143(1)	3,76,000	–	–
Total	8,66,000	8,66,000	81,58,000
Add: Adjustment at the time of assessment/reassessment –			
- Addition because of misrepresentation or suppression of facts (*a*)	–	70,00,000	23,00,000
- Addition on estimation basis (accounts are correct and complete but method employed is such that income cannot be properly deduced therefrom) (*b*)	–	12,000	22,000
- Addition on account of under-reported income (*c*)	–	2,80,000	6,10,000
Assessed income	–	81,58,000	1,10,90,000

Penalty proceeding has been initiated by the Assessing Officer in scrutiny assessment under section 143(3). Determine the amount of penalty under section 270A.

●

In this case, addition (*a*) is on account of misreporting of income as per section 270A(9). Addition (*b*) is not treated as under-reported income. Addition (*c*) is treated as under-reported income. Under-reported income is Rs. 72,80,000 (out of which Rs. 70,00,000 is misreporting of income). Tax on under-reported income/misreporting of income will be calculated as per *Case 3* given above. Penalty under section 270A may be calculated as follows –

	Rs.
x = Amount of tax computed on [under-reported income + total income determined under section 143(1)(*a*) or total income assessed/reassessed/ recomputed in a preceding order] Tax on [under-reported income : Rs. 72,80,000 + total income as per intimation under section 143(1) : Rs. 8,66,000], *i.e.*, tax on Rs. 81,46,000 + SC + HEC	25,81,207
y = Amount of tax computed on total income determined under section 143(1)(*a*) or total income assessed/reassessed/recomputed in a preceding order Tax on total income as per intimation under section 143(1) : Rs. 8,66,000, *i.e.*, tax on Rs. 8,66,000 + HEC	89,128
Tax on under-reported income [*x* – *y*]	24,92,079

Computation of penalty –			
	Under-reported income Rs.	*Misre-porting of income Rs.*	*Total Rs.*
Under-reported income/misreporting of income	2,80,000	70,00,000	72,80,000
Tax on under-reported income/misreporting of income	95,849*	23,96,230**	24,92,079
Penalty leviable under section 270A (50% of tax on under-reported income, 200% of tax on misreporting income)	47,925***	47,92,460	48,40,385

* 2,80,000/72,80,000 × Rs. 24,92,079, **70,00,000/72,80,000 × Rs. 24,92,079.

***X may apply under section 270AA for grant of immunity from imposition of penalty.

138.1-3E5 In the above example, the Assessing Officer in reassessment initiated penalty proceedings under section 270A. Determine the amount of penalty which can be imposed.

•

In this case, addition (*a*) is on account of misreporting of income as per section 270A(9). Addition (*b*) is not treated as under-reported income. Addition (*c*) is treated as under-reported income. Under-reported income is Rs. 29,10,000 (out of which Rs. 23,00,000 is misreporting of income). Tax on under-reported income/misreporting of income will be calculated as per *Case 3* given in para 138.1-3. Penalty under section 270A may be calculated as follows –

	Rs.
x = Amount of tax computed on [under-reported income + total income determined under section 143(1)(*a*) or total income assessed/reassessed/ recomputed in a preceding order] Tax on [under-reported income : Rs. 29,10,000 + total income as per assessment under section 143(3) : Rs. 81,58,000], *i.e.*, tax on Rs. 1,10,68,000 + SC+HEC	37,46,948
y = Amount of tax computed on total income determined under section 143(1)(*a*) or total income assessed/reassessed/recomputed in a preceding order Tax on total income as per assessment under section 143(3) : Rs. 81,58,000, *i.e.*, tax on Rs. 81,58,000 + SC + HEC	25,85,326
Tax on under-reported income [$x – y$]	11,61,623

Computation of penalty –			
	Under-reported income Rs.	*Misre-porting of income Rs.*	*Total Rs.*
Under-reported income/misreporting of income	6,10,000	23,00,000	29,10,000
Tax on under-reported income/misreporting of income	2,43,502*	9,18,121**	11,61,623
Penalty leviable under section 270A (50% of tax on under-reported income, 200% of tax on misreporting income)	1,21,751***	18,36,242	19,57,993

* 6,10,000/29,10,000 × Rs. 11,61,623, ** 23,00,000/29,10,000 × Rs. 11,61,623.

***X may apply under section 270AA for grant of immunity from imposition of penalty.

138.1-3E6 The following information is noted from the records of X Ltd. for the assessment year 2019-20 (annual turnover of X Ltd. is more than Rs. 250 crore since 2009-10) –

	General provisions Rs.	MAT Rs.
Income/book profit as per return of income	9,00,000	21,00,000
Add: Addition on estimated basis (not representing under-reported income)	20,000	Nil
Add: Misreporting of income (sale to D Ltd. not recorded correctly in books of account as discovered by the Assessing Officer) (as per assessment order)	40,000	40,000
Add: Under-reported income (weighted deduction is wrongly claimed under section 35) (as per assessment order)	50,000	Nil
Add: Under-reported income (deferred tax which appeared on the debit side of profit and loss account, not added by X Ltd.) (as per assessment order)	Nil	60,000
Net income/book profit (as per assessment order)	10,10,000	22,00,000

Determine the amount of penalty under section 270A.

•

Under-reported income will be calculated as follows –

	Rs.
A = Total income assessed under general provisions	10,10,000
B = A – under-reported income – misreporting of income (Rs. 10,10,000 – Rs. 40,000 – Rs. 50,000)	9,20,000
C = Book profit	22,00,000
D = Book profit – under-reported income – misreporting of income (Rs. 22,00,000 – Rs. 60,000) (Rs. 40,000 which is deducted under B will not be deducted again from D)	21,40,000
Under-reported income = (*A* – *B*) + (*C* – *D*) (out of which Rs. 40,000 is misreporting of income)	1,50,000

Tax on under-reported income -Tax on under-reported income/misreporting of income will be calculated as per *Case 3* given above. As the assessee is a company, tax on under-reported income is calculated at the applicable rate without separately calculating value of *x* and *y* –

Computation of penalty under section 270A –	
Tax on under-reported income –	
- 31.2% of Rs. 1,10,000	34,320
- 31.2% of Rs. 40,000	12,480
Penalty leviable under section 270A	
- 50% of tax payable (under-reported income) [*see* Note]	17,160
- 200% of tax payable (misreporting of income)	24,960

Note : X Ltd. may apply under section 270AA for grant of immunity from imposition of penalty.

138.1-3E7 In the assessment of X for the assessment year 2018-19 (previous year 2017-18), the Assessing Officer makes the following observations in his assessment order under section 143(3) –

- X has purchased diamonds for Rs. 18 lakh on September 6, 2017 for which he is unable to offer any explanation (investment not recorded in books of account).
- Car maintenance expenses debited in the books of account is Rs. 7,18,000. X has declared that 10 per cent of the expenditure pertains to personal use of car (and the same is added to net profit to calculate taxable income as submitted in the return of income). The Assessing Officer, however, does not agree to it and he treats 30 per cent of Rs. 7,18,000 on account of personal use of the car.

1. Can the Assessing Officer levy penalty under section 270A ?

2. Is it possible for the assessee to argue in the penalty proceedings that the aforesaid investment in diamonds has been made out of following additions made by the Department in earlier years —

Assessment years	*Additions made (in Rs.)*	*Whether penalty was levied earlier*
2017-18	5,00,000	Misreporting of income penalty levied under section 270A on Rs. 5,00,000
2016-17	2,00,000	Concealment penalty levied under section 271(1)(c) on Rs. 2,00,000
2015-16	*Nil*	—
2014-15	8,00,000	Concealment penalty levied on Rs. 8,00,000
2013-14	4,15,000	Concealment penalty levied under section 271(1)(*c*) on Rs. 3,00,000

•

The Assessing Officer cannot levy penalty under section 270A on account of disallowance of car expenditure on an estimated basis. Moreover, unexplained/unrecorded investment in diamond attracts provision of section 69. When income is taxed under sections 68 to 69D, tax is calculated as per provisions of section 115BBE. Under section 115BBE(1), Rs. 18,00,000 will be taxable @ 60%. The amount of tax shall be increased by surcharge (@ 25% of tax) and education cess. The effective amount of tax is 77.25%[88] of Rs. 18,00,000. When income is taxed under sections 68 to 69D, penalty under section 270A cannot be imposed. However, penalty can be imposed under section 271AAC. The amount of tax and penalty pertaining to unexplained/unrecorded investment of Rs. 18,00,000 will be calculated as follows –

88. It is 78 per cent for the assessment years 2019-20 and 2020-21.

	Rs.
Tax on Rs. 18,00,000 under section 115BBE(1) (60% of Rs. 18,00,000)	10,80,000
Add: Surcharge @ 25% of Rs. 10,80,000	2,70,000
Tax and surcharge	13,50,000
Add: Education cess @ 3% of 13,50,000	40,500
Tax liability	13,90,500
Penalty under section 271AAC [10% of tax under section 115BBE(1)] (*i.e.* 10% of Rs. 10,80,000)	1,08,000
Tax and penalty payable on unexplained investment	14,98,500

Penalty under section 271AAC cannot be levied, if the assessee pays advance tax during the previous year and submits return of income under section 139 after including the aforesaid income.

138.1-3E8 X does not agree with the calculation of penalty given above. He insists that penalty is not leviable because of the following reasons –

1. Investment in diamond was made out of additions made to his taxable income by the Assessing Officer in earlier years, as given in the table in the Example 138.1-3E7. No penalty in the current year should be levied when unrecorded investment was financed by income in respect of which concealment penalty was levied by the department in preceding years – *Anantharam Veerasinghaiah & Co.* v. *CIT* [1980] 123 ITR 457 (SC).

2. The scheme of section 270A(4)/(5) permits levy of penalty only if investment of the current year was financed out of additions made in earlier years and on those additions concealment penalty was not imposed. As given in the data above, the entire investment of Rs. 18,00,000 was made out of additions of earlier years and in respect of these additions concealment penalty was imposed.

•

Section 271AAC has been inserted by Taxation Laws (Second Amendment) Act, 2016. It is applicable from the assessment year 2017-18. By virtue of this amendment, penalty under section 270A cannot be imposed if income is taxable under sections 68 to 69D. In such cases, tax is payable within the parameters of section 115BBE and penalty can be imposed only under section 271AAC. The contention of X is, therefore, not tenable in law. The scheme of adjustment given under section 270A(4)/(5) does not have role to play in the case of unexplained cash credit/unexplained investment/investment not recorded in the books of account/unexplained expenditure.

138.1-4 *IMMUNITY FROM IMPOSITION OF PENALTY [SEC. 270AA]* - An assessee may make an application under section 270AA (applicable from the assessment year 2017-18) to the Assessing Officer for grant of immunity from imposition of penalty under section 270A and initiation of proceedings under section 276C/276CC. The benefit of section 270AA is available only if the assessee pays tax and interest payable [as per the order of assessment/reassessment order under section 143(3) or 147] within the period specified in such notice of demand and does not prefer an appeal against such assessment order. The assessee can make such application in Form No. 68 within 1 month from the end of the month in which the order of assessment or reassessment is received.

• The Assessing Officer shall, on fulfilment of the above conditions and after the expiry of period of filing appeal as specified in section 249(2), grant immunity from penalty/prosecution, where the penalty proceedings under section 270A have not been initiated on account of the circumstances of misreporting of income [as laid in section 270A(9)].

• The Assessing Officer is required to pass an order accepting (or rejecting) such application, within a period of 1 month from the end of the month in which such application is received. However, the Assessing Officer shall pass no order rejecting the application unless the assessee has been given an opportunity of being heard and the said order shall be final.

• No appeal under section 246A or an application for revision under section 264 shall be admissible against the order of the assessment/reassessment in a case where the order granting immunity is passed.

• The CBDT has clarified that where an assessee makes an application under section 270AA (seeking immunity from penalty proceedings in case of under-reporting of income), the Assessing Officer shall not take an adverse view in penalty proceedings under section 271(1)(*c*) in earlier assessment years just because the assessee has agreed on the issue in later assessment year by preferring an immunity under section 270AA – Circular No. 5/2018, dated August 16, 2018.

138.1-4E1 In example 138.1-3E1, X pays tax and interest immediately after service of notice of demand by the Assessing Officer. Can he avail of the benefit of section 270AA pertaining to grant of immunity from imposition of penalty under section 270A?

•

As assessment is completed under section 144, X cannot avail of the benefit of immunity from imposition of penalty by filing a petition to the Assessing Officer under section 270AA. This benefit is available if tax is computed under section 143(3) or under section 147.

138.2 ***Concealment penalty in search cases [Sec. 271(1),* Explanations 5 *and* 5A, *Secs. 271AAA, 271AAB]*** - These provisions are given below—

138.2-1 *PENALTY PROVISIONS, WHERE SEARCH IS INITIATED BEFORE JUNE 1, 2007* - *Explanation* 5 to section 271(1) is applicable if search is initiated before June 1, 2007.

138.2-2 *PENALTY PROVISIONS, WHERE SEARCH IS INITIATED ON OR AFTER JUNE 1, 2007 BUT BEFORE JULY 1, 2012* - If search is initiated on or after June 1, 2007 but before July 1, 2012, *Explanation 5A* to section 271(1) and section 271AAA are applicable.

138.2-2a SECTION 271AAA - Section 271AAA is applicable if—

a. a search[89] is initiated under section 132 on or after June 1, 2007, but before July 1, 2012;

b. there is some "undisclosed income"; and

c. undisclosed income pertains to a "specified previous year".

• *What is the quantum of concealment penalty* - If the above conditions are satisfied, 10 per cent of "undisclosed income" of the "specified previous year" is concealment penalty which can be imposed by the Assessing Officer in addition to tax. If section 271AAA is applicable, penalty under section 271(1)(*c*) cannot be imposed.

• *Is it possible to avoid the aforesaid penalty [Sec. 271AAA(2)]* - The aforesaid penalty of 10 per cent of "undisclosed income" of the "specified previous year" can be avoided if the following conditions are satisfied—

1. If the assessee in a statement under section 132(4) in the course of the search, admits the undisclosed income.

2. Further, he specifies the manner in which such income has been derived.

3. He substantiates the manner in which the undisclosed income was derived.

4. He pays the tax, together with interest[90], if any, in respect of the undisclosed income.

If the above 4 conditions are satisfied penalty under section 271AAA (*i.e.*, 10 per cent of "undisclosed income" of the "specified previous year") can be avoided.

• *What is "specified previous year"* - The aforesaid provisions of imposition of 10 per cent concealment penalty and the manner of avoiding it are applicable only when "undisclosed income" pertains to a "specified previous year". For this purpose "specified previous year" is any one or both of the following—

"Specified previous year" one	It is a previous year which satisfies all the following conditions— *a.* it ends before the date of search; *b.* the due date of filing return of income under section 139(1) has not expired before the date of search; *c.* before the date of search, the assessee has not submitted return of income for the above previous year
"Specified previous year" two	It is the previous year in which search is conducted.

It may be noted that in the cases given below, section 271AAA is not applicable as the previous year does not fall in any of the above stated "specified previous year". Consequently, in the cases given below, the normal provisions of section 271(1)(*c*) will be applicable—

Case 1 - Undisclosed income pertains to a previous year which has ended before the date of search and on the date of search the due date of filing return of income has expired. For instance, search is conducted on December 12, 2010 and undisclosed income pertains to the previous year 2009-10.

89. Where only there is a survey under section 133A, penalty under section 271AAA cannot be levied – *Sarat Chandra Sahoo* v. *CIT* [2015] 152 ITD 326 (Ctk.).

90. It is not the requirement that entire tax (along with interest) should be paid before filing of income-tax return—*CIT* v. *Pioneer Marbles & Interiors (P.) Ltd.* [2012] 50 SOT 571 (Kol.). In fact there is no time-limit for this purpose for payment of tax along with interest. Consequently, it is not open to the Assessing Officer to read a condition of time-limit into scheme of section 271AAA—*CIT* v. *Pioneer Online Ltd.* [2012] 52 SOT 94 (Kol.).

Case 2 - Undisclosed income pertains to a previous year which has ended before the date of search, on the date of search return of income has been submitted without disclosing undisclosed income, though due date of filing of return of income has not expired on the date of search. For instance, search is conducted on June 25, 2010. Undisclosed income pertains to previous year 2009-10. Return of income for the previous year 2009-10 has been submitted without disclosing undisclosed income on June 24, 2010.

- *What is undisclosed income* - For the purposes of section 271AAA, "undisclosed income" has been defined so as to mean—

1. Any income of the "specified previous years" represented, either wholly or partly, by any money, bullion, jewellery or other valuable article or thing or any entry in the books of account or other documents or transactions found in the course of a search under section 132, which has not been recorded on or before the date of search in the books of account or other documents maintained in the normal course relating to such previous year; or which has otherwise not been disclosed to the Commissioner before the date of the search.

2. Any income of the "specified previous years" represented, either wholly or partly, by any entry in respect of an expense recorded in the books of account or other documents maintained in the normal course relating to the specified previous year which is found to be false and would not have been found to be so had the search not been conducted.

138.2-2b EXPLANATION 5A TO SECTION 271 - If the following conditions are satisfied it will be assumed that the taxpayer has concealed the particulars of his income or furnished inaccurate particulars of income. In other words, if these conditions are satisfied normal concealment penalty (*i.e.*, 100 per cent - 300 per cent of tax sought to be evaded) can be imposed—

1. Search is conducted on or after June 1, 2007 but before July 1, 2012.

2. In the course of search the assessee is found to be the owner of (*a*) any money, bullion, jewellery or other valuable article or thing (referred to as "assets" in the *Explanation 5A*); or (*b*) any income based on any entry in any books of account or other documents or transactions and he claims that such assets or entry in the books of account or other documents or transactions represents his income (wholly or in part) for a previous year given below.

3. The above "assets" or income pertains to a previous year which has ended before the date of the search, the due date for filing the return of income for such year has expired and the assessee has not filed the return or return has been furnished without disclosing "undisclosed income".

If the above conditions are satisfied *Explanation 5A* will assume that the taxpayer has concealed the particulars of his income or furnished inaccurate particulars of his income and concealment penalty (100 per cent - 300 per cent of tax sought to be evaded) can be imposed under section 271(1)(*c*) even if such income is declared by the taxpayer in any return of income which is furnished on or after the date of search.

138.2-3 *PENALTY PROVISIONS WHERE SEARCH IS INITIATED ON OR AFTER JULY 1, 2012 [SEC. 271AAB(1)/(1A)]* - Section 271AAB is applicable if search is initiated on or after July 1, 2012, there is some "undisclosed income" and it pertains to a "specified previous year"[91]. In such a case, the assessee shall pay a penalty under section 271AAB in addition to tax as follows –

- *Quantum of penalty* - The quantum of penalty under section 271AAB is as follows –

Search is initiated on or after July 1, 2012 before but December 15, 2016 [Sec. 271AAB(1)]	*Search is initiated on or after December 15, 2016 [Sec. 271AAB(1A)]*
Case 1 - If undisclosed income is admitted during the course of search, the taxpayer will be liable for penalty at the rate of 10 per cent of undisclosed income provided the following conditions are satisfied— *a.* the assessee in the course of the search, in a statement under section 132(4) admits the undisclosed income and specifies the manner in which such income has been derived; *b.* he substantiates the manner in which the undisclosed income was derived; *c.* he pays the tax, together with interest, if any, in respect of the undisclosed income; and *d.* he furnishes the return of income for the specified previous year declaring such undisclosed income therein.	***Case 1*** - If the assessee satisfies conditions (*a*), (*b*), (*c*) and (*d*) given in *Column 1*, the penalty will be levied @ 30 per cent. ***Case 2*** - In any other case, penalty will be levied @ 60 per cent.

91. If these conditions are satisfied, penalty will be imposed under section 271AAB. In such a case, penalty under section 271(1)(*c*) or section 270A is not applicable.

Search is initiated on or after July 1, 2012 before but December 15, 2016 [Sec. 271AAB(1)]	*Search is initiated on or after December 15, 2016 [Sec. 271AAB(1A)]*
Case 2 - If undisclosed income is not admitted during the course of search but he satisfies conditions (*c*) and (*d*) (*supra*), he will be liable for penalty at the rate of 20 per cent of undisclosed income. ***Case 3*** - In a case not covered under (*1*) and (*2*) (*supra*), the taxpayer will be liable for penalty as follows – - Not less than 30 per cent (but not more than 90 per cent) of the "undisclosed income" of the "specified previous year" (up to the assessment year 2016-17). - 60 per cent of the "undisclosed income" of the "specified previous year" (with effect from the assessment year 2017-18).	

Note - Where the assessee, in course of search, made a statement under section 132(4) in which he admitted an undisclosed income and specified manner in which such income was earned and has also paid tax along with interest, he will be liable for penalty under *Case 1* (*supra*) (and not as per provisions of *Case 2* or *Case 3*) – *CIT* v. *Vishal Agarwal* [2018] 100 taxmann.com 283 (Kol.).

• *Is it possible to avoid penalty* - Unlike section 271AAA, penalty under section 271AAB cannot be avoided.

• *Specified previous year* - "Specified previous year" means the previous year in which search is conducted. It also includes the previous year which has ended before the date of search but the due date of furnishing return of income under section 139(1) has not expired before the date of search and the assessee has not furnished his return of income for the previous year.

Penalty for failure to furnish quarterly TDS/TCS return [Sec. 271H]

139. The Finance Act, 2012 has inserted section 271H with effect from July 1, 2012. Under section 271H, a person has to pay a penalty of not less than Rs. 10,000. It may be extended to Rs. 1,00,000. Penalty under section 271H is in addition to fees payable under section 234E. Penalty under section 271H is applicable in the following cases—

Case 1 - If a person fails to submit quarterly TDS/TCS return on or before the due date [sec. 271H(1)(*a*)].

Case 2 - If a person furnishes incorrect information in these quarterly returns [sec. 271H(1)(*b*)].

139.1 ***Is it possible to reduce or avoid penalty under section 271H*** - By virtue of sub-section (3) of section 271H, no penalty shall be levied for delay in furnishing of TDS/TCS quarterly return if such return is submitted within one year of the due date after payment of tax deducted/collected along with applicable interest and fee. This concession is given only in *Case 1* [*i.e.*, penalty under section 271H(1)(*a*)] and not in *Case 2*.

• *Provisions illustrated* - X Ltd. deducts tax under section 194-I on May 20, 2018 (rent paid Rs. 5,78,600, tax deducted Rs. 57,860). No other tax is deducted by X Ltd. during 2018-19. Due date of deposit of TDS is June 7, 2018. However, tax is deposited on June 18, 2018. Interest under section 201(1A)(*ii*) is Rs. 867 (*i.e.*, interest at the rate of 1.5 per cent per month for 1 months on Rs. 57,800). Quarterly return should be submitted for the first quarter of 2018-19 on or before July 31, 2018. However, the first quarter return is submitted on April 20, 2019.

Delay in submission of quarterly return is of 263 days. X Ltd. will have to pay fees of Rs. 52,600 under section 234E before submission of quarterly return. In this case, return is submitted within 1 year from the due date. TDS is deposited along with interest and fees before submission of quarterly return on April 20, 2019. Consequently, penalty under section 271H(1)(*a*) cannot be imposed.

If, however, the return is submitted on August 3, 2019 (and not on April 4, 2019), fees under section 234E will be Rs. 57,860 [*i.e.*, Rs. 200 per day × delay of 368 days comes to Rs. 73,600, which cannot be more than tax deducted]. X Ltd. will have to pay TDS, interest and fees before submission of quarterly return on August 3, 2019. The Assessing Officer can impose a minimum penalty of Rs. 10,000 under section 271H(1)(*a*). It may be extended to Rs. 1,00,000. Provisions of sub-section (3) of section 271H are not applicable, as return is submitted after 1 year from the regular due date. However, Commissioner can waive this penalty under section 273A(4). Alternatively, X Ltd. can seek relief under section 273B, if there is a reasonable cause for the said failure.

Interest

In certain circumstances the assessee becomes liable to pay interest to the revenue [para 142], while in certain cases the revenue is required to pay interest to the assessee [para 143]

Interest payable by the assessee from the assessment year 1989-90 onwards

142. Interest is payable by the assessee in the following cases :

142.1 ***For defaults in furnishing return of income [Sec. 234A]*** - If a return of income is furnished after the due date or is not furnished, the assessee is liable to pay interest under section 234A.

142.1-1 *HOW TO CALCULATE INTEREST* - Interest is calculated as under :

1. Rate of interest	1 per cent[92] per month or part of month (simple interest).
2. Period for which interest is payable.	Commencing on the date immediately following the due date for filing the return of income and ending on— *a.* the date of furnishing the return (where return has been filed after the due date) ; or *b.* the date of completion of assessment under section 144 (where no return has been furnished).
3. Amount on which interest is payable	It is calculated as under : *1.* Find out the tax on total income as determined under section 143(1) or on assessment under section 143(3) or section 147 or 153A (if the assessment is made for the first time under section 147 or 153A)[93] *2.* From the tax so determined, advance tax paid[94], tax deducted or collected at source, relief under section **89**/90/90A/91 and MAT/AMT credit under section 115JAA/115JD (but not tax paid under section 140A) shall be deducted.

142.1-2 *OTHER POINTS* - The following points shall also be kept in view :

142.1-2a SELF-ASSESSMENT TAX PAID BEFORE THE DUE DATE AND RETURN SUBMITTED AFTER DUE DATE - Interest would not be payable in a case where tax has been deposited prior to due date of filing of income-tax return even if the return of income is filed after the due date of furnishing such return —*CIT* v. *Dr. Prannoy Roy* [2009] 179 Taxman 53 (SC). It is not open to the Assessing Officer to charge interest under section 234A in a situation where the assessee has paid due taxes and merely filing of income-tax return is delayed.

142.1-2b WHEN ASSESSMENT IS MADE FOR THE FIRST TIME UNDER SECTION 147 - A belated return cannot be submitted after the expiry of one year from the end of the assessment year. If an assessment is made for the first time under section 147, then the assessee cannot be made liable to pay interest for the period during which it was not possible on the part of the assessee to file return (*i.e.*, after one year from the end of the assessment year) till issuance of notice under section 148—*Priti Pithawala* v. *ITO* [2003] 129 Taxman 79 (Bom.) (Mag.).

142.1-2c INTEREST IN THE CASE OF REASSESSMENT - Section 234A(3) is applicable if return of income is not submitted or submitted belatedly in the course of reassessment proceedings. Interest in such a case is payable by the assessee at the rate of 1 per cent per month (for part thereof) for the period of default. The period of default commences on the date immediately following the expiry of time given by notice under section 148 or 153A and ends on the date of furnishing of return (or on the date of completion of reassessment

---

92. 2 per cent upto May 31, 1999, 1.5 per cent from June 1, 1999 to May 31, 2001 and 1.25 per cent from June 1, 2001 to September 7, 2003.

93. If one has to calculate interest under section 234A for the purpose of self-assessment under section 140A, tax on returned income shall be taken.

94. Any instalment of advance tax paid in respect of fringe benefits for the assessment year 2010-11 shall be treated as advance income-tax paid by the concerned assessee for the assessment year 2010-11—Circular No. 2/2010, dated January 29, 2010.

under section 147 or 153A where no return has been furnished). Interest is payable on the amount by which the tax on the total income as reassessed exceeds the tax on the total income determined on the basis of the earlier assessment.

142.1-2d INCREASE/REDUCTION IN INTEREST - If as a result of an order under section 154, 155, 250, 254, 260, 262, 263, 264 or 245D(4), the tax payable is increased or reduced, as the case may be, the interest shall be increased/reduced accordingly.

142.1-2e REDUCTION OF INTEREST - There is no provision for reduction or waiver of interest [*see*, however, para 145].

142.1-2f DELAY DUE TO STRIKE - Interest should not be charged where delay in filing return is due to strike of personnel of Income-tax Department—*Income-tax Bar Association* v. *Chief CIT* [1990] 182 ITR 43 (Guj.).

142.1-2g NO OPPORTUNITY OF HEARING - The liability to pay interest under sections 234A, 234B and 234C is automatic and the question of granting opportunity of being heard does not arise—*CIT* v. *R. Ramalingair* [2000] 108 Taxman 1 (Ker.).

142.1-2h INTEREST MUST BE CHARGED IN THE ASSESSMENT ORDER - While charging interest under section 234A, 234B or 234C, the Assessing Officer is required to pass a specific order to this effect in its assessment order. When the assessment order is silent, as to whether any interest is leviable, the notice of demand under section 156 cannot be beyond the assessment order and the assessee cannot be served with any such notice demanding the interest. Interest cannot be charged by mere observation like charge interest as per law. It has to be by means of a speaking order—*CIT* v. *Inchcape India (P.) Ltd.* [2002] 124 Taxman 744 (Delhi), *CIT* v. *Ranchi Club Ltd.* [2001] 247 ITR 209/114 Taxman 414 (SC), *Tej Kumari* v. *CIT* [2001] 247 ITR 210/114 Taxman 404 (Pat.).

142.1-2i BOOKS OF ACCOUNT IN CUSTODY OF INCOME-TAX AUTHORITY - During the period when the books of account are in the custody of the concerned income-tax authorities, it is not possible for the taxpayer, to submit the return of income. Consequently, he cannot be saddled with liability to pay penal interest under section 234A for that period—*Paras Bansilal Patel* v. *B.M. Jindel* [2004] 135 Taxman 125 (Guj.).

142.1-2j ISSUE OF NOTICE UNDER SECTION 142(1) - Issue of notice under section 142(1)(*ii*) and 142(1)(*iii*) does not give the Assessing Officer jurisdiction to levy interest under section 234A—*CIT* v. *Ranchi Club Ltd.* [2001] 114 Taxman 414 (SC).

142.1-E1 Determine the amount of interest under section 234A in the following cases :

	X (22 years)	*Y (62 years)*	*X (P.) Ltd.*	*X(HUF)*
Due date of filing return for the assessment year 2019-20 (*a*)	July 31, 2019	July 31, 2019	November 30, 2019	September 30, 2019
Date of filing return (*b*)	Not filed	September 4, 2019	March 10, 2020	December 17, 2019
Date of payment of entire self assessment tax (*c*)	Not paid	September 1, 2019	January 3, 2020	November 20, 2020
Date of completion of assessment (*d*)	January 7, 2020	September 4, 2019	April 15, 2020	December 17, 2020
	Rs.	*Rs.*	*Rs.*	*Rs.*
Income declared	—	9,80,070	3,50,100	21,87,170
Income assessed	9,79,210	9,85,930	3,61,560	22,01,670
Advance tax paid during 2018-19	46,400	26,500	95,000	1,000
Tax deducted or collected at source	120	1,188	2,240	500
•				
Interest will be determined as under :				
Period of default (a part of month is taken as full month) [it is (*d*)–(*a*) in the case of X and (*c*)–(*a*) in other cases]	6 months	2 months	2 months	2 months
	Rs.	*Rs.*	*Rs.*	*Rs.*
Income assessed	9,79,210	9,85,930	3,61,560	22,01,670
Tax	1,08,342	1,07,186	1,08,468	4,73,001

	X (22 years)	Y (62 years)	X (P.) Ltd.	X(HUF)
Add: Surcharge	*Nil*	*Nil*	*Nil*	*Nil*
Tax and surcharge	1,08,342	1,07,186	1,08,468	4,73,001
Add: Health and education cess	4,333	4,287	4,339	18,920
Tax payable on assessed income	1,12,676	1,11,473	1,12,806	4,91,921
Less: Advance tax paid and tax deducted or collected at source	46,520	27,688	97,240	1,500
Shortfall	66,156	83,785	15,567	4,90,421
Shortfall (rounded off) (*e*)	66,100	83,700	15,500	4,90,400
Interest on (*e*) at the rate of 1% per month	3,966	1,674	310	9,808

142.1-E2 Determine the amount of interest under section 234A in the following cases —

	X Rs.	Y Rs.	Z Rs.
Due date of filing of return of income (*a*)	July 31, 2019	July 31, 2019	September 30, 2019
Actual date of filing of return of income (*b*)	November 6, 2019	November 6, 2019	December 15, 2019
Tax on income declared in the return (*c*)	56,000	56,000	68,000
Tax on income assessed by the Assessing Officer (*d*)	79,000	79,000	69,000
Advance tax paid during the financial year 2018-19 (*e*)	40,000	40,000	30,000
Tax deducted at source during the financial year 2018-19 (*f*)	4,000	4,000	9,000
Self-assessment tax paid (*g*)	36,000	10,000	12,000
Date of payment of self-assessment tax (*h*)	July 25, 2019	July 25, 2019	October 10, 2019

•

	X Rs.	Y Rs.	Z Rs.
Tax on assessed income after deducting advance tax and TDS [(*d*) – (*e*) – (*f*)]	35,000	35,000	30,000
Less: Self-assessment tax	36,000	10,000	12,000
Balance	(-) 1,000	25,000	18,000
Period of default (a part of month is taken as one month) [(*b*) – (*a*)]	4 months	4 months	3 months

In the case of X, the entire outstanding amount is paid by way of self-assessment tax on July 25, 2019 (*i.e.*, before the due date of submission of return of income). However, return of income is submitted after due date. Consequently, interest under section 234A is not applicable—*CIT* v. *Pranoy Roy* [2009] 179 Taxman 53 (SC).

In the case of Y, self-assessment tax is partly paid before the due date of submission of the return of income and return of income is submitted belatedly. Interest on Rs. 25,000 is payable under section 234A at the rate of 1 per cent per month for 4 months which comes to Rs. 1,000.

In the case of Z, self-assessment tax is paid partly but after the due date of submission of return of income. Interest is payable under section 234A on Rs. 30,000 for 1 month [*i.e.*, (*h*) – (*a*)] and on Rs. 18,000 for 2 months [*i.e.*, (*b*) – (*a*) – 1 month] at the rate of 1 per cent per month which comes to Rs. 660. In the case of *Pranoy Roy* (*supra*), the Court held that interest under section 234A was applicable if self-assessment tax was paid after the due date of submission of return of income. However, the Court's ruling did not indicate that in such a situation section 234A interest is applicable till the date of submission of return of income.

142.2 ***For failure to deduct or collect and pay tax at source [Sec. 201(1A) or 206C(7)]*** - The provisions are given below—

• *Default* - Interest is payable in respect of any of the following defaults—

1. If the person responsible for deducting/collecting tax at source does not deduct/collect tax at source, wholly or partly, under sections 192 to 196C and 206C.

2. After deducting/collecting tax, he fails to pay the same as required by the Act.

142.2-1 *INTEREST FOR FAILURE TO DEDUCT TAX AT SOURCE [SEC. 201(1A)]* - [$]In the above two cases, the person responsible for deducting tax at source is liable to pay interest as follows –

Rate of interest (per month or part)	*Period for which interest is payable*
1 per cent	From the date on which tax was deductible to the date on which tax is actually deducted
1.5 per cent	From the date on which tax was actually deducted to the date on which tax is actually paid

142.2-2 *INTEREST FOR FAILURE TO COLLECT TAX AT SOURCE [SEC. 206C(7)]* - In the above two cases [given in para 142.2], the person responsible for collecting tax at source is liable to pay. Interest is calculated at the rate of 1 per cent per month (or part thereof). Interest is payable on short payment or non-payment. It is payable from the date on which such tax was collectible to the date on which the tax is actually paid.

142.2-3 *RELIEF APPLICABLE FROM JULY 1, 2012* - The Finance Act, 2012 has amended the aforesaid provisions, with effect from July 1, 2012.

• *Relief for default in tax deduction* - After this amendment, the payer shall not be deemed to be an assessee in default if–

a. the resident recipient has included such income in the return submitted under section 139 and the recipient has paid tax on such income; and

b. the payer submits a certificate (in Form No. 26A[$$]) to this effect from a chartered accountant.

In such a case, interest shall be payable at the rate of 1 per cent from the date on which tax was deductible to the date of furnishing of return of income by the resident recipient.

• *Relief for default in tax collection* - Similar rule is applicable from July 1, 2012 in the case of non-collection of tax at source. However, the certificate of chartered accountant should be taken in Form No. 27BA[$$].

• *Date of applicability of relief* - The aforesaid relaxation given by the Finance Act, 2012 is applicable only when the recipient (or the purchaser in the case of tax collection) is resident and the default pertains to the period commencing on or after July 1, 2012. If the recipient (or the purchaser in the case of tax collection) is a non-resident (or if such recipient/purchaser is a resident but default pertains to the period prior to July 1, 2012), the amendment made by the Finance Act, 2012 is not applicable. In such a case, one can take shelter of judicial rulings where the Courts held that interest cannot be recovered for non-deduction or short-deduction from the payer for any period which falls after the date of payment of tax by the recipient – *CIT* v. *Rishikesh Apartments Co-op. Housing Society Ltd.* [2001] 119 Taxman 239 (Guj.), *CIT* v. *Eli Lilly & Co. (India) (P.) Ltd.* [2009] 178 Taxman 505 (SC).

142.2-4 *OTHER POINTS* - One should keep in view the following points—

• *Time limit* - No time-limit is fixed for passing orders under section 201(1A)—*U.P. State Industrial Development Corpn. Ltd.* v. *ITO* [2002] 81 ITD 173 (Lucknow), *Thai Airways International Public Co. Ltd.* v. *CIT* [2005] 2 SOT 389 (Delhi). However, Courts have held that action under section 201 would be possible by a competent authority under the Act within period of four years—*CIT* v. *NHK Japan Broadcasting Corpn.* [2008] 172 Taxman 230 (Delhi). Where the Assessing Officer did not know such default or the assessee delayed the proceedings, there can be some extension to the said limit of four years. The Assessing Officer is required to pass a speaking order for charging interest under section 201(1A)—*Mittal Bhai Investment (P.) Ltd.* v. *ITO* [2005] 92 TTJ (Jp.) 286.

• *When tax is not deducted under section 192 on a uniform basis for each month* - If there is no overall short deduction of tax under section 192 but a few months tax deducted is lower as compared to other months, interest on the basis of monthly shortage cannot be charged under section 201. There is an express provision under section 192(3) authorising the person responsible for deducting tax to increase or reduce the amount to be deducted under section 192 for the purpose of adjusting any excess or deficiency arising out of any previous deduction or failure to deduct during the financial year—*Hero Honda Motors Ltd.* v. *ITO* [2000] 112 Taxman 154 (Delhi) (Mag.), *Vinsons* v. *Third ITO* [2004] 89 ITD 267 (Mum.).

[$] CBDT *via* Circular No. 11/2017, dated March 24, 2017 has issued guidelines to reduce or waived off the interest charged under section 201(1A)(*i*) in case of assessee's failure to deduct tax at source in some specified cases. For these guidelines, log on to *taxmann.com/readyreckoner.aspx.*

[$$] Electronic submission of Form No. 26A/27BA is required. For detailed procedure, log on to *taxmann.com/readyreckoner.aspx.*

If performance incentive can be qualified in the month of March of the financial year and tax is deducted from April to February on the basis of average rate of tax (which is calculated without considering the amount of performance incentive which was not qualified), interest under section 201(1A) for short deduction cannot be imposed—*CIT* v. *Marubeni India (P.) Ltd.* [2007] 165 Taxman 467 (Delhi).

• *Bona fide estimation of income* - Section 192 is very categorical to state that tax has to be deducted from income under the head 'Salaries' computed on the estimated income of the assessee under this head. What has to be seen is whether the employer company has acted *bona fide* or not while computing the tax liability of its employees for the purpose of deducting tax at source—*Associated Cement Co. Ltd.* v. *ITO* [2000] 74 ITD 369/111 Taxman 251 (Mum.) (Mag.). In a step further the Gujarat High Court in a similar fashion in *CIT* v. *Oil & Natural Gas Corpn. Ltd.* [2002] 125 Taxman 698 held that any addition or disallowance in the hands of the employee does not reflect in any manner on the estimate of the employer.

• *Meaning of "month"* - For calculating interest under section 201(1A), term "month" must be given ordinary meaning of term of 30 days period and not British calendar month—*Navayuga Quazigund Expressway (P.) Ltd.* v. *CIT* [2015] 64 taxmann.com 212 (Hyd.). Consider this example—Date of tax deduction : July 12, 2018, due date of deposit : August 7, 2018, actual date of deposit : August 10, 2018, interest of only one month can be charged under section 201(1A).

142.3 ***Interest for default in payment of advance tax [Sec. 234B]*** - Under section 234B(1), interest is payable as follows :

When interest is payable	*Amount on which interest is payable*	*Rate of interest*	*Period for which interest is payable*
(1)	*(2)*	*(3)*	*(4)*
An assessee who is liable to pay advance tax, has failed to pay such tax	Interest is payable on assessed tax	Simple interest @ 1 per cent[95] for every month or part of month	From April 1 of the assessment year to the date of determination of total income under section 143(1) or where regular assessment is made to the date of such regular assessment.[96]
An assessee who has paid advance tax but the amount of advance tax paid by him is less than 90 per cent of assessed tax	Assessed tax *minus* advance tax[97]	Simple interest @ 1 per cent[95] for every month or part of month	From April 1 of the assessment year to the date of determination of total income under section 143(1) or where regular assessment is made to the date of such regular assessment[96]

• *Assessed tax - Meaning of* - 'Assessed tax' means the tax on the total income determined under section 143(1) and where regular assessment is made, the tax on total income determined under such regular assessment as reduced by (*a*) tax deducted/collected at source on any income which is subject to such deduction or collection and which is taken into account in computing such total income, (*b*) relief/deduction of tax claimed under section **89**/90/90A/91 and (*c*) tax credit claimed under section 115JAA or 115JD.

• *Reduction or waiver of interest - See* para 145.

• *Adjustment when tax is paid before regular assessment under section 140A* - If before the date of determination of total income under section 143(1) or completion of a regular assessment, tax is paid on the basis of self-assessment under section 140A, the interest shall be calculated as under :

a. up to the date of payment of tax under section 140A, interest will be calculated as mentioned in the table above; and

95. 2 per cent before June 1, 1999, 1.5 per cent from June 1, 1999 to May 31, 2001 and 1.25 per cent from June 1, 2001 to September 7, 2003.

96. Wherever a regular assessment is made under section 143(3), date of intimation under section 143(1) is not relevant and interest under section 234B would be charged up to date of regular assessment—*Manish D. Shah* v. *C.M. Betgeri, CIT* [2009] 185 Taxman 247 (Bom.).

97. Any instalment of "advance tax paid in respect of fringe benefits" for assessment year 2010-11 shall be treated as advance income-tax paid by the concerned assessee for assessment year 2010-11— Circular No. 2/2010, dated January 29, 2010.

b. from the date of payment of tax under section 140A, interest will be calculated on the amount by which advance tax and tax paid under section 140A falls short of the assessed tax.

From the amount of interest computed above, amount paid under section 140A towards interest chargeable under section 234B shall be deducted.

• *Adjustment in the case of reassessment/re-computation under section 147 or 153A [Sec. 234B(3)]* - If as a result of reassessment/re-computation under section 147or 153A, the amount on which interest was initially payable is increased, the taxpayer will be liable to pay additional interest at the rate of 1 per cent per month (or part of month). This additional interest is payable for the following period –

- *Up to May 31, 2015* - For the period starting from the date of determination of total income under section 143(1) or regular assessment and ending on the date of reassessment/re-computation.
- *From June 1, 2015* - For the period commencing on the first day of the assessment year and ending on the date of reassessment/re-computation.

• *Where an application for settlement is made under section 245C(1) [Sec. 234B(2A)]* - Sub-section (2A) has been inserted with effect from June 1, 2015. It provides that where an application for settlement is made under section 245C(1), the assessee shall be liable to pay simple interest at the rate of 1 per cent for every month (or part of a month) comprised in the period commencing on the first day of April of such assessment year and ending on the date of making such application, on the additional amount of income-tax. Further, where as a result of an order of the Settlement Commission under section 245D(4) for any assessment year, the amount of total income disclosed in the application under section 245C(1) is increased, the assessee shall be liable to pay simple interest at the rate of 1 per cent for every month (or part of a month) comprised in the period commencing on the first day of April of such assessment year and ending on the date of such order, on the amount by which the tax on the total income determined on the basis of such order exceeds the tax on the total income disclosed in the application filed under section 245C(1). Where, as a result of a rectification order under section 245D(6B), the amount on which interest was payable under the above provisions has been increased or reduced, as the case may be, the interest shall be increased or reduced accordingly.

• *Adjustment in the case of rectification/revision/modification under sections 154, 155, 250, 254, 260, 262, 263, 264, 245D(4)* - If as a result of an order under section 154, 155, 250, 254, 260, 262, 263, 264 or 245D(4), the amount on which interest was payable under section 234B(1)/(3) has been increased/reduced, the interest shall be increased/reduced accordingly. In the case of increase in interest liability, the Assessing Officer will serve on the assessee a notice of demand specifying the sum payable. In the case where interest is reduced, the excess interest shall be refunded.

• *Shipping business of non-residents* - The Board is of the opinion that non-resident assessees engaged in the business of carriage by shipping of passengers and goods, etc., shall be liable to pay interest under sections 234B and 234C or entitled to interest under section 244A in respect of their income attributable to the business of such carriage of passengers and goods, etc.—Circular No. 9/2001[$], dated July 9, 2001.

• *Payment by cheque* - A harmonious reading of provisions of rule 7 of the Central Government Account (Receipts and Payment) Rules, 1983 and rules 79 and 80 of the Treasury Rules of the Central Government, makes it clear that Government dues can be presented in the form of cheque into the accredited bank. Upon tendering of a cheque, if it is not dishonoured later, it shall be deemed that payment has been made on the date when it was handed over to the Government's bankers—*K. Saraswatty* v. *P.S.S. Somasundram Chettiar* [1989] 4 SCC 527 (SC), *CIT* v. *Kumudam Publications (P.) Ltd.* [1981] 128 ITR 617 (Mad.), *Sahara Airlines Ltd.* v. *CIT (Appeals)* [2000] 110 Taxman 378 (Govt. of India).

• *Shortfall because of legal interpretation* - If short payment of advance tax is mainly because of *bona fide* dispute regarding interpretation of law, interest under section 234B is not applicable—*CIT* v. *Sedco Forex International Drilling Co. Ltd.* [2004] 134 Taxman 109 (Uttaranchal).

• *Interest under sections 234B and 234C in the case of non-resident assessee* - In the case of a non-resident/foreign company, all payments received from Indian sources are subject to TDS and hence, such assessee is not liable to interest under section 234B/234C—*Cable News Network LP, LLLP* v. *DIT* [2010] 129 TTJ (Delhi) 177.

• *Tax deductible but not actually deducted* - If tax is deductible at source but the payer has not deducted it, the recipient cannot be burdened with interest under sections 234B and 234C. However, section 209 has been amended from the financial year 2012-13 to the effect that where a person has received any income without deduction or collection of tax, he shall be liable to pay advance tax in respect of such income.

[$] For Circular No. 9/2001, log on to *taxmann.com/readyreckoner.aspx.*

142.4 ***For deferment of advance tax [Sec. 234C]*** - Interest is payable under section 234C [for reduction/waiver of interest - *see* para 145] if an assessee has not paid advance tax or underestimated instalments of advance tax. Interest is to be computed on the following basis from the assessment year 1995-96 onwards.

142.4-1 *CATEGORY A* - This category covers the following assessees—

- Any non-corporate assessee (up to the assessment year 2016-17).

In this case, interest under section 234C is payable as follows -

When interest is payable under section 234C	*Rate of interest*	*Period of interest*	*Amount on which interest is payable*
If advance tax paid on or before September 15 is less than 30% (*a—b*)	Simple interest @ 1 per cent per month[99]	3 months	30% (*a—b*)—*c*
If advance tax paid on or before December 15 is less than 60% (*a—b*)	Simple interest @ 1 per cent per month[99]	3 months	60% (*a—b*)—*d*
If advance tax paid on or before March 15 is less than 100% (*a—b*)	Simple interest @ 1 per cent[99]	—	100% (*a—b*)—*e*

Notes :

a. Tax on the total income declared in the return filed by the assessee.

b. Total of (*i*) tax deducted/collected at source on any income which is subject to such deduction or collection and which is taken into account in computing such total income, (*ii*) relief/deduction of tax claimed under section **89**/90/90A/91; and (*iii*) tax credit under section 115JD.

c. Amount of advance tax paid[98] on or before September 15 of the financial year immediately preceding the relevant assessment year.

d. Amount of advance tax paid[98] on or before December 15 of the financial year immediately preceding the relevant assessment year.

e. Amount of advance tax paid[98] on or before March 15 of the financial year immediately preceding the relevant assessment year.

142.4-2 *CATEGORY B* - This category covers the following assessees—

- A corporate assessee.
- A non-corporate assessee (from the assessment year 2017-18) [but not being an assessee who declares his business/professional income in accordance with the provisions of section 44AD(1)/44ADA(1) and discussed in para 142.4-3].

In these cases, interest under section 234C is payable as follows -

When interest is payable under section 234C	*Rate of interest*	*Period of interest*	*Amount on which interest is payable*
If advance tax paid on or before June 15 is less than 12% (*a—b*)	Simple interest @ 1 per cent per month[99]	3 months	15% (*a—b*)—*c*
If advance tax paid on or before September 15 is less than 36% (*a—b*)	Simple interest @ 1 per cent per month[99]	3 months	45% (*a—b*)—*d*
If advance tax paid on or before December 15 is less than 75% (*a—b*)	Simple interest @ 1 per cent per month[99]	3 months	75% (*a—b*)—*e*
If advance tax paid on or before March 15 is less than 100% (*a—b*)	Simple interest @ 1 per cent[99]	—	100% (*a—b*)—*f*

98. Any instalment of "advance tax paid in respect of fringe benefits" for assessment year 2010-11 shall be treated as advance income-tax paid by assessee concerned for assessment year 2010-11— Circular No. 2/2010, dated January 29, 2010.

99. 1.5 per cent up to May 31, 2001 and 1.25 per cent from June 1, 2001 to September 7, 2003.

Notes :

a. Tax on the total income declared in the return filed by the assessee.

b. Total of (*i*) tax deducted/collected at source on any income which is subject to such deduction or collection and which is taken into account in computing such total income, (*ii*) relief/deduction of tax claimed under section **89**/90/90A/91; and (*iii*) tax credit under section 115JAA or 115JD.

c. Amount of advance tax paid[1] on or before June 15 of the financial year immediately preceding the relevant assessment year.

d. Amount of advance tax[1] paid on or before September 15 of the financial year immediately preceding the relevant assessment year.

e. Amount of advance tax[1] paid on or before December 15 of the financial year immediately preceding the relevant assessment year.

f. Amount of advance tax[1] paid on or before March 15 of the financial year immediately preceding the relevant assessment year.

142.4-3 *CATEGORY C* - This category covers the following assessees—

- An assessee who declares his business/professional income in accordance with the provisions of section 44AD(1)/ section 44ADA(1) (applicable from the assessment year 2017-18)

In the case of an assessee, who declares his business/professional income in accordance with the provisions of section 44AD(1)/section 44ADA(1), interest under section 234C is payable (in respect of non-payment or short payment of advance tax pertaining to eligible business/profession) as follows—

When interest is payable under section 234C	*Rate of interest*	*Period of interest*	*Amount on which interest is payable*
If advance tax paid on or before March 15 is less than 100% (*a*—*b*)	Simple interest @ 1 per cent	—	100% (*a*—*b*)—*c*

Notes:

a. Tax on the total income declared in the return filed by the assessee.

b. Total of (*i*) tax deducted/collected at source on any income which is subject to such deduction or collection and which is taken into account in computing such total income, (*ii*) relief/deduction of tax claimed under section 90 or 91 on account of tax paid in a country outside India, (*iii*) relief of tax claimed under section 90A on account of tax paid in any specified territory outside India; and (*iv*) tax credit under section 115JD.

c. Amount of advance tax paid on or before March 15 of the financial year immediately preceding the relevant assessment year.

142.4-4 *SHORT PAYMENT OF ADVANCE TAX IN CASE OF CAPITAL GAINS/CASUAL INCOME/INCOME FROM NEW BUSINESS OR PROFESSION/DIVIDEND INCOME [FIRST PROVISO TO SEC. 234C(1)]* - No interest will be levied in respect of any shortfall in the payment of advance tax due on the returned income if—

a. the shortfall is on account of an underestimate or failure to estimate the amount of capital gains or income of the nature referred to in section 2(*24*)(*ix*) (*i.e.*, lottery income, gambling income, etc.) or (with effect from the assessment year 2017-18) income from new business/profession or dividend income; and

b. the assessee has paid the whole of the amount of tax payable in respect of such income, as part of the remaining instalments of advance tax which are immediately due (after accrual of such income), or if no instalment is due, then such tax is paid before the end of the financial year.

Examples illustrating computation of interest

142-E1 During the financial year 2018-19, X (36 years) pays the following instalments of advance tax :

	Rs.
First instalment on June 15, 2018	52,000
Second instalment on September 15, 2018	1,02,000
Third instalment on December 10, 2018	1,60,000
Fourth instalment on March 13, 2019	30,000
Fifth instalment on March 20, 2019	20,000

1. Any instalment of "advance tax paid in respect of fringe benefits" for assessment year 2010-11 shall be treated as advance income-tax paid by assessee concerned for assessment year 2010-11— Circular No. 2/2010, dated January 29, 2010.

The regular assessment for the assessment year 2019-20 is completed on January 10, 2020 and income determined by the Assessing Officer is Rs. 20,30,740 (income as per income-tax return : Rs. 20,18,140, addition made by the Assessing Officer : Rs. 12,600). He is also entitled to tax credit of Rs. 2,800 on account of tax deducted at source.

Self assessment tax is not paid. Is he liable for interest under section 234B or 234C?

●

Interest liability under section 234B :

	Rs.
Income computed by the Assessing Officer	20,30,740
Tax on Rs. 20,30,740 [for rates, *see* Annex 1]	4,38,590
Less : Tax deducted at source	2,800
Assessed tax	4,35,790
90% of assessed tax	3,92,211
Advance tax paid during the financial year 2018-19 (Rs. 52,000 + Rs. 1,02,000 + Rs. 1,60,000 + Rs. 30,000 + Rs. 20,000)	3,64,000
Since advance tax paid during the financial year is less than 90% of assessed tax, X is liable to pay interest under section 234B as follows –	
Assessed tax	4,35,790
Less: Advance tax paid during the financial year 2018-19	3,64,000
Short fall	71,790
Short fall (rounded off)	71,700
Period for which interest is payable (from April 1, 2019 to January 10, 2020)	9 months (and a few days)
Period for which interest is payable (rounded off)	10 months
Rate of interest	1% per month
Amount of interest under section 234B (Rs. 71,700 × 1% × 10)	7,170
Interest liability under section 234C –	
Income as per return of income	20,18,140
Tax on Rs. 20,31,670 (for rates, *see* Appendix 1)	4,34,660
Less : Tax deducted at source	2,800
Assessed tax	4,31,860
First instalment (due date : June 15, 2018)	
15% of assessed tax	64,779
12% of assessed tax	51,823
Advance tax actually paid up to June 15, 2018	52,000
Since advance tax paid is not less than 12% of assessed tax, interest is not payable for short payment of first instalment of advance tax.	
Second instalment (due date : September 15, 2018)	
45% of assessed tax	1,94,337
36% of assessed tax	1,55,470
Advance tax actually paid up to September 15, 2018 (Rs. 52,000 + Rs. 1,02,000)	1,54,000
Since advance tax paid is less than 36% of assessed tax, interest is payable for short payment of second instalment of advance tax.	
Short fall (45% of assessed tax : Rs. 1,94,337 – advance tax paid up to September 15, 2018 : Rs. 1,54,000)	40,337
Short fall (rounded off)	40,300
Interest for short payment of second instalment (Rs. 40,300 × 1% × 3 months)	1,209
Third instalment (due date : December 15, 2018)	
75% of assessed tax	3,23,895
Advance tax actually paid up to December 15, 2018 (Rs. 52,000 + Rs. 1,02,000 + 1,60,000)	3,14,000
Since advance tax paid is less than 75% of assessed tax, interest is payable for short payment of third instalment of advance tax.	
Short fall (75% of assessed tax : Rs. 3,23,895 – advance tax paid up to December 15, 2018 : Rs. 3,14,000)	9,895
Short fall (rounded off)	9,800
Interest for short payment of third instalment (Rs. 9,800 × 1% × 3 months)	294

	Rs.
Fourth instalment (due date : March 15, 2019)	
100% of assessed tax	4,31,860
Advance tax actually paid up to March 15, 2019 (Rs. 52,000 + Rs. 1,02,000 + Rs. 1,60,000 + Rs. 30,000)	3,44,000
Since advance tax paid is less than 100% of assessed tax, interest is payable for short payment of fourth instalment of advance tax.	
Short fall (100% of assessed tax : Rs. 4,31,860 – advance tax paid up to March 15, 2019 : Rs. 3,14,000)	87,860
Short fall (rounded off)	87,800
Interest for short payment of fourth instalment (Rs. 87,800 × 1%)	878
Interest payable under section 234C (Rs. 1,209 + Rs. 294 + Rs. 878)	2,381

142-E2 X (50 years) is a business person. For the previous year 2018-19, he reports the following transactions in his return of income –

	Rs.
Income from brokerage and commission (business was established in 1982)	14,64,970
Long-term capital gain on sale of gold on September 18, 2018	3,00,000
Income from commission agency business (new business started on November 4, 2018)	6,69,560
Amount deposited in PPF on March 20, 2019	1,50,000
Prepaid tax –	
TDS/TCS	23,400
Advance tax paid on –	
- June 13, 2018	21,000
- September 15, 2018	49,000
- December 14, 2018	1,50,000
- March 15, 2019	2,00,000

Calculate the amount of interest payable under section 234C.

•

Interest under section 234C for short payment of first instalment of advance tax (i.e., on or before June 15, 2018) - For this purpose, long-term capital gain generated after June 15, 2018 and new business started after June 15, 2018 shall not be considered. Short fall will be calculated as follows –

	Rs.
Income from brokerage and commission	14,64,970
Any other income	*Nil*
Gross total income	14,64,970
Less: Deduction under section 80C	1,50,000
Net income	13,14,970
Tax (including health and education cess)	2,15,270
Less: TDS/TCS	23,400
Assessed tax	1,91,870
15% of assessed tax	28,781
12% of assessed tax	23,025
Advance tax paid up to June 15, 2018	21,000
Short fall (for short payment of first instalment of advance tax, interest under section 234C is not applicable if advance tax paid up to June 15, 2018 is not less than 12% of assessed tax. In this case, X has paid advance tax of Rs. 21,000 which is less than 12% of assessed tax of Rs. 23,025. In such a case, interest is payable under section 234C. Short fall will be calculated as the difference between 15% of assessed tax and advance tax paid up to June 15, 2018, *i.e.*, Rs. 28,781 – Rs. 21,000. It comes to Rs. 7,781) (rounded off)	7,700
Interest under section 234C for short payment of first instalment of advance tax (interest on Rs. 7,700 @ 1% per month for 3 months)	231

Interest under section 234C for short payment of second instalment of advance tax (i.e., on or before September 15, 2018) - For this purpose, long-term capital gain generated after September 15, 2018 and new business started after September 15, 2018 shall not be considered. Short fall will be calculated as follows –

	Rs.
Assessed tax	1,91,870
45% of assessed tax	86,342
36% of assessed tax	69,074
Advance tax paid up to September 15, 2018 (Rs. 21,000 + Rs. 49,000)	70,000
Short fall (for short payment of second instalment of advance tax, interest under section 234C is not applicable if advance tax paid up to September 15, 2018 is not less than 36% of assessed tax. In this case, X has paid advance tax of Rs. 70,000 which is more than 36% of assessed tax of Rs. 69,074. If advance tax paid up to September 16, 2018 is shorter than Rs. 69,074, short fall will be calculated by taking the difference between 45% of assessed tax and advance tax paid up to September 15, 2018)	*Nil*
Interest under section 234C for short payment of second instalment of advance tax	*Nil*

Interest under section 234C for short payment of third instalment of advance tax (i.e., on or before December 15, 2018) - Short fall will be calculated as follows –

	Rs.
Income from brokerage and commission	14,64,970
Income from business newly set-up on November 4, 2018	6,69,560
Long-term capital gain	3,00,000
Gross total income	24,34,530
Less: Deduction under section 80C	1,50,000
Net income	22,84,530
Tax (including education cess)	4,86,573
Less: TDS/TCS	23,400
Assessed tax	4,63,173
75% of assessed tax	3,47,380
Advance tax paid up to December 15, 2018 (Rs. 21,000 + Rs. 49,000 + Rs. 1,50,000)	2,20,000
Short fall (rounded off)	1,27,300
Interest under section 234C for short payment of third instalment of advance tax (interest on Rs. 1,27,300 @ 1% per month for 3 months)	3,819

Interest under section 234C for short payment of fourth instalment of advance tax (i.e., on or before March 15, 2019) - Short fall will be calculated as follows –

	Rs.
Assessed tax	4,63,173
Advance tax paid up to March 15, 2019 (Rs. 21,000 + Rs. 49,000 + Rs. 1,50,000 + Rs. 2,00,000)	4,20,000
Short fall (rounded off)	43,100
Interest under section 234C for short payment of fourth instalment of advance tax (interest on Rs. 43,100 @ 1%)	431

Interest payable under section 234C : Rs. 4,481.

142-E3 X (40 years) owns a manufacturing business. Turnover of the business for the previous year 2018-19 is Rs. 1,79,09,060 (Rs. 40,80,000 received by cheque and balance in cash). He does not maintain books of account. The following transactions are noted from his return of income (which he will upload in ITR-4) for the assessment year 2019-20 –

	Rs.
Business income under section 44AD (6% of Rs. 40,80,000 + 8% of balance of Rs. 1,38,29,060) (TDS/TCS : Rs. 9,000)	13,51,125
Rental income from a commercial property purchased on December 18, 2018 (let out @ Rs. 3,00,000 per month from January 1, 2019, municipal tax : nil, interest : nil, tax deducted by tenant : Rs. 90,000 @ 10 per cent)	9,00,000
Interest on bank FD (tax deducted by bank : Rs. 4,00,000)	40,00,000
PPF deposit on March 20, 2019	1,50,000

	Rs.
Advance tax paid on –	
- June 14, 2018	1,08,000
- July 15, 2018	1,62,000
- December 15, 2018	2,70,000
- March 15, 2019	4,00,000
- March 31, 2019	3,00,000

Calculate the amount of interest payable under section 234C.

●

	Rs.
Income from house property (Rs. 9,00,000 – deduction under section 24 @ 30%)	6,30,000
Business income under section 44AD	13,51,125
Bank interest	40,00,000
Gross total income	59,81,125
Less: Deduction under section 80C	1,50,000
Net income	58,31,130
Tax on net income	17,86,744

Section 234C does not provide method of calculating tax separately on business income (covered by section 44AD) and other incomes. In this case, business income is Rs. 13,51,125 and gross total income is Rs. 59,81,125. Tax pertaining to business income may be calculated on the basis of these figures which comes to Rs. 4,03,622 (*i.e.,* Rs. 17,86,744 × Rs. 13,51,125 ÷ Rs. 59,81,125).

	Tax pertaining to –	
	Income u/s 44AD	*Other incomes*
	Rs.	*Rs.*
Tax on income	4,03,622	13,83,122
Less: TDS/TCS	9,000	4,90,000
Assessed tax	3,94,622	8,93,122
15% of assessed tax (12% of assessed tax : Rs. 1,07,175)	–	1,33,968
45% of assessed tax (36% of assessed tax : Rs. 3,21,524)	–	4,01,905
75% of assessed tax	–	6,69,842
100% of assessed tax	3,94,622	8,93,122

Computation of interest under section 234C –

	Rs.
First instalment (advance tax paid up to June 15, 2018 is not less than 12% of assessed tax, interest under section 234C is not applicable for short payment of first instalment)	*Nil*
Second instalment (advance tax paid up to September 15, 2018 is less than 36% of assessed tax, interest under section 234C is applicable) (short-fall : Rs. 4,01,905 – Rs. 1,08,000 – Rs. 1,62,000 = Rs. 1,31,905) (Rs. 1,31,900 × 0.01 × 3 months)	3,957
Third instalment (short-fall : Rs. 6,69,842 – Rs. 1,08,000 – Rs. 1,62,000 – Rs. 2,70,000 = Rs. 1,29,842) (Rs. 1,29,800 × 0.01 × 3 months)	3,894
Fourth instalment (short-fall : Rs. 3,94,622 + Rs. 8,93,122 – Rs. 1,08,000 – Rs. 1,62,000 – Rs. 2,70,000 – Rs. 4,00,000 = Rs. 3,47,742) (Rs. 3,47,700 × 0.01)	3,477
Total	11,328

142-E4 X (28 years) (a businessman whose turnover is Rs. 30 lakh) pays Rs. 10,000 as advance tax on March 15, 2019 (no instalment of advance tax is paid on September 15, 2018 and December 15, 2018). He further paid advance tax of Rs. 12,000 on March 31, 2019. He files his return of income on November 10, 2019 (income declared : Rs. 6,28,150). On November 10, 2019, he pays Rs. 10,600 (Rs. 8,600 by way of tax and Rs. 2,000 by way of interest for not paying advance tax in time and for late filing of return of income). His assessment for the year 2019-20 is completed on March 14, 2020 (income assessed : Rs. 6,43,000). He is also entitled for tax credit of Rs. 5,230 on account of tax deducted at source. Is he liable for interest under sections 234A, 234B and 234C ?

●

Interest liability under section 234A

	As per return of income	*As per assessment order*
Due date of return	July 31, 2019	July 31, 2019
Date of filing of return	November 10, 2019	November 10, 2019
Period of default (a part of month is taken as full month)	4 months	4 months
	Rs.	*Rs.*
Income	6,28,150	6,43,000
Tax on income	38,130	41,100
Add : Surcharge[2]	—	—
Tax	38,130	41,100
Add : Health and education cess	1,525	1,645
Tax payable	39,655	42,745
Less : Advance payment of tax	22,000	22,000
Tax deducted at source	5,230	5,230
Assessed tax	12,425	15,515
Assessed tax (rounded off)	12,400	15,500
Interest on assessed tax @ 1% per month for 4 months	496	620
Interest liability under section 234B		
Assessed tax (as computed above)	34,425	37,515
90% of assessed tax	—	33,764
Advance tax paid during 2018-19	22,000	22,000
Shortfall from April 1, 2019 to November 10, 2019	12,425	15,515
Shortfall (rounded off)	12,400	15,500
Period of default (April 1, 2019 to November 10, 2019)	8 months	8 months
Interest @ 1% per month for 8 months on shortfall	992	1,240
Shortfall from November 10, 2019 to March 14, 2020 [*i.e.*, Rs. 37,515— Rs. 22,000 (advance tax) — Rs. 7,479, self-assessment tax under section 140A paid on November 10, 2019—*see* Note 1]	—	8,036
Shortfall (rounded off)	—	8,000
Period of default (December 1, 2019 to March 14, 2020, in the shortfall of 8 months period up to November 30, 2019 is included)	—	4 months
Interest on Rs. 8,000 for 4 months @ 1% per month	—	320
Interest under section 234B	—	1,560
Interest liability under section 234C		
Income as per return	6,28,150	
Tax on Rs. 6,28,150 (*a*)	39,655	
Less : Tax deducted at source (*b*)	5,230	
Assessed tax (*a—b*)	34,425	
Advance tax paid on or before June 15, 2018 (*c*)	*Nil*	
Advance tax paid on or before September 15, 2018 (*d*)	*Nil*	
Advance tax paid on or before December 15, 2018 (*e*)	*Nil*	
Advance tax paid on or before March 15, 2019 (*f*)	10,000	
Interest on 15% (*a—b*)—(*c*) [*i.e.*, Rs. 5,164 @ 1% per month for 3 months (Rs. 5,100 × 3 × 1/100)]	153	
Interest on 45% (*a—b*)—(*d*) [*i.e.*, Rs. 15,491 @ 1% per month for 3 months (Rs. 15,400 × 3 × 1/100)]	462	
Interest on 75% (*a—b*)—(*e*) [*i.e.* Rs. 25,819 @ 1% per month for 3 months (Rs. 25,800 × 3 × 1/100)]	774	
Interest on (*a—b—f*) (*i.e.*, Rs. 24,425) @ 1% (Rs. 24,400 × 1/100)	244	
Total	1,633	

2. Surcharge is not applicable as income does not exceed Rs. 50 lakh.

Notes :

1. In this example, X has paid Rs. 10,600 on November 10, 2019 under section 140A. Out of Rs. 10,600, Rs. 2,000 is paid towards interest under sections 234A, 234B and 234C. As per calculation given below, interest liability comes to Rs. 3,121. Hence, as per *Explanation* to section 140A(1), Rs. 3,121 shall be adjusted towards payment of interest and the balance Rs. 7,479 (*i.e.*, Rs. 10,600 — Rs. 3,121) is to be adjusted towards the tax payable.

	Rs.
Interest under section 234A as per return of income up to November 10, 2019	496
Interest under section 234B as per return of income up to November 10, 2019	992
Interest under section 234C	1,633
Total interest as per return of income	3,121

2. Net tax and interest payable is to be computed as under :

Tax on Rs. 5,82,500	42,745
Add : Interest	
❑ Under section 234A	620
❑ Under section 234B	1,560
❑ Under section 234C	1,633
Total	46,558
Less : Prepaid tax	
❑ Tax deduction at source	5,230
❑ Advance tax	22,000
❑ Self-assessment tax under section 140A	10,600
Balance payable (rounded off)	8,730

142.5 ***Interest on excess refund [Sec. 234D]*** - Section 234D was inserted (with effect from June 1, 2003[3]) to charge interest on excess refund granted at the time of summary assessment.

• *Interest under section 234D(1)* - In any of the following two cases, interest is attracted under section 234D(1)—

Case one - If any refund is granted under section 143(1) but no refund is due on regular assessment.

Case two - If any refund is granted to the assessee under section 143(1) and the refund so granted exceeds the amount refundable on regular assessment.

For the aforesaid purpose, regular assessment means assessment under section 143(3) or 144. If an assessment is made for the first time under section 147 or section 153A, the assessment so made shall be regarded as a regular assessment.

• *Computation of interest* - In any of the above two cases, interest is payable under section 234D(1) as follows—

Rate of interest	0.5 per cent (from June 1, 2003 to September 7, 2003 : 2/3 per cent) per month or part of a month
Period for which interest is payable	The period commencing from the date of grant of refund under section 143(1) to date of regular assessment
Amount on which interest is payable	In *Case One* on whole of the amount refunded; in *Case Two* on the excess of amount refunded under section 143(1) over the amount refundable on regular assessment.

• *Adjustment under section 234D(2)*[4] - Where, as a result of an order under section 154 or 155 or 250 or 254 or 260 or 262 or 263 or 264 or an order of the Settlement Commission under section 254D(4) the amount of

3. It has been clarified (by inserting an *Explanation* to section 234D) that the provisions of this section will be applicable to any proceeding which is completed on or after June 1, 2003, irrespective of the assessment year to which it pertains.

4. For the purpose of section 234D, where there is no regular assessment, then assessment made for first time under section 147 or 153A shall be regarded as a regular assessment. Conversely, where assessment had already been completed under section 143(3), reassessment done under section 147 cannot be held as regular assessment and in such a case interest under section 234D cannot be charged—*Dredging Corporation of India Ltd.* v. *CIT* [2011] 13 taxmann.com 37 (Visakha.), *K. Anji Reddy* v. *CIT* [2013] 59 SOT 92 (Hyd.). Likewise, where refund is not granted to assessee under section 143(1) but it is granted pursuant to orders passed by the Commissioner (Appeals), section 234D is not applicable—*DIT* v. *Delta Air Lines Inc.* [2012] 21 taxmann.com 511 (Bom.).

refund granted under section 143(1) is held to be correctly allowed, either in whole or in part, as the case may be, then the interest chargeable under section 234D(1), shall be reduced accordingly.

142.5-E1 For the assessment year 2019-20, X files return of income on September 30, 2019 (income declared in the return Rs. 4,55,000, advance tax : Rs. 47,940). The Assessing Officer refunds under section 143(1) the excess tax paid by X on July 20, 2020 as follows—

	Rs.
Tax on Rs. 4,55,000	10,250
Add : Health and education cess	410
Tax	10,660
Add : Interest under different sections	3,500
Total	14,160
Less : Prepaid tax	42,533
Refund	28,373
Add : Interest under section 244A	2,264
Amount refunded (rounded off)	30,640

The Assessing Officer issues notice under section 143(2) on August 16, 2020. The assessment is completed under section 143(3) on March 26, 2021. Income assessed is (a) Rs. 4,55,000, (b) Rs. 4,80,000; or (c) Rs. 7,85,000. Assume that interest under section 234C etc., is (a) Rs. 3,500, (b) Rs. 3,630 or (c) Rs. 6,550, respectively in the three cases, find out interest under section 234D.

●

	If assessed income is		
	Rs. 4.55 lakh	*Rs. 4.8 lakh*	*Rs. 7.85 lakh*
	Rs.	*Rs.*	*Rs.*
Income-tax on assessed income	10,250	11,500	69,500
Add : Surcharge	—	—	—
Tax and surcharge	10,250	11,500	69,500
Add : Health and education cess	410	460	2,780
Tax payable	10,660	11,960	72,280
Add : Interest	3,500	3,630	6,550
Total	14,160	15,590	78,830
Less : Prepaid tax	42,533	42,533	42,533
Tax refund due	28,373	26,940	-
Add : Interest under section 244A	2,264	2,152	-
Refund (rounded off)	30,640	29,090	-
Amount refunded under section 143(1) on July 20, 2020 (*a*)	30,640	30,640	30,640
Amount of tax or refund as per assessment order under section 143(3) dated March 26, 2021 (*b*)	30,640	29,090	
Excess refund given earlier [*a* - *b*]	-	1,550	30,640
Rounded off	-	1,500	30,600
Period from July 20, 2020 to March 26, 2021	-	9 months	9 months
Interest @ 0.5 per cent per month under section 234D	-	67.50	1,377

142.6 ***For making late payment of income-tax [Sec. 220(2)]*** - If any assessee fails to pay any tax (other than advance tax) specified in a demand notice within 30 days of the service of notice of demand, he is liable to pay interest at the rate of 1 per cent[5] for every month or a part of a month from the expiry of 30 days of the service of the demand notice.

The following points should also be kept in view :

• The Chief Commissioner (or Commissioner) may reduce or waive the amount of interest payable by an assessee under section 220(2), if, he is satisfied that payment of such interest would cause genuine hardship to the assessee; the default in the payment of the amount on which interest was payable due to circumstances beyond the control of the assessee; and the assessee has co-operated in any inquiry relating to the assessment or in any proceeding for the recovery of any amount due from him.

• Where an assessment order is cancelled under section 146 or cancelled/set aside by an appellate/revisional authority and the cancellation/setting aside becomes final (*i.e.*, it is not varied as a result of further appeals/revisions), no interest under section 220(2) can be charged in pursuance to the original demand notice. The necessary corollary of this point will be that even when the assessment is reframed, interest can be charged only after the expiry of 35 days from the date of service of demand notice pursuant to such fresh assessment order—Circular No. 334, dated April 3, 1982.

• Section 220 has been amended (with effect from July 1, 2012) to provide that when interest is charged under section 201(1A) on the amount specified in the intimation issued under section 200A(1), then no interest will be charged for the same amount for the same period under section 220(2).

• Where the assessment made originally by the Assessing Officer is either varied or even set aside by one appellate authority but on further appeal, the original order of the Assessing Officer is restored either in part or wholly, the interest payable under section 220(2) will be computed with reference to the due date reckoned from the original demand notice and with reference to the tax finally determined. The fact that during an intervening period, there was no tax payable by the assessee under any operative order would make no difference to this position—Circular No. 334, dated April 3, 1982.

The observation given in Circular No. 334 does not find support in the judicial pronouncement given by the Apex Court in *Vikrant Tyres Ltd.* v. *First ITO* [2001] 115 Taxman 202. In this case, the assessee deposits the demand made by the Assessing Officer and goes in appeal. The appellate authority decides the issue in favour of the assessee and the tax collected is refunded. In further appeal by the revenue before the High Court, the assessee loses the case. Fresh demand notices are issued to the assessee demanding interest under section 220(2) for the period commencing from the refund of tax consequent upon the first appellate order. The assessee disputes the charge of interest from back date when he has satisfied with all the demands raised from time to time.

The Supreme Court held that for invoking section 220 one of the conditions is that if there is a default in payment of amount demanded under a notice by the revenue within the time stipulated therein and if such a demand is not satisfied, interest is leviable under section 220(2). However, Court held that the section cannot be invoked to revive a demand notice, which has already been fully satisfied. However, landmark ruling of the Supreme Court has been superseded by the finance (No. 2) Act, 2014 with effect from October 1, 2014. The amended provisions provide that where any notice of demand has been served upon an assessee and any appeal or other proceeding, as the case may be, is filed or initiated in respect of the amount specified in the said notice of demand, then such demand shall be deemed to be valid till the disposal of appeal by the last appellate authority or disposal of proceedings, as the case may be and such notice of demand shall have effect as provided in section 3 of the Taxation Laws (Continuation and Validation of Recovery Proceedings) Act, 1964.

142.6-E1 For the assessment year 2007-08, X is served on January 23, 2009, with a demand notice for payment of Rs. 16,000 as tax. Determine the amount of interest payable if (*1*) tax of Rs. 16,000 is paid on April 16, 2009, or (*2*) if X is allowed to pay tax in equal instalments of Rs. 4,000 on April 16, 2009, May 1, 2009, June 1, 2009 and July 1, 2009.

•

In this case, demand notice is served on January 23, 2009. The grace period of 30 days expires on February 22, 2009. Interest is, therefore, payable from February 22, 2009 to the date of actual payments, as under :

1. Under situation (*1*), interest is chargeable at the rate of 1% per annum on Rs. 16,000 from February 23, 2009 to April 16, 2009 at the rate of 1% per month.

2. Under situation (*2*), interest is chargeable at the rate of 1% per month on Rs. 16,000 from February 23, 2009 to April 16, 2009.

Further, he is liable for interest @ 1% per month on Rs. 12,000 from April 16, 2009 to April 30, 2009; on Rs. 8,000 from May 1, 2009 to May 31, 2009 and on Rs. 4,000 from June 1, 2009 to June 30, 2009.

---

5. Up to May 31, 2001 : 1.5 per cent from June 1, 2001 to September 7, 2003 : 1.25 per cent.

142.7 ***Fees for default in furnishing quarterly TDS/TCS returns [Sec. 234E, applicable from July 1, 2012]*** - Where a person fails to furnish quarterly TDS/TCS return, he shall be liable to pay, by way of fee, a sum of Rs. 200 for every day during which the failure continues. This provision will be applicable from July 1, 2012. This fees will be in addition to other consequences under the Act. However, the fees shall not exceed the amount of tax deductible/collectible. After July 1, 2012, it will not be possible to submit belatedly quarterly TDS/TCS return without payment of fees under section 234E. *See* also para 137.3.

142.8 ***Fee for default in furnishing return of income [Sec. 234F, applicable from the assessment year 2018-19]*** - A fee for delay in furnishing of return shall be levied for assessment year 2018-19 under section 234F where the return is not filed within the due dates given under section 139(1). The amount of fee under section 234F is as follows –

1. A fee of Rs. 5,000 shall be payable, if the return is furnished after the due date but on or before December 31 of the assessment year.

2. A fee of Rs. 10,000 shall be payable in any other case.

3. However, in a case where the total income does not exceed Rs. 5 lakh, the fee amount shall not exceed Rs. 1,000.

Interest payable to assessee [Sec. 244A]

143. Interest is payable where any refund arises due to any excess payment of tax. Under the provisions there is no need for making claim for refund. When refund is of any advance tax (including tax deducted or collected at source), the interest is payable at the rate of 0.5 per cent (2/3 per cent from June 1, 2002 to September 7, 2003, 0.75 per cent from June 1, 2001 to May 31, 2002 and 1 per cent up to May 31, 2001) per month or part of a month from the first day of the assessment year to the date of grant of refund. No interest is, however, payable if the excess payment is less than 10 per cent of the tax determined on regular assessment, or under section 143(1).

Where refund is of tax other than advance tax or tax deducted or collected at source, interest is payable at the rates given above from the date of payment of such tax or penalty up to the date on which the refund is granted[6].

143.1 ***Provisions applicable from June 1, 2016*** -The above mode of computation of interest under section 244A has been modified with effect from June 1, 2016 on the following lines -

• *Category 1 - Refund out of TDS, TCS and advance tax* - Where refund arises out of TDS, TCS or advance tax paid during the financial year immediately prior to the assessment year, interest shall be calculated at the rate of 0.5 per cent per month (or part thereof) for the following period—

Situation 1 [if return of income is submitted on or before the due date of submission of return of income given under section 139(1)] - In this case, interest is payable from the first day of the assessment year to the date on which refund is granted.

Situation 2 [in any other case] - In this case, interest is payable from the date of furnishing of return of income to the date on which refund is granted.

• *Category 2 - Refund out of self-assessment tax paid under section 140A* - Where the refund is out of self-assessment tax paid under section 140A, such interest shall be calculated at the rate of 0.5 per cent per month (or part thereof) from the date of furnishing of return of income or the date of payment of self-assessment tax, whichever is later, to the date on which the refund is granted.

• *Category 3 - Refund which arises out of appeal effect* - Where a refund arises out of appeal effect being delayed beyond the time prescribed under section 153(5) (*i.e.*, 3 months from the end of the month in which appellate order is received by CIT), the assessee shall be entitled to receive an additional interest (over and above interest given under *Category 1* or *Category 2*). Additional interest on such refund shall be calculated at the rate of 3 per cent per annum, for the period beginning from the date following the date of expiry of the time allowed under section 153(5) to the date on which the refund is granted. Where extension is

---

6. The Delhi High Court in the case of *CIT* v. *Sutlej Industries Ltd.* [2010] 190 Taxman 136 and the Kolkata Tribunal in the case of *DIT* v. *The Royal Bank of Scotland* [2010] 8 taxmann.com 278 held that the assessee is on principle entitled to interest on self-assessment tax paid in terms of section 244A(1)(*b*) from the date of payment of such amount up to the date on which refund is actually granted. For calculating interest under section 244A(1)(*b*) relevant date is date of payment of tax and not date on which amount of tax collected is credited to account of Central Government by an agent of the Central Government—*CIT* v. *Asian Paints Ltd.* [2011] 12 taxmann.com 484 (Bom.).

granted by the Principal CIT/CIT by invoking proviso to section 153(5), the period of additional interest, if any, shall begin from the expiry of such extended period.

• *Category 4 - Refund of TDS to deductor (applicable from April 1, 2017)* - Section 244A(1B) has been inserted from April 1, 2017[7]. It provides that where refund of any amount becomes due to the deductor, such person shall be entitled to receive, in addition to the refund, simple interest on such refund. Interest will be calculated at the rate of 0.5 per cent per month (or part of a month). Interest will be available from the date on which claim for refund is made in the prescribed form to the date on which the refund is granted. Where refund arises on account of giving effect to an appellate order under section 250/254/260/262, interest will be available from the date of deposit of TDS to the date on which refund is granted. However, interest shall not be allowed for the period for which the delay (in the proceedings resulting in the refund) is attributable to the deductor.

143.1-1 *NO INTEREST IN SOME CASES* - No interest under *Category 1* or *Category 2* shall be payable, if the amount of refund is less than 10 per cent of the tax as determined under section 143(1) or on regular assessment.

143.1-E1 X is a businessman. Tax audit under section 44AB is applicable. Due date of submission of return of income for the assessment year 2019-20 is September 30, 2019. Return is, however, uploaded on September 27, 2019. Intimation under section 143(1) is received by e-mail on October 8, 2020. Date of intimation and date of grant of refund is October 6, 2020. Refund is calculated as follows –

	Rs.
Tax on income assessed	2,92,430
Add: Interest under section 234C	18,000
Total	3,10,430
Less: Credit for prepaid tax –	
- TDS, TCS and tax paid in advance	4,70,000
- Self-assessment tax paid on August 18, 2019	9,000
Refund due	1,68,570

Determine the amount of interest payable by the Government under section 244A.

•

Refund of Rs. 1,68,570 may be segregated as follows –

Option 1 - Rs, 9,000 may be taken as refund of self-assessment tax (SAT) and the balance of Rs. 1,59,570 may be taken as refund of TDS/TCS/advance tax (TDS/TCS/AT).

Option 2 - As no formula for segregation is provided, one can also assume that the entire refund pertains to refund of TDS/TCS/advance tax (TDS/TCS/AT).

In the two alternatives given above, interest under section 244A will be calculated as follows –

	Option 1		*Option 2*
Nature of refund	SAT	TDS/TCS/AT	TDS/TCS/AT
Amount of refund (in Rs.)	9,000	1,59,570	1,68,570
Amount of refund (in Rs.) (rounded off for the purpose of calculation of interest)	9,000	1,59,500	1,68,500
Period for which interest is available	From 27-9-19 to 6-10-20	From 1-4-19 to 6-10-20	From 1-4-19 to 6-10-20
No. of months (a part of month is taken as full month)	13	19	19
Interest @ 0.5% per month (in Rs.)	585	15,152.50	16,007.50

Amount of interest is higher in *Option 2.* Interest payable by the Government is Rs. 16,007.50.

143.1-E2 Assume that the amount of TDS/TCS/advance tax is Rs. 3,20,000 in the above example. Determine the amount of interest payable under section 244A.

•

7. For earlier period, one can claim interest under Circular No. 11/2016[$], dated April 26, 2016.

[$] For Circular No. 11/2016, log on to *taxmann.com/readyreckoner.aspx*.

If TDS/TCS/advance tax is Rs. 3,20,000, amount due for refund is Rs. 18,570. It is less 10% of tax determined under section 143(1). Therefore, no interest is payable by the Government under section 244A.

143.1-E3 Assume in example 143.1-E1 that return is uploaded on November 4, 2019 after due date of submission of return of income. No other change in data, determine interest under section 244A.

•

	Option 1		*Option 2*
Nature of refund	SAT	TDS/TCS/AT	TDS/TCS/AT
Amount of refund (in Rs.)	9,000	1,59,570	1,68,570
Amount of refund (in Rs.) (rounded off for the purpose of calculation of interest)	9,000	1,59,500	1,68,500
Period for which interest is available	From 4-11-19 to 6-10-20	From 4-11-19 to 6-10-20	From 4-11-19 to 6-10-20
No. of months (a part of month is taken as full month)	12	12	12
Interest @ 0.5% per month (in Rs.)	540	9,570	10,110

143.1-E4 X Ltd. is entitled to a refund of Rs. 11,76,790 for the assessment year 2014-15. This refund arises because of a favourable verdict given by the Karnataka High Court on February 10, 2019. The judgment is received by the CIT on March 3, 2019. The concerned Assessing Officer grants refund on July 25, 2019 (*Situation 1*) or August 17, 2019 (*Situation 2*). The Commissioner gives no extension under section 153(5). Determine the amount of interest payable by the Government under section 244A(1A).

•

By virtue of section 153(5), the Assessing Officer is supposed to give appeal effect within 3 months from the end of the month in which the Commissioner receives the appeal order. This time-limit expires on June 30, 2019. Refund is given after June 30, 2019. Additional interest is payable by the Government under section 244(1A) as follows –

	Situation 1	*Situation 2*
Date of expiry of time-limit under section 153(5)	June 30, 2019	June 30, 2019
Period for which interest is payable under section 244A(1A)	July 1, 2019 to July 25, 2019	July 1, 2019 to August 17, 2019
No. of months (a part of month is ignored when interest is payable on per annum basis as per rule 119A)	0	1 month
Amount of refund (rounded off) (in Rs.)	11,76,700	11,76,700
Interest @ 3% per annum (in Rs.)	*Nil*	2,941.75

143.2 ***Other points*** -The following points should be noted (where interest is payable for the period commencing June 1, 2016 or otherwise) -

• If as a result of an order under section 143(3), 144, 147, 154, 155, 250, 254, 260, 262, 263, 264 or 245D(4), the amount on which interest was payable has been increased/reduced, the interest shall be increased/reduced accordingly. If interest is reduced, the Assessing Officer will send a notice of demand in the prescribed form specifying the amount of the excess interest paid and requiring him to pay such amount.

• *Vide* Instruction No. 2/2007, dated March 28, 2007, the Board has reminded all Assessing Officers that while granting refund to the assessees, care should be taken to ensure that any interest payable under section 244A on the amount of refund due should be granted simultaneously with the grant of refund and there should, in no case, be any omission or delay in the grant of such interest. Failure to do so will be viewed adversely by the Board and the officer concerned will be held personally accountable, inviting appropriate action from the Board.

• Section 244A(2) provides that in the event the proceeding resulting in refund has been delayed for some reasons attributable to the assessee, the period of delay so attributable shall be excluded from the period for which the interest is payable. The Bombay High Court in the case of *CIT* v. *Larsen & Toubro Ltd.* [2010] 235 CTR (Bom.) 108 held that interest under section 244A could not be denied merely on the ground that the TDS certificates were not furnished with the return of income-tax (while tax was deducted and deposited in the exchequer in time).

• In *Universal Cables Ltd.* v. *CIT* [2010] 191 Taxman 370 (MP), the assessee deducted tax at source erroneously under section 194A in respect of payment to IDBI, though no tax was required to be deducted from such payment. On assessee's request, the department granted refund of amount so deducted. The Court held that on such refund, interest was not available under section 244A. The assessee was not liable to deduct tax and it did so on its own on an erroneous impression, it did not become a deemed assessee and, therefore, section 244A did not get attracted.

• MAT credit is not refundable. If refund becomes due after credit of MAT, TDS and advance tax, refund is attributable to refund of TDS and advance tax only. In such a case, the assessee should be paid interest on such excess payment of TDS and advance tax—*Hyundai Motor India Ltd.* v. *CIT* [2010] 123 ITD 445 (Chennai).

• An assessee is entitled to interest on refund of excess deduction or erroneous deduction of tax at source – *Union of India* v. *Tata Chemicals Ltd.* [2014] 222 Taxman 225 (SC).

• Interest is available if mismatch is not attributable to the recipient of income and the fault solely lay with the deductor – *Rakesh Kumar Gupta* v. *Union of India* [2014] 225 Taxman 198 (All.).

Procedure to be followed in calculation of interest [Rule 119A]

144. In calculating interest payable by the assessee or interest payable by the Central Government to the assessee, the amount of tax, penalty or other sum in respect of which interest is to be calculated will be rounded off to the nearest multiple of Rs. 100 ignoring any fraction of Rs. 100.

Waiver or reduction of interest under sections 234A, 234B and 234C which arises due to operation of any order of Court

145. In exercise of the powers conferred under section 119(2)(*a*), the Central Board of Direct Taxes have directed (*vide* order dated June 2, 1994) that in cases where any income accrues or arises for any previous year due to the operation of any order of a Court, statutory authority or of the Government (other than an order of assessment, appeal, reference or revision passed under the provisions of the Income-tax Act) passed after the close of the said previous year (such income and the order hereinafter referred to as the "relevant income" and the "relevant order" respectively) interest under sections 234A, 234B and 234C shall be reduced or waived by the Chief Commissioner/Director General subject to certain conditions.

145.1 ***Conditions*** - The following conditions shall be satisfied—

a. the relevant income is disclosed in a return of income furnished for the said previous year or is otherwise disclosed to the Assessing Officer; and

b. the tax attributable to such income has been paid.

145.2 ***Period*** - Reduction/waiver of interest is given in respect of the following period :

a. in respect of interest under section 234A from the date immediately following the due date for furnishing the return of income for the relevant assessment year till the end of the month in which the relevant order giving rise to the relevant income is passed;

b. in respect of the interest under section 234B, from the first day of April of the relevant assessment year till the end of the month in which the relevant order giving rise to the relevant income is passed; and

c. in respect of interest under section 234C, for the period mentioned in that section.

145.3 ***Extent of interest to be reduced or waived*** - The quantum of interest to be reduced or waived shall be the difference between :

a. the interest computed for the period mentioned in para 145.2 above with reference to the tax on the total income inclusive of the relevant income; and

b. the interest computed for the same period with reference to the tax on the total income as reduced by the relevant income.

Waiver or reduction under this order shall be allowed with reference to the relevant orders passed on or after April 1, 1989.

Chief Commissioner/Director General (Investigation) to reduce penal interest in certain cases

146. The Central Board of Direct Taxes has decided to authorise Chief Commissioners and Directors General (Investigation) to reduce or waive penal interest under sections 234A, 234B and 234C. However, no reduction or waiver of such interest shall be ordered unless the assessee has filed the return of income for the relevant assessment year and paid the entire income-tax (principal component of demand) due on the income as assessed. The Chief Commissioner of Income-tax or Director-General of Income-tax may also impose any other conditions as deemed fit for the said reduction or waiver of interest. Penal interest charged under the aforesaid sections may be reduced or waived in the following circumstances, namely :

1. Where, in the course of search and seizure operation, books of account have been taken over by the Department and were not available to the taxpayer to prepare his return of income.[8]

2. Any income other than capital gains which was received or accrued after the date of first or subsequent instalment of advance tax, which was neither anticipated nor contemplated by the taxpayer and on which advance tax was paid by taxpayer after the receipt of such income.

3. Where, as a result of any retrospective amendment of law or the decisions of the Supreme Court, certain receipts which were hitherto treated as exempt, become taxable. Since no advance tax would normally be paid in respect of such receipts during the relevant financial year, penal interest is levied for the default in payment of advance tax.

4. Where a return of income is filed voluntarily without detection by the Income-tax Department and due to circumstances beyond the control of the taxpayer such return of income was not filed within the stipulated time-limit or advance tax was not paid at the relevant time.[8]

• CBDT has power to make relaxation in cases covered by sections 234A, 234B and 234C and where assessee makes an application for waiver of interest under these sections. Board cannot decline the assessee's request by a cryptic order that it was unable to interfere in matter—*Sant Lal* v. *UOI* [1996] 89 Taxman 272/222 ITR 375 (Punj. & Har.).

• Instances given above may be taken as illustrative and not exhaustive—*Dr. Mahesh D. Singhvi, In re* [1998] 97 Taxman 58 (ITSC).

Advance payment of tax[9]

Though income of the previous year is taxable in the immediately following assessment year, yet an assessee is required to pay tax during the financial year preceding the assessment year on the basis of his own computation of income

Income liable for advance tax

147. All items of income (including capital gains, winnings from lotteries, crossword puzzles, etc.) are liable for payment of advance tax.

Liability to advance tax - When arises

148. Section 208 makes it obligatory to pay advance tax in every case where the advance tax payable is Rs. 10,000[10] or more.

• A senior citizen (*i.e.*, a resident individual who is at least 60 years of age at any time during the financial year) not having any income from business/profession, is not liable to pay advance tax with effect from the financial year 2012-13 (*i.e.*, the assessment year 2013-14 onwards).

Due dates of payment of advance tax

149. Advance tax is payable[10a] as follows :

• *Due date of payment of advance tax on or after June 1, 2016 (applicable from the advance tax for the assessment year 2017-18 onwards) -*

---

8. In these cases, only interest under section 234A can be waived.

9. Any instalment of "advance tax paid in respect of fringe benefits" for the assessment year 2010-11 shall be treated as advance income-tax paid by the concerned assessee for the assessment year 2010-11—Circular No. 2/2010, dated January 29, 2010.

10. Rs. 5,000 up to the financial year 2008-09.

10a. After March 31, 2008, all corporate assessees and other assessees (who are subject to compulsory audit under section 44AB) will have to make electronic payment of tax through internet banking facility offered by authorized banks. Alternatively, these taxpayers can make electronic payment of tax through internet by way of credit or debit cards. It is not necessary for the assessee to make payment of taxes from his own account in an authorized bank. An assessee can make electronic payment of taxes also from the account of any other person. However, the challan for making such payment must clearly indicate the Permanent Account Number (PAN) of the assessee on whose behalf the payment is made. - Circular No. 5/2008, dated July 17, 2008.

Due date of payment of advance tax	*For any assessee (except an eligible assessee given in Column 3)*	*An assessee who declares his business/professional income in accordance with the provisions of section 44AD(1) or section 44ADA(1)*
On or before June 15 of the previous year	Up to 15 per cent of advance tax payable	—
On or before September 15 of the previous year	Up to 45 per cent of advance tax payable	—
On or before December 15 of the previous year	Up to 75 per cent of advance tax payable	—
On or before March 15 of the previous year	Up to 100 per cent of advance tax payable	Up to 100 per cent of advance tax payable

• *Due date of payment of advance tax before June 1, 2016 (applicable for the advance tax up to the assessment year 2016-17) -*

	In the case of a corporate assessee	*In the case of a non-corporate assessee*
On or before June 15 of the previous year	Up to 15 per cent of advance tax payable	—
On or before September 15 of the previous year	Up to 45 per cent of advance tax payable	Up to 30 per cent of advance tax payable
On or before December 15[11] of the previous year	Up to 75 per cent of advance tax payable	Up to 60 per cent of advance tax payable
On or before March 15[12] of the previous year	Up to 100 per cent of advance tax payable	Up to 100 per cent of advance tax payable

An assessee who has opted for the scheme of computing business income under section 44AD on presumptive basis at the rate of 8 per cent of turnover, is exempted from payment of advance tax related to such business for the assessment years 2011-12 to 2016-17.

149.1 ***Other points*** -The following points should be noted -

1. Where advance tax is payable by virtue of the notice of demand issued by the Assessing Officer, the whole or the appropriate part of the advance tax shall be payable in the remaining instalments. Any payment of advance tax made on or before March 31 shall also be treated as advance tax paid during the financial year.

2. If the last day for payment of any instalments of advance tax is a day on which the receiving bank is closed, the assessee can make the payment on the next immediately following working day, and in such cases, the mandatory interest leviable under sections 234B and 234C would not be charged.

Payment of advance tax by the assessee of his own account

150. An assessee who is liable to pay advance tax will be required to estimate his current income and pay advance tax thereon without having to submit any estimate or statement of income to the assessing authorities.

After making payment of first/second instalment of advance tax, the assessee can revise the remaining instalment(s) of advance tax in accordance with his revised estimate of current income and pay tax accordingly without any requirement of filing the revised estimate of advance tax.

COMPUTATION OF TAX - Tax can be computed on the current income (estimated by the taxpayer) at the rates in force during the financial year. From the tax so computed, tax deducted/collected[13] at source will be deducted. Calculation can be made on similar lines in the case of upward/downward revision of current income.

11. For the financial year 2013-14, extended to December 17, 2013.

12. For the financial year 2013-14, extended to March 18, 2014.

13. Tax deductible or collectible at source has to be excluded from tax payable while computing advance tax liability as provided in section 209(1)(*d*), even if tax had not actually been deducted—*CIT* v. *Pride Foramer SAS* [2008] 24 SOT 59 (Delhi). However, section 209 has been amended from the financial year 2012-13 to the effect that where a person has received any income without deduction or collection of tax, he shall be liable to pay advance tax in respect of such income.

Payment of advance tax in pursuance of order of Assessing Officer

151. If, despite the legal obligation cast upon a taxpayer (who had earlier been assessed to income-tax), he fails to pay advance tax (or advance tax is lower than the correct amount), the Assessing Officer may pass an order requiring him to pay advance tax on his current year's income (specifying the amount of instalments in which tax has to be paid). Such an order must be passed during the financial year but not later than the last day of February.

On receipt of the notice from the Assessing Officer to pay advance tax the assessee can submit his own estimate of lower current income/advance tax and pay tax accordingly. In such a case he has to send an intimation in Form No. 28A to the Assessing Officer.

Alternatively, if the advance tax on current income as per own estimate of the assessee is likely to be higher than the amount estimated by the Assessing Officer, the assessee shall pay higher tax in accordance with his own calculation. In such case, no intimation to the Assessing Officer is required.

COMPUTATION OF TAX BY ASSESSING OFFICER - The total income of the latest previous year in respect of which the assessee has been assessed by way of regular assessment or the total income returned by the assessee in any return of income furnished by him for any subsequent previous year, whichever is higher, shall be taken as current income by the Assessing Officer.

Tax on the current income at the rates in force during the financial year *minus* tax deducted or collected at source, is the amount of advance tax payable by the assessee. Calculation can be made on similar lines when the assessee wants to make upward/downward revision of current income.

151.1 ***Payment of advance tax in pursuance of revised order of Assessing Officer*** - The order passed by the Assessing Officer to pay advance tax can be revised by him, under section 210(4) if subsequent to the making of an order to pay advance tax but before March 1 of the relevant financial year, a return of income in respect of any later year has been furnished or any assessment for any later year has been completed at a higher figure. On receipt of the revised order, the assessee will have to pay advance tax accordingly.

The assessee can, however, submit his own estimate of lower current income/advance tax and pay tax accordingly. In such a case he has to send an intimation in Form No. 28A to the Assessing Officer.

If, alternatively, the advance tax on current income as per own estimate is likely to be higher than the amount re-estimated by the Assessing Officer, the assessee shall pay higher tax in accordance with his own calculation. In such a case, intimation to the Assessing Officer is not required.

COMPUTATION OF TAX - The total income declared in the return furnished by the assessee for the later previous year or total income in respect of which the regular assessment is made after passing an order by the Assessing Officer but before March 1, shall be taken and income-tax thereon shall be calculated at the rates in force in the financial year. From the tax so determined, tax deducted at source will be deducted.

151-E1 X, an individual (29 years), estimates his current income for the financial year 2019-20 as follows :

	Rs.
Profits and gains of business or profession	6,87,000
Capital gains (short-term)	3,000
Income from other sources	26,000
Gross total income	7,16,000
Less : Deduction under sections 80C and 80D (public provident fund : Rs. 30,000 + mediclaim insurance premium : Rs. 500)	30,500
Net income	6,85,500
Tax	49,600
Add : Surcharge	*Nil*
Total	49,600
Add: Health and education cess	1,984
Total	51,584
Less : Tax deducted at source	590
Balance to be paid as advance tax	50,994

Without sending any estimate of advance tax, X must pay advance tax as follows :

First instalment [on or before June 15, 2019] (15% of Rs. 50,994)	7,649
Second instalment [on or before September 15, 2019] (30% of Rs. 50,994)	15,298

He pays Rs. 7,700 on June 15, 2019 and Rs. 15,300 on September 15, 2019. On October 10, 2019 he takes an endowment insurance policy of Rs. 1,00,000 by paying quarterly instalment of premium of Rs. 940. Second quarterly instalment of premium of Rs. 940 is paid on January 10, 2020.

The computation of income-tax requires revision. He can recalculate advance tax liability as follows :

	Rs.
Gross total income	7,16,000
Less : Deduction	
Under section 80C [Rs. 30,000 + Rs. 940 + Rs. 940]	31,880
Under section 80D	500
Net income	6,83,620
Tax	49,224
Add: Surcharge	*Nil*
Total	49,224
Add : Health and education cess	1,969
Total	51,193
Less : Tax deducted at source	590
Balance payable as advance tax	50,603
Computation of remaining instalments of advance tax	
Third instalment payable on or before December 15, 2019 [*i.e.,* 75% of Rs. 50,603 – Rs. 7,700 – Rs. 15,300]	14,952

X pays Rs. 15,000 on December 15, 2019 (no estimate/revised estimate has to be filed).

Without any prior plan on January 20, 2020, he sells gold (owned by him since 1982-83) for Rs. 7,50,000 (indexed cost of acquisition: Rs. 32,881). He also gets a lottery prize of Rs. 6,00,000 (tax deducted at source Rs. 1,80,000) on March 1, 2020. Besides, X gets dividend of Rs. 11,00,000 from domestic companies during January 2020.

He will have to recalculate his income and advance tax liability as follows :

	Rs.	*Rs.*
Business income		6,87,000
Capital gain		
❑ Original computation	3,000	
❑ On sale of gold (Rs. 7,50,000—Rs. 32,881)	7,17,119	7,20,119
Income from other sources		
❑ Original computation	26,000	
❑ Dividend from domestic companies in excess of Rs. 10,00,000	1,00,000	
❑ Winning from lottery	6,00,000	7,26,000
Gross total income		21,33,119
Less : Deduction		
Under section 80C		31,880
Under section 80D		500
Net income		21,00,740
Tax		
- On Rs. 6,00,000 @ 30%		1,80,000
- On Rs. 7,17,119 @ 20%		1,43,424
- On Rs. 1,00,000 @ 10%		10,000
- On the balance of Rs. 6,83,620 (at usual rates)		49,224
Total		3,82,648
Add : Surcharge		*Nil*
Total		3,82,648
Add : Health and education cess		15,306
Total		3,97,954
Less : Tax deducted at source (*i.e.,* Rs. 590 + Rs. 1,80,000)		1,80,590
Balance		2,17,364
Amount of fourth instalment of advance tax—		
Total tax		2,17,364
Less:		
First instalment of advance tax paid on June 15, 2019		7,700
Second instalment of advance tax paid on September 15, 2019		15,300

	Rs.
Third instalment of advance tax paid on December 15, 2019	15,000
Fourth instalment of advance tax payable on or before March 15, 2020	1,79,364

X should pay Rs. 1,79,360 on or before March 15 2020.

Deduction or collection of tax at source

Persons responsible for making payment of income covered by the scheme of tax deduction [paras 153 to 171] are required to deduct tax at source at the prescribed rates [para 0.6]. Tax so deducted should be deposited within the prescribed time [para 172]. Moreover, returns of tax deduction at source should be submitted within the specified time [para 172]

Scheme of tax deduction at source

152. Under the scheme of tax deduction at source (TDS), persons responsible for making payment of income, covered by the scheme, are responsible to deduct tax at source and deposit the same to the Government's treasury within the stipulated time. The recipient of income—though he gets only the net amount (after deduction of tax at source)—is liable to tax on the gross amount and the amount deducted at source is adjusted against his final tax liability.

152.1 ***TDS rates during the financial year 2019-20*** - Normal TDS rates are summarized in Referencer 1, para 0.6.

• *When recipient does not furnish his/its PAN [Sec. 206AA]* - If the recipient does not furnish his PAN to the deductor, tax will be deducted by virtue of section 206AA[14] (with effect from April 1, 2010) at the normal rate or at the rate of 20 per cent, whichever is higher. However, this rule is subject to following modifications –

- *Case 1* - The provisions of section 206AA are not applicable in respect of payment of interest to a non-resident under section 194LC in the following cases –
  a. interest on long-term infrastructure bonds (from June 1, 2013 to September 30, 2014); and
  b. interest on long-term bonds including infrastructure bonds (from October 1, 2014).
- *Case 2* - Where tax is deductible on the strength of the provisions of DTAAs which is lower than 20 per cent, the provisions of section 206AA cannot be invoked (to compel the assessee to deduct tax at the rate of 20 per cent) even if the recipient does not have PAN – *DIT* v. *Serum Institute of India Ltd.* [2015] 56 taxmann.com 1 (Pune - Trib.), *CIT (International Taxation)* v. *Infosys BPO Ltd.* [2015] 60 taxmann.com 465 (Bang.).
- *Case 3* - If the recipient does not furnish PAN, tax will be deducted under section 192A at the maximum marginal rate of tax (*i.e.*, **42.744** per cent for the financial year 2019-20) and not at the rate of 20 per cent given by section 206AA.
- *Case 4* - With effect from June 1, 2016, provisions of section 206AA are not applicable, if conditions of rule 37BC are satisfied. The benefit of rule 37BC[$] is available, if the recipient is non-resident, he/it does not have PAN and the payment/credit subject to TDS is interest, royalty, fees for technical service or payment on transfer of a capital asset. In such a case, tax will be deducted at the regular rate (and not at the rate of 20 per cent given by section 206AA), if the non-resident recipient furnishes the following details/documents to the payer –
  - name, e-mail id, contact number;
  - address in the home country;
  - certificate of being a resident in the home country, if the law of the country provides such a certificate; and
  - Tax Identification Number (TIN) in the home country. Where TIN is not available, a unique identification number through which the deductee is identified in the home country.

---

14. Section 206AA is unconstitutional if income of payee is below taxable limit – *A. Kowsalya Bai* v. *Union of India* [2012] 22 taxmann.com 157 (Kar.).

$ For rule 37BC, log on to *taxmann.com/readyreckoner.aspx.*

PAN of the deductee should be mentioned in any correspondence and document which is exchanged between the deductor and deductee.

• *When recipient is located in a notified jurisdictional area [Sec. 94A(5)]*-Where any person located in a notified jurisdictional area[15] is entitled to receive any sum on which tax is deductible under any provision of the Act, the payer will deduct tax (with effect from June 1, 2011)—

a. at the rates in force or at the rate specified in the relevant provision of the Act (*i.e.*, rates given in Referencer 1); or

b. at the rate of 30 per cent, whichever is higher.

152.2 ***Consequences of default*** - Where a person who is required to deduct tax at source, does not deduct, or does not pay, or after deducting fails to pay, the whole or any part of tax, as required by the Act, then such person shall be deemed to be an assessee-in-default in respect of such tax under section 201(1). He will be liable for payment of tax, interest [*see* para 142.2], penalty and prosecution. Besides, disallowance under section 40(*a*) will be attracted [*see* paras 49.1-1, 49.1-2 and 49.1-7].

• *Time-limit (applicable up to September 30, 2014)* - An order under section 201(1) for failure to deduct the whole or any part of the tax as required under the Act, if the deductee is a resident taxpayer, shall be passed within the time-limit given below—

1. In case statement is filed by the deductor under section 200 - Within 2 years from the end of the financial year in which statement is filed under section 200.

2. In case no such statement is filed, within 4 years (6 years applicable from April 1, 2010) from the end of the financial year in which payment is made or credit is given.

However, an order pertaining to the financial year 2007-08 (or earlier years) can be passed at any time up to March 31, 2011.

• *Time-limit* - No order shall be made under section 200(1) deeming a person to be an assessee in default for failure to deduct the whole or any part of the tax from a person resident in India, at any time after the time-limit given below -

- After expiry of 7 years from the end of the financial year in which payment is made or credit is given (applicable during October 1, 2014 and August 31, 2019).
- After expiry of 7 years from the end of the financial year in which payment is made or credit is given or **2 years from the end of the financial year in which the correction statement is delivered** [under proviso to section 200(3)], whichever is later (applicable with effect from September 1, 2019).

• *Relaxation given when tax is paid by the recipient (applicable from July 1, 2012)* - Section 201 was amended by the Finance Act, 2012 with effect from July 1, 2012. Under the amended version, the payer shall not be deemed to be an assessee-in-default if the resident recipient has included such income in the return submitted under section 139 and the recipient has paid tax on such income. The payer will have to submit a certificate in Form No. 26A to this effect from a chartered accountant.

• *When tax is paid by recipient and it pertains to the period preceding July 1, 2012* - The aforesaid relaxation given by the Finance Act, 2012 is applicable only when the recipient is resident and the default pertains to the period commencing on or after July 1, 2012. If the recipient is a non-resident (or if the recipient is resident but default pertains to the period prior to July 1, 2012), the amendment made by the Finance Act, 2012 is not applicable. In such a case, one can take shelter of the Supreme Court ruling in the case of *Hindustan Coca Cola Beverage (P.) Ltd.* v. *CIT* [2007] 163 Taxman 355. In this case, the Supreme Court held that where the payer has failed to deduct tax but the deductee (*i.e.*, recipient of income) has paid tax on the amount received from the deductor, the department once again cannot recover tax from the deductor on same income by treating the deductor to be an assessee-in-default for non-deduction/short-deduction of tax. Moreover, the Gujarat High Court in the case of *CIT* v. *Rishikesh Apartments Co-op. Housing Society Ltd.* [2001] 119 Taxman 239 held that in such a situation interest cannot be recovered from the deductor for short-deduction/non-deduction of tax.

• *Whether reimbursement to an agent/associate enterprise is again subject to TDS when tax was properly deducted by the agent/associate enterprise* - Where technical fees (or any other expenditure like rent, commission, royalty, professional fees, etc.) is paid by an agent or associate enterprise on behalf of the assessee and tax is deducted properly within the legal parameters by the agent/associate enterprise, reimbursement later on by the assessee of the expenditure to his agent/associate enterprise is not again subject to tax deduction at source—*see Metro Railway Kolkata* v. *ITO* (TDS) [2013] 32 taxmann.com 232 (Kol.), *Temasek Holdings Advisors (I) (P.) Ltd.* v. *CIT* [2013] 60 SOT 134 (Mum.), *CIT* v. *Harbanslal Malhotra & Sons (P.) Ltd.* [2013] 217 Taxman 112 (Cal.), *CIT* v. *Gujarat Narmada Valley Fertilizers Co. Ltd.* [2013] 217

15. 'Cyprus' was specified as notified jurisdictional area for purposes of section 94A *vide* Notification No. SO 3307(E), dated November 1, 2013. However, this notification has been rescinded with effect from November 1, 2013 (except as respects things done or omitted to be done before such rescission) *vide* Notification No. SO 4033(E)[$], dated December 14, 2016.

[$] For Circular No. 5/2002 and Notification No. SO 4033(E), log on to *taxmann.com/readyreckoner.aspx*.

Taxman 114 (Guj.), *CIT* v. *Vector Shipping Services (P.) Ltd.* [2013] 218 Taxman 93 (All.)[16]. The same proposition is given by Circular No. 5/2002[$], dated July, 30, 2002.

• *No TDS on GST/service tax* - The Central Board of Direct Taxes has decided that wherever in terms of the agreement/contract between the payer and the payee, the GST/service tax component comprised in the amount payable to a resident is indicated separately, tax shall be deducted at source under any section on the amount paid/payable without including such GST/service tax component – Circular No. 1/2014, dated January 13, 2014, Circular No. 23/2017, dated July 19, 2017.

Deduction of tax from salaries [Sec. 192]

153. Any person responsible for paying any income chargeable under the head "Salaries" is required to deduct tax at source on the amount payable. Tax is to be calculated at the rates prescribed for the financial year in which the payment to employees is made. The person responsible for paying the salary may, at the time of deducting tax at source, increase or decrease, the amount to be deducted for the purpose of adjusting any previous deficiency or excess deduction.

153.1 ***Computation of salary and tax thereon*** - Tax deducted at source from salary payable in a foreign currency is to be calculated in accordance with rule 26[$]. For computing taxable salary, refer to paras 10 to 23 and para 107. At the time of deducting tax at source during the financial year 2019-20, the person responsible for paying salary should keep the following points in view :

• *Exemption limit* - No tax is required to be deducted at source unless the estimated salary exceeds the amount not chargeable to tax. This rule is applicable even if the employee does not have PAN.

• *Leave encashment* - The amount received on account of encashment of leave due to an employee on retirement is eligible for exemption under section 10(*10AA*) [*see* para 12.1].

• *Notified allowances* - Notified allowances under section 10(*14*) are not subject to tax deduction at source [*see* para 13.3].

• *House rent allowance exemption* - Exemption pertaining to house rent allowance shall be calculated by the employer on the basis of specified limits provided by section 10(*13A*). These limits have been given in the Reckoner in para 13.1. This exemption depends upon rent paid by the employee. The concerned employee should submit to the employer a written statement pinpointing rent paid, name of landlord, address of the property and PAN of landlord (PAN is required only if rent paid is more than Rs. 1,00,000 per annum) along with rent receipt given by the landlord.

Though incurring actual expenditure on payment of rent is a prerequisite for claiming deduction under section 10(*13A*), the Board has decided as an administrative measure that salaried employees drawing house rent allowance up to Rs. 3,000 per month will be exempted from production of rent receipt. It may, however, be noted that this concession is only for the purpose of tax deduction at source and, in the regular assessment of the employee, the Assessing Officer will be free to make such enquiry as he deems fit for the purpose of satisfying himself that the employee has incurred actual expenditure on payment of rent.

• *Perquisites* - The value of the perquisites by way of free residential accommodation and amenities provided by the employers to their employees are determined under rule 3 [*see* para 15] and should be taken into account for computing taxable salary.

• *Donation by employees deductible under section 80G* - Section 80G provides for deductions on account of donation made to various funds, charitable organizations etc. In cases where employees make donations to the Prime Minister's National Relief Fund, the Chief Minister's Relief Fund or the Lieutenant Governor's Relief Fund through their respective employers, it is not possible for such funds to issue separate certificate to every such employee in respect of donations made to such funds as contributions made to these funds are in the form of a consolidated cheque. An employee who makes donations towards these funds is eligible to claim deduction under section 80G. CBDT has clarified that the claim in respect of such donations as indicated above will be admissible under section 80G on the basis of the certificate issued by the Drawing and Disbursing Officer (DDO)/Employer in this behalf. Moreover, no deduction under this section is allowable in case of amount of donation if exceeds Rs. 10,000 unless the amount is paid by any mode other than cash.

• *Other deductions* - The person responsible for making payment of salary should also take into consideration other admissible deductions under sections 80C, 80CCC, 80CCD, 80CCG, 80D, 80DD, 80DDB, 80E, 80EE, 80GG, 80GGA, 80TTA and 80U.

---

16. SLP of the Department against the ruling of the Allahabad High Court has been rejected by the Supreme Court on July 2, 2014.

$ For rule 26, log on to *taxmann.com/readyreckoner.aspx*.

• *Estimated salary* - The total salary should be rounded off to the nearest multiple of rupees ten by ignoring the fraction of less than five rupees and increasing the fraction of five rupees or more.

• *Tax* - On the estimated taxable salary, tax during the financial year 2019-20 is to be deducted at the rates mentioned in para 0.1-1, Referencer 1[17]. *See* also Salary Tables at pages B-51 and B-52.

153.2 *Other points* - One should also keep in view the following points—

153.2-1 *TAX ON PERQUISITE PAID BY EMPLOYER* - Section 192(1A) (inserted with effect from June 1, 2002) provides that the person responsible for paying any income in the nature of a perquisite (not provided for by way of monetary payment) referred to in section 17(*2*) may pay at his option, tax on the whole or part of such income without making any deduction therefrom at the time when such tax was otherwise deductible under the provisions of section 192(1).

For this purpose, tax shall be determined at the average of income-tax computed on the basis of the rates in force for the financial year, on the income chargeable under the head "Salaries" and the tax so payable shall be construed as if it were a tax deductible at source from the income under the head "Salaries".

153.2-2 *HOW TO DEDUCT TAX WHEN A PERSON IS EMPLOYED BY MORE THAN ONE EMPLOYER* - Section 192(2) provides the method of tax deduction at source when a person is employed by more than one employer during the financial year. In such a case, tax will be deducted on the aggregate salary by one of the employers (being the employer as the employee may choose, having regard to the circumstances of his case) by submitting the information in Form No. 12B.

Where an employee has more than one employer, he is required by section 192(2) to furnish in Form No. 12B to one of the employers (as selected by the employee having regard to the circumstances of the case) the details of salary due/received by him from other employers. Only after submission of information in Form No. 12B, it becomes the obligation of the employer (to whom Form No. 12B is submitted) to deduct tax at source after considering the information submitted by the employee. If information is submitted in the month of October, only from October onwards tax shall be deducted at the average rate determined after considering the details submitted in Form No. 12B—*CIT* v. *Marubeni India (P.) Ltd.* [2007] 165 Taxman 467 (Delhi).

• *Provisions illustrated* - The following illustrations are given to have better understanding—

1. X is employed simultaneously by A Ltd. (salary: Rs. 50,000 per month, URPF contribution 10 per cent of salary) and B Ltd. (salary: Rs. 62,000 per month, URPF contribution 10 per cent of salary) on part-time basis during the previous year 2019-20. X may select any of the two companies for deducting tax at source on aggregate salary. Suppose, X selects B Ltd., then tax will be deducted as follows :

	Tax deduction by A Ltd. on salary paid by it
	Rs.
Taxable salary by A Ltd. [(Rs. 50,000 × 12) – standard deduction : Rs. 50,000]	5,50,000
Tax on taxable salary to be deducted at source by A Ltd.	23,400

The above information pertaining to A Ltd. will be submitted by X to B Ltd. in Form No. 12B. B Ltd. will deduct tax on the aggregate salary as follows—

	Tax deduction by B Ltd.
	Rs.
Taxable salary [(Rs. 50,000 × 12 + Rs. 62,000 × 12) – standard deduction : Rs. 50,000]	12,94,000
Tax on taxable salary	2,08,728
Less: Tax deducted by A Ltd.	23,400
Tax to be deducted by B Ltd.	1,85,330

2. Y is employed by C Ltd. up to June 30, 2019 (salary being Rs. 70,000 per month). On July 1, 2019, he joins D Ltd. (salary being Rs. 95,000 per month). Tax will be deducted at source as follows:

17. For the purpose of TDS from salary during the financial year 2019-20, surcharge is applicable only if taxable income of the employee exceeds Rs. 50 lakh. However, health and education cess at the rate of 4 per cent (of tax and surcharge) is applicable in all cases. If any employee does not furnish his PAN to the employer, tax will be deducted either at the normal rates or at the rate of 20 per cent, whichever is higher. PAN of the employee should be mentioned on any correspondence and document which is exchanged between the employer and the employee.

	Tax deduction by C Ltd. on salary paid by it
	Rs.
Taxable salary by C Ltd. [(Rs. 70,000 × 3) – standard deduction : Rs. 50,000]	1,60,000
Tax on taxable salary deducted at source by C Ltd.	18,330

The above information pertaining to C Ltd. will be submitted by Y to D Ltd. in Form No. 12B. D Ltd. will deduct tax on the aggregate salary as follows (Y should not select the old employer for deducting tax in respect of aggregate salary)—

	Tax deduction by D Ltd.
	Rs.
Taxable salary [(Rs. 70,000 × 3 + Rs. 95,000 × 9) – standard deduction : Rs. 50,000]	10,15,000
Tax on taxable salary	1,21,680
Less: Tax deducted by C Ltd.	18,330
Tax to be deducted by D Ltd.	1,03,350

153.2-3 *RELIEF UNDER SECTION 89* - If the employee furnishes information in Form No. 10E[18] to the employer, relief under section 89 should be given to the concerned employee while deducting tax at source under section 192. However, this facility is available only if the employer is Government or public sector undertaking or company, co-operative society, local authority, university, institution or association or body.

153.2-4 *CAN THE EMPLOYER DEDUCT TAX IN RESPECT OF OTHER INCOMES OF EMPLOYEE* - The provisions are given below—

1. The employee may (or may not) declare his other incomes to the employer.

2. If the employee wants to declare his other incomes to the employer, then such information should be given on a plain paper to the employer. A verification shall be annexed to the statement of other income given on plain paper as follows—

"I.............(name of employee) do declare that what is stated above is true to the best of my information and belief."

3. The employee may declare details of his other incomes (including loss[19] from self-occupied or let out property or properties under the head "Income from house property" but not any other loss) and tax deducted thereon by others. If such information is not submitted by the employee to the employer, then employer cannot take into consideration other incomes of the employee (even if the quantum of other incomes is otherwise known to the employer).

4. After receipt of such information, the employer should deduct (out of salary payment) tax due on total income as follows—

Computation one [on the basis of (a) salary and (b) other incomes[£] declared by the employee]	*Computation two [on the basis of salary and ignoring the other incomes[20] declared by the employee]*
a. Find out salary income *b.* *Add*: Other incomes declared by the employee (in case of loss, only house property loss would be considered; no other loss would be taken into consideration) *c.* Find out aggregate of (*a*) and (*b*) *d.* *Less*: Deduction under sections 80C to 80U *e.* Find out (*c*) - (*d*) *f.* Find out tax on (*e*) *g.* *Add*: Surcharge [if (*e*) exceeds Rs. 50 lakh] and health and education cess (@ 4 per cent of tax and surcharge) *h.* *Less*: Tax deducted by others as per information given by the employee *i.* Find out tax liability [(*f*) + (*g*) – (*h*)]	*j.* Find out salary income *k.* *Less*: Loss under the head "Income from house property" as declared by the employee *l.* Find out (*j*) – (*k*) *m.* *Less*: Deduction under sections 80C to 80U *n.* Find out (*l*) – (*m*) *o.* Find out tax on (*n*) *p.* *Add*: Surcharge [if (*n*) exceeds Rs. 50 lakh] and health and education cess (@ 4 per cent of tax and surcharge) *q.* *Less*: Tax deducted from rent by others (if there is loss of house property) as per information given by the employee *r.* Find out tax liability [(*o*) + (*p*) – (*q*)]

18. The department insists that the concerned employee should submit electronically Form No. 10E along with his return of income to claim rebate under section 89 (however, there is no such legal requirement under the Income-tax Act or Income-tax Rules).

19. While taking into account the loss from house property, the DDO shall ensure that the employee files the declaration referred to above and encloses therewith a computation of such loss from house property. The following details shall be obtained and kept by the employer in respect of loss claimed under the head "Income from house property" separately for each house property –

(Contd. on next page)

The tax deductible at source from salary payment is amount determined at (*i*) or (*r*), whichever is higher.

153.2-5 *PARTICULARS OF PERQUISITE* - Section 192(1C) provides that any person responsible for paying salary shall furnish to person (who receives salary) a statement giving particulars of perquisites or profits in lieu of salary provided to him in Form No. 12BA.

Form No. 12BA is required only if salary exceeds Rs. 1,50,000. In other cases the information shall be provided in Form No. 16.

153.2-6 *ADJUSTMENTS* - If there is no overall short deduction of tax under section 192 but a few months tax deducted is lower as compared to other months, interest on the basis of monthly shortage cannot be charged under section 201. There is an express provision under section 192(3) authorising the person responsible for deducting tax to increase or reduce the amount to be deducted under section 192 for the purpose of adjusting any excess or deficiency arising out of any previous deduction or failure to deduct during the financial year—*see Hero Honda Motors Ltd.* v. *ITO* [2000] 112 Taxman 154 (Delhi) (Mag.).

Intention of section 192(3) is not that an employer can casually take deduction of tax from payments of salary in different months and resort to a lump sum deduction at the end of relevant financial year for making good deficiency—*Madhya Gujarat Vij Co. Ltd.* v. *ITO* [2011] 14 taxmann.com 156 (Ahd. - Trib.).

153.2-7 *SUPPORTING EVIDENCE FOR HRA/LTC/INTEREST ON HOME LOAN/DEDUCTIONS UNDER CHAPTER VI-A* - Rule 26C$ has been inserted with effect from June 1, 2016. Under this rule, an employee shall furnish supporting evidence pertaining to the following in Form No. 12BB for the purpose of estimation of his income and tax deduction at source. This form should be submitted to the person responsible for tax deduction under section 192–

Nature of claim	*Evidence or particulars*
House rent allowance	- Name and address of landlord/landlords - Amount of rent paid/payable - PAN of landlord/landlords (where the aggregate rent paid during the financial year exceeds Rs. 1 lakh)
Leave travel concession or assistance	Expenditure and evidence pertaining to expenditure
Deduction of interest under the head "Income from house property"	Name, address, PAN of the lender and interest paid/payable
Deduction under sections 80C, 80CCC, 80CCD, 80CCG, 80D, 80DD, 80DDB, 80E, 80EE, 80GG, 80GGA, 80TTA, 80TTB and 80U	Amount of investment/expenditure and evidence of investment/expenditure

Time-limit for submission of Form No. 12BB by employee to employer - No time-limit has been specified for submission of Form No. 12BB.

Submission of above information by employer to income-tax department - The above information collected by an employer in Form No. 12BB from his employees shall be retained by the employer. However, PAN of landlord (in the case of house rent allowance) and PAN of lender (in the case of interest on housing loan) shall be submitted by the employer in *Columns 357* and *358* in Form No. 24Q (Annexure II) every year in the TDS statements pertaining to the fourth quarter.

153.2-8 *REIMBURSEMENT OF LTC/MEDICAL EXPENDITURE IN ADVANCE* - In *ITO* v. *Goodrich Aerospace Services (P.) Ltd.* [2014] 64 SOT 27 (Bang.), the assessee paid to its employees every month certain amount in advance towards leave travel concession (LTC). Once the concerned employee completed his travel, he had to submit evidence for having incurred expenditure and it was on basis of such evidence exemption was worked out by assessee in accordance with provisions of section 10(5) read with rule 2B.

(Contd. from previous page)

a. gross annual rent/value;
b. municipal taxes paid, if any;
c. deduction claimed for interest paid, if any;
d. other deductions claimed;
e. address of the property;
f. amount of loan, if any, and
g. name and address of the lender (loan provider) – Circular No. 8/2012, dated October 5, 2012.

20. Only house property loss from self-occupied or let out property or properties declared by the assessee would be considered.

$ For rule 26C, log on to *taxmann.com/readyreckoner.aspx.*

Similarly, the assessee paid to its employees every month an amount of Rs. 1,250 (*i.e.*, Rs. 15,000 per annum) in advance towards medical reimbursement. The said amount was treated as exempt only if supported by bills and whenever bills were not submitted the amount was treated as taxable salary and tax is deducted accordingly at the end of the year. The Tribunal held that in peculiar facts of case the assessee was not obliged to deduct tax at source on amount paid in advance towards LTC and medical reimbursement at time of making payment. A similar ruling is given by the Tribunal in the case of *CIT* v. *Infosys BPO* [2014] 64 SOT 36 (Bang.).

153.2-9 *SALARY PAID IN FOREIGN CURRENCY* - For the purposes of deduction of tax on salary payable in foreign currency, the value in rupees of such salary shall be calculated at the "telegraphic transfer buying rate" of such currency as on the date on which tax is required to be deducted at source [*see* rule 26[$]] – Circular No. 29/2017, dated December 5, 2017.

153.3 *When tax is deductible at lower rate* - *See* para 175.5.

Tax deduction at source from withdrawal from employees provident fund scheme [Sec. 192A]

153A. Under the Employees' Provident Fund and Miscellaneous Provisions Act, 1952 (EPF & MP Act, 1952), certain specified employers are required to comply with the Employees' Provident Fund Scheme, 1952 (EPFS). Under this scheme, provident fund contributions of the employer and employees are transferred to the Provident Fund Commissioner. Provident fund is managed by the Provident Fund Commissioner and at the time of retirement employees get payment from the trustees of Employees' Provident Fund Scheme (EPFS). This provident fund is known as recognised provident fund (RPF). Alternatively, some employers are also permitted to establish and manage their own private provident fund scheme (PPFS) subject to fulfilment of certain conditions given under section 17 of EPF & MP Act, 1952. PPFS exempted under section 17 of the said Act and recognised under Part A of the Fourth Schedule to the Income-tax Act is also termed as recognised provident fund (RPF). Under PPFS, a provident fund trust is created by the employer and employees. Provident fund is managed by the trust and at the time of retirement employees get payment from provident fund trust.

• *Withdrawal of accumulated balance at the time of retirement or at the time of leaving job* - Under the provisions of rule 8 of Part A to the Fourth Schedule, the withdrawal of accumulated balance by an employee from the RPF is exempt in the hands of employee in the following situations–

- If the employee has rendered continuous service with his employer for a period of 5 years or more. For the purpose of calculating 5-year time-limit, service rendered with the previous employer shall be included, if the previous employer also maintained recognized provident fund and the provident fund balance of the employee was transferred by him to the current employer.
- If the employee has been terminated because of certain reasons which are beyond his control (*e.g.*, ill health of the employee, discontinuation of business by employer, completion of project for which the employee was employed, etc.).
- If the employee has resigned before completion of 5 years but has joined another employer (who maintains recognized provident fund and provident fund amount with the current employer is transferred to the new employer).
- If the entire balance standing to the credit of the employee is transferred to his account under a pension scheme referred to in section 80CCD and notified by the Central Government (*i.e.*, NPS).

If the employee makes withdrawal before continuous service of 5 years (other than the cases given above), such withdrawal shall be treated as withdrawal from unrecognized provident fund. Unrecognized provident fund withdrawal (excluding employee's contribution) is taxable (hereinafter referred to as "taxable premature withdrawal"). Exact tax liability in such cases can be ascertained only after recomputation of income of earlier years (deduction given earlier under section 80C will be taken back). Rule 9 of Schedule IV-A provides computation mechanism for determining tax liability of the employee. For ensuring collection of tax in respect of these withdrawals, rule 10 of Schedule IV-A provides that the trustees of the RPF, at the time of payment, shall deduct tax.

• *Mechanism of tax deduction under section 192A* - Section 192A has been inserted with effect from June 1, 2015. Under this section tax is deductible (notwithstanding anything contained under other provisions of the Act) as follows –

1. Who is deductor - Tax is to be deducted by the trustees of Employees' Provident Fund Scheme, 1952 or any other person authorised under the scheme to make payment of accumulated sum to employees. When payment is made by trustees of private provident fund scheme (PPFS), section 192A is not applicable (tax is to be deducted within the parameters of section 192 only).

[$] For rule 26 and Circular No. 29/2017, log on to *taxmann.com/readyreckoner.aspx*.

2. Which amount is subject to tax deduction under section 192A - Tax is deductible from "taxable premature withdrawal". In other words, tax is deductible from accumulated lump sum payment (at the time of retirement or at the time of leaving job) in case the employee has not rendered continuous service of 5 years (and he does not fall in any of the 3 cases given above). Out of the lump sum payment, only amount includible in the total income of the employee is subject to tax deduction at source.

3. Time of tax deduction - Tax is deductible at the time of payment.

4. Rate of TDS under section 192A - Tax is deductible under section 192A at the rate of 10 per cent of "taxable premature withdrawal". If recipient is resident, there is no surcharge or Health and education cess. If recipient is non-resident, the rate of 10 per cent will be increased by surcharge[21] and health and education cess.

If PAN of the recipient is not available, tax is deductible at the maximum marginal rate of tax (*i.e.*, at **42.744** per cent for the financial year 2019-20).

5. What is threshold limit under section 192A - Tax is not deductible if "taxable premature withdrawal" is less than Rs. 50,000. (Rs. 30,000 before May 31, 2016).

6. Is it possible to get lower TDS certificate under section 197 - Section 197 has not been amended. Consequently, lower rate TDS certificate cannot be obtained to get payment without TDS or with lower TDS by submitting Form No. 13 to the Assessing Officer.

7. Is it possible to avoid TDS by submitting Form No. 15G/15H under section 197A - An employee can submit a declaration in Form No. 15G to the effect that his total income including taxable premature withdrawal from provident fund does not exceed the maximum amount not chargeable to tax and on furnishing of such declaration, no tax will be deducted. Similar facility of filing self-declaration in Form No. 15H for non-deduction of tax under section 197A is also extended to the senior citizen employees receiving pre-mature withdrawal.

153A-E1 X joins A Chemicals Ltd. on April 16, 2018 (salary being Rs. 1,00,000 per month). A Chemicals Ltd. contributes 12 per cent of salary towards recognised provident fund. X makes a matching contribution. Besides, he annually contributes Rs. 1,20,000 towards public provident fund and annually pays mediclaim insurance premium of Rs. 10,000 on September 30. He resigns on December 31, 2019.

Interest credited to provident fund account of X during the previous years 2018-19 and 2019-20 is Rs. 20,000 and Rs. 30,000 respectively (rate of interest being less than 9.5 per cent). According to the provident fund records, the amount accumulated in provident fund account of X up to December 31, 2019 is Rs. 5,30,000 (*i.e.*, contribution by A Chemicals Ltd. : Rs. 2,40,000, interest thereon : Rs. 25,000, contribution by X : Rs. 2,40,000, interest thereon : Rs. 25,000). The accumulated balance is paid on January 10, 2020. Determine the amount of tax deduction under sections 192 and 192A for the financial year 2019-20 under the following situations –

Situation 1 - Provident fund is managed by the Provident Fund Commissioner under Employees' Provident Fund Scheme, 1952 (EPFS).

Situation 2 - A Chemicals Ltd. has taken exemption under section 17 and provident fund is managed by it through provident fund trust (*i.e.*, A Chemicals PF Trust). It is recognised by the Commissioner of Income-tax.

•

X leaves the employment of A Chemicals Ltd. before rendering continuous service for 5 years. It is assumed that the following conditions are satisfied –

1. Before joining A Chemicals Ltd. on May 1, 2018, X was not employed by any other person (if he was employed by any other person before May 1, 2018 and provident fund accumulated amount was transferred from the old employer to the current employer, the period of previous employment would also be considered for the purpose of 5 year time-limit).

2. After resigning from the service of A Chemicals Ltd. before 5 years on December 31, 2019, he is not going to join another employer who maintains recognized provident fund (if he joins some other employer and provident fund amount is transferred to the new employer, nothing would be taxable on account of provident fund withdrawal).

3. The service of X has not been terminated on December 31, 2019 because of reasons which are beyond his control (*e.g.*, ill health of the employee, discontinuation of business by employer, completion of project for which the employee was employed, etc.).

4. The entire balance standing to the credit of X on December 31, 2019 is not transferred by him to his NPS account.

In the above 4 cases, nothing will be taxable on pre-mature withdrawal of provident fund and benefit of section 80C will not be taken back even if service is lesser than 5 years (no tax deduction under section 192 or 192A on account of pre-mature withdrawal of provident fund). If none of the 4 cases is applicable, the provident fund scheme for X will be treated as unrecognised provident fund since the date of his joining X Chemicals Ltd. Consequently, pre-mature withdrawal of provident fund (excluding contribution by X) will be chargeable to tax in the financial year 2019-20. Moreover, the tax benefit which X has availed in respect of his contribution to recognised provident fund in any of the earlier years will be added to the tax liability of the current year.

---

21. If recipient is non-resident, surcharge is applicable when the amount subject to TDS exceeds Rs. 50 lakh.

Recomputation of tax liability of X of the previous year 2018-19 - X leaves the employment of A Chemicals Ltd. before rendering continuous service for 5 years. Tax benefit which X has availed in any of the earlier years under section 80C will be taken back as follows –

	Tax liability as originally calculated (provident fund is RPF) Rs.	*Recomputation of tax liability (provident fund is UnRPF)* Rs.
Salary (Rs. 1,00,000 × 11.5 months *minus* standard deduction : Rs. 40,000)	11,10,000	11,10,000
Any other income	*Nil*	*Nil*
Gross total income	11,10,000	11,10,000
Less: Deduction		
Under section 80C		
- Public provident fund contribution on September 30	(1,20,000)	(1,20,000)
- Employees provident fund (12% of Rs. 11,50,000)	(1,38,000)	*Nil*
Amount deductible under section 80C (subject to maximum of Rs. 1,50,000)	1,50,000	1,20,000
Under section 80D	10,000	10,000
Net income	9,50,000	9,80,000
Tax	1,06,600	1,12,840

The difference of Rs. 6,240 (*i.e.*, Rs. 1,12,840 – Rs. 1,06,600) will be recovered by the employer by way of TDS under section 192 in the financial year 2019-20.

Tax deduction under Situation 1 - Under *Situation 1*, tax on salary will be deducted by employer under section 192 and tax on premature withdrawal of taxable provident fund will be deducted by the trustees of Employees' Provident Fund Scheme (EPFS) under section 192A as follows –

	TDS by employer under section 192	*TDS by EPFS under section 192A*
	Rs.	*Rs.*
Salary [(Rs. 1,00,000 × 9) – standard deduction : Rs. 50,000]	8,50,000	–
Any other income (premature withdrawal of provident fund excluding contribution by X) (Rs. 2,40,000 + Rs. 25,000 + Rs. 25,000)	–	2,90,000
Gross total income	8,50,000	–
Less: Deduction		
Under section 80C		
- Public provident fund contribution on September 30	(1,20,000)	–
- Employees provident fund (provident fund is treated as unrecognised PF)	(*Nil*)	–
Amount deductible under section 80C	1,20,000	–
Under section 80D	10,000	–
Income subject to TDS	7,20,000	2,90,000
Tax on regular rate on Rs. 7,30,000	58,760	–
Tax on withdrawal of deduction under section 80C for the earlier year(s) (as calculated above)	6,240	–
Tax to be deducted (*10% of Rs. 2,90,000)	65,000	29,000*

Note - Overall tax liability of X for the previous year 2019-20 will be higher than tax deducted under sections 192 and 192A. X will have to pay advance tax (or alternatively, the above information may be given to the new employer, if any, to deduct tax on cumulative basis).

Tax deduction under Situation 2 - Under *Situation 2* provident fund is maintained by X Chemicals Provident Fund Trust. Tax deduction under section 192A is not applicable. Tax deduction under section 192 by the employer-company will be as follows –

	Rs.
Salary (Rs. 1,00,000 × 9 months)	9,00,000
Provident fund withdrawal (contribution by employer)	2,40,000
Interest on above	25,000
Gross salary	11,65,000
Less: Standard deduction	50,000

	Rs.
Salary income	11,15,000
Income from other sources (interest on provident fund contribution by X)	25,000
Gross total income	11,40,000
Less: Deduction	
Under section 80C	
- Public provident fund contribution on September 30	(1,20,000)
- Employees provident fund (provident fund is treated as unrecognised PF)	(*Nil*)
Amount deductible under section 80C	1,20,000
Under section 80D	10,000
Income subject to TDS	10,10,000
Tax on regular rate on Rs. 10,10,000	1,20,120
Tax on withdrawal of deduction under section 80C for the earlier year(s) (as calculated above)	6,240
Tax to be deducted	1,26,360

Deduction of tax at source from interest on securities [Sec. 193]

154. Any person responsible for paying any interest on securities to a resident is required, at the time of credit of such income to the account of the payee or interest payable account or suspense account [*see* also para 154.1-7] or at the time of payment of interest in cash, by cheque/draft, whichever is earlier to deduct income-tax at the rates in force[22]. No tax is, however, deductible at source from the amount of interest payable on :

1. 4¼% National Defence Bonds, 1972, where the bonds are held by any resident individual.

2. 4¼% National Defence Loan, 1968, or 4¾% National Defence Loan, 1972.

3. National Development Bonds.

4. 7 year National Savings Certificates (IV Issue).

5. Debentures issued by any co-operative society (including a co-operative land mortgage bank or a co-operative land development bank) or any other institution or authority (including a public sector company with effect from June 1, 1986) notified by the Central Government.

6. 6½% Gold Bonds, 1977 or 7% Gold Bonds, 1980, held by a resident individual provided conditions in section 193 are fulfilled.

7. Any security of the Central Government or a State Government [however, interest exceeding Rs. 10,000 (from June 1, 2007[23]) on 8 per cent Savings (Taxable) Bonds, 2003 or (from April 1, 2018) on 7.75 per cent Savings (Taxable) Bonds, 2018 during the financial year, shall be subject to tax deduction under section 193].

8. Securities beneficially owned by the Life Insurance Corporation of India or the General Insurance Corporation of India or to any of the four companies formed by virtue of the schemes framed under section 16(1) of the General Insurance Business (Nationalisation) Act, 1972 or any other insurer (applicable from June 1, 2002).

9. Any listed Demat security.

154.1 ***Cases where tax is not deductible or deductible at lower rates*** - In the following cases, tax is not deducted or deducted at lower rates :

154.1-1 *APPLY IN FORM NO. 13 - See* para 175.5.

154.1-2 *DECLARATION TO THE PAYER IN FORM NO. 15G OR 15H - See* para 175.4.

154.1-3 *INTEREST UP TO Rs. 2,500/Rs. 5,000* - It is not necessary to deduct tax at source from any interest on debentures paid to a resident individual (or a resident Hindu undivided family, applicable from July 1, 2012), if the following conditions are fulfilled :

a. the debentures have been issued by a company in which the public are substantially interested;

22. For the financial year 2019-20, TDS rate is 10 per cent (no surcharge or health and education cess). If the recipient does not furnish his PAN to the deductor, tax will be deducted at the rate of 20 per cent. PAN of the deductee should be mentioned in any correspondence and document which is exchanged between the deductor and deductee.

23. The date of investment is not relevant. In other words, tax is deductible even if bonds were issued before June 1, 2007.

b. the debentures are listed in a recognised stock exchange in India (this condition is not applicable from July 1, 2012);

c. the interest is paid by the company by an account payee cheque ; and

d. the aggregate amount of interest paid or likely to be paid by the company to the holder of the debentures during the financial year does not exceed Rs. 5,000 (Rs. 2,500 before July 1, 2012).

154.1-4 *INTEREST PAYABLE TO FUNDS ESTABLISHED FOR THE BENEFITS OF ARMED FORCES* - The matter with regard to regimental fund or non-public fund established by Armed Forces has been examined in the Board. Since the income of these organisations is exempt under section 10(*23AA*), the Board has decided that no tax may be deducted at source under section 193 from the income of such Funds— Circular No. 735, dated January 30, 1996.

154.1-5 *INTEREST TO PROVIDENT FUNDS* - The Board has decided that in the case of a provident fund whose income is exempt under section 10(*25*)(*ii*) established under a scheme under the Employees' Provident Fund and Miscellaneous Provisions Act, 1952, the income by way of interest on securities of Central and State Governments may be paid to such provident funds without deduction of income-tax at source—Circular No. 741, dated April 18, 1996.

154.1-6 *DEEP DISCOUNT BOND* - Tax is deductible at the time of redemption [*see* Circular No. 4/2004, dated May 13, 2004]. If the recipient has paid tax on interest on accrual basis, he can take relief under section 197 [*see* para 175.5] or 197A [*see* para 175.4].

154.1-7 *TRANSFER TO INTEREST PAYABLE ACCOUNT - WHEN PAYEE IS NOT IDENTIFIABLE* - *Explanation* to section 193 lays down that even when an income is credited to any account in the books of account of the person liable to pay such income, such crediting shall be deemed to be credit of such income to the account of the payee and the provisions of tax deduction shall apply accordingly, but the fact that the credit to any account is to be deemed to be credit to the payee's account also presupposes that identity of the payee can be ascertained. Therefore, this deeming fiction can only be activated when the identity of the payee can be ascertained. Therefore, the *Explanation* to section 193 cannot be invoked in a case where the person who is to receive the interest cannot be identified at the stage at which the provision for interest accrued but not due is made. This position is also accepted by the CBDT in its letter dated July 5, 1996 addressed to the Tata Iron & Steel Co. Ltd. [Letter No. 275 126/96 IT(B)]. Accordingly, no tax is required to be deducted at source in respect of the provision for interest payable made by the assessee which reflected provision for 'interest accrued but not due' in a situation where the ultimate recipient of such 'interest accrued but not due' could not have been ascertained at the point of time when the provision was made—*Industrial Development Bank of India* v. *ITO* [2006] 10 SOT 497 (Mum.).

154.1-8 *TDS ON 8 PER CENT SAVINGS (TAXABLE) BONDS, 2003* - The following clarifications have been given in respect of application of TDS on 8 per cent Savings (Taxable) Bonds, 2003—

- Tax deduction at source on 8 per cent Savings (Taxable) Bonds, 2003 is effective from June 1, 2007. Any interest credited or paid on 8 per cent Savings (Taxable) Bonds, 2003 on or after June 1, 2007 will attract TDS if the amount of interest exceeds Rs. 10,000 for the financial year. Therefore, the date of investment is not a relevant factor. TDS would, thus, apply to existing bond holders also.
- The recipient can submit Form No. 15G or 15H to get interest without TDS [for the relevant conditions *see* para 175.4].
- On 'cumulative' type of investments, if the interest is credited every year, tax deduction has to be made if the interest credited during the financial year exceeds the threshold limit of Rs. 10,000. Thus, in the case of 'cumulative' type of investments, though the interest is payable on the date of maturity, tax deduction is still to be made whenever the interest credited or paid exceeds the threshold limit during the financial year.
- A certificate issued by the Assessing Officer under section 197 [*see* para 175.5] for deduction of tax at a lower rate or *Nil* rate is required in the case of charitable institutions and trusts. No special dispensation is allowed to charitable institutions and trusts as far as TDS discipline is concerned.

Deduction of tax at source from dividends [Sec. 194]

155. The principal officer of an Indian company or a company which has made the prescribed arrangements for the declaration and payment of dividends within India is required, before making any payment, to deduct tax at source from the amount of dividend at the prescribed rate [*see* para 0.6, Referencer 1][24]. Tax is deductible under section 194 only if a shareholder is resident in India.

155.1 ***Cases where tax is not deductible or deductible at lower rates*** - In the following cases, tax is not deducted or deducted at lower rates :

155.1-1 *DIVIDENDS COVERED BY SECTION 115-O* - No tax is deductible from June 1, 1997 to March 31, 2002 and from April 1, 2003 in the case of dividend referred to in section 115-O [*see* para 207.2].

155.1-2 *APPLICATION IN FORM No. 13* - *See* para 175.5.

155.1-3 *DECLARATION TO THE PAYER IN FORM NO. 15G OR 15H* - *See* para 175.4.

Deduction of tax at source from interest other than interest on securities [Sec. 194A]

156. Any person, not being an individual or a Hindu undivided family[25], who is responsible for paying to a resident any income by way of interest, other than interest on securities, is required to deduct income-tax thereon at the rates in force [*see* Referencer 1][26] at the time of credit of such income to the account of payee or interest payable account or suspense account [*see* also para 154.1-7] or at the time of payment thereof, in cash or by issue of a cheque or draft or by any other mode, whichever is earlier.

The provisions of this section are, however, not applicable in the following cases :

a. where the aggregate amount of interest credited or paid (or likely to be credited or paid) during the financial year does not exceed the limit given in para 156.1;

b. where interest is credited or paid to any banking company, co-operative society engaged in banking business, public financial institutions, the Life Insurance Corporation, the Unit Trust of India, a company or a co-operative society carrying on the business of insurance, or notified institutions [*see Taxmann's Direct Taxes Circulars*];

c. where interest is credited or paid by a firm to its partners;

d. where interest is credited or paid by a co-operative society (other than a co-operative bank, with effect from June 1, 2015) to its members [it covers interest on time deposits/other deposits to members holding at least one share—Circular No. 9/2002[27], dated September 11, 2002] or to any other co-operative society;

e. where interest is credited or paid in respect of deposits under the schemes of Post Office (Time Deposits), Post Office (Recurring Deposits), Post Office Monthly Income Account, Kisan Vikas Patra, National Savings Certificates and Indira Vikas Patra;

f. where interest is credited or paid in respect of deposits (other than time deposits made on or after July 1, 1995) with a banking company or (interest to non-members on deposits) with a co-operative society engaged in carrying on the business of banking;

g. where interest is credited or paid in respect of deposits (by non-members) with a primary agricultural credit society or co-operative land mortgage bank or co-operative land development bank;

h. where interest is credited or paid by the Central Government under different provisions of the direct taxes;

---

24. TDS is not required if the payer company is subject to dividend tax under section 115-O. After April 1, 2018, even deemed dividend under section 2(22)(*e*) is subject to dividend tax under section 115-O. Consequently, after April 1, 2018, tax deduction provisions of section 194 do not have any practical application.

25. The provisions of sections 194A, 194C(2)[28], 194H, 194-I and 194J were amended from June 1, 2002 to provide that an individual or a Hindu undivided family, whose total sales, turnover or gross receipts from the business or profession carried on by him exceed the monetary limits specified under section 44AB during the financial year immediately preceding the financial year in which the income is to be credited or paid, shall be liable to deduct income-tax under the relevant provisions of the aforementioned sections.

26. For the financial year 2019-20, TDS rate is 10 per cent (no surcharge or health and education cess). If the recipient does not furnish his PAN to the deductor, tax will be deducted at the rate of 20 per cent. PAN of the deductee should be mentioned in any correspondence and document which is exchanged between the deductor and deductee.

27. Circular No. 9 of 2002, making a distinction between nominal member and duly registered member with regard to their rights and privileges, is outside scope of Board's power under section 119—*Jalgaon District Central Co-operative Bank Ltd.* v. *Union of India* [2004] 134 Taxman 1 (Bom.), *Gujarat Urban Co-operative Bank Federation* v. *Union of India* [2012] 209 Taxman 340 (Guj.)

28. A similar amendment has been made in section 194C(1) with effect from June 1, 2007.

i. where the interest is paid (or, up to May 31, 2015, credited) on compensation[29] awarded by the Motor Accidents Claims Tribunal if the amount of payment or the aggregate amount of such payment does not exceed Rs. 50,000[30];

j. where income is payable in relation to zero coupon bonds;

k. interest referred to in section 10(*23FC*); and

l. interest paid/payable by an Offshore Banking Unit on deposits or borrowing made after March 31, 2005 to a resident but not ordinarily resident.

156.1 ***No tax deduction if interest does not exceed a specified amount*** - Tax under section 194A is not deductible where the aggregate amount of interest credited or paid (or likely to be credited or paid) during a financial year does not exceed the amount given below—

Who is payer	*Interest is payable on* ↓	*During June 1, 2007 and March 31, 2018 Rs.*	*From April 1, 2018*		
			When payee is a senior citizen Rs.	*When payee is any other person*	
				During 2018-19 Rs.	*From April 1, 2019 Rs.*
Banking company	Time deposit	10,000	50,000	10,000	**40,000**
A co-operative society engaged in carrying on the banking business	Time deposit	10,000	50,000	10,000	**40,000**
Post office	Notified scheme (*i.e.*, Senior Citizen Savings Scheme, 2004)	10,000	50,000	10,000	**40,000**
Any other person	–	5,000	5,000	5,000	5,000

Notes –

1. The aforesaid limits shall be computed with reference to the income credited or paid by a branch of the banking company or the co-operative society, as the case may be. However, branch-wise computation system is discontinued from June 1, 2015. From June 1, 2015, section 194A has been amended to provide that for computing threshold limit (given above) interest credited or paid by the banking company/co-operative bank which has adopted core banking solutions (CBS), shall be considered.

2. The expression "time deposits" has been defined to mean deposits, excluding recurring deposits, repayable on the expiry of fixed period. The scope of TDS provisions has been extended (with effect from June 1, 2015) to cover interest on recurring deposits within its scope for the purposes of deduction of tax under section 194A.

3. The interest on time deposits made with a primary agricultural credit society or a primary credit society or a co-operative land mortgage bank or a co-operative land development bank, will not be subject to the requirement of deduction of income-tax at source.

156.2 ***Cases where tax is deducted at lower rates or when no tax is deducted*** - In the following cases, tax is not deductible or deductible at lower rates :

156.2-1 *APPLICATION IN FORM NO. 13* - *See* para 175.5.

156.2-2 *DECLARATION TO THE PAYER IN FORM NO. 15G OR 15H* - *See* para 175.4.

156.2-3 *PAYMENT UNDER A HIRE PURCHASE AGREEMENT* - When a part of purchase instalment is paid by a hirer to the owner under a hire purchase contract, the provisions of section 194A are not attracted—Instruction No. 1425, dated November 16, 1981.

156.2-4 *CHIT FUND* - Discount distributed to subscribers of a chit fund in form of bid amount offered by the successful bidder who takes chit, is not interest under section 2(*28A*) and, consequently, tax is not deductible under section 194A—*CIT* v. *Sahib Chits (Delhi) (P.) Ltd.* [2009] 185 Taxman 34 (Delhi).

156.2-5 *INTEREST ON TIME DEPOSIT BY BANK ON DAILY/MONTHLY BASIS IN CBS SOFTWARE* - Since no constructive credit to the depositor's/payee's account takes place while calculating interest on time deposits on daily or monthly basis in the CBS software used by banks, tax need not be deducted at source

---

29. Compensation awarded by Motor Vehicle Accident Claims Tribunal or interest accruing therein, cannot be subjected to TDS as said amounts are not incomes as defined in Income-tax Act—*Tamil Nadu State Transport Corpn. (Salem) Ltd.* v. *Chinnadurai* [2016] 240 Taxman 162 (Mad.).

30. The threshold limit of Rs. 50,000 is applicable separately where interest is to be shared by 2 or more claimants—*National Insurance Co. Ltd.* v. *Draupadibai* [2011] 11 taxmann.com 65 (MP).

on such provisioning of interest by banks for the purposes of macro monitoring only. In such cases, tax shall be deducted at source on accrual of interest at the end of financial year or at periodic intervals as per practice of the bank or as per the depositor's/payee's requirement or on maturity or on encashment of time deposits; whichever event takes place earlier—Circular No. 3/2010, dated March 2, 2010.

156.2-6 *NOTIONAL PROVISION OF HALF-YEARLY/QUARTERLY INTEREST* - In *Bank of Maharashtra* v. *ITO* [2010] 38 SOT 432 (Ahd.), the branch accounts of the assessee were finalized at the end of each financial year. However, as per instruction from the central office, a notional provision for half yearly interest on account of cumulative deposit was shown in general ledger as on September 29, 2001 and same was reversed on October 1, 2001. The Tribunal held that interest credited as per notional entry dated September 29, 2001 was only provisioning in accounts for purposes of macro-monitoring and it was not actual credit or payment of interest to depositors and said provision was reversed on next working day, it could be said that amount so credited never accrued to payees. Section 194A, in such a case is not applicable.

156.2-7 *TAX DEDUCTION ON THE DEPOSITS IN BANKS IN THE NAME OF THE REGISTRAR TO THE SUPREME COURT/HIGH COURT DURING PENDENCY OF LITIGATION*- The Board has issued Circular No. 8/2011[$], dated October 14, 2011. This Circular is applicable where one (or more) litigant is directed by the Court that a specified amount be deposited in the bank directly or through the court. However, in the case of *UCO Bank* v. *Union of India* [2014] 51 taxmann.com 253 (Delhi), the Court has quashed Circular No. 8/2011[$]. Subsequently, the Board has clarified that interest on FDRs made in the name of Registrar General of the Court or the depositor of the fund on the directions of the Court, will not be subject to TDS till the matter is decided by the Court. However, once the Court decides the ownership of the money lying in the fixed deposit, the provisions of section 194A will apply to the recipient of the income—Circular No. 23/2015[$], dated December 28, 2015.

156.2-8 *JUDGMENT DEBTOR* - Judgment debtor is not liable to deduct tax at source on interest component of decree — *Madhusudan Shrikrishna* v. *Emkay Exports* [2010] 188 Taxman 195 (Bom.).

156.2-9 *TDS ON DEPOSITS UNDER THE CAPITAL GAINS ACCOUNTS SCHEME* - In case of deposits under the Capital Gains Accounts Scheme, 1988 where the depositor has deceased –

a. TDS on the interest income accrued for and up to the period of death of the depositor is required to be deducted and reported against PAN of the depositor, and

b. TDS on the interest income accrued for the period after death of the depositor is required to be deducted and reported against PAN of the legal heir,

unless a declaration is filed under rule 37BA(2) to that effect – Notification No. 8/2017, dated September 13, 2017.

Deduction of tax at source from winnings from lotteries or crossword puzzles [Sec. 194B]

157. A person responsible for paying to any person any income by way of winnings from lotteries or crossword puzzles or winnings from card games or other games, exceeding Rs. 10,000 (Rs. 5,000 up to June 30, 2010) is required, at the time of such payment, to deduct income-tax thereon at the rates in force[31]. Where the prize is given partly in cash and partly in kind, tax is deductible from cash prize with reference to the aggregate amount of the cash prize and the value of the prize in kind. Moreover, where the lottery or crossword puzzle prize is paid in instalments, the deduction is to be made at the time of actual payment of each instalment. Likewise, tax is deductible from the amount of the prize money paid to the owner of lucky ticket with reference to the amount paid to him. No tax is, however, deductible from the income by way of bonus or commission paid to the lottery agents or sellers of lottery tickets on the sale made by them—Circular No. 257, dated June 4, 1979 [*see* also para 164].

• With effect from June 1, 1997, where the winnings are wholly in kind or where they are partly in cash and partly in kind but the part in cash is not sufficient to meet the liability for tax deduction in respect of the whole of the winnings, the person responsible for paying shall, before releasing the winnings either in cash or in kind ensure that tax has been paid in respect of the winnings.

Deduction of tax at source from winnings from horse races [Sec. 194BB]

158. Tax is deductible at source from any income by way of winnings from the horse races at prescribed rates[31]. Deduction of tax at source can be made only in cases where the income by way of winnings from horse races to be paid to a person exceeds Rs. 10,000 (Rs. 5,000 during July 1, 2010 to May 31, 2016, Rs. 2,500 up to June 30, 2010). The obligation to deduct tax at source applies only where such winnings are

---

31. Under sections 194B and 194BB, if recipient is a resident, tax is deductible during the financial year 2019-20 at the rate of 30 per cent (no surcharge or health and education cess). If, however, recipient is non-resident tax is deductible at the rate of 30 per cent [+SC+HEC].

$ For Circular Nos. 8/2011 and 23/2015, log on to *taxmann.com/readyreckoner.aspx*.

paid by a bookmaker or a person to whom a licence has been granted by the Government under any law for the time being in force for horse racing in any race course or for arranging for wagering or betting in any race course.

Deduction of tax at source from payments to contractors or sub-contractors [Sec. 194C]

159. The provisions of section 194C are given below—

159.1 ***Who is responsible for tax deduction*** - Any person responsible for paying any sum to any resident contractor for carrying out any work (including supply of labour for carrying out any work) in pursuance of a contract between a *specified person* and the resident contractor is required to deduct tax at source.

Specified person - Meaning of - Tax is deductible under section 194C(1) only if payment is made in pursuance of a contract between a specified person and a resident contractor. The following are "specified persons" for this purpose :

a. the Central Government or any State Government; or

b. any local authority; or

c. any corporation established by or under a Central, State or Provincial Act; or

d. any company; or

e. any co-operative society; or

f. any authority constituted in India by or under any law, engaged either for the purpose of dealing with and satisfying the need for housing accommodation or for the purpose of planning, development or improvement of cities, towns and villages, or for both; or

g. any society registered under the Societies Registration Act, 1860 or under any law corresponding to that Act in force in any part of India; or

h. any trust; or

i. any University established or incorporated by or under a Central, State or Provincial Act and an institution declared to be a University under section 3 of the University Grants Commission Act, 1956; or

j. any foreign Government or a foreign enterprise or any association or body established outside India (applicable from October 1, 2009); or

k. any firm; or

l. any individual or HUF whose books of account are required to be audited under section 44AB(*a*)/(*b*) during the immediately preceding financial year and sum credited/paid is not exclusively for personal purposes; or

m. (with effect from June 1, 2008) AOP/BOI whose books of account are required to be audited under section 44AB(*a*)/(*b*) during the immediately preceding financial year.

159.2 ***When tax has to be deducted at source*** - Tax is to be deducted either at the time of credit of such sum to the account of the payee, or at the time of payment thereof in cash or by issue of cheque or by any other mode, whichever is earlier. For this purpose, any sum credited to any account, whether called "Suspense account" or by any other name in the books of account of the payer, is treated as credit of such income to the account of the payee. Accordingly, tax has to be deducted if amount payable to resident contractor or sub-contractor is transferred to a "Suspense account" by the payer in his books of account. *See* also para 154.1-7.

159.3 ***When no tax is deductible*** - The provisions are given below—

• *Provisions applicable from October 1, 2004 - In insignificant cases* - Tax is required to be deducted at source where the amount credited or paid to a contractor or sub-contractor exceeds Rs. 30,000 in a single payment or Rs. 1,00,000 (Rs. 75,000 during July 1, 2010 to May 31, 2016) in the aggregate during a financial year. In other words, tax shall not be deductible under section 194C if the following two conditions are satisfied—

a. the amount of any (single) sum credited or paid (or likely to be credited or paid) to the contractor does not exceed Rs. 30,000; and

b. the aggregate of the amounts of such sums credited or paid (or likely to be credited or paid) during the financial year does not exceed Rs. 1,00,000 (Rs. 75,000 during July 1, 2010 to May 31, 2016).

• *Payment or credit to transport operators (applicable during October 1, 2009)* - If recipient (maybe an individual, firm, company, or any other person) is a transport contractor (who is in the business of plying, hiring or leasing goods carriages) and satisfies the following conditions, tax is not deductible –

- *During October 1, 2009 and May 31, 2015* - Recipient furnishes his PAN to the deductor.

- *From June 1, 2015* - Recipient owns 10 (or less than 10) goods carriages at any time during the financial year. He gives a declaration[31a] to this effect to the deductor. Besides, he furnishes his PAN to the deductor.

Deductors who make payments to transporters without deducting TDS (as they have quoted PAN) will be required to intimate these PAN details to the Income-tax Department in the prescribed format (*i.e.*, Form No. 26Q).

• *Personal purposes* - Payment by an individual or HUF to a resident contractor for personal purposes is not subject to tax deduction.

• *Small transport sub-contractor (applicable during June 1, 2005 and September 30, 2009)* - Tax is not deductible at source under section 194C during June 1, 2005 and September 30, 2009 if the following conditions are satisfied—

1. Consideration for work contract is paid or payable by a resident contractor to a resident sub-contractor.

2. The resident sub-contractor is an individual.

3. The aforesaid amount is paid or payable to the sub-contractor during the course of business of plying, hiring or leasing goods carriages.

4. The resident sub-contractor does not own more than two goods carriages at any time during the previous year.

5. The resident sub-contractor submits a declaration to the payer in Form No. 15-I.

If the above conditions are satisfied, the payer (*i.e.*, resident contractor) will not deduct tax at source under section 194C. The payer shall furnish the details of above payment to the prescribed income-tax authority in Form No. 15J on or before June 30 after the expiry of the financial year.

159.4 ***Who is a contractor/sub-contractor*** - In order to reduce the scope for disputes regarding classification of contract as sub-contract, the same rate of TDS has been specified (with effect from October 1, 2009) for payments to both contractors as well as sub-contractors.

159.5 ***Meaning of work contract*** - Provisions of section 194C relating to tax deduction from payment to contractors/sub-contractors are applicable only where contract is either a "work contract" or a "contract for supply of labour for works contract". These provisions are, therefore, not applicable for payments made under contract for sale of goods.

• *"Work" as defined in section 194C* - The expression "work", shall include (*a*) advertising, (*b*) broadcasting and telecasting including production of programmes for such broadcasting or telecasting, (*c*) carriage of goods and passengers by any mode of transport other than by railway, and (*d*) catering.

With effect from October 1, 2009, the expression "work" shall also include manufacturing or supplying a product according to the requirement or specification of a customer by using material purchased from such customer. However, it will not include manufacturing or supplying a product according to the requirement or specification of a customer by using material purchased from a person, other than such customer.

159.6 ***TDS rates*** - The following TDS rates are applicable under section 194C—

If the recipient is an individual/HUF	1%
If the recipient is any other person	2%

159.6-1 *OTHER POINTS* - The following points should be noted—

1. Surcharge or health and education cess is not applicable.

2. If the recipient does not furnish his PAN to the deductor, tax will be deducted (with effect from April 1, 2010) at the rate of 20 per cent. PAN of the deductee should be mentioned in any correspondence and document which is exchanged between the deductor and deductee.

31a. The following format for furnishing declaration is specified by the Board *vide* Circular No. 19/2015, dated November 27, 2015—

Declaration under section 194C(6) of the Income-tax Act, 1961

No...... (*To be provided by payee*) Date...............

From: (*Name and address of the payee*)

To : (*Name and address of the payer*)

The freight/transport charges amounting to Rs............for transportation of goods by goods carriages having Registration Number ....may be paid or credited to my account without deduction of tax under section 194C of the Income-tax Act, 1961. I/We, ... in the capacity of ....hereby declare that I/We do not own more than ten goods carriage and also did not own more than ten goods carriage at any time during the period from 1st April .... to ....My Permanent Account Number (PAN) is ....I hereby enclose a self-attested photocopy of my PAN Card.

....

Place: Signature of the person making declaration

3. In the case of work contract being manufacturing or supplying product according to the specification of customer (by using material purchased from such customer), TDS shall be deducted on the invoice value excluding the value of material purchased from such customer, if such value is mentioned separately in the invoice. Where the material component has not been separately mentioned in the invoice, TDS shall be deducted on the whole of the invoice value.

159.7 ***Judicial pronouncements/Board's clarifications*** -The following judicial pronouncements/Board's clarifications should be kept in view -

159.7-1 *ADVERTISING CONTRACT* - If an advertising agency gives a consolidated bill (including charges for art work and other related jobs as well as payment to *media*) the deduction will have to be made under section 194C. The advertising agencies shall have to deduct tax at source at the rate of 10 per cent under section 194J while making payments to artists, actors, models, etc.—Circular No. 715[$], dated August 8, 1995.

• *Payment directly to print media/Doordarshan for release to advertisements* - The payments made directly to print and electronic *media* would be covered under section 194C as these are in the nature of payments for purposes of advertising. It may, however, be noted that the payments made directly to Doordarshan may not be subjected to tax deduction as Doordarshan, being a Government agency, is not liable to income-tax—Circular No. 715[$], dated August 8, 1995.

• *Payment by an advertising agency to print media/electronic media* - It is not subject to tax deduction under section 194C—Circular No. 717[$], dated August 14, 1995.

• *Sponsorship of debates is advertisements* - The agreement of sponsorship of debates, seminars and other functions in schools/colleges/associations is in essence an agreement for carrying out a work of advertisement. Therefore, provisions of section 194C shall apply—Circular No. 715[$], dated August 8, 1995.

• *Advertisement in souvenirs* - Tax has to be deducted on payments for cost of advertisements issued in the souvenirs brought out by various organisations—Circular No. 715[$], dated August 8, 1995.

• *Payment of putting up a hoarding* - The contract for putting up a hoarding is in the nature of advertising contract and provisions of section 194C would be applicable. If, however, a person has taken a particular space on rent and thereafter sublets the same fully or in part for putting up a hoarding, he would be liable to tax deduction under section 194-I and not 194C—Circular No. 715[$], dated August 8, 1995.

• *Payment made by broadcasters/telecasters to production houses for production of content or programme for broadcasting/telecasting* - Where the content is produced as per the specifications provided by the broadcaster/telecaster and the copyright of the content/programme also gets transferred to the telecaster/broadcaster, such contract is covered by the definition of the term "work" and subject to TDS under section 194C. Where, however, the telecaster/broadcaster acquires only the telecasting/broadcasting rights of the content already produced by the production house, there is no contract for "carrying out any work". Such payments are not liable for TDS under section 194C. However, payments of this nature may be liable for TDS under other provisions of the Act – Circular No. 4/2016[$], dated February 29, 2016.

159.7-2 *BROADCASTING/TELECASTING CONTRACTS* - Once there is a specific provision introduced by way of an *Explanation* to section 194C, to bring within its ambit contractual work concerning 'broadcasting and telecasting', the revenue cannot resort to section 194J, which is in more general terms for purpose of tax deduction at source from income from such contractual work—*CIT* v. *Prasar Bharati (Broadcasting Corpn. of India)* [2007] 158 Taxman 470/292 ITR 580 (Delhi).

• Payment made by a cable operator to get license of TV channels is payment for a work contract pertaining telecasting rights and covered by section 194C—*Kurukshetra Darpans (P.) Ltd.* v. *CIT* [2008] 169 Taxman 344 (Punj. & Har.).

159.7-3 *PAYMENT MADE TO TRAVEL AGENT/OR AN AIRLINE* - The payments made to a travel agent or an airline for purchase of a ticket for travel would not be subject to tax deduction at source as the privity of the contract is between the individual passenger and the airline/travel agent, notwithstanding the fact that the payment is made by an entity mentioned in section 194C(1). The provision of section 194C shall, however, apply when a plane or a bus or any other mode of transport is chartered by one of the entities mentioned in section 194C—Circular No. 715[$], dated August 8, 1995.

The above provision shall apply *mutatis mutandis* to the tickets for travel of individuals by any other mode of transport also—Circular No. 713[$], dated August 2, 1995.

• *Payment to clearing/forwarding agents* vis-a-vis *payment to travel agents* - Payments to clearing and forwarding agents for carriage of goods is subject to tax deduction at source under section 194C. The travel agent, issuing tickets on behalf of the airlines for travel of individual passengers, would not be required to

[$] For Circular Nos. 713, 715, 717 and 4/2016, log on to *taxmann.com/readyreckoner.aspx*.

deduct tax at source as he acts on behalf of the airlines. The position of clearing and forwarding agents is different. They act as independent contractors. Any payment made to them would, hence, be liable for deduction of tax at source. They would also be liable to deduct tax at source while making payments for carriage of goods—Circular No. 715$, dated August 8, 1995.

• *Payment made for carriage of documents* - The carriage of documents, letters, etc., is in the nature of carriage of goods and, therefore, provisions of section 194C would be attracted in respect of payments made to the couriers—Circular No. 715$, dated August 8, 1995.

• *Whether each GR is a separate contract* - Normally, each GR can be said to be a separate contract, if the goods are transported at one time. But if the goods are transported continuously in pursuance of a contract for a specific period or quantity, each GR will not be a separate contract and all GRs relating to that period or quantity will be aggregated for the purpose of the tax deduction—Circular No. 715$, dated August 8, 1995.

• *Non-resident shipping companies* - Section 172 is a self-contained code for the levy and recovery of the tax, ship-wise, and journey-wise, and requires the filing of the return within a maximum time of thirty days from the date of departure of the ship.

The provisions of section 172 are to apply, notwithstanding anything contained in other provisions of the Act. Therefore, in such cases, the provisions of sections 194C and 195 relating to tax deduction at source are not applicable. The recovery of tax is to be regulated, for a voyage undertaken from any port in India by a ship under the provisions of section 172.

Section 194C deals with work contracts including carriage of goods and passengers by any mode of transport other than railways. This section applies to payments made by a person referred to in clauses (*a*) to (*j*) of sub-section (1) to any "resident" (termed as contractor). It is clear from the section that the area of operation of TDS is confined to payments made to any "resident". On the other hand, section 172 operates in the area of computation of profits from shipping business of non-residents. Thus, there is no overlapping in the areas of operation of these sections.

There would, however, be cases where payments are made to shipping agents of non-resident ship-owners or charterer for carriage of passengers, etc., shipped at a port in India. Since, the agent acts on behalf of the non-resident ship-owner or charterer, he steps into the shoes of the principal. Accordingly, provisions of section 172 shall apply and those of sections 194C and 195 will not apply—Circular No. 723$, dated September 19, 1995.

• *Goods received on "freight to pay basis"* - Payment of freight[32] would be subject to tax deduction even when goods are received on "freight to pay basis"—Circular No. 715$, dated August 8, 1995.

159.7-4 *DOES CATERING INCLUDE SERVING FOODS IN RESTAURANT* - Tax deduction at source is not required to be made when payment is made for serving food in a restaurant in the normal course of running of the restaurant/cafe—Circular No. 715$, dated August 8, 1995.

159.7-5 *PAYMENT TO AN ELECTRICIAN* - The payments made to an electrician or to a contractor who provides the service of an electrician will be in the nature of payment made in pursuance of a contract for carrying out any work. Accordingly, provisions of section 194C will apply in such cases—Circular No. 715$, dated August 8, 1995.

159.7-6 *MAINTENANCE CONTRACTS* - Routine, normal maintenance contracts which include supply of spares will be covered under section 194C. However, where technical services are rendered, the provisions of section 194J will apply in regard to tax deduction at source—Circular No. 715$, dated August 8, 1995.

159.7-7 *FIXED DEPOSIT COMMISSION* - FD commission/brokerage cannot be covered by section 194C—Circular No. 715$, dated August 8, 1995.

159.7-8 *PROCUREMENT OF ORDERS* - Rendering services for procurement of orders is not covered by section 194C but by section 194J—Circular No. 715$, dated August 8, 1995.

159.7-9 *REIMBURSEMENT* - Section 194C refers to any sum paid. Reimbursements cannot be deducted out of the bill amount for the purpose of tax deduction at source—Circular No. 715$, dated August 8, 1995 [*see*, however, para 166.7].

---

32. A seller sold certain goods to the assessee (buyer). Under contract of sale, the seller was bound to send goods to the buyer and to pay transportation charges to goods transport agency. Seller was, however, entitled to recover transportation charges from the buyer. On reimbursement of freight by the buyer to the seller, TDS provisions of section 194C are not applicable – *Hightension Switchgears (P.) Ltd.* v. *CIT* [2016] 240 Taxman 582 (Cal.).

$ For Circular Nos. 715 and 723, log on to *taxmann.com/readyreckoner.aspx.*

159.7-10 *BIDI MANUFACTURING* - In the case of *bidi* manufacturing industry, payments made to *munshis* (who give the work to the workers who work at home) are subject to tax deduction at source under section 194C—Circular No. 433, dated September 25, 1985. No tax is, however, deductible under section 194C if the worker (employed through the medium of agency such as *munshis*) bring *bidi* to the factory for quality check and for getting payments—Circular No. 487, dated June 8, 1987.

159.7-11 *TDS CERTIFICATES TO CONSIGNEE* - Where the truck or such other goods carriages is booked by the consignor but the payment is made by the consignee on delivery of the goods, the consignee shall issue TDS certificate in the cases of the truck/goods-carriage operators within the prescribed time and in favour of such truck/goods-carriage operators—Circular No. 6/2006, dated June 23, 2006.

159.7-12 *HOTELS* - Services rendered by a hotel to its customers by providing different facilities/amenities do not constitute 'work' within meaning of section 194C — *East India Hotels Ltd* v. *Central Board of Direct Taxes* [2009] 179 Taxman 17 (Bom.).

159.7-13 *PAYMENTS SPECIFIED UNDER SECTION 197A(1F)* - In exercise of the powers conferred by section 197A(1F), the Central Government has notified that tax deduction shall not be applicable on the payment of the nature specified below, if such payment is made by a person to a bank (listed in the Second Schedule to the RBI Act, other than a foreign bank) or to any payment systems company authorised by RBI under section 4(2) of the Payment and Settlement Systems Act, 2007—

a. bank guarantee commission;

b. cash management service charges;

c. depository charges on maintenance of DEMAT accounts;

d. charges for warehousing services for commodities;

e. underwriting service charges;

f. clearing charges (MICR charges) including interchange fee or any other similar charges by whatever name called charged at the time of settlement or for clearing activities under the Payment and Settlement Systems Act, 2007;

g. credit card or debit card commission for transaction between merchant establishment and acquirer bank– Notification No. SO 2143(E), dated June 17, 2016.

159.7-14 *LANDING AND PARKING CHARGES PAYABLE BY AIRLINES* - Landing and parking charges payable by airlines in respect of aircrafts are not for the "use of land" *per se* but the charges are in respect of number of facilities provided by the Airport Authority of India. Thus, landing and parking charges payable by airlines attract TDS under section 194C and not under section 194-I—*Japan Airlines Co. Ltd.* v. *CIT* [2015] 60 taxmann.com 71 (SC).

159.8 ***When tax is not deducted or deducted at lower rate [Sec. 197]*** - *See* para 175.5.

Deduction of tax at source from insurance commission [Sec. 194D]

160. Person responsible for paying to a resident any income by way of remuneration or reward, whether by way of commission or otherwise, for soliciting or procuring insurance business including business relating to the continuance, renewal or revival of policies of insurance is required, at the time of credit of such income to the account of the resident or the payment thereof (by whatever mode), whichever is earlier, to deduct income-tax thereon at the rates in force [*i.e.*, 5 per cent[33] (with effect from April 1, 2016) if recipient is a resident other than a domestic company and 10 per cent[33] in all other cases]. No deduction shall, however, be made in a case where the amount of such income or, as the case may be, the aggregate of the amounts of such income credited or paid or likely to be credited or paid during the financial year to the account of, or to, the payee, does not exceed Rs. 15,000 (Rs. 20,000 during July 1, 2010 to May 31, 2016).

At the time of deducting tax from the insurance commission credited to an agent's account, adjustment for any debits made in this account in respect of excess commission credited or paid to him earlier is not permissible and income-tax must be deducted from the full amount of commission credited to this account—Circular No. 277[$], dated July 21, 1980.

160.1 ***When tax is not deducted or deducted at lower rate*** - *See* paras 175.4 and 175.5.

160.2 ***Reinsurance not covered by section 194D*** - Reinsurance differs from insurance in a number of ways and the most important is that there is no contractual relationship between the direct insured and

---

33. For the financial year 2019-20, there is no surcharge or health and education cess. If the recipient does not furnish his PAN to the deductor, tax will be deducted at the rate of 20 per cent. PAN of the deductee should be mentioned in any correspondence and document which is exchanged between the deductor and deductee.

[$] For Circular No. 277, log on to *taxmann.com/readyreckoner.aspx.*

the reinsurer. There are separate contracts involved—one between the insured and the insurer and another between the insurer and the reinsurer. Insurer has to pay all valid claims to the insured, irrespective of whether the insurer can recover the same from his reinsurer.

When an reinsurance company gets business from insurance company at premium less "commission", the "commission" is not subject to TDS under section 194D, as it is not payable to an agent for procuring insurance business. Similarly, when "profit commission" is payable by an reinsurance company to an insurance company, after the expiry of the term of insurance, in respect of such cases where there is no claim during the operation of the reinsurance treaty, TDS under section 194D is not required—*General Insurance Corpn. of India* v. *CIT* [2009] 28 SOT 453 (Mum.).

Tax deduction from payment of life insurance policy [Sec. 194DA, applicable from October 1, 2014]

160A. Any person responsible for paying to a resident any sum under a life insurance policy (including bonus) shall deduct income-tax thereon, in the cases given below –

• *When TDS under section 194DA is applicable* - If exemption is available to the recipient under section 10(*10D*), then TDS provisions of section 194DA are not applicable. Consequently, in the following cases TDS provisions of section 194DA are applicable [in these cases, exemption under section 10(*10DA*) is not available] —

a. any payment under a keyman insurance policy;

b. any payment under section 80DD(3) or section 80DDA(3);

c. any payment under insurance policy issued during April 1, 2003 to March 31, 2012 where annual insurance premium is more than 20 per cent of capital sum assured;

d. any payment under insurance policy issued after March 31, 2012 where annual insurance premium is more than 10 per cent of capital sum assured; or

e. any payment under insurance policy issued after March 31, 2013 to a person covered under section 80U or 80DDB where annual insurance premium is more than 15 per cent of capital sum assured.

In cases covered by (*c*), (*d*) or (*e*), tax is not deductible if the payment is made on the death of a person.

• *Rate of TDS* - In the aforesaid cases, tax is deductible under section 194DA at the rates given below –

- 2 per cent of payment (applicable during October 1, 2014 and May 31, 2016).
- 1 per cent[34] of payment (applicable during June 1, 2016 and August 31, 2019).
- **5 per cent[34] of the amount of income comprised in payment** (applicable with effect from September 1, 2019).

• *Other points* - Tax is deductible at the time of payment. No TDS is required if the amount payable during the financial year is less than Rs. 1,00,000. Lower TDS certificate provisions of section 197 are not applicable. However, self-declaration in Form No. 15G/15H can be submitted under section 197A (with effect from June 1, 2015).

Payment to non-resident sportsman or sports association or entertainer [Sec. 194E]

161. Person responsible for paying any income referred to in section 115BBA to a non-resident foreign citizen-sportsman (including an athlete) or (with effect from July 1, 2012) an entertainer or a non-resident sports association/institution shall deduct tax at source at the rate of 20 per cent† (10 per cent† up to May 31, 2012). The tax is to be deducted at the time of credit of such income to the account of the payee or at the time of payment thereof in cash or by issue of cheque or draft or by other mode, whichever is earlier. The following points should be noted—

• Obligation to deduction under section 194E is not affected by DTAA—*PILCOM* v. *CIT* [2011] 198 Taxman 555 (Cal.).

• Section 194E nowhere requires to check whether in the hands of recipient income is chargeable to tax in India. This is the requirement of section 195 and not of section 194E—*PILCOM (supra).*

• Payments to an umpire/referee do not come within the purview of section 115BBA or 194E—*Indcom* v. *CIT* [2011] 200 Taxman 40 (Cal.). Payment to a resident umpire is covered by section 194J and payment to a non-resident umpire is subject to tax deduction under section 195 if it is taxable in India in the hands of non-resident umpire in India.

34. For the financial year 2019-20, there is no surcharge or health and education cess. If the recipient does not furnish his PAN to the deductor, tax will be deducted at the rate of 20 per cent. PAN of the deductee should be mentioned in any correspondence and document which is exchanged between the deductor and deductee.

Deduction of tax from payments in respect of National Savings Scheme [Sec. 194EE]

162. Under this section, the person responsible for paying any amount referred to in clause (*a*) of sub-section (2) of section 80CCA will deduct income-tax thereon at the rate of 10 per cent[35] (20 per cent up to May 31, 2016) at the time of payment.

162.1 ***When tax is not deductible*** - In the following cases, tax is not deductible :–

162.1-1 *PAYMENT UP TO RS. 2,500* - Where the amount of payment or the aggregate amount of payments in a financial year is less than Rs. 2,500, tax is not deductible under section 194EE.

162.1-2 *PAYMENT TO LEGAL HEIRS* - Where the payment is made to the heirs of the deceased assessee (depositor), no tax shall be deducted at source.

162.1-3 *DECLARATION TO THE PAYER IN FORM NO. 15G OR 15H* - *See* para 175.4.

Deduction of tax at source on payments on account of repurchase of units by Mutual Funds or UTI [Sec. 194F]

163. The person responsible for paying to any person any amount referred to in section 80CCB shall, at the time of payment thereof, deduct income-tax thereon at the rate of 20 per cent[35].

Deduction of tax from commission, etc., on sale of lottery tickets [Sec. 194G]

164. The person responsible for paying any income by way of commission, remuneration or prize (by whatever name called) on lottery ticket in an amount exceeding Rs. 15,000 (Rs. 1,000 up to May 31, 2016) shall deduct income-tax thereon at the rate of 5 per cent[35] (10 per cent[35] up to May 31, 2016). Tax shall be deducted at the time of credit of such income to the account of the payee or at the time of payment of such income in cash or by issue of cheque/draft or by any other mode, whichever is earlier. *See* also para 154.1-7.

164.1 ***When tax is deductible at lower rate [Sec. 197]*** - *See* para 175.5.

Deduction of tax at source from commission or brokerage [Sec. 194H]

164A. Section 194H was inserted with effect from June 1, 2001.

164A.1 ***Who is responsible for tax deduction*** - Any person (other than an individual or Hindu undivided family[36]) who is responsible for paying commission or brokerage to a resident shall deduct tax at source.

164A.2 ***When tax has to be deducted*** - Tax shall be deducted at the time of credit of such income to the account of the payee or at the time of payment of such income in cash or by the issue of a cheque or draft or by any other mode, whichever is earlier. Where any income is credited to any account, whether called "Suspense account" or by any other name, in the books of account of the person liable to pay such income, such crediting shall be deemed to be credit of such income to the account of the payee. *See* also para 154.1-7.

• *PAYMENT IN EXCESS OF RS. 5,000/RS. 15,000 IS SUBJECT TO TAX DEDUCTION* - No tax is deductible if the amount of commission or brokerage paid/credited during the financial year does not exceed Rs. 15,000 (Rs. 5,000 up to May 31, 2016).

• *COMMISSION OR BROKERAGE AS DEFINED IN SECTION 194H* - Commission or brokerage for this purpose includes any payment (not being insurance commission referred to in section 196D) received or receivable, directly or indirectly, by a person acting on behalf of another person for services rendered (not being professional services) or for any services in the course of buying or selling of goods or in relation to any transaction relating to any asset, valuable article or thing, not being securities. The expression "professional services" means services rendered by a person in the course of carrying on a legal, medical, engineering or architectural profession or the profession of accountancy or technical consultancy or interior decoration or such other profession as is notified by the Board for the purposes of section 44AA (*i.e.*, authorised representative, film artist, company secretary and information technology).

164A.3 ***Rate of tax deduction*** - 5 per cent[35] (10 per cent up to May 31, 2016).

164A.4 ***When tax is deducted at lower rate*** - *See* para 175.5.

---

35. For the financial year 2019-20, there is no surcharge or health and education cess, if the recipient is a resident. If recipient is non-resident, it will be increased by surcharge and health and education cess. If the recipient does not furnish his PAN to the deductor, tax will be deducted at the rate of 20 per cent. PAN of the deductee should be mentioned in any correspondence and document which is exchanged between the deductor and deductee.

36. In some cases, tax is deductible from June 1, 2002 even by an individual or a Hindu undivided family, *see* para 156, footnote.

164A.5 ***When commission is retained by agent*** - A question may arise whether there would be deduction of tax under section 194H where commission or brokerage is retained by the consignee/agent and not remitted to the consignor/principal while remitting the sale consideration. Since the retention of commission by the consignee/agent amounts to constructive payment of the same to him by the consignor/principal, deduction of tax at source is required to be made from the amount of commission. Therefore, the consignor/principal will have to deposit the tax deductible on the amount of commission income—Circular No. 619[$], dated December 4, 1991.

164A.6 ***Other points*** - The following proposition should be noted –

• *Turnover commission* - The work of receipt of tax payments and issue of refunds is conducted by the Bank authorised for such purposes by the Reserve Bank of India (RBI). As a compensation for the work so conducted, the Central Government pays to the Banks, through RBI, commission termed as "Turnover Commission". Tax would not be required to be deducted by RBI on the amount of Turnover Commission paid or credited by it—Circular No. 6/2003[$], dated September 3, 2003.

• *No TDS in the case of amount payable by BSNL/MTNL to PCOs* - Tax is not deductible in respect of commission or brokerage paid or payable by BSNL/MTNL to their PCO franchises.

• *Travel agents* - Commission and supplementary commission received by the travel agents from Airlines are liable to tax deduction at source under section 194H—Letter F. No. 275/70/2009-IT(B), dated December 22, 2009, *Around the World Travels & Tours (P.) Ltd.* v. *Union of India* [2004] 141 Taxman 53 (Mad.), *CIT* v. *Singapore Airlines Ltd.* [2009] 180 Taxman 128 (Delhi).

• *SIM cards* - Discount given by a mobile cellular operator to its distributors in the course of selling of SIM cards and recharge coupons under pre-paid scheme of getting a connection is, in substance, a payment for services to be rendered by distributors to the assessee and covered by section 194H—*Vodafone Essar Cellular Ltd.* v. *CIT* [2010] 194 Taxman 518 (Ker.).

• *Advertisement commission paid by Doordarshan* - Advertisement commission paid by Doordarshan to its agents is subject to tax deduction at source under section 194H—*CIT* v. *Director, Prasarbharti, Doordarshan Kendra* [2010] 189 Taxman 315 (Ker.).

• *Discount given to stamp vendors* - No TDS is applicable on discount given to Stamp Vendors for purchasing stamps in bulk quantity – *CIT* v. *Ahmedabad Stamp Vendors Association* [2012] 25 taxmann.com 201 (SC).

• *Payment made by television channels/newspapers to advertising agency* - No TDS is attracted on payments made by television channels/newspaper companies to the advertising agency for booking or procuring of or canvassing for advertisements. It is trade discount but not commission – Circular No. 5/2016[$], dated February 29, 2016.

Deduction of tax at source from income by way of rent [Sec. 194-I]

165. Section 194-I was inserted with effect from June 1, 1994.

165.1 ***Who is responsible for tax deduction*** - Any person (not being an individual or a Hindu undivided family[36]) responsible for paying rent to a resident is required to deduct tax at source under the provisions of section 194-I. For this purpose, payer himself is treated as person responsible for paying rent. If, however, payer is a company, the company itself, including the principal officer thereof, is the person responsible for paying rent.

165.2 ***When tax has to be deducted*** - The person responsible for paying rent should deduct tax at source. Tax is to be deducted at source either :

a. at the time of credit of such income to the account of payee; or

b. at the time of payment thereof in cash or by issue of a cheque or draft or by any other mode, whichever is earlier.

Where any income by way of rent is credited to any account (whether called "Suspense account" or by any other name) in the books of account of the person liable to pay such rent, such crediting shall be deemed to be credit of such income to the account of the payee. *See* also para 154.1-7.

• *No tax is deductible if payment during a financial year does not exceed Rs.* ***2,40,000***[37] - No tax is deductible if the amount of rent credited/paid during the financial year does not exceed Rs. **2,40,000**[37].

• *No tax deduction when rent is paid/credited to real estate investment trust* - With effect from June 1, 2015, no tax deduction shall be made under section 194-I where the income by way of rent is credited or paid to

---

36. In some cases, tax is deductible from June 1, 2002 even by an individual or a Hindu undivided family, *see* para 156, footnote.

37. **Rs. 2,40,000** is applicable from April 1, 2019. It was Rs. 1,80,000 during July 1, 2010 and March 31, 2019. Up to June 30, 2010, it was Rs. 1,20,000.

$ For Circular Nos. 619, 6/2003 and 5/2016, log on to *taxmann.com/readyreckoner.aspx.*

a business trust, being a real estate investment trust, in respect of any real estate asset, referred to in section 10(*23FCA*), owned directly by such business trust.

165.2-1 *RENT IS DEFINED IN SECTION 194-I* - *Explanation (i)* to section 194-I defines rent as follows :

(*i*) 'rent' means any payment, by whatever name called, under any lease, sub-lease, tenancy or any other agreement or arrangement for the use of (either separately or together) any,—

(*a*) land; or
(*b*) building (including factory building); or
(*c*) land appurtenant to a building (including factory building); or
(*d*) machinery; or
(*e*) plant; or
(*f*) equipment; or
(*g*) furniture; or
(*h*) fittings,

whether or not any or all of the above are owned by the payee.

As per the aforesaid definition, the following are essential features of "rent"—

1. Payment is made under any lease, sub-lease, tenancy or any other agreement or arrangement.

2. Payment is made either for the use of only land or building (including factory building). After the modification of the definition of "rent" under section 194-I, with effect from July 13, 2006, TDS provisions will also be applicable in respect of rent (paid or payable) of machinery, plant, equipment, furniture or fittings.

3. It is immaterial whether or not such asset is owned by the person to whom rent is paid.

165.2-2 *BROAD INFERENCES* - On the basis of the aforesaid definition and clarifications given by the Board, the following broad inferences one can draw :

• *When building is let out along with furniture/fittings* - If a building is let out along with furniture/fittings but rent is payable under two separate agreements (one for building and another for furniture/fittings) the composite rent is subject to tax deduction under section 194-I.

• *Rent of "any" building is covered* - Rent of any building is covered by section 194-I.

• *The payee may not be owner of the building* - Section 194-I is applicable even if the person to whom rent is paid is not the owner of the building. In other words, tax is deductible even in the case of sub-lease of a building.

• *Advance rent* - Where an advance rent is paid before June 1, 1994, tax is not deductible—Circular No. 718$, dated August 22, 1995. If, however, advance rent is paid on or after May 31, 1994, it is subject to tax deduction at the time of "payment".

• *Non-refundable deposit* - In cases where the tenant makes a non-refundable deposit, tax would have to be deducted at source as such deposit represents the consideration for the use of the land or the building, etc., and, therefore, partakes the nature of rent as defined in section 194-I. If, however, the deposit is refundable, no tax is deductible at source. If the deposit carries interest, the tax to be deducted on the amount of interest will be governed by section 194A—Circular No. 718$, dated August 22, 1995.

• *Lump-sum premium or one-time upfront lease charges* - Lump sum lease premium or one-time upfront lease charges (which are not adjustable against periodic rent) paid or payable for acquisition of long-term leasehold rights over land (or any other property) are not payments in the nature of rent within the meaning of section 194-I. Such payments are not liable for TDS under section 194-I– Circular No. 35/2016$, dated October 13, 2016.

• *Warehousing charges* - The term "rent" as defined in *Explanation (i)* below section 194-I means any payment by whatever name called, under any lease, sub-lease, tenancy or any other agreement or arrangement for the use of any building or land. Therefore, the warehousing charges will be subject to deduction of tax under section 194-I—Circular No. 718, dated August 22, 1995.

• *Payment to cold store* - The main function of the cold storage is to preserve perishable goods by means of a mechanical process, and storage of such goods is only incidental in nature. The customer is also not given any right to use any demarcated space/place or the machinery of the cold storage and thus does not become a tenant. Therefore, the provisions of section 194-I is not applicable to the cooling charges paid by the customers of the cold storage. Since the arrangement between the customers and cold storage owners are basically contractual in nature, the provision of section 194C will be applicable to the amounts paid as cooling charges by the customers of the cold storage—Circular No. 1/2008$, dated January 10, 2008.

$ For Circular Nos. 718, 1/2008 and 35/2016, log on to *taxmann.com/readyreckoner.aspx.*

• *Rent inclusive of municipal tax, ground rent* - The basis of tax deduction at source under section 194-I is "income by way of rent". Rent has been defined to mean any payment under any lease, tenancy, agreement, etc., for the use of any land or building. Thus, if the municipal taxes, ground rent, etc., are borne by the tenant, no tax will be deducted on such sum—Circular No. 718$, dated August 22, 1995.

• *Rent of a part of building* - Even if a part or portion of building is given on rent, section 194-I is applicable—Circular No. 718$, dated August 22, 1995.

• *Payment to hotel* - Payments made by persons, other than individuals and HUFs, for hotel or accommodation taken on *regular basis* will be in the nature of rent subject to tax deduction under section 194-I.

• *When payees are different* - Under section 194-I, the tax is deductible from payment by way of rent, if such payment to the payee during the year is likely to be Rs. **2,40,000**[38] or more. If there are a number of payees, each having definite and ascertainable share in the property, the limit of Rs. **2,40,000**[38] will apply to each of the payee/co-owner separately. The payers and payees are, however, advised not to enter into sham agreements to avoid tax deduction provisions.

• *Tax deduction does not depend upon nomenclature* - The tax is to be deducted from rent paid, by whatever name called, for hire of a property (for instance, payments made by a company, taking premises on rent but styling the agreement as a business centre agreement, would attract the provisions of section 194-I). The incidence of deduction of tax at source does not depend upon the nomenclature, but on the contents of the agreement as mentioned in clause (*i*) of *Explanation* to section 194-I—Circular No. 715$, dated August 8, 1995.

• *Amount payable to funds established for the benefit of armed forces* - The matter with regard to regimental fund or non-public fund established by Armed Forces has been examined in the Board. Since the income of these organisations is exempt under section 10(*23AA*), it has been decided that no tax may be deducted at source under sections 193 and 194-I from the income of such funds—Circular No. 735$, dated January 30, 1996.

• *Cinema house* - In the case of sharing of the proceeds of film exhibition between film distributor and a film exhibitor owning a cinema theatre, the Board are of the view that the provisions of section 194-I are not attracted to such payment because :

a. the exhibitor does not let out the cinema hall to the distributor ;
b. generally, the share of the exhibitor is on account of composite services ; and
c. the distributor does not take cinema building on lease or sub-lease or tenancy or under any agreement of similar nature—Circular No. 736$, dated February 13, 1996.

• *When composite agreement is in essence of the tenancy agreement* - If the composite agreement is in essence of the agreement for taking premises on rent, the tax will be deducted under section 194-I from payments thereof. For instance, in a case of composite arrangement for user of premises and provision of manpower for which consideration is paid as a specified percentage of turnover, section 194-I would be attracted if the agreement is in essence the agreement for taking premises on rent at source—Circular No. 715$, dated August 8, 1995.

• *Landing and parking charges* - Payments made by an airline for landing charges and parking charges to Airport Authority of India are in nature of rent, and, hence, assessee-airline would be liable to deduct tax at source under section 194-I and not under section 194C—*CIT* v. *Asiana Airlines* [2008] 175 Taxman 177 (Delhi). Contrary ruling is given by the Madras High Court in the case of *CIT* v. *Singapore Airlines Ltd.* [2012] 24 taxmann.com 200.

• *Passengers service fees* - The normal meaning of the word "rent" is that the payment must be for the use of land and building and mere incidental/minor/insignificant use of the same while providing other facilities and service would not make it a payment for use of land and buildings. Passenger service fees charges in the case of airlines are not subject to TDS provisions of section 194-I – Circular No. 21/2017$, dated June 12, 2017.

165.3 ***TDS rates*** - With effect from October 1, 2009, tax is deductible at source under section 194-I at the rates given below—

38. **Rs. 2,40,000** is applicable from April 1, 2019 [Rs. 1,80,000 (during July 1, 2010 and March 31, 2019) or Rs. 1,20,000 (up to June 30, 2010)].

$ For Circular Nos. 715, 718, 735, 736 and 21/2017, log on to *taxmann.com/readyreckoner.aspx*.

For the use of any machinery or plant or equipment	2%[39]
For the use of any land or building or furniture or fittings for all persons.	10%[39]

165.4 ***No tax deduction if payee is Government/local authorities*** - There is no requirement to deduct income-tax at source on income by way of 'rent' if the payee is the Government. In the case of local authorities and statutory authorities referred to in section 10(*20A*)/10(*20*), there will be no requirement to deduct income-tax at source from income by way of rent if the person responsible for paying it is satisfied about their tax-exempt status under clause (*20*) or (*20A*) of section 10 on the basis of a certificate to this effect given by the said authorities—Circular No. 699, dated January 30, 1995.

165.5 ***When tax is not deducted or deducted at lower rate*** - *See* paras 175.4 and 175.5.

165.6 ***Tax credit when rent is paid in advance*** - The recipient of rent can claim tax credit in respect of tax deducted at source. *Vide* Circular No. 5/2001[$], dated March 2, 2001, tax credit in respect of tax deducted on advance rent will be available as under—

Tax deduction under different situation	*Tax credit*
• Tax is deducted at source under the provisions of section 194-I on advance rent pertaining to more than one financial year to be adjusted against future rent.	Where advance rent is spread over more than one financial year and tax is deducted thereon, credit shall be allowed in the same proportion in which such income is offered for taxation for different assessment years based on the single certificate furnished for tax so deducted on the entire advance rent.
• Subsequent to the deduction of tax at source on advance rent pertaining to one or more financial years : - rent agreement gets terminated/cancelled resulting into refund of balance amount of advance rent to the tenant - rented property is transferred by way of sale, lease, gift, etc. with tenant in occupation or otherwise resulting into refund of balance amount of advance rent to the transferee or the tenant, as the case may be.	Credit for the entire balance of tax deducted at source, which has not been given credit so far, shall be allowed in the assessment year relevant to the financial year during which the rent agreement gets terminated/cancelled or rented property is transferred and balance of advance rent is refunded to the transferee or the tenant, as the case may be.

Tax deduction from payment on transfer of certain immovable properties (other than agricultural land) [Sec. 194-IA, applicable from June 1, 2013]

165A. Section 194-IA is applicable with effect from June 1, 2013.

• *Who is responsible for tax deduction* - Any person (being a transferee) responsible for paying (other than the person referred to in section 194LA) to a resident transferor any sum by way of consideration for transfer of any immovable property (other than rural agricultural land), is liable to deduct tax at source under section 194-IA.

• *Time of deduction* - Tax shall be deducted at the time of payment or at the time of giving credit to the transferor, whichever is earlier.

• *Rate of tax deduction* - Tax is deductible at the rate of 1 per cent[40].

• *Threshold limit* - No tax is deductible where the consideration for the transfer of immovable property is less than Rs. 50,00,000. **With effect from September 1, 2019, consideration for transfer of immovable property shall include all charges of the nature of club membership fee, car parking fee, electricity or water facility fee, maintenance fee, advance fee or any other charges of similar nature, which are incidental to transfer of the immovable property.**

• *Provisions of TAN not applicable* - Provisions of section 203A (pertaining to TAN) shall not apply in respect of tax deducted under section 194-IA.

39. No surcharge or health and education cess during the financial year 2019-20. Tax is not deductible on GST. If PAN is not furnished, then tax will be deductible at the rate of 20 per cent. PAN of the deductee should be mentioned in any correspondence and document which is exchanged between the deductor and deductee.

40. No surcharge or health and education cess during the financial year 2019-20. If PAN is not furnished, then tax will be deductible at the rate of 20 per cent. PAN of the deductee should be mentioned in any correspondence and document which is exchanged between the deductor and deductee.

$ For Circular No. 5/2001, log on to *taxmann.com/readyreckoner.aspx*.

Tax deduction from payment of rent by certain individuals/HUFs [Sec. 194-IB, applicable from June 1, 2017]

165B. Section 194-IB is applicable with effect from June 1, 2017.

• *Who is responsible for tax deduction* - Any individual/HUF [whose books of account are not required to be audited in the immediately preceding financial year under section 44AB(*a*)/(*b*)] responsible for paying to a resident rent of land or building, is liable to deduct tax under section 194-IB. Tax is deductible under this section if the quantum of rent is more than Rs. 50,000 per month (or part of month).

• *Time of deduction* - Tax shall be deducted only at the time of credit of rent (for the last month of the previous year or last month of tenancy if the property is vacated during the year) to the account of payee or at the time of payment thereof in cash or by cheque/draft, whichever is earlier.

• *Rate of tax deduction* - Tax is deductible at the rate of 5 per cent of rent paid/credited during the financial year. However, no tax is deductible where rent is Rs. 50,000 per month (or less). If PAN of recipient is not available, tax is deductible at the rate of 20 per cent (however, in such a case amount of TDS cannot exceed rent payable for the last month of the previous year or last month of tenancy).

• *Provisions of TAN not applicable* - Provisions of section 203A (pertaining to TAN) shall not apply in respect of tax deducted under section 194-IB.

165B-E1 X owns a building situated at T Nagar, Chennai. It is given on rent to Y (rent being Rs. 60,000 per month). Discuss whether TDS provisions are applicable for the financial year 2019-20 in the following three different situations –

Situation 1 - Y is a businessman and his annual turnover from business is more than Rs. 5 crore since 2005. However, building is used by him for his residential purposes.

Situation 2 - Y is a businessman. His turnover for the financial year 2018-19 is Rs. 90 lakh (compulsory tax audit under section 44AB is not required).

Situation 3 - Y is a salaried employee. He gets house rent allowance from the employer. On the basis of rent paid to X, he claims exemption under section 10(*13A*) pertaining to house rent allowance.

•

In *Situation 1,* tax is deductible every month (at the time of payment/credit of rent) at the rate of 10% under section 194-I.

In *Situations 2* and *3,* section 194-I is not applicable. However, Y is required to deduct tax at source under section 194-IB. Tax is deductible at the time of payment/credit of rent for the last month during the financial year 2019-20. Suppose, rent of March is paid on March 5, 2020. Tax is deductible on March 5, 2020 [TDS being Rs. 36,000 (*i.e.,* 5% of Rs. 60,000 × 12 months, from April 1, 2019 to March 31, 2020)].

If the recipient of rent does not have PAN, tax will deductible at the rate of 20% by virtue of section 206AA. Total rent of the financial year is Rs. 7,20,000 (*i.e.,* Rs. 60,000 per month for 12 months). 20% of Rs. 7,20,000 comes to Rs. 1,44,000. TDS of Rs. 1,44,000 cannot be deducted from rent of Rs. 60,000 payable on March 5, 2020. For such a situation, section 194-IB(4) gives a relief (tax deductible by virtue of section 206AA cannot exceed the amount of rent payable for the last month of the financial year or last month of tenancy). To put it differently, Y should deduct tax of Rs. 60,000 out of rent of Rs. 60,000 payable to X (who does not have PAN) on March 5, 2020. Consequently, amount of rent after TDS (for the month of March 2020) payable to X will be *nil.*

Tax deduction from payment under joint development agreement [Sec. 194-IC, applicable from April 1, 2017]

165C. Section 194-IC is applicable with effect from April 1, 2017.

• *Who is responsible for tax deduction* - Any person responsible for paying to a resident any sum by way of consideration (not being consideration in kind) under a joint development agreement, is responsible for tax deduction under section 194-IC.

• *Time of tax deduction* - Tax is deductible at the time of credit of such sum to the account of the payee or at the time of payment thereof in cash or by issue of a cheque/draft or by any other mode, whichever is earlier.

• *Threshold limit - Nil.*

• *Rate of tax deduction* - Tax is deductible at the rate of 10 per cent. If PAN of recipient is not available, tax is deductible at the rate of 20 per cent.

• *Meaning of joint development agreement* - It is a registered agreement in which a land owner (*i.e.,* a person who owns land or building or both) agrees to allow another person to develop a real estate project on such land or building or both, in consideration of a share (being land or building or both) in such project, whether with or without payment of part of the consideration in cash.

165C-E1 Find out whether TDS is applicable in Example 69.18-E1.

•

A Ltd. (the developer) will deduct tax at source under section 194-IC. Tax will be deducted on April 20, 2017 (*i.e.*, the date of payment of cash consideration to X). Applicable TDS rate is 10% (TDS being Rs. 2,00,000 out of payment of cash consideration of Rs. 20,00,000). Tax will be deducted in the financial year 2017-18 but income will be taxable in the hands of X only in the previous year 2018-19 (*i.e.*, the year of issue of completion certificate).

Tax deduction at source on fees for professional or technical services [Sec. 194J]

166. Section 194J was inserted with effect from July 1, 1995.

166.1 ***Who is liable to deduct tax at source under section 194J*** - Any person, who is responsible for paying to a resident any sum by way of fees for professional services, fees for technical services, royalty, non-compete fees referred to in section 28(*va*) or (with effect from July 1, 2012) director's fees, shall deduct tax at source.

The provisions in brief are given below—

Whether tax is deductible under section 194J	*During July 1, 1995 to May 31, 2002*	*During June 1, 2002 to May 31, 2003*	*From June 1, 2003 onwards*
When payer or deductor is a person other than an individual or HUF	*Yes*[41]	*Yes*[41]	*Yes*[41]
When payer or deductor is an individual or HUF and books of account of the payer are required to be audited [under section 44AB(*a*)/(*b*)] in the immediately preceding year			
- Payment or credit of royalty/non-compete fees referred to in section 28(*va*)	*No*	*No*	*No*
- Payment or credit of professional fees for personal purposes	*No*	*Yes*	*No*
- Payment or credit of professional fees (not being for personal purposes)	*No*	*Yes*	*Yes*
- Payment or credit of technical fees	*No*	*Yes*	*Yes*
When payer or deductor is an individual or HUF and books of account of the payer are not required to be audited [under section 44AB(*a*)/(*b*)] in the immediately preceding year	*No*	*No*	*No*

166.2 ***Time of tax deduction*** - Tax shall be deducted at the time of credit of such sum to the account of the payee or at the time of payment thereof in cash or by issue of a cheque or draft or by any other mode, whichever is earlier.

Where any such sum is credited to any account, whether called "Suspense account" or by any other name, in the books of account of the person liable to pay such amount, such crediting shall be deemed to be credit of such sum to the account of the payee. *See* also para 154.1-7.

166.3 ***Rate of tax deduction*** - Tax shall be deducted at the rate of 10 per cent. With effect from June 1, 2017, tax shall be deducted at the rate of 2 per cent in case of a payee who is engaged only in the business of operation of call centre. The above rate is applicable to the total payment (reimbursement cannot be deducted out of bill amount)—Circular No. 715, dated August 8, 1995.

166.4 ***When tax is not deductible*** - Where the amount of such sum or, as the case may be, the aggregate of the amounts of such sums credited or paid or likely to be credited and paid during the financial year by the aforesaid person to the account of, or to, the payee, does not exceed Rs. 30,000[42] in case of fees for professional services or Rs. 30,000[42] in the case of fees for technical services, or Rs. 30,000[42] in the case of royalty or Rs. 30,000[42] in the case of any sum referred to in section 28(*va*), tax is not deductible. No threshold limit is provided in the case of director's fees.

166.5 ***When tax is deductible at lower rate [Sec. 197]*** - *See* para 175.5.

166.6 ***Meaning of professional/technical services/royalty*** - These meanings are given below—

---

41. Payment/credit of technical fees and professional fees is subject to tax deduction at source under section 194J. Payment/credit of royalty/non-compete fees is subject to tax deduction only from July 13, 2006.

42. Rs. 20,000 up to June 30, 2010.

166.6-1 *PROFESSIONAL SERVICES* - The expression "professional services" has been defined to mean services rendered by a person in the course of carrying on legal, medical, engineering or architectural profession or the profession of accountancy or technical consultancy or interior decoration or advertising (*i.e.*, models, artists, photographers providing services to an advertising agency) or such other profession as is notified by the Board for the purposes of section 44AA (*i.e.*, authorised representative, film artist or company secretary or information technology) or of this section.[43]

166.6-2 *ROYALTY* - Royalty for this purpose is defined by *Explanation 2* to section 9(1)(*vi*). It includes consideration for the transfer of any right in respect of a patent, invention, model, design, secret formula, or process or trademark or similar property. Apart from a few other points, royalty as per *Explanation 2* also includes consideration for the use of any patent, invention, model, design, secret formula or process or trade mark or similar property. This definition of royalty has been amended by inserting *Explanations 4, 5* and *6* to section 9(1)(*vi*) by the Finance Act, 2012 with retrospective[44] effect from June 1, 1976. These *Explanations* are given below –

Explanation 4 clarifies that royalty includes transfer of all or any right for use (or right to use) a computer software (including granting of a licence) irrespective of the medium through which such right is transferred.

Explanation 5 clarifies that royalty includes any consideration in respect of any right, property or information, whether or not—

a. the possession or control of such right, property or information is with the payer;

b. such right, property or information is used directly by the payer;

c. the location of such right, property or information is in India.

Explanation 6 clarifies that expression "process" includes transmission by satellite (including up-linking, amplification, conversion for down-linking of any signal), cable, optic fibre or by any other similar technology, whether or not such process is secret.

• *Relief given by Notification No. 21/2012* - In exercise of the power given by section 197A(1F), the Central Government has given a relief *vide* Notification No. 21/2012[$], dated June 13, 2012, which is explained with the help of an example given below –

1. A Ltd. (a resident taxpayer) purchased software and at the time of purchase it deducted tax at source under section 194J or 195.

2. Without any modification A Ltd. transfers software to B Ltd.

3. A Ltd. gives a declaration (giving its PAN) that tax was deducted by it at the time of purchase under section 194J/195.

If these conditions are satisfied B Ltd. will not deduct tax at source under section 194J (with effect from July 1, 2012).

• *Reference of Explanations 4, 5 and 6 missing in the definition of royalty given in sections 194J, 195 and 40(*a*)(*i*)/(*ia*)* - For the purpose of sections 194J, 195 and 40(*a*)(*i*)/(*ia*), "royalty" means royalty as given in *Explanation 2* to section 9(1)(*vi*). When *Explanations 4, 5* and *6* were inserted in section 9(1)(*vi*) by the Finance Act, 2012, a reference of these *Explanations* was not simultaneously incorporated in sections 194J, 195 and 40(*a*)(*i*)/(*ia*). Consequently, the application of *Explanations 4, 5* and *6* to section 9(1)(*vi*) for the purpose of sections 194J, 195 and 40(*a*)(*i*)/(*ia*) is questionable (one should legally challenge it if the Assessing Officer does not agree) – *see Sonata Information Technology Ltd.* v. *CIT* [2012] 54 SOT 233 (Mum.).

---

43. The Board has notified the following persons in relation to the sports activities as "professional services" for the purpose of section 194J namely - (*a*) sports persons, (*b*) umpires and referees, (*c*) coaches and trainers, (*d*) team physicians and physiotherapists, (*e*) event managers, (*f*) commentators, (*g*) anchors and (*h*) sports columnists.

44. *Vide* Letter [F.No. 500/111/2009-FTD-1(PT.)], dated May 29, 2012, the Board has pointed out that the amendment has been made with retrospective effect in order to clarify the legislative intent and state the position of law from the date of coming into effect of these sections in the Act. Further the Board has directed that where assessment proceedings have been completed under section 143(3) before April 1, 2012, and no notice for reassessment has been issued prior to that date, then such case shall not be reopened under section 147/148 on account of the abovementioned clarificatory amendments introduced by the Finance Act, 2012. However, assessment or any other order which stand validated due to the said clarificatory amendments in the Finance Act, 2012 would of course be enforced.

[$] For Notification No. 21/2012, log on to *taxmann.com/readyreckoner.aspx.*

166.7 ***Reimbursement of expenses*** - The Delhi Bench of the Income-tax Appellate Tribunal in *ITO* v. *Dr. Willmar Schwabe India (P.) Ltd.* [2005] 3 SOT 71 examined the scope of Circular No. 715, dated August 8, 1995 on the subject of deduction of tax at source on expenses reimbursement and upon perusal of the same, it held that reimbursement of expenses for which bill is separately raised did not attract the provisions of section 194J.

In their answer to the relevant question No. 30, the Board explained as under :

Q. No. 30. Whether the deduction of tax at source under sections 194C and 194J has to be made out of the gross amount of the bill including reimbursements or excluding reimbursement for actual expenses ?

Ans. Sections 194C and 194J refer to any sum paid obviously, reimbursements cannot be deducted out of the bill amount for the purpose for tax deduction at source.

In other words, if a consolidated bill is given by a professional/consultant for his fees as well as out of pocket expenditure, then the entire amount is subject to TDS. If a separate bill is given for reimbursement of out of pocket expenditure, then reimbursement of expenditure is not subject to tax deduction.

166.8 ***Fees for human resources development*** - Where assessee paid certain amount to its holding company for rendering advice or service in respect of human resources development, maintenance of accounts and finance, service rendered would definitely amount to providing service in managerial/technical field as defined in *Explanation 2* to section 9(1)(*vii*) and, therefore assessee is liable to deduct tax at source under section 194J on payments made to holding company—*Tecumseh Products (I) Ltd.* v. *CIT* [2007] 13 SOT 489 (Hyd.).

166.9 ***Stock exchange charges*** - Service made available by the Bombay Stock Exchange [BSE Online Trading (BOLT) System] for which transaction charges are paid by members of BSE are common services that every member of the stock exchange is necessarily required to avail of to carry out trading in securities. Such services do not amount to "technical services" and not subject to TDS under section 194J – *CIT* v. *Kotak Securities Ltd.* [2016] 239 Taxman 139 (SC).

166.10 ***Payment to hospital by TPAs*** - The services rendered by hospitals to various patients are primarily medical services and, therefore, provisions of section 194J are applicable on payments made by Third Party Administrators (TPAs) to hospitals, etc. Further for invoking provisions of section 194J, there is no stipulation that the professional services have to be necessarily rendered to the person who makes payment to hospital. Therefore TPAs who are making payment on behalf of insurance companies to hospitals for settlement of medical/insurance claims, etc., under various schemes including cashless schemes are liable to deduct tax at source under section 194J—Circular No. 8/2009[$], dated November 24, 2009.

166.11 ***Payments specified under section 197A(1F)*** - In exercise of the powers conferred by section 197A(1F), the Central Government has notified that no deduction of tax shall be applicable on or after January 1, 2013 on the payments of the nature specified below, if such payment is made by a person to a bank listed in the Second Schedule to the RBI Act, excluding a foreign bank or to any payment systems company authorised by RBI under section 4(2) of the Payment and Settlement Systems Act, 2007—

a. bank guarantee commission;

b. cash management service charges;

c. depository charges on maintenance of DEMAT accounts;

d. charges for warehousing services for commodities;

e. underwriting service charges;

f. clearing charges (MICR charges) including interchange fee or any other similar charges by whatever name called charged at the time of settlement or for clearing activities under the Payment and Settlement Systems Act, 2007;

g. credit card or debit card commission for transaction between merchant establishment and acquirer bank- Notification No. SO 2143(E), dated June 17, 2016.

166.12 ***Transmission charges*** - Where an assessee, engaged in buying and selling electricity, pays transmission charges of power, TDS under section 194J is not applicable—*CIT* v. *Delhi Transco Ltd.* [2015] 62 taxmann.com166 (Delhi)[45].

---

45. SLP dismissed against High Court's ruling – *CIT* v. *Delhi Transco Ltd.* [2016] 239 Taxman 263 (SC).

[$] For Circular No. 8/2009, log on to *taxmann.com/readyreckoner.aspx*.

Tax deduction from compensation payable on compulsory acquisition of immovable property [Sec. 194LA]

167. Section 194LA was inserted with effect from October 1, 2004. The provisions of section 194LA are given below—

167.1 ***Who is responsible for tax deduction*** - Any person responsible for paying to a resident any compensation or enhanced compensation or consideration or enhanced consideration on account of compulsory acquisition of any immovable property (but other than agricultural land) is responsible for deduction of tax at source.

• Under section 194LA, tax cannot be deducted in respect of compensation/enhanced compensation payable on account of compulsory acquisition of agricultural land (whether land is situated in urban area or rural area)—*Mysore Urban Development Authority* v. *ITO* [2008] 175 Taxman 307 (Kar.).

• With effect from April 1, 2017, tax is not deductible under section 194LA in respect of any award or agreement which has been exempted from levy of income-tax under section 96 of the Right to Fair Compensation and Transparency in Land Acquisition, Rehabilitation and Resettlement Act, 2013.

167.2 ***Time of tax deduction*** - Tax is deductible at the time of payment of aforesaid sum in cash or by issue of a cheque or draft or by any other mode, whichever is earlier.

167.3 ***Rate of tax deduction*** - Tax is deductible at the rate of 10 per cent[46]. However, tax is not deductible if the aforesaid sum or the aggregate amount during a financial year does not exceed Rs. 2,50,000 (Rs. 2,00,000 during July 1, 2012 and May 31, 2016, Rs. 1,00,000 up to June 30, 2012).

167.4 ***Is it possible to get payment without tax deduction or with lower tax deduction*** - *See* para 175.5.

Tax deduction from interest payable to non-resident by an infrastructure debt fund [Sec. 194LB, applicable from June 1, 2011]

167A. Section 194LB was inserted with effect from June 1, 2011.

• *Who is responsible to deduct tax* - Any person who is responsible to pay any interest by an infrastructure debt fund [referred to in section 10(*47*)] to a non-resident or a foreign company, shall deduct tax at source with effect from June 1, 2011.

• *Time of deduction* - Tax shall be deducted at the time of payment in cash or by cheque/draft or at the time of credit of such income to the account of payee (whichever is earlier).

• *Rate of TDS* - Tax shall be deducted at the rate of 5 per cent [+SC+HEC].

Tax deduction from income from units of business trust [Sec. 194LBA, applicable from October 1, 2014]

167AA. The provisions of section 194LBA, applicable from October 1, 2014, are given below –

• *Time of tax deduction* - Tax deduction is applicable if a business trust distributes any income referred to in section 115UA [being of the nature referred to in section 10(*23FC*) or (with effect from June 1, 2015) section 10(*23FCA*) or (with effect from June 1, 2016) section 10(*23FC*)(*a*)] to its unit holder. Tax is deductible at the time of credit of such payment to the account of the payee or at the time of payment thereof in cash or by the issue of a cheque or draft or by any other mode, whichever is earlier.

• *Rate of TDS* -Tax is deductible at the following rates –

- *If the recipient is resident* - If the recipient unitholder is resident in India, tax is deductible at the rate of 10 per cent[46].
- *If the recipient is non-resident* - If the recipient unitholder is a non-resident or a foreign company, tax is deductible at the rate of 5 per cent (+SC+HEC). If, however, rental income (received by a real estate investment trust) is distributed to unitholders, tax shall be deducted at rate in force as applicable for deduction of tax on payment to the non-resident of any sum chargeable to tax (*i.e.,* 40 per cent (+SC+HEC)[47] if recipient is a foreign company and 30 per cent (+SC+HEC)[47] if recipient is non-resident other than foreign company) (applicable from June 1, 2015).

If the recipient does not have PAN, tax is deductible at the rate of 20 per cent or the rate given above, whichever is more. Provisions of section 197 or section 197A are not applicable.

Tax deduction from income in respect of units of investment fund [Sec. 194LBB]

167AB. Section 194LBB has been inserted with effect from June 1, 2015. Provisions of this section are given below –

---

46. No surcharge or health and education cess during the financial year 2019-20. If PAN is not furnished, then tax will be deductible at the rate of 20 per cent. PAN of the deductee should be mentioned in any correspondence and document which is exchanged between the deductor and deductee.

47. Subject to rate given under DTA.

• *Time of tax deduction* - Tax deduction is applicable if a business trust distributes any income referred to in section 115UB [not being business income of the nature referred to in section 10(*23FBB*)] to its unitholders. Tax is deductible at the time of credit of such payment to the account of the payee or at the time of payment thereof in cash or by the issue of a cheque or draft or by any other mode, whichever is earlier.

• *Rate of TDS* - Tax is deductible at the rate of 10 per cent[48] (during June 1, 2015 and May 31, 2016). From June 1, 2016 is deductible as follows -

a. 10 per cent[48] (where the payee is resident);

b. 40 per cent (+SC[49]+HEC)[47] (where the payee is foreign company);

c. 30 per cent (+SC[49]+HEC)[47] (where the payee is non-resident, not being a foreign company).

• *Gross income subject to TDS* - Where the payee is a non-resident/foreign company, no deduction shall be made in respect of any income that is not chargeable to tax in India (applicable from June 1, 2016).

• *Lower TDS certificate* - Provisions of section 197A are not applicable. However, lower TDS certificate provisions under section 197 are applicable from June 1, 2016.

Tax deduction from income in respect of investment in securitization fund [Sec. 194LBC]

167AC. Section 194LBC has been inserted with effect from June 1, 2016. Provisions of this section are given below -

• *Time of tax deduction* - Tax deduction is applicable if income is payable to an investor in respect of an investment in a securitization trust. Tax is deductible at the time of credit of such payment to the account of the payee or at the time of payment thereof in cash or by the issue of a cheque or draft or by any other mode, whichever is earlier.

• *Rate of TDS* - Tax is deductible at the rate given below -

a. 25 per cent[48] (where the payee is a resident individual/HUF);

b. 30 per cent[48] (where the payee is a resident but other than individual/HUF;

c. 40 per cent (+SC[49]+HEC)[47] (where the payee is foreign company);

d. 30 per cent (+SC[49]+HEC)[47] (where the payee is non-resident, not being a foreign company).

• *Lower TDS certificate* - Provisions of section 197 are applicable. However, section 197A is not applicable.

Tax deduction by an Indian specified company or business trust from interest to a non-resident/foreign company [Sec. 194LC, applicable from July 1, 2012]

167B. Section 194LC is applicable with effect from July 1, 2012.

• *Who is responsible for tax deduction* - Specified company (*i.e.*, an Indian company) or business trust (with effect from October 1, 2014) is responsible for tax deduction under section 194LC in respect of interest paid or payable to a non-resident/foreign company. This section is applicable if interest is paid or payable at approved rate. Interest should pertain to money borrowed in foreign currency from a source outside India—

a. under a loan agreement (at any time on or after July 1, 2012 but before July 1, 2020); or

b. by way of issue of long-term infrastructure bonds (at any time on or after July 1, 2012 but before October 1, 2014); or

c. by way of issue of long-term bonds including long-term infrastructure bonds (at any time on or after October 1, 2014 but before July 1, 2020); or

d. in respect of monies borrowed from a source outside India by way of issue of rupee denominated bond before July 1, 2020.

• *Time of deduction* - Tax shall be deducted at the time of payment or at the time of giving credit to the other party, whichever is earlier.

• *Rate of tax deduction* - Tax is deductible at the rate of 5 per cent [+SC[49]+HEC]. If the recipient does not have PAN, tax is deductible at the rate of 20 per cent by virtue of section 206AA. However, the provisions of section 206AA will not be applicable in respect of payment of –

---

47. Subject to rate given in DTA.

48. No surcharge or health and education cess during the financial year 2019-20. If PAN is not furnished, then tax will be deductible at the rate of 20 per cent. PAN of the deductee should be mentioned in any correspondence and document which is exchanged between the deductor and deductee.

49. If recipient is non-resident, it will be increased by surcharge and health and education cess. If the recipient does not furnish his PAN to the deductor, tax will be deducted at the normal rate or at the rate of 20 per cent, whichever is higher. PAN of the deductee should be mentioned in any correspondence and document which is exchanged between the deductor and deductee.

a. interest on long-term infrastructure bonds (from June 1, 2013 to September 30, 2014); and

b. interest on long-term bonds including infrastructure bonds (from October 1, 2014).

167B.1 ***Approval by Central Government*** - If the following conditions (given by Circular No. 7/2012[$], dated September 21, 2012) are satisfied, loan agreement/long-term infrastructure bonds and rate of interest shall be deemed as approved for the purpose of section 194LC by the Central Government –

• *In respect of agreements for loan* - These conditions are given below –

1. The borrowing of money should be under a loan agreement.

2. Money borrowed under the loan agreement by the Indian company should comply with section 6(3)(*d*) of the Foreign Exchange Management Act, 1999 (read with Notification No. FEMA 3/2000-RB, dated May 3, 2000) (popularly known as ECS Regulations) either under the automatic route or under the approval route.

3. The borrowing company should have obtained a Loan Registration Number (LRN) issued by RBI in respect of the agreement.

4. No part of the borrowing has taken place under the said agreement before July 1, 2012.

5. The agreement should not be restructuring of an existing agreement for borrowing in foreign currency solely for taking benefit of reduced withholding tax rates.

6. The end use of the funds and other conditions as laid out by the RBI under ECB regulations should be followed during the entire term of the loan agreement under which the borrowing has been made.

• *In respect of issue of Bonds* - The relevant conditions are –

1. The bond issue by the Indian company should be authorized under ECB regulations either under the automatic route or under the approval route.

2. The bond issue should have a loan Registration Number issued by the RBI.

3. The term "long term" means that the bond to be issued should have original maturity term of 3 years or more.

4. The bond issue proceeds should be utilized in the "infrastructure sector" only.

5. The term "infrastructure sector" shall have same meaning as is assigned to it by RBI under the ECB regulations.

• *Rate of interest* - Any rate of interest which is within the all-in-cost ceilings specified by the RBI under ECB regulations as is applicable to the borrowing by loan agreement or through a bond issue, as the case may be, having regard to the tenure thereof.

• *Automatic approval without approaching CBDT* - Any loan agreement or bond issue, which satisfies the above conditions, would be treated as approved by the Central Government for the purposes of section 194LC.

• *Approval to be taken from CBDT* - In the case of other long-term infrastructure bonds where the Indian company receives subscription of such bonds in foreign currency and such bond issue is not covered under ECB regulations, the approval, for purpose of section 194LC shall be on case to case basis. In such case, application should be filed with Member (IT), Central Board of Direct Taxes with the relevant details of the purpose, period and rate of interest.

TDS on interest on bonds/Government securities [Sec. 194LD]

167C. Section 194LD has been inserted with effect from June 1, 2013—

Who is deductor - Any person who is responsible for making payment (as given below) should deduct tax at source.

Who is deductee - A foreign institution investor or a qualified foreign investor[50].

Payment covered by section 194LD - Interest on a rupee denominated bond of an Indian company (interest not to exceed notified[51] rate of interest) or Government security which is payable after May 31, 2013 but before July 1, 2020.

---

50. "Qualified Foreign Investor" shall have the meaning assigned to it in the Circular No. Cir/IMD/DF/14/2011, dated August 9, 2011, as amended from time to time, issued by the SEBI under section 11 of the SEBI Act.

51. Notified rate of interest for this purpose is as follows—

a. in case of bonds issued before July 1, 2010, the rate of interest shall not exceed 500 basis points (bps) over the Base Rate of SBI as on July 1, 2010.

b. in case of bonds issued on or after July 1, 2010, the rate of interest shall not exceed 500 basis points (bps) over the Base Rate of SBI applicable on the date of issue of the said bonds.

[$] For Circular No. 7/2012, log on to *taxmann.com/readyreckoner.aspx*.

Time of tax deduction - At the time of payment or at the time giving credit to the recipient, whichever is earlier.
Rate of TDS - 5 per cent (+SC+HEC). If recipient does not have PAN, tax is deductible at the rate of 20 per cent.
Lower TDS certificate under section 197 - Not possible.

TDS on certain payments by an individual/HUF [Sec. 194M, applicable from September 1, 2019]

167D. Provisions of section 194M (applicable from September 1, 2019) are given below –

• *Who is deductor* - An individual/HUF (who is not required to deduct tax at source under sections 194C, 194H or 194J) is required to deduct tax under section 194M. Consequently, **an individual/HUF is required to deduct tax at source in respect of the following under section 194M** –

- **Payment/credit to a resident contractor or resident professional, when such payment is for personal use.**
- **Payment/credit to a resident contractor or resident professional or to a resident by way of commission (not being insurance commission) or brokerage [where payer is an individual/HUF who carries on business or profession and books of account are not subject to audit under section 44AB(*a*)/(*b*) in the immediately preceding financial year].**

• *Threshold limit* - Tax is not deductible if the aggregate amount paid or payable during the financial year to a resident **does not exceed Rs. 50 lakh.**

• *Payment covered* - TDS under section 194M is applicable in respect of amount paid/payable to a resident for **carrying out any work** (including supply of labour for carrying out any work) in pursuance of a contract or **by way of commission (not being insurance commission) or brokerage or by way of fees for professional services.**

• *When deductible* - Tax is deductible at the time of credit of aforesaid sum or at the time of payment of the aforesaid sum in cash or by issue of a cheque or draft or by any other mode, whichever is earlier.

• *Rate of TDS* - **Tax is deductible at the rate of 5 per cent of the aforesaid payment or credit.**

• *Lower TDS certificate* - Recipient can apply for *nil*/lower TDS certificate under section 197.

• *TAN not necessary* - Individual/HUF (who is required to deduct tax under section 194M) shall be able to deposit tax deducted using his PAN and shall not be required to obtain TAN.

TDS on payment of certain amounts in cash [Sec. 194N, applicable from September 1, 2019]

167E. Provisions of section 194N (applicable from September 1, 2019) are given below –

• *Who is deductor* - **A bank, co-operative bank or a post office, who is responsible for paying any sum in cash to an accountholder, is required to deduct tax at source** under section 194N.

• *Threshold limit* - It is **Rs. 1 crore.** In other words, tax is deductible by a bank (or co-operative bank or post office) if aggregate payment in cash from one or more accounts during a previous year to an accountholder, exceeds Rs. 1 crore.

• *When deductible* - Tax is deductible at the time of payment in cash.

• *Rate of TDS* - Tax is deductible at the rate of **2 per cent of payment (or aggregate payment) in cash exceeding Rs. 1 crore.**

• *Lower TDS certificate* - Not possible.

• *Cash payment to certain recipients without TDS* - Exemption is available, when payment is made to certain recipients, such as the Government, banking company, co-operative society engaged in carrying on the business of banking, post office, banking correspondents and white label ATM operators, who are involved in the handling of substantial amounts of cash as a part of their business operation. Moreover, the Central Government can exempt other recipients, through a notification in the official Gazette in consultation with the RBI.

• *Tax deducted under section 194N, not to be treated as deemed receipt* - Tax deducted (under section 194N) shall not be deemed to be income received (for the purpose of section 198) for computing income of recipient.

Deduction of tax at source from other sums [Sec. 195]

168. A person responsible for making payment to a non-corporate non-resident assessee or to a company other than a domestic company, of any interest or any other sum (not being salary) is required, at the time of payment or at the time of credit[52] to the account of payee, interest payable account, or suspense account, or at the time of payment, whichever is earlier [*see* also para 154.1-7] to deduct income-tax thereon

52. Only at the time of payment thereof in cash or by issue of cheque/draft or by any other mode, in the case of interest of Mutual Fund payable by the Government/public sector bank or financial institution.

at the rates prescribed by the relevant Finance Act [*see* Referencer 1]. No tax is deductible in the case of dividend referred to in section 115-O [*see* para 207.2]. Moreover, tax is not deductible in respect of interest paid/credited by an offshore banking unit on deposits made after March 31, 2005 by a non-resident. Further, tax is not deductible under section 195 in the case of payment/credit of interest which is covered by sections 194LB, 194LC and 194LD.

168.1 ***Furnishing of information relating to payment to non-resident/foreign company [Sec. 195(6)]*** - With effect from June 1, 2015, the person responsible for paying to a non-resident/foreign company, any sum (whether or not chargeable under the provisions of this Act in the hands of recipient) shall furnish the information relating to payment of such sum, in such form and manner, as may be prescribed.

168.2 ***Income of recipient taxable in India is subject to tax deduction, not the entire payment*** - Under section 195, income of non-resident which is taxable in India is subject to tax deduction. Where the payer of income (other than salary) considers that the whole of such sum would not be income chargeable in the case of the recipient, he may make an application under section 195(2)[52a] to the Assessing Officer to determine by general or special order the appropriate proportion of such sum so chargeable, and upon such determination, tax shall be deducted under section 195 only on that proportion of the sum which is so chargeable.

• *Only in case of doubt, deductor can approach Assessing Officer under section 195(2)* - The application of section 195(2) pre-supposes that the person responsible for making the payment to the non-resident is in no doubt that tax is payable in respect of some part of the amount to be remitted to a non-resident but is not sure as to what should be the portion so taxable or is not sure as to the amount of tax to be deducted. In such a situation, he is required to make an application to the ITO (TDS) for determining the amount. It is only when these conditions are satisfied and an application is made to the ITO (TDS), that the question of making an order under section 195(2) will arise.

It is incorrect to state that section 195(2) is merely a provision to provide information to the ITO (TDS). Section 195(2) is based on the 'principle of proportionality'. The said sub-section gets attracted only in cases where the payment made is a composite payment in which certain proportion of payment has an element of 'income' chargeable to tax in India—*GE India Technology Cen. (P.) Ltd.* v. *CIT* [2010] 193 Taxman 234 (SC).

• *No prescribed form* - It has been held by the Delhi High Court in the case of *CIT* v. *Jay Engg. Works Ltd.* [1984] 149 ITR 425/19 Taxman 525 that as no form is prescribed for application under section 195(2).[52a] An assessee can approach the Assessing Officer by merely stating that an order under section 195(2) may be made.

168.3 ***Procedure for refund of tax deducted at source under section 195 to the person deducting tax at source*** - The Board have revised (*vide* Circular No. 7/2007, dated October 23, 2007 and Circular No. 7/2011, dated September 27, 2011) the procedure for refund of tax deducted at source under section 195 to the deductor—

• *Cases covered* - In the following cases, tax deducted at source under section 195 can be refunded to the deductor—

1. The contract is cancelled and no remittance is made to the non-resident.

2. The remittance is duly made to the non-resident, but the contract is cancelled. In such cases, the remitted amount has been returned to the person responsible for deducting tax at source.

3. The contract is cancelled after partial execution and no remittance is made to the non-resident for the non-executed part.

4. The contract is cancelled after partial execution and remittance related to non-executed part is made to the non-resident. In such cases, the remitted amount has been returned to the person responsible for deducting the tax at source or no remittance is made but tax was deducted and deposited when the amount was credited to the account of the non-resident.

5. There occurs exemption of the remitted amount from tax either by amendment in law or by notification under the provisions of Act.

6. An order is passed under section 154 or 248 or 264 reducing the tax deduction liability of a deductor under section 195.

52a. **The relevant provision has been amended to allow online application facility for this purpose (applicable from November 1, 2019).**

7. There occurs deduction of tax twice from the same income by mistake.

8. There occurs payment of tax on account of grossing up which was not required under the provisions of the Act.

9. There occurs payment of tax at a higher rate under the domestic law while a lower rate is prescribed in the relevant double taxation avoidance treaty entered into by India or *vice versa*.

• *Refund* - In the cases given above, where no income has accrued to the non-resident due to cancellation of contract or where income has accrued but no tax is due on that income or tax is due at a lesser rate, the amount deposited to the credit of Government to that extent under section 195, can be refunded, with prior approval of the Chief Commissioner or the Director General concerned, to the person who deducted it from the payment to the non-resident.

• *Other points* - The following should also be noted—

1. In case of refund being made to the person who made the payment under section 195, the Assessing Officer may, after giving intimation to the deductor, adjust it against any existing tax liability of the deductor under the Income-tax Act, Wealth-tax Act, or any other direct tax law. The balance amount, if any, should be refunded to the person who made such payment under section 195.

2. A refund should be granted only after obtaining an undertaking that no certificate in form No. 16A has been issued to the non-resident. In cases where such a certificate has been issued, the person making the claim of refund either obtain it or should indemnify the Income-tax Department from any possible loss on account of any separate claim of refund for the same amount by the non-resident.

3. A refund should be granted only if the deductee has not filed return of income and the time for filing of return of income has expired.

4. The limitation for making a claim of refund shall be two years from the end of the financial year in which tax is deducted at source.

5. If a resident deductor is entitled for the refund of tax deposited under section 195, then it has to be refunded with interest under section 244A, from the date of payment of such tax – Circular No. 11/2016[$], dated April 26, 2016 [*see* para 143.1]. From April 1, 2017, interest on such refund will be governed by section 244A(1B) [*see* para 143.1].

168.4 ***Furnishing information regarding remittance to non-resident*** - A person making remittance to a non-resident/foreign company is required to furnish an undertaking in digital mode in Form No. 15CA. In some cases, an online certificate of a chartered accountant in Form No. 15CB has to be taken before uploading Form No. 15CA. The relevant provisions (applicable from April 1, 2016) are given below –

• *Category A - Amount (which is to be remitted abroad) is not chargeable to tax in the hands of recipient in India—*

1. Undertaking in Form No. 15CA and certificate in Form No. 15CB is not required, if remittance pertains to 33 items specified in rule 37BB[$].

2. Undertaking in Form No. 15CA and certificate in Form No. 15CB is not required, if—

a. the remittance is made by an individual; and

b. prior RBI approval is not required[53] by virtue of section 5 of FEMA read with Schedule III to the Foreign Exchange (Current Account Transaction) Rules, 2000.

3. In any other case, certificate in Form No. 15CB is not required. However, undertaking in Form No. 15CA (Part D) should be uploaded.

• *Category B - Amount (which is to be remitted abroad) is chargeable to tax in the hands of recipient in India -*

4. If remittance (or aggregate amount of remittance during the financial year) does not exceed Rs. 5,00,000, Form No. 15CB is not required. However, undertaking in Form No. 15CA (Part A) should be uploaded.

5. If lower TDS certificate is received under section 197 or order of the Assessing Officer is received under section 195(2)/(3), information is to be uploaded in Form No. 15CA (Part B). Certificate from a chartered accountant in Form No. 15CB is not required.

---

53. Prior RBI approval is not required for remittance by an individual within the limit of US $ 5,00,000 for - (*a*) Private visits to any country (except Nepal and Bhutan); (*b*) Gift or donation; (*c*) Going abroad for employment; (*d*) Emigration; (*e*) Maintenance of close relatives abroad; (*f*) Travel for business/conference/specialised training/medical treatment/studies abroad; and (*g*) Any other current account transaction.

$ For rule 37BB and Circular No. 11/2016, log on to *taxmann.com/readyreckoner.aspx*.

6. In any other case of remittance outside India, the person making remittance will have to take a chartered accountant certificate in Form No. 15CB and, subsequently, he/it will have to furnish an undertaking in Form No. 15CA (Part C).

168.4-1 *OTHER POINTS* - The following points should be noted -

1. The information in Form No. 15CA shall be furnished,—

a. electronically under digital signature and thereafter printout of the said form shall be submitted to the authorised dealer, prior to remitting the payment; or

b. electronically in accordance with specified procedures, formats and standards and thereafter signed printout of the said form shall be submitted to the authorised dealer, prior to remitting the payment.

2. An income-tax authority may require the authorised dealer to furnish the signed printout of Form No. 15CA for the purposes of any proceedings under the Act.

3. The certificate of chartered accountant in Form No. 15CB shall be furnished and verified electronically.

4. The authorised dealer shall electronically furnish a quarterly statement for each quarter of the financial year in Form No.15CC to the Principal Director General of Income-tax (Systems) or the person authorised by the Principal Director General of Income-tax (Systems) electronically under digital signature within 15 days from the end of each quarter.

5. A certificate issued by a Chartered Accountant in Form No. 15CB, on the question of taxability of payment to non-resident in India, has no decisive impact on the determination of tax liability of the recipient non-resident in India—*CIT* v. *Rediff.com India Ltd.* [2011] 13 taxmann.com 61 (Mum.).

168.5 ***Reimbursement*** - There is no income element in the case of reimbursement of expenditure actually incurred by a non-resident or a foreign company. In such a case, section 195(2) is not applicable—*Bangalore International Airport Ltd.* v. *ITO* [2008] 24 SOT 26 (Bang.).

168.6 ***Transfer of controlling interest in a foreign company having assets in India*** - Shareholding in companies incorporated outside India is property located outside India. Where such shares become subject matter of offshore transfer between two non-residents, there is no liability for capital gains tax in India. In such a case, tax deduction under section 195 is not applicable—*Vodafone International Holdings B.V.* v. *Union of India* [2012] 204 Taxman 408 (SC). The aforesaid provisions have been amended (with retrospective[54] effect from the assessment year 1962-63) to clarify that an asset or a capital asset being any share (or interest) in a company (or entity) registered (or incorporated) outside India shall be deemed to be situated in India, if the share (or interest) derives (directly or indirectly) its value substantially from the assets located in India.

Deduction of tax at source from interest or dividend or other sums payable to Government, Reserve Bank or certain corporations [Secs. 196 and 197A(1D), (1E), (1F)]

169. Tax is not deductible in the following cases –

- *Section 196* - By virtue of section 196, tax is not deductible in respect of amount payable to the following –

a. Central Government or State Government;

b. the Reserve Bank of India;

c. a statutory corporation whose income is exempt from income-tax[55]; or

d. a mutual fund; or

---

54. Vide Letter [F.No.500/111/2009-FTD-1(PT.)], dated May 29, 2012, the Board has pointed out that the amendment has been made with retrospective effect in order to clarify the legislative intent and state the position of law from the date of coming into effect of these sections in the Act. Further the Board has directed that where assessment proceedings have been completed under section 143(3) before April 1, 2012, and no notice for reassessment has been issued prior to that date, then such case shall not be reopened under section 147/148 on account of the abovementioned clarificatory amendments introduced by the Finance Act, 2012. However, assessment or any other order which stand validated due to the said clarificatory amendments in the Finance Act, 2012 would of course be enforced.

55. Vide Circular No. 4/2002, dated July 16, 2002, Circular No. 7/2008, dated August 1, 2008, Circular No. 7/2015, dated April 23, 2015 and Circular No. 18/2017, dated May 29, 2017, the Board has decided that in case of those funds/authorities/Boards/bodies (by whatever name called), whose income is unconditionally exempt under section 10 and who are statutorily not required to file return of income as per section 139, there would be no requirement for tax deduction at source since their income is anyway exempt. The institutions whose income is unconditionally exempt under section 10 and who are statutorily not required to file return of income and who can receive payment without TDS or who can purchase goods without TCS are –

- local authority [sec. 10(*20*)];
- Regimental Fund or Non-public Fund [sec. 10(*23AA*)];

(Contd. on next Page)

If any person makes payment to the aforesaid, no tax is deductible at source.

• *Section 197A(1D)* - Tax is not deductible by off-shore banking unit from interest paid to non-resident or not ordinarily resident[56].

• *Section 197A(1E)* - With effect from April 1, 2009, no deduction of tax shall be made from any payment to any person for, or on behalf of, the New Pension System Trust.

• *Section 197A(1F)* -Tax is not deductible from a specified payment to a notified institution, association or body or class of institutions, associations or bodies. Notified payment/institutions are—

- Certain payments given by a person to a bank [*see* para 159.7-13];
- Payments pertaining to software, if a few conditions given in Notification No. 21/2012$, dated June 13, 2012 are satisfied [*see* para 166.6-2];
- Any income (other than business income) given to an investment trust (referred to in section 115UB) which is exempt under section 10(*23FBA*).
- Payment of interest or rent (covered by section 193, 194A or 194-I) to the Tirumala Tirupati Devasthanams, Tirupati, Andhra Pradesh.
- Payments of the nature specified in section 10(*23DA*) to securitisation trust.

Deduction of tax at source from income of Mutual Fund [Sec. 196A]

170. Tax is not deductible under section 196A from April 1, 2003.

Deduction of tax at source in respect of units referred to in section 115AB [Sec. 196B]

171. Section 196B was inserted with effect from October 1, 1991. Where any income (including long-term capital gain) is payable in respect of units referred to in section 115AB to an Off-shore Fund, the person responsible for making the payment shall, at the time of credit of such income to the account of the payee [*see* also para 154.1-7] or at the time of payment thereof in cash or by the issue of a cheque or draft or by any other mode, whichever is earlier, deduct income-tax thereon at the rate of 10 per cent[57].

(Contd. from Pre-Page)

- Fund, by whatever name called, set up by LIC [sec. 10(*23AAB*)];
- Khadi and Village Industries Board [sec. 10(*23BB*)];
- Body or authority for administration of public religious charitable trust [sec. 10(*23BBA*)];
- SAARC Fund for Regional Projects [sec. 10(*23BBC*)];
- IRDA [sec. 10(*23BBE*)];
- Central Electricity Regulatory Commission [sec. 10(*23BBG*)];
- Prasar Bharati [sec. 10(*23BBH*)];
- Prime Minister's National Relief Fund [sec. 10(*23C*)(*i*)];
- Prime Minister's Fund (Promotion of Folk Art) [sec. 10(*23C*)(*ii*)];
- Prime Minister's Aid to Students Fund [sec. 10(*23C*)(*iii*)];
- National Foundation for Communal Harmony [sec. 10(*23C*)(*iiia*)];
- Swachh Bharat Cess [sec. 10(*23C*)(*iiiaa*)];
- Clean Ganga Fund [sec. 10(*23C*)(*iiiaaa*)];
- Statutory provident fund, recognised provident fund, approved superannuation fund, approved gratuity fund [sec. 10(*25*)];
- Employees' State Insurance Fund (up to the assessment year 2017-18) [sec. 10(*25A*)];
- Agricultural Produce Marketing Committee [sec. 10(*26AAB*)];
- Corporation/body/institution/association established for promoting interests of members of Scheduled Castes or Scheduled Tribes or backward classes [sec. 10(*26B*)];
- Corporations for promoting interest of members of minority community [sec. 10(*26BB*)];
- Corporation for the welfare and economic upliftment of ex-servicemen [sec. 10(*26BBB*)];
- New Pension System Trust [sec. 10(*44*)].

56. CBDT has clarified that tax is not required to be deducted on interest paid by first International Financial Services Centre (*IFSC*) *Banking Unit* (IBU) on deposits made (on or after April 1, 2005) by non-residents or a person who is not ordinarily resident in India, or on borrowings made on or after April 1, 2005 from such persons - Circular No. 26/2016$, dated July 4, 2016.

57. If recipient is non-resident, it will be increased by surcharge and health and education cess. If the recipient does not furnish his PAN to the deductor, tax will be deducted at the normal rate or at the rate of 20 per cent, whichever is higher. PAN of the deductee should be mentioned in any correspondence and document which is exchanged between the deductor and deductee.

$ For Notification No. 21/2012 and Circular No. 18/2017, log on to *taxmann.com/readyreckoner.aspx*.

Deduction of tax at source from income from foreign currency bonds [Sec. 196C]

172. Section 196C was inserted with effect from June 1, 1992. Under this section any person responsible for paying any income (including long-term capital gain) payable in respect of bonds or global depository receipts referred to in section 115AC to a non-resident shall deduct tax at the rate of 10 per cent[58] of such income. The deduction is required to be made either at the time of credit of such income to the account of the payee [*see* also para 154.1-7] or at the time of payment thereof in cash or at the time of issue of a cheque or draft or by any other mode, whichever is earlier.

• No tax is deductible from June 1, 1997 to March 31, 2002 and from April 1, 2003, in respect of dividends referred to in section 115-O.

Deduction of tax from income of Foreign Institutional Investors from securities [Sec. 196D]

173. Section 196D was inserted with effect from June 1, 1993, to provide that any person responsible for paying any income in respect of securities referred to in section 115AD(1)(*a*) (not being income referred to section 194LD) to a Foreign Institutional Investor shall deduct tax thereon at the rate of 20 per cent[58]. The deduction is required to be made either at the time of credit of such income to the account of the payee [*see* also para 154.1-7] or at the time of payment thereof in cash or at the time of issue of a cheque or draft or by any other mode, whichever is earlier. No deduction of tax is to be made from any income by way of capital gains arising from the transfer of such securities.

• No tax is deductible from June 1, 1997 to March 31, 2002 and from April 1, 2003 in respect of dividends referred to in section 115-O.

Time of deposit of TDS, quarterly return, etc.

174. These provisions are given below –

174.1 ***Time of deposit of TDS/TCS*** - Tax deducted/collected by a person shall be deposited to Government account as follows—

Different situations	*Time of deposit of TDS/TCS (applicable in the case of tax deducted/collected on or after April 1, 2010)*	
	Time of deposit of TDS	*Time of deposit of TCS*
1. Tax is deducted/collected by an office of the Government and tax is paid without production of an income-tax challan	On the same day on which tax is deducted	On the same day on which tax is collected
2. Tax is deducted/collected by an office of the Government and tax deposit is accompanied by an income-tax challan [Challan No. ITNS 281]	On or before 7 days from the end of the month in which tax is deducted	On or before 7 days from the end of the month in which tax is collected
3. Tax is deducted/collected by a person (not being an office of the Government) [Challan No. ITNS 281]	• *Where income or amount is paid or credited in the month of March* : Tax should be deposited by April 30 • *Where income or amount is paid or credited before March 1* : Tax should be deposited within 7 days from the end of the month in which tax is deducted	Within one week from the last day of the month in which tax is collected
4. Tax is deducted by a person (not being an office of the Government) and the Assessing Officer (with prior approval of Joint Commissioner) has permitted quarterly deposit of tax deducted under sections 192, 194A, 194D and 194H [Challan No. ITNS 281]	• *For the quarter ending June 30* : Tax should be deposited by July 7 • *For the quarter ending September 30* : Tax should be deposited by October 7 • *For the quarter ending December 31* : Tax should be deposited by January 7 • *For the quarter ending March 31* : Tax should be deposited by April 30	–
5. Tax is deducted by a person under section 194-IA [Challan No. : Form 26QB]	• *Applicable from June 1, 2016* - Within 30 days from the last date of month in which tax is deducted. • *Applicable up to May 31, 2016* - Within 7 days from the last date of month in which tax is deducted.	-

58. See footnote No. 57.

Different situations	*Time of deposit of TDS/TCS (applicable in the case of tax deducted/collected on or after April 1, 2010)*	
	Time of deposit of TDS	*Time of deposit of TCS*
6. Tax is deducted by a person under section 194-IB [Challan No. : Form 26QC]	• Within 30 days from the last date of month in which tax is deducted.	–

174.2 ***Mode of deposit of TDS/TCS*** - Tax deducted/collected on or after April 1, 2010 shall be deposited as follows—

• *When tax is deducted/collected by a Government office and paid without production of a challan* - The following procedure should be followed—

1. Tax will be deducted/collected by the person responsible for tax deduction/collection (*i.e.*, tax deductor or collector).

2. The deductor/collector shall report tax so deducted/collected to the Pay and Accounts Officer or the Treasury Officer or the Cheque Drawing and Disbursing Officer or any other person (by whatever name called) who is responsible for crediting such sum to the credit of the Central Government.

3. The person to whom tax deduction/collection is reported by the deductors/collectors, shall submit a statement in Form No. 24G. It should be submitted to a notified agency [*i.e.*, an agency authorized by the Director General of Income-tax (Systems)].

It should be submitted within the time-limit given below –

	Time-limit (with effect from June 1, 2016)	*Time-limit (up to May 31, 2016)*
Where statement relates to month of March	On or before 30 days*	On or before 10 days*
Where statement relates to any other month	On or before 15 days*	On or before 10 days*

*From the end of the month in respect of tax deducted/collected by the deductors/collectors and reported to him for that month.

4. When Form No. 24G is submitted to the authorized agency, the agency will generate "Book identification number" in respect of each of the deductors/collectors.

5. The person submitting Form No. 24G shall intimate the "Book identification number" generated by the agency to each of the deductors/collectors in respect of whom the sum deducted/collected has been credited.

• *When tax deducted/collected is deposited accompanied by an income-tax challan* - The tax deducted/collected shall be deposited within the time-limit given above. It can be deposited into any branch of the Reserve Bank of India or the State Bank of India or of any authorized bank.

After March 31, 2008, all corporate assessees and other assessees (who are subject to compulsory audit under section 44AB) will have to make electronic payment of tax (including TDS) through internet banking facility offered by authorized banks. Alternatively, these taxpayers can make electronic payment of tax through internet by way of credit or debit cards. It is not necessary for the assessee to make payment of taxes from his own account in an authorized bank. An assessee can make electronic payment of taxes also from the account of any other person. However, the challan for making such payment must clearly indicate the Permanent Account Number (PAN) of the assessee on whose behalf the payment is made—Circular No. 5/2008[$], dated July 17, 2008.

174.3 ***Quarterly statement of tax deduction/collection*** - In respect of tax deducted/collected on or after April 1, 2010, quarterly TDS/TCS statements shall be submitted in the following forms—

	Form No.
Tax deduction from salary under section 192	24Q
Tax deduction when deductees are non-resident (not being a company), foreign company and persons who are resident but not ordinarily resident	27Q

[$] For Circular No. 5/2008, log on to *taxmann.com/readyreckoner.aspx*.

	Form No.
Tax deduction under section 194-IA	26QB[59]
Tax deduction under section 194-IB	26QC
Tax deduction in any other case	26Q
Tax collection	27EQ

• *Other requirements* - The deductor or collector at the time of preparation of quarterly return of TDS/TCS shall—

a. quote his/its TAN;

b. quote his/its PAN (except in the case where deductor/collector is an office of the Government);

c. quote PAN of all deductees/collectees;

d. furnish particulars of tax paid to the Central Government including book identification number or challan identification number;

e. furnish particulars of amount paid/credited without TDS in view of issue of certificate by the Assessing Officer under section 197;

f. furnish particulars of amount paid/credited to transport contractors (who have intimated their PAN) without TDS in view of the provisions of section 194C(6);

g. furnish particulars of amount paid/credited without TDS after obtaining declaration in Form No. 15G/15H in view of provisions of section 197A(1A)/(1C);

h. furnish particulars of amount paid/credited without TDS in view of the notifications issued under section 197A(1F); and

i. furnish particulars of amount received or debited on which tax was not collected in view of the furnishing of declaration by buyer under section 206C(1A).

• *Correction statements* - A deductor is allowed to file correction statement for rectification/updation of the information furnished in the original TDS statement as per the Centralised Processing of Statements of Tax Deducted at Source Scheme, 2013 notified *vide* Notification No. 3/2013, dated January 15, 2013. With effect from October 1, 2014, sections 200 and 200A have been amended to allow deductors to file correction statements. Further, section 206C has been amended (with effect from June 1, 2015) to allow collectors to file correction statements.

174.3-1 *DUE DATE OF SUBMISSION OF QUARTERLY RETURNS* - In respect of tax deducted/collected the quarterly returns shall be submitted within the time-limit given below—

For the quarter ending	*Due date of submission of quarterly statements*	
	TDS returns	*Quarterly TCS returns*
June 30	July 31	July 15
September 30	October 31	October 15
December 31	January 31	January 15
March 31	May 31[60]	May 15

Note - The time-limit given above is not applicable in the case of TDS under section 194-IA/194-IB. In these cases, challan of electronic deposit of TDS (*i.e.*, Form No. 26QB/26QC) is itself taken as quarterly statement of TDS (no separate statement of TDS is to be submitted).

174.3-2 *MODE OF FURNISHING QUARTERLY RETURNS* - These provisions are given below –

• *Who is required to submit TDS/TCS statements electronically* - The following persons shall submit quarterly TDS/TCS returns electronically –

1. When deductor or collector is an office of the Government.

2. When deductor/collector is the principal officer of a company.

3. When deductor/collector is a person who is required to get his account audited under section 44AB in the immediately preceding financial year.

4. When the number of deductee's/collectee's records in a statement for any quarter of the financial year are 20 or more.

---

59. CPC-TDS has enabled functionality for online correction in Form No. 26QB with effect from February 29, 2016 - Letter F.No. DIT(s)-2/Form 26QB/100/2015, dated March 22, 2016.

60. Extended in the case of Form No. 24Q from May 31, 2019 to June 30, 2019.

Barring the cases given above, any other deductor/collector can submit quarterly TDS/TCS returns either in paper format or electronically.

• *Mode of uploading return* - With effect from February 19, 2013, the aforesaid electronic return can be submitted/uploaded under any one of the following options –

Option 1 - Uploading quarterly returns with digital signature.

Option 2 - Furnishing quarterly return electronically along with the verification of the statement in Form No. 27A.

Option 3 - Furnishing quarterly return electronically along with electronic verification of the statement in Form No. 27A.

174.3-3 *HOW TO OBTAIN REFUND* - A claim for refund for TDS paid to the credit of the Central Government under Chapter XVII-B, shall be furnished by the deductor in Form No. 26B[$] electronically under digital signature.

174.3-4 *CLARIFICATION ON FORM NO. 24Q* - The following clarifications are given by NSDL—

• *Particulars to be filled in Annexures I and III* - It is as follows—

1. In Annexure I, actual figures for the relevant quarter should be reported.

2. Annexure II should have actual figures for the whole financial year in and Annexure II should be submitted for the whole year in Quarter 4.

• *Particulars of employees whose income is below the threshold limit/the income after giving deductions for savings etc. is below the threshold limit* - Particulars of only those employees are to be reported in whose case the estimated income for the whole year is above the threshold limit.

1. In case the estimated income for the whole year of an employee, after allowing deduction for various savings like PPF, GPF, NSC, etc., comes below the taxable limit, his particulars need not be included in Form No. 24Q.

2. In case due to some reason, estimated annual income of an employee exceeds the exemption limit during the course of the year, tax should be deducted in that quarter and his particulars be reported from that quarter onwards.

• *Particulars of those employees, who are with the employer for a part of the year* - It is as follows—

1. Where an employee has worked with a deductor for part of the financial year only, the deductor should deduct tax at source from his salary and report the same in the quarterly statement of the respective quarter(s) up to the date of employment with him. Further, while submitting Form No. 24Q for the last quarter, the deductor should include particulars of that employee in Annexures II and III irrespective of the fact that the employee was not under his employment on the last day of the year.

2. Similarly, where an employee joins employment with deductor during the course of the financial year, his particulars should be reported by the current deductor in Form No. 24Q of the relevant quarter. Further, while submitting Form No. 24Q for the last quarter, the deductor should include particulars of such employee for the actual period of employment under him in Annexures II and III.

• *Explanation for lower/no deduction of tax* - Certificate for lower or no deduction of tax from salary is given by the Assessing Officer on the basis of an application made by the deductee. In case where the Assessing Officer has issued such a certificate to a deductee, deductor has to mention whether no tax has been deducted or tax has been deducted at lower rate on the basis of such a certification in column 326.

174.4 ***Certificate of tax deduction/collection at source*** - TDS/TCS certificate shall be issued (Form No. 16 for TDS from salary, Form No. 16B for TDS under section 194-IA, Form No. 16C for TDS under section 194-IB, Form No. 16A for TDS from other than salary and Form No. 27D for TCS)

174.4-1 *TIME-LIMIT FOR ISSUE OF TDS/TCS CERTIFICATE* - Time-limit for issue of TDS/TCS certificates in new forms has been modified. However, the new limits are applicable only in respect of tax deducted/collected on or after April 1, 2010. The new time-limits are given below—

[$] For requirement of Form No. 26B, log on to *taxmann.com/readyreckoner.aspx.*

Form No. (new format)	*Periodicity*	*Due date*		
Form No. 16	Annual	On or before June 15 of the financial year[61] immediately following the financial year in which tax is deducted.		
Form No. 16A/ Form No. 27D	Quarterly	Within 15 days from the due date of furnishing quarterly TDS/TCS returns. In other words—		
		For the quarter ending	*TDS/TCS certificate should be given on or before*	
			Form No. 16A	*Form No. 27D*
		June 30	August 15	July 30
		September 30	November 15	October 30
		December 31	February 15	January 30
		March 31	June 15	May 30
Form No. 16B	–	Within 15 days of furnishing challan in Form No. 26QB		
Form No. 16C	–	Within 15 days of furnishing challan in Form No. 26QC		

174.4-2 *SALARY TDS CERTIFICATE IN NEW FORM NO. 16* - New Form No. 16 is divided into different parts as follows—

Form No. 16	*Contents*	*How to generate different parts of Form No. 16*
Part A (Form No. 16 and Form No. 12BA)	This part contains information of employer and employee (like name and address of employer, PAN/TAN of deductor, name and address of employee, PAN of employee), assessment year, period of employment, address of CIT (TDS), summary of tax deduction at source (like quarter wise information of receipt numbers of original quarterly TDS returns in Form No. 24Q, amount paid, amount of tax deducted and amount of tax deposited or remitted). Besides, Part A includes details of tax deducted and deposited with the Central Government (like, tax deposited, BSR code of bank, date of deposit, challan serial number, status of challan matching with OLTAS). In verification, the deductor will have to certify the amount of tax deducted and deposited by him.	All deductors (including Government deductors who deposit TDS in the Central Government Account through book entry) shall issue the Part A of Form No. 16, by generating and subsequently downloading through TRACES Portal, in respect of all sums deducted on or after April 1, 2012 – Circular No. 4/2013, dated April 17, 2013. Part A of Form No. 16 shall have a unique TDS certificate number.
Part B (Form No. 16)	Part B includes details of salary paid, other incomes, amount deductible under Chapter VI-A, tax payable and relief under section 89. Part B also includes a separate verification. In verification the deductor will certify that salary/tax details are complete and correct on the basis of account books and other available records/documents/statements.	All deductors (including Government deductors) shall issue Part B of Form No. 16 by generating and downloading through TRACES Portal)[62] in respect of all sums deducted on or after April 1, 2018 under section 192. The TRACES generated Form No. 16 shall have a unique TDS certificate number.

• *When a person is employed by more than one employer during a financial year* - If a person is employed under more than one employer during the year, each of the employers shall issue Part A of Form No. 16 pertaining to the period for which such person was employed with each of the employers. Part B may be issued by each of the employers or the last employer at the option of the employee.

• *Form No. 16 with digital signature* - Part A of Form No. 16 shall be issued only by downloading it from the TRACES Portal. Further, Part B of Form No. 16 (in respect of all sums deducted on or after April 1, 2018) shall be issued only by downloading it from TRACES portal. However, Item Nos. 2(*f*) and 10(*k*) in Part B (Annexure) of Form No. 16 shall be filled in by the deductor manually and it should be printed at the bottom of the TRACES generated Form No. 16 (Part B). Before issuing Part A and Part B to the deductee, deductor shall authenticate the correctness of contents of these parts. Authentication can be verified either by using manual signature or by using digital signature.

61. Extended in the case of Form No. 16 from June 15, 2019 to July 10, 2019.

62. However, Item Nos. 2(*f*) and 10(*k*) in Part B (Annexure) of Form No. 16 shall be filled in by the deductor manually and it should be printed at the bottom of the TRACES generated Form No. 16 (Part B) before furnishing it to employees.

• *Form No. 16 along with statement of perquisites in Form No. 12BA* - Information relating to the nature and value of perquisites shall be provided by the employer in Form No. 12BA in case of salary paid or payable is above Rs. 2,00,000. In other cases, the information would have to be provided by the employer in Form No. 16 itself - Circular No. 8/2012[$], dated October 5, 2012.

174.4-3 *TDS CERTIFICATE IN FORM NO. 16A* - TDS certificates in Form No. 16A shall be issued by downloading from TIN website (now TRACES Portal) by the following deductors—

a. any deductor (including a Government deductor who deposits TDS in the Central Government Account through book entry), if tax is deducted on or after April 1, 2012, and

b. any company (including a banking company), if tax is deducted during 2011-12.

• *Option to non-corporate deductors (if tax is a deducted during 2011-12)* - A non-corporate deductor (including a Government deductor who deposits TDS in the Central Government Account through book entry) has an option to generate (or not to generate) Form No. 16A by downloading from TIN website (now TRACES Portal). This option is available only if tax is deducted during 2011-12. A certificate in Form No. 16A with digital signature is not possible, if it is issued without downloading from TIN website (now TRACES Portal).

• *Authentication of TDS certificate in Form No. 16A* - Deductors, issuing the TDS certificates in Form No. 16A by downloading from the TIN website (now TRACES Portal), shall authenticate these certificates by either using digital signature or manual signature.

• *Other points* - The following points should be noted in respect of new TDS/TCS certificates in Form Nos. 16, 16A and 27D. These certificates should specify—

a. valid PAN of deductee/collectee;

b. valid TAN of deductor/collector;

c. book identification number (numbers) where TDS/TCS is deposited without production of challan in the case of an office of Government;

d. challan identification number (numbers) in the case of deposit of TDS/TCS through bank;

e. receipt number of relevant quarterly TDS/TCS return; and

f. receipt numbers of all the relevant quarterly returns in Form No. 24Q in the case of TDS certificate in Form No. 16.

174.4-4 *TDS CERTIFICATE IN FORM NO. 16B* - If tax is deducted under section 194-IA by a person purchasing an immovable property, TDS certificate shall be issued in Form No. 16B by downloading from TRACES Portal.

Other points

175. One should also note the following—

175.1 ***Rates for deduction of tax at source*** - *See* para 0.6, Referencer 1.

175.2 ***Refund/adjustment of tax deducted at source*** - The following procedure is laid down to regulate the refund of excess payment of tax deducted at source :

• The excess payment would be the difference between the actual payment made by the deductor and the tax deducted at source or that deductible, whichever is more. This excess amount is first adjusted against the existing tax liability of the deductor under any of the Direct Tax Acts and after meeting such liability the balance amount, if any, is refunded to the assessee.

• Where the tax is deducted at source and paid by the branch office of the assessee and the quarterly statement/annual return (in case of salaries) of tax deduction at source is filed by the branch, such branch office would be treated as a separate unit independent of the head office. After meeting any existing tax liability of such a branch (which would normally be in relation to the deduction of tax at source), the balance amount may be refunded to the said branch office. The ITO, who will refund the amount, would be the one who receives the quarterly statement/annual return (in case of salary) of tax deduction at source from that branch office and keeps record of the payments of tax deduction at source made by that branch.

• Since the adjustment/refund of the amount paid in excess would arise in relation to the deduction of tax at source, the recording of the particulars of adjustment/refund is to be done in the quarterly statement of TDS/annual return (in case of salaries) under the signatures of the ITO at the end of the statement, *i.e.*, below the signatures of the person furnishing the statement—Circular No. 285, dated October 21, 1980.

175.3 ***Tax deduction and collection account number (TAN) [Sec. 203A]*** - Every person, deducting tax or collecting tax, who has not been allotted a tax deduction account number or, as the case may be, a tax collection account number, shall, within one month from the end of the month in which tax was deducted

[$] For Circular No. 8/2012, log on to *taxmann.com/readyreckoner.aspx.*

or collected or January 31, 2005, whichever is later, apply to the Assessing Officer in Form No. 49B[63] for the allotment of a "tax deduction and collection account number" (TAN). Where a "tax deduction account number" or "tax collection account number" or "tax deduction and collection account number" (TAN) has been allotted to a person, such person shall quote such number—

a. in all challans for the payment of any sum in accordance with the provisions of section 200 or section 206C(3);

b. in all certificates furnished under section 203 or section 206C(5);

c. in all the returns, delivered in accordance with the provisions of section 206 or section 206C(5A)/(5B); and

d. in all other documents pertaining to such transactions as may be prescribed.

• *Cases when TAN is not required* - For reporting of tax deducted under section 194-IA, the deductor is not required to obtain and quote TAN and he is allowed to report the tax deducted by quoting his PAN. Moreover, section 203A has been amended (with effect from June 1, 2015) so as to provide that the requirement of obtaining and quoting of TAN shall not apply to the notified deductors or collectors.

175.4 ***Provisions of section 197A*** - If a declaration is submitted under section 197A by the recipient to the payer, then no tax is deductible in a few cases. The provisions of section 197A are given in the table (*infra*)—

	Taxable premature withdrawal from provident fund [Sec. 192A][64]	*Interest [Secs. 193 and 194A] or rent [Sec. 194-I*[65]*] or insurance commission [Sec. 194D*[66]*]*	*Dividend [Sec. 194]*	*Payment in respect of life insurance policy [Sec. 194DA]*[64]	*National Saving Scheme [Sec. 194EE]*
Condition 1 - Who is recipient	Individual	Other than a company or firm	Resident individual	Other than a company or firm	Resident individual
Condition 2 - What is tax on total income of the previous year	*Nil*	*Nil*	*Nil*	*Nil*	*Nil*
Condition 3 - How much is total of income covered by sections 192A, 193, 194, 194A, 194D, 194DA, 194EE and 194-I	Not exceeding the maximum amount not chargeable to tax [Note 7]				

Notes—

1. If the above conditions are satisfied and the recipient gives a declaration to the payer of income along with his PAN, the payer will not deduct tax at source. Such declaration should be given in Form No. 15G (Form No. 15H for senior citizen) [senior citizen is a resident individual who is at least 60 years of age (65 years is applicable up to June 30, 2012) during the financial year]. In the case of Senior Citizens Savings Scheme, 2004 (SCSS), investors can submit the aforesaid declaration. Nominees of investors of SCSS can also produce Form No. 15G at the time of payment after the death of the depositor. If this declaration is given to a bank, bank will give an acknowledgement at the time of receipt of Form No. 15G/15H.

2. Condition 3 is not applicable up to May 31, 2002.

3. Condition 3 is not applicable from June 1, 2002 if the income of recipient is exempt under section 10(*20*), (*23AA*), (*23AAB*), (*23BB*), (*23BBA*), (*23BBC*), (*23BBD*), (*23BBE*), (*23C*), (*23EB*), (*25*), (*25A*), (*26BB*) and (*29A*)—Circular No. 4/2002, dated July 16, 2002.

4. Condition 3 is not applicable if the recipient is a senior citizen [senior citizen is a resident individual who is at least 60 years of age (65 years is applicable up to June 30, 2012) during the financial year].

5. From April 1, 2003, no tax is deductible under section 194 in respect of dividend referred to in section 115-O.

6. From April 1, 2003, no tax is deductible under section 194K.

7. Exemption limit for the financial year 2019-20 is Rs. 2,50,000 [higher exemption limit (*a*) in the case of a resident senior citizen born on or after April 2, 1940 but on or before April 1, 1960: Rs. 3,00,000; and (*b*) in the case of a resident super senior citizen born on or before April 1, 1940: Rs. 5,00,000].

---

63. A company (which is not registered under the Companies Act, 2013) can apply for TAN in Form No. INC-7 specified under section 7(1) of the Companies Act.

64. Applicable from June 1, 2015.

65. Applicable from June 1, 2016.

66. Applicable from June 1, 2017.

175.4-1 *MODE OF SUBMISSION OF FORM No. 15G/15H BY THE RECIPIENT OF INCOME* - If the above conditions are satisfied, the recipient of income can submit Form No. 15G (for senior citizen Form No. 15H) to the payer of income. It can be furnished in paper format. Alternatively, it can be furnished electronically after duly verifying through an electronic process (the facility of electronic furnishing Form No. 15G/15H is provided on the website of different banks/payers). The declarant shall mandatorily quote his/her PAN in Form No.15G/15H in accordance with the provisions of section 206AA(2).

175.4-2 *MODE OF FURNISHING FORM No. 15G/15H BY PAYER OF INCOME TO INCOME-TAX AUTHORITY* - The payer shall be responsible for proper verification of the declarant through an electronic process and shall implement the verification process after due diligence to ensure non-repudiation of the declarant. The payer shall be responsible to establish the identity and credentials of the declarant in case of any dispute.

- *Allotment of UIN* - The UIN shall consist of following fields—

a. Sequence Number (10 alphanumeric for Form 15G/15H)

b. Financial year for which declaration is being furnished

c. TAN of the payer

- *Digitization of paper declaration by the payer* -Paper declaration of Form No. 15G/15H received by the payer of income shall be digitized by him/it and the same shall bear sequence number out of the same "running sequence number (Field 'a' of UIN) series", as used for online submission. UIN running sequence number series shall be reset to 1 in case of each TAN of the payer at the start of each financial year.
- *Furnishing the declaration in Form No. 15G/15H by the payer to the income-tax authority* - The payer shall upload all declarations in Form No. 15G/15H (*i.e.*, electronic declarations and digitized declarations) received during a quarter on quarterly basis (within 15 days from the end of first, second and third quarter and within 30 days from the end of fourth quarter) in the given file format on the e-filing site (www.incometaxindiaefiling.gov.in).[67]
- *Quarterly TDS statements in Form No. 26Q, etc.* - Apart from uploading declarations in Form No. 15G/15H (as stated above), the payer of income will have to include the transactions in the quarterly TDS statement (in Form No. 26Q, etc.), even if no TDS is deducted during the quarter. The payer shall quote "sequence number" (Field 'a' of UIN) in quarterly TDS statement (in Form No. 26Q, etc.) against the transaction covered under Form No. 15G/15H declaration. The payer will be responsible for reconciliation of the allotted UINs *vis-a-vis* reported UINs to the Income-tax department through reporting in quarterly TDS statement as well as through uploading of declarations on quarterly basis.
- *Declarations in Form No. 15G/15H to be retained by payer for 7 years* - An income-tax authority may (before the end of 7 years from the end of the financial year in which the declaration in Form No. 15G/15H has been received), require the person responsible for payment to furnish or make available the declaration for the purposes of verification or any proceeding under the Act.
- *Fresh declaration in the case of change/new investment* - When the income for each year changes, new Form No. 15G/15H has to be filed. Whenever the estimated total income/aggregate income changes and new investments are made, one needs to file new Form No. 15G/15H. The amended format of Form No. 15G/15H requires the depositor to furnish the details of all investments up to that date including the current fixed deposit for which the Form No. 15G/15H is being given and which are to be listed in Form No. 15G/15H to enable the deductor to ascertain, whether the Form No. 15G/15H can be accepted – Notification No. 6/2017, dated May 30, 2017.

175.5 ***Obtaining a certificate of lower rate from the Assessing Officer [Sec. 197]*** - The provisions of section 197 are given below—

1. Tax is deductible under sections 192, 193, 194, 194A, 194C, 194D, 194G, 194H, 194-I, 194J, 194K, 194LA, 194LBB (with effect from June 1, 2016), 194LBC (with effect from June 1, 2016), **194M** (with effect from September 1, 2019) or 195.

2. The recipient can apply[68] in Form No. 13 to the Assessing Officer to get a certificate authorizing the payer to deduct tax at lower or deduct no tax as may be appropriate.

3. If the recipient does not have PAN, he cannot apply for the aforesaid certificate under section 197.

67. Time-limit has been extended as follows – For the period October 1, 2015 to June 30, 2016 : extended time-limit : October 31, 2016, for the period July 1, 2016 to September 30, 2016 : December 31, 2016.

68. There is no time-limit for application in Form No. 13. Application can be filed at any time before actual deduction of tax at source (it may be filed in the current financial year or even before the commencement of the financial year)— *Indus Towers Ltd.* v. *CIT* [2014] 220 Taxman 402 (Delhi).

175.5-1 *ADDITIONAL CONDITIONS FOR CHARITABLE TRUST, SCIENTIFIC RESEARCH ASSOCIATION, ETC. [RULE 28AB]* - With effect from April 1, 2004, if the recipient of income is one of the two entities given below, then a few additional conditions should be satisfied to make the above application in Form No. 13 :

a. it is in receipt of income (or deemed income) derived from property held under trust wholly for charitable or religious purposes and it claims exemption under section 11 or section 12; or

b. it is required to file a return in respect of a scientific research association, news agency, association or institution, fund or trust or university or other educational institution or any hospital or other medical institution or trade union referred to in section 139(4C).

Additional conditions - In any of the above cases, application in Form No. 13 can be made if the following conditions are satisfied—

a. the person concerned has furnished the returns of income for all assessment years for which such returns became due on or before the date on which the above application in Form No. 13 is made;

b. the trust, scientific research association, news agency, association or institution, fund or trust or university or other educational institution or any hospital or other medical institution or trade union referred to above is for the time being approved for the purpose of exemption from income-tax; and

c. the applicant gives a list of deductors from whom amounts are to be received without deduction of tax at source every six months along with the names, addresses and the amounts received.

175.5-2 *HOW LOWER RATE IS DETERMINED* - Lower rate of tax deduction shall be determined within the parameters of rule 28AA. Rule 28AA has been amended with effect from April 1, 2011. The legal position before and after the amendment is given below—

175.5-2a *Provisions applicable from April 1, 2011* - The amended provisions of rule 28AA (applicable on or after April 1, 2011) provides that the Assessing Officer will issue a certificate for lower tax deduction or no tax deduction on the basis of existing and estimated tax liability of the recipient. The existing and estimated liability of the recipient shall be determined by the Assessing Officer after taking into consideration the following—

1. Tax payable on estimated income of the previous year relevant to the assessment year.

2. Tax payable on the assessed or returned income, as the case may be, of the last 4 previous years (up to October 24, 2018 : last 3 previous years).

3. Existing liability of the recipient under the Income-tax Act and Wealth-tax Act.

4. Advance tax payment, tax deducted at source and tax collected at source for the assessment year relevant to the previous year till the date of making application in Form No. 13.

5. The certificate for deduction of tax at *nil* rate (or lower rate) shall be issued direct to the person responsible for deducting the tax under advice to the person who made the application for issue of such certificate. This certificate shall be valid only with regard to the person responsible for deducting the tax and named therein.

6. Where, however, the number of persons responsible for deducting the tax is likely to exceed 100 (and the details of such persons are not available at the time of making application with the person making such application), the certificate for *nil* deduction (or lower deduction) may be issued to the person who made the application, authorising him to receive income/sum after lower deduction or *nil* deduction. This certificate shall be valid with regard to the person who made the application for issue of such certificate.

175.5-3 *OTHER POINTS* - One should also keep in view the following propositions,—

• Certificate under section 197 cannot be issued with retrospective effect, it can be effective only prospectively.

• Where the application is allowed, that application culminates in the grant of a certificate in accordance with the provisions of section 197(1). Conversely, if the application is rejected, the Assessing Officer is bound to indicate reasons or a basis for the rejection of the application. The Assessing Officer cannot be heard to urge that, though an assessee fulfils all the requirements (which are stipulated in rule 28AA or, as the case may be, in rule 29B), he possesses an unguided discretion to reject the application. Consequently, the Assessing Officer, when he rejects an application, is bound to furnish reasons which would demonstrate an application of mind by him to the circumstances which are mandated both by the statute and by the rules to be taken into consideration—*Larsen & Toubro Ltd.* v. *CIT* [2010] 190 Taxman 373 (Bom.).

• If an Assessing Officer rejects an application of an assessee submitted under section 197, it can be revised by the Commissioner under section 264—*Larsen & Toubro Ltd.* (*supra*).

• If PAN of the applicant is not available, relief under section 197 is not available [sec. 206AA].

• The Board has directed all Assessing Officers to ensure that all certificates under section 197(1) are issued by them strictly as per the manner prescribed above. No certificate under section 197(1) shall be issued under circumstances, which are not covered by the above provisions, howsoever genuine and compelling such circumstances may be. Moreover, the Assessing Officer shall obtain prior administrative approval in each case. Prior administrative approval of the Commissioner of Income-tax (TDS) shall be taken where the cumulative amount of tax foregone by non-deduction/lesser rate of deduction of tax arising out of certificate under section 197 during a financial year for a particular assessee exceeds Rs. 50 lakh in Delhi, Mumbai, Chennai, Kolkata, Bangalore, Hyderabad, Ahmedabad and Pune stations and Rs. 10 lakh for other stations. In other cases, prior approval should be taken from the Range Jt. CIT/Addl. CIT before issuing a certificate under section 197(1). The Jt. CIT/Addl. CIT or CIT (TDS) shall satisfy himself of the fact that the certificate is being issued strictly in accordance with by the above provisions, before according his approval for issuance of the certificate. A record of such certificate issued should be maintained in the office of the Assessing Officer. Once the CIT(TDS) or Addl. CIT/Jt. CIT gives administrative approval of the above, a copy of it has to be endorsed invariably to the jurisdictional CIT also—Instruction No. 4/2010, dated July 21, 2010.

175.6 ***Furnishing of quarterly returns regarding the details of non-deduction of tax by certain persons [Sec. 206A, applicable from June 1, 2005]*** - Section 206A was inserted with effect from June 1, 2005. It has two sub-sections :

• *Sub-section (1)* - Sub-section (1) is applicable if the following conditions are satisfied—

1. The person who is otherwise responsible for deducting tax at source is (*a*) any banking company, (*b*) a co-operative society, (*c*) a public company.

2. It is responsible for paying to a resident, interest other than interest on securities.

3. Such interest, other than interest on securities, paid or payable during the financial year does not exceed threshold limit prescribed for the purpose of section 194A.

If the above three conditions are satisfied, the person responsible for making payment, is not required to deduct tax at source under section 194A. However, with effect from June 1, 2005, a banking company[69] shall prepare quarterly returns (*i.e.*, consolidated return for all branches) for the period ending on June 30, September 30, December 31 and March 31 in each financial year and deliver the same to the prescribed income-tax authority (or the person authorized by such authority). Such return should be submitted within one month[70] from the end of each quarter (June 30 in the case of last quarter) in digital format on a floppy, diskette, magnetic cartridge tape, CD-ROM or any other computer readable media [Form No. 26QAA[71]].

• *Sub-section (2)* - Sub-section (2) is applicable if the following conditions are satisfied—

1. The payer is a person other than the person who is covered by sub-section (1).

2. Such person is responsible for paying to a resident any income which is liable for deduction of tax at source under sections 192 to 194N.

If the above two conditions are satisfied, the Central Government may require (by notification in the Official Gazette) such person to prepare and deliver quarterly returns in the prescribed digital format. Such return should be submitted to the prescribed income-tax authority (or the person authorised by such authority) on a floppy, diskette, magnetic cartridge tape, CD-ROM or any other computer readable media.

• *Electronic filing of statement of aforesaid transactions (with effect from September 1, 2019)* - **The above provisions have been modified to provide for electronic filing of statement** (where tax has not been deducted on payment of interest to residents). **Further, this modification also provides for correction of such statements for rectification of any mistake or to add, delete or update the information furnished.**

175.7 ***Tax deducted - To be treated as income of deductee and available for tax credit [Secs. 198 and 199]*** - Tax deducted at source is deemed as income of the deductee. Further, the same amount is available as tax credit in the hands of deductee subject to the following propositions—

1. Credit for tax deducted at source and paid to the Central Government, shall be given to the deductee for the assessment year for which such income is assessable.

---

69. Only a banking company is required to submit this return as per Rules 31AC and 31ACA.

70. For the quarters ending on June 30, 2005, September 30, 2005 and December 31, 2005, such return can be submitted up to April 30, 2006.

71. Each branch of a banking company which is required to submit quarterly return under section 206A in respect of interest on time deposit without TDS shall keep and maintain the particular of such time deposit in Form No. 26QA.

2. Where tax has been deducted at source and paid to the Central Government and the income is assessable over a number of years, credit for tax deducted at source shall be allowed across those years in the same proportion in which the income is assessable to tax.

3. If the income on which tax has been deducted is assessable in the hands of a person other than the deductee, then tax credit will be given to such other person if—

a. the deductee files a declaration with the deductor (the declaration should contain the name, address, PAN of the person to whom credit is to be given and reasons for giving credit to such person);

b. the deductor shall keep the declaration in safe custody and report the tax deduction in the name of such other person in Form Nos. 16A, 17, 24C, 26Q, etc.

• Where though tax at source has been deducted from the assessee's salary but no TDS certificate is issued to the assessee by the employer despite repeated requests by the assessee, in view of section 205, income-tax authorities, under no circumstances, can make the assessee liable to make payment of any tax to the extent to which such tax had been deducted at source by the person paying salary to the assessee—*Capt. J.G. Joseph* v. *CIT* [2005] 92 ITD 358 (Mum.), *Yashpal Sahni* v. *CIT* [2007] 165 Taxman 144 (Bom.).

• An assessee (from whose receipts tax has been deducted at source and who is also in possession of Form No. 16/16A) must get credit of tax deducted at source and such credit cannot be declined merely on the ground that person who has issued tax deduction certificate has been refunded tax which he had deposited with the Government - *Lucent Technologies GRL LLC* v. *DIT* [2011] 45 SOT 311 (Mum.).

175.8 ***Processing of statements of tax deducted at source [Sec. 200A]*** - Section 200A was inserted with effect from April 1, 2010 to provide for processing of statements of tax deducted at source on computer so that liabilities on account of interest, fee under section 234E and other defaults in TDS payment are promptly calculated and intimated to the deductor.

The following adjustments can be made during the computerized processing of statements of tax deducted at source—

a. any arithmetical error in the statement; or

b. an incorrect claim, if such incorrect claim is apparent from any information in the statement, for example, in respect of rate of deduction of tax at source where such rate is not in accordance with the provisions of the Act.

After making adjustments, tax and interest would be calculated and sum payable by the deductor or refund due to the deductor will be determined. An intimation will be sent to the deductor informing him of his tax liability or granting him the refund due within one year from the end of the financial year in which the statement is filed. Further, it is provided that the processing of these statements can be undertaken in a centralized processing centre.

175.9 ***Assessee in default*** - Where a person who is required to deduct tax at source, does not deduct, or does not pay, or after deducting fails to pay, the whole or any part of tax, as required by the Act, then such person shall be deemed to be an assessee in default in respect of such tax under section 201(1). He will be liable for payment of tax, interest, penalty and prosecution. Besides, disallowance under section 40(*a*) will be attracted.

• *Time-limit* - An order under section 201(1) for failure to deduct the whole or any part of the tax as required under the Act, if the deductee is a resident taxpayer, shall be passed within the time-limit given below—

1. In case statement is filed by the deductor under section 200, within 2 years from the end of the financial year in which statement is filed under section 200;

2. In case no such statement is filed, within 4 years (6 years applicable from April 1, 2010) from the end of the financial year in which payment is made or credit is given.

However, an order pertaining to the financial year 2007-08 (or earlier years) can be passed at any time up to March 31, 2011.

• *Relaxation given with effect from July 1, 2012* - With effect from July 1, 2012, the payer shall not be deemed to be an assessee in default, if the resident recipient has included such income in the return submitted under section 139 and the recipient has paid tax on such income. The payer will have to submit a certificate in Form No. 26A to this effect from a chartered accountant.

Tax collection at source [Sec. 206C]

176. Under section 206C in some cases tax has to be collected at source.

176.1 ***In which case tax has to be collected at source*** - Under section 206C, tax has to be collected at source in the following cases[72] –

Nature of goods	*Percentage rate of tax collection at source (TCS) applicable*
Category A (sale of the following) –	
A1. Alcoholic liquor for human consumption (other than Indian made foreign liquor)	1
A2. Indian made foreign liquor	1
A3. Tendu leaves	5
A4. Timber obtained under a forest lease	2.50
A5. Timber obtained by any mode other than under a forest lease	2.50
A6. Any other forest produce not being timber or tendu leaves	2.50
A7. Scrap	1
A8. Minerals, being coal or lignite or iron ore	1
Category B (grant of lease/license[73] of the following) –	
B1. Parking lot, toll plaza, mining and quarrying (other than mining and quarrying of mineral oil, petroleum and natural gas)	2
Category D (sale of the following whether payment is received by cheque or by any other mode) –	
D1. Motor vehicle of the value exceeding Rs. 10 lakh	1

Note - In some cases, these rates are subject to surcharge and health and education cess. If the purchaser or the licensee is a foreign company and the amount subject to tax collection is more than Rs. 1 crore, but not more than Rs. 10 crore, surcharge is 2 per cent of TCS during 2019-20 (it is 5 per cent of TCS if such amount is more than Rs. 10 crore). If purchaser/licensee is non-resident firm/co-operative society, surcharge @ 12 per cent is applicable only if amount subject to TCS is more than Rs. 1 crore. If purchaser/licensee is non-resident individual/HUF/AOP/BOI, surcharge is 10 per cent of TCS (if amount subject to TCS is more than Rs. 50 lakh but not more than Rs. 1 crore), 15 per cent of TCS (if amount subject to TCS is more than Rs. 1 crore but not more than Rs. 2 crore), 25 per cent of TCS (if amount subject to TCS is more than Rs. 2 crore but not more than Rs. 5 crore) or 37 per cent of TCS (if amount subject to TCS is more than Rs. 5 crore). If purchaser or licensee is a non-resident or a foreign company, health and education cess of 4 per cent (of TCS+SC) is applicable. In no other case, surcharge and health and education cess shall be added.

176.1-1 *TAX COLLECTION IN CATEGORY A* - In *Category A*, "seller" shall collect tax from the "buyer" of goods.

176.1-1a *WHO IS SELLER IN CATEGORY A* - For this purpose, "seller" means the Central Government, a State Government or any local authority or corporation or authority established by or under a Central, State or Provincial Act, or any company or firm or co-operative society. "Seller" also includes an individual or a Hindu undivided family whose books of account are required to be audited under section 44AB(*a*)/(*b*) during the financial year immediately preceding the financial year in which goods are sold. Consequently, tax will be collected at source by such individuals/Hindu undivided families.

176.1-1b *WHO IS BUYER IN CATEGORY A* - "Buyer" means a person who obtains in any sales by way of auction, tender or any other mode, goods of the nature specified under *Category A* or the right to receive any such goods. It, however, does not include the following :

72. Tax shall be collected under section 206C at the rates given in the table (*supra*). If PAN of collectee is not intimated to the collector, tax will be collected by virtue of section 206CC either at twice the rate specified in the table (*supra*) or at the rate of 5 per cent, whichever is higher. However, the provisions of section 206CC shall not apply in the case of a non-resident collectee who does not have any permanent establishment in India.

73. 'Tehbazari' does not come within the ambit of this provision – *Apar Mukhya Adhikari* v. *ITO* [2018] 97 taxmann.com 107 (All.).

a. a public sector company, the Central Government, a State Government, and an Embassy, a High Commission, Legation, Commission, Consulate and the trade representation, of a foreign State and a club; or

b. a buyer in the retail sale of such goods purchased by him for personal consumption.

• *Purchase for personal consumption from retailer* - A buyer in the retail sale of *Category A* goods purchased by him for 'personal consumption' shall be excluded from being treated as a 'buyer'. This means that if a retailer sells *Category A* goods to a customer for personal consumption only (and not for any other purpose), the purchasing customer will not be treated as a 'buyer'. The resultant effect will be that the retailer need not collect tax from the customer, provided he is satisfied that the customer is purchasing the goods for personal consumption.

• *Mere licensee is not a "buyer"* - When the Government issues a licence, it only enables the licensee to carry on trade or business in that item. The payment made by the licensee by way of licence fee does not *ipso facto* entitle the licensee to lift the goods. For obtaining the goods mentioned in *Category A*, the licensee has to place an order to the manufacturer or the supplier of the said goods and it is at that point of time that section 206C would get attracted. To put it differently, 'buyer' would mean where a person by virtue of the payment gets a right to receive specific goods and not where he is merely allowed/permitted to carry on business in that trade. 'Buyer' has to be buyer of goods and not merely a person who acquires a licence to carry on the business—*Union of India* v. *Om Prakash S.S. & Co.* [2001] 115 Taxman 325 (SC).

• *When income of buyer is exempt* - If income of buyer is exempt under section 10(*26*), then tax cannot be collected at source.

176.1-1c *MEANING OF "SCRAP"* - In the case of sale of "scrap" tax shall be collected by the seller. "Scrap" for this purpose has been defined as waste and scrap from the manufacture or mechanical working of materials which is definitely not usable as such because of breakage, cutting up, wear and other reasons.

It would include only such waste and scrap which arises from manufacture or mechanical working of materials. Further, such waste should not be usable as such. Accordingly, it would not include any waste or scrap—

a. which does not arise from manufacture or mechanical working of materials; or

b. which is usable as such.

Thus, the following are not covered—

a. waste or scrap arising from packing materials, newspapers, old machinery scrapped, etc., which cannot be said to arise from manufacture;

b. by-products generated from the manufacturing process as the same could be used as such; or

c. scrap derived from dismantling of constructed buildings.

It can be inferred that, in case of sale of waste and scrap, the provisions of section 206C will apply to only those sellers who are engaged in the business of manufacturing or mechanical working of materials—*Navine Fluorine International Ltd.* v. *CIT* [2011] 45 SOT 86 (Ahd.).

176.1-1d *WHEN TAX HAS TO BE COLLECTED IN CATEGORY A* - Tax has to be collected by the seller at the time of debiting of the amount payable by the buyer to the account of the buyer or at the time of receipt of such amount from the buyer in cash or by issue of cheque/draft, or by any other mode, whichever is earlier.

• *When purchase price is to be received by different agencies* - The Patna High Court in *Ramjee Prasad Sahu* v. *Union of India* 1993 Tax LR 593, *Bharat Prasad Choudhary* v. *Union of India* [1978] 229 ITR 363, the Punjab and Haryana High Court in *Fairdeal Trading Co.* v. *Union of India* [1993] 70 Taxman 121 and Madhya Pradesh High Court in *Harvach & Sons* v. *UOI* [2003] 133 Taxman 926 have held that tax can be collected under section 206C only in respect of the cost price paid by vendors of country liquor to the wholesalers and not in respect of the excise duty paid to the Government.

The Excise Department of a State Government grants licence to a taxpayer for purchasing country liquor from distilleries or wholesalers. On the licence fees charged by the Excise Department, tax cannot be collected at source under section 206C. The Excise Department in such a case cannot be termed as a "seller" as goods are not sold by the Excise Department —*Naresh Kumar & Co.* v. *Union of India* [2000] 110 Taxman 420 (Punj. & Har.), *Chander Bhan & Co.* v. *Union of India* [2000] 112 Taxman 517 (Punj. & Har.).

176.1-1e *GOODS UTILISED FOR MANUFACTURING/PROCESSING IN CATEGORY A IS NOT SUBJECT TO TAX COLLECTION* - No tax will be collected at source from a resident buyer who purchases goods for the purposes of manufacturing, processing or producing any article or thing (or for the purpose of generation of power) and not for the purpose of trading. This rule is applicable only in *Category A*, if the resident buyer gives a declaration in duplicate in Form No. 27C[74] to the seller that the goods to be purchased are to be utilised in the carrying on of any of the activities referred to above.

• *Form No. 27C in duplicate* - The declaration furnished by the buyer shall be obtained in duplicate by the seller.

• *Declaration without PAN not valid* - The above declaration shall not be valid unless the person filing the declaration furnishes his PAN in such declaration.

• *Copy of Form No. 27C to be submitted to Commissioner by seller* - The seller shall deliver one copy of each Form No. 27C to the jurisdictional Commissioner. All the forms collected in a month should be delivered up to 7th of each succeeding month. For instance for forms collected in April, 2017, the last date of submission to the Commissioner is May 7, 2017.

Buyer shall fill in and sign part I of the declaration Form. Seller shall fill in and sign part II of the declaration Form before furnishing both parts of the Form to the Commissioner.

The last date of delivering the form to the jurisdictional Commissioner is counted from the month in which the declaration is furnished by the buyer to the seller and not from the month in which the goods are sold. However, a declaration should be obtained along with the sale of goods as far as possible.

• *Fresh form every time* - Buyer should furnish fresh declaration every time he buys timber for the purpose of manufacturing, processing or producing articles or things.

• *A builder is not competent to submit Form No. 27C* - A builder is not authorized to furnish Form No. 27C. A builder does not buy timber for the purpose of manufacturing, processing or producing articles or things. A builder generally purchases timber for the purpose of construction of a building. A building is not an article or thing. The doors, frames made by the builder for the purpose of fixing them in the building do not qualify "for the purpose of manufacturing". Building is a construction activity and not a manufacturing activity.

176.1-2 *TAX COLLECTION IN CATEGORY B* - In *Category B*, every person, who grants a lease or a licence or enters into a contract or otherwise, transfers any right or interest in any parking lot or toll plaza or mine or quarry, to another person (hereafter referred to as "licensee or lessee") for the use of such parking lot or toll plaza or mine or quarry, for the purpose of business, shall collect tax at source.

• *Public sector company* - If the licensee or lessee is a public sector company, tax is not collectible.

176.1-3 *TAX COLLECTION IN CATEGORY C* - *Category C* is not applicable from April 1, 2017[$].

176.1-4 *TAX COLLECTION IN CATEGORY D* - In *Category D*, tax is collected by seller who receives any amount as consideration for sale of motor vehicle of value exceeding Rs. 10,00,000. Tax is collected at the rate of 1 per cent of the sale consideration. This tax collection is required with effect from June 1, 2016, regardless of the fact whether consideration is received in cash or by cheque or by any other mode.

• The following points should be noted –

---

74. No time limit is provided in section 206C(1A) to make a declaration in Form 27C collected from buyers (mere minor delay in furnishing Form 27C would not make assessee liable for non-collection of TCS) – *CIT* v. *Siyaram Metal Udyog (P.) Ltd.* [2016] 71 taxmann.com 204 (Guj.).

$ For the provisions of *Category C* (applicable during July 1, 2012 and March 31, 2017), log on to *taxmann.com/readyreckoner.aspx.*

1. The above tax collection provision is applicable only in the case of sale of motor vehicles in transactions of retail sales. In other words, the above provision is not applicable on sale of motor vehicles by manufacturers to dealers/distributors.

2. The above provision is applicable if the amount of sale consideration of a motor vehicle is more than Rs. 10 lakh (irrespective of the fact whether the motor vehicle is a luxury car or any other car).

3. The above provision is not applicable if buyer is the Central Government, a State Government, an Embassy/High Commission/consulate/trade representation of a Foreign Government, local authority or a public sector company which is engaged in the business of carrying of passengers.

4. The above provision is applicable on each sale of motor vehicle of value exceeding Rs. 10 lakh (not on aggregate value of sale made during the year). For instance, a car dealer sells a car to an individual for Rs. 24 lakh. Rs. 1 lakh is received at the time of booking and balance Rs. 23 lakh at the time of delivery. Tax will be collected at the rate of 1 per cent of Rs. 1 lakh at the time of booking and 1 per cent of Rs. 23 lakh at the time of delivery. This rule is applicable whether mode of payment is cash or by cheque. Suppose, at the time of delivery Rs. 5 lakh is received in cash and balance Rs. 18 lakh is received by cheque. Tax will be collected by the seller at the rate of 1 per cent of Rs. 23 lakh at the time of delivery under *Category D* (provisions of *Category C* are not applicable). If, however, sale price of a motor vehicle of Rs. 10 lakh (or less) (suppose sale price is Rs. 9 lakh) and consideration received in cash is more than Rs. 2 lakh, tax collection at the rate of 1 per cent of cash consideration is applicable under *Category C* (*Category C* is applicable only up to March 31, 2017).

176.2 ***Tax collection at lower rate*** - Where the Assessing Officer is satisfied that the total income of the buyer justifies the collection of the tax at any lower rate than the relevant rate specified in para 176.1 (*Category A, Category B* or *Category C*), he can give a certificate for collection of tax at lower rate. For obtaining this certificate, the buyer shall make an application in Form No. 13 (without PAN of the buyer, the application in Form No. 13 remains invalid). Where certificate of lower tax collection is given, the person responsible for collecting the tax shall, until such certificate is cancelled by the Assessing Officer, collect the tax at the rates specified in such certificate. The certificate shall be valid for the assessment year specified in that certificate, unless it is cancelled by the Assessing Officer at any time before the expiry of the specified period. An application for a fresh certificate may be made, if required, after the expiry of the period of validity of the earlier certificate. The certificate shall be valid only for the person named therein. The certificate shall be issued direct to the person responsible for collecting the tax under advice to the buyer who made an application for issue of such certificate.

176.3 ***Deposit of tax*** - *See* paras 174.1 and 174.2.

176.4 ***Issue of certificate*** - *See* para 174.4.

Duplicate certificate - Where the certificate for tax collected at source is lost, the person collecting tax at source may issue a duplicate certificate of collection of tax at source on a plain paper giving necessary details as contained in Form No. 27D. However, the Assessing Officer (before giving credit for the tax collected at source on the basis of duplicate certificate) shall get the payment certified from the Assessing Officer designated in this behalf by the Chief Commissioner or Commissioner and shall also obtain an Indemnity Bond from the assessee.

176.5 ***Quarterly returns to Government*** - *See* para 174.3.

176.5-1 *PROCESSING OF QUARTERLY TCS STATEMENTS [SEC. 206CB]* - Section 206CB has been inserted (with effect from June 1, 2015) to provide for processing of TCS statements on the line of existing provisions for processing of TDS statement contained in section 200A. This provision also incorporates the mechanism for computation of fee payable under section 234E. After processing of TCS statement, an intimation is generated specifying the amount payable or refundable. This intimation generated after processing of TCS statement will be (*i*) subject to rectification under section 154; (*ii*) appealable under section 246A; and (*iii*) deemed as notice of demand under section 156.

176.6 ***Tax credit to one who pays*** - The amount collected is deemed as payment of tax on behalf of the person from whom the amount has been collected. A tax credit is given to him for the amount so collected on production of certificate [Form No. 27D] in the assessment for which the income is assessable. The scheme of giving credit to the collectees has been modified with effect from April 1, 2008 so that the manner in which credit of TCS is to be given will be governed by Rules to be framed. In other words, the Board may make such rules as may be necessary for the purpose of giving credit in respect of TCS or tax paid by employer on perquisite under section 192(1A).

176.7 ***Consequences if tax is not collected or paid*** - If a seller does not collect or after collecting fails to pay the tax, he shall be deemed to be an assessee in default in respect of the tax and the amount of the tax together with the amount of simple interest, calculated at the rate of 1 per cent per month, or part thereof, shall be a charge upon all the assets of the seller. Section 276BB provides for prosecution of a person who fails to pay the tax collected at source for a period which shall not be less than 3 months but which may extend up to 7 years and with fine.

176.8 ***Tax collection account number*** - *See* para 175.3.

176.9 ***If income of buyer is exempt*** - The Gauhati High Court in the case of *Sing Killing* v. *ITO* [2002] 255 ITR 444/125 Taxman 403 has held that no tax is to be collected at source where the income of the buyer is itself exempt.

176.10 ***Assessee-in-default*** - Where a person who is required to collect tax at source, does not collect, or does not pay, or after collecting fails to pay, the whole or any part of tax, as required by the Act, then such person shall be deemed to be an assessee in default in respect of such tax under section 206C(6A). He will be liable for payment of tax, interest, penalty and prosecution.

▪ *Relaxation given with effect from July 1, 2012* - With effect from July 1, 2012, the aforesaid person (but not being a seller of jewellery/bullion) shall not be deemed to be an assessee in default, if the buyer has included such income in the return submitted under section 139 and the buyer has paid tax on such income. The collector will have to submit a certificate in Form No. 27BA to this effect from a chartered accountant.

176.11 ***Requirement to furnish PAN by collectee [Sec. 206CC, applicable from April 1, 2017]*** - In order to strengthen the PAN mechanism, section 206CC has been inserted. The provisions of section 206CC are given below –

• *Tax collection at higher rate* - Collectee shall furnish his PAN to the person responsible for collecting such tax at source. If PAN is not intimated, tax shall be collected at the twice the normal rate or at the rate of 5 per cent, whichever is higher.

• *Declaration without PAN under section 206C(1A) not valid* - The declaration filed under section 206C(1A) shall not be valid unless the person filing the declaration furnishes his PAN in such declaration.

• *Lower tax collection certificate* - Lower tax collection certificate shall not be granted unless application in Form No. 13 by the collectee contains his PAN.

• *PAN to be quoted in all correspondence* - The collectee shall furnish his PAN to the collector and both shall indicate the same in all correspondence, bills and vouchers exchanged between them.

• *Invalid PAN* - Where the PAN provided by the collectee is invalid or it does not belong to the collectee, then it shall be deemed that PAN has not been furnished to the collector.

• *Not applicable if collectee is non-resident* - The above provisions of section 206CC shall not apply in the case of a non-resident collectee who does not have any permanent establishment in India.

How to compute tax liability

Assessment of different taxpayers involves the practical application of various provisions of the Act in a given situation. While different deductions are summarized in Referencer 7, tax rates are given in paras 0.1 to 0.5, Referencer 1

INDIVIDUALS

Tax liability

177. An individual is liable to pay tax in respect of his own income, and the income of certain other persons by virtue of sections 60 to 65.

How to compute taxable income

178. First, ascertain gross total income, ignoring income exempted under section 10, 10A or 10B or 10BA, etc., if any. Then deduct admissible deductions under sections 80C, 80CCC, 80CCD, 80CCG, 80D, 80DD, 80DDB, 80E, 80EE, 80G, 80GG, 80GGA, 80GGC, 80-IA, 80-IAB, 80-IB, 80-IC, 80-ID, 80-IE, 80JJA, 80JJAA, 80QQB, 80RRB, 80TTA, 80TTB and 80U [*see* para 107]. For ready reference of different deductions available to individuals under the Income-tax Act, *see* Referencer 7.

Rates of tax

179. For rates applicable to the assessment years 2019-20 and 2020-21 *see* para 0.1-1, Referencer 1 [*see* Tax Tables at pages B-1 to B-37]. Rates applicable to assessment year prior to 2019-20 are given in Referencer 3 [*see* Tax Tables at pages D-1 to D-12].

• *Non resident* - For special provision relating to non-resident under sections 115C to 115-I, *see* para 179.1.

• *Alternate minimum tax* - From the assessment year 2013-14, tax payable by a non-corporate assessee cannot be less than 18.5 per cent[75] [+ SC + (EC + SHEC) or HEC] of "adjusted total income". The effective rate (as percentage of adjusted total income) for the assessment years 2019-20 and 2020-21 is as follows –

	Assessment year 2019-20	*Assessment year 2020-21*
If adjusted total income is Rs. 50 lakh or less	19.24%	19.24%
If adjusted total income is more than Rs. 50 lakh but not more than Rs. 1 crore	21.164%	21.164%
If adjusted total income is more than Rs. 1 crore but not more than Rs. 2 crore	22.126%	22.126%
If adjusted total income is more than Rs. 2 crore but not more than Rs. 5 crore	22.126%	**24.05%**
If adjusted total income is more than Rs. 5 crore	22.126%	**26.3588%**

For detailed discussion, *see* para 190.1.

179.1 ***Special provisions relating to non-residents [Sections 115C to 115-I]*** - 'Non-resident Indians' can take the benefit of special provisions under sections 115C to 115-I :

179.1-1 *WHO CAN CLAIM THE BENEFIT OF SPECIAL PROVISIONS* - The benefit of special provisions can be claimed by non-resident Indians. The following are "non-resident Indians" for this purpose :

a. citizen of India who is a non-resident ; or

b. a person of Indian origin who is a non-resident.

A person shall be deemed to be of Indian origin if he, or either of his parents or any of his grand-parents, was born in undivided India.

179.1-2 *INCOMES WHICH ARE QUALIFIED FOR SPECIAL TREATMENT* - The provisions under sections 115C to 115-I are applicable only in respect of the following incomes derived by a non-resident Indian :

a. investment income derived from a "foreign exchange assets", not being dividends covered under section 115-O;

b. long-term capital gains on sale or transfer of "foreign exchange assets".

---

75. 9 per cent in case the assessee is a unit located in an International Financial Services Centre and derives its income solely in convertible foreign exchange (applicable from the assessment year 2019-20).

Foreign exchange asset - It means those "specified assets" (which are given below) which the assessee has acquired or purchased with, or subscribed to in, convertible foreign exchange.

The following are "specified assets" for this purpose :

a. shares in an Indian company (public or private) ;

b. debentures issued by an Indian company which is not a private company ;

c. deposits with an Indian company which is not a private company (for instance, deposit with Indian public limited companies, banks, etc.) ;

d. any security of the Central Government ; and

e. such other assets as the Central Government may specify in this behalf by notification in the Official Gazette [no notification has been issued so far].

179.1-2a HOW TO CALCULATE INVESTMENT INCOME - In computing the investment income of a non-resident Indian, no deduction in respect of any expenditure or allowance shall be allowed under any provision of the Act. Moreover, no deduction under sections 80C to 80U shall be allowed in respect of investment income of non-resident Indians.

179.1-2b HOW TO CALCULATE LONG-TERM CAPITAL GAIN - Long-term capital gain on sale or transfer for foreign exchange assets shall be calculated subject to the following points :

1. The benefit of indexation under second proviso to section 48 is not available in respect of sale or transfer of foreign exchange assets [*see* para 69.5].

2. No deduction is permissible in respect of long-term capital gain under sections 80C to 80U.

3. By investing sale consideration in another asset, the non-resident Indian can claim exemption under section 115F [*see* para 69.5-1 for detailed discussion].

179.1-3 *TAX ON INVESTMENT INCOME AND LONG-TERM CAPITAL GAIN* - Non-resident Indians are chargeable to tax on investment income at the rate of 20 per cent[76] and long-term capital gain (as computed above) at the rate of 10[77] per cent[76].

• Long term capital gain which arises on transfer of bonus shares (in case bonus shares were allotted to a non-resident Indian on his original investments made out of convertible foreign exchange) is eligible for the aforesaid 10 per cent tax rate – *Deivanayagam Maruthini* v. *DIT (International Taxation)* [2012] 51 SOT 163 (Chennai).

179.1-4 *RETURN OF INCOME NOT TO BE FILED IN CERTAIN CASES* - In cases where a non-resident Indian has income only from a foreign exchange asset or income by way of long-term capital gains arising on transfer of a foreign exchange asset, or both, and tax deductible at source from such income has been deducted, he is not required to file the return of income under section 139(1).

The income from foreign exchange assets and long-term capital gains arising on transfer of such assets would be treated as a separate block and charged to tax at a flat rate as explained above. If the non-resident Indian has other income in India, such other income is treated as an altogether separate block and charged to tax in accordance with the other provisions of the Act.

179.1-5 *BENEFIT AVAILABLE EVEN AFTER THE ASSESSEE BECOMES RESIDENT* - Where a person, who is a non-resident Indian in any previous year, becomes assessable as resident in India in any subsequent year, he may furnish to the Assessing Officer a declaration in writing (along with his return of income under section 139 for the assessment year for which he is so assessable) to the effect that the special provisions shall continue to apply to him in relation to the investment income derived from any foreign exchange asset being debentures of and deposits with, an Indian public limited company and Central Government securities. If he does so, the special provisions shall continue to apply to him in relation to such income for that assessment year (and for every subsequent assessment year) until the transfer or conversion (otherwise than by transfer) into money of such assets.

• So long as the original source of deposit was convertible foreign exchange, transfer of such deposit from one bank to another bank would not affect its identity as a "foreign exchange asset" and, consequently, the assessee is entitled to concessional rate of tax on interest earned from such deposits—*CIT* v. *M.C. George* [2011] 198 Taxman 466 (Ker.).

179.1-6 *SPECIAL PROVISIONS NOT TO APPLY IF THE ASSESSEE SO CHOOSES [SECTION 115-I]* - A non-resident Indian may opt that the special provisions relating to taxation of the investment income and long-term capital gains at a flat rate should not apply to him. This option is exercisable by a taxpayer by making

76. For surcharge/health and education cess, *see* Referencer 1.

77. 20 per cent up to assessment year 1997-98.

a declaration to that effect in his return of income for the relevant assessment year. In cases where such an option is exercised by a non-resident Indian, the whole of his total income (including income from foreign exchange assets and long-term capital gains arising on transfer of a foreign exchange asset) is charged to tax under the general provisions of the Income-tax Act.

179.1-E1 X, Y and Z are persons (aged 32 years) of Indian origin, though their residential status is non-resident. During the previous year relevant for the assessment year 2019-20, their income from investment in India is as follows :

	X Rs.	Y Rs.	Z Rs.
a. Interest on deposits with public limited companies received on March 31, 2019	30,000	60,000	2,80,000
b. Interest on Government securities received on December 31, 2018	1,95,000	2,40,000	2,40,000
c. Interest on deposits with private limited companies on September 30, 2018	—	2,30,000	7,25,000
Tax deducted at source, *i.e.*, @ 20.8 per cent in respect of foreign exchange assets (a) and (*b*); and @ 31.2 per cent in respect of (*c*)	46,800	1,34,160	3,34,360

Determine the amount of tax liability/refund for the assessment year 2019-20. Also discuss whether the assessee should opt under section 115-I, *i.e.*, not to be governed by provisions of sections 115C to 115-I.

•

Tax liability if the assessee opts under section 115-I, not to be governed under the provisions of sections 115C to 115-I :

	X Rs.	Y Rs.	Z Rs.
Gross total income	2,25,000	5,30,000	12,45,000
Less : Deduction	—	—	—
Net income	2,25,000	5,30,000	12,45,000
Tax (including education cess and secondary and higher education cess) (*d*)	*Nil*	19,240	1,93,440
Tax deducted at source (*e*)	46,800	1,34,160	3,34,360
Final tax liability [*i.e.*, (*d*) – (*e*)] (rounded off)	(–) 46,800	(-) 1,14,920	(-)1,40,920
Tax liability if provisions of sections 115C to 115-I are applicable :			
Income from foreign exchange assets eligible for provisions of sections 115C to 115-I [*i.e., (a) + (b)*]	2,25,000	3,00,000	5,20,000
Tax on income from foreign exchange assets [*i.e.*, @ 20.8% in the case of X, Y and Z] (*f*)	46,800	62,400	1,08,160
Other income [*i.e.*, (*c*)]	—	2,30,000	7,25,000
Less : Deduction	—	*Nil*	*Nil*
Taxable income	—	2,30,000	7,25,000
Tax (including Health and education cess) (*g*)	—	—	59,800
Tax liability [*i.e.*, (*f*) + (*g*)] (*h*)	46,800	62,400	1,67,960
Tax deducted at source (*i*)	46,800	1,34,160	3,34,360
Final tax liability [*i.e.*, (*h*) – (*i*)] (rounded off)	*Nil*	(-) 71,760	(-) 1,66,400

Note : In the problem given above, X and Y should opt under section 115-I (*i.e.*, not to be governed by special provisions of sections 115C to 115-I) by furnishing return of income under section 139. Z should take the benefit of special provisions of sections 115C to 115-I.

HINDU UNDIVIDED FAMILIES

How to compute taxable income

181. First ascertain gross total income ignoring incomes exempted under section 10, 10A, 10B or 10BA, if any. Then, deduct admissible deductions under sections 80C, 80D, 80DD, 80DDB, 80G, 80GGA, 80GGC, 80-IA, 80-IAB, 80-IB, 80-IC, 80-ID, 80-IE, 80JJA, 80JJAA and 80TTA. For ready reference of different deductions available to HUFs under the Income-tax Act, *see* Referencer 7.

Rates of tax

182. For rates applicable to the assessment years 2019-20 and 2020-21, *see* para 0.1-1, Referencer 1 [*see* Tax Tables at pages B-1 to B-37]. Rates applicable to assessment year prior to the assessment year 2019-20 are given in Referencer 3 [*see* Tax Tables at pages D-1 to D-12].

• *Alternate minimum tax* - From the assessment year 2013-14, tax payable by a non-corporate assessee cannot be less than 18.5 per cent[78] [+ SC + (EC + SHEC) or HEC] of "adjusted total income". The effective rate (as percentage of adjusted total income) for the assessment years 2019-20 and 2020-21 is as follows –

	Assessment year 2019-20	*Assessment year 2020-21*
If adjusted total income is Rs. 50 lakh or less	19.24%	19.24%
If adjusted total income is more than Rs. 50 lakh but not more than Rs. 1 crore	21.164%	21.164%
If adjusted total income is more than Rs. 1 crore but not more than Rs. 2 crore	22.126%	22.126%
If adjusted total income is more than Rs. 2 crore but not more than Rs. 5 crore	22.126%	**24.05%**
If adjusted total income is more than Rs. 5 crore	22.126%	**26.3588%**

For detailed discussion, *see* para 190.1.

FIRMS[79]

Scheme of taxation of firms

183. The salient features of the scheme are as under :

• A firm is taxed as a separate entity. There is no distinction between registered and unregistered firms.

• The share of the partner in the income of the firm is not to be included in computing his total income.

• Any salary, bonus, commission or remuneration by whatever name called, which is due to or received by partner is allowed as a deduction subject to certain restrictions.

• Where a firm pays interest to any partner, the firm can claim deduction of such interest from its total income. However, the maximum rate at which interest can be allowed to a partner is 12 per cent per annum (18 per cent up to assessment year 2002-03).

• The income of a firm is taxed at a flat rate of 30 per cent (+SC+HEC).

• A limited liability partnership (from the assessment year 2012-13) or any firm (from the assessment year 2013-14) is subject to alternate minimum tax at the rate of 18.5 per cent[78] (+SC+EC/SHEC or HEC) of "adjusted total income".

For detailed discussion, *see* para 190.1.

When remuneration/interest is deductible

184. Every assessee (including a firm) has to establish, in the first instance, its right to claim deduction in respect of an expenditure under one of the sections between sections 30 to 38 and in the case of the firm, if it claims special deduction in respect of remuneration and interest, it has also to prove that it satisfies the requirement of sections 184 and 40(*b*)—*Munjal Sales Corpn.* v. *CIT* [2008] 168 Taxman 44 (SC). In other words, remuneration and interest to partners are deductible only if—

1. These are otherwise deductible under sections 36 and 37.

2. Conditions of section 184 are satisfied [*see* para 185].

3. Conditions of section 40(*b*) are satisfied [*see* para 186 for remuneration and para 187 for interest].

Conditions a firm should fulfil under section 184

185. There are five basic conditions which a firm has to satisfy—

185.1 ***A firm must be evidenced by an instrument [Section 184(1)(i)]*** - The firm should be evidenced by an "instrument". The word "instrument" means a document of legal nature by which any right or liability is or purports to be created, transferred, limited, extended, extinguished or recorded.

"Instrument" does not mean only a regular partnership deed but it may constitute any other formal document. If the terms of a partnership are contained in a number of documents or in the correspondence

78. 9 per cent in case the assessee is a unit located in an International Financial Services Centre and derives its income solely in convertible foreign exchange (applicable from the assessment year 2019-20).

79. From the assessment year 2010-11, these provisions are also applicable in the case of limited liability partnership.

between the parties, the documents or letters would constitute "instrument" for the purpose of section 184(1)(*i*).

185.2 ***Individual share of partners must be specified in instrument*** - The instrument of partnership (*i.e.*, partnership deed) must specify the individual shares of partners in profits of the partnership. Evidence regarding the shares of the partners should be afforded within the four corners of the instrument and should not be made to depend on a reference and scrutiny of a number of documents. In other words, instrument of partnership must specify the individual shares of partners in the profits of the partnership.

185.3 ***Certified copy of the instrument should be submitted*** - This condition requires that a certified copy of the instrument of partnership should accompany the first return of income[80] of a firm.

The instrument for the purpose would include all documents and deeds if the arrangement is reflected in more than one deed or documents. Accordingly, certified copies of all documents/deeds will have to be submitted[80]. For the purpose of section 184, the copy of the instrument (maybe xeroxed copy), shall be certified in writing by all partners (other than minors). If, however, the return is made after the dissolution of the firm, it should be certified by all partners (other than minors) who were partners in the firm immediately before the dissolution and by the legal representative of any such partner who is deceased.

185.4 ***Revised instrument should be submitted whenever there is change in the constitution of firm/ profit-sharing ratio*** - If there is any change in the constitution of the firm or the profit-sharing ratio during any previous year, a certified copy of the revised instrument of partnership should be filed[80] along with return of income of the relevant assessment year. Even if, there is a change in remuneration/payment of interest to partners but there is no change in profit-sharing ratio, a copy of the revised instrument of partnership should be submitted[80] along with return to comply with the provisions of section 40(*b*).

185.5 ***There should not be any failure as is mentioned in section 144*** - There should not be any failure as is mentioned in section 144. What is important is type of failure in section 144 and not an assessment under section 144. Filing of a return against notice (issued under section 148) itself is not the same as filing a return under section 139 and, so much so, a failures referred to in section 144(1) which attract disallowance of deductions under section 184(5) are absolute failures which cannot be remedied by filing returns based on notice under section 148—*Radha Picture Palace* v. *CIT* [2011] 9 taxmann.com 16 (Ker.).

Remuneration paid to partners

186. To obtain deduction of remuneration paid to partners, conditions given by sections 184 and 40(*b*) should be satisfied.

186.1 ***Conditions of section 40(b)*** - The following specific conditions, as prescribed by section 40(*b*), should be satisfied :

- Remuneration should be paid only to a working partner [*see* para 186.1-1].
- Remuneration must be authorised by the partnership deed [*see* para 186.1-2]
- Remuneration should not pertain to period prior to partnership deed [*see* para 186.1-3]
- Remuneration should not exceed the permissible limit [*see* para 186.1-4].

186.1-1 *PAYMENT SHOULD BE TO A WORKING PARTNER* - Any payment of salary, bonus, commission or remuneration to any partner who is not a working partner is not allowable as deduction.

For this purpose, "working partner" means an individual who is actively engaged in conducting the affairs of the business or profession of the firm of which he is a partner [*Explanation* to section 40(*b*)].

As per the aforesaid definition, a "working partner" means :

a. an individual who is a partner of a firm ; and

b. such an individual is actively engaged in conducting the affairs of the business/profession of the firm.

Broadly speaking, a partnership firm would usually have to fulfil the following functions :

- Establishing business policies
- Implementing business policies
- Effecting transactions
- Conducting day-to-day administration
- Attending to routine jobs.

---

80. It is not possible to attach any certificate, statement or report with new income-tax return forms. The assessee should himself retain the certified copy of the instrument or revised instrument with it. It may be furnished whenever the Assessing Officer wants to examine it in assessment proceedings or otherwise.

The above functions would involve the (*a*) planning, (*b*) organising, (*c*) directing, (*d*) staffing, and (*e*) controlling of the core area of business, namely : production, marketing, finance and personnel.

The following persons would qualify as being working partners :

a. partner carrying out all or most of the above functions ;

b. a partner who attends to framing of business policies even though he does not participate in their implementation and other routine jobs ;

c. a partner who attends to business decision-making even though he is not attending to business administration and routine jobs ;

d. a partner who is effecting business transactions even though he is not attending to administration and routine jobs ;

e. a partner who attends to general administration of the firm whether or not he participates in decision-making;

f. a partner who attends to routine job whether or not he participates in decision-making.

The most important and noteworthy observation is that there is no requirement of "full time" attendance to any/all the above tasks. A mere consideration of the total time devoted to the business is not a relevant criterion.

The following persons would not qualify as being "working partners" :

a. a partner who does not have any knowledge of the business and is a partner on account of relationship and/or capital ;

b. a partner who does not take part/or interest in the business ;

c. a partner carrying out some business tasks temporarily, in the absence of the regular working partner.

186.1-2 *REMUNERATION MUST BE AUTHORISED BY PARTNERSHIP DEED* - Any payment of salary, bonus, commission or remuneration by whatever name called to a working partner is not allowed as deduction in the following cases :

a. if the payment is not authorised by the partnership deed; or

b. if it is not in accordance with the terms of the partnership deed.

To claim deduction of remuneration paid to a partner, it should not only be authorised by the partnership deed, but should also be in accordance with the terms of the partnership deed.

• Quantum of remuneration or the manner of computation of quantum of remuneration should be stated in the partnership deed and should not be left undetermined, undecided or to be determined or decided on a future date—*Sood Brij & Associates* v. *CIT* [2011] 203 Taxman 188 (Delhi).

186.1-2a BOARD'S CLARIFICATION - The Board have received representations seeking clarification regarding disallowance of remuneration paid to the working partners as provided under section 40(*b*)(*v*). In particular, the representations have referred to two types of clauses which are generally incorporated in the partnership deeds. These are :

a. the partners have agreed that the remuneration to a working partner will be the amount of remuneration allowable under the provisions of section 40(*b*)(*v*) of the Income-tax Act; and

b. the amount of remuneration to working partner will be as may be mutually agreed upon between partners at the end of the year.

It has been represented that the Assessing Officers are not allowing deduction on the basis of these and similar clauses in the course of scrutiny assessments for the reason that they neither specify the amount of remuneration to each individual nor lay down the manner of quantifying such remuneration.

The Board have considered the representations. Since the amended provisions of section 40(*b*) have been introduced only with effect from the assessment year 1993-94 and these may not have been understood correctly the Board are of the view that a liberal approach may be taken for the initial years. It has been decided that for the assessment years 1993-94 to 1996-97 deduction for remuneration to a working partner may be allowed on the basis of clauses of type mentioned at (*a*) *supra.*

In cases where neither the amount has been quantified nor even the limit of total remuneration has been specified but the same has been left to be determined by the partners at the end of the accounting period, in such cases payment of remuneration to partners cannot be allowed as deduction in the computation of firm's income.

It is clarified that for the assessment years subsequent to the assessment year 1996-97, no deduction under section 40(*b*)(*v*) will be admissible unless the partnership deed either specifies the amount of remuneration payable to each individual working partner or lays down the manner of quantifying such remuneration—

Circular No. 739, dated March 25, 1996. Since section 40(*b*) uses the term 'authorise' and not 'quantify', the Assessing Officer cannot disallow salary to partners mainly because of reasons that salary is not quantified by the partnership deed. CBDT has no jurisdiction to substitute the term 'authorise' occurring in section 40(*b*) by the term 'quantify' in its Circular No. 739, dated March 25, 1996—*CIT* v. *Suman Construction* [2009] 34 SOT 495 (Pune).

186.1-3 *IT SHOULD NOT PERTAIN TO THE PERIOD PRIOR TO PARTNERSHIP DEED* - The remuneration to the working partners as per the partnership deed, should be payable after the date of deed. In other words, if such payment is made from a date prior to the date of partnership deed, it would not be allowed as deduction, unless the earlier deed provides for such payment.

• *Provisions illustrated* - A and B enter into a partnership agreement on April 1, 2018. Each of them will be entitled for salary at the rate of Rs. 10,000 per month apart from profit. The agreement of partnership is amended on July 1, 2018 to increase the salary to Rs. 30,000 per month with effect from May 1, 2018.

In this case, salary will be deductible as follows subject to the satisfaction of other conditions :

	X *Rs.*	*Y* *Rs.*
From April 1, 2018 to June 30, 2018	10,000 per month	10,000 per month
From July 1, 2018 onwards	30,000 per month	30,000 per month

186.1-4 *REMUNERATION SHOULD NOT EXCEED THE PERMISSIBLE LIMIT*[81] - Where any salary, bonus, commission or other remuneration is paid to any working partner, in accordance with, and as authorised by, the terms of the partnership deed and in relation to any period falling after the date of the partnership deed, it may be allowed as deduction in the hands of the firm. However, the maximum amount of such payment to all the partners during the previous year should not exceed the limits given below :

186.1-4a FROM THE ASSESSMENT YEAR 2010-11 ONWARDS - Uniform limits have been provided for both professional firm and non-professional firm. Further, these limits will be applicable whether the firm is a limited liability partnership firm or otherwise. The revised limits are as follows—

Book profit	*Amount deductible in respect of remuneration to partners under section 40(b) with effect from the assessment year 2010-11*
• If book profit is negative	Rs. 1,50,000
• In case book profit is positive—	
On first Rs. 3 lakh of book profit	Rs. 1,50,000 or 90 per cent of book profit, whichever is more
On the balance of the book profit	60 per cent of book profit

186.1-4b UP TO THE ASSESSMENT YEAR 2009-10 - Up to the assessment year 2009-10, professional firms or non-professional firms have different limits given below—

• *In case of a firm carrying on a profession referred to in section 44AA or which is notified for the purpose of that section—*	
a. On the first Rs. 1,00,000 of the book profit or in case of a loss	Rs. 50,000 or at the rate of 90 per cent of the book-profit, whichever is more
b. On the next Rs. 1,00,000 of the book-profit	at the rate of 60 per cent
c. On the balance of the book-profit	at the rate of 40 per cent
• *In the case of any other firm—*	
a. On the first Rs. 75,000 of the book-profit, or in case of a loss	Rs. 50,000 or at the rate of 90 per cent of the book-profit, whichever is more
b. On the next Rs. 75,000 of the book-profit	at the rate of 60 per cent
c. On the balance of the book-profit	at the rate of 40 per cent

• *Profession referred to in section 44AA* - The following professions have been referred to in section 44AA : legal, medical, engineering or architectural profession or the profession of accountancy or technical consultancy or interior decoration or any other profession as is notified by the Board (*i.e.*, the profession of an authorised representative, film artist, company secretary and information technology).

81. If remuneration payable to partners is within the ceiling limit prescribed under section 40(*b*), section 40A(2) is not attracted—*CIT* v. *Great City Manufacturing Co.* [2009] 33 SOT 31 (Delhi).

186.1-4c BOOK PROFIT - HOW TO COMPUTE - It would be determined as under :

- *Step one* - Find out the net profit of the firm as per the Profit and Loss Account.
- *Step two* - Make adjustments as provided by sections 28 to 44D.
- *Step three* - *Add* remuneration to partners, if debited to the Profit and Loss Account.

The resulting amount is "book profit".

It may be noted that under Step Two, only adjustments as specified under sections 28 to 44D will be made and, consequently,—

a. income chargeable to tax under the heads "Income from house property", "Capital gains" and "Income from other sources" will not be a part of "book profit";

b. brought forward business losses will not be deducted from "book profit"; and

c. permissible deductions from gross total income under sections 80C to 80U shall be ignored from computing "book profit".

186.1-4E1 Profit and Loss Account of X Co. (a partnership firm) for the year ending March 31, 2019 is as follows :

	Rs.		*Rs.*
Cost of goods sold	70,00,000	Sales	86,00,000
Remuneration to partners	11,45,000	Rent of house property	60,000
Interest to partners	40,000	Interest on company deposit	1,70,000
Municipal tax of house property	25,000		
Other expenses	2,40,000		
Net profit	3,80,000		
	88,30,000		88,30,000

Other information :

1. Out of interest paid to partners, Rs. 10,000 is not deductible by virtue of section 40*(b).*
2. Out of other expenses, Rs. 18,400 is not deductible under sections 36, 37(1) and 43B.
3. On January 15, 2019, the firm pays an outstanding sales tax liability of Rs. 54,700 of the previous year 2013-14. As this amount pertains to the previous year 2013-14, it has not been debited to the aforesaid profit and loss account.
4. Brought forward losses and unabsorbed depreciation are as follows :

	Previous years		
	2016-17	*2015-16*	*2014-15*
	Rs.	*Rs.*	*Rs.*
Business loss	11,64,000	31,000	15,000
Capital loss	18,000	19,000	—
Unabsorbed depreciation	1,13,000	28,000	19,000

•

Computation of remuneration deductible under section 40(b) :	*Rs.*
Net profit as per Profit and Loss account	3,80,000
Less : Income not chargeable to tax under section 28 :	
Rent	(–)60,000
Interest on company deposit	(–)1,70,000
Balance	1,50,000
Add: Expenses debited to Profit and Loss Account but which are not deductible :	
Remuneration (taken separately)	(+)11,45,000
Interest to partners	(+)10,000
Municipal taxes of house property	(+)25,000
Other expenses	(+)18,400
Balance	13,48,400
Less : Outstanding sales tax paid during 2018-19 (deductible by virtue of section 43B)	54,700
	12,93,700

		Rs.
Less: Depreciation brought forward from earlier years [*i.e.*, Rs. 1,13,000 + Rs. 28,000 + Rs. 19,000; however, Rs. 12,93,700 will be notionally reduced to the extent of brought forward business loss (*i.e.*, Rs. 12,10,000) as given by section 32(2) read with section 72(2), and the balancing amount, *i.e.*, Rs. 83,700 would be available for setting off of unabsorbed depreciation]		83,700
Book profit		12,10,000
Maximum amount which is deductible on account of payment of remuneration to partners :		
	Rs.	
First Rs. 3,00,000 @ 90%	2,70,000	
Balance of Rs. 9,10,000 @ 60%	5,46,000	8,16,000

186.1-4E2 Profit and Loss Account of A Co. (a partnership firm of chartered accountants) for the year ending March 31, 2019 is as follows :

	Rs.		Rs.
Expenses	88,000	Receipts from clients for tax advice	1,60,000
Depreciation	32,000	Audit fees	72,000
Remuneration to partners	1,75,000	Net loss	68,000
Interest on capital to partners	5,000		
	3,00,000		3,00,000

Other information :

1. Out of expenses of Rs. 88,000, Rs. 17,250 is not deductible under sections 36 and 37.

2. Depreciation as per section 32 is Rs. 33,100.

3. Interest on capital to partners, not deductible under section 40(*b*) is Rs. 700.

•

Computation of remuneration deductible under section 37(1) read with section 40(b)

	Rs.
Net profit as per profit and loss account	(-)68,000
Add: Expenses (other than remuneration) not deductible	
Expenses	(+)17,250
Interest on capital to partners	(+)700
	(-)50,050
Less: Depreciation as per section 32 (*i.e.*, Rs. 33,100 – Rs. 32,000 debited in profit and loss account)	(-)1,100
	(-)51,150
Add: Remuneration to partner debited to profit and loss account	(+)1,75,000
Book profit	1,23,850
Maximum permissible remuneration (*i.e.*, 90% of Rs. 1,23,850 or Rs. 1,50,000, whichever is more)	1,50,000
Computation of income of the firm	
Book profit	1,23,850
Less: Remuneration to partners	(-)1,50,000
Loss to be carried forward by firm	(-)26,150

186.2 ***Whether remuneration paid and allowable can be disallowed under section 40A(2)*** - Technically even if remuneration to partners is deductible under section 37(1), read with section 40(*b*), it may be disallowed by the Assessing Officer under section 40A(2).

186.2-1 *ASSURANCE GIVEN BY THE FINANCE MINISTER* - While moving the Finance Bill, 1992, in Lok Sabha on April 30, 1992, the Finance Minister gave the following assurance regarding invoking of section 40A(2) in respect of payment of remuneration to partners :

> "There seems to be some apprehension that the provisions of section 40A(2) of the Income-tax Act may be indiscriminately resorted to by the Assessing Officers to make disallowance out of salary paid to the partners as being excessive. The Central Board of Direct Taxes will be asked to issue instructions to the Assessing Officers so as to ensure that this power is not used in the case of small firms and even otherwise, it should be used sparingly" — [1992] 195 ITR (St.) 128.

On the basis of the aforesaid statement one may conclude that only in the case of big sized firms, section 40A(2) may be invoked. Section 40A does not have overriding effect over the provisions of section 40(*b*)—*Syntholab Chemicals & Research* v. *CIT* [2008] 172 Taxman 38 (ITAT).

186.2-2 *PROVISIONS OF SECTION 40A(2)* - *See* para 49.2.

Interest payable to partners

187. Deductibility of interest paid to partners by a firm depends upon the fulfilment of conditions of sections 184 and 40(*b*)[82].

187.1 ***Compliance of section 40(b)***[82] - The following specific conditions should be fulfilled to obtain deduction of interest paid to the partners :

- Payment of interest should be authorised by the partnership deed - *See* para 186.1-2.
- Payment of interest should pertain to the period after the partnership deed - *See* para 186.1-3.
- Rate of interest should not exceed 12 per cent‡ - *See* paras 187.1-1 to 187.1-3.

187.1-1 *RATE OF INTEREST SHOULD NOT EXCEED 12 PER CENT*[83] - Interest paid to a partner is deductible if it does not exceed simple interest @ 12 per cent[83] per annum. If, however, interest payable exceeds simple interest of 12 per cent[83] per annum, the excess amount is not deductible. The Assessing Officer is not entitled to disallow payment of interest to partners by reworking capital account balances of partners under section 40(*b*). He can only verify whether the payment of interest to any partner is authorised by and is in accordance with the terms of partnership deed and also whether it relates to the period falling after the date of partnership deed—*Swaraj Enterprises* v. *ITO* [2011] 10 taxmann.com 270 (Vishakha. - ITAT).

187.1-2 *WHEN RECIPIENT OF INTEREST ACTS IN A REPRESENTATIVE CAPACITY* - *Explanations 1* and *2* to section 40(*b*) deal with cases where the recipient of the interest acts in a representative capacity.

187.1-2a EXPLANATION 1 - *Explanation 1* provides that where an individual is a partner in a firm on behalf, or for the benefit of any other person, interest paid by the firm to such individual otherwise than as partner in a representative capacity, is not taken into account, for the purpose of section 40(*b*).

It is also provided that in such cases, interest paid by the firm to such individual as partner in a representative capacity and interest paid by the firm to the person so represented, is taken into account for the purpose of section 40(*b*).

For instance, X is a partner in a firm on behalf of his HUF. The firm pays to X, interest on deposit and capital—Rs. 4,000 to X (otherwise than as partner in a representative capacity) and Rs. 5,000 to X (for HUF).

In this case, section 40(*b*) will not be applicable in respect of payment of Rs. 4,000, it will be deductible under sections 36(1)(*iii*), 40(*a*)(*i*) and 40A(2). However, the payment of Rs. 5,000 will be subject to application of section 40(*b*) [and it will be deductible subject to conditions of sections 36(1)(*iii*), 40(*a*)(*i*), 40(*b*) and 40A(2)].

187.1-2b EXPLANATION 2 - *Explanation 2* provides that where an individual is a partner in a firm, otherwise than in a representative capacity, interest paid by the firm to such individual will not be taken into account for the purposes of section 40(*b*), if such interest is received by him, on behalf, or for the benefit, of any other person.

For instance, a partner receives Rs. 10,000 from the firm as interest on deposit made by his minor son, Rs. 10,000 will be allowed subject to the provisions of sections 36(1)(*iii*), 40(*a*)(*i*) and 40A(2) while computing income of the firm. Similarly, if X is a partner in a firm in his personal capacity, interest paid by the firm to X (not in his personal capacity but, say as representing the HUF of which he is karta) is not taken into account for the purpose of section 40(*b*).

187.1-3 *INTEREST CHARGED BY FIRM ON DRAWINGS* - Where a firm pays as well as receives interest from the same partner, interest received by the firm will be chargeable to tax. Interest paid to the same partner will be allowed within the four corners of section 40(*b*).

---

82. It may be noted that interest is allowable as deduction only when it comes within the parameters of section 36(1)(*iii*) read with section 14A. In the case of a firm, deductibility of interest also depends upon section 40(*b*). Section 40(*b*) restricts and regulates deduction allowable to a firm on account of payment of interest to partners and is not an allowing section. For instance, if the capital borrowed from partners is invested by the firm for earning exempt income, it will not be allowed as deduction by virtue of section 36(1)(*iii*) read with section 14A, even if such interest is not hit by section 40(*b*) —*Shankar Chemicals Works* v. *CIT* [2011] 47 SOT 121 (Ahd.).

83. 18 per cent up to the assessment year 2002-03.

187.2 ***Disallowance of interest under section 40A(2)*** - Even if interest paid to a partner is deductible under section 36(1)(*iii*), read with section 40(*a*)(*i*) and 40(*b*), it may be disallowed under section 40A(2). However, the Bombay Tribunal in the case of *ITO* v. *M.M. Textiles* [2010] 122 ITD 435 (Mum.) held that interest payments to partners as per section 40(*b*) could not be disallowed under section 40A(2) as excessive or unreasonable.

187.2-1 *NO ASSURANCE BY THE FINANCE MINISTER* - An assurance was given by the Finance Minister in respect of deductibility of remuneration *vis-a-vis* application of section 40A(2). No such assurance is given in respect of interest.

187.2-2 *PROVISION OF SECTION 40A(2)* - *See* para 49.2.

Carry forward and set off of loss in the case of change in the constitution of firm

188. Section 78 provides that where there is a change in the constitution of the firm on account of death/ retirement, the firm shall not be entitled to carry forward so much of the loss as is attributable to such partner. This provision covers the case when a partner goes out of the firm (*i.e.*, the case of retirement or death). It does not, however, cover the case of change in profit sharing ratio or the case of admission of a partner.

188.1 ***Carry forward of house property loss, business loss, capital loss and loss from the activity of owning and maintaining race horses*** - These losses can be set off and carried forward by a firm in the case of a change in the constitution of the firm, as follows, as per the modified provisions of section 78:

1. First ascertain the share of the outgoing partner in the profit/loss of the firm in the year of change in the constitution of the firm.

2. Compute the share of loss of outgoing partner in the brought forward loss.

3. The difference between the two (in the case of profit in the year of change) or the aggregate of the two (if there is loss in the year of change in the constitution of the firm) cannot be allowed to be set off and carried forward.

188.2 ***Carry forward of unabsorbed depreciation*** - As section 78 is not applicable in the case of unabsorbed depreciation, the entire unabsorbed depreciation (without deducting share of outgoing partner) will be carried forward by the reconstituted firm.

How to find out income of a firm

189. First find out the taxable income of a firm under the following steps :

1. Find out income under the different heads of income (*viz.*, "Income from house property", "Profits and gains of business or profession", "Capital gains" and "Income from other sources") ignoring incomes exempt under sections 10 to 13A.

2. Make adjustment on account of brought forward losses/disallowances. The total income under the aforesaid heads is gross total income.

3. From the "gross total income" make deductions under sections 80G, 80GGA, 80GGC, 80-IA, 80-IAB, 80-IB, 80-IC, 80-ID, 80-IE, 80JJA and 80JJAA.

189.1 ***Other points*** - The following other points one should also keep in mind—

1. Where at the time of assessment, it is found that a change has occurred in the constitution of a firm, only one assessment shall be made in respect of the entire previous year in which change in the constitution has occurred. A change in the constitution of a firm is said to take place :

a. if one or more of the partners cease to be partners or one or more new partners are admitted, provided that at least one of the partners of the firm before the change continues as partners after the change [it does not cover a case where a firm is dissolved on the death of any of its partners];

b. where all the partners continue with a change in their respective shares or change in the shares of some of them.

2. Where a firm carrying on a business/profession is succeeded by another firm and the case is not covered by the aforesaid provision, separate assessments shall be made on the predecessor firm and the successor firm.

3. Every person who was, during the previous year, a partner of a firm, and the legal representative of any such person who is deceased, shall be jointly and severally liable along with the firm for the amount of tax, penalty or other sum payable by the firm for the assessment year.

How to find out tax liability

190. On the income computed above, tax is payable at the following rates by a firm for the assessment years 2019-20 and 2020-21:

	Tax rate [surcharge and education cess/secondary and higher education cess or health and education cess, shall be added]
Short-term capital gain under section 111A	15%
Long-term capital gain	20%
Winnings from lottery	30%
Other income (not being income which is subject to special tax rate)	30%

Tax liability shall be calculated as follows—

1. Find out income-tax on net income.

2. Add: Surcharge @ 12 per cent if total income exceeds Rs. 1 crore.

3. Find out total of (*1*) and (*2*).

4. Add: Health and education cess [4% of (*3*)].

5. Tax liability is (*1*) + (*2*) + (*4*) [*see* Tax table at pages B-38 to B-40].

190.1 ***Alternate minimum tax [Secs. 115JC to 115JF]*** - Alternate minimum tax provisions are applicable for different non-corporate assessees for different assessment years as follows—

	Up to the assessment year 2011-12	*Assessment year 2012-13*	*Assessment year 2013-14 onwards*
• Limited liability partnership	Not applicable	Applicable	Applicable[84]
• Any other firm	Not applicable	Not applicable	Applicable[84]
• Individual, HUF, AOP, BOI, artificial juridical person	Not applicable	Not applicable	Applicable if adjusted total income exceeds Rs. 20 lakh[84]
• Any other person (not being a company)	Not applicable	Not applicable	Applicable[84]

A corporate-assessee is subject to the provisions of MAT (*i.e.*, minimum alternate tax given by section 115JB).

190.1-1 *LEVY OF ALTERNATE MINIMUM TAX* - A limited liability partnership (from the assessment year 2012-13) or any other non-corporate assessee (from the assessment year 2013-14) is subject to alternate minimum tax which shall be determined as follows—

• *Step 1* - Find out the regular income-tax liability of the non-corporate assessee ignoring the provisions of sections 115JC to 115JF.

• *Step 2* - Find out adjusted total income of the non-corporate assessee. Adjusted total income is net income or total income of the non-corporate assessee as increased by—

a. amount claimed as deduction by the non-corporate assessee under sections 80H to 80RRB, (not being section 80P);

b. amount claimed as deduction by the non-corporate assessee under section 10AA; and

c. (from the assessment year 2015-16) deduction claimed, if any, under section 35AD (as reduced by the amount of depreciation allowable in accordance with the provisions of section 32 as if no deduction under section 35AD was allowed in respect of the assets on which the deduction under that section is claimed).

If the assessee is an individual, HUF, AOP, BOI or an artificial juridical person and the adjusted total income is Rs. 20 lakh (or less), then the provisions of alternate minimum tax are not applicable.

---

84. Provisions pertaining to computation of alternate minimum tax liability are applicable in the case of a non-corporate assessee only if the assessee has claimed any deduction under –

a. section 10AA or sections 80H to 80RRB (except section 80P) (for the assessment year 2013-14 or 2014-15); or

b. section 10AA or section 35AD or sections 80H to 80RRB (except section 80P) (for the assessment year 2015-16 onwards).

• *Step 3* - Find out 18.5 per cent[85] [+ SC + HEC] of "adjusted total income" computed under *Step 2*. The effective rate (as percentage of adjusted total income) for the assessment years 2019-20 and 2020-21 is as follows –

	Firm/co-operative society	*Individual/HUF/AOP/BOI/ artificial juridical person*	
	AY 2019-20 and 2020-21	*AY 2019-20*	*AY 2020-21*
If adjusted total income is Rs. 50 lakh or less	19.24%	19.24%	19.24%
If adjusted total income is more than Rs. 50 lakh but not more than Rs. 1 crore	19.24%	21.164%	21.164%
If adjusted total income is more than Rs. 1 crore but not more than Rs. 2 crore	21.5488%	22.126%	22.126%
If adjusted total income is more than Rs. 2 crore but not more than Rs. 5 crore	21.5488%	22.126%	**24.05%**
If adjusted total income is more than Rs. 5 crore	21.5488%	22.126%	**26.3588%**

• *Step 4* - If amount computed under *Step 1* is equal to or more than amount determined under *Step 3*, then the provisions of alternate minimum tax will not be applicable. If, however, amount computed under *Step 3* is more than the regular tax liability determined under *Step 1*, then—

a. adjusted total income determined under *Step 2* will be deemed as total income of the non-corporate assessee for such previous year; and

b. 18.5 per cent[85] [+ SC + HEC] of adjusted total income will be deemed as tax liability of the non-corporate assessee for such previous year.

• *Step 5* - The excess of the amount computed under *Step 3* over the amount computed under *Step 1* will be available as credit for alternate minimum tax[86]. It can be carried forward and can be set off against regular tax liability of the non-corporate assessee of the next year or subsequent year [but not beyond 10th assessment year (up to the assessment year 2017-18) and not beyond 15th assessment year (from the assessment year 2018-19)]. No interest is payable on such credit. Tax credit shall be allowed to be set off for an assessment year in which the regular income-tax exceeds the alternate minimum tax to the extent of the excess of the regular income-tax over the alternate minimum tax.

• *Step 6* - If provisions of alternate minimum tax are applicable, the assessee will have to obtain a report in Form No. 29C from a chartered accountant.

190.1-E1 The assessee is a non-corporate-assessee for the assessment year 2019-20. Income of the assessee is calculated as follows –

	Rs.
Net profit as per profit and loss account	67,60,000
Add: Excess depreciation (*i.e.*, excess of depreciation debited to profit and loss account over depreciation available under section 32)	2,000
Add: Disallowance under section 37(1) and under section 43B	60,000
Total	68,22,000
Less: Deduction under section 10AA	65,00,000
Business income under section 28	3,22,000
Long-term capital gain (on transfer of gold)	1,50,000
Gross total income	4,72,000
Less: Deductions	
Under section 80G	3,000
Under section 80-IB	48,000
Net income	4,21,000

•

85. 9 per cent in case the assessee is a unit located in an International Financial Services Centre and derives its income solely in convertible foreign exchange (applicable from the assessment year 2019-20).

86. However, from the assessment year 2018-19, the amount of tax credit in respect of AMT shall not be allowed to be carried forward to subsequent year to the extent such credit relates to the difference between the amount of foreign tax credit (FTC) allowed against AMT and FTC allowable against the tax computed under regular provisions of Act other than the provisions relating to AMT.

	*Individual/ HUF/AOP/BOI**	*Firm/LLP*
	Rs.	*Rs.*
Tax computation under normal provisions –		
Tax on long-term capital gain of Rs. 1,50,000 @ 20%	30,000	30,000
Tax on remaining income of Rs. 2,71,000	1,050	81,300
Total	31,050	1,11,300
Add: HEC	1,242	4,452
Tax liability (*a*)	32,292	1,15,752
Computation of adjusted total income		
Net income	4,21,000	4,21,000
Add: Deduction claimed under section 80-IB	48,000	48,000
Add: Deduction claimed under section 10AA	65,00,000	65,00,000
Adjusted total income	69,69,000	69,69,000
Computation of alternate minimum tax		
18.5% of adjusted total income	12,89,265	12,89,265
Add: Surcharge	1,28,927	—
Total	14,18,192	12,89,265
Add: HEC	56,728	51,571
Alternate minimum tax (*b*)	14,74,920	13,40,836
Tax payable [(*a*) or (*b*) whichever is more] (rounded off)	14,74,920	13,40,840
Alternate minimum tax credit	14,42,628	12,25,084

190.1-E2 X & Co. is a partnership firm. The firm is eligible for deduction under section 35AD of Rs. 14,00,000 (because of this deduction the firm cannot claim depreciation under section 32 of Rs. 80,000). Business income of the firm before deduction under section 35AD and before depreciation of Rs. 80,000 is Rs. 15,00,000. Deduction available under section 80-IB is Rs. 50,000. Income from other sources is Rs. 1,00,000. The firm has given a donation of Rs. 90,000 to a political party. Find out the tax liability of the firm for the assessment year 2019-20.

●

	Rs.
Business income (Rs. 15,00,000 - Rs. 14,00,000)	1,00,000
Any other income	1,00,000
Gross total income	2,00,000
Less: Deductions	
Under section 80GGC	90,000
Under section 80-IB	50,000
Net income	60,000
Tax on net income	
Tax on net income @ 30% (normally a firm is taxable @ 30%)	18,000
Add: Surcharge (not applicable as net income does not exceed Rs. 1 crore)	*Nil*
Tax and surcharge	18,000
Add: Health and education cess	720
Normal tax liability	18,720

Computation of adjusted total income - X & Co. is a non-corporate assessee. It has claimed deduction under section 80-IB. It will be subject to the provisions of alternate minimum tax. To find out alternate minimum tax, one has to first calculate adjusted total income. Adjusted total income shall be calculated as follows –

	Rs.
Net income or normal taxable income	60,000
Add: Deduction claimed under section 10AA or under sections 80HHH to 80RRB (except section 80P)	50,000
Add: Deduction under section 35AD as reduced by depreciation which is not available because of section 35AD deduction [*i.e.*, Rs. 14,00,000 - depreciation : Rs. 80,000]	13,20,000
Adjusted total income	14,30,000

Adjusted total income is not more than Rs. 20,00,000. But the check of Rs. 20,00,000 is applicable only in the case of an individual, HUF, AOP, BOI or artificial juridical person. A firm is subject to the provisions of alternate minimum tax even if adjusted total income is Rs. 20,00,000 or less. Alternate minimum tax liability shall be calculated as follows–

	Rs.
18.5% of adjusted total income	2,64,550
Add: Surcharge (not applicable as adjusted total income does not exceed Rs. 1 crore)	*Nil*
Tax and surcharge	2,64,550
Add: Health and education cess @ 4%	10,582
Alternate minimum tax	2,75,132

Tax payable is Rs. 2,75,130 (*i.e.*, normal tax or minimum alternate tax, whichever is higher). Tax credit (if any) pertaining to TDS/TCS, double taxation relief under sections 90, 90A and 91, tax relief under sections 86 and 89, shall be deducted from the tax payable of Rs. 2,75,132.

How to find out taxable income of partners of a firm

191. The provisions are given below—

191.1 ***Share of profit*** - Section 10(*2A*) provides that in the case of a partner (including a minor admitted for the benefit of the firm) of a firm, his share in the total income of the firm shall be exempt from tax[87].

191.2 ***Remuneration or interest*** - Any interest, salary, bonus, commission or remuneration, by whatever name called, which is due to (or received by) a partner of a firm from the firm is taxable in his hands under section 28(*v*), under the head "Profits and gains of business or profession". It is not taxable under section 15 under the head "Salaries" (*Explanation 2* to section 15). Hence, standard deduction cannot be claimed in respect of such remuneration. However, any expenditure incurred in order to earn such income can be claimed as a deduction from such income under sections 32 to 37. For instance, if a partner borrows money to make his capital contribution to the firm and he is paid interest on his capital contribution, the amount of such interest will be taxed under the head "Profits and gains of business or profession", but the interest paid by him on the borrowed money is allowed as a deduction.

Consequences when remuneration/interest is disallowed in firm's hands - If any remuneration/interest (or part thereof) has not been allowed as deductible by virtue of section 40(*b*)[read with section 184], in the hands of the firm, it shall not be chargeable to tax in the hands of partners.

Example on computation of taxable income of a firm and partners

192-E1 X (58 yrs.) and Y (64 yrs.) are two partners of XY Co. (a firm of chartered accountants). On March 31, 2018, there is no provision for payment of salary and interest to partners. On April 1, 2018, the deed of partnership has been amended to provide salary and interest as follows :

	X *Rs.*	*Y* *Rs.*
Salary	60,000 per month	50,000 per month
Interest	24 per cent per annum	24 per cent per annum

The income and expenditure account of XY Co. for the year ending March 31, 2019 is as follows :

	Rs.		*Rs.*
Office expenses	3,10,000	Receipt from clients	23,23,000
Salary to employees	70,000		
Salary to X	7,20,000		
Salary to Y	6,00,000		
Interest on capital to X @ 24%	6,000		
Interest on capital to Y @ 24%	9,000		
Net profit	6,08,000		
	23,23,000		23,23,000

Other information :

1. Out of office expenses, Rs. 800 are not deductible by virtue of sections 30 to 37.
2. During the previous year, the firm sells a capital asset for Rs. 2,10,000 (indexed cost of acquisition being Rs. 44,960).
3. Personal income and investment of partners are as follows :

---

87. Share of profit received by a partner from his partnership firm is not taxable in the hands of partner. This rule is applicable whether share of profit pertains to income which is taxable (or exempt) in the hands of firm – Circular No. 8/2014[$], dated March 31, 2014.

[$] For Circular No. 8/2014, log on to *taxmann.com/readyreckoner.aspx.*

	X	Y
	Rs.	*Rs.*
Interest on Government securities	82,000	57,000
Bank interest	3,10,000	12,00,000
Deposit in public provident fund	1,10,000	1,11,000
Mediclaim insurance premium on the life of father/mother	32,000	31,000
Mediclaim insurance premium on the life of X and Y	26,000	27,000

Find out the net income and tax liability of the firm and partners for the assessment year 2019-20.

•

Computation of net income/tax liability of the firm

Net profit as per income and expenditure account		6,08,000
Add:		
Office expenses		800
Salary to X and Y (entire amount)		13,20,000
Interest to X and Y [to the extent not allowed as deduction, *i.e.*, 12/24 of (Rs. 6,000 + Rs. 9,000)]		7,500
Book profit		19,36,300
Less : Remuneration to partners [maximum deductible amount is 90% of Rs. 3,00,000 + 60% of Rs. 16,36,300]		12,51,780
Income from the profession		6,84,520
Capital gains		
Sale proceeds	2,10,000	
Less: Indexed cost of acquisition	44,960	1,65,040
Net income		8,49,560
Tax		
Income-tax on long-term capital gain [20% of Rs. 1,65,040]		33,008
Income-tax on balancing amount [30% of Rs. 6,84,520]		2,05,356
Tax		2,38,364
Add: Surcharge		*Nil*
Tax and surcharge		2,38,364
Add: Health and education cess		9,535
Tax liability (rounded off)		2,47,900

Computation of net income and tax liability of partners

	X	Y
	Rs.	*Rs.*
Profits and gains of business or profession		
Interest from the firm (to the extent allowed is deduction, *i.e.*, 12/24 of Rs. 6,000 and 9,000)	3,000	4,500
Salary received from the firm (to the extent allowed as deduction, *i.e.*, Rs. 12,51,780 distributed in the ratio of 72 : 60)	6,82,789	5,68,991
Income from profession	6,85,789	5,73,491
Income from other sources	3,92,000	12,57,000
Gross total income	10,77,789	18,30,491
Less : Deductions :		
Under section 80C	1,10,000	1,11,000
Under section 80D	57,000	58,000
Net income (rounded off)	9,10,790	16,61,490
Tax on income		
Income-tax[88]	94,658	3,08,447
Add: Surcharge	—	—
Tax and surcharge	94,658	3,08,447
Add : Health and education cess	3,786	12,338
Tax liability (rounded off)	98,440	3,20,780

88. Rebate under section 87A is not available, as net income exceeds Rs. 3,50,000.

How to compute income of association of persons (AOP) or body of individuals (BOI)

193. In the case of AOP[89]/BOI, income will be determined as under :

1. If any salary, bonus, commission or remuneration (by whatever name called) is paid by the AOP/BOI to its members, it is not deductible [section 40(*ba*)—*see* para 193.1].

2. Similarly, any interest paid by AOP/BOI to its members (on loan, capital, or borrowing) by whatever name called is not deductible [section 40(*ba*)—*see* para 193.2].

3. Total income of the AOP/BOI is taxable either at the rates applicable to an individual, or at the maximum marginal rate or at a rate higher than maximum marginal rate [*see* para 194].

193.1 ***Remuneration not allowed as deduction*** - In the case of AOP/BOI, salary, bonus, commission or remuneration to members (by whatever name called), is not allowed as deduction in the computation of income of the AOP/BOI. Even remuneration for actual services is not deductible.

193.2 ***Interest not allowed as deduction*** - Interest paid by AOP/BOI to its members is not allowed as deduction by virtue of section 40(*ba*).

193.2-1 *WHEN INTEREST IS PAID ON CAPITAL AND CHARGED ON DRAWING* - *Explanation 1* to section 40(*ba*) provides that where interest is paid by AOP/BOI to a member who has also paid interest to the AOP/BOI, the amount of interest to be disallowed under section 40(*ba*) is limited to the net amount of interest paid by the AOP/BOI to the member, that is the amount by which the payment of interest by the AOP/BOI to the member exceeds the payment of interest by the member to the AOP/BOI. For instance, if a AOP/BOI pays interest of Rs. 40,000 to a member A and receives Rs. 13,000 from the same member as interest on withdrawals, the amount which is to be disallowed as deduction under section 40(*ba*) is Rs. 27,000. If, on the other hand, an AOP/BOI pays interest of Rs. 5,000 to a member and that member pays interest of Rs. 8,000 to the AOP/BOI in the same previous year, no disallowance of interest is required to be made under section 40(*ba*). There is, however no provision in the Act permitting an adjustment of interest received from a member against interest paid to other members. Where AOP/BOI pays interest to three of its members and receives interest from the fourth member, the entire amount of interest paid to the three members will be disallowed under section 40(*ba*), while interest received from the fourth member is taxable as income in the hands of the AOP/BOI—*Sugar Dealers* v. *CIT* [1980] 122 ITR 826 (All.).

193.2-2 *WHEN RECIPIENT OF INTEREST ACTS IN REPRESENTATIVE CAPACITY* - *Explanations 2* and *3* deal with cases where the recipient of interest acts in a representative capacity.

193.2-2a EXPLANATION 2 - *Explanation 2* provides that where an individual is a member in an AOP/BOI on behalf, or for the benefit of any other person, interest paid by the AOP/BOI to such individual, otherwise than as member in a representative capacity, is not taken into account, for the purpose of section 40(*ba*). It is also provided that in such cases, interest paid by the AOP/BOI to such individual, as member in a representative capacity and interest paid by the AOP/BOI to the person, so represented, is taken into account for the purposes of section 40(*ba*).

For instance, X is a member in AOP/BOI on behalf of his HUF. The AOP/BOI pays interest on deposit and capital—Rs. 23,000 to X (otherwise than as member in a representative capacity) and Rs. 15,000 to X (for HUF).

In this case, section 40(*ba*) will not be applicable in respect of payment of Rs. 23,000 ; it will be deductible. However, the payment of Rs. 15,000 will be subject to application of section 40(*ba*) (and consequently, it will not be deducted).

193.2-2b EXPLANATION 3 - *Explanation 3* provides that where an individual is a member in AOP/BOI (otherwise than in a representative capacity) interest paid by the AOP/BOI to such individual will not be taken into account for the purpose of section 40(*ba*), if such interest is received by him, on behalf, or for the benefit, of any other person.

For instance X, a member, receives Rs. 10,000 from the AOP/BOI as interest on deposit made by his minor son, Rs. 10,000 will be allowed subject to the provisions of sections 36(1)(*iii*), 40(*a*)(*i*) and 40A(2) while computing income of the AOP/BOI. Similarly, if X is a partner in a AOP/BOI in his personal capacity interest paid by the AOP/BOI to X (not in his personal capacity, but say, as representing the HUF of which he is karta) is not taken into account for the purpose of section 40(*ba*).

---

89. CBDT has decided that a consortium arrangement for executing engineering procurement and construction contracts/turnkey contracts which has certain specified attributes (*i.e.* there is a clear demarcation in the work and costs between the consortium members and each member incurs expenditure only in its specified area of work, each member earns profit or incurs losses, based on performance of the contract falling strictly within its scope of work, the men and materials used for any area of work are under the risk and control of respective consortium members, the control and management of the consortium is not unified and common management is only for the *inter se* co-ordination between the consortium members for administrative convenience), may not be treated as an AOP – Circular No. 7/2016$, dated March 7, 2016.

$For Circular No. 7/2016, log on to *taxmann.com/readyreckoner.aspx.*

How to compute taxable income of an AOP/BOI

194. First find out the taxable income of the AOP/BOI under the following steps :

1. Find out income under the different heads of income (*viz.*, "Income from house property", "Profits and gains of business or profession", "Capital gains" and "Income from other sources", ignoring incomes exempt under sections 10 to 13A.

2. Make adjustments on account of brought forward losses/allowances. The total income under the aforesaid heads is "Gross total income".

3. From the "gross total income" make deductions under sections 80G, 80GGA, 80GGC, 80-I, 80-IA, 80-IB, 80-IC and 80JJA.

4. The balancing amount is total income or taxable income.

How to find out tax liability of an AOP/BOI[90]

195. Tax incidence on an AOP/BOI depends upon whether (or not) shares of members are determinate.

195.1 ***Where shares of members are determinate*** - Tax liability is determined as under :

195.1-1 *IF NONE OF THE MEMBER OF THE AOP/BOI HAS INCOME IN EXCESS OF THE MAXIMUM AMOUNT WHICH IS NOT CHARGEABLE TO TAX[91] IN THE HANDS OF MEMBERS* - In this case, tax is chargeable on the income of the AOP/BOI at the same rate as is applicable in the case of an individual.

195.1-1a WHEN A COMPANY IS A MEMBER - Where in the case discussed in para 195.1-1, total income of any member of AOP/BOI is taxable at a rate higher than the maximum marginal rate [*i.e.*, 35.88 per cent (for the assessment year 2019-20) and **42.744** per cent (for the assessment year 2020-21)] (this is possible when a company is a partner), tax will be chargeable on that portion of the income of the AOP/BOI which is relatable to the share of such member at such higher rate and the balance of the income is taxable at the maximum marginal rate of tax.

195.1-2 *IF ANY MEMBER OF THE AOP/BOI HAS INCOME IN EXCESS OF THE MAXIMUM AMOUNT WHICH IS NOT CHARGEABLE TO TAX[91]* - In such case, tax will be chargeable at the maximum marginal rate [*i.e.*, 35.88 per cent (for the assessment year 2019-20) and **42.744** per cent (for the assessment year 2020-21)].

195.1-2a WHEN A COMPANY IS A MEMBER - When in the case discussed in para 195.1-2, the total income of any member of the AOP/BOI is chargeable to tax at a rate higher than the maximum marginal rate (for instance when a foreign company is a member), tax will be charged on that portion of the total income of the AOP/BOI which is relatable to the share of such member, at such higher rate and the balance of the total income shall be taxed at the maximum marginal rate of tax [*i.e.*, 35.88 per cent (for the assessment year 2019-20) and **42.744** per cent (for the assessment year 2020-21)].

195.2 ***When shares of members are indeterminate*** - Where the individual shares of the member of the AOP/BOI in the whole or in any part of the income of the AOP/BOI are indeterminate or unknown, tax will be charged on the total income of the AOP/BOI at the maximum marginal rate [*i.e.*, 35.88 per cent (for the assessment year 2019-20) and **42.744** per cent (for the assessment year 2020-21)]. Where the income of any member of the AOP/BOI is taxable at a rate higher than the maximum marginal rate, tax will be chargeable on the total income of the AOP/BOI at such higher rate.

The individual shares of the member of the AOP/BOI in the whole or any part of the income of the AOP/BOI will be deemed to be indeterminate or unknown if such shares (in relation to the whole or any part of such income) are indeterminate or unknown on the date of formation of the AOP/BOI or at any time thereafter.

How to determine taxable income of members of AOP/BOI

196. The following procedure is to be followed in order to compute the share of a member of AOP/BOI (in which the shares of the members are determinate and known) in the total income of the AOP/BOI [sec. 67A(1)].

1. From the total income of the AOP/BOI, any interest, salary, bonus, commission or remuneration by whatever name called, is to be deducted.

---

90. From the assessment year 2013-14, tax payable by a non-corporate assessee cannot be less than 18.5[92] per cent [+ SC + (EC + SHEC) or HEC] of "adjusted total income".

91. Exemption limit for the assessment year 2019-20 is Rs. 2,50,000 [higher exemption limit (*a*) in the case of a resident senior citizen born on or after April 2, 1939 but on or before April 1, 1959: Rs. 3,00,000; and (*b*) in the case of a resident super senior citizen born on or before April 1, 1939: Rs. 5,00,000].

Exemption limit for the assessment year 2020-21 is Rs. 2,50,000 [higher exemption limit (*a*) in the case of a resident senior citizen born on or after April 2, 1940 but on or before April 1, 1960: Rs. 3,00,000; and (*b*) in the case of a resident super senior citizen born on or before April 1, 1940: Rs. 5,00,000].

92. 9 per cent in case the assessee is a unit located in an International Financial Services Centre and derives its income solely in convertible foreign exchange (applicable from the assessment year 2019-20).

2. The balance is to be apportioned among the members in the proportions in which they are entitled to share in the income of the AOP/BOI.

3. Where the amount apportioned as in (2) above to a member is a profit, any interest, salary, bonus, commission or other remuneration paid to the member by the AOP/BOI in respect of the previous year is to be added to such apportioned amount and the resulting amount will be treated as the member's share in the income of the AOP/BOI.

4. Where, however, the amount apportioned as in (2) above to a member is a loss, any interest salary, bonus, commission or other remuneration paid to the member by the AOP/BOI in respect of the previous year will be adjusted against such apportioned loss and the resultant sum will be the member's share in the income of the AOP/BOI.

5. For the purpose of assessment, the share of a member in the income or loss of the AOP/BOI as computed under section 67A(1) is to be apportioned under the various heads of income in the same manner in which the income or loss of the AOP/BOI has been determined under each head of income [sec. 67A(2)].

196.1 ***Interest paid by member on capital borrowed [Sec. 67A(3)]*** - In computing the income of a member chargeable under the head "Profits and gains of business or profession" in respect of his share in the income of the AOP/BOI, any interest paid by the member on capital borrowed by him for the purpose of investment in the AOP/BOI can be deducted from his share.

196.2 ***Meaning of word 'paid' [Explanation to sec. 67A]*** - The word paid used in section 67A means actually paid or incurred according to the method of accounting upon the basis of which the profits or gains are computed under the head "Profits and gains of business or profession".

196.3 ***Non-availability of certain deduction under Chapter VI-A [Sec. 80A(3)]*** - In computing the total income of AOP/BOI if any deduction is admissible under section 80G or 80GGA or 80GGC or 80HHA or 80-I or 80-IA or 80-IB or 80-IC or 80-ID or 80-IE no deduction under that section can be claimed while computing the total income of a member of the AOP/BOI in relation to the share of that member in the income of AOP/BOI.

Computation of tax of members

197. The share of a member in the income of the AOP/BOI is treated in three different ways, depending upon whether the AOP/BOI is chargeable to tax at the maximum marginal rate or at the normal rate or is not chargeable to tax at all. These are :

1. Where the AOP/BOI is chargeable to tax at the maximum marginal rate [*i.e.*, 35.88 per cent (for the assessment year 2019-20) and **42.744** per cent (for the assessment year 2020-21)] or at a rate higher than the maximum marginal rate, the share of a member therein shall not be included in his total income at all.

2. Where the AOP/BOI is chargeable to tax at the normal rate applicable to individuals, etc., the share of a member, therein shall be included in his total income, but a rebate shall be given on the same under section 86.

3. Where no income-tax is chargeable on the total income of the AOP/BOI, the shares of a member therein shall be fully chargeable to tax as part of his total income and no rebate shall be given thereon. Thus, where an AOP/BOI is taxable at the normal rates applicable to individuals, etc., but has income below taxable limit so that no income-tax is chargeable on the total income of AOP/BOI, member in such AOP/BOI shall be fully taxable in his own assessment without any tax rebate.

197-E1 X (26 years), Y (28 years) and Z (62 years) are three members of B & Co. (an AOP). Profit and loss account of the firm for the year ending March 31, 2019 is as follows :

	Rs.		*Rs.*
Cost of goods sold	1,34,000	Sales	4,00,000
Interest on capital to members :		Short-term capital gain (on transfer of land)	2,10,000
❑ X	9,000	Interest on drawings	
❑ Y	27,000	recovered from members	
❑ Z	35,000	X	2,000
Salary to members		Y	1,000
❑ Y	65,000	Z	3,000
❑ Z	70,000		
Other expenses	60,000		
Net profit	2,16,000		
	6,16,000		6,16,000

Other information :

1. The AOP gives a donation of Rs. 46,000 to a public charitable trust (not debited to P & L A/c) which is eligible for section 80G deduction.

2. Out of other expenses, Rs. 26,000 is not deductible by virtue of section 43B.

Find out the tax liability of the AOP and members for the assessment year 2019-20 under the following situations :

Situation 1 - The profit-sharing ratio of X, Y and Z is 2 : 3 : 5. Other incomes of members are given below :

	Amount Rs.	*Nature of income*	*Investment for the purpose of section 80D*	*PPF contribution* Rs.
X	2,70,000	Bank FD interest	Rs. 6,000 mediclaim insurance premia	14,000
Y	3,50,000	Interest on Government securities	—	1,15,000
Z	3,20,000	Interest on company deposit	Rs. 3,000 mediclaim insurance premia	28,000

Situation 2 - The profit-sharing ratio of X, Y and Z is 3:1:6. Other incomes of members are as follows :

	Amount of income Rs.	*Donation* Rs.	*PPF deposit* Rs.
X	1,51,000	10,000	2,000
Y	2,95,000	36,000	16,000
Z	1,65,000	16,000	6,000

Situation 3 - One of the members X is a closely-held foreign company and the profit-sharing ratio of X Ltd., Y and Z is 2 : 3 : 5. Other income of the members is as follows :

	Rs.
X Ltd.	*Nil*
Y	1,52,000
Z	2,30,000

Situation 4 - One of the members X is a closely-held foreign company and the profit-sharing ratio is 2 : 3 : 5. Other income of the members is as follows :

	Rs.
X Ltd.	2,80,000
Y	11,40,000
Z	1,70,000

Situation 5 - From the available information, it is not possible to find out the profit-sharing ratio. Other income of members is :

	Amount Rs.	*Nature of income*
X	90,000	Bank fixed deposit interest
Y	1,90,000	Rent (taxable)
Z	2,95,000	Interest on company deposit
Z	15,000	Being 60 per cent share from D & Co. (an AOP which has not paid tax because its taxable income is lower than Rs. 2,50,000)

Situation 6 - It is not possible to determine the profit-sharing ratio of members. One of the members, X is a foreign company. Other income of members is as follows :

	Rs.
X Ltd.	1,17,800
Y	4,30,000
Z	16,30,000

•

Computation of taxable income of AOP

Net profit as per P&L A/c	2,16,000
Add :	
Interest to members [being net interest disallowed under section 40(*ba*) (*i.e.*, X : Rs. 9,000 — Rs. 2,000; Y : Rs. 27,000 — Rs. 1,000; Z : Rs. 35,000 — Rs. 3,000)]	65,000
Remuneration to members [disallowed under section 40(*ba*)]	1,35,000

	Rs.
Other expenses [not deductible under section 43B]	26,000
	4,42,000
Less : Capital gains	2,10,000
Business income	2,32,000
Capital gain (short-term)	2,10,000
Gross total income	4,42,000
Less : Deduction under section 80G (50% of Rs. 44,200)	22,100
Net income	4,19,900

Situation 1 - Since shares of members are determinate and none of the members is a foreign company and none of the members has taxable income exceeding Rs. 2,50,000 (in the case of senior citizen Rs. 3,00,000), income of the AOP will be taxable at the rates applicable to an individual as follows :

	Rs.
Tax on Rs. 4,19,900 at the rate applicable to an individual	8,495
Add : Surcharge	*Nil*
Tax	8,495
Add : Health and education cess	340
Tax liability of AOP	8,840

Allocation of income to the members

	Salary	*Interest*	*Balance in the ratio of 2 : 3 : 5*	*Total*
	Rs.	*Rs.*	*Rs.*	*Rs.*
X	*Nil*	7,000	43,980	50,980
Y	65,000	26,000	65,970	1,56,970
Z	70,000	32,000	1,09,950	2,11,950
Total	1,35,000	65,000	2,19,900	4,19,900

Computation of income/tax liability of members :

	X *Rs.*	*Y* *Rs.*	*Z* *Rs.*
Business income (share of profit from AOP)	50,980	1,56,970	2,11,950
Income from other sources	2,70,000	3,50,000	3,20,000
Gross total income	3,20,980	5,06,970	5,31,950
Less : Deductions			
Under section 80C	14,000	1,15,000	28,000
Under section 80D	6,000	—	3,000
Net income	3,00,980	3,91,970	5,00,950
Income-tax on net income	2,549	7,099	10,190
Less: Rebate under section 87A (100% of tax or Rs. 2,500, whichever is less, applicable only in the case of a resident individual if net income does not exceed Rs. 3,50,000)	2,500	–	*Nil*
Balance	49	7,099	10,190
Add: Surcharge	*Nil*	*Nil*	*Nil*
Tax and surcharge	49	7,099	10,190
Add: Health and education cess	2	284	408

	X Rs.	Y Rs.	Z Rs.
Tax	51	7,382	10,598
Less : Rebate under section 86 in respect of share of profit from the AOP	9[93]	2,956[94]	4,484[95]
Tax liability of members (rounded off)	40	4,430	6,110

Situation 2 - Since in this case taxable income of Y exceeds Rs. 2,50,000, the entire income of AOP will be taxable @ 35.88%.

	Rs.
Net income of AOP	4,19,900
Tax @ 35.88%	1,50,660

Assessment of members :

	X Rs.	Y Rs.	Z Rs.
Share of income from AOP (not to be included as tax is payable @ 35.88% by AOP)	—	—	—
Other income	1,51,000	2,95,000	1,65,000
Gross total income	1,51,000	2,95,000	1,65,000
Less : Deduction under section 80C	2,000	16,000	6,000
Less : Deduction under section 80G	5,000	13,950	7,950
Net income	1,44,000	2,65,050	1,51,050
Income-tax on net income	—	753	—
Less: Rebate under section 87A (100% of tax or Rs. 2,500, whichever is less, applicable only in the case of a resident individual if net income does not exceed Rs. 3,50,000)	-	753	-
Balance	-	*Nil*	-
Add : Surcharge	—	—	—
Tax and surcharge	—	—	—
Add : Health and education cess	—	—	—
Tax liability (rounded off)	—	—	—

Situation 3 - Since one of the members X Ltd. is taxable at the rate of 41.60%, the share attributable to X Ltd. is taxable at the rate of 41.6% and the balancing amount is taxable at the rate of 35.88%.

	Rs.
Tax on Rs. 50,980 (being share of X Ltd. which is taxable at a rate higher than 35.88%, 41.6% of Rs. 50,980)	21,208
Tax on the balance (*i.e.*, Rs. 4,19,900 — Rs. 50,980) 35.88% of Rs. 3,68,920	1,32,368
Tax (rounded off)	1,53,580

Tax liability of the member :

	X Ltd. *Rs.*	Y *Rs.*	Z *Rs.*
Share of profit from AOP (not included)	—	—	—
Other income	*Nil*	1,52,000	2,30,000
Net income	*Nil*	1,52,000	2,30,000
Tax liability	*Nil*	*Nil*	*Nil*

93. Rs. 51 ÷ Rs. 3,00,980 × Rs. 50,980.
94. Rs. 7,382 ÷ Rs. 3,91,970 × Rs. 1,56,970.
95. Rs. 10,598 ÷ Rs. 5,00,950 × Rs. 2,11,950.

Situation 4 - While tax liability of the AOP will be Rs. 1,53,580 as computed in *Situation 3*, tax liability of the members will be as under :

	X Ltd. *Rs.*	*Y* *Rs.*	*Z* *Rs.*
Share of profit from the AOP (not to be included)	—	—	—
Other income	2,80,000	11,40,000	1,70,000
Net income	2,80,000	11,40,000	1,70,000
Income-tax[96]	1,12,000	1,54,500	*Nil*
Add : Surcharge	*Nil*	*Nil*	—
Tax	1,12,000	1,54,500	*Nil*
Add : Health and education cess [1% of tax]	4,480	6,180	—
Tax liability (rounded off)	1,16,480	1,60,680	*Nil*

Situation 5 - Since shares of members are unknown, the entire income of the AOP will be taxable @ 35.88% (which comes to Rs. 1,50,660)

Taxable income and tax liability of the members will be as follows :

	X *Rs.*	*Y* *Rs.*	*Z* *Rs.*
Rent	—	1,90,000	—
Share of profit from D & Co. (AOP)	—	—	15,000
Bank interest	90,000	—	—
Interest on company deposit	—	—	2,95,000
Gross total income	90,000	1,90,000	3,10,000
Less : Deduction	—	—	—
Net income	90,000	1,90,000	3,10,000
Tax on net income	*Nil*	*Nil*	500
Less: Rebate under section 87A (100% of tax or Rs. 2,500, whichever is less, applicable only in the case of a resident individual if net income does not exceed Rs. 3,50,000)	*Nil*	*Nil*	500
Balance	*Nil*	*Nil*	*Nil*
Add : Surcharge	—	—	—
Tax	*Nil*	*Nil*	*Nil*
Add : Health and education cess	*Nil*	*Nil*	*Nil*
Tax liability (rounded off)	*Nil*	*Nil*	*Nil*

Note : Z is not entitled for any tax rebate under section 86, as D & Co. has not paid any tax.

Situation 6 - Since one of the members is a foreign company taxable at the rate of 41.6% and shares of members are not known, the entire income of the AOP will be taxable at the rate of 41.6%.

	Rs.
Net income of AOP	4,19,900
Tax on Rs. 4,19,900 @ 40%	1,67,960
Add : Surcharge	*Nil*
Tax and surcharge	1,67,960
Add : Health and education cess	6,718
Tax liability of AOP (rounded off)	1,74,680

96. Rebate under section 87A is not available in the case of Y, as his income exceeds Rs. 3.50 lakh.

Tax liability of members :

	X Ltd. Rs.	Y Rs.	Z Rs.
Net income	1,17,800	4,30,000	16,30,000
Tax	47,120	9,000	2,99,000
Less: Rebate under section 87A (100% of tax or Rs. 2,500, whichever is less, applicable only in the case of a resident individual if net income does not exceed Rs. 3,50,000)	*Nil*	*Nil*	*Nil*
Balance	47,120	9,000	2,99,000
Add: Surcharge	*Nil*	*Nil*	*Nil*
Tax and surcharge	47,120	9,000	2,99,000
Add: Health and education cess	1,885	360	11,960
Tax	49,000	9,360	3,10,960

COMPANIES

Types of companies

205. For the purpose of computation of taxable income and tax liability, companies are of the following types:

205.1 ***Companies in which the public are substantially interested [Sec. 2(18)]*** - A company is regarded as company in which the public are substantially interested in the following cases where :

a. it is a company owned by the Government or the Reserve Bank or in which not less than 40 per cent shares are held by the Government or the Reserve Bank or a corporation owned by the Reserve Bank; or

b. it is a company registered under section 25 of the Companies Act, 1956; or

c. it is a company having no share capital and it is declared by the Board to be a company in which the public are substantially interested; or

d. it is a mutual benefit finance company, that is to say, a company which mainly carries on the business of deposit from its members and which is declared by the Central Government under section 620A of the Companies Act to be a *Nidhi* or Mutual Benefit Society; or

e. it is a company in which shares carrying not less than 50 per cent of the voting power have been allotted unconditionally to or acquired unconditionally by, and are throughout the relevant previous year held by one or more co-operative societies [applicable from the assessment year 1993-94 onwards].

f. it is a company which is not a private company and its equity shares are listed in a recognised stock exchange in India; or

g. it is a company which is not a private company and whose equity shares carrying not less than 50 per cent (40 per cent in case of industrial companies) of the voting power, are held by the Government, a statutory corporation, or another widely-held company or a wholly-owned subsidiary of such company (shares held by the public are not considered for this purpose).

205.2 ***Domestic company*** - "Domestic company" means an Indian company or any other company which, in respect of its income liable to tax under the Act, has made prescribed arrangements for the declaration and payment of dividends within India in accordance with section 194.

205.3 ***Foreign company*** - Foreign company means a company which is not a domestic company.

205.4 ***Industrial company*** - Industrial company means a company :

a. which is mainly engaged in the business of generation or distribution of electricity or any other form of power or in the construction of ships or in the manufacture or processing of goods or in mining, even if its total income from such activities is less than 51 per cent of its total income; and

b. which even though not mainly so engaged, derives in any year 51 per cent or more of its income from such activities.

How to compute taxable income of companies

206. First ascertain gross total income, ignoring incomes exempted under sections 10 to 13B, if any. Then deduct permissible deductions under sections 80G, 80GGA, 80GGB, 80-IA, 80-IAB, 80-IB, 80-IC, 80-ID, 80-IE, 80JJA, 80JJAA and 80LA. [*see* para 107]. For ready reference of different deductions available to companies under the Income-tax Act, *see* Referencer 7.

Rates of tax

207. For rates applicable to the assessment years 2019-20 and 2020-21, *see* para 0.1-4, Referencer 1 [*see* also Tax Tables at pages B-41 to B-48]. Rates applicable to the assessment years prior to the assessment year 2019-20 are given in Referencer 3.

• *Dividend income of an Indian company received from a specified foreign company [Sec. 115BBD]* - Income of an Indian company by way of dividend declared, distributed or paid by a specified foreign company, shall be taxable at the rate of 15 per cent from the assessment year 2012-13 onwards. "Specified foreign company" means a foreign company in which the Indian company holds 26 per cent or more in nominal value of the equity share capital of the company.

207.1 ***Minimum alternate tax*** - Section 115JB regulates the provisions regarding minimum alternate tax. Up to the assessment year 2001-02, these provisions were given by section 115JA. These provisions in brief are given below—

Section	*Applicability for which assessment year*	*When these provisions are applicable*	*Consequences*
115JA	1997-98 to 2000-01	If income of a company under normal provisions is lower than 30 per cent of "book profit"	30 per cent of "book profit" shall be deemed as total income of the company
115JB	2001-02 onwards	If tax liability of a company under normal provisions is lower than 18.5 per cent[97] [+ SC + (EC + SHEC) or HEC] of "book profit"	"Book profit" shall be deemed as total income and 18.5 per cent[97] of "book profit" should be deemed as tax liability

• *Exceptions* - The provisions of minimum alternate tax are not applicable in the following cases –

Nature of income	*Time frame when MAT provisions are not applicable*
1. Income from any business/services in the hands of entrepreneur/developer in a special economic zone	Income arising after March 31, 2005 but before April 1, 2011
2. Income of a shipping company which is subject to the provisions of "tonnage income" of Chapter XII-G (*i.e.*, sections 115V to 115VZC)	Income arising after March 31, 2004 (*i.e.*, assessment year 2005-06 onwards)
3. Income which accrues and arises to a company from life insurance business referred to in section 115B	Income arising after March 31, 2000 (*i.e.*, assessment year 2001-02 onwards)
4. In the case of a foreign company where its total income comprises solely of profits and gains referred to in sections 44B, 44BB, 44BBA and 44BBB	Income arising after March 31, 2000 (*i.e.*, assessment year 2001-02 onwards)

• *Principle of mutuality* - Once income is found to be covered by principle of mutuality, the same cannot be brought to tax even under provisions of section 115JB—*Delhi Gymkhana Club Ltd.* v. *CIT* [2010] 35 SOT 335 (Delhi).

• *Computation of book profit in the case of insurance, banking and electricity companies* - Book profit is calculated by making a few adjustments in the net profit disclosed under the profit and loss account prepared by the company in accordance with the Schedule VI of the Companies Act, 1956. Schedule VI of the Companies Act is not applicable in the case of insurance, banking and electricity companies. In the case of these companies, the provisions of minimum alternate tax are not applicable—*Krung Thai Bank PCL* v. *DIT* [2012] 49 SOT 70 (Mum.), *Kerala State Electricity Board* v. *CIT* [2011] 196 Taxman 1 (Ker.), *Union Bank of India* v. *CIT* [2012] 49 SOT 32 (Mum.).

Superseding the ruling given above, section 115JB was amended (with effect from the assessment year 2013-14) to align the provisions of Income-tax Act with the Companies Act, 1956. The amended version of section 115JB provides that the book profit in the case of—

a. any insurance or banking company or any company engaged in the generation or supply of electricity (or any other class of company for which a form of profit and loss account has been specified in or under the Act governing such class of company), shall be calculated on the basis of profit and loss

97. 7.5 per cent for the assessment years 2001-02 to 2006-07, 10 per cent for the assessment years 2007-08 to 2009-10, 15 per cent for the assessment year 2010-11 and 18 per cent for the assessment year 2011-12. Moreover, with effect from the assessment year 2017-18, it is 9 per cent in case the assessee is a unit located in an International Financial Services Centre and derives its income solely in convertible foreign exchange.

account prepared in accordance with the provisions of their regulatory Acts [however, for the assessment year 2012-13 (or any earlier year) these companies have an option to prepare profit and loss account either in accordance with the provisions of Schedule VI to the Companies Act or in accordance with the provisions of the Act governing such companies], or

b. any other company shall be calculated on the basis of profit and loss account prepared in accordance with Schedule VI of the Companies Act, 1956 or statement of profit and loss prepared in accordance with Schedule III of the Companies Act, 2013.

• *Foreign company* - With effect from the assessment year 2001-02, the provisions of minimum alternate tax are not applicable to a foreign company in the following two cases—

a. the assessee is a resident of a country/specified territory with which India has an agreement under section 90/90A and the assessee does not have a permanent establishment in India in accordance with the provisions of such agreement;

b. the assessee is a resident of a country with which India does not have an agreement referred to above and the assessee is not required to seek registration under any law for the time being in force relating to companies.

207.1-1 *BOOK PROFIT - HOW TO DETERMINE [SEC. 115JB]* - For computation of book profit, one may proceed as follows –

• *Step 1* - Find out net profit [before other comprehensive income (OCI)] as per statement of profit and loss of the company [*see* para 207.1-1a].

• *Step 2* -Make adjustments which are given under *Explanation 1* to section 115JB(2) [*see* paras 207.1-1b to 207.1-1b$].

• *Step 3* - Make specific adjustments in the case of demerger as given by sub-section (2B) to section 115JB$.

• *Step 4* - Make further adjustment pertaining to OCI items that will be permanently recorded in reserves (*i.e.*, never to be reclassified to the statement of profit and loss)$.

207.1-1a ASSESSING OFFICER'S POWER TO ALTER NET PROFIT - Only in the following two cases, the Assessing Officer can rewrite the profit and loss account —

• *If profit and loss account is not prepared according to the Companies Act* - If it is discovered that the profit and loss account is not drawn up in accordance with the provisions of the Companies Act, the Assessing Officer can recalculate the net profit. In a case where there is no allegation of fraud or misrepresentation but only a difference of opinion as to the question whether a particular amount should be properly shown in the profit and loss account or in the balance sheet, the provisions of section 115JB do not empower the Assessing Officer to disturb the profit as shown by the assessee.

• *If accounting policies, accounting standards or rates or method of depreciation are different* - According to the first proviso to section 115JB(2), the accounting policies, the accounting standards adopted for preparing such accounts, the method and rates of depreciation which have been adopted for preparation of the profit and loss account laid before the annual general meeting, should be followed while preparing profit and loss account for the purpose of computing book profit under section 115JB.

Some companies follow an accounting year under the Companies Act which is different from financial year (*i.e.*, previous year ending March 31) under the Income-tax Act. These companies generally prepare two sets of accounts—one for the Companies Act and another for the Income-tax Act. Different accounting policies/standards, and method or rate of depreciation are adopted in two sets of account so that higher profits is reported to shareholders and lower profit is disclosed to tax authorities.

To curb the aforesaid practice, second proviso to section 115JB(2) has been incorporated to ensure that accounting policies, accounting standards, depreciation method and rates of depreciation for two sets of account shall be the same. In case it is not so, the Assessing Officer can recalculate net profit after adopting the same accounting policies, accounting standards and depreciation method and rates which have been adopted for reporting profit to shareholders.

207.1-1b ADJUSTMENT TO NET PROFIT TO CONVERT IT INTO BOOK PROFIT - Net profit as shown in profit and loss account shall be adjusted as follows—

Positive adjustments - Net profit as shown in profit and loss account (prepared in accordance with the provisions of Parts II and III of the Sixth Schedule to the Companies Act, 1956) or statement of profit and loss (prepared in accordance with Schedule III of the Companies Act, 2013) is to be increased by the following amounts if debited to the profit and loss account –

$ For these adjustments, log on to *taxmann.com/readyreckoner.aspx*.

Amount to be added back if debited to profit and loss account	*Comments*
1. Income-tax paid or payable and the provisions therefor	Income-tax, interest under the Income-tax Act, dividend tax under section 115-O, distribution tax under section 115R including surcharge, education cess and secondary and higher education cess/health and education cess if debited to profit and loss account shall be added back. No adjustment is required in respect of the following taxes (including interest, penalty, fine, surcharge, education cess, etc.) : Securities transaction tax, banking cash transaction tax, wealth-tax, gift-tax, fringe benefit tax, indirect taxes. Moreover, no adjustment is required in respect of penalty/time under the Income-tax Act.
2. Amounts carried to any reserves, by whatever name called	No adjustment is required in respect of reserve created under section 33AC with effect from the assessment year 2003-04.
3. Amount or amounts set aside to provisions made for meeting liabilities, other than ascertained liabilities	
4. Amount by way of provision for losses of subsidiary companies	
5. Amount or amounts of dividends paid or proposed	
6. Amount of expenditure relatable to certain incomes (if such income is not subject to minimum alternate tax)	Expenses pertaining to income given under (*10*) below if debited to profit and loss account shall be added back.
7. (From the assessment year 2007-08), the amount of depreciation	*See* para 207.1-1b[4]
8. Amount of deferred tax and the provisions therefor and the amount or amounts set aside as provision for diminution in the value of any asset.[98]	Inserted with retrospective effect from the assessment year 2001-02
8A. Amount standing in revaluation reserve relating to revalued asset on the retirement or disposal of such asset	Applicable from the assessment year 2013-14
8B. Amount of income/loss in the case of units referred to in section 47(*xvii*)	*See* para 207.1-1b[5].

Negative adjustments - Net profit as shown in the profit and loss account is to be reduced by the following amounts :

Amount to be deducted from net profit	*Comments*
9. Amount withdrawn from reserves or provisions, if any such amount is credited to the profit and loss account	*See* para 207.1-1b[1]
10. Income exempt from tax	The following income, if credited to profit and loss account, shall be deducted– *a.* long-term capital gain exempt under section 10(*38*) for the assessment years 2005-06 and 2006-07; *b.* income exempt under section 10(*23G*) up to the assessment year 2004-05; *c.* income exempt under other clauses of section 10; *d.* income exempt under sections 10A and 10B up to the assessment year 2007-08; *e.* income exempt under sections 11 and 12; *f.* share of profit from an AOP on which no income-tax is payable in accordance with the provisions of section 86 (applicable from the assessment year 2016-17);

98. Law does not require that some value of the asset must remain after diminution, as a precondition for adding it to the net profit - *ITO* v. *TCFC Finance Limited* [2011] 10 taxmann.com 144 (Mum. - ITAT).

Amount to be deducted from net profit	*Comments*
	g. (in the case of a foreign company) interest, royalty or technical fees chargeable to tax under sections 115A to 115BBE, or capital gain arising on transactions in securities, if income-tax payable in respect of these incomes under normal provisions (other than provisions governing MAT) is less than the rate of MAT (applicable from the assessment year 2016-17); and *h.* royalty in respect of patent chargeable to tax under section 115BBF. The above incomes are not subject to minimum alternate tax. Moreover, there is no minimum alternate tax (*a*) in respect of income arising after March 31, 2005 (but up to the assessment year 2011-12) from special economic zone to a developer or entrepreneur, (*b*) in respect of income of shipping companies subject to the provisions of "tonnage income", (*c*) income from life insurance business of a company (arising after March 31, 2000) and income of a foreign company taxable under sections 44B, 44BB, 44BBA and 44BBB (arising after March 31, 2000).
11. Depreciation (other than because of revaluation of assets) debited to profit and loss account (applicable from the assessment year 2007-08 onwards)	*See* para 207.1-1b[4]
12. Amount withdrawn from revaluation reserve credited to profit and loss account to the extent it does not exceed the amount of depreciation on account of revaluation of assets [applicable from the assessment year 2007-08]	*See* para 207.1-1b[4]
12A. Aggregate amount of unabsorbed depreciation and loss brought forward if corporate insolvency resolution process has been started	*See* para 207.1-1b[6]
13. Amount of loss (before depreciation) brought forward or unabsorbed depreciation, whichever is less, as per books of account [not being a company which is covered by *Item 12A* (supra)]	*See* para 207.1-1b[2]
14. Amount of profit eligible for deduction under sections 80HHC, 80HHE and 80HHF	This adjustment does not have any practical utility now a days[99] and the reference of sections 80HHB, 80HHE and 80HHF have been omitted with effect from the assessment year 2005-06.
15. Profit of sick industrial unit	*See* para 207.1-1b[3]
16. The amount of deferred tax, if any such amount is credited to the profit and loss account.	Inserted with effect from the assessment year 2001-02.
16A. Amount of income/loss in the case of units referred to in section 47(*xvii*)	*See* para 207.1-1b[5].

No adjustment is required in respect of capital profit credited to profit and loss account even if it is exempt under section 54EC—*N.J. Jose & Co. (P.) Ltd.* v. *CIT* [2008] 174 Taxman 141 (Ker.).

207.1-1b[1] *Reserves or provision credited to profit and loss account* - The amount withdrawn from reserves/provision and credited to profit and loss account shall be reduced as follows—

99. However, the Apex Court in the case of *Ajanta Pharma Ltd.* v. *CIT* [2010] 194 Taxman 358 has held that amount computed under section 80HHC will be deducted from net profit to convert it into book profit, even if deduction under section 80HHC is not available now-a-days while calculating taxable income. To supersede the ruling of Apex Court in the case of *Ajanta Pharma Ltd.* (*supra*), clauses (*iv*), (*v*) and (*vi*) have been omitted by the Finance Act, 2011 (with effect from the assessment year 2005-06) in *Explanation 1* to section 115JB(2).

a. the amount withdrawn from any reserve created before April 1, 1997 otherwise than by way of a debit to the profit and loss account, shall not be reduced from the book profits; and

b. the amount withdrawn from any reserves or provisions created on or after April 1, 1997, which are credited to the profit and loss account, shall not be reduced from the book profits, unless the book profits were increased by the amount transferred to such reserves or provisions in the year of creation of such reserves (out of which the said amount was withdrawn).

207.1-1b[2] *Brought forward depreciation or loss* - Section 115JB provides that in computing book profit, the amount of "loss" brought-forward or unabsorbed depreciation, whichever is less as per books of account, shall be reduced from net profit.

For this purpose, "loss" does not include depreciation and, therefore, in a case where an assessee has shown profit in a year, but after adjustment of depreciation, it results in loss, no adjustment in book profit is allowed.

Where a company does not have both brought forward losses and unabsorbed depreciation but has only one of them, nothing is deductible, since one of the two figures is *nil.*

The table below highlights the above provisions—

(*Rs. in thousand*)

	Brought forward loss before depreciation as per books of account	*Brought forward depreciation as per books of account*	*Brought forward loss after depreciation as per books of account*	*Amount to be deducted from net profit to convert it into book profit*
Case 1	-40	-10	-50	10
Case 2	-30	-40	-70	30
Case 3	-25	0	-25	0
Case 4	0	-10	-10	0
Case 5	+5	-70	-65	0

• *Consolidated loss and depreciation for earlier years in totality to be considered* - The reference to the "amount of brought forward loss or unabsorbed depreciation, whichever is less" shows the intention of the legislature for considering one consolidated figure of brought forward loss or unabsorbed depreciation for the earlier years in totality and not on year to year basis—*Amline Textiles Pvt. Ltd.* v. *ITO* [2009] 27 SOT 155 (Mum.).

• *Adjustment is required even if deduction is not permissible under the Income-tax Act* - In arriving at book profit, lower of amount of brought forward loss or unabsorbed depreciation which is appearing in books of account of assessee has to be allowed, irrespective of the fact whether or not the same is allowable under other provisions of the Income-tax Act—*Fascel Ltd.* v. *ITO* [2008] 117 TTJ (Ahd.) 891.

207.1-1b[3] *Profit of sick industrial undertaking* - Profit of sick industrial undertaking is not subject to the provisions of minimum alternate tax. Consequently if such profit appears in the profit and loss account, it shall be deducted from net profit to find out book profit.

This adjustment is required only in respect of the amount of profits of sick industrial company for the assessment year—

a. commencing from the assessment year relevant to the previous year in which the said company has become a sick industrial company under section 17(1) of the Sick Industrial Companies (Special Provisions) Act, 1985; and

b. ending with the assessment year during which the entire net worth (*i.e.,* paid-up capital *plus* free reserves) of such company becomes equal to or exceeds the accumulated losses.

"Free reserves" for this purpose means all reserves created out of the profits and share premium account but does not include reserves credited out of revaluation of assets, write back of depreciation provisions and amalgamation.

207.1-1b[4] *Depreciation* - Depreciation debited to profit and loss account shall be added back. However, depreciation (not being depreciation which arises because of revaluation of assets) shall be deducted as given in (*11*) (*supra*).

The cumulative impact of the addition and deduction is that book profit will be increased by depreciation (pertaining to revaluation of assets). Some relief is available if there is a withdrawal from the revaluation reserve account and it appears on the credit side of the profit and loss account [*see* (*12*) (*supra*)].

Provisions illustrated - Profit and loss account of 5 companies are given below—

(*Rs. in lakhs*)

Debit side						*Credit side*					
	A	*B*	*C*	*D*	*E*		*A*	*B*	*C*	*D*	*E*
Purchase	37	37	37	37	37	Sales	90	90	90	90	90
Depreciation (normal)	6	6	6	6	6	Withdrawal from reserve (1)	10	10	10	10	10
Depreciation (because of revaluation)	4	4	4	4	0	Withdrawal from reserve (2)	9	9	9	9	9
Other expenses	5	5	5	5	5	Withdrawal from revaluation reserve	0	4	1	11	11
Net profit	57	61	58	68	72						
	109	113	110	120	120		109	113	110	120	120

Reserve (1) was initially created on January 3, 1998 by debiting profit and loss account. However, reserve (2) was initially created on April 2, 1990 without debiting profit and loss account.

Computation of book profit—

	Adjustment No.	*A*	*B*	*C*	*D*	*E*
Net profit as per P&L account		57	61	58	68	72
Add: Depreciation debited to P&L account (total, *i.e.,* normal as well as extra because of revaluation) (Rs. 6 lakh + Rs. 4 lakh)	(7)	10	10	10	10	6
Less: Withdrawal from reserve which was initially created by debiting P&L account	(9)	10	10	10	10	10
Less: Depreciation (normal)	(11)	6	6	6	6	6
Less: Withdrawal from revaluation reserve to the extent it does not exceed revaluation depreciation	(12)	0	4	1	4	0
Book profit		51	51	51	58	62

207.1-1b[5] *Gain/loss on transfer of shares in SPV to business trust (applicable from the assessment year 2016-17)* - The following income will not be subject to MAT –

a. notional capital gain on transfer of a share in a special purpose vehicle (SPV) to a business trust in exchange of units allotted by that trust referred to in section 47(*xvii*); or

b. notional gain resulting from any change in carrying amount of said units.

The above incomes shall be excluded while computing book profit (if these are credited to profit and loss account). Any notional loss [pertaining to (*a*) or (*b*) (*supra*)] shall be added back to convert net profit into book profit (whether or not such notional losses are debited to profit and loss account).

• *Gain or loss on transfer of units referred to in section 47(*xvii*)* - In respect of transfer of units referred to in section 47(*xvii*) the following adjustments will be made –

1. Gain on transfer of units referred to in section 47(*xvii*) shall be deducted from net profit (if it is credited to profit and loss account).

2. Loss on transfer of units referred to in section 47(*xvii*) shall be added to net profit (whether or not it appears in profit and loss account).

3. The amount of loss on transfer of units referred to in section 47(*xvii*) computed by taking into account the cost of the shares exchanged with units referred to in the said clause or the carrying amount of the shares at the time of exchange where such shares are carried at a value other than the cost through profit or loss account, as the case may be, shall be deducted from net profit to convert it into book profit.

4. Amount of gain [if any, pertaining to transaction mentioned in (*3*) (*supra*)] shall be added to net profit to convert it into book profit.

• *Provisions illustrated* - A Ltd. holds 100 shares in B Ltd. [*i.e.,* a Special Purpose Vehicle (SPV)]. In the books of A Ltd., these shares are recorded at Rs. 2,000 per share as on April 1, 2015. During the financial year 2015-16, these 100 shares are exchanged with the 100 units of DEF Trust (*i.e.,* a business trust) and the exchange transaction is recorded (as per Accounting Standard 13) at the fair value of Rs. 3,000 per share. Consequently, it results into a notional gain of Rs. 1,000 per share. At the end of financial year 2016-17, the carrying amount of the units of business trust has been recorded at Rs. 2,500 per unit (which results into a notional loss of Rs.500 per unit). During the financial year 2017-18, these units are transferred for Rs. 4,000 per unit.

In this case, the notional gain of Rs. 1,000 per share shall be excluded from the book profit of the financial year 2015-16. Similarly, the notional loss of Rs. 500 per unit shall be excluded from the book profit of the financial year 2016-17. For computation of book profit for the financial year 2017-18, the actual gain of Rs. 2,000 per share [*i.e.*, actual sale price : Rs. 4,000 per unit *minus* cost of share : Rs. 2,000 per share] shall be included in the section 115JB.

207.1-1b[6] *In case of corporate insolvency/suspension of Board of Directors* - The aggregate amount of unabsorbed depreciation and loss brought forward (before depreciation) shall be excluded in the following cases –

- **Company, and its subsidiary and the subsidiary of such subsidiary, where, the Tribunal, on an application moved by the Central Government under section 241 of the Companies Act, has suspended the Board of Directors** of such company and has appointed new directors (who are nominated by the Central Government under section 242 of the said Act) (applicable with effect from the assessment year 2020-21).
- Company against whom an application for corporate insolvency resolution process has been admitted by the Adjudicating Authority under section 7/9/10 of the Insolvency and Bankruptcy Code (applicable from the assessment year 2018-19).

207.1-2 *MINIMUM INCOME AND TAX* - In the case of a company if tax payable as computed under other provisions (*i.e.*, all provisions ignoring section 115JB) is lower than the amount given below, then book profit is taken as taxable income and the amount given below is taken as tax payable by the company for the assessment year 2019-20[1] —

	If book profit does not exceed Rs.1 crore				*If book profit is in the range of Rs. 1 crore – Rs. 10 crore*				*If book profit exceeds Rs. 10 crore*			
	IT	*SC*	*HEC*	*Total*	*IT*	*SC*	*HEC*	*Total*	*IT*	*SC*	*HEC*	*Total*
Domestic company	18.5[2]	–	0.74	19.24	18.5[2]	1.295	0.7918	20.5868	18.5[2]	2.22	0.8288	21.5488
Foreign company	18.5[2]	–	0.74	19.24	18.5[2]	0.37	0.7548	19.6248	18.5[2]	0.925	0.777	20.202

Note - If book profit of a company exceeds Rs. 1 crore but does not exceed Rs. 10 crore, the minimum alternate tax cannot exceed the following : (Rs. 18.5 lakh + book profit – Rs. 1 crore) + HEC. If, however, book profit exceeds Rs. 10 crore, the minimum alternate tax cannot exceed the following –

a. in the case of domestic company, (Rs. 197.95 lakh + book profit – Rs. 10 crore) + HEC; or

b. in the case of a foreign company, (Rs. 188.7 lakh + book profit – Rs. 10 crore) + HEC.

207.1-3 *REPORT FROM A CHARTERED ACCOUNTANT* - Every company to which section 115JB applies, shall furnish[3] a report (in Form No. 29B) from a chartered accountant certifying that the book profit has been computed in accordance with the provisions of section 115JB along with the return of income filed under section 139(1) or along with the return of income furnished in response to a notice under section 142(1)(*i*).

207.1-4 *LOSS WHICH CAN BE CARRIED FORWARD* - In respect of the relevant previous year, the amounts determined under the provisions of sub-section (2) of section 32 or sub-section (3) of section 32A or clause (*ii*) of sub-section (1) of section 72 or section 73 or section 74 or sub-section (3) of section 74A, shall be allowed to be carried forward to the subsequent year or years.

207.1-5 *CREDIT IN RESPECT OF MAT* - Section 115JAA is applicable for assessment years 1997-98 to 2000-01 and from assessment year 2006-07. It provides that where tax is paid in any assessment year in relation to the deemed income under section 115JA, a tax credit shall be allowed in subsequent years.

207.1-5a SCHEME OF TAX CREDIT - WHEN APPLICABLE - One can find out the amount of tax credit under section 115JAA under the following steps —

1. Find out total income of the company (ignoring the provisions of section 115JA or 115JB) and tax liability (including surcharge and education cess/secondary and higher education cess or health and education cess).

1. For the assessment year 2020-21, *see* Referencer 1.
2. 9 per cent, if the assessee is a unit located in an International Financial Services Centre and derives its income solely in convertible foreign exchange (applicable from the assessment year 2017-18).
3. From April 1, 2014, audit report should be submitted electronically. Provisions pertaining to electronic submission of audit report were not applicable prior to April 1, 2014 (for period prior to April 1, 2014, audit report may be retained by the assessee and it may be furnished in original whenever the Assessing Officer wants to examine it in assessment proceedings or otherwise).

2. Find out 18.5 per cent[4] of book profit (+SC+EC/SHEC or HEC). No tax credit is available under section 115JAA if tax (as computed under step *1*) is equal to or more than tax computed under step 2.

3. The amount of tax credit[5] is equal to the tax paid under step *2* as reduced by the tax computed under step *1*. In other words, the extra tax which is paid only because of provisions of section 115JA or 115JB will be qualified for tax credit under section 115JAA. However, from the assessment year 2018-19, the amount of tax credit in respect of MAT shall not be allowed to be carried forward to subsequent year to the extent such credit relates to the difference between the amount of foreign tax credit (FTC) allowed against MAT and FTC allowable against the tax computed under regular provisions of Act other than the provisions relating to MAT.

Tax credit computed under the above steps can be carried forward for being set off against future tax liability.

207.1-5b CARRY FORWARD AND SET OFF OF TAX CREDIT - The amount of tax credit under section 115JAA shall be carried forward and set off subject to the following propositions —

1. No interest is payable in respect of tax credit.

2. Tax credit shall be allowed set off in a future year in which tax becomes payable on the total income computed in accordance with the provisions other than section 115JA or 115JB.

3. Set off in respect of brought forward tax credit will be allowed for any assessment year to the extent of—

a. tax computed on total income (ignoring section 115JA or 115JB) ; *minus*

b. 18.5 per cent[6] [+ SC + (EC + SHEC) or HEC] of book profit.

It may be noted that set off is not allowed in the year in which tax computed under (*a*) *supra* is lower than (*b*) *supra*.

4. Carry forward shall not be allowed beyond the 10th assessment year (up to the assessment year 2017-18)/ 15th assessment year (from the assessment year 2018-19)] immediately succeeding the assessment year in which tax credit becomes allowable.

5. Carry forward and set off of MAT credit shall not apply to a limited liability partnership which has been converted from a private company or unlisted public company. This rule will be applicable whether or not conversion takes place by satisfying the requirement of section 47(*xiiib*).

6. There is no other condition to claim the benefit of set off of tax credit. For instance, there is no provision for submission of return of income within the time limit prescribed by section 139, or for payment of tax in time. Tax credit is allowed even if tax was paid late. Moreover, there is no provision that the Assessing Officer should determine the tax credit which shall be carried forward.

207.1-5c PROVISIONS ILLUSTRATED - The following case study is given to have a better understanding of the provisions of section 115JAA discussed above.

Assessment years *(Rs. in thousand)*

	2006-07	*2007-08*	*2008-09*	*2009-10*	*2010-11*	*2011-12*	*2012-13*
1. Book profit	670	750	1200.97	171.55	925.95	296.82	750.77
2. Taxable income (ignoring section 115JB)	120	150	420.46	(-)40	435.73	186.28	648.16
3. Tax on (*1*) @ 18.5%[7] (+ SC + EC + SHEC)	56.38	84.15	123.70	17.67	143.06	55.03	143.06
4. Tax on (*2*) @ 30% (+SC+EC+SHEC)	40.39	50.49	129.93	*Nil*	134.64	57.56	200.28
5. Whether tax credit is available (up to which year)	*Yes* (2016-17)	*Yes* (2017-18)	*No*	*Yes* (2019-20)	*Yes*	*No*	*No*
6. Amount of credit which is available [*i.e.*, (*3*)—(*4*)]	15.99	33.66	*Nil*	17.67	8.42	*NA*	*NA*

4. 7.5 per cent for the assessment years 2001-02 to 2006-07, 10 per cent for the assessment years 2007-08 to 2009-10, 15 per cent for the assessment year 2010-11 and 18 per cent for the assessment year 2011-12. Moreover, with effect from the assessment year 2017-18, it is 9 per cent in case the assessee is a unit located in an International Financial Services Centre and derives its income solely in convertible foreign exchange.
5. It is inclusive of surcharge and education cess – *Consolidated Securities Ltd.* v. *CIT* [2018] 96 taxmann.com 418 (Delhi).
6. 9 per cent in case the assessee is a unit located in an International Financial Services Centre and derives its income solely in convertible foreign exchange (applicable from the assessment year 2017-18).
7. 7.5 per cent for the assessment year 2006-07, 10 per cent for the assessment years 2007-08 to 2009-10, 15 per cent for the assessment year 2010-11 and 18 per cent for the assessment year 2011-12.

	2006-07	*2007-08*	*2008-09*	*2009-10*	*2010-11*	*2011-12*	*2012-13*
7. Cumulative credit for being set off	15.99	49.65	49.65	61.09	69.51	69.51	66.98
8. Whether brought forward tax credit can be set off during the current year [only if *(4)* is more than *(3)*]	*NA*	*NA*	*Yes*	*NA*	*NA*	*Yes*	*Yes*
9. Maximum amount which can be set off during the current year [*i.e.*, the excess of *(4)* over *(3)*, subject to maximum of *(7)*]	*NA*	*NA*	6.23	*NA*	*NA*	2.53	57.22
10. Credit which is lapsed	*NA*	*NA*	*Nil*	*NA*	*NA*	*Nil*	*Nil*
11. How much can be carried forward [*i.e.*, *(7)*—*(9)*—*(10)*]	15.99	49.65	43.42	61.09	69.51	66.98	9.76
12. Tax payable for the current year	56.38	84.15	123.7	17.67	143.06	55.03	143.06

207-E1 X Ltd. is engaged in the business of manufacture of garments.

	Rs.
Sale proceeds of goods (domestic sale)	22,23,900
Sale proceeds of goods (export sale)	5,76,100
Amount withdrawn from general reserve (reserve was created in 1996-97 by debiting P&L A/c)	2,00,000
Amount withdrawn from revaluation reserve	1,50,000
Total	31,50,000
Less : Expenses	
Depreciation (normal)	6,16,000
Depreciation (extra depreciation because of revaluation)	2,70,000
Salary and wages	2,20,000
Income-tax	3,50,000
Outstanding customs duty (not paid as yet)	17,500
Proposed dividend	60,000
Consultation fees paid to a tax expert	21,000
Other expenses	1,39,000
Net profit	14,56,500

For tax purposes the company wants to claim the following :

- Deduction under section 80-IB (30 per cent of Rs. 14,56,500).
- Depreciation under section 32 (Rs. 5,36,000)

The company wants to set off the following losses/allowances :

	For tax purposes *Rs.*	*For accounting purposes* *Rs.*
Brought forward loss of 2010-11	14,70,000	4,00,000
Unabsorbed depreciation	—	70,000

Compute the net income and tax liability of X Ltd. for the assessment year 2019-20 assuming that X Ltd. has a (deemed) long-term capital gain of Rs. 60,000 under proviso (*i*) to section 54D(2) which is not credited in profit and loss account.

•

	Rs.
Net profit as per P&L a/c	14,56,500
Add :	
Excess depreciation [*i.e.*, Rs. 6,16,000+Rs. 2,70,000 — Rs. 5,36,000]	3,50,000
Income-tax	3,50,000
Customs duty which is not paid	17,500
Proposed dividend	60,000
Total	22,34,000
Less : Amount withdrawn from reserve (*i.e.*, Rs. 2,00,000 + Rs. 1,50,000)	3,50,000
Business income	18,84,000
Less : Unabsorbed loss	14,70,000
Business income	4,14,000
Long-term capital gain	60,000

	Rs.
Gross total income	4,74,000
Less : Deductions under section 80-IB [30% of Rs. 4,14,000]	1,24,200
Net income (rounded off)	3,49,800
Tax liability (under normal provisions) [20% of Rs. 60,000 + 30% of Rs. 2,89,800, *plus* 4% of tax as HEC]	1,02,900
Book profit	
Net profit	14,56,500
Add :	
Depreciation [*i.e.*, Rs. 6,16,000 + Rs. 2,70,000]	8,86,000
Income-tax	3,50,000
Proposed dividend	60,000
Less :	
Amount withdrawn from general reserve	(–) 2,00,000
Unabsorbed depreciation	(–) 70,000
Depreciation (normal)	(–)6,16,000
Amount withdrawn from revaluation reserve to the extent it does not exceed extra depreciation because of revaluation	(–) 1,50,000
Book profit	17,16,500
Tax liability (19.24% of book profit)	3,30,250

X Ltd. will pay Rs. 3,30,250 as tax for the assessment year 2019-20 as per section 115JB. Tax credit is however, available in respect of excess tax (*i.e.*, Rs. 2,27,350) under section 115JB.

207.2 ***Tax on distributed profit [applicable from June 1, 1997 to March 31, 2002 and from April 1, 2003 onwards]*** - It is applicable during June 1, 1997 to March 31, 2002 and from April 1, 2003 onwards.

207.2-1 *BASIS OF CHARGE [SEC. 115-O(1)]* - A separate and additional charge has been created by section 115-O(1). It is subject to the following propositions—

1. Tax on distributed profit is in addition to income-tax chargeable in respect of total income.

2. Only a domestic company (not a foreign company) is liable for above tax [*see* para 205.2].

3. Any amount declared, distributed or paid by a domestic company by way of dividend shall be charged to additional tax.

4. It is applicable whether the dividend is interim or otherwise.

5. It is applicable only if such dividend is declared, distributed or paid on or after June 1, 1997 but before April 1, 2002 or on or after April 1, 2003. However, dividend tax is not applicable in the case of—

a. dividend declared, distributed or paid during April 1, 2005 and May 31, 2011 by a developer/enterprise out of current income from a special economic zone;

b. the amount of dividend paid on or after April 1, 2009 to any person for, or on behalf of, the new pension system trust;

c. (with effect from June 1, 2016), any amount declared, distributed or paid by the specified domestic company by way of interim/final dividend to a business trust out of its current income on or after a specified date;

d. any interim/final dividend declared, distributed or paid on or after April 1, 2017 by a company (being a unit established on or after April 1, 2016 in an International Financial Services Centre) deriving income solely in convertible foreign exchange out of its current income (or **income accumulated as a unit of International Financial Services Centre** after April 1, 2017);

e. any dividend distributed by the recipient out of (*d*) (*supra*); and

f. any loan or advance which is deemed as dividend (before April 1, 2018) under section 2(*22*)(*e*).

6. It is applicable whether such dividend is paid out of current profit or accumulated profit.

• *Relief in the case of inter-corporate dividend in some cases* - Section 115-O(1A) provides a relief when a holding company has received dividend from its subsidiary company and in the same financial year the holding company declares dividends to its shareholders. When dividend is declared, distributed or paid by the holding company to its shareholders, dividend tax shall be payable on the following amount –

	Rs.
Dividend declared, distributed or paid by the holding company to its shareholders (*a*)	*xxx*
Less: Dividend received by holding company from its subsidiary company in the same financial year (*b*)	*xxx*
Balance [*i.e.*, (*a*) – (*b*)] on which dividend tax is payable by the holding company	*xxx*

The aforesaid relief is available only in the situations given below –

1. Subsidiary company is a domestic company and it has paid tax under section 115-O when dividend is paid to the holding company and holding company is not subsidiary of any other company (applicable from April 1, 2008 to June 30, 2012).

2. Subsidiary company is a domestic company and it has paid tax under section 115-O when dividend is paid to the holding company (applicable from July 1, 2012).

3. Subsidiary company is a foreign company and dividend received by the holding company from the subsidiary company is taxable in the hands of holding company under section 115BBD (applicable from June 1, 2013).

For the aforesaid purposes, a company shall be a subsidiary of another company, if such other company holds more than half in nominal value of the equity share capital of the company.

207.2-2 *WHAT IS "DIVIDEND"* - Dividend declared, distributed or paid on or after June 1, 1997 but before April 1, 2002 or on or after April 1, 2003 is subject to additional tax. For the purpose of section 115-O the expression "dividend" shall have the same meaning as is given to "dividend" under section 2(*22*) but it shall not include (up to March 31, 2018) sub-clause (*e*) of section 2(*22*).

207.2-3 *TAX RATE* - The rate of dividend tax is as follows :

	Dividend tax (as a % of dividend)	*Surcharge (as a % of dividend tax)*	*EC/SHEC or HEC (as a % of dividend tax and surcharge)*	*Total (as a % of dividend)*
• April 1, 2000 to May 31, 2000	10	10	*Nil*	11
• June 1, 2000 to January 3, 2001	20	10	*Nil*	22
• January 4, 2001 to February 2, 2001	20	11	*Nil*	22.20
• February 3, 2001 to March 31, 2001	20	13	*Nil*	22.60
• April 1, 2001 to May 31, 2001	20	2	*Nil*	20.40
• June 1, 2001 to March 21, 2002	10	2	*Nil*	10.20
• April 1, 2002 to March 31, 2003	NA	NA	NA	NA
• April 1, 2003 to March 31, 2004	12.5	2.5	*Nil*	12.8125
• From April 1, 2004 to March 31, 2005	12.5	2.5	2	13.06875
• From April 1, 2005 to March 31, 2007	12.5	10	2	14.025
• From April 1, 2007 to March 31, 2010	15	10	3	16.995
• From April 1, 2010 to March 31, 2011	15	7.5	3	16.60875
• From April 1, 2011 to March 31, 2013	15	5	3	16.2225
• From April 1, 2013 to September 30, 2014	15	10	3	16.995
• From October 1, 2014 to March 31, 2015	17.64706	10	3	19.99412
• From April 1, 2015 to March 31, 2018	17.64706	12	3	20.357647
• From April 1, 2018 [not being deemed dividend under section 2(*22*)(*e*)]	17.64706	12	4	20.555294
• From April 1, 2018 [being deemed dividend under section 2(*22*)(*e*)]	30	12	4	34.944

207.2-4 *NATURE OF TAX* - The levy of additional tax is in addition to normal tax payable by a company. This additional tax incidence cannot be avoided even if no income-tax is payable by a domestic company on its total income computed under the provisions of the Act. Moreover, brought forward MAT credit under section 115JAA cannot be adjusted against the additional tax on dividend.

207.2-5 *WHEN THE DIVIDEND TAX SHOULD BE PAID* - The tax on distributed profit shall be paid within 14 days from the date of—

a. declaration of any dividend; or

b. distribution of any dividend; or

c. payment of any dividend,

whichever is the earliest.

Who is liable to pay tax - The principal officer of the domestic company and the company shall be liable to pay the aforesaid tax.

207.2-6 *DIVIDEND TAX - IS IT FINAL LEVY* - Tax on dividend paid by a domestic company shall be taken as the final tax payment in respect of the amount declared, distributed or paid as dividend. In respect of tax so paid, no credit is available to the company paying tax, or the recipient of dividend or to any other person. By virtue of section 10(*34*), dividend income (in respect of which dividend tax is applicable under section 115-O) is exempt in the hands of recipient shareholders. However, this rule is subject to an exception given below—

- *Tax on certain dividends under section 115BBDA in the hands of shareholders* - In the case of a resident individual/HUF/firm[8], aggregate dividend income from domestic companies in excess of Rs. 10 lakh is chargeable to tax at the rate of 10 per cent [+ SC + (EC + SHEC) or HEC] with effect from the assessment year 2017-18. This additional tax in the hands of shareholders under section 115BBDA is applicable even if the company (which declares dividend) is subject to dividend distribution tax under section 115-O. However, tax under section 115BBDA is not applicable in the case of deemed dividend under section 2(*22*)(*e*).

207.2-7 *DIVIDEND TAX IS NOT DEDUCTIBLE* - The company (or the shareholders) cannot claim any deduction from taxable income in respect of dividend tax levied under section 115-O. Moreover, no deduction is available from the tax on dividend under any provision.

207.2-8 *INTEREST FOR NON-PAYMENT OF TAX [SEC. 115P]* - If the company or the principal officer fails to pay the whole or any part of dividend tax within the specified time-limit, then it or he shall be liable to interest in addition to dividend tax as follows—

Rate of interest	1 per cent (up to May 31, 2000 : 2 per cent, 1.5 per cent from June 1, 2000 to May 31, 2001 and 1.25 per cent from June 1, 2001 to September 7, 2003) per month or part thereof.
Amount on which interest is chargeable	Amount of tax as reduced by the amount paid within the time-limit
Period for which interest is payable	Interest is chargeable for the period commencing from the next date after the last date of payment and ending on the date of actual payment.

207.2-9 *WHEN COMPANY IS DEEMED TO BE IN DEFAULT [SEC. 115Q]* - In case of domestic company or principal officer of a domestic company does not pay tax on distributed profits within the specified time-limit, then he or it shall be deemed to be an assessee in default in respect of the amount of tax payable by him or it. Consequently, all provisions regarding collection and recovery of tax contained in the Act would apply.

207.2-10 *PENALTY UNDER SECTION 271C* - Section 271C has been amended with effect from June 1, 1997 to provide that if any person fails to comply with the provisions of section 115-O, he shall be liable to pay penalty of a sum equal to the amount of tax which he has failed to pay. The penalty is, however, not applicable, if the assessee proves that there was reasonable cause for failure.

207.2-11 *PROSECUTION* - Section 276B has been amended with effect from June 1, 1997 to provide that if a person fails to pay to the credit of the Central Government the tax payable by him, as required by or under the provisions of section 115-O, he shall be punishable with rigorous imprisonment for a term which shall not be less than three months but which may extend to seven years and with fine.

However, no person shall be punishable if he proves that there was a reasonable cause for the default/failure.

Tax on income distributed to unit holders [Secs. 115R, 115S and 115T, applicable from June 1, 1999 to March 31, 2002 and from April 1, 2003 onwards]

207A. The provisions of these sections are given below. These provisions are applicable for June 1, 1999 to March 31, 2002 and from April 1, 2003 onwards—

1. The income distributed to a unit holder of the Unit Trust of India or a Mutual Fund shall be charged to tax under section 115R at a flat rate [*see* Referencer 1] to be payable by the Unit Trust of India or the Mutual Fund, as the case may be. This tax liability of the Unit Trust of India or Mutual Funds is notwithstanding the existing provisions of the Unit Trust of India Act, 1963, which states that the Unit Trust of India is not liable to tax on its income, profits or gains, or section 10(*23D*) which exempts the income of a Mutual Fund from income-tax.

2. The person responsible for making the payment of income distributed by the UTI or a Mutual Fund and the UTI or the Mutual Fund itself, as the case may be, shall be liable to pay the tax to the credit of the Central Government within 14 days from the date of distribution or payment of such income, whichever is earlier.

---

8. From the assessment year 2018-19, this provision will be applicable if the shareholder is any person [but other than a domestic company, a fund/trust/institute whose income is exempt under section 10(*23C*)(*iv*)/(*v*)/(*vi*)/(*via*), or a trust or institute registered under section 12A/12AA].

3. No deduction under any other provision of the Act shall be allowed to the Unit Trust of India or to a Mutual Fund in respect of the income which has been charged to the aforesaid tax.

4. If the person or UTI or Mutual Fund liable to make the payment fails to so pay the tax to the credit of the Central Government, he or it shall be liable to pay simple interest at the rate of 1 per cent (2 per cent up to May 31, 2000, 1.5 per cent from June 1, 2000 to May 31, 2001 and 1.25 per cent from June 1, 2001 to September 7, 2003) every month or part thereof on such amount of tax which has not been paid or was not paid in time.

5. If the person or UTI or Mutual Fund liable to make the payment fails to so pay the tax to the credit of the Central Government, he or it shall be deemed to be an assessee in default in respect of the amount of tax payable and all the provisions of the Act for the collection and recovery of income-tax shall apply.

6. The person responsible for making payment of the income distributed by the Unit Trust of India or the Mutual Fund and the Unit Trust of India or the Mutual Fund, as the case may be, shall be liable to file a statement of distributed income in Form No. 63 (for UTI)[9] or Form No. 63A (for mutual fund)[9], giving details of income distributed to unit holders, tax paid thereon and other relevant details. The statement should be submitted on or before September 15 giving details of amount distributed during the immediately preceding previous year.

Tax on distributed income of domestic company for buy-back of shares [Sec. 115QA, applicable from June 1, 2013]

207B. Amount distributed by a domestic company for buy-back of shares is subject to an additional tax under section 115QA with effect from June 1, 2013. Provisions of this section are given below –

1. Section 115QA is applicable when amount is distributed by a domestic company for buy-back of its shares.

2. Such shares are –

- Not listed in any recognized stock exchange (applicable up to July 4, 2019).
- **Listed or not unlisted** in any recognised stock exchange (applicable on or after July 5, 2019).

3. For this purpose, buy-back means purchase by a company of its own shares in accordance with the provisions of section 77A of the Companies Act or (with effect from June 1, 2016) any law for the time being in force relating to companies.

4. 20 per cent [+ SC + (EC + SHEC) or HEC] of "distributed income" is additional tax payable under section 115QA by the company purchasing its own shares. "Distributed income" means the consideration paid by the company on buy-back of shares as reduced by the amount which was received by the company for issue of such shares, determined in the manner as may be prescribed.

5. The aforesaid tax is payable even if regular tax is not payable by the company on its income. For instance, even if the entire income of the company is exempt under section 10, the aforesaid tax is applicable.

6. The aforesaid tax is payable within 14 days from the date of payment of any consideration to the shareholders on buy-back of shares.

7. The aforesaid tax shall be treated as final payment of tax and no credit will be available to the company or shareholders.

8. Income which is chargeable to tax under the aforesaid provisions will not be deductible under any provision of the Act in the hands of the company or shareholders.

9. For short payment or non-payment of the aforesaid tax, the company (as well as the principal officer of the company) shall be liable for interest at the rate of 1 per cent per month (or part thereof).

10. Any income arising to shareholders on account of buy back of shares (covered by the aforesaid provisions) is exempt under section 10(*34A*).

CO-OPERATIVE SOCIETIES

Meaning of co-operative society [Sec. 2(19)]

208. "Co-operative society" means a society registered under the Co-operative Societies Act, 1912, or under any other law for the time being in force in any State for the registration of co-operative societies. For the purpose of the Income tax Act, a regional rural bank is deemed to be a co-operative society— Circular No. 319, dated January 11, 1982.

9. Form Nos. 63 and 63A are to be submitted electronically.

How to arrive at taxable income

209. First, compute gross total income, ignoring income exempt from tax under section 10, if any. Then, deduct permissible deductions under sections 80G, 80GGA, 80GGC, 80-IA, 80-IB, 80-IC, 80JJA, 80JJAA and 80P [*see* para 107]. For ready reference of different deductions available to a co-operative society under the Income-tax Act, *see* Referencer 7.

209.1 ***Deductions under section 80P***[10] - The following amounts are allowed as deduction under this section. However, from the assessment year 2007-08 onwards, deduction under section 80P is not available to a co-operative bank. A primary agricultural credit society, a primary co-operative agricultural and rural development bank will continue to get deduction under section 80P.

• The whole of the amount of the profits attributable to any one or more of the following activities in the case of a co-operative society engaged in—

a. carrying on the business of banking or providing credit facilities to its member ; or

b. a cottage industry ; or

c. the marketing of the agricultural produce grown by its members ; or

d. the purchase of agricultural implements, seeds, livestock or other articles intended for agriculture for the purposes of supplying them to its members ; or

e. the processing, without the aid of power, of the agricultural produce of its members ; or

f. the collective disposal of the labour of its members ; or

g. fishing or allied activities, that is to say, the catching, curing, processing, preserving, storing or marketing of fish or the purchase of materials and equipment in connection therewith for the purpose of supplying them to its members.

In the case of a co-operative society falling under (*f*) and (*g*), deduction is available subject to the condition that the rules and bye-laws of the society restrict the voting rights to the following classes of its members, *viz.*, the individuals who contribute their labour or, as the case may be, carry on the fishing or allied activities, the co-operative credit societies which provide financial assistance to the society, and the State Government.

• The whole of the amount of profits in the case of a co-operative society, being a primary society engaged in supplying milk raised by its members to a federal milk co-operative society or, with effect from the assessment year 1979-80, to the Government or a local authority or a Government company or corporation established under the Central, State or Provincial Act. Scope of deduction under section 80P is extended with effect from the assessment year 1984-85 to cover primary co-operative societies which are engaged in the supply of oil seeds, fruits and vegetables. Accordingly, profits derived by a primary co-operative society engaged in supplying oil seeds, fruits or vegetables raised or grown by its members to a federal oil seeds, fruits or vegetables co-operative society, Government, local authority or a Government company or a statutory corporation engaged in supplying oil seeds, fruits or vegetables to the public will be deductible.

• So much of the profits of a co-operative society, engaged in the activities other than those mentioned above, either independently or in addition to all or any of the activities so specified, as does not exceed Rs. 50,000[11] (Rs. 1,00,000[12] in the case of a consumers' co-operative society with effect from the assessment year 1980-81.

• The whole of the interest and dividend income derived by a co-operative society from its investment in any other co-operative society.

• The whole of the income derived by a co-operative society from the letting of godowns or warehouses, for storage, or processing or facilitating the marketing of commodities.

• The whole of the interest income from securities and property income in the case of a co-operative society other than housing society or an urban consumers' society or a society carrying on transport business or a society engaged in manufacturing operations with the aid of power provided gross total income of such co-operative society does not exceed Rs. 20,000.

---

10. Deduction under section 80P is not available unless it is claimed in the return of income (applicable from the assessment year 2003-04 onwards).

11. Rs. 20,000 up to the assessment year 1998-99.

12. Rs. 40,000 up to the assessment year 1998-99.

209.1-1 *WHAT IS COTTAGE INDUSTRY* - What constitutes a "cottage industry" has been the subject-matter of discussion in a number of cases decided by various courts. Based on the ratio of these decisions, a co-operative society engaged in a cottage industry is required to satisfy the following criteria for availing of the benefits under section 80P(2)(*a*)(*ii*) :

a. a cottage industry is one which is carried on small scale with a small amount of capital and a small number of workers and has a turnover which is correspondingly limited;

b. it should not be required to be registered under the Factories Act;

c. it should be owned and managed by the co-operative society;

d. the activities should be carried on by the members of the society and their families. [For this purpose, a family would include self, spouse, parents, children, spouses of the children and any other relative who customarily lives with such a member. Outsiders (*i.e.*, persons other than members and their families) should not work for the society. In other words, the co-operative society should not engage outside hired labour];

e. a member of a co-operative society means a shareholder of the society;

f. the place of work could be an artisan shareholder's residence or it could be a common place provided by the co-operative society;

g. the cottage industry must carry on activity of manufacture, production or processing; it should not be engaged merely in trade, *i.e.*, purchase and sale of the same commodity.

In the case of a weaver's society, so long as weaving is done by the members of the society at their residence or at a common place provided by the society, without any outside labour, such a society will be eligible for deduction under section 80P(2)(*a*)(*ii*) even if certain payments have been made to an outside agency for dyeing, bleaching, transport arrangements, etc., provided it satisfies all other conditions necessary for availing the deduction under section 80P(2)(*a*)(*ii*)—Circular No. 722, dated September 19, 1995.

209.1-2 *OTHER POINTS* - The following points should be noted—

• *Regional rural banks* - Regional Rural Banks are not eligible for deduction under section 80P—Circular No. 6/2010, dated September 20, 2010.

• *Interest on funds not immediately required for business purposes* - If a society regularly earns interest on funds (not required immediately for business purposes), such interest income is taxable under section 56 under the head "Income from other sources" and not eligible for deduction under section 80P—*Totgars' Co-operative Sale Society Ltd.* v. *ITO* [2010] 188 Taxman 282 (SC).

• *Interest on income-tax refund* - Interest received on income-tax refund is subject to deduction under section 80P(2)(*a*)(*i*)—*Maharashtra State Co-operative Bank Ltd.* v. *CIT* [2010] 38 SOT 325 (Mum.)(SB).

Rate of tax

210. For rates applicable to the assessment years 2019-20 and 2020-21, *see* para 0.1-4 [*see* also Tax Table at pages B-49 and B-50]. Rates for the preceding assessment year are given in Referencer 3.

• *Alternate minimum tax* - From the assessment year 2013-14, tax payable by a non-corporate assessee cannot be less than 18.5 per cent[13] [+ SC + (EC + SHEC) or HEC] of "adjusted total income". For detailed discussion, *see* para 190.1.

---

13. 9 per cent in case the assessee is a unit located in an International Financial Services Centre and derives its income solely in convertible foreign exchange (applicable from the assessment year 2019-20).

Tax incidence on trusts

In order to ascertain the tax incidence on a trust, it is necessary to know the nature and character of trust and also the specific mode of computation of its income and exemption. Besides, there are certain incomes which do not qualify for exemption. Moreover, in some cases income of a trust is taxable at maximum marginal rate of tax

Exemption from tax

211. Income of a charitable trust is exempt according to the provisions of sections 11, 12, 12A and 13. The trust should be one established in accordance with law and its objects should fall within the definition of the term "charitable purpose".

Charitable purpose [Sec. 2(*15*)]

212. It is defined to include relief to the poor, education, (with effect from the assessment year 2016-17) yoga[14], medical relief, preservation of environment (including watersheds, forests and wildlife) and preservation of monuments or places or objects of artistic or historic interest, and the advancement of any other object of general public utility.

• *Sports or games* - Promotion of sports and games is considered to be a charitable purpose within the meaning of section 2(*15*). Therefore, an association or institution engaged in the promotion of sports and games can claim exemption under section 11 even if it is not approved under section 10(*23*) — Circular No. 395, dated September 24, 1984.

• *Advancement of any other object of general public utility* - From the assessment year 2009-10, "advancement of any other object of general public utility" shall not be a charitable purpose, if it involves the carrying on of any activity in the nature of trade, commerce or business, or any activity of rendering any service in relation to any trade, commerce or business, for a cess or fee or any other consideration. This restriction is, however, not applicable if the total receipts from any activity in the nature of trade, commerce or business, or any activity of rendering any service in relation to any trade, commerce or business does not exceed the limits given below –

For the assessment years 2009-10 to 2011-12	Rs. 10 lakh during the relevant previous year
For the assessment years 2012-13 to 2015-16	Rs. 25 lakh during the relevant previous year
From the assessment year 2016-17 onwards	20 per cent of total receipts of the relevant previous year of the trust undertaking such activities*

*The above benefit (from the assessment year 2016-17) is available only if such activity is undertaken in the course of actual carrying out of such advancement or any other object of general public utility, regardless of nature of use or application, or retention, of the income from such activity.

Board's Circular No. 11/2008[$], *dated December 19, 2008* – The above restriction does not apply in respect of the first five limbs of section 2(*15*), *i.e.*, relief of the poor, education, yoga, medical relief or preservation of environment, etc. Consequently, where the purpose of a trust or institution is relief of the poor, education, yoga, medical relief or preservation of environment, etc., it will constitute 'charitable purpose' even if it incidentally involves the carrying on of commercial activities. The above restriction applies only to entities whose purpose is "advancement of any other object of general public utility", *i.e.*, the sixth limb of the definition of "charitable purpose" contained in section 2(*15*). Hence, such entities are not eligible for exemption under section 11 or under section 10(*23C*) if they carry on commercial activities and receipts from such activities exceed the limits given in the table above. Whether such an entity is carried on as an activity in the nature of trade, commerce or business, is a question of fact. The decision in such cases depends upon

14. It is well established fact that the practice of yoga gives positive relief in the cases of asthma, migraine, hyper tension, stress, etc. Thus, even for assessment years prior to assessment year 2016-17, yoga qualifies as "medical relief" – *Patanjali Yogpeeth (Nyas)* v. *DIT* [2017] 78 taxmann.com 128 (Delhi).

$ For Circular No. 11/2008, log on to *taxmann.com/readyreckoner.aspx*.

the nature, scope, extent and frequency of the activity. Where industry or trade associations claim both to be charitable institutions as well as mutual organizations and their activities are restricted to contributions from and participation of only their members, these would not fall under the purview of the above restrictions owing to the principle of mutuality. However, if such organizations have dealings with non-members, their claim to be charitable organizations are governed by the additional conditions stipulated in the provisos to section 2(*15*) and given in the table above.

Essential conditions for exemption

213. The compliance of the following main conditions is essential for claiming exemption under section 11 :

- The property from which income is derived should be held under a trust or other legal obligation.
- The property should be held for charitable or religious purposes. In the case of a charitable trust created on or after April 1, 1962, the further conditions are :

a. the trust should not be created for the benefit of any particular religious community or caste ;

b. no part of the income should ensure directly or indirectly for the benefit of the settlor or other specified persons ;

c. the property should be held wholly for charitable purposes.

The conditions mentioned at (*b*) and (*c*) also apply to religious trust created on or after April 1, 1962.

- The exemption is confined to only such portion of the trust's income which is applied to charitable or religious purposes or is accumulated for applying to such purposes within the limits of accumulation permitted under section 11(1) and (2) [*see* paras 214 and 215].
- The exemption is restricted to such portion of the income as is applied to charitable or religious purposes in India except in the cases covered by section 11(1)(*c*).
- Where trust property comprises a business undertaking, the income shown in the books of account should not be less than the income determined by the Assessing Officer according to the provisions of the Act. However, the exemption from tax will not be available to any religious or charitable trust or institution in respect of business profits, unless—

a. the business is carried on by the trust wholly for public religious purposes and the business consists of printing and publication of books or publication of books or is of a kind notified by the Government ; or

b. the business is carried on by the institution wholly for charitable purposes and the work in connection with the business is mainly carried on by the beneficiaries of the institution ;

and the separate books of account are maintained by the trust/institution of such business. From the assessment year 1992-93, trusts or institutions can carry out business activities if business activities are incidental to the attainment of its objectives and separate books of account are maintained. In other words, irrespective of whether any business is carried on by such a trust or institution or the business undertaking itself is held in trust, in either case, the trust or institution is charged to tax on such profits and gains at the rates of tax applicable in the case of individuals, association of persons, body of individuals, etc., if the above conditions are not satisfied.

- The trust should get itself registered[15] [Form No. 10A for application[$]] with the Commissioner of Income-tax.

There is no time-limit for this purpose (if application is made after May 31, 2007). However, if a trust applies for registration (after May 31, 2007), the registration shall be effective only prospectively (*i.e.*, after registration, exemption under section 11 will be available only from the previous year in which application is made). Non-application of registration for the period prior to the year of registration causes genuine hardship to charitable organisations. Due to absence of registration, tax liability gets attached even though they may otherwise be eligible for exemption and fulfil other substantive conditions. The power of condonation of delay in seeking registration is not available under the section.

In order to provide relief to such trusts and remove hardship in genuine cases, section 12A has been amended (with effect from October 1, 2014[16]). Under the amended provisions, the benefit of sections 11 and 12 shall be available in respect of any income derived from property held under trust in any assessment proceeding for an earlier assessment year which is pending before the Assessing Officer as on the date of such registration, if the objects and activities of such trust or institution in the relevant earlier assessment year are the same as those on the basis of which such registration has been granted. Further, no action for reopening of an assessment under section 147 shall be taken by the Assessing Officer in the case of such trust or institution for any

15. Where a trust/institution has been granted registration under section 12A/12AA and, subsequently, it has adopted or undertaken modifications of the objects which do not conform to the conditions of registration, it shall be required to obtain fresh registration by making an application within a period of 30 days from the date of such adoption or modifications of the objects in the prescribed form and manner (applicable from the assessment year 2018-19).

16. It is applicable retrospectively or even for period prior to October 1, 2014 – *Punjab Educational Society* v. *ITO* [2018] 168 ITD 109 (Asr.).

[$] Application in Form No. 10A is required to be submitted online. For attachments and other procedures, log on to *taxmann.com/readyreckoner.aspx.*

assessment year preceding the first assessment year for which the registration applies, merely for the reason that such trust or institution has not obtained the registration under section 12AA for the said assessment year. However, the above benefits would not be available in case of any trust or institution which at any time had applied for registration and the same was refused under section 12AA or a registration once granted was cancelled.

❑ The Commissioner shall call for documents and information and hold enquiries regarding the genuineness of the trust or institution. **The Commissioner can also (with effect from September 1, 2019) satisfy himself about the compliance of the trust or institution to requirements of any other law which is material for the purpose of achieving its objects.** After he is satisfied about the charitable or religious nature of the objects and genuineness of the activities of the trust or institution, he will pass an order granting registration and if he is not so satisfied, he will pass an order refusing registration, subject to the condition that an opportunity of being heard shall be provided to the applicant before an order of refusal to grant registration is passed by the Commissioner and the reasons for refusal of registration shall be mentioned in such order. The order granting or refusing registration has to be passed within six months[17] from the end of the month in which the application for registration is received by the Commissioner and a copy of such order shall be sent to the applicant. If the Commissioner does not respond within 6 months, registration shall be deemed to have been granted. For instance, registration application is made on February 24, 2018 and the concerned Commissioner does not respond till August 23, 2018. Registration shall be deemed to have been granted on August 24, 2018 – *CIT* v. *Society for Promn. of Edn.* [2016] 238 Taxman 330 (SC). The grant of registration shall be one of the conditions for grant of income-tax exemption.

❑ If after registration, the activities of the trust or the institution are being carried out in a manner that the provisions of sections 11 and 12 do not apply to exclude either whole (or any part) of the income due to operation of section 13(1) (*i.e.*, income does not enure for the benefit of general public, it is for the benefit of particular religious community or caste, income/property is utilised for the benefit of specified persons, like author of trust, trustee, etc., or funds are invested in prohibited modes), then the Commissioner or Principal Commissioner may by order in writing cancel the registration of such trust or institution[18]. **Moreover, (with effect from September 1, 2019), cancellation provisions can also be invoked if it is noticed that the trust or institution has violated requirements of any other law which was material for the purpose of achieving its objects, and the order (direction or decree), holding that such violation has occurred, has either not been disputed (or has attained finality).** However, the registration shall not be cancelled if the assessee proves that there was a reasonable cause for the activities to be carried out in the said manner.

❑ Where a trust or an institution has been granted registration for purposes of availing exemption under section 11, and the registration is in force for a previous year, then such trust or institution cannot claim any exemption under any provision of section 10 [other than that relating to exemption of agricultural income and income exempt under section 10(*23C*)] for that previous year (applicable from the assessment year 2015-16).

• The accounts of the trust should be audited [Form No. 10B][19] for such accounting year in which its income (without giving effect to the provisions of sections 11 and 12) exceeds the exemption limit.

• The funds of the trust should be invested or deposited in any one or more of the modes or forms mentioned in section 11(5) [*see* para 213.1].

• Return of income of the trust/institution should be submitted within the time allowed under section 139(1), if the total income of the trust/institution (before giving exemption under sections 11 and 12) exceeds the maximum amount which is not chargeable to tax (applicable from the assessment year 2018-19).

213.1 ***Forms or modes of investment [Sec. 11(5)]*** - A uniform pattern of investment is laid down, with effect from April 1, 1983, for all categories of funds belonging to charitable and religious trusts or institutions. The same pattern of investment will apply in relation to accumulation of income in excess of 15 per cent. The uniform forms or modes for investing funds of charitable and religious trusts and institutions are given below :

a. investment in Government savings certificates[20];

---

17. The time-limit of 6 month is applicable even in the case of invalid application—*Sahitya Sadawart Samiti* v. *CIT* [2008] 23 SOT 49 (Jp.).

18. The temporary excess of commercial receipts beyond the specified cut-off in one year (*i.e.*, 20 per cent of total receipts) may not necessarily be the outcome of alteration in the very nature of the activities of the trust or institution requiring cancellation of registration already granted to the trust or institution. The Board has advised its field authorities not to cancel registration of trust just because proviso to section 2(*15*) comes into play—Circular No. 21/2016$, dated May 27, 2016.

19. From April 1, 2014, audit report should be submitted electronically. Provisions pertaining to electronic submission of audit report were not applicable prior to April 1, 2014 (for period prior to April 1, 2014, audit report may be retained by the assessee and it may be furnished in original whenever the Assessing Officer wants to examine it in assessment proceedings or otherwise).

20. It has been clarified that the investment in "Indira Vikas Patra (IVP)" and "Kisan Vikas Patra (KVP)" is in accordance with the norms and modes specified in section 11(5)—Circular No. 566, dated July 17, 1990. However, after an amendment to small savings schemes in 2005, a trust cannot invest in IVP or KVP.

$ For Circular No. 21/2016, log on to *taxmann.com/readyreckoner.aspx.*

b. deposit in any Post Office Savings Bank Account;

c. deposit in any account (*i.e.*, current account or any other account) with any scheduled bank or a co-operative society engaged in carrying on the business of banking (including a co-operative land mortgage bank or a co-operative land development bank);

d. investment in units of the Unit Trust of India;

e. investment in any Central Government or State Government securities;

f. investment in debentures[21] of any corporate body, the principal whereof and the interest whereon are guaranteed by the Central or a State Government;

g. investment or deposit in any public sector company [a proviso was inserted in clause (*vii*) of section 11(5) with effect from the assessment year 2001-02. It provides that where an investment is made in the shares of any public sector company and such public sector company ceases to be a public sector company, the investment so made shall be deemed to be an investment made for a period of 3 years from the date such company ceases to be a public sector company and in the case of any other investment or deposit, it shall be deemed to be an investment made for the period up to the date on which such investment or deposit becomes repayable by such company];

h. deposits with or investment in any bonds issued by any financial corporation engaged in providing long-term funds for industrial development in India, if the corporation is eligible for deduction under section 36(1)(*viii*);

i. deposits with or investment in any bonds issued by any public company carrying on the business of providing long-term finance for construction or purchase of house in India for residential purposes, if the company is eligible for deduction under section 36(1)(*viii*);

j. deposits with Industrial Development Bank of India;

k. immovable property;

l. any other prescribed form or mode of investment[22]; and

m. from the assessment year 2001-02, deposit with or investment in any bonds issued by a public company formed and registered in India with the main object of carrying on the business of providing long-term finance for urban infrastructure in India (for this purpose "long-term finance" means any loan or advance where the terms under which money is loaned or advanced provide for repayment along with interest thereof during a period of not less than 5 years. "Urban infrastructure" means a project for providing potable water supply, sanitation and sewerage, drainage, solid waste management, roads, bridges and flyovers or urban transport).

Application of income [Sec. 11(1)]

214. In order to claim tax exemption, a charitable trust or institution will have to apply at least 85 per cent[23] of the income to charitable or religious purposes. Voluntary contributions or donations (not being contributions made with a specific direction that they will form a part of the corpus of the trust/institution) will be deemed to be a part of the income derived from property held under trust. If the income applied to charitable or religious purposes, during the previous year, falls short of 85 per cent[23] of the income derived during the year, either because (*a*) the income has not been received in the relevant previous year, or (*b*) because of any other reason, the charitable trust or institution has been given an option to spend such income for charitable or religious purposes in the following manner. In the case of (*a*) either during the previous year in which the income is so received or during the previous year immediately following such year; and in the case of (*b*), during the previous year immediately following the previous year in which the income was derived.

For availing of the benefit of extended time beyond the relevant previous year, the charitable trust or institution, in either case, has to exercise the option under clause (*2*) of *Explanation* to section 11(1)[24]. Income

21. The expression "debentures" includes bonds—*DIT* v. *Shree Visheshwar Nath Memorial Public Ch. Trust* [2010] 194 Taxman 280 (Delhi).

22. Investment in (*a*) units issued under any scheme of mutual fund referred to in section 10(*23D*), (*b*) any transfer of deposit to the Public Account of India, (*c*) deposits made with an authority constituted in India by or under any law enacted either for the purpose of dealing with and satisfying the need for housing accommodation or for the purpose of planning, development or improvement of cities, towns and villages, or for both, (*d*) investment by way of acquiring equity shares of a depository as defined in section 2(*1*)(*e*) of the Depositories Act, 1996, (*e*) investment in certain securities by a recognized stock exchange, (*f*) investment by way of acquiring equity shares of an incubatee by an incubator, (*g*) investment by way of acquiring shares of National Skill Development Corporation, and (*h*) investment in debt instruments issued by any infrastructure finance company registered with the RBI, and investment in "stock certificate" as defined in paragraph 2(*c*) of the Sovereign Gold Bonds Scheme, 2015.

23. 75 per cent up to the assessment year 2002-03.

24. This option can be exercised by uploading Form No. 9A (either under digital signature or electronic verification code) before the expiry of time allowed for submission of return of income under section 139(1).

applied to such purposes during the extended time will be deemed to have been applied to such purposes during the previous year in which it was derived. Where, however, any income in respect of which an option is exercised under clause (*2*) of *Explanation* to section 11(1) is not applied for charitable or religious purposes in India during the extended time, such income is liable to be taxed as the income in the case of (*a*) *supra* of the previous year immediately following the previous year in which the income was received (where the income was not received in the previous year in which it was derived) or in the case of (*b*) *supra* of the previous year immediately following the previous year in which income was derived.

• Where any income is required to be applied (or accumulated or set apart for application), then, for such purposes the income shall be determined without any deduction or allowance by way of depreciation (or otherwise) in respect of any asset, acquisition of which has been claimed as an application of income under section 11 in the same or any other previous year (applicable from the assessment year 2015-16).

• A donation or contribution given by a charitable trust to another charitable trust, is treated as "application of income" in the hands of trust which gives donation. Consequently, exemption under section 11(1)(*a*) is available to the donor trust. This exemption is available to the donor trust, even if nothing is spent by the done trust out of such donation during the current year – *CIT* v. *Thanthi Trust* [1999] 239 ITR 502 (SC). However, the donor trust will not be able to avail exemption under section 11(1)(*a*) (with effect from the assessment year 2018-19), in respect of donations given with a specific direction that they shall form part of the corpus of the donee trust.

• For the purposes of determining "application of income" under section 11(1), the provisions of section 40(*a*)(*ia*) and section 40A(3)/(3A) shall, *mutatis mutandis*, apply as they apply in computing the income chargeable under the head "Profits and gains of business or profession" (applicable from the assessment year 2019-20).

214-E1 During the accounting period ending March 31, 2019, a charitable trust derived (*a*) income from property held for charitable purposes : Rs. 3,00,000 (Rs. 1,70,000 received in cash and the remaining balance of Rs. 1,30,000 is to be received in the year 2020-21), (*b*) voluntary contribution : Rs. 2,00,000 with no specific direction, and (*c*) Rs. 20,00,000 with specific direction that it shall form corpus of the trust.

During the previous year 2018-19, the trust spends only Rs. 1,40,000 for charitable purposes. Determine its taxable income on the assumption that the trust has obtained extension of time for applying the unrealised income of Rs. 1,30,000 in the year of receipt, *i.e.*, 2020-21 whereas it actually spends Rs. 30,000 in the year 2020-21 and Rs. 40,000 in the year 2021-22.

•

Taxable income of the trust will be computed as under :

For the assessment year 2019-20 (previous year 2018-19)	*Rs.*
Income from property held under trust for charitable purposes	3,00,000
Voluntary contributions with no specific direction	2,00,000
Total income	5,00,000
Less : 15% set apart for future	75,000
Balance	4,25,000
Less : Amount spent during the previous year	1,40,000
Shortfall	2,85,000
Less : Amount not realised during the previous year	1,30,000
Taxable income	1,55,000

For the assessment year 2022-23 (previous year 2021-22, *i.e.*, the year next following previous year in which the unrealised income of the previous year 2018-19 is received) :

	Rs.	*Rs.*
Income received during the previous year 2020-21		1,30,000
Less : Amount spend during		
❑ previous year 2020-21	30,000	
❑ previous year 2021-22	40,000	70,000
Taxable income		60,000

Note : Voluntary contributions received with specific direction that they shall form corpus of the trust are not treated as income of the trust.

Accumulation of income [Sec. 11(2)]

215. Where 85 per cent[25] of the income is not applied to charitable or religious purposes in the aforesaid manner, the charitable trust or institution may accumulate or set apart either the whole or part of its

25. 75 per cent up to the assessment year 2002-03.

income for future application for such purposes in India. Such income so accumulated or set apart will not be included in the total income of the trust or institution in the year of receipt of income, provided such trust or institution has specified by means of a notice[26] to the Assessing Officer, in Form No. 10, the purpose and period (which in no case can exceed 5 years)[27] for which the income is accumulated or set apart. Further, the money so set apart or accumulated should be invested in any one or more of the modes/forms specified in section 11(5).

• The following should be noted—

1. The benefit of accumulation is not available (with effect from the assessment year 2016-17) if return of income is not furnished before the due date of filing return of income under section 139(1).

2. If in any year, income accumulated for a specified purpose or purposes of the trust is applied to purposes other than charitable or religious purposes or ceases to be accumulated or set apart for application to such purposes, it will become chargeable to tax as the income of that year.

3. If in any year, the accumulations cease to remain invested in securities specified above, then also the income so accumulated will become chargeable to tax as the income of that year.

4. If the accumulations are not utilised for the specified purposes during the period of accumulation or in the year immediately following the expiry of that period, then the accumulations, to the extent they are not so utilised, will become chargeable to tax as income of the previous year immediately following the expiry of that period.

5. Sometimes, failure to apply the income so accumulated or set apart in the specified manner may arise due to circumstances beyond the control of the trustees. In such a case, the Assessing Officer may, on the receipt of an application from the person in receipt of the income, allow such income to be applied for such other charitable/religious purposes in India as are in conformity with the objects of the trust/institution.

6. Any amount paid or credited out of accumulated income to any trust or institution registered under section 12AA or to any fund or institution or trust or any university or other educational institution or any hospital or other medical institution either during the period of accumulation or thereafter, shall not be treated as application of income for charitable or religious purposes. Thus, payment to other trusts and institutions out of income from property held under trust in the year of receipt will continue to be treated as application of income. However, any such payment out of the accumulated income shall not be treated as application of income and will be taxed in the year in which such payment/credit is made out of accumulated income (inserted by the Finance Act, 2002 with effect from the assessment year 2003-04).

Sometimes failure to apply the income so accumulated or set apart in the specified manner may arise due to circumstances beyond the control of trustees. In such case, the Assessing Officer may, on the receipt of an application from the person in receipt of the income, allow such income to be applied for such other charitable/religious purposes in India as are in conformity with the objects of the trust/institution.

Forfeiture of exemption [Sec. 13]

216. The following incomes of charitable/religious trusts/institutions do not qualify for exemption by virtue of section 13 :

216.1 ***Income for private religious purposes*** - Any part of income from a property held under a trust for private religious purposes which does not enure for the benefit of the public is not eligible for exemption under section 11 or 12.

216.2 ***Income for the benefit of particular religious community*** - Entire income of a charitable trust/institution (established on or after April 1, 1962) created for the benefit of any particular religious community or caste is not eligible for exemption under section 11 or 12. A trust or institution created or established for the benefit of Scheduled Castes, Backward Classes, Scheduled Tribes or women and children shall not be deemed to be a trust or institution created or established for the benefit of a religious community or caste for this purpose.

216.3 ***Income for the benefit of interested persons*** - If religious/charitable trust/institution is created or established after March 31, 1962 and any part of its income enures directly or indirectly under the

---

26. With effect from April 1, 2014, notice in Form No. 10 should be submitted electronically. From the assessment year 2016-17, the benefit of accumulation is not available if Form No. 10 is not uploaded (either under digital signature or electronic verification code) before the due date of filing return of income specified under section 139(1) for the fund or institution.

27. In computing the period of 5 years, the period during which the income could not be applied for the purposes for which it was accumulated or set apart due to an order or injunction of any court shall be excluded. The maximum period for which accumulation is permitted is 10 years in respect of any income accumulated or set apart before April 1, 2001.

rules governing the trust, for the benefit of any person specified in section 13(3) [*see* para 216.3-1] then the entire income of such trust is not eligible for exemption under section 11 or 12.

Entire income of a trust/institution created/established after March 31, 1962 is also not eligible for exemption under section 11 or 12 if the income/property is used/applied, during the relevant year, for the direct/indirect benefit of the author of the trust and other persons mentioned in section 13(3) [*see* para 216.3-1]. This provision is also applicable in the case of a trust/institution created/established prior to April 1, 1962 but in such case exemption is not forfeited if such use of the trust income/property is in compliance with a mandatory provision in the terms of the trust or mandatory rule governing the institution.

216.3-1 *MEANING OF INTERESTED PERSON* - For the purposes of section 13, the following are interested persons :

a. the author of the trust or the founder of the institution ;

b. any person who had made a total contribution (up to the end of the relevant previous year) of an amount exceeding Rs. 50,000[28] (substantial contributor) ;

c. any member of the HUF (or any relative of such member) where such author or founder or substantial contributor is a HUF ;

d. any trustee of the trust or manager (by whatever name called) of the institution ;

e. any relative of such author, founder, substantial contributor, member, trustee or manager ;

f. any concern in which any of the persons referred to above has a substantial interest.

216.3-1a RELATIVE - MEANING OF - A "relative" in relation to an individual means :

a. spouse of the individual ;

b. brother or sister of the individual ;

c. brother or sister of the spouse of the individual ;

d. any lineal ascendant or descendant of the individual ;

e. any lineal ascendant or descendant of the spouse of the individual ;

f. spouse of a person referred to in (*b*), (*c*), (*d*) or (*e*) above ;

g. any lineal ascendant or descendant of a brother or sister of either the individual or of the spouse of the individual.

216.3-1b SUBSTANTIAL INTEREST - MEANING OF - For the aforesaid provisions, a person will be deemed to have substantial interest in a company if he (or along with "interested persons" mentioned above) beneficially holds at least 20 per cent equity share capital of the company at any time during the previous year. In the case of a concern other than a company, a person will be deemed to have substantial interest, if he (or along with "interested persons" mentioned above) is entitled to at least 20 per cent of the profits of such concern at any time during the previous year.

216.3-2 *CONFERMENT OF BENEFIT, AMENITY OR PERQUISITE ON AN INTERESTED PERSON* - The income or the property of the trust (or institution) shall be deemed to have been used (or applied) in a manner which results (directly or indirectly) in conferring any benefit, amenity or perquisite (whether convertible into money or not) on any interested person, in the following cases :

- Where any part of the income or property of the trust (or institution) is (or continues to be) lent to any interested person for any period during the previous year without either adequate security or adequate interest or both.
- Where any land, building or other property of the trust (or institution) is (or continues to be) made available for the use of any interested person for any period during the previous year without charging adequate rent or other compensation.

Where any amount is paid by way of salary, allowance or otherwise during the previous year to any interested person out of the resources of the trust (or institution) for services rendered by that person to such trust (or institution) and the amount so paid is more than what may be reasonably paid for such services.

- Where the services of the trust or institution are made available to any interested person during the previous year without adequate remuneration or compensation.
- Where any share, security or other property is purchased by or on behalf of the trust (or institution) from any interested person during the previous year for more than adequate consideration.
- Where any share, security or other property is sold by or on behalf of the trust (or institution) to any interested person during the previous year for less than adequate consideration.

---

28. Rs. 25,000 up to the assessment year 1994-95.

• Where any income or property of the trust (or institution) is diverted during the previous year in favour of any interested person. Where, however, the aggregate of income or the value of the property so diverted does not exceed Rs. 1,000 this provision is not applicable.

• Where any funds of the trust (or institution) are (or continue to remain) invested for any period during the previous year in any concern in which any interested person has a substantial interest. Where, however, the aggregate of the funds of the trust (or institution) invested in a concern in which any interested person has a substantial interest does not exceed 5 per cent of the capital of that concern, exemption under section 11 will not be denied in relation to the application of any income other than the income arising to the trust or institution from such investment.

216.4 ***Fund not invested in section 11(5) securities/deposits*** - Income of a trust/institution is not eligible for exemption under section 11 or 12 if its funds are invested/deposited otherwise than in the forms specified in section 11(5).

In this regard the following points should be noted :

1. The exemption under section 11(1)(*a*) is available only if at least 85 per cent of the income is applied for charitable/religious purposes in India during the year and the remaining amount is invested in the forms/modes specified under section 11(5). Thus, both the requirements will have to be fulfilled before the trust can claim and avail of the exemption under section 11(1)(*a*). For instance, a trust derives income from property held for charitable purposes to the extent of Rs. 40,000 in a year. Under section 11(1)(*a*) it has to spend at least Rs. 30,000[29] on the charitable purposes. The balance of Rs. 10,000 will have to be invested in the forms/modes prescribed under section 11(5). It is only then that the entire income of the trust will get exemption— Circular No. 335, dated April 13, 1982.[30]

2. Any charitable or religious trust or institution will forfeit exemption from tax if any funds of the trust or institution are invested or deposited, after February 28, 1983, otherwise than in any one or more of the modes specified in section 11(5). Such trusts and institutions will also forfeit exemption from tax if any part of their funds invested before March 1, 1983 otherwise than in any one or more of the forms or modes specified in section 11(5), continue to remain so invested or deposited after November 30, 1983. Trusts or institutions which continue to hold any shares in a company [other than shares in a public sector company or shares which are prescribed as mode of investment under section 11(5)(*xii*)] after the said date will also forfeit exemption from income-tax.

216.4-1 *EXCEPTION* - In the cases given below, exemption is not forfeited even if funds are invested otherwise than in the modes specified in section 11(5) :

1. The exemption is not denied in relation to assets held by the trust or institution where such assets form a part of the corpus of the trust or institution as on June 1, 1973.

2. Similarly, exemption is not denied in relation to any accretion to the assets, being shares of a company forming part of the corpus of the trust or institution as on June 1, 1973, where such accretion arises by way of allotment of bonus shares.

3. Exemption is not forfeited in relation to debentures[31] acquired by the trust or institution before March 1, 1983. Where debentures[31] of an Indian company are acquired by the trust or institution after February 28, 1983 but before July 25, 1991, the exemption from tax under section 11 will be denied only in respect of interest on such debentures[31]. If, however, such debentures[31] are not disinvested by March 31, 1992, the trust or institution will lose exemption under section 11.

4. Exemption is not forfeited in relation to any funds representing the profits and gains of a business, if the trust/institution maintains separate books of account in respect of such business.

5. Acceptance of donations in kind or acquiring any asset not conforming to the provision of section 11(5) will not make the fund or trust or institution lose tax exemption. The trust or institution shall be required to dispose of or convert the asset not conforming to the requirement of section 11(5) into permissible investment within one year[32] from the end of the financial year in which such assets are acquired or March 31, 1993, whichever is later.

216.5 ***Educational and medical facilities to specified persons [Secs. 12(2) and 13(6)]*** - Sections 12(2) and 13(6) provide as follows—

---

29. Now Rs. 34,000 (*i.e.,* 85 per cent of Rs. 40,000).

30. *See,* however, *CIT* v. *A.L.N. Rao Charitable Trust* [1995] 216 ITR 697 (SC).

31. The expression "debentures" includes bonds—*DIT* v. *Shree Visheshwar Nath Memorial Public Ch. Trust* [2010] 194 Taxman 280 (Delhi).

32. Where, however, the assessee is restrained from converting shares held by it in a private limited company to other forms of permissible investment by virtue of a High Court restraint order, it cannot be held liable for violation of the aforesaid provision – *CIT* v. *Dr. Bhai Mohan Singh Foundation* [2018] 95 taxmann.com 332 (Delhi).

1. Income of a charitable or religious trust will not be exempt if any part of such income or any property of the trust is used or applied directly or indirectly for the benefit of any person such as the author of the trust, trustee or any relative of such persons or any concerns in which such persons have a substantial interest [referred to as interested person, *see* para 216.3-1]. Sub-section (6) was inserted in section 13 with effect from the assessment year 2001-02. It provides that a charitable or religious trust running an educational institution or a medical institution or a hospital shall not be denied the benefit of exemption under section 11 or section 12, in relation to any income by reason only that such trust has provided educational or medical facilities to interested persons.

2. Sub-section (2) was inserted in section 12 with effect from the assessment year 2001-02. It provides that the value of any medical or educational services made available by any charitable or religious trust running a hospital or medical institution or an educational institution to any interested person shall be deemed to be the income of such trust or institution derived from property held under trust wholly for charitable or religious purposes during the previous year in which such services are so provided and shall be chargeable to income-tax notwithstanding the provisions of section 11(1).

216.6 ***Anonymous donation [Sec. 13(7)]*** - Section 13 has been amended from the assessment year 2007-08 to the effect that any anonymous donation will not be eligible for deduction under sections 11 and 12.

216.6-1 *WHAT IS ANONYMOUS DONATION [SEC. 115BBC(3)]* - The expression "anonymous donation" has been defined as follows—

1. It is a voluntary contribution referred to in section 2(*24*)(*iia*).

2. The person receiving such contribution does not maintain a record of—

a. the identity indicating the name and address of the person making such contribution[33] ; and

b. such other records as may be prescribed.

216.6-2 *SPECIAL RATE OF TAX [SEC. 115BBC(1)]* - "Anonymous donation" would be taxable at the rate of 30 per cent[34]. However, from the assessment year 2010-11, anonymous donations are taxable only to the extent such donation exceeds Rs. 1,00,000 or 5 per cent of total donations received by the trust, whichever is higher.

216.6-3 *INSTITUTIONS AFFECTED BY THE ABOVE PROVISIONS [SEC. 115BBC(1)]* - The above provisions are applicable in the case of following—

a. any trust or institution referred to in section 11;

b. any university or other educational institution referred to in section 10(*23C*)(*iiiad*) and (*vi*);

c. any hospital or other institution referred to in section 10(*23C*)(*iiiae*) and (*via*);

d. any fund or institution referred to in section 10(*23C*)(*iv*); and

e. any trust or institution referred to in section 10(*23C*)(*v*).

216.6-4 *DONATIONS NOT AFFECTED BY THE ABOVE PROVISIONS [SEC. 115BBC(2)]* - The following anonymous donations shall not be covered by the provisions of section 115BBC—

i. donations received by any trust or institution created or established wholly for religious purposes; and

ii. donations received by any trust or institution created or established for both religious as well as charitable purposes.

However, donation mentioned in (*ii*) (*supra*) does not include any anonymous donation made with a specific direction that such donation is for any university or other educational institution or any hospital or other medical institution run by such trust or institution.

• There is no line of demarcation in the Hindu system between religion and charity. The "religious purpose" also includes relief to the poor, education, and medical relief, etc. Thus, where the objects of a trust exhibits the dual tenor of religious and charitable purpose and activities and anonymous donation is received by it without any specific direction that such donation is for any university or other educational institutions or any hospital or other medical institutions run by the trust, such donation cannot be taxed by invoking provisions of section 115BBC—*CIT* v. *All India Pingalwara Charitable Society* [2016] 67 taxmann.com 338 (Asr.).

---

33. Amount of offerings put by various devotees in donation boxes of a trust (maybe a sidh peeth/deity) cannot be treated as anonymous donations taxable under section 115BBC merely on the ground that the assessee has not maintained any records of such offerings—*Gurudev Siddha Peeth* v. *ITO* [2015] 59 taxmann.com 400 (Mum.).

34. It is subject to surcharge and health and education cess.

216.6-5 *CONCLUSIONS* - The following conclusions can be drawn from the aforesaid discussion—

Institution receiving anonymous donations	*Tax treatment*
Case 1 - Wholly religious entities	Section 115BBC is not applicable
Case 2 - Partly religious and partly charitable entities	If anonymous donation is made to an educational or medical institution run by such entity, such anonymous donation is taxable at the rate of 30 per cent[35] [*see* Notes]. Any other anonymous donation is not subject to tax under section 115BBC
Case 3 - Wholly charitable entities	All anonymous donations are taxed at the rate of 30 per cent[35] [*see* Notes] under section 115BBC

Notes - The following points are applicable from the assessment year 2010-11 onwards—

1. If aggregate anonymous donation is Rs. 1 lakh or less, section 115BBC will not be applicable.

2. If aggregate anonymous donation is more than Rs. 1 lakh but it is not more than 5 per cent of the total donations received by the assessee, section 115BBC will not be applicable.

3. If aggregate amount of anonymous donation is more than Rs. 1 lakh or 5 per cent of the total donations received, whichever is higher, the excess amount will be subject to tax at the rate of 30 per cent[35] under section 115BBC. However, it will be taxable only in the cases of *Case 2* and *Case 3* noted above.

216.6-E1 Consider the following situations for the assessment year 2019-20—

		Situation 1	*Situation 2*	*Situation 3*	*Situation 4*	*Situation 5*	*Situation 6*
		Rs.	*Rs.*	*Rs.*	*Rs.*	*Rs.*	*Rs.*
Aggregate amount of anonymous donation	(*a*)	6,00,000	2,50,000	10,00,000	30,000	2,70,000	2,60,000
Other donation	(*b*)	3,00,000	60,00,000	70,00,000	7,50,000	59,05,000	55,00,000
Total donation [(*a*) + (*b*)]	(*c*)	9,00,000	62,50,000	80,00,000	7,80,000	61,75,000	57,60,000
Total income [*i.e.*, (*c*) + other incomes – exemption under section 11]	(*d*)	14,00,000	73,00,000	95,00,000	9,00,000	6,00,000	4,39,000
5% of total donation [*i.e.*, (*c*)] or Rs. 1,00,000, whichever is higher	(*e*)	1,00,000	3,12,500	4,00,000	1,00,000	3,08,750	2,88,000
Amount of anonymous donation in excess of (*e*) [*i.e.*, (*a*) - (*e*)], which is taxable at the rate of 30% + SC +HEC under section 115BBC(*i*)	(*f*)	5,00,000	*Nil*	6,00,000	*Nil*	*Nil*	*Nil*
Balance amount of income which is taxable at normal rate under section 115BBC(*ii*) [*i.e.*, (*d*) - (*f*)]	(*g*)	9,00,000	73,00,000	89,00,000	9,00,000	6,00,000	4,39,000
Tax on (*f*)	(*h*)	1,56,000	*Nil*	2,05,920	*Nil*	*Nil*	*Nil*
Tax on (*g*)	(*i*)	96,200	22,90,860	28,39,980	96,200	33,800	9,828
Total tax [(*h*) + (*i*), rounded off]	(*j*)	2,52,200	22,90,860	30,45,900	96,200	33,800	9,830

Note - It is assumed that in the aforesaid cases the assessee is (*a*) partly religious and partly charitable entity and anonymous donation is for educational or medical institute run by the assessee, or (*b*) wholly charitable entity.

If, however, the assessee is (*a*) wholly religious entity, or (*b*) partly religious and partly charitable entity and anonymous donation is not for educational/medical institute run by the assessee, then section 115BBC will not be applicable and, consequently, the total income [*i.e.*, (*d*)] will be chargeable to tax at the normal rate which will come to Rs. 2,41,800 (*Situation 1*), Rs. 22,90,860 (*Situation 2*), Rs. 30,45,900 (*Situation 3*), Rs. 96,200 (*Situation 4*), Rs. 33,800 (*Situation 5*), Rs. 9,830 (*Situation 6*).

35. It is subject to surcharge and health and education cess.

216.6-E2 A trust gives the following information for the assessment year 2019-20—

	Income *Rs.*	*How much is applied for charitable purposes* *Rs.*
Income from property held for charitable purposes	15,00,000	6,00,000
Voluntary contribution for corpus of the trust (names and addresses of donors available)	80,00,000	*Nil*
Voluntary contribution without any direction (names and addresses of donors available)	40,00,000	12,75,000
Voluntary contribution without any direction (names and addresses of donors not available)	30,00,000	26,00,000

•

In this case, Rs. 80,00,000 (being voluntary contribution for corpus of the trust) is not chargeable to tax. Anonymous donation is Rs. 30,00,000 (names and addresses of donors are not available). In respect of anonymous donation, exemption under section 11 is not available. Taxable income and tax liability will be calculated as follows—

	Rs.
Income from property held for charitable purposes	15,00,000
Voluntary contribution for corpus of the trust (not taxable)	—
Voluntary contribution without any direction	40,00,000
Anonymous donation	30,00,000
Total	85,00,000
Less : Anonymous donation taxable under section 115BBC @ 30% (as calculated below)	26,50,000
Income subject to exemption under section 11	58,50,000
Less: Exemption under section 11 (15% of Rs. 58,50,000 + Rs. 6,00,000 + Rs. 12,75,000)	27,52,500
Balance	30,97,500
Add: Anonymous donation (taxable @ 30% under section 115BBC)	26,50,000
Taxable income	57,47,500
Computation of tax	
Tax on anonymous donation (total donation is Rs. 40,00,000 + Rs. 30,00,000, *i.e.*, Rs. 70,00,000. 5% of total donation is Rs. 3,50,000. 5% of total donation or Rs. 1,00,000, whichever is higher, is Rs. 3,50,000. Anonymous donation in excess of Rs. 3,50,000 is Rs. 26,50,000 which will be taxable @ 30%)	7,95,000
Tax on income other than anonymous donation (*i.e.*, normal tax on Rs. 30,97,500)	7,41,750
Total	15,36,750
Add: Surcharge @ 10%	1,53,675
Tax and surcharge	16,90,425
Add: Health and education cess	67,617
Tax liability	17,58,040

Note - The above calculations are applicable only if the trust is wholly charitable entity (or it is partly religious and partly charitable and anonymous donations are received for educational/medical institution run by such entity). In other cases, section 115BBC is not applicable and taxable income and tax liability will be calculated as under —

	Rs.
Income from property held for charitable purposes	15,00,000
Voluntary contribution for corpus of the trust (not taxable)	-
Voluntary contribution without any direction	40,00,000
Voluntary contribution without any direction (names and addresses of donors not available)	30,00,000
Total	85,00,000
Less: Exemption under section 11 (15% of Rs. 85,00,000 + Rs. 6,00,000 + Rs. 12,75,000 + Rs. 26,00,000)	57,50,000
Taxable income	27,50,000
Computation of tax	
Tax on income (*i.e.*, normal tax on Rs. 27,50,000)	6,37,500
Add: Health and education cess	25,500
Tax liability	6,63,000

216.7 ***When commercial receipts exceeds the specified threshold [Sec. 13(8)]*** - Where the activity of any trust or institution is of the nature of advancement of any other object of general public utility, it involves carrying on of any activity in the nature of trade, commerce or business and the aggregate value of receipts from the commercial activities exceeds Rs. 25,00,000 in the previous year, then the purpose of such institution shall not be considered as charitable. Such trust or institution will not be entitled to get benefit of exemption with effect from the assessment year 2009-10 under sections 11 and 12 [and also section 10(*23C*)] in respect of its income for that previous year for which such receipts exceed Rs. 25,00,000.

Public charitable/religious trust - How chargeable to tax

217. Subject to the rule mentioned in para 217.1, in the following cases income of a charitable/religious trust which is not exempt under section 11 or 12 is chargeable to tax as if it is the income of an association of persons :

a. income from property held under trust wholly for charitable or religious purposes;

b. voluntary contributions without any direction that they shall form a part of the corpus of trust; or

c. income of trust or institution being profits and gains of business which is incidental to the attainment of the objectives of trust and separate books of account are maintained.

217.1 ***Levy of tax at maximum marginal rate in case of public charitable and religious trusts which forfeit tax exemption*** - Charitable or religious trusts, which may otherwise be eligible for tax exemption, are liable to forfeit this exemption in the following circumstances, namely :

1. Where the trust is created after March 31, 1962, any part of the income of the trust enures, under the terms of the trust deed, directly or indirectly, for the benefit of specified categories of persons such as, the author of the trust, trustee or manager of the trust, substantial contributor to the trust and any relative of such author, trustee, etc. [*see* para 216.3].

2. Any part of the income or any property of the trust (whenever created) is used or applied during the relevant year, directly or indirectly, for the benefit of specified categories of persons [*see* para 216.3].

3. The trust funds (with certain exceptions) are invested in contravention of the investment pattern of such funds [*see* para 216.4].

Where a charitable or religious trust forfeits tax exemption in the circumstances mentioned at (*1*) to (*3*) above, the trust shall be charged to tax at the maximum marginal rate [*i.e.*, 35.88 per cent (for the assessment year 2019-20) and **42.744** per cent (for the assessment year 2020-21)].

217.2 ***Levy of tax at the maximum marginal rate where a charitable trust ceases to exist or converts into a non-charitable entity [Sec. 115TD, applicable from June 1, 2016]*** - Section 115TD is inserted with effect from June 1, 2016. This section provides for levy of additional income-tax in case of conversion into, or merger with, any non-charitable form or on transfer of assets of a charitable organisation on its dissolution to a non-charitable institution. The elements of the regime are—

1. The accretion in income (accreted income) of the trust or institution shall be taxable on conversion of trust or institution into a form not eligible for registration under section 12AA or on merger into an entity not having similar objects and registered under section 12AA or on non-distribution of assets on dissolution to any charitable institution registered under section 12AA or approved under section 10(*23C*) within a period of 12 months from dissolution.

2. For the above purpose, a trust or institution shall be deemed to have been converted into any form (not eligible for registration under section 12AA) in a previous year, if—

a. the registration granted to it under section 12AA has been cancelled; or

b. it has modified its objects and not applied for fresh registration (or fresh registration application has been rejected).

2. Accreted income shall be amount of aggregate of total assets as reduced by the liability as on the specified date (mode of valuation is yet to be notified). The asset and the liability of the charitable organisation which have been transferred to another charitable organisation within specified time will be excluded while calculating accreted income.

3. So much of the accreted income as is attributable to the following asset and liability, if any, related to such asset shall be ignored for the purposes of computation of accreted income—

- Any asset which is established to have been directly acquired by the trust or institution out of agricultural income as is referred to in section 10(*1*).

- Any asset acquired by the trust/institution during the period beginning from the date of its creation and ending on the date from which the registration under section 12AA became effective or deemed effective (however, this rule is valid only if the trust/institution has not been allowed any benefit of sections 11 and 12 during the said period). "Deemed" effective covers a case where due to first proviso to section 12A(2) the benefit of sections 11 and 12 have been allowed to the trust/institution in respect of any previous year prior to the year of registration.

4. The taxation of accreted income shall be at the maximum marginal rate [*i.e.*, 35.88 per cent (for the assessment year 2019-20) and **42.744** per cent (for the assessment year 2020-21)].

5. This levy shall be in addition to any income chargeable to tax in the hands of the entity.

6. This tax shall be final tax for which no credit can be taken by the trust or institution or any other person, and like any other additional tax, it shall be leviable even if the trust or institution does not have any other income chargeable to tax in the relevant previous year.

7. In case of failure of payment of tax within the prescribed time a simple interest @ 1 per cent per month (or part of it) shall be applicable for the period of non-payment.

8. For the purpose of recovery of tax and interest, the principal officer or the trustee and the trust or the institution shall be deemed to be assessee in default and all provisions related to the recovery of taxes shall apply. Further, the recipient of assets of the trust, which is not a charitable organisation, shall also be liable to be held as assessee in default in case of non-payment of tax and interest. However, the recipient's liability shall be limited to the extent of the assets received.

Business trust

Special provisions pertaining to business trust [Sec. 115UA]

218. The Securities and Exchange Board of India (SEBI) has come out with two new categories of investment vehicles, namely, the Real Estate Investment Trust (REIT) and Infrastructure Investment Trust (Invit). The income-investment model of such REITs and Invits (referred to as business trusts) has the following distinctive elements –

1. The trust would raise capital by way of issue of units (to be listed on a recognised stock exchange) and can also raise debts directly both from resident as well as non-resident investors.

2. The income bearing assets would be held by the trust by acquiring controlling or other specific interest in an Indian company (SPV) from the sponsor.

The expansion of asset delivery through the public-private partnership (PPP) model has increased the number of assets available for financing. The Indian infrastructure and the PPPs are currently in a challenging phase, with development of existing projects delayed, and diminishing attractiveness of new projects to private sector funds and strategic operators. In order to meet these challenges, new investment vehicle structure, an Infrastructure Investment Trust needs to be facilitated. Similarly, securitization of income earning real estate assets needs to be facilitated. Certainty in the taxation aspects of these trusts is necessary.

• *Salient features of new taxation regime* - Keeping in view the aforesaid, a few amendments have been made by the Finance (No. 2) Act, 2014 (from the assessment year 2015-16) and the Finance Act, 2015 (from the assessment year 2016-17) to incorporate a specific taxation regime for providing the way the income in the hands of such trusts is to be taxed and the taxability of the income distributed by such business trusts in the hands of the unit holders of such trusts. Such regime has the following main features –

1. The listed units of a business trust, when traded on a recognised stock exchange, would attract same levy of securities transaction tax (STT), and would be given the same tax benefits in respect of taxability of capital gains as equity shares of a company, *i.e.*, long term capital gains, would be exempt and short term capital gains would be taxable at the rate of 15 per cent [+ SC + (EC + SHEC) or HEC].

2. In case of capital gains arising to the sponsor at the time of exchange of shares in SPVs with units of the business trust, the taxation of gains shall be deferred and taxed at the time of disposal of units by the sponsor. However, the preferential capital gains regime (consequent to levy of STT) available in respect of units of business trust is not available to the sponsor in respect of these units at the time of disposal for (only for) the assessment year 2015-16. Further, for the purpose of computing capital gain, the cost of these units shall be considered as cost of the shares to the sponsor. The holding period of shares shall also be included in the holding period of such units.

3. The income by way of interest received by the business trust from SPV is accorded pass through treatment, *i.e.*, there is no taxation of such interest income in the hands of the trust and no withholding tax at the level of SPV. However, TDS at the rate of 5 per cent (+SC+HEC) in case of payment of interest component of income distributed to non-resident unit holders and at the rate of 10 per cent in respect of payment of interest component of distributed income to a resident unit holder, shall be effected by the trust.

4. In case of external commercial borrowings by the business trust, the benefit of reduced rate of 5 per cent [+ SC + (EC + SHEC) or HEC] tax on interest payments to non-resident lenders shall be available on similar conditions, for such period as is provided in section 194LC.

5. The dividend received by the trust shall be subject to dividend distribution tax at the level of SPV but will be exempt in the hands of the trust and the dividend component of the income distributed by the trust to unit holders will also be exempt.

6. The income by way of capital gains on disposal of assets by the trust shall be taxable in the hands of the trust at the applicable rate. However, if such capital gains are distributed, then the component of distributed income attributable to capital gains would be exempt in the hands of unit holder. Any other income of the trust shall be taxable at the maximum marginal rate.

7. The business trust is required to furnish its return of income.

8. A business trust is required to e-file statement of income distributed to unitholders, in Form No. 64A, by November 30 immediately after the end of the previous year in which income is distributed. Moreover, a statement is also required to be furnished to the unitholders in Form No. 64B, by June 30 of financial year following the previous year in which income is distributed.

• *Rental income of Real Estate Investment Trust (REIT)* - In case of a business trust, being REIT, the income is predominantly in the nature of rental income. This rental income arises from the assets held directly by REIT or held by it through an SPV. The rental income received at the level of SPV gets passed through by way of interest or dividend to the REIT; the rental income directly received by the REIT is taxable at REIT level and does not get pass through benefit.

Amendments - In order to provide pass through to the rental income arising to REIT from real estate property directly held by it, the following amendments have been made by the Finance Act, 2015 from the assessment year 2016-17 –

1. Any income of a business trust, being REIT by way of renting or leasing or letting out any real estate asset (owned directly by such business trust) shall be exempt under section 10(*23FCA*).

2. The distributed income (or any part thereof) received by a unitholder from the REIT, which is in the nature of income by way of renting or leasing or letting out any real estate asset owned directly by such REIT, shall be deemed to be income of such unitholder and shall be charged to tax.

3. The REIT shall deduct tax at source on rental income allowed to be passed through. In case of resident unitholder, tax shall deducted at the rate of 10 per cent under section 194LBA and in case of distribution to non-resident unitholder, the tax shall be deducted at rate in force as applicable for deduction of tax on payment to the non-resident of any sum chargeable to tax [*i.e.*, at 30 per cent (+SC+HEC) if the recipient is a non-resident (not being a foreign company) or at 40 per cent (+SC+HEC) if the recipient is a foreign company].

4. No tax deduction shall be made under section 194-I where the income by way of rent is credited or paid by a tenant to a business trust, being a REIT, in respect of any real estate asset held directly by such REIT.

Alternative Investment Funds

Pass through status to Category I and Category II Alternative Investment Funds [Sec. 115UB]

219. The existing provisions of section 10(*23FB*) provide that any income of a Venture Capital Company (VCC) or a Venture Capital Fund (VCF) from investment in a Venture Capital Undertaking (VCU) shall be exempt from taxation. Section 115U provides that income accruing or arising or received by a person out of investment made in a VCC or VCF shall be taxable in the same manner, on current year basis, as if the person had made direct investment in the VCU.

These sections provide a tax pass through (*i.e.*, income is taxable in the hands of investors instead of VCF/VCC) only to the funds, being set-up as a company or a trust, which are registered (*i*) before May 21, 2012 as a VCF under SEBI (Venture Capital Funds) Regulations, 1996, or (*ii*) as venture capital fund [being one of the sub-categories under Category-I Alternative investment fund (AIF) regulated by SEBI (AIF) Regulations, 2012] with effect from May 21, 2012. The existing pass through is available only in respect of income which arises to the fund from investment in VCU, being a company which satisfies the conditions provided in SEBI (VCF) Regulations, 1996 or SEBI (AIF) Regulations, 2012 (AIF regulations).

Under the AIF regulations, various types of AIFs have been classified under three separate categories as Category I, II and III AIFs –

- Category I includes AIFs that invest in start-ups or early stage ventures or social ventures or small and medium enterprises (SMEs) or infrastructure or other sectors or areas, which the Government or regulators consider as socially or economically desirable. Category I AIFs are the funds which have positive spillover effects on economy and for which the Government/SEBI/other regulators in India might consider providing incentives or concessions.
- Category II AIFs are funds including private equity funds or debt funds which do not fall in Category I and III and which do not undertake leverage or borrowing other than to meet day-to-day operational requirements.
- Category III AIFs are funds which employ diverse or complex trading strategies and may employ leverage including through investment in listed or unlisted derivatives. These AIFs are hedge funds or funds, which trade with a view to making short-term returns, or such other funds, which are open ended, for which no specific incentives or concessions are given by the Government or any other regulators.

These funds can be set-up as a trust, company, limited liability partnership and any other body corporate. Similarly, investment by AIFs can be in entities which can be a company, firm, etc.

Pooled investment vehicles (other than hedge funds) engaged in making passive investments have been accorded pass through in certain tax jurisdictions. In order to rationalize the taxation of Category I and Category II AIFs (hereafter referred to as investment fund), a special tax regime has been provided under section 115UB. The salient features of the special regime are given below –

• Income of a person (being a unit holder of an investment fund) out of investments made in the investment fund shall be chargeable to income-tax in the same manner as if it was the income accruing or arising to (or received by) such person, had the investments (made by the investment fund) been made directly by him.

• Income in the hands of investment fund, other than income from profits and gains of business, shall be exempt from tax. The income in the nature of profits and gains of business or profession shall be taxable in the case of investment fund. If investment fund is a company or a firm, such business income will be taxable at the rate applicable to the company or firm. Conversely, if such fund is a person other than company or firm, business income will be taxable at the maximum marginal rate of tax [*i.e.*, 35.88 per cent (for the assessment year 2019-20) and **42.744** per cent (for the assessment year 2020-21)].

• Income in the hands of investor which is of the same nature as income by way of profits and gains of business at investment fund level shall be exempt.

• Where any income, other than income which is taxable at investment fund level, is payable to a unit holder by an investment fund, the fund shall deduct income-tax under section 194LBB.

• The income paid or credited by the investment fund shall be deemed to be of the same nature and in the same proportion in the hands of the unit holder as if it had been received by, or had accrued or arisen to, the investment fund.

• If in any year there is a loss at the fund level (either current loss or the loss which remained to be set off), the loss shall not be allowed to be passed through to the investors but would be carried over at fund level to be set off against income of the next year in accordance with the provisions of Chapter VI (applicable up to the assessment year 2019-20). From the assessment year 2020-21, section 115UB(2) has been amended to provide that –

- **the business loss of the investment fund shall be allowed to be carried forward by the fund and it shall not be passed onto the unit holder;**
- **the loss (other than business loss) shall also be ignored for the purposes of pass through to its unit holders, if such loss has arisen in respect of a unit which has not been held by the unit holder for a period of at least 12 months;**
- **the loss (other than business loss) accumulated at the level of investment fund as on March 31, 2019, shall be deemed to be the loss of a unit holder who held the unit on March 31, 2019 in respect of the investments made by him in the investment fund and allowed to be carried forward by him for the remaining period calculated from the year in which the loss had occurred for the first time taking that year as the first year and it shall be set-off by him in accordance with the provisions of Chapter VI;**

- **the loss so deemed in the hands of unit holders shall not be available to the investment fund for the purposes of Chapter VI.**

• The provisions of dividend distribution tax under section 115-O or tax on distributed income under section 115R shall not apply to the income paid by an investment fund to its unit holders.

• The income received by the investment fund would be exempt from TDS requirement [a notification to this effect has been issued under section 197A(1F)].

• It shall be mandatory for the investment fund to file its return of income. The investment fund shall also provide to the prescribed income-tax authority and the investors, the details of various components of income, etc., for the purposes of the scheme as follows—

a. statement of income distributed by investment fund in Form No. 64D to the Principal CIT/CIT (Form No. 64D should be uploaded on or before November 30 immediately after the end of the financial year);

b. statement of income distributed by an investment fund to its unitholders in Form No. 64C (Form No. 64C should be given on or before June 30 immediately after the end of the financial year).

• The existing pass through regime shall continue to apply to VCF/VCC which had been registered under SEBI (VCF) Regulations, 1996. Remaining VCFs (being part of Category I AIFs) shall be subject to the new pass through regime.

Special procedure for assessment of search cases

Assessment in the case of search or requisition [Sec. 153A, applicable from June 1, 2003]

220. Section 153A was inserted with effect from June 1, 2003 to provide for assessment in case of search or making requisition.

220.1 ***Notice for submission of return of six assessment years*[36]** - Section 153A provides the procedure for completion of assessment where a search is initiated under section 132 or books of account, or other documents or any assets are requisitioned under section 132A after May 31, 2003. In such cases, the Assessing Officer shall issue notice to such person requiring him to furnish, within such period as may be specified in the notice, return of income in respect of six assessment years[36] immediately preceding the assessment year relevant to the previous year in which the search was conducted under section 132 or requisition was made under section 132A.

For instance if search is conducted under section 132 on June 20, 2014, the Assessing Officer shall issue notice requiring the assessee to furnish return of income in respect of assessment years 2009-10 to 2014-15.

220.1-1 *EXTENSION OF SCOPE OF SECTION 153A TO ASSESS INCOME FOR A PERIOD BEYOND 6 YEARS* - The scope of section 153A has been enlarged by the Finance Act, 2017with effect from April 1, 2017. After this amendment, the Assessing Officer can issue notice for 6 preceding assessment years and for "the relevant assessment year or years". For this purpose, "relevant assessment year" shall mean an assessment year preceding the assessment year relevant to the previous year in which search is conducted or requisition is made which falls beyond 6 assessment years but not later than 10 assessment years from the end of the assessment year relevant to the previous year in which search is conducted or requisition is made. However, for the "relevant assessment year", notice can be issued if –

36. And for "relevant assessment year/years". For this purpose, "relevant assessment year" shall mean an assessment year preceding the assessment year relevant to the previous year in which search is conducted or requisition is made which falls beyond six assessment years but not later than ten assessment years from the end of the assessment year relevant to the previous year in which search is conducted or requisition is made. However, for the "relevant assessment year", notice can be issued if –

a. the Assessing Officer has in his possession books of account or other documents or evidence which reveal that the income which has escaped assessment amounts to or is likely to amount to Rs. 50 lakh (or more) in one year or in aggregate in the relevant four assessment years (falling beyond the sixth year);

b. such income escaping assessment is represented in the form of asset;

c. the income escaping assessment or part thereof relates to such year or years.

These provisions pertaining to "relevant assessment year" shall apply where search under section 132 is initiated or requisition under section 132A is made on or after April 1, 2017.

a. the Assessing Officer has in his possession books of account or other documents or evidence which reveal that the income which has escaped assessment amounts to (or is likely to amount) to Rs. 50 lakh (or more) in one year or in aggregate in the relevant 4 assessment years (falling beyond the 6th year);

b. such income escaping assessment is represented in the form of asset (for this purpose "asset" shall include[37] immovable property being land or building or both, shares and securities, loans and advances, deposits in bank account);

c. the income escaping assessment or part thereof relates to such year or years; and

d. search under section 132 is initiated or requisition under section 132A is made on or after April 1, 2017.

Provisions illustrated - Search is conducted on the premises of X Ltd. on May 20, 2018. The Assessing Officer can issue notice requiring X Ltd. to furnish return of income in respect of 6 preceding assessment years (*i.e.*, assessment years 2013-14 to 2018-19). The Assessing Officer has documents in his possession which reveal that X Ltd. has undisclosed income (represented in the form of asset) pertaining to earlier assessment years as follows –

(Rs. in lakh)

Assessment years	*Undisclosed income*		
	Situation 1	*Situation 2*	*Situation 3*
2012-13 (7th year)	10	5	40
2011-12 (8th year)	12	12	0
2010-11 (9th year)	13	13	1
2009-10 (10th year)	15	15	9
2008-09 (11th year)	5	10	150

Situation 1 - Notice can also be issued under section 153A for the assessment years 2009-10 to 2012-13 (as the aggregate undisclosed income for these assessment years is Rs. 50 lakh). However, notice cannot be issued for years earlier than 10th year (*i.e.*, assessment year 2008-09 or earlier).

Situation 2 - Notice cannot be issued for the assessment years 2009-10 to 2012-13 (as the aggregate undisclosed income for these assessment years is less than Rs. 50 lakh). Even for earlier years, notice cannot be issued.

Situation 3 - Notice can also be issued for the assessment years 2009-10, 2010-11 and 2012-13. For earlier years, notice cannot be issued.

220.2 ***Pending assessment*** - The Assessing Officer shall assess or reassess the total income of each of these six assessment years[38]. Assessment or reassessment, if any, relating to any assessment year falling within the period of six assessment years[38] pending on the date of initiation of the search under section 132 or requisition under section 132A, as the case may be, shall abate.

220.3 ***Existing provisions for reassessment vis-a-vis section 153A*** - Save as otherwise provided in sections 153A, 153B and 153C, all other provisions of the Act shall apply to the assessment made under section 153A. Section 153A authorises issue of notice for reassessment or recomputation for six earlier assessments[38], without the necessity of satisfaction of the superior officers, required under section 151. Moreover, there is no need for income concealment for longer or shorter time-limit under section 147, since provisions of sections 147 and 148 will not be applicable in search cases. On the mere fact of search, all the precautions given to the taxpayer against re-opening of back assessment have been set aside.

220.4 ***Prior approval necessary for assessment in cases of search [Sec. 153D]*** - Section 153D was inserted with effect from June 1, 2007. In search cases, assessment order cannot be passed by the Assessing Officer below the rank of Joint Commissioner except with the prior approval of the Joint Commissioner.

Time-limit for completion of assessment year under section 153A [Sec. 153B applicable from June 1, 2003]

221. *See* Referencer 11.

Assessment of income of any other person [Sec. 153C applicable from June 1, 2003]

222. Section 153C inserted from June 1, 2003 provides that where an Assessing Officer is satisfied that any money, bullion, jewellery or other valuable article belongs to; or thing or books of account or documents seized or requisitioned belongs to (or, from June 1, 2015, relates to) a person other than the person referred to in section 153A, then the books of account, or documents or assets seized or requisitioned shall be handed

37. The definition of "asset" is inclusive. Any asset (whether movable or immovable), though not specifically included in the definition, may fall under the definition of asset.

38. *See* Foot Note 36 (previous page).

over to the Assessing Officer having jurisdiction over such other person and that Assessing Officer shall proceed against such other person and issue such other person notice and assess or reassess income of such other person in accordance with the provisions of section 153A for the relevant assessment year or years referred to in section 153A(1).

The following points should be noted—

• In case of "other person", the reference to the date of initiation of the search under section 132 or making of requisition under section 132A in the second proviso to section 153A shall be construed as reference to the date of receiving the books of account or documents or assets seized or requisitioned by the Assessing Officer having the jurisdiction over such other person.

• In respect of the assessment year relevant to the previous year in which search is conducted under section 132 or requisition is made under section 132A, in case of other person, where—

a. no return of income has been furnished by such person and no notice under section 142(1) has been issued to him, or

b. a return of income has been furnished by such person but no notice under section 143(2) has been served and limitation of serving the notice under section 143(2) has expired, or

c. assessment or reassessment, if any, has been made,

before the date of receiving of books of account or documents or assets seized or requisitioned by the Assessing Officer having jurisdiction over such other person, such Assessing Officer shall issue the notice and assess or reassess total income of such other person for such assessment year in the manner provided in section 153A.

The above provisions would apply where books of account or documents or assets seized or requisitioned referred to in sub-section (1) have been received by the Assessing Officer having jurisdiction over such other person after the due date for furnishing the return of income for the assessment year relevant to the previous year in which search is conducted under section 132 or requisition is made under section 132A.

Tax clearance certificate

Tax clearance certificate

223. The scheme of section 230 has been modified with effect from June 1, 2003.

223.1 ***When a person is not domiciled in India [Sec. 230(1)]*** - The provisions of section 230(1) are given below—

223.1-1 *CONDITIONS* - Section 230(1) is applicable if the following conditions are satisfied—

1. The concerned person is not domiciled in India.

2. He has come to India in connection with business, profession or employment.

3. He has income which is generated from any source in India.

223.1-2 *NO OBJECTION CERTIFICATE* - No objection certificate shall be issued as follows—

• *Undertaking from employer/payer of income* - If the aforesaid conditions are satisfied, the concerned person shall not leave India by land, sea or air unless he furnishes an undertaking as follows—

a. the undertaking should be in Form No. 30A from his employer or through whom such person is in receipt of the income ; and

b. such undertaking should be to the effect that tax payable by such person shall be paid by the employer or the person through whom any income is received.

• *No objection certificate* - If such person submits the undertaking to the prescribed authority (*i.e.*, CCIT or DG who has jurisdiction over the person not domiciled in India or other authority/authorities by CCIT/DG) satisfying the above conditions, the prescribed authority shall on receipt of the undertaking, immediately give to such person a no objection certificate in Form No. 30B, for leaving India. A copy of Form No. 30A and certificate in Form No. 30B should be forwarded to CCIT or DG having jurisdiction over person mentioned in (*a*) *supra*.

223.1-3 *EXCEPTIONS* - The aforesaid requirement is not applicable in the following two cases—

• *Exception one* - If a person who is not domiciled in India but visits India as a foreign tourist or for any other purpose not connected with business, profession or employment.

• *Exception two* - If the case is covered by such exceptions as the Central Government may, by notification in the Official Gazette, specify in this behalf.

223.2 ***When a person is domiciled in India [Sec. 230(1A)]*** - If a person is domiciled in India, then he would be covered by the requirement of section 230 in one or both of the following two cases—

• *Case one - A self-declaration* - A self-declaration is necessary if the person who wants to leave the country is domiciled in India. The self-declaration should satisfy the following conditions—

a. it should be in Form No. 30C;

b. it should be given to the income-tax authority or a prescribed authority (*i.e.*, CCIT);

c. it should contain the permanent account number allotted under section 139A (in case no such permanent account number has been allotted to him, or his total income is not chargeable to income-tax or he is not required to obtain a permanent account number under the Act, such person shall furnish a certificate in the prescribed form, *i.e.*, Annexure to Form No. 30C);

d. it should disclose the purpose of visit outside India; and

e. it should also disclose the estimated period of his stay outside India.

Every domiciled person should submit the aforesaid self-declaration at the time of departure (a few exception may be notified by the Central Government). Such person can leave the country without obtaining a certificate from income-tax authorities, unless he comes in *case two* (*infra*).

• *Case two - Obtaining a certificate from income-tax authority* - A certificate should be obtained from the concerned income-tax authority if the following conditions are satisfied—

1. The person is domiciled in India at the time of departure. (Application should be in Form No. 31)

2. The concerned income-tax authority (*i.e.*, Assessing Officer) is of the opinion that in respect of such person certain circumstances exist[39] which render it necessary for such person to obtain a certificate under section 230(1A).

3. Such income-tax authority records the reasons for the circumstances mentioned above.

4. Prior approval of the Chief Commissioner is obtained by the income-tax authority.

If the above four conditions are satisfied, then such person cannot leave India by land, sea or air, unless he obtains a certificate in Form No. 33 from the concerned income-tax authority. Such certificate should state—

a. the person who wants to leave the country has no liabilities under Income-tax Act, or Wealth-tax Act, Gift-tax Act, Expenditure-tax Act; or

b. that satisfactory arrangements have been made for the payment of all or any of such taxes which are or may become payable by that person.

223.3 ***Clarifications from Board*** - Contractors are now not required to obtain income-tax clearance certificate from the Income-tax Department and there is no need to furnish such certificate while submitting tenders or obtaining commercial contracts. Further, income-tax clearance certificate shall also not be required for any other purposes such as registration or renewal of registration of contractors, renewal of import/export licences, renewal of post licences and renewal of shipping licences. However, all such persons shall quote their Permanent Account Number in their tender or other relevant documents—Circular No. 2/2004, dated February 10, 2004.

Tonnage tax

Introduction of Tonnage Tax [Secs. 115V to 115VZC]

224. To make the Indian shipping industry more competitive, a tonnage tax scheme for taxation of shipping profits has been introduced. Many maritime nations have introduced tonnage based taxation. Some of the basic features of the tonnage tax scheme are as follows:—

• It is a scheme of presumptive taxation whereby the notional income arising from the operation of a ship is determined based on the tonnage of the ship.

39. In this regard, the Board has directed that tax clearance certificate, may be required to be obtained by persons domiciled in India in the following circumstances :

a. where the person is involved in serious financial irregularities and his presence is necessary in investigation of cases under the Income-tax Act or the Wealth-tax Act and it is likely that a tax demand will be raised against him, or

b. where the person has direct tax arrears exceeding Rs. 10 lakh outstanding against him which have not been stayed by any authority.

• The notional income is taxed at the normal corporate rate applicable for the year.

• Tax is payable even if there is a loss in a year.

• A company may opt for the scheme and once such option is exercised, there is a lock-in-period of 10 years. If a company opts out, it is debarred from re-entry for ten years.

• Since this is a preferential regime of taxation, certain conditions like creation of reserves, training, etc., are required to be met.

• A company may be expelled in certain circumstances.

Chapter XII-G was inserted in the Income-tax Act containing sections 115V to 115VZC which provides for special provisions relating to taxation of the income of shipping companies.

224.1 *Salient features* - The salient features of the scheme which is applicable from the assessment year 2005-06 are as follows:

• A company owning at least one qualifying ship may join. A qualifying ship is one with a minimum tonnage of 15 tons and having a valid certificate. The company has to opt for the scheme within 3 months, *i.e.*, any time between October 1, 2004 to December 31, 2004 by making an online application in Form No. 65 to the concerned Joint Commissioner who may pass an appropriate order. A new company can make application within three months of the date of its incorporation or the date on which it became a qualifying company, as the case may be.

• Certain types of ships like fishing vessels, pleasure crafts, harbour and river ferries, etc., are excluded in terms of section 115VD which gives details of as to what ships will qualify for the scheme.

• The business of operating qualifying ships is to be considered a separate business and separate accounts are to be maintained. Section 115VG gives the manner of computation of the daily tonnage income as follows—

Qualifying ship having net tonnage	*Amount of daily tonnage income (for the assessment years 2005-06 to 2012-13)*	*Amount of daily tonnage income (from the assessment year 2013-14 onwards)*
Up to 1,000	Rs. 46 for each 100 tons	Rs. 70 for each 100 tons
Exceeding 1,000 but not more than 10,000	Rs. 460 *plus* Rs. 35 for each 100 tons exceeding 1,000 tons	Rs. 700 *plus* Rs. 53 for each 100 tons exceeding 1,000 tons
Exceeding 10,000 but not more than 25,000	Rs. 3,610 *plus* Rs. 28 for each 100 tons exceeding 10,000 tons	Rs. 5,470 *plus* Rs. 42 for each 100 tons exceeding 10,000 tons
Exceeding 25,000	Rs. 7,810 *plus* Rs. 19 for each 100 tons exceeding 25,000 tons.	Rs. 11,770 *plus* Rs. 29 for each 100 tons exceeding 25,000 tons

The daily tonnage income shall be multiplied by the number of days the ship operated. The resulting amount would be the annual tonnage income from the ship. A company owning at least one ship may charter in ships subject to certain limits for the purpose of operation. Relevant shipping income, which replaces the actual income from the operations, is defined in section 115VI. Section 115VJ gives the treatment of common costs.

• A company opting for the scheme is not allowed any set-off of loss nor is any depreciation allowed. However, both loss and depreciation are deemed to have been allowed and notional adjustments are made against the relevant shipping income. Although depreciation is not allowed, it is necessary to bifurcate the qualifying ships and non-qualifying ships at the time a company joins the scheme. Section 115VK lays down the method for allocating the written down value amongst qualifying and non-qualifying ships. Any income from transfer of qualifying assets is treated in the same manner as for any other business asset in terms of section 115VN.

• The profits from the business of operating qualifying ships will not be taken into consideration for the purpose of MAT as per section 115VO.

• Section 115VP relates to method and time of opting for tonnage tax scheme. A qualifying company may opt for the tonnage tax scheme by making an application to the Joint Commissioner having jurisdiction over the company in Form No. 65 and manner prescribed in rule 11P. A Certificate of Registration under Merchant Shipping Act, 1958 and International Tonnage Certificate should accompany application in Form No. 65. The initial period in which a company will be able to opt for the scheme will be for a period of three months starting from October 1, 2004 and ending on December 31, 2004. After the end of the initial period, only those companies which are incorporated after the initial period or which become qualifying companies after the initial period for the first time (in case of existing companies) shall be able to opt for the scheme. In such cases, however, the application for exercising the option will have to be made within three months[40] of the date of the incorporation or, as the case may be, the date on which the company became a qualifying company—Circular No. 5/2005, dated July 15, 2005.

• Section 115VQ lays down that once a company opts for the scheme, the option remains in force for 10 years except in certain circumstances. Section 115VS provides for the circumstances in which the tonnage tax company is prohibited from opting for the scheme. Such prohibition is for a period of 10 years. Sections 115VT, 115VU, 115VS and 115VW lay down the conditions for the applicability of the scheme. In terms of section 115VT, a tonnage tax company has to create a reserve of at least 20 per cent of its book profits to be utilized for the purpose of acquisition of new ships. As per section 115VU a tonnage tax company has to comply with a minimum training requirement in accordance with the guidelines to be issued by the DG (Shipping). The company will be expelled if the training requirements are not met for 5 consecutive years. Section 115VV lays down that every company which has opted for tonnage tax scheme, not more than 49 per cent of the net tonnage of the qualifying ships operated by it during any previous year shall be chartered in. In terms of section 115VW, maintenance of separate books of account and the audit [Form No. 66][41] of the same is compulsory for a company opting for the scheme. Section 115VX lays down the details regarding valid certificate which indicates the net tonnage of ships. Sections 115VY and 115VZ provide for the contingencies of amalgamation and demerger. Section 115VZB enjoins upon a company not to abuse the preferential tax regime and section 115VZC provides for expulsion of a company in case of abuse.

Securities transaction tax

Securities transaction tax

225. Securities transaction tax has been levied on the value of taxable securities transactions. The provisions relating to the transaction tax are contained in Chapter VII of the Finance (No. 2) Act, 2004, and shall take effect from October 1, 2004.

225.1 ***Charge of security transaction tax*** - Securities transaction tax is applicable in respect of the following transactions—

1. Purchase or sale of an equity share in a company or a derivative or a unit of an equity oriented fund or unit of a business trust, entered into in a recognized stock exchange.

2. Sale of unlisted equity shares under an offer for sale to the public included in an initial public offer (applicable from July 1, 2012).

3. Sale of unlisted units of a business trust by any holder of such units which were acquired in consideration of a transfer referred to in section 47(*xvii*) of the Income-tax Act under an offer for sale to the public included in an initial offer and where such units are subsequently listed on a recognised stock exchange (applicable from June 1, 2015).

4. Sale of unit of an equity oriented fund to the mutual fund.

• *Equity oriented fund* - Equity oriented fund means a fund set up under a scheme of a mutual fund specified under section 10(*23D*) and, —

a. in a case where the fund invests in the units of another fund which is traded on a recognised stock exchange, —
   - a minimum of 90 per cent of the total proceeds of such fund is invested in the units of such other fund; and
   - such other fund also invests a minimum of 90 per cent of its total proceeds in the equity shares of domestic companies listed on a recognised stock exchange; and

b. in any other case, a minimum of 65 per cent of the total proceeds of such fund is invested in the equity shares of domestic companies listed on a recognised stock exchange.

---

40. If an assessee had filed the application under section 115VP in time but Tonnage Certificate was submitted belatedly at the time of assessment (and the delay in submission of the valid Tonnage Certificate was under the circumstances beyond its control), the benefit of tonnage scheme as per the provisions of section 115VP cannot be denied—*CIT* v. *EPSOM Shipping (I) (P.) Ltd.* [2008] 24 SOT 192 (Mum.).

41. From April 1, 2014, audit report should be submitted electronically. Provisions pertaining to electronic submission of audit report were not applicable prior to April 1, 2014 (for period prior to April 1, 2014, audit report may be retained by the assessee and it may be furnished in original whenever the Assessing Officer wants to examine it in assessment proceedings or otherwise).

The percentage of equity shareholding or unit held in respect of the fund, as the case may be, shall be computed with reference to the annual average of the monthly averages of the opening and closing figures.

However, securities transaction tax is not applicable in the following cases –

a. in respect of transactions entered into by any person for, or on behalf of, the New Pension System Trust (applicable with effect from October 1, 2009); or

b. in respect of transaction entered into by any person on a recognised stock exchange located in an International Financial Services Centre where the consideration for such transaction is paid or payable in foreign currency (applicable with effect from June 1, 2016).

225.2 ***Value of taxable securities*** - The value of a taxable securities transaction is to be computed as follows:—

a. in the case of a taxable securities transaction relating to a derivative (being "option in securities"), it shall be the aggregate of the strike price and the option premium of such "option in securities";

b. in the case of any other taxable securities transaction relating to a derivative (being future), it shall be the price at which such "futures" is traded; and

c. in the case of any other taxable securities transaction, it shall be the price at which such securities are purchased or sold.

The Board may specify (having regard to the manner in which taxable securities transactions are settled in a recognised stock exchange), the method of determining the price of securities for the aforesaid purpose.

225.3 ***Rate of tax*** - Securities Transaction Tax (STT) rates and other relative issues are given in para 0.10 Referencer 1.

225.4 ***Collection and recovery of tax*** - Every recognized stock exchange shall collect the securities transaction tax from every person being a purchaser and seller of taxable securities in that stock exchange at the rates stated above. However, in the case of sale of units to the mutual fund, it shall be collected by the prescribed person in the mutual fund and in the case of initial public offer, it shall be collected by the lead merchant banker. The amount of securities transaction tax collected by the recognised stock exchange/mutual fund has to be paid to the credit of the Government by 7th day of the month following the month in which the securities transaction tax is collected.

225.5 ***Return*** - A recognised stock exchange/prescribed person in every mutual fund shall be responsible for submission of a return in the prescribed form [Form No. 1 in the case of recognised stock exchange and Form No. 2 in the case of a Mutual Fund] of all taxable securities transactions entered into during a financial year on that stock exchange or, as the case may be, in respect of all taxable securities transactions, being sale of units to such mutual fund during such financial year. A revised return can be submitted before the assessment is made, in case of discovery of any omission or wrong statement in the return earlier furnished.

225.6 ***Issue of notice*** - The Assessing Officer may issue notice requiring any assessee who is responsible for collection of securities transaction tax, and has not furnished the return, to furnish such return within such time as may be specified in the notice.

225.7 ***Assessment*** - Section 102 of the Finance (No. 2) Act, 2004 contains provisions relating to assessment of the value of taxable securities transactions and securities transaction tax payable or refundable on the basis of such assessment. It also provides that no assessment shall be made after the expiry of 2 years from the end of the relevant financial year.

225.8 ***Rectification*** - Mistakes apparent from record of any order passed by the Assessing Officer can be rectified within 1 year from the end of the financial year in which the order sought to be amended was passed. The Assessing Officer may rectify mistakes either *suo motu* or at the instance of the assessee. Further, any amendment which has the effect of enhancing an assessment or reducing a refund or otherwise increasing the liability of the assessee shall be made only after giving the assessee a reasonable opportunity of being heard.

225.9 ***Interest*** - A simple interest at the rate of 1 per cent, for every month (or part of a month) is applicable where the securities transaction tax collected is not credited to the account of the Central Government within the period specified above.

225.10 ***Penalty*** - The following penalties may be imposed on a recognized stock exchange/mutual fund—

If the recognized stock exchange/mutual fund fails to collect whole or any part of securities transaction tax	In addition of paying tax and interest, a penalty which is equal to 100 per cent of the amount of tax which is not collected may be imposed

If after collecting such tax, it is not paid to the credit of the Government within the specified time	In addition of paying tax and interest, a sum of Rs. 1,000 for each day during which the default continues may be imposed
If the recognized stock exchange/mutual fund fails to furnish return within the time given under section 91(1) or in response to notice	Rs. 100 per day for which the default continues
If any person has failed to comply with a notice under section 92(1)	In addition of paying tax and interest, a sum of Rs. 10,000 for each day during which the default continues may be imposed

Notes :

1. If the assessee proves that there was reasonable cause for the above failure, penalty cannot be imposed.

2. No order of imposing penalty can be made unless the assessee has been given a reasonable opportunity of being heard.

225.11 ***Application of certain provisions of the Income-tax Act*** - Sections 120, 131, 133A, 156, 178, 220 to 227, 229, 232, 260A, 261, 262, 265 to 269, 278B, 282 and 288 to 293 of the Income-tax Act which, *inter alia*, relate to issue of notice of demand, recovery and collection of tax, appeals to High Courts and Supreme Court, appearance of authorised representatives, etc., will, so far as may be, apply in relation to securities transaction tax.

225.12 ***Appeals*** - Section 110 of the Finance (No. 2) Act, 2004 provides for an appeal to the Commissioner of Income-tax (Appeals) [Form No. 4] when the assessee denies its liability to be assessed or against any order passed by an Assessing Officer. This clause contains provisions relating to time-limit for filing appeal, etc., and provides that provisions of sections 249 to 251 of the Income-tax Act will, as far as may be, apply in such cases. Likewise, the provisions of sections 252 to 255 of the Income-tax Act shall apply for appeal to the Appellate Tribunal [Form No. 5] against an order passed by a Commissioner of Income-tax (Appeals).

225.13 ***Prosecution*** - Section 112 provides for punishment, by way of imprisonment up to a period of 3 years and with fine, for submitting any statement in any verification, account or statement which is false. It also provides that an offence punishable under these provisions shall be deemed to be non-cognisable within the meaning of the Code of Criminal Procedure, 1973. However, no prosecution shall be initiated except with the prior sanction of the Chief Commissioner of the Income-tax.

Restriction on cash transactions

Restriction on cash transactions [Secs. 269ST and 271DA]

226. In order to achieve the mission of the Government to move towards a less cash economy to reduce generation and circulation of black money, sections 269ST and 271DA have been inserted with effect from April 1, 2017.

226.1 ***Mode of undertaking transaction [Sec. 269ST]*** - Section 269ST provides that no person shall receive an amount of Rs. 2 lakh (or more) otherwise than by an account-payee cheque or account-payee bank draft or use of electronic clearing system through a bank account (**or through prescribed electronic mode**). This provision is applicable whether the recipient is seller of goods or service provider or transferor of a capital asset (or any other person). The ceiling of Rs. 2 lakh is calculated as follows –

1. Same payer in a day - The aggregate amount received [other than by an account-payee cheque/draft/use of electronic clearing system through a bank account (**or through prescribed electronic mode**)] from the same person in a day should not be Rs. 2 lakh or more.

2. Same transaction - Amount received [other than by an account-payee cheque/draft/use of electronic clearing system through a bank account (**or through prescribed electronic mode**)] in respect of a single transaction should not be Rs. 2 lakh or more.

3. Same event/occasion - Amount received [other than by an account payee cheque/draft/use of electronic clearing system through a bank account (**or through prescribed electronic mode**)] in respect of a transaction relating to one event/occasion from a person should not be Rs. 2 lakh or more.

226.2 ***When section 269ST is not applicable*** - Section 269ST is not applicable in the cases given below –

- *When recipient is banking company, post office, etc.* - The above restriction shall not apply when recipient is Government, any banking company, post office savings bank or co-operative bank.

• *Withdrawal from bank/post office* - The restriction on cash transaction imposed by section 269ST is not applicable to withdrawal of cash from a bank, co-operative bank or a post office savings bank – Notification No. SO 1057(E)[$], dated April 5, 2017.

• *Cash payment to a few notified persons* - CBDT has notified the list of the persons who are exempt from receiving cash payments of Rs. 2 lakh or more as specified in section 269ST. CBDT has exempted 5 entities from the purview of section 269ST. The list of the persons is as follows (section 269ST is not applicable if the recipients are given below) –

1. Receipt by business correspondent on behalf of banking company or co-operative bank in accordance with guidelines issued by RBI.

2. Receipt by White Label ATM Operator from retail outlet sources on behalf of banking company or co-operative bank, in accordance with the authorization issued by RBI.

3. Receipt from an agent by an issuer of prepaid payment instruments, in accordance with the authorization issued by RBI.

4. Receipt by a company or institution issuing credit cards against bills raised in respect of one or more credit cards.

5. Receipt pertaining to award/reward which is not includible in the total income under section 10(*17A*) – Notification No. 57/2017[$], dated July 3, 2017.

• *Loan repayment received by NBFC/HFC* - CBDT has clarified that in respect of receipt in the nature of repayment of loan by non-banking finance companies (NBFCs) or Housing Finance Companies (HFCs), all the instalments of loan repayment shall not be aggregated for the purpose of determining applicability of provisions of section 269ST. Provision of this section shall be applicable on one instalment of loan – Circular No. 22/2017[$], dated July 3, 2017. In other words, the receipt of one instalment of loan repayment in respect of a loan shall constitute a "single transaction" as specified in section 269ST(*b*).

226.3 ***Penalty for failure to comply with provisions of section 269ST [Sec. 271DA]*** - Section 271DA provides for levy of penalty. If a person receives any sum in contravention of the provisions of section 269ST, he shall be liable to pay, by way of penalty, a sum equal to the amount of such receipt. However, penalty shall not be imposable if such person proves that there were good and sufficient reasons for the contravention. Penalty under this section shall be imposed by the Joint Commissioner.

226-E1 X is a wholesale dealer in computer hardware in Cuttack. On April 17, 2018, he sells goods on credit to Y (vide Invoice No. 3/47, amount being Rs. 16,70,000). Payment is made by Y as follows –

1. Payment of Rs. 1,30,000 in cash on April 20, 2018.
2. Payment of Rs. 4,00,000 by RTGS (from SBI account of Y to HDFC account of X) on April 25, 2018.
3. Payment of Rs. 1,80,000 in cash on April 26, 2018 (afternoon).
4. Payment of Rs. 1,10,000 by bearer cheque on April 26, 2018 (late evening).
5. Payment of Rs. 20,000 by bearer cheque on April 27, 2018.
6. Payment of Rs. 100 in cash on April 28, 2018.
7. Payment of Rs. 8,29,900 by account-payee draft on March 28, 2018.

What are the tax consequences of aforesaid payments?

•

Tax consequences for recipient - X, the recipient, is subject to the following tax consequences –

- Payment received [otherwise than by account-payee cheque/draft/use of electronic clearing through a bank account (or through prescribed electronic mode)] is Rs. 4,40,100 (*i.e.,* Rs. 1,30,000 + Rs. 1,80,000 + Rs. 1,10,000 + Rs. 20,000 + Rs. 100). It is covered by section 269ST (even if cash payment/bearer cheque payment in a single day is less than Rs. 2,00,000). The Assessing Officer can impose 100% of Rs. 4,40,100 as penalty under section 271DA.
- Consideration received in cash is Rs. 3,10,100 (*i.e.,* Rs. 1,30,000 on April 20, 2018 + Rs. 1,80,000 on April 26, 2018 + Rs. 100 on April 28, 2018). However, section 206C(1D) has been omitted with effect from April 1, 2017. TCS provisions are not applicable.
- X has received more than Rs. 2,00,000 in cash pertaining to Invoice No. 3/47. He is required to report this transaction in Form No. 61A (*i.e.,* statement of financial transaction under section 285BA), if he is subject to tax audit under section 44AB.

[$] For Notification No. SO 1057(E), Notification No. 57/2017 and Circular No. 22/2017, log on to *taxmann.com/readyreckoner.aspx.*

Tax consequences for payer - Payment made in cash/bearer cheque/crossed cheque is covered by disallowance under section 40A(3), if such payment in aggregate in a day exceeds Rs. 10,000. Consequently, payment of Rs. 1,30,000, Rs. 1,80,000, Rs. 1,10,000 and Rs. 20,000 will be disallowed in the hands of Y under section 40A(3).

226-E2 X Ltd. provides tax consultancy in Bhopal. On June 5, 2018, it gets cash payment of Rs. 3,70,000 from Y Ltd. (out of which Rs. 2,10,000 is for part payment of Invoice No. 5/2018, dated April 6, 2018; Rs. 1,40,000 is for part payment of Invoice No. 23/2018, dated May 28, 2018 and Rs. 20,000 for part payment of Invoice No. 29/2018, dated June 1, 2018). The balance payment of Invoice No. 5/2018, Invoice No. 23/2018 and Invoice No. 29/2018 is received on July 20, 2018 by RTGS. Discuss tax consequences.

●

Tax consequences for X Ltd. - X Ltd. will be subject to the following –

- Payment received [otherwise than by account-payee cheque/draft/use of electronic clearing through a bank account (or through prescribed electronic mode)] from Y Ltd. on June 5, 2018 is Rs. 3,70,000. It is covered by section 269ST (even if payment for Invoice No. 23/2018 is less than Rs. 2,00,000). The Assessing Officer can impose 100% of Rs. 3,70,000 as penalty under section 271DA.
- Cash consideration of Rs. 2,10,000 is received in respect of Invoice No. 5/2018. However, section 206C(1D) has been omitted with effect from April 1, 2017. TCS provisions are not applicable.
- X Ltd. will have to report the above transaction of cash receipt of Rs. 2,10,000 in Form No. 61A (*i.e.*, statement of financial transaction under section 285BA), if it is subject to tax audit under section 44AB.

Tax consequences for Y Ltd. - Cash payment of Rs. 2,10,000, Rs. 1,40,000 and Rs. 20,000 will be disallowed under section 40A(3).

226-E3 X Ltd. is a wedding planner. Different functions pertaining to the wedding of Y's son are arranged by X Ltd. For this event, four different invoices are issued by X Ltd. to Y (Invoice 1 for ring ceremony: Rs. 17,25,000, Invoice 2 for sagan ceremony: Rs. 21,00,000, Invoice 3 for marriage ceremony: Rs. 35,00,000 and Invoice 4 for reception: Rs. 28,00,000). Rs. 2,10,000 (*i.e.*, Rs. 1,95,000 for Invoice 1 paid on June 3, 2018 and Rs. 15,000 for Invoice 2 paid on June 5, 2018) is received in cash/bearer cheque/crossed cheque. The balance is received on August 19, 2018 by RTGS (in the current account of X Ltd. from the savings bank account of Y). Discuss whether provisions of sections 269ST and 271DA are applicable.

●

As the payment pertaining to one event/occasion (*i.e.*, marriage of Y's son) received in cash/bearer cheque/crossed cheque is Rs. 2,10,000, it is covered by section 269ST. The Assessing Officer can impose 100% of Rs. 2,10,000 as penalty on X Ltd. under section 271DA.

226-E4 In 226-E3 the recipient of service in Invoice 2 is Mrs. Y. In all other invoices, recipient of service is Y. Payment of Rs. 15,000 is received from Mrs. Y and the balance payment is made by Y. Discuss whether provisions of sections 269ST and 271DA are applicable.

●

Cash payment of Rs. 1,95,000 is received from Y and another cash payment Rs. 15,000 is received from Mrs. Y. Recipient is X Ltd. The two payments pertain to one event/occasion (*i.e.*, marriage of Y's son). However, section 269ST is not applicable, as cash payment pertaining to an event received from "a person" is less than Rs. 2,00,000.

226-E5 In 226-E4, A Ltd. is a subsidiary of X Ltd. Invoice 2 is issued by A Ltd. (recipient of service: Y). Other invoices are issued by X Ltd. (recipient of service: Y). Mode of payment is same. Discuss whether provisions of sections 269ST and 271DA are applicable.

●

Payment received in cash/bearer cheque/crossed cheque by X Ltd. for the event pertaining to marriage of Y's son is less than Rs. 2,00,000. Provisions of sections 269ST and 271DA are not applicable. Likewise, these provisions are not applicable in the hands of A Ltd.

Banking cash transaction tax

Banking cash transaction tax

227. The provisions of banking cash transaction tax are applicable during June 1, 2005 and March 31, 2009.

Equalisation levy

What is equalisation levy

228. Business may be conducted in digital domain without regard to national boundaries. This may dissolve the link between an income-producing activity and a specific location. To tackle taxation issues in transaction conducted in cyber space, equalisation levy has been imposed. Salient features of this levy are given below –

1. *Date of enforcement* - This levy shall come into force on June 1, 2016.

2. *Charge of equalisation levy* - Equalisation levy shall be charged at the rate of 6 per cent of the amount of consideration for specified services received or receivable by a non-resident from a person resident in India and carrying on business or profession or from a non-resident having a permanent establishment in India.

"Specified service" for this purpose, means online advertisement, any provision for digital advertising space or any other facility or service for the purpose of online advertisement and includes any other service as may be notified by the Central Government in this behalf.

3. *When equalisation levy is not applicable* - In the following cases equalisation levy is not applicable –

a. if the non-resident service provider has a permanent establishment in India and income from such specified services is effectively connected to this permanent establishment;

b. where the payment for specified service by the person resident in India (or the permanent establishment in India) is not for the purpose of carrying out business or profession;

c. if the aggregate amount of consideration for specified services received or receivable by a non-resident from a person resident in India (or from a non-resident having a permanent establishment in India) does not exceed Rs. 1 lakh in any previous year.

4. *Collection and recovery* - Every person, being a resident and carrying on business or profession or a non-resident having a permanent establishment in India (here for the purpose of equalisation levy referred to as "assessee") shall deduct equalisation levy from the amount paid or payable to the non-resident in respect of specified services. The amount of equalisation levy so deducted by the payer has to be paid to the credit of the Government by 7th day of the month following the month in which the equalisation levy is collected. Even if equalisation levy is not deducted, the payer is liable to pay the levy to the credit of Central Government.

5. *Furnishing of statement* - Payer responsible for deduction of equalisation levy shall furnish a statement electronically in Form No. 1[$] in respect of all specified services entered into during a financial year. Such statement shall be furnished on or before June 30 immediately following the financial year.

6. *Processing of statement* - Provisions have been made relating to processing of the value of specified services and equalisation levy payable or refundable on the basis of such processing. It further provides for computation mechanism. It also provides that no intimation shall be made after the expiry of 1 year from the end of the relevant financial year. Further, rectification order can be passed by the Assessing Officer within 1 year from the end of the financial year in which the order sought to be amended was passed. The Assessing Officer may rectify mistakes either *suo motu* or at the instance of the assessee. Further, any amendment which has the effect of enhancing the liability or reducing a refund of the assessee shall be made only after giving the assessee a reasonable opportunity of being heard.

7. *Interest* - Simple interest at the rate of 1 per cent for every month (or part of a month) shall be payable where the equalisation levy collected is not credited to the account of the Central Government within the due date of payment.

8. *Penalty* - An assessee will be liable for penalty as follows –

Different situations	*Penalty (in addition to paying equalisation levy and interest)*
Failure to deduct equalisation levy (wholly or partly)	A penalty equal to amount of equalisation levy
Failure to deposit equalisation levy with Government	Rs. 1,000 for each day of default (not to exceed amount of equalisation levy)
Failure to furnish statement	Rs. 100 for each day of default

Penalty is not imposable if the assessee proves to the satisfaction of the Assessing Officer that there was reasonable cause for the failure given above.

9. *Other provisions* - Other provisions pertaining to appeal[$$], punishment, power to make rule, power to remove difficulties have been incorporated.

[$] For Form No. 1, log on to *taxmann.com/readyreckoner.aspx.*

[$$] For appeal to Commissioner (Appeals), online submission of Form No. 3 is required. For attachments and other procedures, log on to *taxmann.com/readyreckoner.aspx.*

HOW TO USE TABLES

Example 1 : Salary of X (55 years) for the previous years 2018-19 and 2019-20 is Rs. 8,55,000 (before standard deduction). During the previous years 2018-19 and 2019-20 he has made the following investment/contribution : *(a)* PPF : Rs. 1,00,000, *(b)* mediclaim insurance premium for his father Rs. 21,000, *(c)* NSC (VIII Issue) : Rs. 60,000 and *(d)* NPS : Rs. 50,000.

•

	AY 2019-20 Rs.	*AY 2020-21 Rs.*
Salary (Rs. 8,55,000 *minus* standard deduction)	8,15,000	8,05,000
Any other income	*Nil*	*Nil*
Gross total income	8,15,000	8,05,000
Less : Deduction		
Under section 80C	1,50,000	1,50,000
Under section 80D	21,000	21,000
Under section 80CCD	50,000	50,000
Total income	5,94,000	5,84,000
Income-tax	31,300	29,300
Less : Rebate under section 87A	*Nil*	*Nil*
Income-tax [page B-11 or page B-27]	31,300	29,300
Add: Surcharge	*Nil*	*Nil*
Income-tax and surcharge	31,300	29,300
Add: Health and education cess @ 4%	1,252	1,172
Total tax (rounded off)	32,550	30,470

Example 2 : Gross total income of X is Rs. 14,26,000 for the assessment year 2020-21. Deduction under sections 80C, 80CCD, 80D is Rs. 1,50,000, Rs. 50,000 and Rs. 25,000 respectively. Age of X is *(a)* 81 years, *(b)* 68 years, *(c)* 62 years, *(d)* 34 years.

	If age of X is		
	81 years Rs.	*68/62 years Rs.*	*34 years Rs.*
Gross total income	14,26,000	14,26,000	14,26,000
Less: Deduction under section 80C	1,50,000	1,50,000	1,50,000
Less: Deduction under section 80CCD	50,000	50,000	50,000
Less: Deduction under section 80D	25,000	25,000	25,000
Net income	12,01,000	12,01,000	12,01,000
Income-tax	1,60,300	1,70,300	1,72,800
Less : Rebate under section 87A	—	—	—
Income-tax [page B-29]	1,60,300	1,70,300	1,72,800
Add : Surcharge	*Nil*	*Nil*	*Nil*
Income-tax and surcharge	1,60,300	1,70,300	1,72,800
Add: Health and education cess @ 4%	6,412	6,812	6,912
Total tax (rounded off)	1,66,710	1,77,110	1,79,710

Income-tax : 1.1

INDIVIDUAL

HUF and AOP

Net Income Range : Rs. 2,50,000 - Rs. 2,83,000

Assessment year : 2019-20

Slab rate : 5%
Surcharge : *Nil*
HEC : 4%

NI Rs.	IT Rs. P.	HEC Rs. P.	Total Rs. P.	NI Rs.	IT Rs.	HEC Rs. P.	Total Rs. P.	NI Rs.	IT Rs.	HEC Rs. P.	Total Rs. P.
10	0.50	0.02	0.52	**100**	5	0.20	5.20	**100**	5	0.20	5.20
20	1.00	0.04	1.04	**200**	10	0.40	10.40	**200**	10	0.40	10.40
30	1.50	0.06	1.56	**300**	15	0.60	15.60	**300**	15	0.60	15.60
40	2.00	0.08	2.08	**400**	20	0.80	20.80	**400**	20	0.80	20.80
50	2.50	0.10	2.60	**500**	25	1.00	26.00	**500**	25	1.00	26.00
60	3.00	0.12	3.12	**600**	30	1.20	31.20	**600**	30	1.20	31.20
70	3.50	0.14	3.64	**700**	35	1.40	36.40	**700**	35	1.40	36.40
80	4.00	0.16	4.16	**800**	40	1.60	41.60	**800**	40	1.60	41.60
90	4.50	0.18	4.68	**900**	45	1.80	46.80	**900**	45	1.80	46.80

	Resident senior citizen**			***Resident super senior citizen******			***Any other resident individual****			***Non-resident individual/ any HUF or AOP***		
NI Rs.	IT Rs.	HEC Rs.	Total Rs.	IT Rs.	HEC Rs.	Total Rs.	IT# Rs.	HEC Rs.	Total Rs.	IT Rs.	HEC Rs. P.	Total Rs. P.
250000	-	-	-	-	-	-	-	-	-	-	-	-
251000	-	-	-	-	-	-	-	-	-	50	2	52
252000	-	-	-	-	-	-	-	-	-	100	4	104
253000	-	-	-	-	-	-	-	-	-	150	6	156
254000	-	-	-	-	-	-	-	-	-	200	8	208
255000	-	-	-	-	-	-	-	-	-	250	10	260
256000	-	-	-	-	-	-	-	-	-	300	12	312
257000	-	-	-	-	-	-	-	-	-	350	14	364
258000	-	-	-	-	-	-	-	-	-	400	16	416
259000	-	-	-	-	-	-	-	-	-	450	18	468
260000	-	-	-	-	-	-	-	-	-	500	20	520
261000	-	-	-	-	-	-	-	-	-	550	22	572
262000	-	-	-	-	-	-	-	-	-	600	24	624
263000	-	-	-	-	-	-	-	-	-	650	26	676
264000	-	-	-	-	-	-	-	-	-	700	28	728
265000	-	-	-	-	-	-	-	-	-	750	30	780
266000	-	-	-	-	-	-	-	-	-	800	32	832
267000	-	-	-	-	-	-	-	-	-	850	34	884
268000	-	-	-	-	-	-	-	-	-	900	36	936
269000	-	-	-	-	-	-	-	-	-	950	38	988
270000	-	-	-	-	-	-	-	-	-	1000	40	1040
271000	-	-	-	-	-	-	-	-	-	1050	42	1092
272000	-	-	-	-	-	-	-	-	-	1100	44	1144
273000	-	-	-	-	-	-	-	-	-	1150	46	1196
274000	-	-	-	-	-	-	-	-	-	1200	48	1248
275000	-	-	-	-	-	-	-	-	-	1250	50	1300
276000	-	-	-	-	-	-	-	-	-	1300	52	1352
277000	-	-	-	-	-	-	-	-	-	1350	54	1404
278000	-	-	-	-	-	-	-	-	-	1400	56	1456
279000	-	-	-	-	-	-	-	-	-	1450	58	1508
280000	-	-	-	-	-	-	-	-	-	1500	60	1560
281000	-	-	-	-	-	-	-	-	-	1550	62	1612
282000	-	-	-	-	-	-	-	-	-	1600	64	1664
283000	-	-	-	-	-	-	-	-	-	1650	66	1716

Note - For how to use table, *see* page B-1.

After rebate under section 87A.

*If the individual was born on or after April 2, 1959.

**If the individual was born on or after April 2, 1939 but before April 2, 1959.

***If the individual was born before April 2, 1939.

Income-tax : 1.2

INDIVIDUAL

HUF and AOP

Net Income Range : Rs. 2,83,000 - Rs. 3,16,000

Assessment year : 2019-20

Slab rate : 5%
Surcharge : *Nil*
HEC : 4%

NI Rs.	*IT Rs. P.*	*HEC Rs. P.*	*Total Rs. P.*	*NI Rs.*	*IT Rs.*	*HEC Rs. P.*	*Total Rs. P.*	*NI Rs.*	*IT Rs.*	*HEC Rs. P.*	*Total Rs. P.*
10	0.50	0.02	0.52	**100**	5	0.20	5.20	**100**	5	0.20	5.20
20	1.00	0.04	1.04	**200**	10	0.40	10.40	**200**	10	0.40	10.40
30	1.50	0.06	1.56	**300**	15	0.60	15.60	**300**	15	0.60	15.60
40	2.00	0.08	2.08	**400**	20	0.80	20.80	**400**	20	0.80	20.80
50	2.50	0.10	2.60	**500**	25	1.00	26.00	**500**	25	1.00	26.00
60	3.00	0.12	3.12	**600**	30	1.20	31.20	**600**	30	1.20	31.20
70	3.50	0.14	3.64	**700**	35	1.40	36.40	**700**	35	1.40	36.40
80	4.00	0.16	4.16	**800**	40	1.60	41.60	**800**	40	1.60	41.60
90	4.50	0.18	4.68	**900**	45	1.80	46.80	**900**	45	1.80	46.80

	Resident senior citizen**			***Resident super senior citizen******			***Any other resident individual****			***Non-resident individual/ any HUF or AOP***		
NI Rs.	*IT# Rs.*	*HEC Rs.*	*Total Rs.*	*IT Rs.*	*HEC Rs.*	*Total Rs.*	*IT# Rs.*	*HEC Rs. P.*	*Total Rs. P.*	*IT Rs.*	*HEC Rs.*	*Total Rs.*
283000	-	-	-	-	-	-	-	-	-	1650	66	1716
284000	-	-	-	-	-	-	-	-	-	1700	68	1768
285000	-	-	-	-	-	-	-	-	-	1750	70	1820
286000	-	-	-	-	-	-	-	-	-	1800	72	1872
287000	-	-	-	-	-	-	-	-	-	1850	74	1924
288000	-	-	-	-	-	-	-	-	-	1900	76	1976
289000	-	-	-	-	-	-	-	-	-	1950	78	2028
290000	-	-	-	-	-	-	-	-	-	2000	80	2080
291000	-	-	-	-	-	-	-	-	-	2050	82	2132
292000	-	-	-	-	-	-	-	-	-	2100	84	2184
293000	-	-	-	-	-	-	-	-	-	2150	86	2236
294000	-	-	-	-	-	-	-	-	-	2200	88	2288
295000	-	-	-	-	-	-	-	-	-	2250	90	2340
296000	-	-	-	-	-	-	-	-	-	2300	92	2392
297000	-	-	-	-	-	-	-	-	-	2350	94	2444
298000	-	-	-	-	-	-	-	-	-	2400	96	2496
299000	-	-	-	-	-	-	-	-	-	2450	98	2548
300000	-	-	-	-	-	-	-	-	-	2500	100	2600
301000	-	-	-	-	-	-	50	2	52	2550	102	2652
302000	-	-	-	-	-	-	100	4	104	2600	104	2704
303000	-	-	-	-	-	-	150	6	156	2650	106	2756
304000	-	-	-	-	-	-	200	8	208	2700	108	2808
305000	-	-	-	-	-	-	250	10	260	2750	110	2860
306000	-	-	-	-	-	-	300	12	312	2800	112	2912
307000	-	-	-	-	-	-	350	14	364	2850	114	2964
308000	-	-	-	-	-	-	400	16	416	2900	116	3016
309000	-	-	-	-	-	-	450	18	468	2950	118	3068
310000	-	-	-	-	-	-	500	20	520	3000	120	3120
311000	-	-	-	-	-	-	550	22	572	3050	122	3172
312000	-	-	-	-	-	-	600	24	624	3100	124	3224
313000	-	-	-	-	-	-	650	26	676	3150	126	3276
314000	-	-	-	-	-	-	700	28	728	3200	128	3328
315000	-	-	-	-	-	-	750	30	780	3250	130	3380
316000	-	-	-	-	-	-	800	32	832	3300	132	3432

Note - For how to use table, *see* page B-1.

\# After rebate under section 87A.

*If the individual was born on or after April 2, 1959.

**If the individual was born on or after April 2, 1939 but before April 2, 1959.

***If the individual was born before April 2, 1939.

Income-tax : 1.3

INDIVIDUAL

HUF and AOP

Net Income Range : Rs. 3,16,000 - Rs. 3,50,000

Assessment year : 2019-20

Slab rate : 5%
Surcharge : *Nil*
HEC : 4%

NI Rs.	*IT Rs. P.*	*HEC Rs. P.*	*Total Rs. P.*	*NI Rs.*	*IT Rs.*	*HEC Rs. P.*	*Total Rs. P.*	*NI Rs.*	*IT Rs.*	*HEC Rs. P.*	*Total Rs. P.*
10	0.50	0.02	0.52	**100**	5	0.20	5.20	**100**	5	0.20	5.20
20	1.00	0.04	1.04	**200**	10	0.40	10.40	**200**	10	0.40	10.40
30	1.50	0.06	1.56	**300**	15	0.60	15.60	**300**	15	0.60	15.60
40	2.00	0.08	2.08	**400**	20	0.80	20.80	**400**	20	0.80	20.80
50	2.50	0.10	2.60	**500**	25	1.00	26.00	**500**	25	1.00	26.00
60	3.00	0.12	3.12	**600**	30	1.20	31.20	**600**	30	1.20	31.20
70	3.50	0.14	3.64	**700**	35	1.40	36.40	**700**	35	1.40	36.40
80	4.00	0.16	4.16	**800**	40	1.60	41.60	**800**	40	1.60	41.60
90	4.50	0.18	4.68	**900**	45	1.80	46.80	**900**	45	1.80	46.80

	Resident senior citizen*			***Resident super senior citizen*****			***Any other resident individual****			***Non-resident individual/ any HUF or AOP***		
NI Rs.	*IT# Rs.*	*HEC Rs.*	*Total Rs.*	*IT Rs.*	*HEC Rs.*	*Total Rs.*	*IT# Rs.*	*HEC Rs.*	*Total Rs.*	*IT Rs.*	*HEC Rs.*	*Total Rs.*
316000	-	-	-	-	-	-	800	32	832	3300	132	3432
317000	-	-	-	-	-	-	850	34	884	3350	134	3484
318000	-	-	-	-	-	-	900	36	936	3400	136	3536
319000	-	-	-	-	-	-	950	38	988	3450	138	3588
320000	-	-	-	-	-	-	1000	40	1040	3500	140	3640
321000	-	-	-	-	-	-	1050	42	1092	3550	142	3692
322000	-	-	-	-	-	-	1100	44	1144	3600	144	3744
323000	-	-	-	-	-	-	1150	46	1196	3650	146	3796
324000	-	-	-	-	-	-	1200	48	1248	3700	148	3848
325000	-	-	-	-	-	-	1250	50	1300	3750	150	3900
326000	-	-	-	-	-	-	1300	52	1352	3800	152	3952
327000	-	-	-	-	-	-	1350	54	1404	3850	154	4004
328000	-	-	-	-	-	-	1400	56	1456	3900	156	4056
329000	-	-	-	-	-	-	1450	58	1508	3950	158	4108
330000	-	-	-	-	-	-	1500	60	1560	4000	160	4160
331000	-	-	-	-	-	-	1550	62	1612	4050	162	4212
332000	-	-	-	-	-	-	1600	64	1664	4100	164	4264
333000	-	-	-	-	-	-	1650	66	1716	4150	166	4316
334000	-	-	-	-	-	-	1700	68	1768	4200	168	4368
335000	-	-	-	-	-	-	1750	70	1820	4250	170	4420
336000	-	-	-	-	-	-	1800	72	1872	4300	172	4472
337000	-	-	-	-	-	-	1850	74	1924	4350	174	4524
338000	-	-	-	-	-	-	1900	76	1976	4400	176	4576
339000	-	-	-	-	-	-	1950	78	2028	4450	178	4628
340000	-	-	-	-	-	-	2000	80	2080	4500	180	4680
341000	-	-	-	-	-	-	2050	82	2132	4550	182	4732
342000	-	-	-	-	-	-	2100	84	2184	4600	184	4784
343000	-	-	-	-	-	-	2150	86	2236	4650	186	4836
344000	-	-	-	-	-	-	2200	88	2288	4700	188	4888
345000	-	-	-	-	-	-	2250	90	2340	4750	190	4940
346000	-	-	-	-	-	-	2300	92	2392	4800	192	4992
347000	-	-	-	-	-	-	2350	94	2444	4850	194	5044
348000	-	-	-	-	-	-	2400	96	2496	4900	196	5096
349000	-	-	-	-	-	-	2450	98	2548	4950	198	5148
350000	-	-	-	-	-	-	2500	100	2600	5000	200	5200

Note - For how to use table, *see* page B-1.

\# After rebate under section 87A.

*If the individual was born on or after April 2, 1959.

**If the individual was born on or after April 2, 1939 but before April 2, 1959.

***If the individual was born before April 2, 1939.

Income-tax : 1.4

INDIVIDUAL

HUF and AOP

Net Income Range : Rs. 3,50,000 - Rs. 3,85,000

Assessment year : 2019-20

Slab rate : 5%
Surcharge : *Nil*
HEC : 4%

NI Rs.	IT Rs. P.	HEC Rs. P.	Total Rs. P.	NI Rs.	IT Rs.	HEC Rs. P.	Total Rs. P.	NI Rs.	IT Rs.	HEC Rs. P.	Total Rs. P.
10	0.50	0.02	0.52	**100**	5	0.20	5.20	**100**	5	0.20	5.20
20	1.00	0.04	1.04	**200**	10	0.40	10.40	**200**	10	0.40	10.40
30	1.50	0.06	1.56	**300**	15	0.60	15.60	**300**	15	0.60	15.60
40	2.00	0.08	2.08	**400**	20	0.80	20.80	**400**	20	0.80	20.80
50	2.50	0.10	2.60	**500**	25	1.00	26.00	**500**	25	1.00	26.00
60	3.00	0.12	3.12	**600**	30	1.20	31.20	**600**	30	1.20	31.20
70	3.50	0.14	3.64	**700**	35	1.40	36.40	**700**	35	1.40	36.40
80	4.00	0.16	4.16	**800**	40	1.60	41.60	**800**	40	1.60	41.60
90	4.50	0.18	4.68	**900**	45	1.80	46.80	**900**	45	1.80	46.80

	Resident senior citizen**			***Resident super senior citizen******			***Any other resident individual*/any non-resident individual/ any HUF or AOP***		
NI Rs.	IT Rs.	HEC Rs.	Total Rs.	IT Rs.	HEC Rs.	Total Rs.	IT Rs.	HEC Rs.	Total Rs.
350000	2500	100	2600	-	-	-	5000	200	5200
351000	2550	102	2652	-	-	-	5050	202	5252
352000	2600	104	2704	-	-	-	5100	204	5304
353000	2650	106	2756	-	-	-	5150	206	5356
354000	2700	108	2808	-	-	-	5200	208	5408
355000	2750	110	2860	-	-	-	5250	210	5460
356000	2800	112	2912	-	-	-	5300	212	5512
357000	2850	114	2964	-	-	-	5350	214	5564
358000	2900	116	3016	-	-	-	5400	216	5616
359000	2950	118	3068	-	-	-	5450	218	5668
360000	3000	120	3120	-	-	-	5500	220	5720
361000	3050	122	3172	-	-	-	5550	222	5772
362000	3100	124	3224	-	-	-	5600	224	5824
363000	3150	126	3276	-	-	-	5650	226	5876
364000	3200	128	3328	-	-	-	5700	228	5928
365000	3250	130	3380	-	-	-	5750	230	5980
366000	3300	132	3432	-	-	-	5800	232	6032
367000	3350	134	3484	-	-	-	5850	234	6084
368000	3400	136	3536	-	-	-	5900	236	6136
369000	3450	138	3588	-	-	-	5950	238	6188
370000	3500	140	3640	-	-	-	6000	240	6240
371000	3550	142	3692	-	-	-	6050	242	6292
372000	3600	144	3744	-	-	-	6100	244	6344
373000	3650	146	3796	-	-	-	6150	246	6396
374000	3700	148	3848	-	-	-	6200	248	6448
375000	3750	150	3900	-	-	-	6250	250	6500
376000	3800	152	3952	-	-	-	6300	252	6552
377000	3850	154	4004	-	-	-	6350	254	6604
378000	3900	156	4056	-	-	-	6400	256	6656
379000	3950	158	4108	-	-	-	6450	258	6708
380000	4000	160	4160	-	-	-	6500	260	6760
381000	4050	162	4212	-	-	-	6550	262	6812
382000	4100	164	4264	-	-	-	6600	264	6864
383000	4150	166	4316	-	-	-	6650	266	6916
384000	4200	168	4368	-	-	-	6700	268	6968
385000	4250	170	4420	-	-	-	6750	270	7020

Note - For how to use table, *see* page B-1.

*If the individual was born on or after April 2, 1959.

**If the individual was born on or after April 2, 1939 but before April 2, 1959.

***If the individual was born before April 2, 1939.

Income-tax : 1.5

INDIVIDUAL

HUF and AOP

Net Income Range : Rs. 3,85,000 - Rs. 4,20,000

Assessment year : 2019-20

Slab rate : 5%
Surcharge : *Nil*
HEC : 4%

NI Rs.	IT Rs. P.	HEC Rs. P.	Total Rs. P.	NI Rs.	IT Rs.	HEC Rs. P.	Total Rs. P.	NI Rs.	IT Rs.	HEC Rs. P.	Total Rs. P.
10	0.50	0.02	0.52	**100**	5	0.20	5.20	**100**	5	0.20	5.20
20	1.00	0.04	1.04	**200**	10	0.40	10.40	**200**	10	0.40	10.40
30	1.50	0.06	1.56	**300**	15	0.60	15.60	**300**	15	0.60	15.60
40	2.00	0.08	2.08	**400**	20	0.80	20.80	**400**	20	0.80	20.80
50	2.50	0.10	2.60	**500**	25	1.00	26.00	**500**	25	1.00	26.00
60	3.00	0.12	3.12	**600**	30	1.20	31.20	**600**	30	1.20	31.20
70	3.50	0.14	3.64	**700**	35	1.40	36.40	**700**	35	1.40	36.40
80	4.00	0.16	4.16	**800**	40	1.60	41.60	**800**	40	1.60	41.60
90	4.50	0.18	4.68	**900**	45	1.80	46.80	**900**	45	1.80	46.80

	Resident senior citizen**			***Resident super senior citizen******			***Any other resident individual*/any non-resident individual/ any HUF or AOP***		
NI Rs.	*IT Rs.*	*HEC Rs.*	*Total Rs.*	*IT Rs.*	*HEC Rs.*	*Total Rs.*	*IT Rs.*	*HEC Rs.*	*Total Rs.*
385000	4250	170	4420	-	-	-	6750	270	7020
386000	4300	172	4472	-	-	-	6800	272	7072
387000	4350	174	4524	-	-	-	6850	274	7124
388000	4400	176	4576	-	-	-	6900	276	7176
389000	4450	178	4628	-	-	-	6950	278	7228
390000	4500	180	4680	-	-	-	7000	280	7280
391000	4550	182	4732	-	-	-	7050	282	7332
392000	4600	184	4784	-	-	-	7100	284	7384
393000	4650	186	4836	-	-	-	7150	286	7436
394000	4700	188	4888	-	-	-	7200	288	7488
395000	4750	190	4940	-	-	-	7250	290	7540
396000	4800	192	4992	-	-	-	7300	292	7592
397000	4850	194	5044	-	-	-	7350	294	7644
398000	4900	196	5096	-	-	-	7400	296	7696
399000	4950	198	5148	-	-	-	7450	298	7748
400000	5000	200	5200	-	-	-	7500	300	7800
401000	5050	202	5252	-	-	-	7550	302	7852
402000	5100	204	5304	-	-	-	7600	304	7904
403000	5150	206	5356	-	-	-	7650	306	7956
404000	5200	208	5408	-	-	-	7700	308	8008
405000	5250	210	5460	-	-	-	7750	310	8060
406000	5300	212	5512	-	-	-	7800	312	8112
407000	5350	214	5564	-	-	-	7850	314	8164
408000	5400	216	5616	-	-	-	7900	316	8216
409000	5450	218	5668	-	-	-	7950	318	8268
410000	5500	220	5720	-	-	-	8000	320	8320
411000	5550	222	5772	-	-	-	8050	322	8372
412000	5600	224	5824	-	-	-	8100	324	8424
413000	5650	226	5876	-	-	-	8150	326	8476
414000	5700	228	5928	-	-	-	8200	328	8528
415000	5750	230	5980	-	-	-	8250	330	8580
416000	5800	232	6032	-	-	-	8300	332	8632
417000	5850	234	6084	-	-	-	8350	334	8684
418000	5900	236	6136	-	-	-	8400	336	8736
419000	5950	238	6188	-	-	-	8450	338	8788
420000	6000	240	6240	-	-	-	8500	340	8840

Note - For how to use table, *see* page B-1.

*If the individual was born on or after April 2, 1959.

**If the individual was born on or after April 2, 1939 but before April 2, 1959.

***If the individual was born before April 2, 1939.

Income-tax : 1.6

INDIVIDUAL

HUF and AOP

Net Income Range : Rs. 4,20,000 - Rs. 4,60,000

Assessment year : 2019-20

Slab rate : 5%

Surcharge : *Nil*

HEC : 4%

NI Rs.	*IT Rs. P.*	*HEC Rs. P.*	*Total Rs. P.*	*NI Rs.*	*IT Rs.*	*HEC Rs. P.*	*Total Rs. P.*	*NI Rs.*	*IT Rs.*	*HEC Rs. P.*	*Total Rs. P.*
10	0.50	0.02	0.52	**100**	5	0.20	5.20	**100**	5	0.20	5.20
20	1.00	0.04	1.04	**200**	10	0.40	10.40	**200**	10	0.40	10.40
30	1.50	0.06	1.56	**300**	15	0.60	15.60	**300**	15	0.60	15.60
40	2.00	0.08	2.08	**400**	20	0.80	20.80	**400**	20	0.80	20.80
50	2.50	0.10	2.60	**500**	25	1.00	26.00	**500**	25	1.00	26.00
60	3.00	0.12	3.12	**600**	30	1.20	31.20	**600**	30	1.20	31.20
70	3.50	0.14	3.64	**700**	35	1.40	36.40	**700**	35	1.40	36.40
80	4.00	0.16	4.16	**800**	40	1.60	41.60	**800**	40	1.60	41.60
90	4.50	0.18	4.68	**900**	45	1.80	46.80	**900**	45	1.80	46.80

	Resident senior citizen**			***Resident super senior citizen******			***Any other resident individual*/any non-resident individual/ any HUF or AOP***		
NI Rs.	*IT Rs.*	*HEC Rs.*	*Total Rs.*	*IT Rs.*	*HEC Rs.*	*Total Rs.*	*IT Rs.*	*HEC Rs.*	*Total Rs.*
420000	6000	240	6240	-	-	-	8500	340	8840
421000	6050	242	6292	-	-	-	8550	342	8892
422000	6100	244	6344	-	-	-	8600	344	8944
423000	6150	246	6396	-	-	-	8650	346	8996
424000	6200	248	6448	-	-	-	8700	348	9048
425000	6250	250	6500	-	-	-	8750	350	9100
426000	6300	252	6552	-	-	-	8800	352	9152
427000	6350	254	6604	-	-	-	8850	354	9204
428000	6400	256	6656	-	-	-	8900	356	9256
429000	6450	258	6708	-	-	-	8950	358	9308
430000	6500	260	6760	-	-	-	9000	360	9360
431000	6550	262	6812	-	-	-	9050	362	9412
432000	6600	264	6864	-	-	-	9100	364	9464
433000	6650	266	6916	-	-	-	9150	366	9516
434000	6700	268	6968	-	-	-	9200	368	9568
435000	6750	270	7020	-	-	-	9250	370	9620
436000	6800	272	7072	-	-	-	9300	372	9672
437000	6850	274	7124	-	-	-	9350	374	9724
438000	6900	276	7176	-	-	-	9400	376	9776
439000	6950	278	7228	-	-	-	9450	378	9828
440000	7000	280	7280	-	-	-	9500	380	9880
441000	7050	282	7332	-	-	-	9550	382	9932
442000	7100	284	7384	-	-	-	9600	384	9984
443000	7150	286	7436	-	-	-	9650	386	10036
444000	7200	288	7488	-	-	-	9700	388	10088
445000	7250	290	7540	-	-	-	9750	390	10140
446000	7300	292	7592	-	-	-	9800	392	10192
447000	7350	294	7644	-	-	-	9850	394	10244
448000	7400	296	7696	-	-	-	9900	396	10296
449000	7450	298	7748	-	-	-	9950	398	10348
450000	7500	300	7800	-	-	-	10000	400	10400
451000	7550	302	7852	-	-	-	10050	402	10452
452000	7600	304	7904	-	-	-	10100	404	10504
453000	7650	306	7956	-	-	-	10150	406	10556
454000	7700	308	8008	-	-	-	10200	408	10608
455000	7750	310	8060	-	-	-	10250	410	10660
456000	7800	312	8112	-	-	-	10300	412	10712
457000	7850	314	8164	-	-	-	10350	414	10764
458000	7900	316	8216	-	-	-	10400	416	10816
459000	7950	318	8268	-	-	-	10450	418	10868
460000	8000	320	8320	-	-	-	10500	420	10920

Note - For how to use table, *see* page B-1.

*If the individual was born on or after April 2, 1959.

**If the individual was born on or after April 2, 1939 but before April 2, 1959.

***If the individual was born before April 2, 1939.

Income-tax : 1.7

INDIVIDUAL

HUF and AOP

Net Income Range : Rs. 4,60,000 - Rs. 5,00,000

Assessment year : 2019-20

Slab rate : 5%
Surcharge : *Nil*
HEC : 4%

NI Rs.	*IT Rs. P.*	*HEC Rs. P.*	*Total Rs. P.*	*NI Rs.*	*IT Rs.*	*HEC Rs. P.*	*Total Rs. P.*	*NI Rs.*	*IT Rs.*	*HEC Rs. P.*	*Total Rs. P.*
10	0.50	0.02	0.52	**100**	5	0.20	5.20	**100**	5	0.20	5.20
20	1.00	0.04	1.04	**200**	10	0.40	10.40	**200**	10	0.40	10.40
30	1.50	0.06	1.56	**300**	15	0.60	15.60	**300**	15	0.60	15.60
40	2.00	0.08	2.08	**400**	20	0.80	20.80	**400**	20	0.80	20.80
50	2.50	0.10	2.60	**500**	25	1.00	26.00	**500**	25	1.00	26.00
60	3.00	0.12	3.12	**600**	30	1.20	31.20	**600**	30	1.20	31.20
70	3.50	0.14	3.64	**700**	35	1.40	36.40	**700**	35	1.40	36.40
80	4.00	0.16	4.16	**800**	40	1.60	41.60	**800**	40	1.60	41.60
90	4.50	0.18	4.68	**900**	45	1.80	46.80	**900**	45	1.80	46.80

	Resident senior citizen**			***Resident super senior citizen******			***Any other resident individual*/any non-resident individual/ any HUF or AOP***		
NI Rs.	*IT Rs.*	*HEC Rs.*	*Total Rs.*	*IT Rs.*	*HEC Rs.*	*Total Rs.*	*IT Rs.*	*HEC Rs.*	*Total Rs.*
460000	8000	320	8320	-	-	-	10500	420	10920
461000	8050	322	8372	-	-	-	10550	422	10972
462000	8100	324	8424	-	-	-	10600	424	11024
463000	8150	326	8476	-	-	-	10650	426	11076
464000	8200	328	8528	-	-	-	10700	428	11128
465000	8250	330	8580	-	-	-	10750	430	11180
466000	8300	332	8632	-	-	-	10800	432	11232
467000	8350	334	8684	-	-	-	10850	434	11284
468000	8400	336	8736	-	-	-	10900	436	11336
469000	8450	338	8788	-	-	-	10950	438	11388
470000	8500	340	8840	-	-	-	11000	440	11440
471000	8550	342	8892	-	-	-	11050	442	11492
472000	8600	344	8944	-	-	-	11100	444	11544
473000	8650	346	8996	-	-	-	11150	446	11596
474000	8700	348	9048	-	-	-	11200	448	11648
475000	8750	350	9100	-	-	-	11250	450	11700
476000	8800	352	9152	-	-	-	11300	452	11752
477000	8850	354	9204	-	-	-	11350	454	11804
478000	8900	356	9256	-	-	-	11400	456	11856
479000	8950	358	9308	-	-	-	11450	458	11908
480000	9000	360	9360	-	-	-	11500	460	11960
481000	9050	362	9412	-	-	-	11550	462	12012
482000	9100	364	9464	-	-	-	11600	464	12064
483000	9150	366	9516	-	-	-	11650	466	12116
484000	9200	368	9568	-	-	-	11700	468	12168
485000	9250	370	9620	-	-	-	11750	470	12220
486000	9300	372	9672	-	-	-	11800	472	12272
487000	9350	374	9724	-	-	-	11850	474	12324
488000	9400	376	9776	-	-	-	11900	476	12376
489000	9450	378	9828	-	-	-	11950	478	12428
490000	9500	380	9880	-	-	-	12000	480	12480
491000	9550	382	9932	-	-	-	12050	482	12532
492000	9600	384	9984	-	-	-	12100	484	12584
493000	9650	386	10036	-	-	-	12150	486	12636
494000	9700	388	10088	-	-	-	12200	488	12688
495000	9750	390	10140	-	-	-	12250	490	12740
496000	9800	392	10192	-	-	-	12300	492	12792
497000	9850	394	10244	-	-	-	12350	494	12844
498000	9900	396	10296	-	-	-	12400	496	12896
499000	9950	398	10348	-	-	-	12450	498	12948
500000	10000	400	10400	-	-	-	12500	500	13000

Note - For how to use table, *see* page B-1.

*If the individual was born on or after April 2, 1959.

**If the individual was born on or after April 2, 1939 but before April 2, 1959.

***If the individual was born before April 2, 1939.

Income-tax : 1.8

INDIVIDUAL

HUF and AOP

Net Income Range : Rs. 5,00,000 - Rs. 5,40,000

Assessment year : 2019-20

Slab rate : 20%
Surcharge : *Nil*
HEC : 4%

NI Rs.	IT Rs. P.	HEC Rs. P.	Total Rs. P.	NI Rs.	IT Rs.	HEC Rs. P.	Total Rs. P.	NI Rs.	IT Rs.	HEC Rs. P.	Total Rs. P.
10	2	0.08	2.08	**100**	20	0.80	20.80	**100**	20	0.80	20.80
20	4	0.16	4.16	**200**	40	1.60	41.60	**200**	40	1.60	41.60
30	6	0.24	6.24	**300**	60	2.40	62.40	**300**	60	2.40	62.40
40	8	0.32	8.32	**400**	80	3.20	83.20	**400**	80	3.20	83.20
50	10	0.40	10.40	**500**	100	4.00	104.00	**500**	100	4.00	104.00
60	12	0.48	12.48	**600**	120	4.80	124.80	**600**	120	4.80	124.80
70	14	0.56	14.56	**700**	140	5.60	145.60	**700**	140	5.60	145.60
80	16	0.64	16.64	**800**	160	6.40	166.40	**800**	160	6.40	166.40
90	18	0.72	18.72	**900**	180	7.20	187.20	**900**	180	7.20	187.20

	Resident senior citizen**			***Resident super senior citizen******			***Any other resident individual*/any non-resident individual/ any HUF or AOP***		
NI Rs.	**IT Rs.**	**HEC Rs.**	**Total Rs.**	**IT Rs.**	**HEC Rs.**	**Total Rs.**	**IT Rs.**	**HEC Rs.**	**Total Rs.**
500000	10000	400	10400	0	0	0	12500	500	13000
501000	10200	408	10608	200	8	208	12700	508	13208
502000	10400	416	10816	400	16	416	12900	516	13416
503000	10600	424	11024	600	24	624	13100	524	13624
504000	10800	432	11232	800	32	832	13300	532	13832
505000	11000	440	11440	1000	40	1040	13500	540	14040
506000	11200	448	11648	1200	48	1248	13700	548	14248
507000	11400	456	11856	1400	56	1456	13900	556	14456
508000	11600	464	12064	1600	64	1664	14100	564	14664
509000	11800	472	12272	1800	72	1872	14300	572	14872
510000	12000	480	12480	2000	80	2080	14500	580	15080
511000	12200	488	12688	2200	88	2288	14700	588	15288
512000	12400	496	12896	2400	96	2496	14900	596	15496
513000	12600	504	13104	2600	104	2704	15100	604	15704
514000	12800	512	13312	2800	112	2912	15300	612	15912
515000	13000	520	13520	3000	120	3120	15500	620	16120
516000	13200	528	13728	3200	128	3328	15700	628	16328
517000	13400	536	13936	3400	136	3536	15900	636	16536
518000	13600	544	14144	3600	144	3744	16100	644	16744
519000	13800	552	14352	3800	152	3952	16300	652	16952
520000	14000	560	14560	4000	160	4160	16500	660	17160
521000	14200	568	14768	4200	168	4368	16700	668	17368
522000	14400	576	14976	4400	176	4576	16900	676	17576
523000	14600	584	15184	4600	184	4784	17100	684	17784
524000	14800	592	15392	4800	192	4992	17300	692	17992
525000	15000	600	15600	5000	200	5200	17500	700	18200
526000	15200	608	15808	5200	208	5408	17700	708	18408
527000	15400	616	16016	5400	216	5616	17900	716	18616
528000	15600	624	16224	5600	224	5824	18100	724	18824
529000	15800	632	16432	5800	232	6032	18300	732	19032
530000	16000	640	16640	6000	240	6240	18500	740	19240
531000	16200	648	16848	6200	248	6448	18700	748	19448
532000	16400	656	17056	6400	256	6656	18900	756	19656
533000	16600	664	17264	6600	264	6864	19100	764	19864
534000	16800	672	17472	6800	272	7072	19300	772	20072
535000	17000	680	17680	7000	280	7280	19500	780	20280
536000	17200	688	17888	7200	288	7488	19700	788	20488
537000	17400	696	18096	7400	296	7696	19900	796	20696
538000	17600	704	18304	7600	304	7904	20100	804	20904
539000	17800	712	18512	7800	312	8112	20300	812	21112
540000	18000	720	18720	8000	320	8320	20500	820	21320

Note - For how to use table, *see* page B-1.

*If the individual was born on or after April 2, 1959.

**If the individual was born on or after April 2, 1939 but before April 2, 1959.

***If the individual was born before April 2, 1939.

Income-tax : 1.9

INDIVIDUAL

HUF and AOP

Net Income Range : Rs. 5,40,000 - Rs. 5,80,000

Assessment year : 2019-20

Slab rate : 20%
Surcharge : *Nil*
HEC : 4%

NI Rs.	*IT Rs. P.*	*HEC Rs. P.*	*Total Rs. P.*	*NI Rs.*	*IT Rs.*	*HEC Rs. P.*	*Total Rs. P.*	*NI Rs.*	*IT Rs.*	*HEC Rs. P.*	*Total Rs. P.*
10	2	0.08	2.08	**100**	20	0.80	20.80	**100**	20	0.80	20.80
20	4	0.16	4.16	**200**	40	1.60	41.60	**200**	40	1.60	41.60
30	6	0.24	6.24	**300**	60	2.40	62.40	**300**	60	2.40	62.40
40	8	0.32	8.32	**400**	80	3.20	83.20	**400**	80	3.20	83.20
50	10	0.40	10.40	**500**	100	4.00	104.00	**500**	100	4.00	104.00
60	12	0.48	12.48	**600**	120	4.80	124.80	**600**	120	4.80	124.80
70	14	0.56	14.56	**700**	140	5.60	145.60	**700**	140	5.60	145.60
80	16	0.64	16.64	**800**	160	6.40	166.40	**800**	160	6.40	166.40
90	18	0.72	18.72	**900**	180	7.20	187.20	**900**	180	7.20	187.20

	Resident senior citizen**			***Resident super senior citizen******			***Any other resident individual*/any non-resident individual/ any HUF or AOP***		
NI Rs.	*IT Rs.*	*HEC Rs.*	*Total Rs.*	*IT Rs.*	*HEC Rs.*	*Total Rs.*	*IT Rs.*	*HEC Rs.*	*Total Rs.*
540000	18000	720	18720	8000	320	8320	20500	820	21320
541000	18200	728	18928	8200	328	8528	20700	828	21528
542000	18400	736	19136	8400	336	8736	20900	836	21736
543000	18600	744	19344	8600	344	8944	21100	844	21944
544000	18800	752	19552	8800	352	9152	21300	852	22152
545000	19000	760	19760	9000	360	9360	21500	860	22360
546000	19200	768	19968	9200	368	9568	21700	868	22568
547000	19400	776	20176	9400	376	9776	21900	876	22776
548000	19600	784	20384	9600	384	9984	22100	884	22984
549000	19800	792	20592	9800	392	10192	22300	892	23192
550000	20000	800	20800	10000	400	10400	22500	900	23400
551000	20200	808	21008	10200	408	10608	22700	908	23608
552000	20400	816	21216	10400	416	10816	22900	916	23816
553000	20600	824	21424	10600	424	11024	23100	924	24024
554000	20800	832	21632	10800	432	11232	23300	932	24232
555000	21000	840	21840	11000	440	11440	23500	940	24440
556000	21200	848	22048	11200	448	11648	23700	948	24648
557000	21400	856	22256	11400	456	11856	23900	956	24856
558000	21600	864	22464	11600	464	12064	24100	964	25064
559000	21800	872	22672	11800	472	12272	24300	972	25272
560000	22000	880	22880	12000	480	12480	24500	980	25480
561000	22200	888	23088	12200	488	12688	24700	988	25688
562000	22400	896	23296	12400	496	12896	24900	996	25896
563000	22600	904	23504	12600	504	13104	25100	1004	26104
564000	22800	912	23712	12800	512	13312	25300	1012	26312
565000	23000	920	23920	13000	520	13520	25500	1020	26520
566000	23200	928	24128	13200	528	13728	25700	1028	26728
567000	23400	936	24336	13400	536	13936	25900	1036	26936
568000	23600	944	24544	13600	544	14144	26100	1044	27144
569000	23800	952	24752	13800	552	14352	26300	1052	27352
570000	24000	960	24960	14000	560	14560	26500	1060	27560
571000	24200	968	25168	14200	568	14768	26700	1068	27768
572000	24400	976	25376	14400	576	14976	26900	1076	27976
573000	24600	984	25584	14600	584	15184	27100	1084	28184
574000	24800	992	25792	14800	592	15392	27300	1092	28392
575000	25000	1000	26000	15000	600	15600	27500	1100	28600
576000	25200	1008	26208	15200	608	15808	27700	1108	28808
577000	25400	1016	26416	15400	616	16016	27900	1116	29016
578000	25600	1024	26624	15600	624	16224	28100	1124	29224
579000	25800	1032	26832	15800	632	16432	28300	1132	29432
580000	26000	1040	27040	16000	640	16640	28500	1140	29640

Note - For how to use table, *see* page B-1.

*If the individual was born on or after April 2, 1959.

**If the individual was born on or after April 2, 1939 but before April 2, 1959.

***If the individual was born before April 2, 1939.

Income-tax : 1.10

INDIVIDUAL

HUF and AOP

Net Income Range : Rs. 5,80,000 - Rs. 6,20,000

Assessment year : 2019-20

Slab rate : 20%
Surcharge : *Nil*
HEC : 4%

NI Rs.	*IT Rs. P.*	*HEC Rs. P.*	*Total Rs. P.*	*NI Rs.*	*IT Rs.*	*HEC Rs. P.*	*Total Rs. P.*	*NI Rs.*	*IT Rs.*	*HEC Rs. P.*	*Total Rs. P.*
10	2	0.08	2.08	**100**	20	0.80	20.80	**100**	20	0.80	20.80
20	4	0.16	4.16	**200**	40	1.60	41.60	**200**	40	1.60	41.60
30	6	0.24	6.24	**300**	60	2.40	62.40	**300**	60	2.40	62.40
40	8	0.32	8.32	**400**	80	3.20	83.20	**400**	80	3.20	83.20
50	10	0.40	10.40	**500**	100	4.00	104.00	**500**	100	4.00	104.00
60	12	0.48	12.48	**600**	120	4.80	124.80	**600**	120	4.80	124.80
70	14	0.56	14.56	**700**	140	5.60	145.60	**700**	140	5.60	145.60
80	16	0.64	16.64	**800**	160	6.40	166.40	**800**	160	6.40	166.40
90	18	0.72	18.72	**900**	180	7.20	187.20	**900**	180	7.20	187.20

	Resident senior citizen*			***Resident super senior citizen*****			***Any other resident individual*/any non-resident individual/ any HUF or AOP***		
NI Rs.	*IT Rs.*	*HEC Rs.*	*Total Rs.*	*IT Rs.*	*HEC Rs.*	*Total Rs.*	*IT Rs.*	*HEC Rs.*	*Total Rs.*
580000	26000	1040	27040	16000	640	16640	28500	1140	29640
581000	26200	1048	27248	16200	648	16848	28700	1148	29848
582000	26400	1056	27456	16400	656	17056	28900	1156	30056
583000	26600	1064	27664	16600	664	17264	29100	1164	30264
584000	26800	1072	27872	16800	672	17472	29300	1172	30472
585000	27000	1080	28080	17000	680	17680	29500	1180	30680
586000	27200	1088	28288	17200	688	17888	29700	1188	30888
587000	27400	1096	28496	17400	696	18096	29900	1196	31096
588000	27600	1104	28704	17600	704	18304	30100	1204	31304
589000	27800	1112	28912	17800	712	18512	30300	1212	31512
590000	28000	1120	29120	18000	720	18720	30500	1220	31720
591000	28200	1128	29328	18200	728	18928	30700	1228	31928
592000	28400	1136	29536	18400	736	19136	30900	1236	32136
593000	28600	1144	29744	18600	744	19344	31100	1244	32344
594000	28800	1152	29952	18800	752	19552	31300	1252	32552
595000	29000	1160	30160	19000	760	19760	31500	1260	32760
596000	29200	1168	30368	19200	768	19968	31700	1268	32968
597000	29400	1176	30576	19400	776	20176	31900	1276	33176
598000	29600	1184	30784	19600	784	20384	32100	1284	33384
599000	29800	1192	30992	19800	792	20592	32300	1292	33592
600000	30000	1200	31200	20000	800	20800	32500	1300	33800
601000	30200	1208	31408	20200	808	21008	32700	1308	34008
602000	30400	1216	31616	20400	816	21216	32900	1316	34216
603000	30600	1224	31824	20600	824	21424	33100	1324	34424
604000	30800	1232	32032	20800	832	21632	33300	1332	34632
605000	31000	1240	32240	21000	840	21840	33500	1340	34840
606000	31200	1248	32448	21200	848	22048	33700	1348	35048
607000	31400	1256	32656	21400	856	22256	33900	1356	35256
608000	31600	1264	32864	21600	864	22464	34100	1364	35464
609000	31800	1272	33072	21800	872	22672	34300	1372	35672
610000	32000	1280	33280	22000	880	22880	34500	1380	35880
611000	32200	1288	33488	22200	888	23088	34700	1388	36088
612000	32400	1296	33696	22400	896	23296	34900	1396	36296
613000	32600	1304	33904	22600	904	23504	35100	1404	36504
614000	32800	1312	34112	22800	912	23712	35300	1412	36712
615000	33000	1320	34320	23000	920	23920	35500	1420	36920
616000	33200	1328	34528	23200	928	24128	35700	1428	37128
617000	33400	1336	34736	23400	936	24336	35900	1436	37336
618000	33600	1344	34944	23600	944	24544	36100	1444	37544
619000	33800	1352	35152	23800	952	24752	36300	1452	37752
620000	34000	1360	35360	24000	960	24960	36500	1460	37960

Note - For how to use table, *see* page B-1.

*If the individual was born on or after April 2, 1959.

**If the individual was born on or after April 2, 1939 but before April 2, 1959.

***If the individual was born before April 2, 1939.

Income-tax : 1.11

INDIVIDUAL

HUF and AOP

Net Income Range : Rs. 6,20,000 - Rs. 10,00,000

Assessment year : 2019-20

Slab rate : 20%

Surcharge : *Nil*

HEC : 4%

NI Rs.	*IT Rs. P.*	*HEC Rs. P.*	*Total Rs. P.*	*NI Rs.*	*IT Rs.*	*HEC Rs. P.*	*Total Rs. P.*	*NI Rs.*	*IT Rs.*	*HEC Rs. P.*	*Total Rs. P.*
10	2	0.08	2.08	**100**	20	0.80	20.80	**1000**	200	8	208
20	4	0.16	4.16	**200**	40	1.60	41.60	**2000**	400	16	416
30	6	0.24	6.24	**300**	60	2.40	62.40	**3000**	600	24	624
40	8	0.32	8.32	**400**	80	3.20	83.20	**4000**	800	32	832
50	10	0.40	10.40	**500**	100	4.00	104.00	**5000**	1000	40	1040
60	12	0.48	12.48	**600**	120	4.80	124.80	**6000**	1200	48	1248
70	14	0.56	14.56	**700**	140	5.60	145.60	**7000**	1400	56	1456
80	16	0.64	16.64	**800**	160	6.40	166.40	**8000**	1600	64	1664
90	18	0.72	18.72	**900**	180	7.20	187.20	**9000**	1800	72	1872

	Resident senior citizen**			***Resident super senior citizen******			***Any other resident individual*/any non-resident individual/ any HUF or AOP***		
NI Rs.	*IT Rs.*	*HEC Rs.*	*Total Rs.*	*IT Rs.*	*HEC Rs.*	*Total Rs.*	*IT Rs.*	*HEC Rs.*	*Total Rs.*
620000	34000	1360	35360	24000	960	24960	36500	1460	37960
630000	36000	1440	37440	26000	1040	27040	38500	1540	40040
640000	38000	1520	39520	28000	1120	29120	40500	1620	42120
650000	40000	1600	41600	30000	1200	31200	42500	1700	44200
660000	42000	1680	43680	32000	1280	33280	44500	1780	46280
670000	44000	1760	45760	34000	1360	35360	46500	1860	48360
680000	46000	1840	47840	36000	1440	37440	48500	1940	50440
690000	48000	1920	49920	38000	1520	39520	50500	2020	52520
700000	50000	2000	52000	40000	1600	41600	52500	2100	54600
710000	52000	2080	54080	42000	1680	43680	54500	2180	56680
720000	54000	2160	56160	44000	1760	45760	56500	2260	58760
730000	56000	2240	58240	46000	1840	47840	58500	2340	60840
740000	58000	2320	60320	48000	1920	49920	60500	2420	62920
750000	60000	2400	62400	50000	2000	52000	62500	2500	65000
760000	62000	2480	64480	52000	2080	54080	64500	2580	67080
770000	64000	2560	66560	54000	2160	56160	66500	2660	69160
780000	66000	2640	68640	56000	2240	58240	68500	2740	71240
790000	68000	2720	70720	58000	2320	60320	70500	2820	73320
800000	70000	2800	72800	60000	2400	62400	72500	2900	75400
810000	72000	2880	74880	62000	2480	64480	74500	2980	77480
820000	74000	2960	76960	64000	2560	66560	76500	3060	79560
830000	76000	3040	79040	66000	2640	68640	78500	3140	81640
840000	78000	3120	81120	68000	2720	70720	80500	3220	83720
850000	80000	3200	83200	70000	2800	72800	82500	3300	85800
860000	82000	3280	85280	72000	2880	74880	84500	3380	87880
870000	84000	3360	87360	74000	2960	76960	86500	3460	89960
880000	86000	3440	89440	76000	3040	79040	88500	3540	92040
890000	88000	3520	91520	78000	3120	81120	90500	3620	94120
900000	90000	3600	93600	80000	3200	83200	92500	3700	96200
910000	92000	3680	95680	82000	3280	85280	94500	3780	98280
920000	94000	3760	97760	84000	3360	87360	96500	3860	100360
930000	96000	3840	99840	86000	3440	89440	98500	3940	102440
940000	98000	3920	101920	88000	3520	91520	100500	4020	104520
950000	100000	4000	104000	90000	3600	93600	102500	4100	106600
960000	102000	4080	106080	92000	3680	95680	104500	4180	108680
970000	104000	4160	108160	94000	3760	97760	106500	4260	110760
980000	106000	4240	110240	96000	3840	99840	108500	4340	112840
990000	108000	4320	112320	98000	3920	101920	110500	4420	114920
1000000	110000	4400	114400	100000	4000	104000	112500	4500	117000

Note - For how to use table, *see* page B-1.

*If the individual was born on or after April 2, 1959.

**If the individual was born on or after April 2, 1939 but before April 2, 1959.

***If the individual was born before April 2, 1939.

Income-tax : 1.12

INDIVIDUAL

HUF and AOP

Net Income Range : Rs. 10,00,000 - Rs. 50,00,000

Assessment year : 2019-20

Slab rate	:	30%
Surcharge	:	*Nil*
HEC	:	4%

NI Rs.	*IT Rs. P.*	*HEC Rs. P.*	*Total Rs. P.*	*NI Rs.*	*IT Rs.*	*HEC Rs. P.*	*Total Rs. P.*	*NI Rs.*	*IT Rs.*	*HEC Rs. P.*	*Total Rs. P.*
10	3	0.12	3.12	**100**	30	1.20	31.20	**1000**	300	12	312
20	6	0.24	6.24	**200**	60	2.40	62.40	**2000**	600	24	624
30	9	0.36	9.36	**300**	90	3.60	93.60	**3000**	900	36	936
40	12	0.48	12.48	**400**	120	4.80	124.80	**4000**	1200	48	1248
50	15	0.60	15.60	**500**	150	6.00	156.00	**5000**	1500	60	1560
60	18	0.72	18.72	**600**	180	7.20	187.20	**6000**	1800	72	1872
70	21	0.84	21.84	**700**	210	8.40	218.40	**7000**	2100	84	2184
80	24	0.96	24.96	**800**	240	9.60	249.60	**8000**	2400	96	2496
90	27	1.08	28.08	**900**	270	10.80	280.80	**9000**	2700	108	2808

	Resident senior citizen**			***Resident super senior citizen******			***Any other resident individual*/any non-resident individual/ any HUF or AOP***		
NI Rs.	*IT Rs.*	*HEC Rs.*	*Total Rs.*	*IT Rs.*	*HEC Rs.*	*Total Rs.*	*IT Rs.*	*HEC Rs.*	*Total Rs.*
1000000	110000	4400	114400	100000	4000	104000	112500	4500	117000
1100000	140000	5600	145600	130000	5200	135200	142500	5700	148200
1200000	170000	6800	176800	160000	6400	166400	172500	6900	179400
1300000	200000	8000	208000	190000	7600	197600	202500	8100	210600
1400000	230000	9200	239200	220000	8800	228800	232500	9300	241800
1500000	260000	10400	270400	250000	10000	260000	262500	10500	273000
1600000	290000	11600	301600	280000	11200	291200	292500	11700	304200
1700000	320000	12800	332800	310000	12400	322400	322500	12900	335400
1800000	350000	14000	364000	340000	13600	353600	352500	14100	366600
1900000	380000	15200	395200	370000	14800	384800	382500	15300	397800
2000000	410000	16400	426400	400000	16000	416000	412500	16500	429000
2100000	440000	17600	457600	430000	17200	447200	442500	17700	460200
2200000	470000	18800	488800	460000	18400	478400	472500	18900	491400
2300000	500000	20000	520000	490000	19600	509600	502500	20100	522600
2400000	530000	21200	551200	520000	20800	540800	532500	21300	553800
2500000	560000	22400	582400	550000	22000	572000	562500	22500	585000
2600000	590000	23600	613600	580000	23200	603200	592500	23700	616200
2700000	620000	24800	644800	610000	24400	634400	622500	24900	647400
2800000	650000	26000	676000	640000	25600	665600	652500	26100	678600
2900000	680000	27200	707200	670000	26800	696800	682500	27300	709800
3000000	710000	28400	738400	700000	28000	728000	712500	28500	741000
3100000	740000	29600	769600	730000	29200	759200	742500	29700	772200
3200000	770000	30800	800800	760000	30400	790400	772500	30900	803400
3300000	800000	32000	832000	790000	31600	821600	802500	32100	834600
3400000	830000	33200	863200	820000	32800	852800	832500	33300	865800
3500000	860000	34400	894400	850000	34000	884000	862500	34500	897000
3600000	890000	35600	925600	880000	35200	915200	892500	35700	928200
3700000	920000	36800	956800	910000	36400	946400	922500	36900	959400
3800000	950000	38000	988000	940000	37600	977600	952500	38100	990600
3900000	980000	39200	1019200	970000	38800	1008800	982500	39300	1021800
4000000	1010000	40400	1050400	1000000	40000	1040000	1012500	40500	1053000
4100000	1040000	41600	1081600	1030000	41200	1071200	1042500	41700	1084200
4200000	1070000	42800	1112800	1060000	42400	1102400	1072500	42900	1115400
4300000	1100000	44000	1144000	1090000	43600	1133600	1102500	44100	1146600
4400000	1130000	45200	1175200	1120000	44800	1164800	1132500	45300	1177800
4500000	1160000	46400	1206400	1150000	46000	1196000	1162500	46500	1209000
4600000	1190000	47600	1237600	1180000	47200	1227200	1192500	47700	1240200
4700000	1220000	48800	1268800	1210000	48400	1258400	1222500	48900	1271400
4800000	1250000	50000	1300000	1240000	49600	1289600	1252500	50100	1302600
4900000	1280000	51200	1331200	1270000	50800	1320800	1282500	51300	1333800
5000000	1310000	52400	1362400	1300000	52000	1352000	1312500	52500	1365000

Note - For how to use table, *see* page B-1.

*If the individual was born on or after April 2, 1959.

**If the individual was born on or after April 2, 1939 but before April 2, 1959.

***If the individual was born before April 2, 1939.

Income-tax : 1.13

INDIVIDUAL

HUF and AOP

Net Income Range : Rs. 50,00,010 – Rs. 51,95,520/
Rs. 51,94,020/Rs. 51,95,890

Assessment year : 2019-20

Slab rate	:	30%
Surcharge	:	10%
HEC	:	4%

NI Rs.	*IT Rs.*	*SC Rs.*	*HEC Rs.*	*Total Rs.*	*NI Rs.*	*IT Rs.*	*SC Rs.*	*HEC Rs.*	*Total Rs.*	*NI Rs.*	*IT Rs.*	*SC Rs.*	*HEC Rs.*	*Total Rs.*
10	3	7	0.40	10.40	**100**	30	70	4	104	**1000**	300	700	40	1040
20	6	14	0.80	20.80	**200**	60	140	8	208	**2000**	600	1400	80	2080
30	9	21	1.20	31.20	**300**	90	210	12	312	**3000**	900	2100	120	3120
40	12	28	1.60	41.60	**400**	120	280	16	416	**4000**	1200	2800	160	4160
50	15	35	2.00	52.00	**500**	150	350	20	520	**5000**	1500	3500	200	5200
60	18	42	2.40	62.40	**600**	180	420	24	624	**6000**	1800	4200	240	6240
70	21	49	2.80	72.80	**700**	210	490	28	728	**7000**	2100	4900	280	7280
80	24	56	3.20	83.20	**800**	240	560	32	832	**8000**	2400	5600	320	8320
90	27	63	3.60	93.60	**900**	270	630	36	936	**9000**	2700	6300	360	9360

	Resident senior citizen**				***Resident super senior citizen******				***Any other resident individual*/any non-resident individual/any HUF or AOP***			
NI Rs.	*IT Rs.*	*SC Rs.*	*HEC Rs.*	*Total Rs.*	*IT Rs.*	*SC Rs.*	*HEC Rs.*	*Total Rs.*	*IT Rs.*	*SC Rs.*	*HEC Rs.*	*Total Rs.*
5000010	1310003	7	52400	1362410	1300003	7	52000	1352010	1312503	7	52500	1365010
5010000	1313000	7000	52800	1372800	1303000	7000	52400	1362400	1315500	7000	52900	1375400
5020000	1316000	14000	53200	1383200	1306000	14000	52800	1372800	1318500	14000	53300	1385800
5030000	1319000	21000	53600	1393600	1309000	21000	53200	1383200	1321500	21000	53700	1396200
5040000	1322000	28000	54000	1404000	1312000	28000	53600	1393600	1324500	28000	54100	1406600
5050000	1325000	35000	54400	1414400	1315000	35000	54000	1404000	1327500	35000	54500	1417000
5060000	1328000	42000	54800	1424800	1318000	42000	54400	1414400	1330500	42000	54900	1427400
5070000	1331000	49000	55200	1435200	1321000	49000	54800	1424800	1333500	49000	55300	1437800
5080000	1334000	56000	55600	1445600	1324000	56000	55200	1435200	1336500	56000	55700	1448200
5090000	1337000	63000	56000	1456000	1327000	63000	55600	1445600	1339500	63000	56100	1458600
5100000	1340000	70000	56400	1466400	1330000	70000	56000	1456000	1342500	70000	56500	1469000
5110000	1343000	77000	56800	1476800	1333000	77000	56400	1466400	1345500	77000	56900	1479400
5120000	1346000	84000	57200	1487200	1336000	84000	56800	1476800	1348500	84000	57300	1489800
5130000	1349000	91000	57600	1497600	1339000	91000	57200	1487200	1351500	91000	57700	1500200
5140000	1352000	98000	58000	1508000	1342000	98000	57600	1497600	1354500	98000	58100	1510600
5150000	1355000	105000	58400	1518400	1345000	105000	58000	1508000	1357500	105000	58500	1521000
5160000	1358000	112000	58800	1528800	1348000	112000	58400	1518400	1360500	112000	58900	1531400
5170000	1361000	119000	59200	1539200	1351000	119000	58800	1528800	1363500	119000	59300	1541800
5180000	1364000	126000	59600	1549600	1354000	126000	59200	1539200	1366500	126000	59700	1552200
5190000	1367000	133000	60000	1560000	1357000	133000	59600	1549600	1369500	133000	60100	1562600
5194020	—	—	—	—	1358206	135814	59761	1553781	—	—	—	—
5195520	1368656	136864	60221	1565741	—	—	—	—	—	—	—	—
5195890	—	—	—	—	—	—	—	—	1371267	137123	60336	1568726

Note - For how to use table, *see* page B-1.

*If the individual was born on or after April 2, 1959.

**If the individual was born on or after April 2, 1939 but before April 2, 1959.

***If the individual was born before April 2, 1939.

Income-tax : 1.14

INDIVIDUAL

HUF and AOP

Net Income Range : Rs. 51,95,530/Rs. 51,94,030/
Rs. 51,95,900 – Rs. 1,00,00,000

Assessment year : 2019-20

Slab rate : 30%
Surcharge : 10%
HEC : 4%

NI Rs.	IT Rs.	SC Rs.	HEC Rs.	Total Rs.	NI Rs.	IT Rs.	SC Rs.	HEC Rs.	Total Rs.	NI Rs.	IT Rs.	SC Rs.	HEC Rs.	Total Rs.
10	3	0.30	0.13	3.43	**100**	30	3	1.32	34.32	**1000**	300	30	13.20	343.20
20	6	0.60	0.26	6.86	**200**	60	6	2.64	68.64	**2000**	600	60	26.40	686.40
30	9	0.90	0.40	10.30	**300**	90	9	3.96	102.96	**3000**	900	90	39.60	1029.60
40	12	1.20	0.53	13.73	**400**	120	12	5.28	137.28	**4000**	1200	120	52.80	1372.80
50	15	1.50	0.66	17.16	**500**	150	15	6.60	171.60	**5000**	1500	150	66.00	1716.00
60	18	1.80	0.79	20.59	**600**	180	18	7.92	205.92	**6000**	1800	180	79.20	2059.20
70	21	2.10	0.92	24.02	**700**	210	21	9.24	240.24	**7000**	2100	210	92.40	2402.40
80	24	2.40	1.06	27.46	**800**	240	24	10.56	274.56	**8000**	2400	240	105.60	2745.60
90	27	2.70	1.19	30.89	**900**	270	27	11.88	308.88	**9000**	2700	270	118.80	3088.80

	Resident senior citizen**				***Resident super senior citizen******				***Any other resident individual*/any non-resident individual/any HUF or AOP***			
NI Rs.	IT Rs.	SC Rs.	HEC Rs.	Total Rs.	IT Rs.	SC Rs.	HEC Rs.	Total Rs.	IT Rs.	SC Rs.	HEC Rs.	Total Rs.
5194030	—	—	—	—	1358209	135821	59761	1553791	—	—	—	—
5195530	1368659	136866	60221	1565746	—	—	—	—	—	—	—	—
5195900	—	—	—	—	—	—	—	—	1371270	137127	60336	1568733
5200000	1370000	137000	60280	1567280	1360000	136000	59840	1555840	1372500	137250	60390	1570140
5400000	1430000	143000	62920	1635920	1420000	142000	62480	1624480	1432500	143250	63030	1638780
5600000	1490000	149000	65560	1704560	1480000	148000	65120	1693120	1492500	149250	65670	1707420
5800000	1550000	155000	68200	1773200	1540000	154000	67760	1761760	1552500	155250	68310	1776060
6000000	1610000	161000	70840	1841840	1600000	160000	70400	1830400	1612500	161250	70950	1844700
6200000	1670000	167000	73480	1910480	1660000	166000	73040	1899040	1672500	167250	73590	1913340
6400000	1730000	173000	76120	1979120	1720000	172000	75680	1967680	1732500	173250	76230	1981980
6600000	1790000	179000	78760	2047760	1780000	178000	78320	2036320	1792500	179250	78870	2050620
6800000	1850000	185000	81400	2116400	1840000	184000	80960	2104960	1852500	185250	81510	2119260
7000000	1910000	191000	84040	2185040	1900000	190000	83600	2173600	1912500	191250	84150	2187900
7200000	1970000	197000	86680	2253680	1960000	196000	86240	2242240	1972500	197250	86790	2256540
7400000	2030000	203000	89320	2322320	2020000	202000	88880	2310880	2032500	203250	89430	2325180
7600000	2090000	209000	91960	2390960	2080000	208000	91520	2379520	2092500	209250	92070	2393820
7800000	2150000	215000	94600	2459600	2140000	214000	94160	2448160	2152500	215250	94710	2462460
8000000	2210000	221000	97240	2528240	2200000	220000	96800	2516800	2212500	221250	97350	2531100
8200000	2270000	227000	99880	2596880	2260000	226000	99440	2585440	2272500	227250	99990	2599740
8400000	2330000	233000	102520	2665520	2320000	232000	102080	2654080	2332500	233250	102630	2668380
8600000	2390000	239000	105160	2734160	2380000	238000	104720	2722720	2392500	239250	105270	2737020
8800000	2450000	245000	107800	2802800	2440000	244000	107360	2791360	2452500	245250	107910	2805660
9000000	2510000	251000	110440	2871440	2500000	250000	110000	2860000	2512500	251250	110550	2874300
9200000	2570000	257000	113080	2940080	2560000	256000	112640	2928640	2572500	257250	113190	2942940
9400000	2630000	263000	115720	3008720	2620000	262000	115280	2997280	2632500	263250	115830	3011580
9600000	2690000	269000	118360	3077360	2680000	268000	117920	3065920	2692500	269250	118470	3080220
9800000	2750000	275000	121000	3146000	2740000	274000	120560	3134560	2752500	275250	121110	3148860
10000000	2810000	281000	123640	3214640	2800000	280000	123200	3203200	2812500	281250	123750	3217500

Note - For how to use table, *see* page B-1.

*If the individual was born on or after April 2, 1959.

**If the individual was born on or after April 2, 1939 but before April 2, 1959.

***If the individual was born before April 2, 1939.

Income-tax : 1.15

INDIVIDUAL

HUF and AOP

Net Income Range : Rs. 1,00,00,010 – Rs. 1,02,14,500/
Rs. 1,02,13,740/Rs. 1,02,14,690

Assessment year : 2019-20

Slab rate : 30%
Surcharge : 15%
HEC : 4%

NI Rs.	IT Rs.	SC Rs.	HEC Rs.	Total Rs.	NI Rs.	IT Rs.	SC Rs.	HEC Rs.	Total Rs.	NI Rs.	IT Rs.	SC Rs.	HEC Rs.	Total Rs.
10	3	7	0.40	10.40	**100**	30	70	4	104	**1000**	300	700	40	1040
20	6	14	0.80	20.80	**200**	60	140	8	208	**2000**	600	1400	80	2080
30	9	21	1.20	31.20	**300**	90	210	12	312	**3000**	900	2100	120	3120
40	12	28	1.60	41.60	**400**	120	280	16	416	**4000**	1200	2800	160	4160
50	15	35	2.00	52.00	**500**	150	350	20	520	**5000**	1500	3500	200	5200
60	18	42	2.40	62.40	**600**	180	420	24	624	**6000**	1800	4200	240	6240
70	21	49	2.80	72.80	**700**	210	490	28	728	**7000**	2100	4900	280	7280
80	24	56	3.20	83.20	**800**	240	560	32	832	**8000**	2400	5600	320	8320
90	27	63	3.60	93.60	**900**	270	630	36	936	**9000**	2700	6300	360	9360

	Resident senior citizen*				***Resident super senior citizen*****				***Any other resident individual*/any non-resident individual/any HUF or AOP***			
NI Rs.	IT Rs.	SC Rs.	HEC Rs.	Total Rs.	IT Rs.	SC Rs.	HEC Rs.	Total Rs.	IT Rs.	SC Rs.	HEC Rs.	Total Rs.
10000010	2810003	281007	123640	3214650	2800003	280007	123200	3203210	2812503	281257	123750	3217510
10010000	2813000	288000	124040	3225040	2803000	287000	123600	3213600	2815500	288250	124150	3227900
10020000	2816000	295000	124440	3235440	2806000	294000	124000	3224000	2818500	295250	124550	3238300
10030000	2819000	302000	124840	3245840	2809000	301000	124400	3234400	2821500	302250	124950	3248700
10040000	2822000	309000	125240	3256240	2812000	308000	124800	3244800	2824500	309250	125350	3259100
10050000	2825000	316000	125640	3266640	2815000	315000	125200	3255200	2827500	316250	125750	3269500
10060000	2828000	323000	126040	3277040	2818000	322000	125600	3265600	2830500	323250	126150	3279900
10070000	2831000	330000	126440	3287440	2821000	329000	126000	3276000	2833500	330250	126550	3290300
10080000	2834000	337000	126840	3297840	2824000	336000	126400	3286400	2836500	337250	126950	3300700
10090000	2837000	344000	127240	3308240	2827000	343000	126800	3296800	2839500	344250	127350	3311100
10100000	2840000	351000	127640	3318640	2830000	350000	127200	3307200	2842500	351250	127750	3321500
10110000	2843000	358000	128040	3329040	2833000	357000	127600	3317600	2845500	358250	128150	3331900
10120000	2846000	365000	128440	3339440	2836000	364000	128000	3328000	2848500	365250	128550	3342300
10130000	2849000	372000	128840	3349840	2839000	371000	128400	3338400	2851500	372250	128950	3352700
10140000	2852000	379000	129240	3360240	2842000	378000	128800	3348800	2854500	379250	129350	3363100
10150000	2855000	386000	129640	3370640	2845000	385000	129200	3359200	2857500	386250	129750	3373500
10160000	2858000	393000	130040	3381040	2848000	392000	129600	3369600	2860500	393250	130150	3383900
10170000	2861000	400000	130440	3391440	2851000	399000	130000	3380000	2863500	400250	130550	3394300
10180000	2864000	407000	130840	3401840	2854000	406000	130400	3390400	2866500	407250	130950	3404700
10190000	2867000	414000	131240	3412240	2857000	413000	130800	3400800	2869500	414250	131350	3415100
10200000	2870000	421000	131640	3422640	2860000	420000	131200	3411200	2872500	421250	131750	3425500
10210000	2873000	428000	132040	3433040	2863000	427000	131600	3421600	2875500	428250	132150	3435900
10213740	—	—	—	—	2864122	429618	131750	3425490	—	—	—	—
10214500	2874350	431150	132220	3437720	—	—	—	—	—	—	—	—
10214690	—	—	—	—	—	—	—	—	2876907	431533	132338	3440778

Note - For how to use table, *see* page B-1.

*If the individual was born on or after April 2, 1959.

**If the individual was born on or after April 2, 1939 but before April 2, 1959.

***If the individual was born before April 2, 1939.

Income-tax : 1.16

INDIVIDUAL

HUF and AOP

Slab rate : 30%
Surcharge : 15%
HEC : 4%

Net Income Range : Rs. 1,02,14,510/Rs. 1,02,13,750/
Rs. 1,02,14,700 – Rs. 1,30,00,000

Assessment year : 2019-20

NI Rs.	*IT Rs.*	*SC Rs.*	*HEC Rs.*	*Total Rs.*	*NI Rs.*	*IT Rs.*	*SC Rs.*	*HEC Rs.*	*Total Rs.*	*NI Rs.*	*IT Rs.*	*SC Rs.*	*HEC Rs.*	*Total Rs.*
10	3	0.45	0.14	3.59	**100**	30	4.50	1.38	35.88	**1000**	300	45	13.80	358.80
20	6	0.90	0.28	7.18	**200**	60	9.00	2.76	71.76	**2000**	600	90	27.60	717.60
30	9	1.35	0.41	10.76	**300**	90	13.50	4.14	107.64	**3000**	900	135	41.40	1076.40
40	12	1.80	0.55	14.35	**400**	120	18.00	5.52	143.52	**4000**	1200	180	55.20	1435.20
50	15	2.25	0.69	17.94	**500**	150	22.50	6.90	179.40	**5000**	1500	225	69.00	1794.00
60	18	2.70	0.83	21.53	**600**	180	27.00	8.28	215.28	**6000**	1800	270	82.80	2152.80
70	21	3.15	0.97	25.12	**700**	210	31.50	9.66	251.16	**7000**	2100	315	96.60	2511.60
80	24	3.60	1.10	28.70	**800**	240	36.00	11.04	287.04	**8000**	2400	360	110.40	2870.40
90	27	4.05	1.24	32.29	**900**	270	40.50	12.42	322.92	**9000**	2700	405	124.20	3229.20

	Resident senior citizen**				***Resident super senior citizen******				***Any other resident individual*/any non-resident individual/any HUF or AOP***			
NI Rs.	*IT Rs.*	*SC Rs.*	*HEC Rs.*	*Total Rs.*	*IT Rs.*	*SC Rs.*	*HEC Rs.*	*Total Rs.*	*IT Rs.*	*SC Rs.*	*HEC Rs.*	*Total Rs.*
10213750	—	—	—	—	2864125	429619	131750	3425494	—	—	—	—
10214510	2874353	431153	132220	3437726	—	—	—	—	—	—	—	—
10214700	—	—	—	—	—	—	—	—	2876910	431537	132338	3440785
10300000	2900000	435000	133400	3468400	2890000	433500	132940	3456440	2902500	435375	133515	3471390
10400000	2930000	439500	134780	3504280	2920000	438000	134320	3492320	2932500	439875	134895	3507270
10500000	2960000	444000	136160	3540160	2950000	442500	135700	3528200	2962500	444375	136275	3543150
10600000	2990000	448500	137540	3576040	2980000	447000	137080	3564080	2992500	448875	137655	3579030
10700000	3020000	453000	138920	3611920	3010000	451500	138460	3599960	3022500	453375	139035	3614910
10800000	3050000	457500	140300	3647800	3040000	456000	139840	3635840	3052500	457875	140415	3650790
10900000	3080000	462000	141680	3683680	3070000	460500	141220	3671720	3082500	462375	141795	3686670
11000000	3110000	466500	143060	3719560	3100000	465000	142600	3707600	3112500	466875	143175	3722550
11100000	3140000	471000	144440	3755440	3130000	469500	143980	3743480	3142500	471375	144555	3758430
11200000	3170000	475500	145820	3791320	3160000	474000	145360	3779360	3172500	475875	145935	3794310
11300000	3200000	480000	147200	3827200	3190000	478500	146740	3815240	3202500	480375	147315	3830190
11400000	3230000	484500	148580	3863080	3220000	483000	148120	3851120	3232500	484875	148695	3866070
11500000	3260000	489000	149960	3898960	3250000	487500	149500	3887000	3262500	489375	150075	3901950
11600000	3290000	493500	151340	3934840	3280000	492000	150880	3922880	3292500	493875	151455	3937830
11700000	3320000	498000	152720	3970720	3310000	496500	152260	3958760	3322500	498375	152835	3973710
11800000	3350000	502500	154100	4006600	3340000	501000	153640	3994640	3352500	502875	154215	4009590
11900000	3380000	507000	155480	4042480	3370000	505500	155020	4030520	3382500	507375	155595	4045470
12000000	3410000	511500	156860	4078360	3400000	510000	156400	4066400	3412500	511875	156975	4081350
12100000	3440000	516000	158240	4114240	3430000	514500	157780	4102280	3442500	516375	158355	4117230
12200000	3470000	520500	159620	4150120	3460000	519000	159160	4138160	3472500	520875	159735	4153110
12300000	3500000	525000	161000	4186000	3490000	523500	160540	4174040	3502500	525375	161115	4188990
12400000	3530000	529500	162380	4221880	3520000	528000	161920	4209920	3532500	529875	162495	4224870
12500000	3560000	534000	163760	4257760	3550000	532500	163300	4245800	3562500	534375	163875	4260750
12600000	3590000	538500	165140	4293640	3580000	537000	164680	4281680	3592500	538875	165255	4296630
12700000	3620000	543000	166520	4329520	3610000	541500	166060	4317560	3622500	543375	166635	4332510
12800000	3650000	547500	167900	4365400	3640000	546000	167440	4353440	3652500	547875	168015	4368390
12900000	3680000	552000	169280	4401280	3670000	550500	168820	4389320	3682500	552375	169395	4404270
13000000	3710000	556500	170660	4437160	3700000	555000	170200	4425200	3712500	556875	170775	4440150

Note - For how to use table, *see* page B-1.

*If the individual was born on or after April 2, 1959.

**If the individual was born on or after April 2, 1939 but before April 2, 1959.

***If the individual was born before April 2, 1939.

Income-tax : 2.1

INDIVIDUAL

HUF and AOP

Net Income Range : Rs. 2,50,000 - Rs. 2,83,000

Assessment year : 2020-21

Slab rate : 5%
Surcharge : *Nil*
HEC : 4%

NI Rs.	*IT Rs. P.*	*HEC Rs. P.*	*Total Rs. P.*	*NI Rs.*	*IT Rs.*	*HEC Rs. P.*	*Total Rs. P.*	*NI Rs.*	*IT Rs.*	*HEC Rs. P.*	*Total Rs. P.*
10	0.50	0.02	0.52	**100**	5	0.20	5.20	**100**	5	0.20	5.20
20	1.00	0.04	1.04	**200**	10	0.40	10.40	**200**	10	0.40	10.40
30	1.50	0.06	1.56	**300**	15	0.60	15.60	**300**	15	0.60	15.60
40	2.00	0.08	2.08	**400**	20	0.80	20.80	**400**	20	0.80	20.80
50	2.50	0.10	2.60	**500**	25	1.00	26.00	**500**	25	1.00	26.00
60	3.00	0.12	3.12	**600**	30	1.20	31.20	**600**	30	1.20	31.20
70	3.50	0.14	3.64	**700**	35	1.40	36.40	**700**	35	1.40	36.40
80	4.00	0.16	4.16	**800**	40	1.60	41.60	**800**	40	1.60	41.60
90	4.50	0.18	4.68	**900**	45	1.80	46.80	**900**	45	1.80	46.80

	Resident senior citizen**			***Resident super senior citizen******			***Any other resident individual****			***Non-resident individual/ any HUF or AOP***		
NI Rs.	*IT Rs.*	*HEC Rs.*	*Total Rs.*	*IT Rs.*	*HEC Rs.*	*Total Rs.*	*IT# Rs.*	*HEC Rs.*	*Total Rs.*	*IT Rs.*	*HEC Rs. P.*	*Total Rs. P.*
250000	-	-	-	-	-	-	-	-	-	-	-	-
251000	-	-	-	-	-	-	-	-	-	50	2	52
252000	-	-	-	-	-	-	-	-	-	100	4	104
253000	-	-	-	-	-	-	-	-	-	150	6	156
254000	-	-	-	-	-	-	-	-	-	200	8	208
255000	-	-	-	-	-	-	-	-	-	250	10	260
256000	-	-	-	-	-	-	-	-	-	300	12	312
257000	-	-	-	-	-	-	-	-	-	350	14	364
258000	-	-	-	-	-	-	-	-	-	400	16	416
259000	-	-	-	-	-	-	-	-	-	450	18	468
260000	-	-	-	-	-	-	-	-	-	500	20	520
261000	-	-	-	-	-	-	-	-	-	550	22	572
262000	-	-	-	-	-	-	-	-	-	600	24	624
263000	-	-	-	-	-	-	-	-	-	650	26	676
264000	-	-	-	-	-	-	-	-	-	700	28	728
265000	-	-	-	-	-	-	-	-	-	750	30	780
266000	-	-	-	-	-	-	-	-	-	800	32	832
267000	-	-	-	-	-	-	-	-	-	850	34	884
268000	-	-	-	-	-	-	-	-	-	900	36	936
269000	-	-	-	-	-	-	-	-	-	950	38	988
270000	-	-	-	-	-	-	-	-	-	1000	40	1040
271000	-	-	-	-	-	-	-	-	-	1050	42	1092
272000	-	-	-	-	-	-	-	-	-	1100	44	1144
273000	-	-	-	-	-	-	-	-	-	1150	46	1196
274000	-	-	-	-	-	-	-	-	-	1200	48	1248
275000	-	-	-	-	-	-	-	-	-	1250	50	1300
276000	-	-	-	-	-	-	-	-	-	1300	52	1352
277000	-	-	-	-	-	-	-	-	-	1350	54	1404
278000	-	-	-	-	-	-	-	-	-	1400	56	1456
279000	-	-	-	-	-	-	-	-	-	1450	58	1508
280000	-	-	-	-	-	-	-	-	-	1500	60	1560
281000	-	-	-	-	-	-	-	-	-	1550	62	1612
282000	-	-	-	-	-	-	-	-	-	1600	64	1664
283000	-	-	-	-	-	-	-	-	-	1650	66	1716

Note - For how to use table, *see* page B-1.

\# After rebate under section 87A.

*If the individual was born on or after April 2, 1960.

**If the individual was born on or after April 2, 1940 but before April 2, 1960.

***If the individual was born before April 2, 1940.

Income-tax : 2.2

INDIVIDUAL

HUF and AOP

Net Income Range : Rs. 2,83,000 - Rs. 3,16,000

Assessment year : 2020-21

Slab rate : 5%
Surcharge : *Nil*
HEC : 4%

NI Rs.	*IT Rs. P.*	*HEC Rs. P.*	*Total Rs. P.*	*NI Rs.*	*IT Rs.*	*HEC Rs. P.*	*Total Rs. P.*	*NI Rs.*	*IT Rs.*	*HEC Rs. P.*	*Total Rs. P.*
10	0.50	0.02	0.52	**100**	5	0.20	5.20	**100**	5	0.20	5.20
20	1.00	0.04	1.04	**200**	10	0.40	10.40	**200**	10	0.40	10.40
30	1.50	0.06	1.56	**300**	15	0.60	15.60	**300**	15	0.60	15.60
40	2.00	0.08	2.08	**400**	20	0.80	20.80	**400**	20	0.80	20.80
50	2.50	0.10	2.60	**500**	25	1.00	26.00	**500**	25	1.00	26.00
60	3.00	0.12	3.12	**600**	30	1.20	31.20	**600**	30	1.20	31.20
70	3.50	0.14	3.64	**700**	35	1.40	36.40	**700**	35	1.40	36.40
80	4.00	0.16	4.16	**800**	40	1.60	41.60	**800**	40	1.60	41.60
90	4.50	0.18	4.68	**900**	45	1.80	46.80	**900**	45	1.80	46.80

	Resident senior citizen**			***Resident super senior citizen******			***Any other resident individual****			***Non-resident individual/ any HUF or AOP***		
NI Rs.	*IT# Rs.*	*HEC Rs.*	*Total Rs.*	*IT Rs.*	*HEC Rs.*	*Total Rs.*	*IT# Rs.*	*HEC Rs. P.*	*Total Rs. P.*	*IT Rs.*	*HEC Rs.*	*Total Rs.*
283000	-	-	-	-	-	-	-	-	-	1650	66	1716
284000	-	-	-	-	-	-	-	-	-	1700	68	1768
285000	-	-	-	-	-	-	-	-	-	1750	70	1820
286000	-	-	-	-	-	-	-	-	-	1800	72	1872
287000	-	-	-	-	-	-	-	-	-	1850	74	1924
288000	-	-	-	-	-	-	-	-	-	1900	76	1976
289000	-	-	-	-	-	-	-	-	-	1950	78	2028
290000	-	-	-	-	-	-	-	-	-	2000	80	2080
291000	-	-	-	-	-	-	-	-	-	2050	82	2132
292000	-	-	-	-	-	-	-	-	-	2100	84	2184
293000	-	-	-	-	-	-	-	-	-	2150	86	2236
294000	-	-	-	-	-	-	-	-	-	2200	88	2288
295000	-	-	-	-	-	-	-	-	-	2250	90	2340
296000	-	-	-	-	-	-	-	-	-	2300	92	2392
297000	-	-	-	-	-	-	-	-	-	2350	94	2444
298000	-	-	-	-	-	-	-	-	-	2400	96	2496
299000	-	-	-	-	-	-	-	-	-	2450	98	2548
300000	-	-	-	-	-	-	-	-	-	2500	100	2600
301000	-	-	-	-	-	-	-	-	-	2550	102	2652
302000	-	-	-	-	-	-	-	-	-	2600	104	2704
303000	-	-	-	-	-	-	-	-	-	2650	106	2756
304000	-	-	-	-	-	-	-	-	-	2700	108	2808
305000	-	-	-	-	-	-	-	-	-	2750	110	2860
306000	-	-	-	-	-	-	-	-	-	2800	112	2912
307000	-	-	-	-	-	-	-	-	-	2850	114	2964
308000	-	-	-	-	-	-	-	-	-	2900	116	3016
309000	-	-	-	-	-	-	-	-	-	2950	118	3068
310000	-	-	-	-	-	-	-	-	-	3000	120	3120
311000	-	-	-	-	-	-	-	-	-	3050	122	3172
312000	-	-	-	-	-	-	-	-	-	3100	124	3224
313000	-	-	-	-	-	-	-	-	-	3150	126	3276
314000	-	-	-	-	-	-	-	-	-	3200	128	3328
315000	-	-	-	-	-	-	-	-	-	3250	130	3380
316000	-	-	-	-	-	-	-	-	-	3300	132	3432

Note - For how to use table, *see* page B-1.

After rebate under section 87A.

*If the individual was born on or after April 2, 1960.

**If the individual was born on or after April 2, 1940 but before April 2, 1960.

***If the individual was born before April 2, 1940.

Income-tax : 2.3

INDIVIDUAL

HUF and AOP

Net Income Range : Rs. 3,16,000 - Rs. 3,50,000

Assessment year : 2020-21

Slab rate : 5%
Surcharge : *Nil*
HEC : 4%

NI Rs.	IT Rs. P.	HEC Rs. P.	Total Rs. P.	NI Rs.	IT Rs.	HEC Rs. P.	Total Rs. P.	NI Rs.	IT Rs.	HEC Rs. P.	Total Rs. P.
10	0.50	0.02	0.52	**100**	5	0.20	5.20	**100**	5	0.20	5.20
20	1.00	0.04	1.04	**200**	10	0.40	10.40	**200**	10	0.40	10.40
30	1.50	0.06	1.56	**300**	15	0.60	15.60	**300**	15	0.60	15.60
40	2.00	0.08	2.08	**400**	20	0.80	20.80	**400**	20	0.80	20.80
50	2.50	0.10	2.60	**500**	25	1.00	26.00	**500**	25	1.00	26.00
60	3.00	0.12	3.12	**600**	30	1.20	31.20	**600**	30	1.20	31.20
70	3.50	0.14	3.64	**700**	35	1.40	36.40	**700**	35	1.40	36.40
80	4.00	0.16	4.16	**800**	40	1.60	41.60	**800**	40	1.60	41.60
90	4.50	0.18	4.68	**900**	45	1.80	46.80	**900**	45	1.80	46.80

	Resident senior citizen**			***Resident super senior citizen******			***Any other resident individual****			***Non-resident individual/ any HUF or AOP***		
NI Rs.	IT# Rs.	HEC Rs.	Total Rs.	IT Rs.	HEC Rs.	Total Rs.	IT# Rs.	HEC Rs.	Total Rs.	IT Rs.	HEC Rs.	Total Rs.
316000	-	-	-	-	-	-	-	-	-	3300	132	3432
317000	-	-	-	-	-	-	-	-	-	3350	134	3484
318000	-	-	-	-	-	-	-	-	-	3400	136	3536
319000	-	-	-	-	-	-	-	-	-	3450	138	3588
320000	-	-	-	-	-	-	-	-	-	3500	140	3640
321000	-	-	-	-	-	-	-	-	-	3550	142	3692
322000	-	-	-	-	-	-	-	-	-	3600	144	3744
323000	-	-	-	-	-	-	-	-	-	3650	146	3796
324000	-	-	-	-	-	-	-	-	-	3700	148	3848
325000	-	-	-	-	-	-	-	-	-	3750	150	3900
326000	-	-	-	-	-	-	-	-	-	3800	152	3952
327000	-	-	-	-	-	-	-	-	-	3850	154	4004
328000	-	-	-	-	-	-	-	-	-	3900	156	4056
329000	-	-	-	-	-	-	-	-	-	3950	158	4108
330000	-	-	-	-	-	-	-	-	-	4000	160	4160
331000	-	-	-	-	-	-	-	-	-	4050	162	4212
332000	-	-	-	-	-	-	-	-	-	4100	164	4264
333000	-	-	-	-	-	-	-	-	-	4150	166	4316
334000	-	-	-	-	-	-	-	-	-	4200	168	4368
335000	-	-	-	-	-	-	-	-	-	4250	170	4420
336000	-	-	-	-	-	-	-	-	-	4300	172	4472
337000	-	-	-	-	-	-	-	-	-	4350	174	4524
338000	-	-	-	-	-	-	-	-	-	4400	176	4576
339000	-	-	-	-	-	-	-	-	-	4450	178	4628
340000	-	-	-	-	-	-	-	-	-	4500	180	4680
341000	-	-	-	-	-	-	-	-	-	4550	182	4732
342000	-	-	-	-	-	-	-	-	-	4600	184	4784
343000	-	-	-	-	-	-	-	-	-	4650	186	4836
344000	-	-	-	-	-	-	-	-	-	4700	188	4888
345000	-	-	-	-	-	-	-	-	-	4750	190	4940
346000	-	-	-	-	-	-	-	-	-	4800	192	4992
347000	-	-	-	-	-	-	-	-	-	4850	194	5044
348000	-	-	-	-	-	-	-	-	-	4900	196	5096
349000	-	-	-	-	-	-	-	-	-	4950	198	5148
350000	-	-	-	-	-	-	-	-	-	5000	200	5200

Note - For how to use table, *see* page B-1.

\# After rebate under section 87A.

*If the individual was born on or after April 2, 1960.

**If the individual was born on or after April 2, 1940 but before April 2, 1960.

***If the individual was born before April 2, 1940.

Income-tax : 2.4

INDIVIDUAL

HUF and AOP

Net Income Range : Rs. 3,50,000 - Rs. 3,85,000

Assessment year : 2020-21

Slab rate : 5%

Surcharge : *Nil*

HEC : 4%

NI Rs.	*IT Rs. P.*	*HEC Rs. P.*	*Total Rs. P.*	*NI Rs.*	*IT Rs.*	*HEC Rs. P.*	*Total Rs. P.*	*NI Rs.*	*IT Rs.*	*HEC Rs. P.*	*Total Rs. P.*
10	0.50	0.02	0.52	**100**	5	0.20	5.20	**100**	5	0.20	5.20
20	1.00	0.04	1.04	**200**	10	0.40	10.40	**200**	10	0.40	10.40
30	1.50	0.06	1.56	**300**	15	0.60	15.60	**300**	15	0.60	15.60
40	2.00	0.08	2.08	**400**	20	0.80	20.80	**400**	20	0.80	20.80
50	2.50	0.10	2.60	**500**	25	1.00	26.00	**500**	25	1.00	26.00
60	3.00	0.12	3.12	**600**	30	1.20	31.20	**600**	30	1.20	31.20
70	3.50	0.14	3.64	**700**	35	1.40	36.40	**700**	35	1.40	36.40
80	4.00	0.16	4.16	**800**	40	1.60	41.60	**800**	40	1.60	41.60
90	4.50	0.18	4.68	**900**	45	1.80	46.80	**900**	45	1.80	46.80

	Resident senior citizen*			***Resident super senior citizen*****			***Any other resident individual****			***Non-resident individual/ any HUF or AOP***		
NI Rs.	*IT# Rs.*	*HEC Rs.*	*Total Rs.*	*IT Rs.*	*HEC Rs.*	*Total Rs.*	*IT# Rs.*	*HEC Rs.*	*Total Rs.*	*IT Rs.*	*HEC Rs. P.*	*Total Rs. P.*
350000	-	-	-	-	-	-	-	-	-	5000	200	5200
351000	-	-	-	-	-	-	-	-	-	5050	202	5252
352000	-	-	-	-	-	-	-	-	-	5100	204	5304
353000	-	-	-	-	-	-	-	-	-	5150	206	5356
354000	-	-	-	-	-	-	-	-	-	5200	208	5408
355000	-	-	-	-	-	-	-	-	-	5250	210	5460
356000	-	-	-	-	-	-	-	-	-	5300	212	5512
357000	-	-	-	-	-	-	-	-	-	5350	214	5564
358000	-	-	-	-	-	-	-	-	-	5400	216	5616
359000	-	-	-	-	-	-	-	-	-	5450	218	5668
360000	-	-	-	-	-	-	-	-	-	5500	220	5720
361000	-	-	-	-	-	-	-	-	-	5550	222	5772
362000	-	-	-	-	-	-	-	-	-	5600	224	5824
363000	-	-	-	-	-	-	-	-	-	5650	226	5876
364000	-	-	-	-	-	-	-	-	-	5700	228	5928
365000	-	-	-	-	-	-	-	-	-	5750	230	5980
366000	-	-	-	-	-	-	-	-	-	5800	232	6032
367000	-	-	-	-	-	-	-	-	-	5850	234	6084
368000	-	-	-	-	-	-	-	-	-	5900	236	6136
369000	-	-	-	-	-	-	-	-	-	5950	238	6188
370000	-	-	-	-	-	-	-	-	-	6000	240	6240
371000	-	-	-	-	-	-	-	-	-	6050	242	6292
372000	-	-	-	-	-	-	-	-	-	6100	244	6344
373000	-	-	-	-	-	-	-	-	-	6150	246	6396
374000	-	-	-	-	-	-	-	-	-	6200	248	6448
375000	-	-	-	-	-	-	-	-	-	6250	250	6500
376000	-	-	-	-	-	-	-	-	-	6300	252	6552
377000	-	-	-	-	-	-	-	-	-	6350	254	6604
378000	-	-	-	-	-	-	-	-	-	6400	256	6656
379000	-	-	-	-	-	-	-	-	-	6450	258	6708
380000	-	-	-	-	-	-	-	-	-	6500	260	6760
381000	-	-	-	-	-	-	-	-	-	6550	262	6812
382000	-	-	-	-	-	-	-	-	-	6600	264	6864
383000	-	-	-	-	-	-	-	-	-	6650	266	6916
384000	-	-	-	-	-	-	-	-	-	6700	268	6968
385000	-	-	-	-	-	-	-	-	-	6750	270	7020

Note - For how to use table, *see* page B-1.

#After rebate under section 87A.

*If the individual was born on or after April 2, 1960.

**If the individual was born on or after April 2, 1940 but before April 2, 1960.

***If the individual was born before April 2, 1940.

Income-tax : 2.5

INDIVIDUAL

HUF and AOP

Net Income Range : Rs. 3,85,000 - Rs. 4,20,000

Assessment year : 2020-21

Slab rate : 5%
Surcharge : *Nil*
HEC : 4%

NI Rs.	*IT Rs. P.*	*HEC Rs. P.*	*Total Rs. P.*	*NI Rs.*	*IT Rs.*	*HEC Rs. P.*	*Total Rs. P.*	*NI Rs.*	*IT Rs.*	*HEC Rs. P.*	*Total Rs. P.*
10	0.50	0.02	0.52	**100**	5	0.20	5.20	**100**	5	0.20	5.20
20	1.00	0.04	1.04	**200**	10	0.40	10.40	**200**	10	0.40	10.40
30	1.50	0.06	1.56	**300**	15	0.60	15.60	**300**	15	0.60	15.60
40	2.00	0.08	2.08	**400**	20	0.80	20.80	**400**	20	0.80	20.80
50	2.50	0.10	2.60	**500**	25	1.00	26.00	**500**	25	1.00	26.00
60	3.00	0.12	3.12	**600**	30	1.20	31.20	**600**	30	1.20	31.20
70	3.50	0.14	3.64	**700**	35	1.40	36.40	**700**	35	1.40	36.40
80	4.00	0.16	4.16	**800**	40	1.60	41.60	**800**	40	1.60	41.60
90	4.50	0.18	4.68	**900**	45	1.80	46.80	**900**	45	1.80	46.80

	Resident senior citizen**			***Resident super senior citizen******			***Any other resident individual****			***Non-resident individual/ any HUF or AOP***		
NI Rs.	*IT# Rs.*	*HEC Rs.*	*Total Rs.*	*IT Rs.*	*HEC Rs.*	*Total Rs.*	*IT# Rs.*	*HEC Rs.*	*Total Rs.*	*IT Rs.*	*HEC Rs. P.*	*Total Rs. P.*
385000	-	-	-	-	-	-	-	-	-	6750	270	7020
386000	-	-	-	-	-	-	-	-	-	6800	272	7072
387000	-	-	-	-	-	-	-	-	-	6850	274	7124
388000	-	-	-	-	-	-	-	-	-	6900	276	7176
389000	-	-	-	-	-	-	-	-	-	6950	278	7228
390000	-	-	-	-	-	-	-	-	-	7000	280	7280
391000	-	-	-	-	-	-	-	-	-	7050	282	7332
392000	-	-	-	-	-	-	-	-	-	7100	284	7384
393000	-	-	-	-	-	-	-	-	-	7150	286	7436
394000	-	-	-	-	-	-	-	-	-	7200	288	7488
395000	-	-	-	-	-	-	-	-	-	7250	290	7540
396000	-	-	-	-	-	-	-	-	-	7300	292	7592
397000	-	-	-	-	-	-	-	-	-	7350	294	7644
398000	-	-	-	-	-	-	-	-	-	7400	296	7696
399000	-	-	-	-	-	-	-	-	-	7450	298	7748
400000	-	-	-	-	-	-	-	-	-	7500	300	7800
401000	-	-	-	-	-	-	-	-	-	7550	302	7852
402000	-	-	-	-	-	-	-	-	-	7600	304	7904
403000	-	-	-	-	-	-	-	-	-	7650	306	7956
404000	-	-	-	-	-	-	-	-	-	7700	308	8008
405000	-	-	-	-	-	-	-	-	-	7750	310	8060
406000	-	-	-	-	-	-	-	-	-	7800	312	8112
407000	-	-	-	-	-	-	-	-	-	7850	314	8164
408000	-	-	-	-	-	-	-	-	-	7900	316	8216
409000	-	-	-	-	-	-	-	-	-	7950	318	8268
410000	-	-	-	-	-	-	-	-	-	8000	320	8320
411000	-	-	-	-	-	-	-	-	-	8050	322	8372
412000	-	-	-	-	-	-	-	-	-	8100	324	8424
413000	-	-	-	-	-	-	-	-	-	8150	326	8476
414000	-	-	-	-	-	-	-	-	-	8200	328	8528
415000	-	-	-	-	-	-	-	-	-	8250	330	8580
416000	-	-	-	-	-	-	-	-	-	8300	332	8632
417000	-	-	-	-	-	-	-	-	-	8350	334	8684
418000	-	-	-	-	-	-	-	-	-	8400	336	8736
419000	-	-	-	-	-	-	-	-	-	8450	338	8788
420000	-	-	-	-	-	-	-	-	-	8500	340	8840

Note - For how to use table, *see* page B-1.

#After rebate under section 87A.

*If the individual was born on or after April 2, 1960.

**If the individual was born on or after April 2, 1940 but before April 2, 1960.

***If the individual was born before April 2, 1940.

Income-tax : 2.6

INDIVIDUAL

HUF and AOP

Net Income Range : Rs. 4,20,000 - Rs. 4,60,000

Assessment year : 2020-21

Slab rate : 5%
Surcharge : *Nil*
HEC : 4%

NI Rs.	IT Rs. P.	HEC Rs. P.	Total Rs. P.	NI Rs.	IT Rs.	HEC Rs. P.	Total Rs. P.	NI Rs.	IT Rs.	HEC Rs. P.	Total Rs. P.
10	0.50	0.02	0.52	**100**	5	0.20	5.20	**100**	5	0.20	5.20
20	1.00	0.04	1.04	**200**	10	0.40	10.40	**200**	10	0.40	10.40
30	1.50	0.06	1.56	**300**	15	0.60	15.60	**300**	15	0.60	15.60
40	2.00	0.08	2.08	**400**	20	0.80	20.80	**400**	20	0.80	20.80
50	2.50	0.10	2.60	**500**	25	1.00	26.00	**500**	25	1.00	26.00
60	3.00	0.12	3.12	**600**	30	1.20	31.20	**600**	30	1.20	31.20
70	3.50	0.14	3.64	**700**	35	1.40	36.40	**700**	35	1.40	36.40
80	4.00	0.16	4.16	**800**	40	1.60	41.60	**800**	40	1.60	41.60
90	4.50	0.18	4.68	**900**	45	1.80	46.80	**900**	45	1.80	46.80

	Resident senior citizen**			***Resident super senior citizen******			***Any other resident individual****			***Non-resident individual/ any HUF or AOP***		
NI Rs.	*IT# Rs.*	*HEC Rs.*	*Total Rs.*	*IT Rs.*	*HEC Rs.*	*Total Rs.*	*IT# Rs.*	*HEC Rs.*	*Total Rs.*	*IT Rs.*	*HEC Rs. P.*	*Total Rs. P.*
420000	-	-	-	-	-	-	-	-	-	8500	340	8840
421000	-	-	-	-	-	-	-	-	-	8550	342	8892
422000	-	-	-	-	-	-	-	-	-	8600	344	8944
423000	-	-	-	-	-	-	-	-	-	8650	346	8996
424000	-	-	-	-	-	-	-	-	-	8700	348	9048
425000	-	-	-	-	-	-	-	-	-	8750	350	9100
426000	-	-	-	-	-	-	-	-	-	8800	352	9152
427000	-	-	-	-	-	-	-	-	-	8850	354	9204
428000	-	-	-	-	-	-	-	-	-	8900	356	9256
429000	-	-	-	-	-	-	-	-	-	8950	358	9308
430000	-	-	-	-	-	-	-	-	-	9000	360	9360
431000	-	-	-	-	-	-	-	-	-	9050	362	9412
432000	-	-	-	-	-	-	-	-	-	9100	364	9464
433000	-	-	-	-	-	-	-	-	-	9150	366	9516
434000	-	-	-	-	-	-	-	-	-	9200	368	9568
435000	-	-	-	-	-	-	-	-	-	9250	370	9620
436000	-	-	-	-	-	-	-	-	-	9300	372	9672
437000	-	-	-	-	-	-	-	-	-	9350	374	9724
438000	-	-	-	-	-	-	-	-	-	9400	376	9776
439000	-	-	-	-	-	-	-	-	-	9450	378	9828
440000	-	-	-	-	-	-	-	-	-	9500	380	9880
441000	-	-	-	-	-	-	-	-	-	9550	382	9932
442000	-	-	-	-	-	-	-	-	-	9600	384	9984
443000	-	-	-	-	-	-	-	-	-	9650	386	10036
444000	-	-	-	-	-	-	-	-	-	9700	388	10088
445000	-	-	-	-	-	-	-	-	-	9750	390	10140
446000	-	-	-	-	-	-	-	-	-	9800	392	10192
447000	-	-	-	-	-	-	-	-	-	9850	394	10244
448000	-	-	-	-	-	-	-	-	-	9900	396	10296
449000	-	-	-	-	-	-	-	-	-	9950	398	10348
450000	-	-	-	-	-	-	-	-	-	10000	400	10400
451000	-	-	-	-	-	-	-	-	-	10050	402	10452
452000	-	-	-	-	-	-	-	-	-	10100	404	10504
453000	-	-	-	-	-	-	-	-	-	10150	406	10556
454000	-	-	-	-	-	-	-	-	-	10200	408	10608
455000	-	-	-	-	-	-	-	-	-	10250	410	10660
456000	-	-	-	-	-	-	-	-	-	10300	412	10712
457000	-	-	-	-	-	-	-	-	-	10350	414	10764
458000	-	-	-	-	-	-	-	-	-	10400	416	10816
459000	-	-	-	-	-	-	-	-	-	10450	418	10868
460000	-	-	-	-	-	-	-	-	-	10500	420	10920

Note - For how to use table, *see* page B-1.

#After rebate under section 87A.

*If the individual was born on or after April 2, 1960.

**If the individual was born on or after April 2, 1940 but before April 2, 1960.

***If the individual was born before April 2, 1940.

Income-tax : 2.7

INDIVIDUAL

HUF and AOP

Net Income Range : Rs. 4,60,000 - Rs. 5,00,000

Assessment year : 2020-21

Slab rate : 5%
Surcharge : *Nil*
HEC : 4%

NI Rs.	*IT Rs. P.*	*HEC Rs. P.*	*Total Rs. P.*	*NI Rs.*	*IT Rs.*	*HEC Rs. P.*	*Total Rs. P.*	*NI Rs.*	*IT Rs.*	*HEC Rs. P.*	*Total Rs. P.*
10	0.50	0.02	0.52	**100**	5	0.20	5.20	**100**	5	0.20	5.20
20	1.00	0.04	1.04	**200**	10	0.40	10.40	**200**	10	0.40	10.40
30	1.50	0.06	1.56	**300**	15	0.60	15.60	**300**	15	0.60	15.60
40	2.00	0.08	2.08	**400**	20	0.80	20.80	**400**	20	0.80	20.80
50	2.50	0.10	2.60	**500**	25	1.00	26.00	**500**	25	1.00	26.00
60	3.00	0.12	3.12	**600**	30	1.20	31.20	**600**	30	1.20	31.20
70	3.50	0.14	3.64	**700**	35	1.40	36.40	**700**	35	1.40	36.40
80	4.00	0.16	4.16	**800**	40	1.60	41.60	**800**	40	1.60	41.60
90	4.50	0.18	4.68	**900**	45	1.80	46.80	**900**	45	1.80	46.80

	Resident senior citizen**			***Resident super senior citizen******			***Any other resident individual****			***Non-resident individual/ any HUF or AOP***		
NI Rs.	*IT# Rs.*	*HEC Rs.*	*Total Rs.*	*IT Rs.*	*HEC Rs.*	*Total Rs.*	*IT# Rs.*	*HEC Rs.*	*Total Rs.*	*IT Rs.*	*HEC Rs. P.*	*Total Rs. P.*
460000	-	-	-	-	-	-	-	-	-	10500	420	10920
461000	-	-	-	-	-	-	-	-	-	10550	422	10972
462000	-	-	-	-	-	-	-	-	-	10600	424	11024
463000	-	-	-	-	-	-	-	-	-	10650	426	11076
464000	-	-	-	-	-	-	-	-	-	10700	428	11128
465000	-	-	-	-	-	-	-	-	-	10750	430	11180
466000	-	-	-	-	-	-	-	-	-	10800	432	11232
467000	-	-	-	-	-	-	-	-	-	10850	434	11284
468000	-	-	-	-	-	-	-	-	-	10900	436	11336
469000	-	-	-	-	-	-	-	-	-	10950	438	11388
470000	-	-	-	-	-	-	-	-	-	11000	440	11440
471000	-	-	-	-	-	-	-	-	-	11050	442	11492
472000	-	-	-	-	-	-	-	-	-	11100	444	11544
473000	-	-	-	-	-	-	-	-	-	11150	446	11596
474000	-	-	-	-	-	-	-	-	-	11200	448	11648
475000	-	-	-	-	-	-	-	-	-	11250	450	11700
476000	-	-	-	-	-	-	-	-	-	11300	452	11752
477000	-	-	-	-	-	-	-	-	-	11350	454	11804
478000	-	-	-	-	-	-	-	-	-	11400	456	11856
479000	-	-	-	-	-	-	-	-	-	11450	458	11908
480000	-	-	-	-	-	-	-	-	-	11500	460	11960
481000	-	-	-	-	-	-	-	-	-	11550	462	12012
482000	-	-	-	-	-	-	-	-	-	11600	464	12064
483000	-	-	-	-	-	-	-	-	-	11650	466	12116
484000	-	-	-	-	-	-	-	-	-	11700	468	12168
485000	-	-	-	-	-	-	-	-	-	11750	470	12220
486000	-	-	-	-	-	-	-	-	-	11800	472	12272
487000	-	-	-	-	-	-	-	-	-	11850	474	12324
488000	-	-	-	-	-	-	-	-	-	11900	476	12376
489000	-	-	-	-	-	-	-	-	-	11950	478	12428
490000	-	-	-	-	-	-	-	-	-	12000	480	12480
491000	-	-	-	-	-	-	-	-	-	12050	482	12532
492000	-	-	-	-	-	-	-	-	-	12100	484	12584
493000	-	-	-	-	-	-	-	-	-	12150	486	12636
494000	-	-	-	-	-	-	-	-	-	12200	488	12688
495000	-	-	-	-	-	-	-	-	-	12250	490	12740
496000	-	-	-	-	-	-	-	-	-	12300	492	12792
497000	-	-	-	-	-	-	-	-	-	12350	494	12844
498000	-	-	-	-	-	-	-	-	-	12400	496	12896
499000	-	-	-	-	-	-	-	-	-	12450	498	12948
500000	-	-	-	-	-	-	-	-	-	12500	500	13000

Note - For how to use table, *see* page B-1.

#After rebate under section 87A.

*If the individual was born on or after April 2, 1960.

**If the individual was born on or after April 2, 1940 but before April 2, 1960.

***If the individual was born before April 2, 1940.

Income-tax : 2.8

INDIVIDUAL

HUF and AOP

Net Income Range : Rs. 5,00,010 - Rs. 5,40,000

Assessment year : 2020-21

Slab rate : 20%
Surcharge : *Nil*
HEC : 4%

NI Rs.	*IT Rs. P.*	*HEC Rs. P.*	*Total Rs. P.*	*NI Rs.*	*IT Rs.*	*HEC Rs. P.*	*Total Rs. P.*	*NI Rs.*	*IT Rs.*	*HEC Rs. P.*	*Total Rs. P.*
10	2	0.08	2.08	**100**	20	0.80	20.80	**100**	20	0.80	20.80
20	4	0.16	4.16	**200**	40	1.60	41.60	**200**	40	1.60	41.60
30	6	0.24	6.24	**300**	60	2.40	62.40	**300**	60	2.40	62.40
40	8	0.32	8.32	**400**	80	3.20	83.20	**400**	80	3.20	83.20
50	10	0.40	10.40	**500**	100	4.00	104.00	**500**	100	4.00	104.00
60	12	0.48	12.48	**600**	120	4.80	124.80	**600**	120	4.80	124.80
70	14	0.56	14.56	**700**	140	5.60	145.60	**700**	140	5.60	145.60
80	16	0.64	16.64	**800**	160	6.40	166.40	**800**	160	6.40	166.40
90	18	0.72	18.72	**900**	180	7.20	187.20	**900**	180	7.20	187.20

	Resident senior citizen**			***Resident super senior citizen******			***Any other resident individual*/any non-resident individual/ any HUF or AOP***		
NI Rs.	*IT Rs.*	*HEC Rs.*	*Total Rs.*	*IT Rs.*	*HEC Rs.*	*Total Rs.*	*IT Rs.*	*HEC Rs.*	*Total Rs.*
500010	10002	400.08	10402	2	0	2	12502	500.08	13002
501000	10200	408	10608	200	8	208	12700	508	13208
502000	10400	416	10816	400	16	416	12900	516	13416
503000	10600	424	11024	600	24	624	13100	524	13624
504000	10800	432	11232	800	32	832	13300	532	13832
505000	11000	440	11440	1000	40	1040	13500	540	14040
506000	11200	448	11648	1200	48	1248	13700	548	14248
507000	11400	456	11856	1400	56	1456	13900	556	14456
508000	11600	464	12064	1600	64	1664	14100	564	14664
509000	11800	472	12272	1800	72	1872	14300	572	14872
510000	12000	480	12480	2000	80	2080	14500	580	15080
511000	12200	488	12688	2200	88	2288	14700	588	15288
512000	12400	496	12896	2400	96	2496	14900	596	15496
513000	12600	504	13104	2600	104	2704	15100	604	15704
514000	12800	512	13312	2800	112	2912	15300	612	15912
515000	13000	520	13520	3000	120	3120	15500	620	16120
516000	13200	528	13728	3200	128	3328	15700	628	16328
517000	13400	536	13936	3400	136	3536	15900	636	16536
518000	13600	544	14144	3600	144	3744	16100	644	16744
519000	13800	552	14352	3800	152	3952	16300	652	16952
520000	14000	560	14560	4000	160	4160	16500	660	17160
521000	14200	568	14768	4200	168	4368	16700	668	17368
522000	14400	576	14976	4400	176	4576	16900	676	17576
523000	14600	584	15184	4600	184	4784	17100	684	17784
524000	14800	592	15392	4800	192	4992	17300	692	17992
525000	15000	600	15600	5000	200	5200	17500	700	18200
526000	15200	608	15808	5200	208	5408	17700	708	18408
527000	15400	616	16016	5400	216	5616	17900	716	18616
528000	15600	624	16224	5600	224	5824	18100	724	18824
529000	15800	632	16432	5800	232	6032	18300	732	19032
530000	16000	640	16640	6000	240	6240	18500	740	19240
531000	16200	648	16848	6200	248	6448	18700	748	19448
532000	16400	656	17056	6400	256	6656	18900	756	19656
533000	16600	664	17264	6600	264	6864	19100	764	19864
534000	16800	672	17472	6800	272	7072	19300	772	20072
535000	17000	680	17680	7000	280	7280	19500	780	20280
536000	17200	688	17888	7200	288	7488	19700	788	20488
537000	17400	696	18096	7400	296	7696	19900	796	20696
538000	17600	704	18304	7600	304	7904	20100	804	20904
539000	17800	712	18512	7800	312	8112	20300	812	21112
540000	18000	720	18720	8000	320	8320	20500	820	21320

Note - For how to use table, *see* page B-1.

*If the individual was born on or after April 2, 1960.

**If the individual was born on or after April 2, 1940 but before April 2, 1960.

***If the individual was born before April 2, 1940.

Income-tax : 2.9

INDIVIDUAL

HUF and AOP

Net Income Range : Rs. 5,40,000 - Rs. 5,80,000

Assessment year : 2020-21

Slab rate : 20%
Surcharge : *Nil*
HEC : 4%

NI Rs.	*IT Rs. P.*	*HEC Rs. P.*	*Total Rs. P.*	*NI Rs.*	*IT Rs.*	*HEC Rs. P.*	*Total Rs. P.*	*NI Rs.*	*IT Rs.*	*HEC Rs. P.*	*Total Rs. P.*
10	2	0.08	2.08	**100**	20	0.80	20.80	**100**	20	0.80	20.80
20	4	0.16	4.16	**200**	40	1.60	41.60	**200**	40	1.60	41.60
30	6	0.24	6.24	**300**	60	2.40	62.40	**300**	60	2.40	62.40
40	8	0.32	8.32	**400**	80	3.20	83.20	**400**	80	3.20	83.20
50	10	0.40	10.40	**500**	100	4.00	104.00	**500**	100	4.00	104.00
60	12	0.48	12.48	**600**	120	4.80	124.80	**600**	120	4.80	124.80
70	14	0.56	14.56	**700**	140	5.60	145.60	**700**	140	5.60	145.60
80	16	0.64	16.64	**800**	160	6.40	166.40	**800**	160	6.40	166.40
90	18	0.72	18.72	**900**	180	7.20	187.20	**900**	180	7.20	187.20

	Resident senior citizen**			***Resident super senior citizen******			***Any other resident individual*/any non-resident individual/ any HUF or AOP***		
NI Rs.	*IT Rs.*	*HEC Rs.*	*Total Rs.*	*IT Rs.*	*HEC Rs.*	*Total Rs.*	*IT Rs.*	*HEC Rs.*	*Total Rs.*
540000	18000	720	18720	8000	320	8320	20500	820	21320
541000	18200	728	18928	8200	328	8528	20700	828	21528
542000	18400	736	19136	8400	336	8736	20900	836	21736
543000	18600	744	19344	8600	344	8944	21100	844	21944
544000	18800	752	19552	8800	352	9152	21300	852	22152
545000	19000	760	19760	9000	360	9360	21500	860	22360
546000	19200	768	19968	9200	368	9568	21700	868	22568
547000	19400	776	20176	9400	376	9776	21900	876	22776
548000	19600	784	20384	9600	384	9984	22100	884	22984
549000	19800	792	20592	9800	392	10192	22300	892	23192
550000	20000	800	20800	10000	400	10400	22500	900	23400
551000	20200	808	21008	10200	408	10608	22700	908	23608
552000	20400	816	21216	10400	416	10816	22900	916	23816
553000	20600	824	21424	10600	424	11024	23100	924	24024
554000	20800	832	21632	10800	432	11232	23300	932	24232
555000	21000	840	21840	11000	440	11440	23500	940	24440
556000	21200	848	22048	11200	448	11648	23700	948	24648
557000	21400	856	22256	11400	456	11856	23900	956	24856
558000	21600	864	22464	11600	464	12064	24100	964	25064
559000	21800	872	22672	11800	472	12272	24300	972	25272
560000	22000	880	22880	12000	480	12480	24500	980	25480
561000	22200	888	23088	12200	488	12688	24700	988	25688
562000	22400	896	23296	12400	496	12896	24900	996	25896
563000	22600	904	23504	12600	504	13104	25100	1004	26104
564000	22800	912	23712	12800	512	13312	25300	1012	26312
565000	23000	920	23920	13000	520	13520	25500	1020	26520
566000	23200	928	24128	13200	528	13728	25700	1028	26728
567000	23400	936	24336	13400	536	13936	25900	1036	26936
568000	23600	944	24544	13600	544	14144	26100	1044	27144
569000	23800	952	24752	13800	552	14352	26300	1052	27352
570000	24000	960	24960	14000	560	14560	26500	1060	27560
571000	24200	968	25168	14200	568	14768	26700	1068	27768
572000	24400	976	25376	14400	576	14976	26900	1076	27976
573000	24600	984	25584	14600	584	15184	27100	1084	28184
574000	24800	992	25792	14800	592	15392	27300	1092	28392
575000	25000	1000	26000	15000	600	15600	27500	1100	28600
576000	25200	1008	26208	15200	608	15808	27700	1108	28808
577000	25400	1016	26416	15400	616	16016	27900	1116	29016
578000	25600	1024	26624	15600	624	16224	28100	1124	29224
579000	25800	1032	26832	15800	632	16432	28300	1132	29432
580000	26000	1040	27040	16000	640	16640	28500	1140	29640

Note - For how to use table, *see* page B-1.

*If the individual was born on or after April 2, 1960.

**If the individual was born on or after April 2, 1940 but before April 2, 1960.

***If the individual was born before April 2, 1940.

Income-tax : 2.10

INDIVIDUAL

HUF and AOP

Net Income Range : Rs. 5,80,000 - Rs. 6,20,000

Assessment year : 2020-21

Slab rate : 20%
Surcharge : *Nil*
HEC : 4%

NI Rs.	IT Rs. P.	HEC Rs. P.	Total Rs. P.	NI Rs.	IT Rs.	HEC Rs. P.	Total Rs. P.	NI Rs.	IT Rs.	HEC Rs. P.	Total Rs. P.
10	2	0.08	2.08	**100**	20	0.80	20.80	**100**	20	0.80	20.80
20	4	0.16	4.16	**200**	40	1.60	41.60	**200**	40	1.60	41.60
30	6	0.24	6.24	**300**	60	2.40	62.40	**300**	60	2.40	62.40
40	8	0.32	8.32	**400**	80	3.20	83.20	**400**	80	3.20	83.20
50	10	0.40	10.40	**500**	100	4.00	104.00	**500**	100	4.00	104.00
60	12	0.48	12.48	**600**	120	4.80	124.80	**600**	120	4.80	124.80
70	14	0.56	14.56	**700**	140	5.60	145.60	**700**	140	5.60	145.60
80	16	0.64	16.64	**800**	160	6.40	166.40	**800**	160	6.40	166.40
90	18	0.72	18.72	**900**	180	7.20	187.20	**900**	180	7.20	187.20

NI Rs.	Resident senior citizen**			Resident super senior citizen***			Any other resident individual*/any non-resident individual/ any HUF or AOP		
	IT Rs.	HEC Rs.	Total Rs.	IT Rs.	HEC Rs.	Total Rs.	IT Rs.	HEC Rs.	Total Rs.
580000	26000	1040	27040	16000	640	16640	28500	1140	29640
581000	26200	1048	27248	16200	648	16848	28700	1148	29848
582000	26400	1056	27456	16400	656	17056	28900	1156	30056
583000	26600	1064	27664	16600	664	17264	29100	1164	30264
584000	26800	1072	27872	16800	672	17472	29300	1172	30472
585000	27000	1080	28080	17000	680	17680	29500	1180	30680
586000	27200	1088	28288	17200	688	17888	29700	1188	30888
587000	27400	1096	28496	17400	696	18096	29900	1196	31096
588000	27600	1104	28704	17600	704	18304	30100	1204	31304
589000	27800	1112	28912	17800	712	18512	30300	1212	31512
590000	28000	1120	29120	18000	720	18720	30500	1220	31720
591000	28200	1128	29328	18200	728	18928	30700	1228	31928
592000	28400	1136	29536	18400	736	19136	30900	1236	32136
593000	28600	1144	29744	18600	744	19344	31100	1244	32344
594000	28800	1152	29952	18800	752	19552	31300	1252	32552
595000	29000	1160	30160	19000	760	19760	31500	1260	32760
596000	29200	1168	30368	19200	768	19968	31700	1268	32968
597000	29400	1176	30576	19400	776	20176	31900	1276	33176
598000	29600	1184	30784	19600	784	20384	32100	1284	33384
599000	29800	1192	30992	19800	792	20592	32300	1292	33592
600000	30000	1200	31200	20000	800	20800	32500	1300	33800
601000	30200	1208	31408	20200	808	21008	32700	1308	34008
602000	30400	1216	31616	20400	816	21216	32900	1316	34216
603000	30600	1224	31824	20600	824	21424	33100	1324	34424
604000	30800	1232	32032	20800	832	21632	33300	1332	34632
605000	31000	1240	32240	21000	840	21840	33500	1340	34840
606000	31200	1248	32448	21200	848	22048	33700	1348	35048
607000	31400	1256	32656	21400	856	22256	33900	1356	35256
608000	31600	1264	32864	21600	864	22464	34100	1364	35464
609000	31800	1272	33072	21800	872	22672	34300	1372	35672
610000	32000	1280	33280	22000	880	22880	34500	1380	35880
611000	32200	1288	33488	22200	888	23088	34700	1388	36088
612000	32400	1296	33696	22400	896	23296	34900	1396	36296
613000	32600	1304	33904	22600	904	23504	35100	1404	36504
614000	32800	1312	34112	22800	912	23712	35300	1412	36712
615000	33000	1320	34320	23000	920	23920	35500	1420	36920
616000	33200	1328	34528	23200	928	24128	35700	1428	37128
617000	33400	1336	34736	23400	936	24336	35900	1436	37336
618000	33600	1344	34944	23600	944	24544	36100	1444	37544
619000	33800	1352	35152	23800	952	24752	36300	1452	37752
620000	34000	1360	35360	24000	960	24960	36500	1460	37960

Note - For how to use table, *see* page B-1.

*If the individual was born on or after April 2, 1960.

**If the individual was born on or after April 2, 1940 but before April 2, 1960.

***If the individual was born before April 2, 1940.

Income-tax : 2.11

INDIVIDUAL

HUF and AOP

Net Income Range : Rs. 6,20,000 - Rs. 10,00,000

Assessment year : 2020-21

Slab rate : 20%

Surcharge : *Nil*

HEC : 4%

NI Rs.	*IT Rs. P.*	*HEC Rs. P.*	*Total Rs. P.*	*NI Rs.*	*IT Rs.*	*HEC Rs. P.*	*Total Rs. P.*	*NI Rs.*	*IT Rs.*	*HEC Rs. P.*	*Total Rs. P.*
10	2	0.08	2.08	**100**	20	0.80	20.80	**1000**	200	8	208
20	4	0.16	4.16	**200**	40	1.60	41.60	**2000**	400	16	416
30	6	0.24	6.24	**300**	60	2.40	62.40	**3000**	600	24	624
40	8	0.32	8.32	**400**	80	3.20	83.20	**4000**	800	32	832
50	10	0.40	10.40	**500**	100	4.00	104.00	**5000**	1000	40	1040
60	12	0.48	12.48	**600**	120	4.80	124.80	**6000**	1200	48	1248
70	14	0.56	14.56	**700**	140	5.60	145.60	**7000**	1400	56	1456
80	16	0.64	16.64	**800**	160	6.40	166.40	**8000**	1600	64	1664
90	18	0.72	18.72	**900**	180	7.20	187.20	**9000**	1800	72	1872

	Resident senior citizen**			***Resident super senior citizen******			***Any other resident individual*/any non-resident individual/ any HUF or AOP***		
NI Rs.	*IT Rs.*	*HEC Rs.*	*Total Rs.*	*IT Rs.*	*HEC Rs.*	*Total Rs.*	*IT Rs.*	*HEC Rs.*	*Total Rs.*
620000	34000	1360	35360	24000	960	24960	36500	1460	37960
630000	36000	1440	37440	26000	1040	27040	38500	1540	40040
640000	38000	1520	39520	28000	1120	29120	40500	1620	42120
650000	40000	1600	41600	30000	1200	31200	42500	1700	44200
660000	42000	1680	43680	32000	1280	33280	44500	1780	46280
670000	44000	1760	45760	34000	1360	35360	46500	1860	48360
680000	46000	1840	47840	36000	1440	37440	48500	1940	50440
690000	48000	1920	49920	38000	1520	39520	50500	2020	52520
700000	50000	2000	52000	40000	1600	41600	52500	2100	54600
710000	52000	2080	54080	42000	1680	43680	54500	2180	56680
720000	54000	2160	56160	44000	1760	45760	56500	2260	58760
730000	56000	2240	58240	46000	1840	47840	58500	2340	60840
740000	58000	2320	60320	48000	1920	49920	60500	2420	62920
750000	60000	2400	62400	50000	2000	52000	62500	2500	65000
760000	62000	2480	64480	52000	2080	54080	64500	2580	67080
770000	64000	2560	66560	54000	2160	56160	66500	2660	69160
780000	66000	2640	68640	56000	2240	58240	68500	2740	71240
790000	68000	2720	70720	58000	2320	60320	70500	2820	73320
800000	70000	2800	72800	60000	2400	62400	72500	2900	75400
810000	72000	2880	74880	62000	2480	64480	74500	2980	77480
820000	74000	2960	76960	64000	2560	66560	76500	3060	79560
830000	76000	3040	79040	66000	2640	68640	78500	3140	81640
840000	78000	3120	81120	68000	2720	70720	80500	3220	83720
850000	80000	3200	83200	70000	2800	72800	82500	3300	85800
860000	82000	3280	85280	72000	2880	74880	84500	3380	87880
870000	84000	3360	87360	74000	2960	76960	86500	3460	89960
880000	86000	3440	89440	76000	3040	79040	88500	3540	92040
890000	88000	3520	91520	78000	3120	81120	90500	3620	94120
900000	90000	3600	93600	80000	3200	83200	92500	3700	96200
910000	92000	3680	95680	82000	3280	85280	94500	3780	98280
920000	94000	3760	97760	84000	3360	87360	96500	3860	100360
930000	96000	3840	99840	86000	3440	89440	98500	3940	102440
940000	98000	3920	101920	88000	3520	91520	100500	4020	104520
950000	100000	4000	104000	90000	3600	93600	102500	4100	106600
960000	102000	4080	106080	92000	3680	95680	104500	4180	108680
970000	104000	4160	108160	94000	3760	97760	106500	4260	110760
980000	106000	4240	110240	96000	3840	99840	108500	4340	112840
990000	108000	4320	112320	98000	3920	101920	110500	4420	114920
1000000	110000	4400	114400	100000	4000	104000	112500	4500	117000

Note - For how to use table, *see* page B-1.

*If the individual was born on or after April 2, 1960.

**If the individual was born on or after April 2, 1940 but before April 2, 1960.

***If the individual was born before April 2, 1940.

Income-tax : 2.12

INDIVIDUAL

HUF and AOP

Net Income Range : Rs. 10,00,000 - Rs. 50,00,000

Assessment year : 2020-21

Slab rate	:	30%
Surcharge	:	*Nil*
HEC	:	4%

NI Rs.	*IT Rs. P.*	*HEC Rs. P.*	*Total Rs. P.*	*NI Rs.*	*IT Rs.*	*HEC Rs. P.*	*Total Rs. P.*	*NI Rs.*	*IT Rs.*	*HEC Rs. P.*	*Total Rs. P.*
10	3	0.12	3.12	**100**	30	1.20	31.20	**1000**	300	12	312
20	6	0.24	6.24	**200**	60	2.40	62.40	**2000**	600	24	624
30	9	0.36	9.36	**300**	90	3.60	93.60	**3000**	900	36	936
40	12	0.48	12.48	**400**	120	4.80	124.80	**4000**	1200	48	1248
50	15	0.60	15.60	**500**	150	6.00	156.00	**5000**	1500	60	1560
60	18	0.72	18.72	**600**	180	7.20	187.20	**6000**	1800	72	1872
70	21	0.84	21.84	**700**	210	8.40	218.40	**7000**	2100	84	2184
80	24	0.96	24.96	**800**	240	9.60	249.60	**8000**	2400	96	2496
90	27	1.08	28.08	**900**	270	10.80	280.80	**9000**	2700	108	2808

	Resident senior citizen**			***Resident super senior citizen******			***Any other resident individual*/any non-resident individual/ any HUF or AOP***		
NI Rs.	*IT Rs.*	*HEC Rs.*	*Total Rs.*	*IT Rs.*	*HEC Rs.*	*Total Rs.*	*IT Rs.*	*HEC Rs.*	*Total Rs.*
1000000	110000	4400	114400	100000	4000	104000	112500	4500	117000
1100000	140000	5600	145600	130000	5200	135200	142500	5700	148200
1200000	170000	6800	176800	160000	6400	166400	172500	6900	179400
1300000	200000	8000	208000	190000	7600	197600	202500	8100	210600
1400000	230000	9200	239200	220000	8800	228800	232500	9300	241800
1500000	260000	10400	270400	250000	10000	260000	262500	10500	273000
1600000	290000	11600	301600	280000	11200	291200	292500	11700	304200
1700000	320000	12800	332800	310000	12400	322400	322500	12900	335400
1800000	350000	14000	364000	340000	13600	353600	352500	14100	366600
1900000	380000	15200	395200	370000	14800	384800	382500	15300	397800
2000000	410000	16400	426400	400000	16000	416000	412500	16500	429000
2100000	440000	17600	457600	430000	17200	447200	442500	17700	460200
2200000	470000	18800	488800	460000	18400	478400	472500	18900	491400
2300000	500000	20000	520000	490000	19600	509600	502500	20100	522600
2400000	530000	21200	551200	520000	20800	540800	532500	21300	553800
2500000	560000	22400	582400	550000	22000	572000	562500	22500	585000
2600000	590000	23600	613600	580000	23200	603200	592500	23700	616200
2700000	620000	24800	644800	610000	24400	634400	622500	24900	647400
2800000	650000	26000	676000	640000	25600	665600	652500	26100	678600
2900000	680000	27200	707200	670000	26800	696800	682500	27300	709800
3000000	710000	28400	738400	700000	28000	728000	712500	28500	741000
3100000	740000	29600	769600	730000	29200	759200	742500	29700	772200
3200000	770000	30800	800800	760000	30400	790400	772500	30900	803400
3300000	800000	32000	832000	790000	31600	821600	802500	32100	834600
3400000	830000	33200	863200	820000	32800	852800	832500	33300	865800
3500000	860000	34400	894400	850000	34000	884000	862500	34500	897000
3600000	890000	35600	925600	880000	35200	915200	892500	35700	928200
3700000	920000	36800	956800	910000	36400	946400	922500	36900	959400
3800000	950000	38000	988000	940000	37600	977600	952500	38100	990600
3900000	980000	39200	1019200	970000	38800	1008800	982500	39300	1021800
4000000	1010000	40400	1050400	1000000	40000	1040000	1012500	40500	1053000
4100000	1040000	41600	1081600	1030000	41200	1071200	1042500	41700	1084200
4200000	1070000	42800	1112800	1060000	42400	1102400	1072500	42900	1115400
4300000	1100000	44000	1144000	1090000	43600	1133600	1102500	44100	1146600
4400000	1130000	45200	1175200	1120000	44800	1164800	1132500	45300	1177800
4500000	1160000	46400	1206400	1150000	46000	1196000	1162500	46500	1209000
4600000	1190000	47600	1237600	1180000	47200	1227200	1192500	47700	1240200
4700000	1220000	48800	1268800	1210000	48400	1258400	1222500	48900	1271400
4800000	1250000	50000	1300000	1240000	49600	1289600	1252500	50100	1302600
4900000	1280000	51200	1331200	1270000	50800	1320800	1282500	51300	1333800
5000000	1310000	52400	1362400	1300000	52000	1352000	1312500	52500	1365000

Note - For how to use table, *see* page B-1.

*If the individual was born on or after April 2, 1960.

**If the individual was born on or after April 2, 1940 but before April 2, 1960.

***If the individual was born before April 2, 1940.

Income-tax : 2.13

INDIVIDUAL

HUF and AOP

Net Income Range : Rs. 50,00,010 – Rs. 51,95,520/ Rs. 51,94,020/Rs. 51,95,890

Assessment year : 2020-21

Slab rate : 30%

Surcharge : 10%

HEC : 4%

NI Rs.	*IT Rs.*	*SC Rs.*	*HEC Rs.*	*Total Rs.*	*NI Rs.*	*IT Rs.*	*SC Rs.*	*HEC Rs.*	*Total Rs.*	*NI Rs.*	*IT Rs.*	*SC Rs.*	*HEC Rs.*	*Total Rs.*
10	3	7	0.40	10.40	**100**	30	70	4	104	**1000**	300	700	40	1040
20	6	14	0.80	20.80	**200**	60	140	8	208	**2000**	600	1400	80	2080
30	9	21	1.20	31.20	**300**	90	210	12	312	**3000**	900	2100	120	3120
40	12	28	1.60	41.60	**400**	120	280	16	416	**4000**	1200	2800	160	4160
50	15	35	2.00	52.00	**500**	150	350	20	520	**5000**	1500	3500	200	5200
60	18	42	2.40	62.40	**600**	180	420	24	624	**6000**	1800	4200	240	6240
70	21	49	2.80	72.80	**700**	210	490	28	728	**7000**	2100	4900	280	7280
80	24	56	3.20	83.20	**800**	240	560	32	832	**8000**	2400	5600	320	8320
90	27	63	3.60	93.60	**900**	270	630	36	936	**9000**	2700	6300	360	9360

	Resident senior citizen**				***Resident super senior citizen******				***Any other resident individual*/any non-resident individual/any HUF or AOP***			
NI Rs.	*IT Rs.*	*SC Rs.*	*HEC Rs.*	*Total Rs.*	*IT Rs.*	*SC Rs.*	*HEC Rs.*	*Total Rs.*	*IT Rs.*	*SC Rs.*	*HEC Rs.*	*Total Rs.*
5000010	1310003	7	52400	1362410	1300003	7	52000	1352010	1312503	7	52500	1365010
5010000	1313000	7000	52800	1372800	1303000	7000	52400	1362400	1315500	7000	52900	1375400
5020000	1316000	14000	53200	1383200	1306000	14000	52800	1372800	1318500	14000	53300	1385800
5030000	1319000	21000	53600	1393600	1309000	21000	53200	1383200	1321500	21000	53700	1396200
5040000	1322000	28000	54000	1404000	1312000	28000	53600	1393600	1324500	28000	54100	1406600
5050000	1325000	35000	54400	1414400	1315000	35000	54000	1404000	1327500	35000	54500	1417000
5060000	1328000	42000	54800	1424800	1318000	42000	54400	1414400	1330500	42000	54900	1427400
5070000	1331000	49000	55200	1435200	1321000	49000	54800	1424800	1333500	49000	55300	1437800
5080000	1334000	56000	55600	1445600	1324000	56000	55200	1435200	1336500	56000	55700	1448200
5090000	1337000	63000	56000	1456000	1327000	63000	55600	1445600	1339500	63000	56100	1458600
5100000	1340000	70000	56400	1466400	1330000	70000	56000	1456000	1342500	70000	56500	1469000
5110000	1343000	77000	56800	1476800	1333000	77000	56400	1466400	1345500	77000	56900	1479400
5120000	1346000	84000	57200	1487200	1336000	84000	56800	1476800	1348500	84000	57300	1489800
5130000	1349000	91000	57600	1497600	1339000	91000	57200	1487200	1351500	91000	57700	1500200
5140000	1352000	98000	58000	1508000	1342000	98000	57600	1497600	1354500	98000	58100	1510600
5150000	1355000	105000	58400	1518400	1345000	105000	58000	1508000	1357500	105000	58500	1521000
5160000	1358000	112000	58800	1528800	1348000	112000	58400	1518400	1360500	112000	58900	1531400
5170000	1361000	119000	59200	1539200	1351000	119000	58800	1528800	1363500	119000	59300	1541800
5180000	1364000	126000	59600	1549600	1354000	126000	59200	1539200	1366500	126000	59700	1552200
5190000	1367000	133000	60000	1560000	1357000	133000	59600	1549600	1369500	133000	60100	1562600
5194020	—	—	—	—	1358206	135814	59761	1553781	—	—	—	—
5195520	1368656	136864	60221	1565741	—	—	—	—	—	—	—	—
5195890	—	—	—	—	—	—	—	—	1371267	137123	60336	1568726

Note **-** For how to use table, *see* page B-1.

*If the individual was born on or after April 2, 1960.

**If the individual was born on or after April 2, 1940 but before April 2, 1960.

***If the individual was born before April 2, 1940.

Income-tax : 2.14

INDIVIDUAL

HUF and AOP

Net Income Range : Rs. 51,95,530/Rs. 51,94,030/ Rs. 51,95,900 – Rs. 1,00,00,000

Assessment year : 2020-21

Slab rate : 30%
Surcharge : 10%
HEC : 4%

NI Rs.	IT Rs.	SC Rs.	HEC Rs.	Total Rs.	NI Rs.	IT Rs.	SC Rs.	HEC Rs.	Total Rs.	NI Rs.	IT Rs.	SC Rs.	HEC Rs.	Total Rs.
10	3	0.30	0.13	3.43	**100**	30	3	1.32	34.32	**1000**	300	30	13.20	343.20
20	6	0.60	0.26	6.86	**200**	60	6	2.64	68.64	**2000**	600	60	26.40	686.40
30	9	0.90	0.40	10.30	**300**	90	9	3.96	102.96	**3000**	900	90	39.60	1029.60
40	12	1.20	0.53	13.73	**400**	120	12	5.28	137.28	**4000**	1200	120	52.80	1372.80
50	15	1.50	0.66	17.16	**500**	150	15	6.60	171.60	**5000**	1500	150	66.00	1716.00
60	18	1.80	0.79	20.59	**600**	180	18	7.92	205.92	**6000**	1800	180	79.20	2059.20
70	21	2.10	0.92	24.02	**700**	210	21	9.24	240.24	**7000**	2100	210	92.40	2402.40
80	24	2.40	1.06	27.46	**800**	240	24	10.56	274.56	**8000**	2400	240	105.60	2745.60
90	27	2.70	1.19	30.89	**900**	270	27	11.88	308.88	**9000**	2700	270	118.80	3088.80

	Resident senior citizen**				***Resident super senior citizen******				***Any other resident individual*/any non-resident individual/any HUF or AOP***			
NI Rs.	IT Rs.	SC Rs.	HEC Rs.	Total Rs.	IT Rs.	SC Rs.	HEC Rs.	Total Rs.	IT Rs.	SC Rs.	HEC Rs.	Total Rs.
5194030	—	—	—	—	1358209	135821	59761	1553791	—	—	—	—
5195530	1368659	136866	60221	1565746	—	—	—	—	—	—	—	—
5195900	—	—	—	—	—	—	—	—	1371270	137127	60336	1568733
5200000	1370000	137000	60280	1567280	1360000	136000	59840	1555840	1372500	137250	60390	1570140
5400000	1430000	143000	62920	1635920	1420000	142000	62480	1624480	1432500	143250	63030	1638780
5600000	1490000	149000	65560	1704560	1480000	148000	65120	1693120	1492500	149250	65670	1707420
5800000	1550000	155000	68200	1773200	1540000	154000	67760	1761760	1552500	155250	68310	1776060
6000000	1610000	161000	70840	1841840	1600000	160000	70400	1830400	1612500	161250	70950	1844700
6200000	1670000	167000	73480	1910480	1660000	166000	73040	1899040	1672500	167250	73590	1913340
6400000	1730000	173000	76120	1979120	1720000	172000	75680	1967680	1732500	173250	76230	1981980
6600000	1790000	179000	78760	2047760	1780000	178000	78320	2036320	1792500	179250	78870	2050620
6800000	1850000	185000	81400	2116400	1840000	184000	80960	2104960	1852500	185250	81510	2119260
7000000	1910000	191000	84040	2185040	1900000	190000	83600	2173600	1912500	191250	84150	2187900
7200000	1970000	197000	86680	2253680	1960000	196000	86240	2242240	1972500	197250	86790	2256540
7400000	2030000	203000	89320	2322320	2020000	202000	88880	2310880	2032500	203250	89430	2325180
7600000	2090000	209000	91960	2390960	2080000	208000	91520	2379520	2092500	209250	92070	2393820
7800000	2150000	215000	94600	2459600	2140000	214000	94160	2448160	2152500	215250	94710	2462460
8000000	2210000	221000	97240	2528240	2200000	220000	96800	2516800	2212500	221250	97350	2531100
8200000	2270000	227000	99880	2596880	2260000	226000	99440	2585440	2272500	227250	99990	2599740
8400000	2330000	233000	102520	2665520	2320000	232000	102080	2654080	2332500	233250	102630	2668380
8600000	2390000	239000	105160	2734160	2380000	238000	104720	2722720	2392500	239250	105270	2737020
8800000	2450000	245000	107800	2802800	2440000	244000	107360	2791360	2452500	245250	107910	2805660
9000000	2510000	251000	110440	2871440	2500000	250000	110000	2860000	2512500	251250	110550	2874300
9200000	2570000	257000	113080	2940080	2560000	256000	112640	2928640	2572500	257250	113190	2942940
9400000	2630000	263000	115720	3008720	2620000	262000	115280	2997280	2632500	263250	115830	3011580
9600000	2690000	269000	118360	3077360	2680000	268000	117920	3065920	2692500	269250	118470	3080220
9800000	2750000	275000	121000	3146000	2740000	274000	120560	3134560	2752500	275250	121110	3148860
10000000	2810000	281000	123640	3214640	2800000	280000	123200	3203200	2812500	281250	123750	3217500

Note - For how to use table, *see* page B-1.

*If the individual was born on or after April 2, 1960.

**If the individual was born on or after April 2, 1940 but before April 2, 1960.

***If the individual was born before April 2, 1940.

Income-tax : 2.15

INDIVIDUAL

HUF and AOP

Net Income Range : Rs. 1,00,00,010 – Rs. 1,02,14,500/ Rs. 1,02,13,740/Rs. 1,02,14,690

Assessment year : 2020-21

Slab rate : 30%
Surcharge : 15%
HEC : 4%

NI Rs.	*IT Rs.*	*SC Rs.*	*HEC Rs.*	*Total Rs.*	*NI Rs.*	*IT Rs.*	*SC Rs.*	*HEC Rs.*	*Total Rs.*	*NI Rs.*	*IT Rs.*	*SC Rs.*	*HEC Rs.*	*Total Rs.*
10	3	7	0.40	10.40	**100**	30	70	4	104	**1000**	300	700	40	1040
20	6	14	0.80	20.80	**200**	60	140	8	208	**2000**	600	1400	80	2080
30	9	21	1.20	31.20	**300**	90	210	12	312	**3000**	900	2100	120	3120
40	12	28	1.60	41.60	**400**	120	280	16	416	**4000**	1200	2800	160	4160
50	15	35	2.00	52.00	**500**	150	350	20	520	**5000**	1500	3500	200	5200
60	18	42	2.40	62.40	**600**	180	420	24	624	**6000**	1800	4200	240	6240
70	21	49	2.80	72.80	**700**	210	490	28	728	**7000**	2100	4900	280	7280
80	24	56	3.20	83.20	**800**	240	560	32	832	**8000**	2400	5600	320	8320
90	27	63	3.60	93.60	**900**	270	630	36	936	**9000**	2700	6300	360	9360

	Resident senior citizen*				***Resident super senior citizen*****				***Any other resident individual*/any non-resident individual/any HUF or AOP***			
NI Rs.	*IT Rs.*	*SC Rs.*	*HEC Rs.*	*Total Rs.*	*IT Rs.*	*SC Rs.*	*HEC Rs.*	*Total Rs.*	*IT Rs.*	*SC Rs.*	*HEC Rs.*	*Total Rs.*
10000010	2810003	281007	123640	3214650	2800003	280007	123200	3203210	2812503	281257	123750	3217510
10010000	2813000	288000	124040	3225040	2803000	287000	123600	3213600	2815500	288250	124150	3227900
10020000	2816000	295000	124440	3235440	2806000	294000	124000	3224000	2818500	295250	124550	3238300
10030000	2819000	302000	124840	3245840	2809000	301000	124400	3234400	2821500	302250	124950	3248700
10040000	2822000	309000	125240	3256240	2812000	308000	124800	3244800	2824500	309250	125350	3259100
10050000	2825000	316000	125640	3266640	2815000	315000	125200	3255200	2827500	316250	125750	3269500
10060000	2828000	323000	126040	3277040	2818000	322000	125600	3265600	2830500	323250	126150	3279900
10070000	2831000	330000	126440	3287440	2821000	329000	126000	3276000	2833500	330250	126550	3290300
10080000	2834000	337000	126840	3297840	2824000	336000	126400	3286400	2836500	337250	126950	3300700
10090000	2837000	344000	127240	3308240	2827000	343000	126800	3296800	2839500	344250	127350	3311100
10100000	2840000	351000	127640	3318640	2830000	350000	127200	3307200	2842500	351250	127750	3321500
10110000	2843000	358000	128040	3329040	2833000	357000	127600	3317600	2845500	358250	128150	3331900
10120000	2846000	365000	128440	3339440	2836000	364000	128000	3328000	2848500	365250	128550	3342300
10130000	2849000	372000	128840	3349840	2839000	371000	128400	3338400	2851500	372250	128950	3352700
10140000	2852000	379000	129240	3360240	2842000	378000	128800	3348800	2854500	379250	129350	3363100
10150000	2855000	386000	129640	3370640	2845000	385000	129200	3359200	2857500	386250	129750	3373500
10160000	2858000	393000	130040	3381040	2848000	392000	129600	3369600	2860500	393250	130150	3383900
10170000	2861000	400000	130440	3391440	2851000	399000	130000	3380000	2863500	400250	130550	3394300
10180000	2864000	407000	130840	3401840	2854000	406000	130400	3390400	2866500	407250	130950	3404700
10190000	2867000	414000	131240	3412240	2857000	413000	130800	3400800	2869500	414250	131350	3415100
10200000	2870000	421000	131640	3422640	2860000	420000	131200	3411200	2872500	421250	131750	3425500
10210000	2873000	428000	132040	3433040	2863000	427000	131600	3421600	2875500	428250	132150	3435900
10213740	—	—	—	—	2864122	429618	131750	3425490	—	—	—	—
10214500	2874350	431150	132220	3437720	—	—	—	—	—	—	—	—
10214690	—	—	—	—	—	—	—	—	2876907	431533	132338	3440778

***Note* -** For how to use table, *see* page B-1.

*If the individual was born on or after April 2, 1960.

**If the individual was born on or after April 2, 1940 but before April 2, 1960.

***If the individual was born before April 2, 1940.

Income-tax : 2.16

INDIVIDUAL

HUF and AOP

Net Income Range : Rs. 1,02,14,510/Rs. 1,02,13,750/
Rs. 1,02,14,700 – Rs. 2,00,00,000

Assessment year : 2020-21

Slab rate : 30%
Surcharge : 15%
HEC : 4%

NI Rs.	IT Rs.	SC Rs.	HEC Rs.	Total Rs.	NI Rs.	IT Rs.	SC Rs.	HEC Rs.	Total Rs.	NI Rs.	IT Rs.	SC Rs.	HEC Rs.	Total Rs.
10	3	0.45	0.14	3.59	**100**	30	4.50	1.38	35.88	**1000**	300	45	13.80	358.80
20	6	0.90	0.28	7.18	**200**	60	9.00	2.76	71.76	**2000**	600	90	27.60	717.60
30	9	1.35	0.41	10.76	**300**	90	13.50	4.14	107.64	**3000**	900	135	41.40	1076.40
40	12	1.80	0.55	14.35	**400**	120	18.00	5.52	143.52	**4000**	1200	180	55.20	1435.20
50	15	2.25	0.69	17.94	**500**	150	22.50	6.90	179.40	**5000**	1500	225	69.00	1794.00
60	18	2.70	0.83	21.53	**600**	180	27.00	8.28	215.28	**6000**	1800	270	82.80	2152.80
70	21	3.15	0.97	25.12	**700**	210	31.50	9.66	251.16	**7000**	2100	315	96.60	2511.60
80	24	3.60	1.10	28.70	**800**	240	36.00	11.04	287.04	**8000**	2400	360	110.40	2870.40
90	27	4.05	1.24	32.29	**900**	270	40.50	12.42	322.92	**9000**	2700	405	124.20	3229.20

	Resident senior citizen**				***Resident super senior citizen******				***Any other resident individual*/any non-resident individual/any HUF or AOP***			
NI Rs.	IT Rs.	SC Rs.	HEC Rs.	Total Rs.	IT Rs.	SC Rs.	HEC Rs.	Total Rs.	IT Rs.	SC Rs.	HEC Rs.	Total Rs.
10213750	—	—	—	—	2864125	429619	131750	3425494	—	—	—	—
10214510	2874353	431153	132220	3437726	—	—	—	—	—	—	—	—
10214700	—	—	—	—	—	—	—	—	2876910	431537	132338	3440785
10300000	2900000	435000	133400	3468400	2890000	433500	132940	3456440	2902500	435375	133515	3471390
10400000	2930000	439500	134780	3504280	2920000	438000	134320	3492320	2932500	439875	134895	3507270
10500000	2960000	444000	136160	3540160	2950000	442500	135700	3528200	2962500	444375	136275	3543150
10600000	2990000	448500	137540	3576040	2980000	447000	137080	3564080	2992500	448875	137655	3579030
10700000	3020000	453000	138920	3611920	3010000	451500	138460	3599960	3022500	453375	139035	3614910
10800000	3050000	457500	140300	3647800	3040000	456000	139840	3635840	3052500	457875	140415	3650790
10900000	3080000	462000	141680	3683680	3070000	460500	141220	3671720	3082500	462375	141795	3686670
11000000	3110000	466500	143060	3719560	3100000	465000	142600	3707600	3112500	466875	143175	3722550
11100000	3140000	471000	144440	3755440	3130000	469500	143980	3743480	3142500	471375	144555	3758430
11200000	3170000	475500	145820	3791320	3160000	474000	145360	3779360	3172500	475875	145935	3794310
11300000	3200000	480000	147200	3827200	3190000	478500	146740	3815240	3202500	480375	147315	3830190
11400000	3230000	484500	148580	3863080	3220000	483000	148120	3851120	3232500	484875	148695	3866070
11500000	3260000	489000	149960	3898960	3250000	487500	149500	3887000	3262500	489375	150075	3901950
11600000	3290000	493500	151340	3934840	3280000	492000	150880	3922880	3292500	493875	151455	3937830
11700000	3320000	498000	152720	3970720	3310000	496500	152260	3958760	3322500	498375	152835	3973710
11800000	3350000	502500	154100	4006600	3340000	501000	153640	3994640	3352500	502875	154215	4009590
11900000	3380000	507000	155480	4042480	3370000	505500	155020	4030520	3382500	507375	155595	4045470
12000000	3410000	511500	156860	4078360	3400000	510000	156400	4066400	3412500	511875	156975	4081350
13000000	3710000	556500	170660	4437160	3700000	555000	170200	4425200	3712500	556875	170775	4440150
14000000	4010000	601500	184460	4795960	4000000	600000	184000	4784000	4012500	601875	184575	4798950
15000000	4310000	646500	198260	5154760	4300000	645000	197800	5142800	4312500	646875	198375	5157750
16000000	4610000	691500	212060	5513560	4600000	690000	211600	5501600	4612500	691875	212175	5516550
17000000	4910000	736500	225860	5872360	4900000	735000	225400	5860400	4912500	736875	225975	5875350
18000000	5210000	781500	239660	6231160	5200000	780000	239200	6219200	5212500	781875	239775	6234150
19000000	5510000	826500	253460	6589960	5500000	825000	253000	6578000	5512500	826875	253575	6592950
20000000	5810000	871500	267260	6948760	5800000	870000	266800	6936800	5812500	871875	267375	6951750

Note - For how to use table, *see* page B-1.

*If the individual was born on or after April 2, 1960.

**If the individual was born on or after April 2, 1940 but before April 2, 1960.

***If the individual was born before April 2, 1940.

Income-tax : 2.17

INDIVIDUAL

HUF and AOP

Net Income Range : Rs. 2,00,00,010 – Rs. 2,09,29,600/ Rs. 2,09,28,000/Rs. 2,09,30,000

Assessment year : 2020-21

Slab rate : 30%
Surcharge : 25%
HEC : 4%

NI Rs.	IT Rs.	SC Rs.	HEC Rs.	Total Rs.	NI Rs.	IT Rs.	SC Rs.	HEC Rs.	Total Rs.	NI Rs.	IT Rs.	SC Rs.	HEC Rs.	Total Rs.
10	3	7	0.40	10.40	**100**	30	70	4	104	**1000**	300	700	40	1040
20	6	14	0.80	20.80	**200**	60	140	8	208	**2000**	600	1400	80	2080
30	9	21	1.20	31.20	**300**	90	210	12	312	**3000**	900	2100	120	3120
40	12	28	1.60	41.60	**400**	120	280	16	416	**4000**	1200	2800	160	4160
50	15	35	2.00	52.00	**500**	150	350	20	520	**5000**	1500	3500	200	5200
60	18	42	2.40	62.40	**600**	180	420	24	624	**6000**	1800	4200	240	6240
70	21	49	2.80	72.80	**700**	210	490	28	728	**7000**	2100	4900	280	7280
80	24	56	3.20	83.20	**800**	240	560	32	832	**8000**	2400	5600	320	8320
90	27	63	3.60	93.60	**900**	270	630	36	936	**9000**	2700	6300	360	9360

	Resident senior citizen**				***Resident super senior citizen******				***Any other resident individual*/any non-resident individual/any HUF or AOP***			
NI Rs.	*IT Rs.*	*SC Rs.*	*HEC Rs.*	*Total Rs.*	*IT Rs.*	*SC Rs.*	*HEC Rs.*	*Total Rs.*	*IT Rs.*	*SC Rs.*	*HEC Rs.*	*Total Rs.*
20000010	5810003	871507	267260	6948770	5800003	870007	266800	6936810	5812503	871882	267375	6951760
20030000	5819000	892500	268460	6979960	5809000	891000	268000	6968000	5821500	892875	268575	6982950
20060000	5828000	913500	269660	7011160	5818000	912000	269200	6999200	5830500	913875	269775	7014150
20090000	5837000	934500	270860	7042360	5827000	933000	270400	7030400	5839500	934875	270975	7045350
20120000	5846000	955500	272060	7073560	5836000	954000	271600	7061600	5848500	955875	272175	7076550
20150000	5855000	976500	273260	7104760	5845000	975000	272800	7092800	5857500	976875	273375	7107750
20180000	5864000	997500	274460	7135960	5854000	996000	274000	7124000	5866500	997875	274575	7138950
20210000	5873000	1018500	275660	7167160	5863000	1017000	275200	7155200	5875500	1018875	275775	7170150
20240000	5882000	1039500	276860	7198360	5872000	1038000	276400	7186400	5884500	1039875	276975	7201350
20270000	5891000	1060500	278060	7229560	5881000	1059000	277600	7217600	5893500	1060875	278175	7232550
20300000	5900000	1081500	279260	7260760	5890000	1080000	278800	7248800	5902500	1081875	279375	7263750
20330000	5909000	1102500	280460	7291960	5899000	1101000	280000	7280000	5911500	1102875	280575	7294950
20360000	5918000	1123500	281660	7323160	5908000	1122000	281200	7311200	5920500	1123875	281775	7326150
20390000	5927000	1144500	282860	7354360	5917000	1143000	282400	7342400	5929500	1144875	282975	7357350
20420000	5936000	1165500	284060	7385560	5926000	1164000	283600	7373600	5938500	1165875	284175	7388550
20450000	5945000	1186500	285260	7416760	5935000	1185000	284800	7404800	5947500	1186875	285375	7419750
20480000	5954000	1207500	286460	7447960	5944000	1206000	286000	7436000	5956500	1207875	286575	7450950
20510000	5963000	1228500	287660	7479160	5953000	1227000	287200	7467200	5965500	1228875	287775	7482150
20540000	5972000	1249500	288860	7510360	5962000	1248000	288400	7498400	5974500	1249875	288975	7513350
20570000	5981000	1270500	290060	7541560	5971000	1269000	289600	7529600	5983500	1270875	290175	7544550
20600000	5990000	1291500	291260	7572760	5980000	1290000	290800	7560800	5992500	1291875	291375	7575750
20630000	5999000	1312500	292460	7603960	5989000	1311000	292000	7592000	6001500	1312875	292575	7606950
20660000	6008000	1333500	293660	7635160	5998000	1332000	293200	7623200	6010500	1333875	293775	7638150
20690000	6017000	1354500	294860	7666360	6007000	1353000	294400	7654400	6019500	1354875	294975	7669350
20720000	6026000	1375500	296060	7697560	6016000	1374000	295600	7685600	6028500	1375875	296175	7700550
20750000	6035000	1396500	297260	7728760	6025000	1395000	296800	7716800	6037500	1396875	297375	7731750
20780000	6044000	1417500	298460	7759960	6034000	1416000	298000	7748000	6046500	1417875	298575	7762950
20810000	6053000	1438500	299660	7791160	6043000	1437000	299200	7779200	6055500	1438875	299775	7794150
20840000	6062000	1459500	300860	7822360	6052000	1458000	300400	7810400	6064500	1459875	300975	7825350
20870000	6071000	1480500	302060	7853560	6061000	1479000	301600	7841600	6073500	1480875	302175	7856550
20900000	6080000	1501500	303260	7884760	6070000	1500000	302800	7872800	6082500	1501875	303375	7887750
20928000	—	—	—	—	6078400	1519600	303920	7901920	—	—	—	—
20929600	6088880	1522220	304444	7915544	—	—	—	—	—	—	—	—
20930000	—	—	—	—	—	—	—	—	6091500	1522875	304575	7918950

Note - For how to use table, *see* page B-1.

*If the individual was born on or after April 2, 1960.

**If the individual was born on or after April 2, 1940 but before April 2, 1960.

***If the individual was born before April 2, 1940.

Income-tax : 2.18

INDIVIDUAL

HUF and AOP

Net Income Range : Rs. 2,09,29,610/Rs. 2,09,28,010/
Rs. 2,09,30,010 – Rs. 5,00,00,000

Assessment year : 2020-21

Slab rate : 30%
Surcharge : 25%
HEC : 4%

NI Rs.	IT Rs.	SC Rs.	HEC Rs.	Total Rs.	NI Rs.	IT Rs.	SC Rs.	HEC Rs.	Total Rs.	NI Rs.	IT Rs.	SC Rs.	HEC Rs.	Total Rs.
10	3	0.75	0.15	3.90	**100**	30	7.50	1.50	39	**1000**	300	75	15	390
20	6	1.50	0.30	7.80	**200**	60	15.00	3.00	78	**2000**	600	150	30	780
30	9	2.25	0.45	11.70	**300**	90	22.50	4.50	117	**3000**	900	225	45	1170
40	12	3.00	0.60	15.60	**400**	120	30.00	6.00	156	**4000**	1200	300	60	1560
50	15	3.75	0.75	19.50	**500**	150	37.50	7.50	195	**5000**	1500	375	75	1950
60	18	4.50	0.90	23.40	**600**	180	45.00	9.00	234	**6000**	1800	450	90	2340
70	21	5.25	1.05	27.30	**700**	210	52.50	10.50	273	**7000**	2100	525	105	2730
80	24	6.00	1.20	31.20	**800**	240	60.00	12.00	312	**8000**	2400	600	120	3120
90	27	6.75	1.35	35.10	**900**	270	67.50	13.50	351	**9000**	2700	675	135	3510

	*Resident senior citizen***				*Resident super senior citizen****				*Any other resident individual*/any non-resident individual/any HUF or AOP*			
NI Rs.	IT Rs.	SC Rs.	HEC Rs.	Total Rs.	IT Rs.	SC Rs.	HEC Rs.	Total Rs.	IT Rs.	SC Rs.	HEC Rs.	Total Rs.
20928010	—	—	—	—	6078403	1519601	303920	7901924	—	—	—	—
20929610	6088883	1522221	304444	7915548	—	—	—	—	—	—	—	—
20930010	—	—	—	—	—	—	—	—	6091503	1522876	304575	7918954
21000000	6110000	1527500	305500	7943000	6100000	1525000	305000	7930000	6112500	1528125	305625	7946250
22000000	6410000	1602500	320500	8333000	6400000	1600000	320000	8320000	6412500	1603125	320625	8336250
23000000	6710000	1677500	335500	8723000	6700000	1675000	335000	8710000	6712500	1678125	335625	8726250
24000000	7010000	1752500	350500	9113000	7000000	1750000	350000	9100000	7012500	1753125	350625	9116250
25000000	7310000	1827500	365500	9503000	7300000	1825000	365000	9490000	7312500	1828125	365625	9506250
26000000	7610000	1902500	380500	9893000	7600000	1900000	380000	9880000	7612500	1903125	380625	9896250
27000000	7910000	1977500	395500	10283000	7900000	1975000	395000	10270000	7912500	1978125	395625	10286250
28000000	8210000	2052500	410500	10673000	8200000	2050000	410000	10660000	8212500	2053125	410625	10676250
29000000	8510000	2127500	425500	11063000	8500000	2125000	425000	11050000	8512500	2128125	425625	11066250
30000000	8810000	2202500	440500	11453000	8800000	2200000	440000	11440000	8812500	2203125	440625	11456250
31000000	9110000	2277500	455500	11843000	9100000	2275000	455000	11830000	9112500	2278125	455625	11846250
32000000	9410000	2352500	470500	12233000	9400000	2350000	470000	12220000	9412500	2353125	470625	12236250
33000000	9710000	2427500	485500	12623000	9700000	2425000	485000	12610000	9712500	2428125	485625	12626250
34000000	10010000	2502500	500500	13013000	10000000	2500000	500000	13000000	10012500	2503125	500625	13016250
35000000	10310000	2577500	515500	13403000	10300000	2575000	515000	13390000	10312500	2578125	515625	13406250
36000000	10610000	2652500	530500	13793000	10600000	2650000	530000	13780000	10612500	2653125	530625	13796250
37000000	10910000	2727500	545500	14183000	10900000	2725000	545000	14170000	10912500	2728125	545625	14186250
38000000	11210000	2802500	560500	14573000	11200000	2800000	560000	14560000	11212500	2803125	560625	14576250
39000000	11510000	2877500	575500	14963000	11500000	2875000	575000	14950000	11512500	2878125	575625	14966250
40000000	11810000	2952500	590500	15353000	11800000	2950000	590000	15340000	11812500	2953125	590625	15356250
41000000	12110000	3027500	605500	15743000	12100000	3025000	605000	15730000	12112500	3028125	605625	15746250
42000000	12410000	3102500	620500	16133000	12400000	3100000	620000	16120000	12412500	3103125	620625	16136250
43000000	12710000	3177500	635500	16523000	12700000	3175000	635000	16510000	12712500	3178125	635625	16526250
44000000	13010000	3252500	650500	16913000	13000000	3250000	650000	16900000	13012500	3253125	650625	16916250
45000000	13310000	3327500	665500	17303000	13300000	3325000	665000	17290000	13312500	3328125	665625	17306250
46000000	13610000	3402500	680500	17693000	13600000	3400000	680000	17680000	13612500	3403125	680625	17696250
47000000	13910000	3477500	695500	18083000	13900000	3475000	695000	18070000	13912500	3478125	695625	18086250
48000000	14210000	3552500	710500	18473000	14200000	3550000	710000	18460000	14212500	3553125	710625	18476250
49000000	14510000	3627500	725500	18863000	14500000	3625000	725000	18850000	14512500	3628125	725625	18866250
50000000	14810000	3702500	740500	19253000	14800000	3700000	740000	19240000	14812500	3703125	740625	19256250

Note - For how to use table, *see* page B-1.

*If the individual was born on or after April 2, 1960.

**If the individual was born on or after April 2, 1940 but before April 2, 1960.

***If the individual was born before April 2, 1940.

Income-tax : 2.19

INDIVIDUAL

HUF and AOP

Net Income Range : Rs. 5,00,00,010 – Rs. 5,30,17,310/ Rs. 5,30,15,280/Rs. 5,30,17,820

Assessment year : 2020-21

Slab rate : 30%
Surcharge : 37%
HEC : 4%

NI Rs.	IT Rs.	SC Rs.	HEC Rs.	Total Rs.	NI Rs.	IT Rs.	SC Rs.	HEC Rs.	Total Rs.	NI Rs.	IT Rs.	SC Rs.	HEC Rs.	Total Rs.
10	3	7	0.40	10.40	**100**	30	70	4	104	**1000**	300	700	40	1040
20	6	14	0.80	20.80	**200**	60	140	8	208	**2000**	600	1400	80	2080
30	9	21	1.20	31.20	**300**	90	210	12	312	**3000**	900	2100	120	3120
40	12	28	1.60	41.60	**400**	120	280	16	416	**4000**	1200	2800	160	4160
50	15	35	2.00	52.00	**500**	150	350	20	520	**5000**	1500	3500	200	5200
60	18	42	2.40	62.40	**600**	180	420	24	624	**6000**	1800	4200	240	6240
70	21	49	2.80	72.80	**700**	210	490	28	728	**7000**	2100	4900	280	7280
80	24	56	3.20	83.20	**800**	240	560	32	832	**8000**	2400	5600	320	8320
90	27	63	3.60	93.60	**900**	270	630	36	936	**9000**	2700	6300	360	9360

	Resident senior citizen**				Resident super senior citizen***				Any other resident individual*/any non-resident individual/any HUF or AOP			
NI Rs.	IT Rs.	SC Rs.	HEC Rs.	Total Rs.	IT Rs.	SC Rs.	HEC Rs.	Total Rs.	IT Rs.	SC Rs.	HEC Rs.	Total Rs.
50000010	14810003	3702507	740500	19253010	14800003	3700007	740000	19240010	14812503	3703132	740625	19256260
50100000	14840000	3772500	744500	19357000	14830000	3770000	744000	19344000	14842500	3773125	744625	19360250
50200000	14870000	3842500	748500	19461000	14860000	3840000	748000	19448000	14872500	3843125	748625	19464250
50300000	14900000	3912500	752500	19565000	14890000	3910000	752000	19552000	14902500	3913125	752625	19568250
50400000	14930000	3982500	756500	19669000	14920000	3980000	756000	19656000	14932500	3983125	756625	19672250
50500000	14960000	4052500	760500	19773000	14950000	4050000	760000	19760000	14962500	4053125	760625	19776250
50600000	14990000	4122500	764500	19877000	14980000	4120000	764000	19864000	14992500	4123125	764625	19880250
50700000	15020000	4192500	768500	19981000	15010000	4190000	768000	19968000	15022500	4193125	768625	19984250
50800000	15050000	4262500	772500	20085000	15040000	4260000	772000	20072000	15052500	4263125	772625	20088250
50900000	15080000	4332500	776500	20189000	15070000	4330000	776000	20176000	15082500	4333125	776625	20192250
51000000	15110000	4402500	780500	20293000	15100000	4400000	780000	20280000	15112500	4403125	780625	20296250
51100000	15140000	4472500	784500	20397000	15130000	4470000	784000	20384000	15142500	4473125	784625	20400250
51200000	15170000	4542500	788500	20501000	15160000	4540000	788000	20488000	15172500	4543125	788625	20504250
51300000	15200000	4612500	792500	20605000	15190000	4610000	792000	20592000	15202500	4613125	792625	20608250
51400000	15230000	4682500	796500	20709000	15220000	4680000	796000	20696000	15232500	4683125	796625	20712250
51500000	15260000	4752500	800500	20813000	15250000	4750000	800000	20800000	15262500	4753125	800625	20816250
51600000	15290000	4822500	804500	20917000	15280000	4820000	804000	20904000	15292500	4823125	804625	20920250
51700000	15320000	4892500	808500	21021000	15310000	4890000	808000	21008000	15322500	4893125	808625	21024250
51800000	15350000	4962500	812500	21125000	15340000	4960000	812000	21112000	15352500	4963125	812625	21128250
51900000	15380000	5032500	816500	21229000	15370000	5030000	816000	21216000	15382500	5033125	816625	21232250
52000000	15410000	5102500	820500	21333000	15400000	5100000	820000	21320000	15412500	5103125	820625	21336250
52100000	15440000	5172500	824500	21437000	15430000	5170000	824000	21424000	15442500	5173125	824625	21440250
52200000	15470000	5242500	828500	21541000	15460000	5240000	828000	21528000	15472500	5243125	828625	21544250
52300000	15500000	5312500	832500	21645000	15490000	5310000	832000	21632000	15502500	5313125	832625	21648250
52400000	15530000	5382500	836500	21749000	15520000	5380000	836000	21736000	15532500	5383125	836625	21752250
52500000	15560000	5452500	840500	21853000	15550000	5450000	840000	21840000	15562500	5453125	840625	21856250
52600000	15590000	5522500	844500	21957000	15580000	5520000	844000	21944000	15592500	5523125	844625	21960250
52700000	15620000	5592500	848500	22061000	15610000	5590000	848000	22048000	15622500	5593125	848625	22064250
52800000	15650000	5662500	852500	22165000	15640000	5660000	852000	22152000	15652500	5663125	852625	22168250
52900000	15680000	5732500	856500	22269000	15670000	5730000	856000	22256000	15682500	5733125	856625	22272250
53000000	15710000	5802500	860500	22373000	15700000	5800000	860000	22360000	15712500	5803125	860625	22376250
53015280	—	—	—	—	15704584	5810696	860611	22375891	—	—	—	—
53017310	15715193	5814617	861192	22391002	—	—	—	—	—	—	—	—
53017820	—	—	—	—	—	—	—	—	15717846	5815599	861338	22394783

Note - For how to use table, *see* page B-1.

*If the individual was born on or after April 2, 1960.

**If the individual was born on or after April 2, 1940 but before April 2, 1960.

***If the individual was born before April 2, 1940.

Income-tax : 2.20

INDIVIDUAL

HUF and AOP

Net Income Range : Rs. 5,30,17,320/Rs. 5,30,15,290/
Rs. 5,30,17,830 – Rs. 7,00,00,000

Assessment year : 2020-21

Slab rate : 30%
Surcharge : 37%
HEC : 4%

NI Rs.	IT Rs.	SC Rs.	HEC Rs.	Total Rs.	NI Rs.	IT Rs.	SC Rs.	HEC Rs.	Total Rs.	NI Rs.	IT Rs.	SC Rs.	HEC Rs.	Total Rs.
10	3	1.11	0.16	4.27	**100**	30	11.10	1.64	42.74	**1000**	300	111	16.44	427.44
20	6	2.22	0.33	8.55	**200**	60	22.20	3.29	85.49	**2000**	600	222	32.88	854.88
30	9	3.33	0.49	12.82	**300**	90	33.30	4.93	128.23	**3000**	900	333	49.32	1282.32
40	12	4.44	0.66	17.10	**400**	120	44.40	6.58	170.98	**4000**	1200	444	65.76	1709.76
50	15	5.55	0.82	21.37	**500**	150	55.50	8.22	213.72	**5000**	1500	555	82.20	2137.20
60	18	6.66	0.99	25.65	**600**	180	66.60	9.86	256.46	**6000**	1800	666	98.64	2564.64
70	21	7.77	1.15	29.92	**700**	210	77.70	11.51	299.21	**7000**	2100	777	115.08	2992.08
80	24	8.88	1.32	34.20	**800**	240	88.80	13.15	341.95	**8000**	2400	888	131.52	3419.52
90	27	9.99	1.48	38.47	**900**	270	99.90	14.80	384.70	**9000**	2700	999	147.96	3846.96

	Resident senior citizen**				***Resident super senior citizen******				***Any other resident individual*/any non-resident individual/any HUF or AOP***			
NI Rs.	IT Rs.	SC Rs.	HEC Rs.	Total Rs.	IT Rs.	SC Rs.	HEC Rs.	Total Rs.	IT Rs.	SC Rs.	HEC Rs.	Total Rs.
53015290	—	—	—	—	15704587	5810697	860611	22375895	—	—	—	—
53017320	15715196	5814623	861193	22391011	—	—	—	—	—	—	—	—
53017830	—	—	—	—	—	—	—	—	15717849	5815604	861338	22394791
53100000	15740000	5823800	862552	22426352	15730000	5820100	862004	22412104	15742500	5824725	862689	22429914
54000000	16010000	5923700	877348	22811048	16000000	5920000	876800	22796800	16012500	5924625	877485	22814610
55000000	16310000	6034700	893788	23238488	16300000	6031000	893240	23224240	16312500	6035625	893925	23242050
56000000	16610000	6145700	910228	23665928	16600000	6142000	909680	23651680	16612500	6146625	910365	23669490
57000000	16910000	6256700	926668	24093368	16900000	6253000	926120	24079120	16912500	6257625	926805	24096930
58000000	17210000	6367700	943108	24520808	17200000	6364000	942560	24506560	17212500	6368625	943245	24524370
59000000	17510000	6478700	959548	24948248	17500000	6475000	959000	24934000	17512500	6479625	959685	24951810
60000000	17810000	6589700	975988	25375688	17800000	6586000	975440	25361440	17812500	6590625	976125	25379250
61000000	18110000	6700700	992428	25803128	18100000	6697000	991880	25788880	18112500	6701625	992565	25806690
62000000	18410000	6811700	1008868	26230568	18400000	6808000	1008320	26216320	18412500	6812625	1009005	26234130
63000000	18710000	6922700	1025308	26658008	18700000	6919000	1024760	26643760	18712500	6923625	1025445	26661570
64000000	19010000	7033700	1041748	27085448	19000000	7030000	1041200	27071200	19012500	7034625	1041885	27089010
65000000	19310000	7144700	1058188	27512888	19300000	7141000	1057640	27498640	19312500	7145625	1058325	27516450
66000000	19610000	7255700	1074628	27940328	19600000	7252000	1074080	27926080	19612500	7256625	1074765	27943890
67000000	19910000	7366700	1091068	28367768	19900000	7363000	1090520	28353520	19912500	7367625	1091205	28371330
68000000	20210000	7477700	1107508	28795208	20200000	7474000	1106960	28780960	20212500	7478625	1107645	28798770
69000000	20510000	7588700	1123948	29222648	20500000	7585000	1123400	29208400	20512500	7589625	1124085	29226210
70000000	20810000	7699700	1140388	29650088	20800000	7696000	1139840	29635840	20812500	7700625	1140525	29653650

Note - For how to use table, *see* page B-1.

*If the individual was born on or after April 2, 1960.

**If the individual was born on or after April 2, 1940 but before April 2, 1960.

***If the individual was born before April 2, 1940.

Income-tax : 3.1

FIRMS

Slab rate : 30%
Surcharge : *Nil*
HEC : 4%

Net Income Range : Rs. 100 - Rs. 1,00,00,000
Assessment years : 2019-20 and 2020-21

NI Rs.	IT Rs.	HEC Rs.	Total Rs.	NI Rs.	IT Rs.	HEC Rs.	Total Rs.	NI Rs.	IT Rs.	HEC Rs.	Total Rs.
100	30	1.20	31.20	**1000**	300	12	312	**10000**	3000	120	3120
200	60	2.40	62.40	**2000**	600	24	624	**20000**	6000	240	6240
300	90	3.60	93.60	**3000**	900	36	936	**30000**	9000	360	9360
400	120	4.80	124.80	**4000**	1200	48	1248	**40000**	12000	480	12480
500	150	6.00	156.00	**5000**	1500	60	1560	**50000**	15000	600	15600
600	180	7.20	187.20	**6000**	1800	72	1872	**60000**	18000	720	18720
700	210	8.40	218.40	**7000**	2100	84	2184	**70000**	21000	840	21840
800	240	9.60	249.60	**8000**	2400	96	2496	**80000**	24000	960	24960
900	270	10.80	280.80	**9000**	2700	108	2808	**90000**	27000	1080	28080
100000	30000	1200	31200	**3400000**	1020000	40800	1060800	**6700000**	2010000	80400	2090400
200000	60000	2400	62400	**3500000**	1050000	42000	1092000	**6800000**	2040000	81600	2121600
300000	90000	3600	93600	**3600000**	1080000	43200	1123200	**6900000**	2070000	82800	2152800
400000	120000	4800	124800	**3700000**	1110000	44400	1154400	**7000000**	2100000	84000	2184000
500000	150000	6000	156000	**3800000**	1140000	45600	1185600	**7100000**	2130000	85200	2215200
600000	180000	7200	187200	**3900000**	1170000	46800	1216800	**7200000**	2160000	86400	2246400
700000	210000	8400	218400	**4000000**	1200000	48000	1248000	**7300000**	2190000	87600	2277600
800000	240000	9600	249600	**4100000**	1230000	49200	1279200	**7400000**	2220000	88800	2308800
900000	270000	10800	280800	**4200000**	1260000	50400	1310400	**7500000**	2250000	90000	2340000
1000000	300000	12000	312000	**4300000**	1290000	51600	1341600	**7600000**	2280000	91200	2371200
1100000	330000	13200	343200	**4400000**	1320000	52800	1372800	**7700000**	2310000	92400	2402400
1200000	360000	14400	374400	**4500000**	1350000	54000	1404000	**7800000**	2340000	93600	2433600
1300000	390000	15600	405600	**4600000**	1380000	55200	1435200	**7900000**	2370000	94800	2464800
1400000	420000	16800	436800	**4700000**	1410000	56400	1466400	**8000000**	2400000	96000	2496000
1500000	450000	18000	468000	**4800000**	1440000	57600	1497600	**8100000**	2430000	97200	2527200
1600000	480000	19200	499200	**4900000**	1470000	58800	1528800	**8200000**	2460000	98400	2558400
1700000	510000	20400	530400	**5000000**	1500000	60000	1560000	**8300000**	2490000	99600	2589600
1800000	540000	21600	561600	**5100000**	1530000	61200	1591200	**8400000**	2520000	100800	2620800
1900000	570000	22800	592800	**5200000**	1560000	62400	1622400	**8500000**	2550000	102000	2652000
2000000	600000	24000	624000	**5300000**	1590000	63600	1653600	**8600000**	2580000	103200	2683200
2100000	630000	25200	655200	**5400000**	1620000	64800	1684800	**8700000**	2610000	104400	2714400
2200000	660000	26400	686400	**5500000**	1650000	66000	1716000	**8800000**	2640000	105600	2745600
2300000	690000	27600	717600	**5600000**	1680000	67200	1747200	**8900000**	2670000	106800	2776800
2400000	720000	28800	748800	**5700000**	1710000	68400	1778400	**9000000**	2700000	108000	2808000
2500000	750000	30000	780000	**5800000**	1740000	69600	1809600	**9100000**	2730000	109200	2839200
2600000	780000	31200	811200	**5900000**	1770000	70800	1840800	**9200000**	2760000	110400	2870400
2700000	810000	32400	842400	**6000000**	1800000	72000	1872000	**9300000**	2790000	111600	2901600
2800000	840000	33600	873600	**6100000**	1830000	73200	1903200	**9400000**	2820000	112800	2932800
2900000	870000	34800	904800	**6200000**	1860000	74400	1934400	**9500000**	2850000	114000	2964000
3000000	900000	36000	936000	**6300000**	1890000	75600	1965600	**9600000**	2880000	115200	2995200
3100000	930000	37200	967200	**6400000**	1920000	76800	1996800	**9700000**	2910000	116400	3026400
3200000	960000	38400	998400	**6500000**	1950000	78000	2028000	**9800000**	2940000	117600	3057600
3300000	990000	39600	1029600	**6600000**	1980000	79200	2059200	**9900000**	2970000	118800	3088800
3400000	1020000	40800	1060800	**6700000**	2010000	80400	2090400	**10000000**	3000000	120000	3120000

Note - For how to use table, *see* page B-1.

Income-tax : 3.2

FIRMS

Slab rate : 30%
Surcharge : 12%
HEC : 4%

Net Income Range : Rs. 1,00,00,010 - Rs. 1,05,42,160

Assessment years : 2019-20 and 2020-21

NI Rs.	IT Rs.	SC Rs.	HEC Rs.	Total Rs.	NI Rs.	IT Rs.	SC Rs.	HEC Rs.	Total Rs.	NI Rs.	IT Rs.	SC Rs.	HEC Rs.	Total Rs.
10	3	7	0.40	10.40	**100**	30	70	4	104	**1000**	300	700	40	1040
20	6	14	0.80	20.80	**200**	60	140	8	208	**2000**	600	1400	80	2080
30	9	21	1.20	31.20	**300**	90	210	12	312	**3000**	900	2100	120	3120
40	12	28	1.60	41.60	**400**	120	280	16	416	**4000**	1200	2800	160	4160
50	15	35	2.00	52.00	**500**	150	350	20	520	**5000**	1500	3500	200	5200
60	18	42	2.40	62.40	**600**	180	420	24	624	**6000**	1800	4200	240	6240
70	21	49	2.80	72.80	**700**	210	490	28	728	**7000**	2100	4900	280	7280
80	24	56	3.20	83.20	**800**	240	560	32	832	**8000**	2400	5600	320	8320
90	27	63	3.60	93.60	**900**	270	630	36	936	**9000**	2700	6300	360	9360
10000010	3000003	7	120000	3120010	**10180000**	3054000	126000	127200	3307200	**10365000**	3109500	255500	134600	3499600
10005000	3001500	3500	120200	3125200	**10185000**	3055500	129500	127400	3312400	**10370000**	3111000	259000	134800	3504800
10010000	3003000	7000	120400	3130400	**10190000**	3057000	133000	127600	3317600	**10375000**	3112500	262500	135000	3510000
10015000	3004500	10500	120600	3135600	**10195000**	3058500	136500	127800	3322800	**10380000**	3114000	266000	135200	3515200
10020000	3006000	14000	120800	3140800	**10200000**	3060000	140000	128000	3328000	**10385000**	3115500	269500	135400	3520400
10025000	3007500	17500	121000	3146000	**10205000**	3061500	143500	128200	3333200	**10390000**	3117000	273000	135600	3525600
10030000	3009000	21000	121200	3151200	**10210000**	3063000	147000	128400	3338400	**10395000**	3118500	276500	135800	3530800
10035000	3010500	24500	121400	3156400	**10215000**	3064500	150500	128600	3343600	**10400000**	3120000	280000	136000	3536000
10040000	3012000	28000	121600	3161600	**10220000**	3066000	154000	128800	3348800	**10405000**	3121500	283500	136200	3541200
10045000	3013500	31500	121800	3166800	**10225000**	3067500	157500	129000	3354000	**10410000**	3123000	287000	136400	3546400
10050000	3015000	35000	122000	3172000	**10230000**	3069000	161000	129200	3359200	**10415000**	3124500	290500	136600	3551600
10055000	3016500	38500	122200	3177200	**10235000**	3070500	164500	129400	3364400	**10420000**	3126000	294000	136800	3556800
10060000	3018000	42000	122400	3182400	**10240000**	3072000	168000	129600	3369600	**10425000**	3127500	297500	137000	3562000
10065000	3019500	45500	122600	3187600	**10245000**	3073500	171500	129800	3374800	**10430000**	3129000	301000	137200	3567200
10070000	3021000	49000	122800	3192800	**10250000**	3075000	175000	130000	3380000	**10435000**	3130500	304500	137400	3572400
10075000	3022500	52500	123000	3198000	**10255000**	3076500	178500	130200	3385200	**10440000**	3132000	308000	137600	3577600
10080000	3024000	56000	123200	3203200	**10260000**	3078000	182000	130400	3390400	**10445000**	3133500	311500	137800	3582800
10085000	3025500	59500	123400	3208400	**10265000**	3079500	185500	130600	3395600	**10450000**	3135000	315000	138000	3588000
10090000	3027000	63000	123600	3213600	**10270000**	3081000	189000	130800	3400800	**10455000**	3136500	318500	138200	3593200
10095000	3028500	66500	123800	3218800	**10275000**	3082500	192500	131000	3406000	**10460000**	3138000	322000	138400	3598400
10100000	3030000	70000	124000	3224000	**10280000**	3084000	196000	131200	3411200	**10465000**	3139500	325500	138600	3603600
10105000	3031500	73500	124200	3229200	**10285000**	3085500	199500	131400	3416400	**10470000**	3141000	329000	138800	3608800
10110000	3033000	77000	124400	3234400	**10290000**	3087000	203000	131600	3421600	**10475000**	3142500	332500	139000	3614000
10115000	3034500	80500	124600	3239600	**10295000**	3088500	206500	131800	3426800	**10480000**	3144000	336000	139200	3619200
10120000	3036000	84000	124800	3244800	**10300000**	3090000	210000	132000	3432000	**10485000**	3145500	339500	139400	3624400
10125000	3037500	87500	125000	3250000	**10305000**	3091500	213500	132200	3437200	**10490000**	3147000	343000	139600	3629600
10130000	3039000	91000	125200	3255200	**10310000**	3093000	217000	132400	3442400	**10495000**	3148500	346500	139800	3634800
10135000	3040500	94500	125400	3260400	**10315000**	3094500	220500	132600	3447600	**10500000**	3150000	350000	140000	3640000
10140000	3042000	98000	125600	3265600	**10320000**	3096000	224000	132800	3452800	**10505000**	3151500	353500	140200	3645200
10145000	3043500	101500	125800	3270800	**10325000**	3097500	227500	133000	3458000	**10510000**	3153000	357000	140400	3650400
10150000	3045000	105000	126000	3276000	**10330000**	3099000	231000	133200	3463200	**10515000**	3154500	360500	140600	3655600
10155000	3046500	108500	126200	3281200	**10335000**	3100500	234500	133400	3468400	**10520000**	3156000	364000	140800	3660800
10160000	3048000	112000	126400	3286400	**10340000**	3102000	238000	133600	3473600	**10525000**	3157500	367500	141000	3666000
10165000	3049500	115500	126600	3291600	**10345000**	3103500	241500	133800	3478800	**10530000**	3159000	371000	141200	3671200
10170000	3051000	119000	126800	3296800	**10350000**	3105000	245000	134000	3484000	**10535000**	3160500	374500	141400	3676400
10175000	3052500	122500	127000	3302000	**10355000**	3106500	248500	134200	3489200	**10540000**	3162000	378000	141600	3681600
10180000	3054000	126000	127200	3307200	**10360000**	3108000	252000	134400	3494400	**10542160**	3162648	379512	141686	3683846

Note - For how to use table, *see* page B-1.

Income-tax : 3.3
FIRMS

Slab rate : 30%
Surcharge : 12%
HEC : 4%

Net Income Range : Rs. 1,05,42,170 - Rs. 1,70,00,000
Assessment years : 2019-20 and 2020-21

NI Rs.	IT Rs.	SC Rs.	HEC Rs.	Total Rs.	NI Rs.	IT Rs.	SC Rs.	HEC Rs.	Total Rs.	NI Rs.	IT Rs.	SC Rs.	HEC Rs.	Total Rs.
10	3	0.36	0.13	3.49	**100**	30	3.60	1.34	34.94	**1000**	300	36	13.44	349.44
20	6	0.72	0.27	6.99	**200**	60	7.20	2.69	69.89	**2000**	600	72	26.88	698.88
30	9	1.08	0.40	10.48	**300**	90	10.80	4.03	104.83	**3000**	900	108	40.32	1048.32
40	12	1.44	0.54	13.98	**400**	120	14.40	5.38	139.78	**4000**	1200	144	53.76	1397.76
50	15	1.8	0.67	17.47	**500**	150	18.00	6.72	174.72	**5000**	1500	180	67.20	1747.20
60	18	2.16	0.81	20.97	**600**	180	21.60	8.06	209.66	**6000**	1800	216	80.64	2096.64
70	21	2.52	0.94	24.46	**700**	210	25.20	9.41	244.61	**7000**	2100	252	94.08	2446.08
80	24	2.88	1.08	27.96	**800**	240	28.80	10.75	279.55	**8000**	2400	288	107.52	2795.52
90	27	3.24	1.21	31.45	**900**	270	32.40	12.10	314.50	**9000**	2700	324	120.96	3144.96
10542170	3162651	379518	141687	3683856	**12700000**	3810000	457200	170688	4437888	**14900000**	4470000	536400	200256	5206656
10600000	3180000	381600	142464	3704064	**12800000**	3840000	460800	172032	4472832	**15000000**	4500000	540000	201600	5241600
10700000	3210000	385200	143808	3739008	**12900000**	3870000	464400	173376	4507776	**15100000**	4530000	543600	202944	5276544
10800000	3240000	388800	145152	3773952	**13000000**	3900000	468000	174720	4542720	**15200000**	4560000	547200	204288	5311488
10900000	3270000	392400	146496	3808896	**13100000**	3930000	471600	176064	4577664	**15300000**	4590000	550800	205632	5346432
11000000	3300000	396000	147840	3843840	**13200000**	3960000	475200	177408	4612608	**15400000**	4620000	554400	206976	5381376
11100000	3330000	399600	149184	3878784	**13300000**	3990000	478800	178752	4647552	**15500000**	4650000	558000	208320	5416320
11200000	3360000	403200	150528	3913728	**13400000**	4020000	482400	180096	4682496	**15600000**	4680000	561600	209664	5451264
11300000	3390000	406800	151872	3948672	**13500000**	4050000	486000	181440	4717440	**15700000**	4710000	565200	211008	5486208
11400000	3420000	410400	153216	3983616	**13600000**	4080000	489600	182784	4752384	**15800000**	4740000	568800	212352	5521152
11500000	3450000	414000	154560	4018560	**13700000**	4110000	493200	184128	4787328	**15900000**	4770000	572400	213696	5556096
11600000	3480000	417600	155904	4053504	**13800000**	4140000	496800	185472	4822272	**16000000**	4800000	576000	215040	5591040
11700000	3510000	421200	157248	4088448	**13900000**	4170000	500400	186816	4857216	**16100000**	4830000	579600	216384	5625984
11800000	3540000	424800	158592	4123392	**14000000**	4200000	504000	188160	4892160	**16200000**	4860000	583200	217728	5660928
11900000	3570000	428400	159936	4158336	**14100000**	4230000	507600	189504	4927104	**16300000**	4890000	586800	219072	5695872
12000000	3600000	432000	161280	4193280	**14200000**	4260000	511200	190848	4962048	**16400000**	4920000	590400	220416	5730816
12100000	3630000	435600	162624	4228224	**14300000**	4290000	514800	192192	4996992	**16500000**	4950000	594000	221760	5765760
12200000	3660000	439200	163968	4263168	**14400000**	4320000	518400	193536	5031936	**16600000**	4980000	597600	223104	5800704
12300000	3690000	442800	165312	4298112	**14500000**	4350000	522000	194880	5066880	**16700000**	5010000	601200	224448	5835648
12400000	3720000	446400	166656	4333056	**14600000**	4380000	525600	196224	5101824	**16800000**	5040000	604800	225792	5870592
12500000	3750000	450000	168000	4368000	**14700000**	4410000	529200	197568	5136768	**16900000**	5070000	608400	227136	5905536
12600000	3780000	453600	169344	4402944	**14800000**	4440000	532800	198912	5171712	**17000000**	5100000	612000	228480	5940480

Note - For how to use table, *see* page B-1.

Income-tax : 4.1

DOMESTIC COMPANIES

Net Income Range : Rs. 1,000 - Rs. 1,00,00,000

Assessment years : 2019-20 and 2020-21

Surcharge : *Nil*

HEC : 4%

	Domestic company whose turnover/gross receipt does not exceed Rs. 250 crore† (Slab rate : 25%)			*Any other domestic company (Slab rate : 30%)*		
NI Rs.	*IT Rs.*	*HEC Rs.*	*Total Rs.*	*IT Rs.*	*HEC Rs.*	*Total Rs.*
1000	250	10	260	300	12	312
2000	500	20	520	600	24	624
3000	750	30	780	900	36	936
4000	1000	40	1040	1200	48	1248
5000	1250	50	1300	1500	60	1560
6000	1500	60	1560	1800	72	1872
7000	1750	70	1820	2100	84	2184
8000	2000	80	2080	2400	96	2496
9000	2250	90	2340	2700	108	2808
10000	2500	100	2600	3000	120	3120
20000	5000	200	5200	6000	240	6240
30000	7500	300	7800	9000	360	9360
40000	10000	400	10400	12000	480	12480
50000	12500	500	13000	15000	600	15600
60000	15000	600	15600	18000	720	18720
70000	17500	700	18200	21000	840	21840
80000	20000	800	20800	24000	960	24960
90000	22500	900	23400	27000	1080	28080
100000	25000	1000	26000	30000	1200	31200
200000	50000	2000	52000	60000	2400	62400
300000	75000	3000	78000	90000	3600	93600
400000	100000	4000	104000	120000	4800	124800
500000	125000	5000	130000	150000	6000	156000
600000	150000	6000	156000	180000	7200	187200
700000	175000	7000	182000	210000	8400	218400
800000	200000	8000	208000	240000	9600	249600
900000	225000	9000	234000	270000	10800	280800
1000000	250000	10000	260000	300000	12000	312000
2000000	500000	20000	520000	600000	24000	624000
3000000	750000	30000	780000	900000	36000	936000
4000000	1000000	40000	1040000	1200000	48000	1248000
5000000	1250000	50000	1300000	1500000	60000	1560000
6000000	1500000	60000	1560000	1800000	72000	1872000
7000000	1750000	70000	1820000	2100000	84000	2184000
8000000	2000000	80000	2080000	2400000	96000	2496000
9000000	2250000	90000	2340000	2700000	108000	2808000
10000000	2500000	100000	2600000	3000000	120000	3120000

† Rate of 25% is applicable –

- for the assessment year 2019-20 (if turnover/gross receipt during the financial year 2016-17 does not exceed Rs. 250 crore),
- for the assessment year 2020-21 (if turnover/gross receipt during the financial year 2017-18 does not exceed Rs. 250 crore).

Income-tax : 4.2

DOMESTIC COMPANIES

Net Income Range : Rs. 1,00,00,010 - Rs. 1,02,38,900/ Rs. 1,03,09,270

Assessment years : 2019-20 and 2020-21

Surcharge : 7%
HEC : 4%

	Domestic company whose turnover/gross receipt does not exceed Rs. 250 crore†				*Any other domestic company*			
	Slab rate : 25%				*Slab rate : 30%*			
NI Rs.	*IT Rs.*	*SC Rs.*	*HEC Rs.*	*Total Rs.*	*IT Rs.*	*SC Rs.*	*HEC Rs.*	*Total Rs.*
1000	250	750	40	1040	300	700	40	1040
2000	500	1500	80	2080	600	1400	80	2080
3000	750	2250	120	3120	900	2100	120	3120
4000	1000	3000	160	4160	1200	2800	160	4160
5000	1250	3750	200	5200	1500	3500	200	5200
6000	1500	4500	240	6240	1800	4200	240	6240
7000	1750	5250	280	7280	2100	4900	280	7280
8000	2000	6000	320	8320	2400	5600	320	8320
9000	2250	6750	360	9360	2700	6300	360	9360
10000010	2500003	8	100000	2600011	3000003	7	120000	3120010
10010000	2502500	7500	100400	2610400	3003000	7000	120400	3130400
10020000	2505000	15000	100800	2620800	3006000	14000	120800	3140800
10030000	2507500	22500	101200	2631200	3009000	21000	121200	3151200
10040000	2510000	30000	101600	2641600	3012000	28000	121600	3161600
10050000	2512500	37500	102000	2652000	3015000	35000	122000	3172000
10060000	2515000	45000	102400	2662400	3018000	42000	122400	3182400
10070000	2517500	52500	102800	2672800	3021000	49000	122800	3192800
10080000	2520000	60000	103200	2683200	3024000	56000	123200	3203200
10090000	2522500	67500	103600	2693600	3027000	63000	123600	3213600
10100000	2525000	75000	104000	2704000	3030000	70000	124000	3224000
10110000	2527500	82500	104400	2714400	3033000	77000	124400	3234400
10120000	2530000	90000	104800	2724800	3036000	84000	124800	3244800
10130000	2532500	97500	105200	2735200	3039000	91000	125200	3255200
10140000	2535000	105000	105600	2745600	3042000	98000	125600	3265600
10150000	2537500	112500	106000	2756000	3045000	105000	126000	3276000
10160000	2540000	120000	106400	2766400	3048000	112000	126400	3286400
10170000	2542500	127500	106800	2776800	3051000	119000	126800	3296800
10180000	2545000	135000	107200	2787200	3054000	126000	127200	3307200
10190000	2547500	142500	107600	2797600	3057000	133000	127600	3317600
10200000	2550000	150000	108000	2808000	3060000	140000	128000	3328000
10238900	2559725	179175	109556	2848456	—	—	—	—
10309270	—	—	—	—	3092781	216489	132371	3441641

† Rate of 25% is applicable –

- for the assessment year 2019-20 (if turnover/gross receipt during the financial year 2016-17 does not exceed Rs. 250 crore),
- for the assessment year 2020-21 (if turnover/gross receipt during the financial year 2017-18 does not exceed Rs. 250 crore).

Income-tax : 4.3

DOMESTIC COMPANIES

Surcharge : 7%
HEC : 4%

Net Income Range : Rs. 1,02,38,910/Rs. 1,03,09,280 - Rs. 10,00,00,000

Assessment years : 2019-20 and 2020-21

NI Rs.	*Domestic company whose turnover/gross receipt does not exceed Rs. 250 crore†* — Slab rate : 25% — IT Rs.	SC Rs.	HEC Rs.	Total Rs.	*Any other domestic company* — Slab rate : 30% — IT Rs.	SC Rs.	HEC Rs.	Total Rs.
1000	250	17.50	10.70	278.20	300	21	12.84	333.84
2000	500	35.00	21.40	556.40	600	42	25.68	667.68
3000	750	52.50	32.10	834.60	900	63	38.52	1001.52
4000	1000	70.00	42.80	1112.80	1200	84	51.36	1335.36
5000	1250	87.50	53.50	1391.00	1500	105	64.20	1669.20
6000	1500	105.00	64.20	1669.20	1800	126	77.04	2003.04
7000	1750	122.50	74.90	1947.40	2100	147	89.88	2336.88
8000	2000	140.00	85.60	2225.60	2400	168	102.72	2670.72
9000	2250	157.50	96.30	2503.80	2700	189	115.56	3004.56
10238910	2559728	179181	109556	2848465	—	—	—	—
10309280	—	—	—	—	3092784	216495	132371	3441650
15000000	3750000	262500	160500	4173000	4500000	315000	192600	5007600
20000000	5000000	350000	214000	5564000	6000000	420000	256800	6676800
25000000	6250000	437500	267500	6955000	7500000	525000	321000	8346000
30000000	7500000	525000	321000	8346000	9000000	630000	385200	10015200
35000000	8750000	612500	374500	9737000	10500000	735000	449400	11684400
40000000	10000000	700000	428000	11128000	12000000	840000	513600	13353600
45000000	11250000	787500	481500	12519000	13500000	945000	577800	15022800
50000000	12500000	875000	535000	13910000	15000000	1050000	642000	16692000
55000000	13750000	962500	588500	15301000	16500000	1155000	706200	18361200
60000000	15000000	1050000	642000	16692000	18000000	1260000	770400	20030400
65000000	16250000	1137500	695500	18083000	19500000	1365000	834600	21699600
70000000	17500000	1225000	749000	19474000	21000000	1470000	898800	23368800
75000000	18750000	1312500	802500	20865000	22500000	1575000	963000	25038000
80000000	20000000	1400000	856000	22256000	24000000	1680000	1027200	26707200
85000000	21250000	1487500	909500	23647000	25500000	1785000	1091400	28376400
90000000	22500000	1575000	963000	25038000	27000000	1890000	1155600	30045600
95000000	23750000	1662500	1016500	26429000	28500000	1995000	1219800	31714800
100000000	25000000	1750000	1070000	27820000	30000000	2100000	1284000	33384000

† Rate of 25% is applicable –

- for the assessment year 2019-20 (if turnover/gross receipt during the financial year 2016-17 does not exceed Rs. 250 crore),
- for the assessment year 2020-21 (if turnover/gross receipt during the financial year 2017-18 does not exceed Rs. 250 crore).

Income-tax : 4.4

DOMESTIC COMPANIES

Net Income Range : Rs. 10,00,00,010 - Rs. 10,17,36,110/ Rs. 10,22,59,030

Assessment years : 2019-20 and 2020-21

Surcharge : 12%
HEC : 4%

	Domestic company whose turnover/gross receipt does not exceed Rs. 250 crore†				*Any other domestic company*			
	Slab rate : 25%				*Slab rate : 30%*			
NI Rs.	*IT Rs.*	*SC Rs.*	*HEC Rs.*	*Total Rs.*	*IT Rs.*	*SC Rs.*	*HEC Rs.*	*Total Rs.*
1000	250	750	40	1040	300	700	40	1040
2000	500	1500	80	2080	600	1400	80	2080
3000	750	2250	120	3120	900	2100	120	3120
4000	1000	3000	160	4160	1200	2800	160	4160
5000	1250	3750	200	5200	1500	3500	200	5200
6000	1500	4500	240	6240	1800	4200	240	6240
7000	1750	5250	280	7280	2100	4900	280	7280
8000	2000	6000	320	8320	2400	5600	320	8320
9000	2250	6750	360	9360	2700	6300	360	9360
100000010	25000003	1750000	1070000	27820003	30000003	2100000	1284000	33384003
100100000	25025000	1825000	1074000	27924000	30030000	2170000	1288000	33488000
100200000	25050000	1900000	1078000	28028000	30060000	2240000	1292000	33592000
100300000	25075000	1975000	1082000	28132000	30090000	2310000	1296000	33696000
100400000	25100000	2050000	1086000	28236000	30120000	2380000	1300000	33800000
100500000	25125000	2125000	1090000	28340000	30150000	2450000	1304000	33904000
100600000	25150000	2200000	1094000	28444000	30180000	2520000	1308000	34008000
100700000	25175000	2275000	1098000	28548000	30210000	2590000	1312000	34112000
100800000	25200000	2350000	1102000	28652000	30240000	2660000	1316000	34216000
100900000	25225000	2425000	1106000	28756000	30270000	2730000	1320000	34320000
101000000	25250000	2500000	1110000	28860000	30300000	2800000	1324000	34424000
101100000	25275000	2575000	1114000	28964000	30330000	2870000	1328000	34528000
101200000	25300000	2650000	1118000	29068000	30360000	2940000	1332000	34632000
101300000	25325000	2725000	1122000	29172000	30390000	3010000	1336000	34736000
101400000	25350000	2800000	1126000	29276000	30420000	3080000	1340000	34840000
101500000	25375000	2875000	1130000	29380000	30450000	3150000	1344000	34944000
101600000	25400000	2950000	1134000	29484000	30480000	3220000	1348000	35048000
101700000	25425000	3025000	1138000	29588000	30510000	3290000	1352000	35152000
101736110	25434028	3052083	1139444	29625555	—	—	—	—
102259030	—	—	—	—	30677709	3681321	1374361	35733391

† Rate of 25% is applicable –

- for the assessment year 2019-20 (if turnover/gross receipt during the financial year 2016-17 does not exceed Rs. 250 crore),
- for the assessment year 2020-21 (if turnover/gross receipt during the financial year 2017-18 does not exceed Rs. 250 crore).

Income-tax : 4.5

DOMESTIC COMPANIES

Surcharge : 12%
HEC : 4%

Net Income Range : Rs. 10,17,36,120/
Rs. 10,22,59,040 - Rs. 30,00,00,000

Assessment years : 2019-20 and 2020-21

	Domestic company whose turnover/gross receipt does not exceed Rs. 250 crore†				Any other domestic company			
	Slab rate : 25%				Slab rate : 30%			
NI Rs.	IT Rs.	SC Rs.	HEC Rs.	Total Rs.	IT Rs.	SC Rs.	HEC Rs.	Total Rs.
1000	250	30	11.20	291.20	300	36	13.44	349.44
2000	500	60	22.40	582.40	600	72	26.88	698.88
3000	750	90	33.60	873.60	900	108	40.32	1048.32
4000	1000	120	44.80	1164.80	1200	144	53.76	1397.76
5000	1250	150	56.00	1456.00	1500	180	67.20	1747.20
6000	1500	180	67.20	1747.20	1800	216	80.64	2096.64
7000	1750	210	78.40	2038.40	2100	252	94.08	2446.08
8000	2000	240	89.60	2329.60	2400	288	107.52	2795.52
9000	2250	270	100.80	2620.80	2700	324	120.96	3144.96
101736120	25434030	3052084	1139445	29625558	—	—	—	—
102259040	—	—	—	—	30677712	3681325	1374361	35733399
110000000	27500000	3300000	1232000	32032000	33000000	3960000	1478400	38438400
120000000	30000000	3600000	1344000	34944000	36000000	4320000	1612800	41932800
130000000	32500000	3900000	1456000	37856000	39000000	4680000	1747200	45427200
140000000	35000000	4200000	1568000	40768000	42000000	5040000	1881600	48921600
150000000	37500000	4500000	1680000	43680000	45000000	5400000	2016000	52416000
160000000	40000000	4800000	1792000	46592000	48000000	5760000	2150400	55910400
170000000	42500000	5100000	1904000	49504000	51000000	6120000	2284800	59404800
180000000	45000000	5400000	2016000	52416000	54000000	6480000	2419200	62899200
190000000	47500000	5700000	2128000	55328000	57000000	6840000	2553600	66393600
200000000	50000000	6000000	2240000	58240000	60000000	7200000	2688000	69888000
210000000	52500000	6300000	2352000	61152000	63000000	7560000	2822400	73382400
220000000	55000000	6600000	2464000	64064000	66000000	7920000	2956800	76876800
230000000	57500000	6900000	2576000	66976000	69000000	8280000	3091200	80371200
240000000	60000000	7200000	2688000	69888000	72000000	8640000	3225600	83865600
250000000	62500000	7500000	2800000	72800000	75000000	9000000	3360000	87360000
260000000	65000000	7800000	2912000	75712000	78000000	9360000	3494400	90854400
270000000	67500000	8100000	3024000	78624000	81000000	9720000	3628800	94348800
280000000	70000000	8400000	3136000	81536000	84000000	10080000	3763200	97843200
290000000	72500000	8700000	3248000	84448000	87000000	10440000	3897600	101337600
300000000	75000000	9000000	3360000	87360000	90000000	10800000	4032000	104832000

† Rate of 25% is applicable –

- for the assessment year 2019-20 (if turnover/gross receipt during the financial year 2016-17 does not exceed Rs. 250 crore),
- for the assessment year 2020-21 (if turnover/gross receipt during the financial year 2017-18 does not exceed Rs. 250 crore).

Income-tax : 4.6

FOREIGN COMPANIES

Net Income Range : Rs. 1,000 - Rs. 1,00,00,000

Assessment years : 2019-20 and 2020-21

NI	Dividend and interest (Note 1)	Interest on infrastructure debt fund/bonds (Note 2)	Royalty/technical fees if agreement is made before April 1, 1976 (Note 3)	Royalty/technical fees if agreement is made on or after April 1, 1976 (Note 4)	Other income (Note 5)
	IT + HEC 20.80%	*IT + HEC 5.20%*	*IT + HEC 52%*	*IT + HEC 10.40%*	*IT + HEC 41.6%*
Rs.	*Rs.*	*Rs.*	*Rs.*	*Rs.*	*Rs.*
1000	208	52	520	104	416
2000	416	104	1040	208	832
3000	624	156	1560	312	1248
4000	832	208	2080	416	1664
5000	1040	260	2600	520	2080
6000	1248	312	3120	624	2496
7000	1456	364	3640	728	2912
8000	1664	416	4160	832	3328
9000	1872	468	4680	936	3744
10000	2080	520	5200	1040	4160
20000	4160	1040	10400	2080	8320
30000	6240	1560	15600	3120	12480
40000	8320	2080	20800	4160	16640
50000	10400	2600	26000	5200	20800
60000	12480	3120	31200	6240	24960
70000	14560	3640	36400	7280	29120
80000	16640	4160	41600	8320	33280
90000	18720	4680	46800	9360	37440
100000	20800	5200	52000	10400	41600
200000	41600	10400	104000	20800	83200
300000	62400	15600	156000	31200	124800
400000	83200	20800	208000	41600	166400
500000	104000	26000	260000	52000	208000
600000	124800	31200	312000	62400	249600
700000	145600	36400	364000	72800	291200
800000	166400	41600	416000	83200	332800
900000	187200	46800	468000	93600	374400
1000000	208000	52000	520000	104000	416000
2000000	416000	104000	1040000	208000	832000
3000000	624000	156000	1560000	312000	1248000
4000000	832000	208000	2080000	416000	1664000
5000000	1040000	260000	2600000	520000	2080000
6000000	1248000	312000	3120000	624000	2496000
7000000	1456000	364000	3640000	728000	2912000
8000000	1664000	416000	4160000	832000	3328000
9000000	1872000	468000	4680000	936000	3744000
10000000	2080000	520000	5200000	1040000	4160000

Notes -

1. It covers dividend and interest as specified in section 115A(1)(*a*)(*i*)/(*ii*).

2. It covers interest on infrastructure debt fund/bonds as specified in section 115A(1)(*a*)(*iia*)/(*iiaa*) read with section 194LC.

3. It covers royalty and technical fees in pursuance of an agreement made before April 1, 1976 as specified in the First Schedule to the Finance Bill/Act.

4. It covers royalty and technical fees in pursuance of an agreement made on or after April 1, 1976 as specified in section 115A(1)(*b*)(*A*)/(*B*).

5. It covers any other income which is not subject to any special rate of tax.

Income-tax : 4.7

FOREIGN COMPANIES

Net Income Range : Rs. 1,00,00,000 - Rs. 10,00,00,000

Assessment years : 2019-20 and 2020-21

NI	Dividend and interest (Note 1)	Interest on infrastructure debt fund/bonds (Note 2)	Royalty/technical fees if agreement is made before April 1, 1976 (Note 3)	Royalty/technical fees if agreement is made on or after April 1, 1976 (Note 4)	Other income (Note 5)
Rs.	*IT + SC + HEC* 21.216% *Rs.*	*IT + SC + HEC* 5.304% *Rs.*	*IT + SC + HEC* 53.04% *Rs.*	*IT + SC + HEC* 10.608% *Rs.*	*IT + SC + HEC* 42.432% *Rs.*
1000	212.16	53.04	530.40	106.08	424.32
2000	424.32	106.08	1060.80	212.16	848.64
3000	636.48	159.12	1591.20	318.24	1272.96
4000	848.64	212.16	2121.60	424.32	1697.28
5000	1060.80	265.20	2652.00	530.40	2121.60
6000	1272.96	318.24	3182.40	636.48	2545.92
7000	1485.12	371.28	3712.80	742.56	2970.24
8000	1697.28	424.32	4243.20	848.64	3394.56
9000	1909.44	477.36	4773.60	954.72	3818.88
10000	2121.60	530.40	5304.00	1060.80	4243.20
20000	4243.20	1060.80	10608.00	2121.60	8486.40
30000	6364.80	1591.20	15912.00	3182.40	12729.60
40000	8486.40	2121.60	21216.00	4243.20	16972.80
50000	10608.00	2652.00	26520.00	5304.00	21216.00
60000	12729.60	3182.40	31824.00	6364.80	25459.20
70000	14851.20	3712.80	37128.00	7425.60	29702.40
80000	16972.80	4243.20	42432.00	8486.40	33945.60
90000	19094.40	4773.60	47736.00	9547.20	38188.80
100000	21216	5304	53040	10608	42432
200000	42432	10608	106080	21216	84864
300000	63648	15912	159120	31824	127296
400000	84864	21216	212160	42432	169728
500000	106080	26520	265200	53040	212160
600000	127296	31824	318240	63648	254592
700000	148512	37128	371280	74256	297024
800000	169728	42432	424320	84864	339456
900000	190944	47736	477360	95472	381888
10000000*	2121600	530400	5304000	1060800	4243200
20000000	4243200	1060800	10608000	2121600	8486400
30000000	6364800	1591200	15912000	3182400	12729600
40000000	8486400	2121600	21216000	4243200	16972800
50000000	10608000	2652000	26520000	5304000	21216000
60000000	12729600	3182400	31824000	6364800	25459200
70000000	14851200	3712800	37128000	7425600	29702400
80000000	16972800	4243200	42432000	8486400	33945600
90000000	19094400	4773600	47736000	9547200	38188800
100000000	21216000	5304000	53040000	10608000	42432000

Notes -

1. It covers dividend and interest as specified in section 115A(1)(*a*)(*i*)/(*ii*).
2. It covers interest on infrastructure debt fund/bonds as specified in section 115A(1)(*a*)(*iia*)/(*iiaa*) read with section 194LC.
3. It covers royalty and technical fees in pursuance of an agreement made before April 1, 1976 as specified in the First Schedule to the Finance Bill/Act.
4. It covers royalty and technical fees in pursuance of an agreement made on or after April 1, 1976 as specified in section 115A(1)(*b*)(*A*)/(*B*).
5. It covers any other income which is not subject to any special rate of tax.

* The total amount payable as income-tax and surcharge cannot exceed the total amount payable as income-tax on a total income of Rs. 1,00,00,000 by more than the amount of income that exceeds Rs. 1,00,00,000 (generally it is known as marginal relief).

Income-tax : 4.8

FOREIGN COMPANIES

Net Income Range : Above Rs. 10,00,00,000

Assessment years : 2019-20 and 2020-21

NI	Dividend and interest (Note 1)	Interest on infrastructure debt fund/bonds (Note 2)	Royalty/technical fees if agreement is made before April 1, 1976 (Note 3)	Royalty/technical fees if agreement is made on or after April 1, 1976 (Note 4)	Other income (Note 5)
	IT + SC + HEC 21.84%	*IT + SC + HEC* 5.46%	*IT + SC + HEC* 54.60%	*IT + SC + HEC* 10.92%	*IT + SC + HEC* 43.68%
Rs.	*Rs.*	*Rs.*	*Rs.*	*Rs.*	*Rs.*
1000	218.40	54.60	546.00	109.20	436.80
2000	436.80	109.20	1092.00	218.40	873.60
3000	655.20	163.80	1638.00	327.60	1310.40
4000	873.60	218.40	2184.00	436.80	1747.20
5000	1092.00	273.00	2730.00	546.00	2184.00
6000	1310.40	327.60	3276.00	655.20	2620.80
7000	1528.80	382.20	3822.00	764.40	3057.60
8000	1747.20	436.80	4368.00	873.60	3494.40
9000	1965.60	491.40	4914.00	982.80	3931.20
10000	2184	546	5460	1092	4368
20000	4368	1092	10920	2184	8736
30000	6552	1638	16380	3276	13104
40000	8736	2184	21840	4368	17472
50000	10920	2730	27300	5460	21840
60000	13104	3276	32760	6552	26208
70000	15288	3822	38220	7644	30576
80000	17472	4368	43680	8736	34944
90000	19656	4914	49140	9828	39312
100000	21840	5460	54600	10920	43680
200000	43680	10920	109200	21840	87360
300000	65520	16380	163800	32760	131040
400000	87360	21840	218400	43680	174720
500000	109200	27300	273000	54600	218400
600000	131040	32760	327600	65520	262080
700000	152880	38220	382200	76440	305760
800000	174720	43680	436800	87360	349440
900000	196560	49140	491400	98280	393120
100000000*	21840000	5460000	54600000	10920000	43680000
200000000	43680000	10920000	109200000	21840000	87360000
300000000	65520000	16380000	163800000	32760000	131040000
400000000	87360000	21840000	218400000	43680000	174720000
500000000	109200000	27300000	273000000	54600000	218400000

Notes -

1. It covers dividend and interest as specified in section 115A(1)(*a*)(*i*)/(*ii*).
2. It covers interest on infrastructure debt fund/bonds as specified in section 115A(1)(*a*)(*iia*)/(*iiaa*) read with section 194LC.
3. It covers royalty and technical fees in pursuance of an agreement made before April 1, 1976 as specified in the First Schedule to the Finance Bill/Act.
4. It covers royalty and technical fees in pursuance of an agreement made on or after April 1, 1976 as specified in section 115A(1)(*b*)(*A*)/(*B*).
5. It covers any other income which is not subject to any special rate of tax.

* The total amount payable as income-tax and surcharge cannot exceed the total amount payable as income-tax and surcharge on a total income of Rs. 10,00,00,000 by more than the amount of income that exceeds Rs. 10,00,00,000 (generally it is known as marginal relief).

Income-tax : 5.1

CO-OPERATIVE SOCIETY

Net Income Range : Rs. 10 - Rs. 20,000

Assessment years : 2019-20 and 2020-21

When net income is in the range of Rs. 10 - Rs. 10,000
Slab rate : 10% SC : *Nil*
HEC : 4%

NI Rs.	*IT Rs.*	*HEC Rs.*	*Total Rs.*	*NI Rs.*	*IT Rs.*	*HEC Rs.*	*Total Rs.*
10	1	0.04	1.04	**110**	11	0.44	11.44
20	2	0.08	2.08	**120**	12	0.48	12.48
30	3	0.12	3.12	**130**	13	0.52	13.52
40	4	0.16	4.16	**140**	14	0.56	14.56
50	5	0.20	5.20	**150**	15	0.60	15.60
60	6	0.24	6.24	**160**	16	0.64	16.64
70	7	0.28	7.28	**170**	17	0.68	17.68
80	8	0.32	8.32	**180**	18	0.72	18.72
90	9	0.36	9.36	**190**	19	0.76	19.76
100	10	0.40	10.40	**200**	20	0.80	20.80
200	20	0.80	20.80	**5200**	520	20.80	540.80
400	40	1.60	41.60	**5400**	540	21.60	561.60
600	60	2.40	62.40	**5600**	560	22.40	582.40
800	80	3.20	83.20	**5800**	580	23.20	603.20
1000	100	4.00	104.00	**6000**	600	24.00	624.00
1200	120	4.80	124.80	**6200**	620	24.80	644.80
1400	140	5.60	145.60	**6400**	640	25.60	665.60
1600	160	6.40	166.40	**6600**	660	26.40	686.40
1800	180	7.20	187.20	**6800**	680	27.20	707.20
2000	200	8.00	208.00	**7000**	700	28.00	728.00
2200	220	8.80	228.80	**7200**	720	28.80	748.80
2400	240	9.60	249.60	**7400**	740	29.60	769.60
2600	260	10.40	270.40	**7600**	760	30.40	790.40
2800	280	11.20	291.20	**7800**	780	31.20	811.20
3000	300	12.00	312.00	**8000**	800	32.00	832.00
3200	320	12.80	332.80	**8200**	820	32.80	852.80
3400	340	13.60	353.60	**8400**	840	33.60	873.60
3600	360	14.40	374.40	**8600**	860	34.40	894.40
3800	380	15.20	395.20	**8800**	880	35.20	915.20
4000	400	16.00	416.00	**9000**	900	36.00	936.00
4200	420	16.80	436.80	**9200**	920	36.80	956.80
4400	440	17.60	457.60	**9400**	940	37.60	977.60
4600	460	18.40	478.40	**9600**	960	38.40	998.40
4800	480	19.20	499.20	**9800**	980	39.20	1019.20
5000	500	20.00	520.00	**10000**	1000	40.00	1040.00

When net income is in the range of Rs. 10,000 - Rs. 20,000
Slab rate: 20% SC : *Nil*
HEC : 4%

NI Rs.	*IT Rs.*	*HEC Rs.*	*Total Rs.*	*NI Rs.*	*IT Rs.*	*HEC Rs.*	*Total Rs.*
10	2	0.08	2.08	**110**	22	0.88	22.88
20	4	0.16	4.16	**120**	24	0.96	24.96
30	6	0.24	6.24	**130**	26	1.04	27.04
40	8	0.32	8.32	**140**	28	1.12	29.12
50	10	0.40	10.40	**150**	30	1.20	31.20
60	12	0.48	12.48	**160**	32	1.28	33.28
70	14	0.56	14.56	**170**	34	1.36	35.36
80	16	0.64	16.64	**180**	36	1.44	37.44
90	18	0.72	18.72	**190**	38	1.52	39.52
100	20	0.80	20.80	**200**	40	1.60	41.60
10200	1040	41.60	1081.60	**15200**	2040	81.60	2121.60
10400	1080	43.20	1123.20	**15400**	2080	83.20	2163.20
10600	1120	44.80	1164.80	**15600**	2120	84.80	2204.80
10800	1160	46.40	1206.40	**15800**	2160	86.40	2246.40
11000	1200	48.00	1248.00	**16000**	2200	88.00	2288.00
11200	1240	49.60	1289.60	**16200**	2240	89.60	2329.60
11400	1280	51.20	1331.20	**16400**	2280	91.20	2371.20
11600	1320	52.80	1372.80	**16600**	2320	92.80	2412.80
11800	1360	54.40	1414.40	**16800**	2360	94.40	2454.40
12000	1400	56.00	1456.00	**17000**	2400	96.00	2496.00
12200	1440	57.60	1497.60	**17200**	2440	97.60	2537.60
12400	1480	59.20	1539.20	**17400**	2480	99.20	2579.20
12600	1520	60.80	1580.80	**17600**	2520	100.80	2620.80
12800	1560	62.40	1622.40	**17800**	2560	102.40	2662.40
13000	1600	64.00	1664.00	**18000**	2600	104.00	2704.00
13200	1640	65.60	1705.60	**18200**	2640	105.60	2745.60
13400	1680	67.20	1747.20	**18400**	2680	107.20	2787.20
13600	1720	68.80	1788.80	**18600**	2720	108.80	2828.80
13800	1760	70.40	1830.40	**18800**	2760	110.40	2870.40
14000	1800	72.00	1872.00	**19000**	2800	112.00	2912.00
14200	1840	73.60	1913.60	**19200**	2840	113.60	2953.60
14400	1880	75.20	1955.20	**19400**	2880	115.20	2995.20
14600	1920	76.80	1996.80	**19600**	2920	116.80	3036.80
14800	1960	78.40	2038.40	**19800**	2960	118.40	3078.40
15000	2000	80.00	2080.00	**20000**	3000	120.00	3120.00

Note: For how to use the table, *see* page B-1.

Income-tax : 5.2

CO-OPERATIVE SOCIETY

Slab rate : 30%
Surcharge : *Nil*
HEC : 4%

Net Income Range : Rs. 20,000 - Rs. 1,00,00,000
Assessment years : 2019-20 and 2020-21

NI Rs.	IT Rs.	HEC Rs.	Total Rs.	NI Rs.	IT Rs.	HEC Rs.	Total Rs.	NI Rs.	IT Rs.	HEC Rs.	Total Rs.
100	30	1.20	31.20	**1000**	300	12	312	**10000**	3000	120	3120
200	60	2.40	62.40	**2000**	600	24	624	**20000**	6000	240	6240
300	90	3.60	93.60	**3000**	900	36	936	**30000**	9000	360	9360
400	120	4.80	124.80	**4000**	1200	48	1248	**40000**	12000	480	12480
500	150	6.00	156.00	**5000**	1500	60	1560	**50000**	15000	600	15600
600	180	7.20	187.20	**6000**	1800	72	1872	**60000**	18000	720	18720
700	210	8.40	218.40	**7000**	2100	84	2184	**70000**	21000	840	21840
800	240	9.60	249.60	**8000**	2400	96	2496	**80000**	24000	960	24960
900	270	10.80	280.80	**9000**	2700	108	2808	**90000**	27000	1080	28080
20000	3000	120	3120	**2900000**	867000	34680	901680	**6500000**	1947000	77880	2024880
30000	6000	240	6240	**3000000**	897000	35880	932880	**6600000**	1977000	79080	2056080
40000	9000	360	9360	**3100000**	927000	37080	964080	**6700000**	2007000	80280	2087280
50000	12000	480	12480	**3200000**	957000	38280	995280	**6800000**	2037000	81480	2118480
60000	15000	600	15600	**3300000**	987000	39480	1026480	**6900000**	2067000	82680	2149680
70000	18000	720	18720	**3400000**	1017000	40680	1057680	**7000000**	2097000	83880	2180880
80000	21000	840	21840	**3500000**	1047000	41880	1088880	**7100000**	2127000	85080	2212080
90000	24000	960	24960	**3600000**	1077000	43080	1120080	**7200000**	2157000	86280	2243280
100000	27000	1080	28080	**3700000**	1107000	44280	1151280	**7300000**	2187000	87480	2274480
200000	57000	2280	59280	**3800000**	1137000	45480	1182480	**7400000**	2217000	88680	2305680
300000	87000	3480	90480	**3900000**	1167000	46680	1213680	**7500000**	2247000	89880	2336880
400000	117000	4680	121680	**4000000**	1197000	47880	1244880	**7600000**	2277000	91080	2368080
500000	147000	5880	152880	**4100000**	1227000	49080	1276080	**7700000**	2307000	92280	2399280
600000	177000	7080	184080	**4200000**	1257000	50280	1307280	**7800000**	2337000	93480	2430480
700000	207000	8280	215280	**4300000**	1287000	51480	1338480	**7900000**	2367000	94680	2461680
800000	237000	9480	246480	**4400000**	1317000	52680	1369680	**8000000**	2397000	95880	2492880
900000	267000	10680	277680	**4500000**	1347000	53880	1400880	**8100000**	2427000	97080	2524080
1000000	297000	11880	308880	**4600000**	1377000	55080	1432080	**8200000**	2457000	98280	2555280
1100000	327000	13080	340080	**4700000**	1407000	56280	1463280	**8300000**	2487000	99480	2586480
1200000	357000	14280	371280	**4800000**	1437000	57480	1494480	**8400000**	2517000	100680	2617680
1300000	387000	15480	402480	**4900000**	1467000	58680	1525680	**8500000**	2547000	101880	2648880
1400000	417000	16680	433680	**5000000**	1497000	59880	1556880	**8600000**	2577000	103080	2680080
1500000	447000	17880	464880	**5100000**	1527000	61080	1588080	**8700000**	2607000	104280	2711280
1600000	477000	19080	496080	**5200000**	1557000	62280	1619280	**8800000**	2637000	105480	2742480
1700000	507000	20280	527280	**5300000**	1587000	63480	1650480	**8900000**	2667000	106680	2773680
1800000	537000	21480	558480	**5400000**	1617000	64680	1681680	**9000000**	2697000	107880	2804880
1900000	567000	22680	589680	**5500000**	1647000	65880	1712880	**9100000**	2727000	109080	2836080
2000000	597000	23880	620880	**5600000**	1677000	67080	1744080	**9200000**	2757000	110280	2867280
2100000	627000	25080	652080	**5700000**	1707000	68280	1775280	**9300000**	2787000	111480	2898480
2200000	657000	26280	683280	**5800000**	1737000	69480	1806480	**9400000**	2817000	112680	2929680
2300000	687000	27480	714480	**5900000**	1767000	70680	1837680	**9500000**	2847000	113880	2960880
2400000	717000	28680	745680	**6000000**	1797000	71880	1868880	**9600000**	2877000	115080	2992080
2500000	747000	29880	776880	**6100000**	1827000	73080	1900080	**9700000**	2907000	116280	3023280
2600000	777000	31080	808080	**6200000**	1857000	74280	1931280	**9800000**	2937000	117480	3054480
2700000	807000	32280	839280	**6300000**	1887000	75480	1962480	**9900000**	2967000	118680	3085680
2800000	837000	33480	870480	**6400000**	1917000	76680	1993680	**10000000**	2997000	119880	3116880

Note - For how to use table, *see* page B-1.

Income-tax : 6.1

SALARIED EMPLOYEES (other than senior citizens)

Slab rate : *Nil* up to Rs. 5,00,000
20% above Rs. 5,00,000

Surcharge : *Nil*

HEC : 4%

Monthly Taxable Salary Range : Rs. 41,500 - Rs. 77,200

Annual Taxable Salary Range : Rs. 4,98,000 - Rs. 9,26,400

Assessment year : 2020-21

Monthly		Annual		Monthly		Annual		Monthly		Annual	
Sl Rs.	Tax† Rs.	Sl Rs.	Tax Rs.	Sl Rs.	Tax Rs.	Sl Rs.	Tax Rs.	Sl Rs.	Tax Rs.	Sl Rs.	Tax Rs.
41500	0.00	**498000**	0.00†	**53500**	3544.67	**642000**	42536.00	**65500**	6040.67	**786000**	72488.00
41800	1111.07	**501600**	13332.80	**53800**	3607.07	**645600**	43284.80	**65800**	6103.07	**789600**	73236.80
42100	1173.47	**505200**	14081.60	**54100**	3669.47	**649200**	44033.60	**66100**	6165.47	**793200**	73985.60
42400	1235.87	**508800**	14830.40	**54400**	3731.87	**652800**	44782.40	**66400**	6227.87	**796800**	74734.40
42700	1298.27	**512400**	15579.20	**54700**	3794.27	**656400**	45531.20	**66700**	6290.27	**800400**	75483.20
43000	1360.67	**516000**	16328.00	**55000**	3856.67	**660000**	46280.00	**67000**	6352.67	**804000**	76232.00
43300	1423.07	**519600**	17076.80	**55300**	3919.07	**663600**	47028.80	**67300**	6415.07	**807600**	76980.80
43600	1485.47	**523200**	17825.60	**55600**	3981.47	**667200**	47777.60	**67600**	6477.47	**811200**	77729.60
43900	1547.87	**526800**	18574.40	**55900**	4043.87	**670800**	48526.40	**67900**	6539.87	**814800**	78478.40
44200	1610.27	**530400**	19323.20	**56200**	4106.27	**674400**	49275.20	**68200**	6602.27	**818400**	79227.20
44500	1672.67	**534000**	20072.00	**56500**	4168.67	**678000**	50024.00	**68500**	6664.67	**822000**	79976.00
44800	1735.07	**537600**	20820.80	**56800**	4231.07	**681600**	50772.80	**68800**	6727.07	**825600**	80724.80
45100	1797.47	**541200**	21569.60	**57100**	4293.47	**685200**	51521.60	**69100**	6789.47	**829200**	81473.60
45400	1859.87	**544800**	22318.40	**57400**	4355.87	**688800**	52270.40	**69400**	6851.87	**832800**	82222.40
45700	1922.27	**548400**	23067.20	**57700**	4418.27	**692400**	53019.20	**69700**	6914.27	**836400**	82971.20
46000	1984.67	**552000**	23816.00	**58000**	4480.67	**696000**	53768.00	**70000**	6976.67	**840000**	83720.00
46300	2047.07	**555600**	24564.80	**58300**	4543.07	**699600**	54516.80	**70300**	7039.07	**843600**	84468.80
46600	2109.47	**559200**	25313.60	**58600**	4605.47	**703200**	55265.60	**70600**	7101.47	**847200**	85217.60
46900	2171.87	**562800**	26062.40	**58900**	4667.87	**706800**	56014.40	**70900**	7163.87	**850800**	85966.40
47200	2234.27	**566400**	26811.20	**59200**	4730.27	**710400**	56763.20	**71200**	7226.27	**854400**	86715.20
47500	2296.67	**570000**	27560.00	**59500**	4792.67	**714000**	57512.00	**71500**	7288.67	**858000**	87464.00
47800	2359.07	**573600**	28308.80	**59800**	4855.07	**717600**	58260.80	**71800**	7351.07	**861600**	88212.80
48100	2421.47	**577200**	29057.60	**60100**	4917.47	**721200**	59009.60	**72100**	7413.47	**865200**	88961.60
48400	2483.87	**580800**	29806.40	**60400**	4979.87	**724800**	59758.40	**72400**	7475.87	**868800**	89710.40
48700	2546.27	**584400**	30555.20	**60700**	5042.27	**728400**	60507.20	**72700**	7538.27	**872400**	90459.20
49000	2608.67	**588000**	31304.00	**61000**	5104.67	**732000**	61256.00	**73000**	7600.67	**876000**	91208.00
49300	2671.07	**591600**	32052.80	**61300**	5167.07	**735600**	62004.80	**73300**	7663.07	**879600**	91956.80
49600	2733.47	**595200**	32801.60	**61600**	5229.47	**739200**	62753.60	**73600**	7725.47	**883200**	92705.60
49900	2795.87	**598800**	33550.40	**61900**	5291.87	**742800**	63502.40	**73900**	7787.87	**886800**	93454.40
50200	2858.27	**602400**	34299.20	**62200**	5354.27	**746400**	64251.20	**74200**	7850.27	**890400**	94203.20
50500	2920.67	**606000**	35048.00	**62500**	5416.67	**750000**	65000.00	**74500**	7912.67	**894000**	94952.00
50800	2983.07	**609600**	35796.80	**62800**	5479.07	**753600**	65748.80	**74800**	7975.07	**897600**	95700.80
51100	3045.47	**613200**	36545.60	**63100**	5541.47	**757200**	66497.60	**75100**	8037.47	**901200**	96449.60
51400	3107.87	**616800**	37294.40	**63400**	5603.87	**760800**	67246.40	**75400**	8099.87	**904800**	97198.40
51700	3170.27	**620400**	38043.20	**63700**	5666.27	**764400**	67995.20	**75700**	8162.27	**908400**	97947.20
52000	3232.67	**624000**	38792.00	**64000**	5728.67	**768000**	68744.00	**76000**	8224.67	**912000**	98696.00
52300	3295.07	**627600**	39540.80	**64300**	5791.07	**771600**	69492.80	**76300**	8287.07	**915600**	99444.80
52600	3357.47	**631200**	40289.60	**64600**	5853.47	**775200**	70241.60	**76600**	8349.47	**919200**	100193.60
52900	3419.87	**634800**	41038.40	**64900**	5915.87	**778800**	70990.40	**76900**	8411.87	**922800**	100942.40
53200	3482.27	**638400**	41787.20	**65200**	5978.27	**782400**	71739.20	**77200**	8474.27	**926400**	101691.20

†After rebate under section 87A.

Income-tax : 6.2

SALARIED EMPLOYEES (other than senior citizens)

Slab rate : 20% up to Rs. 10,00,000
30% above Rs. 10,00,000

Surcharge : *Nil*

HEC : 4%

Monthly Taxable Salary Range : Rs. 77,500 - Rs. 1,13,200
Annual Taxable Salary Range : Rs. 9,30,000 - Rs. 13,58,400
Assessment year : 2020-21

Monthly		Annual		Monthly		Annual		Monthly		Annual	
SI Rs.	Tax Rs.	SI Rs.	Tax Rs.	SI Rs.	Tax Rs.	SI Rs.	Tax Rs.	SI Rs.	Tax Rs.	SI Rs.	Tax Rs.
77500	8536.67	**930000**	102440.00	**89500**	11674.00	**1074000**	140088.00	**101500**	15418.00	**1218000**	185016.00
77800	8599.07	**933600**	103188.80	**89800**	11767.60	**1077600**	141211.20	**101800**	15511.60	**1221600**	186139.20
78100	8661.47	**937200**	103937.60	**90100**	11861.20	**1081200**	142334.40	**102100**	15605.20	**1225200**	187262.40
78400	8723.87	**940800**	104686.40	**90400**	11954.80	**1084800**	143457.60	**102400**	15698.80	**1228800**	188385.60
78700	8786.27	**944400**	105435.20	**90700**	12048.40	**1088400**	144580.80	**102700**	15792.40	**1232400**	189508.80
79000	8848.67	**948000**	106184.00	**91000**	12142.00	**1092000**	145704.00	**103000**	15886.00	**1236000**	190632.00
79300	8911.07	**951600**	106932.80	**91300**	12235.60	**1095600**	146827.20	**103300**	15979.60	**1239600**	191755.20
79600	8973.47	**955200**	107681.60	**91600**	12329.20	**1099200**	147950.40	**103600**	16073.20	**1243200**	192878.40
79900	9035.87	**958800**	108430.40	**91900**	12422.80	**1102800**	149073.60	**103900**	16166.80	**1246800**	194001.60
80200	9098.27	**962400**	109179.20	**92200**	12516.40	**1106400**	150196.80	**104200**	16260.40	**1250400**	195124.80
80500	9160.67	**966000**	109928.00	**92500**	12610.00	**1110000**	151320.00	**104500**	16354.00	**1254000**	196248.00
80800	9223.07	**969600**	110676.80	**92800**	12703.60	**1113600**	152443.20	**104800**	16447.60	**1257600**	197371.20
81100	9285.47	**973200**	111425.60	**93100**	12797.20	**1117200**	153566.40	**105100**	16541.20	**1261200**	198494.40
81400	9347.87	**976800**	112174.40	**93400**	12890.80	**1120800**	154689.60	**105400**	16634.80	**1264800**	199617.60
81700	9410.27	**980400**	112923.20	**93700**	12984.40	**1124400**	155812.80	**105700**	16728.40	**1268400**	200740.80
82000	9472.67	**984000**	113672.00	**94000**	13078.00	**1128000**	156936.00	**106000**	16822.00	**1272000**	201864.00
82300	9535.07	**987600**	114420.80	**94300**	13171.60	**1131600**	158059.20	**106300**	16915.60	**1275600**	202987.20
82600	9597.47	**991200**	115169.60	**94600**	13265.20	**1135200**	159182.40	**106600**	17009.20	**1279200**	204110.40
82900	9659.87	**994800**	115918.40	**94900**	13358.80	**1138800**	160305.60	**106900**	17102.80	**1282800**	205233.60
83200	9722.27	**998400**	116667.20	**95200**	13452.40	**1142400**	161428.80	**107200**	17196.40	**1286400**	206356.80
83500	9802.00	**1002000**	117624.00	**95500**	13546.00	**1146000**	162552.00	**107500**	17290.00	**1290000**	207480.00
83800	9895.60	**1005600**	118747.20	**95800**	13639.60	**1149600**	163675.20	**107800**	17383.60	**1293600**	208603.20
84100	9989.20	**1009200**	119870.40	**96100**	13733.20	**1153200**	164798.40	**108100**	17477.20	**1297200**	209726.40
84400	10082.80	**1012800**	120993.60	**96400**	13826.80	**1156800**	165921.60	**108400**	17570.80	**1300800**	210849.60
84700	10176.40	**1016400**	122116.80	**96700**	13920.40	**1160400**	167044.80	**108700**	17664.40	**1304400**	211972.80
85000	10270.00	**1020000**	123240.00	**97000**	14014.00	**1164000**	168168.00	**109000**	17758.00	**1308000**	213096.00
85300	10363.60	**1023600**	124363.20	**97300**	14107.60	**1167600**	169291.20	**109300**	17851.60	**1311600**	214219.20
85600	10457.20	**1027200**	125486.40	**97600**	14201.20	**1171200**	170414.40	**109600**	17945.20	**1315200**	215342.40
85900	10550.80	**1030800**	126609.60	**97900**	14294.80	**1174800**	171537.60	**109900**	18038.80	**1318800**	216465.60
86200	10644.40	**1034400**	127732.80	**98200**	14388.40	**1178400**	172660.80	**110200**	18132.40	**1322400**	217588.80
86500	10738.00	**1038000**	128856.00	**98500**	14482.00	**1182000**	173784.00	**110500**	18226.00	**1326000**	218712.00
86800	10831.60	**1041600**	129979.20	**98800**	14575.60	**1185600**	174907.20	**110800**	18319.60	**1329600**	219835.20
87100	10925.20	**1045200**	131102.40	**99100**	14669.20	**1189200**	176030.40	**111100**	18413.20	**1333200**	220958.40
87400	11018.80	**1048800**	132225.60	**99400**	14762.80	**1192800**	177153.60	**111400**	18506.80	**1336800**	222081.60
87700	11112.40	**1052400**	133348.80	**99700**	14856.40	**1196400**	178276.80	**111700**	18600.40	**1340400**	223204.80
88000	11206.00	**1056000**	134472.00	**100000**	14950.00	**1200000**	179400.00	**112000**	18694.00	**1344000**	224328.00
88300	11299.60	**1059600**	135595.20	**100300**	15043.60	**1203600**	180523.20	**112300**	18787.60	**1347600**	225451.20
88600	11393.20	**1063200**	136718.40	**100600**	15137.20	**1207200**	181646.40	**112600**	18881.20	**1351200**	226574.40
88900	11486.80	**1066800**	137841.60	**100900**	15230.80	**1210800**	182769.60	**112900**	18974.80	**1354800**	227697.60
89200	11580.40	**1070400**	138964.80	**101200**	15324.40	**1214400**	183892.80	**113200**	19068.40	**1358400**	228820.80

Market Quotation

GOLD AND SILVER

	MARKET QUOTATIONS ON		
	1-4-1981	1-4-2001	31-3-2019
	Rs.	Rs.	Rs.
Gold Standard 24 Carats (for 10 grams)	1,670	4,190	31,640
Silver 999 (for 1 Kg.)	2,715	7,215	37,245

Income-tax : 1.1

INDIVIDUALS

HUF and AOP

Net Income Range : Rs. 2,00,000 - Rs. 2,20,000

Assessment Years : 2013-14 to 2018-19

Assessment Years	2013-14		2014-15		2015-16 to 2018-19
	Resident senior citizen**	Any other	Resident Individual	Non-resident individual or any HUF/AOP	
Slab rate	—	10%	—	10%	—
Surcharge	—	—	—	—	—
EC	—	3%	—	3%	—
NI Rs.	IT Rs.	IT+EC Rs.	IT† Rs.	IT+EC Rs.	IT+EC Rs.
10	—	1.03	—	1.03	—
20	—	2.06	—	2.06	—
30	—	3.09	—	3.09	—
40	—	4.12	—	4.12	—
50	—	5.15	—	5.15	—
60	—	6.18	—	6.18	—
70	—	7.21	—	7.21	—
80	—	8.24	—	8.24	—
90	—	9.27	—	9.27	—
100	—	10.30	—	10.30	—
200	—	20.60	—	20.60	—
300	—	30.90	—	30.90	—
400	—	41.20	—	41.20	—
500	—	51.50	—	51.50	—
600	—	61.80	—	61.80	—
700	—	72.10	—	72.10	—
800	—	82.40	—	82.40	—
900	—	92.70	—	92.70	—
1000	—	103.00	—	103.00	—
2000	—	206.00	—	206.00	—
3000	—	309.00	—	309.00	—
4000	—	412.00	—	412.00	—
200000	—	0	—	0	—
205000	—	515	—	515	—
210000	—	1030	—	1030	—
215000	—	1545	—	1545	—
220000	—	2060	—	2060	—

**Senior citizen is a resident individual who is at least 60 years of age at any time during the previous year.

†After rebate under section 87A.

Income-tax : 1.2

INDIVIDUALS

HUF and AOP

Net Income Range : Rs. 2,20,000 - Rs. 2,40,000

Assessment Years : 2013-14 to 2018-19

Assessment Years	2013-14		2014-15			2015-16 to 2018-19
	Resident senior citizen**	Any other	Resident senior citizen**	Any other resident Individual	Non-resident individual or any HUF/AOP	
Slab rate	—	10%	—	10%	10%	—
Surcharge	—	—	—	—	—	—
EC	—	3%	—	3%	3%	—
NI Rs.	IT Rs.	IT+EC Rs.	IT† Rs.	IT†+EC Rs.	IT+EC Rs.	— Rs.
10	—	1.03	—	1.03	1.03	—
20	—	2.06	—	2.06	2.06	—
30	—	3.09	—	3.09	3.09	—
40	—	4.12	—	4.12	4.12	—
50	—	5.15	—	5.15	5.15	—
60	—	6.18	—	6.18	6.18	—
70	—	7.21	—	7.21	7.21	—
80	—	8.24	—	8.24	8.24	—
90	—	9.27	—	9.27	9.27	—
100	—	10.30	—	10.30	10.30	—
200	—	20.60	—	20.60	20.60	—
300	—	30.90	—	30.90	30.90	—
400	—	41.20	—	41.20	41.20	—
500	—	51.50	—	51.50	51.50	—
600	—	61.80	—	61.80	61.80	—
700	—	72.10	—	72.10	72.10	—
800	—	82.40	—	82.40	82.40	—
900	—	92.70	—	92.70	92.70	—
1000	—	103.00	—	103.00	103.00	—
2000	—	206.00	—	206.00	206.00	—
220000	0	2060	0	0	2060	0
222000	0	2266	0	206	2266	0
224000	0	2472	0	412	2472	0
226000	0	2678	0	618	2678	0
228000	0	2884	0	824	2884	0
230000	0	3090	0	1030	3090	0
232000	0	3296	0	1236	3296	0
234000	0	3502	0	1442	3502	0
236000	0	3708	0	1648	3708	0
238000	0	3914	0	1854	3914	0
240000	0	4120	0	2060	4120	0

**Senior citizen is a resident individual who is at least 60 years of age at any time during the previous year.

†After rebate under section 87A.

Income-tax : 1.3

INDIVIDUALS

HUF and AOP

Net Income Range : Rs. 2,40,000 - Rs. 2,50,000

Assessment Years : 2013-14 to 2018-19

Assessment Years	2013-14		2014-15			2015-16 to 2018-19
	Resident senior citizen**	Any other	Resident senior citizen**	Any other resident Individual	Non-resident individual or any HUF/AOP	
Slab rate Surcharge EC	— — —	10% — 3%	— — —	10% — 3%	10% — 3%	— — —
NI Rs.	IT Rs.	IT+EC Rs.	IT Rs.	IT†+EC Rs.	IT+EC Rs.	— Rs.
10	—	1.03	—	1.03	1.03	—
20	—	2.06	—	2.06	2.06	—
30	—	3.09	—	3.09	3.09	—
40	—	4.12	—	4.12	4.12	—
50	—	5.15	—	5.15	5.15	—
60	—	6.18	—	6.18	6.18	—
70	—	7.21	—	7.21	7.21	—
80	—	8.24	—	8.24	8.24	—
90	—	9.27	—	9.27	9.27	—
100	—	10.30	—	10.30	10.30	—
200	—	20.60	—	20.60	20.60	—
300	—	30.90	—	30.90	30.90	—
400	—	41.20	—	41.20	41.20	—
500	—	51.50	—	51.50	51.50	—
600	—	61.80	—	61.80	61.80	—
700	—	72.10	—	72.10	72.10	—
800	—	82.40	—	82.40	82.40	—
900	—	92.70	—	92.70	92.70	—
240000	—	4120	—	2060	4120	—
241000	—	4223	—	2163	4223	—
242000	—	4326	—	2266	4326	—
243000	—	4429	—	2369	4429	—
244000	—	4532	—	2472	4532	—
245000	—	4635	—	2575	4635	—
246000	—	4738	—	2678	4738	—
247000	—	4841	—	2781	4841	—
248000	—	4944	—	2884	4944	—
249000	—	5047	—	2987	5047	—
250000	—	5150	—	3090	5150	—

**Senior citizen is a resident individual who is at least 60 years of age at any time during the previous year.

†After rebate under section 87A.

Income-tax : 1.4

INDIVIDUALS

HUF and AOP

Net Income Range : Rs. 2,50,000 - Rs. 2,70,000

Assessment Years : 2013-14 to 2018-19

Assess-ment Years	2013-14				2014-15				2015-16 to 2017-18				2018-19			
	Any other	Resident senior citizen**	Resident super senior citizen***	Any other	Resident senior citizen**	Resident super senior citizen***	Any other resident Individual	Non-resident individual or any HUF/ AOP	Resident senior citizen**	Resident super senior citizen***	Any other resident individual	Non-resident individual or any HUF/ AOP	Resident senior citizen**	Resident super senior citizen***	Any other resident individual	Non-resident individual or any HUF/ AOP
Slab rate Surcharge EC	10% – 3%	10% – 3%	– – –	10% – 3%	— — —	— — —	10% — 3%	10% — 3%	— — —	— — —	— — —	10% — 3%	– – –	– – –	– – –	5% – 3%
NI Rs.	IT+EC Rs.	IT+EC Rs.	IT Rs.	IT+EC Rs.	IT Rs.	IT Rs.	IT†+EC Rs.	IT+EC Rs.	IT Rs.	IT Rs.	IT† Rs.	IT+EC Rs.	IT Rs.	IT Rs.	IT† Rs.	IT + EC Rs.
10	1.03	1.03	–	1.03	—	—	1.03	1.03	—	—	—	1.03	–	–	–	0.52
20	2.06	2.06	–	2.06	—	—	2.06	2.06	—	—	—	2.06	–	–	–	1.03
30	3.09	3.09	–	3.09	—	—	3.09	3.09	—	—	—	3.09	–	–	–	1.55
40	4.12	4.12	–	4.12	—	—	4.12	4.12	—	—	—	4.12	–	–	–	2.06
50	5.15	5.15	–	5.15	—	—	5.15	5.15	—	—	—	5.15	–	–	–	2.58
60	6.18	6.18	–	6.18	—	—	6.18	6.18	—	—	—	6.18	–	–	–	3.09
70	7.21	7.21	–	7.21	—	—	7.21	7.21	—	—	—	7.21	–	–	–	3.61
80	8.24	8.24	–	8.24	—	—	8.24	8.24	—	—	—	8.24	–	–	–	4.12
90	9.27	9.27	–	9.27	—	—	9.27	9.27	—	—	—	9.27	–	–	–	4.64
100	10.30	10.30	–	10.30	—	—	10.30	10.30	—	—	—	10.30	–	–	–	5.15
200	20.60	20.60	–	20.60	—	—	20.60	20.60	—	—	—	20.60	–	–	–	10.30
300	30.90	30.90	–	30.90	—	—	30.90	30.90	—	—	—	30.90	–	–	–	15.45
400	41.20	41.20	–	41.20	—	—	41.20	41.20	—	—	—	41.20	–	–	–	20.60
500	51.50	51.50	–	51.50	—	—	51.50	51.50	—	—	—	51.50	–	–	–	25.75
600	61.80	61.80	–	61.80	—	—	61.80	61.80	—	—	—	61.80	–	–	–	30.90
700	72.10	72.10	–	72.10	—	—	72.10	72.10	—	—	—	72.10	–	–	–	36.05
800	82.40	82.40	–	82.40	—	—	82.40	82.40	—	—	—	82.40	–	–	–	41.20
900	92.70	92.70	–	92.70	—	—	92.70	92.70	—	—	—	92.70	–	–	–	46.35
1000	103.00	103.00	–	103.00	—	—	103.00	103.00	—	—	—	103.00	–	–	–	51.50
2000	206.00	206.00	–	206.00	—	—	206.00	206.00	—	—	—	206.00	–	–	–	103.00
3000	309.00	309.00	–	309.00	—	—	309.00	309.00	—	—	—	309.00	–	–	–	154.50
4000	412.00	412.00	–	412.00	—	—	412.00	412.00	—	—	—	412.00	–	–	–	206.00
5000	515.00	515.00	–	515.00	—	—	515.00	515.00	—	—	—	515.00	–	–	–	257.50
250000	7210	0	–	5150	—	—	3090	5150	—	—	—	0	–	–	–	0.00
255000	7725	515	–	5665	—	—	3605	5665	—	—	—	515	–	–	–	257.50
260000	8240	1030	–	6180	—	—	4120	6180	—	—	—	1030	–	–	–	515.00
265000	8755	1545	–	6695	—	—	4635	6695	—	—	—	1545	–	–	–	772.50
270000	9270	2060	–	7210	—	—	5150	7210	—	—	—	2060	–	–	–	1030.00

**Senior citizen is a resident individual who is at least 60 years of age at any time during the previous year but less than 80 years on the last day of the previous year.

***Super senior citizen is a resident individual who is at least 80 years of age at any time during the previous year.

†After rebate under section 87A.

Income-tax : 1.5

INDIVIDUALS

HUF and AOP

Net Income Range : Rs. 2,70,000 - Rs. 3,00,000

Assessment Years : 2013-14 to 2018-19

Assessment Years	2013-14			2014-15				2015-16 and 2016-17				2017-18				2018-19			
	Resident senior citizen**	Resident super senior citizen***	Any other	Resident senior citizen**	Resident super senior citizen***	Any other resident Individual	Non-resident individual or any HUF/ AOP	Resident senior citizen**	Resident super senior citizen***	Any other resident individual	Non-resident individual or any HUF/ AOP	Resident senior citizen**	Resident super senior citizen***	Any other resident individual	Non-resident individual or any HUF/AOP	Resident senior citizen**	Resident super senior citizen***	Any other resident individual	Non-resident individual or any HUF/AOP
Slab rate	10%	–	10%	–	–	10%	10%	–	–	10%	10%	–	–	–	10%	–	–	–	5%
Surcharge	–	–	–	–	–	–	–	–	–	–	–	–	–	–	–	–	–	–	–
EC	3%	–	3%	–	–	3%	3%	–	–	3%	3%	–	–	–	3%	–	–	–	3%
NI Rs.	IT+EC Rs.	IT Rs.	IT+EC Rs.	IT Rs.	IT Rs.	IT†+EC Rs.	IT+EC Rs.	IT Rs.	IT Rs.	IT†+EC Rs.	IT+EC Rs.	IT Rs.	IT Rs.	IT† Rs.	IT+EC Rs.	IT Rs.	IT Rs.	IT† Rs.	IT + EC Rs.
10	1.03	–	1.03	–	–	1.03	1.03	–	–	1.03	1.03	–	–	–	1.03	–	–	–	0.52
20	2.06	–	2.06	–	–	2.06	2.06	–	–	2.06	2.06	–	–	–	2.06	–	–	–	1.03
30	3.09	–	3.09	–	–	3.09	3.09	–	–	3.09	3.09	–	–	–	3.09	–	–	–	1.55
40	4.12	–	4.12	–	–	4.12	4.12	–	–	4.12	4.12	–	–	–	4.12	–	–	–	2.06
50	5.15	–	5.15	–	–	5.15	5.15	–	–	5.15	5.15	–	–	–	5.15	–	–	–	2.58
60	6.18	–	6.18	–	–	6.18	6.18	–	–	6.18	6.18	–	–	–	6.18	–	–	–	3.09
70	7.21	–	7.21	–	–	7.21	7.21	–	–	7.21	7.21	–	–	–	7.21	–	–	–	3.61
80	8.24	–	8.24	–	–	8.24	8.24	–	–	8.24	8.24	–	–	–	8.24	–	–	–	4.12
90	9.27	–	9.27	–	–	9.27	9.27	–	–	9.27	9.27	–	–	–	9.27	–	–	–	4.64
100	10.30	–	10.30	–	–	10.30	10.30	–	–	10.30	10.30	–	–	–	10.30	–	–	–	5.15
200	20.60	–	20.60	–	–	20.60	20.60	–	–	20.60	20.60	–	–	–	20.60	–	–	–	10.30
300	30.90	–	30.90	–	–	30.90	30.90	–	–	30.90	30.90	–	–	–	30.90	–	–	–	15.45
400	41.20	–	41.20	–	–	41.20	41.20	–	–	41.20	41.20	–	–	–	41.20	–	–	–	20.60
500	51.50	–	51.50	–	–	51.50	51.50	–	–	51.50	51.50	–	–	–	51.50	–	–	–	25.75
600	61.80	–	61.80	–	–	61.80	61.80	–	–	61.80	61.80	–	–	–	61.80	–	–	–	30.90
700	72.10	–	72.10	–	–	72.10	72.10	–	–	72.10	72.10	–	–	–	72.10	–	–	–	36.05
800	82.40	–	82.40	–	–	82.40	82.40	–	–	82.40	82.40	–	–	–	82.40	–	–	–	41.20
900	92.70	–	92.70	–	–	92.70	92.70	–	–	92.70	92.70	–	–	–	92.70	–	–	–	46.35
1000	103.00	–	103.00	–	–	103.00	103.00	–	–	103.00	103.00	–	–	–	103.00	–	–	–	51.50
2000	206.00	–	206.00	–	–	206.00	206.00	–	–	206.00	206.00	–	–	–	206.00	–	–	–	103.00
3000	309.00	–	309.00	–	–	309.00	309.00	–	–	309.00	309.00	–	–	–	309.00	–	–	–	154.50
4000	412.00	–	412.00	–	–	412.00	412.00	–	–	412.00	412.00	–	–	–	412.00	–	–	–	206.00
5000	515.00	–	515.00	–	–	515.00	515.00	–	–	515.00	515.00	–	–	–	515.00	–	–	–	257.50
270000	2060	–	7210	0	–	5150	7210	–	–	0	2060	–	–	–	2060	–	–	–	1030.00
275000	2575	–	7725	515	–	5665	7725	–	–	515	2575	–	–	–	2575	–	–	–	1287.50
280000	3090	–	8240	1030	–	6180	8240	–	–	1030	3090	–	–	–	3090	–	–	–	1545.00
285000	3605	–	8755	1545	–	6695	8755	–	–	1545	3605	–	–	–	3605	–	–	–	1802.50
290000	4120	–	9270	2060	–	7210	9270	–	–	2060	4120	–	–	–	4120	–	–	–	2060.00
295000	4635	–	9785	2575	–	7725	9785	–	–	2575	4635	–	–	–	4635	–	–	–	2317.50
300000	5150	–	10300	3090	–	8240	10300	–	–	3090	5150	–	–	–	5150	–	–	–	2575.00

**Senior citizen is a resident individual who is at least 60 years of age at any time during the previous year but less than 80 years on the last day of the previous year.

***Super senior citizen is a resident individual who is at least 80 years of age at any time during the previous year.

†After rebate under section 87A.

Income-tax : 1.6

INDIVIDUALS

HUF and AOP

Net Income Range : Rs. 3,00,000 - Rs. 3,20,000

Assessment Years : 2013-14 to 2018-19

Assess-ment Years	2013-14			2014-15				2015-16 and 2016-17				2017-18				2018-19			
	Resident senior citizen**	Resident super senior citizen***	Any other	Resident senior citizen**	Resident super senior citizen***	Any other resident Individual	Non-resident individual or any HUF/ AOP	Resident senior citizen**	Resident super senior citizen***	Any other resident individual	Non-resident individual or any HUF/ AOP	Resident senior citizen**	Resident super senior citizen***	Any other resident individual	Non-resident individual or any HUF/ AOP	Resident senior citizen**	Resident super senior citizen***	Any other resident individual	Non-resident individual or any HUF/AOP
Slab rate	10%	–	10%	10%	–	10%	10%	–	–	10%	10%	–	–	10%	10%	–	–	5%	5%
Surcharge	–	–	–	–	–	–	–	–	–	–	–	–	–	–	–	–	–	–	–
EC	3%	–	3%	3%	–	3%	3%	–	–	3%	3%	–	–	3%	3%	–	–	3%	3%
NI Rs.	IT+EC Rs	IT –	IT+EC Rs	IT† Rs.	IT Rs.	IT†+EC Rs.	IT+EC Rs.	IT† Rs.	IT Rs.	IT†+EC Rs.	IT+EC Rs.	IT† Rs.	IT Rs.	IT†+EC Rs.	IT+EC Rs.	IT† Rs.	IT Rs.	IT† + EC Rs.	IT + EC Rs.
10	1.03	–	1.03	1.03	–	1.03	1.03	–	–	1.03	1.03	–	–	1.03	1.03	–	–	0.52	0.52
20	2.06	–	2.06	2.06	–	2.06	2.06	–	–	2.06	2.06	–	–	2.06	2.06	–	–	1.03	1.03
30	3.09	–	3.09	3.09	–	3.09	3.09	–	–	3.09	3.09	–	–	3.09	3.09	–	–	1.55	1.55
40	4.12	–	4.12	4.12	–	4.12	4.12	–	–	4.12	4.12	–	–	4.12	4.12	–	–	2.06	2.06
50	5.15	–	5.15	5.15	–	5.15	5.15	–	–	5.15	5.15	–	–	5.15	5.15	–	–	2.58	2.58
60	6.18	–	6.18	6.18	–	6.18	6.18	–	–	6.18	6.18	–	–	6.18	6.18	–	–	3.09	3.09
70	7.21	–	7.21	7.21	–	7.21	7.21	–	–	7.21	7.21	–	–	7.21	7.21	–	–	3.61	3.61
80	8.24	–	8.24	8.24	–	8.24	8.24	–	–	8.24	8.24	–	–	8.24	8.24	–	–	4.12	4.12
90	9.27	–	9.27	9.27	–	9.27	9.27	–	–	9.27	9.27	–	–	9.27	9.27	–	–	4.64	4.64
100	10.30	–	10.30	10.30	–	10.30	10.30	–	–	10.30	10.30	–	–	10.30	10.30	–	–	5.15	5.15
200	20.60	–	20.60	20.60	–	20.60	20.60	–	–	20.60	20.60	–	–	20.60	20.60	–	–	10.30	10.30
300	30.90	–	30.90	30.90	–	30.90	30.90	–	–	30.90	30.90	–	–	30.90	30.90	–	–	15.45	15.45
400	41.20	–	41.20	41.20	–	41.20	41.20	–	–	41.20	41.20	–	–	41.20	41.20	–	–	20.60	20.60
500	51.50	–	51.50	51.50	–	51.50	51.50	–	–	51.50	51.50	–	–	51.50	51.50	–	–	25.75	25.75
600	61.80	–	61.80	61.80	–	61.80	61.80	–	–	61.80	61.80	–	–	61.80	61.80	–	–	30.90	30.90
700	72.10	–	72.10	72.10	–	72.10	72.10	–	–	72.10	72.10	–	–	72.10	72.10	–	–	36.05	36.05
800	82.40	–	82.40	82.40	–	82.40	82.40	–	–	82.40	82.40	–	–	82.40	82.40	–	–	41.20	41.20
900	92.70	–	92.70	92.70	–	92.70	92.70	–	–	92.70	92.70	–	–	92.70	92.70	–	–	46.35	46.35
1000	103.00	–	103.00	103.00	–	103.00	103.00	–	–	103.00	103.00	–	–	103.00	103.00	–	–	51.50	51.50
2000	206.00	–	206.00	206.00	–	206.00	206.00	–	–	206.00	206.00	–	–	206.00	206.00	–	–	103.00	103.00
3000	309.00	–	309.00	309.00	–	309.00	309.00	–	–	309.00	309.00	–	–	309.00	309.00	–	–	154.50	154.50
4000	412.00	–	412.00	412.00	–	412.00	412.00	–	–	412.00	412.00	–	–	412.00	412.00	–	–	206.00	206.00
5000	515.00	–	515.00	515.00	–	515.00	515.00	–	–	515.00	515.00	–	–	515.00	515.00	–	–	257.50	257.50
300000	5150	0	10300	3090	0	8240	10300	–	–	3090	5150	–	–	0	5150	–	–	0.00	2575.00
305000	5665	0	10815	3605	0	8755	10815	–	–	3605	5665	–	–	515	5665	–	–	257.50	2832.50
310000	6180	0	11330	4120	0	9270	11330	–	–	4120	6180	–	–	1030	6180	–	–	515.00	3090.00
315000	6695	0	11845	4635	0	9785	11845	–	–	4635	6695	–	–	1545	6695	–	–	772.50	3347.50
320000	7210	0	12360	5150	0	10300	12360	–	–	5150	7210	–	–	2060	7210	–	–	1030.00	3605.00

**Senior citizen is a resident individual who is at least 60 years of age at any time during the previous year but less than 80 years on the last day of the previous year.

***Super senior citizen is a resident individual who is at least 80 years of age at any time during the previous year.

†After rebate under section 87A.

Income-tax : 1.7

INDIVIDUALS

HUF and AOP

Net Income Range : Rs. 3,20,000 - Rs. 3,50,000

Assessment Years : 2013-14 to 2018-19

Assess-ment Years	2013-14			2014-15				2015-16 and 2016-17				2017-18				2018-19			
	Resident senior citizen**	Resident super senior citizen***	Any other	Resident senior citizen**	Resident super senior citizen***	Any other resident Individual	Non-resident individual or any HUF/ AOP	Resident senior citizen**	Resident super senior citizen***	Any other resident individual	Non-resident individual or any HUF/ AOP	Resident senior citizen**	Resident super senior citizen***	Any other resident individual	Non-resident individual or any HUF/AOP	Resident senior citizen**	Resident super senior citizen***	Any other resident individual	Non-resident individual or any HUF/AOP
Slab rate	10%	–	10%	10%	–	10%	10%	10%	–	10%	10%	–	–	10%	10%	–	–	5%	5%
Surcharge	–	–	–	–	–	–	–	–	–	–	–	–	–	–	–	–	–	–	–
EC	3%	–	3%	3%	–	3%	3%	3%	–	3%	3%	–	–	3%	3%	–	–	3%	3%
NI Rs.	IT+EC Rs.	IT –	IT+EC Rs.	IT† Rs.	IT† Rs.	IT†+EC Rs.	IT+EC Rs.	IT†+EC Rs.	IT Rs.	IT†+EC Rs.	IT+EC Rs.	IT† Rs.	IT Rs.	IT†+EC Rs.	IT+EC Rs.	IT† Rs.	IT Rs.	IT† + EC Rs.	IT + EC Rs.
10	1.03	–	1.03	1.03	–	1.03	1.03	1.03	–	1.03	1.03	–	–	1.03	1.03	–	–	0.52	0.52
20	2.06	–	2.06	2.06	–	2.06	2.06	2.06	–	2.06	2.06	–	–	2.06	2.06	–	–	1.03	1.03
30	3.09	–	3.09	3.09	–	3.09	3.09	3.09	–	3.09	3.09	–	–	3.09	3.09	–	–	1.55	1.55
40	4.12	–	4.12	4.12	–	4.12	4.12	4.12	–	4.12	4.12	–	–	4.12	4.12	–	–	2.06	2.06
50	5.15	–	5.15	5.15	–	5.15	5.15	5.15	–	5.15	5.15	–	–	5.15	5.15	–	–	2.58	2.58
60	6.18	–	6.18	6.18	–	6.18	6.18	6.18	–	6.18	6.18	–	–	6.18	6.18	–	–	3.09	3.09
70	7.21	–	7.21	7.21	–	7.21	7.21	7.21	–	7.21	7.21	–	–	7.21	7.21	–	–	3.61	3.61
80	8.24	–	8.24	8.24	–	8.24	8.24	8.24	–	8.24	8.24	–	–	8.24	8.24	–	–	4.12	4.12
90	9.27	–	9.27	9.27	–	9.27	9.27	9.27	–	9.27	9.27	–	–	9.27	9.27	–	–	4.64	4.64
100	10.30	–	10.30	10.30	–	10.30	10.30	10.30	–	10.30	10.30	–	–	10.30	10.30	–	–	5.15	5.15
200	20.60	–	20.60	20.60	–	20.60	20.60	20.60	–	20.60	20.60	–	–	20.60	20.60	–	–	10.30	10.30
300	30.90	–	30.90	30.90	–	30.90	30.90	30.90	–	30.90	30.90	–	–	30.90	30.90	–	–	15.45	15.45
400	41.20	–	41.20	41.20	–	41.20	41.20	41.20	–	41.20	41.20	–	–	41.20	41.20	–	–	20.60	20.60
500	51.50	–	51.50	51.50	–	51.50	51.50	51.50	–	51.50	51.50	–	–	51.50	51.50	–	–	25.75	25.75
600	61.80	–	61.80	61.80	–	61.80	61.80	61.80	–	61.80	61.80	–	–	61.80	61.80	–	–	30.90	30.90
700	72.10	–	72.10	72.10	–	72.10	72.10	72.10	–	72.10	72.10	–	–	72.10	72.10	–	–	36.05	36.05
800	82.40	–	82.40	82.40	–	82.40	82.40	82.40	–	82.40	82.40	–	–	82.40	82.40	–	–	41.20	41.20
900	92.70	–	92.70	92.70	–	92.70	92.70	92.70	–	92.70	92.70	–	–	92.70	92.70	–	–	46.35	46.35
1000	103.00	–	103.00	103.00	–	103.00	103.00	103.00	–	103.00	103.00	–	–	103.00	103.00	–	–	51.50	51.50
2000	206.00	–	206.00	206.00	–	206.00	206.00	206.00	–	206.00	206.00	–	–	206.00	206.00	–	–	103.00	103.00
3000	309.00	–	309.00	309.00	–	309.00	309.00	309.00	–	309.00	309.00	–	–	309.00	309.00	–	–	154.50	154.50
4000	412.00	–	412.00	412.00	–	412.00	412.00	412.00	–	412.00	412.00	–	–	412.00	412.00	–	–	206.00	206.00
5000	515.00	–	515.00	515.00	–	515.00	515.00	515.00	–	515.00	515.00	–	–	515.00	515.00	–	–	257.50	257.50
320000	7210	0	12360	5150	0	10300	12360	0	0	5150	7210	0	0	2060	7210	–	–	1030	3605
330000	8240	0	13390	6180	0	11330	13390	1030	0	6180	8240	0	0	3090	8240	–	–	1545	4120
340000	9270	0	14420	7210	0	12360	14420	2060	0	7210	9270	0	0	4120	9270	–	–	2060	4635
350000	10300	0	15450	8240	0	13390	15450	3090	0	8240	10300	0	0	5150	10300	–	–	2575	5150

**Senior citizen is a resident individual who is at least 60 years of age at any time during the previous year but less than 80 years on the last day of the previous year.

***Super senior citizen is a resident individual who is at least 80 years of age at any time during the previous year.

†After rebate under section 87A.

Income-tax : 1.8

INDIVIDUALS

HUF and AOP

Net Income Range : Rs. 3,50,000 - Rs. 5,00,000

Assessment Years : 2013-14 to 2018-19

Assessment Years	2013-14			2014-15				2015-16 and 2016-17				2017-18				2018-19		
	Resident senior citizen**	Resident super senior citizen***	Any other	Resident senior citizen**	Resident super senior citizen***	Any other resident Individual	Non-resident individual or any HUF/AOP	Resident senior citizen**	Resident super senior citizen***	Any other resident individual	Non-resident individual or any HUF/ AOP	Resident senior citizen**	Resident super senior citizen***	Any other resident individual	Non-resident individual or any HUF/ AOP	Resident senior citizen**	Resident super senior citizen***	Any other
Slab rate Surcharge EC	10% – 3%	– – –	10% – 3%	10% – 3%	– – –	10% – 3%	10% – 3%	10% – 3%	– – –	10% – 3%	10% – 3%	10% – 3%	– – –	10% – 3%	10% – 3%	5% – 3%	– – –	5% – 3%
NI Rs.	IT+EC Rs.	IT –	IT+EC Rs.	IT† Rs.	IT† Rs.	IT†+EC Rs.	IT+EC Rs.	IT†+EC Rs.	IT Rs.	IT†+EC Rs.	IT+EC Rs.	IT†+EC Rs.	IT Rs.	IT†+EC Rs.	IT+EC Rs.	IT + EC Rs.	IT Rs.	IT + EC Rs.
10	1.03	–	1.03	1.03	–	1.03	1.03	1.03	–	1.03	1.03	1.03	–	1.03	1.03	0.52	–	0.52
20	2.06	–	2.06	2.06	–	2.06	2.06	2.06	–	2.06	2.06	2.06	–	2.06	2.06	1.03	–	1.03
30	3.09	–	3.09	3.09	–	3.09	3.09	3.09	–	3.09	3.09	3.09	–	3.09	3.09	1.55	–	1.55
40	4.12	–	4.12	4.12	–	4.12	4.12	4.12	–	4.12	4.12	4.12	–	4.12	4.12	2.06	–	2.06
50	5.15	–	5.15	5.15	–	5.15	5.15	5.15	–	5.15	5.15	5.15	–	5.15	5.15	2.58	–	2.58
60	6.18	–	6.18	6.18	–	6.18	6.18	6.18	–	6.18	6.18	6.18	–	6.18	6.18	3.09	–	3.09
70	7.21	–	7.21	7.21	–	7.21	7.21	7.21	–	7.21	7.21	7.21	–	7.21	7.21	3.61	–	3.61
80	8.24	–	8.24	8.24	–	8.24	8.24	8.24	–	8.24	8.24	8.24	–	8.24	8.24	4.12	–	4.12
90	9.27	–	9.27	9.27	–	9.27	9.27	9.27	–	9.27	9.27	9.27	–	9.27	9.27	4.64	–	4.64
100	10.30	–	10.30	10.30	–	10.30	10.30	10.30	–	10.30	10.30	10.30	–	10.30	10.30	5.15	–	5.15
200	20.60	–	20.60	20.60	–	20.60	20.60	20.60	–	20.60	20.60	20.60	–	20.60	20.60	10.30	–	10.30
300	30.90	–	30.90	30.90	–	30.90	30.90	30.90	–	30.90	30.90	30.90	–	30.90	30.90	15.45	–	15.45
400	41.20	–	41.20	41.20	–	41.20	41.20	41.20	–	41.20	41.20	41.20	–	41.20	41.20	20.60	–	20.60
500	51.50	–	51.50	51.50	–	51.50	51.50	51.50	–	51.50	51.50	51.50	–	51.50	51.50	25.75	–	25.75
600	61.80	–	61.80	61.80	–	61.80	61.80	61.80	–	61.80	61.80	61.80	–	61.80	61.80	30.90	–	30.90
700	72.10	–	72.10	72.10	–	72.10	72.10	72.10	–	72.10	72.10	72.10	–	72.10	72.10	36.05	–	36.05
800	82.40	–	82.40	82.40	–	82.40	82.40	82.40	–	82.40	82.40	82.40	–	82.40	82.40	41.20	–	41.20
900	92.70	–	92.70	92.70	–	92.70	92.70	92.70	–	92.70	92.70	92.70	–	92.70	92.70	46.35	–	46.35
1000	103.00	–	103.00	103.00	–	103.00	103.00	103.00	–	103.00	103.00	103.00	–	103.00	103.00	51.50	–	51.50
2000	206.00	–	206.00	206.00	–	206.00	206.00	206.00	–	206.00	206.00	206.00	–	206.00	206.00	103.00	–	103.00
3000	309.00	–	309.00	309.00	–	309.00	309.00	309.00	–	309.00	309.00	309.00	–	309.00	309.00	154.50	–	154.50
4000	412.00	–	412.00	412.00	–	412.00	412.00	412.00	–	412.00	412.00	412.00	–	412.00	412.00	206.00	–	206.00
5000	515.00	–	515.00	515.00	–	515.00	515.00	515.00	–	515.00	515.00	515.00	–	515.00	515.00	257.50	–	257.50
350000	10300	0	15450	8240	0	13390	15450	3090	0	8240	10300	0	0	5150	10300	2575	–	5150
380000	13390	0	18540	11330	0	16480	18540	6180	0	11330	13390	3090	0	8240	13390	4120	–	6695
410000	16480	0	21630	14420	0	19570	21630	9270	0	14420	16480	6180	0	11330	16480	5665	–	8240
440000	19570	0	24720	17510	0	22660	24720	12360	0	17510	19570	9270	0	14420	19570	7210	–	9785
470000	22660	0	27810	20600	0	25750	27810	15450	0	20600	22660	12360	0	17510	22660	8755	–	11330
500000	25750	0	30900	23690	0	28840	30900	18540	0	23690	25750	15450	0	20600	25750	10300	–	12875

**Senior citizen is a resident individual who is at least 60 years of age at any time during the previous year but less than 80 years on the last day of the previous year.

***Super senior citizen is a resident individual who is at least 80 years of age at any time during the previous year.

†After rebate under section 87A.

Income-tax : 1.9

INDIVIDUALS

HUF and AOP

Net Income Range : Rs. 5,00,000 - Rs. 8,00,000

Assessment Years : 2013-14 to 2018-19

Assessment Years	2013-14 and 2014-15			2015-16 to 2017-18			2018-19		
	Resident senior citizen**	Resident super senior citizen***	Any other	Resident senior citizen**	Resident super senior citizen***	Any other	Resident senior citizen**	Resident super senior citizen***	Any other
Slab rate	20%	20%	20%	20%	20%	20%	20%	20%	20%
Surcharge	—	—	—	—	—	—	–	–	–
EC	3%	3%	3%	3%	3%	3%	3%	3%	3%
NI Rs.	IT+EC Rs.	IT+EC Rs.	IT+EC Rs.	IT+EC Rs.	IT Rs.	IT+EC Rs.	IT + EC Rs.	IT + EC Rs.	IT + EC Rs.
10	2.06	2.06	2.06	2.06	2.06	2.06	2.06	2.06	2.06
20	4.12	4.12	4.12	4.12	4.12	4.12	4.12	4.12	4.12
30	6.18	6.18	6.18	6.18	6.18	6.18	6.18	6.18	6.18
40	8.24	8.24	8.24	8.24	8.24	8.24	8.24	8.24	8.24
50	10.30	10.30	10.30	10.30	10.30	10.30	10.30	10.30	10.30
60	12.36	12.36	12.36	12.36	12.36	12.36	12.36	12.36	12.36
70	14.42	14.42	14.42	14.42	14.42	14.42	14.42	14.42	14.42
80	16.48	16.48	16.48	16.48	16.48	16.48	16.48	16.48	16.48
90	18.54	18.54	18.54	18.54	18.54	18.54	18.54	18.54	18.54
100	20.60	20.60	20.60	20.60	20.60	20.60	20.60	20.60	20.60
200	41.20	41.20	41.20	41.20	41.20	41.20	41.20	41.20	41.20
300	61.80	61.80	61.80	61.80	61.80	61.80	61.80	61.80	61.80
400	82.40	82.40	82.40	82.40	82.40	82.40	82.40	82.40	82.40
500	103.00	103.00	103.00	103.00	103.00	103.00	103.00	103.00	103.00
600	123.60	123.60	123.60	123.60	123.60	123.60	123.60	123.60	123.60
700	144.20	144.20	144.20	144.20	144.20	144.20	144.20	144.20	144.20
800	164.80	164.80	164.80	164.80	164.80	164.80	164.80	164.80	164.80
900	185.40	185.40	185.40	185.40	185.40	185.40	185.40	185.40	185.40
1000	206.00	206.00	206.00	206.00	206.00	206.00	206.00	206.00	206.00
2000	412.00	412.00	412.00	412.00	412.00	412.00	412.00	412.00	412.00
3000	618.00	618.00	618.00	618.00	618.00	618.00	618.00	618.00	618.00
4000	824.00	824.00	824.00	824.00	824.00	824.00	824.00	824.00	824.00
5000	1030.00	1030.00	1030.00	1030.00	1030.00	1030.00	1030.00	1030.00	1030.00
500000	25750	0	30900	20600	0	25750	10300	0	12875
550000	36050	10300	41200	30900	10300	36050	20600	10300	23175
600000	46350	20600	51500	41200	20600	46350	30900	20600	33475
650000	56650	30900	61800	51500	30900	56650	41200	30900	43775
700000	66950	41200	72100	61800	41200	66950	51500	41200	54075
750000	77250	51500	82400	72100	51500	77250	61800	51500	64375
800000	87550	61800	92700	82400	61800	87550	72100	61800	74675

**Senior citizen is a resident individual who is at least 60 years of age at any time during the previous year but less than 80 years on the last day of the previous year.

***Super senior citizen is a resident individual who is at least 80 years of age at any time during the previous year.

Income-tax : 1.10

INDIVIDUALS

HUF and AOP

Net Income Range : Rs. 8,00,000 - Rs. 10,00,000

Assessment Years : 2013-14 to 2018-19

Assessment Years		2013-14 and 2014-15			2015-16 to 2017-18			2018-19		
	Any other	Resident senior citizen**	Resident super senior citizen***	Any other	Resident senior citizen**	Resident super senior citizen***	Any other	Resident senior citizen**	Resident super senior citizen***	Any other
Slab rate Surcharge EC	30% — 3%	20% — 3%	20% — 3%	20% — 3%	20% — 3%	20% — 3%	20% — 3%	20% — 3%	20% – 3%	20% – 3%
NI Rs.	IT+EC Rs.	IT+EC Rs.	IT+EC Rs.	IT+EC Rs.	IT+EC Rs.	IT Rs.	IT+EC Rs.	IT + EC Rs.	IT + EC Rs.	IT + EC Rs.
10	3.09	2.06	2.06	2.06	2.06	2.06	2.06	2.06	2.06	2.06
20	6.18	4.12	4.12	4.12	4.12	4.12	4.12	4.12	4.12	4.12
30	9.27	6.18	6.18	6.18	6.18	6.18	6.18	6.18	6.18	6.18
40	12.36	8.24	8.24	8.24	8.24	8.24	8.24	8.24	8.24	8.24
50	15.45	10.30	10.30	10.30	10.30	10.30	10.30	10.30	10.30	10.30
60	18.54	12.36	12.36	12.36	12.36	12.36	12.36	12.36	12.36	12.36
70	21.63	14.42	14.42	14.42	14.42	14.42	14.42	14.42	14.42	14.42
80	24.72	16.48	16.48	16.48	16.48	16.48	16.48	16.48	16.48	16.48
90	27.81	18.54	18.54	18.54	18.54	18.54	18.54	18.54	18.54	18.54
100	30.90	20.60	20.60	20.60	20.60	20.60	20.60	20.60	20.60	20.60
200	61.80	41.20	41.20	41.20	41.20	41.20	41.20	41.20	41.20	41.20
300	92.70	61.80	61.80	61.80	61.80	61.80	61.80	61.80	61.80	61.80
400	123.60	82.40	82.40	82.40	82.40	82.40	82.40	82.40	82.40	82.40
500	154.50	103.00	103.00	103.00	103.00	103.00	103.00	103.00	103.00	103.00
600	185.40	123.60	123.60	123.60	123.60	123.60	123.60	123.60	123.60	123.60
700	216.30	144.20	144.20	144.20	144.20	144.20	144.20	144.20	144.20	144.20
800	247.20	164.80	164.80	164.80	164.80	164.80	164.80	164.80	164.80	164.80
900	278.10	185.40	185.40	185.40	185.40	185.40	185.40	185.40	185.40	185.40
1000	309.00	206.00	206.00	206.00	206.00	206.00	206.00	206.00	206.00	206.00
800000	94760	87550	61800	92700	82400	61800	87550	72100	61800	74675
820000	100940	91670	65920	96820	86520	65920	91670	76220	65920	78795
840000	107120	95790	70040	100940	90640	70040	95790	80340	70040	82915
860000	113300	99910	74160	105060	94760	74160	99910	84460	74160	87035
880000	119480	104030	78280	109180	98880	78280	104030	88580	78280	91155
900000	125660	108150	82400	113300	103000	82400	108150	92700	82400	95275
920000	131840	112270	86520	117420	107120	86520	112270	96820	86520	99395
940000	138020	116390	90640	121540	111240	90640	116390	100940	90640	103515
960000	144200	120510	94760	125660	115360	94760	120510	105060	94760	107635
980000	150380	124630	98880	129780	119480	98880	124630	109180	98880	111755
1000000	156560	128750	103000	133900	123600	103000	128750	113300	103000	115875

**Senior citizen is a resident individual who is at least 60 years of age at any time during the previous year but less than 80 years on the last day of the previous year.

***Super senior citizen is a resident individual who is at least 80 years of age at any time during the previous year.

Income-tax : 1.11

INDIVIDUALS

HUF and AOP

Net Income Range : Rs. 10,00,000 - Rs. 20,00,000

Assessment Years : 2013-14 to 2018-19

Assessment Years		2013-14 and 2014-15			2015-16 to 2017-18			2018-19		
	Any other	Resident senior citizen**	Resident super senior citizen***	Any other	Resident senior citizen**	Resident super senior citizen***	Any other	Resident senior citizen**	Resident super senior citizen***	Any other
Slab rate	30%	30%	30%	30%	30%	30%	30%	30%	30%	30%
Surcharge	—	—	—	—	—	—	—	–	–	–
EC	3%	3%	3%	3%	3%	3%	3%	3%	3%	3%
NI Rs.	IT+EC Rs.	IT+EC Rs.	IT+EC Rs.	IT+EC Rs.	IT+EC Rs.	IT Rs.	IT+EC Rs.	IT + EC Rs.	IT + EC Rs.	IT + EC Rs.
10	3.09	3.09	3.09	3.09	3.09	3.09	3.09	3.09	3.09	3.09
20	6.18	6.18	6.18	6.18	6.18	6.18	6.18	6.18	6.18	6.18
30	9.27	9.27	9.27	9.27	9.27	9.27	9.27	9.27	9.27	9.27
40	12.36	12.36	12.36	12.36	12.36	12.36	12.36	12.36	12.36	12.36
50	15.45	15.45	15.45	15.45	15.45	15.45	15.45	15.45	15.45	15.45
60	18.54	18.54	18.54	18.54	18.54	18.54	18.54	18.54	18.54	18.54
70	21.63	21.63	21.63	21.63	21.63	21.63	21.63	21.63	21.63	21.63
80	24.72	24.72	24.72	24.72	24.72	24.72	24.72	24.72	24.72	24.72
90	27.81	27.81	27.81	27.81	27.81	27.81	27.81	27.81	27.81	27.81
100	30.90	30.90	30.90	30.90	30.90	30.90	30.90	30.90	30.90	30.90
200	61.80	61.80	61.80	61.80	61.80	61.80	61.80	61.80	61.80	61.80
300	92.70	92.70	92.70	92.70	92.70	92.70	92.70	92.70	92.70	92.70
400	123.60	123.60	123.60	123.60	123.60	123.60	123.60	123.60	123.60	123.60
500	154.50	154.50	154.50	154.50	154.50	154.50	154.50	154.50	154.50	154.50
600	185.40	185.40	185.40	185.40	185.40	185.40	185.40	185.40	185.40	185.40
700	216.30	216.30	216.30	216.30	216.30	216.30	216.30	216.30	216.30	216.30
800	247.20	247.20	247.20	247.20	247.20	247.20	247.20	247.20	247.20	247.20
900	278.10	278.10	278.10	278.10	278.10	278.10	278.10	278.10	278.10	278.10
1000	309.00	309.00	309.00	309.00	309.00	309.00	309.00	309.00	309.00	309.00
2000	618.00	618.00	618.00	618.00	618.00	618.00	618.00	618.00	618.00	618.00
3000	927.00	927.00	927.00	927.00	927.00	927.00	927.00	927.00	927.00	927.00
4000	1236.00	1236.00	1236.00	1236.00	1236.00	1236.00	1236.00	1236.00	1236.00	1236.00
5000	1545.00	1545.00	1545.00	1545.00	1545.00	1545.00	1545.00	1545.00	1545.00	1545.00
6000	1854.00	1854.00	1854.00	1854.00	1854.00	1854.00	1854.00	1854.00	1854.00	1854.00
7000	2163.00	2163.00	2163.00	2163.00	2163.00	2163.00	2163.00	2163.00	2163.00	2163.00
8000	2472.00	2472.00	2472.00	2472.00	2472.00	2472.00	2472.00	2472.00	2472.00	2472.00
9000	2781.00	2781.00	2781.00	2781.00	2781.00	2781.00	2781.00	2781.00	2781.00	2781.00
1000000	156560	128750	103000	133900	123600	103000	128750	113300	103000	115875
1100000	187460	159650	133900	164800	154500	133900	159650	144200	133900	146775
1200000	218360	190550	164800	195700	185400	164800	190550	175100	164800	177675
1300000	249260	221450	195700	226600	216300	195700	221450	206000	195700	208575
1400000	280160	252350	226600	257500	247200	226600	252350	236900	226600	239475
1500000	311060	283250	257500	288400	278100	257500	283250	267800	257500	270375
1600000	341960	314150	288400	319300	309000	288400	314150	298700	288400	301275
1700000	372860	345050	319300	350200	339900	319300	345050	329600	319300	332175
1800000	403760	375950	350200	381100	370800	350200	375950	360500	350200	363075
1900000	434660	406850	381100	412000	401700	381100	406850	391400	381100	393975
2000000	465560	437750	412000	442900	432600	412000	437750	422300	412000	424875

**Senior citizen is a resident individual who is at least 60 years of age at any time during the previous year but less than 80 years on the last day of the previous year.

***Super senior citizen is a resident individual who is at least 80 years of age at any time during the previous year.

Income-tax : 1.12

INDIVIDUALS

HUF and AOP

Net Income Range : Rs. 20,00,000 - Rs. 30,00,000

Assessment Years : 2013-14 to 2018-19

Assessment Years		2013-14 and 2014-15			2015-16 to 2017-18			2018-19		
	Any other	Resident senior citizen**	Resident super senior citizen***	Any other	Resident senior citizen**	Resident super senior citizen***	Any other	Resident senior citizen**	Resident super senior citizen***	Any other
Slab rate	30%	30%	30%	30%	30%	30%	30%	30%	30%	30%
Surcharge	—	—	—	—	—	—	—	–	–	–
EC	3%	3%	3%	3%	3%	3%	3%	3%	3%	3%
NI Rs.	IT+EC Rs.	IT+EC Rs.	IT+EC Rs.	IT+EC Rs.	IT+EC Rs.	IT Rs.	IT+EC Rs.	IT + EC Rs.	IT + EC Rs.	IT + EC Rs.
10	3.09	3.09	3.09	3.09	3.09	3.09	3.09	3.09	3.09	3.09
20	6.18	6.18	6.18	6.18	6.18	6.18	6.18	6.18	6.18	6.18
30	9.27	9.27	9.27	9.27	9.27	9.27	9.27	9.27	9.27	9.27
40	12.36	12.36	12.36	12.36	12.36	12.36	12.36	12.36	12.36	12.36
50	15.45	15.45	15.45	15.45	15.45	15.45	15.45	15.45	15.45	15.45
60	18.54	18.54	18.54	18.54	18.54	18.54	18.54	18.54	18.54	18.54
70	21.63	21.63	21.63	21.63	21.63	21.63	21.63	21.63	21.63	21.63
80	24.72	24.72	24.72	24.72	24.72	24.72	24.72	24.72	24.72	24.72
90	27.81	27.81	27.81	27.81	27.81	27.81	27.81	27.81	27.81	27.81
100	30.90	30.90	30.90	30.90	30.90	30.90	30.90	30.90	30.90	30.90
200	61.80	61.80	61.80	61.80	61.80	61.80	61.80	61.80	61.80	61.80
300	92.70	92.70	92.70	92.70	92.70	92.70	92.70	92.70	92.70	92.70
400	123.60	123.60	123.60	123.60	123.60	123.60	123.60	123.60	123.60	123.60
500	154.50	154.50	154.50	154.50	154.50	154.50	154.50	154.50	154.50	154.50
600	185.40	185.40	185.40	185.40	185.40	185.40	185.40	185.40	185.40	185.40
700	216.30	216.30	216.30	216.30	216.30	216.30	216.30	216.30	216.30	216.30
800	247.20	247.20	247.20	247.20	247.20	247.20	247.20	247.20	247.20	247.20
900	278.10	278.10	278.10	278.10	278.10	278.10	278.10	278.10	278.10	278.10
1000	309.00	309.00	309.00	309.00	309.00	309.00	309.00	309.00	309.00	309.00
2000	618.00	618.00	618.00	618.00	618.00	618.00	618.00	618.00	618.00	618.00
3000	927.00	927.00	927.00	927.00	927.00	927.00	927.00	927.00	927.00	927.00
4000	1236.00	1236.00	1236.00	1236.00	1236.00	1236.00	1236.00	1236.00	1236.00	1236.00
5000	1545.00	1545.00	1545.00	1545.00	1545.00	1545.00	1545.00	1545.00	1545.00	1545.00
6000	1854.00	1854.00	1854.00	1854.00	1854.00	1854.00	1854.00	1854.00	1854.00	1854.00
7000	2163.00	2163.00	2163.00	2163.00	2163.00	2163.00	2163.00	2163.00	2163.00	2163.00
8000	2472.00	2472.00	2472.00	2472.00	2472.00	2472.00	2472.00	2472.00	2472.00	2472.00
9000	2781.00	2781.00	2781.00	2781.00	2781.00	2781.00	2781.00	2781.00	2781.00	2781.00
2000000	465560	437750	412000	442900	432600	412000	437750	422300	412000	424875
2100000	496460	468650	442900	473800	463500	442900	468650	453200	442900	455775
2200000	527360	499550	473800	504700	494400	473800	499550	484100	473800	486675
2300000	558260	530450	504700	535600	525300	504700	530450	515000	504700	517575
2400000	589160	561350	535600	566500	556200	535600	561350	545900	535600	548475
2500000	620060	592250	566500	597400	587100	566500	592250	576800	566500	579375
2600000	650960	623150	597400	628300	618000	597400	623150	607700	597400	610275
2700000	681860	654050	628300	659200	648900	628300	654050	638600	628300	641175
2800000	712760	684950	659200	690100	679800	659200	684950	669500	659200	672075
2900000	743660	715850	690100	721000	710700	690100	715850	700400	690100	702975
3000000	774560	746750	721000	751900	741600	721000	746750	731300	721000	733875

**Senior citizen is a resident individual who is at least 60 years of age at any time during the previous year but less than 80 years on the last day of the previous year.

***Super senior citizen is a resident individual who is at least 80 years of age at any time during the previous year.